FROMMER'S
DOLLARWISE GUIDE TO
JAPAN & HONG KONG

by Beth Reiber

1988–89 Edition

Published by Prentice Hall Press
A Division of Simon & Schuster, Inc.
Gulf + Western Building
One Gulf +Western Plaza
New York, NY 10023

ISBN 0–13–217647–5

Manufactured in the United States of America

CONTENTS

MAPS

To Joan and Fritz, my parents in Kansas,
who always encouraged me
to look farther than my own backyard

ACKNOWLEDGMENTS

I would like to thank a number of fine and very special people
who graciously offered their help in preparation of this book:
Toshinobu Ikubo, Mary Testa, and Seiko Taniguchi of the
Japan National Tourist Organization; Morris Simoncelli of
Japan Air Lines; David Tsugoshi of ANA enterprises; Jun Oda
of Miyako Hotels; Karisa Yuen-Ha Lui of the Hong Kong
Tourist Association; Debbie Howard, Janie Spencer, and
Evelyn Lenzen for their moral support and editorial advice;
and Paul Pasmantier, Marilyn Wood, and all the other people
at Frommer Books who helped make this book a reality.

INFLATION ALERT: We don't have to tell you that inflation has hit Japan & Hong Kong as it has everywhere else. In researching this book, we have made every effort to obtain up-to-the-minute prices, but even the most conscientious researcher cannot keep up with the current pace of inflation. As we go to press, we believe we have obtained the most reliable data possible. Nonetheless, in the lifetime of this edition—particularly its second year (1989)—the wise traveler will add 15% to 20% to the prices quoted throughout these pages.

A DISCLAIMER: Although every effort was made to ensure the accuracy of the prices and travel information appearing in this book, it should be kept in mind that prices can and do fluctuate in the course of time, and that information does change under the impact of the varied and volatile factors that affect the travel industry.

A NOTE ON JAPANESE SYMBOLS: Many hotels, restaurants, and other establishments in Japan do not have signs showing their names in English letters. Appendix II lists the Japanese symbols for all such places appearing in this guide. Each establishment name in Japanese symbols is numbered, and the same number appears in brackets in the text following the boldfaced establishment name. For example, in the text the Osaka hotel, Hokke Club [161], is number 161 in the Japanese symbol list in Appendix II.

DOLLARWISE GUIDE TO JAPAN & HONG KONG

HARDLY A DAY GOES BY that you don't hear something about Japan, whether it's about trade or business, cars or computers. And yet despite the fact that Japan has become one of the most advanced industrialized nations in the world, it still remains something of an enigma to people in the Western world. What is Japan? Is it computers and robots, cars and cameras? Or is it still the land of the *geisha* and the *bonsai,* the tea ceremony and flower arranging? Has Japan become more Westernized than Japanese?

The fact is that Japan is a blend of both East and West, and it is not an easy nation for Westerners to comprehend. Discovering Japan is much like peeling an onion—you uncover one layer only to find many more. Thus no matter how long you stay in Japan you never stop learning, and to me that's one of the most fascinating aspects of being in Japan. One American journalist who has lived in Japan more than 20 years and is the author of several books on Japan told me that she still doesn't understand all the nuances of Japanese culture and customs, and that she is amazed to find new aspects of the country almost daily.

This book is designed as an aid to your own discoveries of this truly wonderful and interesting country. According to the Japan National Tourist Organization, the average length of stay for tourists visiting Japan is 10½ days. To see all the places I've listed in this book you would need approximately three months. It's obvious, therefore, that you must be selective in planning your itinerary. Decide beforehand what your priorities are: whether they're temples, hot-spring spas, landscape gardens, or mountain scenery. Although the Japanese archipelago consists of more than 3,000 islands, I've limited the scope of this book to Japan's four main islands, where you'll find all of Japan's major cities and historical sights.

One aspect of this guidebook that sets it apart from most others is that in Appendix II it lists the written Japanese equivalent for restaurants and hotels that do not have signs in English. After all, nothing is more frustrating than walking down a street where everything is written only in Japanese and you can't distinguish one locale from the other. Most Japanese consists of pictographs called *kanji,* and with a little practice you can probably match up identical kanji. Appendix I, on Japanese vocabulary, should further help you in your travels through Japan.

But don't worry—even though you don't know the language you'll find Japan navigable. Japan rates as one of the safest countries in the world, much safer than the United States or even European countries. You don't have to worry about muggers, pickpockets, or crooks. The Japanese are honest and extremely helpful toward foreign visitors. Indeed, it's the people themselves who make traveling in Japan such a delight.

Readers of this book will also find a chapter devoted to the British colony of Hong Kong, known throughout the world as a mecca for shopping bargains. Many airlines that fly to Hong Kong (such as Japan Air Lines) allow stopovers in Japan, making it easy to combine a trip to both destinations. Seeing Japan and Hong Kong will give you the opportunity to observe both Japanese and Chinese culture, providing you with a well-rounded view of the Orient.

A WORD ABOUT COSTS: No doubt you've heard horror stories about how expensive Japan can be. The truth is, hardly anyone comes to Japan without suffering an initial shock at how expensive everything is—simply because almost everything *is* shockingly expensive. With the dramatic fall of the dollar against the yen, Tokyo has emerged as one of the most expensive—if not *the* most expensive—cities in the world. Food and lodging, for example, are much costlier in Tokyo than what you'd pay for the same thing in New York, and if you insist on living and eating exactly as you do back home, the costs will be astronomical.

The secret is to live and eat much as the Japanese do. This book will help you do exactly that, with descriptions on out-of-the-way eateries and Japanese-style inns that cater to the Japanese. By following the advice in this book and exercising a little caution on your own, you should be able to cut down needless expenses and learn even more about Japan in the process. While you may never find Japan cheap, you will find it richly rewarding for all those other reasons that brought you here in the first place.

And how much should you expect to spend every day for food and accommodations? If you want to travel rock-bottom and are willing to stay in youth hostels and eat inexpensive Japanese food, you can travel in Japan on ¥5,000 ($36) a day, excluding transportation costs. It's best, however, to allow yourself at least ¥10,000 ($71) to ¥14,000 ($100) a day, plus extra for occasional splurges, shopping, and emergencies. That's the budget I follow when I travel in Japan, and by sticking to the recommendations in this book you should be able to do it too.

However, in this book I haven't neglected the finest and most expensive places—after all, even though you may flinch at spending $200 on a meal, many such restaurants do exist and you may be interested simply in reading about them. Recommendations in this book are generally listed in a descending order from the most expensive down to the cheapest—skip to the end of the list, therefore, for a rundown of budget recommendations.

Keep in mind, however, that although every effort was made to be as accurate as possible, prices do change—which means that they go up. Always inquire about prices before checking into a hotel to avoid embarrassment when it comes time to pay the bill. Furthermore, keep in mind that places close and change ownership or management.

AN INVITATION TO READERS: In researching this book I have come across many wonderful establishments, the best of which I've included here. However, I being only one person and you readers being many, I'm sure that you'll run across other great hotels, inns, restaurants, shops, and attractions during your own travels in Japan and Hong Kong. Please don't keep them to yourself. Share them so that others might benefit from your experiences. You might also wish to comment on places I *have* covered in this book—especially if the place has changed for the worse. You can write to me, Beth Reiber, c/o Frommer Books, Gulf + Western Building, One Gulf + Western Plaza, New York, NY 10023. Thanks for your help!

THE $35-A-DAY TRAVEL CLUB—HOW TO SAVE MONEY ON ALL YOUR TRAVELS

In this book we'll be looking at how to get your money's worth in Japan and Hong Kong, but there is a "device" for saving money and determining value on *all* your trips. It's the popular, international $35-A-Day Travel Club, now in its 26th successful year of operation. The Club was formed at the urging of numerous readers of the $-A-Day and Dollarwise Guides, who felt that such an organization could provide continuing travel information and a sense of community to value-minded travelers in all parts of the world. And so it does!

In keeping with the budget concept, the annual membership fee is low and is immediately exceeded by the value of your benefits. Upon receipt of $18 (U.S. residents), or $20 U.S. by check drawn on a U.S. bank or via international postal money order in U.S. funds (Canadian, Mexican, and other foreign residents) to cover one year's membership, we will send all new members the following items.

(1) Any *two* of the following books

Please designate in your letter which two you wish to receive:

Frommer's $-A-Day Guides
   Europe on $30 a Day
   Australia on $25 a Day
   Eastern Europe on $25 a Day
   England on $40 a Day
   Greece (including Istanbul and Turkey's Aegean Coast) on $30 a Day
   Hawaii on $50 a Day
   India on $25 a Day
   Ireland on $30 a Day
   Israel on $30 & $35 a Day
   Mexico (plus Belize and Guatemala) on $20 a Day
   New York on $50 a Day
   New Zealand on $40 a Day
   Scandinavia on $50 a Day
   Scotland and Wales on $40 a Day
   South America on $30 a Day
   Spain and Morocco (plus the Canary Is.) on $40 a Day
   Turkey on $25 a Day
   Washington, D.C., & Historic Virginia on $40 a Day

Frommer's Dollarwise Guides
   Dollarwise Guide to Austria and Hungary
   Dollarwise Guide to Belgium, Holland, & Luxembourg
   Dollarwise Guide to Bermuda and The Bahamas
   Dollarwise Guide to Canada
   Dollarwise Guide to the Caribbean
   Dollarwise Guide to Egypt

Dollarwise Guide to England and Scotland
Dollarwise Guide to France
Dollarwise Guide to Germany
Dollarwise Guide to Italy
Dollarwise Guide to Japan and Hong Kong
Dollarwise Guide to Portugal, Madeira, and the Azores
Dollarwise Guide to the South Pacific
Dollarwise Guide to Switzerland and Liechtenstein
Dollarwise Guide to Alaska
Dollarwise Guide to California and Las Vegas
Dollarwise Guide to Florida
Dollarwise Guide to the Mid-Atlantic States
Dollarwise Guide to New England
Dollarwise Guide to New York State
Dollarwise Guide to the Northwest
Dollarwise Guide to Skiing USA—East
Dollarwise Guide to Skiing USA—West
Dollarwise Guide to the Southeast and New Orleans
Dollarwise Guide to the Southwest
Dollarwise Guide to Texas
(Dollarwise Guides discuss accommodations and facilities in all price ranges, with emphasis on the medium-priced.)

Frommer's Touring Guides
Egypt
Florence
London
Paris
Venice
(These new, color illustrated guides include walking tours, cultural and historic sites, and other vital travel information.)

Serious Shopper's Guides
Italy
London
Los Angeles
Paris
(Practical and comprehensive, each of these handsomely illustrated guides lists hundreds of stores, selling everything from antiques to wine, conveniently organized alphabetically by category.)

Arthur Frommer's New World of Travel
(From America's #1 travel expert, a sourcebook with the hottest news and latest trends that's guaranteed to change the way you travel—and save you hundreds of dollars. Jam-packed with alternative new modes of travel will lead you to vacations that cater to the mind, the spirit, and a sense of thrift.)

A Shopper's Guide to the Caribbean
(Two experienced Caribbean hands guide you through this shopper's paradise, offering witty insights and helpful tips on the wares and emporia of more than 25 islands.)

Beat the High Cost of Travel
(This practical guide details how to save money on absolutely all travel items—

accommodations, transportation, dining, sightseeing, shopping, taxes, and more. Includes special budget information for seniors, students, singles, and families.)

Bed & Breakfast—North America
(This guide contains a directory of over 150 organizations that offer bed & breakfast referrals and reservations throughout North America. The scenic attractions, and major schools and universities near the homes of each are also listed.)

Dollarwise Guide to Cruises
(This complete guide covers all the basics of cruising—ports of call, costs, fly-cruise package bargains, cabin selection booking, embarkation and debarkation and describes in detail over 60 or so ships cruising the waters of Alaska, the Caribbean, Mexico, Hawaii, Panama, Canada, and the United States.)

Dollarwise Guide to Skiing Europe
(Describes top ski resorts in Austria, France, Italy, and Switzerland. Illustrated with maps of each resort area plus full-color trail maps.)

Guide to Honeymoon Destinations
(A special guide for that most romantic trip of your life, with full details on planning and choosing the destination that will be just right in the U.S. [California, New England, Hawaii, Florida, New York, South Carolina, etc.], Canada, Mexico, and the Caribbean.)

Marilyn Wood's Wonderful Weekends
(This very selective guide covers the best mini-vacation destinations within a 175-mile radius of New York City. It describes special country inns and other accommodations, restaurants, picnic spots, sights, and activities—all the information needed for a two- or three-day stay.)

Motorist's Phrase Book
(A practical phrase book in French, German, and Spanish designed specifically for the English-speaking motorist touring abroad.)

Swap and Go—Home Exchanging Made Easy
(Two veteran home exchangers explain in detail all the money-saving benefits of a home exchange, and then describe precisely how to do it. Also includes information on home rentals and many tips on low-cost travel.)

The Candy Apple: New York for Kids
(A spirited guide to the wonders of the Big Apple by a savvy New York grandmother with a kid's-eye view to fun. Indispensable for visitors and residents alike.)

Travel Diary and Record Book
(A 96-page diary for personal travel notes plus a section for such vital data as passport and traveler's check numbers, itinerary, postcard list, special people and places to visit, and a reference section with temperature and conversion charts, and world maps with distance zones.)

Where to Stay USA
(By the Council on International Educational Exchange, this extraordinary

guide is the first to list accommodations in all 50 states that cost anywhere from $3 to $30 per night.)

(2) A one-year subscription to *The Wonderful World of Budget Travel*

This quarterly eight-page tabloid newspaper keeps you up to date on fast-breaking developments in low-cost travel in all parts of the world bringing you the latest money-saving information—the kind of information you'd have to pay $25 a year to obtain elsewhere. This consumer-conscious publication also features columns of special interest to readers: **Hospitality Exchange** (members all over the world who are willing to provide hospitality to other members as they pass through their home cities); **Share-a-Trip** (offers and requests from members for travel companions who can share costs and help avoid the burdensome single supplement); and **Readers Ask . . . Readers Reply** (travel questions from members to which other members reply with authentic firsthand information).

(3) A copy of *Arthur Frommer's Guide to New York*

This is a pocket-size guide to hotels, restaurants, nightspots, and sightseeing attractions in all price ranges throughout the New York area.

(4) Your personal membership card

Membership entitles you to purchase through the Club all Arthur Frommer publications for a third to a half off their regular retail prices during the term of your membership.

So why not join this hardy band of international budgeteers and participate in its exchange of travel information and hospitality? Simply send your name and address, together with your annual membership fee of $18 (U.S. residents) or $20 U.S. (Canadian, Mexican, and other foreign residents), by check drawn on a U.S. bank or via international postal money order in U.S. funds to: $35-A-Day Travel Club, Inc., Frommer Books, Gulf + Western Building, One Gulf + Western Plaza, New York, NY 10023. And please remember to specify which *two* of the books in section (1) above you wish to receive in your initial package of members' benefits. Or, if you prefer, use the last page of this book, simply checking off the two books you select and enclosing $18 or $20 in U.S. currency.

Once you are a member, there is no obligation to buy additional books. No books will be mailed to you without your specific order.

Chapter I

GETTING TO AND AROUND JAPAN

1. Getting There
2. Traveling Within Japan
3. Tips for the Traveler
4. The ABCs of Japan

A HOLIDAY IN JAPAN, for most readers of this book, must first begin with a trans-Pacific trip to Japan. That necessitates a brief examination of the available transportation.

1. Getting There

There is infrequent ferry service connecting ports in Japan with Shanghai, Nakhodka in Russia, Taiwan, and South Korea, but the overwhelming majority of visitors to Japan arrive by air. There are a number of airlines, including major U.S. carriers, that fly to Japan, but to get a headstart on your travel adventure it seems only appropriate to fly Japan's own Japan Air Lines (JAL). An introduction to Japanese culture begins as soon as you enter the plane and are greeted with a bow and a smile by the flight crew. After your craft leaves the ground you are given a hot, steaming towel called *oshibori* with which to refresh yourself, and your meal will include both Japanese and Western cuisine selections. Of course, everyone has heard about the legendary Japanese hospitality—and on JAL the flight attendants live up to the legend. They are gracious, efficient, and conscientious, a real plus when you're spending a dozen or so hours up in the air.

Japan Air Lines serves 60 cities in 34 countries on all continents, with particular emphasis on Japan, China, the Orient, and Europe. Gateways include New York, Atlanta, Chicago, Los Angeles, San Francisco, Seattle, Mexico City, Vancouver, Anchorage, Honolulu, Rio de Janeiro (served through Los Angeles), London, and Sydney. Almost all JAL international flights from North America and Europe arrive at the New Tokyo International Airport in Narita, about 41 miles from Tokyo's center. Another international gateway is Osaka, which is the most convenient gateway if you plan to go straight to either Osaka or Kyoto. The flying time to Tokyo is about 14 hours from New York or Chicago, 10 hours from Seattle, almost 11 hours from San Francisco, and about 11 hours 20 minutes from Los Angeles.

PLANE FARES: Japan Air Lines has a wide range of various fares available, from its exclusive first-class to APEX budget fares. Listed below are some of the options in fares to Japan from New York, Chicago, and the West Coast as of August 1987. Be sure to contact your travel agent or Japan Air Lines for an update in prices once you've decided on your exact travel plans. If you plan to include Hong Kong on your trip to the Orient—and I strongly urge that you do—you should purchase a ticket that will allow you a stopover in Japan on your way to Hong Kong. (All JAL flights operating between North America and Hong Kong make stopovers in Japan.) Consult the Hong Kong "Getting There" section for fares to Hong Kong from North America.

First Class
The royal treatment on JAL's first class begins as soon as you step up to the airport counter. After checking in at the special first-class check-in counter where your baggage is given doorside priority, you'll be given an invitation to use the Sakura Lounge, a special waiting area with free alcoholic drinks, coffee, and soda. On board the plane you'll have a comfortable, fully padded seat that will recline to a 60° angle, and you'll be offered a Japanese *happi* coat and slippers for in-flight wear. You'll be given champagne, a choice of five entrées of Western or Japanese cuisine, and fine wines and liqueurs. Free travel kits are passed out, and you'll be given electronic earphones for music and the in-flight movie. Round-trip fares to Tokyo are $3,982 from New York, $3,980 from Chicago, and $3,282 from Seattle, San Francisco, or Los Angeles.

JAL Executive Class
Traveling at the normal economy-class fare on JAL between North America and Japan automatically gives you seating in the airline's business executive class, a private, separate cabin with seats that recline 37°. In addition to your own special check-in counter at the airport, you'll receive complimentary champagne, cocktails, and wines, a choice of Western or Japanese cuisine, free use of electronic headphones, and a complimentary travel kit.

JAL's economy-class round-trip fares to Tokyo are $2,266 from New York, $2,264 from Chicago, and $1,684 from Seattle, Los Angeles, or San Francisco.

A Warning
Remember that all fares, rules, and regulations are subject to change. Be sure to contact your travel agent or JAL (tel. 800/525-3663) for current information.

APEX (Advance Purchase) Fares
One way to cut the cost of your flight to Japan is to purchase your ticket in advance and comply with certain restrictions. Reservations, ticketing, and payment for the APEX fare usually must be completed no later than 21 days prior to departure, but rules vary depending on the airline. There's a minimum time you can stay in Japan, usually one to two weeks; the maximum stay may be up to six months. Rates vary according to the season, with peak season rates applied June through October. Contact your travel agent for the latest fares and airlines.

Other Carriers
Other airlines with routes between Japan and the United States include **All Nippon Airways** (tel. 800/235-9262), **American Airlines** (tel. 800/433-7300), **China Airlines** (tel. 800/227-5118), **Delta Air Lines** (tel. 800/221-1212), **Korean**

Air (tel. 800/223-1155), **Northwest Orient** (tel. 800/225-2525), **Philippine Airlines** (tel. 800/435-9725), **Singapore Airlines** (tel. 800/742-3333), **Thai Airways International** (tel. 800/426-5204), and **United Airlines** (tel. 800/241-6522). Contact your travel agent or specific carrier for current information.

NARITA AIRPORT: Most likely you'll arrive at the New Tokyo International Airport in Narita. Once you've gone through Customs you'll exit through automatic doors into the arrival waiting lobby. The arrival lobby is divided into a south and a north wing, where you'll find counters for hotel reservations, limousine bus service into Tokyo, and the Keisei Skyliner train to Ueno Station. If you've purchased a Japan Rail Pass, you can turn in your voucher at the arrival lobby at the JR Information and Ticket Office, which is open from 7 a.m. to 11 p.m.

The **Tourist Information Office** is located in the south wing and is open from 9 a.m. to 8 p.m. (closed on Sunday, holidays, and Saturday afternoon). You can pick up a map here and ask for directions to your hotel or inn. If you need to change money, there is a counter located just after you clear Customs and *before* you enter the arrival lobby. If you forget to change money here, there are also counters in the arrival lobby and a bank in the departure lobby up on the fourth floor. Other facilities include a post office in the basement (open from 9 a.m. to 5 p.m. Monday through Friday, to 12:30 p.m. on Saturday), a post office on the fourth floor of the north wing (open from 9 a.m. to 8:30 p.m.), and a **KDD (Kokusai Denshin Denwa)** office on the fourth floor, where you can make an international call or send a telegram 24 hours a day.

Getting from Narita to Tokyo

Everyone grumbles about the Narita airport because it's so far away from Tokyo when compared to the airports of other capital cities. Obviously, jumping into a **taxi** and driving straight to your hotel is the easiest way to get to Tokyo, but it's also the most expensive—and may not even be the quickest if it's during rush hour. Expect to spend ¥22,000 ($157) or more for a taxi from the Narita airport for a ride that will take from one to two hours.

The most popular way to get from Narita to Tokyo is via the **Airport Limousine Bus.** Buses operate most frequently to the Tokyo City Air Terminal, and the trip takes about 70 minutes. Buses also go to more than a dozen of Tokyo's major hotels, but service is less frequent. Check with the staff at the Airport Limousine Bus counter to inquire as to which bus is most convenient to your hotel. If you take a bus to the Tokyo City Air Terminal there are plenty of taxis available that can deliver you to your final destination. Fares for the Limousine Bus range from ¥2,700 ($19.29) to ¥3,000 ($21.43), according to the distance.

There's another company that operates buses to more than 20 hotels in Tokyo, called **Airport Express**. Fares for this service begin at ¥2,800 ($20), and the counter is in the arrival lobby.

Another way to reach Tokyo is the privately owned **Keisei Skyliner** train. It's the way I always get to and from the Narita airport, but keep in mind that you have to make several transfers—which may not be practical if you have lots of baggage. There are porters available, however, who charge ¥200 ($1.43) per bag. At any rate, there's a Keisei Skyliner counter in the north and south wings of the arrival lobby. The fare from the Narita airport to Ueno Station in Tokyo is ¥1,800 ($12.86), and includes the cost of the shuttle bus that takes you from the airport to Narita Airport Station. The bus stop is located just outside the arrival doors. The bus ride takes only five minutes and the ride on the Skyliner train to

Ueno Station takes one hour. Trains depart approximately every 30 minutes between 7:52 a.m. and 10 p.m. At Ueno Station you can take either the subway or JR Yamanote Line to other parts of Tokyo (refer to "Getting Around" in Chapter III). There are also plenty of taxis available.

If you've bought a voucher for a Japan Rail Pass (described more fully in the "Traveling Within Japan" section that follows), you can exchange it for the **train** pass right in the arrival lobby at the JR Information and Ticket Office, which is open from 7 a.m. to 11 p.m. Then you can use your pass to get to Tokyo via a shuttle bus from outside the arrival lobby to Narita Station (it takes 25 minutes) and from there by train to Tokyo Station. You can also go by shuttle bus to Narita Airport Station and from there take a train to Ueno Station. The route you choose should depend on which hotel you're staying in. Keep in mind, however, that these routes are not as convenient or fast as the modes of transportation listed above, and should be used only if you want to economize.

If you don't have a rail pass, the fare is ¥870 ($6.21) from Narita Airport Station to Ueno Station. The trip takes 75 minutes on the limited express and 90 minutes on the express. From Narita Station (in the city of Narita) to Tokyo Station the limited express costs ¥2,700 ($19.29) and takes 63 minutes; the rapid train costs ¥1,160 ($8.29) and takes approximately 75 minutes.

HANEDA AIRPORT: If you're connecting to a domestic flight, more than likely you'll need to transfer to Haneda Airport. The Airport Limousine Bus makes runs between Narita and Haneda airports. The fare is ¥2,900 ($20.71), and the trip takes an hour or more depending on the traffic. If perchance you're arriving in Haneda Airport, you can also take the Airport Limousine Bus to Shinjuku and Akasaka. The locals, however, are more likely to take the monorail from Haneda Airport to Hamamatsucho Station on the Yamamote Line, for which the fare is ¥290 ($2.07). The trip takes only 15 minutes, and if you have a validated rail pass you can use it here.

OSAKA AIRPORT: Osaka Airport is convenient to Osaka and Kyoto. Taxis to hotels in Osaka average about ¥4,500 ($32.14) and are the most convenient way to get into the city. There's also frequent bus service from the airport to Osaka Station and to Shin-Osaka, which is the terminus for the Shinkansen bullet train (more about that later). The trip to Osaka Station takes about 30 minutes and costs ¥380 ($2.71), while the journey to Shin-Osaka takes 25 minutes and costs ¥290 ($2.07).

If you're going to Kyoto, there is frequent bus service from Osaka Airport directly to Kyoto Station and to major hotels. The trip takes from 60 to 90 minutes, depending on traffic and your destination, and fares average about ¥800 ($5.71).

2. Traveling Within Japan

BY TRAIN: The most convenient way to travel around Japan is by train. Whether you're being whisked through the countryside aboard the famous Shinkansen bullet train or are winding your way up a wooded mountainside in a two-car electric tram, trains in Japan are punctual, comfortable, dependable, and clean. And because train stations are usually located in the heart of the city next to the city bus terminal, arriving in a city by train is usually the most convenient way to begin your stay there. What's more, most train stations in Japan's major cities and resort areas have tourist offices that can help with directions to your hotel. The staff may not speak English, but they often have maps or brochures in English. Train stations also often have a counter where hotel reservations can be made. Most of Japan's trains are run by **Japan Railways (JR)**, which operates as many as 28,000 trains daily, including more than 500 Shinkansen bullet trains.

The **Shinkansen** is probably Japan's best-known train. With a front car that resembles a space rocket, the Shinkansen hurtles 140 miles per hour through the countryside on its own special tracks (new trains are being built now that will increase speeds up to 190 miles per hour).

There are three Shinkansen lines operating in Japan. The most widely used line for tourists is the **Tokaido–Sanyo Shinkansen**, which runs from Tokyo Station west to such cities as Nagoya, Kyoto, Osaka, Kobe, Himeji, Okayama, and Hiroshima before reaching its final destination of Hakata / Fukuoka, on the island of Kyushu. The **Tohoku Shinkansen** line runs from Ueno Station to Morioka in northern Japan, while the **Joetsu Shinkansen** connects Ueno with Niigata on the Japan Sea coast. There are two types of Shinkansen running along these tracks, one that stops only at the major cities and one that makes more stops and is therefore slightly slower. If your destination is a smaller city on the Shinkansen line, make sure the train you're on stops there. As a plus, telephone calls can be made to and from the bullet trains. To reach someone on a bullet train, you can call 107 from anywhere in Japan, providing you know the exact train; announcements are made only in Japanese.

In addition to the Shinkansen, there are also two long-distance trains which operate on regular tracks. The **limited express trains (Tokkyu)** are the fastest after the Shinkansen, while the **express trains (Kyuko)** are slightly slower and make more stops. To serve the everyday needs of Japan's commuting population, **local trains (Futsu)** stop at all stations and are the trains most widely used for side trips outside the major cities.

In addition to JR trains there are also some privately owned lines that operate from major cities to tourist destinations. No matter which train you ride be sure to hang on to your ticket—you'll be required to give it up at the end of your trip as you exit through the gate.

As for finding out the various **train schedules**, the Tourist Information Center in Tokyo has a *Condensed Railway Timetable* that gives details in English for the Shinkansen and some other major lines. If you plan to do a lot of traveling by train, however, I recommend that you purchase *JTB's Mini-Timetable (Speedo Jikokuhyo)* for ¥300 ($2.14) published monthly and available at bookstores or Japan Travel Bureau offices in big cities. It covers the schedules in both English and Japanese for all JR long-distance trains, including the Shinkansen, and for private trains, planes, ferries, and even express buses. It also has maps of Japan with various destinations served by trains written in both Japanese and English. I find this handy little guide invaluable during my trips through Japan.

Train Reservations

You can reserve a seat in advance for Shinkansen, limited express, and express trains at any major JR station for a small fee. The larger stations have special reservation counters or offices that are easily recognizable by their green signs with "Reservation Tickets" written on them. They're open daily from 10 a.m. to 6 p.m. If there is no special reservation office at the JR station, you can reserve your seat at one of the regular ticket windows. I recommend that you reserve your seats for your entire trip through Japan as soon as you know your itinerary if you'll be traveling during peak times. However, all trains have nonreserved cars as well that work on a first-come, first-served basis.

Japan Rail Pass

The Japan Rail Pass is without a doubt the most convenient and most economical way to travel throughout Japan by train. With the rail pass you don't

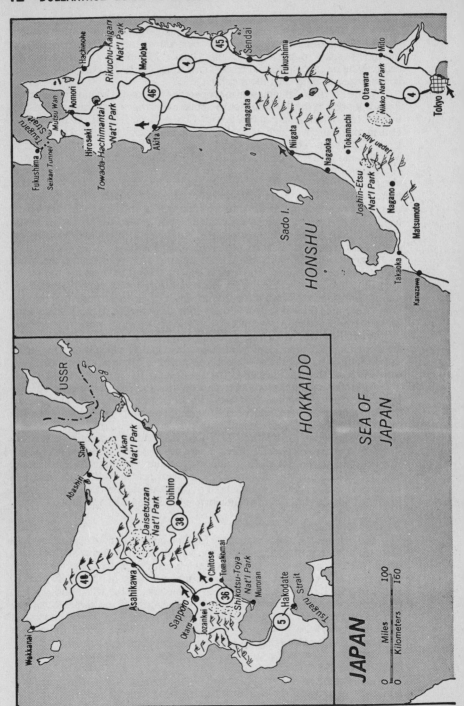

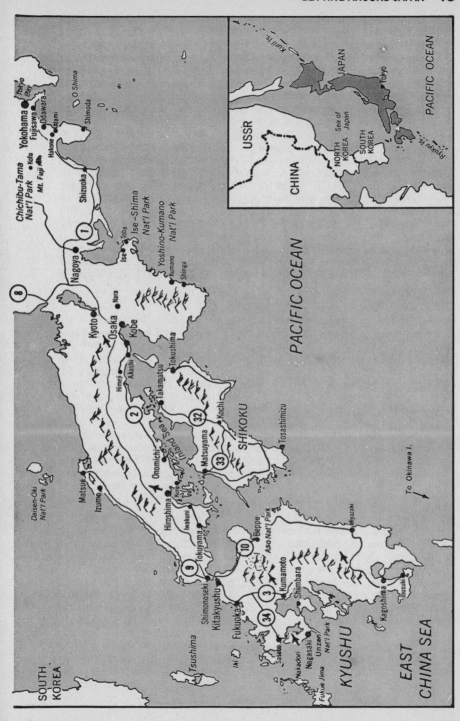

have to hassle with buying individual tickets, and you can reserve all your seats on all JR trains for free. The rail pass entitles you to unlimited travel on all JR train lines, including the Shinkansen, and on JR buses and ferries.

The Japan Rail Pass is available only to foreigners visiting Japan on a tourist or transit visa, and can be purchased only outside Japan. *You cannot buy a rail pass once you're in Japan.* You can purchase the pass from an authorized travel agent or from Japan Air Lines. You'll be issued a voucher which you then exchange for the pass itself after you've arrived in Japan. This can be done at the JR Information and Ticket Office at the Narita airport or at any of the 12 JR Travel Service Centers in Japan, including Tokyo Station and JR stations in Osaka, Kyoto, Hiroshima, and Sapporo.

There are two types of Japan Rail Passes available—for ordinary coach class or for the first-class Green Car—and you can purchase passes good for one, two, or three weeks. Rates for the ordinary pass as of September 1987 are ¥27,000 ($193) for 7 days, ¥43,000 ($307) for 14 days, and ¥55,000 ($393) for 21 days. Rates for the Green Car are ¥37,000 ($264) for 7 days, ¥60,000 ($429) for 14 days, and ¥78,000 ($557) for 21 days. And how much can you save by purchasing a rail pass? Quite a bit if you plan to do even just a little traveling. If you were to buy a round-trip ticket on the Shinkansen from Tokyo to Kyoto, for example, it would cost you ¥24,000 ($171), which is almost as much as a week's ordinary rail pass. If you plan to see more than just Tokyo and Kyoto, it pays to use a rail pass.

JAL Room & Rail

If the idea of a rail pass appeals to you and you'd like to make life even simpler by paying for your hotels in advance, **Japan Air Lines' Room & Rail package** may be the thing for you. Offered only to passengers of Japan Air Lines, this do-it-yourself package combines the Japan Rail Pass described above with hotel coupons good for more than 80 hotels in more than 50 cities in Japan. These hotel coupons are valid for one or two weeks. The coupons for seven nights cost approximately ¥42,500 ($304) per person for a twin room and ¥49,500 ($354) for a single. The 14-night coupons cost ¥85,000 ($607) per person for a twin room and ¥99,000 ($707) for a single.

You can combine the rail pass and hotel coupons in any combination you wish. For example, if you want to spend your time leisurely you might want to purchase a one-week rail pass and combine it with two weeks of hotel coupons.

Hotel coupons can be purchased only in conjunction with the rail pass, and *the whole package must be purchased outside Japan* at least one week prior to your first night's stay in Japan. Contact your travel agent or JAL for more details.

BY AIR: Because it takes the better part of a day and night to get from Tokyo down to southern Kyushu or up to northern Hokkaido, you may find it more convenient to fly at least one stretch of your journey in Japan. You may, for example, take a leisurely two weeks to travel by train from Tokyo through Honshu and Kyushu, and then fly back to Tokyo from Kagoshima. I don't advise flying for shorter distances—say, from Tokyo to Osaka—because of the time spent getting to and from airports. By the way, departures on domestic flights from Tokyo leave from the much more conveniently located Haneda Airport, reached by monorail from Hamamatsucho Station on the Yamanote Line.

Two major domestic airlines are **Japan Air Lines** and **All Nippon Airways (ANA)**, with networks that stretch all the way from Okinawa to northern Hokkaido. ANA carries more than half of all domestic passengers in Japan and flies to 30 cities throughout the country, including Tokyo, Sapporo, Fukuoka, Hakodate, Takamatsu, Nagasaki, Kagoshima, and Osaka.

Although it's subject to change, the cost of flying from Tokyo to Sapporo in Hokkaido runs about ¥25,500 ($182) one way, while the flight from Tokyo to Kagoshima is about ¥31,500 ($225). It's cheaper, however, if you plan ahead and purchase your domestic flight in conjunction with your international flight to Japan. Contact your travel agent.

BY BUS: Buses often run where trains don't—and may be the only way to get to the more remote areas of Japan. Buses are used extensively, for example, in Hokkaido, and the only way to get to Shirakawa in the Japan Alps is by bus. Although the procedure may vary, there's generally a ticket machine by the entry door of the bus. Take a ticket, which is number-coded with a board displayed at the front of the bus. The board shows the various fares, which increase with the distance traveled. You pay your fare upon departure.

In addition to serving the remote areas of the country, buses also operate between major cities in Japan. There is, for example, a special bus that leaves Tokyo Station every night for Nagoya (¥6,600, or $47), Kyoto (¥8,500, or $61), and Osaka (¥9,000, or $64), arriving the next morning. Similarly, there's also a night bus from Osaka, Kyoto, and Nagoya to Tokyo. If you're on a budget, this is certainly the cheapest way to travel between Tokyo and Kyoto.

BY BOAT: Because Japan is an island nation, it has an extensive ferry network linking the string of islands. Although it takes longer to travel by ferry, it's also cheaper. You can, for example, take the ferry from Tokyo all the way to Hokkaido for ¥12,500 ($89). There are also many ferries plying the waters of the Seto Inland Sea. From Osaka you can take a ferry in late evening and arrive in Beppu on Kyushu the next morning for ¥6,200 ($44). Contact the Tourist Information Office for more details concerning ferries, prices, and schedules.

BY CAR: With the exception of perhaps the Izu Peninsula and Hokkaido, driving is not recommended as a means for touring Japan. For one thing, signs are invariably in Japanese only, and cars are driven British style, on the left side of the road. (The government is slowly replacing Japanese signs with bilingual Japanese / English ones on major highways, but the process won't be completed until the turn of the decade.) In cities, streets are often hardly wide enough for a rickshaw let alone a car. Many roads do not have sidewalks, so you have to dodge people, streetlamps, and telephone poles. But that's not all—it's not even economical to drive in Japan. All Japan's expressways charge high tolls. The one-way toll from Tokyo to Kyoto, for example, is almost the same as the price of a ticket to Kyoto on the Shinkansen. But whereas the Shinkansen takes only three hours to get to Kyoto, driving takes about eight. So unless there are four of you to split the costs and you are not limited by time, it doesn't make sense to drive.

Rates vary, but the average cost for 24 hours with unlimited mileage (but not including gasoline) ranges from ¥8,500 ($61) for a subcompact to ¥17,000 ($121) for a standard-size car. Both **Hertz** and **Avis** can accept reservations for their affiliated car-rental companies in Japan.

Note: If you intend to drive in Japan, you'll need either an international or a Japanese driving license.

3. Tips for the Traveler

PLANNING YOUR ITINERARY: If you want to see everything Honshu, Hokkaido, Kyushu, and Shikoku have to offer, plan on spending at least a year traveling about. Barring that, it's obvious you'll have to be selective in planning your itinerary. Decide beforehand what your priorities are.

If you're interested in feudal castles, you'll find them in Osaka, Nagoya, Matsue, Matsumoto, Himeji, Kumamoto, Okayama, Hiroshima, and Matsuyama. Japan's most famous gardens are Kenrokuen Garden in Kanazawa, Korakuen Garden in Okayama, and Kairakuen in Mito. Other beautiful gardens are Ritsurin in Takamatsu on the island of Shikoku, and Suizenji in Kumamoto and Iso Garden in Kagoshima, both on the island of Kyushu. Japan's most famous rock garden is probably the one at Ryoanji Temple in Kyoto.

If you're a camera buff, my own personal list of picturesque towns and villages in Japan includes Kyoto, Kamakura, Takayama, Shirakawa-go, Kurashiki, Mount Koya, and the tiny village of Chiran, south of Kagoshima. As for towns with historical significance, nothing can beat Kyoto, Nara, or Kamakura, three ancient capitals of Japan. These three towns are also where you'll find a majority of the country's temples and shrines. Other important Shinto shrines in Japan include the Meiji Shrine in Tokyo, Ise Jingu Shrines located in Ise-Shima National Park, and Itsukushima Shrine on Miyajima Island. Mount Koya is the place to head if you're interested in spending the night in a genuine Buddhist temple.

And last but not least, Japan is blessed with a number of hot-spring spas, from its southern to northern tips. In fact, tourism in Japan began when bathing enthusiasts started traveling to hot springs simply for the joys of the bath. There are open-air spas in forests, sand baths, gigantic public baths, mud baths, sulphur baths, and just plain hot tubs. The closest hot springs to Tokyo are in Hakone and Izu Peninsula. Other famous hot springs include Matsuyama's Dogo Spa on Shikoku Island; Beppu, Ibusuki, and Unzen on Kyushu; and Noboribetsu, Toyako Spa, Sounkyo, and Akanko Onsen in Hokkaido.

One- and Two-Week Itineraries

If you have only one week in Japan—what can I say, I feel sorry for you. I suppose if I were faced with such a limited amount of time, I would spend it this way:

Day 1: Most likely you'll arrive in Narita airport, from which it's about a two-hour trip to your hotel in Tokyo. Spend the first day recuperating from your flight, settling in, and getting a feel for the city. Top off the day with a meal in a traditional restaurant.

Day 2: Because of the difference in time zones, most visitors from the Western Hemisphere find themselves wide awake in the wee hours of the morning. That's the perfect time to get up and head for Tsukiji Fish Market, the largest wholesale fish market in Japan. After a breakfast of fresh sushi at the market, take the Hibiya Line to Ueno, where you'll find the Tokyo National Museum. From Ueno hop on the Ginza Line for Asakusa and its famous Nakamise Dori lane, with shops selling traditional products and the popular Sensoji Temple. If you have time, take a stroll down Ginza's fashionable shopping district or head for Harajuku for its inexpensive clothing boutiques and Oriental Bazaar, one of the best places to shop for Japanese souvenirs. Spend the evening in Shinjuku, Roppongi, or another one of Tokyo's famous nightlife areas.

Day 3: Take the three-hour Shinkansen bullet train to Kyoto early in the morning. Spend the afternoon on a self-guided walk from Kiyomizu Temple to Heian Shrine and the Silver Pavilion, followed by shopping at the Kyoto Handicraft Center. Spend the night in one of Kyoto's many traditional Japanese-style inns.

Day 4: Take in Nijo Castle, Ryoanji Temple, the Golden Pavilion, and a few other sights of your choosing. If you want to see more temples in one of

Japan's ancient capitals, head for Nara, where you'll want to spend at least two to three hours to see the Great Buddha, Nara Park, and Kasuga Shrine.

Day 5: From Kyoto there are several destinations good for a one-night trip, but you should leave Kyoto very early in the morning. If you want to spend the night in a Buddhist temple atop Japan's most sacred mountain, take the Kintetsu Railways private line (there are only a couple of departures daily, so plan ahead) to Kintetsu Namba Station, in Osaka, transferring there to the Nankai Koya Line for the two-hour trip to Mount Koya. If you'd rather spend the night in a quaint, picturesque town with some museums, board the Shinkansen for Kurashiki—less than two hours away, although along the way it's worth your while to make a two-hour stopover in Himeji, where you'll find Himeji Castle, considered by many to be the most beautiful feudal castle in Japan. And finally, if all you want to do is relax at a hot-spring resort, take the Shinkansen back towards Tokyo to Odawara, where you should transfer to a local train bound for Hakone.

Day 6: Spend the day sightseeing, departing by late afternoon for Tokyo. If your plane leaves early the next morning, you may wish to spend the night at Narita.

Day 7: Departure.

If you have two weeks, I would expand the above schedule as follows:

Day 1: Arrival in Narita, settling into your hotel, and becoming acclimated to Tokyo.

Day 2: Same as in the one-week itinerary.

Day 3: If you'd like to spend another day in Tokyo, refer to the Tokyo chapter. If you'd rather make an excursion to one of the sites outside Tokyo, foremost on the list are day trips to either Kamakura, with its many temples, or Nikko, which is famous for the colorful mausoleum of Shogun Ieyasu Tokugawa.

Day 4: Tokyo to Takayama. Early in the morning take the Shinkansen to Nagoya (about two hours), from which it's a three-hour train ride to Takayama, in the Japan Alps. Take time to explore the picturesque, narrow streets of this old castle town.

Day 5: Takayama to Shirakawa-go. Before departing Takayama, be sure tovisit the morning market by the river. Take the 2½-hour bus ride along a winding mountain road to Shirakawa-go, a tiny village of rice paddies and thatched farmhouses. Spend the night in one of these farmhouses.

Day 6: Shirakawa-go to Kyoto. Since Shirakawa-go is rather remote, it takes the better part of a day to reach Kyoto. Luckily, the scenery is magnificent. From Shirakawa-go you can take a bus either back to Takayama or to Nagoya. In any case, you must afterwards transfer to a train for the rest of the journey to Kyoto.

Days 7 and 8: Same as one-week itinerary above, except save Nara for the next day.

Day 9: Kyoto to Mount Koya: Early in the morning, set out for Nara, visiting the Great Buddha, Nara Park, and Kasuga Shrine. From Nara you can take the Kintetsu Railways private line (departing from Nara Kintetsu Station) to Kintetsu Namba Station in Osaka, transferring there to the Nankai Koya Line bound for Mount Koya. If you have a rail pass, you can take JR trains to Hashimoto, there transferring to the private Nankai Koya Line. Spend the night on Mount Koya, one of Japan's most sacred Buddhist retreats, in a Buddhist temple.

Day 10: Mount Koya to Kurashiki. After paying your respects at Okunoin, the burial grounds of Kobo Daishi, return to Osaka and transfer to the Shinkansen bullet train at Shin-Osaka Station or a JR train at Osaka Station.

bound for Kurashiki. It's worth your while to make a two-hour stopover in Himeji along the way to see the beautiful Himeji Castle. Spend the night in one of Kurashiki's varied accommodations and take an evening stroll along the canal.

Day 11: Take in Kurashiki's sights, including its many museums. Leave for Hiroshima late in the day (about an hour away by Shinkansen).

Day 12: Hiroshima to Beppu: Spend the morning at Peace Memorial Park, with its museum and statues erected in memory of those who lost their lives when an atomic bomb was dropped over Hiroshima on August 6, 1945. In the afternoon take an excursion to the tiny island of Miyajima, with its famous Itsukushima Shrine. Take the overnight ferry from Hiroshima to Beppu.

Day 13: Spend a relaxing day in the hot-spring resort of Beppu, where you can visit the huge baths of Suginoi Palace or take a sand bath at Takegawara Bathhouse. Visit the Hells, boiling ponds created by volcanic activity.

Day 14: Beppu to Tokyo. Take an early morning flight from nearby Oita (¥27,000, or $193) airport to Haneda Airport in Tokyo, transferring to Narita Airport for the flight home.

Needless to say, this is something of a whirlwind trip, but it allows you to take in some of the best that Honshu island has to offer. If you want to get off the beaten track or have more time, refer to the chapters on Shikoku, Kyushu, and northern Japan for more ideas in planning your itinerary.

THE LANGUAGE BARRIER: Without a doubt the hardest part of traveling in Japan is the language barrier. Suddenly you find yourself transported to a crowded land of 120 million people where you can neither speak nor read the language. To make matters worse, few Japanese speak English, and outside the major cities the signs are usually only in Japanese. Menus, signs at train stations, and shop names are often only in Japanese.

However, millions of foreign visitors before you who didn't speak a word of Japanese have traveled throughout Japan on their own with great success. In fact, I've talked to foreign tourists who told me they thought it was actually quite easy getting around in Japan. Much of the anxiety travelers have in other countries is eliminated in Japan because the country is so safe and the people are so kind and helpful to foreigners. In addition, the Japan National Tourist Organization (JNTO) does a super job of publishing brochures, leaflets, and maps on various aspects of Japan.

A NOTE ON JAPANESE CHARACTERS: Many hotels, restaurants, and other establishments in Japan do not have signs showing their names in English letters. Appendix II lists the Japanese symbols for all such places appearing in this guide. Each establishment name in Japanese symbols is numbered, and the same number appears in brackets in the text following the boldfaced establishment name. For example, in the text the Osaka hotel, Hokke Club [161], is number 161 in the Japanese symbol list in Appendix II.

If you need to ask directions of a stranger in Japan, your best bet is to ask younger people. They have all studied English in school and are most likely to be able to help you. Japanese businessmen also often know some English. And as strange as it sounds, if you're having problems communicating with someone, write it down so they can read it. The emphasis in schools tends to be written rather than oral, with the result that Japanese who can't understand a word you say may know all the subtleties of syntax and English grammar. If you still have problems communicating you can always call the Travel-Phone, a toll-free nationwide helpline set up by JNTO to help foreigners in distress or in need of information. (Information on the Travel-Phone is given in the following section, "The ABCs of Japan.")

If you're heading out for a particular restaurant, shop, or sight, it helps to have your destination written out in Japanese. Have someone at your hotel do that for you. If you get lost along the way, look for a police box. Called a *koban,* these are spread throughout neighborhoods virtually everywhere in Japan. They have maps of the district and can pinpoint exactly where you want to go if you have the address with you. Remember too that train stations in major cities and tourist resort areas have tourist information offices *(kanko annaisho),* which can help you with everything from directions to hotel reservations. The staff may not speak any English, but I don't think you'll have trouble communicating your needs.

For specific words and phrases in Japanese, refer to Appendix I at the back of this book. In addition, *The Tourist's Handbook,* distributed free by JNTO, lists phrases in both English and Japanese for situations that may arise, from eating at a restaurant to staying in a Japanese inn.

WHAT TO BRING: A friend and I once spent the better part of an hour trying to list items travelers may need that they wouldn't be able to find in Japan. We finally gave up. With the exception of perhaps some medicines, we decided that virtually everything is available in Japan—the problem lies in choosing the brand. Even bleach to make your hair blond is available in this nation of black-haired people. It doesn't make sense, therefore, to pack king-size supplies of toothpaste, shampoo, and other daily necessities. If you run out of something, you'll have no problem finding it in Japan.

One item you should absolutely bring with you is a pair of good walking shoes. Shoe sizes in Japan are much smaller than in the West and chances are you won't be able to find Japanese shoes that fit. Keep in mind, too, that because you have to remove your shoes to enter Japanese homes, inns, shrines, and temples, you should bring a pair that's easy to slip on and off. And since you may be walking around in stockinged feet, save yourself embarrassment by packing socks and hose without holes.

As for traveling around Japan, you'll want to have a folding umbrella. It's also good to carry a supply of pocket tissues since most public rest rooms don't have toilet paper. You can pick up pocket tissues at newspaper stands near and in train stations. In the summer when the weather is hot and humid you'll see women walking around with wet cotton handkerchiefs that they use to wipe their faces. Try it; it helps keep you cooler.

Although most hotels and Japanese-style inns provide guests with towels, soap, washcloths, toothbrushes and toothpaste, and a cotton kimono called a *yukata,* some of the budget-priced inns do not. If you're traveling on a budget, therefore, carry these items with you. Many hotels and inns also provide a Thermos of hot water or a water heater as well as some tea bags. If you're a coffee addict, you can save money by buying instant coffee and drinking your morning cup in your hotel room.

And at the risk of sounding perverse, I also recommend traveling with your own portable cassette player and headphones. Buy one once you get to Japan—they're inexpensive, and they may help preserve your sanity. Many of the buses traveling scenic routes (and tourist boats as well) run continuous commentaries in Japanese at a pitch so high it drives me crazy. I'd much rather look at the scenery to the accompaniment of my own choice of noise. And if you're staying in a budget accommodation, chances are there won't be a radio, but only a TV with programs in Japanese. You can buy all kinds of attachments for portable cassette players, including tiny speakers and even a cord with outlets for two headphones so that both you and your companion can listen to the music.

Although it might seem superfluous to say this, pack lightly. Struggling through crowded train stations with big bags is no fun, and stations often consist of multitudes of stairways and overhead and underground passageways. In addition, trains in Japan do not have large overhead racks.

While traveling you'll probably pick up souvenirs, gifts, and other items. I deal with this problem of accumulation by mailing boxes home to myself every two weeks or so while I'm on the road. All international post offices in Japan sell three sizes of cardboard boxes that come with everything you need for mailing packages abroad, which makes sending packages a snap. I simply show up with my bag, empty it of all unneeded items, buy a box, and leave the post office feeling pounds lighter. And, believe me, traveling with a lighter bag is almost like getting a new lease on life.

POSTCARDS: Unless you have a photographic memory and can remember places, names, and how to spell them, chances are all those snapshots of temples, shrines, and gardens will look distressingly alike once you get your film developed. My mother's solution: buy postcards of every place you visit. That way you can match snapshots with postcards, many of which may have such useful information as name, location, and correct spelling of the object in question. And if your pictures don't turn out, well, you always have those postcards.

DATES TO AVOID: The Japanese have a passion for travel, and generally they all travel at the same time. Trains and hotels are jam-packed at these times. Refer to the section in Chapter II on festivals and annual events for dates you should avoid. The worst times of year are the New Year's period, from December 28 to January 4, the so-called Golden Week, from April 29 to May 5, and the Obon Festival time, in mid-August—avoid traveling at all costs on these dates.

CUTTING EXPENSES: During your first few days in Japan—particularly if you're in Tokyo—money will seem to flow out of your pockets like water. In fact, money has a tendency to disappear so quickly that many people become convinced they must have *lost* some of it somehow. At this point almost everyone panics (I've seen it happen again and again), but then slowly comes the realization that values are different here and that all it takes is a bit of readjustment in thinking and habits. Coffee, for example, is somewhat of a luxury, and some Japanese are astonished at the thought of drinking four or five cups a day. By following the advice here, you'll be able to cut down on needless expenses, saving your money for those splurges that are really worth it.

If you're on a budget, avoid eating breakfast at your hotel. Coffeeshops offer what is called "morning service" until about 10 a.m., which generally consists of a cup of coffee, a small salad, a boiled egg, and toast for about ¥400 ($2.86). That's a real bargain when you consider the fact that just one cup of coffee usually costs ¥300 ($2.14) to ¥500 ($3.57). If you're addicted to coffee in the morning, you can save money by purchasing instant coffee and drinking it in your hotel room. Many hotels and inns in Japan provide a Thermos of hot water or a water heater. Since jars of instant coffee tend to be heavy and bulky, you might want to buy individual packets of coffee, which come complete with powdered cream and sugar and are available at all large grocery stores. Called "coffee sticks," popular brands are Astoria and UCC.

Eat your biggest meal at lunch. Many restaurants offer a daily set lunch, called *teishoku,* at a fraction of what their set dinners might be. Usually ranging in price from ¥700 ($5) to ¥1,500 ($10.71), they're generally available from 11 or 11:30 a.m. to 2 p.m. A Japanese teishoku will often include the main course (such as tempura, grilled fish, or the specialty of the house), soup, pickled vegetables, rice, and tea, while the set menu in a Western-style restaurant usually consists of an entrée, salad, bread, and coffee. Places to look for inexpensive restaurants include department stores (often one whole floor will be devoted to various kinds of restaurants), underground shopping arcades, around train and subway stations, and in nightlife districts. Some of the cheapest establishments for a night out on the town are the countless *yakitori-ya* across the nation, which are drinking locales that also sell skewered meats and vegetables.

And if you really want to save money, you can avoid restaurants altogether. Japan is one of the most accomplished countries in the world when it comes to the preparation, packaging, and selling of pre-prepared foods. The *obento,* or box lunch, is a complete meal usually costing between ¥500 ($3.57) and ¥1,000 ($7.14) and commonly sold on express trains, at train stations, and in tiny neighborhood shops throughout Japan. In the basements of department stores are counters after counters of pre-prepared foods, including grilled meats, salads, sushi, and desserts. More information on inexpensive meals is given in the food section in Chapter II.

Another way to cut costs is to cut short your time spent in Tokyo. Accommodations in Kyushu, for example, are much more reasonably priced than they are in the capital. Your best bet is to stay in a *minshuku,* a private home that offers rooms—usually Japanese style—to tourists. These average ¥5,000 ($35.71) to ¥6,000 ($42.86) per person and include both breakfast and dinner. And as for your travels in Japan, avoid taxis when possible and purchase a Japan Rail Pass if you plan on covering long distances.

ORGANIZED CITY TOURS: With the exception of Tokyo and Kyoto, few city tours are conducted in English. This book is designed for the individual traveler who prefers sightseeing on his or her own, but if you're pressed for time or don't want to deal with public transportation to sights that may be spread throughout a city, consider joining a Japanese tour. It's certainly the easiest way to get to the various attractions, and perhaps there will even be a Japanese along who won't mind providing some translations.

TOURIST BROCHURES: The Tourist Information Centers in Tokyo and Kyoto have a number of leaflets available on destinations throughout Japan, along with information on train, bus, and ferry schedules. Unfortunately such leaflets are almost never available at the destination itself, so you must pick them up at the T.I.C. *before* leaving Tokyo or Kyoto. Below is a partial list of leaflets available:

Sapporo and Vicinity	*Nagoya and Vicinity*
Southern Hokkaido	*Ise-Shima*
Morioka and Rikuchu Kaigan	*Tokyo, Walking Tour Courses*
(Coast) National Park	*Kyoto, Walking Tour Courses*
Sendai and Matsushima	*Nara, Walking Tour Courses*
Nikko and Mashiko	*Okayama and Kurashiki*
Narita	*Matsue and Izumo-Taisha*
Hakone and Kamakura	*Hiroshima and Miyajima*

Mt. Fuji and Fuji Lakes	*Fukuoka*
Izu Peninsula	*Beppu, Mt. Aso, and*
Matsumoto and Kamikochi	*Kumamoto*
Kanazawa and the Noto	*Nagasaki and Unzen*
Peninsula	*Miyazaki, Kagoshima, and*
Takayama and Vicinity	*Ibusuki*
The Inland Sea and Shikoku	*Kobe, Himeji, and Takarazuka*

4. The ABCs of Japan

Arriving in Japan for the first time can be rather overwhelming, primarily because of the language barrier. For one thing, assuming that you don't know any Japanese you won't be able to read any of the signs, which means that in the beginning you won't be able to tell the difference between even a post office and a bank, much less read the hours and days of the week they're open. In addition, because few Japanese speak fluent English, if you make what's intended to be a quick and casual telephone inquiry it's likely to turn into moments of pure frustration. In other words, finding information in Japan is sometimes a true test of ingenuity. To make your stay in Japan as problem-free as possible, this section is designed to answer some questions you might have before and during your trip with regard to such items as visa requirements, whether you should tip, business hours, and electric voltage of the country. For information pertaining to a particular city, be sure to check under the individual chapter headings. The Tokyo ABCs section, for example, tells you where the main post office is, the address of the American Express office, and where in Tokyo you can buy books in English.

Remember also that much information can be gleaned from the staff of your hotel. Many of the larger first-class hotels even have guest relations officers who are there to answer any questions tourists may have. Finally, if you don't know where else to turn, the **Japan National Tourist Organization** has set up a tourist telephone helpline with English-speaking staff members who can help you with everyday problems you may encounter. I've used this telephone service for such diverse problems as how to find the Tokyo office of the Hong Kong Tourist Association, where to go for a visa extension, and the date and the time of the next sumo match. You can call them if you're bewilderingly lost, are having communication problems with a store clerk or hotelier, or simply want information about sightseeing. Look under the heading "Travel-Phone."

CURRENCY NOTE: The prices quoted in this book were figured at ¥140=US$1. However, due to fluctuations in the exchange rate of the yen (it was ¥126 to the dollar at presstime and there were indications that it might rise further), the U.S. dollar equivalents given might vary during the lifetime of this edition. Be sure to check current exchange rates when planning your trip.

BANKS AND EXCHANGES: Banks are open from 9 a.m. to 3 p.m. on weekdays and from 9 a.m. to noon on Saturday. They're closed on the second and third Saturday of each month, and on Sunday. If you need to exchange money outside these hours, inquire at one of the larger first-class hotels—some of them will cash traveler's checks or exchange money even if you're not their guest. If you're arriving at the Narita airport outside Tokyo, you can exchange money there from 9 a.m. until the arrival of the last flight.

BUSINESS HOURS: Government offices and private companies are generally open from about 9 a.m. to 5 p.m. Monday through Friday, and many are open on Saturday morning as well. In reality, however, Japanese businessmen in the private sector tend to work long hours and it's not unusual to find someone in the office as late as 7, 8, or even 10 p.m. To be on the safe side, however, it's best to conduct business before 5 p.m.

CIGARETTES: A wide variety of both domestic and imported brands are readily available throughout Japan. There are even outdoor vending machines on what seems to be every major city street in Japan. There isn't a major campaign against smoking as there is in the United States, with the result that there are few no-smoking sectors in restaurants or public places. The cost for Japanese brands, of which Mild Seven is among the most popular, is about ¥220 ($1.57) per pack, while imported brands, such as Marlboro, cost about ¥280 ($2).

CLIMATE: Most of Japan's islands lie in a temperate seasonal wind zone similar to the East Coast of the United States, which means that there are four distinct seasons. **Summer**, which begins in June, is heralded by the rainy season, which lasts from about mid-June to mid-July. Although it doesn't rain every day, it does rain a lot and umbrellas are imperative. As you walk through all those puddles, remember that this is when Japan's farmers are out planting their rice seedlings. After the rains stop it turns very hot (in the 80s) and humid throughout the country, with the exception of the northern island of Hokkaido, such mountaintop resorts as Hakone, and the Japan Alps.

The end of August and September is typhoon season, though most storms stay out at sea and generally vent their fury on land only in thunderstorms. **Autumn**, which lasts until about November, is one of the best times to travel in Japan. The days are pleasant and slightly cool, with the changing reds and scarlets of leaves giving brilliant contrast to deep-blue skies. A photographer I know says that autumn is the best season for landscape photography in Japan.

Lasting from about December to March, **winter** is marked by snow in much of Japan, especially in the mountain ranges, where the skiing is superb. The climate is generally dry, and on the Pacific coast the skies are often blue. Tokyo, where the mean temperature is about 40°F, doesn't get much snow.

Spring is brought in with a magnificent fanfare of plum and cherry blossoms in March and April, an exquisite time when all Japan is set ablaze in whites and pinks. The cherry blossom season starts in southern Kyushu toward the end of March and travels slowly northward until it reaches northern Japan in about mid-April. The blossoms themselves last only a few days, symbolizing to the Japanese the fragile nature of beauty and life itself.

Remember that because Japan's four main islands stretch from north to south at about the same latitudes as Boston and Atlanta, you can travel in Japan virtually any time of the year. Winters in southern Kyushu are mild and pleasant, while summers in Hokkaido in the north are cool. In addition there is no rainy season in Hokkaido.

CLOTHING SIZES: Talking in stereotypes, the Japanese are generally of slighter build than most Westerners, with sizes to match. If you're a basketball player, of large build, or simply have big feet, you're going to be tormented by all the wonderful, well-made, and often bargain-priced merchandise you can't fit into. Be sure to pack accordingly.

CREDIT CARDS AND CHECKS: Major hotels, tourist shops, and well-known restaurants generally accept such credit cards as American Express, MasterCard, or VISA. The majority of Japan's smaller shops, however, do not. Traveler's checks can be exchanged for yen at banks, but personal checks are virtually useless in Japan. Even if you have an account at a Japanese bank, it costs about $20 and takes a couple of weeks to process a personal check. Most Japanese pay with cash—and because the country has such a low crime rate, you can feel safe walking around with lots of money. When I worked as editor of a travel magazine in Tokyo, I was paid in cash; I often left the office for a night on the town with a whole month's salary in my purse and never once was I afraid I would be mugged, and I certainly wasn't the only one. Because the Japanese feel so safe in their own society and carry lots of cash with them, sadly enough they're often easy targets when they travel abroad. The only time you should be alert to possible pickpockets is when you're riding a crowded subway during rush hour.

CURRENCY: The currency in Japan is called the yen, symbolized by ¥. Coins come in ¥1, ¥5, ¥10, ¥50, ¥100, and ¥500. Bills come in ¥1,000, ¥5,000, and ¥10,000 denominations. Although the conversion rate varies daily, the prices in this book are based on ¥140 to $1. In your own rough calculations, therefore, you can generally approximate what things cost by figuring roughly $7 to every ¥1,000. If something costs ¥5,000, for example, you know it's around $35.

CUSTOMS: You can bring duty-free into Japan up to 200 non-Japanese cigarettes or 250 grams of tobacco or 50 cigars; three bottles (760 cc each) of alcoholic beverages; and two ounces of perfume. In addition to the items above you can also bring in gifts and souvenirs whose total market value is less than ¥200,000 ($1,429).

A word of catuion: Make sure you do not take any pornographic material with you; American magazines such as *Playboy, Penthouse,* and others are not allowed into Japan because it's prohibited to show pubic hair. The Japanese equivalent of these magazines are either much more modest or have the offensive parts blacked out. As for drugs, don't even think about it. A number of musicians, including Paul McCartney, have been busted at the Narita airport and are prohibited from returning to Japan. Penalties for offenders are severe and strict.

Upon returning to the United States, you're allowed to bring back free of duty $400 worth of goods purchased abroad. Beyond that the next $1,000 worth of goods is assessed at 10% duty. If you're shipping purchases home by mail, you're allowed to send up to $50 per package duty-free.

READER'S CUSTOMS SUGGESTION: "I would highly recommend that fellow tourists keep a traveler's diary, especially regarding their purchases. When handed the customs slip en route to Honolulu, it was hard to remember all the things I bought and the dollar value of each. Travelers should keep all their papers—passports, customs slip, and reciepts—together, and if possible, all the purchases in one bag. It would help for a smoother exit from customs" (Sharon Nakata, Los Angeles, Calif.).

DOCUMENTS FOR ENTRY: In addition to a valid passport, Americans and Australians must obtain a tourist visa at a Japanese embassy or consulate before entry to Japan. The two completed visa application forms must be accompanied by a valid passport, a passport-size photo, and evidence of a ticket to and from Japan. The visa is issued free of charge. Canadians do not need visas for stays up to 90 days, while citizens of the United Kingdom can stay up to 180 days without a visa.

If you want to extend your tourist visa, you can do so at the nearest immigration bureau in Japan. U.S. citizens can apply for another three months and the charge is ¥4,000 ($28.57) In Tokyo the place to go is the **Tokyo Regional Immigration Bureau**, 1-3-1 Otemachi, Chiyoda-ku (tel. 03/213-8111). The nearest station is Otemachi. Hours are 9 a.m. to 5 p.m. (closed from noon to 1 p.m. for lunch) and from 9 a.m. to noon on Saturday. After you've extended your visa you must also apply for an alien registration card, which all foreigners must carry if they stay in Japan longer than three months. Apply at the ward office closest to your hotel. The registration card is free but you'll need two passport-size photos.

If you intend to drive in Japan, you'll need either an international or a Japanese driver's license.

DRINKING WATER: The water is safe to drink anywhere in Japan, though some people claim it's too highly chlorinated. Bottled water is also readily available.

ELECTRICAL APPLIANCES: The electrical current throughout Japan is 100 volts A.C., but there are two different cycles in use. In Tokyo and to the northeast it's 50 cycles, while in Nagoya, Kyoto, Osaka, and all points to the southwest it's 60. Leading hotels in Tokyo often have two outlets, for 110 and 220 volts; many of them also have hair dryers that you can use for free. Actually you can use many American appliances such as radios or hair dryers in Japan because the American current of 110 volts and 60 cycles is close enough that the only difference is that they'll run a little slower than back in the States. For sensitive equipment, either have it adjusted or try to see whether it can run on batteries.

EMBASSIES: Embassies for most countries are located in Tokyo, and are generally open from 8:30 or 9 a.m. to about 5 or 5:30 p.m. Monday through Friday. Most of them close for an hour or so for lunch, and the visa or passport sections are open only at certain times during the day. It's best to call in advance. The **American Embassy and Consulate** is located at 1-10-5 Akasaka, Minato-ku (tel. 03/583-7141), close to Toranomon subway station. The **Canadian Embassy** is at 7-3-38 Akasaka, Minato-ku (tel. 03/408-2101), near Aoyama-Itchome subway station; the **British Embassy and Consulate**, 1 Ichibancho, Chiyoda-ku (tel. 03/265-5511), is close to Ichigaya, Kojimachi, and Hanzomon stations; and the **Australian Embassy**, at 2-1-14 Mita, Minato-ku (tel. 03/453-0251), is closest to either Mita or Shiba-Koen station.

EMERGENCIES: The national emergency numbers are 110 for police and 119 for both **ambulances** and **fire** reports. Be sure to speak slowly and precisely.

FILM AND CAMERAS: Probably no one is surprised to hear that Japan is one of the best countries to be in if you're nuts about photographic equipment. Check the Tokyo shopping section in Chapter IV to find out where to shop. As for film, you won't have trouble finding Kodak or the Japanese brand Fuji in major cities for most types of film. Outside the big cities, however, and especially around tourist attractions, it's sometimes difficult to find anything other than Fuji film for color prints. If you prefer taking slides, be sure to stock up before setting out for more remote areas. You'll probably want to wait until you return to Tokyo or home to process Kodak film. Shops outside Tokyo send Kodak film to the capital city for developing, which can take as long as a week.

GAS: Gas stations are found readily along Japan's major highways. As of this writing, the average cost for regular gasoline is about $3.43 per gallon.

HIKING: Day hiking and backpacking are popular summer recreation sports in Japan, particularly in the Japan Alps and in Hokkaido, where there are cabins in which hikers can stay overnight. Another popular trek is up to the summit of Mount Fuji, covered later in this book. Check with the Tourist Information Center about details for different parts of the country.

HITCHHIKING: Hitchhiking is not common in Japan; in fact, foreigners who have hitchhiked in Japan tell me that some drivers stop simply because they're curious as to what the foreigners could possibly want. But even though hitchhiking is uncommon, Japan is probably one of the safest and easiest countries in the world for hitchhiking. Stories abound of how drivers have gone hours out of their way to deposit passengers at their destination.

HOLIDAYS: National holidays are January 1 (New Year's Day); January 15 (Adults' Day); February 11 (National Foundation Day); March 20 or 21 (Vernal Equinox Day); April 29 (Emperor's Birthday); May 3 (Constitution Memorial Day); May 5 (Children's Day); September 15 (Respect-for-the-Aged Day); September 23 or 24 (Autumn Equinox Day); October 10 (Health and Sports Day); November 3 (Culture Day); November 23 (Labor Thanksgiving Day). When a national holiday falls on a Sunday, the following Monday becomes a holiday.

Although government offices and some businesses will be closed on public holidays, restaurants and most stores remain open. The exception is during the New Year's celebration from January 1 to 3, when almost all restaurants, public and private offices, and stores close up shop; during that time you'll have to dine in hotels. Keep in mind that the New Year season is peak travel time for the Japanese, who all seem to make a mass exodus for their respective hometowns. Another peak travel time is so-called Golden Week, at the end of April and beginning of May, when there are three public holidays in a row. And finally, from about August 10 to 18 is Obon, a time when many Japanese will return to their hometowns to pay respects to their ancestors. Trains, ferries, and hotels are often fully booked during these three peak times, so be sure to plan far in advance.

As for regional peak travel times, be sure to check the section on festivals and annual events in the next chapter for dates when particular cities might be crowded due to festivals. Some festivals are so popular that you must book a hotel room at least six months in advance.

HONG KONG TOURIST ASSOCIATION: If you plan to go to Hong Kong from Japan, you might want to stop off at the Hong Kong Tourist Association, on the fourth floor of the Toho Twin Tower Building, 1-5-2 Yurakucho (tel. 03/503-0731), close to Hibiya subway station in Tokyo. Although its main function is to provide the Japanese with information on Hong Kong, it does have some publications in English and can answer questions you might have.

LAUNDRY: All the upper-bracket hotels and even some of the hotels for businessmen have laundry service. Since this tends to be expensive, you may want to wash your clothes yourself. Not everyone has a washing machine in Japan, so laundromats are abundant. The cost is about ¥150 ($1.07) to ¥200 ($1.43) per load for the washer; dryers are about ¥100 (71¢) for 30 minutes.

Some of the inexpensive Japanese inns described in this book that cater largely to young travelers also have coin laundry machines on their premises.

MAIL DELIVERY: Citizens of Canada, the United Kingdom, and Australia can have their mail forwarded to them at their respective embassies in Japan. The American Embassy, however, told me that they stopped such a policy in the 1970s and will no longer hold mail. If you don't know where you'll be staying, you can always have your mail sent to the central post office of the major cities you'll be visiting. In Tokyo, have your mail sent c/o *Poste Restante,* Central Post Office, Tokyo, Japan, which is located just southwest of Tokyo Station.

METRIC MEASURES: Japan uses the metric system.

Weights

U.S.		Japan
1 ounce	=	28.3 grams
1 pound	=	454 grams
2.2 pounds	=	1 kilo (1,000 grams)
1 pint	=	0.47 liter
1 quart	=	0.94 liter
1 gallon	=	3.78 liters

Measures

U.S.		Japan
1 inch	=	2.54 centimeters
1 foot	=	0.3 meters
1 yard	=	0.91 meters
1.09 yards	=	1 meter
1 mile	=	1.61 kilometers
0.62 mile	=	1 kilometer
1 acre	=	0.40 hectare
2.47 acres	=	1 hectare

Before the metric system came into use in Japan, the country had its own standards for measuring length and weight. There's no reason for you to learn these nowadays, but you will hear one way of measuring that is still common— rooms in Japan are still measured by the number of tatami straw mats that will fit in them. A six-tatami room, for example, is the size of six tatami mats. A tatami is roughly three feet wide and six feet long.

NEWSPAPERS AND PERIODICALS: Four English-language newspapers are published daily in Japan. They're the *Japan Times,* the *Mainichi Daily News,* the *Daily Yomiuri,* and the *Asahi Evening News.* Hotels and major bookstores also carry the international edition of such news magazines as *Time* and *Newsweek.* For regional publications detailing what's going on in a city, check with the local tourist information office listed in the individual city chapters.

PASSPORT: Foreigners are required to carry with them *at all times* either their passport or their alien registration card. The police generally do not stop foreigners, but if you're caught without the proper identification you'll be taken to the local police headquarters. It happened to me once and, believe me, I can think of better ways to spend an hour and a half. I had to explain in detail who I was, what I was doing in Japan, where I lived, and what I planned on doing the rest of my life. I then had to write a statement explaining how it was that I rushed out that day without my passport, apologizing and promising never to do such a thoughtless thing again. The policemen at the station were very nice and polite —they were simply doing their duty.

POLITICS: Japan has both an emperor, who acts as head of state, and a prime minister, who is head of the government. The constitution, which was adopted in 1947, stipulates that the supreme power of the country resides with the people, who vote for members of the National Diet, the legislative body in Japan. The constitution also renounces war, which is at least one reason why the Japanese have been reluctant to build up their own military since World War II.

POSTAL SERVICE: Although all post offices are open from 9 a.m. to 5 p.m. on weekdays and 9 a.m. to 12:30 p.m. on Saturday (the smaller ones are closed the second and third Saturday of the month), international post offices are open much later, often until 7 or 8 p.m. It's only at international post offices that you can mail packages abroad, and these are often found close to the city's main train station. Keep in mind also that these branches sell cardboard boxes in three sizes that come with the necessary tape and string, which is certainly much easier than going out and buying all that stuff. Packages mailed abroad cannot weigh more than ten kilograms.

If you're mailing a letter, your hotel may be able to do it for you or direct you to the nearest post office. Airmail letters up to 10 grams cost ¥130 (93¢) to North America and ¥150 ($1.07) to Europe. Postcards are ¥90 (64¢) and ¥100 (71¢) respectively. Domestic letters up to 25 grams are ¥60 (43¢); postcards are ¥40 (29¢).

Post offices are easily recognizable by the red symbol of a capital "T" with a horizontal line above it.

RADIO AND TELEVISION: If you enjoy watching television you've come to the wrong country. Almost nothing is broadcast in English—even foreign films are dubbed in Japanese and the only way to hear them in English is if you have what's called a bilingual television. A few of the best hotels in Tokyo and other major cities do have bilingual televisions, and there are generally one to three English movies on television each week. Major hotels in Tokyo, Osaka, and Kyoto also have cable TV with English-language programs, including CNN broadcasts from America. But even if you don't understand the language I suggest that you watch television in Japan at least once. Maybe you'll catch a samurai series, which is very popular. Commercials are also worth watching—often they're what I call "mood" advertising in which the scenery simply sets a mood that has very little to do with the actual product.

As for radio, the Far East Network (FEN, 810 kHz) is the U.S. military station, with broadcasts of music, talk shows, sports broadcasts from the U.S., and Tokyo sumo matches. Upper-bracket hotels in Tokyo also have KTYO, a cable radio station broadcasting music, news, and sports around the clock.

REST ROOMS: If you're in need of a rest room your best bet is at train and subway stations, big hotels, and department stores. Many toilets in Japan, especially those at train stations, are Japanese-style. They're holes in the ground over which you squat facing the end that has a raised hood. Men stand and aim for the hole. Although Japanese lavatories may seem uncomfortable at first, they're actually much more sanitary because none of your body touches anything. Who knows, you may even come to prefer it over Western-style toilets. To find out if a stall is empty, knock on the door. If it's occupied someone will knock back. Similarly, if you're inside a stall and someone knocks, answer with a knock back or else they'll just keep on knocking persistently and try to get in.

Don't be surprised if you go into a rest room and find men's urinals and individual private stalls in the same room. Women are supposed to simply walk right past the urinals without giving them notice.

SAFETY: Japan is one of the safest countries in the world. Although crime is slowly on the increase, it's still negligible compared with that in the United States. Although it doesn't hurt to exercise caution, you'll notice shortly after arrival that the country is safe and the people are honest. Those are two of Japan's best attributes.

SHOP HOURS: Most stores in Japan don't open until 10 a.m. and they close about 8 p.m. Often they're closed one day a week, and it's not unusual for almost all the shops in a particular neighborhood to be closed on the same day. Some shops, especially those around major train stations and entertainment areas, stay open until 10 p.m. Some convenience stores are open 24 hours.

Department stores are open from 10 a.m. to 6 or 7 p.m. They close one day a week, but it's different for each store so you can always find one that's open, even on Sundays.

SHOPPING: It probably won't take you long to figure out that the number-one hobby in Japan is shopping. Stores both mammoth and miniature are everywhere, offering everything you can and can't imagine. Traditional Japanese crafts and souvenirs that make good buys include woodblock prints *(ukiyoe)*, products made of Japanese paper *(washi)*, such as umbrellas, lanterns, boxes, wallets and stationery, toys and kites, bamboo window blinds, Japanese dolls, carp banners, swords, lacquerware, ceramics, fans, masks, knives and scissors, sake, and silk and cotton kimonos. Japan is also famous for its workmanship in electronic products, including cameras, stereo and video equipment, computers and typewriters. However, because of the present exchange rate, you can probably find these products just as cheaply in the United States. If you think you want to shop for electronic products, therefore, it pays to do some comparison shopping before you leave home so that you know what the prices are.

SKIING: With about 75% of Japan's land space consisting of mountains, you can bet that skiing is the country's most popular winter sport. The skiing is so good here that Hokkaido, Japan's big northern island, was selected as the site of the 1972 Winter Olympics. With the ski season generally lasting from about mid-December to early April, keep in mind that the slopes can be very crowded during weekends and holidays, especially those close to a large city. Also, although shops where you can rent skis, boots, and poles for about ¥4,500 ($32) to ¥5,500 ($39) a day are plentiful, most shops don't have shoes larger than about size 9 in men's. Day passes for ski lifts generally average about ¥3,000 ($21) to ¥3,300 ($24). For more information, the Tourist Information Centers in both Tokyo and Kyoto have a pamphlet called *Skiing in Japan,* which gives information about ski resorts in northern and central Japan. There are also a number of skiing areas within easy access to Tokyo and Sapporo. A great plus of many of Japan's ski resorts is that they're situated around hot springs—what could be better than soaking in a hot tub after a day out on the slopes?

TAXES AND SERVICE CHARGE: If you stay overnight at lodgings that cost more than ¥5,000 ($36) per person per night, a 10% tax will be added to your bill after ¥2,500 ($18) is deducted per person for each night that you stay. Thus, if you stay one night in a single room for ¥6,500 ($46.43) per night, your tax will be 10% of ¥4,000, which is ¥400 ($2.86). In restaurants, a 10% tax will be added to your bill if your meal costs more than ¥2,500 ($17.86) per person.

In addition to tax, a 10% to 15% service charge will be added to your bill in lieu of tipping at most of the fancier restaurants and at many hotels. Thus, the 25% in tax and service charge that will be added to your bill in the more expensive locales can really add up. Most *ryokan,* or Japanese-style inns, and many of the businessmen's hotels and cheaper inns include tax and service charge in their rates. If you're not sure, ask.

As for shopping, Japan does not have a sales tax, but for some luxury goods a commodity tax is incorporated into the retail price tag. Nonresidents are exempt from this tax if they buy the goods at an authorized tax-free shop and present their passport. The best buys are cameras and electronic goods; check the Tokyo shopping section in Chapter IV.

If you depart Japan from the Narita airport outside Tokyo, you will be charged a ¥2,000 ($14.29) service facility fee (there is no departure tax at any of the other international airports in Japan).

TELEGRAMS: Your hotel may be able to handle telegrams. If not, you can send a telegram from a **KDD (Kokusai Denshin Denwa)** office. Ask the hotel clerk where the office nearest your hotel is. If you need to send a telegram in the middle of the night, the Tokyo KDD office at 1-8-1 Otemachi (tel. 03/211-5588) is open 24 hours a day. In Osaka, a KDD office open day and night is at 1-25 Bingo-machi, Higashi-ku (tel. 06/228-2151). Both offices can handle facsimiles and phototelegrams, and have booths for ISD calls and Telex. The cost of sending a telegram to the United States is ¥118 (84¢) per word.

TELEPHONES: If you're staying in a medium- or upper-range hotel, most likely you can make an **international call** from your room. Alternatives are to go to a KDD office or purchase a disposable telephone credit card and use it in one of the international green telephones (described below). If you want to make a collect call or call through an operator, dial 0051. An operator-assisted, station-to-station call to the United States costs ¥1,890 ($13.50) for the first three minutes.

Cheaper are calls made without the assistance of an operator, either through an international public telephone or telephones that offer direct dialing service (most first-class and some medium-priced hotels now offer direct dialing). The direct dial number for calls to the United States is 001 + 1 + area code + telephone number. These cost ¥500 ($3.57) for the first minute in a call to the United States and ¥370 ($2.64) for each minute after that. Between 11 p.m. and 4 a.m. Japan time, international direct calls are only ¥300 ($2.14) for the first minute to the United States. Rates are also cheaper on Sunday.

As for **local and domestic phone calls,** there are a number of different telephones, all color coded. You can find these telephones virtually everywhere—on stands in front of little shops, on train station platforms, in restaurants and coffeeshops. There are even telephones in Japan's bullet trains. The red, pink, and blue phones take only ¥10 coins, while the yellow and green ones take both ¥10 and ¥100 coins. A local call costs ¥10 (7¢) for three minutes, and after that a warning chime will come on to tell you to insert more coins or else you'll be disconnected. I usually insert two or three coins when I make a phone call so that I don't have to worry about being disconnected—coins that aren't used are always returned at the end of the call. If you don't want to deal with coins, you can purchase a disposable telephone credit card that can be inserted into a slot on many of the newer green telephones. These can be bought at telephone offices and at some station kiosks for values of ¥500 ($3.57) to ¥5,000 ($35.71). If the green telephone is equipped to handle international calls, there will be a sign that reads "International & Domestic Card/Coin Telephone." Note that not all green telephones that accept credit cards are capable of international calls.

Area codes for all of Japan's cities begin with a zero. Tokyo's area code, for example, is 03, while Osaka's is 06. For other area codes, check the "Orientation" section in each city. Use the area code only when dialing from outside the area.

TIME: Japan is 9 hours ahead of Greenwich Mean Time, 14 hours ahead of New York, 15 hours ahead of Chicago, and 17 hours ahead of Los Angeles. Since Japan does not go on Daylight Savings Time, subtract one hour from the above times if you're calling the United States in the summer. Because Japan is on the other side of the International Dateline, you lose one day when traveling from the United States to Asia. Returning to North America, however, you gain a day, which means that you arrive on the same day you left. In fact, it often happens that you arrive in the States at an earlier hour than you departed Japan.

TIPPING: One of the delights of being in Japan is that there is *no* tipping, not even to waitresses, taxi drivers, or bellboys. If you try to tip them they'll probably be confused or embarrassed. Instead of individual tipping a 10% to 15% service charge will be added to your bill at the higher-priced hotels and restaurants.

TOURIST INFORMATION: Nearly all of Japan's cities and towns have tourist offices, most of them located at or near the main train station. Although the staff does not always speak English and they may not have maps in English, they can point you in the right direction to your hotel, and in many cases even make bookings for you. Your best bet for information is at the **Tourist Information Centers (T.I.C.)** in Tokyo, Kyoto, and the Narita airport. They have literature and information not only on their own cities but on the rest of Japan as well. Before setting out on your travels, be sure to pick up any pamphlets or maps they may have on the areas you want to visit; in most cases these pamphlets are not available outside Tokyo or Kyoto. For more information on tourist information centers, see the individual listings for each city.

Overseas, you'll find the **Japan National Tourist Organization** offices at 630 Fifth Ave., New York, NY 10111 (tel. 212/757-5640); at 333 N. Michigan Ave., Chicago, IL 60601 (tel. 312/332-3975); at 1519 Main St., Suite 200, Dallas, TX 75201 (tel. 214/741-4931); at 360 Post St., Suite 401, San Francisco, CA 94108 (tel. 415/989-7140); and at 624 S. Grand Ave., Los Angeles, CA 90017 (tel. 213/623-1952). Other offices are at 165 University Ave., Toronto, ON M5H 3B8, Canada (tel. 416/366-7140); 167 Regent St., London, W.1, England (tel. 01/734-9638); and 115 Pitt St., Sydney, N.S.W. 2000, Australia (tel. 02/232-4522).

TRAVEL-PHONE: If you're having problems communicating with someone in Japan, are lost, or need information, the Japan National Tourist Organization operates a nationwide toll-free system that provides service every day throughout the year from 9 a.m. to 5 p.m. If you're outside Tokyo or Kyoto, all you have to do is insert a ¥10 coin into a yellow, blue, or green phone (the coin will be returned to you at the end of the call) and dial one of two numbers. If you want to know something about eastern Japan (Tokyo, Yokohama, Matsumoto, Hokkaido, etc.), dial 0120-222800. If you have any questions that pertain to western Japan (Nagoya, Kanazawa, Kyoto, western Honshu, Shikoku, and Kyushu) dial 0120-444800. Toll-free calls can be made only if you're outside Tokyo or Kyoto. If you're in Tokyo, the number to dial is 502-1461; in Kyoto it's 371-5649. In these two cities you have to pay for the call, which is ¥10 (7¢) per three minutes.

VACCINATIONS: You don't need any inoculations for entry into Japan.

Chapter II

AN INTRODUCTION TO JAPAN

1. Geography
2. History
3. The People
4. The Language
5. Meeting the Japanese
6. Japanese Etiquette and Manners
7. A Word About Japanese Inns
8. Other Types of Accommodation
9. Food and Drink
10. Religion, Shrines, and Temples
11. Festivals and Annual Events
12. Cultural Activities
13. Recommended Reading

BEING INFORMED ABOUT JAPAN, its history, people, and culture, will greatly enhance your trip. This chapter should serve only as an introduction to the wealth of information available. At the end of the chapter is a recommended reading list for books on Japan.

1. Geography

Separated from mainland China and Korea by the Sea of Japan, the nation of Japan stretches in a sliver of an arc about 1,860 miles long from northeast to southwest. Only 250 miles wide at its widest point, Japan consists primarily of four main islands—Honshu, Hokkaido, Kyushu, and Shikoku—which account for 97% of its 145,000 square miles. Surrounding these four islands are more than 3,000 islands and islets, most of them tiny and uninhabited, as well as a group of islands much farther to the south known collectively as the Okinawan islands, perhaps best-known because of the fierce fighting that took place there during World War II. If you were to superimpose Japan's four main islands onto a map of the United States, they would stretch all the way from Maine down to northern Florida, which should give you at least some idea of the diversity of Japan's climate, flora, and scenery.

Of the four main islands, **Honshu** is the largest, has always been the most important both historically and culturally, and is where most visitors to Japan spend the bulk of their time. Honshu is the home of the ancient capitals of Nara, Kyoto, and Kamakura, as well as such bustling metropolises as Osaka, Nagoya, Hiroshima, and the modern capital of Japan, Tokyo. **Hokkaido**, the next largest island, lies to the north of Honshu and is regarded as Japan's last frontier, with its wide-open pastures, wildlife, and national parks of mountains, woods, and lakes. The southernmost of the four main islands is **Kyushu**, with a mild subtropical climate, active volcanoes, and hot-spring spas. Because it's the closest to Korea and China, Kyushu served as a gateway to the continental mainland throughout much of Japan's history, later becoming the springboard for both traders and Christian missionaries from the West. **Shikoku**, the smallest of the four islands, remains fairly undeveloped and is famous for its 88 Buddhist temples founded by one of Japan's most interesting historical figures, the Buddhist priest Kukai, known posthumously as Kobo Daishi.

As much as 75% of Japan consists of mountains, most of them volcanic in origin. Altogether there are some 265 volcanoes in Japan, more than 30 of them still considered active. Mount Fuji, now dormant, is Japan's most famous volcano, while Mount Aso on the island of Kyushu is the largest volcano in the world. Because of its volcanic origins, Japan throughout the centuries has been plagued by earthquakes (the last huge earthquake struck in 1923). Today Japan's buildings are constructed to withstand the shakes, quakes, and tremors that used to leave towns and villages in ruins.

At any rate, even though Japan is only slightly smaller in size than California, it has more than half the population of the United States. And because three-fourths of the nation is mountainous and therefore uninhabitable, Japan's people are concentrated primarily in what amounts to only 10% of the country's land mass, with the rest of the land devoted to agriculture. Thus, as an island nation physically isolated from the rest of the world, struck repeatedly through the centuries by earthquakes, fires, and typhoons, and with only limited space for harmonious living, Japan's geography and topography have played major roles in the country's development and in shaping its culture, customs, and the arts.

2. History

ANCIENT HISTORY (ca. 30,000 B.C. to A.D. 710): According to Japanese mythology, the history of Japan began when the sun goddess, Amaterasu, sent one of her descendants down to the island of Kyushu to unify Japan. This unification was realized a few generations later when Jimmu, an offspring of this descendant, succeeded in bringing all of Japan under his rule. It's at this point that legend fuses with fact, for in the fourth century there was a family known as Yamato who did indeed succeed in expanding its kingdom and unifying Japan. At the core of this unification was the Japanese belief in Shintoism, a religion indigenous to Japan which worships nature and ancestors, and which believes in the divinity of the emperor. At any rate, considered to be descended from the gods, Jimmu became Japan's first emperor and his descendants have continued to occupy the throne ever since. Japan's imperial family is the longest-running imperial family in the world.

Of course, the real history of Japan begins before the emperor came to the throne. Although the exact origin of the Japanese people is unknown, we know that Japan was once connected to the Asian mainland by a land bridge and that the territory was occupied as early as 30,000 B.C. From about 10,000 to 300

B.C., hunters and gatherers called the Jomon people were thriving in small communities primarily in central Honshu. They are best known for their hand-formed pottery decorated with cord patterns. The Jomon Period was followed by the Yayoi Period, marked by metalworking, the pottery wheel, and the mastering of irrigated rice cultivation, a period that lasted until about A.D. 300. It was after this that the Yamato family succeeded in unifying the state for the first time. Yamato became the ancient name of Japan, which began turning its cultural feelers toward its great neighbor to the west, China.

In the sixth century, Buddhism, which originated in India, was brought to Japan via China and Korea. This was the beginning of many cultural and scholarly ideas imported from China, including Chinese characters for writing, art, and architecture. Although the Japanese subsequently adapted the Chinese form of art and architecture, and even Buddhism, into its own cultural mold, the influence that China had on early Japan cannot be overstated. In 604 the Prince Regent Shotoku, greatly influenced by the teachings of Buddhism and Confucianism, drafted a document calling for political reforms and a constitutional government. By 607 he was sending multitudes of Japanese scholars to China to study Buddhism. Under Shotoku's guidance a number of Buddhist temples were built, the most famous of which was Horyuji Temple near Nara, said today to be the oldest existing wooden structure in the world.

THE NARA PERIOD (A.D. 710–794): Before the 700s, the site of Japan's capital changed every time a new emperor came to the throne. In 710, however, a permanent capital was established in Nara. Although it remained the capital only 74 years, seven successive emperors ruled from Nara and the period was graced with the expansion of Buddhism and a flourishing of temple construction throughout the country. Buddhism also inspired the arts, including sculpture, metalcasting, painting, and lacquerware. It was during this time that the huge bronze statue of Buddha was cast and erected in Nara. Known as the Daibutsu, this huge statue remains Nara's biggest attraction.

THE HEIAN PERIOD (A.D. 794–1192): In 784 the capital was moved from Nara to Nagaoka. Ten years later it was moved once again to Heiankyo (present-day Kyoto), where it remained until Tokyo was made the new capital in 1868. Following the example of cities in China, Kyoto was laid out in a grid pattern with broad roads and canals.

The Heian Period, which lasted from 794 until 1192, was a peaceful time in Japanese history, and in fact "Heiankyo" means "capital of peace and tranquillity." It was a glorious time, a time of luxury and prosperity, during which court life reached new heights in artistic pursuits. The Chinese alphabet was blended with a new Japanese writing system, allowing for the first time the flowering of Japanese literature and poems. The life of the times was captured in the works of two women: Sei-Shonagon, who wrote a collection of essays known as the *Pillow Book,* and Murasaki-Shikibu, who wrote the world's first novel, *The Tale of Genji.*

Because the nobles were completely engrossed in their own luxurious lifestyles, however, they failed to notice the growth of military clans in the provinces. The two most powerful warrior clans were the Taira and the Minamoto, who fought fierce civil wars that tore the nation apart until finally a young warrior named Yoritomo Minamoto triumphed and established supremacy.

THE KAMAKURA PERIOD (A.D. 1192–1333): Wishing to set up rule far away from Kyoto, Yoritomo Minamoto established his capital in a remote and easily defendable fishing village called Kamakura, not far from today's Tokyo. He created a military government, ushering in a new era in Japan's history in which the power of the country passed from the aristocratic court into the hands of the warrior class. In becoming the nation's first *shogun,* or military dictator, Yoritomo laid the groundwork for military governments in Japan, which lasted for some 700 years, until the imperial court was restored in 1868.

The Kamakura Period is perhaps best known for the unrivaled ascendancy of the warrior caste, known as the *samurai.* Ruled by a rigid code of honor, the samurai were bound in loyalty to their feudal lord, and as the centuries wore on they became the only caste allowed to carry weapons. They were supposed to give up their lives for their lord without hesitation, and if they failed in their duty they could gain back their honor by committing ritualistic suicide, known as *seppuku.* Spurning the soft life led by the noble court in Kyoto, the samurai embraced a harsher and simpler set of ideals marked by a spartan lifestyle. When Zen Buddhism with its tenets of mental and physical discipline was introduced to Japan from China in the 1190s, it appealed greatly to the samurai class.

In 1274 Mongolian forces under Kublai Khan attempted to invade Japan. They failed but returned in 1281 with an even larger fleet. Luck was on Japan's side, however, when a typhoon blew in and destroyed the whole fleet. Regarding it as a gift from the gods, the Japanese called it *kamikaze,* meaning "divine wind," a term that took on a different significance at the end of World War II when Japanese pilots flew suicide missions in an attempt to turn the tide of war. More important, however, is the fact that until American occupation forces entered Japan at the end of World War II, Japan was never once invaded or occupied by a foreign nation.

THE MUROMACHI AND AZUCHI-MOMOYAMA PERIODS (A.D. 1336–1603):
After the fall of the Kamakura shogunate, a new feudal government was set up at Muromachi in Kyoto. The next 200 years, however, were marred by bloody civil wars and confusion as *daimyo* (feudal lords) staked out their fiefdoms throughout the land. Similar to the barons of Europe, the daimyo owned tracts of land with complete rule over the people who lived on them. To help serve him each lord had his retainers, the samurai, who helped in waging war against his enemies.

But even though these centuries were characterized by strife, they also saw a blossoming of art and culture. Kyoto witnessed the construction of the extravagant Golden and Silver Pavilions as well as the artistic arrangements of the famous rock garden at Ryoanji Temple. Noh drama, the tea ceremony, flower arranging, and landscape gardening became the passions of the upper class. The end of the 16th century also saw a flurry of castles built across the land, both as a show of a daimyo's strength and might as well as a defense against the firearms that had been introduced in Japan around 1543.

In the second half of the 16th century, a brilliant military strategist by the name of Nobunaga Oda almost succeeded in ending the civil wars by unifying Japan. Before he could succeed, however, in 1582 he was assassinated by one of his own retainers. His campaign was taken up by one of his best generals, Hideyoshi Toyotomi, who had been born a peasant instead of a samurai but who had risen up in the ranks of Nobunaga's army. Hideyoshi built a magnificent castle in Osaka, crushed all rebellion, and was finally able to unify Japan before he died in 1598.

THE EDO PERIOD (A.D. 1603–1867):
Upon Hideyoshi's death, power was seized by Ieyasu Tokugawa, a statesman so shrewd and skillful in eliminating

enemies that his Tokugawa heirs would continue to rule Japan for the next 250 years. In 1603 Ieyasu set up his shogunate government in Edo (present-day Tokyo), leaving the emperor intact but virtually powerless in Kyoto.

Meanwhile Western influence in Japan was spreading. Japan had already had its first contact with the Western world back in 1543 with the arrival of the Portuguese, who were followed by Christian missionaries. In 1549 Saint Francis Xavier arrived in Kyushu where he remained for two years, converting thousands of Japanese into Christians. By 1580 there were perhaps as many as 150,000 Christians in Japan. Although the rulers of Japan at first welcomed the foreigners and trade, they gradually became alarmed at the influence of the Christian missionaries. Hearing about the power of the Catholic church in Rome and fearing the expansionist policies of the European nations, the shogunate banned Christianity at the end of the 1500s. In 1597 some 26 Japanese and European Christians were crucified in Nagasaki.

The Tokugawa shogunate intensified the campaign against the Christians and carried it a step further when in 1633 it closed all its ports to foreign trade. Adopting a policy of total isolation, the Tokugawas subsequently forbade foreigners to land in Japan and forbade the Japanese to leave. Even those Japanese who had been living abroad in overseas trading posts were not allowed to return to their native homes and were therefore forced to live the rest of their days in exile. Those who defied the strict decrees paid for it with their lives. The only exception to this policy of isolation was in Nagasaki, where there was a colony of tightly controlled Chinese merchants and a handful of Dutch who were confined to a small trading post on a tiny island.

Thus began an amazing time in Japanese history, during which its doors were virtually closed to the rest of the world for more than 200 years. It was a time of political stability but also a time when personal freedom was strictly controlled by the Tokugawa government. Japanese society was divided into four distinct classes: the court nobles, the samurai, the farmers, and the merchants. Although the nobles occupied the most exalted social position, the real power lay with the samurai, and it was probably during the Tokugawa Period that the samurai class reached the zenith of its glory. At the bottom of the social ladder were the merchants, but as peace reigned on and they began accumulating wealth, new forms of entertainment arose to occupy their time. Kabuki drama and woodblock prints became the new rage, while stone and porcelain ware, silk brocade for elaborate and gorgeous kimonos, and lacquer ware improved in quality.

To ensure that no daimyo in the distant provinces might grow powerful enough to usurp the shogun's power, the Tokugawa government ordered that each daimyo leave his family in Edo to serve as a kind of hostage. Furthermore, each daimyo was required to spend every other year in Edo. In exerting so much time and money traveling back and forth and maintaining residences both in the provinces and in Edo, the daimyo was left with nothing extra with which to wage a rebellion. To serve these elaborate processions as the daimyo traveled with his retainers back and forth between Edo and the provinces, inns and townships sprang up along Japan's major highways. What a sight these constant processions must have been with their palanquins, samurai, and footmen as they made their way through the rough terrain of Japan's mountains.

But even though the Tokugawa government took measures to ensure its supremacy, by the mid-19th century it was clear that the feudal system was outdated. With the economic power in the hands of the merchants, money rather than rice became the primary means of exchange. Many samurai families found themselves on the brink of poverty and discontent with the shogunate grew widespread.

In 1853 Commodore Matthew C. Perry of the U.S. Navy sailed to Japan to force the nation to grant America trading rights. Returning a year later, he finally succeeded in forcing the shogun to sign an agreement despite the disapproval of the emperor, thus ending Japan's two centuries of isolation. In 1867 some powerful families succeeded in toppling the Tokugawa regime and restoring the emperor as ruler. The feudal era drew to an end.

MODERN JAPAN (A.D. 1868–PRESENT): In 1868 Emperor Meiji moved his imperial government to Edo, renamed it Tokyo (which means "Eastern Capital"), and made it the official capital of the nation. The ensuing years, known as the Meiji Restoration, were nothing short of amazing as Japan rapidly progressed from a feudal agricultural society of samurai and peasants to an industrial nation in only a few decades. The samurai were stripped of their power and no longer allowed to carry swords, a prime minister and cabinet were appointed, a constitution was drafted, and a parliament, called the Diet, was elected. With the enthusiastic support of Emperor Meiji for the modernization and Westernization of Japan, all the latest in technology and know-how was imported to Japan, including the railway, postal system, and even specialists and advisers. Between 1881 and 1898 as many as 6,177 British, 2,764 Americans, 913 Germans, and 619 French were retained by the Japanese government to help in the transformation of Japan into a modern society.

Meanwhile, Japan was testing its new wings with forays into neighboring lands. In 1894 Japan fought China and won, and in 1905 Japan attacked and defeated Russia. In 1910 Japan annexed Korea. After militarists gained control of the government in the 1930s, these expansionist policies continued when Japan went to war with China in 1937. On December 7, 1941, Japan attacked Pearl Harbor, entering World War II against the United States. Although victories continued as Japan conquered Hong Kong, Singapore, Burma, Malaysia, the Philippines, Dutch East Indies, and Guam, the tide eventually turned. American bombers reduced to rubble every major city in Japan with the exception of Kyoto. On August 6, 1945, the United States dropped over Hiroshima the world's first atomic bomb, followed on August 9 by a second atomic bomb over Nagasaki. Japan submitted to unconditional surrender on August 14 and soon thereafter American occupational forces arrived in Japan, where they remained until 1952. For the first time in Japan's history it had suffered defeat and occupation by a foreign power.

Adopting a new constitution that renounced war and set up a democratic government, Japan quickly began rebuilding its cities and economy. By the time the Olympic Games were held in Tokyo in 1964, Japan had become an economic phenomenon. Considering the fact that today Japan is one of the most industrialized nations in the world, its progress in the past century is indeed nothing short of remarkable. What's more, Japan is ready, eager, and able to lead the rest of the world into the 21st century.

3. The People

As an island nation with few natural resources, Japan's greatest asset is its 120 million people. Hard-working, honest, and proud about performing a task well no matter how insignificant it might seem, the Japanese are well known for their politeness and helpfulness to strangers. Hardly anyone returns from a trip to Japan without stories of the extraordinary goodness and kindness extended to them by the Japanese.

With approximately 99.5% of the population consisting of Japanese, Japan is one of the most homogeneous nations in the world. Originally of Mongoloid stock with strains of a few other Asian peoples thrown in, the Japanese have had remarkably little influx of other gene pools into the country ever since the eighth century. That, coupled with Japan's actual physical isolation as an island nation, has more than anything else led to a feeling among the Japanese that they belong to one huge tribe different from any other people on earth. You'll often hear a Japanese preface a statement or opinion with the words "We Japanese," the implications of which are that all Japanese think alike and that all people can basically be divided into two worlds, Japanese and non-Japanese.

One characteristic of the Japanese that has received much publicity in recent years, and that is regarded as at least one reason why their nation has become so powerful economically, is their group mentality. In Japan, consideration of the group—whether it be family, friends, co-workers, or Japanese society as a whole—always wins out over the desire of the individual. In fact, I have had Japanese tell me that they consider individuality to be synonymous with selfishness and a complete disregard for the feelings and consideration of others.

Whereas in the West the attainment of "happiness" seems to be the elusive goal for a full and rewarding life, in Japan it's the satisfactory performance of duty and obligation. From the time they are born the Japanese are instilled with a sense of duty that extends toward their parents, their husband or wife, their children, their boss and co-workers, their neighbors, and the rest of Japanese society as a whole.

In a nation as crowded as Japan, such consideration of others is essential. The average Japanese family lives in what Westerners would regard as intolerably tiny living quarters, especially in the larger cities like Tokyo or Osaka where space is at a premium. And in most cases it's still customary for retired parents to live with their eldest son.

The son, however, has very little time to spend at home. If he lives in Tokyo he probably spends two to three hours a day commuting to and from work on the city's trains and subways. He works long hours, sometimes until 7 or 8 p.m., often followed by an evening out with his fellow workers, which he considers necessary for promoting understanding, closeness, and a more harmonious working condition. Most likely he'll work for the same company his entire life, taking only national holidays and one week's vacation a year. In return he is assured of lifetime employment (unless his company goes bankrupt, which is not too terribly uncommon), a pay raise according to his age, and promotion according to the number of years he has worked for the company. Although he may secretly complain of the long hours he has to work, he basically accepts it because everyone else is doing the same thing.

Being a housewife and full-time mother is considered the most honored position a woman can have. Although more and more women are working outside the home than ever before, they are generally confined to low-paying menial and part-time jobs. Take a look at the employment opportunities in the classified section of the *Japan Times*. There you'll see that employers can discriminate on the basis of sex, age, and race. Jobs for women are typically as secretaries, waitresses, and teachers, with few jobs open to those over 30. It's still pretty much a man's society when it comes to business in Japan, and a woman's primary obligation and function is in the home. With few exciting career opportunities easily open to them, it's perhaps understandable why the main goal of most Japanese women is to get married and have children. Those who fail to find a mate during college or the early working years can always find one through an arranged marriage, which still make up about 30% of the matches in Japan. The Japanese go all out when it comes to marriage ceremonies—believe it or not, the cost of an average wedding in Japan, including the honeymoon, is a whopping $30,000.

Of course, the situation is changing in Japan, as elsewhere, and it's no longer safe to talk in stereotypes. In 1986 a new law, the Equal Employment Opportunity Act, went into effect, thereby overturning an earlier law which had limited the number of hours women could work overtime—and if you don't work overtime in Japan, there's hardly any chance for promotion. Although rare, you can now find female politicians, doctors, and lawyers who juggle both family and career. Day-care centers for children are on the increase, young people are moving away and living far from their hometowns, and some young couples are determined to lead different, and separate, lives from their parents.

But change evolves slowly in Japan. Those who advocate change are in danger of ridicule or, even worse, rejection from the group. It's especially difficult for Japanese who have lived abroad and then return home—unless they slip back quietly into their old mold they are regarded with suspicion and resentment, as though they have somehow become tainted and are no longer quite Japanese.

As for foreigners, even though treated with extreme kindness during a visit, they soon realize that they will never be totally accepted in Japanese society: they will always be considered outsiders, even if they speak fluent Japanese. In fact, Japanese-speaking foreigners will tell you that they are often met with suspicion and coldness simply because, to the Japanese mind, foreigners aren't supposed to be able to speak their language. Among the groups most discriminated against are probably the Koreans, many of them second and third generation and the descendants of Koreans who were brought to Japan in forced labor before World War II.

On the positive side, on a personal level the Japanese are among the most likeable in the world. They are kind, thoughtful, and adept in perceiving another's needs. The fact that the country is so safe from violent crime speaks highly of the people. And as for aestheticism, the Japanese have an unerring eye for pure beauty, whether it be in food, architecture, or landscaped gardens. I don't think it would be possible to visit Japan and not have some of the Japanese appreciation of beauty rub off. As a people who have produced both the bonsai and Toyota, the robot, the sumo wrestler, and the geisha, the Japanese are such a fascinating people that it's impossible not to get hooked. Quite a few foreigners living in Japan came to the country with the intention of staying only a short while—and they end up living here for years. I was one of them.

In short, Japan, like every nation in the world, has both its good and bad sides, and the informed visitor should be aware of both. On the whole, however, the visitor will be overwhelmed by the wonderful aspects of the country and the kindness of the people, which makes traveling in Japan such a delight. By the time you go home, no doubt you'll have your own extraordinary stories to tell.

4. The Language

No one knows the exact origins of the Japanese language, but we do know that it existed only in spoken form until the sixth century. It was then that the Japanese borrowed the Chinese characters, called *kanji*, and used them to develop their own form of written language. Later, two additional character systems, *hiragana* and *katakana*, were added to kanji to form the existing Japanese writing system. Thus both Chinese and Japanese use some of the same pictographs, but otherwise there is no similarity between the two languages. While they may be able to recognize some of each other's language, the Chinese and Japanese cannot communicate verbally.

There are at least two ways of pronouncing most kanji in Japanese—one is a Chinese pronunciation from the sixth century and the other is a Japanese pronunciation. This leads to the problem that one often can't tell by looking at the characters which pronunciation is the proper one except by context. Similarly, if you don't know the characters of, say, a restaurant, it may be impossible to find out the telephone number.

A NOTE ON JAPANESE SYMBOLS: Many hotels, restaurants, and other establishments in Japan do not have signs showing their names in English letters. Appendix II lists the Japanese symbols for all such places appearing in this guide. Each establishment name in Japanese symbols is numbered, and the same number appears in brackets in the text following the boldfaced establishment name. For example, in the text the Osaka hotel, Hokke Club [161], is number 161 in the Japanese symbol list in Appendix II.

There are about 10,000 Japanese characters, but the average adult knows only 2,500 or so, which is enough to read newspapers, most books and novels, etc. Hiragana and katakana, phonetic alphabets consisting of 46 symbols each, came into use because kanji was considered inadequate to express everything in Japanese thought. Hiragana is used for writing words not expressed in kanji and for verb endings. Katakana is the alphabet used for all foreign words and for telegrams. As a foreigner, for example, if you have visiting cards made up in Japanese, your name will be written in the katakana syllabary.

The Japanese written language—a combination of kanji, hiragana, and katakana—is probably one of the most difficult systems of written communication in the modern world. And as for the spoken language, there are all kinds of levels of speech and forms of expression that relate to your own social status and whether you're male or female. It's little wonder that Saint Francis Xavier, a Jesuit missionary who came to Japan in the 16th century, wrote that Japanese was an invention of the devil designed to thwart the spread of Christianity. And yet the most astounding thing is that literacy in Japan is estimated at around 99%.

But despite the fact that Japanese are able to learn their own complicated language, they have much difficulty when it comes to English. Although most students are required to take English for six years in school, these studies lean primarily toward entrance exams at universities, which require extensive reading comprehension of the language and grammar but almost no practical application. Thus while many Japanese can read English, few are able to understand spoken English. As I've mentioned elsewhere, if you're having problems communicating with a Japanese it sometimes helps to write everything down.

Realizing the difficulties foreigners have with the language barrier in Japan, the Japan National Tourist Organization has put out a nifty booklet called *The Tourist's Handbook* with sentences written in English and Japanese equivalents for everything from asking directions to shopping to ordering in a restaurant and staying in a Japanese inn. Foreigners traveling around Japan on their own should pick up a copy of this valuable booklet at the Tourist Information Center in either Tokyo or Kyoto. Appendix I in the back of this guide also lists some common phrases and words in Japanese to help you get around on your own.

Finally, if you are having difficulty communicating with a Japanese, it may help to pronounce an English word in a Japanese way. Foreign words, especially

English, have penetrated the Japanese language to such an extent that they are now estimated to make up 20% of the words used by the Japanese. The problem is that these words change in Japanese pronunciation because words always end in either a vowel or "n," and because two consonants in one syllable are usually separated by a vowel. Would you recognize *terebi* as "television," *koohi* as "coffee," or *rajio* as "radio"?

I'd like to mention here that English words are quite fashionable in Japanese advertising, with the result that you'll often see English on shop signs, posters, shopping bags, and T-shirts. However, words are often wonderfully misspelled or used in such unusual contexts that you can only guess at the original intent. I don't know how many times my day has been brightened with the discovery of some zany or unfathomable English. What, for example, could possibly be the meaning behind "Today birds, tomorrow men" which appeared under a picture of birds on a shopping bag? In Matsue there's a "Beauty Saloon," which conjures up all kinds of images of beauties getting their hair cut while chugging down mugs of beer, and in Gifu one can only guess at the pleasures to be had at the Hotel Joybox. In Okayama I saw a shop whose name was a stern admonition to its customers to "Grow Up," while in Kyoto there's the "Selfish" coffeeshop and the "Pitiful Pub." How about a "sandwitch" or "Creap" coffee creamer? Popular advertising slogans such as "I feel Coke" and "Speak Lark" have puzzled many a resident foreigner.

Certainly the best sign I saw was at the Narita airport. At all the check-in counters was a sign telling passengers that they would be required to pay a service facility charge at "the time of check-in for your fright." Unable to control my giggles, I explained the reason for my breakdown to the perplexed man behind the counter. Two weeks later when I came back through the airport, all the signs had been corrected. That's Japanese efficiency.

5. Meeting the Japanese

If you've been invited to Japan by some organization or business, you will receive the royal treatment, most likely being wined and dined so wonderfully and thoroughly that you'll never want to return home. If you've come to Japan on your own as an ordinary tourist, however, chances are your experiences will be much different. Except for those who have lived or traveled a lot abroad, few Japanese have had much contact with foreigners. In fact even in Tokyo there are Japanese who have never spoken to a foreigner and would be quite embarrassed and uncomfortable if suddenly confronted with the possibility. And even though most of them have studied English, few of them have had the opportunity to use it and most feel totally unable to communicate in it. That's one reason why the empty seat beside you in the subway is the last one to be occupied—most Japanese are deathly afraid you'll ask them a question they won't be able to understand.

In many respects, therefore, it's much harder to meet the inhabitants than in many other countries, where the people tend to be more gregarious, openly curious, and forward. The Japanese are simply much more shy. Although they will sometimes approach you to ask whether they might practice some English with you, for the most part you are left pretty much on your own unless you make the first move. And for the most part your experiences in Japan will depend on you and your own initiative.

Recognizing the difficulty foreigners may face in meeting the Japanese, the Japanese National Tourist Organization has launched a super program called the **Home Visit System**, which offers overseas visitors the chance to visit an English-speaking Japanese family in their home. It doesn't cost anything and the visit usually takes place for a few hours in the evening (dinner is *not* served).

It's a good idea to bring a small gift, such as flowers, fruit, or something from your hometown. The system is operating in the following 15 cities, for which I've provided the contact telephone numbers: Tokyo (tel. 03/502-1461); Sapporo (tel. 011/211-3341); Narita (tel. 0476/32-8711 or 24-3198); Yokohama (tel. 045/641-5824); Nagoya (tel. 052/581-5678); Otsu (tel. 0775/23-1234); Kyoto (tel. 075/752-0215); Osaka (tel. 06/345-2189); Kobe (tel. 078/303-1010); Okayama (tel. 0862/32-2255); Kurashiki (tel. 0864/22-5141); Hiroshima (tel. 082/247-6738); Fukuoka (tel. 092/291-0777); Nagasaki (tel. 0958/24-1111); and Kagoshima (tel. 0992/24-1111 or 53-2500). To apply, call the appropriate city at least one day in advance of the intended visit. If you have any other questions, the Tourist Information Center in Tokyo (tel. 03/502-1461) can answer them.

Another good way to meet the Japanese is to stay in a *minshuku,* inexpensive lodging in a Japanese home. Usually small with only a handful of rooms, minshuku often afford the opportunity to meet both the family running the place as well as the other guests, since meals are usually served in a communal dining room. More information is given about minshuku in the section on accommodation later in this chapter.

I've found that one of the best ways to meet Japanese is to visit a so-called **English conversation lounge.** These are informal affairs, often attached to English schools for the Japanese to give them the opportunity for unstructured conversations in English with anyone who is there. Most are open in the evenings and offer the chance to play games or read magazines and have drinks of coffee or beer. Usually foreigners are admitted free of charge; at some lounges you must pay an entrance fee of ¥400 ($2.86) or so, but it's always less than what the Japanese pay. At any rate, the Japanese who come to these lounges often speak excellent English and will be delighted to talk to you. When I first came to Japan I visited one of these lounges about five times, learning much about Japanese society as we talked about everything from the role of women in Japan to homosexuality to opinions about interracial marriages. I was told that the Japanese feel much more comfortable talking about such subjects in English and would be unable to express themselves as openly in Japanese. Regardless, it's an excellent way to meet Japanese and learn about the country. The *Tokyo Journal,* published monthly to describe what's going on in the capital city, lists conversation lounges in its classified section.

And finally, another way to meet Japanese is to go where they play, namely the country's countless bars and eateries. There you'll often encounter Japanese who will want to speak to you if they understand English, and even some slightly inebriated Japanese who will speak to you if they don't. If you're open to it, such chance encounters may prove to be the highlight of your trip, or at the very least an evening of just plain fun.

6. Japanese Etiquette and Manners

Much of Japan's etiquette and manners for behavior stem from its feudal days, when the social hierarchy dictated how a person spoke, sat, bowed, ate, walked, and lived. Failure to comply with the rules could bring severe punishment, sometimes even death.

Of course, nowadays it's quite different, though the Japanese still attach much importance to proper behavior. As a foreigner, however, you can get away with a lot. After all, you're just a "barbarian" and as such can be forgiven for not knowing the rules. There are **two cardinal sins**, however, that you should never commit. One is that you should never wear your shoes inside a Japanese home, traditional inn, or temple, and the other is that you should never, ever wash with soap inside a Japanese bathtub. Except for committing either of these two horrors, you will probably be forgiven for any other social blunder.

As a sensitive traveler, however, you should try to familiarize yourself with the social etiquette for Japan, the basics of which are given below. The Japanese are very appreciative of foreigners who take the time to learn about their country and are quite patient in helping you learn. And, remember, if you do commit a faux pas, apologize profusely and smile. They don't chop off heads anymore.

BOWING: The main form of greeting in Japan is the bow rather than the handshake. Although at first glance it might seem simple enough, the bow and its implications are actually quite complicated, with the depth of the bow, the number of seconds, and the total number of bows dependent on who you are and who you're bowing to. In addition to bowing in greeting, the Japanese also bow upon departing and to express deep gratitude. The proper form for a bow is to bend from the waist with a straight back and to keep your arms at your sides, but as a foreigner a simple nod of the head is enough. Knowing that foreigners shake hands, a Japanese may extend his hand, though he probably won't be able to stop himself from giving a little bow as well. In my travels in Japan I've even seen Japanese businessmen shake hands among themselves, although it is still quite rare.

VISITING CARDS: You're a nonentity in Japan if you don't have a visiting card, called a *meishi* in Japanese. Everyone from housewives to plumbers to secretaries to bank presidents carries meishi with them to give out upon introduction. If you're trying to conduct business in Japan, you'll be regarded suspiciously as a phony if you don't have business cards. As a tourist you don't have to have business cards, but it certainly doesn't hurt and the Japanese will be greatly impressed by your preparedness. The card should have your address and occupation on it. As a nice souvenir you might consider having your meishi made in Japan with the Japanese syllabic script (katakana) written on the reverse side.

DINING: One of the great customs in Japan is that as soon as you're seated in a Japanese restaurant you'll be given a wet towel, which will be steaming hot in winter or pleasantly cool in summer. Called an *oshibori*, it's for wiping your hands. In all but the fancy restaurants men can get away with wiping their faces as well, but women are not supposed to (I ignore this one if I'm hot and sweaty). The oshibori is one custom you'll wish would be adopted back home.

The next thing you'll probably be confronted with are chopsticks. The proper way to use them is to place the first chopstick between the base of the thumb and the top of the ring finger (this chopstick remains stationary) and the second one between the top of the thumb and the middle and index fingers. This second chopstick is what you move to pick up food. The best way to learn is to have a Japanese show you how. It's not difficult to learn, but if you find it impossible some restaurants might have a fork as well. How proficiently foreigners handle chopsticks is a matter of great curiosity for the Japanese and they're surprised if you know how to use them; even if you were to live in Japan 20 years you would never stop receiving compliments on how talented you are with chopsticks.

As for etiquette involving chopsticks, if you're taking something from a communal bowl or tray you're supposed to turn your chopsticks upside down and use the part that hasn't been in your mouth. After transferring the food to your plate you turn the chopsticks back to their proper position. Never stick your chopsticks down vertically into your bowl of rice and leave them there—

that is done only when a person has died. Similarly you're not supposed to pass anything between chopsticks since that's how cremated bones are passed in a Buddhist funeral.

If you're eating soup you won't use a spoon, but rather will pick up the bowl and drink from it. It's considered in good taste to slurp with gusto, especially if you're eating noodles. Noodle shops in Japan are always well orchestrated with slurps and smacks. And, by the way, it's considered bad manners to walk down the street in Japan eating or drinking. You'll notice that if a Japanese buys a drink from a vending machine, he'll stand there, gulp it down, and throw away the container before going on.

If you're drinking in Japan, the main thing to remember is that you never pour your own glass. Bottles of beer in Japan are so large that people often share one. The rule is that, in turn, one person pours for everyone else in the group, so be sure to hold up your glass when someone is pouring for you. Only as the night progresses do the Japanese get sloppy about this rule. It took me a while to figure this one out, but if no one notices that your glass is empty, the best thing to do is to pour everyone else a drink so that someone will pour yours. If someone wants to pour you a drink and your glass is full, the proper thing to do is to take a few gulps so that he or she can fill your glass. Because each person is continually filling everyone else's glass you never know exactly how much you've had to drink, which (depending on how you look at it) is very good or very bad.

SHOES: Nothing is so distasteful to the Japanese as the bottoms of shoes, and as such they are taken off before entering a home, a Japanese-style inn, a temple, and even some museums and restaurants. Usually there will be some plastic slippers at the entranceway for you to slip on, but whenever you encounter tatami you should take off even these slippers—only bare feet or socks are allowed to tread upon tatami.

Rest rooms present a whole other set of slippers. If you're in a home or Japanese inn you'll notice another pair of slippers—again plastic or rubber—sitting right inside the rest room at the door. Step out of the hallway plastic shoes and into the bathroom slippers, and wear these the whole time you're in the rest room. When you're finished, change back into the hallway slippers. If you forget this last changeover you'll regret it—nothing is as embarrassing as walking down the hall in the bathroom slippers and not realizing what you've done until you see the mixed looks of horror and mirth on the faces of the Japanese. Although it might seem like a lot of bother to go through all this ritual with the shoes, it actually does make sense once you get used to it.

THE JAPANESE BATH: On my very first trip to Japan I was certain that I would never get into a Japanese bath. I was under the misconception that men and women bathed together and I couldn't imagine getting into a tub with a group of smiling and bowing Japanese men. I needn't have worried. The good news (or, I suppose, bad news for some of you) is that in almost all circumstances bathing is segregated for men and women in Japan. There are some exceptions, primarily outdoor hot-spring spas in the countryside, but the women who go to these are usually grandmothers who couldn't care less. Young Japanese women wouldn't dream of jumping into a tub with a group of male strangers. And, by the way, whoever said that the Japanese are very good at averting their eyes and don't stare must have been blind. I once went to an outdoor sulfurous hot-spring spa with a group of friends where there were little pools spread throughout the hillside. We finally found a deserted pool and bathed, but as we were getting dressed we discovered a group of hikers in the distance observing us with binoculars. Honestly!

Anyway, Japanese baths are delightful—and I, for one, am addicted to them. You find them at Japanese-style inns, hot-spring spas, and at neighborhood baths (not everyone has his own bath in Japan). Sometimes they're elaborate affairs with many tubs, plants, and statues, and sometimes they're nothing more than a tiny tub. The procedure at all of them is the same. After completely disrobing in the changing room and putting your clothes in either a locker or basket, hold your wash cloth in front of you so that it covers the vital parts and walk into the bath area. There you'll find a plastic basin (they used to be wood), a plastic stool, and faucets along the wall. Sit on the stool in front of the faucet and repeatedly fill your basin with water, splashing it all over you. If there's no hot water from the faucet it's acceptable to dip your plastic basin into the hot bath. Soap yourself down and completely—and I mean *completely*—rinse away all traces of soap. After you're squeaky clean you're ready to get into the bath.

Your first attempt at a Japanese bath may be painful—simply too scalding for comfort. It helps if you ease in gently and then sit perfectly still. You'll notice all tension and stiffness ebbing away, a decidedly relaxing way to end the day. The Japanese are so fond of baths that many take them every night, especially in the winter when a hot bath keeps one toasty warm for hours afterward. Who knows, with time you'll probably become addicted too.

TIPS ON BEHAVIOR: Most forms of behavior and etiquette in Japan developed to allow relationships to be as frictionless as possible, a pretty good idea in crowded Japan. The Japanese don't like confrontations, and although I'm told they occur, I've never seen a fight in Japan.

The Japanese are an emotional people but they're very good at covering almost all unpleasantness with a smile. Foreigners find the smile hard to read, but a smiling Japanese face can mean happiness, sadness, embarrassment, even anger. My first lesson in this happened on a subway in Tokyo where I saw a middle-aged Japanese woman who was about to board the subway brutally knocked out of the way by a Japanese man rushing off the train. She almost lost her balance but she gave a little laugh, smiled, and got on the train. A few minutes later as the train was speeding through the tunnel I stole a look at her and was able to read her true feelings on her face. Lost in her own thoughts, her brow was knitted in consternation and she looked most upset and unhappy. The smile had been a put-on.

Another aspect of Japanese behavior that sometimes causes difficulty for foreigners is that the Japanese find it very difficult to say no. They're much more apt to say that your request is very difficult to fulfill or they'll simply beat around the bush without giving a definite answer. At this point you're expected to let the subject drop. Showing impatience, anger, or aggressiveness rarely gets you anywhere in Japan. Apologizing sometimes does. And if someone does give in to your request, you can't say thank you enough.

MISCELLANEOUS ETIQUETTE: If you are invited to a Japanese home, you should know that it is a rarity and an honor. Most Japanese consider their homes too small and humble for entertaining guests, which is why there are so many restaurants, coffeeshops, and bars. If you are invited to a home, don't show up empty-handed. Bring a small gift such as candy, fruit, or flowers. Alcohol is also appreciated. You don't have to fly to Japan more than once to realize that—it seems like every Japanese on board is laden down with his or her three-bottle quota of alcohol. Take your cue from them and stock up on a few bottles on the flight over if you know you'll be visiting someone. Whisky and brandy seem to be the favorites.

When the Japanese give back change, they hand it back to you in a lump sum rather than counting it out. Trust them. It's considered insulting for you to sit there and count it in front of them because it insinuates that you think they might be trying to cheat you. The Japanese are honest. It's one of the great pleasures of being in their country.

Don't blow your nose in public if you can help it and never at the dinner table. It's considered most disgusting. On the other hand, even though the Japanese are very hygienic they are not at all averse to spitting on the sidewalk. And, even more peculiar, the men urinate when and where they want, usually against a tree or a wall and most often after a night of carousing in the bars.

This being a man's society, men will walk in and out of doors and elevators before women, and in subways will often sit down while their wives stand. Some Japanese men who have had contact with the Western world and who know that in the West it's women before men will make a gallant show of allowing a Western woman to step out of the elevator, etc., first. For the sake of Western women living in Japan, such men should be warmly thanked and their behavior greatly encouraged.

7. A Word About Japanese Inns

Even though it can be very expensive, it's worth it to splurge at least once during your trip to Japan to spend the night in an old Japanese-style inn. Nothing conveys the mood, simplistic beauty, and atmosphere of old Japan better than these small enclaves of gleaming polished wood, tatami floors, rice-paper sliding doors, meticulously pruned Japanese gardens, and kimono-clad hostesses. Personalized service and exquisitely prepared meals are the trademarks of a Japanese inn, called *ryokan* in Japanese, and staying in one of these is like taking a trip back in time.

Ideally made of wood with tile roofs, most ryokan are small, only one or two stories high with about 10 to 30 rooms. The entrance is often through a gate and small garden, whereupon you are met by a bowing woman in a kimono. Take off your shoes, slide on the plastic slippers, and follow your hostess down long wooden corridors until you reach the sliding door of your room. After taking off your slippers, step into your tatami room almost void of furniture—a low table in the middle of the room, floor cushions, an antique scroll hanging in an alcove, a simple flower arrangement, and best of all, a view past rice-paper sliding screens of a Japanese landscaped garden with bonsai, stone lanterns, and a meandering pond filled with carp. You notice that there's no bed in the room.

Almost immediately your hostess brings you a welcoming hot tea and a sweet, served at your low table so that you might sit there for a while and appreciate the view, the peace, and solitude. Next comes your hot bath, either in your own room (if you have one) or in the communal bath. (Be sure to follow the procedure outlined in the previous section on Japanese etiquette, soaping and rinsing yourself *before* getting into the tub.) After bathing and soaking away all tension, aches, and pains, change into your *yukata,* a cotton kimono provided by the ryokan.

When you return to your room you'll find the maid ready to serve your dinner, which consists of locally grown vegetables, fish, and various regional specialties all spread out on many tiny plates. There is no menu in a ryokan but rather one or more set courses determined by the chef. Admire how each dish is in itself a delicate piece of artwork, adorned with slices of ginger, a maple leaf, or a flower. It all looks too wonderful to eat, but finally hunger takes over. If you want, you can order sake or beer to accompany your meal.

After you've finished eating, your maid will return to clear away the dishes and to lay out your bed. Called a *futon*, it's a kind of mattress with quilts and is laid out on the tatami floor. The next morning the maid will wake you up, put away the futon, and serve a breakfast of fish, pickled vegetables, soup, dried seaweed, rice, and a raw egg to be mixed with the rice. Feeling rested, well fed, and pampered, you are then ready to pack your bags and pay your bill. Your hostess sees you off at the front gate, smiling and bowing as you set off for the rest of your travels.

Such is life at a good ryokan. Sadly enough, however, the number of upper-class ryokan diminishes each year. Unable to compete with the more profitable high-rise hotels, many ryokan in Japan's large cities have had to close down, with the result that there are very few left in such cities as Tokyo or Osaka. If you want to stay in a Japanese inn, it's best to do so at a resort or hot-spring spa. Altogether there are approximately 90,000 ryokan still operating in Japan in a variety of different price ranges. Although ideally a ryokan is an old wooden structure at least 100 years old and perhaps once the home of a samurai or a wealthy merchant, many—especially those in hot-spring resort areas—are modern concrete affairs with as many as 100 or more rooms. What they lack in intimacy, however, is made up for in modern bathrooms and the added attractions of perhaps a bar and outdoor recreational facilities. Most guest rooms are fitted with color television, phone, and a safe for locking up valuables.

Unlike Western-style hotels, rates in a ryokan are based on a per-person charge rather than a straight room charge, and they include breakfast and dinner, tax, and service charge. Although rates can vary from ¥8,000 ($57) to ¥60,000 ($429) per person, the average cost is generally ¥10,000 ($71) to ¥20,000 ($143). Even within a single ryokan the rates can vary greatly, depending on the room you choose, the dinner course you select, and the number of people in your room. If you're paying the highest rate you can be certain you are getting the best view of the garden, or perhaps even your own private garden, as well as a better meal than the lower-paying guests. All the rates for ryokan in this book are based on double occupancy; if there are more than two of you in one room you can generally count on a slightly cheaper per-person rate.

Although I heartily recommend that you try spending at least one night in a ryokan, there are a number of disadvantages to this style of accommodation. In my estimation, however, the experience itself far outweighs the disadvantages. The most obvious problem may be that you will find it uncomfortable sitting on the floor. And because the futon is put away during the day, there's no place except the hard tatami-covered floor on which to lie down for an afternoon nap or rest. In addition, some of the older ryokan, though quaint, are bitterly cold in the winter and may have only Japanese-style toilets. As for breakfast, some foreigners might find it difficult to swallow raw egg, rice, and seaweed in the morning. Sometimes you can get a Western-style breakfast if you order it the night before, but more often than not the fried or scrambled eggs will arrive cold, leading you to suspect that they were cooked right after you ordered them.

A ryokan is also quite rigid in its schedule. You're expected to arrive sometime after 4 p.m., take your bath, and then eat at around 6 or 7 p.m. Breakfast is served early, usually by 8 a.m., and checkout is by 10 a.m. That means you can't sleep in late, and because the maid is continually coming in and out you have a lot less privacy than you would in a hotel.

The main drawback of the ryokan, however, is that the majority of them will not take you. They simply do not want to deal with the problems inherent in accepting a foreign guest, including the language barrier and differing customs. I saw a number of beautiful old ryokan that I would have liked to include in this book, but I was turned away at the door. The ryokan in this guide, therefore, are ones willing to take in foreigners, but because management and policies can change, it's best to call beforehand. In fact you should always make a reservation if you want to stay in a first-class ryokan, and even in most medium-priced ones, because the chef has to shop for and prepare your meals. They do not look kindly upon unannounced strangers turning up on their doorstep.

You can book a reservation for a ryokan through any travel agency in Japan, such as the Japan Travel Bureau (JTB), or by calling a ryokan directly, though it's best if the call is conducted in Japanese and you may be required to pay a deposit.

8. Other Types of Accommodation

Besides ryokan there are a number of other kinds of accommodation available in Japan, ranging from inexpensive Japanese-style to large Western-style hotels. Although theoretically you can travel throughout Japan without making reservations beforehand, it's essential to do so if you're traveling during peak travel seasons, and recommended at other times. These peak times are the end of April through the first week of May (called Golden Week), New Year's holiday from about December 27 to January 4, and mid-July through August, particularly around mid-August.

If you find all my recommendations for a certain city fully booked, there are several ways to find alternative accommodations. Easiest is to book through a travel agency, such as the Japan Travel Bureau. If you arrive at your destination and need help obtaining an accommodation, most major train stations in Japan have a hotel and ryokan reservation office that will find you a place to stay. Although policies may differ from office to office, you generally don't have to pay a fee for their services, though you usually do have to pay a percentage of your overnight charge as a deposit. The disadvantage is that you don't see the locale beforehand, and if there's space left here even in peak tourist season you can guess that there's probably a pretty good reason for it. The two worst places I've stayed in in Japan were through one of these reservation offices at a train station (don't worry, I don't recommend them in this book!). Although these offices can be a real lifesaver in a pinch and in most cases may be able to recommend quite reasonable and pleasant places in which to stay, it certainly pays to plan in advance.

By the way, during your travels you may come across rooms in both Western- and Japanese-style establishments that offer video programs with their televisions. These programs are either coin-operated or are charged automatically to your bill. Since the explanations for these programs are usually in Japanese only, I will clear up the mystery—they're generally "adult entertainment" programs. Now you know.

JAPANESE-STYLE ACCOMMODATIONS: If you want to experience a Japanese-style inn but can't afford the prices of a ryokan, there are a number of other types of accommodation available. Though they don't offer the personalized service and beautiful setting of a ryokan, they do offer the chance to stay in a simple tatami room, sleep on a futon, and in some cases eat Japanese food. Similarly to ryokan, prices are per person and include tax and service charge, and often two meals as well. English is rarely spoken.

Japanese Inn Group

The Japanese Inn Group is a special group of more than 60 Japanese-style inns throughout Japan that offer inexpensive lodging and cater largely to foreigners. Although at first thought you may balk at the idea of staying at a place filled mainly with foreigners, you must remember that most of the cheap Japanese-style inns in Japan are not accustomed to guests from abroad and may be quite reluctant to take you in. I have covered many of these Japanese Inn Group members in this guidebook and have found the owners for the most part to be an exceptional group of friendly people eager to offer foreigners the chance to experience life on tatami and futon. In many cases these are good places in which to exchange information with other world travelers, and are popular with both young people and families.

A NOTE ON JAPANESE SYMBOLS: Many hotels, restaurants, and other establishments in Japan do not have signs showing their names in English letters. Appendix II lists the Japanese symbols for all such places appearing in this guide. Each establishment name in Japanese symbols is numbered, and the same number appears in brackets in the text following the boldfaced establishment name. For example, in the text the Osaka hotel, Hokke Club [161], is number 161 in the Japanese symbol list in Appendix II.

Although they call themselves ryokan, they are not ryokan in the true sense of the word because they do not offer personalized service and many of them do not serve food. However, they do offer simple tatami rooms which generally come with a coin-operated TV and sometimes with a coin-operated air conditioner as well. Some of them have towels and the cotton *yukata* kimono for your use. Facilities generally include a coin-operated washer and dryer and a public bath, and the average cost of a one-night stay is about ¥4,000 ($29) per person, without meals.

Upon your arrival in Japan, you can pick up a pamphlet at the Tourist Information Center in Tokyo called *Japanese Inn Group,* which lists the members of this organization. You should make reservations directly with the ryokan in which you wish to stay. In some cases you will be asked to pay a deposit (equal to one night's stay), which you can do with a personal check, traveler's check, money order, or bank check, but the easiest way is with American Express. If you want more information, the Inn Group's office headquarters is at 314, Hayao-cho, Kaminoguchi-agaru, Ninomiyacho-dori, Shimogyo-ku, Kyoto 600 (tel. 075/351-6748). If you're in Tokyo, there's a liaison office at 03/822-2251, but the T.I.C. may be able to answer your questions.

Minshuku

Technically, a *minshuku* is an inexpensive lodging in a private home. The average per-person cost for one night is about ¥5,000 ($36) to ¥6,000 ($43), including two meals. Because minshuku are family-run affairs, you are expected to lay out your own futon at night, supply your own towel and nightgown, and tidy up your room in the morning. Rooms do not have their own private bathroom, but there is a public bath. Meals are served in a communal dining room. Minshuku can range from thatched farmhouses to old rickety wooden buildings to modern concrete structures. Although, officially, the difference between a ryokan and a minshuku is that the ryokan is supposedly more expensive and provides more services, the difference is sometimes very slight. I've stayed in cheap ryokan that provided almost no service at all and in minshuku too large and modern to be considered a private home.

Since minshuku cater primarily to Japanese travelers, they're often excellent places in which to meet the locals, and I've included in this guide a number of minshuku willing to take in foreigners. For more information, contact the **Japan Minshuku Center**, Kotsu Kaikan Building, Basement 1, 2–10–1 Yurakucho, Chiyoda-ku, Tokyo (tel. 03/216-6556). It's open from 10 a.m. to 7 p.m. every day except Sunday and holidays, and you can make reservations here for member minshuku across the country.

Kokumin Shukusha

A *kokumin shukusha* is public lodging found primarily in resort and vacation areas. Established by the government, there are more than 300 of these facilities throughout Japan. Catering largely to Japanese school groups and families, they offer basic, Japanese-style rooms at an average daily rate of about ¥6,000 ($43) per person, including two meals. Although you don't have to have a reservation to stay here, they are usually quite full during summer and peak seasons. Reservations can be made through a travel agency. The drawback to many of these lodges is that because they are often located in national parks and in scenic spots, the best way to reach them is by car.

Kokumin Kyuka Mura

Similar to kokumin shukusha, the *kokumin kyuka mura* is a "vacation village" that is government run and located in a national park, but the difference is that it is more expensive, generally around ¥8,500 ($61) per person with two meals, and offers more recreational facilities. Apply through a travel agency.

Shukubo

These are lodgings in a Buddhist temple. Japanese-style rooms, they are similar to inexpensive ryokan except that they're attached to temples and serve vegetarian food. There is usually an early-morning service at 6 a.m. in which you are welcome to join. Probably the best place to experience life in a temple is at Mount Koya (described in Chapter VIII). Prices at a shukubo range from about ¥5,000 ($36) to ¥11,000 ($79) per person, including two meals.

WESTERN-STYLE ACCOMMODATIONS: Lodging in this category ranges from large first-class hotels to inexpensive ones catering primarily to Japanese businessmen. Remember in figuring out your bill that accommodations that cost more than ¥5,000 ($36) per person per night will add a 10% tax after reducing the rate by ¥2,500 ($17.86). There will also be a 10% to 15% service charge added to your bill. Although ryokan and some of the less expensive types of lodging include both tax and service in their price, most hotels do not. Unless otherwise stated, therefore, you can assume that 25% will be added to the prices quoted in this book for hotels costing more than ¥5,000 ($36) per person per night.

Hotels

Both first-class and medium-priced hotels in Japan are known for their excellent service and cleanliness. The first-class hotels in the larger cities can compete with the best hotels in the world, and offer a wide range of services, which may include a health club (for which there's an extra charge), an executive business center with secretarial services, a guest relations officer to help with any problems you may have, a travel agency, shopping arcade, cocktail lounges with live music, and fine Japanese- and Western-style restaurants. Rooms have their own private bathroom and color television, and usually a radio, hot-water Thermos with tea bags, and a mini-bar. Because they're accustomed to foreigners, most hotels in this category employ an English-speaking staff. The most expensive hotels in Japan are in Tokyo, where you will pay at least ¥18,000 ($129) for a single room in a first-class hotel. Outside Tokyo, single rooms in this category generally range from about ¥9,000 ($64) to ¥12,000 ($86), while in medium-priced hotels rooms are usually about ¥2,000 ($14.29) less.

Business Hotels

Catering primarily to traveling Japanese businessmen, a "business hotel" is a no-frills establishment with tiny, sparsely furnished rooms, most of them singles, but usually with some twin or double rooms also available. Primarily just a place to crash for the night, these rooms usually have everything you need but in miniature form—minuscule bathrooms, tiny bathtubs, small beds, and barely enough space to unpack your bags. After a while these business hotels all start to look alike. If you're a large person you may have trouble sleeping in a place like this. There's no room service, no bellboys, and sometimes not even a lobby or coffeeshop, although usually there are vending machines that dispense beer and soda. The advantages to staying in business hotels is that they're inexpensive—usually starting at ¥5,000 ($36) for a single—and are often conveniently located next to train and subway stations. Although check-in is usually not until 3 or 4 p.m. and checkout is usually at 10 a.m., you can leave your bags at the front desk. The most sophisticated business hotels can be found in Tokyo, where because of high prices they make up the bulk of medium-priced accommodation.

Pensions

If you see an accommodation listed as a pension, you know that it is the Western equivalent of a minshuku. Usually containing no more than ten rooms, these Western-style lodges come with beds and, on the average, charge ¥6,000 ($43) to ¥8,000 ($57) per person, including two meals. Many seem geared to young Japanese girls and are thus done up in rather feminine-looking decor with lots of pinks and flower prints. They're most often located in ski resorts and in the countryside, sometimes making access a problem.

Youth Hostels

There are more than 500 youth hostels in Japan, most of them privately run and operating in locations ranging from temples to concrete blocks. There is no age limit, and although most of them require a youth hostel membership card from the Japan Youth Hostel Association, they often let foreigners stay without one for about ¥500 ($3.57) extra per night. Although there are usually such restrictions as a 9 or 10 p.m. curfew, meals at fixed times, and rooms with many bunkbeds or futons, youth hostels are quite cheap, costing only ¥2,500 ($17.86) to ¥3,000 ($21.43) per day, including two meals. They're certainly the cheapest places to stay in Japan, though one Norwegian I met compared life in a youth hostel to that in the military. They're not quite that regimented, but you get the picture.

I've included youth hostels throughout my guide just in case you want to try some of them to keep down costs. If you plan on staying exclusively in youth hostels, however, you should pick up a pamphlet available at the Tourist Information Centers in Tokyo or Kyoto called *Youth Hostels in Japan.* You should also get a youth hostel membership card. If you fail to get one in your own country, you can get one in Japan for ¥2,200 ($15.71). The **Japan Youth Hostel Association** is located in the Hoken Kaikan Honkan Building, 1–2 Ichigaya-Sadohara-cho, Shinjuku-ku, Tokyo 162 (tel. 03/269-5831). Other places in Tokyo where you can buy a youth hostel card are at YH information counters on the sixth floor of Keio Department Store in Shinjuku, the second basement of Sogo Department Store in front of Yurakucho Station, and on the eighth floor of Seibu Department Store in Ikebukuro.

9. Food and Drink

Whenever I leave Japan it's the food I miss the most. Sure, there are sushi bars and other Japanese specialty restaurants spread throughout the United States, but they don't offer nearly the variety you can get in Japan. For just as America has more to offer than hamburgers and steaks, Japan has more than just sushi and tempura. For both the gourmet and the uninitiated, Japan is a treasure trove of culinary surprises.

Altogether there are more than a dozen different and distinct types of Japanese cuisine, as well as countless regional specialties. A good deal of what you eat may be completely new to you as well as completely unidentifiable. No need to worry. I've found that sometimes the Japanese don't even know what they're eating, so varied and so wide is the range of Japanese edibles. The rule is simply to enjoy, and the joy of Japanese food begins even before it enters your mouth. To the Japanese, presentation of food is as important as the food itself, and dishes are designed to appeal to the eye as well as to the palate. In contrast to the American way of piling as much food as possible onto a single plate, the Japanese use lots of small plates, each arranged artfully with bite-size morsels of food. After you've seen what can be done with maple leaves, flowers, bits of bamboo, and even pebbles to enhance the appearance of food, your relationship with what you eat may be changed forever.

The biggest problem facing the hungry foreigner in Japan is ordering, because few restaurants have English menus. This book alleviates that problem to a large extent by giving some sample dishes and prices for specific restaurants throughout Japan. Another custom in Japan that simplifies ordering is the use of plastic food models in glass display cases either outside or just inside the front door. Sushi, tempura, daily specials, spaghetti—they're all there in mouthwatering plastic replicas, along with the corresponding prices. The use of such food models began after Japan opened its doors a century ago and was inundated by all kinds of strange, foreign things. Food was one of them, and the models eased the problems of ordering. Today those plastic dishes work in reverse by saving the hungry lives of visiting foreigners. Simply decide what you want and point it out to your waitress.

Unfortunately, not all restaurants in Japan have plastic display cases. When that's the situation, the best thing to do is to look at what people around you are eating and order what looks best. An alternative is to simply order the *teishoku,* or the daily special. These are set courses and often include an entire meal with soup, rice, appetizer, and main dish. Although some restaurants have special set courses for dinner as well, lunch is the usual time for teishoku, and you can help keep your costs down by eating your big meal in the middle of the day. Even a restaurant that may be prohibitive to your budget at dinnertime may be perfect for a lunchtime splurge, when specials may cost as little as a fourth of what a dinner would be. The usual time for teishoku is from about 11 or 11:30 a.m. to 2 p.m.

Keep in mind that on restaurant charges more than ¥2,500 ($17.86) per person, a 10% tax will be added to your bill. First-class restaurants will also add a 10% to 15% service charge.

For those of you who may not want to eat Japanese food every day, I've included suggestions throughout this book for non-Japanese restaurants as well. The most popular Western-style restaurants in Japan are Italian and French, although more often than not they cook for the Japanese rather than the Western palate. French nouvelle cuisine matches well the Japanese style of cooking, since both stress presentation, textures, and flavor, and the most expensive foreign restaurants in Japan are nearly all French. Other popular restaurants in Japan include Indian and Chinese, as well as numerous steakhouses.

Below are explanations of some of Japan's most common types of cuisine and foods. Generally speaking, only one type of cuisine is served in a given restaurant—that is, only raw seafood is served in a sushi bar. There are some exceptions to this, especially in those restaurants where raw fish may be served as an appetizer. In addition, some of Japan's drinking establishments offer a wide range of foods, from soups to salads to sushi to skewered pieces of chicken.

RICE: There are no problems here—everyone is familiar with rice. The difference, however, is that in Japan it is quite sticky, making it easier to pick up with chopsticks. It's also just plain white rice (called *gohan*)—no salt, no butter, no soy sauce. Like other Asians, the Japanese have used rice as a staple in their diet for about 2,000 years, though not everyone in the old days could afford the expensive white kind. The peasants had to be satisfied with a mixture of white and brown rice, millet, and greens. Today some Japanese still eat rice three times a day, though the younger ones are now just as apt to have bread and coffee for breakfast.

KAISEKI CUISINE: *Kaiseki* is the king of Japanese cuisine, the epitome of delicately and exquisitely arranged food, the ultimate in Japanese aesthetic appeal. It's also among the most expensive and can cost ¥20,000 ($143) per person. Some restaurants, however, do offer mini-kaiseki courses that are much more affordable. The reason kaiseki is expensive is that much time and skill is involved in preparing each of the many dishes, with the ingredients cooked so as to preserve their natural flavor. Even the plates are chosen with great care, meant to enhance the color, texture, and shape of each piece of food.

Kaiseki cuisine is based on the four seasons, with the selection of food and its presentation dependent on the time of the year. In fact, so strongly does a kaiseki preparation convey the mood of a particular season that the kaiseki gourmet can tell what season it is just by looking at his meal. The roots of kaiseki go back to the development of the tea ceremony, when monks ate small morsels of food to protect the stomach against the effects of strong tea.

A kaiseki meal is usually a lengthy affair, with various dishes appearing in set order. First comes the appetizer, clear broth, and one uncooked dish. That's followed by boiled, broiled, fried, steamed, heated, and vinegared dishes, and finally by another soup, rice, pickled vegetables, and fruit. Since kaiseki is always a set course there's no problem in ordering. Let your budget be your guide.

SUSHI AND SASHIMI: It is estimated that the average Japanese eats 70 pounds of seafood a year, six times the amount Americans do. Although this seafood may be served in any number of ways, from grilled to boiled, a great deal of it is eaten raw. Granted, the idea of eating raw fish might seem a little strange at first, but if you'll just try it you'll probably like it.

Sashimi is simply raw seafood. A good choice to start out with if you've never eaten it is *maguro,* or lean tuna. Contrary to what you might think, it doesn't taste fishy at all and is so delicate in texture that it almost melts in your mouth. The way to eat sashimi is first to mix *wasabi* (pungent green horseradish) into a small dish of soy sauce and then dip the raw fish into the sauce.

Sushi, also called *nigiri-zushi*, is raw fish, seafood, or vegetables placed on top of vinegared rice with just a touch of wasabi. It's also dipped into soy sauce. Use chopsticks or your fingers to eat sushi; remember that you're supposed to eat each piece in one bite—quite a mouthful but about the only way to keep it from falling apart. Another trick is to turn it upside down when you dip it into the sauce so that only the fish and not the rice touches the sauce.

Typical sushi includes flounder *(hirame)*, sea bream *(tai)*, squid *(ika)*, octopus *(tako)*, shrimp *(ebi)*, and omelet *(tamago)*. Ordering is easy because you usually sit at the sushi bar, where you can see all the food in a refrigerated glass case in front of you. You also get to see all the action of the sushi chefs at work. The typical meal begins with sashimi and is followed by sushi, but if you don't want to order separately there are always various set courses.

TEMPURA: Today a well-known Japanese food, tempura was actually introduced by the Portuguese, who came to Japan in the 16th century. Tempura is deep-fried food that has been coated in a batter of egg, water, and wheat flour and is served piping hot. To eat it, dip it into a soy sauce that has been mixed with a fish stock base and flavored with radish *(daikon)* and grated ginger. Various tempura specialties may include eggplant, mushroom, sweet potato, green pepper, slices of lotus root, shrimp, squid, and many kinds of fish. Again, the easiest thing to do is to order the set course, the *teishoku*. If you're still hungry you can always order something extra à la carte.

SUKIYAKI: Until about a hundred years ago the Japanese could think of nothing so disgusting as eating the flesh of animals (fish was okay). Considered unclean by the Buddhists, meat consumption was banned by the emperor way back in the seventh century. Imagine the horror of the Japanese to discover that Western "barbarians" ate bloody meat! It wasn't until Emperor Meiji himself made a public announcement a century ago that he was going to eat meat that the Japanese accepted the idea. Today the Japanese have become skilled in preparing a number of beef dishes. And according to a survey conducted a couple of years back by the Japan Fisheries Association, grilled meat, curried rice, and hamburger were the three favorite dishes among senior high school boys living in Tokyo. The girls, by the way, still preferred sushi.

Sukiyaki is one of Japan's best-known beef dishes and is one many Westerners seem to prefer. Actually its origins are more Western than Japanese (it was introduced in the last century as a new Western cuisine). To the Western palate, however, it seems distinctly Japanese and today enjoys immense popularity in Japan. Whenever I'm invited to a Japanese home, this is the meal most often served. Like fondue, it's cooked at the table, which makes for an intimate and cozy setting.

Sukiyaki is thinly sliced beef cooked in a broth of soy sauce, stock, and sake, along with scallions, spinach, mushrooms, tofu, bamboo shoots, and other vegetables. All diners serve themselves by taking what they want out of the simmering pot and then dipping it into their own bowl of raw egg. You can skip the raw egg if you want, but it adds to the taste and also cools the food down enough so it doesn't burn your tongue.

SHABU-SHABU: Similar to sukiyaki, shabu-shabu is also prepared at your table and consists of thinly sliced beef cooked in a broth with vegetables. The main difference between the two is the broth. Whereas in sukiyaki it consists of stock flavored with soy sauce and sake and is slightly sweet, the broth of shabu-shabu is relatively clear and has little taste of its own. The pots used are also different.

Named for the swishing sound the beef supposedly makes when it's cooking, shabu-shabu is a meal in which you hold your own piece of meat in the watery broth with your chopsticks until it cooks, usually only a few seconds.

Vegetables are left in longer to swim around until you fish them out. Sauces are either sesame with diced green onions or a more bitter sauce made from fish stock. Restaurants serving sukiyaki usually serve shabu-shabu as well.

TEPPANYAKI: A teppanyaki restaurant is a Japanese steakhouse. As in the famous Benihana restaurants in many cities in the United States, the chef slices, dices, and cooks your meal of tenderloin or sirloin steak and vegetables on a smooth hot grill right in front of you. Because beef is relatively new in Japanese cooking, some people categorize teppanyaki restaurants as "Western" cuisine. However, I consider its style of cooking and presentation unique enough that throughout this book I refer to such restaurants as Japanese.

ROBATAYAKI: Robatayaki refers to restaurants in which seafood and vegetables are cooked over a *robata* grill. In the olden days an open fireplace (robata) in the middle of an old Japanese house was the center of activity for cooking, eating, socializing, and simply keeping warm. So today's robatayaki restaurants are like nostalgia trips back into Japan's past. They are often decorated in rustic farmhouse style with the staff dressed in traditional clothing. Many robatayaki restaurants are open only in the evenings and are popular among office workers for both eating and drinking.

There's no special menu in a robatayaki restaurant—rather, it includes just about everything eaten in Japan. The difference is that most of the foods will be grilled. Favorites of mine include gingko nuts, asparagus, green peppers, mushrooms, potatoes, and just about any kind of fish. You can also usually get skewers of beef or chicken as well as a stew of meat and potatoes *(nikujaga)*, delicious in cold winter months. Since ordering is à la carte, you'll just have to look and point.

YAKITORI: Yakitori is chunks of chicken or chicken parts basted in a sweet soy sauce and grilled over a charcoal fire on thin skewers. A place that serves yakitori (sometimes called a *yakitori-ya* and often identifiable by a red paper lantern outside its front door) is technically not a restaurant but rather a drinking establishment. It usually doesn't open until 5 p.m., and most are extremely popular with the working crowd as an inexpensive place to drink, eat, and be merry.

Although you can order a set dish of various yakitori, I usually refrain because this will often include various parts of the chicken like the skin, heart, and liver. You may like such exotica but it's definitely not for me. If you're ordering by the stick, you might want to try chicken meatballs *(tsukune)*, green peppers *(piman)*, chicken and leeks *(negima)*, mushrooms *(shitake)*, gingko nuts *(ginnan)*, or chicken breast *(sasami)*.

KUSHIAGE: Kushiage foods (also called *kushikatsu* or *kushiyaki*) are deep-fried on skewers and include chicken, beef, seafood, and lots of seasonal vegetables (snowpeas, gingko nuts, lotus root, and the like). The result is delicious and I highly recommend trying it. I don't understand why this style of cooking isn't better known—maybe someday it will be. Ordering the set menu is easiest, and what you get is often determined by both the chef and the season.

TONKATSU: Tonkatsu is the Japanese word for "pork cutlet" and it's made by dredging pork in wheat flour, moistening it with egg and water, dipping it in bread crumbs, and deep-frying it in vegetable oil. Restaurants serving tonkatsu are generally inexpensive and therefore popular with office workers and families. The easiest order is the teishoku, and the most common is with either the pork filet *(hirekatsu)* or the pork loin *(rosukatsu)*. In any case, your tonkatsu is served on a bed of lettuce or shredded cabbage, and two different sauces will be at your table.

FUGU: Known as the blowfish, pufferfish, or globefish in English, fugu is perhaps one of the most exotic and adventurous foods in Japan, primarily because if it's not prepared properly it means almost certain death for the consumer. In the past decade or so as many as 200 people in Japan have died from fugu poisoning, usually because they tried preparing it at home. The ovaries and intestines of the fugu are deadly and must be entirely removed, without puncturing them. So why eat fugu if it can kill you? Well, for one thing it's delicious, and for another, fugu chefs are strictly licensed by the government and greatly skilled in preparing fugu dishes. You can eat fugu raw *(sashimi)* or in a stew *(fugu-chiri)* cooked with vegetables at your table. The season for fresh fugu is from October or November through March, but some restaurants serve it throughout the year.

UNAGI: I'll bet that if you ate unagi without knowing what it was you'd find it very tasty. In fact, you'd probably be very surprised to find out that you had just eaten eel. Popular as a health food because of its high vitamin A content, eel is supposed to help fight fatigue during the hot summer months but is eaten year round. Broiled eel *(kabayaki)* is prepared by grilling filet strips over a charcoal fire; the eel is repeatedly dipped in a sweetened barbecue soy sauce while cooking. A favorite way to eat broiled eel is on top of rice, in which case it's called *unaju.* Do yourself a favor and try it.

NOODLES: The Japanese love eating noodles but I suspect that at least part of the fascination stems from the *way* they eat them—they slurp and suck them in with a speed that defies gravity. If you ask me, *Gone in 60 Seconds* could describe the way a businessman attacks his lunchtime bowl of noodles. At any rate, you're *supposed* to slurp noodles: it's considered proper etiquette. Fearing that it would stick with me forever, however, slurping is a technique I never quite mastered.

There are many different kinds of noodles—some are eaten plain, some in combination with other foods; some hot and some cold. *Soba,* made from buckwheat flour, is eaten hot or cold. *Udon* is a thick, white noodle originally from Osaka and is usually served hot. *Somen* is a fine, white noodle that is eaten cold in the summer and dunked in a cold sauce.

Noodle shops are generally inexpensive, ranging from stand-up stalls seen around train stations to more traditional restaurants, where guests sit at low tables on tatami.

OKONOMIYAKI: Meaning literally "as you like it," okonomiyaki originated in Osaka and is sort of like a Japanese pizza. Basically it's a kind of pancake to which meat or fish, shredded cabbage, and vegetables are added. Since it's a popular fare of street vendors, restaurants specializing in this type of cuisine are very reasonably priced. At some locales the cook makes it for you, but in others it's do-it-yourself, which can be quite fun if you're with a group.

OTHER TYPES OF CUISINE: During your travels you might also run into other types of Japanese cuisine. *Kamameshi* is a rice casserole with different kinds of toppings that might include seafood, meat, or vegetables. *Nabe* cuisine is a stew cooked in an earthenware pot at your table with ingredients that might consist of chicken, sliced beef, pork, or seafood, and vegetables. *Oden* is fish cakes, tofu, and vegetables steeped in broth, served with hot mustard.

Although technically a Chinese fast-food restaurant, *ramen* shops are so much a part of dining in Japan that I feel compelled to include them here. Serving what I consider to be generic Chinese noodles, soups, and other dishes, ramen shops can be found everywhere in Japan, easily recognizable by their red signs, flashing lights, and quite often pictures of various dishes displayed right by the front door. In addition to ramen, noodle and vegetable soup, you can also get such things as fried noodles or—my favorite—*gyoza,* which are fried pork dumplings. What these places lack in atmosphere is made up for in price: most dishes average about ¥500 ($3.57).

BUDGET CHOICES: Although some of the above types of restaurants (such as noodle and ramen shops) are already rock-bottom choices, you can save even more money by avoiding restaurants altogether. There are all kinds of pre-prepared foods you can buy, and some of them are complete meals in themselves, perfect for picnics in the park or right in your hotel room.

Perhaps the best-known is the *obento,* or box lunch, commonly sold on express trains, on train station platforms, and at counter windows of tiny shops throughout Japan. Costing usually between ¥500 ($3.57) and ¥1,000 ($7.14), the basic obento contains a piece of meat (generally fish or chicken), rice, and pickled vegetables. Sushi boxed lunches are also available.

Department stores usually sell pre-prepared foods in their basements in their food and produce sections, including such items as tempura, yakitori, sushi, salads, and desserts. These places are very popular with housewives. By the way, most department stores also have inexpensive restaurants, usually on one of the top floors. Since they almost always have plastic food displays, ordering is easy.

Street vendors are also good sources for inexpensive meals. They sell a variety of foods, including oden, okonomiyaki, and fried noodles *(yakisoba).* And finally, if you find yourself in real financial woes, you can always subsist on "cup noodle," which you can buy in any food store. Eaten by poor students and workingmen who don't have the time to sit down to a real meal, it's a dried soup that springs to life (well, sort of) when you add hot water—usually readily available if you're staying in a ryokan. It comes in a variety of choices, such as curry or chili tomato, and usually costs less than ¥200 ($1.43). Eat too much of it, though, and you'll probably disintegrate.

In case you're interested, Japan also has American fast-food chains such as McDonald's (where Big Macs cost about ¥400 or $2.86), Wendy's, and Kentucky Fried Chicken, as well as Japanese chains—Morninaga and First Kitchen among them—which also sell hamburgers and french fries.

DRINKS: All Japanese restaurants serve complimentary Japanese green tea with meals. If that's a little too weak, Japanese *sake* made from rice is an alcoholic beverage, served either hot or cold, that goes well with most forms of Japanese cuisine. Japanese beer is also very popular. The biggest sellers are Suntory, Kirin, and Sapporo, but ironically enough Budweiser is a big hit among young Japanese. Japanese businessmen are fond of whisky, which they usually drink with ice and water. Although cocktails are available in discos, hotel lounges, and fancier bars, most Japanese stick with beer, sake, or whisky. Popular in recent years is *shochu,* an alcoholic beverage usually made from rice but sometimes from wheat or sweet potato. It used to be considered a drink of the lower classes, but its sales have increased so much that it's threatening the sake and whisky business. A clear liquid, it's often combined with soda water in a drink called *chu-hi,* but watch out—the stuff can be deadly.

10. Religion, Shrines, and Temples

The main religions in Japan are Shintoism and Buddhism, and many Japanese consider themselves believers in both. Whereas a Westerner might find it difficult to belong to two completely different religious organizations, the Japanese find nothing unusual about it and incorporate both into their lifestyles. Most Japanese, for example, are married in a Shinto ceremony, but when they die, they'll probably have a Buddhist funeral.

Unlike in the West where churches have religious services weekly, the Japanese generally visit a temple or shrine only for a specific purpose. On New Year's, for example, many Japanese throng to shrines to pray for good fortune in the coming year, while in mid-July or mid-August they go to pay respect to their ancestors. As such, neither religion has a great influence in the everyday life of the Japanese. Rather, religion is more a way of thinking, a way of relating to one's world, environment, and family. The Japanese appreciation of natural beauty and strong sense of duty and obligation, for example, have religious roots.

SHINTOISM: A native religion of Japan, Shintoism is the worship of ancestors and national heroes, as well as all natural things, both animate and inanimate. These natural things are thought to embody gods, called *kami,* and can be anyone or anything: mountains, trees, the moon, stars, rivers, seas, fires, animals, a rock, even vegetables. In this respect it resembles beliefs of some American Indian tribes. Shintoism also embraces much of Confucianism, which entered Japan in the fifth century and stressed the importance of family and loyalty. There are no scriptures in Shintoism, no set of morals or ethics.

The most important goddess in Shintoism is Amaterasu, the sun goddess, who is considered the progenitor of the Japanese imperial family. Central to the principles of Shintoism through the centuries, therefore, was the belief that the emperor was a living god. The emperor held this revered position for more than 1,500 years, until the end of World War II. It was then that the emperor was forced to renounce his claim to divinity and admit that he was a regular human being just like everyone else. At this time Shintoism also lost its official status as the national religion, a position it had held since the Meiji Restoration (1868). However, Shintoism has not lost its popularity and claims more than 80 million followers in Japan. As for the imperial family, they still occupy a special place in the hearts of the Japanese.

The place of worship in Shintoism is called a shrine, *jinja* in Japanese. Every city, town, village, and hamlet has at least one shrine, and to most inhabitants they embody the soul of their district. The most famous shrines are Meiji Shrine in Tokyo, the Ise Shrines in the Ise-Shima National Park (dedicated to the sun goddess), and Itsukushima Shrine on Miyajima Island.

The most obvious telltale sign of a shrine is its *torii,* an entrance usually of wood that consists of two tall poles topped with either one or two crossbeams. Sometimes there will be several of these torii spread out over the pathway leading to the shrine, reminding visitors that they are approaching a shrine and giving them time to achieve the proper frame of mind. Before reaching the shrine itself you'll pass a water trough with communal cups where the Japanese will rinse out their mouths and wash their hands. Purification and cleanliness are important in Shintoism because they show respect to the gods, aspects that have carried over even today in the Japanese custom of bathing and removing shoes indoors.

At the shrine itself the worshipper will throw a few coins into a money box, clap his hands three times to get the attention of the gods, and then bow his head and pray. Sometimes there will be a rope attached to a gong that's even louder in calling the gods. And what do worshippers pray for? Good health, protection, safe delivery of a child, that sons get into good universities and that daughters get good husbands. Some shrines are considered lucky for love while others are good against certain ailments. You can ask any favor of the gods. Shrines are also the sites of many festivals and are visited on important occasions throughout one's life, including marriage and on certain birthdays.

BUDDHISM: Whereas they're called shrines in Shintoism, in Buddhism they're called temples *(otera* in Japanese). Instead of *torii,* temples will often have an entrance gate with a raised doorsill and heavy doors. Temples may also have a cemetery on their grounds, which Shinto shrines never have, and a pagoda.

Founded in India in the fifth century, Buddhism came to Japan in the sixth century via China and Korea, introducing to Japan the concept of eternal life. By the end of the sixth century Buddhism had gained such popularity that Prince Shotoku, one of Japan's most remarkable historical figures, declared Buddhism the state religion and based many of his governmental policies on its tenets. Another important Buddhist leader to emerge was a priest called Kukai, known posthumously as Kobo Daishi. After studying Buddhism in China in the early 800s, he returned to Japan, where he founded the Shingon sect of Buddhism and established his mission atop Mount Koya. The temples he built throughout Japan, including the famous 88 temples on Shikoku Island and those on Mount Koya, continue to attract millions of pilgrims even today.

Probably the Buddhist sect best known to the West, however, is Zen Buddhism. Considered the most Japanese form of Buddhism, Zen is the practice of meditation and a strictly disciplined lifestyle in the belief that it helps rid oneself of desire so that one can achieve enlightenment. There are no rites in Zen Buddhism, no dogmas nor a theological conception of divinity. You do not analyze rationally but rather are supposed to know things intuitively. The strict and simple lifestyle of Zen appealed greatly to Japan's samurai warrior class, and many of Japan's arts, including the tea ceremony, arose from the practice of Zen.

Visitors to Japan who are interested in Buddhism and temples should try to spend at least one night in a temple. The best place for this is Mount Koya, known as Koya-san to the Japanese, where approximately 50 temples have opened their doors to overnight guests, offering them simple tatami rooms, vegetarian meals, and the opportunity to join in the 6 a.m. service.

11. Festivals and Annual Events

With both Shintoism and Buddhism as the major religions in Japan it seems as though there's a festival going on somewhere in the country almost every day. Every major shrine and temple in the land has at least one annual festival, with events that might include traditional dances, archery, or colorful processions in which portable shrines are carried through the streets by groups of chanting Japanese dressed in traditional costumes.

There are also a number of national holidays observed throughout the country, as well as such annual events as cormorant fishing and cherry-blossom viewing. During the summer, festivals are held seemingly everywhere, and you may stumble on to a neighborhood festival just by accident.

As for the larger, better-known festivals, they may be exciting for the visitor but do take some planning since hotel rooms may be booked six months in advance. If you haven't made prior arrangements, you may want to let the following schedule be your guide in avoiding certain cities on certain days. You won't find a hotel room anywhere near Takayama, for example, on the days of its two big festivals. If you plan your trip around a certain festival, be sure to double-check the exact dates with the Japan Tourist Office, since these dates can change. And remember, if a national holiday falls on a Sunday, the following Monday becomes a holiday.

January

1—New Year's Day. This is the most important national holiday in Japan. Like Christmas in the West, it's a time of family reunions, and it's a time when friends get together to drink sake and eat special New Year dishes. Streets and homes are decorated with straw ropes and pine or plum branches. Because this is a time that Japanese spend together with their families, and because almost all businesses, restaurants, and shops close down, it's not a particularly rewarding time of the year for foreigners.

3—Tamaseseri (Ball-Catching Festival), held at Hakozakigu Shrine in Fukuoka on Kyushu. The main attraction here is a struggle between two groups of youths who try to capture a sacred wooden ball. The team that wins is supposed to have good luck the whole year.

6—Dezome-shiki (New Year's Parade of Firemen), held in Harumi Chuo Dori in Tokyo. Agile firemen dressed in traditional costumes prove their worth with acrobatic stunts atop tall bamboo ladders—you'd certainly feel safe being rescued by one of them.

7—Usokae (Bullfinch Exchange Festival), at Dazaifu Temmangu Shrine outside Fukuoka City. The trick here is to get hold of the bullfinches made of gilt wood that are given away by priests—they're supposed to bring good luck.

9 to 11—Toka Ebisu Festival, held at Imamiya Ebisu Shrine in Osaka. Ebisu is considered the patron saint of business and good fortune, so this is the time when businesspeople pray for a successful year. The highlight of the festival is a parade of women dressed in colorful kimonos and carried through the streets in palanquins.

15—Adults' Day. A national holiday in Japan, this day honors young people who have reached the age of 20, when they can vote and assume other responsibilities.

15—Grass Fire Ceremony, on Wakakusayama Hill in Nara. As evening approaches Wakakusayama Hill is set ablaze and fireworks are displayed. The celebration marks a time more than a thousand years ago when a dispute over the boundary of two major temples in Nara was settled peacefully.

15—Toshi-ya, a traditional Japanese archery contest held at Sanjusangendo Hall in Kyoto.

February

Wednesday to Saturday of the first week—Snow Festival, in Sapporo. This famous festival features huge, elaborate statues and figures carved of snow and ice.

First Sunday—Oyster Festival, held in Matsushima at the seaside park along the bay. Matsushima is famous for its oysters, and this is the time they're considered at their best. Booths are set up and oysters are given out free.

3 or 4—Setsubun (Bean-Throwing Festival), held at leading temples throughout Japan. According to the lunar calendar this is the last day of winter, and people throng to temples to participate in the traditional ceremony of throwing beans to drive away imaginary devils.

3 or 4—Lantern Festival, at Kasuga Shrine in Nara. This is a beautiful sight in which more than 3,000 stone and bronze lanterns are lit.

11—National Foundation Day *(Kigensetsu)*, a national holiday.

March

1 to 14—Omizutori (Water-Drawing Festival), at Todaiji Temple in Nara. This festival includes a solemn rite performed in the evenings in which young ascetics brandish large burning torches and draw circles of fire. The biggest ceremony takes place on March 12th, and on the 13th the ceremony of drawing water is held to the accompaniment of ancient Japanese music.

3—Hinamatsuri (Doll Festival). Observed throughout Japan, it's held in honor of young girls to wish them a future of happiness. In homes where there are girls, dolls dressed in ancient costumes representing the emperor, empress, and dignitaries are set up on a tier of shelves along with miniature household articles.

13—Kasuga Matsuri, at Kasuga Shrine in Nara. This festival has a history stretching back 1,100 years and features traditional costumes and classical dances.

20 or 21—Vernal Equinox Day, a national holiday. Throughout the week Buddhist temples hold ceremonies to pray for the souls of the departed.

Late March to May—The **cherry-blossom season** begins in late March on the southern islands of Kyushu and Shikoku, travels up Honshu through April and reaches Hokkaido by the beginning of May. Early to mid-April is when the blossoms burst forth in Tokyo and Kyoto. Popular cherry-viewing spots in Kyoto include Maruyama Park, the garden of Heian Shrine, the Imperial Palace, Nijo Castle, Kiyomizu Temple, and Arashiyama, while in Tokyo people throng to Ueno Park, Yasukuni Shrine, and the moat encircling the Imperial Palace.

April

8—Buddha's Birthday. Ceremonies are held at all Buddhist temples.

Second to third Sunday—Kamakura Matsuri, at Tsurugaoka Hachimangu Shrine in Kamakura. This festival honors heroes from the past, including Yoritomo Minamoto, who made Kamakura his shogunate capital back in 1192. Highlights are horseback archery (truly spectacular to watch), a parade of portable shrines, and sacred dances.

13 to 17—Yayoi Matsuri, at Futarasan Shrine in Nikko. This festival features a parade of decorated floats.

14 and 15—Takayama Festival, at Hie Shrine in Takayama. This festival supposedly dates back to the 15th century and features a procession of huge, gorgeous floats.

Mid-April—Gumonji-do (Firewalking Ceremonies). These rites and ancient shrine dances called *bugaku* are held atop Mount Misen on Miyajima. Walking on fire is meant to show devotion and is also for purification.

29—The Emperor's Birthday, a national holiday.

April 29 to May 5—Golden Week. Many Japanese offices and businesses close down and families go on vacation. It's a crowded time to travel, making reservations a must.

May

3—Constitution Memorial Day, a national holiday.

3 and 4—Hakata Dontaku, in Fukuoka. Citizens dressed as deities ride through the streets on horseback to the accompaniment of flutes, drums, and traditional instruments.

5—Children's Day, a national holiday. This festival honors young boys, and the most common sight are colorful streamers of carp flying from poles throughout Japan. These fish symbolize attributes desirable for young boys— perseverance and strength.

11 and 12—Takigi Noh performances, at Kofukuji Temple in Nara. Noh plays are presented on stage after dark under the blaze of torches.

11 to October 15—Cormorant fishing, on the Nagara River near Gifu. Visitors board small wooden boats at night to watch cormorants dive into the water to catch *ayu*, a kind of trout. Cormorant fishing is also held on the Katsura (also called Oi) River outside Kyoto.

15—Aoi Matsuri (Hollyhock Festival), of Shimogamo and Kamigamo shrines in Kyoto. This is one of Kyoto's biggest festivals, a colorful pageant commemorating the days when the imperial procession visited the city's shrines. It supposedly dates from the seventh century, when a ceremony was held to appease the gods following severe storms.

Saturday and Sunday closest to the 15th—Kanda Festival, held at Kanda Myojin Shrine in Tokyo every other year. Portable shrines are carried through the district.

Mid-May—Kobe Matsuri, in Kobe. This relatively new festival celebrates Kobe's international past with fireworks at Kobe Port, street markets, and a parade on Flower Road, with participants wearing native costumes.

17 and 18—Grand Festival of Toshogu Shrine, in Nikko. This festival commemorates the day in 1617 when Ieyasu Tokugawa's remains were brought to his mausoleum in Nikko, accompanied by 1,000 people. This festival re-creates the drama with more than 1,000 armor-clad people escorting three palanquins through the streets.

Third Saturday and Sunday—Sanja Matsuri, at Asakusa Shrine in Tokyo. About 100 portable shrines are carried through the district on the shoulders of men and women in traditional garb.

Third Sunday—Mifune Matsuri, held on the Oi River outside Kyoto in Arashiyama. In a reproduction of an ancient boat festival, the days of the Heian Period are reenacted, when the imperial family used to take pleasure rides on the river.

June

1 and 2—Takigi Noh performances, at Heian Shrine in Kyoto. Evening performances of Noh are presented on an open-air stage in the shrine's compound.

10 to 16—Sanno Festival, at Hie Shrine in Tokyo. This festival, which first began in the Edo Period (1603–1867), features the usual portable shrines transported through the busy streets of the Akasaka district.

14—Rice-planting Festival, at Sumiyoshi Shrine in Osaka. In hopes of a successful harvest, young girls in traditional farmers' costumes transplant rice seedlings in the shrine's rice paddy to the sound of music and traditional songs.

Mid-June—Hyakuman-goku Festival, in Kanazawa. Held only since 1952, the Hyakuman-goku Festival commemorates the arrival of Maeda, a feudal lord who laid the foundations of the Kaga clan, in this castle town. The highlight of the festival is a procession, and in the evening paper lanterns float down the Asano River.

July

1 to 15—Hakata Yamagasa, at Fukuoka. The main event takes place on the 15th, when a giant fleet of floats topped with elaborate decorations is paraded through the streets.

7—Tanabata (Star Festival), celebrated throughout Japan. According to myth, the two stars Vega and Altair, representing a weaver and a shepherd, are allowed to meet once a year on this day. If the skies are cloudy, however, the celestial pair cannot meet and must wait another year.

13 to 15—Obon Festival. This festival takes place in either mid-July or mid-August, depending on the area in Japan, and is held in memory of the dead, who, according to Buddhist belief, revisit the world during this period. Many Japanese return to their hometowns for the event, especially if a member of the family has died recently. As one Japanese, whose grandmother had died a few months before, told me, "I have to go back to my hometown—it's my grandmother's first Obon."

17—Gion Matsuri, at Yasaka Shrine in Kyoto. This festival is one of the most famous festivals in Japan. It dates back to the ninth century, when the head priest at Yasaka Shrine organized a procession in an attempt to ask the gods' assistance against a plague that was raging in the city. Although the festival is actually celebrated the whole month of July, the highlight is on the 17th, when spectacular floats wind their way through the city streets. Many foreigners plan their trip to Japan around this event.

25—Tenjin Matsuri, at Temmangu Shrine in Osaka. This is one of Osaka's biggest festivals. It dates back to the tenth century, when the people of Osaka visited Temmangu Shrine to pray for protection against the diseases prevalent during the long, hot summer. They would take pieces of paper cut in the form of human beings and, while the Shinto priest said prayers, would rub the paper over themselves in ritual cleansing. Afterward the pieces of paper were taken by boat to the mouth of the river and disposed of. Today the festival reenacts the boat procession with a fleet of more than 100 sacred boats making its way down the river, followed by a fireworks display.

Late July or early August—Kangensai Music Festival, at Itsukushima Shrine in Miyajima. There's classical court music and *bugaku* dancing and three barges carrying portable shrines, priests, and musicians across the bay, along with a flotilla of other boats. Because this festival takes place according to the lunar calendar, the actual date changes each year.

Late July or early August—Fireworks display over the Sumida River in Asakusa, Tokyo. This is Tokyo's largest, and everyone sits on blankets along the banks of the river. Great fun!

August

First Saturday and Sunday—Oshiro Matsuri, in Himeji. This festival is famous for its Noh dramas performed on a special stage constructed on the Himeji Castle grounds. On Sunday there's a procession from the castle to the city center, with participants dressed in traditional costumes.

6—Peace Ceremony, in Hiroshima. Held at Peace Memorial Park, this annual ceremony is in memory of the victims who died from the atomic bomb dropped over Hiroshima on August 6, 1945. A similar ceremony is held on August 9 in Nagasaki.

5 and 6—Waraku Odori, in Nikko. This is a good opportunity to see some of Japan's folk dances.

6 to 8—Tanabata Festival, at Sendai. Sendai holds its Star Festival one month later than the rest of Japan. It's the country's largest, and the whole town is decorated with colored paper streamers.

11 to 13—Matsuyama Festival, in Matsuyama on Shikoku. Festivities include dances, fireworks, and a night fair.

12 to 14—Takamatsu Festival, in Takamatsu on Shikoku. About 6,000 people participate in a dance procession which threads its way along Chuo-dori Street. Anyone can join in.

15—Toronagashi and Fireworks Display in Matsushima. Held in the evening, first there's a fireworks display, followed by the setting adrift of about 5,000 small boats with lanterns on the bay. Another 3,000 lanterns are lit on islets in the bay, which illuminate the water. The lanterns are thought to console the souls of the dead.

16—Daimonji Bonfire, on Mount Nyoigadake in Kyoto. A huge bonfire in the shape of the Chinese character *dai,* which means "large," is lit near the peak as part of the Obon festival.

September

15—Respect-for-the-Aged Day, a national holiday.

16—Yabusame, at Tsurugaoka Hachimangu Shrine in Kamakura. Archery performed on horseback recalls the days of the samurai.

23 or 24—Autumnal Equinox Day, a national holiday.

October

7 to 9—Okunchi Festival, at Suwa Shrine in Nagasaki. This festival illustrates the influence Nagasaki's Chinese population has had on the city through the centuries. A parade of floats and dragon dances are highlights.

8 to 10—Marimo Matsuri, on Lake Akan, Hokkaido. *Marimo* is a spherical green weed that grows in Lake Akan. This festival is put on by the native Ainu population.

9 and 10—Takayama Matsuri, of Hachiman Shrine in Takayama. Similar to the festival held here in April, huge floats are paraded through the streets.

10—Health-Sports Day, a national holiday.

9 to 11—Great Festival of Kotohiragu Shrine, near Takamatsu on Shikoku. The climax of this festival is a parade of *mikoshi* (portable shrines).

14 and 15—Mega Kenka Matsuri (Roughhouse Festival), at Matsubara Shrine in Himeji. Portable shrines shouldered by youths jostle each other as the youths attempt to show their skill in balancing the heavy shrines.

17—Autumn Festival, at Toshogu Shrine in Nikko. Armor-clad parishioners escort a sacred portable shrine.

22—Jidai Matsuri (Festival of the Ages), at Heian Shrine in Kyoto. Another of Kyoto's grand festivals, this is one of the most interesting because it features a procession of more than 2,000 people dressed in ancient costumes representing different epochs of Kyoto's 1,200-year history. The festival is held in commemoration of the founding of Kyoto in 794.

22—Fire Festival, at Yuki Shrine, Kyoto. Long rows of torches are embedded along the approach to the shrine to illuminate a procession of children.

November

2 and 3—Ohara Matsuri, in Kagoshima. About 15,000 people parade through the town in cotton *yukata,* dancing to the tune of popular Kagoshima folk songs. A sort of Japanese Mardi Gras, this event attracts several hundred thousand spectators a year.

3—Culture Day, a national holiday.

3—Daimyo Gyoretsu, in Hakone. The old Tokaido Highway that used to link Kyoto and Tokyo comes alive again with a long parade that is a faithful reproduction of a feudal lord's procession in the olden days.

15—Shichi-go-san (Children's Shrine-Visiting Day), held throughout Japan. *Shichi-go-san* literally means "seven-five-three," and refers to children of these ages who are taken to shrines by their elders to express thanks and pray for their future.

23—Labor Thanksgiving Day, a national holiday.

December

17—On-Matsuri, at Kasuga Shrine in Nara. This festival features a parade of people dressed as courtiers, retainers, and wrestlers of long ago.

31—New Year's Eve. At midnight many temples ring huge bells 108 times to signal the end of the old year and the beginning of the new. Many families visit temples and shrines on New Year's Eve to pray for the coming year.

12. Cultural Activities

Japan is known around the world for its aestheticism, apparent in everything from its food to its gardens to its art. Rich in its cultural history, the nation has produced widely divergent forms of expression—the tea ceremony, sumo, Kabuki, and flower arranging, to name a few—all of which command a large audience even today. In fact, the Japanese think so highly of their artists and performers that masters in many fields have been designated National Living Treasures.

Although it's possible to see the performing arts as well as sumo and the tea ceremony in other parts of Japan, Tokyo is your best bet for offering the most at any one time. Several of the larger first-class hotels in Tokyo, for example, offer a few hours' instruction in English in the tea ceremony, and sumo matches and Kabuki performances are held several times during the year. For specific information on cultural entertainment in the capital city, refer to Chapter IV.

KABUKI: Probably Japan's best-known traditional stage art, Kabuki theater is also one of the country's most popular forms of entertainment. Visit a performance and it's easy to see why. In a word, Kabuki is *fun!* The plays are dramatic, the costumes are gorgeous, the stage settings are often fantastic, and the themes are about things everyone can identify with—love, revenge, and conflicts between duty and personal feelings. Probably one of the reasons Kabuki is so popular even today is that it developed centuries ago as a form of entertainment for the common people in feudal Japan, particularly the merchants. And one of the interesting aspects of Kabuki is that all roles—even those of women—are portrayed only by men.

It didn't start out that way. Kabuki was actually originated by a group of women in Kyoto in the early 1600s who began by giving performances of erotic dances. Needless to say, the dances were enthusiastically received by the audience and it wasn't long before there were troupes of women of rather questionable repute giving all kinds of lewd performances. Finally the shogun decided that the dances were too vulgar, and he banned all women from performing. Kabuki was then taken over by all-male companies, who transformed it into the drama it is today.

Kabuki has changed little in the past century. Altogether there are more than 300 Kabuki plays, all written before this century. One of the most interesting things about going to a Kabuki play lies in watching the audience. Because this has always been entertainment for the masses, the audience can get quite lively, with yells from spectators, guffaws, and laughter. In fact, old woodcuts showing cross-eyed men apparently stem from Kabuki—actors would stomp their feet and strike a cross-eyed pose in an attempt to get the audience's attention when things got a little too rowdy.

Of course you won't be able to understand what's being said, but it doesn't matter. Because much of Kabuki drama dates from the 18th century, even the Japanese have a hard time understanding the language. This has led to a good system of programs and/or earphones that describe the plots in minute detail, often available in English as well. Thus you can follow the story and enjoy Kabuki just as much as everyone around you.

NOH: Whereas Kabuki developed as a form of entertainment for the masses, Noh was a much more traditional and aristocratic form of theater. In contrast to Kabuki's extroverted liveliness, Noh is very calculated, slow, and restrained. Noh is the oldest form of theater in Japan and there has been very little change in Noh presentations in the past 600 years. In fact the language is so archaic that Japanese cannot understand it today, which explains in part why Noh does not have the following that Kabuki does.

As in Kabuki, all the performers in Noh are men. The subject matter of Noh's some 240 surviving plays is usually about supernatural beings, beautiful women, mentally confused people, or tragic-heroic epics. Performers usually wear masks.

Because the action in Noh is so slow, watching an entire evening can be quite tedious unless you are particularly interested in Noh dance and music. You may just want to drop in for a short while. In between Noh plays are short comic reliefs called *kyogen* which usually make fun of life in the 1600s.

BUNRAKU: Bunraku is traditional Japanese puppet theater. But contrary to what you might expect, Bunraku is for adults rather than children, with themes centering on love and revenge, sacrifice and suicide. Many dramas now used in Kabuki were first written for the Bunraku stage.

Popular in Japan since the 17th century and at times even more popular than Kabuki, Bunraku is fascinating to watch because the puppeteers are right on stage with their puppets, dressed in black and wonderfully skilled in making the puppets seem like living beings. Usually there are three puppeteers for each puppet, which is about three-fourths the size of a human being. One is responsible for the head, the expression on the puppet's face, and the right arm and hand. The second operates the puppet's left arm and hand, while the third one moves the legs. Although at first the puppeteers are somewhat distracting, after a while you forget they're even there as the puppets assume personalities of their own. All the talking of Bunraku is provided by a narrator, who tells the story and speaks all the various parts as well. The narrator is accompanied by the *shamisen,* a three-stringed traditional Japanese instrument. By all means try to see Bunraku if possible. The most famous Bunraku presentations are at the Osaka Bunraku Theater, but there are performances in Tokyo and other major cities as well.

TEA CEREMONY: Brought to Japan from China more than 1,000 years ago, tea first became popular among Japanese Buddhist priests as a means to stay awake during long hours of meditation. Gradually its use filtered down among the upper classes, and in the 16th century the tea ceremony was perfected by a merchant by the name of Sen-no-Rikyu. Using the principles of Zen and the spiritual discipline of the samurai, the tea ceremony became a highly stylized ritual with exact detail given to how tea was prepared, served, and drunk. The simplicity of movement and tranquillity of setting was meant to free the mind from everyday life and allow the spirit to enjoy peace.

The tea ceremony, *cha-no-yu,* is still practiced in Japan today and is regarded as a form of disciplinary training for mental composure as well as a good way to learn etiquette and manners. There are many schools with different methods for performing the tea ceremony throughout the country. Several of Japan's more famous landscape gardens have tea houses on their grounds where you can sit on tatami, drink the frothy green tea and eat some sweets (meant to counteract the bitter taste of the tea), and contemplate the view.

IKEBANA: Whereas a Westerner is likely to put a bunch of flowers into a vase and be done with it, the Japanese consider the arrangement of flowers paramount to an art. Most young girls have at least some training in flower arranging, known as *ikebana* in Japanese, and there are various schools and differing methods on the subject. First becoming popular among the aristocrats during the Heian Period (8th to 12th centuries) and spreading to the common people in the 14th to 16th centuries, traditional ikebana in its simplest form is supposed to represent heaven, man, and earth. Department store galleries sometimes have ikebana exhibitions; otherwise check with the local tourist office.

GARDENS: Nothing is left to chance in a Japanese landscape garden. The shape of hills, of trees, the placement of rocks and waterfalls—everything is skillfully arranged by the gardener in a faithful reproduction of nature. To the Westerner, perhaps, it may seem a bit strange to arrange nature to look like nature. But to the Japanese even nature can be improved upon to make it more beautiful and more pleasing, with the best possible use of limited space. The Japanese are masters at this, as a visit to any of their famous gardens will testify.

The Japanese have been sculpting gardens for more than 1,000 years. At first the gardens were designed as pleasure gardens for walking and boating, with ponds, man-made islands, and pavilions. As with almost everything else in Japanese life, however, Zen Buddhism exerted an influence on the style of Japanese gardens, making them simpler and attempting to create the illusion of boundless space within a small area. To the Buddhist a garden was not for merriment but rather for contemplation, an uncluttered and simple landscape on which to rest the eyes.

Basically there are three styles of Japanese gardens. One style uses ponds, hills, and streams to depict nature in miniature. Another uses stones and raked sand in the place of water and is often seen at Zen Buddhist temples. The third style emerged with the tea ceremony and is built around a tea house with an eye toward simplicity and tranquillity. Japanese gardens often use the principle of "borrowed landscape," that is, using the surrounding mountains and landscape by incorporating them into the overall design and impact of the garden.

Famous gardens in Japan include Kenrokuen and Suizenji parks in Kanazawa, Korakuen Park in Okayama, and Ritsurin Park in Takamatsu. Kyoto alone has about 50 gardens, including the famous Zen rock gardens at Daitokuji and Ryoanji temples, the gardens at both the Golden and Silver Pavilions, and those at Heian Shrine, Nijo Castle, and the Katsura Imperial Villa.

ZAZEN: Zazen, or meditation, is practiced by Zen Buddhists as a form of mental or spiritual training. Laymen meditate to relieve stress and clear the mind.

Zazen is accomplished sitting down in a cross-legged lotus position, with the neck and back straight and the eyes slightly open. Usually done by a group in a semi-dark room with cushions facing the wall, meditation is helped along by a monk who stalks noiselessly behind the meditators—if someone squirms or moves, that person is whacked on the shoulders with a stick, which is supposed to help him get back to meditating.

There are several Zen temples at which foreigners can join in zazen. Through a notice in the *Japan Times,* I spent a weekend at a Zen temple outside Tokyo and tried zazen, ate vegetarian meals, and helped in household chores. If you'd like to try zazen yourself, contact the Tourist Information Center in either Tokyo or Kyoto. Check the *Japan Times* also to see whether a session of zazen is being organized with instruction in English for foreigners.

SUMO: The Japanese form of wrestling known as sumo began perhaps as long as 2,000 years ago, becoming immensely popular by the sixth century. Today it's still popular, and the best wrestlers are revered as national heroes in Japan, much as baseball players are in the United States. Often taller than six feet and well over 200 pounds, sumo wrestlers follow a vigorous training period that usually begins in their teens. Unmarried wrestlers even live together at their training schools, called sumo stables.

A sumo match takes place on a sandy-floored ring less than 15 feet in diameter. The object of sumo is for a wrestler either to eject his opponent from the ring or cause him to touch the ground with any part of his body other than his feet. This is accomplished by shoving, slapping, tripping, throwing, and even carrying the opponent. Altogether there are 48 holds and throws, and sumo fans know all of them.

There are six 15-day sumo tournaments in Japan every year. Three are held in Tokyo (in January, May, and September), and the others are held in Osaka (March), Nagoya (July), and Fukuoka (November). Matches are widely covered on television as well as on the American armed forces FEN radio station. If there's no match being held during your stay, you may want to drop in on a sumo stable to watch the training. See Chapter IV for more details.

13. Recommended Reading

Japanese history, culture, life, society, and the arts are so rich and extensive that I have been able to give only a short overview in this book. Fortunately there are vast numbers of books in English covering every aspect of Japan, so you shouldn't have any problem reading up on subjects in more detail. In particular, Kodansha International, a Japanese publishing company, has probably published more books on Japan in English than any other company. Available at major bookstores in Japan, its books are distributed in the United States through Harper & Row, 10 E. 53rd St., New York, NY 10022.

For an introduction to Japan's history, a standard work is George B. Sansom's *Japan: A Short Cultural History* (Prentice-Hall, 1962), which covers the country's history from antiquity to modern times. A former United States ambassador to Japan, Edwin O. Reischauer gives a detailed look at Japan's history in *Japan: The Story of a Nation* (Knopf, 1974). If you're interested in Japan since World War II, *A History of Postwar Japan*, by Masataka Kosaka (Kodansha, 1982), takes in the enormous changes that have occurred in the country in the past few decades.

A general overview of Japanese history, politics, and society is provided in Edwin O. Reischauer's *The Japanese* (Harvard University Press, 1977). Delving deeper into Japanese society and psychology are Kurt Singer's *Mirror, Sword and Jewel: The Geometry of Japanese Life* (Kodansha, 1981) and Chie Nakane's *Japanese Society* (University of California Press, 1970).

A classic in describing the Japanese and their culture is the brilliantly written book by Ruth Benedict called *The Chrysanthemum and the Sword: Patterns of Japanese Culture* (New American Library, 1967), first written in the 1940s but reprinted many times. A more contemporary book on the Japanese is *The Japanese Mind: The Goliath Explained* (Linden Press/Simon & Schuster, 1983), by Robert C. Christopher. I consider this book compulsory reading for anyone traveling to Japan because it describes so accurately the Japanese, the role history has played in developing the Japanese psyche, and problems facing the nation today.

In a more lighthearted vein, a delightful account of the Japanese and their customs is given by the irrepressible George Mikes in *The Land of the Rising Yen.* Because it was published in the early 1970s, I doubt you'll be able to find a copy in the United States; it's in major bookstores in Japan, however, and would make light and enjoyable reading during your trip.

Likewise, the Japan Travel Bureau puts out some nifty pocket-size booklets on things Japanese, including *Eating in Japan* and *Festivals of Japan.* My favorite, however, is *Salaryman in Japan* (JTB, 1986), which describes the private and working lives of those guys in the look-alike business suits, Japan's army of white-collar workers who receive set salaries. The book is illustrated throughout and includes a picture of the typical salaryman, from his metal-framed square-rimmed glasses down to his dark-red necktie with diagonal stripes and black leather shoes. The endearing thing about this book is that it was written in complete seriousness, with chapters devoted to life in the salaryman's company, the etiquette of business cards, company trips, the wife of a salaryman, and even the "salaryman blues." Easy to read, this book is both entertaining and enlightening.

If you're interested in women's issues in Japan, read Alice Cooks and Hiroko Hayashi's *Working Women in Japan: Discrimination, Resistance and Reform* (ILR Press, 1980). A book seemingly from another era is *Geisha* (Kodansha, 1983), written by Liza Crihfield Dalby and describing her year living as a geisha in Kyoto as part of a research project.

For information on Japanese religions, two beautifully illustrated books are *Shinto: Japan's Spiritual Roots* (Kodansha, 1980) and *Buddhism: Japan's Cultural Identity* (Kodansha, 1982), both by Stuart D. B. Picken with introductions by Edwin O. Reischauer.

If you find yourself becoming addicted to Japanese food, you might want to invest in a copy of *Japanese Cooking: A Simple Art* (Kodansha, 1980), by Shizuo Tsuji. Written by the proprietor of one of the largest cooking schools in Japan, this book contains more than 220 recipes as well as information on food history and table etiquette. The history and philosophy of the tea ceremony, beginning with its origins in the 12th century, is given in *The Tea Ceremony,* by Sen'o Tanaka (Kodansha, 1983).

An introduction to Japanese art is provided in Langdon Warner's *Enduring Art of Japan* (Grove Press, 1958). Kabuki and other stage arts are covered in Faubion Bowers's *Japanese Theater* (Greenwood Press, 1976).

Reading fiction is certainly one of the most relaxing and fun ways to learn about a country. Whenever I travel in Japan I especially enjoy reading fictional accounts of the country because it puts me more in tune with my surroundings and increases my awareness and perception. The world's first novel was written by a Japanese woman, Murasaki-Shikibu, whose classic *The Tale of Genji* (Knopf, 1978) was written in the 11th century and describes the aristocratic life of Prince Genji. Lafcadio Hearn, a prolific writer of things Japanese in the late 1800s, describes life in Japan around the turn of the century in *Writings from Japan* (Penguin, 1985), while Isabella Bird, an Englishwoman who traveled alone to Hokkaido in the 1870s, writes a vivid account of what life was like for rural Japanese in *Unbeaten Tracks in Japan* (Virago Press Limited, 1984). An overview of Japanese classical literature is provided in *Anthology of Japanese Literature* (Grove Press, 1955), edited by Donald Keene.

And finally, because it was also made into a television mini-series, most Westerners are familiar with James Clavell's *Shogun* (Dell, 1975), a fictional account based on the lives of Englishman William Adams and military leader

Ieyasu Tokugawa around 1600. In addition, a vivid history of Japanese woodblock prints from the 17th to 19th centuries comes alive in a first-person account written by James Michener in *The Floating World* (University of Hawaii Press, 1983).

For more recent, personal accounts of what it's like for Westerners living in Japan, two entertaining novels are *Ransom* by Jay McInerney (Vintage, 1985) and *Pictures from the Water Trade* by John D. Morley (Harper & Row, 1986).

Chapter III

GETTING SETTLED IN TOKYO

1. Introducing Tokyo
2. Orientation and Getting Around
3. Accommodations
4. Where to Dine
5. The ABCs of Tokyo

TO THE UNINITIATED, Tokyo may seem like a whirlwind of traffic and people, so confusing that visitors might swear they had somehow landed on another planet. This chapter should make getting settled in Tokyo not only less confusing but more enjoyable as well.

1. Introducing Tokyo

First-time visitors to Tokyo are almost invariably disappointed. They come expecting an exotic and Oriental city, but instead they find a city that has been Westernized and modernized to the point of ugliness, much of it a drab concrete jungle of unimaginative buildings clustered so close together there's hardly room to breathe.

Simply stated, Tokyo is a crush of humanity. Its subways are often packed, its sidewalks are crowded, its streets are congested, and its air is filled with an irritating amount of noise, pollution, and what can only be called "mystery smells." Almost 12 million people live in Tokyo's 770 square miles, many of them in so-called bedroom towns where they have to commute to work an average of two to three hours every day. No matter where you go in Tokyo, you are never alone. After you've been here for a while, Paris, London, and even New York will seem like deserted cities.

Tokyo's crowdedness and ugliness, however, is what you'll see only if you don't bother to scratch beneath its surface. Beautiful in its own way, Tokyo is most definitely a state of mind, and if you open yourself to it you'll find a city humming with energy and vitality, a city unlike any other in the world. People rush around here with such purpose, with such determination, it's hard not to feel that you're in the midst of something important, that you're witnessing history in the making.

But before I begin discussing Tokyo's merits, it might help to put the city into historical perspective.

Although today the nation's capital, Tokyo is a relative newcomer to the pages of Japanese history. For centuries it was nothing more than a rather unimportant village called Edo, which means simply "mouth of the estuary." Then, in 1603 Edo got a shot in the arm when the new shogun, Ieyasu Tokugawa, made the sleepy village the seat of his shogunate government. From then on the town grew quickly, and by 1787 the population had grown to 1.3 million, making Edo even then one of the largest cities in the world.

The Tokugawas ruled Japan for about 250 years, following a policy of isolation from the rest of the world. When the Tokugawas were overthrown in 1868, the Japanese emperor was restored to power. Although the imperial family had been living in Kyoto all these years, they decided to move their capital to Edo, which they renamed Tokyo, "Eastern Capital." Thus Japan's feudal era came to an end. Its policy of isolation from the rest of the world ground to an abrupt halt and its doors were flung open to the West in a scramble to modernize itself.

As the nation's capital, Tokyo was the hardest hit in this new era of modernization as fashions, architecture, food, department stores, and even people were imported from the West. West was best, and things Japanese were forgotten or ignored. It didn't help that Tokyo was almost totally destroyed twice in the first half of this century. In 1923 a huge earthquake struck the city, followed by tidal waves. Almost 150,000 people died and half of Tokyo was in ruins. Disaster struck again during World War II in 1945, when incendiary bombs destroyed most of the city.

I guess that's why most visitors are disappointed with Tokyo—there's almost nothing of historical importance to match Kyoto or Kamakura. So put your notions of "quaint Japan" out of your mind and plunge headfirst into the 21st century. Because that's what Tokyo is all about. The city is so wired and electric you can feel it in the air.

As the financial nerve center of Japan, Tokyo is where it's happening in Asia. In a nation of overachievers, Tokyo has more than its fair share of intelligentsia, academics, politicians, and artists, and it's the country's showcase for technology, fashion, art, music, and advertising.

But even though Tokyo has a fast-paced, somewhat zany, and sometimes crazy side to it, it also has a quieter and often overlooked side that makes the city both loveable and liveable. Although formidable at first glance, Tokyo is nothing more than a series of small towns and neighborhoods clustered together, each with its own narrow, winding streets, ma-and-pa shops, fruit stands, and stores. Look for the small things and you'll notice the carefully pruned bonsai sitting on the sidewalks, women in kimonos bowing and shuffling down the streets, old wooden houses, neatness and order.

Tokyo is both new and old, both Western and Japanese—but it's definitely more Japanese than Western. I myself love Tokyo. Despite the fact that it's overcrowded and that it's sometimes frustrating being a foreigner here, I find Tokyo exhilarating, often exciting, and always interesting. And perhaps best of all, Tokyo is one of the safest cities in the world. In a city of almost 12 million, it's remarkable indeed that you can walk safely anywhere, anytime, night or day. The only thing you have to watch out for are those Japanese businessmen who have had too much to drink—reserve thrown off, they may want to practice their English on you.

2. Orientation and Getting Around

Your most frustrating moments in Tokyo will probably occur when you find that you are totally lost. Maybe it will be in a subway or train station when all you see are signs in Japanese. Or perhaps it will be on a street somewhere as you search for a museum, restaurant, or bar. At any rate, accept here and now that

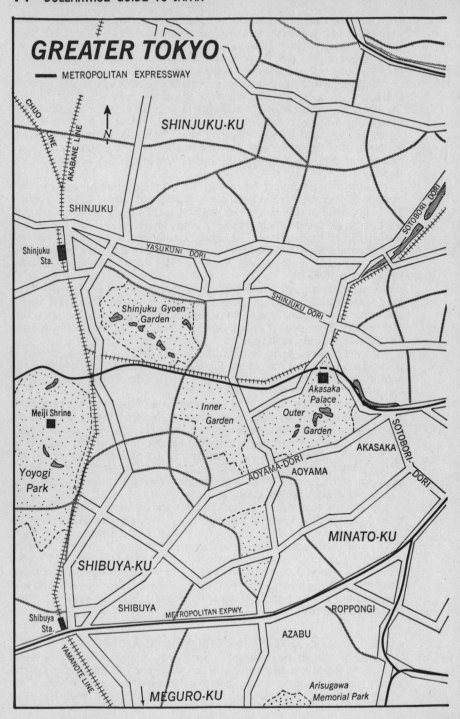

GREATER TOKYO

— METROPOLITAN EXPRESSWAY

SHINJUKU-KU

CHUO LINE
AKABANE LINE
N

SHINJUKU

Shinjuku Sta.

YASUKUNI DORI

SHINJUKU DORI

SOTOBORI DORI

Shinjuku Gyoen Garden

Akasaka Palace

Meiji Shrine

Inner Garden

Outer Garden

AKASAKA

SOTOBORI-DORI

Yoyogi Park

AOYAMA-DORI
AOYAMA

MINATO-KU

SHIBUYA-KU

SHIBUYA

METROPOLITAN EXPWY.

ROPPONGI

Shibuya Sta.

YAMANOTE LINE

AZABU

MEGURO-KU

Arisugawa
Memorial Park

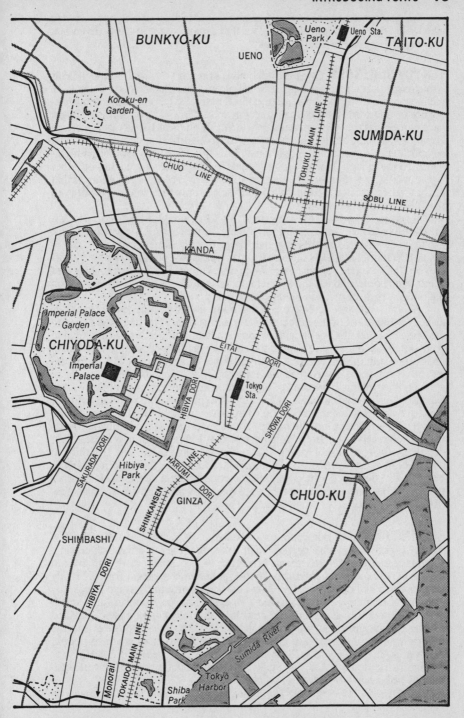

you *will* get lost if you are at all adventurous and strike out on your own. It's inevitable. But take comfort in the fact that Japanese get lost too. Even taxi drivers get lost and bewildered in Tokyo.

TOKYO ADDRESSES: One factor that makes finding your way around difficult is that hardly any streets are named. Think about what that means in Tokyo—12 million people living in a huge metropolis of nameless streets. Oh, major thoroughfares and some well-known streets in areas like Ginza or Shinjuku might have names that they received after World War II on the insistence of American occupation forces, but for the most part Tokyo's address system is based on a complicated number scheme that must make the postman's job here a nightmare. To make matters worse, most streets in Tokyo aren't straight but rather zigzag around, apparently left over from olden days to confuse any enemies that might attack. Today streets in Tokyo confuse not only foreign tourists but even the Tokyo residents themselves.

A typical Tokyo address might read 7-8-4 Roppongi, Minato-ku, which is the address of the Inakaya restaurant. Minato-ku is the name of the ward, which encompasses a large area (altogether there are 23 wards, known as *ku,* in Tokyo). Within that area is the district, in this case Roppongi. Roppongi is further broken down into *chome,* here 7-*chome.* Number 8 refers to a smaller area within the *chome,* and 4 is the actual building. Addresses are usually posted on buildings, beside doors, and on telephone poles.

As you walk around Tokyo you will notice maps posted beside sidewalks giving a breakdown of the number system for the area. The first time I tried to use one I stopped first one Japanese, and then later another, and asked them to point out on the map where a particular address was. They both studied the map and pointed out the direction. Both turned out to be wrong. Not very encouraging, but if you learn how to read these maps they're invaluable.

Another invaluable source of information are the numerous police boxes, called *koban,* spread throughout the city. The policemen have maps of their areas and are very helpful. You should also never hesitate to ask a Japanese the way, but be sure to ask more than one. You'll be amazed at the conflicting directions you'll receive. Apparently the Japanese would rather hazard a guess than impolitely shrug their shoulders and leave you standing there. The best thing to do is ask directions from several Japanese and then follow the majority opinion. You can also duck into a shop and ask someone where a nearby address is, although it's been my experience that employees may not even know the address of their own store.

GETTING AROUND: Before setting out on your own, arm yourself with a few maps. Maps are so much a part of life in Tokyo that they're often included in a shop or restaurant advertisement, brochure, on a business card, and even in private party invitations. Even though I've spent several years in Tokyo, I rarely venture forth without a map. One I find particularly useful is issued free by the Tourist Information Center; it's called *Tourist Map of Tokyo* and includes smaller, detailed maps of several districts (such as Shinjuku) as well as subway and greater Tokyo train maps. With this map you should be able to locate at least the general vicinity of every place mentioned in the Tokyo chapters of this book. Another source for maps is *Tour Companion,* a free weekly publication for tourists distributed at T.I.C. and major hotels that includes area maps with locations of well-known restaurants and nightspots.

At any rate, the best policy for getting around Tokyo is to take the subway to the station nearest your destination. From there you can either walk, asking directions along the way, or take a taxi.

By Subway

To get around Tokyo on your own it's imperative that you learn how to ride its subways. Fortunately, Tokyo's subway system is efficient, modern, clean, and easy to use, and all station names are written in English. Altogether there are ten subway lines crisscrossing underneath the city, and each line is color coded. The Ginza Line, for example, is orange, which means that all its coaches are orange. If you're transferring to the Ginza Line from another line, just follow the orange signs and circles to the Ginza Line platform.

Vending machines at all subway stations sell tickets, which begin at ¥120 (86¢) for the shortest distance and increase according to how far you're traveling. Vending machines give change and some even accept ¥1,000 notes. A large subway map above the vending machines will tell you your fare, but it's in Japanese only. Major stations also post a smaller map listing fares in English, but you may have to search for it. An alternative is to look at your T.I.C. subway map—it lists stations in both Japanese and English. Once you know what the Japanese characters look like, you may be able to locate your station and the corresponding fare on the huge subway map above the vending machines.

If you still don't know the fare, just buy a basic fare ticket for ¥120 (86¢). When you exit at the other end, the ticket collector will tell you how much you owe. In any case, be sure to hang on to your ticket since you must give it up at the end of your journey. If you're confused about which exit to take from the station, ask the ticket collector. Taking the right exit can make a world of difference, especially in Shinjuku where there are more than 60 exits from the station.

If you think you're going to be using the subways a lot, you can purchase a one-day ticket (¥600, or $4.29, for an adult; ¥300, or $2.14, for children), which allows unlimited travel on the Ginza, Marunouchi, Hibiya, Tozai, Chiyoda, Yurakucho, and Hanzomon subway lines. These lines pass through 132 stations in Tokyo, including Hibiya, Ginza, Shinjuku, Tsukiji, Ueno, and major sightseeing destinations. One-day tickets are valuable, however, only if you plan on using the subways for very long distances or more than five times in one day. If so, you can purchase a one-day ticket at more than two dozen subway stations, including Ginza, Shinjuku, Shibuya, and Akasaka-mitsuke. Contact the T.I.C. for more information.

Most subways run from about 5 a.m. to midnight, though the times of the first and last trains depend on the line, the station, and whether it's a weekday or weekend. There are schedules posted in the stations, and through most of the day trains run every three to five minutes. Avoid taking the subway during the morning rush hour, from 8 to 9 a.m. The stories you've heard about commuters packed into trains like sardines are all true. There are even "platform pushers," men wearing white gloves who push people into compartments so that the doors can close. If you want to witness Tokyo at its craziest, go to Shinjuku station at 8:30 a.m.—but go by taxi unless you want to experience the crowding firsthand.

By Train

In addition to subway lines, there are also electric trains operated by Japan Railways that run above ground. These are also color coded and fares also begin at ¥120 (86¢). Buy your ticket the same as you would for the subway. The Yamanote Line (green-colored coaches) is the best-known and convenient JR line. It makes a loop around the city, stopping at 29 stations along the way. In

TOKYO SUBWAYS

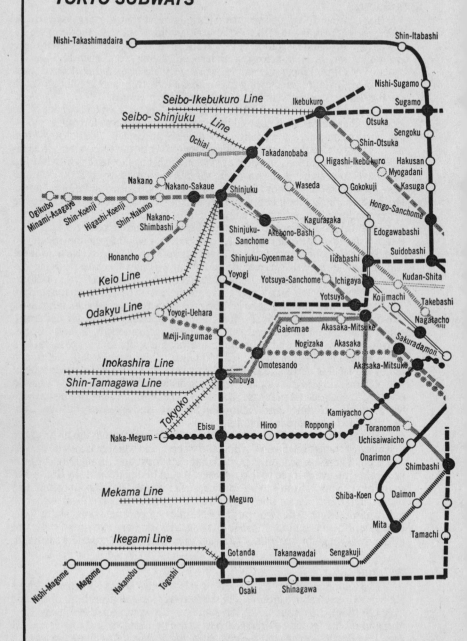

Nishi-Takashimadaira

Shin-Itabashi

Nishi-Sugamo

Seibo-Ikebukuro Line — Ikebukuro — Sugamo

Seibo- Shinjuku Line — Otsuka

Sengoku

Ochiai — Takadanobaba — Shin-Otsuka

Higashi-Ikebukuro — Hakusan

Nakano — Waseda — Myogadani

Nakano-Sakaue — Shinjuku — Gokokuji — Kasuga

Ogikubo — Hongo-Sanchome

Minami-Asagaya — Shin-Koenji — Higashi-Koenji — Shin-Nakano — Nakano-Shimbashi — Kagurazaka — Edogawabashi

Shinjuku-Sanchome — Akebono-Bashi — Suidobashi

Honancho — Shinjuku-Gyoenmae — Iidabashi — Kudan-Shita

Keio Line — Yoyogi — Yotsuya-Sanchome — Ichigaya — Takebashi

Odakyu Line — Yoyogi-Uehara — Yotsuya — Kojimachi — Nagatacho

Meiji-Jingumae — Gaienmae — Akasaka-Mitsuke — Sakuradamon

Nogizaka — Akasaka

Inokashira Line — Omotesando — Akasaka-Mitsuke

Shin-Tamagawa Line — Shibuya

Tokyoko — Kamiyacho

Naka-Meguro — Ebisu — Hiroo — Roppongi — Toranomon

Uchisaiwaicho

Onarimon — Shimbashi

Mekama Line — Meguro — Shiba-Koen — Daimon

Mita — Tamachi

Ikegami Line — Gotanda — Takanawadai — Sengakuji

Nishi-Magome — Magome — Nakanobu — Togoshi

Osaki — Shinagawa

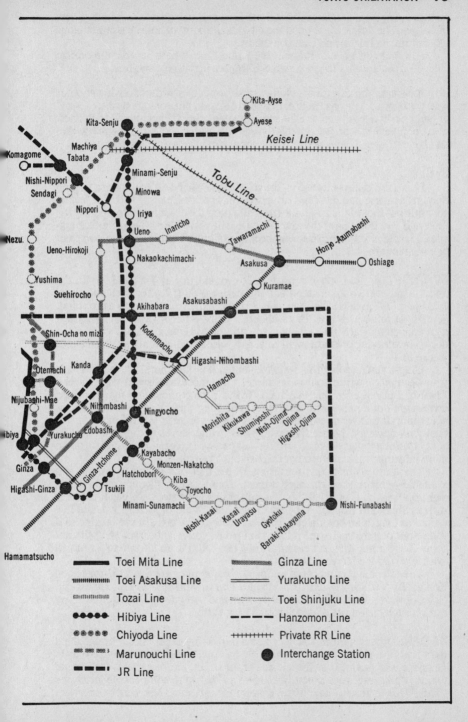

fact, you may want to take the Yamanote Line and stay on it for a roundup view of Tokyo. The entire trip around the city takes about an hour, passing stations like Shinjuku, Tokyo, and Ueno on the way.

Another convenient JR line is the Chuo Line, whose coaches are orange colored. It cuts across Tokyo between Shinjuku and Tokyo stations.

Transfers: You can transfer between subway lines without buying another ticket. Likewise, you can transfer between JR train lines on one ticket. However, your ticket does not allow a transfer between subway lines and JR train lines. You don't have to worry about this though, because if you exit through a wicket and have to give up your ticket, you'll know you have to buy another one.

By Bus

Buses are difficult to use in Tokyo because their destinations are written only in Japanese and most bus drivers do not speak English. If you're feeling adventurous, board the bus at the front and drop the exact fare into a box by the driver. If you don't have the exact fare (usually ¥160, or $1.14), another machine located next to the driver will accept coins only. Your change will come out below, minus the fare.

BY TAXI: Taxis are fairly expensive in Tokyo, starting at ¥470 ($3.36) for the first 1¼ miles (two kilometers) and increasing ¥80 (57¢) for each additional 1,034 feet (307 meters). You can hail a taxi from the street or go to a taxi stand. A red light will show above the dashboard if a taxi is free to pick up a passenger; a green light indicates the taxi is already occupied. Be sure to stand clear of the door—it will swing open automatically. Likewise, it will automatically shut once you're in.

Unless you're going to a well-known landmark or hotel, it's best to have your destination written out in Japanese, since most taxi drivers do not speak English. But not even that may help. Tokyo is so complicated that even taxi drivers are not familiar with much of it, although they do have detailed maps with them. If a driver doesn't understand where you're going, he may refuse to take you, however. Notice the taxi drivers' white gloves and the way they're always writing things down on a roster—Japanese taxi drivers must write down more information than any other taxi drivers on earth.

There are so many taxis cruising Tokyo that one is always around and available—except when you need it most. That is, when it's raining and late at night on weekends after all subways and trains have stopped. Nightlife areas such as Shinjuku, Roppongi, Ginza, and Akasaka are especially bad, and I've waited as long as an hour in each of these places for a taxi after midnight. So if you're out past midnight on Friday or Saturday, you might as well stay out until about 2 or 3 a.m., when it's easier to get a taxi. And from 11 p.m. to 5 a.m., an extra 20% is added to your fare.

The telephone numbers of major taxi companies are 586-2151 for Nihon Kotsu; 491-6001 for Kokusai; 563-5151 for Daiwa; and 814-1111 for Hinomaru. Note, however, that only Japanese is spoken and that you will be required to pay extra (usually not more than ¥550, or $3.93, extra).

BY CAR: Driving a car in Tokyo can be a harrowing experience. For one thing the streets are crowded and unbelievably narrow, street signs are often only in Japanese, and driving is on the left side of the street. Parking spaces can be hard to find, and garages are expensive. However, if you're still not convinced, see "The ABCs of Tokyo" later in this chapter for car-rental agencies.

3. Accommodations

Tokyo has no old, grand hotels. In fact, it doesn't have many old hotels, period. But what Tokyo's hotels may lack in quaintness or old grandeur is more than made up for in the excellent service for which the Japanese are legendary, and in cleanliness and efficiency. Be prepared, however, for small rooms. Space is at a premium in Tokyo, so with the exception of some of the upper-range hotels, rooms seem to come in only three sizes: minuscule, small, and adequate.

Unfortunately, Tokyo does not have many *ryokan,* or Japanese-style inns. So I suggest that you wait for your travels around Japan to have your ryokan experience. However, realizing that not all visitors have the opportunity to travel outside Tokyo, I've listed medium- and budget-range ryokan that are enthusiastic and willing to take in foreigners. In fact, if you're traveling on a budget, a ryokan is often the cheapest way to go. As for upper-range ryokan in Tokyo, none of them accepts foreigners. They prefer that guests be introduced through someone they know and simply do not want to deal with the inconveniences and difficulties caused by cultural and language barriers.

Most of the upper-bracket hotels offer at least a few Japanese-style rooms, with tatami mats, Japanese bathtubs (which are deeper and narrower than Western ones), and futons. Although these rooms tend to be expensive, they are usually large enough for four people.

For each hotel or ryokan listed I've given the nearest subway station and the walking time required. Remember that in addition to the prices quoted below, a 10% tax and a 10% to 15% service charge will be added to your bill. If your room charge is less than ¥5,000 ($35.71), no additional tax will be added.

A word about costs: Because of the unfavorable dollar/yen exchange rate, the price of a hotel room in Tokyo is truly astronomical. Recognizing the difficulty foreigners have making ends meet, some hotels that cater largely to Americans have kept their tariffs at the same level for the past two years. Some hotels have even lowered their rates. Hopefully, the yen amount given here is the most you'll have to pay.

THE UPPER BRACKET: The hotels in this category can rival upper-range hotels anywhere in the world. Although many of Tokyo's best hotels may not show much character from the outside, inside they are oases of subdued simplicity where service and hospitality reign supreme. Rooms in this category are adequate in size, some of them even large by Tokyo's standards, and they all come with such amenities as mini-bar, bilingual television with English-language cable, clock, radio, cotton kimono, hot water for tea, and countless other personal touches that make staying in Japan a pleasure.

The **Imperial Hotel,** 1-1-1 Uchisaiwaicho, Chiyoda-ku (tel. 03/504-1111), is one of Tokyo's best-known hotels. About 65% of its guests are foreigners, mostly business executives. Located across from Hibiya Park within walking distance of Ginza, the Imperial's trademark is excellent and impeccable service, where guests are treated like royalty and where the atmosphere throughout is subdued and dignified. Although the present hotel dates from 1970 with a 31-story tower added in 1983, the Imperial's history goes back to 1922, when it opened as a small hotel made of brick and stone with intricate designs carved into its façade —all designed by Frank Lloyd Wright. The Imperial won lasting fame when it survived almost intact the 1923 earthquake that destroyed much of the rest of the city. Although the old structure was torn down in 1968 to make way for a larger building, part of it was moved to Meiji-Mura, a museum village outside Nagoya.

The Imperial's 1,143 rooms are located in both the main building and the tower. Rooms in the main building are quite large for Tokyo, running from ¥24,750 ($177) to ¥46,000 ($329) for one person and ¥29,000 ($207) to ¥50,000 ($357) for two. They are currently being renovated, a process that will be completed by 1990. Tower rooms, while slightly smaller, are higher up, bright and cheerful, and from their floor-to-ceiling bay windows offer fantastic views of either the Imperial Palace or Ginza and the harbor. Prices here run ¥26,500 ($189) to ¥46,000 ($329) for one person and ¥30,800 ($220) to ¥50,000 ($357) for two. Facilities at the hotel include 13 restaurants and four bars, an impressive shopping arcade, and Tokyo's most dramatic swimming pool, located on the 20th floor with a breathtaking view of Tokyo Bay. The closest subway station is Hibiya Station, about a minute's walk away.

Another venerable hotel in Tokyo is the **Hotel Okura**, 2-10-4 Toranomon, Minato-ku (tel. 03/582-0111), built just before the 1964 Olympic Summer Games were held in Tokyo. Located across the street from the American Embassy, it's the favorite hotel of visiting U.S. dignitaries as well as such celebrities as rock star David Bowie and pianist Vladimir Horowitz. Conservative and traditional in decor, the Okura combines Western comfort with Japanese design in the use of shoji screens, flower displays, and a beautifully sculptured garden. The hotel has both indoor and outdoor swimming pools, eight restaurants and four bars, and a shopping arcade of exclusive boutiques from Hanae Mori to Mikimoto pearls.

Rooms here are ¥25,000 ($179) to ¥34,000 ($243) for one person and ¥31,900 ($228) to ¥55,000 ($393) for two. The more expensive rooms are on the fifth floor just off the lobby. Conveniently located, they have good-sized balconies overlooking the Japanese garden. The Okura also has 11 Japanese-style rooms with tatami floors, shoji screens, and Japanese tubs, costing ¥36,000 ($257) to ¥71,000 ($507). Nearest subway stations: Toranomon and Kamiyacho, each about ten minutes away.

Since its grand opening in 1986, the **ANA Hotel Tokyo**, 1-12-33 Akasaka, Minato-ku (tel. 03/505-1111), has given the Hotel Okura stiff competition. A gleaming white building rising 37 stories high above the crossroads of Akasaka, Roppongi, Toranomon, and Kasumigaseki, the ANA Hotel is Tokyo's newest luxury hotel. Its lobby, located on the second floor and of cool, cream-colored marble with a water fountain serving as a focal point, is both impressive and spacious, and the lobby lounge is a favorite among Tokyoites for people-watching. Restaurants, rooms, and even corridors are superbly decorated with artwork and vases. Facilities at the hotel include a business center with secretarial services, a travel desk, shopping arcade, barbershop and beauty salon, sauna (for men only), a swimming pool, and a babysitter's room. Restaurants serve Japanese, Chinese, and Western cuisine; the Astral bar on the 37th floor provides fantastic views of the city.

Rooms are large, with views of Tokyo Bay, Mount Fuji, or the Imperial Palace and come with TV, pay video, mini-bar. English-language newspapers delivered twice a day, and other thoughtful amenities. Various types of rooms and suites are available, with prices starting at ¥19,000 ($136) for single occupancy and ¥26,500 ($189) for double occupancy. For ¥4,000 ($28.57) more, you can opt to stay on the executive floor, which offers the services of a concierge, free continental breakfast, and an evening cocktail hour. Nearest subway stations: Roppongi, Akasaka, Kamiyacho, Toranomon, and Kokkai Gijido-mae.

The **Capitol Tokyu**, 2-10-3 Nagata-cho, Chiyoda-ku (tel. 03/581-4511), is another one of Tokyo's hotels built just before the Olympics. It used to be the Tokyo Hilton, but in 1984 the current owner, the Tokyu hotel chain, took over the management. A cozy establishment, it has only 479 guest rooms—a small hotel by Tokyo's standards—and has the unique ability of making foreign guests feel like they are in the Orient and at home all at the same time. With more than 892 full-time employees, service is at a premium. There are, for example, no cigarette machines in the hotel—instead, guests are requested to ask any hotel employee to fetch them a pack of cigarettes. The hotel boasts a meticulously pruned Japanese garden complete with a pond and golden carp, an outdoor swimming pool, a small shopping arcade, and Japanese, Chinese, and Western restaurants. The hotel is located in the Akasaka district within walking distance of the moat-encircled Imperial Palace. If you stay here, be sure to check out Hie Shrine, next door.

Double and twin rooms, which are comfortably large, start at ¥25,800 ($184) for single occupancy and ¥29,000 ($207) for double. There are also 50 single rooms available for ¥22,000 ($157) to ¥25,000 ($179), but they're smaller and it may be worth springing for the additional couple of thousand yen for a double room. Three Japanese-style rooms are available for ¥62,000 ($443). Nearest subway station: Kokkai Gijido-mae, one minute away.

The **Miyako Hotel Tokyo**, 1-1-50 Shiroganedai, Minato-ku (tel. 03/447-3111), is an affiliate of the famous Miyako Hotel in Kyoto and was designed by Minoru Yamasaki, the architect of the World Trade Center in New York and the Century Plaza in Los Angeles. The Japanese themselves account for 70% of its guests, and although it's a bit inconveniently located, it offers a free bus shuttle to Tamachi and Hamamatsucho stations and to Ginza. The lobby overlooks 5½ acres of lush gardens that once belonged to the father of a foreign prime minister. The hotel's rooms are large, with huge floor-to-ceiling windows that have views of either the hotel's own garden, a garden next door, or Tokyo Tower. All rooms were recently recarpeted, and all single beds are semi-double in size. There are nine restaurants and bars, a huge indoor pool that is great for swimming laps, and even a chapel. Double rooms start at ¥21,000 ($150) for single occupancy and ¥23,000 ($164) for double, while twin rooms start at ¥18,500 ($132) and ¥22,000 ($157) respectively. Although there are nine single rooms, each for ¥17,500 ($125), these are usually booked. Five Japanese-style rooms are available for ¥21,000 ($150) for one person and ¥25,000 ($179) for two. Closest subway station: Takanawadai, about an eight-minute walk.

Hotel Seiyo Ginza, 1-11-2 Ginza, Chuo-ku (tel. 03/535-1111), opened in 1987 as Ginza's newest luxury hotel. Its room rates, which begin at ¥42,000 ($300) for a double and go all the way up to ¥275,000 ($1,964) for its premier suite, are the most expensive in Tokyo, if not in all of Japan. Its market is targeted at foreign executives, and with only 80 guest rooms, service is at a premium. The hotel is not open to the public—that is, you must either be a hotel guest or have a reservation at one of its exclusive restaurants to enter the main entrance. A hush prevails throughout the hotel, and instead of a front desk there is a comfortable reception room that resembles a living room. As one hotel employee explained, "The hardware is a Western-style hotel, but the software is traditional Japanese service."

Rooms are large for Japan and come with safes, humidity-control dials, and video-cassette players. With the busy executive in mind, telephones have two lines and there are computerized "Do Not Disturb" and "Maid Service" buttons linked to hotel personnel so that they can respond immediately to the desires of their guests. Bathrooms are huge, with separate shower and tub units and even mini-TV. The hotel is located about a five-minute walk from the Ginza 4-chome Crossing and two minutes from the Ginza-Itchome subway station.

Japan's largest hotel is the **Hotel New Otani**, 4-1 Kioi-cho, Chiyoda-ku (tel. 03/265-1111), with more than 2,000 rooms. Its facilities are incredible: more than 27 restaurants and bars, 120 stores, medical offices, a post office, health club, tea ceremony room, outdoor swimming pool and tennis courts, and a babysitting room. Most splendid of all, however, is its 400-year-old Japanese garden that sprawls over ten acres of ponds, waterfalls, bridges, bamboo groves, and manicured bushes. Standard single rooms, which are extremely small, begin at ¥23,000 ($164) while double and twin rooms go for ¥26,000 ($186) to ¥40,000 ($486). If you're booking a standard double or twin room, request that it be in the 40-story tower (it was built in 1974 and has slightly larger rooms). Japanese suites start at ¥49,000 ($350). Nearest subway stations: Akasaka-mitsuke, about three minutes away, and Yotsuya, about five.

Across the street from the New Otani is the **Akasaka Prince Hotel**, 1-2 Kioicho, Chiyoda-ku (tel. 03/234-1111), a 40-story, gleaming white skyscraper of remarkable modern design. Its lobby is intentionally spacious and empty, lined with almost 12,000 slabs of white marble. When the hotel opened in 1983 it caused quite a stir, as some Tokyoites complained that it was too cold and sterile. In my opinion, however, the Akasaka Prince is just ahead of its time. Japanese style, after all, has always called for simplicity—and this hotel's design is a projection of that Japanese simplicity into the world of the 21st century.

Designed by Kenzo Tange, the hotel's 761 rooms are set on a 45° angle from the center axis of the core of the building, giving each room a corner view with expansive windows overlooking the city. Room color schemes are a soothing powder-blue and white, bright with a lot of sunshine. The single rooms, which start at ¥21,000 ($150), are among the nicest in Tokyo, with three windows forming a pleasant alcove around a sofa. Sinks and vanity desks are located away from the toilet and bath area. Twin rooms start at ¥28,000 ($200) and doubles at ¥33,000 ($236). Request a room overlooking the Akasaka side and you'll have a view of neon lights down below and Tokyo Tower off in the distance. Japanese suites go for ¥85,000 ($607) and ¥90,000 ($643). Facilities include 12 international restaurants and bars. Nearest subway station: Akasaka-mitsuke, a three-minute walk.

Also located in Akasaka, but with slightly lower prices, is the **Akasaka Tokyu Hotel**, 2-14-3 Nagata-cho, Chiyoda-ku (tel. 03/580-2311). Built in 1969 and easily recognizable from the outside by its candy striped exterior, this 566-room hotel boasts an 89% average occupancy, attributed in part to its ideal location. Its 184 single rooms go for ¥17,500 ($125) to ¥21,000 ($150), but the lower-priced ones are pretty small. Double rooms are ¥27,000 ($193), while twins start at ¥27,000 ($193) and go to ¥38,000 ($271). Try to get a twin or double room facing Akasaka—the windows can open, a rarity in Tokyo. There are more than 14 restaurants in the building, and the first and second floors are devoted to shops and boutiques. The lobby is on the third floor—and be prepared for the huge poster of a semi-nude woman in the lobby lounge. Nearest subway station: Akasaka-mitsuke, one minute away.

Because of its proximity to Tokyo's business district, the **Palace Hotel**, 1-1-1 Marunouchi, Chiyoda-ku (tel. 03/211-5211), is a favorite among foreign businessmen, and foreigners account for 65% of its hotel guests. Located across the street from the Imperial Palace and gardens, the hotel's deluxe twin rooms—which are large, face the gardens, and have balconies—are highly recommended. They go for ¥43,000 ($307). Otherwise, the standard single rooms, which are adequate in size, start at a low of ¥17,000 ($121) and double rooms start at ¥27,000 ($193). Built in 1961, the hotel is small, with only 404 rooms, and repeat guests are rewarded with monogram slippers. Of its seven restaurants, the French Crown Restaurant on the tenth floor is the best, offering superb views of the Imperial Palace. Nearest subway station: Otemachi Station, three minutes away.

Shinjuku's newest deluxe hotel is the **Tokyo Hilton International**, 6-6-2 Nishi-Shinjuku, Shinjuku-ku (tel. 03/344-5111), which opened in 1984. As with all Hiltons, its room decor reflects traditional native style: shoji screens instead of curtains and simple yet elegant furniture. The largest Hilton in the Asia/Pacific area, the S-shaped, 38-story structure houses 839 rooms, which offer views of either Shinjuku's skyscrapers (a pretty sight at night) or (on clear days) Mount Fuji. Room rates are based on both size and location, with the more expensive rooms higher up. Single occupancy runs ¥23,000 ($164) to ¥33,000 ($236), while double occupancy costs ¥26,500 ($189) to ¥38,000 ($271). A good value are the Japanese-style rooms, which range from ¥44,000 ($314) to ¥52,000 ($371). The hotel boasts an excellent fitness center, tennis courts, indoor and outdoor pools, and seven restaurants and bars. Nearest subway station: Shinjuku, a ten-minute walk.

Across the street from the Hilton is the **Century Hyatt Tokyo**, 2-7-2 Nishi-Shinjuku, Shinjuku-ku (tel. 03/349-0111). Its lobby is an impressive seven-story atrium with three massive chandeliers and an inlaid marble floor. Its adequately sized rooms are attractively appointed in soft pastels, and the bathrooms feature bright lights that are great for applying makeup. There are single rooms available for ¥18,500 ($132), but the windows are at such an angle in the corner of the rooms that you can hardly see out of them. The twin rooms are better, with big windows that let in a lot of sunshine. These range from ¥20,000 ($143) to ¥26,500 ($189). Japanese suites are ¥49,500 ($354). Diversions here include a swimming pool on the 28th floor, a disco, and twelve restaurants and bars. Closest subway station: Shinjuku, a ten-minute walk.

The **Keio Plaza Inter-Continental Hotel**, 2-2-1 Nishi-Shinjuku, Shinjuku-ku (tel. 03/344-0111), has the distinction of being the first skyscraper built in Japan, and at 47 stories it's still Tokyo's tallest hotel. Built in 1971, its brilliant white exterior is composed of precast concrete panels, the first application of this technique in Japan. With 1,485 rooms and 29 restaurants and bars, it's one of Tokyo's largest hotels. The room rates are based on size rather than location, so ask for a room higher up where the view is better. Singles range from ¥23,000 ($164) to ¥29,500 ($211), and doubles cost ¥25,000 ($179) to ¥33,000 ($236). The hotel is just a few minutes' walk from Shinjuku Station.

A subsidiary of Air France, the **Hotel Pacific Meridien**, 3-13-3 Takanawa, Minato-ku (tel. 03/445-6711), is built on grounds that once belonged to Japan's imperial family and has a coffee lounge that looks out onto a peaceful and tranquil garden. Its Blue Pacific lounge on the 30th floor has dynamite views of Tokyo Bay. Restaurants include Japanese, Chinese, and excellent French cuisine, and there's an outdoor pool. The hotel's 954 rooms are of adequate size and begin at ¥18,500 ($132) for singles and ¥21,000 ($150) for doubles and twins. Nearest subway station: Shinagawa, only two minutes away.

The **Takanawa Prince Hotel**, 3-13-1 Takanawa, Minato-ku (tel. 03/447-1111), has a subdued, comfortable lobby with dark colors and low ceilings. Known for its beautiful ten-acre traditional Japanese garden, this hotel caters largely to Japanese, both businessmen and tourists. Single rooms begin at ¥18,500 ($132), doubles at ¥24,000 ($171), and twins at ¥22,000 ($157). The guest rooms are slightly small but are quiet and comfortable and were renovated in 1986. Eighteen Japanese tatami rooms and suites are also available for ¥38,000 ($271) to ¥60,000 ($429). There are two outdoor swimming pools and French, Chinese, and Japanese restaurants. Nearest subway station: Shinagawa, a five-minute walk.

The **Roppongi Prince Hotel**, 3-1-7 Roppongi, Minato-ku (tel. 03/587-1111), opened in 1984—a welcome event in Roppongi, which still woefully lacks in hotels. The Roppongi Prince attracts young Japanese vacationers aged 20 to 25 and caters to them throughout with a young and cheerful staff, modern designs, and bold colors. The hotel is built around an inner courtyard, which features an outdoor swimming pool with a heated deck; a solar mirror on the hotel's roof directs sunrays down on sunbathers below. The pool is open year-round. Rooms are small, but are bright and colorful and come with the usual mini-bar, desk, color TV, clock, and radio. Singles here are ¥20,000 ($143); twins, ¥21,500 ($154) to ¥24,700 ($176); and doubles, ¥22,500 ($161) to ¥24,500 ($175). A good place to be if you want to be close to the action in Roppongi. Roppongi Station is a 15-minute walk away.

Another relatively new hotel on the Tokyo scene is the **Asakusa View Hotel**, 3-17-1 Nishi-Asakusa, Taito-ku (tel. 03/842-2111), which opened in the fall of 1985. It's the only upper-bracket and modern hotel in the Asakusa area and looks almost out of place rising among this famous district's older buildings. This is a good place to stay if you want to be in Tokyo's old downtown rather than in the spanking newness of its business districts. The lobby exudes cool elegance, with a marble floor, atrium, and hanging chandeliers. Its 350 guest rooms are very pleasant, with contemporary Japanese furnishings of sleek lines and wallpaper with a fan motif. Bay windows give rooms plenty of sunshine, and rooms that face the front have views of the famous Asakusa Kannon Temple. Facilities include an indoor swimming pool and French, Chinese, Italian, and Japanese restaurants. Singles are ¥17,500 ($125), doubles and twins are ¥22,000 ($157). Prices include tax and service charge. If you want to stay in a Japanese-style room, eight are available, each costing ¥50,000 ($357) and sleeping up to five persons. Nearest subway station: Tawaramachi Station on the Ginza Line, an eight-minute walk away.

THE MEDIUM BRACKET: Accommodations in this price range vary from Western-style hotels to business hotels to ryokan, with business hotels making up the majority in this category. Popular with Japanese businessmen, business hotels are generally quite small and offer just the basics but are usually situated in a convenient location. There's very little to differentiate one business hotel from another—they all look pretty much the same. If you're more interested in a clean and functional place to sleep rather than in roomy comfort, a business hotel may be the way to go, although the distinction between a hotel and a business hotel is sometimes a fine one. Unless otherwise stated, all rooms in this category come with private bath and toilet and air conditioning. Remember, too, that unless otherwise stated, a tax and service charge will be added to the quoted room rate.

Hotels

The 212-room **President Hotel**, 2-2-3 Minami Aoyama, Minato-ku (tel. 03/497-0111), is one of the best deals in town. Although a small hotel, it offers some of the same conveniences as the larger and more expensive hotels (like Telex and room service) and has a great location between Akasaka, Shinjuku, and Roppongi. Its rooms are small but clean, comfortable, and pleasant. They come with mini-bar, hot water for tea, hair dryer, TV with English cable, radio, and cotton kimono. The lobby is pleasingly elegant but unpretentious and has a somewhat European atmosphere. The President has two very good restaurants, one Japanese and one French. Foreigners constitute 50% of the hotel's clientele. Room rates begin at ¥10,000 ($71) for a single, ¥12,000 ($86) for a twin, and ¥14,300 ($102) for a double. Nearest subway station: Aoyama-Itchome, one minute away.

The **Fairmont Hotel**, 2-1-17 Kudan Minami, Chiyoda-ku (tel. 03/262-1151), is another good choice in this category. It's beautifully located on a quiet street opposite the Imperial Palace moat, which is lined with cherry trees—a real treat when the blossoms burst forth in spring. Guests like the Fairmont because it's an older hotel (built in 1952) with only 250 rooms and because it's located away from the hustle and bustle of downtown Tokyo. Both of the hotel's restaurants look out onto a pleasant small garden with a waterfall, and there's a swimming pool on the hotel roof. Singles here range from ¥10,900 ($78) to ¥12,300 ($88), twins run ¥20,500 ($146), to ¥29,800 ($213), and doubles cost ¥20,500 ($146) to ¥23,100 ($165). Prices include tax and service. The more expensive rooms are larger and face the palace moat—definitely worth it during cherry-blossom season. Nearest subway station: Kudanshita, a ten-minute walk.

The **Hilltop Hotel**, 1-1 Surugadai, Kanda, Chiyoda-ku (tel. 03/293-2311), is located, as the name implies, on a hill. An old-fashioned, unpretentious hotel with character, its main building dates back to 1937, and together with its annex contains a total of only 75 rooms. The hotel's brochure maintains that "oxygen and negative ions are circulated into the rooms and its refreshing atmosphere is accepted by many, including prominent individuals, as most adequate for work and rest." I'm not sure exactly what that means but it probably doesn't do any harm. Its double rooms are fairly small, and although nothing fancy, they're pleasant and come with cherry-wood furniture, color TV, radio and clock, desk, table and chairs, and old-fashioned heaters with intricate grillwork. Prices are ¥18,700 ($134) to ¥21,000 ($150) for a double and ¥18,700 ($134) to ¥24,000 ($171) for a twin. There are also small singles starting at ¥12,000 ($86). The hotel's six restaurants are all tastefully decorated and offer Italian, French, Chinese, and Japanese cuisine. Closest subway stations: Ochanomizu and Shin-Ochanomizu, each eight minutes away.

The **Tokyo Holiday Inn**, 1-13-7 Hatchobori, Chuo-ku (tel. 03/553-6161), is similar to Holiday Inns back home. As many as 30% of its guests are Americans, mainly individual travelers. A red-brick building with the familiar Holiday Inn sign, it's located on Shin Ohashi-dori Avenue. The rooms are what you'd expect and come with the usual mini-bar, desk, clock, radio, and TV. They're priced at ¥12,800 ($91) for one and ¥20,300 ($145) for two persons. The hotel is small, with only 120 rooms, and has an outdoor swimming pool. It's about a 20-minute walk to Ginza. Nearest subway station: Hatchobori, a three-minute walk.

The 800-room **Ginza Dai-ichi Hotel**, 8-13-1 Ginza, Chuo-ku (tel. 03/542-5311), is located on the southern edge of Ginza and offers such facilities as a sauna, beauty salon, barbershop, shopping arcade, travel agency, bar, coffeeshop, and a sushi bar. French and Japanese restaurants are located on the 15th floor, with good views of Tokyo Bay by day and the lights of Ginza by night. The lobby is on the second floor. The guest rooms are unexciting but comfortable enough, and the bathrooms are tiny, one-piece plastic units. Those with the best views face Tokyo Bay. The price for one person is ¥12,900 ($92), twins start at ¥17,000 ($121), and triples start at ¥22,500 ($161). Nearest subway station: Shimbashi, five minutes away.

Located right next to Tokyo Station near its Yaesu North Exit, **Hotel Kokusai Kanko**, 1-8-3 Marunouchi, Chiyoda-ku (tel. 03/215-3281), is convenient for visitors who are staying in Tokyo only one or two nights before departing for southern Japan on the Shinkansen from Tokyo Station. With a total of 94 rooms, it's a combination business and tourist hotel and caters primarily to the Japanese. Rooms are fairly quiet despite its noisy location, though higher-priced rooms are more shielded from traffic noise. Room rates range from ¥11,300 ($81) to ¥13,500 ($96) for a single; ¥20,900 ($149) to ¥22,000 ($157) for a double; and ¥21,500 ($154) to ¥22,000 ($157) for a twin. Restaurants serve both Western and Japanese food. Nearest station: Tokyo Station, one minute away.

An older, rather eccentric-looking hotel, the **Gajoen Kanko Hotel,** 1-8-1 Shimo-Meguro, Meguro-ku (tel. 03/491-0111), was built in the early 1930s. It has a decidedly Oriental atmosphere, with wood paneling and Japanese prints on its lobby ceiling and intricately inlaid shell designs in its two old elevators. In its early years it was a hospital; after World War II American army personnel were stationed here for ten years. Now the hotel caters to a large Chinese clientele. In any case, for several years the hotel was becoming more and more run-down, but in 1986 extensive renovations cleaned up the lobby and guest rooms and added a new wing, bringing the total number of rooms to 104. Singles start at ¥8,000 ($57) and twins begin at ¥13,200 ($94). The best rooms are those on a corner or those facing the backyard, where there are lots of trees. Nearest station: Meguro, an eight-minute walk.

Business Hotels

An attractive hotel, the **Mitsui Urban Hotel Ginza,** 8-6-15 Ginza, Chuo-ku (tel. 03/572-4131), is a cross between a business hotel and a regular hotel. Because of its location, convenient to Ginza and to the Kasumigaseki and Marunouchi business centers, it caters to both businessmen and tourists. The lobby is on the second floor and is manned by a friendly staff. The guest rooms are small and come with hot water for tea, alarm clock, radio, cotton kimono, and color TV offering English programs and adult entertainment for an extra ¥550 ($2.75) a day. The bathrooms are larger than in other business hotels. Rooms vary in size, beginning at ¥10,500 ($75) for a single and ¥16,500 ($118) for a twin or double. I suggest asking for a room away from the highway overpass beside the hotel. Nearest subway station: Shimbashi, only one minute on foot.

The **Ginza Capital Hotel,** 3-1-5 Tsukiji, Chuo-ku (tel. 03/543-8211), and its newer annex, called the New Ginza Capital Hotel, offer a total of 528 rooms within a ten-minute walk of Ginza. A modern and efficient establishment with a friendly staff, its rooms are clean and bright even though they are minuscule in size. If being able to look out a window is a big deal to you, stay away from rooms in the annex that face north—they have a glazed covering about a foot out from the building so you can't see anything (heaven knows why). Rooms come with the usual hot water for tea, cotton kimono, and TV with adult movies, but a plus here are the full-length mirrors. The annex has a Japanese restaurant and the main building a Western one. Rates in the main building start at ¥7,600 ($54) for a single and ¥13,100 ($94) for a twin; in the annex it's ¥8,500 ($61) for a single, ¥13,900 ($99) for a double, and ¥14,500 ($104) for a twin. Triples are ¥17,000 ($121). Prices include service charge and tax. Nearest subway station: Shintomicho, two minutes away.

A red-brick building, **Hotel Ginza Dai-ei,** 3-12-2 Ginza Chuo-ku (tel. 03/541-0111), is a typical business hotel with minuscule rooms and the usual TV, hot-water heater, cotton kimono, clock, and desk. A plus, however, is that its windows open. It also has Japanese-style rooms available at ¥12,000 ($86) for one person, ¥14,300 ($102) for two, and ¥16,700 ($119) for three. Otherwise, rooms start at ¥8,200 ($59) for one and ¥12,400 ($89) for two. Because of the miserable state of the dollar, the hotel has been offering discounted rates to foreigners that amount to about ¥1,000 ($7.14) off the regular room rates quoted above, so be sure to ask whether you're getting a discount. Three restaurants serve Japanese, Western, and Chinese food. The hotel is just a few minutes' walk from Higashi-Ginza Station.

There's nothing fancy or out of the ordinary about the **Ginza Nikko Hotel,**

8-4-21 Ginza, Chuo-ku (tel. 03/571-4911), but it's clean and conveniently located in southern Ginza. A small and personable business hotel with only 112 rooms, it's more than a quarter of a century old, making it one of the oldest hotels in the area. Facilities include a coffeeshop, two restaurants, and a bar. Singles start at ¥10,600 ($76), doubles at ¥16,700 ($119), twins at ¥19,200 ($137), and triples at ¥25,900 ($185). It's a four-minute walk to Shimbashi Station.

Miyako Inn Tokyo, 3-7-8 Mita, Minato-ku (tel. 03/454-3111), is a combination business and city hotel rising 14 stories high in southern Tokyo. Rooms on the top floor have the best views and face either Tokyo Bay or Tokyo Tower in the distance. All rooms come with the usual refrigerator, TV with extra charges for movies, cotton kimono, alarm clock, and hot-water Thermos and tea. Facilities include Japanese, Chinese, and Western restaurants. Prices range from ¥8,500 ($60) to ¥9,300 ($66) for a single and ¥14,300 ($102) to ¥19,800 ($141) for a twin. Differences in room rates are reflected in the size of the room and the bed. Double rooms are ¥15,400 ($110). Nearest stations: Tamachi, Mita, and Sengakuji, all within a six-minute walk.

Tokyo City Hotel, 1-9 Nihombashi Honcho, Chuo-ku (tel. 03/270-7671), is a fine, no-nonsense business hotel with all the usuals. Its one restaurant serves Western food. Although the single rooms are quite small, the twin rooms are adequate. Singles start at ¥6,600 ($47), doubles begin at ¥9,700 ($69), and twins at ¥9,900 ($71). Nearest subway station: Mitsukoshi-mae, two minutes away.

The bottom ten floors of the **Shinjuku Prince Hotel**, 1-30-1 Kabuki-cho, Shinjuku-ku (tel. 03/205-1111), include shopping arcades and restaurants, while the 10th through 24th floors hold the hotel's 571 rooms. A smart-looking, streamlined brick building in the heart of Shinjuku, this business hotel has 13 restaurants and bars and 24-hour room service. The standard rooms go for ¥13,200 ($94) for a single and ¥15,900 ($114) for a double or a twin. Deluxe rooms are twice as large as the standards and start at ¥20,900 ($149) for a twin and ¥23,000 ($164) for a double. This hotel has a great location, just a five-minute walk north of Shinjuku Station. The Seibu Shinjuku Line begins in the hotel itself.

The **Hotel Sunroute Tokyo**, 2-3-1 Yoyogi, Shibuya-ku (tel. 03/375-3211), attracts a 40% foreign clientele and calls itself a "city hotel," but its rooms resemble a business hotel rather than tourist accommodation. A 15-story white building, it has five restaurants serving French, Chinese, and Japanese cuisine. The guest rooms are small but clean, cozy and attractive and start at ¥9,300 ($66) for a single, ¥15,400 ($110) for a double, and ¥17,600 ($126) for a twin. Nearest train station: it's a two-minute walk south of Shinjuku Station.

In 1985 **Hotel Sunlite**, 5-15-8 Shinjuku, Shinjuku-ku (tel. 03/356-0391), moved across the street from its old location into a spanking new building. As for the older building, it was turned into the Hotel Sunlite Annex and offers much lower rates than the newer location. At any rate, all 192 rooms are cheerful and clean, though those in the Annex are small and its singles are minuscule. Feelings of claustrophobia are somewhat mitigated, however, by the fact that all windows can be opened. The best rooms are the new building's twin rooms that are situated on the corners, which have windows on two sides. Rates in the Annex start at ¥6,500 ($46) for a single and ¥10,000 ($71) for a twin. Charges in the new building start at ¥7,500 ($54) for a single, ¥13,200 ($94) for a twin, and ¥12,000 ($86) for a double. All rates include tax and service charge. Incidentally, if you like to stay out late, beware. Doors here close at 2 a.m. and don't reopen until 5:30 a.m. It's about a 15-minute walk to Shinjuku Station.

If you like electronic gadgetry and the benefits of the Space Age, you might like staying at **Shinjuku Washington Hotel**, 3-2-9 Nishi-Shinjuku, Shinjuku-ku (tel. 03/343-3111). Opened in West Shinjuku in 1984 with an annex added in 1987, this huge white building reminds me of an ocean liner—even the hotel's tiny windows look like a ship's portholes. It has an interesting interior design with a lot of open spaces, and everything is bright and white. Make your way up to the third floor to the lobby—a row of machines provides for automated check-in and check-out. There are a few humans there, however, to help you with the process. You'll receive a "card key" resembling a credit card, which also activates the bedside controls for such things as the TV, radio, and room lights. There are no bellboys here, no room service. The guest rooms remind me of cabins in a ship and are small, but everything you need is there—fridge, TV with video programs, and radio. It's rather comical to see older women shuffling down the corridor of this thoroughly modern and automated hotel, but the place seems to attract all kinds. It also has a reputation for serving as a "love hotel" for young couples—an interesting place. Singles start at ¥7,500 ($54), doubles at ¥13,200 ($94), twins at ¥12,600 ($90), and triples at ¥21,000 ($150). Prices in the annex are slightly different, starting at ¥7,700 ($55) for a single, ¥12,600 ($90) for a double, and ¥16,000 ($114) for a twin. The annex has its own check-in desk, and be sure to check out the annex toilets. Instructions are in Japanese only, but with the right push of a switch a spray of water is sent shooting into the air. A Japanese version of the French bidet. Nearest station: Shinjuku, about ten minutes away.

A pleasant, small business hotel, the **Hotel Yoko Akasaka**, 6-14-12 Akasaka, Minato-ku (tel. 03/586-4050), caters primarily to Japanese. In a handy location close to the nightlife in both Roppongi and Akasaka, its singles start at ¥7,500 ($54) and twins begin at ¥13,200 ($94). Prices include tax and service charge. For a couple dollars more in each category you can get a slightly larger room, which may be worth it if you're claustrophobic. In any case, the bathrooms are barely large enough for even one person. Nearest subway station: Akasaka Station, five minutes away, on Akasaka Dori Street.

Not far from the Hotel Yoko Akasaka is **Shanpia**, 7-6-13 Akasaka, Minato-ku (tel. 03/586-0811). The special feature of this hotel is that 228 of its 250 rooms are singles. The other 22 rooms are twins only—no double beds. Singles go for ¥7,900 ($56) and ¥8,300 ($59), and twins run ¥14,700 ($105), including tax and service charge. Closest subway station: Akasaka is about a five-minute walk.

Hotel Tokyukanko, 2-21-6 Akasaka, Minato-ku (tel. 03/583-4741), is located close to the ANA Hotel, about a ten-minute walk from either the Roppongi or Akasaka subway station. An older, 48-room hotel built at the time of the Olympics, in 1964, it's a bit worn in places and shows its age but is still popular because of its location. Single rooms with showers are ¥7,000 ($50), but these face an inner courtyard and have glazed windows. If you like the light of day, spring for a single with bath for ¥9,000 ($64). Twins start at ¥13,500 ($96), while doubles are ¥14,000 ($100). Rooms are larger than in some other business hotels, and bathrooms are tiled instead of being the usual plastic units.

If you want to stay closer to the night action of Roppongi, the **Hotel Ibis**, 7-4-14 Roppongi, Minato-ku (tel. 03/403-4411), is about as close as you can get, and you can't beat it for its location. It caters to both businessmen and to couples who came to Roppongi's discos and didn't make (or didn't want to make) the last subway home. Prices start at ¥9,300 ($66) for a single room, ¥13,200 ($94) for a double, and ¥16,500 ($118) for a twin. The lobby is on the fifth floor. On the 13th floor is the Sky Restaurant, an inexpensive French restaurant offering a good view of the surrounding area. Closest subway station: Roppongi, one minute away.

All 1,016 rooms in the main building of the **Shinagawa Prince Hotel,** 4-10-30 Takanawa, Minato-ku (tel. 03/440-1111), are singles. In 1986 an annex of 257 twin and double rooms was added. The best feature of this huge hotel complex is its adjoining sports complex, where you can use tennis courts, an ice-skating rink, bowling lanes, and an outdoor pool for an extra charge. The hotel has 13 restaurants and bars, and in the summer it has an outdoor beer garden. Catering to Japanese businessmen on weekdays and students on weekends and holidays, the Shinagawa Prince charges ¥9,620 ($69) for singles. If there are two of you but you still want to stay in the hotel's main building, an extra bed can be added for a total of ¥11,500 ($82). That gives you hardly room to walk, but the price is certainly reasonable. Ask for a room above the tenth floor, where you have a view of either mountains on the west side or the sea on the east. As for rooms in the annex, twins go for ¥15,300 ($109) and doubles for ¥16,000 ($114); all of these have the extra benefit of a refrigerator. The views, however, are unexciting. Prices include tax and service. Nearest station: Shinagawa, a one-minute walk.

A NOTE ON JAPANESE SYMBOLS: Many hotels, restaurants, and other establishments in Japan do not have signs showing their names in English letters. Appendix II lists the Japanese symbols for all such places appearing in this guide. Each establishment name in Japanese symbols is numbered, and the same number appears in brackets in the text following the boldfaced establishment name. For example, in the text the Osaka hotel, Hokke Club [161], is number 161 in the Japanese symbol list in Appendix II.

The **Hotel Ohgaiso,** 3-3-21 Ikenohata, Taito-ku (tel. 03/822-4611), is an inexpensive and clean, if rather unimaginative, place to stay. Its 85 rooms all have private bath and toilet, and come with desk, coin-operated TV, refrigerator, radio, and clock. There's no closet but there's a bar for hanging up clothes. Front doors close at 2 a.m. Rates are ¥6,600 ($47) for a single room and ¥11,500 ($82) for a twin. The hotel is located close to Ueno Park and has bicycles for rent. Its one restaurant serves both Japanese- and Western-style breakfasts, tempura, sashimi, and sukiyaki. Closest subway station: the Ohgaiso is a three-minute walk from Nezu and a five-minute walk from the Ikenohata Exit of the Keisei (Skyliner) Ueno Station.

Ryokan

Seifuso [1], 1-12-15 Fujimi, Chiyoda-ku (tel. 03/263-0681), is an excellent choice for travelers wishing to experience a ryokan for the first time. It's run by Setsuko Fukushima, a friendly woman who doesn't speak a lot of English but who compensates for it with warmth and with a sheet of instructions written in English about such things as etiquette of the Japanese bath and where and when to wear slippers. More than 30 years old, Seifuso has a total of 17 rooms, most of which have their own small alcove with chairs overlooking a small Japanese garden. If you'd like to have the experience of staying in a ryokan but don't relish the idea of sleeping on the floor, there's one Western-style room with a double bed available. There are also public baths that are separated for men and women.

Rooms without bath begin at ¥6,600 ($47) for one, ¥11,000 ($79) for two, and ¥16,500 ($118) for three. If you want a room with private bath, it's ¥12,000

($86) for one, ¥22,000 ($157) for two, and ¥27,000 ($193) for three. These prices include tax and service charge, but no meals. Meals range from ¥1,320 ($9.43) for tempura to ¥5,000 ($36) for a Japanese-style dinner, and are served in a dining area that looks out onto the garden. Nearest subway station: Iidabashi, about a seven-minute walk. However, because Seifuso is a bit hard to find and has a sign only in Japanese, I suggest taking a taxi from Iidabashi.

Shimizu Bekkan [2], 1-30-29 Hongo, Bunkyo-ku (tel. 03/812-6285), is another ryokan that accepts foreigners and has had American guests. It has a variety of rooms available, and its prices, which include tax and service charge, are on a per-person rather than per-room basis. A variety of meal options are offered. Rooms without bath and toilet are ¥6,600 ($47) with no meals, ¥7,700 ($55) with breakfast only, ¥8,800 ($63) with dinner only, and ¥9,900 ($71) with dinner and breakfast. For rooms with private bath and toilet, add ¥1,000 ($7.14) to the charges above. Meals are served in your room, and there are separate public baths for men and women. Nearest subway station: Hongo Sanchome is about eight minutes away; it's best to take a taxi.

A bit far from the station, but a good medium-price ryokan as far as Tokyo goes, is **Tokiwa**, 7-27-9 Shinjuku, Shinjuku-ku (tel. 03/202-4321). An older building surrounded by a white wall and gate on Meiji Dori Street, this place is divided into two parts, a hotel and a ryokan, but all its 50 rooms are Japanese style. I suggest staying in the ryokan part—it's more than 40 years old and has a lot more character, with wooden beams, the earthy smell of tatami, and an old rock-enclosed and quaint public bath. Like most older Japanese buildings, it's cold and drafty in winter, but rooms have *kotatsu*—a low table with a heating element underneath and a blanket spread all around it. By sitting at the table with your legs stuck under the quilt you can stay pretty toasty. Rates are per person and include tax and service charge. The charge is ¥4,800 ($34) for a room without bath or meals, ¥7,700 ($55) for a room without meals but with its own bathroom. Rooms with their own private bath and meals range from ¥11,000 ($79) to ¥16,500 ($118). Nearest subway station: Shin-Okubo, a ten-minute walk.

Meguro Gajoen Ryokan [3], 1-8-1 Shimo-Meguro, Meguro-ku (tel. 03/491-4111), is a rambling, 60-year old building surrounded by a massive gate and towering trees. Made of Japanese cypress, cedar, bamboo, and timber imported from China, South America, and the United States, Meguro Gajoen is used mainly for wedding receptions and has a number of exquisite banquet halls with designs in mother-of-pearl. It also has a couple dozen Japanese-style rooms available for ¥15,400 ($110) per person, including breakfast and dinner (served in your room), tax and service. You can wander around through endlessly long corridors with wooden floors and high ceilings where walls are decorated with either Japanese prints or inlaid shell. Rooms are large, with wooden beams and big windows. All in all it's a lovely place, but it lacks the intimacy of the usually small ryokan. I got lost here and wandered around for what seemed like an eternity, wondering whether I was ever going to find the exit or see another living soul again. Hardly anyone here speaks English so try to have a Japanese make your room reservation for you. Nearest subway station: Meguro, about five minutes away.

THE BUDGET CATEGORY: It's difficult to find inexpensive lodging in Tokyo the way you can in other big cities in Asia. The price of land is simply too prohibitive. You can, however, find rooms—tiny though they might be—for less than $30 a night, which is pretty good considering that you're in one of the most expensive cities in the world. Accommodation in this category is basic: a bed and usually a phone, television, heating, and air conditioning. Facilities are generally spotless, and prices include tax and service charge. Inexpensive Japanese-style rooms make up the majority of this category.

Western Style

Asia Center of Japan, 8-10-32 Akasaka, Minato-ku (tel. 03/402-6111), is top choice in this category if you're looking for Western-style accommodation in the center of town. The only problem is that it's so popular it's often fully booked. Everyone from businessmen to students to travelers to foreigners teaching English stay here. (I know one teacher who has lived here for years.) Resembling a college dormitory, it has 172 rooms with and without private bath; a cafeteria and a lobby are located on the second floor. Rooms are basic, no frills, and in the singles you can almost reach out and touch all four walls. They come with bed, desk, telephone, air-conditioner, heater, and pay TV. Rooms without bath are ¥4,620 ($33) for a single, ¥5,800 ($41) for a twin, and ¥9,800 ($70) for a triple. If you want your own bath, it's ¥5,500 ($39) for a single, ¥9,200 ($66) for a twin, and ¥12,000 ($86) for a triple. The average price of meals served in the cafeteria is ¥550 ($3.93) for breakfast, ¥660 ($4.71) for lunch, and ¥1,300 ($9.29) for dinner. Nearest station: Aoyama-Itchome, about three minutes away. It's about a 15-minute walk to Roppongi, where all the night action is.

The **YMCA Asia Youth Center,** 2-5-5 Sarugaku-cho, Chiyoda-ku (tel. 03/233-0611), is a relatively new and modern-looking facility, which opened in 1980. Its concrete structure houses a total of 55 rooms, all with their own private bathrooms. Both men and women of any age are accepted, and about 30% of its guests are Korean. Rooms are very simple and go for ¥6,600 ($47) for a single, ¥11,000 ($79) for a twin, and ¥14,800 ($106) for a triple. YMCA members receive a discount of ¥500 ($3.57) on the above rates. Western- or Japanese-style breakfasts are available for ¥900 ($6.43), lunches start at ¥1,000 ($7.14), and dinners start at ¥1,650 ($11.79). Facilities include an indoor swimming pool. Closest station: Suidobashi or Jimbocho, each about a five-minute walk away.

Close to Ichigaya Station are two YWCAs. If you've already made reservations, make sure you're headed for the right one. The **National YWCA of Japan** [4], 4-8-8 Kudan-Minami, Chiyoda-ku (tel. 03/264-0661), is located about two minutes by foot from the Kudan exit of the station. It accepts women only. An exceptionally clean, cheerful, and rather modern establishment, it has nine Western-style rooms (eight singles and one twin) and two Japanese-style rooms, all without private bath. The charge is ¥5,000 ($36) for one person staying in a room, and ¥10,000 ($71) for the twin room. There's a small living room with a kitchenette for personal use and a TV. There's no cafeteria, and front doors close at 11 p.m.

At the opposite end of Ichigaya Station, close to the Ichigaya exit, is the **Tokyo YWCA Sadowara Center** [5], 3-1-1 Ichigaya Sadowara-cho, Shinjuku-ku (tel. 03/268-7313). It accepts married couples as well as single women. The rates here are ¥5,200 ($37) for one person and ¥10,500 ($75) for two.

Ryokan

Ryokan Mikawaya Bekkan, 1-31-11 Asakusa, Taito-ku (tel. 03/843-2345), is located just off Nakamise Dori, a colorful, shop-lined pedestrian street leading to the famous Asakusa Kannon Temple. This is a pleasant area in which to stay because it gives you more of a feel for older Japan. Owned by Katsuo Tobita, who speaks good English, Mikawaya Bekkan has been a ryokan for more than half a century. Its 12 tatami rooms are all different and come with pay TV, floor cushions with backrests, and Japanese-style vanity mirrors. The ryokan is built around a small inner courtyard with a goldfish pond, where you can sit outside in warm weather. Room rates are ¥5,000 ($36) for one person and ¥9,500 ($68) for two. A Japanese breakfast is available for ¥550 ($3.93), but if you're tired of fish, rice, and vegetables in the morning, a Western-style breakfast of eggs, toast, salad, fruit, and coffee can be arranged for the same price. Doors close at 11:30 p.m. and guests are requested to leave their rooms from 10 a.m. to noon daily for cleaning. Nearest subway station: the ryokan is just a few minutes from Asakusa.

Another good place to stay in Asakusa is **Namiju**, 2-24-4 Asakusa, Taito-ku (tel. 03/841-9126), located just northwest of Hanayashiki Amusement Park. Entrance to the ryokan is through a traditional Japanese front gate and tiny garden. Throughout the house, part of which has been recently remodeled, modern conveniences have been combined with traditional touches, such as pebbles inlaid in the entryway and bamboo-latticed windows. Check-in is at 4 p.m., check-out is at 10 a.m., and the front doors lock up for the night at 11:30 p.m. All rooms are Japanese-style, and rates start at ¥4,400 ($31.43) for one person, ¥7,700 ($55) for two, and ¥10,200 ($73) for three. By the way, all those other discreet-looking establishments you see in the surrounding neighborhood are so-called "love hotels," at which rooms are rented by the hour to couples who have no privacy at home. In Japan it's not uncommon for couples to live with in-laws and extended families. Namiju is a seven-minute walk from Tawaramachi Station.

If the above ryokan are full, another place to stay in Asakusa is **Kikuya Ryokan**, 2-18-9 Nishi Asakusa, Taito-ku (tel. 03/841-6404). A modern red-brick building with eight Japanese-style rooms, it's located just off Kappabashi Dori Avenue, lined with shops selling those plastic-food displays you see in restaurants throughout Japan. Sensoji Temple is about a ten-minute walk away. Rates for rooms without private bathroom are ¥3,800 ($27) for one person, ¥5,500 ($39) for two, and ¥7,700 ($55) for three. Rooms with private bathroom range from ¥4,200 ($30) to ¥5,000 ($36) for one person, ¥6,000 ($43) to ¥8,200 ($59) for two persons, and are ¥11,000 ($79) for three persons. The front doors close at midnight, and the closest station is Tawaramachi, about an eight-minute walk away.

Another great place to stay if you want to get away from the glitter and neon of Tokyo is the area around Ueno Park. **Ryokan Sawanoya**, 2-3-11 Yanaka, Taito-ku (tel. 03/822-2251), is located northwest of Ueno Park. Although the ryokan itself is relatively modern-looking and unexciting, it's surrounded by a delightful part of old Tokyo—narrow streets lined with potted plants and bonsai, temples and old wooden houses tucked behind walls with wood gates, ma-and-pa shops selling everything from Japanese paper to rice crackers. To help in your exploration of the area, the ryokan will give you a map outlining places of interest.

As for the ryokan itself, it has a nice feeling to it. It has pamphlets and lots of information on other inexpensive ryokan and accommodations throughout Japan, and if you pay for the call, the owner here will even make your next reservation for you. It's a good place to meet other travelers and exchange information. There's instant coffee and tea available free in the lobby/dining area throughout the day. Unlike most ryokan, you wear your shoes inside, taking them off only before entering your tatami room. All 12 rooms are Japanese style, but only two come with private bath. Along with the usual pay TV, phone, heater, and air-conditioner, each room has its own sink. The best rooms, in my opinion, are those on the third floor because they have their own small balcony. A breakfast of toast and fried eggs is available for ¥330 ($2.36), and if you order it the day before you can have a Japanese-style breakfast for ¥880 ($6.29). Facilities include a vending machine dispensing beer and soda, a coin-operated washing machine and dryer (with free laundry detergent), a refrigerator, and a public bath. Room rates begin at ¥3,900 ($28) for one person, ¥7,500 ($54) for two, and ¥9,900 ($71) for three. Nearest subway station: the Yanaka exit of Nezu Station is about a seven-minute walk.

In the same neighborhood but located a few minutes farther south is **Katsutaro,** 4-16-8 Ikenohata, Taito-ku (tel. 03/821-9808). All of its seven rooms are Japanese style, and four of these have their own private bathroom. Rooms are quite large and have coin-operated TVs, but try to avoid rooms that face the main street, as these can be quite noisy. The building itself is about 35 years old, and at least half the guests staying here are Japanese. A continental breakfast costs ¥380 ($2.71). Rooms without bath are ¥3,900 ($28) for one person, ¥7,400 ($53) for two, and ¥9,900 ($71) for three. Rooms with bath are ¥4,800 ($34), ¥8,300 ($59), and ¥11,500 ($82) respectively.

A third ryokan close to Ueno Park is **Suigetsu,** 3-3-21 Ikenohata, Taito-ku (tel. 03/822-4611). It's located next to the Hotel Ohgaiso, a Western-style hotel described above. They are under the same management but have their own front desks. Suigetsu has 66 Japanese-style rooms (some with balconies) in a hotel-like setting, and caters mainly to Japanese families and tour groups. The rooms come with coin-operated TV with adult video, refrigerator, safe, mirror, and table. There are three public baths: one for women, one for men, and one for families. You can rent bicycles here. A restaurant serves Japanese food and Japanese- and Western-style breakfasts. Most rooms are without bath and start at ¥4,400 ($31) for a single, ¥7,700 ($55) for a twin, and ¥9,900 ($71) for a triple. Rooms with private bath are for four or five people only and cost ¥8,800 ($63) per person. Nearest subway stations: the Ikenohata exit of Keisei (Skyliner) Ueno Station (a ten-minute walk) and Nezu Station (a five-minute walk).

The small (only nine rooms) **Sansuiso** is at 2-9-5 Higashi Gotanda, Shinagawa-ku (tel. 03/441-7475). The friendly and accommodating couple who run this place don't speak any English but they have a poster answering all pertinent questions, such as how many nights, whether you want breakfast, etc. The ryokan is very clean and rooms come with the usual hot water and tea bags, cotton kimono and towel, mirror, heater and air-conditioner, and pay TV. Some rooms have Japanese toilet and bath. A Japanese breakfast costs ¥880 ($6.29). Rooms start at ¥4,200 ($30) for one, ¥7,400 ($53) for two, and ¥9,900 ($71) for three. Nearest subway station: Sansuiso is a five-minute walk east of Gotanda Station.

Okayasu, 1-7-11 Shibaura, Minato-ku (tel. 03/452-5091), is typical of larger homes built in Tokyo about two decades ago. It has a total of 13 rooms, two of which are Western style, with beds; none have a private bath. Amenities include coin-operated TV, cotton kimono, heater, and air-conditioner. Japanese-style breakfasts are ¥880 ($6.29). Rates start at ¥3,900 ($28) for one person, ¥7,200 ($51) for two, and ¥9,200 ($66) for three. The nearest stations are Mita, Tamachi, and Hamamatsucho, all about a 15-minute walk away.

Inabaso Ryokan, 5-6-13 Shinjuku, Shinjuku-ku (tel. 03/341-9581), first began receiving foreign guests during the 1964 Olympics and since then has had many travelers from North America, Australia, and Europe. All 13 rooms (two of them Western style) have their own private bath and Western-style toilet, TV, and refrigerator. A Japanese breakfast of rice, bean-paste soup, fish, and ham and eggs is available for ¥660 ($4.71); coffee, toast, and eggs cost ¥330 ($2.36), and a Japanese dinner runs ¥1,650 ($11.79). Room rates here begin at ¥4,200 ($30) for one person, ¥7,700 ($55) for two, and ¥9,900 ($71) for three. Nearest subway stations: it's ten minutes from Shinjuku, three minutes from either Shinjuku Sanchome or Shinjuku Gyoen-mae.

Kimi Ryokan, 2-1034 Ikebukuro, Toshima-ku (tel. 03/971-3766), underwent extensive remodeling in 1986 and reopened as a completely new structure. In place of the old, rambling building that used to stand here is a five-story cement building with whitewashed walls, wooden corridors, and tatami-style guest rooms. The place is spotlessly clean, and although it's modern in every sense of the word, care has been given to add such Japanese touches as sliding screens and traditional Japanese music playing softly in the hallways. Owned by three brothers who speak excellent English, Kimi began attracting overseas visitors in the late 1970s and now caters exclusively to foreigners, many of whom are working in Tokyo as English teachers or in other professions and some of whom are living here while searching for more permanent places to stay. There's a bulletin board with various jobs available (mainly as English teachers). This place is so popular, in fact, that there's sometimes a waiting list to get in. All rooms are without private bath but are cheerful and clean and come with telephone and coin-operated heater and air-conditioner. Prices start at ¥2,800 ($20) for a single, ¥4,900 ($35) for a double, and ¥5,500 ($39) for a twin. Facilities include a lounge with TV, a vending machine for drinks, and a pay telephone from which you can make international calls. Free tea is available throughout the day. Nearest station: about a five-minute walk from the west exit of Ikebukuro Station. The tiny police station located to your right as you exit the station has maps available that will guide you to Kimi.

One of the least expensive places to stay in Shinjuku is **Keiunso Ryokan** [6], 2-4-2 Yoyogi, Shibuya-ku (tel. 03/370-0333 or 370-3751). However, the English-speaking woman who runs this place expressed some reluctance about taking in foreigners who had never stayed in a ryokan before. Another disadvantage to staying here is that guests are requested to leave during the day from 10 a.m. to 5 p.m. However, this place has such a good location that it's worth a try. There are a total of 30 rooms in two buildings and are all Japanese style with just the basics of pay TV and phone. Most also have their own sink, but the bath is communal. The price per person is ¥6,000 ($43) if there's one of you and ¥4,400 ($31) if there are two. Nearest station: the south exit of Shinjuku Station is only three minutes away.

If the ryokan listed above are full, you might try **Okubo House**, 1-11-32 Hyakunincho, Shinjuku-ku (tel. 03/361-2348). You have to leave during the day from 9:30 a.m. to 5 p.m., the front doors are locked at 11 p.m., and the people who run this place are sometimes curt and gruff, but it's one of the cheapest places to stay in Tokyo. The rooms are the smallest I've seen—just two- or three-tatami-mat rooms—but at least they all have windows. Room prices are ¥3,000 ($21) for one person and ¥4,100 ($29) for two. There are also two dormitory-style rooms with bunk beds, for men only, for ¥1,650 ($12). Children are not accepted in this ryokan. Cotton kimonos and Japanese tea are provided, but there's no kitchen or meals. There are separate public baths for men and women. Nearest subway station: Shin-Okubo., about a two-minute walk. To get there, turn left out of the station's only exit, then turn left again on the first side street, which runs right past the station and parallels the train tracks. Okubo is on this street and is easy to identify, having a sign in English.

Youth Hostels

Opened in 1984, the **Tokyo International Youth Hostel**, 21-1 Kaguragashi, Shinjuku-ku (tel. 03/235-1107), is definitely the best place to stay in its price range. The lobby is on the 18th floor of the new Central Plaza Building and you just can't beat this place—it's new, spotlessly clean, modern, and offers a great view of Tokyo. And the best thing is that you don't even need a youth hostel card to stay here, and there is no age limit. All 138 beds are dormitory style, with two, four, or five bunk beds to a room. The rooms are very pleasant, with big windows and wooden and metal bunk beds of modern design. Each bed even has its own curtain you can draw around it for privacy. Lodging costs ¥1,800 ($13) per night; for students it's ¥1,000 ($7.14). If you need to rent sheets and blankets there's a one-time fee of ¥150 ($1.07). There's an extra charge of ¥240 ($1.71) for heating and ¥250 ($1.79) for air conditioning.

There are, however, some restrictions and rules. Officially you can stay here a maximum of only three days, although if there are vacancies you can stay longer. The place is so popular in summer that it's necessary to make reservations about three months in advance. At 10:30 p.m. the front door is locked and it's lights out. The hostel is closed during the day from 10 a.m. to 3 p.m. A plus, however, is that you have free use of a washer and dryer. Nearest subway station: Iidabashi is one minute away.

Only youth hostel members can stay at the **Tokyo Yoyogi Youth Hostel**, National Olympic Memorial Youth Center, 3-1 Yoyogi-Kamizono, Shibuya-ku (tel. 03/467-9163), on the west side of Meiji Shrine Outer Garden. Located in an enclosed complex of buildings surrounded by a fence, the hostel is in Building 14. The whole compound used to house American occupation troops after World War II and was then used to accommodate athletes during the 1964 Olympics. It's now devoted to a number of youth activities. There are 150 beds here and the cost is ¥1,850 ($13) per night. No meals are served but there are cooking facilities. There's a large Japanese-style bath in a neighboring building. The hostel is closed daily from 10 a.m. to 5 p.m., and the front gate closes at 10 p.m. Closest station: Sangubashi, about five minutes away.

Capsule Hotels

So-called capsule hotels became popular in the early 1980s and are used primarily by Japanese businessmen who have spent an evening out drinking with fellow workers and missed their last train home—a capsule hotel is cheaper than a taxi home. At any rate, accommodation in one of these establishments is a small unit no larger than a coffin consisting of a bed and private color TV, alarm clock, and radio. These are usually stacked two deep in rows down a corridor, and the only thing separating you from your probably inebriated neighbor is a curtain. A cotton kimono and locker are provided, and bath and toilets are communal.

Most capsule hotels do not accept women; the two listed here are no exception. **Fontaine Akasaka**, 4-3-5 Akasaka, Minato-ku (tel. 03/583-6554), is located right in the heart of Akasaka's nightlife. It offers a total of 332 capsule beds, a sauna and public bath, and nonsmoking floors. Check-in is after 5 p.m., checkout is at 10 a.m. and the charge is ¥4,000 ($29) per person. Closest subway stations: a two-minute walk from Akasaka Station or a five-minute walk from Akasaka-mitsuke.

Capsule Inn Akasaka, 6-14-1 Akasaka, Minato-ku (tel. 03/588-1811), is located just off Akasaka Dori Street, about a five-minute walk from Akasaka subway station. It also offers a sauna and public bath and has the same check-in and check-out times as the capsule hotel listed above. The charge here is ¥3,300 ($24) per night.

ACCOMMODATIONS AT NARITA: If you find yourself on a stopover at Narita International Airport for one or two nights you may not want to take the one- to two-hour trip to a hotel in Tokyo. There are a number of Western-style hotels close by that operate free shuttle buses to and from the airport. Rooms are soundproofed and have the usual conveniences of private bath and toilet, TV,

phone, and radio, but otherwise there's nothing that really distinguishes one hotel from the next. Reservations for these hotels can be made at the hotel counter located in the arrival wing of the airport. The telephone prefix for Narita is 0476, which you needn't dial if you're calling from the airport.

If you find yourself with some spare time, be sure to visit Shinshoji Temple, popularly known as Narita-san, which is located close to the train station in downtown Narita. It's a Buddhist temple dedicated to Fudo, god of fire, and is visited by more than seven million people each year—usually when they have a favor to ask, whether it be good health, a happy marriage, or success in passing a university entrance exam. Behind the temple is a 40-acre Japanese garden that has three ponds and many flowering trees and bushes, including wisteria, plum, and cherry.

Narita International Hotel, 650-35 Nanae, Tomisato-mura Inba-gun, Chiba (tel. 0476/93-1234), is located 15 minutes away from the airport via shuttle bus. An affiliate of Northwest Orient Airlines, its 212 rooms are large for Japan, and the hotel is surrounded by greenery, woods, and fields. Facilities include an outdoor swimming pool, tennis courts, and Japanese and Western restaurants. There's free shuttle bus service daily to Narita-san temple. Room rates are ¥11,500 ($82) for a single, ¥17,500 ($125) for a double, and ¥20,000 ($143) for a twin.

Narita Airport Rest House (tel. 0476/32-1212) is a square white building located right beside the airport terminal. Its singles are ¥12,200 ($87), and twins and doubles start at ¥16,600 ($119), including tax and service. The 210 rooms are rather sterile but they have everything you need. Four TV screens in the hotel give all the latest information on arrival and departure times for all airlines. There's a Japanese and a Western restaurant and a bar in the hotel.

Holiday Inn–Narita, 320-1 Tokko, Narita-shi, Chiba (tel. 0476/32-1234), is located just a mile away from the airport and is similar to Holiday Inns in the United States. Its rooms are pleasantly decorated in powder blue and white. Facilities include an outdoor swimming pool, sauna, restaurants serving Japanese, Chinese, and Western cuisine, and a bar/restaurant on the ninth floor with views of the airport. Rates begin at ¥11,000 ($79) for one person and ¥14,300 ($102) for two.

Narita View Hotel, 700 Kosuge, Narita City (tel. 0476/32-1111), is located ten minutes away from both the airport and Narita train station. Facilities here include four restaurants and one bar, sauna, tennis courts, indoor and outdoor pools, a garden, and gym. Singles are ¥12,000 ($86), doubles run ¥15,500 ($111), and twins cost ¥18,700 ($134).

Hotel Nikko Narita, 500 Tokko, Narita (tel. 0476/32-0032), is located about five minutes from the airport by free shuttle bus. It offers an outdoor swimming pool, tennis courts, and two bars and four restaurants serving Japanese, French, Chinese, and Western cuisine. Its 525 rooms cost ¥12,000 ($86) for a single, ¥20,300 ($145) for a double, and ¥20,300 ($145) to ¥24,000 ($171) for a twin.

4. Where to Dine

From stand-up noodle shops at train stations to rustic farmhouses serving country cooking Japanese style, restaurants in Tokyo number at least 45,000, which gives you at least some idea of how fond the Japanese are of food and of eating out. In a city where apartments are so small and cramped that entertaining at home is almost unheard of, restaurants serve as places for socializing, meeting friends, and wooing business associates—as well as excuses for drinking a lot of beer, sake, and whisky. I know people in Tokyo who claim they haven't cooked in years—and that doesn't mean that they're millionaires (though it could mean that they're bad cooks). It just means that they take advantage of one of the best deals in Tokyo, the *teishoku*, or set lunch course. Even the most prohibitive restaurants in Tokyo often offer set lunch menus by which you can dine in style at very reasonable prices. To keep your costs down, therefore, try eating your bigger meal at lunch.

Although Japanese food is varied, healthy, and delicious, even the most dedicated Japanophile starts craving Western food after a while. In fact, even the Japanese themselves crave Western food, as shown by the increase in Western restaurants in Tokyo in the past decade. So I have included a goodly number of restaurants serving food other than Japanese. The most popular Western restaurants are French and Italian, which can be quite expensive. Other international cuisines tend to be more reasonably priced, including Mexican, Chinese, Greek, and American. Ethnic restaurants have literally mushroomed in popularity in the past few years and have become somewhat of an epidemic. The result is that you can dine at French, Indian, and other international restaurants that rival ethnic restaurants anywhere else in the world.

In addition to the restaurants recommended in this section, there are a number of bars and nightspots listed in the Chapter IV "Tokyo After Dark" section that serve food. Remember that if your meal exceeds ¥2,500 ($17.86), a 10% government tax will be added to your bill. Many first-class restaurants also add a 10% to 15% service charge. Unless otherwise stated, the prices I've given do not include the extra tax and charges.

Street maps for the Ginza, Asakusa, Shinjuku, and Akasaka/Roppongi areas are provided in Chapter IV, in the "Tokyo Sights" and "After Dark" sections. Use them to plan your restaurant journeys.

RESTAURANTS AT A GLANCE: Below is a partial list of restaurants covered in the Tokyo dining section, divided into various areas for easy reference. You may, for example, find yourself in Asakusa with an appetite for sukiyaki but not a desire to read through the entire restaurant section to find a sukiyaki restaurant in Asakusa. I've therefore selected eight of the most commonly visited areas in Tokyo and listed restaurants in those areas, along with each locale's price bracket (upper, medium, or budget) and the type of cuisine served. More information on these restaurants is given in the extensive dining section that follows, which also covers restaurants outside these eight areas.

Name of Restaurant	Price Bracket	Type of Cuisine
GINZA		
Japanese Food		
Kisso	Upper	Kaiseki
Kinsen	Upper	Kaiseki
Ten-ichi	Upper	Tempura
Sushiko	Upper	Sushi
Tsubohan	Medium	Home-style cooking
Ohmatsuya	Medium	Grilled foods
Suehiro	Medium	Steaks, sukiyaki
Benihana of New York	Medium	Teppanyaki
Kushi Colza	Medium	Yakitori, kushiyaki
Ginza Benkay	Medium	Teppanyaki, sushi, kaiseki
Ohmatsuya	Budget	Rice casseroles
Munakata	Budget	Mini-kaiseki
Torigin	Budget	Yakitori, rice casseroles
Atariya	Budget	Yakitori
Hyotanya	Budget	Eel, yakitori

Donto	Budget	Varied, including noodles, tempura, sashimi

Non-Japanese Food

Maxim's	Upper	French
Shakey's	Budget	Pizza

AKASAKA
Japanese Food

Hayashi	Upper	Grilled foods
Inakaya	Upper	Grilled foods
Sekishin-tei	Upper	Teppanyaki
Zakuro	Upper	Shabu-shabu, sukiyaki, teppanyaki
Misono	Upper	Kobe beefsteaks
Hayashi	Budget	Rice casseroles
Torijoh	Budget	Yakitori
Kushinobo	Budget	Kushikatsu

Non-Japanese Food

Tour D'Argent	Upper	French
Kana Uni	Upper	French
Trader Vic's	Upper	Seafood, steaks
Le Chalet	Upper	French
Tiger Seafood Restaurant	Medium	Seafood
Moti	Budget	Indian

ROPPONGI
Japanese Food

Takamura	Upper	Kaiseki
Kisso	Upper	Kaiseki
Inakaya	Upper	Grilled foods
Fukuzushi	Upper	Sushi
Seryna	Upper	Shabu-shabu, sukiyaki
Sushi Sei	Medium	Sushi
Momiji-ya	Medium	Seafood
Hassan	Medium	Shabu-shabu, sukiyaki
Shabu Zen	Medium	Shabu-shabu, sukiyaki
Gonin Byakusho	Medium	Varied, including grilled foods, obento
Chisen	Medium	Kushiage
Roppongi Colza	Medium	Teppanyaki, seafood
Ganchan	Medium	Yakitori
Torigin	Budget	Yakitori, rice casseroles
Kamakura	Budget	Yakitori
Tanuki	Budget	Noodles
Roppongi Shokudo	Budget	Home-style cooking
Ichioku	Budget	Original creations

Non-Japanese Food

Chianti	Upper	Italian
Spago	Upper	Californian

Atantot	Medium	French
Metropole	Medium	Chinese
Victoria Station	Medium	Hamburgers, steaks
Nicola's	Budget	Italian
Moti	Budget	Indian
Samrat	Budget	Indian

SHINJUKU
Japanese Food

Kakiden	Upper	Kaiseki
Shirakawago	Upper	Regional specialties
Mon Cher Ton Ton	Upper	Shabu-shabu, teppanyaki
Hayashi	Medium	Grilled foods
Tsunahachi	Medium	Tempura
Irohanihoheto	Budget	Yakitori

Non-Japanese Food

La Primavera	Medium	Italian
Shakey's	Budget	Pizza
Spaghetti Factory	Budget	Spaghetti
Healthmagic	Budget	Sandwiches, salads

HARAJUKU and AOYAMA
Japanese Food

| Genrokusushi | Budget | Sushi |

Non-Japanese Food

L'Orangerie de Paris	Upper	French, Sunday brunch
Sabatini	Upper	Italian
Mominoki House	Medium	Japanese/French
Sabatini Pizzeria Romana	Budget	Italian
Shakey's	Budget	Pizza
Central Park	Budget	Chinese
El Amigo	Budget	Mexican
Brasserie D	Budget	Sunday brunch
Spiral Cafe	Budget	Sunday brunch

TSUKIJI
Japanese Food

Tamura	Upper	Kaiseki
Edogin	Medium	Sushi
Tentake	Medium	Blowfish
Sushi Dai	Budget	Sushi

ASAKUSA
Japanese Food

Chinya	Medium	Shabu-shabu, sukiyaki
Komagata Dojo	Medium	Dojo (a sardine-like river fish)
Mugitoro	Medium	Yam
Tatsumiya	Budget	Varied, traditional dishes

| Keyaki | Budget | Eel |
| Namiki | Budget | Noodles |

SHIBUYA
Japanese Food

Furusato	Upper	Shabu-shabu, sukiyaki
Irohanihoheto	Budget	Yakitori
Tenmi	Budget	Macrobiotic vegetarian

Non-Japanese Food

| The Prime | Budget | Sandwiches, salads, curries, Chinese, sushi |

THE UPPER BRACKET: Japanese patrons in Tokyo's top restaurants almost never spend their own money. Most of them are on expense accounts, without which many of these establishments would dry up and die out tomorrow. If you're not on an expense account, however, don't despair. The restaurants I've listed in this category will allow you to splurge and experience some of Japan's most exquisite and finest cuisine without having to mortgage your house upon your return home. And don't forget about those set lunch courses—great bargains by any standards.

Japanese Food

Takamura [7], 3-4-27 Roppongi (tel. 585-6600), is a must for everyone who can afford it. Located on the edge of the hot spot that is Roppongi, this wonderful 42-year-old house is like a peaceful oasis that time forgot. Each of the eight rooms in this house is different, with windows looking out onto miniature gardens and bamboo, and with charcoal hearths built into the floor. Takamura has a very Japanese feel to it, a feeling that expands proportionately with the arrival of your meal—seasonal kaiseki food arranged so artfully that you almost hate to destroy it. Your pleasure increases, however, as you savor the various textures and flavors of the food. Specialties here may include quail, sparrow, or duck, grilled on the hearth in your own private tatami room. Seating, by the way, is on the floor as it is in most traditional Japanese restaurants. Reservations are a must, and with dinners ranging from ¥14,300 ($102.14) to ¥20,000 ($142.86), the price of dinner here usually averages about ¥25,000 ($178.57) to ¥30,000 ($214) by the time you add drinks, tax, and service charge. If you are a party of four or more, you can also come here for lunch if you make reservations one day in advance. Special lunches cost ¥14,000 ($100), taxes and service charge included. Hours here are noon to 3 p.m. and 5 to 10:30 p.m., with last orders taken at 8 p.m. It's closed Sunday. Nearest subway station: Roppongi is about five minutes away by foot. There are two entrances to Takamura, marked by wooden gates complete with little roofs. The sign on the restaurant is in Japanese only, but look for the credit card signs.

At the other extreme from Takamura is the thoroughly modern **Kisso** (tel. 582-4191), located in the basement of the Axis Building, at 5-17-1 Roppongi. A combination shop/restaurant, Kisso sells Japanese gourmet cookware, including expensive ceramics, utensils, and lacquerware of contemporary design. The dining area is simple but elegant, with sprigs of flowers, heavy tables, and soft lighting. The food is kaiseki and comes only in set courses, served (as you might guess) in beautifully lacquered bowls, trays, and ceramic plates. I love eating here because to me Kisso represents all the best that is modern Japan—

understated elegance, a successful marriage between the contemporary and the traditional. There should be more places like this in Tokyo. Dinner courses range from ¥8,800 ($62.86) to ¥13,200 ($94.29), with a complete meal consisting of an appetizer, soup, sashimi, a seasonal dish, baked dish, boiled dish, tea, rice, and dessert. If you want to come here for lunch, it's very reasonable, with set courses ranging from ¥1,300 ($9.29) to ¥3,850 ($27.50). Lunch is served from 11:30 a.m. to 2 p.m. and dinner from 5:30 to 10 p.m.; closed Sunday. Closest subway station: Roppongi. From Roppongi Station, walk toward Tokyo Tower; after about four minutes the Axis Building will be on your right.

If you're in Ginza, there's a second branch of Kisso at 4-6-18 Ginza (tel. 535-5035), with courses similar to those described above. Hours are from 11:30 a.m. to 2 p.m. and from 5 to 9 p.m., closed Sunday and public holidays. Very modern in decor, it's located on Chuo Dori Avenue between Mitsukoshi and Matsuya department stores and is up on the fifth floor.

Another kaiseki restaurant is **Kakiden** [8], 3-37-11 Shinjuku (tel. 352-5121), on the eighth floor of Yasuyo Building on the east side of Shinjuku Station next to My City shopping complex. This is a sister restaurant to one in Kyoto that was founded more than 260 years ago as a catering service for the elite. Although located in a rather uninspiring building, Kakiden has a relaxing tea house atmosphere, with low chairs, shoji screens, bamboo trees, and soothing traditional Japanese music playing softly in the background. The menu is in Japanese only, but since meals are set courses, simply pick one to fit your budget. Dinners range from ¥6,600 ($47.14) to ¥16,500 ($117.86), and, as with all kaiseki, meals vary daily according to what's available and fresh. Some of the more common dishes here will include fish, vegetables, eggs, sashimi, shrimp, and mushrooms, but don't worry if you can't identify everything. I've found that even the Japanese don't always know what they're eating. Special lunches are available until 5 p.m. for ¥2,750 ($19.64) to ¥6,600 ($47.14). Kakiden is open daily beginning at 11 a.m.; the last order is at 9 p.m.

Tamura [9], 2-12-11 Tsukiji (tel. 541-2591), is a modern kaiseki restaurant with four floors of smiling and bowing kimono-clad waitresses and hostesses. The very friendly staff here make you feel as though they've been waiting all this time just for you. Although the menu is only in Japanese, they'll help you decide what to order, and you have your choice of either tatami or table-and-chairs dining. Dinner, served daily from 5:30 to 10 p.m. (last orders taken at 7:30 p.m.), starts at ¥33,000 ($235.71) and reservations are necessary.

If you want to come for lunch, however, reservations are not necessary. This place is popular with Japanese housewives, and there's even a tatami room for women only and a special menu for ladies only for ¥5,500 ($39.29), including tax. Men can order it too, but for some reason have to pay an additional 10%. Other courses are available for ¥7,700 ($55) and ¥11,000 ($78.57). Lunch is served from noon to 3 p.m. daily. Closest subway station: Tsukiji, about a two-minute walk.

A conveniently located, modern kaiseki restaurant in the heart of Ginza is **Kinsen,** 4-4-10 Ginza (tel. 561-8708). It's located on Harumi Dori Avenue on the fifth floor of the Ginza Kintetsu Building, just across the street from Jena Bookstore. There's no English menu, but various courses are available so simply choose one to fit your budget. Lunch courses range from ¥4,200 ($30) to ¥8,800 ($62.86), while dinners cost from ¥7,700 ($55) to ¥11,000 ($78.57). Food is served artistically arranged in various bowls and boxes. Incidentally, an English pamphlet describes this restaurant as "homely," but don't let that deter you—it means the same as homey. It's open every day from 11:30 a.m. to 2 p.m. and from 5 to 8:30 p.m. Nearest subway: one minute from Ginza Station.

One of the most delightful old-time restaurants I've been to is **Hayashi** [10], on the fourth floor of the Sanno Kaikan Building, 2-14-1 Akasaka (tel. 582-4078). Serving home-style country cooking, this cozy, rustic-looking restaurant specializes in grilled food, which you do yourself over your own square hibachi. Altogether there are ten grills in this small place, some of them surrounded by tatami mats and some by wooden stools or chairs. As the evening wears on the one-room main dining area can get quite smoky, but somehow that just adds to the atmosphere (sorry, couldn't resist saying that), and nice touches are the big gourds and memorabilia hanging around and the waiter in traditional baggy pants. The owner of Hayashi, which opened in 1965, is almost always present and told me that it was his philosophy that the fire in the grills brought people more in touch with their basic feelings. "All mankind loves fire," he said. "For many years man has had a close relationship with fire. It opens our hearts and makes us relax."

Open every day except Sunday from 5:30 to 11 p.m., Hayashi serves just three set menus, which change with the seasons. The ¥5,500 ($39.29) meal—which will cost about ¥8,800 ($62.86) by the time you add drinks, tax, and service charge—may include such items as sashimi and vegetables, chicken, scallops, and gingko nuts, which you grill yourself. The ¥7,700 ($55) and ¥10,000 ($71.43) meals have more items, and may include oysters, abalone, beef, or fresh fish. Since this place is small it's safest to make a reservation. You can also come here for lunch from 11:30 a.m. to 2 p.m. Monday through Friday, when only *oyakodomburi* is served. Literally "parent and child," it's a simple rice dish with egg and chicken on top costing only ¥850 ($6.07). Nearest subway: Akasaka Station, only one minute away, near the Akasaka Dori and Misuji Dori intersection.

Shirakawago [11], 2-29-10 Kabuki-cho, Shinjuku-ku (tel. 200-5255), is a 300-year-old farmhouse brought to Tokyo from the Shirakawa region in the Japan Alps (minus the thatched roof, which would probably be a major fire hazard in crowded Tokyo). A massive house with heavy wooden beams and tatami floors, this place serves food native to the Hida Shirakawa region, chiefly river fish, such as rainbow trout, from Nagara River, as well as wild fowl and game. Other items on the menu, which is written in English, include chicken teriyaki, a one-pot tofu dish, green-tea buckwheat noodles, sashimi, tempura, grilled smelt, and deep-fried whole river crab. It may be easier to order one of the set courses. These start at ¥3,300 ($23.57) for five dishes and go up to ¥4,400 ($31.43) for nine dishes. Expect to spend at least ¥6,000 ($42.86) per person once you add tax, service charge, and drinks, and don't neglect to visit the upstairs floor with its eclectic collection of kitsch and antiques, including farm implements, straw shoes, a bowling trophy, and even a statue of the Virgin Mary. Hours are 1 to 11 p.m. daily. Nearest subway station: it's about a 10- to 15-minute walk from Shinjuku Station on the northern edge of Kabuki-cho, but it may be best to go by taxi. There's no sign in English, but the farmhouse is easy to recognize and there are credit cards displayed outside.

Along the same lines as Shirakawago is **Furusato** [12], 3-4-1 Aobadai, Meguro-ku (tel. 463-2310). Also a 300-year-old farmhouse transported to Tokyo more than 30 years ago (don't ask me how they do it), Furusato specializes in shabu-shabu and sukiyaki. The food is good, but it's mainly for the atmosphere that I like to come here. The waitress will give you a tour of the place, including upstairs where you can see how the roof beams are held together with ropes rather than nails. There are also farm implements on display. The house used to be the home of about 30 to 40 people in an extended family, with living quarters on the ground floor and silk production on the second.

The main dining area is a large room on the ground floor, with shoji screens that are pushed open in summer to reveal a small garden. You sit on the floor at low tables, but the cushions here have backs to them which make them more comfortable for uninitiated Westerners. The place is a little touristy—which you'll figure out for yourself as soon as your waitress asks you which country you're from and then promptly returns with your country's miniature flag, which she proudly places on your table. (She assured me they had a flag for every country in the world, which should tempt at least some of you to come up with a hard one.) At any rate, this is a good place to come if your time in Japan is limited. Shabu-shabu and sukiyaki cost ¥6,000 ($42.86) per person. There's also roast duck for ¥7,500 ($53.57) and a duck sukiyaki meal for the same price. Other courses start at ¥5,000 ($35.71). Dinner is served daily from 5:30 to 10:30 p.m. You can also come for lunch from 11:30 a.m. to 2 p.m. for noodles starting at ¥650 ($4.64), or box lunches for ¥1,300 ($9.29) to ¥2,750 ($19.64), tempura, and sashimi. Nearest subway station: Shibuya Station is a 15-minute walk away. A big statue of a beaver guards the entrance to this place on Tamagawa Dori Avenue.

Whenever I'm playing hostess to foreign visitors in Tokyo I always take them to **Inakaya** [13], 7-8-4 Roppongi (tel. 405-9866), and they've never been disappointed. What I like about this place is the drama of it. You sit at a counter and in front of you are mountains of fresh vegetables, beef, and seafood. In the middle of all the food are two male cooks (cooks in Japan are almost always male), who can sit for inordinate amounts of time on pillows with their legs tucked neatly underneath them. They cook on a grill in front of them in a style called robatayaki. To order, simply point at what you want. Your waiter shouts it out and then all the other waiters repeat it in shouted unison, with the result that there is always this excited yelling going on. No way to order quietly here. Food offerings may include yellowtail, red snapper, sole, king crab legs, giant shrimp, steak, meatballs, gingko nuts, potatoes, eggplant, and asparagus, all piled high in wicker baskets. Sometimes there are tiny, crunchy crabs you pop whole in your mouth—they tickle all the way down. A meal here costs at least ¥12,000 ($85.71) per person and no reservations are accepted. Hours are 5 p.m. to 5 a.m. daily. Inakaya is about a five-minute walk from Roppongi Station toward Aoyama-Itchome on Gaien-Higashi Dori Avenue.

If you want to make reservations, you can do so at the two other Inakaya restaurants up to 7 p.m. (whenever a restaurant proves successful in Japan, branches open immediately). The **Roppongi East Branch**, 5-3-4 Roppongi (tel. 408-5040), is also open from 5 p.m. to 5 a.m. **Inakaya in Akasaka**, 3-12-7 Akasaka (tel. 586-3054), is open only until 11 p.m.

Ten-ichi, Ginza 6-chome on Namiki Dori Street (tel. 571-1949), is the main shop of a restaurant chain that first began serving tempura in Tokyo more than 50 years ago and helped this style of cooking gain worldwide recognition by serving important foreign customers. Today there are more than ten Ten-ichi restaurants in Tokyo. Hours may vary, but generally they're 11:30 a.m. to 9:30 p.m.—it's best to call beforehand and make a reservation. Ten-ichi has one of the best reputations in town for serving the most delicately fried foods. Set menus range from ¥5,500 ($39.29) to ¥13,200 ($94.29), and you can sit at a counter to watch the chef prepare your food. Closest subway station: Ginza is a few minutes away.

Other Ten-ichi restaurants can be found in the Ginza Sony Building (tel. 571-3837), the Imperial Hotel's Tower basement (tel. 503-1001), Akasaka 3-chome, Misujidori (tel. 583-0107), and both the Shibuya and Ikebukuro Seibu department stores.

Fukuzushi [14], 5-7-8 Roppongi (tel. 402-4116), is one of the classiest sushi bars in town. Tucked underneath Spago's restaurant behind the Roi Building in Roppongi, this sushi bar has an entrance through a small courtyard and an interior of red and black. Some people in town swear it has the best sushi in Tokyo, although with 7,000 sushi bars in the city I'd be hard pressed to say which one is tops. Certainly you can't go wrong here. Open for dinner daily from 5 to 11 p.m., it has an English menu which opens up like a fan and offers a variety of choices of sashimi and nigiri-sushi. Dinner will cost anywhere from ¥8,800 ($62.86) to ¥16,500 ($117.86), although if you're careful about your drinks and the amount you order you can do it for much less. Another alternative is the set lunch, served from 11:30 a.m. to 2 p.m. every day except Sunday and holidays in two courses costing ¥2,750 ($19.64). Nearest subway station: Roppongi.

If you're in pursuit of exclusive sushi shops in Tokyo, your search will eventually take you to **Sushiko** [15], 6-3-8 Ginza (tel. 571-1968). There's no menu and its counter seating is for 11 customers only, so reservations are imperative. Owned by a fourth-generation restaurateur, this establishment doesn't display its fish as in most sushi bars but rather keeps the fish freshly refrigerated until the moment it meets the swift blade of the expert chefs. A meal here averages about ¥15,000 ($107.14), and hours are from noon to 2 p.m. and from 4 to 9:30 p.m., closed Sunday and public holidays. Nearest subway station: Ginza.

Seryna, 3-12-2 Roppongi (tel. 403-6211), is the name usually associated with this well-known large, modern establishment, but actually there are four restaurants here, all under the same ownership. Japanese often entertain foreign visitors here, and menus are in English. Seryna Honkan serves Kobe beef shabu-shabu and sukiyaki. Saraebo, on the third floor, specializes in yaki-shabu and Chinese cuisine. Mon Cher Ton Ton, in the basement, serves Kobe beef, shrimp, fish, shellfish, and vegetables grilled teppanyaki style right before your eyes. Kani Seryna offers crab and seafood dishes, including crab shabu-shabu, Maine lobster, and steamed fish. It also has the famous Kobe beefsteak that is cooked at your table on a heated stone. The average dinner at these places will range from ¥14,000 ($100) to ¥20,000 ($142.86). All restaurants are open from 5 to 11:30 p.m. (10:30 p.m. on Sunday and holidays) with the exception of Kani Seryna, which opens at noon. Nearest subway station: Roppongi is three minutes away.

If you're in Shinjuku there's another branch of Seryna and **Mon Cher Ton Ton** on the 52nd floor of the Shinjuku Sumitomo Building, 2-6-1 Nishi-Shinjuku (tel. 344-6761). It serves Kobe beefsteaks starting at ¥5,500 ($39.29) and various meals of shabu-shabu starting at ¥8,800 ($62.86), and there's an English menu. Teppanyaki courses begin at ¥7,000 ($50). Hours here are 11:30 a.m. to 10:30 p.m., and needless to say the view is great. It's a good place to stop off if you're exploring the west side of Shinjuku. Nearest station: Shinjuku is about a seven-minute walk.

Sekishin-tei, 4-1 Kioi-cho, Chiyoda-ku (tel. 265-1111), located in the New Otani Hotel's 400-year-old garden, is a glass-enclosed teppanyaki restaurant where Kobe beef, fish, lobster, and vegetables are cooked on a grill right in front of you. Meals begin at ¥4,000 ($28.57) for lunch and ¥7,900 ($56.43) for dinner, and if you order a salad, try the soy sauce dressing—it's delicious. This place, with peaceful views surrounding you, is open daily from noon to 2 p.m. and 6 to 9 p.m. Nearest subway stations: Yotsuya or Akasaka-mitsuke.

Serving shabu-shabu, sukiyaki, teppanyaki, and tempura, **Zakuro** [16] is conveniently located in the basement of the TBS Kaikan Building, 5-3-3 Akasaka (tel. 582-6841). Open every day from 11 a.m. to 11 p.m. (last order at 10 p.m.), it has an English menu which lists a special sukiyaki lunch for ¥1,800 ($12.86) and shabu-shabu, sukiyaki, and teppanyaki beginning at ¥6,900 ($49.29). Japanese-style set courses, which might include such items as sashimi, charcoal-broiled fish, soup, rice, and pickled vegetables, begin at ¥7,400 ($52.86). By the time you add tax, service charge, and drinks, most dinner checks average ¥10,000 ($71.43). Nearest subway station: Akasaka, a minute from the TBS exit.

Not far from Zakuro and near the easily recognizable Kentucky Fried Chicken is **Misono,** 2-14-31 Akasaka (tel. 583-3389), probably the oldest steakhouse in Tokyo. Opened more than 30 years ago, it serves marbled beef from Kobe, with set dinner courses priced at ¥11,000 ($78.57) and set lunches at ¥3,300 ($23.57). With its small garden, moss-covered rocks, and fish pond, it's a welcome oasis of tranquillity in the heart of Akasaka. It's open weekdays from noon to 2 p.m. and for dinner from 5 to 11 p.m. On weekends and holidays it's open only for dinner. Nearest subway station: a minute away from the TBS exit of Akasaka Station.

Although Japanese restaurants usually specialize in only one type of cooking, **Yamatoya Sangen,** in the Miyako Hotel, 1-1-50 Shiroganedai (tel. 445-0058), serves a variety of foods, from shabu-shabu, tempura, kaiseki, and sushi to eel. This is a good place to come if there are several of you and you can't make up your mind what you want to eat. The restaurant overlooks the hotel's Japanese garden and is simply decorated with shoji screens and slats of wood. Dinners range from ¥7,000 ($50) to ¥20,000 ($142.86), and are served daily from 5 to 10 p.m. There are also special lunch menus averaging ¥3,000 ($21.43) to ¥8,800 ($62.86), served from 11:30 a.m. to 2 p.m. If you've been intimidated by the thought of eating eel, this may be the best place to try it for the first time, although it's available only for lunch. Closest subway station: Takanawadai.

Another hotel restaurant with a good selection of Japanese food served in a charming setting is the **Unkai,** in the ANA Hotel Tokyo, 1-12-33 Akasaka (tel. 459-6921). With its stone pathway leading through the restaurant and a replica of a thatched-roof house built as a facade into one of the walls, the atmosphere is one of a country village. The restaurant, open from 11:30 a.m. to 2:30 p.m. and 5:30 to 10 p.m., overlooks a pond and a waterfall. There are various set courses available for lunch beginning at ¥3,300 ($23.57), as well as à la carte selections of tempura, sashimi, seasonal vegetables, and other dishes. Dinner will probably cost at least ¥6,000 ($42.86) per person. Nearest stations: Roppongi, Akasaka, Kamiyacho, Toranomon, and Kokkai Gijido-mae.

Western Food

When **Tour D'Argent,** 4-1 Kioi-cho, Chiyoda-ku (tel. 239-3111), opened in the New Otani Hotel in 1984 there were rumors flying around Tokyo that it was the most expensive restaurant in town. I doubt it, especially when I consider those exclusive and highly elusive Japanese restaurants with geisha entertainment patronized by Japan's top corporate management. Still, the cost of a meal here with wine ranges from ¥27,500 ($196.43) to ¥33,000 ($235.71) per person. Tour D'Argent is the sister restaurant to the one in Paris, which opened back in 1582 and which has been visited twice by Japan's emperor.

Entrance to the Tour D'Argent in Tokyo is through an impressive hallway with a plush interior and displays of tableware which have been used in the Paris restaurant through the centuries. The dining hall looks like a Parisian drawing room, with an elegance a bit too overstated for my taste. The service, however, is superb and the food is excellent. The specialty here is duckling—it meets its untimely end at the age of three weeks and is flown to Japan from Brittany. Other dishes on the menu, which changes with the seasons, may include sea bass, médaillons of veal in light curry sauce, young pigeon, beef tenderloin, or fricassee of lobster and morels. For appetizers I recommend either duck or goose foie gras. Closed Monday, the restaurant opens at 5:30 p.m., with the last order taken at 9:30 p.m. If you can afford to come here you probably won't come by subway, but the nearest stations are Akasaka-mitsuke and Yotsuya.

It's hard to imagine a more romantic setting than the **Rose Room** in the ANA Hotel Tokyo, 1-12-33 Akasaka (tel. 459-6921). Small and intimate with a huge vase of roses in the center of the dining room, this French restaurant is perfect for a tête-à-tête as classical or instrumental music plays softly in the background. The menu changes twice a year but may include such selections as Beluga caviar, turtle soup lightly seasoned with curry, lobster, rack of lamb, chicken, and steak. Meals here cost upwards of ¥15,000 ($107.14) and are served daily from 11:30 a.m. to 2:30 p.m. and from 5:30 to 10 p.m. After dinner you may wish to retire to the Astral lounge up on the 37th floor, where you have a good view of the city. The lounge is open until 2 a.m. Nearest stations: Roppongi, Akasaka, Kamiyacho, Toranomon, and Kokkai Gijido-mae.

It may seem kind of strange to find a top-class restaurant in the third basement of the Sony Building, but then this is Japan. **Maxim's**, 5-3-1 Ginza (tel. 572-3621), opened in 1966 and is an exact copy of Paris's famous Maxim's, which opened its doors in 1893. Decorated in art nouveau style, the small dining room is one of the most romantic in town—very French, with gilded mirrors, cut-glass panels, mahogany paneling, and crimson cushions. Service is discreet and professional, as waiters bring you such specialties as goose liver pâté, sole cooked in French vermouth, sautéed tenderloin with truffle sauce, roast duckling with peaches, or grilled prime rib of Kobe beef. If you order à la carte it will cost around ¥25,000 ($178.57). There is also a set dinner for ¥22,000 ($157.14) and a set lunch menu for ¥6,600 ($47.14), both of which change daily and include tax and service charge. Maxim's is open for lunch from 11:30 a.m. to 2:30 p.m. and for dinner from 5:30 to 11 p.m.; closed Sunday. Nearest subway station: Ginza is a minute away.

Another French restaurant with a sister in Paris is **L'Orangerie de Paris**, 3-6-1 Kita-Aoyama, Minato-ku (tel. 407-7461), located in the chic area of Omote Sando, on the fifth floor of the Hanae Mori Building, which houses fashion designer Hanae Mori's entire collection. The building was designed by Kenzo Tange, who also designed the controversial Akasaka Prince Hotel as well as a score of other buildings around town. Check out the front shop windows—they're always interesting. There's a set dinner menu here for ¥8,800 ($62.86) and a set lunch menu for ¥4,400 ($31.43), which change every two weeks. Hours are 11:30 a.m. to 2:30 p.m. and 5:30 to 10 p.m. (last order: 9:30 p.m.) every day except Sunday. Very popular, Sunday brunch is held here from 11 a.m. to 2:30 p.m. It costs ¥4,200 ($30) and seems to attract half the foreign population in Tokyo. Nearest subway station: Omote Sando is one minute away.

One more French restaurant, this one not far from Akasaka's nightlife district, **Kana Uni**, 1-1-16 Moto-Akasaka (tel. 404-4776), is a cozy and intimate restaurant/bar. It's owned and managed by a brother and sister who speak excellent English and who love to have foreign guests. In fact, because the place is a little hard to find they'll even come and fetch you if you call from Akasakamitsuke Station. Open since 1966, it has an English menu and entrées include sliced raw tenderloin, steaks, beef stew, grilled fish, sautéed scallops, and poached filet of sole with caviar. Expect to spend about ¥8,000 ($57.14) for dinner. It's open only in the evening from 6 p.m. to 2:30 a.m.; closed Sunday and national holidays. It's one of the few restaurants in Akasaka still serving food after midnight, and there's even live jazz nightly from 7 to 11 p.m. After dinner, relax with cocktails and enjoy the ambience. Cocktails run from ¥1,000 ($7.14) to ¥1,400 ($10). Nearest subway station: Akasaka-mitsuke.

Sabatini, located in the basement of the Suncrest Building, 2-13-5 Kita-Aoyama, Minato-ku (tel. 402-3812), is owned by three Italian brothers who have had a restaurant in Rome for more than 30 years. They take turns overseeing the Tokyo store, so one of them is always here, serving food or helping out in the kitchen. This restaurant, with its Italian furniture and tableware and strolling musicians, seems like it was moved intact from the Old World. In fact, the only thing to remind you you're in Tokyo are the Japanese waiters. The menu includes soups, spaghetti, seafood, veal, steak, lamb, and a variety of vegetables. Dinner ranges from about ¥15,000 ($107.14) to ¥19,000 ($135.71), but you can do it cheaper at lunch with the ¥5,000 ($35.71) set menu, which gives you a choice of soup or pasta, fish or meat, and salad and coffee. Hours are 11:30 a.m. to 2:30 p.m. and 5:30 p.m. to 11 p.m. Nearest subway station: Sabatini is two minutes from Gaienmae.

Established in 1960, **Chianti**, 3-1-7 Azabudai (tel. 583-7546), is one of the oldest Italian restaurants in Tokyo. Founded by two Japanese who had been living in Europe and who wanted to introduce Western food to the Japanese, through the years it became popular with Tokyo's foreign community as well. Dining is in two separate areas, although the menu is the same. On the second floor it's the requisite red-and-white-checkered tablecloth, an informal atmosphere. In the basement it's more formal, more intimate, better for couples. The menu includes such entrées as grilled chicken in spicy tomato sauce, veal scallop sautéed with vegetables, Milanese veal cutlet, Hungarian beef stew, and braised veal shank in tomato sauce. The average price per dish runs between ¥3,500 ($25) and ¥4,400 ($31.43), though most people end up spending about ¥13,000 ($92.86) including wine and appetizers. On the ground floor there's a coffeeshop where you can have snacks, salads, and sandwiches. There's also an additional restaurant that opened a few years back called **Chianti Nishi-Azabu**, 3-17-26 Nishi-Azabu (tel. 404-6500), where the food is about 20% cheaper, with entrées under ¥3,000 ($21.43). It caters to a slightly younger crowd. Hours for both are noon to 3 a.m. daily, and the nearest subway station is Roppongi.

Spago, 5-7-8 Roppongi (tel. 423-4025), serves California cuisine created by its owner, Wolfgang Puck, an Austrian-born chef who has a similar restaurant in Los Angeles. The atmosphere here is bright, airy, and cheerful, very Californian, with huge bouquets of flowers, potted palms, ferns, white walls, and a colorful mural. The menu changes every three months to reflect what's in season, but examples of what's been offered in the past include spicy fettuccine with grilled shrimp and fresh basil; sliced breast of duck with Japanese *oba* leaves and plum wine sauce; angel hair noodles with goat cheese, broccoli, and thyme; grilled spicy chicken with garlic and Italian parsley; and roasted baby lamb with a Cabernet, mustard, and rosemary sauce. If you order pizza, it will come not with tomato sauce but with olive oil, making it much lighter, so the emphasis is on the toppings. Needless to say, the entrées are always imaginative, and the service is great. Dining here is a pleasure, and as you might expect, Spago has the largest selection of California wines in town. For dessert try the restaurant's homemade ice cream. An average meal here, including wine, runs about ¥11,000 ($79.57), but there's also a set course offered Monday through Saturday for ¥8,800 ($62.86). The most economical day to dine here is on Sunday, when a special set menu is offered for ¥5,200 ($37.14). Spago is open daily from 5:30 p.m. to 11 p.m., with last orders taken at 10:30 p.m. Nearest subway: two minutes from Roppongi, located behind the Roi Building.

Trader Vic's, in the New Otani Hotel, 4-1 Kioi-cho, Chiyoda-ku (tel. 265-4708), is part of an American chain operating out of California. The decor, as always, is Polynesian, and there are views of the hotel's 400-year-old landscaped garden. The extensive menu offers salads, seafood, Chinese dishes, curries, and steak, fish, and chicken dishes, with entrées running about ¥4,500 ($32.14) to ¥9,000 ($64.29). Hours are 11:30 a.m. to 2:30 p.m. and 5 to 10 p.m. Its bar is open throughout the day, from 11:30 a.m. to 2 a.m. Cocktails start at ¥1,500 ($10.71).

THE MEDIUM-PRICED RANGE: So many of Tokyo's good restaurants fall into this category that it's tempting simply to eat your way through the city—and the range of cuisine is so great that you could eat something different with each meal. Be sure to read the list of restaurants in the upper-bracket category— many have great set courses for lunch at very reasonable prices.

Japanese Food

Sushi Sei [17], 7-14-15 Roppongi (tel. 401-0578), is a typical medium-priced sushi bar serving tender cuts of raw fish, making it a good place to go for both novice and appreciative sushi fans. The decor is simple here—just a long counter with stools for about 25 people sitting elbow to elbow. Behind a glass case on the counter you can see what's fresh and available, and on the other side of that the sushi experts deftly slice fish and make sushi according to your instructions. Just point at what you want. Ordering à la carte is the fun way to do it, and an evening spent here drinking sake or beer won't cost more than ¥5,000 ($35.71). If that's too formidable, however, take the easy way out and order a *seto*, or set meal. This costs only ¥1,300 ($9.29), is available anytime night and day, and comes with six pieces of sushi with various selections of raw fish and six pieces of *makizushi* (raw fish, cucumber, and rice rolled inside a sheet of seaweed). The chef will prepare your food and place it on a raised platform on the counter in front of you. This is your plate, and it's proper etiquette to use your fingers. Hours are noon to 2 p.m. and 5 to 11 p.m.; closed Sunday and holidays. Nearest subway station: Sushi Sei is one minute from Roppongi. There are many branches of this restaurant throughout the city, and a couple more addresses are: Dainana Kanai Building, 8-2-13 Ginza (tel. 572-4770), and Aoyama Bell Commons, fifth floor (tel. 475-8053).

Close to Tsukiji's famous fish market is **Edogin** [18], 4-5-1 Tsukiji (tel. 543-4401). Actually there are four Edogin sushi restaurants in Tsukiji, all located within walking distance of one another, and in any of them you can be assured that the fish is fresh since it's close to the market. There's nothing aesthetic about Edogin—the lights are bright, it's packed with the locals, and it's noisy and busy, with waitresses constantly bustling around. Open every day except Sunday from 11 a.m. to 9:30 p.m., it's particularly packed during lunch- and dinnertime. All this points to one thing: the food is dependably good and plentiful. The menu is in Japanese only, but there's a glass case outside with some of the dishes displayed. As an alternative, look at what the people around you are eating. The lunch teishoku range from ¥880 ($6.29) to ¥1,300 ($9.29), and if you come here for dinner you can eat a satisfying meal with beer or sake for less than ¥5,000 ($35.71). Nearest subway station: three minutes from Tsukiji Station. Anyone in the neighborhood will be able to point you in the right direction; look for the building with a string of Japanese lanterns adorning its facade.

People who really know their *fugu*, or blowfish, will tell you that the only time to eat it is from October through March, when it's fresh. You can eat fugu all year round, however, and a good place to try this Japanese delicacy is at **Tentake** [19], 6-16-6 Tsukiji (tel. 541-3881). This is also a popular place with the Tsukiji working crowd. The menu is in Japanese, so if you want suggestions try the fugu sushi, which costs ¥2,700 ($19.29), or fugu-chiri for the same price. The latter is a do-it-yourself meal whereby you cook raw blowfish, cabbage, dandelion leaves, and tofu in a pot of boiling water in front of you. This is what I had and it was more than I could eat. There are also fugu dishes for ¥4,400 ($31.43) and ¥6,300 ($45) that come with a variety of other dishes as well. You can also order tempura, eel, and crab dishes here. The restaurant is open from noon to 10 p.m. (from April through September it's closed on Sunday, and from

October through March it's closed the first and third Wednesdays of the month). Nearest subway station: Tsukiji is about a seven-minute walk.

Momiji-ya, Asano Building, 6-1-12 Roppongi (tel. 479-0400), is one of Roppongi's newest seafood restaurants. A gigantic round fish tank adorns the front facade, along with a list of the fresh catches of the day. Inside, the dominant feature is another fish tank in the middle of the dining room. Fish is scooped directly from this tank, so you know your meal is fresh. Other seafood selections available include cuttlefish, scallops, live lobster, and, of course, sashimi. Dinner courses start at ¥6,600 ($47.14), while a special lunch menu is only ¥1,100 ($7.86). It's open daily from 11:30 a.m. to 2 p.m. and from 5 to 11 p.m. Last order is at 10 p.m. Closest station: Roppongi Station, about two minutes away.

Hassan [20], in the basement of the Denki Building, 6-1-20 Roppongi (tel. 403-8333), serves shabu-shabu and sukiyaki. Seating is either in chairs or on tatami, waitresses wear kimonos, and *koto* music plays in the background. Open seven days a week from 11:30 a.m. to 2 p.m. and 4:30 to 11 p.m. (last order: 10 p.m.), Hassan has an all-you-can-eat beef shabu-shabu meal for just ¥4,700 ($33.57) per person. Sukiyaki starts at ¥4,100 ($29.29). It also serves kaiseki menus for ¥7,500 ($53.57) to ¥11,000 ($78.57), but you need reservations for these. For lunch you can order the all-you-can-eat shabu-shabu menu for ¥3,900 ($27.86) per person. There's also a sukiyaki plate for ¥1,870 ($13.36), and a shabu-shabu selection for ¥2,200 ($15.71). Kaiseki lunches begin at ¥4,200 ($30), and lunch boxes are ¥2,200 ($15.71). The menu is in English, so it's easy to order here. Closest subway: one minute from Roppongi Station. If you take the road toward Shibuya, Hassan will be on your left.

Shabu Zen [21], 5-17-16 Roppongi (tel. 585-5388), has an English-speaking staff and a menu in English along with color illustrations. For ¥4,700 ($33.57) you can eat all the shabu-shabu or sukiyaki you want. Shabu Zen also has a seafood shabu-shabu for the same price. If you're hungry you might want to order the ¥6,600 ($47.14) shabu-shabu menu, which includes an unlimited amount of meat and vegetables, plus two appetizers, sashimi, egg custard, salad, and dessert. There are also kaiseki menus for ¥5,500 ($39.29), ¥8,800 ($62.86), and ¥11,000 ($78.57), but you must order these at least two days in advance. The restaurant is open daily from 5 p.m. to midnight. Closest subway: a five-minute walk from Roppongi Station; it's located behind the Axis Building.

Established in 1880, **Chinya** [22], 1-3-4 Asakusa (tel. 841-0010), is an old sukiyaki restaurant with a new home in a seven-story building. It's located to the left of the Kaminarimon Gate if you stand facing the famous Asakusa Kannon Temple; look for the sukiyaki sign. The entrance to this place is open-fronted, where all you'll see is a man standing there, waiting. Take off your shoes and step up onto the tatami floor, and a kimono-clad waitress will take you upstairs to one of the restaurant's many rooms. The menu is in Japanese only, but there are pictures to choose from. Most courses are ¥5,500 ($39.29) and up, although there are sukiyaki and shabu-shabu dishes available for ¥2,200 ($15.71). The best time to come is for lunch, when you can order sukiyaki or shabu-shabu for just ¥2,000 ($14.29). If you want to eat even more cheaply, there's another dining area in the basement with slightly lower prices. Hours are 11:30 a.m. to 9 p.m.; closed Wednesday. Closest subway station: Asakusa, about five minutes away.

Also relatively close to the Kaminarimon Gate of Asakusa Kannon Temple is **Komagata Dojo** [23], 1-7-12 Komagata, Taito-ku (tel. 842-4001). Following a tradition that has spanned more than 185 years, this old-style dining hall specializes in *dojo,* a tiny sardine-like river fish. It's served in a variety of styles, from grilled to stewed. Teishoku, available throughout the day, range in price from ¥2,000 ($14.29) to ¥5,500 ($39.29). The dining area is simply one large room of tatami mats, with waitresses moving quietly about dressed in kimonos. Subway station: about a five-minute walk from Asakusa Station. To reach the restaurant, walk south with your back towards Kaminarimon Gate. The restaurant, a large, old-fashioned house on a corner with blue curtains at its door, is located on the right side of the street past the Bank of Tokyo. Hours are from 11 a.m. to 9 p.m. daily.

In the same neighborhood as Komagata Dojo is **Mugitoro** [24], 2-2-4 Kaminarimon (tel. 842-1066). This restaurant, founded about 60 years ago but now housed in a new building, specializes in *tororo-imo,* which is yam. Popular as a health food, yam is featured in most all the dishes and the menu changes monthly. Most courses range from about ¥2,000 ($14.29) to ¥4,000 ($28.57), served daily from 11:30 a.m. to 9 p.m. Nearest station: Asakusa. If you're walking here from Asakusa Kannon Temple, walk south with your back to the temple until you reach the first big intersection. Komagatabashi Bridge will be to your left, and Mugitoro is located right beside the bridge. Look for the big white lanterns hanging outside.

In the midst of all the chic discos in the Roppongi Square Building is **Gonin Byakusho** [25], 3-10-3 Roppongi (tel. 470-1675), which is on the fourth floor. Its name means "five farmers," and the atmosphere here is of a farmhouse in the countryside with the usual heavy beams and thick wooden tables; there's a huge hearth and oven off to one side. You take off your shoes before entering this restaurant and place them in lockers. Most of the food here is grilled, and dinner courses that may include grilled fish or shrimp, sashimi, and vegetables begin at ¥3,300 ($23.57). A la carte items such as yakitori, charcoal-broiled shrimp, assorted sashimi, kamameshi, or tempura begin at ¥600 ($4.29). Dinner à la carte will probably cost about ¥5,000 ($35.71) per person. At lunchtime there are special box lunches for ¥1,650 ($11.79) and ¥2,750 ($19.64), as well as tempura courses. This place is open every day from 11:30 a.m. to 2 p.m. and 5 to 10:30 p.m. (on Sunday from noon to 10 p.m.). Nearest subway station: three minutes from Roppongi Station.

With a rustic interior imported intact from the mountain region of Takayama, **Hayashi** [26], Hide Building, 2-22-5 Shinjuku (tel. 209-5672), specializes in Japanese set courses cooked over your own hibachi grill. A companion restaurant to the Hayashi restaurant described under the upper bracket and budget category sections but under a different ownership, it's a small, cozy place with only five hibachi grills. Women in kimonos oversee the cooking operations like mother hens, taking over the operation if customers seem the least bit hesitant. Four set courses are offered, ranging in price from ¥3,300 ($23.57) to ¥7,700 ($55). I chose the ¥4,400 ($31.43) course, which came with sashimi, yakitori, tofu steak, scallops cooked in their shell, shrimp, and vegetables, all grilled one after the other. Open from 5 p.m. to midnight every day except Sunday and public holidays, this restaurant is about a ten-minute walk from Shinjuku Station on the edge of Kabuki-cho.

If you're looking for a small and quiet restaurant in Ginza you might try **Tsubohan**, 5-3-9 Ginza (tel. 571-3467). It's located on the street behind the Sony Building that parallels Namiki Dori Street. Look for the sign outside that says "Chazuke Tsubohan: The most tasty one among pure Japanese dishes, A Gourmet's Last Goal!" This restaurant has been here since 1950 and is a rickety two-story establishment with six tiny rooms, two with tables and chairs and four with tatami. The elderly women who work here are motherly and eager to please, and the food is home-style cooking. Since the à la carte menu is in Japanese only, it's easier to order the set meal described in English for ¥7,000 ($50).

This includes a variety of vegetables, seafood and broiled fish, and rice. Hours are 4:30 to 11 p.m.; closed Sunday and public holidays. Nearest subway station: two minutes from Ginza Station.

Another country-style restaurant in the heart of Ginza is the delightful **Ohmatsuya** [27], 5-4-18 Ginza (tel. 571-7053). Located also on the small side street behind the Sony Building that parallels Namiki Dori Street, it's up on the second floor of a very ordinary-looking building. Once inside the restaurant, however, you're greeted instantly by waitresses clad in countryside costumes and by an atmosphere that very much evokes the feeling of an old farmhouse. Little wonder: part of the decor was brought from a 17th-century samurai house in northern Japan. Even the style of cooking is traditional, as customers grill their own food over a hibachi and charcoal flame. Sake is served in a length of bamboo and is drunk from bamboo cups. Dinner courses, very reasonably priced from ¥3,300 ($23.57) to ¥5,500 ($39.29), include such delicacies as grilled fish, skewered pieces of meat, and vegetables. Lunches are even cheaper, with *oyakodomburi* (rice with morsels of chicken laid on top) costing just ¥800 ($5.71). The buckwheat noodles for ¥880 ($6.29) are a special treat— you're given a fresh chunk of wasabi that you grate yourself and add to the soy sauce. Ohmatsuya is open from 11:30 a.m. to 2 p.m. and from 5 to 10 p.m. every day except Sunday. Closest subway station: Ginza.

Kushiage, which literally means "skewered cutlets," is a little-known style of cooking whereby food is breaded, deep-fried, and served on skewers. An excellent restaurant serving this delicious food is **Chisen**, 4-12-5 Roppongi (tel. 403-7677), open daily from 5:30 to 11 p.m.—it has more than 25 different kinds of kushiage (also called *kushikatsu*). What's available will change according to the season, but common items include mushrooms, asparagus, shrimp, squid, oysters, and onions. The breading is very light and flaky. There's a menu in English with a few à la carte selections, but I'd advise you to select one of the set meals. The Chisen Set for ¥4,200 ($30) gives you 11 kushiage sticks, fresh vegetables, and rice or soba (noodles). If you choose the Zen menu, kushiage will be served to you one after the other until you say stop, and this option includes small seasonal dishes as well. The Zen menu is what I opted for, and I had three sticks of kushiage, two types of salad, and a bottle of beer for ¥2,500 ($17.86). If you're hungrier, of course, it will cost more. There's another Chisen shop not far away at 7-12-5 Roppongi (tel. 478-6241) in case the first one is full. Nearest subway station: just a few minutes from Roppongi Station.

A restaurant serving tempura, **Tsunahachi** [28], 3-31-8 Shinjuku (tel. 352-1012), first opened in 1923. There are now more than 40 branch restaurants in Japan, including three in Shinjuku Station alone, and others in Ginza, Akasaka, and Roppongi. Hours may vary, but most shops are open daily from 11:30 a.m. to 10 p.m. Tempura à la carte ranges from about ¥350 ($2.50) to ¥1,000 ($7.14). The least expensive set meal begins at ¥1,000 ($7.14) and includes deep-fried shrimp, three kinds of fish, a vegetable, and a shrimp ball. The ¥2,000 ($14.29) meal consists of two deep-fried shrimp, four kinds of fish, three kinds of vegetables, and a shrimp ball. Nearest station: this branch is about a five-minute walk east of Shinjuku Station.

Another successful chain restaurant, **Suehiro** [29], has 23 stores throughout Japan. A steak-and-sukiyaki chain, the main store is at 6-11-2 Ginza (tel. 571-9271) behind the Matsuzakaya department store. Established in 1933, it claims to be the first restaurant in Tokyo to serve sukiyaki and it has its own cattle ranches for its Matsuzaka beef. There are various courses, from sirloin steak for ¥3,300 ($23.57) to Matsuzaka beef sukiyaki for ¥11,000 ($78.57). Open from 11 a.m. to 10 p.m. daily, Suehiro is about a five-minute walk from Ginza Station.

With about 50 Benihana restaurants in the United States, I'm not sure whether anyone is interested in seeking out the one in Tokyo—which, by the way, calls itself **Benihana of New York**, 6-3-7 Ginza (tel. 571-9060). Specializing in teppanyaki steak, this is the place where the cook prepares your meal in front of you with lots of theatrical bravado and karate-like knife chops. Dinners range from ¥3,800 ($27.14) for minute steak and side dishes to ¥11,000 ($78.57) for the sirloin steak "New York Special," with most choices in the ¥7,000 ($50) range. A steak lunch costs ¥2,750 ($19.64). Benihana is open daily from 11 a.m. to 10 p.m., except on Sunday when it closes at 8 p.m. Nearest subway stations: about a five-minute walk from Hibiya Station and a ten-minute walk from Ginza Station.

Kikkoman is a well-known brand of soy sauce in Japan, and the Kikkoman company maintains a few restaurants as well. **Kushi Colza** [30], 6-2-1 Ginza (tel. 571-8228), is one of these, and it serves yakitori and *kushi-yaki* (also grilled meats and vegetables served on skewers) delicately seasoned with—what else, Kikkoman soy sauce. This place is modern and pleasant, and you can watch the chefs at work preparing your food. Open for dinner from 5 to 10 p.m. daily, it serves three dinner menus beginning at ¥3,300 ($23.57). If you come for lunch (between 11:30 a.m. and 1:30 p.m) you will have six courses to choose from, ranging in price from ¥770 ($5.50) to ¥2,200 ($15.71). These consist of various skewered filets of beef, fish, eel, or pork, and include salad, rice, and bean-paste soup. À la carte selections include skewered beef, pork, chicken, prawn, squid, and such vegetables as asparagus and bacon, gingko nuts, and mushrooms. Nearest subway stations: about five minutes from Hibiya or ten minutes from Ginza. It's located in the basement of the Riccar Building, across from the Gekkoso Museum. A sign above the door reads, "Kushi & Wine."

Another Kikkoman restaurant, this time in Roppongi, is **Roppongi Colza**, 7-15-10 Roppongi (tel. 405-5631). Located in the basement of the Clover Building, this locale specializes in teppanyaki steaks and seafood, flavored with Kikkoman condiments. Open daily from 11:30 a.m. to 2 p.m. and from 5 to 10 p.m., it features courses ranging from ¥8,800 ($62.86) to ¥13,200 ($94.29) for various cuts of Matsuzaka beef, along with side dishes and dessert. Lunch set menus begin at ¥1,300 ($9.29). Roppongi Station is about a minute's walk away.

Ginza Benkay, 7-2-17 Ginza (tel. 573-7335), is a Japan Air Lines affiliate and specializes in teppanyaki, sushi, and kaiseki, each served in its own special dining area. Coolly decorated with a stone-and-pebble floor, bamboo, wood, and shoji screens, it offers a variety of set courses in many price ranges. Lunch is the most economical time to come, when teppanyaki courses, an assorted plate of sushi, or a small kaiseki lunch box all start at ¥1,300 ($9.29). Dinner courses of teppanyaki, sushi, or kaiseki begin at around ¥7,000 ($50), while a shabu-shabu course is ¥8,800 ($62.86). An especially good deal is the dinner "lunch box" for ¥3,800 ($27.14). Closest station: Yurakucho. Another Ginza Benkay is located in the basement of the President Hotel in Aoyama (tel. 402-0246).

Ganchan [31], 6-8-23 Roppongi (tel. 478-0092), is one of my favorite *yakitori-ya*. It's small, intimate, and is owned by a friendly and entertaining man who can't speak English worth a darn but keeps trying with the help of a worn-out Japanese-English dictionary he keeps behind the counter. He also keeps an eclectic cassette collection—I never know whether to expect Japanese pop tunes or mellower Simon and Garfunkel. Seating is just along one counter with room for only a dozen or so people. Because the menu is in Japanese I suggest you order the *yakitori seto* for ¥2,200 ($15.71). It comes with salad and soup and eight skewers of such items as chicken, beef, meatballs, green peppers, and asparagus with bacon wrapped around it. When I've ordered à la carte my meal

has come to about ¥4,000 ($28.57), including beer. This place is open daily
from 6 p.m. to 3 a.m., except on Sunday, when it closes at midnight. Nearest
subway station: about four minutes from Roppongi. Take the small street going
downhill on the left side of the Almond Coffee Shop; Ganchan is at the bottom
of the hill on the right—look for the big white paper lantern.

Non-Japanese Food

I'm not sure how to categorize **Mominoki House**, 2-18-5 Jingumae (tel. 405-
9144). Although the menu (written only in Japanese, up on a huge blackboard)
is French, the dishes are the special creations of the chef, who uses lots of soy
sauce, ginger, and Japanese vegetables. Suffice it to say that Mominoki House is
in a category all by itself and is somewhat of a rarity in Tokyo. Serving
macrobiotic foods, this alternative restaurant features hanging plants and split-
level dining, allowing for more privacy than one would think possible in such a
tiny place. Its recorded jazz collection is extensive, and on weekends there's live
music. The menu changes according to what's fresh and what the chef himself
feels like eating, but dishes may include tofu steak, duck, sole, escargots, eggplant gratin (baked in a delicious white sauce), salads, and homemade sorbet.
At any rate, this place seems to always satisfy both vegetarians and meat eaters,
and you'll probably spend about ¥4,000 ($28.57) for dinner. An especially good
deal is the daily lunch special for ¥770 ($5.50), which gives you brown rice, miso
soup, salad, fish or other entrée, and a glass of wine. It's open every day except
Sunday from 11 a.m. to 11 p.m. (last order is at 10 p.m.). Closest stations:
Harajuku or Meiji-Jingu-mae, from which you're best off taking a taxi.

Chez Figaro, 4-4-1 Nishi Azabu (tel. 400-8718), has been serving traditional French cooking for more than 20 years. A small and cozy place popular with
both foreigners and Japanese, its specialties include homemade pâté, escargots,
fish soup, stuffed quail with grapes, steak, and braised sweetbreads with port
wine. À la carte entrées range from about ¥3,300 ($23.57) to ¥4,500 ($32.14),
and there are two dinner courses offered for ¥5,500 ($39.29) and ¥7,700 ($55).
Lunch is reasonable, with three set menus beginning at ¥2,200 ($15.71), served
from noon to 2 p.m. on weekdays only. Dinner is from 6 to 9:30 p.m. (last order)
Sunday through Friday. This is the first time in my life I've come across a restaurant in Japan that is closed on Saturday. Chez Figaro is about a 15-minute walk
from Roppongi Station. From Roppongi Crossing, walk toward Shibuya until
you come to the second major intersection, at the bottom of a hill. Turn left and
after about four minutes you'll see Chez Figaro on your right. Hiro Station is
seven minutes away.

Another French restaurant is the chic **Atantot**, 5-17-1 Roppongi (tel. 586-
4431), located on the third floor of the Axis Building. Its interior is sparse, with
black, brown, and white marble walls and floors and only eight tables. The center attraction is the open kitchen, where you can watch the chefs prepare your
food. The menu changes weekly, and there's a set dinner menu for ¥6,500
($46.43), served daily from 5:30 to 10 p.m. Personally, I prefer to come here for
lunch when the weather is warm and I can sit outside on the terrace. The set
lunch is ¥2,200 ($15.71), and is served from 11:30 a.m. to 5 p.m.—to match the
erratic eating schedule of self-employed artists and designers who frequent this
place. Be sure to check out the battery-powered gadget used to sweep crumbs
off your table. Nearest subway station: Roppongi.

Le Chalet, in the basement of the Shimizu Building, 3-14-9 Akasaka (tel.
584-0080), is a pleasant and modestly priced French restaurant in the heart of
Akasaka. With seating for only 26 persons and decorated in an opulent pink and
red, Le Chalet serves set lunches starting at ¥1,300 ($9.29) and set dinners
ranging from ¥4,400 ($31.43) to ¥8,800 ($62.86). The ¥4,400 course includes

an hors d'oeuvre, soup, fish, a meat dish, dessert, and coffee. Hours here are 11:30 a.m. to 2 p.m. and 5 to 10 p.m. daily. Nearest subway: a minute away from Akasaka Station.

La Patata, 2-9-11 Jingumae, Shibuya-ku (tel. 403-9664), is an Italian restaurant specializing in seafood. It's a cheerful place with lots of windows, plants, and warm, blond furniture, reminding me of health-food restaurants in the States. Served from 6 to 10:30 p.m., the dinner menu includes a fish of the day, broiled shrimp, sole, lamb, sliced veal, and beef filet, with the average dinner costing about ¥7,500 ($53.57), including wine. Lunch specials are ¥1,100 ($7.86) and ¥2,700 ($19.29), available from noon to 2 p.m. The restaurant is closed on Monday. Nearest subway station: about ten minutes from Gaienmae, La Patata is on a street with the intimidating name of Killer Dori Avenue.

The discovery of **La Primavera,** Sanko Building, 2-5-15 Shinjuku (tel. 354-7873), has been a cause for celebration for many an Italian-food lover in Tokyo. The food is great, the prices are reasonable, and the bread is among the best in town. Opened in 1985, its faithful clientele has been growing steadily ever since. An intimate locale with only half a dozen tables, each with candles, and Botticelli reproductions on the wall, it serves pastas starting at ¥750 ($5.36), pizzas from ¥1,000 ($7.14), and main entrées of steak, scallops, or fish, most ranging in price from ¥2,200 ($15.71) to ¥3,300 ($23.57). Set lunch courses, which include steak, stew, homemade sausage, or pasta, range in price from ¥900 ($6.43) to ¥2,200 ($15.71). It's open daily from 11:30 a.m. to 2 p.m. and from 6:30 to 11 p.m. Nearest station: Shinjuku Gyoen-mae, about a four-minute walk away.

If you're hit with a craving for Mexican food, try **Mexico Lindo,** 2-20-7 Akasaka (tel. 583-2095). It has a one-room dining area with Mexican knick-knacks, pleasant waitresses, and Mexican music. The dinner menu includes tacos, flautas, tostados, and enchiladas, soups, and nachos. Most dishes are about ¥1,700 ($12.14), and if you're really hungry you'll probably want to order two. A set lunch for two persons costs ¥2,200 ($15.71) per person. Tacos come in a soft tortilla with only the meat inside—there are then separate bowls of tomatoes, green peppers, onions, cottage cheese, lettuce, and sauce, which you put on the way you like it. Mexico Lindo is open for lunch weekdays only from 11:30 a.m. to 2 p.m. (last order at 1:30 p.m.) and for dinner from 5:30 to 10 p.m.; closed Sunday. Nearest subway station: Akasaka or Roppongi, both about ten minutes away (near the ANA Hotel).

With its black marble walls and innocuous decor, there's little to tip you off that **Z Greek Tavern,** 6-9-11 Minami Aoyama (tel. 499-4958), is a Greek restaurant. No Greek music (at least not during my visit) and no obligatory pictures of the Acropolis. The main menu includes pizza, souvlaki, lobster, moussaka, roast lamb, and stuffed peppers and tomatoes, with most entrées priced under ¥2,300 ($16.43). Dinner courses range from ¥3,500 ($25) to ¥6,600 ($47.14). The special lunch menu lists set meals starting at ¥1,000 ($7.14), which may include a choice of pork, fish, lamb, or vegetable entrée along with salad, soup, rice, and coffee or tea. No lunches are served on Sunday and holidays, but otherwise the hours here are 11:30 a.m. to 3 p.m. and from 5 to 11 p.m. Nearest subway station: Omote Sando. Z is located on Roppongi Dori Street, which runs between Roppongi and Shibuya, near the Fuji Film building.

Metropole, 6-4-5 Roppongi (tel. 405-4400), gets my vote as having the most interesting, eclectic decor in town. A hip Chinese restaurant, it has everything from an old-fashioned double-door entryway to Roman statues and a bar area that looks like an old-world library. Large mirrors on the walls allow you to watch the action even if your back is turned, and the waiters are correct and trendy. All in all, the whole scene looks like a set for a Fellini movie. Open for dining from 11:30 a.m. to 3 p.m. and from 6 to 11:30 p.m. daily, it has a menu with more than 80 offerings, including beef in a lettuce roll, jellyfish, shrimp in spicy chili sauce, braised shark's fin with crab meat, crispy duck, and shredded pork with bamboo shoot. A meal here averages ¥5,000 ($35.71) to ¥8,500 ($60.71). Nearest subway station: Roppongi, about a ten-minute walk away.

If you're hungering for American steaks, salads, and soups, **Victoria Station**, 4-9-2 Roppongi (tel. 479-4601), may be the closest you can come. Similar to the approximately 100 Victoria Stations in the United States, it's decorated like a railroad station and has one of the best salad bars in town. The price for prime rib ranges from ¥2,700 ($19.29) to ¥8,200 ($58.57) and includes as many trips as you want to the salad bar. I prefer to come for lunch, at which time they also serve hamburgers. A hamburger plus a trip to the salad bar costs only ¥1,050 ($7.50). If you're interested mainly in beverages, there's a cocktail bar upstairs with drinks starting at ¥600 ($4.29). It has its own menu, with spaghetti, sandwiches, and snacks available throughout the day. For ¥880 ($6.29) you can go to the salad bar as many times as you wish, and until 2 p.m. you can visit it once for ¥330 ($2.36), one of the best deals in town.

Victoria Station is open from 11 a.m. to midnight, except on Sunday and holidays, when it closes at 11 p.m. It's located close to Roppongi Crossing almost cater-corner from the Almond Coffee Shop.

Tiger Seafood Restaurant, 3-11-3 Akasaka (tel. 582-0105), is an American West Coast chain restaurant serving seafood the way you're used to it back home (that is, cooked instead of raw). Green walls, a red carpet, and brass palm trees are the decor here. Entrées start at ¥2,200 ($15.71), averaging ¥3,500 ($25) for most seafood dishes. Lobster halves cost ¥3,300 ($23.57), and there are also steaks at ¥3,300 ($23.57) and up. Hours are 11 a.m. to 3 a.m., and the nearest stations are Akasaka-mitsuke and Akasaka. There's another Tiger Seafood Restaurant at 3-5-12 Kita-Aoyama (tel. 478-1222) on Aoyama Dori Avenue between Omote Sando and Gaienmae subway stations.

The **Terrace Restaurant** is a pleasant café-style restaurant and coffeehouse in the venerable Okura Hotel, 2-10-4 Toranomon (tel. 582-0111). There are so few restaurants in Tokyo with good views that you might want to come here just to relax and unwind, looking out on a landscape garden with a waterfall and a little stream. The best time to come is at lunch, when there are set meals from ¥2,600 ($18.57). Otherwise, à la carte dishes generally cost about ¥1,400 ($10) to ¥2,400 ($17.14) and include such things as spaghetti, sandwiches, filet of sole, salmon steak, beef Stroganoff, and shrimp or chicken pilaf. For the weight-conscious there's also a diet menu with the calorie count and nutritional value listed beside each dish. It's open from 8 a.m. to 9 p.m. daily.

THE BUDGET CATEGORY: Many of Tokyo's most colorful, noisy, and popular restaurants fall into this category, frequented by the city's huge working population as they catch a quick lunch or socialize with friends after hours. Be sure to read over the restaurants listed in the upper- and medium-range categories—most of them offer great lunches at reasonable prices, which means that you may be able to splurge in style. For the most part, however, keep in mind that you can generally eat more economically at Japanese restaurants than at Western establishments. Remember to check the nightlife section for more suggestions on inexpensive drinking places that serve food.

Japanese Food

Hayashi [10], on the fourth floor of the Sanno Kaikan Building, 2-14-1 Akasaka (tel. 582-4078), was described at length as an upper-bracket restaurant, but I mention it again here simply because I don't want those of you on a budget to miss it. This is one of the coziest and most delightful restaurants in town, and although dinner here can cost you ¥5,500 ($39.29) and up, you can go for lunch and enjoy the same atmosphere for only ¥850 ($6.07). There's only one dish served at lunch and it's called *oyakodomburi* (rice with chunks of chicken and omelet on top). Served with your meal are pickled vegetables, clear soup, and tea. Hours are 11:30 a.m. to 2 p.m. Monday through Friday only.

Similar to Hayashi in atmosphere and food is **Ohmatsuya** [27], 5-4-18 Ginza (tel. 571-7053), also described earlier in the medium-range category of restaurants. It too serves oyakodomburi for ¥800 ($5.71), as well as buckwheat noodles for ¥880 ($6.29), every day except Sundays from 11:30 a.m. to 2 p.m. Nearest station: Ginza.

Another wonderful restaurant, and a great place to stop off for lunch or dinner on your visit to Asakusa, is **Tatsumiya** [32], 1-33-5 Asakusa (tel. 842-7373). Serving home-style cooking, this old farmhouse is jam-packed with antiques—old chests, pots, bags, gourds, hibachis, clocks, cups, rice buckets, and more. You could spend an hour here just looking at everything. Seating is on the floor in a room elevated from the rest of the house and partitioned with sliding shoji screens and wooden-slatted doors. There's an English menu and à la carte dishes include sashimi, yakitori, shrimp, yellowtail tuna, and grilled sole for ¥800 ($4) to ¥1,750 ($8.75). There are two dinner courses: ¥2,400 ($17.14) is for sashimi, boiled vegetables, and grilled fish; ¥4,000 ($28.57) gets you soup, sashimi, boiled vegetables, grilled fish, pickled food, and rice porridge. Lunch is much cheaper, with set meals ranging from ¥680 ($4.86) to ¥1,300 ($9.29) for fried chicken, rice porridge with either crab or chicken, and rice with either beef or chicken. Hours are noon to 2 p.m. and 5 to 10 p.m.; closed Monday. The closest subway station is Asakusa. Tatsumiya is located on the second street that parallels Nakamise Dori Avenue to the east. There's no English sign, but look for the shop windows packed with antiques and blue curtains hanging in front of the door.

Technically a drinking establishment and every bit as interesting as Tatsumiya but a lot more boisterous, **Irohanihoheto** [33], 1-19-3 Jinnan, Shibuya-ku (tel. 476-1682), is extremely popular with university students. It seats 400 people at tables, counters, and on tatami mats, and if you get here after 7 p.m. you may have to wait for a place to sit. The atmosphere is country—Japanese style—with dark-stained heavy wooden ceiling beams held together with big thick ropes (purely for show, since this establishment is located in the basement of a modern building). From the ceiling hang all kinds of kitsch: straw and wooden toys, ornaments, noise-makers, Japanese dolls, paper lanterns, kites, and a million other things. All in all, it's a fun place to go.

The extensive menu of both Japanese and Western food is in Japanese but has pictures, making it easy to order. Try *niku-jaga* (potato and meat soup), fried tofu, or *oden* (a tofu, fishcake, and vegetable stew). You can also order yakitori, fried noodles, potato salad, sashimi, or grilled meatballs. The list is almost endless, and most items are only ¥350 ($2.50) to ¥450 ($3.21). You'll probably want to order several dishes per person. This place is open every day from 5 p.m. to 4 a.m. Less than ten minutes from the subway station near the Parco I and II department stores, it's a little hard to find. Once you get to Parco you'll probably have to stop someone on the street and ask.

There's another Irohanihoheto more conveniently located in Shinjuku, at 3-15-15 Shinjuku (tel. 359-1682). On the sixth floor of a building next to Isetan Kaikan on Yasukuni Dori Avenue, it bills itself as an "Antique Pub," the meaning of which becomes even more evasive once you're inside. The main hall looks imitation barn to me, with rafters, hurricane lamps, and glass lanterns everywhere. A second room is more traditional Japanese, with tatami seating and folkcrafts hanging about. People don't come here for the decor, however, but because of the prices. Its menu is similar to the Irohanihoheto described above, with draft beer starting at ¥380 ($2.71). Nearest stations: Shinjuku and Shinjuku-Sanchome.

Kaiseki cooking is one of the most expensive meals you can have in Japan, but there are some lunch specials that make it quite reasonable. **Munakata**, a Japanese restaurant in the basement of the Mitsui Urban Hotel in Ginza, 8-6-15 Ginza (tel. 574-9356), serves a small kaiseki lunch for ¥2,750 ($19.64). In addition, both **Kisso** and **Kakiden** (described as upper-range restaurants) offer inexpensive kaiseki lunches.

Uogashi [34], 2-2-3 Nihombashi (tel. 271-8833), is a sushi bar for the adventurous. It's difficult to find but the rewards are great—it's one of the cheapest and best sushi places in town. First, look for the restaurant with the number 2-3 on it. You'll see display cases with plastic food in front of it and short blue curtains hanging in front of the sliding door. This is the main restaurant, but not the one you want. The sushi bar is located at the end of a short alley on the right side of this main restaurant.

Uogashi is tiny, just one small counter, and since there are no stools you have to stand. The people around you will be serious sushi eaters. They put away their food with astonishing speed, usually out of consideration for the people who are waiting in line for their turn at the counter. There are no chopsticks, so you just eat with your fingers. Whatever you order will usually come in a set of four, costing a total of only ¥200 ($1.43). When it's time to pay, go to the small closet-like room beside the front door. The man there will give you your change from the shop's cash register, just an old wooden box. Closed on Sunday and holidays, Uogashi is open from 11:30 a.m. to 2 p.m. and again from 4 to 11 p.m. Nearest subway station: three minutes from Nihombashi Station or five minutes from Tokyo Station.

Located right in the Tsukiji fish market, **Sushi Dai** [35] (tel. 542-1111) boasts some of the freshest fish in town. Nestled in a barrack-like building with other tiny shops and restaurants, Sushi Dai consists of just one counter, filled usually with people who work in the vicinity or at the market. This is one of the few places I've seen Japanese drink beer in the morning when they weren't on holiday. The easiest thing to order is the *seto* for ¥880 ($6.29), which usually comes with tuna, eel, shrimp, and other morsels of sushi, along with six rolls of tuna and rice in seaweed *(onigiri)*. Sushi Dai is open every day except Sunday and holidays from 5 a.m. to 1:30 p.m. Closest station: Tsukiji Station. If you're walking from the station, take your first right once you've crossed the bridge leading onto the market grounds (don't enter into the market building itself). If you're uncertain, there's a little guard's box right after the bridge to the left where you can ask for directions. Otherwise, turn right as described above and then take your first left. To your right will be a row of several barrack-like buildings and tiny alleyways. Sushi Dai is located on the third alley and is the third shop on the right side. Look for the blue curtains hanging outside the door.

A sushi bar that's a bit easier to navigate is **Genrokusushi** [36], 5-8-5 Jingumae (tel. 498-3968). Located in Harajuku, this is actually just one of a chain of fast-food sushi bars. The gimmick here is plates of food conducted along the counter on a conveyor belt. Seated at the counter, you simply take the plate you want when it comes by, which makes dining a cinch because you don't have to know the names of anything. Each plate costs ¥130 (92¢) and when you go to pay, just tell the cashier how many plates you had. Hours are 11 a.m. to 9 p.m. daily. Nearest subway stations: one minute from Meiji-Jingumae or five minutes from Harajuku Station. Genrokusushi is on Omote-Sando Dori Avenue close to Oriental Bazaar.

Another chain restaurant, but this time a *yakitori-ya*, **Torigin** [37] has one of its shops located at 4-12-6 Roppongi (tel. 403-5829). The decor in this one is simple, typical of so many of the smaller Japanese restaurants, and the older men working behind the counter look like they've been here since the Edo Period. The *yakimono* ("grilled things") begin at ¥120 (86¢) a stick, but after 9 p.m. prices rise about ¥10 (7¢) to ¥100 (71¢) per item. Yakimono listed in the English menu include gingko nuts, green pepper, quail eggs, and chicken. Not on the menu are some salads, as well as grilled bacon and asparagus (my favorite). Dinner courses range from ¥950 ($6.79) to ¥1,300 ($9.29). Torigin also has *kamameshi*, a rice casserole cooked and served in its own little pot and topped with such things as chicken, bamboo shoots, mushroom, crab, salmon, or shrimp. Prices for these begin at ¥720 ($5.14). Open every day except Sunday from 11:30 a.m. to 2 p.m. and 5 p.m. to 1 a.m. (last order at 12:30 a.m.), Torigin is about a two-minute walk from Roppongi Station.

If Torigin is full, there's another branch not far away at 7-14-14 Roppongi (tel. 401-9854), calling itself Torigin Toka. The atmosphere here isn't quite as good, maybe because it's newer, but the menu is the same. This one closes earlier, at 10 p.m. If you're in Ginza, there's yet another Torigin, at 5-5-7 Ginza (tel. 571-3333), located off Namiki Dori Street.

Much more refined than most *yakitori-ya* is **Kamakura**, 4-10-11 Roppongi (tel. 405-4377). Open from 5 p.m. to 1 a.m. every day except the first and third Tuesdays of the month, it's decorated with paper lanterns and sprigs of fake but cheerful spring blossoms, with traditional koto music playing softly in the background. Its English menu lists yakitori courses starting at ¥2,200 ($15.71). Sticks à la carte include those with shrimp, meatballs, squid, eggplant, and mushrooms, most in the ¥200 ($1.43) range. Beer is ¥550 ($3.93). Closest subway station: Roppongi, about a minute away. Kamakura is located on the side street across from the Ibis hotel.

Another *yakitori-ya* is **Atariya**, [38], 3-5-17 Ginza (tel. 564-0045). You have your choice of table or counter seating on the first floor, while up on the second floor you take off your shoes and sit on split-reed mats. Wearing colorful twisted headbands, the employees here will bring either a yakitori course beginning at ¥1,400 ($10) or individual skewers starting at ¥150 ($1.07). Since courses will include most parts of the chicken including its liver, gizzard, and skin, you might wish to order à la carte for your favorites. The shop's name means to be right on target, to score a bull's eye, and according to its English pamphlet, eating here is certain to bring you good luck. "If you are a businessman, your business will prosper. If you are an artist, your art will become famous. If you are ball players, you will hit many home runs," the pamphlet promises. I'm still waiting. Closed on Sunday, it's open the rest of the week from 5 to 10:30 p.m. Closest station: Ginza.

Torijoh [39], 3-1-10 Akasaka (tel. 583-7600), is another *yakitori-ya*, this one in Akasaka. I stumbled on it once when I was wandering through the area looking for a cheap place to eat, and I was so overwhelmed by the enthusiastic and friendly reception given by the waiters that I've been back several times since. The only way to describe the atmosphere is primitive—the lights are too bright, the place looks like some greasy spoon back home, and there's absolutely nothing about it that's aesthetically appealing. But look around you. It's packed with Japanese businessmen in suits and ties stopping in for food, conversation, and a bottle of beer before battling it on the trains back to the suburbs. What's more, Torijoh has been serving yakitori from this spot for more than 100 years. Skewers begin at ¥130 (93¢) and include the usual fare of chicken, gingko nuts, meatballs, or green peppers. If you want to try a variety of grilled items, ask for the ¥1,000 ($7.14) platter, which includes chicken, meatballs, and quail eggs. Closest subway station: Akasaka-mitsuke in the heart of Akasaka. It's open from 4 to 11 p.m. every day except Sunday.

Not far away, on the third floor of the Akasaka Plaza Building (connected to the Akasaka Tokyu Hotel), is a kushikatsu restaurant called **Kushinobo** [40], 2-14-3 Nagato-cho (tel. 581-5056). With skewers of shrimp, vegetables, and meats deep fried in oil, it's a tiny, popular place and customers will wait in line to eat here. I like ordering the *Omakase* course, or cook's choice, with the cook supplying skewer after skewer until you simply say stop. I've been able to eat mint leaf, beef, mushroom, fish, asparagus, chicken, crab, shrimp, green peppers, and pumpkin before crawling away from the table. You'll have various sauces in which to dip your skewered goodies, including soy sauce, mustard, and vinegar. Lunch courses begin at ¥1,300 ($9.29), while dinner courses start at ¥2,200 ($15.71). If you opt for the Omakase, your bill will probably be between ¥3,000 ($21.43) and ¥5,000 ($35.71), a splurge that's worth it. Nearest subway station: Akasaka-mitsuke, one minute away. Hours here are from 11:30 a.m. to 10 p.m. daily.

Tonki [41], 1-1-2 Shimo Meguro, Meguro-ku (tel. 491-9928), is probably the best-known *tonkatsu* (pork cutlet) restaurant in town, and most likely you'll have to wait to get a seat at the long U-shaped counter. At any rate, as soon as you walk in the door a man will ask you which you want, the *hirekatsu* (a filet cut of lean pork) or *rosukatsu* (loin cut). If you're uncertain he'll hold up the two slabs of meat and you just point to one. No matter which slab you decide on, ask for the teishoku, the set meal, which costs ¥1,300 ($9.29) and includes soup, rice, cabbage, pickled vegetable, and tea. He'll scribble your order down on a piece of paper and put it with all the other scraps of paper, miraculously keeping track not only of which order belongs to whom but also which customers have been waiting for a seat the longest.

The open kitchen behind the counter takes up most of the space in the restaurant, and as you eat you can watch the dozen or so cooks scrambling around turning out orders. Never a dull moment. You can get free refills on tea and cabbage, and when you're ready to go, just pay at the counter where you're sitting. This place is closed Tuesday and open the rest of the week from 4 to 11 p.m. (last order at 10:30 p.m.). Nearest station: one minute from Meguro. Take the west exit from the station and then the first left after the Mitsui Bank building and just before McDonald's. Tonki has blue curtains hanging in front of its sliding glass doors.

Put all your prejudices about eels aside and head for **Hyotanya** [42], 1-5-13 Ginza (tel. 561-5615). This is a plain-looking, small restaurant popular with the Ginza working crowd. It serves four different kinds of eel in set menus ranging in price from ¥1,100 ($7.86) to ¥2,000 ($14.29). All courses come with rice and strips of eel on top, the differences in price reflecting the number of side dishes that come along with them. Open from 11 a.m. to 2 p.m. and again from 5 to 8 p.m., this tiny place also serves yakitori in the evenings. It's closed on Sunday and national holidays. Nearest subway stations: one minute from Ginza Itchome Station and about seven minutes from Ginza Station.

Another eel restaurant, and one that's probably a bit easier to find, is **Keyaki** [43], 1-34-5 Asakusa (tel. 844-9012). It's located on the second street that parallels Nakamise Dori Avenue to the east—look for the brown flag with an eel on it and for the fish tank just inside the door. Small with just a counter, a couple of tables, and an adjoining tatami room, it offers a set eel course *(unagi* *seto)* for ¥2,000 ($14.29) as well as tempura or sashimi courses for ¥1,600 ($11.43). Try the house specialty, a sake called *gingo-shu.* Hours here are 11:30 a.m. to 2 p.m. and 5 to 10 p.m., closed Monday. Nearest station: Asakusa.

If you're in the vicinity of the Tourist Information Center in Hibiya and are looking for an inexpensive place to have lunch, across the street from the T.I.C. is **Donto** [44], located in the basement of the Denki Building, 1-7-1 Yurakucho (tel. 201-3021). Popular with the local working crowd, it's pleasantly decorated with shoji screens, wooden floors, and an open kitchen. Choose what you want from the plastic display case, which shows various teishoku for ¥930 ($6.64). Everything from noodles, sashimi, and tempura to kaiseki is available. Closed on Sunday, it's open the rest of the week from 11 a.m. to 3 p.m. and from 5 to 11 p.m. Nearest subway station: Hibiya.

Soba (noodle) shops are among the least expensive restaurants in Japan, and one of Tokyo's most famous noodle places is **Yabu-Soba** [45], 2-10 Awajicho, Kanda (tel. 251-0287). Established in 1880, it's surrounded by a wooden gate and has a small bamboo and rock garden. The house is Japanese style, with shoji screens and a wooden ceiling, and although it looks old it dates only from the 1940s, the previous building having been flattened during World War II. You'll find the restaurant filled with middle-aged businessmen and housewives, and if you come during lunchtime you may have to wait for a seat. One big room, the dining area is divided into tatami mats and tables, and since there's a menu in English ordering is easy. Listen to the woman sitting at a small counter by the kitchen—she sings out orders to the chef as well as hellos and good-byes to customers. Hot and cold noodles start at ¥550 ($3.93), and you can also get noodles with shredded yam, topped with crispy shrimp tempura, or served with grilled eel. Noodles and beer here will cost you less than ¥2,000 ($14.29). Hours are 11:30 a.m. to 7 p.m.; closed Monday. Nearest subway stations: about five minutes from Awajicho and ten minutes from Akihabara. Located between these two stations, it's on a side street east of Sotobori Dori Avenue. A good place to stop off for a meal or snack if you're in Akihabara looking at electronics.

Tanuki [46], 3-5-6 Azabudai, Minato-ku (tel. 583-0545), is another soba restaurant, this time a wonderful respite from the concrete of Roppongi. Tanuki means "racoon" and there's a stuffed animal in the window vaguely resembling the real thing, but get past that and you'll find yourself in an old farmhouse that looks out onto a walled garden—you can even sit outside when it's warm. The friend who showed me this place said she was here once over New Year's and witnessed distinguished-looking businessmen coming in to bow deeply to the old woman in a kimono who runs this place, clearly a sign of deep respect and admiration. Prices start at ¥550 ($3.93) for buckwheat noodles, and the menu includes warm noodles *(kake soba),* cold noodles *(mori soba),* noodles with tempura *(tempura soba),* with sushi *(soba sushi).* This place is closed Sunday, but otherwise is open from 11:30 a.m. to 4 p.m. and 5 to 8 p.m. Nearest subway station: less than ten minutes from Roppongi Station, across the street from Azabu Post Office as you walk toward Tokyo Tower.

Asakusa's best-known noodle shop is **Namiki** [47], 2-11-9 Kaminarimon (tel. 841-1340). It's a one-room place with tatami and tables and an English menu. Noodles range in price from ¥440 ($3.14) for plain noodles in cold or hot stock to ¥1,200 ($8.57) for tempura and noodles. Hours are 11:30 a.m. to 7:30 p.m.; closed Thursday. Nearest subway station: about five minutes from Asakusa. To reach Namiki, take the road that leads south away from Asakusa Kannon Temple and Kaminarimon Gate. Namiki is a brown building on the right side of the street with some bamboo trees by the front door.

Roppongi Shokudo [48], 3-10-11 Roppongi (tel. 404-2714), means Roppongi "cafeteria or mess hall," and it's patronized by everyone from office workers to construction workers to punkers to students. It's the perfect place to witness the famous ten-minute lunch, which is usually the amount of time a Japanese businessman devotes to eating his noon meal. Just walk to the back of the room, get a tray, and then select the dishes you want from the cafeteria's shelves. After you find a place to sit, a woman will come by to give you some tea and leave your bill. The food is basic, home-style cooking and changes daily, but usually includes fish, sashimi, meat dishes, salads, tofu, soup, and rice. A meal here generally costs between ¥500 ($3.57) and ¥1,000 ($7.14). It's open from 10 a.m. to 2 p.m. and 4 to 7 p.m. every day except Sunday and holidays. Nearest subway: about one minute from Roppongi Station on the right side of the street as you walk toward Tameike. Look for the blue curtains.

Ichioku [49], 4-4-5 Roppongi (tel. 405-9891), is one of my favorite restaurants in Tokyo for casual dining. Opened in the early 1970s, its name means "one-hundred million," supposedly the amount of money the owner hopes to earn eventually. Open from 5 p.m. to 12:30 a.m. every day except Sunday, it's a tiny, cozy place with only eight tables, and you fill out your order yourself. The menu is in English, comes complete with pictures, and is glued onto your table underneath clear glass. The food is difficult to describe and categorize—maybe you could call it Japanese nouveau cooking. There's tuna and ginger sauté, mushroom sauté, shrimp spring rolls, and a dish of crumbled radish and tiny fish. I recommend the tofu steak (fried tofu with flakes of dried fish on it), as well as the cheese *gyoza* (a fried pork dumpling with cheese melted on it). The average meal here will cost ¥2,000 ($14.29) or less. The nearest station is Roppongi, about three minutes away.

If you're a vegetarian or looking for a Japanese health-food restaurant, **Tenmi** [50], on the second floor of Daiichi Iwashita Building, 1-10-6 Jinnan, Shibuya-ku (tel. 496-9703) serves traditional Japanese macrobiotic vegetarian food from 11:30 a.m. to 2:30 p.m. and 4:30 to 8 p.m. except on Sunday and holidays when it's open from 11:30 a.m. to 6 p.m. Tenmi is closed the third Wednesday of the month. Dishes and set menus range from ¥650 ($4.64) to ¥1,700 ($12.14) and include various vegetable, tofu, noodle, and rice combinations. I found the set menu for ¥1,000 ($7.14) that included brown rice, an assortment of boiled vegetables, seaweed, and miso soup very satisfying and delicious. There's a health-food shop on the ground floor. Nearest station: about five minutes from Shibuya.

Non-Japanese Food

If you find yourself in Shibuya, it's worth checking out **The Prime**, 2-29-5 Dogenzaka (tel. 770-0111). Opened a few years back by the Seibu conglomeration, The Prime is a great building filled with restaurants and amusements, including movie theaters, a dance and aerobics studio, and a concert and theater-ticket agency. The second floor is a large cafeteria, with various counters offering dishes from around the world. You can pick up everything from bagels and sandwiches to Indian curries, Chinese food, sushi, salads, and pasta. Most dishes are priced less than ¥1,000 ($7.14), and you pay the cashier at each counter. It's open from 10 a.m. to 11 p.m. daily. Other restaurants in The Prime include those dishing out Korean barbecue, French cuisine, and hearty German fare. In the basement are a number of noodle shops serving Chinese, Singaporean, Kyushu, and Hokkaido styles, with huge bowlfuls priced at ¥500 ($3.57) and up. The Prime is located about two minutes away from Shibuya Station.

The 1984 opening of **Sabatini Pizzeria Romana**, located in the basement of the Suncrest Building, 2-13-5 Kita-Aoyama, Minato-ku (tel. 402-2027), was a cause for rejoicing among pizza lovers in Tokyo. Owned by three brothers from Rome who operate an expensive Italian restaurant (also located in the Suncrest Building), its offering is the closest thing to real Italian pizza in town. Many ingredients are flown in from Italy, including olive oil, huge slabs of parmesan and other cheeses, as well as the restaurant's large wine selection; they even shipped in a pasta machine. Pizzas here start at ¥1,000 ($7.14), and there's also spaghetti, lasagne, and fettuccine. The ¥1,800 ($12.86) lunch special gives you a choice of pizza or lasagne, salad, coffee, and choice of beer or wine. A la carte meals should average about ¥2,000 ($14.29) to ¥2,500 ($17.86). Hours are 11:30 a.m. to 2:30 p.m. and 5:30 to 11 p.m. daily. The pizzeria is one minute from Gaienmae, at the intersection of Aoyama Dori and Killer Dori Avenues.

One of the oldest, if not *the* oldest, pizzerias in town is **Nicola's**, 3-12-6 Roppongi (tel. 401-6936). It claims to have been the first to bring pizza to Japan, more than three decades age. At any rate, it offers more than 50 different kinds of pizza, starting at ¥800 ($5.71) in 6-inch, 9-inch, or 12-inch pans. Other items on the menu include spaghetti, beginning at ¥770 ($5.50); pastas, averaging ¥1,800 ($12.86); and steaks, which start at ¥4,400 ($31.43) and include potato, vegetables, salad, bread, and coffee. If you come for lunch you can get spaghetti with salad and coffee for just ¥700 ($5). With its dimmed lighting and comfortable booths and chairs it's a good place to relax—if you can just ignore the fake grapes hanging from the ceiling. Nicola's is open every day of the week from noon to 3 a.m., closing at 1 a.m. Sundays. Nearest subway station: Roppongi. From Roppongi Station, walk toward Tokyo Tower; Nicola's is on the first alley to the left on the third floor of Roppongi Plaza Building. Look for Nicola's sign.

If you want to gorge yourself on pizza, the best deal in town is at one of the 20 or so **Shakey's** around town. They offer a great all-you-can-eat pizza lunch every day except Sunday and holidays from 11 a.m. to 2 p.m.—for just ¥600 ($4.29) per person. One German I know prides himself on being able to put away 27 pieces in one sitting, but you don't have to eat that much for it to be a bargain. In Shinjuku there's a Shakey's across the street from Isetan department store at 3-30-11 Shinjuku (tel. 341-0322). Others are in Harajuku at 6-1-10 Meiji-Jingumae (tel. 409-2405), on Omote Sando Dori Avenue close to the Oriental Bazaar, and in Ginza at 3-5-8 Ginza (tel. 563-2008), on Chuo-Dori Avenue across the street from Matsuya department store.

Spaghetti with a view is what you'll get at the **Spaghetti Factory**, located on the 29th floor of the N.S. Building in Shinjuku at 2-4-1 Nishi Shinjuku (tel. 348-1393). Open every day from 11:30 a.m. to 9:45 p.m., it offers spaghetti dishes starting at ¥900 ($6.43) with a wide variety of sauces and toppings. Nearest station: about an eight-minute walk west of Shinjuku Station.

A good place for hamburgers is **Ari's Lamp Light**, 7-8-1 Minami Aoyama (tel. 499-1573). Actually a piano bar where Ari himself plays easy-listening music every evening from 9:30 on, this place has hamburgers, sandwiches, and salads for ¥1,000 ($7.14) to ¥1,700 ($12.14). There's also a large cocktail selection with drinks costing between ¥900 ($6.43) and ¥ ($9.29). Hours are 5:30 p.m. to 2 a.m. daily, except Sunday and holidays. Nearest subway station: about a 15- to 20-minute hike from Roppongi. From Roppongi Crossing, walk toward Shibuya. After you pass the big Fuji Film building on your right, look for the "Lamp Light" sign on your left. It's in the basement of the Odakyu Building.

Central Park, 4-30-6 Jingumae (tel. 478-6200), is an interesting restaurant serving Cantonese Chinese dishes, spaghetti, sandwiches, and snacks, with most items costing less than ¥1,000 ($7.14). It has a good selection of juices and cocktails. The interesting thing about this place is that it's located in the middle courtyard of a tall office building, with palm trees and open sky above. In winter a plastic tarp covers the restaurant. Another noteworthy item is that an aerobics class adjoins the restaurant—which means that you can watch women working out as you eat. Hours here are 11:30 a.m. to 10 p.m. daily. Nearest subway station: one minute from Meiji-Jingumae in Harajuku. Central Park is located in Central Apartment Building on the corner of Omote Sando and Meiji Dori Avenues.

Not far from Central Park in Harajuku, **El Amigo**, 4-30-2 Jingumae (tel. 405-9996), is one of the cheapest Mexican restaurants in town. To cut corners they use cabbage instead of lettuce, but otherwise it's the usual tacos and enchiladas, margheritas, and Mexican beer. Unless you become addicted to those margheritas (a lot of people come here just for those) your meal will probably cost less than ¥1,800 ($12.86). A plus here is that there's an outdoor patio of sorts, below street level and smothered in plants. The place is cheerful and often crowded. Hours are 5 p.m. to midnight daily. Nearest subway station: Meiji-Jingumae, one minute away off Omote Sando Dori Avenue on a side street beside Wendy's hamburger shop.

My favorite Indian restaurant in town is **Moti**, 6-2-35 Roppongi (tel. 479-1939), and judging by how crowded it sometimes gets, it must be a lot of other people's favorite as well. Vegetable curries begin at around ¥1,100 ($7.86), chicken and mutton curries at ¥1,200 ($8.57). I usually opt for the sag mutton (lamb with spinach). There are also tandoori chicken dishes beginning at ¥1,500 ($10.71). An especially good deal are the lunches, which are ¥900 ($6.43) and give you a choice of vegetable, chicken or mutton curry, along with Indian bread *(nan)*, and tea or coffee. I recommend the vegetable curry—it's always good. Moti is open seven days a week from 11:30 a.m. to 10 p.m. (lunch is served until 2:30 p.m.). Moti is about three minutes from Roppongi Station, on the left side of the street as you walk from Roppongi Crossing toward Shibuya.

There are also two other Moti restaurants, both in Akasaka: on the second floor of the Akasaka Floral Plaza, 3-8-8 Akasaka (tel. 582-3620), and on the third floor of the Kinpa Building, 2-14-31 Akasaka (tel. 584-6640).

Samrat, Shojikiya Building on the third floor, 4-10-10 Roppongi (tel. 478-5877), is another Indian restaurant, this one located across from the Ibis hotel. Open seven days a week from 11 a.m. to 10 p.m., its curries average ¥1,300 ($9.29), while the tandoori mixed grill is ¥1,650 ($11.79). For ¥2,300 ($16.43) you can have either a vegetarian or meat set course, which gives you three dishes and nan. Until 3 p.m. there's a special lunch set for ¥1,050 ($7.50), with a choice of curries and nan. Closest subway station: a minute away from Roppongi.

Popular with the young Japanese crowd is **Healthmagic**, 3-16-4 Shinjuku (tel. 352-4062). Billing its food as "high-protein, high-mineral, high-vitamin, low-fat, and low-sugar," this restaurant serves salads, soups, pita-bread sandwiches, low-calorie desserts, and fruit and vegetable drinks, with most items ranging in price from ¥750 ($5.36) to ¥1,500 ($10.71). Some foods on the menu sound a bit interesting, such as seaweed salad, pita bread filled with peanut butter and banana, tofu au gratin, and the cottage cheese cake. Open from 11 a.m. to 11 p.m. daily. except on Sunday, when it closes earlier, at 3 p.m., this is a pleasant restaurant with potted palms and large windows. However, the music tends to be too loud, and for some reason everyone here seems to be a fiendish cigarette smoker. About five minutes from Shinjuku's east exit, Healthmagic is located on a back alley to the west and behind the Isetan department store.

Sunday brunches have yet to catch on in Tokyo, but one restaurant that serves a very reasonable Sunday brunch is **Brasserie D**, Ecsaine Plaza Aoyama, 3-15-14 Kita Aoyama, Minato-ku (tel. 470-0203). Served on Sunday from 11:30 a.m. to 3 p.m., brunch here gives you a choice of either beer, wine, kir, or juice, and a choice of either omelet, quiche Lorraine, or eggs Benedict. On the buffet table are a variety of salads, side dishes, and desserts. The cost is ¥3,000 ($21.43) per person. The nearest subway station is Omote Sando, about two minutes away. It's located on the left side of Aoyama Dori Avenue as you walk from Omote Sando toward Gaienmae.

Also in Omote Sando but on the other side of Aoyama Dori Avenue is **Spiral Cafe,** located in the Spiral building, 5-6-23 Minami Aoyama (tel. 498-5791). A beautifully designed white building which opened in 1985, Spiral houses galleries, a concert hall and theater, a shop on the second floor that specializes in well-designed kitchenware and household gadgets, and several restaurants. On Sunday from 11 a.m. to 2 p.m., Spiral Cafe also offers a brunch for ¥2,500 ($17.86), which includes a choice of cocktails and one egg dish and a trip to a buffet. Nearest subway station: less than a minute from Omote Sando Station.

There are ramen (Chinese noodle) shops all over Tokyo, easily recognizable by their red signs, flashing lights, and pictures of various dishes displayed by the front door. In addition to ramen you can also order *gyoza* (fried dumplings), fried noodles, and other Chinese fast food. Since **ramen shops** are found on almost every corner in Tokyo it seems pointless to single any out, but if you want specific addresses there are two in Roppongi that are easy to find. If you walk from Roppongi Crossing toward Tokyo Tower, within a minute there will be a ramen shop on your right at 5-1-6 Roppongi (tel. 403-1448) and farther down, one on your left at 3-14-10 Roppongi (tel. 408-9190). Look for the red signs and pictures (outside by the door) of the various dishes served.

CURRENCY NOTE: The prices quoted in this book were figured at ¥140 = US$1. However, due to fluctuations in the exchange rate of the yen (it was ¥126 to the dollar at presstime and there were indications that it might rise further), the U.S. dollar equivalents given might vary during the lifetime of this edition. Be sure to check current exchange rates when planning your trip.

---

5. The ABCs of Tokyo

As one of the most modern and efficient cities in the world, Tokyo has just about every facility and service you might need. Listed below is practical information and addresses for the capital city. If you can't find what you're looking for here, check "The ABCs of Japan" in Chapter I.

AMERICAN EXPRESS: The American Express office handling currency exchanges is located in the Mitsui Building at 3-8-1 Kasumigaseki, Chiyoda-ku (tel. 03/508-2400). Hours are 9 a.m. to 3 p.m. Monday through Friday, and 9 a.m. to noon on Saturday, closed Sunday and public holidays. Closest subway station: Toranomon. An additional American Express office is located in the Four-Stars Building, 4-4-1 Ginza (tel. 564-4381). It's open Monday through Friday from 10 a.m. to 4:30 p.m. and on Saturday from 10 a.m. to 4:30 p.m.

BANKS: Banking hours are 9 a.m. to 3 p.m. on weekdays and 9 a.m. to noon on Saturday (closed the second and third Saturdays of each month). You can exchange money in major banks throughout Tokyo, often indicated by a sign in English near the front door. The **Bank of America** is located in the Arc Mori Building, 1-12-32 Akasaka, Minato-ku (tel. 587-3111), and the **Chase Manhattan Bank** is in the A.I.U. Building, 1-1-3 Marunouchi, Chiyoda-ku (tel. 214-3361).

BOOKSTORES: There are several very good bookstores in Tokyo where there's a large selection of books written in English about Japan, as well as novels and reference materials. On Shinjuku Station's east side on Shinjuku Dori there's the **Kinokuniya Bookstore**, 3-17-7 Shinjuku (tel. 354-0131). Books in English are located on the sixth floor, and this large store is open from 10 a.m. to 7 p.m. (closed the third Wednesday of the month). Another good bookstore is **Maruzen**, 2-3-10 Nihombashi, Chuo-ku (tel. 272-7211), with its foreign books located on the second floor. Hours are 10 a.m. to 6 p.m.; closed Sunday. The **Yaesu Book Center**, 2-5-1 Yaesu, Chuo-ku (tel. 281-1811), located close to Tokyo Station, is a five-story bookstore with about a million books, including books in English on the fourth floor. It's open from 10 a.m. to 7 p.m. Monday through Saturday; closed Sunday. **Jena**, 5-6-1 Ginza, Chuo-ku (tel. 571-2980), is conveniently located in the heart of Ginza on Harumi Dori Avenue. Open from 10:30 a.m. to 7:50 p.m. Monday through Saturday and from 12:30 to 6:45 p.m. on Sunday, it has English paperbacks, magazines, special-interest books, maps, and travel guides. It's located between the Ginza and Hibiya subway stations. Another place to look for books in English is the area of **Jimbocho-Kanda**, with its many kinds of bookstores, described more fully in the Tokyo shopping section.

CAR RENTALS: As I've stressed before, driving a car in Tokyo can make a roller-coaster ride at the local amusement park seem like tame stuff. If you're still not convinced, there are approximately a dozen major rental-car companies in Tokyo with branch offices spread throughout the city and at Narita airport. The **Avis-Nissan Reservation Center** is in the Landick Iikura Building, 1-5-7 Azabudai, Minato-ku (tel. 03/587-4000); the **Hertz-Nippon Rent-A-Car Service** is in the Jinnan Building, 4-3 Udagawacho, Shibuya-ku (tel. 03/496-0919); and **Toyota Rent-A-Lease** is at 1 Sanban-cho, Chiyoda-ku (tel. 03/264-2834). Prices start at around ¥8,000 ($57.14) for 24 hours. You'll need either an international or Japanese driver's license.

DOCTORS AND DENTISTS: Your embassy can refer you to English-speaking doctors, specialists, and dentists. Otherwise there are a few clinics popular with foreigners living in Tokyo where some of the staff speak English. The **Tokyo Medical & Surgical Clinic**, close to Tokyo Tower in the 32 Mori Building, 3-4-30 Shiba-koen, Minato-ku (tel. 436-3028), is open from 9 a.m. to 4:45 p.m. weekdays (closed 1 to 2 p.m. for lunch) and from 9 a.m. to noon on Saturday. The **International Clinic** is within walking distance of Roppongi Station at 1-5-9 Azabudai, Minato-ku (tel. 582-2646), and is open from 9 a.m. to noon and 2:30 to 5 p.m. Monday through Friday. You can also make appointments to visit doctors in the hospitals listed below under "Hospitals."

DRUGSTORES: There is no 24-hour drugstore in Tokyo, but there are convenience stores throughout the city that carry things like aspirin. (If it's an emergency, I suggest going to one of the hospitals listed below.) If you're looking for specific pharmaceuticals, a good bet is the **American Pharmacy**, in the Hibiya Park Building, 1-8-1 Yurakucho, Chiyoda-ku (tel. 271-4034). Open from 9 a.m. to 7 p.m. every day except Sunday, it has most of the drugs you can find at home, many of them imported from the United States, and can fill American prescriptions. This handy drugstore is located just a minute's walk from the Tourist Information Center at Hibiya Station.

EMERGENCY: The same all over Japan, the national emergency numbers to call are 110 for police and 119 for an ambulance or to report a fire.

HELPLINE: At the end of your rope? Have some problems? The **Tokyo English Life Line** (tel. 03/264-4347) gives free confidential counseling over the telephone, will listen to your problems, and will let you blow off steam.

HOSPITALS: In addition to going to a hospital for an emergency, you can also visit a hospital's clinic to see a doctor. The **International Catholic Hospital (Seibo Byoin)**, 2-5-1 Naka-Ochiai, Shinjuku (tel. 951-1111), has clinic hours from 8:30 to 11 a.m. Monday through Saturday. The cost for a first visit is about ¥4,400 ($31.43); special tests or treatments cost more. The closest subway station is Meijiro on the Yamanote Line.

Other hospitals include **St. Luke's International Hospital (Seiroka Byoin)**, 1-10 Akashicho, Chuo-ku (tel. 541-5151), with clinic hours from 9 to 11 a.m. Monday through Saturday (closest subway: Tsukiji on the Hibiya Line); and the **Japan Red Cross Hospital** (Nisseki Iryo Center), 4-1-22 Hiroo, Shibuya-ku (tel. 400-1311), with hours from 8:30 to 11 a.m. on weekdays and 8:30 to 10:30 a.m. on Saturday (closest subway stations are Roppongi, Hiroo, and Shibuya, from which you should take a taxi).

LOST PROPERTY: If you've forgotten something on a subway, in a taxi, or on a park bench, you don't have to assume it's gone forever. In fact, if you're willing to trace it down you'll probably get it back. If you've lost something along a street or outside, go to the nearest police box, called a *koban*. Items found in the neighborhood will stay there for about three days. After that you should contact the Central Lost and Found Office of the **Metropolitan Police Board**, 1-9-11 Koraku, Bunkyo-ku (tel. 814-4151).

If you've lost something in a taxi or subway, you need to contact the appropriate office: for taxis it's the **Taxi Kindaika Center** at 7-3-3 Minamisuma, Koto-ku (tel. 648-0300); for JR trains it's the **Lost and Found Section** at Tokyo JR Station (tel. 231-1880) or at Ueno Subway Station (tel. 834-5577); and for Tokyo Metropolitan buses, subways, and streetcars it's the Lost and Found Section of the Tokyo Metropolitan Government, fifth floor of the Tokyo Kotsu Kaikan Building, 2-10-1 Yurakucho (tel. 216-2953).

POST OFFICE: If your hotel cannot mail letters for you, ask the concierge where the nearest post office is. The Central Post Office is located just southwest of Tokyo Station. If you need information on postage or mail, contact the Information Office of the **Tokyo International Post Office** at 2-3-3 Otemachi (tel. 241-4891), located north of Tokyo Station.

RAILWAY INFORMATION: You can obtain information and buy tickets for

Japan Railways trains going throughout Japan at any JR station, including those along the Yamanote Line, which loops around Tokyo. For specific train times, call the Tourist Information Center at 502-1461 or call JR directly (best if you have a Japanese speaker with you) at 212-3579.

TELEGRAMS AND TELEPHONES: You can make long-distance calls from your room in most tourist hotels in Tokyo. Otherwise, there are telephone and telegraph offices throughout the city. The **Tokyo Telegraph & Telephone (KDD) office** at 1-8-1 Otemachi (tel. 211-5588), close to Tokyo Station, is open 24 hours a day throughout the year and can handle facsimiles, phototelegrams, ISD calls, and Telex in addition to telegrams and telephone calls. In Shinjuku there's a telephone and telegraph office at 2-3-2 Nishi Shinjuku (tel. 347-5000).

There are several English telephone directories available that provide addresses and telephone numbers for many businesses, companies, shops, and restaurants in Tokyo. They're the *English Telephone Directory,* the *Japan Times Directory,* and the *Japan Telephone Book Yellow Pages.* If your hotel does not have one of these and you're interested in buying one, they're available at the bookstores listed above. For assistance on directory telephone listings in Tokyo, English-speaking operators can help you if you call 201-1010.

If you're calling a number in Tokyo from outside the city, the **area code for Tokyo** is 03.

TOURIST INFORMATION: The Tourist Information Center (T.I.C.), 1-6-6 Yurakucho, Chiyoda-ku (tel. 502-1461), can answer all your questions regarding Tokyo and can give you a map of the city as well as various sightseeing materials. It also has more information than any place else on the rest of Japan, including pamphlets and brochures on major cities and attractions across the nation. Be sure to stop off here if you plan to travel to other destinations, since in many cases information in English is not available at the destination itself. Check the travel tips section in Chapter I for various pamphlets available on Japan.

The tourist office is open from 9 a.m. to 5 p.m. weekdays and from 9 a.m. to noon on Saturday. Although it doesn't make sense in a city as large as Tokyo, it is closed on Sunday and national holidays. The office is located close to both Hibiya and Yurakucho stations (if you're arriving at Hibiya Station, take the A4 or A5 exit). There's also a tourist office at the Narita airport where you can pick up a map and ask how to get to your hotel.

If you want to have a quick rundown of what's happening in Tokyo, you can call 503-2911 for a taped recording in English of what's going on in the city and the vicinity in the way of special exhibitions, performances, festivals, and events.

TOURIST PUBLICATIONS: The best publication for finding out what's going on in Tokyo in terms of contemporary and traditional music and theater, exhibitions in museums and galleries, films, and special events is the *Tokyo Journal.* Published monthly and available for ¥500 ($3.57) at foreign-language bookstores, restaurants, and bars, it also has articles of interest to foreigners in Japan. It even lists department store sales, photography exhibitions, apartments for rent, schools for learning Japanese, and many other services. I don't know how foreigners survived in Tokyo before this publication made its debut in the early 1980s.

Another English publication of interest to tourists is the *Tour Companion,* a weekly distributed free to hotels, travel agencies, and the T.I.C. It tells of up-coming events and festivals, as well as other information useful to the traveler. *Weekender* is also a free weekly and is found in supermarkets, hotels, and other places where foreigners hang out. It's best known for its classified ad section, but has articles and features as well. English-language newspapers such as the *Japan Times* also carry information on the theater, films, and special events.

Chapter IV

WHAT TO DO IN TOKYO

1. The Imperial Palace
2. Ginza
3. Ueno
4. Asakusa
5. Shinjuku
6. Harajuku
7. Sightseeing Miscellany
8. Cultural Entertainments
9. Shopping
10. After Dark in Tokyo

TOKYO HASN'T FARED VERY WELL over the centuries. Fires and earthquakes have taken their toll, old buildings have been torn down in the zeal of modernization, and World War II left most of the city in ruins. The Tokyo of today has very little remaining of historical significance. Save your important sightseeing for places like Kyoto, Nikko, and Kamakura, and consider Tokyo your introduction to Japan's economic miracle, the showcase of the nation's accomplishments in the arts, technology, fashion, and design. Go shopping, explore mammoth department stores, experiment with restaurants, visit museums, walk around the city's various neighborhoods, and take advantage of the city's glittering nightlife. There are plenty of things to do in Tokyo. I can't imagine being bored even for a minute.

If you're so unfortunate as to have only one day in Tokyo, I suggest you spend it going to Tsukiji Fish Market in the wee hours of the morning, followed by a trip to the Tokyo National Museum, the country's largest and most important museum. In the afternoon you could go to Ginza for some shopping, eat dinner at a restaurant in Akasaka, and then spend your evening in either Roppongi or Shinjuku. You might be exhausted by the end of the day but at least you'd have seen a few of the city's highlights and visited a few of its different areas.

Assuming that you have more than one day to spare, however, I am including in this chapter six districts in Tokyo that offer the most to tourists in terms of sightseeing and variety. This chapter also covers shopping, a few offbeat suggestions for sightseeing, Tokyo's nightlife, and cultural events such as sumo and Kabuki.

1. The Imperial Palace

The Imperial Palace can be considered the heart of Tokyo, where Japan's imperial family lives. Built on the very spot where Edo Castle used to stand during the days of the Tokugawa Shogunate, it became the imperial home at its completion in 1888. The present palace, however, isn't even the original—that was destroyed along with almost everything else during air raids in 1945. The palace was rebuilt in 1968, but you can't see much of it. Except on New Year's and on the emperor's birthday (April 29), when the grounds are open to the public, the palace remains off limits to visitors. You'll have to console yourself with a camera shot of the palace taken from the southeast side of Nijubashi Bridge, with the moat and the palace turrets showing above the trees.

But despite the fact that you can't really see the palace, tourists still like to make a brief stop here. Surrounding the palace is a wide moat lined with cherry trees, beautiful in the spring and popular all year round with jogging enthusiasts. If you feel like taking a stroll at a more leisurely pace, you can walk the three miles around the palace in about an hour.

Probably the most worthwhile thing to do in the vicinity of the palace is to visit its **East Garden (Higashi Gyoen)**, located just to the east of the palace grounds and open free to the public from 9 a.m to 4 p.m. (you must enter by 3 p.m.); closed on Monday and Friday. It takes about an hour to wander through this pleasant green oasis in the middle of the city. Be sure to stop by the little pond with its wisteria, stepping stones, and croaking frogs.

In the garden is also what's left of the central keep of old **Edo Castle**—the stone foundation. Built in the first half of the 1600s, Edo Castle was once the largest castle in the world, with an outer perimeter stretching ten miles. The central keep towered 168 feet above its foundations, offering an expansive view of Edo. As you stand there on top of what's left of the keep's foundation, consider how different things used to look back then—a marsh surrounding the Sumida River, a fishing village where Hibiya now stands. You could see the shore of the bay; what's Ginza today used to be completely under water.

North of the Imperial Palace lies **Kitanomaru Koen Park**, formerly the private grounds of the imperial guard and today the home of several museums. The most important museum here is the **National Museum of Modern Art.** (Tokyo Kokuritsu Kindai Bijutsukan; tel. 214-2561), with an excellent collection of modern Japanese art, dating from the Meiji Period. A few Western artists are also represented in the displays of paintings, sculpture, prints, watercolors, and drawings. Open from 10 a.m. to 5 p.m. every day except Monday and during exhibition changes, the museum charges a ¥300 ($2.14) admission fee.

Not far from the art museum is the **Crafts Gallery** (Bijutsukan Kogeikan; tel. 211-7811). Housed in a Gothic-style brick building constructed in 1910 as headquarters of the imperial guard, the gallery has in its custody contemporary crafts including lacquerware, ceramics, textiles, and dolls. Usually, however, the gallery is used for special exhibitions, and while the hours are the same as the modern art museum, the admission charge here is from ¥300 ($2.14) up, depending on the exhibit. The **Japan Science Museum** is also in Kitanomaru Koen Park, open from 9:30 a.m. to 4:50 p.m. daily with a ¥500 ($3.57) admission fee. However, because exhibits are in Japanese only, the museum doesn't have much of interest to the foreigner.

If you have the time and inclination to cover more in this area, northwest of Kitanomaru Koen Park is **Yasukuni Shrine**, built in 1869 and dedicated to the Japanese war dead. Famous for its cherry blossoms in the spring, the shrine is built in classic Shinto style and becomes a center of controversy every August when World War II memorials are held here and the prime minister shows up. Some people think it improper that a prime minister should visit a shrine so closely tied to Japan's nationalistic and militaristic past.

2. Ginza

Ginza is without a doubt the most chic, most sophisticated, and swankiest area in all of Japan. Ginza is Tokyo's Fifth Avenue, its Champs-Élysées. But rather than just a street Ginza is a whole area of expensive boutiques, the city's largest concentration of department stores and galleries, excellent restaurants, hostess bars, and coffeeshops. Elegant and glamorous, Ginza is worth a browse even if you can't afford to buy anything.

Ginza means "silver mint," a name that goes back to the days of Ieyasu Tokugawa, when the area was reclaimed from the sea and became the home of a silver mint in 1612. After Japan opened itself up to the rest of the world in 1868, Ginza was the first place to become modernized, with Western-style buildings, and to display goods from abroad. There were brick buildings, gas streetlamps, and planted trees, a popular place for the upwardly mobile to shop and be seen.

The buildings have changed since then, but Ginza remains the hub of Japan's affluence and the most expensive area in which to shop and entertain. There's no longer a silver mint here, but the coins keep rolling in.

For a tour through Ginza, I suggest that you begin not in Ginza itself but rather in neighboring **Hibiya** on the north side of the Imperial Hotel. If you've been touring the vicinity of Imperial Palace, walking to Hibiya and then on to Ginza can all be combined in an easy day's self-guided tour. By the way, the Tourist Information Center is also located in Hibiya, so you may want to stop by there first before beginning your tour of this area.

At any rate, the **Imperial Hotel**, located above Hibiya Station, is easy to find and is one of the city's landmarks. Today a modern first-class hotel it used to be much smaller and was originally designed by Frank Lloyd Wright. Pressures of space, however, brought the grand old hotel's demise. The original facade is now in Meiji Mura, an architectural museum outside Nagoya. The present Imperial Hotel houses expensive boutiques, such as Gucci, Hanae Mori, Mikimoto, Chanel, Dunhill, and other imported brands, favorites of wealthy Japanese. You might be interested in seeing how the other half lives.

Across the street on the north side of the Imperial Hotel is a small shop selling woodblock prints called **Nakazawa**, 1-2-15 Yurakucho. It also deals in old and new prints and is open from 10 a.m. to 7 p.m. every day except Sunday.

As you leave the print shop and head east toward Ginza, you'll see overhead the tracks of the Yamanote Line. Underneath these tracks is the **International Arcade**, a long arcade of shops where you can look for such tax-free items as watches, kimonos, Noritake china, woodblock prints, pearls, cameras, and other souvenirs, as well as clothing, shoes, and accessories. Although you can find cheaper prices elsewhere, this may be a good place to wander through if you're in a rush and don't have time to hunt around. Who knows, you might find a bargain or two. Be sure to have your passport with you so you qualify for duty-free prices.

Located next to the International Arcade and also under the tracks is the **Nishi Ginza Electric Center,** where you can shop for radios, cassette players, calculators, compact disk players, and televisions. It's closed on Sunday but open the rest of the week from 9:30 a.m. to 7 p.m.

Just on the other (east) side of the tracks is the **Riccar Art Museum**, 6-2-3 Ginza (tel. 571-3254), a delightful little musuem devoted exclusively to *ukiyoe*, or woodblock prints. Located on the seventh floor of the Riccar Building (note

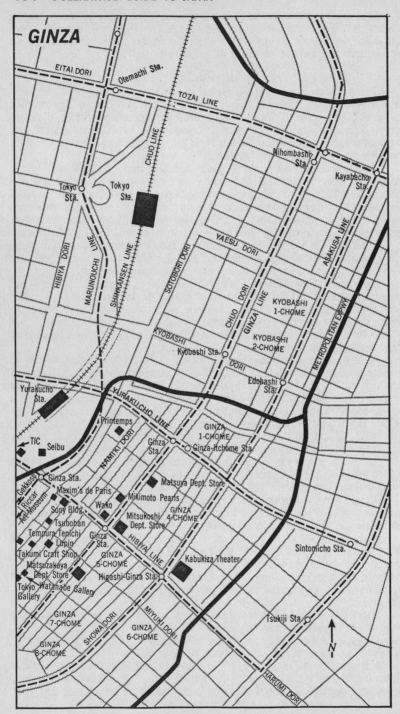

that the entrance to the museum is not through the main entrance of the Riccar Building but rather through a much smaller entrance on a side street called Miyuki Dori), it has approximately 6,000 prints in its collection, which it displays on a rotating basis. Open every day except Monday from 11 a.m. to 6 p.m., it changes exhibits monthly. The place is so tiny it won't take you long to walk through, but it's certainly worth the ¥300 ($2.14) to ¥500 ($3.57) admission.

Ready for some more art? There are lots of galleries in the Ginza area, some of them dealing with old paintings or screens and some in modern art. Right next to the Riccar Art Musuem on Miyuki Dori Street is the **Gallery Center Building**, 6-3-2 Ginza, with seven floors of art galleries. Gallery Hiragi, on the third floor, deals in old scrolls and paintings, while Gekkoso Museum displays changing exhibitions that might include holograms, optical illusions, and modern art. Open daily from 11 a.m. to 8 p.m., it charges a ¥600 ($4.29) admission. An adjoining small shop sells small holograms and novelties.

From Gallery Center Building, walk one more block east to a large street called Sotobori Dori Avenue, where you should take a right and walk a few blocks until you find the **Takumi Craft Shop** on your left (if you reach Ginza Nikko Hotel you've gone too far), located at 8-4-2 Ginza (tel. 571-2017). This crafts store stocks Japanese folk art including ceramics, some kites, umbrellas, lacquerware, textiles, and paper objects. Hours are 11 a.m. to 7 p.m. (to 5:30 p.m. on national holidays); closed Sunday.

Paralleling Sotobori Dori a couple blocks east is Namiki Dori Street. A narrow tree-lined lane, it alternates art galleries and exclusive boutiques with pubs and hostess bars, giving it a wholly different perspective if you were to return here at night. **Tokyo Gallery**, on the second floor of the Dai Go Shuwa Building, 8-6-18 Ginza (tel. 571-1808), is a one-room gallery that specializes in avant-garde art. Since the gallery is so small, it may be that only one artist's work is displayed. Hours are 10 a.m. to 7 p.m.; closed Sunday and holidays. Almost right next door to Tokyo Gallery is **S. Watanabe**, 8-6-19 Ginza (tel. 571-4684), an interesting small shop that deals mostly in modern and old woodcut prints. The staff is friendly and used to foreigners, and the hours here are 9:30 a.m. to 8 p.m. (to 5 p.m. on national holidays); closed Sunday. One more gallery you might want to drop in on is **Yoseido Gallery**, 5-5-15 Ginza (tel. 571-1312), also on Namiki Dori just off Harumi Dori Avenue. Open from 10 a.m. to 6:30 p.m. (closed Sunday and holidays), it specializes in modern Japanese woodblock prints, silkscreens, lithographs, copper plates, and etchings.

Next on the agenda is Harumi Dori Avenue, a busy street that runs from Hibiya through the heart of Ginza. As you come out on this busy avenue you might want to turn left and go two blocks, to the **Sony Building**, 5-3-1 Ginza (tel. 573-2371). This place is always crowded because it acts as a meeting place in Ginza, especially in early evening when couples or friends meet after work to go for a meal or drink. As you might expect, Sony displays its products in showrooms on the first, third, and fourth floors. Stop here to see all the latest in everything from the Walkman to computers to television. There's also a listening room for music and a room with a large video screen showing movies. A good place to stop for a break. It's open from 11 a.m. to 8 p.m. daily.

Catercorner from the Sony Building are two relatively new department stores, **Hankyu** and **Seibu**, both of which opened a couple years back with a lot of fanfare. Altogether there are seven large department stores in the Ginza area. They're closed one day a week, but it's staggered so you can always find a department stores open.

To see more department stores, walk east on Harumi Dori Avenue until you come to Chuo Dori Avenue. This intersection, called the **Ginza 4-chome Crossing**, is the heart of Ginza, the subway staion here is serviced by three subway lines—the Hibiya, Ginza, and Marunouchi lines. The older building with the clock tower is **Wako** department store, famous for its innovative shop windows (and high prices). Across the street is **Mitsukoshi**, and other department stores in the area are **Matsuya, Matsuzaka,** and **Printemps.** (Check the Tokyo shopping section for more information regarding department stores.) There are also many boutiques and shops along Chuo Dori Avenue, including **Mikimoto,** 4-5-5 Ginza (tel. 535-4611), Japan's most famous distributor of cultivated pearls.

Feel like a snack? **Le Carrefour,** on the second floor of Mitsukoshi department store, is a coffeeshop that dishes up bowls of ice cream, pie, fruit salads, and other desserts, including a questionable "creap apple." Open daily from 8 a.m. to midnight, this place with large windows right above the busy intersection of Ginza 4-chome Crossing affords a vantage point from which to watch the bustling crowds, and if you're here at dusk you can witness Ginza explode into colors with the bright lights of neon and signs. It's one of my favorite places to end a successful shopping day in Ginza.

3. Ueno

Ueno, on the northeast edge of the Yamanote Line, is one of the most popular places in Tokyo for Japanese families on a day's outing. In contrast to the chic sophistication of Ginza, Ueno has always been favored by the common people of Tokyo, workers, and immigrants from the north. The atmosphere is more down-to-earth, more casual. The main drawing card is Ueno Park, one of the largest parks in Tokyo and a cultural mecca with a number of museums, including the prestigious Tokyo National Museum, a zoo, and a pond with a bird sanctuary. And close to Ueno Station, the terminus for trains departing for nothern Japan, is a large and lively produce and goods market popular with housewives of the area. Plan on spending at least half a day here to see all the sights, but if you're pressed for time, head straight for the Tokyo National Museum.

UENO PARK: Opened in 1873, Ueno Park was Tokyo's first public park and the first place in Japan to see the establishment of a museum and a zoo. It's not a very large park, especially compared to New York's Central Park, but families and school groups come here for a bit of culture, relaxation, and fun. By the way, along with Shinjuku, Ueno is also a favorite place for Tokyo's down-and-out population. (Yes, even Tokyo has its bums, mainly alcoholics who live tucked away in corners of parks or sleep at entrances to subway stations on sheets of cardboard. They stay politely out of people's way and are left pretty much on their own.)

A landmark in the park is a **statue of Takamori Saigo**, a samurai born in 1827 near Kagoshima on Kyushu island. After helping restore the emperor to power after the downfall of the Tokugawa Shogunate, Saigo subsequently became disenchanted with the Meiji regime when rights enjoyed by the military class were suddenly rescinded. He led a revolt that failed and ended up taking his own life in ritualistic suicide. The statue was erected in 1898 and became the center of controversy when Gen. Douglas MacArthur, leader of the occupation forces in Japan after World War II, demanded that the statue be removed because of its ties to nationalism. The Japanese people protested in a large public outcry and MacArthur finally relented. Today the statue is one of the best known in Tokyo.

The busiest time of the year at Ueno Park is in April, during the cherry blossom season. There's nothing like the bursting forth of cherry blossoms to make one feel that spring is finally here, and people come en masse to Ueno Park to celebrate the birth of the new season. It's not the spiritual communion with nature that you might think, however. In the daytime on a weekday Ueno Park may be peaceful and sane enough, but on the weekends and in the evenings during cherry blossom season all havoc breaks forth as officeworkers break out of their winter shells. Whole companies of workers converge on Ueno Park to sit under the cherry trees on plastic or cardboard. They drink sake and beer, and they get drunk and rowdy. The worst offenders are those who sing loudly into microphones accompanied by cassettes playing background music, a hit in Japan known as *karaoke* music. At any rate, visiting Ueno Park during cherry blossom season is an experience no one should miss. More than likely you'll be invited to join one of the large groups—by all means do. You'll all sit there drinking, being merry, and seemingly totally oblivious to the pink and fragile blossoms shimmering above.

TOKYO NATIONAL MUSEUM: In addition to being the largest museum in Japan, the Tokyo National Museum (Tokyo Kokuritsu Hakubutsukan; tel. 822-1111) has the largest collection of Japanese art in the world. This where you go to see antiques of Japan's past—old kimonos, samurai armor, priceless swords, lacquerware, pottery, scrolls, screens, *ukiyoe* woodblock prints, and more. Altogether the museum has about 86,000 items in its collections, including more than 10,000 paintings, 1,000 sculptures, 15,500 metalworks, 3,000 swords, 3,700 pieces of lacquerware, 27,000 archeological finds, and 7,500 works of foreign Eastern art. Needless to say, it's all too much to be displayed at once, so only about 4,000 items are shown at any one time and are moved on a rotating basis. Thus no matter how many times you visit the museum you'll always see different things.

There are four main buildings with museum displays. The **Main Gallery (Honkan)**, the building straight ahead as you enter the main gate, is the most important one. Just inside the building's entrance is a desk where you can buy the *Tokyo National Museum Handbook* if you want a room-by-room account with explanations of various periods in Japanese art history. You'll feast your eyes on Buddhist sculptures dating from about 538 to 1192; armor, helmets, and decorative sword mountings (armor worn by the nobility was *heavy*—imagine walking around, or worse yet, fighting, with all that stuff on); swords, which throughout Japanese history were considered to embody spirits all their own; textiles; ceramics from prehistoric times; and paintings, calligraphy, and scrolls.

The **Gallery of Eastern Antiquities (Toyokan)** houses art and archeological artifacts from everywhere in Asia outside Japan. There are Buddhas from Pakistan and the second and third centuries; Egyptian relics, including a mummy dating from around 751–656 B.C. and wooden objects from the 20th century B.C.; bronze weapons from Iran; stone reliefs from Cambodia; embroidered wall hangings and cloth from India; Korean bronze and celadon; and Thai and Vietnamese ceramics. The largest part of the collection consists of Chinese art, including jade, glass, stone reliefs, paintings and calligraphy, mirrors, lacquerware, ceramics, and bronzes. Throughout the centuries China played a tremendous role in the development of Japan's art, architecture, and religion.

The **Hyokeikan Gallery** is where you'll find archeological relics of Japan, including pottery and objects found around old burial mounds. One room is devoted to items used in daily life by the Ainu, an indigenous ethnic group now confined mainly to Hokkaido (refer to Chapter XI for more information regarding the Ainu). The fourth building is the **Gallery of Horyuji Treasures**, open only on Thursday if the weather permits. It houses treasures from the Horyuji Temple in Nara, including gilt bronze Buddhist statuettes, religious objects, and paintings.

The Tokyo National Museum is open from 9 a.m. to 4:30 p.m. every day except Monday and charges ¥300 ($2.14) admission. Sometimes it hosts special exhibitions as well, for which it charges a special admission.

THE OTHER MUSEUMS: Not far from the Tokyo National Museum, the **Tokyo Metropolitan Art Museum** (Tokyo-to Bijutsukan; tel. 823-6921) displays modern Japanese works, usually with a number of temporary exhibitions. There are separate admission fees for each exhibit, so unless you're familiar with the particular artists it's just a hit-and-miss thing as far as choosing which exhibit to see. Hours here are 9 a.m. to 5 p.m.; closed Monday and during changing of the exhibits.

Nearby is the **National Museum of Western Art** (Kokuritsu Seiyo Bijutsukan; tel. 828-5131), the main building of which was designed by Le Corbusier. As the name implies, it features Western art, with a concentration on French impressionism. Artists include Renoir, Monet, Sisley, Manet, Delacroix, Cézanne, Degas, El Greco, and Goya. Open daily from 9:30 a.m. to 5 p.m. (except on Monday and during exhibition changes), the museum is famous for its 50 some sculptures by Rodin, the third-largest Rodin collection in the world.

Also in Ueno Park is the **National Science Museum** (Kokuritsu Kagaku Hakubutsukan; tel. 822-0111), open from 9 a.m. to 4:30 p.m. daily except Monday. This sprawling complex covers everything from the evolution of life to electronics in Japan to aircraft and automobiles. Unfortunately not all displays are explained in English but there's an English handbook available for ¥300 ($2.14). The museum is worth visiting because of its exhibits relating to Japan. For example, there are displays on the origin and development of the Japanese people, examples of architecture (no nails were used to join heavy wooden beams), the process of making Japanese lacquerware and paper, a "Zero" fighter plane built during World War II, and an excellent collection of antique Japanese clocks. It charges a ¥350 ($2.50) admission.

TOSHOGU SHRINE: Erected in 1651, Toshogu Shrine is dedicated to Ieyasu Tokugawa, founder of the Tokugawa Shogunate. Stop here to pay respects to the man who made Edo (present Tokyo) the seat of his government and thus elevated the small village to the most important city in the country. The pathway to the shrine is lined with massive stone lanterns that were donated by various feudal lords.

UENO ZOO: Opened back in 1882, Ueno Zoo is small but very popular with Japanese families. The main attractions are two giant pandas which were donated by the Chinese government. These two celebrities are so popular that there are always long lines to their cages on weekends, and there are all kinds of souvenirs you can buy with pandas on them. The zoo also has an aquarium and a large aviary filled with tropical plants that you can walk through, enabling you to observe birds in their natural surroundings. Open from 9:30 a.m. to 4:30 p.m. daily except Monday, the zoo charges ¥400 ($2.86) admission.

SHINOBAZU POND: This marshy pond was constructed in the 17th century so that visitors to the various shrines in the area had a nice view of water on which to rest their eyes; tea houses used to line the pond's banks. Now part of the pond has literally gone to the birds: it's a bird sanctuary. The pond is filled with lotus plants, there are small boats for rent in a corner, and there's also a small temple in the middle of the water attached to the bank with walkways.

SHITAMACHI MUSEUM: At the southeastern edge of Shinobazu Pond is the Shitamachi Museum (Shitamachi Fuzoku Shiryokan; tel. 823-7451). Shitamachi means "downtown" and refers to the area of Tokyo in which commoners used to live, mainly around Ueno and Asakusa. There's very little left of old downtown Tokyo, and with that in mind, this museum seeks to preserve for future generations a way of life that was virtually wiped out first by the great earthquake of 1923 and then by World War II.

On display is a Shitamachi tenement house that was common at the turn of the century, a long narrow building with one roof over a series of dwelling units. The only thing separating one family from another was a thin wooden wall. These were homes of the poorer people, confined to the narrow back alleys. Everyone knew everyone else's business—there were few secrets you could keep in such crowded conditions as these. The alleyways served as communal living rooms. Children played in them and families sat outside in them in the summertime to catch whatever breeze there might be. The museum also displays relics relating to the life of these commoners, including utensils, toys, costumes, and tools, most of which are not behind glass cases but are simply lying around so that you can pick them up and inspect them more closely. There are also shops set up as they might have looked back then, including a merchant's shop and a candy shop.

Admission is ¥200 ($1.43) and hours are 9:30 a.m. to 4:30 p.m. every day except Monday.

AMEYA YOKOCHO: On your way back to Ueno Station you may want to walk through Ameya Yokocho, a narrow shopping street along the west side of the elevated tracks of the Yamanote Line between Ueno and Okachimachi Stations. Originally a wholesale market for candy and snacks and later becoming a black market in U.S. Army goods after World War II, Ameya Yokocho today consists of approximately 400 shops selling discounted items of everything from fish to vegetables to handbags and clothes. Early evening is the most crowded time as workers rush through on their way home and hawkers shout out their wares. The scene retains something of the shitamachi spirit of old Tokyo.

4. Asakusa

East of Ueno is an area called Asakusa, the heart of old downtown Tokyo. It's where the merchants settled back when the Tokugawas made Edo the seat of their shogunate government. In those days merchants were considered quite low on the social ladder and were restricted as to where they could live and even what they could wear. Gradually, however, the merchants acquired wealth, and whole new forms of popular entertainment arose to occupy their time. Theaters for Kabuki and Bunraku were built and flourished in Asakusa. Ukiyoe (woodblock prints) became the latest artistic rage, with scenes depicting daily life in Edo, Kabuki stars, and beauties. To the north of Asakusa was Yoshiwara, the most famous geisha and pleasure district in the city. What a sight Asakusa must have been back then, with its carnival atmosphere of stalls, theaters, and amusements, its bustling crowdedness and liveliness.

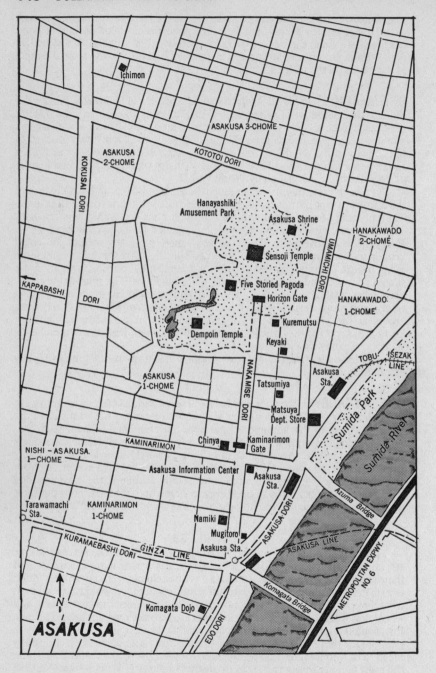

Ichimon

ASAKUSA 3-CHOME

KOTOTOI DORI

ASAKUSA
2-CHOME

KOKUSAI DORI

KAPPABASHI

DORI

Hanayashiki
Amusement Park

Asakusa Shrine

HANAKAWADO
2-CHOME

UNAMICHI DORI

Sensoji Temple

Five Storied Pagoda

Horizon Gate

HANAKAWADO
1-CHOME

Kuremutsu

Keyaki

Dempoin Temple

NAKAMISE DORI

TOBU ISEZAK
LINE

ASAKUSA
1-CHOME

Asakusa
Sta.

Sumida Park

Tatsumiya

Matsuya
Dept. Store

KAMINARIMON

Chinya

Kaminarimon
Gate

Sumida River

NISHI – ASAKUSA.
1-CHOME

Asakusa Information Center

Asakusa
Sta.

ASAKUSA DORI

Tarawamachi
Sta.

KAMINARIMON
1-CHOME

Namiki

Azuma Bridge

Mugitoro
Asakusa Sta.

ASAKUSA LINE

KURAMAEBASHI DORI GINZA LINE

METROPOLITAN EXPWY.
NO. 6

N

Komagata Dojo

Komagata Bridge

EDO DORI

ASAKUSA

Unfortunately, Asakusa has not escaped the modernization that swept through Japan over the past century, but more than anywhere else in Tokyo it still retains the charm of old downtown Edo. It still has a festive atmosphere, crowded with stalls and people. For Japanese, visting Asakusa evokes feelings of nostalgia. For tourists, it provides a glimpse of the way things were.

HOW TO GET THERE: The most dramatic way to arrive in Asakusa is by boat. Departing from Hi no de Sanbashi Pier (closest subway station: Hamamatsucho), the small ferry makes its way along the Sumida River just as in past centuries boats carried wealthy townsmen to the pleasure district of Yoshiwara. Although much of what you see along the river today is only concrete embankments, I recommend the trip because it affords a different perspective of Tokyo —barges making their way down the river, high-rise apartment buildings with laundry fluttering from balconies, warehouses, and superhighways. The boat passes under approximately a dozen bridges during the 40-minute trip, each bridge completely different. Ferryboats ply the waters between Asakusa and Hamamatsucho about every hour, but because schedules change it's best to call ahead (tel. 841-9178 or 457-7830). Cost of the ferry one way is ¥560 ($4).

If you're combining both Ueno and Asakusa into a day's trip, transportation between the two districts is served by either the Ginza subway line or a special double-decker bus. If you arrive in Asakusa via Ueno, you might want to take the boat trip back home.

If you need information on Asakusa upon arrival, stop by the **Asakusa Information Center,** located catercorner from the Kaminarimon Gate. Open from 9:30 a.m. to 8 p.m. daily, it's staffed by English-speaking volunteers.

SENSOJI TEMPLE: The most famous attraction in Asakusa, Sensoji Temple is the oldest temple in Tokyo. You'll know you've reached the main entrance when you see a huge lantern hanging from the front gate, named the Kaminarimon Gate after the god of thunder. Once inside the gate, a pedestrian lane, called Nakamise Dori, leads straight to the temple. This lane is lined on both sides with stalls selling fabrics, shoes, toys, trinkets, bags, umbrellas, Japanese dolls, clothes, fans, masks, and traditional Japanese accessories. How about a brightly decorated straight hairpin? A black hairpiece? A wooden comb? Old Japanese women dressed in kimonos shuffle slowly down the lane, bent over their canes. Perhaps there's a Buddhist monk in gray robes and straw hat, begging and thereby learning humility. At the end of the lane is another gate, and then a square filled with pigeons, and then there's the temple itself.

Founded in the seventh century, Sensoji Temple is dedicated to Kannon, the Buddhist goddess of mercy, and is therefore popularly called the Asakusa Kannon Temple. According to legend, the temple was founded after two fishermen pulled up a golden statue of Kannon from the sea. The sacred statue is still housed in the temple, carefully preserved inside three boxes, and even though it's never on display and none of the public has ever seen it, people still flock to the temple to pay their respects. In front of the temple is a large incense pot where worshippers "wash" themselves to ward off or help against illness. If, for example, you have a sore throat, be sure to rub some of the smoke over your throat for good measure. On the right side of the temple is a shrine, the Asakusa Jinja Shrine.

VICINITY OF THE TEMPLE: West of Sensoji Temple (the area to the left if you stand facing the temple) is a small but interesting area of Asakusa popular among Tokyo's older working class. In addition to tiny shops and more stalls, the area also has pubs, a rather corny amusement park called Hanayashiki (open 10 a.m. to 6 p.m.; closed Friday) and inexpensive strip shows. One of the most famous strip shows is France-za, located on a small street that leads west from Sensoji Temple. With four shows daily, beginning at 11 a.m. and the last show at 7:25 p.m., it charges a ¥2,700 ($19.29) entrance fee—and leaves nothing to the imagination. At any rate, the area of Asakusa is fun just to wander through. If you keep walking west, within ten minutes you'll reach Kappabashi Dori Street, Tokyo's wholesale district for restaurant items. Yes, this is where you can buy models of all that plastic food you've been drooling over in restaurant displays. Mugs foaming with beer, ice cream, pizza, fish, sushi—it's all here, looking like the real thing. Surely you know someone back home who would get a kick out of receiving a gift of plastic food. My favorite is one of spaghetti with a fork hovering above it, supported by a few strands of noodles. In addition to plastic food there is also kitchenware, including frying pans, knives, lunch boxes, lacquerware, and ceramics. This is where restaurant owners come to purchase items wholesale, but retail sales are made to the public as well.

If you want to return to the center of Tokyo by subway, the nearest station to Kappabashi Dori is Tawaramachi, on the Ginza Line. However, first you should take advantage of the number of interesting traditional restaurants (check the restaurant section) and bars in Asakusa. **Kuremutsu** [51], 2-2-13 Asakusa (tel. 842-0906), is a unique watering hole located just southeast of Sensoji Temple. It's actually a tiny house, tucked behind an inviting courtyard with a willow tree, a millstone covered with moss, and an entrance invitingly lit with lanterns. Inside it's like a farmhouse in the countryside, filled with farm implements, old chests, masks, cast-iron tea kettles, hibachis, and other odds and ends. Traditionally dressed to match the mood, waitresses will bring you a dish of hors d'oeuvres (*otsumami*) whether you want it or not—perhaps some roasted soybeans or a small river fish. The food is expensive, so you're best off ordering noodles for ¥550 ($3.79) or a platter of assorted sashimi for ¥2,700 ($19.29). My one beer and the otsumami came to ¥1,400 ($10). Closed Thursday, it's open the rest of the week from 4 to 10 p.m.

Ichimon [52], 3-12-6 Asakusa (tel. 875-6800), takes its name from *mon*, which was the lowest piece of currency used by the common people during the Edo Period. Ichimon means "one mon." At any rate, this establishment has a unique system whereby each customer is required to purchase ¥5,000 ($35.71) worth of mon, issued here in wooden tokens, which are then used to pay for your sake and meal. It's usually enough to cover a couple of small flasks of sake, a tray of appetizers, and a dish or two that might include sashimi, steak, *nabe* (a one-pot stew of meat and vegetables), or chicken. Mon you don't use can be exchanged for the real thing when you leave. Open every day except Sunday from 5 to 11 p.m., this place is cozy and decorated like an old farmhouse, with wooden beams, shoji screens, and koto music playing in the background. The specialty of the house is its 20 different kinds of sake. When you order some, a basket filled with sake cups is brought to your table so you can select the one you want to drink from. Nearest subway station: about a 15-minute walk from Asakusa Station.

5. Shinjuku

A few hundred years ago Shinjuku was nothing more than a fork in the road, a small community with lodgings, painted ladies of the night, and other amusements for passing travelers. Today Shinjuku is a burgeoning satellite center of skyscrapers, office buildings, shops, bars, and sex shows. Such deluxe hotels as the Keio Plaza, Century Hyatt, and Hilton International are found in

Shinjuku, as well as the famous department stores Isetan, Odakyu, Keio, and Mitsubishi.

The nucleus of Shinjuku is **Shinjuku Station**, the largest station in Japan, handling a whopping two million passengers a day. No mater what time of the day or evening you pass through Shinjuku Station you'll find it unbelievably congested, as shoppers and commuters surge through it in rivers of humanity. In fact, it can probably be argued that you haven't seen Tokyo unless you've witnessed its trains and subways during rush hour, and Shinjuku Station is the best place to see it. The most crowded time is around 8:30 a.m. when workers are rushing to their jobs. If you go to the platform of the Yamanote Line, you'll see people packed into train compartments like sardines in a can, and just when you think a compartment is filled to capacity ten more people will push their way in. On the platform, uniformed men wearing white gloves rush up and down pushing arms, legs, and umbrellas far enough in so that the doors can close. Imagine going through that every day. And yet it's not unusual for Tokyo's workers to commute two to three hours a day going to and from their jobs.

As for the station itself, I find myself lost here more than any other place in Tokyo. Nine train and subway lines pass through Shinjuku Station. There are more than 60 exits leading out of the station, made even more confusing by a maze of underground shopping arcades. Your best bet is to head toward either the east or west exit and then go above ground as soon as possible to get your bearings. On the west side of Shinjuku Station is a modern area of skyscrapers and deluxe hotels. The east side features shopping by day and a somewhat seamy but fascinating entertainment district by night.

THE WEST SIDE: In the early 1970s Shinjuku's first skyscraper appeared on the scene with the opening of the 47-story Keio Plaza Hotel. Now there are more than a dozen high-rises tickling the clouds on Shinjuku Station's west side, including office buildings and a couple more hotels. On the top floors of several of the skyscrapers are restaurants providing panoramic views of the city, while in between the buildings are open-air plazas of brick and tile. Shinjuku is Tokyo's newest business hub, an upstart rival of Tokyo's older established business districts around Marunouchi and Akasaka.

This is the area to head to if you're interested in 20th-century architecture. My favorite building is the **Sumitomo Building**, a triangular building that's hollow on the inside. Stand in the middle of the ground-floor lobby and look up— you'll see past the glass roof and more than 50 stories to the sky above. On the ground floor is Jewel Palace, with individual boutiques selling everything from gold and diamonds to pearls and coral. On the 49th to 52nd floors are coffeeshops and restaurants, most of them open from 10 a.m. to 10 p.m., providing outstanding views of the huge metropolis and on clear days of Mount Fuji beyond.

Another interesting building in Shinjuku is the Nihon Seimei Building, popularly called the **N.S. Building**. It also has a hollow interior atrium extending all the way to the top floor. The large open lobby has a 24-foot-tall Seiko clock, and the top two floors sport a number of Japanese and Western restaurants. Computer buffs will enjoy the fifth floor, called the O.A. Center, where more than a dozen computer companies have showrooms displaying all the latest in computers, telephones, printers, copiers, and software. Exhibitors include NEC, Toshiba, Epson, Fujitsu, Hitachi, and Riso, and the hours are generally from about 9:30 to 10 a.m. to 5 or 6 p.m.; closed Sunday.

Shinjuku is also the best place in Tokyo to shop for camera equipment. **Yodobashi,** on Shinjuku's west side, has probably the lowest prices around, with

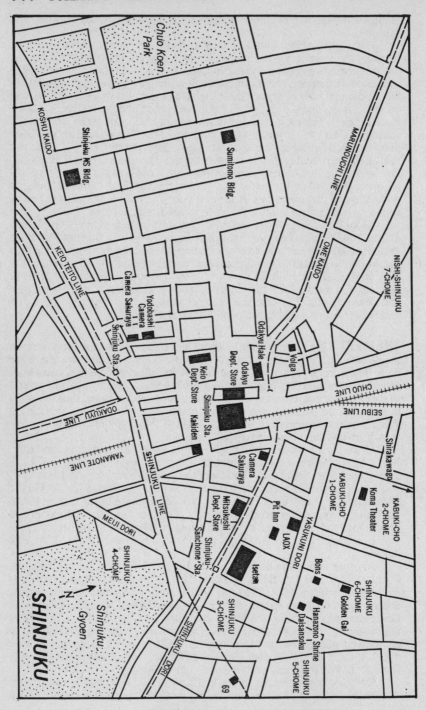

about 30,000 items on stock including every imaginable kind of camera, calculator, watch, and more. **Doi** and **Sakuraya** are other camera shops worth checking out. Refer to Section 9, shopping, in this chapter for more information.

THE EAST SIDE: With department stores and countless boutiques and shops, Shinjuku is a shopping mecca by day. Come night, however, the emphasis shifts to pleasures of a different kind. Located northeast of Shinjuku Station past Yasukuni Dori Avenue, the area of **Kabukicho** is one of the raunchiest, wildest, and most fascinating nightlife districts in all of Japan. There are pachinko pinball parlors, bars, discos, jazz clubs, pornographic shops, sex shows, and things going on you wouldn't believe. The best way to enjoy the atmosphere of this area is simply by walking around. (For specific dining and entertainment recommendations, refer to the dining section in Chapter III and the nightlife section in this chapter.)

In addition to shopping and entertainment, Shinjuku's east side is home also to **Shinjuku Gyoen**, a wonderful park that amazes me every time I go there. Its 144 acres provide changing vistas of Japanese classic gardens, as well as French- and English-style gardens. Each bend in the pathway brings a completely different garden—ponds and sculpted bushes give way to a promenade lined with sycamores which opens up into a rose garden. Cherry blossoms, azaleas, chrysanthemums, and other flowers provide splashes of color from spring through autumn, and also in the park is a greenhouse filled with tropical plants. Formerly the private estate of a feudal lord and then of the imperial family, the park is open every day except Monday from 9 a.m. to 4:30 p.m. and charges admission of ¥150 ($1.07). Although you can walk to Shinjuku Gyoen from Shinjuku Station in about 15 minutes, if you're feeling tired you can also take the Marunouchi Line to Shinjuku Gyoenmae Station.

6. Harajuku

An area south of Shinjuku on the Yamanote Line, Harajuku is one of my favorite neighborhoods in Tokyo. Sure, I'm too old to really fit in. If you're over 25 you're apt to feel ancient here, since this is Tokyo's most popular and trendy place for Japanese high school and college students. But I like Harajuku for its vibrancy, its sidewalk cafés, its street hawkers and fashionable clothing boutiques. Harajuku is where the young come to see and be seen, and there are Japanese punks, girls dressed all in black, and young couples in their fashionable best. Harajuku is also the home of Tokyo's most important Shinto shrine, as well as a woodblock print museum, an excellent souvenir shop of traditional Japanese items, and a park with wide open spaces. Formerly the training grounds of the Japanese army and later the residential area of American families during the Occupation, Harajuku was also the site of the 1964 Olympic Village.

SUNDAY ATTRACTIONS: If at all possible, come to Harajuku on a Sunday. That's when the main thoroughfare, a tree-lined venue bisecting the heart of Harajuku called Omote Sando Dori, is closed to vehicular traffic and becomes a pedestrian promenade. Young Japanese dressed to kill walk up and down holding hands (a rather new phenomenon) and in the shadows of the Olympic stadiums is where the crowds are the thickest—for that's where Sunday's most unusual attraction takes place, an open stage for anyone who wants to perform.

Every Sunday from about noon to 5 p.m., everyone from rock 'n' rollers and breakdancers to roller skaters, rock bands, and pantomime artists converges on **Omote Sando Dori** just south of Yoyogi Park to do their thing on the street. It all started in the 1970s when a group of kids got together and began dancing to music they brought with them on their portable cassette players. Gradually the number of young dancers grew, until by the mid-1980s there were as many as several hundred teenagers dancing in the street, dressed either in styles of the 1950s or in colorful circus-like clothing.

Although today the number of dancers has dwindled, the diehards are still here. Contrary to what you might imagine, however, this isn't just wild and random dancing in the street. Similar to most undertakings in Japan, this is group participation. In other words, you have to belong to one of the dancing groups. Individual dancing is out, and if by chance you simply joined in, the other dancers would regard you with astonishment and consider you slightly weird. Each group has its own cassette player, own music, own leader, and own costumes. The fun consists in simply wandering about, observing group after group. In addition to dancers, you might also come across a roller skating club putting on stunts, young boys performing on trick bicycles, a pantomimist, and rock bands. In this carnival-like atmosphere there are also stalls selling everything from fried noodles to roasted corn on the cob to a kind of Japanese omelet. In nearby Yoyogi Park, families spread their picnic lunches.

If it's the first or fourth Sunday of the month, you might also want to drop by Togo Shrine off Meiji Dori Avenue in the heart of Harajuku. A **flea market** is held here these two days of the month. Everything from old chests, dolls, and inkwells to kitchen utensils and kimonos are for sale, spread out on cloths on a sidewalk that meanders under trees to the shrine. Beginning early in the morning, it usually goes on until about 4 p.m.

Another flea market, held once a month on a Sunday but not a specific Sunday, takes place on a tree-lined pedestrian lane between the Olympic Stadiums and the NHK broadcasting building. It's mainly old clothes and secondhand kitsch. To find out when the next market is, call 226-6800.

Incidentally, you may want to begin your Sunday with brunch at L'Orangerie, Brasserie D, or Spiral Cafe, all described under the Tokyo restaurant section in Chapter III.

MEIJI JINGU SHRINE: The most venerable shrine in Tokyo, Meiji Jingu Shrine opened in 1920, dedicated to Emperor and Empress Meiji, who were instrumental in opening Japan to the outside world a hundred years ago. A fine example of dignified and refined Shinto architecture, this shrine is made of Japanese cypress topped with green copper roofs. Two large *torii* built of cypress wood more than 1,700 years old mark the entrance to the shrine on a shaded pathway lined with trees and dense woods. Almost all of the 100,000 shrubs and trees on the shrine grounds were donated by people from throughout Japan, which means that you can find flora from all over the country. Huge crows like to hang out around here, and on the way to the shrine you can stop off at the **Iris Garden**, spectacular for its irises in late June. A stream meanders through the garden, and if you follow it to its source, you'll find a spring where you can drink the cold water and refresh yourself. North of the shrine complex is the **Treasure Museum** with garments and personal effects of Emperor Meiji and the empress.

OTA MEMORIAL MUSEUM OF ART: This museum, at 1-10-10 Jingumae (tel. 403-0880), just off Omote Sando Dori not far from Harajuku Station, features the private ukiyoe (woodblock prints) collection of the late Ota Seizo. Exhibitions of the museum's 12,000 prints are changed monthly, and hours are 10:30

a.m. to 5:30 p.m. The museum is closed on Monday, New Year's, and from the 25th to the end of every month. Admission is ¥500 ($3.57).

JUST WALKING AROUND: From the north exit of Harajuku Station there's a narrow street extending east that bisects Meiji Dori Avenue. Called **Takeshita Dori Street**, it's always jam-packed with pedestrians—usually young Japanese girls—out hunting for bargains in the shops with doors flung open wide to the crowds. If you're looking for a refuge, a good place to stop for a break is a small café/flowershop located at the top of Takeshita Dori Street next to McDonald's. Called **Sterling Silver** (tel. 404-8787), this glass-enclosed café filled with plants and flowers is a pleasant place from which to contemplate the shoulder-to-shoulder stream of shoppers rushing by. Serving coffee, iced or hot chocolate, beer, and snacks, it's open from 11:30 a.m. to 11 p.m. (to 8 p.m. on Sunday and holidays).

Continuing on Takeshita Dori Street, you'll pass boutiques, record shops, shoe stores, and coffeeshops—it's all there if you can only find it through the crowds. At the end of Takeshita Dori is Meiji Dori Avenue, where you should turn right and walk until you come to the first major intersection. This crossroad of Meiji and Omote Sando Dori Streets is the heart of Harajuku. On the corner is La Foret, a building filled with trendy shoe and clothing stores.

Take a left on Omote Sando Dori, and on your right you'll soon come to the **Oriental Bazaar**, 5-9-13 Jingumae (tel. 400-3933), one of Tokyo's best places to shop for Japanese souvenirs. Three floors offer antique chinaware, old kimonos, Japanese paper products, fans, jewelry, woodblock prints, screens, and more. Shopping hours are 9:30 a.m. to 6:30 p.m. every day except Thursday. Other interesting shops along Omote Sando Dori include **Vivre 21,** open from the 11 a.m. to 8 p.m. daily and boasting boutiques showcasing fashions the designers Kenzo, Takeo Kikuchi, and Kensho Abe, and the **Hanae Mori Building,** with a shop of fashions by this famous fashion designer. In the basement of the Hanae Mori Building is the **Antique Market,** with individual stallkeepers selling china, jewelry, clothing, watches, swords, and items from the 1930s. It's open from 11 a.m. to 8 p.m. daily. Near the Hanae Mori Building is **Shu Uemura,** which features cosmetics, blush, and eyeshadow in incredible rainbow colors.

More fashionable—and expensive—stores can be found along nearby Aoyama Dori Avenue.

SIDEWALK CAFÉS: After you've seen the Sunday dancers of Harajuku, visited Meiji Jingu Shrine, and fought your way through the crowds, you're probably ready to imbibe a drink or two. Although Tokyo does not have many sidewalk cafés, Harajuku is blessed with three of them, all on Omote Sando Dori Avenue. Closest to the Meiji–Omote Sando Dori intersection is **Café de Rope**, 6-1-8 Jingumae (tel. 406-6845). The oldest outdoor café in Harajuku, this has long been a place popular with Tokyo's "beautiful people." In the wintertime a plastic tarp and heaters keep the place in operation. Beers start at ¥550 ($3.93), cocktails at ¥1,000 ($7.14), and coffee at ¥450 ($3.21). There are also cakes and sandwiches. This place is open every day from 10:30 a.m. to 11 p.m.

Farther east on Omote Sando Dori, right next to Shakey's pizza parlor, is **Café Haus Vie Ben**, 5-10-1 Jingumae (tel. 498-2655), a slick sidewalk café that opened in 1985. It features white-tiled floors and sleek black furniture. Hours are 9 a.m. to 11 p.m. If you continue walking east you'll come to **Key West Club**, 5-1-2 Jingumae (tel. 406-8606). Washed in pink inside and out, this drinking establishment is open seven days a week from 11 a.m. to midnight.

Although Harajuku is tremendously popular during the day, it's rather empty in the evenings, primarily due to zoning restrictions (if you look past the shops on Omote Sando Dori, you'll see that all of Harajuku is actually residential). There are, however, a few bars and restaurants in the area in case you feel like spending the evening in Harajuku. For more information, refer to the dining section in Chapter III and the nightlife section in this chapter.

7. Sightseeing Miscellany

In addition to the six districts described above, there are a number of other attractions, museums, and sights to lure you to other parts of Tokyo. In planning your itinerary, try to coordinate your sightseeing, shopping, and dining choices so that you cover Tokyo a section at a time. It takes more time than you think to crisscross the wide expanses of this metropolis.

TSUKIJI FISH MARKET: This huge wholesale fish market—the largest in Japan—is a must for anyone who has never seen such markets in action, and the action here starts *early*. About 3 a.m. boats begin arriving from the seas around Japan, from Africa, and even from America with enough fish to satisfy the demands of a nation where seafood reigns supreme. The king is tuna, huge and frozen, unloaded from the docks, laid out on the ground, and numbered. Wholesalers then walk up and down the rows, jotting down the numbers of the best-looking tuna. By 6 a.m. auctions are well under way, but they're not open to the general public. The wholesalers then transfer the fish they've bought to their own stalls in the market, which they subsequently sell to their regular customers, usually retail stores and restaurants.

This wholesale market is held in a cavernous hangar-like covered building, which means that you can visit it even on a dismal rainy morning. Stall after stall stretches in front of you, selling everything from the sea that the Japanese eat—salmon, shrimp, mackerel, tuna, sardine, squid, octopus, and countless varieties of fish. This market handles almost all the seafood consumed in Tokyo, which should give you at least some idea of its enormity. There's a lot going on—men in black rubber boots rushing wheelbarrows and carts through the aisles, hawkers shouting, knives chopping and slicing. This is a good place to bring your camera if you have a flash—the people working here burst with pride if you single them out for a photograph.

This is also a good place to come if you want sushi for breakfast. Beside the covered market are rows of barrack-like buildings divided into sushi restaurants and shops related to the fish trade. Sushi Dai, for example, described in the restaurant section in Chapter III, offers a *seto* for ¥880 ($6.29) and is open every day except Sunday and holidays from 5 a.m. to 1:30 p.m.

The Tsukiji Fish Market takes place every day except Sunday, holidays, New Year's, and August 15 and 16. You can find something going on anytime between 3 and 10 a.m., but the best hours are between 4 and 8 a.m. Because the floors are wet, leave your fancy shoes at the hotel. The nearest subway station is Tsukiji Station on the Hibiya Line; take the Honganji Temple exit.

As you walk the distance between the Tsukiji subway station and the fish market, you'll find yourself in a delightful district of tiny retail shops and stalls where you can buy the freshest seafood in town, plus dried fish and fish products, seaweed, vegetables, and cooking utensils. In this area and beside the wholesale market are stalls selling cheap sushi, noodles, and fish, catering mainly to buyers and sellers at the market who come for a quick breakfast. There are also a lot of pottery shops and stores that sell plastic and lacquered trays, bowls, and cups. Although they usually sell in great quantities to restaurant owners, shopkeepers will usually sell to the casual tourist as well.

HAMA RIKYU GARDEN: Not far from Tsukiji Fish Market is the Hama Rikyu Garden, making it a logical next stop on your day's itinerary. Open every day except Monday from 9 a.m. to 4:30 p.m., this garden is considered by many Tokyoites to be the best in the city. Once the site of a villa of former Tokugawa shoguns, the garden passed to the imperial family in 1871 and was opened to the public after World War II. Come here to see how the upper classes enjoyed themselves during the Edo Period. In the center of the garden is a tidal pond, spanned by three bridges draped in wisteria. There are also other ponds, a beach lined with pine trees, moon-viewing pavilions, and tea houses. Admission is ¥200 ($1.43).

OBSERVATION PLATFORMS: If you like getting an overview of things, you might want to take a trip to one of the observation decks high above the city. Most famous is **Tokyo Tower**, built in 1958 and modeled after the Eiffel Tower in Paris. Lit up at night, this 1,089-foot tower is a familiar landmark in the city's landscape but has lost its popularity over the decades with the construction of Tokyo's skyscrapers. It's open from 9 a.m. to 8 p.m. (to 6 p.m. from November to March), and the best time of year to go up is supposedly during Golden Week at the beginning of May. With many Tokyoites gone from the city and most plants and businesses closed down, the air is thought to be the cleanest and clearest at this time, affording views of the far reaches of the city—and exactly how far this city stretches will amaze you. Admission to the main observatory (492 feet high) costs ¥650 ($4.64). If you want to go farther up—to the highest place in Tokyo—the special observatory (820 feet) costs ¥450 ($3.21) more. Nearest subway station: Onarimon or Kamiyacho.

If you don't want to dish out money for a view, the **Kasumigaseki Building** at 3-2-5 Kasumigaseki, Chiyoda-ku, has a free observatory on its top floor, the 36th floor. Back when this building was constructed in the 1960s it was Japan's first skyscraper. From here you have a superb view of the Imperial Palace, the harbor, Ginza, and even Shinjuku off in the distance, and there are free binoculars you can use. On the 36th floor is also a restaurant serving such items as pizza, spaghetti, tempura, or desserts from 10:30 a.m. to 10 p.m. Nearest subway station: Toranomon.

At the other end of Tokyo is the city's tallest building, the 60-story-high **Sunshine City Building**, near Ikebukuro Station at 3-1-1 Higanshi. On the top floor is an observatory, open from 10 a.m. to 7:30 p.m. at a charge of ¥650 ($4.64). Even better is the Le Trianon Lounge on the 59th story of this building, where you can sit and relax over a cup of coffee or a cocktail while looking out over the city. Coffee, tea, and desserts are served from 10 a.m. to 5 p.m., while cocktails starting at ¥800 ($5.71) are served from 5 p.m. to 2 a.m.

VISITING A PUBLIC BATH: If you won't have any other opportunity to visit a communal bath in Japan, I suggest you go at least once to a neighborhood *sento* (public bath). Altogether Tokyo has an estimated 2,000 sento, which may sound like a lot but is nothing compared to the 20,000 the city used to have. Easily recognizable by a tall chimney and shoe lockers just inside the door, a sento usually costs about ¥250 ($1.79) and is generally open from about 4 to 11 p.m. You can buy almost everything you need at the bathhouse—soap, shampoo, towels, and even underwear.

Since there are so many public baths spread throughout the city, it's best simply to go to the one most convenient to you. If you prefer a suggestion, however, the **Azabu Juban Onsen**, at 1-5 Azabu Juban in Minato-ku (tel. 404-2610), is the one I used to go to when I lived for a while in an apartment without a tub or shower. Closed on Tuesday but open the rest of the week from 11 a.m. to 9 p.m., it has brownish water that actually comes from a hot spring. The nearest station is Roppongi, from which it's about a ten-minute walk.

The **Asakusa Kannon Onsen**, 2-7-26 Asakusa in Taito-ku (tel. 844-4141), is located just west of the Sensoji Temple described in the Asakusa section above. This one also boasts water from a hot spring and has the atmosphere of a real neighborhood bath. Closed Thursday, it opens early at 6:30 a.m. and closes at 6 p.m. The fee is also slightly higher, at ¥450 ($3.21).

TOKYO DISNEYLAND: I'm not sure why anyone coming to Japan from the United States would want to spend time visiting Tokyo Disneyland, but in case you do this one is virtually a carbon copy of the back-home versions. Here you can find the Jungle Cruise, Pirates of the Caribbean, Haunted Mansion, and Space Mountain (okay, I admit that I've been to Tokyo Disneyland three times). Opened in April 1983, this Disneyland had already had more than 40 million visitors by the end of its fourth year.

Tickets for Tokyo Disneyland can be purchased in advance at Tokyo Station near the Yaesu-guchi exit and at travel agencies, such as JTB. The Disneyland Passport, which includes entrance and use of all attractions, is ¥4,600 ($32.86) for adults, ¥4,100 ($29.29) for junior high and high school students, and ¥3,100 ($22.14) for children. Disneyland is open daily from 8 or 8:30 a.m. to 10 p.m. in summer, with slightly shorter hours in winter.

The easiest way to reach Tokyo Disneyland is via the shuttle buses that run at ten-minute intervals from Tokyo Station directly to Disneyland's front gate. The bus stop is behind the Tekko Building on the Yaesu-guchi side of Tokyo Station, and the one-way fare is ¥600 ($4.29) for adults and ¥300 ($2.14) for children.

A less expensive way to go is to take the Tozai subway line from either Nihonbashi or Otemachi Station to Urayasu Station. From Urayasu you have to walk five minutes to the Disneyland bus terminal and catch a bus that costs ¥200 ($1.43) for adults and half that for children.

WORLD'S MAGAZINE GALLERY: If you're a voracious reader of magazines and miss your favorite publications, chances are you can find them at World's Magazine Gallery, located on the mezzanine floor of the Magazine House, 3-13-10 Ginza (tel. 545-7227). Magazine House is a flashy pink-and-gray-striped building located behind the Kabukiza theater (nearest subway station: Higashi-Ginza). You can't take the magazines out of the gallery, but there are tables and chairs there as well as an adjacent coffeeshop. Altogether there are approximately 1,300 current magazines from about 50 countries, including the United States, Germany, France, England, Italy, Spain, Korea, Russia, China, and countries in Africa and South America. Publications include *The New Yorker, Foreign Affairs, Advertising Age, Billboard, Chicago, Vogue, Bazaar, House and Garden, Ellery Queen's Mystery Magazine, Dog Fancy, Teen Machine, Fly Fishing*—and all kinds of publications you never knew existed. Use of the gallery is free. It's a good place to come if you want a few quiet hours spent catching up on what's going on in the rest of the world. It's open from 10 a.m. to 7 p.m., closed on Monday.

NATIONAL FILM CENTER: If you're a fan of Japanese movies, no doubt you'll be disappointed to discover that the big box office favorites are usually imported from Hollywood. If you're interested in seeing Japanese classics, your best bets are movies shown Saturday and Sunday at the **National Museum of Modern Art**, located in Kitanomaru Koen Park. Movies include both Japanese and foreign films (some with English subtitles), and programs change often so the best thing to do is call the National Film Center (a branch of the museum) to see what's playing (tel. 561-0823) and to check the times. Admission to the movies is ¥380 ($2.71). Nearest subway station: Takebashi Station.

PACHINKO: No doubt you'll notice so-called pachinko parlors as you walk around Tokyo. Usually brightly lit and garish, they're packed with upright pinball-like machines, with row upon row of Japanese businessmen, housewives, and students sitting intently and quietly in front of their machines. Becoming popular after World War II, pachinko is a game in which ball bearings are flung into the machine, one after the other. Humans control the strength with which the ball is released, but otherwise there's very little to do. Points are amassed according to which holes the ball bearings fall into. Just ¥100 (71¢) gives you 20 ball bearings, which don't last for long. If you're good at it, you win ball bearings back, which you can subsequently trade in for food, cigarettes, watches, calculators, and the like. It's illegal to win money in Japan, but outside many pachinko parlors along back alleyways are tiny windows where you can trade in the watches, calculators, etc., that you won for cash. Police just look the other way. At any rate, there are probably more pachinko parlors in Tokyo than there are street lights, so you won't have any problems finding one.

SIGHTSEEING TOURS: Although this book is designed to make it possible for individual travelers to explore Japan on their own, your schedule might make it more advantageous to join a sightseeing tour group. Unsurprisingly, there are a number of tour operators offering group tours of Tokyo and its environs, including companies such as the **Japan Travel Bureau** (JTB, tel. 276-7777), **Japan Gray Line** (tel. 433-5745), **Odakyu Travel Service** (tel. 345-1461), and **Fujita Travel Service** (tel. 573-1417), with bookings easily made at most tourist hotels. Day tours may include such sights as Tokyo Tower, the Imperial Palace district, Asakusa Sensoji Temple, Meiji Shrine, and Ginza. Night tours may take in such things as a Japanese dinner, a visit to a Kabuki theater, and a trip to a geisha party—but keep in mind that it's very touristy. Prices for tours range from about ¥3,600 ($25.71) for a half-day tour to ¥14,200 ($101.43) for a night tour.

One tour you might consider joining because you can't do it on your own is the "Industrial Tokyo" tour offered by JTB three times a week. Plants toured may include the Japan Air Lines maintenance plant, Isuzu Motors factory, the Tokyo stock exchange, or a computer factory. The price of this tour is ¥11,000 ($78.57), including lunch.

ADDITIONAL MUSEUMS: In addition to the museums described previously in the sections on the Imperial Palace, Ginza, Ueno, and Harajuku, there are a number of other museums worth checking out if you have the time. Be sure to pick up a copy of the Japan National Tourist Organization's pamphlet *Museums and Art Galleries* for more information on museums in Tokyo and throughout Japan.

Note that most museums are closed on Monday. If Monday happens to be a national holiday, however, most museums will remain open but will close the next day—Tuesday—instead. Call beforehand to avoid disappointment.

Museums of the Arts

The **Gotoh Art Museum (Gotoh Bijutsukan)**, 3-9-25 Kaminoge, Setagaya-ku (tel. 703-0661), houses fine arts and crafts of ancient Japan, China, and other Asian countries, including calligraphy, paintings, ceramics, and lacquerware. Surrounding the museum is a garden with a tea house. Hours are 9:30 a.m. to 4:30 p.m.; closed Monday and during exhibit changes. Admission is ¥500 ($3.57). Nearest subway station: Kaminoge.

The **Hara Museum of Contemporary Art (Hara Bijutsukan)**, 4-7-25 Kita-Shinagawa, Shinagawa-ku (tel. 445-0651), is open every day except Monday from 11 a.m. to 4:45 p.m. Featuring paintings and sculpture mainly from the 1950s and 1960s by Japanese and foreign artists, this is a pleasant museum housed in a building that used to be the Hara family home. The museum holds exhibitions regularly for rising young artists. Admission: ¥500 ($3.57). The nearest station is Shinagawa.

Hatakeyama Collection, 2-20-12 Shiroganedai, Minato-ku (tel. 447-5787), is behind the garden of the Hannya-en Restaurant, a six-minute walk from Takanawadai subway station. With an emphasis on tea-ceremony ceramics and objects, it also has paintings and calligraphy, sculpture, and lacquerware from ancient Japan and China. Charging ¥500 ($3.57) admission, it's open from 10 a.m. to 5 p.m. (until 4:30 p.m. from October through March); closed Monday and the last two weeks in March, June, September, and December and the first week in January.

The **Nezu Art Museum (Nezu Bijutsukan)**, 6-5-36 Minami Aoyama, Minato-ku (tel. 400-2536), has a fine collection of Oriental art, including Chinese bronzes, Japanese calligraphy, Korean ceramics, and other artwork. The museum is surrounded by a delightful small garden with several tea houses. Hours are 9:30 a.m. to 4:30 p.m.; closed Monday, the day after a national holiday, during exhibition changes, and the whole month of August. Admission is ¥500 ($3.57) and the closest station is Omote Sando Station, from which it's about a ten-minute walk.

The **Suntory Museum of Art (Suntory Bijutsukan)** is on the 11th floor of the Suntory Building, 1-2-3 Moto-Akasaka (tel. 470-1073), only a few minutes' walk from the Akasaka-mitsuke subway station. Exhibitions change regularly and feature ceramics, kimonos, screens, glass objects, lacquerware, paintings, and prints. Closed on Monday and during exhibition changes, it's open otherwise from 10 a.m. to 5 p.m. (until 7 p.m. on Friday). That means you could begin an evening in Akasaka with a visit to this museum. Admission is ¥500 ($3.57).

Specialized Museums

Opened in 1986, the **Fukagawa Edo Museum (Fukagawa Edo Shiryokan)**, 3-3-28 Shirakawa, Koto-ku (tel. 630-8625), is a delightful museum which captures life in Tokyo during the Edo Period. It contains an entire neighborhood—11 houses, shops, and buildings which were brought here from their original locations in Fukagawa and reconstructed. Among them are shops belonging to a vegetable dealer and a fishmonger, two inns, and tenement homes. This museum is open daily from 10 a.m. to 5 p.m., and admission is ¥300 ($5.71). Nearest stations are Monzen-Nakacho or Morishita Station. From either station you can catch bus 33 going in the direction of Kiyosumi Garden; get off at Kiyosumi Teien-mae bus stop, from which it's a three-minute walk.

The **Japan Folk Crafts Museum (Nippon Mingeikan)**, 4-3-33 Komaba (tel. 467-4527), has folk art from all over Japan and includes furniture, pottery, and textiles, many dating from the Edo and Meiji eras. Crafts from other Asian and European countries are also displayed. Admission is ¥700 ($5) and hours are 10 a.m. to 5 p.m.; closed Monday. The museum is about a five-minute walk from Komaba-Todaimae Station on the Keio-Inokashira Line.

The **Furniture Museum (Kagu no Hakubutsukan)**, 3-10 Harumi, Chuo-ku (tel. 533-0098), features—as you might have guessed—old Japanese furniture. On the second floor of the JFC Building, it charges ¥200 ($1.43) and is open from 10 a.m. to 4:30 p.m.; closed Wednesday and national holidays. The closest station is Tsukiji, but from there you should take a taxi. There's also a bus from Ginza.

The **Kite Museum (Tako no Hakubutsukan)**, on the fifth floor of the Taimeiken Building at 1-12-10 Nihombashi (tel. 271-2465), has kites from Japan and other countries. Hours here are 11 a.m. to 5 p.m. (closed Sunday and national holidays), and the entrance fee is only ¥100 (71¢).

If you're interested in Japanese paper, the **Paper Museum (Kami no Hakubutsukan)**, 1-1-8 Horifune, Kita-ku (tel. 911-3545), displays products and utensils used in making Japanese paper by hand. Open from 9:30 a.m. to 4:30 p.m. (closed Monday and national holidays), it charges ¥200 ($1.43) admission and is located about a three-minute walk from Oji Station.

The **Sword Museum**, 4-25-10 Yoyogi, Shibuya-ku (tel. 379-1386), pays tribute to Japanese swords, long considered an art form in the highest degree. Sword makers were respected as masters in feudal Japan. Hours are 9 a.m. to 4 p.m.; closed Monday. Admission is ¥300 ($2.14). The nearest station is Sangubashi Station on the Odakyu Line.

The **Sumo Museum**, 1-3-28 Yokoami, Sumida-ku (tel. 622-0366), is located in the Kokugikan sumo stadium, about a minute's walk from Ryogoku Station. It shows the history of sumo since the 18th century, with portraits and mementos of past grand champions. It's open from 9:30 a.m. to 4:30 p.m., closed Saturday, Sunday, and national holidays. Admission is free, but during tournaments you must have sumo tickets to enter the stadium.

Daimyo Clock Museum, 2-1-27 Yanaka, Taito-ku (tel. 821-6913), houses 260 clocks made during the Edo Period. Only about 50 can be shown at any one time, however, and exhibitions are changed annually. Closed on Monday and from July 1 to September 30 and December 25 to January 15, it's open the rest of the time from 10 a.m. to 4 p.m. Admission is ¥300 ($2.14). It's about a ten-minute walk from Nezu Station in an interesting neighborhood filled with temples and old homes.

The **Sugino Costume Museum**, 4-6-19 Osaki, Shinagawa-ku (tel. 491-8151), exhibits clothing of Western Europe from around the 18th century, as well as clothing worn in Japan and other Asian countries. Included are kimonos, samurai outfits, and costumes worn in Noh and Kyogen plays. It's open from 10 a.m. to 4 p.m., closed Sunday and national holidays. Admission is ¥200 ($1.43). It's about a five-minute walk from Meguro Station.

8. Cultural Entertainment

To find out about current productions, Kabuki performances, and other information relating to the performing arts, check either *Tour Companion* or the *Tokyo Journal,* or contact the Tourist Information Center.

KABUKI: Among the several theaters in Tokyo with regular showings of Kabuki, **Kabukiza**, at 4-12-15 Ginza (tel. 541-3131), is the most famous and best known. Located above the Higashi-Ginza subway station, this theater has about eight or nine Kabuki productions a year, each of which lasts close to 25 days beginning between the first and third of each month (there are no shows in August). Usually there are two different programs being shown; matinees run from about 11 or 11:30 a.m. to 4 p.m., and evening performances run from 4:30 or 5 to about 9 p.m. It's considered perfectly okay to come for only part of a performance. In addition to English programs explaining the plot, which cost ¥800 ($5.71), there are also English earphones you can rent (¥650, or $4.64) that provide a running commentary on the story, the music, actors, stage properties, and other aspects of Kabuki. I strongly suggest that you either buy a program or rent earphones; it will add to your enjoyment of the play immensely.

Tickets generally range from about ¥1,800 ($12.86) to ¥12,000 ($85.71), depending on the program and the seat location. Advance tickets can be purchased at the Advance Ticket Office, to the right side of the Kabukiza's main entrance, from 10 a.m. to 6:30 p.m. Otherwise, tickets for each day's performance are placed on sale one hour before the opening of each matinee and evening performance. For more information, call 541-3131.

If you want to come for only part of a performance (say, for an hour or so), you can do so for as little as ¥600 ($4.29) to ¥800 ($5.71) if you're willing to sit up on the fourth floor. No earphones are available, but you can still buy a program. These seats are on a first-come, first-served basis.

Kabuki performances are also held several times a year at the **National Theatre of Japan**, 4-1 Hayabusacho, Chiyoda-ku (tel. 265-7411). Nearest stations are Hanzomon, Kojimachi, and Nagatacho.

NOH: Noh performances are given at a number of locations in Tokyo, with tickets generally ranging from ¥3,000 ($15) to ¥8,000 ($40). Following is a list of several Noh theaters:

Ginza Nohgakudo, on the eighth floor of the Ginza Nohgakudo Building, 6-5-15 Ginza (tel. 571-0197). Nearest station is Ginza, and it's about 100 yards from Sukiyabashi intersection toward Shimbashi.

Hosho Nohgakudo, about a five-minute walk from Suidobashi Station at 1-5-9 Hongo, Bunkyo-ku (tel. 811-4843).

Kanze Nohgakudo, 1-16-4 Shoto, Shibuya-ku (tel. 469-5241), a 15-minute walk from Shibuya Station in the area behind the Tokyu Main Department Store.

Kita Nohgakudo, 4-6-9 Kami-Osaki, Shinagawa-ku (tel. 491-7773). This theater is a ten-minute walk from the JR Meguro station toward Gajoen.

National Noh Theater (Kokuritsu Nohgakudo), 4-18-1 Sendagaya, Shibuya-ku (tel. 423-1331). Near Sendagaya Station.

Tessenkai Butai, 4-21-29 Minami Aoyama, Minato-ku (tel. 401-2285). About a five-minute walk from Omote Sando Station (take the A4 exit from the station).

Umewaka Nohgakudo, 2-6-14 Higashi-Nakano, Nakano-ku (tel. 363-7748), about a five-minute walk from Nakano Sakaue Station on the Marunouchi subway line, or a seven-minute walk from Higashi-Nakano Station on the JR Sobu Line.

Yarai Nohgakudo, 60 Yaraicho, Shinjuku-ku (tel. 268-7311). This theater is up the hill from the Yarai exit of Kagurazaka Station on the Tozai subway line.

BUNRAKU: The National Theatre of Japan (Kokuritsu Gekijo), 4-1 Hayabusacho, Chiyoda-ku (tel. 265-7411), stages about three Bunraku performances a year with two to three plays daily. Nearest stations are Kojimachi, Nagatacho, and Hanzomon.

TEA CEREMONY: Several first-class hotels in Tokyo hold tea ceremonies with instruction in English. Since they are often booked by groups, be sure to call in advance to see whether you can participate.

The **Seisei-an** is on the seventh floor of the Hotel New Otani, 4-1 Kioi-cho, Chiyoda-ku (tel. 265-1111, ext. 2567), where instruction is given on Thursday, Friday, and Saturday from 11 a.m. to noon and again from 1 to 4 p.m. Cost of the instruction is ¥1,000 ($7.14). Closest station: Yotsuya or Akasaka-mitsuke.

The **Chosho-an**, on the seventh floor of the Hotel Okura, 2-10-4 Toranomon, Minato-ku (tel. 582-0111), gives instruction anytime between 11 a.m. and noon or 1 and 5 p.m. The cost is also ¥1,000 ($7.14). Nearest subway station is Toranomon.

Toko-an is on the fourth floor of the Imperial Hotel, 1-1-1 Uchisaiwaicho, Chiyoda-ku (tel. 504-1111), close to Hibiya Station. Instruction here is from 10 a.m. to 4 p.m. daily except Sunday and holidays. The cost is ¥1,100 ($7.86).

Another place you can enjoy the tea ceremony is at **Sakura Kai**, the Tea Ceremony Service Center, 3-2-25 Shimoochiai, Shinjuku-ku (tel. 951-9043), a short walk from Mejiro Station on the Yamanote Line. Instruction is on Thursday and Friday from 11 a.m. to noon and 1 to 4 p.m. There are various fees, and you can even combine a tea ceremony with a lesson in *ikebana* (flower arranging) for ¥2,700 ($19.29).

IKEBANA: Instruction in *ikebana*—or flower arranging—is available at a number of schools in Tokyo. Information can be obtained from **Ikebana International**, on the second floor of the Shufunotomo Building, 1-6 Surugadai, Kanda (tel. 293-8188). Otherwise, one school particularly good for foreigners is the **Ichiyo School Nakano**, 4-17-5 Nakano (tel. 388-0141). It provides instruction in English at various sites around Tokyo and will give certifications. Other well-known schools include the **Sogetsuryu Ikebana School**, 7-2-21 Akasaka (tel. 408-1126), located close to Aoyama-Itchome Station, with instructions in English every Tuesday from 10 a.m. to noon for ¥3,300 ($23.57); and the **Ohararyu Ikebana School,** 5-7-17 Minami Aoyama (tel. 499-1200), close to Omote Sando Station, where you can join in lessons Monday through Friday from 10 a.m. to noon for ¥3,300 ($23.57) per lesson. Appointments must be made in advance. Flower arranging is also taught for ¥1,650 ($11.79) per lesson at **Sakura Kai**, 3-2-25 Shimoochiai, Shinjuku-ku (tel. 951-9043), described above in the tea ceremony section.

SUMO: A new sumo stadium was completed in 1985 at 1-3-28 Yokoami in Sumida-ku, just north of Ryogoku Station. Matches are held in Tokyo in January, May, and September for 15 consecutive days, beginning at around 10 a.m. and lasting until 6 p.m. The top wrestlers compete after 4 p.m. The best seats are ringside box seats, but they're bought out by companies and friends and families of sumo wrestlers. Balcony seats, which start at about ¥6,000 ($42.86), are usually available and so are bench seats, way up in the back, for ¥1,000 ($7.14). If you don't mind standing you can even get in for only ¥550 ($3.93). Sumo matches are broadcast on Japanese television as well as on the American military FEN radio station.

If no tournament is going on, you might want to visit a sumo stable to watch the wrestlers train. There are more than 30 stables in Tokyo, many of which are located in Ryogoku close to the sumo stadium. Call first to make an appointment and make sure the wrestlers are in town. Stables include **Dewanoumi Beya**, 2-3-15 Ryogoku, Sumida-ku (tel. 631-0090); **Izutsu Beya**, 2-2-7 Ryogoku, Sumida-ku (tel. 633-8920); **Kasugano Beya**, 1-7-11 Ryogoku, Sumida-ku (tel. 631-1871); and **Takasago Beya**, 1-22-5 Yanagibashi, Taito-ku (tel. 861-3210). The Tourist Information Center has a list of other stables as well.

ZAZEN: Sitting meditation is occasionally offered with instruction in English by a few temples in the Tokyo vicinity. **Eiheiji Temple,** 2-21-34 Nishi-Azabu, Minato-ku, holds a zazen every Monday from 7 to 9 p.m. and charges ¥100 (71¢). Instruction here, however, is only in Japanese. For more information, contact the Tourist Information Center. The *Japan Times* also carries announcements of zazen instruction.

ACUPUNCTURE: Although it's not in the same category as Kabuki or sumo, acupuncture can definitely be a cultural experience so I'm including it here. There are acupuncture clinics everywhere in Tokyo, and the staff of your hotel may be able to tell you of the one nearest you. If you want a specific recommendation, try **Kojimachi Rebirth**, on the second floor of the Kur House Building at 4-2-12 Kojimachi, Chiyoda-ku (tel. 262-7561). Hours here are 9:30 a.m. to 9 p.m.; closed on Sunday and holidays. First-time fee is ¥7,700 ($55) for acupuncture and ¥6,000 ($42.86) for a massage.

9. Shopping

One of the delights of being in Japan is shopping, but it's not only the tourists who go crazy shopping in Japan. The Japanese themselves are avid shoppers, and it won't take you long to become as convinced as I am that shopping is the number-one pastime in Tokyo. Women, men, couples, and even whole families go on shopping expeditions in their free time, making Sunday the most crowded shopping day of the week. With such a discriminating, knowledgeable, and enthusiastic domestic market, it's little wonder that Japanese products have earned respect in international markets around the world. Today the label "Made in Japan" is synonymous with quality, reliability, and superb craftsmanship. Japanese workers take great pride in the products they produce, whether toys, lacquerware, computers, or cars.

As for Tokyo, it's the country's showcase for everything from the latest in camera or stereo equipment to original woodblock prints. You don't have to spend a fortune shopping either. You can pick up Japanese handmade paper products or other souvenirs, for example, for a fraction of what they would cost in import shops in the United States. In Harajuku it's possible to buy a fully lined dress of the latest fashionable craze for $35, and I can't even count the number of pairs of shoes I've bought in Tokyo for a mere $14. Used cameras can be picked up for a song, reproductions of famous woodblock prints make great inexpensive gifts, and many items—from pearls to electronic video and audio equipment—can be bought tax free.

If you have only a few hours to spare for shopping in Tokyo—what can I say, I feel sorry for you!—head for either a department store or a shopping arcade. With a wide selection of goods under one roof, they're the most convenient places to shop if you can't afford to waste a single minute. Another good choice if your time is limited is the Japan Taxfree Center, with its wide range of everything from cameras to kimonos to watches and chinaware, while Oriental Bazaar is excellent for traditional Japanese items. Those of you with more time on your hands might want to explore districts in Tokyo that specialize in certain products—Akihabara, for example, for electronic equipment or Kanda for used books.

DEPARTMENT STORES: Japanese department stores are institutions in themselves. Usually enormous, well designed, and chock-full of merchandise, they have about everything you can imagine including art galleries, pet stores, rooftop playgrounds or greenhouses, travel agencies, restaurants, grocery markets, and flower shops. You could easily spend a whole day in a department store, eating, attending cultural exhibitions, planning your next vacation, and exploring the various departments. Microcosms of Japanese society, these department stores reflect the affluence of modern Japan, offering everything from a wedding kimono to fashions by the world's top designers. And one of the most wonderful aspects of the Japanese department store is its service. Sales clerks are everywhere ready to help you, and in many cases you don't even have to go to the cash register once you've made your choice. Just hand over the product along with your money to the sales clerk, who will return with your change, your purchase neatly wrapped, and an *"arigatoo gozaimashita"* (thank you very much). A day spent in a Japanese department store could spoil you for the rest of your life.

Department stores are good and convenient places to shop for traditional Japanese items, including lacquerware, china and kitchenware, trays, gift items, toys, furniture, sporting goods, shoes, cosmetics, jewelry, clothing, sweets, lingerie, belts, hats, and household goods. The basement is usually devoted to foodstuffs: fresh fish, produce, and pre-prepared snacks and dinners. Most department stores include boutiques of such famous Japanese and international fashion designers as Issey Miyake, Rei Kawakubo (whose line is called "Comme des Garçons"), Hanae Mori, Christian Dior, Calvin Klein, or Brooks Brothers, as well as a department devoted to kimonos. To find out what's where, stop by the store's information counter close to the front entrance. Many in the Ginza and Shinjuku areas have floor-by-floor guides in English.

Hours are generally 10 a.m. to 6 or 7 p.m. and since department stores close on different days of the week, you can always find several that are open, even on Sunday and holidays.

The *Tokyo Journal,* the monthly guide to what's going on in Tokyo, lists sales in department stores where you can pick up great bargains in everything from men's suits and electric goods to secondhand cameras, golf clubs, and brand-name clothing. In fact, most of the people I know living in Tokyo buy Japanese designer clothing only during these sales at department stores. You can pick up fantastic clothing at cut-rate prices—but be prepared for the crowds. Items on sale are usually on one of the top floors, with sometimes an entire floor devoted to the sale. Whenever I go to a department store I can't resist riding the escalators up and up until I finally reach the bargain floor. I've come upon sales I never knew existed and ended up buying things I never really needed, but what the heck, it's great fun anyway. The *Tokyo Journal* also lists the various exhibitions being held at department store art galleries.

Stores in Ikebukuro

If you want to visit a department store simply for the cultural experience, you might be interested in knowing that Seibu in Ikebukuro claims to be the largest department store in the world. Just imagine—there are 47 entrances to Seibu, 8,000 sales clerks, 63 restaurants, 12 floors, 31 elevators, and eight escalators. On an average weekday 190,000 shoppers pass through the store, a number that swells to 300,000 on a Sunday.

Located practically on top of Ikebukuro Station, **Seibu**, at 1-28-1 Minami Ikebukuro (tel. 981-0111), devotes two basement floors to foodstuffs alone, where you can buy everything from taco shells to octopus to seaweed. Dishes are set out so that you can nibble and sample the food as you move along, and hawkers yelling out their wares give the place a market-like atmosphere. Fast-food counters sell salads, grilled eel, chicken, sushi, and other dishes ready to eat. The rest of the floors are devoted to clothing, furniture, art galleries, kitchenware, and a thousand other things, and many of the best Japanese and Western designers have boutiques here. It's closed on Thursday.

Other department stores easily spotted from Ikebukuro Station include **Tobu** (tel. 981-2211), which is closed on Wednesday; **Mitsukoshi** (tel. 987-1111), closed on Monday; and **Parco** (tel. 981-2111), open every day.

In Ginza and Nihombashi

The fashionable district of Ginza, along with Nihombashi east of Tokyo Station, has the largest concentration of top-quality department stores in Tokyo. **Wako**, 4-5-11 Ginza (tel. 562-2111), on the corner of Ginza 4-chome Crossing, is one of the few buildings in the area to have survived World War II. Its distinctive clock tower and innovative window displays are Ginza landmarks. Closed on Sunday, it specializes in imported fashions, luxury items, and Seiko timepieces, with prices to match. Certainly one of the classiest stores around.

Also located on Ginza 4-chrome Crossing, **Mitsukoshi**, 4-6-16 Ginza (tel. 562-1111), is a branch of the famous Mitsukoshi in Nihombashi. Popular with young shoppers, it's closed on Monday. **Matsuzakaya**, 6-10-1 Ginza (tel. 572-1111), is located one block from Ginza 4-chome Crossing on Chuo Dori Avenue in the direction of Shimbashi. An older, more established mart, it was the first department store in Japan that did not require customers to take off their shoes at the entrance. It's closed on Wednesday. In the opposite direction from Ginza 4-chome Crossing, on Chuo Dori Avenue, **Matsuya**, 3-6-1 Ginza (tel. 567-1211), is one of my favorite department stores in Tokyo. It has a good selection of Japanese folkcraft items, kitchenware, and beautifully designed contemporary household goods in addition to the usual clothes and accessories. It's closed on Thursday.

Newcomers in the Ginza scene are **Printemps**, 3-2-1 Ginza (tel. 567-0077), closed on Wednesday and a branch of Paris's fashionable Au Printemps; and **Seibu** (tel. 286-0111) and **Hankyu** (tel. 575-2233), two department stores located side by side in Yurakucho between the Hibiya and Ginza subway stations, both closed on Thursday.

In Nihombashi, **Mitsukoshi**, 1-7-4 Nihombashi Muromachi (tel. 241-3311), is one of Japan's oldest department stores. First opened as a kimono shop back in the 1600s, today it has many name-brand boutiques, including Givenchy, Dunhill, Chanel, Hanae Mori, Oscar de la Renta, Christian Dior, and Tiffany. Its kimonos, by the way, are still hot items. The building itself is old, stately, and attractive, making shopping here a pleasure. It's closed on Monday. The nearest station is Mitsukoshimae, which means "In Front of Mitsukoshi."

Takashimaya, 2-4-1 Nihombashi (tel. 211-4111), provides stiff competition for Mitsukoshi, with a history just as long. Closed on Wednesday and located close to Nihombashi Station, it also has boutiques by such famous designers as Chanel, Laroche, Dunhill, Celine, Lanvin, Louis Vuitton, Gucci, Christian Dior, Issey Miyake, and Kenzo.

In Shinjuku

Isetan, 3-14-1 Shinjuku (tel. 352-1111), is a favorite among foreigners living in Tokyo. It has a good line of conservative clothing appropriate for working situations, as well as contemporary and fashionable styles. It's closed on Wednesday and is located about a five-minute walk west of Shinjuku Station on Shinjuku Dori Avenue.

Odakyu, 1-1-3 Nishi Shinjuku (tel. 342-1111), is hard to miss since it's located right above Shinjuku Station. It's closed on Thursday. Another department store right over the station is Keio, 1-1-4 Nishi Shinjuku (tel. 342-2111), which specializes in everyday products and is closed on Thursday.

MORE JAPANESE FASHION: The department stores listed above are all good places for checking the latest in fashion from Japan. A couple more places worth looking into are Parco in Shibuya and La Foret in Harajuku. **Parco**, 15-1 Udagawacho Shibuya (tel. 464-5111), a division of Seibu, is divided into three buildings called Parco 1, 2, and 3. Parco 1 and 2 are filled with designer boutiques for men and women, including such avant-garde Japanese designers and designs as Kansai, Yohji Yamamoto, Nicole, Comme des Garçons, and Issey Miyake, while Parco 3 is devoted to household goods and interiors. Open daily, Parco has two sales a year that you shouldn't miss if you're here—one in January and one in July.

Another good place to shop is **La Foret**, 1-11-6 Jingumae (tel. 475-0411), near Harajuku's main intersection of Omote Sando Dori and Meiji Dori Avenues, the most fashionable clothing store in the area. Although some of the boutiques are expensive, there are some great deals to be found here, particularly in the shops in the basement. Shops are open from 11 a.m. to 8 p.m. every day.

Not far from La Foret is **Vivre 21**, 5-10-1 Jingumae (tel. 498-2221), a sleek white building filled with fashionable boutiques selling designer clothing and jewelry. Nicole, Kenzo, Takeo Kikuchi, Jean Paul Gaultier, and Kensho Abe are just a few of the designers with concessions here, and in the basement is an interesting shop selling kitchenware and interior design products for the home and office. It's open every day from 11 a.m. to 8 p.m.

If you want to pick up some fashions that have the Japanese-designer look without the corresponding price tags, the whole area around Harajuku has hundreds of shops selling inexpensive clothing. Takeshita Dori, described in the sightseeing section on Harajuku, is lined with shops catering to young, fashion-conscious Japanese.

ARCADES AND TAX-FREE SHOPS: Shopping arcades are found in several of Tokyo's first-class hotels. While they don't offer the excitement and challenge of going out and rubbing elbows with the natives, they are convenient, sales clerks speak English, and you can be assured of top-quality merchandise. The **Imperial Hotel Arcade** is one of the best, with shops selling pearls, woodblock prints, toys, antiques, and expensive name-brand clothing like Hanae Mori. The Okura and New Otani hotels also have extensive shopping arcades.

Underground shopping arcades are found around several of Tokyo's train and subway stations, the biggest of which are Tokyo and Shinjuku stations. Serving commuters on their way home, they often have great sales and bargains on clothing, accessories, and electronics.

Another good place to shop if you're short of time are duty-free stores. To qualify, you must present your passport, whereupon you'll be issued a piece of paper which you surrender at the Customs desk when departing Japan (the Customs desk at the Narita airport is well marked, so you can't miss it). At that time you may also be requested to show the product to Customs officials.

Japan Taxfree Center, 5-8-6 Toranomon (tel. 432-4351), has seven floors of merchandise including traditional folkcrafts and electronics. Located close to Kamiyacho Station, it's open from 10 a.m. to 6 p.m. daily.

There are also tax-free stores in the **International Arcade**, 1-7-23 Uchisaiwaicho, Chiyoda-ku (tel. 501-5774), located close to the Imperial Hotel in Hibiya. Stores here are open from 10 a.m. to 6:30 p.m. daily and include merchandise from pearls and cameras to kimonos, china, woodblock prints, and electronics.

TRADITIONAL CRAFTS: If you want to shop for traditional Japanese folkcraft items, a number of stores in Tokyo offer such craftwork as fans, paper products, chinaware, lacquerware, kimonos, and bamboo products. In addition to the shops listed below, remember that department stores have crafts sections with wide selections of everything from kitchenware to lacquerware to kimonos. Also, Nakamise Dori Street (described in the section on Asakusa) is packed with stalls selling everything from wooden *geta* shoes to hairpins worn by geishas.

Even if you can't afford to buy anything, it's worth a trip to the **Japan Traditional Craft Center** (Zenkoku Dentoteki Kogeihin Senta), on the second floor of the Plaza 246 Building, 3-1-1 Minami Aoyama (tel. 403-2460). Just a three-minute walk from the Gaienmae subway station, it's located at the corner of Gaien-nishi Dori Avenue and Aoyama Dori Avenue above a Häagen-Dazs ice-cream parlor. This store is devoted to beauty in all forms of Japanese traditional crafts and is a good introduction to Japanese design. Established to publicize and distribute information on Japanese crafts, the Craft Center has permanent exhibitions as well as items for sale. There's lacquerware, ceramics, fabrics, paper products, bamboo items, dolls, writing brushes, metalwork, and more. Prices are high but rightfully so. In a corner of the shop is a video screen where you can watch the making of Japanese swords, lacquerware, woodblock prints, and other traditional crafts, and some of the displays carry explanations in English about the origin and production of the craftwork exhibited. Crafts include those of traditional design as well as those that are strikingly contemporary. Hours are 10 a.m. to 6 p.m.; closed Thursday.

About a 15-minute hike from the Craft Center is the **Oriental Bazaar**, 5-9-13 Jingumae (tel. 400-3933), located on Omote Sando Dori in Harajuku. With an Oriental-looking façade of orange and green, it's easy to spot. Although it's tourist-oriented, I've always been partial to this store and have found great bargains here in used kimonos. Open from 9:30 a.m. to 6:30 p.m. daily except Thursday, it offers three floors of souvenir and gift items, including cotton and silk kimonos, woodblock prints, paper products, fans, Japanese swords, lamps and vases, Imari chinaware, sake sets, Japanese dolls, and pearls. If you're looking for something to buy for office co-workers, neighbors, or friends, I recommend the Japanese paper wallets (good for checkbooks) in a corner of the basement. They're only ¥100 (71¢) apiece and would easily cost $4 or $5 in the United States. Other good gift buys include cardboard coasters with woodblock prints on them, chopsticks, fans, and small prints, all of which are inexpensive and easy to pack. I've taken all my foreign guests to this shop and they always leave with bags of merchandise. Luckily, this store will also ship things home for you.

In the Ginza area, **Takumi Craft Shop**, 8-4-2 Ginza (tel. 571-2017), is on Sotobori Dori Avenue, close to Hibiya and Ginza Stations. Stocking a variety of Japanese folk art, including rustic ceramics, paper products, fabrics, furniture, and lacquerware, it's open from 11 a.m. to 7 p.m. every day except Sunday. On holidays it closes early at 5:30 p.m.

Also on Sotobori Dori Avenue, but this time almost in front of Tokyo Station, is **Ishizuka**, 1-5-20 Yaesu, Chuo-ku (tel. 275-2991). Open from 9:30 a.m. to 7:30 p.m. daily except Sunday and holidays, its folkcrafts from various regions around Japan include ceramics, a wonderful selection of toys, clay idols, paper products, Japanese workers' pants (called *mompe*), products made of cherry bark, wooden dolls, chopsticks, bamboo products, and glassware. You can even buy the tiny spoon-like sticks the Japanese traditionally use for cleaning out their ears. An attractive tea room is on the second floor.

If you're in Shinjuku, head for **Bingoya** in Wakamatsucho (tel. 202-8778), located about a 15-minute walk from Akebonobashi Station (it's probably easiest to go by taxi from either Shinjuku or Akebonobashi stations). Its five floors hold toys, baskets, rustic furniture, pottery, lacquerware, and fabrics from all over Japan. Hours are 10 a.m. to 7 p.m.; closed Monday.

WOODBLOCK PRINTS: Originals and reproductions of the famous *ukiyoe* woodblock-print masters are available at **Nakazawa**, located across from the Imperial Hotel and described in the Ginza sightseeing section. Another good place to look for prints is at the **Oriental Bazaar**, listed in the traditional crafts section above.

The **Sakai Kokodo Gallery**, 2-7 Awajicho, Kanda (tel. 255-3007), specializes in originals and reproductions of works by famous ukiyoe woodblock-print masters. Claiming to be the longest-running woodblock print shop in Japan, it was opened back in 1870 in Kanda by the present owner's great-grandfather, and altogether four generations of the Sakai family have tended the store (if you're really a woodblock-print fan, you'll want to visit the Sakai family's private and excellent museum in the small town of Matsumoto in the Japan Alps). As for this shop it's open from 10 a.m. to 5 p.m. every day, except Sunday and holidays. Closest stations: Awajicho and Akihabara stations.

ART GALLERIES: Ginza has the highest concentration of art galleries in Tokyo, with shops dealing in everything from old woodblock prints to silk screens to contemporary paintings. Refer to the Ginza sightseeing section for more information regarding particular stores.

JAPANESE PAPER PRODUCTS: Folkcraft shops such as Takumi in Ginza, the Oriental Bazaar in Harajuku, and Ishizuka near Tokyo Station all have items made of Japanese paper.

For a store dealing almost exclusively in handmade Japanese paper and handcrafts from various parts of Japan, visit **Washikobo**, 1-8-10 Nishi Azabu, Minato-ku (tel. 405-1841). It's located about seven minutes on foot from

Roppongi Station on the right side of the street as you walk toward Shibuya. Open from 10 a.m. to 6 p.m. every day except Sunday and national holidays, it sells paper and cardboard boxes, paper wallets, notebooks, paper lamps, toys, and sheets of beautifully crafted paper.

If you're visiting Asakusa, you might want to stop in at **Kurodaya,** 1-2-5 Asakusa (tel. 844-7511), located right beside Kaminarimon Gate just a few minutes' walk from Asakusa Station. First opened back in 1856, it sells traditional Japanese papers, kites, papier mâché masks, boxes, and other products made of paper. It's open from 11 a.m. to 7 p.m. every day except Monday.

SWORDS: The best-known sword shop in **Tokyo, Japan Sword,** 3-8-1 Toranomon (tel. 434-4321), which also deals in sword accessories, sword guards, and kitchen cutlery, is open from 9:30 a.m. to 6 p.m.; closed Sunday and holidays. The closest stations are Toranomon and Kamiyacho.

Other places to look for swords include the Oriental Bazaar and the Tokyo Antiques Hall.

STONE LANTERNS: Some people are so enamored of the huge stone lanterns they see at shrines and landscaped gardens that they want to take one home. If that's you, a good place to go is **Ishikatsu,** 3-4-7 Minami Aoyama (tel. 401-1677). In operation since 1706, they have a catalog of various stone lanterns to choose from and they'll ship it to you. Hours are 10 a.m. to 5 p.m.; closed on Sunday and holidays. The nearest stations are Roppongi and Omote Sando, from which you should take a taxi.

JAPANESE DOLLS: Japanese dolls range from elegant creatures with delicately arranged coiffures and silk kimonos to wooden dolls called *kokeshi.* One of the biggest doll shops in Japan is **Kyugetsu,** 1-20-4 Yanagibashi, Taito-ku (tel. 861-5511). Open from 9 a.m. to 6 p.m. daily, it's located in front of Asakusabashi Station.

Yoshitoku Dolls, 1-9-14 Asakusabashi, Taito-ku (tel. 863-4419), has had a shop at this location since 1711. It sells a variety of Japanese dolls, including Hakata and kokeshi, as well as souvenirs and some antiques. It's open from 9:30 a.m. to 5:30 p.m., closed Sunday and national holidays. Nearest station: Asakusabashi Station.

FLOWER ARRANGING AND TEA CEREMONY ACCESSORIES: Tsutaya, 5-10-4 Minami Aoyama, Minato-ku (tel. 400-3815), has everything you might need for *ikebana* (flower arranging) or the Japanese tea ceremony, including vases of unusual shapes and sizes and tea whisks. Hours here are 9 a.m. to 7 p.m., closed the first and fourth Sundays of the month. Nearest station: Omote Sando.

ANTIQUES AND CURIOS: One place to go for one-stop antique shopping is **Tokyo Antique Hall,** called Komingu Kottokan in Japanese. Located at 3-9-5 Minami Ikebukuro, Toshima-ku Kanda (tel. 982-3433 or 980-8228), this building has more than 35 antique dealers' stalls. Although most articles are marked, it's okay to try bargaining. You could spend hours here, looking over furniture, ceramics, woodblock prints, jewelry, lacquerware, swords, china, hair combs, Japanese army memorabilia, kimonos and fabrics, scrolls and screens, samurai gear, clocks, watches, dolls, and other items too numerous to list. Antiques are both Japanese and Western, and dealers here work the flea markets across the country. Hours are 10 a.m. to 7 p.m. every day except Thursday, but it's best to get here before 5 p.m. because some of the stalls close down early if business is slow. The nearest station is Ikebukuro, a ten-minute walk.

One of the best-known names in fine antiques, **Mayuyama**, 2-5-9 Kyobashi, Chuo-ku (tel. 561-5146), was first established in 1905 and is one of Tokyo's oldest antique shops. A distinguished-looking stone building between Kyobashi and Takaracho, within walking distance of Tokyo Station, Mayuyama deals in ceramics and pottery from Japan, China, and Korea—at expectedly high prices. Hours are 9:30 a.m. to 6 p.m.; closed Sunday and national holidays.

Kurofune, 7-7-4 Roppongi (tel. 479-1552), is owned by an American who has made his home in Japan for more than 18 years. Located in a house about a five-minute walk from Roppongi Station, it specializes in Japanese antique furniture which has not been refinished but rather left in its original condition. The stock also includes fabrics, prints, maps, and folk art. It's open from 10 a.m. to 6 p.m., closed Sunday and national holidays.

The Gallery, 1-11-6 Akasaka (tel. 585-4816), is located close to the Hotel Okura. Run by an American woman who is very knowledgeable about Oriental curios, it is expensive but has quality antiques from Japan, China, and Korea. Open from 10 a.m. to 6 p.m. (11 a.m. to 4 p.m. on holidays), it's closed on Sunday. Nearest stations: Toranomon and Kamiyacho.

Other places to look for antiques include both the Oriental Bazaar, described above, and the **Antique Market** in the basement of the Hanae Mori Building, 3-6-1 Kita-Aoyama, Minato-ku, on Omote Sando Dori. Individual stall holders here sell china, jewelry, clothing, swords, watches, and 1930s kitsch, open from 11 a.m. to 8 p.m. daily.

FLEA MARKETS: Flea markets, of course, are also good opportunities to shop for antiques as well as for delightful junk. Don't expect to find any good buys in furniture, but you can pick up second-hand kimonos, kitchenware, small chests, dolls, household items, and odds and ends. The markets usually begin as early as 6 a.m. and last until 4 p.m. or so, but go early if you want to pick up bargains. Bargaining is expected.

Togo Shrine, described in the Harajuku section, has a flea market on the first and fourth Sundays of the month. Nearest stations are either Meiji-Jingumae or Harajuku. **Nogi Shrine**, located at Nogizaka Station, has a flea market the second Sunday of the month. In Roppongi, the steps of the **Roi Building** (closest station: Roppongi) become a market as dealers lay out their wares on the fourth Thursday and Friday of every month.

On the second and third Sundays of the month, **Hanazono Shrine**, behind the Isetan department store on Yasukuni Dori in Shinjuku, is the site of a flea market, as is the basement of the Sunshine City's **Alpha Shopping Arcade** in Ikebukuro, on the third Saturday and Sunday of every month.

INTERIOR DESIGN: The **department stores** listed above have furniture and interior design sections, of which Seibu in Ikebukuro is especially popular and well known.

My favorite is Ginza's Matsuya department store's Design Collection on the seventh floor, which displays items from around the world selected by the Japan Design Committee as examples of fine design. Included may be such goods as the Alessi teapot from Italy, Braun razors and clocks, and Porsche sunglasses.

A very good place for studying the latest in contemporary Japanese interior design is the **Axis Building**, 5-17-1 Roppongi. Altogether there are more than two dozen shops here, most devoted to high-tech interior design. The majority of the products are Japanese but there are also selected goods from the United States and Europe. Shops feature various aspects of contemporary design, from sleek and unusual lighting fixtures to textiles and linen, clocks, kitchenware, office accessories, and lacquered furniture. Most of the stores are closed on Monday, and don't forget to check out the shops in the basement. Nearest subway station is Roppongi, and the Axis Building is on your right as you walk toward Tokyo Tower.

KITCHEN- AND TABLEWARE: In addition to the department stores listed above, there are two areas in Tokyo with a number of shops filled with items related to cooking and serving. In Tsukiji along the streets stretching between Tsukiji Station and the Tsukiji Fish Market are shops selling pottery, serving trays, bowls, dishes, and lunch boxes. On Kappabashi Street near Tawaramachi subway station are many stores selling cookware, including sukiyaki pots, woks, lunch boxes, pots and pans, and disposable wooden chopsticks. Although stores in Tsukiji and Kappabashi are wholesalers selling mainly to restaurants, you're welcome to browse and purchase as well.

PLASTIC FOOD: As described in the Asakusa sightseeing section, Kappabashi near Tawaramachi subway station is also the place to go if you want to buy the plastic food you see in restaurant displays. Simply wander up and down the street—there's no mistaking stores selling plastic sushi, spaghetti, beer, and more. Buy something here for the person who has everything.

PEARLS: The first really good cultured pearl was produced back in 1913 by a Japanese man named Koichi Mikimoto. Today Mikimoto is one of the most famous names in the world of cultured pearls. The main **Mikimoto** shop is located at 4-5-5 Ginza (tel. 535-4611), not far from Ginza 4-chome Crossing. Closed on Wednesday, it's open from 10:30 a.m. to 6 p.m.

Another good place to shop for pearls is in the **Imperial Hotel Arcade** at 1-1-1 Uchisaiwaicho. Mikimoto has a branch shop here (tel. 591-5001), and there's also the **K. Uyeda** pearl shop (tel. 503-2587). In business since 1884, this shop has a wide selection of pearls in many different price ranges. **Asahi Shoten** (tel. 503-2528) is another pearl shop in the Imperial Hotel Arcade with a good selection in the modest-to-moderate price range. There are also pearl shops in the Hotel Okura shopping arcade and the International Arcade.

CLOISONNÉ: At 5-6-2 Ginza (tel. 572-2261), **Ando** has what is probably the largest selection of cloisonné in town. Opened in 1880, it's located on Harumi Dori Avenue not far from the Ginza subway station. Hours are 9 a.m. to 5:30 p.m. daily; closed Sunday and holidays.

ELECTRONICS: The largest concentration of electronic and electrical shops in Japan is in an area of Tokyo called **Akihabara**. Although you can find good deals on video and audio equipment elsewhere, Akihabara is special simply for its sheer volume. With more than 600 stores, shops, and stalls, Akihabara accounts for one-tenth of the nation's electronic and electrical appliance sales. An estimated 50,000 shoppers come here on a weekday, 100,000 per day on a weekend. It may surprise you to learn that 80% of Japan's consumer electronics market is domestic.

Even if you don't buy anything, it's great fun walking around (and if you do intend to buy something, make sure you know what it would cost back home—with the present exchange rate there are few bargains in Japanese electronic products, but you may be able to pick up something unavailable back home). Most of the stores and stalls are open-fronted, many of them are painted neon green and pink, and inside, lights are flashing, fans are blowing, washing machines are shaking and shimmying, stereos are blasting music. Salesmen yell out their wares, trying to get customers to look at their rice cookers, computers, video equipment, cassette players, TVs, calculators, and watches. This is the best place to go to see the latest models of everything electronic, an educational experience in itself.

If you purchase anything, make sure it is made for export—that is, that there are instructions in English, there's an international warranty, and it has the correct electrical connectors. All the larger shops in Akihabara have duty-free floors where the products are designed for export. Some of these shops include **Yamagiwa**, 3-13-10 Soto-Kanda (tel. 253-2111); **LAOX**, 1-2-9 Soto-Kanda (tel. 253-7111); and **Hirose Musen**, 1-10-5 Soto Kanda (tel. 255-2211). Simply look for signs saying "duty free." Good buys in Akihabara include cassette players, stereo equipment and compact disk players, watches, calculators, video equipment, and portable electronic typewriters. Be sure to bargain, and don't buy at the first place you go to. One woman I know who was looking for a portable cassette player bought it at the third shop she went to for ¥4,000 ($28.57) less than what was quoted to her at the first shop.

The easiest way to get to Akihabara is via the Yamanote Line or Keihin Tohoku Line to the JR Akihabara Station. You can also take the Hibiya subway line to Akihabara Station, but it's farther to walk. Most shops are open from about 10 a.m. to 7 p.m. daily.

If you don't have time to go to Akihabara, in Shinjuku there's a branch of **LAOX** at 3-15-16 Shinjuku (tel. 352-5611), close to the Isetan department store on Shinjuku Station's east side. It also has duty-free prices on video cameras, stereo components, compact disk players, and VCRs. In Ginza there's the **Nishi-Ginza Electric Center**, 2-1-1 Yurakucho (tel. 503-4481), located next to the International Arcade under the train tracks. Shops here sell radios, cassette players, calculators, compact disk players, and other electrical and electronic gadgets duty free. It's open every day except Sunday from 9:30 a.m. to 7 p.m.

CAMERAS: Although you can purchase cameras at many duty-free shops, including those in Akihabara, if you're really serious about photographic equipment you should make a trip to a shop dealing specifically in cameras. Shinjuku is the photographic equipment center for Tokyo, and the biggest store there is **Yodobashi Camera**, 1-11-1 Nishi Shinjuku (tel. 346-1010). Just a block west of Shinjuku Station, it ranks as one of the largest discount camera shops in the world with around 30,000 items in stock and reputedly sells approximately 500 to 600 cameras daily. In addition to cameras it also has watches, calculators, typewriters, and cassette players. Its duty-free section is on the second floor, and even though prices are marked you can bargain here. Hours are 9:30 a.m. to 8:30 p.m. daily.

Another camera shop nearby is **Doi Camera**, 1-15-4 Nishi Shinjuku (tel. 344-2310). On the east side of Shinjuku Station is another Doi Camera shop, as well as three Sakuraya camera shops.

If purchasing a new camera is too formidable an expense, you should consider buying a used camera. New models in just about everything come out so frequently in Japan that older models can be grabbed up for next to nothing. **Camera no Kimura**, 1-18-8 Nishi Ikebukuro (tel. 981-8437), is west of Ikebukuro Station and has a good selection of used cameras. It's open every day from 8 a.m. to 8 p.m. Another shop that deals in used Japanese and foreign cameras is **Matsuzakya Camera**, 1-27-34 Takanawa, Minato-ku (tel. 443-1311), about a 15-minute walk from Shinagawa Station. Hours here are 10 a.m. to 7 p.m. (only until 5 p.m. on Sunday and holidays).

RECORDS: Department stores sell records and cassettes, with the largest selection available at Seibu in Ikebukuro. The largest record shop in town, however, happens to be a branch of Seibu called **Wave**, 6-2-27 Roppongi (tel. 408-0111). This innovative store has a computerized record reference system and a comprehensive selection of records, cassettes, and videos. On the first floor are headphones where you can select from 200 of the top hits, which is one way to keep abreast of what's hot in the music industry. Come to Wave for jazz, German new wave, reggae, heavy metal, classical, vintage, or the latest in Japanese music. In the basement is Cine Vivant, a 194-seat mini-theater that shows foreign films four or five times daily for ¥1,500 ($10.71). Wave is open every day except Wednesday from 11 a.m. to 9 p.m. It's about three minutes from Roppongi Station, on the left side of the street as you walk in the direction of Shibuya.

If for some reason you're desperate for the latest U.S. releases, **Tower Records**, on the second floor of the Village 80 Building, 39-2 Udagawacho (tel. 496-3661) in Shibuya, is usually among the first places in town to get them. It's about a ten-minute walk from Shibuya Station and is open from 10 a.m. to 10 p.m. daily.

BOOKS: In addition to the bookstores listed in the Tokyo ABCs section in Chapter III, there's a whole slew of bookstores along Yasukuni Dori Avenue in Jimbocho-Kanda that no bookworm should pass up. A mecca for both new and used books, there are more than 50 bookstores here, several of which deal in books written in English. The closest station is Jimbocho.

Tuttle Book Shop, 1-3 Jimbocho, Kanda (tel. 291-7072), has a wide selection of books on Japan and the Far East written in English, as well as Japanese-language books. The Tokyo branch of a Vermont firm, it's open from 10:30 a.m. to 6:30 p.m. Monday through Friday and from 11 a.m. to 6 p.m. Saturday and national holidays. Closed on Sunday.

Kitazawa, 2-5 Jimbocho, Kanda (tel. 263-0011), has an overwhelming selection of books on Japan. This is a good place to come if you're looking for the latest books published about this country. It also has old and rare books. Hours here are 10:30 a.m. to 6:30 p.m.; closed Sunday.

Another shop in Kanda is **Ohya Shobo**, 1-1 Jimbocho, Kanda (tel. 291-0062), open from 10 a.m. to 6:30 p.m. every day except Sunday and holidays. It claims to have the largest stock of old Japanese illustrated books, woodblock prints, and maps in the world.

10. After Dark in Tokyo

By day Tokyo is arguably one of the least attractive cities in the world. A congested mass of concrete, it has too many unimaginative buildings, too many cars and people, and not enough trees and greenery.

Come dusk, however, Tokyo comes into its own. The drabness fades and Tokyo blossoms into a profusion of giant neon lights, paper lanterns, and millions of overworked Japanese out to have a good time. If you ask me, Tokyo at night is unequivocally one of the craziest cities in the world. It's a city that never gives up and never seems to sleep. The entertainment district of Roppongi, for example, is as crowded at 3 a.m. as it is at 3 p.m. Many establishments stay open until the first subways start running after 5 a.m. Whether it's jazz, reggae, gay bars, sex shows, discos, mania, or madness that you're searching for, Tokyo has it all.

To understand Tokyo's nightlife, you first have to know that there is no one center of nighttime activity. Rather, there are many nightspots spread throughout the city, each with its own atmosphere, price range, and clientele. Most famous are probably the centers of Ginza, Akasaka, Roppongi, and Shinjuku. Before visiting any of the locals suggested in this guide, be sure to walk around and absorb the atmosphere. The streets will be crowded, the neon lights will be overwhelming, and you never know what you might discover on your own.

Although there are many bars, discos, and restaurants packed with young Japanese men and women, nightlife in Japan is still pretty much a man's domain, just as it has been for centuries. At the high end of this domain are geisha bars, where highly trained women entertain by playing traditional Japanese instruments, singing, and holding witty conversations—and nothing more risqué than that. Generally speaking such places are outrageously expensive and closed to outsiders. As a foreigner you'll have little opportunity to visit such a place unless you're invited by a business associate, in which case you should consider yourself extremely fortunate.

A NOTE ON JAPANESE SYMBOLS: Many hotels, restaurants, and other establishments in Japan do not have signs showing their names in English letters. Appendix II lists the Japanese symbols for all such places appearing in this guide. Each establishment name in Japanese symbols is numbered, and the same number appears in brackets in the text following the boldfaced establishment name. For example, in the text the Osaka hotel, Hokke Club [161], is number 161 in the Japanese symbol list in Appendix II.

More common than geisha bars, and generally not quite as expensive, are the so-called hostess bars, many of which are located in Ginza and Akasaka. And what do you get at a hostess bar? A woman who will sit at your table, talk to you, pour your drinks, listen to your problems, and boost your ego. You buy her drinks as well, which is one reason the tab can be so high. Hostess bars in various forms have been a part of Japanese society for centuries. Most foreigners will probably find the cost of visiting a hostess bar not worth the price, but such places provide Japanese males with sympathetic ears and the chance to escape the world of both work and family. Men usually have their favorite hostess bar, often a small place with just enough room for regular customers. In the more exclusive hostess bars, only those with an introduction are allowed entrance. And in almost all cases, Japanese companies are picking up the tab.

At the low end of the spectrum are Tokyo's topless bars, sex shows, massage parlors, and pornography shops, with the largest concentration of such places in Shinjuku.

Keep in mind that taxis—which are seemingly everywhere during the day —suddenly become very scarce after midnight, especially on weekends. In great demand after the subways stop running, they are impossible to flag down in all entertainment districts of Tokyo, and I've had the unpleasant experience of having to wait two hours in the dead of winter before an empty taxi would finally stop to pick me up. If it's a weekend night, you should plan either to catch the last subway home or else resign yourself to staying out someplace until 2 or 3 a.m. when it becomes easier to catch a taxi. And, of course, you can also simply stay out all night until the first subways start running after 5 a.m. In the section that follows, I've listed a number of establishments that stay open until such an ungodly hour.

In addition to the establishments listed here, be sure to check the Tokyo dining section. If you're counting your yen, for example, the Japanese restaurants listed under the budget category in Chapter III are your best bet for a relatively inexpensive night out on the town. Many places serve as both eateries and watering holes, especially those that dish out skewers of yakitori.

And finally, one more thing you should be aware of is the "table charge" which many bars and cocktail lounges charge their customers. Included in the table charge is usually a small appetizer—maybe nuts, chips, or a vegetable. At any rate, the charge is usually between ¥300 ($2.14) to ¥500 ($3.57) per person. Some establishments levy a table charge only after a certain time in the evening; others may add it only if you don't order food from their menu. If you're not sure and it matters to you, be sure to ask. Some locales call it an *otsumami,* or snack charge.

GINZA: A chic and expensive shopping area by day, at night Ginza transforms itself into a dazzling entertainment district of restaurants, bars, and first-grade hostess bars. Ginza is the most sophisticated of Tokyo's nightlife districts and also one of the most expensive. So you have to exercise great caution in choosing a place in which to settle down for the evening—otherwise you might be paying for the experience for a long time to come. Ginza clubs are notorious for being ridiculously expensive, supported solely by business executives out on expense accounts. Remember that—hardly any of the Japanese businessmen you see out carousing Ginza's expensive hostess bars are paying for it out of their own pockets. The cost is simply too prohibitive, with bills running from $100 to $500 per person. Since I am not wealthy, I personally prefer Shinjuku and Roppongi to Ginza for nighttime entertainment. However, because Ginza does have some fabulous restaurants, I am including some suggestions of things to do in the Ginza area if you find yourself here after dinner. Remember, the cheapest way to absorb the atmosphere in Ginza is to simply wander about.

If you are interested in visiting a hostess bar, one in Ginza that is receptive to foreigners and not too prohibitively expensive is **Club Maiko** [53], located in the heart of Ginza on the fourth floor of the Aster Plaza Building, 7-7-6 Ginza (tel. 574-7745), on Suzuran Dori Street. The hostesses here are geisha and *maiko*, who are young women still training to be geisha. This is a small bar, consisting of a few tables and a long counter. The women here put on dancing shows, talking and sitting with customers in between performances. With its traditional music and atmosphere, this may be the closest you'll get to Japan's geisha bars. Open every night except Sunday and holidays from 6 p.m. to midnight, performances are given by the geisha four times nightly. Foreigners are charged a special package deal of ¥8,800 ($62.86), which includes entrance and show charge, snacks, and two free drinks. Additional drinks are ¥1,000 ($7.14) each.

If you're looking for a quiet place for a drink, you can't find a more subdued place than **Lupin** [54], 5-5-11 Ginza (tel. 571-0750). Located in a tiny alley behind Ketel, a German restaurant, this tiny basement bar first opened back in 1928 and has changed little over the decades. Featuring a long wooden bar and wooden booths and cabinets, it's so quiet here you can hear yourself think. As though the world of jukeboxes and stereos has passed it by, no music is ever played here, making it a good place to come if you want to talk. Open from 5 to 11 p.m. every day except Sunday and holidays, it charges from ¥1,000 ($7.14) to ¥1,650 ($11.79) for cocktails and ¥880 ($6.29) for a bottle of beer.

If you're looking for a more boisterous drinking atmosphere, I recommend **Yagura Chaya** [55], 7-2-22 Ginza (tel. 571-3494). This dining-drinking establishment is in the basement of the Riccar Building not far from the Imperial Hotel. Look for a traditional-looking restaurant with lockers just inside the door where you're supposed to deposit your shoes. Popular with businessmen, couples, and large groups, this place has the great advantage of an English menu. The food includes sashimi, yakitori, fish, oden, and pizza, so technically you could come here for both drinks and dinner. Prices are very reasonable; the average cost of most dishes is about ¥600 ($4.29), beer starts at ¥640 ($4.57) for a bottle, and sake starts at ¥380 ($2.71). Decorated with antiques and traditional craft objects, this pleasant spot is open from 5 p.m. to midnight.

Another lively watering hole is **Nanbantei**, 5-6-6 Ginza (tel. 571-5700), which is actually a chain of yakitori-ya. Open from 5 to 11:30 p.m. daily, it combines the modern with the traditional in its decor. Its à la carte menu lists skewers of pork with asparagus, Japanese mushroom, large shrimp, quail eggs, gingko nuts, and chicken meatballs, among many others, with pairs of skewers ranging from ¥450 ($3.21) to ¥770 ($5.50).

Sapporo beer is the lure of **Sapporo Lion**, 7-9-20 Ginza (tel. 571-2590). Located on Chuo Dori Avenue not far from Matsuzakaya department store, this beer hall with its mock Gothic ceiling is open daily from 11:30 a.m. to 10:30 p.m. Draft beer starts at ¥470 ($3.36), and the English menu lists snacks ranging from yakitori to salads, spaghetti, and shrimp with chili sauce.

Another beer hall, this one featuring Kirin beer, is **Kirin City**, 8-8-1 Ginza (tel. 571-9694). Open daily from 11 a.m. to 11 p.m., this relatively new and modern establishment offers beer starting at ¥450 ($3.21) and snacks that include assorted sausage, chili beans and crackers, and salads. There's also a daily lunch special available for ¥770 ($5.50).

Tokyo is filled with so-called cafébars, which are combination coffeeshops and bars popular with young Japanese women and couples. One such cafébar in Ginza is **Skyair**, 8-6-25 Ginza (tel. 571-7864), easy to find because it's on Namiki Dori Street. Open every day except Sunday and holidays from 11:30 a.m. to 2 a.m., its decor is an eclectic blend of 1950s kitsch and objects of sleek modern design. Coffee starts at ¥500 ($3.57), beer at ¥550 ($3.93), and cocktails at ¥770 ($5.50), but keep in mind that after 10 p.m. a 10% service charge will be added to your bill. This place also serves Häagen-Dazs ice cream and other desserts.

Although actually in neighboring Yurakucho, a visit to the Takarazuka theater could be part of an evening in Ginza since it's not far away. **Takarazuka Kagekidan** is a world-famous all-female troupe that stages elaborate musical revues with dancing, singing, and gorgeous costumes. The first Takarazuka troupe formed back in 1912 in a resort near Osaka and gained instant notoriety because it was all women just as Kabuki is all men. When I went to see this troupe perform I was surprised to see that the audience consisted almost exclusively of women.

Performances are held in Tokyo at the Tokyo Takarazuka Gekijo, 1-1-3 Yurakucho (tel. 591-8100), about six or seven months of the year, generally in March, April, July, August, November, and December and sometimes in June. Occasionally a performance is held in the Kabukiza theater in Higashi-Ginza. Inquire at the Tourist Information Center for more information. Tickets generally range from about ¥1,000 ($7.14) to ¥4,600 ($32.86).

And finally, if you're in Hibiya or Yurakucho, you might like to stop at the **Rainbow Lounge**, located on the 17th floor of the Imperial Hotel's main wing, 1-1-1 Uchisaiwaicho (tel. 504-1111), for a quiet drink and a view of the city lights. It's open from 11:30 a.m. to midnight and cocktails start at ¥1,200 ($8.57).

AKASAKA: Not quite as sophisticated as Ginza, Akasaka nonetheless has its share of exclusive geisha and hostess bars, hidden away behind forbidding walls and exquisite front courtyards. More accessible are the many drinking bars, cabarets, restaurants, and inexpensive holes-in-the-wall. Popular with both executive tycoons and ordinary officeworkers, as well as foreigners staying in one of Akasaka's many hotels, this district stretches from the Akasaka-mitsuke subway station along a couple of narrow streets to the Akasaka subway station and beyond.

Cocktail Lounges and a Beer Garden

Whenever I go to Akasaka I like to start out the evening with a quiet drink at **Top of Akasaka**, on the 40th floor of the Akasaka Prince Hotel, 1-2 Kioi-cho (tel. 234-1111). From here I can watch the day fade into darkness as millions of lights and neon signs twinkle on in the distance. Fancy and romantic, this cocktail lounge with the city of Tokyo as a dramatic backdrop is open daily from 5 p.m. to 2 a.m., with most drinks averaging ¥1,500 ($10.71).

If you'd rather rest your eyes on a Japanese landscape garden than neon lights, the **Garden Lounge**, across the street at the Hotel New Otani, 4-1 Kioi-cho (tel. 265-1111), looks out over a 400-year-old garden complete with waterfall, pond, bridges, and manicured bushes. Cocktails, which start at ¥1,400 ($10), are served every day from 6 to 10 p.m.

If the prices at these two places are a bit out of your range, you can still enjoy a view from the beer garden atop the **Suntory Building**, 1-2-3 Moto-Akasaka, at Akasaka-mitsuke's main intersection above the subway station. Open during the summer months from 5 to 9 p.m., its prices are similar to most beer gardens, the various sizes of foaming mugs ranging from about ¥500 ($3.57) to ¥1,000 ($7.14)

The nearest subway station for all three of these establishments is Akasaka-mitsuke.

A Nightclub

A well-known nightclub in Akasaka is **Cordon Bleu**, 6-6-4 Akasaka (tel. 582-7800 in the evening and 478-3000 before 6 p.m.). Small and intimate, this 150-seat establishment is actually a dinner theater. Former guests have included boxer Muhammad Ali and the late John Lennon. It opens at 6:30 p.m. daily, and shows are performed two times a night, featuring topless Japanese and foreign dancers and singing. Full-course dinners, including free drinks, show, and service charges, run ¥18,000 ($128.57) per person. A 10% tax will be added to your bill. There's also an hors d'oeuvre course that includes snacks, drinks, and service charge for ¥13,200 ($94.29) per person, plus a 10% tax. Closest subway station: Akasaka.

Bars

This **Henry Africa**, on the second floor of the Akasaka Ishida Building, 3-13-14 Akasaka (tel. 585-0149), is one of several Henry Africa pubs in Tokyo. Decorated in the theme of the African hunt, with elephant tusks, potted palms, and Tiffany-style lampshades, this place is very popular with young Japanese male and female officeworkers. Snacks, averaging ¥900 ($6.43) per dish, include sandwiches, tofu steak, and salads, and cocktails begin at ¥850 ($6.07). This place is open daily from 11:45 a.m. to 11:30 p.m., except on Saturday and Sunday when it's open from 6 to 11:30 p.m.

Henry Africa is just a 30-second walk from the Akasaka subway station across from the TBS Kaikan television building on Hitotsugi Street.

Another bar in Akasaka is **Chez Mirabeau**, 3-11-7 Akasaka (tel. 586-3579). With a stark interior with modern artwork decorating the walls, it's open from 11:30 a.m. to 10 p.m.; closed Sunday and holidays. Cocktails start at ¥770 ($5.50), beer at ¥550 ($3.93), and wine by the glass at ¥550 ($3.93). Western-style meals are also served, with set lunches starting at ¥770 ($5.50) and set dinners at ¥2,700 ($19.29).

ROPPONGI: Although perhaps not as well known to the outside world as Ginza and Shinjuku, Roppongi has emerged as the most fashionable and hip place to hang out for Tokyo's younger crowd. It's also a favorite with Tokyo's foreign community, including the many models in the city, businessmen, and English teachers. With more discos than any other place in town, Roppongi also has more than its fair share of jazz houses, restaurants, expatriate bars, and pubs. Some Tokyoites complain that Roppongi is too crowded, too trendy, and too commercialized, but for the casual visitor I think Roppongi offers an excellent opportunity to view what's new and hot in the capital city.

For orientation purposes, the center of Roppongi is Roppongi Crossing intersection, at the corner of which sits the garishly pink Almond Coffee Shop. The coffeeshop itself has mediocre coffee and desserts at terribly inflated prices, but the sidewalk in front of the store is the number-one meeting spot in Roppongi. If you're going to meet a friend in Roppongi, this is probably where it will be.

If you need directions, there's a conveniently located *koban* (police box) catercorner from the Almond Coffee Shop and next to the Mitsubishi Bank. They have a big map of the Roppongi area and someone is always there.

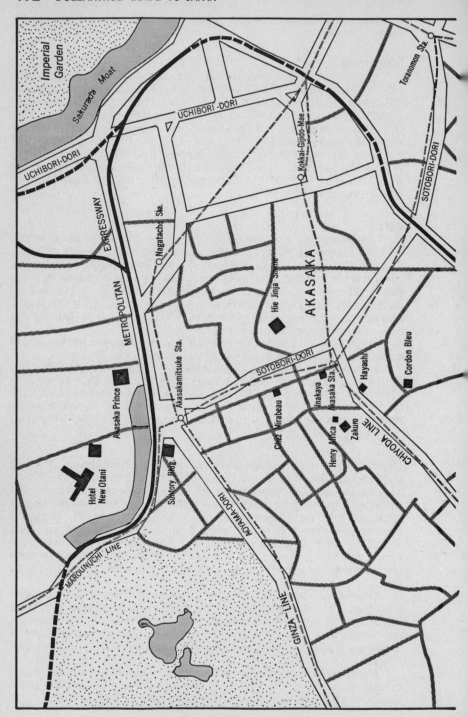

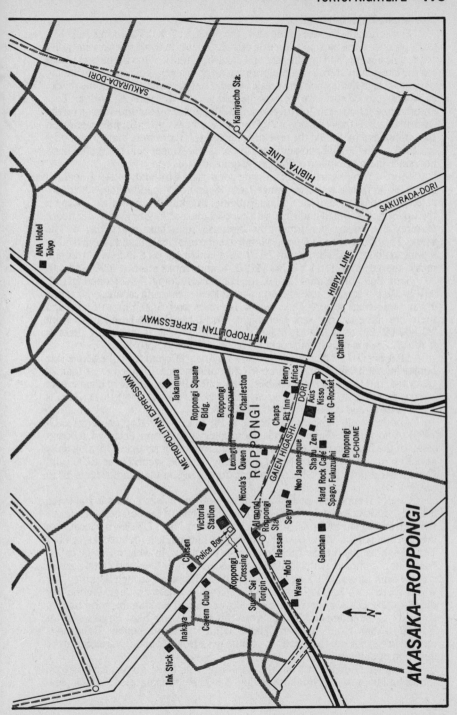

Live Music Entertainment

Presenting the newest of the new, **Ink Stick**, at 7-5-11 Roppongi (tel. 401-0429), is one of the most avant-garde establishments in town, with a steady diet of jazz, new wave, and synthesizer and electronic music. One of the best places for the latest in modern Japanese music, it attracts a very chic crowd, including personalities in the fashion and music world. I enjoy coming here for the music, as well as out of curiosity for how people will be dressed. As with all live-entertainment houses in Tokyo, check the *Tokyo Journal* for information on the current bands as they change several times a week, as well as for information on show times and prices. At the time of going to press there were plans to remodel Ink Stick, with the slight possibility of live music no longer being offered. I hope not, since there's no place in Roppongi quite like this one.

More down-to-earth and featuring good jazz, **Birdland**, 3-10-3 Roppongi (tel. 478-3456), is a welcome refuge from Roppongi's madding crowd. It's located in the basement of the Square Building, well known for its eight discos on the upper floors. Small and cozy with candles and soft lighting, this jazz house features live music performed by Japanese musicians every day of the week. The doors open at 6 p.m., with live entertainment running from 8:30 or 9 p.m. to about 1:45 a.m. (from 7:15 p.m. to midnight on Sunday). Cover and music charges here total ¥2,700 ($19.29), and drinks start at ¥900 ($6.43).

Satin Doll, on the third floor of the Haiyuza Building, 4-9-2 Roppongi (tel. 401-3080), is a comfortable and established locale featuring Japanese jazz singers and musicians seven nights a week. It's open from 5:30 p.m. to 1 a.m. and there are three or four sets each night. The table charge here ranges from ¥1,300 ($9.29) to ¥1,800 ($12.86) depending on who is appearing. Beer is ¥700 ($5), while whisky and cocktails begin at ¥770 ($5.50).

After Six, 3-13-8 Roppongi (tel. 405-7233), is different from the above jazz houses in that its musicians are imported from America. Opened more than 20 years ago, this tiny basement establishment offers live music every night except Sunday from 8 p.m. to 2 a.m. The cover charge here is ¥2,200 ($15.71), beer is ¥650 ($4.64), and cocktails start at ¥880 ($6.29).

Another well-known music house is **Pit Inn**, 3-17-7 Roppongi (tel. 585-1063). A no-frills basement establishment catering to a younger crowd, it boasts some of the finest in native and imported fusion and jazz rock. Opening daily at 6:30 p.m., its first concert is at 7:30 p.m. and the second is at 10:30 p.m. Cover charge is ¥2,700 ($19.29) and up, depending on the band. Beer is ¥550 ($3.93).

One of Roppongi's newest and most innovative jazz houses is **Bohemia**, 3-17-25 Nishi Azabu (tel. 401-8143). The brainchild of fashion designer Takeo Kikuchi and styled by British design revolutionary Nigel Coates, it's located in the basement of the Takeo Kikuchi Building, which made its debut in December 1986. High tech and eccentric, Bohemia is decorated in what might be called "airplane," complete with old airplane seats in its lower level and metal parts of a plane built into a wall. Live jazz is featured Thursday through Saturday, for which there's a ¥1,600 ($11.43) music charge. Monday through Wednesday there's a jazz DJ, for which there's no cover charge, making it a good time to come if you're interested just in what this place looks like. Drinks start at ¥1,100 ($7.86). Hours here are 7 p.m. to 2 a.m., closed Sunday. Bohemia is located in Nishi Azabu, about a ten-minute walk from Roppongi Crossing in the direction of Shibuya.

Completely different from the establishments listed above, **Lollipop**, on the second floor of the Nittaku Building, 3-8-15 Roppongi (tel. 478-0028), features a house band that plays hits from the 1960s, Motown, and twist tunes. The dance floor is small and usually crowded, and there are even mirrored disco balls hanging from the ceiling. It's open from 6 p.m. to 3 a.m. every night except Sunday when it closes earlier at midnight. There's a ¥1,600 ($11.43) cover charge, and you're required to order one food dish from the menu—mixed nuts are the cheapest at ¥660 ($4.71). Beer is ¥550 ($3.93), and the house wine is ¥650 ($4.64) a glass.

Similar to Lollipop but in business many more years, **Kento's**, in the basement of the Daini Building at 5-3-1 Roppongi (tel. 401-5755), is where enthusiasts of yesterday come to hear bands play music of the '50s and '60s. It's decorated with posters of such stars as Elvis and Connie Francis, has waiters with slicked-back hair, and even the microphones here are decades old. Although there's hardly room to dance, that doesn't stop the largely over-30 Japanese audience from doing a kind of rock 'n' roll-twist in the aisles. Open daily from 6 p.m. to 2:30 a.m. (to midnight on Sunday night), it charges ¥1,400 ($10) as a cover. Beer starts at ¥550 ($3.93), while drinks are around ¥700 ($5). If you get hungry you can order such snacks as chicken, pizza, spaghetti, sausage, salads, and a rather peculiar treat consisting of butter and raisins, all within the ¥600 ($4.29) to ¥1,000 ($7.14) price range.

Owned by the same company but with a slightly different twist, the **Cavern Club**, on the third floor of the Hoshiyo Building at 7-14-1 Roppongi (tel. 405-5223), has bands performing exclusively Beatles music. Named after the famous Cavern Club in Liverpool where the Beatles got their start, the bar is an example of how good the Japanese are at imitation. Close your eyes and you might even be inclined to think you've been transported back in time to the real thing. Extremely popular with both Japanese and foreigners, it's packed on weekends with long waiting lines, and unfortunately reservations are not possible. Filled with photos and memorabilia of the famous foursome, the Cavern Club has a ¥1,500 ($10.71) music charge plus a 10% service charge. Beer starts at ¥550 ($3.93), cocktails are ¥770 ($5.50), and such snacks as mixed pizza, various salads, pasta, and rice dishes range from ¥770 ($5.50) to ¥1,100 ($7.86). Hours here are 6 p.m. to 2:30 a.m. daily (to midnight on Sunday and holidays).

If you miss live country-and-western music, Tokyo even has that. The **Lone Star Bar Chaps**, in the basement of the Shimojo Building at 3-14-8 Roppongi (tel. 479-2136), features country music nightly from 8 p.m. to 2 a.m. (until 4 a.m. on weekends). Popular with country-and-western Japanese fans and homesick Americans, it's filled with American relics from the Wild West, including cowboy chaps, cowboy hats, wagon wheels, Union and Confederate flags, an Indian headdress, and posters of John Wayne and Ronald Reagan dressed in cowboy get-ups. Cover charge is ¥1,000 ($7.14) and beer starts at ¥650 ($4.64). A 10% tax will be added to your bill. Grub includes spare ribs, fried chicken, fish and chips (how did that slip in?), pizza, and salads.

If you like your music loud, you won't be disappointed at **Hot Co-Rocket**, 5-18-2 Roppongi (tel. 583-9409), located across from the Porsche dealership as you walk from Roppongi Crossing toward Tokyo Tower. Live reggae bands regale the crowds here, performing in front of a gigantic Jamaican flag, and there's a tiny dance floor. Cover charge is ¥1,100 ($7.86), beer is ¥550 ($3.93), and tropical drinks start at ¥770 ($5.50). It's open from 7 p.m. to 3 a.m. every night except Sunday, when it closes earlier, at midnight.

Discos

Roppongi is disco heaven, with approximately two dozen clustered in the vicinity. Since the set cover charge often includes drinks and food, they're usually the cheapest way to spend an evening.

The most famous disco building in Tokyo is the **Square Building**, at 3-10-3 Roppongi, with its eight discos on various floors. You can check them all out to see which one fits your tastes, but my favorite is **Chakras Mandala** on the seventh floor (tel. 479-5600). I realize it may not be for everyone, but the gimmick here is Filipino men dressed in drag who give three performances nightly, at 7, 9, and 11 p.m. Some of these men are beautiful, and I'll bet that if you saw them on the street you'd never guess they weren't women. Contrary to what you might think, the clientele here is fairly straight, made up mainly of Japanese men in business suits and secretaries out for an evening with office buddies. In between performances the place becomes an ordinary disco. Hours are 5 p.m. to midnight, and the cover charge of ¥3,800 ($27.14) for males and ¥3,300 ($23.57) for females includes all the drinks (excluding beer) and food you can consume. I find the buffet here better than most. On weekends and the night before a holiday the cover charge is raised ¥500 ($3.57) per person.

Also in the Square Building up on the tenth floor is **L'infini Japonesque** (tel. 423-0080), which also offers live floor shows intermixed with disco time. The dancers here are Japanese, with performances that blend a bit of the traditional with modern choreography. Both the audience and the dancers are 20 to 25 years in age, and what the dancers may lack in experience is made up for in enthusiasm. The cover charge is ¥2,200 ($15.71) and drinks start at ¥550 ($3.93). Closed on Monday, it's open the rest of the week from 6 p.m. to 2 a.m., with dancers performing at 7:30, 9:30, and 11:30 p.m.

Lexington Queen, located in the basement of the Daisan Goto Building at 3-13-14 Roppongi (tel. 401-1661), opened back in 1980 and has been swinging ever since. The list of its guests reads like a Who's Who of foreign movie and rock stars who have visited Tokyo—Stevie Wonder, Rod Stewart, Liza Minelli, Sheena Easton, Joe Cocker, Dustin Hoffman, John Denver, Jacqueline Bisset, Spandau Ballet, Duran Duran, and Jennifer Beals, to name a few. One night when I was there the two lead musicians of Wham walked in. Another night it was Duran Duran. Popular with foreign models working in Tokyo, Lexington Queen is managed by Bill Hersey who, appropriately enough, writes a gossip column for the *Weekender*. Evidently the best place to be on Halloween and New Year's if you can stand the crowds, this disco is officially open from 6 p.m. to midnight but usually doesn't shut down until 2 or 3 a.m. The cover charge of ¥3,300 ($23.57) includes free drinks and ¥1,000 ($7.14) worth of sushi. If women come before 8 p.m., they are let in for ¥2,200 ($15.71).

Not far from Lexington Queen is a new disco called **Area**, 3-8-15 Roppongi (tel. 479-3721), an appropriate name for a disco with the highest ceiling in town. Its spaciousness also belies the fact that it's actually in the basement of the Nittaku Building (the same building as Lollipop described above). This is one of the best discos for dancing and observing—there are elevated blocks for the nerviest of dancers who like showing what they can do. The lighting is good, curtains lower and rise on the dance floor, and the ceiling is mirrored. All in all, this place somehow seems a bit wilder than most, and it's popular mainly with young Japanese women. The charge here is ¥3,800 ($27.14) for females and ¥4,400 ($31.43) for males, which includes tickets for about three drinks. On Friday and Saturday and the eve before a national holiday, cover charges increase by ¥500 ($3.57). This place opens at 5 p.m.

I rather like the entrance to **Neo Japonesque**—through an inner courtyard past slinking black panthers with eyes glowing in the dark. The disco itself, however, located in the basement of the Roppongi Forum Building at 5-16-5 Roppongi (tel. 586-0050), is plainly decorated in black and white. The main attraction is laser beams, which are shot through the crowd and bounced off the walls to create a fantastic light show. Messages and designs of dots and lines are flashed against the wall. Catering to a slightly older disco crowd than the usual 20-year-olds, this place is also slightly more expensive, at ¥5,500 ($39.29) for men and ¥4,400 ($31.43) for women, which includes three free drinks. After that, drinks are ¥1,100 ($7.86) apiece. Hours are 7 p.m. to 3 a.m. daily. Note: The sign on the door says that no jeans are allowed and that men unaccompanied by women are not admitted.

Cleo Palazzi, in the basement of the Shadai Building at 3-18-2 Roppongi (tel. 586-8494), is on a back street behind the Crazy Horse. Even though this place is open daily from 9 p.m. to 5 a.m. it doesn't start hopping until after midnight. In other words, this is where people end up after they've been partying their way through Roppongi. A very narrow place, it doesn't look like there's room to do any dancing at all, but if it gets too crowded the unconcerned clientele simply dances on the counter and the tables. A slick establishment with walls of black marble, it charges ¥2,200 ($15.71) for both men and women, which includes three tickets which can be used for either drinks or food. When your tickets have run out, you can purchase two more for ¥1,100 ($7.86), which will buy you two more drinks. Food includes soups, pizza, sandwiches, and that all-time favorite, raisin-butter. Sorry fellows—parties of men only are not admitted.

Bars

Although popular nightspots in Tokyo seem to come and go with both the brilliancy and durability of a shooting star, it's worth mentioning that the hottest place this moment seems to be **Déjàvu**, 3-15-24 Roppongi (tel. 403-8777). Some people find the chaotic and colorful walls gaudy, others find them interesting, but everyone seems to be trying to get into this small place—they'll even line up outside and wait. There's no cover charge, and most drinks are around ¥1,000 ($7.14). It's open Monday through Saturday from 8 p.m. to 4 a.m., and the clientele is mainly foreign.

Much larger is **Paradiso**, 3-13-12 Roppongi (tel. 478-4211), located in the basement of a building next to Lexington Queen disco. Popular, chic, and very avant garde, it goes on and on like some underground cavern. It closes early on Sunday at 11:30 p.m. but is open the rest of the week from 7 p.m. to 4 a.m. It charges a ¥1,000 ($7.14) table charge, but for some reason if you want to sit at one of the counters it's more expensive at ¥2,200 ($15.71). Cocktails start at ¥1,000 ($7.14). Good for people watching, but expensive.

Located in the same building as Ink Stick and run by the same company, the **Mint Bar**, at 7-5-11 Roppongi (tel. 403-1537), is a small cocktail bar featuring some original cocktails. With a cool red-and-gray interior, some of its drinks are green. Try the Mint Bar, which consists of tequila, green mint, and lemon juice. Open daily from 7 p.m. to 4 a.m., it charges an ¥1,800 ($12.86) table charge, which includes one drink. Drinks thereafter are ¥1,000 ($7.14) each.

Red Shoes, located in the basement of Azabu Palace at 2-25-18 Nishi Azabu (tel. 499-4319), is a pleasant bar located on the right side of the street as you walk from Roppongi Crossing toward Shibuya. Its decor is one of my favorites—sleek, with modern lamps, red walls, stark black pillars, and tabletops streaked with white paint in imitation marble. The music, provided by a jukebox, is at a low enough decibel that you can actually carry on a conversation. The table charge here is ¥650 ($4.64), and most drinks range from ¥1,000 ($7.14) to ¥1,300 ($9.29). It's open from 7 p.m. to 7 a.m. daily.

Similar to its counterpart in Akasaka, **Henry Africa**, at 3-15-23 Roppongi (tel. 405-9868), is devoted to the spirit of the hunt and even has a real rhinoceros head, purchased in Hong Kong. The first of the Henry Africa chain bars (there are now four), it's open from 6 p.m. until 2 a.m. Monday through Thursday, until 4 a.m. on Friday and Saturday, and until 11:30 p.m. on Sunday and holidays. Popcorn is served free, there's no table charge, and drinks start at ¥800 ($5.71).

Charleston, 3-8-11 Roppongi (tel. 402-0372), has had its ups and downs in the years it's been open. Starting out as a hip place filled with foreign models, it now has a clientele and corresponding atmosphere that is different every time I've come here. Sometimes it's filled with U.S. military men on leave, sometimes with foreign businessmen dressed in suits, and sometimes with characters that must have dragged themselves up from the deep. At any rate, it's almost always filled with men, which may be just what you're looking for, but the recent opening of Déjàvu has given Charleston some pretty tough competition and has stolen away much of its clientele. Who knows, we may be witnessing the demise of one of Roppongi's oldest establishments. Hours are 6 p.m. to 6 a.m. daily. There's no cover charge, and cocktails start at ¥770 ($5.50).

Run by an Australian woman who knows almost all of her customers by name, **Maggie's Revenge**, at 3-8-12 Roppongi (tel. 479-1096), is another expatriate bar which is also popular with the Japanese. There's live music here every night, usually provided by a guitar or piano soloist. Sometimes the music's good, sometimes not—you take your chances, but since the music charge is only ¥660 ($4.71), what the heck. Open from 6:30 p.m. to 3 a.m. every day except Sunday, Maggie's charges ¥660 ($4.71) for its smallest beer and ¥880 ($6.29) for most cocktails. It also has a good selection of liqueurs, brandy, and champagne.

For a bit of old Germany right in the heart of Tokyo, pay a visit to **Ex**, 7-7-6 Roppongi (tel. 408-5487). Its name, appropriately enough, means "bottoms up," and although this is primarily a beer-drinking establishment, owner Horst serves hearty helpings of German food. There's no menu so you just have to ask Horst what's cooking, but common dishes are schnitzel, various kinds of wurst, boiled ribs of pork, sauerkraut, and fried potatoes. Ex is a tiny place, just a half-circle of a bar with enough seating for 15 people, but it's usually packed with German businessmen and expatriates who don't mind standing to drink their favorite brand of German beer. Eating is usually done good-naturedly in shifts. Hanging from the ceiling and on the walls are such German paraphernalia as beer mugs, soccer pennants, and photos of German celebrities who have visited Ex. A meal and beer here will cost an average of ¥3,000 ($21.43) to ¥4,000 ($28.57), and the hours are 5 p.m. to 2 a.m.; closed Sunday and holidays. The nearest subway station is Roppongi, from which it's about a five-minute walk.

If you like your music loud, the **Hard Rock Café**, at 5-4-20 Roppongi (tel. 408-7018), is the place for you. Easily recognizable by Godzilla scaling an outside wall, the inside looks like a modern Yuppie version of the local hamburger hangout joint. Cocktails start at ¥880 ($6.29), and the food includes pizza, burgers, and fries. Hours are 4 p.m. to 2 a.m.

A very civilized yet casual meeting place is **Inter-National Station**, 6-1-5 Roppongi (tel. 423-4667), located on the diagonal street down from Almond Coffee Shop on the right side (across from With disco). The owner, Hiro, speaks English and serves as the amiable bartender. There are little gadgets and toys to play with if you don't feel like talking, and the music is at a level that allows for conversation if you do. You can come here as a single female and not feel weird. Closed on Sunday, it's open from 6 p.m. to 2 a.m. every night except Friday and Saturday, when it remains open until 6 p.m. Beer starts at ¥700 ($5), and the extensive cocktail selections start at ¥880 ($6.29).

SHINJUKU: Northeast of Shinjuku is an area called Kabuki-cho, which undoubtedly has the craziest nightlife in all of Tokyo. A world of its own, it's sleazy, chaotic, crowded, vibrant, and safe—block after block of strip joints, massage parlors, pornography shops, peep shows, bars, restaurants, and lots of drunk Japanese men. I wouldn't be surprised to hear that (with the possible exception of Munich's Oktoberfest) there are more drunk people per square meter in Shinjuku than anywhere else in the world.

Shinjuku's primary night hot spot is called **Kabuki-cho** but it has nothing to do with Kabuki. Apparently at one time there was a plan to bring some culture to the area by introducing a Kabuki theater. The plan never materialized but the name stuck. To the east of Kabuki-cho is a smaller district called "Goruden Gai," which is pronounced "Golden Guy." It's a neighborhood of tiny alleyways leading past even tinier bars, each consisting of just a counter and a few chairs. Closed to outsiders, these bars cater to regular customers. On hot summer evenings the "mama-san" of these bars sit outside on stools and fan themselves, soft red lights melting out of the open doorways. Things aren't as they appear, however. These aren't brothels, they are simply bars, and the mamasan—well, more likely than not they're men instead of women.

Unfortunately, Goruden Gai sits on such expensive land that many of the bar owners are being forced to sell their shops. Some of them are already boarded up, awaiting land developers who are itching to build a high-rise. It's a shame, because this tiny neighborhood is one of the most fascinating in all of Tokyo. If you feel like a drink, the most accessible establishment in the area is **Bon's**, 1-1-10 Kabuki-cho (tel. 209-6334). It's located on the very eastern edge of Goruden Gai near Hanazono Shrine. Open from 6 p.m. to 5 a.m. every day except Sunday and holidays, when it closes at 2 a.m., it boasts a Mickey Mouse collection behind a glass case. Drinks are under ¥1,000 ($7.14).

Even farther east is Shinjuku 2-chome, officially recognized as the gay bar district of Shinjuku. It's here that I was once taken to a host bar featuring young men in crotchless pants. Strangely enough, the clientele included both gay men and groups of young, giggling office girls. The place has since closed down, but Shinjuku is riddled with places bordering on the absurd.

The best thing to do in Shinjuku is simply walk around. In the glow of neon light, you'll pass everything from smoke-filled restaurants to hawkers trying to get you to step inside so they can part you from your money. If you're looking for strip joints, topless or bottomless coffeeshops, peep shows, or pornography shops, I leave you to your own devices, but you certainly won't have any problems finding them. In Kabuki-cho alone there are an estimated 200 sex businesses in operation, including so-called Turkish baths. A Turkish bath is a bathhouse where women are available for sex, usually at a cost of around ¥25,000 ($178.57) to ¥30,000 ($214.29). Although prostitution is illegal in Japan, everyone seems to ignore what goes on behind closed doors.

In 1985, however, a new law went into effect stipulating that sex-related businesses must close by midnight. Before then Shinjuku's bright lights flamed until the crack of dawn and about 400,000 people visited Kabuki-cho nightly. Now things are closing up early and businesses are complaining about losing customers. Whether the law will continue to be enforced is anybody's guess.

A word for women traveling by themselves—forgo the experience of Shinjuku. Although you're relatively safe here with so many people milling about, you won't feel comfortable with so many inebriated fellows stumbling around. If there are two of you, however, you'll be okay. I took my mother to Kabuki-cho for a spin around the neon and we escaped relatively unscathed.

Besides walking around and dining in Shinjuku (check the Tokyo dining section in Chapter III), you can also hear music and visit inexpensive drinking establishments. **Shinjuku Pit Inn**, 3-16-4 Shinjuku (tel. 354-2024), is one of Tokyo's most famous jazz, fusion, and blues clubs, and features both Japanese and foreign musicians. An institution for more than 20 years, this basement locale with exposed pipes and bare concrete walls places more emphasis on good music than on atmosphere. There are three programs daily, at 11:30 a.m., 2:30 p.m., and 7:30 p.m., making it a great place to stop for a bit of music in the middle of the day. Prices range from ¥880 ($6.29) for the 11:30 a.m. show—¥1,400 ($10) on weekends —to ¥2,700 ($19.29) and up for the evening show and include one drink. After that all drinks cost ¥450 ($3.21) for coffee or beer. Since only a few snacks (like potato chips and sandwiches) are available, eat before you come.

If you're young and don't have much money, head for **Irohanihoheto**, 3-15-15 Shinjuku (tel. 359-1682), located on Yasukuni Dori Avenue next to Isetan Kaikan on the sixth floor. Described earlier in the budget category of restaurants in Chapter III, its draft beer starts at ¥380 ($2.71) and most food items are less than ¥450 ($3.21).

Although most of the night action in Shinjuku is east of the station, the west side also has an area of inexpensive restaurants and bars. Try **Volga** [56], 1-4 Nishi Shinjuku (tel. 342-4996), an ivy-covered two-story brick building on the second alley behind the Odakyu-Halc department store. A yakitori-ya, it has an open grill facing the street. Open from 5 to 11 p.m. every night except Sunday, this smoky and packed drinking hall is typical of older establishments across the country. Rooms are tiny and simply decorated with wooden tables and benches, and the clientele is middle-aged. Very Japanese, it charges ¥520 ($3.71) for a beer.

If you feel like dancing, try **Daisansoku** [57], 5-17-6 Shinjuku (tel. 207-6953). It's located in the basement of the Hanazono Building just off Yasukuni Dori Avenue near the pathway of stone lanterns leading to Hanazono Shrine.

Rather bare in decor but filled with colorful characters, it's open weekends only from 7 p.m. to 3 a.m. The ¥2,700 ($19.29) cover gets you three drinks' worth of tickets.

After midnight foreigners in Shinjuku gravitate toward **69**, located in the basement of the Daini Seiko Building at 2-18-5 Shinjuku (tel. 341-6358). In the heart of the gay district, the clientele here is mostly heterosexual as far as I can tell. Playing primarily reggae music, this dive is tiny, and often so packed it reminds me of the Yamanote Line during rush hour. It usually has a healthy mix of both foreigners and Japanese, with an atmosphere unlike any other place in Tokyo. Hours are 6 p.m. until 3 a.m.

After 69 closes, many who refuse to call it quits migrate around the corner to **New Sazae**, 2-18-5 Shinjuku (tel. 354-1745), located on the second floor of the Ishikawa Building. It's open from 10 p.m. to 6 a.m. Your first drink here will cost you ¥750 ($5.36), except on Saturday and the eve before a national holiday, when the first drink costs ¥1,000 ($7.14). Thereafter drinks cost ¥550 ($3.93). The crowd is a bit rowdy, but if you get this far you're probably where you belong.

HARAJUKU: One of the most popular districts among young Japanese by day, Harajuku doesn't have a nightlife district because of the city zoning laws. There are a few places scattered through the area, however, that are good alternatives if you don't like the crowds or the commercialism of Tokyo's nightlife districts.

Oh God, 6-7-18 Jingumae (tel. 406-3206), is one of the best places to go if you find yourself in Harajuku after nightfall. Located at the end of an alley behind the Café de Rope, this mellow, dimly lit bar uses Japanese umbrellas as lampshades, giving it an Oriental flavor. Open from 6 p.m. to 6 a.m. daily, it shows foreign films every night beginning at 6 p.m. and there's no charge. I've seen everything from James Bond to Fassbinder to grade B movies here. Drinks start at ¥700 ($5). A plus here is a pool table.

Upstairs on the second floor of the same building as Oh God is **Café la Bohème** (tel. 400-3406). As you'd expect, the atmosphere is rather Bohemian, with lots of plants, ceiling fans, antiques, and Tiffany-style lampshades. This bar-restaurant has a long cocktail list—most drinks cost around ¥1,000 ($7.14) —and serves inexpensive pizza, pastas, and salads. It's open seven days a week from 11:30 a.m. to 5 a.m.

Located on Meiji Dori Avenue in the direction of Shibuya, **Crocodile**, 6-18-8 Jingumae (tel. 499-5205), describes itself as a casual rock 'n' roll club with live bands ranging from rock to blues to jazz-fusion, reggae, and experimental. With an interesting interior and good atmosphere, it opens at 6 p.m. with live music played from around 8 p.m. to midnight daily. The cover charge usually ranges from about ¥1,500 ($10.71) to ¥2,500 ($17.86).

About a ten-minute walk from Harajuku and not far from the Omote Sando subway station, **Tokio**, at 5-9-12 Minami Aoyama (tel. 407-1085), is one of the places to be seen if you're a young foreign model working in Tokyo. Although I find the place a bit snobbish and the expressions of perpetual boredom emanating from some of the models a bit much, it's an interesting enough place to go once in your life. Hours are 6 p.m. to 5 a.m. daily, and the cover charge of ¥3,300 ($23.57) includes free drinks.

There's a small dance floor, but the best thing about this place is its video room, where an American movie is shown every night beginning at 7:30 p.m.

SHIBAURA: Close to Tokyo Bay near Tamachi JR Station, Shibaura is an area of canals and warehouses. In the past few years, it has also gained a reputation as Tokyo's newest nightspot. Land prices are cheaper here and there's room to spread out, and even though only a few brave souls have opened up locales, Shibaura may be the place to watch in the future. **Ink Stick**, 2-2-20 Shibaura (tel. 798-3921), is a sister to the older Ink Stick in Roppongi and was one of the first businesses to set up shop in Shibaura. Taking over a warehouse that used to store produce, Ink Stick is empty and spacious, reminding me somehow of a school gymnasium. The music here is rock, new wave, electronic, and synthesizer, with a ¥2,000 ($14.29) to ¥5,500 ($39.29) admission charged when there's a live band. On nights when there's no live music, Ink Stick is a disco and charges ¥2,700 ($19.29) at the door. Drinks are separate and average ¥800 ($5.71). Hours are from 6 to 11:30 p.m. daily.

On your way to or from Ink Stick you might like to stop off for a meal or drink at one of the two establishments right next door. **Tango** (tel. 798-1311) opened in 1986 in a redecorated tin warehouse. Serving Spanish and Andalusian cuisine, it offers daily specials ranging from ¥1,000 ($7.14) to ¥2,000 ($14.29), which are usually fresh seafood. The menu lists paella, ratatouille, sole, grilled fish, and lamb ragoût. Large windows reveal a canal with tugboats moored alongside. It's open every day from 6 p.m. to 4 a.m. (last order is at 3 a.m.), and it's best to make a reservation.

Across the street is **Venice** (tel. 452-3009), which offers the plus of outdoor seating beside another canal. Not exactly Venice, but it is one of the few places in Tokyo where you can sit outside. It's open Sunday through Thursday from 10 a.m. to 2 p.m. and again from 5 p.m. to midnight, while on Friday and Saturday it's open only in the evenings from 5 p.m. to 2 a.m. You can have a meal—mainly seafood, with most entrées less than ¥2,400 ($17.14)— or just drop by for a cocktail. On Monday, Wednesday, and Friday, Venice offers a one-hour cruise on the canals in its own boat for ¥2,700 ($19.29) per person (which includes one drink), for which you should make a reservation.

NIGHTLIFE MISCELLANY: There are a number of organized **evening tours** which take in such activities as Kabuki or a geisha party (see the description in the Tokyo sightseeing sections). If your time is limited you might be interested in such a tour, though be warned that they are very tourist-oriented. Prices range from about ¥6,400 ($45.71) to ¥14,200 ($101.43).

If you're here in the summer months, a lovely place to go for either a meal or drinks is the **Hanezawa Beer Garden**, 3-12-15 Hiro, Shibuya-ku (tel. 400-6500). An outdoor beer garden spread under paper lanterns and trees, this pleasantly traditional-looking place is open from 5 to 9:30 p.m. daily from June to September. A mug of foaming beer starts at ¥550 ($3.93), and such meals as sukiyaki, shabu-shabu, and Mongolian barbecue can be cooked at your table for ¥2,700 ($19.29) to ¥4,400 ($31.43) per person. Note that if you want shabu-shabu or sukiyaki, however, you should notify the restaurant the day before. The nearest station is Ebisu, from which you should take a taxi.

Finally, word should be mentioned here about Tokyo's so-called **love hotels**. Usually found close to large entertainment districts and along major highways, such hotels do not provide sexual services themselves, but rather offer rooms for rent by the hour to lovers. Altogether there are an estimated 35,000 such love hotels in Japan, usually gaudy structures shaped like ocean liners or castles and offering such extras as rotating beds or mirrored walls. The most famous love hotel in Tokyo is the Meguro Emperor, a white castle with turrets that resembles Cinderella's castle at Disneyland. Located beside a river not far from Meguro Station at 2-1 Shimo-Meguro (tel. 494-1211), its rooms are all individually designed and may feature such appurtenances as video equipment so you can film yourself, waterfalls, and all kinds of gadgetry. A quarter of a century old, this love hotel costs from ¥8,300 ($59) to ¥22,000 ($157) for three hours until 6 p.m. After 6 p.m., rooms start at ¥12,000 ($86).

Overnight stays begin at ¥16,500 ($118). Highly recommended for married couples—after all, how many people can tell their grandchildren they stayed at the Meguro Emperor?

Chapter V

EXPLORING THE ENVIRONS OF TOKYO

1. Kamakura
2. Nikko
3. Mashiko
4. Yokohama
5. Kawasaki
6. Mt. Fuji
7. Hakone
8. The Izu Peninsula

IF YOUR STAY IN TOKYO is long enough you should consider taking excursions to some of the sights in the vicinity. Kamakura and Nikko, for example, rank as two of the most important historical sites in Japan, while the Fuji-Hakone-Izu National Park serves as a huge recreational playground for the residents of Tokyo. The Tourist Information Center has a color brochure called *Side Trips from Tokyo* with information on Kamakura, Nikko, Hakone, and the Mount Fuji area. The T.I.C. also has a map of Tokyo's vicinity.

1. Kamakura

If you take only one trip to the environs of Tokyo, it should be to Kamakura, especially if you're unable to include the ancient capitals of Kyoto and Nara in your travels. Located about an hour south of Tokyo by train, Kamakura is a delightful hamlet with no fewer than 65 Buddhist temples and 19 Shinto shrines spread throughout the village and in the surrounding wooded hills. Most of these were built centuries ago, when a warrior named Yoritomo Minamoto seized political power and established his shogunate government in Kamakura back in 1192. Wanting to set up his seat of government as far away as possible from what he considered to be the corrupt imperial court in Kyoto, Yoritomo selected Kamakura because it was easy to defend. The village is enclosed on three sides by wooded hills and on the fourth by the sea, a setting that lends dramatic background to the many temples and shrines.

Although Kamakura remained the military and political center of the na-

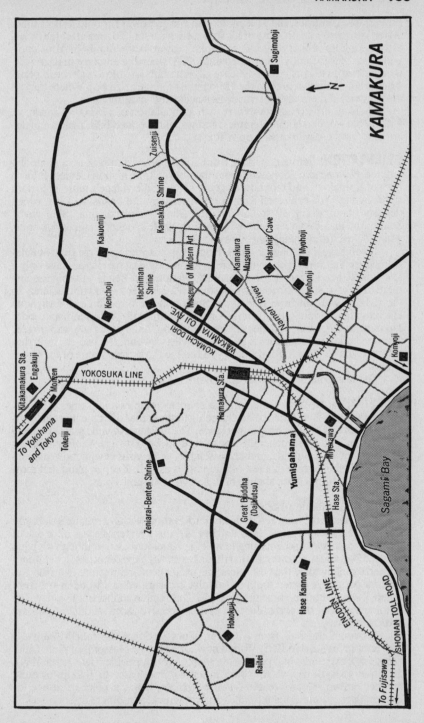

KAMAKURA

Sugimotoji

Zuisenji

Kamakura Shrine

Kakuonji

Kamakura Museum of Modern Art

Kamakura Museum

Harakiri Cave

Myohoji

Myohonji

Yamenu River

Hachman Shrine

Kenchoji

WAKAMIYA OJI AVE.

KOMACHI DORI

Komyoji

Kitakamakura Sta.

Engakuji

Meigetsu-in

YOKOSUKA LINE

Tokeiji

To Yokohama and Tokyo

Kamakura Sta.

Yumigahama

Miyokawa

Zeniarai-Benten Shrine

Hase Sta.

Great Buddha (Daibutsu)

Sagami Bay

Hase Kannon

Hokokuji

ENODEN LINE

SHONAN TOLL ROAD

Raitei

To Fujisawa

tion for 1½ centuries, the Minamoto clan was in power for only a short time. After Yoritomo's death, both of his sons were assassinated, one after the other, after taking up military rule. Power then passed to the family of Yoritomo's widow, the Hojo family. They ruled until 1333, when the emperor in Kyoto dispatched troops to crush the shogunate government. Unable to halt the imperial troops, 800 soldiers retired to the Hojo family temple at Toshoji, where they all disemboweled themselves in ritualistic suicide known as *seppuku*.

Today a thriving seaside resort with a population of 175,000, Kamakura, with its old wooden homes, temples, shrines, and wooded hills, makes a pleasant one- or two-day excursion from Tokyo.

ORIENTATION: Before departing from Tokyo, be sure to pick up a pamphlet entitled *Hakone and Kamakura* from the Tourist Information Center. It has a map of Kamakura and tells how to get to some of the village's most important sights by bus. You can reach Kamakura by train on the Yokosuka Line, which departs about every 10 to 20 minutes from the Yokohama, Shinagawa, Shimbashi, and Tokyo JR stations. The trip from Tokyo Station takes one hour, while the trip from Shinagawa takes 43 minutes.

If you have a full day for sightseeing, I suggest getting off the train at Kita-Kamakura Station, which is just before Kamakura Station. If you have only a few hours, head straight for Kamakura Station and begin your sightseeing there. The tourist information window (tel. 22-3350) is located immediately to the right as you exit from Kamakura Station in the direction of Tsurugaoka Hachimangu Shrine. Open from 9 a.m. to 5 p.m. daily, it has a map in both Japanese and English, and the staff can direct you to the sights you want to see. Transportation in Kamakura is by bus, as well as a wonderful two-car train that will take you to Hase Station where you can see the bronze statue of the Great Buddha.

The **telephone area code** for Kamakura is 0467.

THE SIGHTS: Because Kamakura has so many temples and shrines, it's obvious that visitors must limit their sightseeing to those that offer the most in terms of historical and architectural importance. The most worthwhile places of interest in Kamakura are generally considered to be Tsurugaoka Hachimangu Shrine, the Great Buddha, and Hase Temple, while visitors with more time on their hands should take in a few other temples as well. Keep in mind that most temples and shrines open about 8 a.m. and close around 5 p.m.

Around Kita-Kamakura Station

If you leave the train at Kita-Kamakura Station, within a minute's walk you can reach **Engakuji Temple**. Founded in 1282, this Zen temple was once one of the most important and imposing temples in Kamakura, and although it's been reduced in grandeur by fires and earthquakes through the centuries, it's still considered by many to be the best remaining example of architecture from the Kamakura period. A sacred tooth of Buddha is enshrined in a wooden structure called *Shari-den* on the precinct grounds. This temple sponsors a five-day Zen training course at the end of July, as well as intensive zazen meditation courses several times a year.

A five-minute walk from Kita-Kamakura Station is the **Tokeiji Temple**, a Zen temple founded in 1285. Visited now for its flower blossoms of plum (mid-February), magnolias and peach (late March/April), peonies (late April/May), and irises (May/June), visitors back in feudal times came to Tokeiji for quite another reason. Known as the Divorce Temple, it was a place of refuge for women fleeing from cruel husbands and disagreeable mothers-in-law. Back in those days only men could divorce their wives. Women had no legal recourse, but if they could make it to Tokeiji they were given protection from their husbands and allowed to live among the nuns.

If you feel like walking, you can go on to Tsurugaoka Hachimangu Shrine in about 30 minutes, stopping in at **Kenchoji Temple** on the way, which along with Engakuji is considered to be among the five best Zen temples in Kamakura. Note the magnificent cedars surrounding the temple, as well as the ceremonial gate held together with wooden wedges. If you don't feel like walking, return to Kita-Kamakura Station and go one more stop to Kamakura Station.

Around Kamakura Station

About a ten-minute walk from Kamakura Station, **Tsurugaoka Hachimangu Shrine** is the spiritual heart of Kamakura. It was built by Yoritomo and dedicated to Hachiman, the Shinto god of war who served as the clan deity of the Minamoto family. The pathway to the shrine is along Wakamiya Oji, a cherry tree-lined pedestrian lane that was also constructed by Yoritomo back in the 1180s so that his oldest son's first visit to the family shrine could be accomplished in style with an elaborate procession. Along the pathway are souvenir and antique shops selling lacquerware and folk art, and three massive *torii* gates signal the approach to the shrine.

On the shrine grounds are the **Kanazawa Prefectural Modern Art Museum**, which exhibits contemporary art every day except Monday from 10 a.m. to 5 p.m., and the **Kamakura Municipal Museum**, which displays a collection of carvings, bronzes, swords, calligraphy, lacquerware, and other historical objects from neighboring shrines and temples. This museum is open from 9 a.m. to 4 p.m.; closed Monday.

As you approach the vermillion-painted Hachimangu Shrine, note the gingko tree to the left as you ascend the steps. This is supposedly the site where Yoritomo's second son was ambushed and murdered back in 1219. The gingko tree itself is thought to be about 1,000 years old.

Although it's a little bit far out of the way, it might pay to make a visit to **Zeniarai-Benten Shrine**, about a 20-minute walk west of Kamakura Station. This shrine is dedicated to the goddess of good fortune, and on Oriental zodiac days of the snake, worshippers believe that if you take your money and wash it in spring water in a small cave on the shrine grounds your money will double or triple itself later on. Of course, this being modern Japan, don't be surprised if you see a bit of ingenuity. My Japanese landlady told me that when she visited the shrine she didn't have much cash on her so she washed something she thought would be equally as good—her plastic credit card.

Around Hase Station

To get to the attractions around Hase Station, you can go by bus, which departs from in front of Kamakura Station, or you can go by the Enoden train line, a two-car train that putts its way seemingly through backyards on its way from Kamakura Station to Hase and beyond to Enoshima and Fujisawa. Since there's only one track, trains have to take turns going in either direction. I would suggest taking the bus from Kamakura Station directly to the Great Buddha, walking to Hase Shrine, and then taking the Enoden train back to Kamakura Station.

Probably the most famous attraction in Kamakura is the **Great Buddha**, the Daibutsu, which at 37 feet and 93 tons is the second-largest bronze image in Japan. The largest Buddha is in Nara, but in my opinion the Kamakura Daibutsu is much more impressive. For one thing, whereas the Nara Buddha sits enclosed in a wooden structure which reduces the effectiveness of its size, the Kamakura Buddha sits outside in a dramatic backdrop of wooded hills. Cast in 1252, the Kamakura Buddha was once housed in a temple, but a huge tidal wave destroyed the wooden structure and the statue has sat under the sun, snow, and stars ever since. I also like the face of the Kamakura Buddha better than the statue in Nara. I find it more inspiring and divine, as though with its half-closed eyes and calm, serene face it's somehow above the worries of the world of wars, natural disasters, calamities, and sorrow. It's as though it represents the plane above human suffering, the point at which birth and death, joy and sadness, merge and become one and the same. If you want you can go inside the statue—it's hollow.

Nearby, **Hase Temple**, constructed on a hill with a sweeping view of the sea, is the home of an 11-headed gilt statue of Kannon, the goddess of mercy. At more than 30 feet it's the tallest wooden image in Japan and was made from a single piece of camphorwood back in the eighth century. The legend surrounding this Kannon is quite remarkable. Supposedly two wooden images were made from the wood of a huge camphor tree. One of the images was kept in Hase not far from Nara, while the second image, if you can imagine, was given a short ceremony and then duly tossed into the sea to find a home of its own. The image drifted 300 miles eastward and washed up on shore but was thrown back in again because all who touched it became ill or incurred bad luck. Finally the image reached Kamakura, where it gave the people no trouble. This was interpreted as a sign that the image was content with its surroundings and Hase Temple was erected at its present site.

As you climb up the steps to Hase Temple and its Kannon, you'll encounter statues of a different sort. All around you will be statues of Jizo, the guardian deity of children. Although originally parents came to Hase Temple to set up statues to represent their children in hopes that the deity would protect and watch over them, through the years the purpose of the Jizo has changed. Now they represent miscarried, stillborn, or, most frequently, aborted children. Altogether there are more than 50,000 of these statues here, and some of them, which you can buy on the temple grounds for as much as $100, are fitted with hand-knitted caps and sweaters. The effect is quite chilling.

WHERE TO DINE: A lovely spot for taking lunch is at **Raitei** [58], Takasago (tel. 32-5656), which you can reach by taking a bus departing from platform 3 in front of Kamakura Station (make sure the bus is going to the Takasago bus stop, since not all buses from this platform go there). The wonder of this restaurant is that you can have either an inexpensive meal of *soba* (Japanese noodles) or a princely feast of kaiseki. Situated on the edge of Kamakura in verdant countryside, Raitei commands a fine view of a garden, stone and wooden pagodas, and a wooded ridge in the distance. There's a path circling through the garden that will lead you past a house serving snacks (how about stopping off for a beer here after lunch? There are benches outside where you can enjoy the view), a bamboo grove, stone images, and a miniature shrine. The stroll along the pathway takes about 20 minutes.

But back to your meal. At the entrance gate to the restaurant you pay an entrance fee of ¥550 ($3.93), which counts toward the price of your meal at the restaurant. Noodles are served from 11 a.m. "until the sun goes down" (about 6:30 p.m. in summer) on the bottom floor of an old house. There's no English menu, but dishes available include plain soba for ¥650 ($4.64), soba with chicken in it for ¥1,100 ($7.86), tempura soba for ¥1,450 ($7.25), and a soba teishoku set meal for ¥2,400 ($17.14). Obento lunch boxes are available for ¥3,300 ($23.57).

If you feel like splurging you can also eat kaiseki cuisine here, but you must make a reservation beforehand. Offerings range from ¥3,300 ($23.57) for mini-kaiseki to ¥5,500 ($39.29), ¥7,700 ($55), and ¥11,000 ($78.57) for full meals. Kaiseki meals are served until 8 p.m.

A NOTE ON JAPANESE SYMBOLS: Many hotels, restaurants, and other establishments in Japan do not have signs showing their names in English letters. Appendix II lists the Japanese symbols for all such places appearing in this guide. Each establishment name in Japanese symbols is numbered, and the same number appears in brackets in the text following the boldfaced establishment name. For example, in the text the Osaka hotel, Hokke Club [161], is number 161 in the Japanese symbol list in Appendix II.

Monzen [59], Yamanouchi 407 (tel. 25-1121), is a modern-looking kaiseki restaurant located just across the tracks from Engakuji Temple in Kita-Kamakura. Open from 11 a.m. to 7:30 p.m., the main dining hall is on the second floor and seating is on tatami mats at low tables. Although there's no English menu, there are pictures of various meals available, which start at ¥2,700 ($19.29) for the teishoku. Vegetarian dishes can be ordered, and prices begin at ¥4,800 ($34.29).

The beach of Kamakura, called Yuigahama Beach, is nothing special, consisting of muddy-looking sand often strewn with litter and unbelievably crowded in summer. (One friend of mine told me he came to Kamakura Beach on a hot weekend day and couldn't find enough space in which to spread his towel, the beach was so packed with bodies. Perhaps he was exaggerating but you get the general idea.) Most amusing are the surfers. The waves are usually nothing more than ripples but that doesn't stop the surfing fanatics, who promptly fall off if a big wave does roll along unexpectedly. At any rate, located close to Yuigahama Beach on the main road leading from the beach to Kamakura Station is **Miyokawa** [60], 2-22-5 Yuigahama (tel. 23-0911), a modern restaurant constructed to resemble a country farmhouse with heavy crossbeams and latticed windows. It specializes in shabu-shabu and steaks. The menu is in Japanese only, but there's a pamphlet with pictures of set meals. Shabu-shabu starts at ¥3,500 ($25), while a full-course shabu-shabu meal with sashimi appetizer and dessert costs ¥5,000 ($35.71). Steak courses are ¥3,600 ($25.71). There are also obento lunch boxes costing ¥2,200 ($15.71) and up, which include various items from sashimi to tempura. Hours are 11 a.m. to 10 p.m. daily.

Closer to Kamakura Station, **Kayagi-ya** [61], 2-11-16 Komachi (tel. 22-1460), is situated on Wakamiya Oji Street next to a lumberyard. This modest, older-looking restaurant serves seven different kinds of inexpensive eel dishes. My favorite is the *unagi donburi* (eel served on top of rice) for ¥1,300 ($9.29). Closed on Friday, it's open the rest of the week from noon to 6:30 p.m.

Nakamura-an [62], 1-7-6 Komachi (tel. 25-3500), is a noodle restaurant located on a side street off Wakamiya Oji Avenue between Kamakura Station and Hackimangu Shrine. Open from 11:30 a.m. to 6 p.m. daily except Thursday, it's easy to spot because of the front window where you can watch noodles being made. There's also a front window display of plastic food so it's easy to make your selection. Noodles start at a low ¥600 ($4.29).

WHERE TO STAY: A cheerful, elegant, and cozy ryokan, **Kaihinso**, 4-8-14

Yuigahama (tel. 0467/22-0960), is in a quiet neighborhood not far from the beach. Formerly the Western-style house of a baron, new additions have been grafted onto the old house in a very unobtrusive way and provide a total of 20 guest rooms. Most of the rooms are Japanese-style with tatami mats and deep Japanese bathtubs, but a few Western-style rooms with beds are also available. The management here is very friendly and receptive to foreigners, a tremendous help if you need directions for your sightseeing tours. Rates average ¥15,400 ($110) to ¥16,500 ($118) per person but depend on the number of people per room and whether it's peak season in summer or on weekends. Prices include two meals, tax, and service, and Western breakfasts are available. You can also experience communal bathing in the ryokan's public baths, which are separated for men and women.

Kamakura Hotel [63], 2-22-29 Hase (tel. 0467/22-0029), is an older hotel built around 1920. Located between Hase Station and the sea, some of its rooms have balconies and the more expensive rooms have good views of the sea. Japanese-style rooms range from ¥11,000 ($79) to ¥22,000 ($157) per person including two meals; the higher-priced rooms are very cheerful, with lots of windows and shoji screens. Western-style rooms with either twin or double beds are the same price. If you'd rather not take your meals at the hotel, Western-style rooms range from ¥6,600 ($47) to ¥12,000 ($86) per person.

2. Nikko

Since the publication of James Clavell's *Shogun,* many people have heard of Ieyasu Tokugawa, a real-life powerful shogun of the 1600s on which Clavell's fictional shogun was based. Quashing all rebellions and unifying Japan under his leadership, Tokugawa built such a military stronghold that his heirs continued to rule Japan for the next 250 years without serious challenge.

If you'd like to join the millions of Japanese who through the centuries have paid homage to this great man, travel 87 miles north of Tokyo to Nikko, where a mausoleum was constructed in his honor in the 17th century and where his remains were laid to rest. Nikko means "sunlight," an apt description of the way the sun's rays play upon this sumptuous mausoleum of wood and gold leaf. Surrounding the mausoleum are thousands of cedar trees in a 200,000-acre national park. A trip to Nikko can be combined with a visit to Chuzenji Lake, a jewel of a lake about an hour's bus ride from the mausoleum.

ORIENTATION: Before leaving Tokyo, pick up a leaflet called *Nikko and Mashiko* from the Tourist Information Center. It gives the train schedule for both the Tobu Line, which departs from Asakusa Station, and JR trains that depart from Ueno Station. The T.I.C. also has some color brochures with maps of the Nikko area. The easiest and fastest way to get to Nikko is on the Tobu Line's limited express, which costs ¥2,200 ($15.71) one way and takes almost two hours. If you have a railpass you'll probably want to take one of the JR trains departing from Ueno, in which case you'll have to change trains in Utsunomiya.

At any rate, the Tobu and JR stations in Nikko are located almost side by side in the village's downtown area. Tokugawa's mausoleum is on the edge of town, which you can reach by foot in about a half hour or by bus from either the Tobu or JR station in about ten minutes. When I last checked, no one at the **Nikko Tobu Station tourist information counter** spoke English, but the Japanese maps there have a few sights listed in English. An additional tourist office is located about halfway to Toshogu Shrine from the train stations on the main road leading through town (tel. 0288/54-2496). Closed on Wednesday, it's open the rest of the week from 9 a.m. to 5 p.m.

The **telephone area code** for Nikko is 0288.

THE SIGHTS: The first indication that you're nearing Tokugawa's mausoleum, which is called Toshogu Shrine, is a vermilion-painted bridge arching over the rushing Daiyagawa River. It was built in 1636, and for more than three centuries only shoguns and their emissaries were allowed to cross it. Even today mortal souls like us are prevented from completely crossing it because of a barrier at one end. For a small fee, however, you can walk on the bridge if you like.

As you climb the steps opposite the bridge and across the road which leads into a forest of cedar, the first major group of temple buildings you'll come across belong to **Rinnoji Temple**, whose Sanbutsudo Hall contains three images of Buddha. You can buy a combination ticket here for ¥580 ($4.14), which allows entry to Rinnoji, Toshogu Shrine and neighboring Futarasan Shrine, and another Tokugawa mausoleum. The combination ticket is also sold at Toshogu Shrine. At Rinnoji Temple there's also a small garden and museum, which you can visit for an additional fee of ¥300 ($2.14).

The most important and famous structure in Nikko, of course, is **Toshogu Shrine**, which contains the tomb of Ieyasu Tokugawa. Although Ieyasu died in 1616, construction of the mausoleum did not begin until 1634, when his grandson, Iemitsu Tokugawa, undertook the project as an act of devotion. It seems that no expense was too great in creating the monument. Some 15,000 artists and craftsmen were brought to Nikko from all over Japan, and after two years' work they had succeeded in erecting a group of buildings more elaborate and gorgeous than any other Japanese temple or shrine. Rich in colors and carvings, Toshogu Shrine is bedecked with an incredible amount of gold leaf used in gilding. Altogether 2.4 million sheets of gold leaf (that would cover an area of almost six acres) were used. The mausoleum was completed in 1636, almost 20 years after Ieyasu's death.

Toshogu Shrine is set in a grove of magnificent ancient Japanese cedars planted by a feudal lord named Masatsuna Matsudaira. It took him 20 years to plant these cedars back in the 1600s, and 13,000 of the original trees are still standing. They add a sense of dignity to the mausoleum and the shrine, standing as silent sentinels over Ieyasu's tomb. They seem timeless, adding a continuity to the individual struggles of the men who have passed beneath them and to the faces that come and go.

You enter Toshogu Shrine via a flight of stairs which pass under a huge stone *torii* gateway, one of the largest in Japan. On your left is a five-story, 115-foot-high pagoda. Although normally pagodas are found only at temples, this pagoda is just one example of how both Buddhism and Shintoism are combined at Toshogu Shrine. After climbing a second flight of stairs, turn left, where you'll presently see the Sacred Stable, which houses a sacred white horse. Look for the three monkeys carved above the stable door fixed in the pose of "hear no evil, speak no evil, and see no evil."

At the next flight of stairs is Yomeimon Gate, considered to be the center showpiece of Nikko. It's popularly known as the Twilight Gate, implying that it could take you all day until twilight to see everything carved onto it. Painted in red, blue, and green, and decorated with gilding and lacquerwork, this gate has about 400 carvings of flowers, dragons, birds, and other animals. It's almost too much to take in at once.

To the left of the gate is the hall where the portable shrines are kept, as well as Honchido Hall, famous for its dragon painting on the ceiling. If you clap your hands under the painting, the echo supposedly resembles a dragon's roar. You can visit the shrine's main hall, where guides will explain its history and main features in Japanese. To the right of the main hall is a gate with a carving of a sleeping cat above it. Beyond that are 200 stone steps leading past cedars to Ieyasu's tomb, which costs an additional ¥300 ($2.14).

Directly to the west of Toshogu Shrine is **Futarasan Shrine**, the oldest building in the district (from 1617), which has a pleasant garden. On the shrine's grounds is the so-called ghost lantern, enclosed in a small wooden structure. According to legend it used to come alive at night and sweep around Nikko in the form of a ghost. It apparently scared one of the guards so much that he struck it with his sword, the marks of which are still visible on the lamp's rim.

Past Futarasan Shrine is the **second mausoleum**, that of Iemitsu, grandson of Ieyasu and the third Tokugawa shogun. Completed in 1653, it's not nearly so ornate as the Toshogu Shrine. It's also not as crowded, making it a pleasant last stop on your tour of Nikko.

After touring Nikko's shrines, you can catch a bus not far from the vermillion-painted bridge for **Lake Chuzenji** (you can also board it in front of Tobu Station). The ride takes about 50 minutes, winding higher and higher along hairpin roads. The view is breathtaking—I've even seen bands of monkeys along the side of the road. On Lake Chuzenji are many ryokan, souvenir stores, and coffeeshops, making it a popular holiday resort. Things to do include visiting Chuzenji Temple beside the lake, going on an hour-long boat cruise, and visiting nearby Kegon Falls, a stunning 250-foot waterfall considered to be one of the most beautiful falls in Japan.

FOOD AND LODGING: The most famous hotel in Nikko is the **Nikko Kanaya Hotel**, 1300 Kami-Hatsuishi (tel. 0288/54-0001). First established back in 1873, it has played host to a number of VIPs—Charles Lindbergh, Indira Gandhi, Helen Keller, Eleanor Roosevelt, David Rockefeller, Shirley MacLaine, and Albert Einstein, to name a few. A distinguished-looking, old-fashioned hotel secluded on a hill above the red sacred bridge, it combines the rustic heartiness of a European country lodge with elements of old Japan.

All rooms are Western-style twins and doubles, the differences in their prices based on room size and view. Room rates range from ¥6,600 ($47) to ¥20,000 ($143) for single occupancy and ¥7,700 ($55) to ¥22,000 ($157) for double. During the peak seasons of New Year's, Golden Week in early May, summer vacation in July and August, and in October, rates rise to ¥12,100 ($86) to ¥25,300 ($181) for singles and ¥13,200 ($94) to ¥27,500 ($196) for doubles. Rooms are rather old-fashioned but cozy, giving you the feeling that things haven't changed all that much around here in the past 50 years. Facilities at this grand old hotel include a small outdoor swimming pool, an outdoor skating rink, and a Japanese garden.

Even if you don't spend the night here you might want to come for a meal in the hotel's quaint dining hall. Since it's only a ten-minute walk from Toshogu Shrine, you can easily combine it with your sightseeing tour of Nikko. Lunch is served from noon to 2 p.m. and dinner from 6 to 7:30 p.m. I suggest Nikko's specialty, locally caught rainbow trout, available for ¥3,000 ($21.43) in three different styles of cooking. I had mine cooked Kanaya style, covered with soy sauce, sugar, and sake, grilled and served whole. Other items on the menu include veal cutlet Cordon Bleu, lobster thermidor, king salmon steak, and tenderloin with goose liver and truffle, all in the ¥3,000 ($21.43) to ¥9,000 ($64.29) price range. There are also sandwiches, spaghetti, and pilaf, averaging ¥1,500 ($10.71) per item.

A member of the Japanese Inn Group, **St. Bois**, 1560 Tokorono (tel. 0288/53-3399), is a wooden country house located atop a hill and nestled in among pine trees on the edge of Nikko. About a 15-minute walk north of Tobu Station and a 30-minute walk from Toshogu Shrine, it's very pleasant and peaceful here, making it an inexpensive getaway from Tokyo. Rooms without private bath are ¥4,100 ($29.29) for one person and ¥7,900 ($56.43) for two. Rooms with private bathroom go for ¥4,500 ($32.14) and ¥8,500 ($61) respectively. Of the 11 rooms here, 9 are Western-style with beds and 2 are Japanese-style. Five of the rooms that face the front have their own balconies. Breakfast is available for ¥500 ($3.57) if you let the manager know the night before, and dinner is also available for ¥2,000 ($14.29) if you order it by 3 p.m.

Pension Turtle, 2-16 Takumi-cho (tel. 0288/53-3168), is also a member of the Japanese Inn Group. Although it's not as picturesque as St. Bois, it's closer to Toshogu Shrine and is run by the very friendly Fukuda family. A new two-story house on a quiet side street beside the Daiyagawa River, this 12-room establishment charges ¥3,300 ($23.57) to ¥4,900 ($35) for a single and ¥6,600 ($47) to ¥8,800 ($63) for a double; the higher prices indicate rooms with a private bathroom. Rooms are bright and cheerful, in both Japanese and Western styles. Three rooms on the second floor have their own balconies. Dinners for ¥1,000 ($7.14) to ¥1,500 ($10.71) and breakfasts for ¥500 ($3.57) are available if you order them in advance.

Most ryokan are strung along the shores of Lake Chuzenji. Keep in mind, however, that the majority of them are closed during the winter months and are open only from about mid-April to mid-November. It's best to reserve a room in advance if you want to stay in one of these ryokan, which you can do at a travel agency or upon arrival at Nikko at the accommodation-reservation window inside Nikko Tobu Station. They'll charge a ¥200 ($1.43) to ¥500 ($3.57) fee but will take care of all arrangements for you. Ryokan owners in this area do not speak English and aren't likely to take you in if you simply show up at their door (I've done it this way but I had to try several places before I finally found a sympathetic manager). If it's peak season, you should definitely reserve a room before leaving Tokyo at a travel agency such as the Japan Travel Bureau. Most ryokan start at ¥10,000 ($71) per person and includes two meals, rising to ¥15,000 ($107) on holidays. There's little difference in what they offer: basically a tatami room, coin-operated TV, hot tea, breakfast and dinner served in your room, and a cotton kimono. Be sure to specify if you want a lakeside view.

If you want to stay at Lake Chuzenji but prefer a Western-style hotel, the **Nikko Lakeside Hotel**, 2482 Chugushi (tel. 0288/55-0321), is a conveniently located, modern 100-room hotel on the rim of the lake not far from Kegon Falls. It's open throughout the year. Each room comes with a private bathroom and begins at ¥17,600 ($126) for a twin or double during the winter months, rising to ¥33,000 ($236) during peak seasons. Facilities include tennis courts and a pleasant restaurant with a view of the lake where you can enjoy a meal of lake trout for ¥2,800 ($20).

The **Chuzenji Kanaya Hotel**, 2482 Chugushi (tel. 0288/55-0345), is a member of the same chain as the Nikko Kanaya Hotel and is open from mid-April to mid-November. A two-story wooden building dating from 1950, it's right on the water's edge, surrounded by birch trees. The nearest bus station is Chuzenji Kanaya Hotel Mae. Activities offered include swimming, hiking, boating, fishing, and tennis. There's also an open-door café terrace, and the 31 Western-style rooms come with toilet, bathtub or shower, refrigerator, and TV. Single occupancy rates start at ¥11,000 ($79) off-season and at ¥13,700 ($98) during July, August, and October, while double occupancy begins at ¥13,200 ($94) and ¥16,500 ($118) respectively.

3. Mashiko

Mashiko is a small village known throughout Japan for its *Mashiko-yaki*, distinctive, heavy, country-style pottery. A visit to Mashiko is usually combined with a trip to Nikko, since both are located not far from the town of Utsunomiya north of Tokyo. The T.I.C. leaflet *Nikko and Mashiko* gives directions on how to reach Mashiko, which involves taking the train from either Asakusa or Ueno to Utsunomiya, and from there transferring to a bus. You can also reach Mashiko by taking the Tohoku Line from Ueno as far as Oyama, changing there for a local train to Mashiko. In any case, the trip from Tokyo to Mashiko takes three hours or more. Since the major attraction in Mashiko is its pottery shops and kilns, and there's little in the way of restaurants and accommodations, I suggest coming here just for the day, returning to Tokyo or traveling on to Nikko before nightfall.

Mashiko gained fame back in 1930 when the late Shoji Hamada, designated a National Living Treasure, built a kiln in this tiny village and introduced Mashiko ware throughout Japan. Other potters have since taken up his technique, producing ceramics for everyday use, including plates, cups, vases, and tableware. Altogether there are about 50 pottery shops in Mashiko, along with a number of kilns, where you can simply wander in, watch the craftsmen at work, and even try your own hand at throwing or glazing a pot.

The whole process of making pottery, for example, can be seen at **Tsukamoto Pottery** (tel. 02857/2-3223), and visitors can try their hand at kneading clay, turning the potter's wheel, or hand-molding a pot. At the **Mashiko Reference Collection Museum (Mashiko Sankokan)** (tel. 2-5300), open from 9:30 a.m. to 4:30 p.m. every day except Monday, New Year's, and the month of February, you can see works by Hamada as well as a collection of Eastern and Western glass, ceramics, fabrics, furniture, and paintings. Charging an admission of ¥400 ($2.86), the museum is housed in several thatched-roof structures, which served as Hamada's workshop. His kilns are still there, built along a sloping hill and once heated with wood.

The *Nikko and Mashiko* leaflet contains a map identifying Tsukamoto Pottery, the museum, and other points of interest in Mashiko.

WHERE TO EAT: There are a number of inexpensive restaurants spread along Mashiko's main street, where the pottery shops are located. They all sell the same types of dishes, including tempura, curry rice, and noodles ranging from about ¥600 ($4.29) and up. The **Yamani Restaurant** (tel. 2-4783), for example, located next to the Mashiko Pottery Center, serves the usual tempura starting at ¥1,100 ($7.86), curry rice for ¥600 ($4.29), and noodles for ¥770 ($5.50). Since there's little difference between the restaurants, however, you may want to try the one closest at hand when hunger strikes.

4. Yokohama

There are few attractions in Yokohama to warrant a visit by the short-term traveler to Japan. However, if you find yourself in Tokyo for an extended period of time, Yokohama is a pleasant and easy destination for an afternoon or one-day excursion.

A rather new city in Japan's history books, Yokohama was nothing more than a tiny fishing village when Commodore Perry arrived in the mid-1800s and demanded that Japan open its doors to trade. Nevertheless, the village was selected by the shogun as one of several ports to be opened for international trade, and in 1859 the first foreign settlers arrived. To accommodate them, Yokohama was divided into two parts—Outside the Barrier (Kangai) and Inside the Barrier (Kannai). A canal was dug between the two and the foreigners were placed in Kannai, ostensibly to protect them from irate samurai who were disgruntled with these foreign intruders and might try to assassinate them. It's probably not too far-fetched to assume, however, that this separation between foreigner and Japanese was also meant to isolate the strangers. After all, following more than two centuries of isolation from the rest of the world the Japanese were bound to be at least a little cautious of foreigners and their habits. But as Japan entered the Meiji Period in full swing, relations relaxed and the foreigners moved to a nearby hill known as The Bluff.

Even so, throughout the 19th century the foreigners in Yokohama continued to be a source of great curiosity for the Japanese, who came from as far away as Tokyo to look at them and to see the Western goods that were being imported and unloaded at Yokohama's port. Serving as the capital city's port, Yokohama grew by leaps and bounds, becoming so important that the first railroad in Japan linked Tokyo with Yokohama, reducing the ten-hour journey by foot to less than an hour.

Today Yokohama is still an important international port and still supports a large international community, with many foreigners continuing to reside on The Bluff. Yokohama also has a large Chinese population, descendants of immigrants who moved here shortly after Japan opened itself to trade. With a population of almost three million, Yokohama is Japan's second-largest city.

ORIENTATION: Yokohama is easily reached by train from Tokyo, Shimbashi, Shinagawa, Yurakucho, and Shibuya stations, and most trains take 30 minutes or less. The majority of attractions in Yokohama are centered in the old part of town around Kannai Station, which is connected to Yokohama Station by subway, train, and bus. If you want to go directly to Kannai Station, the Keihin Tohoku Line from Tokyo Station, with stops in Shimbashi and Shinagawa, reaches Kannai in about 45 minutes.

The **Yokohama Municipal Tourist Association** is located in the Silk Center, 1 Yamashita-cho, Naka-ku (tel. 045/641-5824), close to the harbor and an easy walk from Kannai Station. The Silk Center also contains the Silk Museum, an attraction you shouldn't miss. The Yokohama Tourist Association is one of the best and most efficient I've come across in Japan, and its English map is excellent. The staff speaks English and can give you all kinds of brochures on the city. Yokohama also has the Home-Visit System whereby you can visit with a Japanese family. Be sure to call the Yokohama Tourist Association to set up the appointment at least a day in advance of your intended visit.

The **telephone area code** for Yokohama is 045.

THE SIGHTS: Because Yokohama is a relatively new city by Japanese standards, it doesn't have ancient temples or shrines, a castle, or a centuries-old landscape garden. In fact, most Japanese come to Yokohama for the same reason they've always come here—to soak up the cosmopolitan atmosphere created by the city's foreign population. They visit The Bluff, the nearby International Cemetery where many of Yokohama's first international residents are buried, Yokohama port, and Chinatown, where there are a number of fine Chinese restaurants. For the foreigner visiting Yokohama, I would say that Kannai with its Silk Museum, the historical museums, the port, and neighboring Chinatown hold the most attraction, along with a superb park on the outskirts of town.

Around Kannai

Your first stop in Kannai should be the Silk Center, in which you'll find both the tourist office and the **Silk Museum** (tel. 641-0841). For many years after Japan first opened its doors silk was its major export item, and almost all this silk was shipped to the rest of the world from Yokohama, the nation's largest raw silk market. In tribute to the role silk has played in Yokohama's history, this museum has displays showing the metamorphosis of the silkworm and how silk is obtained from cocoons and has exhibits of various kinds of silk fabrics as well as gorgeous kimonos. I was astonished to learn that as many as 10,000 cocoons are needed to make just one kimono. By the way, today Japan produces about 33% of the world's silk, but the Japanese are such avid fans of the expensive fabric that they use 50% of the world's total, which means that they must import silk to satisfy the demand. The Silk Museum is open from 9 a.m. to 4:30 p.m. daily and admission is ¥300 ($2.14).

Just a minute's walk from the Silk Center is the **Yokohama Archives of History**, 3 Nippon O-dori (tel. 201-2100), with exhibits and pictures relating to the opening of Japan and the establishment of Yokohama as an international port. It's a very small museum and can be toured quickly just to get an idea of early Yokohama. Hours are 9:30 a.m. to 4:30 p.m.; closed Monday and days following public holidays. The entrance fee is ¥200 ($1.43).

If you're really a museum buff, you should wander over to the **Kanagawa Prefectural Museum (Kanagawa Kenritsu Hakubutsukan)**, 5-chome Minami-naka-dori (tel. 201-0926). It's close to Sakuragicho Station, about a 20-minute walk from the Silk Center. In a Western-style building constructed in 1904 to house the nation's first modern foreign-exchange bank, it exhibits items related to natural science, archeology, history, and folklore in Kanagawa Prefecture. Yokohama, incidentally, is Kanagawa Prefecture's chief town. The museum is open from 9 a.m. to 4 p.m. (closed on Monday and the last Friday of the month), and entrance is ¥200 ($1.43). Included in the collection are rooms of a traditional Japanese farmhouse, tools for farming and silk production, and models of both Perry's ships and of Japan's first train, which ran between Tokyo and Yokohama.

Not far from the Silk Center is **Yamashita Park**, laid out after the huge earthquake in 1923 that destroyed much of Tokyo and Yokohama. Japan's first seaside park, Yamashita Park is a pleasant place for a stroll along the waterfront, where you have a view of the city's mighty harbor. At one end of the park is the 348-foot-high Marine Tower, with an observation platform which provides an excellent view of the city, port, and sometimes even Mount Fuji. It's open from 10 a.m. to 9 p.m. (6 p.m. in winter) and charges ¥650 ($4.64). Moored at a pier off the park is the *Hikawa Maru*, an old transoceanic liner built in 1930. Its maiden voyage was to Seattle, after which it crossed the Pacific 238 times until it was retired in 1960. Today it houses an aquarium.

From Yamashita Park you can also take a sightseeing **tour of Yokohama harbor** by boat which, according to the boat company's English brochure, "will fill up your complete satisfactions." Tours are operated approximately every half hour or hour from 10:30 a.m. to 6:30 p.m. The 40-minute cruise costs ¥820 ($5.86), the 60-minute tour costs ¥1,300 ($9.29), and the 90-minute cruise costs ¥2,200 ($15.71).

If you're interested in visiting **The Bluff** and the **International Cemetery**, they're located south of Yamashita Park across the Nakamura River. From The Bluff you have another view of the harbor from Harbor View Park. Also of interest is **Chinatown**, with about 100 Chinese restaurants and shops selling Chinese foodstuffs and souvenirs. Refer to the dining section below for information on Chinese restaurants.

Sankei-en Garden

In my opinion Sankei-en Garden is the best reason for visiting Yokohama. Although it's not old, it's a lovely park with a number of old historical buildings that were brought here from other parts of Japan, all situated around streams and ponds. It was laid out back in 1906 by Tomitaro Hara, a local millionaire who made his fortune exporting silk. As you wander along the gently winding pathways, you'll see a villa built in 1649 by the Tokugawa Shogunate clan, tea arbors, a 500-year-old pagoda, and a farmhouse built in 1650 without the use of nails. No matter what the season, the views here are beautiful.

. The easiest way to reach Sankei-en Garden is by bus 8, which departs from Yokohama Station and winds its way through Kannai and past Chinatown before reaching the Sankei-en-mae bus stop. It's therefore easy to combine Sankei-en and Kannai in a day's sightseeing tour. In fact, you may want to come first to Sankei-en Garden and then take the bus back to Kannai, ending up in Chinatown for dinner. Sankei-en is open from 9 a.m. to 4:30 p.m. and admission is ¥400 ($2.86)

WHERE TO EAT: Chinatown consists of one main street and dozens of offshoots, with restaurant after restaurant serving Chinese food. Most of them have plastic food displays or pictures of their menu, so let your budget be your guide.

A typical one is **Yokaro** [64], 102 Yamashita-cho (tel. 681-3466), which is open from 11 a.m. to 9 p.m. daily and serves both Mandarin and Szechuan food. There's no English menu but there is a plastic display case. À la carte dishes come in three sizes—small, medium, and large—with small dishes running from ¥1,300 ($9.29) to ¥2,200 ($15.71).

If you feel like splurging, **Kaseiro** [65], at 164 Yamashita-cho (tel. 661-0661), is much more elegant than most other Chinese restaurants, though it hasn't escaped the stereotypically ornate decor of reds and golds. It serves Pekinese food and you should expect to spend at least ¥4,000 ($28.57) and up per person. Hours are 11:30 a.m. to 8 p.m. daily.

One note I'd like to add is that unless you arrive by taxi it's a bit frustrating searching for a particular restaurant in Chinatown because there are so many of them. You may want simply to wander around and choose one that suits your fancy.

If you'd rather have Japanese food, head for **Janomeya** [66], 126 5-chome Isezaki-cho (tel. 251-0832). It's located toward the end of the Isezaki-cho pedestrian shopping street, which stretches south from Kannai Station. At night this area lights up as one of Yokohama's nightlife districts. The plastic food display in its front window shows various dishes available, which include sukiyaki, shabu-shabu, sashimi, and tempura. Since there's no English menu, you might want to make your choice before going inside. Open every day from 11:30 a.m. to 9:30 p.m., it serves sukiyaki beginning at ¥2,400 ($17.14) and shabu-shabu at ¥3,300 ($23.57). Set meals range from ¥5,200 ($37.14) to ¥8,800 ($62.86).

5. Kawasaki

With a population of almost one million, Kawasaki has pretty much been swallowed up by the Tokyo–Yokohama metropolis, and as you travel by train it's virtually impossible to see where Tokyo ends and Kawasaki begins. A sprawling industrial complex with some of the largest Japanese manufacturing plants located here, Kawasaki is one of those cities better left unseen. However, tucked away in a corner of woods and hills is a delightful open-air museum called **Nihon Minka-en** (tel. 044/922-2181), where traditional thatched houses and other historical buildings have been preserved. If you don't have the chance to visit Takayama or Shirakawa in the Japan Alps or a similar museum in Takamatsu, on the island of Kyushu, this may be your only chance to examine closely the way rural Japanese lived in centuries past.

Altogether 19 structures have been brought here from other parts of Japan and have been artistically situated on various wooded hills. Most of them are heavy-beamed thatched houses, but there are also warehouses, a shrine, and a Kabuki stage from a small fishing village. All the buildings are open to the public so you can wander in and inspect the various rooms. The oldest houses date from about 300 years ago and were usually homes for extended families. Imagine how it must have been to live back then, with the family gathered around the central hearth on cold winter nights. An English pamphlet tells about each of the buildings, and there are many explanations throughout in English.

The Nihon Minka-en is open every day except Monday from 9:30 a.m. to 4:30 p.m. and charges ¥300 ($2.14) admission. To reach the open-air museum, take the Odakyu Line from Shinjuku to the Mukogaoka-yuen Station, which is the 18th stop. Minka-en is about a 15-minute walk from the south exit of the station. Because there are no special restaurants in this area, I suggest you either bring a picnic lunch to eat at the open-air museum or return to Shinjuku to take advantage of the many wonderful restaurants there.

In addition to Nihon Minka-en, there's also one other attraction in Kawasaki you might like to know about, though it takes place only once a year in mid-April. That's when the **Jibeta Matsuri festival** takes place, a rather unusual festival that extolls the joys of sex. This festival points out perhaps better than anything else the differences in attitude that the Japanese and Westerners have had about sex throughout the centuries. Whereas in the West sexuality has a long history of repression expressed largely through religious beliefs, the Japanese have always taken a rather open and natural attitude toward sex without the burden of guilt and without treating it as a moral issue.

At any rate, this festival takes place at Kanayama Shrine, which has on display huge phalluses as well as various sexual objects, and the highlight of the festival is a parade in which various phallic objects are carried through the streets. As with many festivals in Japan, this one is tied to a legend. According to a well-known Japanese myth, a long time ago there was a beautiful maiden who was afflicted by a terrible demon. Twice she tried to marry, but on both wedding nights her grooms died while they tried to consummate the marriage—the demon had bitten off the symbol of their manhood. As you can imagine, the father of the poor girl was unsuccessful in securing her another husband. Finally a blacksmith heard about her story and, taking pity, he resolved to help her and applied to the protective deities of metalsmiths at his local shrine for assistance. There he had a vision in which he was instructed to create a metal phallus and use that to deflower the girl. The plan worked, the demon broke its teeth on the metal phallus, and everyone lived happily ever after. In gratitude to the deities the smith presented the metal phallus to the shrine and from that time on the deities were known as the Deities of the Metal Phallus.

You can get some unusual photographs at this annual event. Inquire at the Tokyo Tourist Information Center for the exact date. To get to the Kanayama Shrine, also known as the Shrine of Kanamara-sama, take the Keihin Kyuko Line from Shinagawa Station to Keihin Kawasaki Station, and transfer to the Kawasaki Daishi Line for the ten-minute trip to Kawasaki Daishi Station. From there it's only a few minutes' walk.

Mt. Fuji

Mount Fuji, affectionately called "Fuji-san" by the Japanese, has been revered as sacred since ancient times. Throughout the centuries Japanese poets have written about it, painters have painted it, pilgrims have flocked to it, and more than a few people have died on it. Without a doubt Mt. Fuji has been photographed more than anything else in Japan.

Visible on a clear day from as far as 100 miles away, Mt. Fuji is stunningly impressive. At 12,388 feet it towers far above anything else around it, a symmetrical cone of almost perfect proportions. Mt. Fuji is majestic, grand, and awe-inspiring. To the Japanese Mt. Fuji symbolizes the very spirit of Japan. However, even though Mt. Fuji is something every visitor to Japan should see, few ever do. Unfortunately, Fuji-san is almost always cloaked in clouds. If you catch a glimpse of this mighty mountain, consider yourself extremely lucky.

The most popular thing to do regarding Mt. Fuji is to climb it. Several well-marked trails leading to the top are open throughout the year, but because of snow and inclement weather from fall through late spring the "official" climbing season from July 1 to August 31 is considered the best time to make an ascent. It's also the most crowded time of the year. Ask any Japanese where he would go if he could travel to only one place in his lifetime, and most likely he will answer Mt. Fuji. Consider the fact that there are approximately 120 million Japanese, most of whom wouldn't dream of climbing the mountain outside the "official" two months it's open, and you begin to get the picture. More specifically, about 400,000 people climb Fuji-san every year, mostly in July and August and mostly on weekends. In other words, if you plan on climbing Mt. Fuji on a Saturday or Sunday in the summer, go to the end of the line, please. I've seen pictures of a trail leading up to Fuji's summit taken on a hot summer's day and it was a solid, unbroken line of hikers stretching all the way up the face of the mountain, one right behind the other. It was as though everyone was waiting in a queue to get into a movie being shown at the top, but I have no doubt in my mind that these Japanese hikers were enjoying themselves immensely, reveling in the togetherness, happy that they were all sharing in the spirit of the climb up old Fuji-san.

In other words, unless you climb Mt. Fuji outside the summer months it will not be a solitary venture. Rather, the experience should be viewed as something you can do together with a determined group of Japanese who are following in their fathers' footsteps by making pilgrimages to the top (women, incidentally, weren't allowed to climb Mt. Fuji until 1868). Climbing Mt. Fuji is not difficult, but it *is* extremely strenuous. You'll be amazed by the number of children and old people doggedly making their way to the top of the highest mountain in Japan.

ORIENTATION: As part of a larger national park called Fuji-Hakone-Izu National Park, Mt. Fuji is only 60 miles away from Tokyo. Of the handful of trails leading to the top, Kawaguchiko is the one most often used by Tokyoites. All trails are divided into ten different stages, and Kawaguchiko Fifth Stage is the starting point for most climbs to the top. It takes about five hours to reach the summit and three hours to descend back to the Fifth Stage.

The easiest way to reach Kawaguchiko Fifth Stage is by direct bus from Hamamatsucho or Shinjuku Bus Terminal, in operation several times daily from July 13 to August 31. The fare from Hamatsucho Bus Terminal is ¥2,500 ($17.86) one way, and from Shinjuku Bus Terminal it's ¥2,300 ($16.43). Reservations for the bus are required and can be made through a travel agency, such as the Japan Travel Bureau. You can also reach the Fifth Stage by taking the bus or train to Kawaguchiko Station and then transferring to a bus. Bus service to the Fifth Stage is suspended, however, from November to April, a time when Mt. Fuji is blanketed in snow and should be considered too dangerous for the novice climber.

More information regarding train and bus schedules to Mt. Fuji and its surrounding area can be obtained from the Tokyo Tourist Information Center in a leaflet called *Mt. Fuji and Fuji Five Lakes*.

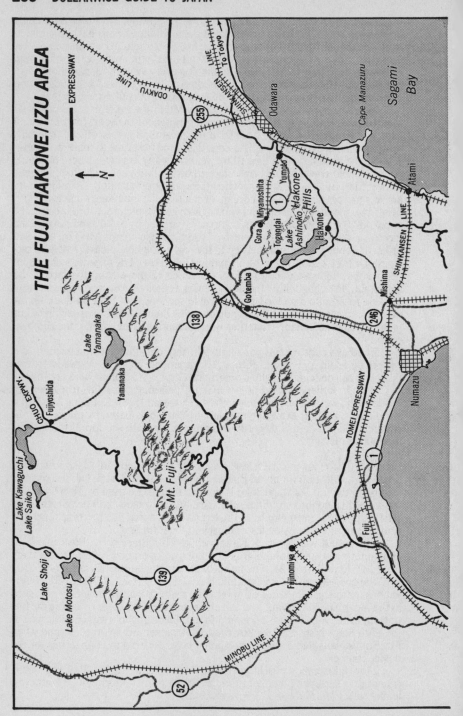

THE FUJI/HAKONE/IZU AREA

— EXPRESSWAY

← N —

ODAKYU LINE

SHINKANSEN LINE
To Tokyo

Odawara

Cape Manazuru

Sagami Bay

255

Yumoto

Miyanoshita

Gora

Togendai

Lake Ashinoko

Hakone

Hakone Hills

Atami

SHINKANSEN LINE

Gotemba

138

Mishima

246

Lake Yamanaka

Yamanaka

Numazu

CHUO EXPWY.

Fujiyoshida

TOMEI EXPRESSWAY

Lake Kawaguchi
Lake Saiko

Mt. Fuji

1

Lake Shoji

Lake Motosu

139

Fuji

Fujinomiya

MINOBU LINE

52

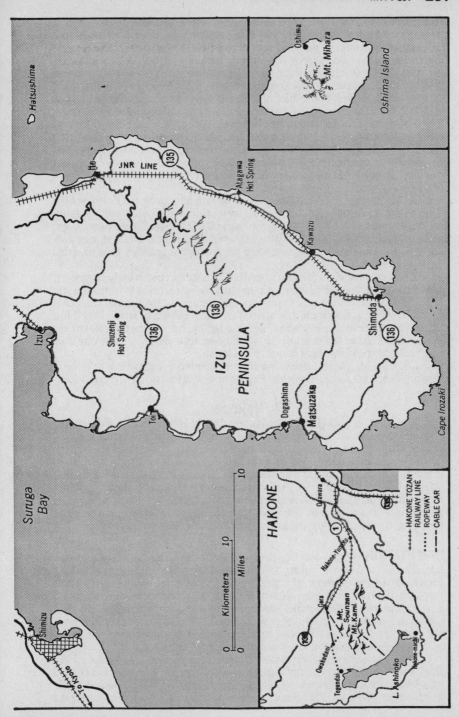

CLIMBING MT. FUJI: Don't be disappointed when your bus deposits you at Kawaguchiko Fifth Stage, where you'll be bombarded with an overflow of souvenir shops, restaurants, and busloads of tourists. Most of these tourists aren't climbing to the top, and as soon as you get past them and the blaring loudspeakers you'll find yourself on a steep rocky path surrounded only by scrub brush and hikers on the path below and above you. After a couple of hours you'll probably find yourself above the roily clouds which stretch in all directions. It will be as if you're on an island, barren and rocky, in the middle of an ocean.

You needn't have climbing experience to ascend Mt. Fuji, but you do need stamina. It goes without saying that you also need good walking shoes. It's possible to do it in tennis shoes, but if rocks are wet they can get awfully slippery. You should also bring a light plastic raincoat (which you can buy at souvenir shops at the Fifth Stage), a sun hat, and a sweater for the evening. It gets very chilly on Mt. Fuji at night.

As for sleeping, there are about 30 mountain huts along the Kawaguchiko Trail above the Fifth Stage, but they're very primitive, providing only a futon and toilet facilities. The cost without meals is ¥4,000 ($28.57) per person, and with meals it's ¥5,100 ($36.43). When I stayed in one of these huts dinner consisted of dried fish, rice, bean-paste soup, and pickled vegetables; breakfast was exactly the same.

The usual procedure for climbing Mt. Fuji is to start out in early afternoon, spend the night near the summit, get up early in the morning to watch the sun rise, climb the rest of the way to the top, and then make the descent. In recent years, however, a new trend has started in which climbers arrive at the Fifth Stage late in the evening and then climb through the night to the top with the aid of flashlights. After the sunrise they then make their descent. That way they don't have to spend the night in one of the huts.

Climbing Mt. Fuji is definitely a unique experience, but there is a saying in Japan: "Everyone should climb Mt. Fuji once; only a fool would climb it twice."

7. Hakone

As part of the Fuji-Hakone-Izu National Park, Hakone is one of the closest and most popular resorts for residents of Tokyo. Blessed with beautiful scenery, Hakone has about everything a vacationer could wish for—hot-spring resorts, mountains, lakes, breathtaking views of Mt. Fuji, and diversions in the form of interesting historical sites. It's located about 50 miles southwest of Tokyo, and you can tour Hakone in a day. An overnight stay near Lake Hakone, or in the mountains, where you can soak in the water of hot springs, is much more pleasant. If you plan to return to Tokyo, I suggest leaving your luggage in storage at your Tokyo hotel and traveling to Hakone with only an overnight bag.

ORIENTATION: Before leaving Tokyo, pick up the *Hakone and Kamakura* leaflet available from the Tourist Information Office. It lists the time schedules for the extensive network of trains, buses, cable cars, and pleasure boats throughout the Hakone area. In fact, it's Hakone's transportation system that makes a trip here so pleasurable. Starting out by train from Tokyo, you can then switch to a small two-car train that zigzags up the mountain, change to a cable car and then a smaller ropeway, and end your trip with a boat ride across Hakone Lake, stopping off to see major attractions along the way.

The most economical way to see Hakone is to purchase the Hakone Free Pass, which despite its name isn't free but does give you a round-trip ticket from Shinjuku Station to Odawara or Hakone Yumoto on the Odakyu Romance Car and includes almost all other modes of transportation in Hakone, including the two-car train, cable car and ropeway, and boat ride. Valid for four days, it costs ¥5,800 ($41.43) if you take the nonstop Romance Car and ¥4,700 ($33.57) if you take the slower, ordinary train. If you have a railpass, you should take the Shinkansen bullet train from Tokyo Station to Odawara. From there, you can travel on the private railways, cable cars, and boats for the ¥3,700 ($26.43) Hakone Free Pass, also valid for four days. Both passes can be purchased at any station of the Odakyu Railway, including Shinjuku Station.

The **telephone area code** for Hakone is 0460.

WHAT TO DO: If you plan on spending only one day in Hakone, you should leave Tokyo by 9 a.m. Otherwise, you can arrange your itinerary in a more leisurely fashion and devote more time to Hakone's attractions, reaching your hotel or ryokan by about 5 or 6 p.m.

The Train Trip

If you leave Tokyo via the Shinkansen, your train will pass through Odawara, the gateway to Hakone. In Odawara, transfer to the Hakone Tozan Railway, a small tram that winds its way through forests and over streams as it travels upward to Gora, making several switchbacks along the way. If you're on the Romance Car, you should switch to the Hakone Tozan Railway at Yumoto Station. At any rate, between Odawara and Gora the Tozan Railway makes almost a dozen stops along the way, including Tonosawa and Miyanoshita, two hot-spring spa resorts with a number of old ryokan and hotels (refer to my food and lodging recommendations). Some of these ryokan date back several centuries, from the days when they were on the main thoroughfare to Tokyo, the old Tokaido Highway. If the train trip has worn you out, you can stop for some open-air bathing at the public baths behind Yumoto Station, called Kappa Tengoku. Probably the closest outdoor baths in the vicinity of Tokyo, they're open from 10 a.m. to 8 p.m. and charge a ¥350 ($2.50) admission.

The next-to-the-last stop is Chokoku-no-mori, first stop on our sightseeing itinerary. Here is where you'll find the **Hakone Open-Air Museum**, with more than 100 sculptures by artists from around the world, including Rodin, Henry Moore, Imoto Atusushi, and Yodoi Toshio. Using nature itself as a dramatic backdrop, this museum spreads through glens and gardens and over ponds. There's also an indoor exhibit of paintings and sculpture. Open from 9 a.m. to 5 p.m. (to 4 p.m. in winter), it charges ¥1,300 ($9.29) admission.

After arriving in Gora, the last stop on the railway, you may want to visit the **Hakone Art Museum**, open from 9 a.m. to 4 p.m. (closed Thursday), charging ¥500 ($3.57). This museum displays ancient Oriental paintings, porcelain, and other works from Japan, China, and Korea. A lovely Japanese landscape garden of moss and bamboo is on the museum grounds. Not far from the museum is **Gora Koen Park**, a rock garden laid out in 1912 in the French style.

By Cable Car and Ropeway

From Gora you can travel by cable car, which leaves every 15 minutes and arrives 9 minutes later at the end station of Sounzan, making several stops along the way. One of the stops is Koen-Kami, which is only a minute away from the Hakone Art Museum. If you've walked to the museum, you may want to board the cable car here rather than walking back to Gora Station.

From Sounzan you board a small ropeway for a long haul down the mountain to Togendai, which lies beside Lake Hakone, known as Lake Ashinoko in Japanese. Before reaching Togendai, however, get off at the first intermediary station, Owakudani. Here you can take a 30-minute hike along a nature path through Owakudani, which means "Great Boiling Valley." Sulfurous steam escapes from fissures in the rock, testimony to volcanic activity still present here. In Owakudani there's also the **Natural Science Museum**, with displays on the fauna, flora, geology, and volcanic origins of Hakone. It's open from 9 a.m. to 5 p.m. and charges an admission of ¥300 ($2.14). Before starting back down on the ropeway, stop off for a snack or drink at the second floor of the ropeway station, where you have fantastic views of Hakone and of Mt. Fuji if it's not being fickle about showing itself.

Lake Ashinoko (Lake Hakone)

From Togendai you can take a pleasure boat across Lake Ashinoko, referred to as "Lake Hakone" in English brochures. Believe it or not, one of the boats crossing the lake is a replica of a centuries-old man-of-war. The trip takes about half an hour to cross the lake to Hakone-machi and Moto Hakone, two resort towns right next to each other on the southern edge of the lake. This end of the lake affords the best view of Mt. Fuji, a view often depicted in tourist publications.

In Hakone-machi you should visit the **Hakone Barrier Gate** (Hakone Sekisho), a reconstructed guardhouse. Originally built in 1618, it served as a checkpoint on the famous **Tokaido Highway**, which connected Edo (present Tokyo) with Kyoto. In feudal days, local lords, called *daimyo*, were required to spend alternate years in Edo, and their wives were kept in Edo as hostages so that the lords wouldn't plan rebellions while in their homelands. This was one of the points along the highway where travelers were checked. Although it was possible to sneak around it, violators who were caught were promptly executed. A nearby museum illustrates the history of the Tokaido Highway.

Between Hakone-machi and Moto-Hakone is part of the Tokaido Highway itself. Lined with ancient and mighty cedars, 1¼ miles of the old highway follows the curve of Lake Ashinoko and makes a pleasant stroll (unfortunately, a road of the 20th century has been built right beside it). In Moto-Hakone is **Hakone Shrine**, revered by samurai until the Meiji Restoration in 1868. Especially picturesque is its red *torii* gate standing in the water.

FOOD AND LODGING: Japan's ryokan sprang into existence to accommodate the stately processions of daimyo and shogun as they traversed the roads between Edo and the rest of Japan. Many of these ryokan were built along the Tokaido Highway, and some of the oldest are found in Hakone.

Ichinoyu [67], 90 Tonosawa (tel. 0460/5-5331), first opened more than 350 years ago and is now in its 14th generation of owners. It claims to be the oldest ryokan in the area and was once honored by the visit of a shogun. Located about a five-minute walk from Tonosawa Station (on the Hakone Tozan Line), this delightful, rambling wooden ryokan is located on a tree-shaded winding road that follows on the track of the old Tokaido Highway. On the one side of the ryokan is a roaring river.

There are 22 rooms here, the oldest dating from the Meiji Period, more than 100 years ago. The two rooms I like the most are called Seseragi and Matsu (rooms are usually named in ryokan). Old-fashioned, they face the river and consist mainly of seasoned and weathered wood. Old artwork, wall hangings, and paintings decorate the ryokan, and some of the rooms have old wooden bathtubs. Both the communal tubs and the tubs in the rooms have hot water supplied from a natural spring. As with all ryokan, prices include two meals, tax, and service, and range from ¥16,000 ($114) to ¥20,000 ($143) per person for rooms with private bath and toilet. Rooms without private bathroom begin at ¥14,000 ($100) per person.

The **Fujiya Hotel**, 359 Miyanoshita (tel. 0460/2-2211), is one of Japan's oldest Western-style hotels and is located within a ten-minute walk of Miyanoshita Station on the Hakone Tozan Line. Established in 1878, it's the grandest and most majestic old hotel in Hakone, a lovely establishment with a Japanese-style roof, lots of windows, and wooden corridors. It consists of five separate buildings, each different and added on at various times in its 100-year history. One is shaped like a pagoda, while another has turrets and a roof shaped like a Japanese temple. In the back of the hotel is a garden with a waterfall and a pond full of carp. There's an outdoor swimming pool as well as an indoor thermal pool fed by water from a hot spring. The hotel even has its own greenhouse. As expected, rooms are old-fashioned with high ceilings and wooden furniture, and all 150 rooms come with a private bathroom. Accustomed to foreign guests, the front-desk personnel speak very good English. The room charge starts at ¥11,000 ($79) for weekdays, increasing to ¥14,300 ($102) on Saturday, the day before a national holiday, and during Golden Week, from April 28 to May 4. During New Year's and the July/August vacation periods, rooms cost ¥19,800 ($141).

Fujiya Hotel is also a good place to come for a meal. Its main dining room, open from noon to 2 p.m. and 6 to 8:30 p.m., is very bright and cheerful, with a high ceiling, large windows with Japanese screens, and a wooden floor. The views are nice and the service is attentive. For lunch you can have such dishes as pilaf, spaghetti, sandwiches, chicken, and hamburger steak, with most dishes averaging ¥1,600 ($11.43). The dinner menu is more expensive and includes steaks, fish, grilled chicken, and stews, most in the ¥2,200 ($15.71) to ¥8,800 ($62.86) price range.

Across the street from the Fujiya Hotel is the **Naraya**, 162 Miyanoshita (tel. 0460/2-2411), a traditional Japanese inn with tiled roof, wooden walls, shoji screens, and hot-spring baths. Although the inn's history stretches back several hundred years, the present building is about a century old. The tatami rooms here, all with bath and toilet, have inspiring views of a large landscape garden and mountains beyond. This is a great place to relax and revel in nature's beauty. Prices begin at ¥33,000 ($236) per person, including two meals, tax, and service charge.

Situated right on Lake Ashinoko on secluded property is the luxurious **Hakone Prince Hotel** [68], 144 Motohakone, Hakone-machi (tel. 0460/3-7111). The various types of rooms available here are in several complexes that sprawl over the well-tended grounds, which include gardens, tennis courts, an outdoor pool, and an arboretum. The public baths overlook the lake. The Ryuguden [69], with its Japanese-style tatami rooms, resembles an Oriental palace, a grand structure built in 1936 with iron lanterns hanging from its wooden upturned eaves and sculptured bushes gracing its manicured lawns. Rooms here begin at ¥33,000 ($236) per person, including two meals, tax, and service charge. During peak seasons (New Year's and summer vacation) the rates increase to ¥38,000 ($271).

Not far from the Ryuguden is the Prince's Western-style hotel, designed by Japanese architect Togo Murano in a circular shape so that each room has a different panoramic view, complete with balcony. Room rates here start at ¥34,000 ($243), rising to ¥42,000 ($300) during the summer season.

And finally, you can also stay in your own pine log cabin, the wood imported from Finland. Spread underneath the trees in a kind of log-cabin village, they range in price from ¥27,000 ($193) for a one-bedroom cabin to ¥46,000 ($329) for a two-bedroom cabin with kitchenette. Summer rates are ¥31,000 ($221) and ¥53,000 ($379) respectively.

Located in the heart of Hakone-machi at the southern tip of Ashinoko is the **Hakone Hotel**, 65 Hakone-machi (tel. 0460/3-6311). Opened more than three decades ago, this older white hotel with traces of Spanish architectural influences is one of the best places in Hakone from which to observe Mt. Fuji on a clear day. Most rooms face the water, and those on the second floor have balconies, but the rooms themselves are a bit old and run down. Basic room rates begin at ¥10,000 ($71) for those without a lake view and without private bathtub, increasing to ¥13,200 ($94) to ¥18,000 ($129) for rooms facing the water and with a private tub. During weekends and national holidays, expect to pay ¥2,000 ($14.29) to ¥3,000 ($21.43) more. And during the peak season in July and August and during New Year's, the cheapest room in the house is ¥20,000 ($143). The dining room of the Hakone Hotel has a sweeping, unobstructed view of the lake and is open from noon to 2 p.m. and 6 to 8 p.m. Only one set course, featuring Western fare, is available, averaging ¥5,500 ($39.29) for lunch and ¥6,600 ($47), for dinner.

Also located at the southern tip of Ashinoko is **Sugiyoshi Ryokan** [70], 56 Moto-Hakone, Hakone-machi (tel. 0460/3-6327). All 12 rooms are Japanese-style and come with the usual coin-operated TV and fridge, and some of them have lake views. The public baths here are natural hot springs. Rates per person, including two meals, tax, and service charge, are ¥10,000 ($71) for rooms without bath or toilet and ¥14,000 ($100) for rooms with a private bathroom. During peak season rates range from ¥13,000 ($93) to ¥17,000 ($121).

Although it's a bit isolated, **Fuji-Hakone Guest House**, 912 Sengoku (tel. 0460/4-6577), is a member of the Japanese Inn Group and offers inexpensive lodging in nine tatami rooms. Opened in 1984 and kept spotlessly clean, this modern house in tranquil surroundings set back from a tree-shaded road is run by a man who speaks very good English. Some of the rooms face the Hakone mountain range. Facilities include a public hot-spring bath, coin-operated laundry and dryer, a large lounge area, and a communal refrigerator. Rates range from ¥4,200 ($30) to ¥5,000 ($36) for one person, and ¥7,700 ($55) to ¥8,800 ($63) for two. Triples range from ¥10,500 ($75) to ¥12,100 ($86). To reach the guest house, take a Hakone Tozan bus from Odawara Station for 45 minutes to Sengoku, getting off at the Senkyoro-mae bus stop. From there it's a one-minute walk. This bus is included in the Hakone Free Pass and continues on to Togendai, from which you can catch either the ropeway or the boat across Ashinoko (described above).

8. The Izu Peninsula

Whenever Tokyoites want to spend a few days at a hot-spring spa on the seashore, they head for the Izu Peninsula. Jutting out into the Pacific Ocean, Izu boasts some fine beaches, verdant and lush countryside, and a dramatic coastline marked in spots by high cliffs and tumbling surf. However, even though the scenery is at times breathtaking there is little of historical interest to lure the short-term visitor to Japan; make sure you've seen both Kamakura and Nikko before coming here. Keep in mind also that Izu's resorts are terribly crowded during the summer vacation period from mid-July to the end of August.

ORIENTATION: The fastest way to reach Izu is by the Shinkansen bullet train from Tokyo Station, which whisks you in less than an hour to Atami, Izu's main gateway on the east side of the peninsula. From Atami you can travel farther south to Shimoda by limited express train.

The west side of the peninsula is much less developed and in my opinion offers the best scenery in Izu. Since there is no rail service here, transportation is either by bus or by boat. A good choice of a place to stay on the west side is Dogashima, a small fishing village with a good beach, clear waters, and interesting rock formations. A pleasant way to reach Dogashima is either by boat from Numazu or by bus along the coast from Shimoda.

But the best way to enjoy Izu is to drive, making this one of the few times when it may be worth it to rent your own car. There's a road that hugs the coast all the way around the peninsula which you can drive easily in a day. If you're traveling by public transportation, an interesting route is to take the Shinkansen to Atami, travel by limited express to Shimoda, take the bus from Shimoda to Dogashima, and from there take a boat to Numazu, where you can catch a train back to Tokyo. Before leaving Tokyo, be sure to pick up the leaflet *The Izu Peninsula* at the Tourist Information Center.

PLACES OF INTEREST IN IZU: If you're traveling during the peak summer season you should make reservations at least several months in advance. Otherwise, there are hotel, ryokan, and minshuku reservation offices in all of Izu's resort towns which will arrange accommodation for you, but be aware that if a place has a room still open in August there's probably a reason for it—poor location, poor service, or unimaginative decor. I took my chances one August and arrived in Atami without prior arrangements. The "ryokan" arranged by the accommodation office at the Atami train station was the worst I've ever stayed in. It pays to plan ahead. Below are recommendations for accommodations in Atami, Shimoda, and Dogashima, three towns that provide a good overview of what the peninsula has to offer.

Atami

Atami means "hot sea." Legend has it that a long time ago there was a hot geyser spewing forth in the sea, killing a lot of fish and marine life. The concerned fishermen asked a Buddhist monk to intervene on their behalf and to pray for a solution to the problem. The prayers paid off when the geyser moved itself to the beach. Not only was the marine life spared, but Atami was blessed with hot spring water the townspeople could henceforth bathe in.

Today Atami, with a population of more than 50,000, is a conglomeration of hotels, ryokan, restaurants, pachinko parlors, souvenir shops, and a sizable red-light district. The city itself is not very interesting, but it's the most easily accessible hot-spring resort from Tokyo. Be sure to see the **MDA Art Museum**, located on top of a hill a short bus ride away from Atami Station. Housed in a modern building at the headquarters of the Church of World Messianity, this museum includes ukiyoe woodblock prints, ceramics, lacquerware, and artwork from the collection of Mokichi Okada, leader of this relatively new religion in Japan. Closed on Thursday, it's open the rest of the week from 9 a.m. to 4 p.m., and admission is ¥1,000 ($7.14).

The **Atami Tourist Information Office** is located at the train station (tel. 0557/81-6002) and is open from 10 a.m. to 6 p.m. daily.

The **telephone area code** for Atami is 0557.

Food and Lodging: One of Atami's oldest ryokan, **Kiunkaku** [71], 4-2 Showacho (tel. 0557/81-3623), has a beautiful garden with a meandering stream, manicured bushes, and stunted pine trees. Although rooms encircle the garden they are artfully concealed from each other and give optimum privacy through the clever use of bushes and mounds. Facilities include hot-spring baths, one of the most pleasant coffeeshops I've seen in a ryokan, and an outdoor pool. There are various styles of rooms available, ranging in price from ¥22,000 ($157) to ¥44,000 ($314) per person, including two meals, tax, and service charge. The most expensive rooms are those with the best view, the most space, and the best meals.

However, there are a few rooms in the lower price range that are real bargains. Tamahime, for example, is the name of one of the ryokan's two Western-style rooms and it's changed little over the decades. It sports stained-glass windows, a paneled ceiling, a fireplace (no longer used), a monstrous old dresser, and cozy furniture—plus a good view of the garden. The only reason it's available for ¥22,000 ($157) is that there is no private bathroom. Another good choice is the room named Aoi, the Blue Room, also available for ¥22,000 but with its own bathroom. There's room for only two people here in a tiny, cute room that extends right out over the pond. Modern tatami rooms with views of the pool in a new wing that opened up in 1983 average ¥27,500 ($196).

The **Hotel New Akao** [72], Atami-cho 1993-250 (tel. 0557/82-5151), is one of the most conspicuous resort hotels on the Izu Peninsula. A large pleasure hotel hemmed in on one side by cliffs and on the other by the blue sea, it has about everything most Japanese want in a vacation: a swimming pool, a fancy dining hall affording an unusual view of surf crashing into cliffs, two discos, a large hot-spring public bath, an outdoor garden complete with Corinthian pillars and arbors, and a small miniature golf area. It even has a roped-off area in the sea where you can swim. Rooms in both Japanese and Western style are available, simply but tastefully done, all with large windows facing the water and a private bath. Obviously, what you're paying for here is use of the facilities rather than luxurious rooms. Per-person rates are ¥21,000 ($150) on weekdays and ¥23,000 ($164) on weekends, including two meals, tax, and service charge. My only complaint about this hotel is that it's so popular and crowded during peak season that the front desk seems too busy to be very accommodating.

On a less grand scale, the **New Fujiya Hotel**, 1-16 Ginza-cho (tel. 0557/81-0111), was built just before the 1964 Olympics. The staff here is friendly and efficient and used to foreigners. Although located a few blocks inland, its top-floor rooms have partial views of the water. The cheapest rooms are doubles that face an inside courtyard. Facilities include an indoor pool, a rooftop playground, a public bath and sauna, and even an outdoor hot-spring spa. In the evening there's a nightclub—usually with performances by women rather scantily clad. Both Japanese- and Western-style rooms are available, beginning at ¥20,000 ($143) per person, including two meals, tax, and service charge. If you want a room without meals, they begin at ¥12,000 ($86).

Shimoda

Located on the southeast end of the Izu Peninsula, Shimoda is famous as the site where Commodore Perry set anchor in 1854 on his trip to Japan to force the nation to open its doors to trade. Shimoda is also where the first American diplomatic representative, Townsend Harris, lived before setting up permanent residence in Yokohama.

Ryosenji Temple, located about a 15-minute walk from Shimoda Station, is where Perry and representatives of the Tokugawa shogunate government agreed upon and signed the treaty to open up Japan. Strangely enough, the temple also houses a small museum of erotica. **Hofukuji Temple**, about a five-minute walk from Shimoda Station, is dedicated to Tojin Okichi, the mistress of Townsend Harris while he lived in Shimoda. Although today no one is exactly certain how it came about that she was chosen, we do know that she ended her life by drowning herself after he left. This temple contains both her tomb and personal artifacts. About 20 minutes south of Shimoda by bus is **Yumigahama Beach**, considered by many to be the best public beach in Izu.

The **Shimoda Tourist Office** is located just outside the train station and is open from 9 a.m. to 5 p.m. daily (tel. 05582/2-1531). They have very good brochures and a map in English.

The **telephone area code** for Shimoda is 05582.

Food and Lodging: A large white hotel situated on top of a hill, the **Shimoda Tokyu Hotel**, 5-12-1 Shimoda-shi (tel. 05582/2-2411), is about a ten-minute taxi ride from Shimoda Station. In addition to a hot-spring spa, it also has an outdoor swimming pool and a bathing area in the sea. From mid-July through August there's an outdoor beer garden. Western-style rooms range from ¥11,000 ($79) to ¥18,700 ($134) for a single, and from ¥13,000 ($93) to ¥35,200 ($251) for a twin or double. The higher prices indicate rates during peak season. Japanese-style rooms start at ¥17,000 ($121), rising to ¥35,000 ($250) during peak season.

Shimoda Onsen Hotel, 6-12 Takegahama (tel. 05582/2-3111), is a reasonably priced ryokan which opened in 1954 with 63 tatami rooms. Located an eight-minute walk from Shimoda Station, it has friendly front-desk personnel and features a small outdoor swimming pool, an outside beer garden (from mid-July to mid-August), and hot-spring baths. Rooms with private bathroom as well as a view of the sea past a ship-repair yard begin at ¥18,000 ($129), while bathless rooms that face inland start at ¥12,000 ($86). Rates are per person and include two meals, tax, and service charge. Western-style breakfasts are available if ordered the night before.

If you're on a budget, head for Sotoura, a small bay on the edge of Shimoda with about 60 minshuku and pensions. It has its own small beach and is popular with young people and families. **Haji** [73] (tel. 05582/2-2597) is a small, clean, and simple minshuku with seven rooms, four which have their own toilet. The owner spent a year in England more than a decade ago but doesn't have much opportunity to practice his English, so he's happy to see foreign guests. Rates are ¥5,000 ($36) per person and include two meals.

If Haji is full, you might try the nearby **Shimoda Pension Ohban** (tel. 05582/2-2953), a new three-story building with "Shimoda Pension" written on the front. I find this place rather impersonal and its dorm-like rooms dull, but connected to the hotel is a place where you can rent surfboards and windsurfers. The charge here is ¥8,000 ($57) per person, including two meals.

Dogashima

With its fishing boats, tiny lanes and back alleyways, sandy beach, clear water, and rock formations jutting out of the sea, Dogashima is one of my favorite villages on Izu's west side. There's not much to do here except relax, swim, and walk around—which may be exactly what you're looking for. The **tourist office** (tel. 05585/2-1268) is located across the street from the bus terminal in a tiny one-room building not far from the boat pier. It's open from 8:30 a.m. to 5 p.m. weekdays, from 8:30 a.m. to noon on Saturday, and is closed on Sunday and national holidays. During the peak season of July and August, it remains open every day from 8:30 a.m. to 5 p.m.

The **telephone area code** for Dogashima is 0558.

Food and Lodging: Dogashima's most exclusive luxury resort ryokan is **Ginsuiso** [74], 2977-1 Nishina, Nishi-Izu-cho (tel. 0558/52-1211). Service here is excellent and begins as soon as you arrive, with staff personnel on hand at the door to greet you. This stunningly white hotel sprawls along a cliff over the sea and has its own private beach and outdoor swimming pool. All 90 rooms are tatami, have a private bathroom and views of the sea, and there's a cabaret show nightly beginning at 8 p.m. The price is ¥22,000 ($157) per person including two meals, tax, and service charge, but because it's popular with large Japanese tour groups you should book well in advance.

Kaikomaru [75], Nishi-Izu-cho, Sawada (tel. 0558/52-1054), is a tiny family-run minshuku on Dogashima's main road. There are only six Japanese-style rooms here and they go for ¥5,000 ($36) per person, including two meals. Use of the hot-spring bath costs ¥200 ($1.43) extra. No one speaks English, but the family, which seems to include everyone from small children to grandparents, is friendly if a bit shy. If you're gregarious and outgoing you'll like this place.

Chapter VI

KYOTO

AS YOUR SHINKANSEN BULLET TRAIN glides into Kyoto Station, your first reaction is likely to be one of great disappointment. There's Kyoto Tower looming in the foreground, looking like some misplaced spaceship. Modern buildings and hotels surround you on all sides, making Kyoto look like just any other Japanese town.

But nestled in between all those buildings are an incredible 1,500 Buddhist temples and 200 Shinto shrines, narrow alleyways and willow-lined canals, gardens of rock and moss, and enough history to fill the pages of 1,000 years. If you stay here long enough, you'll grow to understand why I consider Kyoto to be Japan's most romantic city.

A BRIEF HISTORY: Kyoto served as Japan's capital for more than 1,000 years, from 794 to the Meiji Restoration in 1868. It was laid out in a grid pattern borrowed from the Chinese, with streets running north and south and east and west. Its first few hundred years, from about 800 to the 12th century, were perhaps its grandest, a time when culture blossomed and the court nobility led luxurious and splendid lives. If you have any fantasies about old Japan, perhaps they fit into this time period, known as the Heian Period. There were poetry-composing parties and moon-gazing events. Buddhism flourished and temples were built. A number of learning institutions were set up for the sons and daughters of aristocratic families, and scholars were versed in both Japanese and Chinese.

Toward the end of the Heian Period, however, military clans began clashing for power, resulting in a series of civil wars that eventually pushed Japan into the feudal era of military government that lasted nearly 680 years—until 1868. The first shogun to rise to power was Yoritomo Minamoto, who set up his shogunate government in Kamakura. With the downfall of the Kamakura government in 1336, however, Kyoto once again became the seat of power for the country. The beginning of this era, known as the Muromachi and Azuchi-

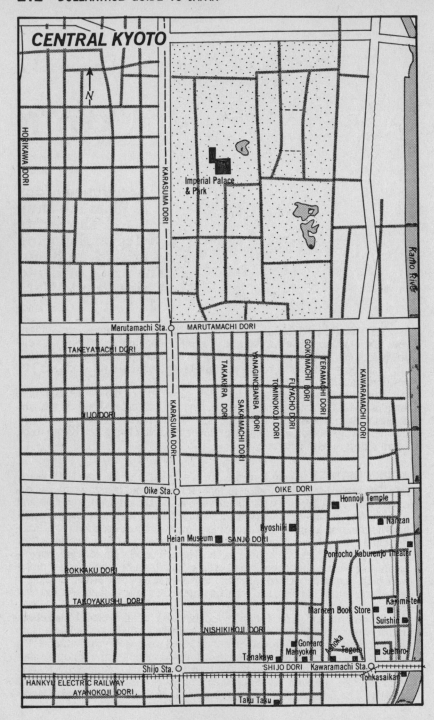

CENTRAL KYOTO

Momoyama Periods, was marked by extravagant prosperity and luxury, expressed in such splendid villas as Kyoto's Gold and Silver Pavilions. Lacquerware, landscape paintings, and the art of metal engraving came into their own. Zen Buddhism was the rage. And despite the civil wars that rocked the nation in the 15th and 16th centuries and destroyed much of Kyoto, culture flourished. It was during these turbulent times that Noh drama, the tea ceremony, flower arranging, and landscape gardening gradually took form.

Emerging as victor in the civil wars, Ieyasu Tokugawa established himself as shogun and set up his military rule in Edo (present Tokyo), far to the east of Kyoto. For the next 250 years Kyoto remained the capital in name only, and in 1868 (which marked the downfall of the Tokugawa shogunate and the restoration of the emperor to power) the capital was officially moved from Kyoto to Tokyo. Thus Tokyo mushroomed into the concrete megalopolis it is today. Kyoto, with a population of about 1½ million people, remains very much a city of the past.

If you go to only one place in all of Japan, Kyoto should be it. As the only major Japanese city spared bombing attacks during World War II, Kyoto is charming, captivating, and spellbinding. As you walk its narrow streets and along its tiny canals, you will be struck with images of yesterday. Old women in kimonos bend over their "garden," which may consist only of a couple of gnarled bonsai beside their front door. An open-fronted shop reveals a man making tatami mats, the musty smell of the rice mats reminiscent of earth itself. Perhaps you'll see a geisha shuffling to her evening appointment in Gion, a small enclave of solemn-brown wooden houses where the sounds of laughter and traditional Japanese music escape through shoji screens. Nijo Castle is still here, built by the Tokugawas and famous for its creaking floorboards designed to warn of enemy intruders. The famous Ryoanji rock garden is here, a Zen garden of pebbles and stones. A pleasant stroll is from Kiyomizu Temple to Heian Shrine, with tea gardens, pottery shops, and temples along the way. In the evening in the summertime, couples sit along the banks of the Kamo River which cuts through the heart of the city.

But as I said before, Kyoto has not escaped the afflictions of the modern age. Kyoto, too, has its share of ugly concrete buildings, the flashing neon of pachinko parlors, telephone lines, and traffic. But, then, Kyoto has always led a rather fragile existence, as a look at any of its temples and shrines will tell you. Made of wood, they have been rebuilt countless times, destroyed through the years by man, fires, and earthquakes.

So perhaps that is the lesson of Kyoto. Life is fleeting, ever-changing, and nothing lasts forever. As a product of the past and the present, Kyoto is a synthesis of all that is Japan in the 20th century. No one who comes to this country should miss the wealth of experience this ancient capital has to offer.

ORIENTATION: One of the major stops on the Shinkansen bullet train, **Kyoto** is three hours away from Tokyo and only 20 minutes from Osaka. If you're arriving in Japan at Osaka International Airport, you can reach Kyoto in about an hour by a special airport bus, for which the fare is ¥840 ($6). Most of Kyoto's attractions and hotels lie to the north of Kyoto Station. The largest concentration of restaurants, shops, bars, and nightlife activity spreads in a radius from the Kawaramachi–Shijo Dori intersection and includes a narrow street called Pontocho and the geisha district of Gion. Temples are sprinkled throughout Kyoto. Be sure to stop off at the **Kyoto Tourist Information Center (T.I.C.)** (tel. 075/371-5649) upon arrival. Located across the street from Kyoto Station's north side (take the Karasuma Central Exit out of Kyoto Station), it has great maps of the city as well as information on sightseeing. Keep in mind, however, that it's closed on Sunday, Saturday afternoon, and weekdays after 5 p.m., so plan your arrival accordingly. Otherwise, there's the local **Kyoto City Information Office**, also located on the station's north side. No one here speaks English, but you can pick up a map and get directions to your hotel. It's open every day from 8:30 a.m. to 5 p.m. You can also call the **Japan Travel-Phone** for any questions you might have regarding Kyoto and the surrounding area at 371-5649 between 9 a.m. and 5 p.m., seven days a week. More information regarding Kyoto is given in Section 6, "The ABCs of Kyoto."

Kyoto's address system is actually quite simple once you understand what the directions mean. Many of its streets are named. Those north of Kyoto Station that run east-west are numbered; for example, the *shi* of Shijo Dori Avenue means "four." *Agaru* means "to the north," *sagaru* means "to the south," *nishi-iru* means "to the west," and *higashi-iru* means "to the east." Thus an address that reads Shijo-agaru means "north of Shijo Dori (or Fourth) Avenue."

GETTING AROUND: The easiest way to get around Kyoto is by bus. The city map given out by the T.I.C. shows major bus routes too. Some of the buses travel in a loop around the city, while others go back and forth between two destinations. At any rate, get on at the back of the bus. If the bus travels a long distance there will be a ticket machine right beside the back door—take the ticket and hold onto it. It has a number on it and will tell the bus driver when you got on and how much you owe. You can see for yourself how much you owe by looking for your number on a panel at the front of the bus. Unsurprisingly, your fare rises the longer you stay on the bus. If you're on a loop bus the fare is the same no matter how long you stay on—¥160 ($1.14)—and you pay when you get off. There are no transfer tickets so you have to pay separately for each ride.

In addition to buses there's also one subway line completed, which is useful only for going to the Imperial Palace. A second line, scheduled for completion in 1989, will be useful primarily to commuters and will run south from Kyoto Station to Takeda.

Taxis in Kyoto come in three different sizes with correspondingly different fares. Small ones are ¥460 ($3.29) for the first two kilometers (1¼ miles), medium-size ones are ¥470 ($3.36), and large ones are ¥490 ($3.50). You can also hire taxis by the half hour, which may not be a bad idea if there are several of you and you don't have much time. Small taxis are available for ¥1,400 ($10) per 30 minutes, medium-size ones are ¥1,750 ($12.50), and large ones are ¥2,000 ($14.29). Make sure your taxi driver understands how long you want him for, and make sure of the price. Note that fares may have changed by the time you arrive in Kyoto.

1. Accommodations

There are many types of accommodation available in Kyoto, ranging from exclusive Japanese inns to business hotels to rock-bottom dormitory-like lodgings. If you've never stayed in a ryokan, Kyoto is probably the best place to do so. With the possible exception of some hot-spring resorts, Kyoto has more choices of ryokan in all price categories than any other city in Japan. Small, usually made of wood, and often situated in delightfully quaint neighborhoods, these ryokan can enrich your stay in Kyoto by putting you in direct touch with the city's traditional past. Remember that in upper- and medium-price ryokan the room charge is per person and includes two meals, tax, and service. Ryokan listed in the budget category, on the other hand, usually do not serve meals unless stated otherwise.

But even if you decide to stay in a hotel, Kyoto has a number of excellent choices in all price ranges (many hotels also have Japanese-style rooms available). Whichever type of accommodation you select, make reservations in advance. Kyoto is a favorite holiday destination for the Japanese, receiving as many as ten million visitors each year. Keep in mind that whereas ryokan include tax and service charges in their prices, hotels in the upper and medium price ranges will add a 10% tax and a 10% service charge to your bill.

Because Kyoto is relatively small and is served by such a good bus system, no matter where you stay you won't be too far away from the city's center. Most hotels and ryokan, however, are concentrated in the center of Kyoto not far from the Kawaramachi–Shijo Dori intersection (called Nakagyo-ku), east of the Kamo River (called Higashiyama-ku), or around Kyoto Station (called Shimogyo-ku).

THE UPPER BRACKET: The service and hospitality at Kyoto's first-class hotels and ryokan are legendary. After all, Kyoto has had centuries of practice catering to members of the imperial court, feudal lords, shoguns, and their emissaries. Following in their footsteps, you too will be treated like royalty. Western-style hotels in this category have the extra benefit of English-language television broadcasts, with CNN newscasts from the United States and information on local sightseeing attractions.

Western Style

One of the newest hotels in Kyoto is the centrally located **ANA Hotel Kyoto**, Nijo-Castle-Mae, Horikawa-dori Avenue, Nakagyo-ku (tel. 075/231-1155). Located just across the street from Nijo Castle—some rooms possess views of the castle grounds—this 303-room property has one of the most stunning lobbies in town, complete with a glass wall overlooking an impressive waterfall and tiny landscape garden. There's a service desk to help you make travel plans for the city and beyond, and facilities include an indoor swimming pool and sauna [which you can use at an extra charge of ¥2,200 ($15.71)]; a nursery room; a beauty salon; and first-rate restaurants serving Japanese, Chinese, and Western cuisine. Rooms are attractive and comfortable, with lots of space in the bathrooms for spreading out cosmetics and toiletries. Singles, none of which face the castle, range from ¥9,300 ($66) to ¥15,400 ($110). Twins start at ¥17,000 ($121), with those facing the castle starting at ¥21,000 ($150).

Another new hotel in Kyoto is the **Kyoto Takaragaike Prince Hotel**, Takaragaike, Sakyo-ku (tel. 075/712-1111). Although it's a bit inconveniently located on the northern fringes of the city, about a 30-minute taxi ride from Kyoto Station, it's useful for those attending conferences in the Kyoto International Conference Hall across the street. Another advantage to staying here is nearby Takaragaike Park, complete with jogging paths, pond, botanical garden, and wood-covered hills. If you want the benefits of being in the countryside but don't want to give up the comforts of a first-class hotel, this may be the place for you. In any case, there are free shuttle buses which depart for Kyoto Station every morning at 8 and 10.

Designed by the famous architect Togo Murano, this imposing circular hotel has the unmistakable touches of a Prince Hotel, including its excellent service, cheerful staff, and its bright color schemes of white, pink, and purple. Restaurants serve French, Chinese, and Japanese cuisine; on the hotel grounds is a traditional tea house, where you can observe a tea-ceremony demonstration for free. For ¥800 ($5.71) you can even partake of the green frothy mixture, along with Japanese sweets. As for the rooms, they are positively spacious, with a sink and vanity area separated from the bathroom. Upon arrival at the hotel, you will be treated to a complimentary tea and sweet, brought to your room by a kimono-clad hostess. Should you have any questions regarding the hotel or

Kyoto during your stay, there's a guest relations officer on duty to help. Rates here start at ¥33,000 ($236) for a double or twin.

If you're looking for an older, more established hotel with a lot more history, one of the best-known hotels in all of Japan is the **Miyako Hotel**, Sanjo Keage, Higashiyama-ku (tel. 075/771-7111), which spreads like an eagle on top of a hill in Higashiyama-ku, commanding a good view of the city. First opened back in 1890, its guests since then read like a Who's Who of visitors to Japan—Queen Elizabeth II, Prince Charles, Anwar El-Sadat, Edward Kennedy, Rosalynn and Amy Carter, Albert Einstein, Charles Lindbergh, Dwight D. Eisenhower, Robert Kennedy, the Dalai Lama of Tibet, Gerald Ford, and Ronald Reagan, to name just a few. In fact, the Miyako Hotel is so well-known around the world that half of its guests are foreigners.

Located about a 20-minute taxi ride from Kyoto Station or just a minute's walk from Keage Station on the Keihen Electric Railway Keishin Line, the Miyako Hotel is spread over 16 acres, including landscaped gardens, a pool, and a sauna. Its Western-style rooms come in a variety of decors and price ranges, but all are cozy, comfortable, and large. English-language newspapers are delivered to your room both morning and evening. Twenty Japanese-style rooms are available in an annex (connected to the main hotel by a covered passageway) that manages to maintain the atmosphere of a traditional ryokan with views of a Japanese garden. Rooms in this Japanese annex range from ¥26,400 ($189) to ¥49,500 ($350), with most in the ¥28,500 ($204) range. Rates for Western-style rooms range from ¥8,200 ($59) to ¥15,400 ($110) for a single and ¥13,200 ($94) to ¥36,000 ($257) for most twins and doubles.

The **Kyoto Grand Hotel**, Shiokoji-Horikawa, Shimogyo-ku (tel. 075/341-2311), was built in 1969 just before Expo was held in Osaka and has been one of Kyoto's grand hotels ever since. I like the architecture of this building—with its flat roof and railed ledges it resembles traditional Japanese architecture. The inside is a successful blend of traditional and modern. The rooms, for example, have shoji screens and fresh-flower arrangements, yet come with bilingual TVs with remote control, soundproof windows, clock, radio, and other modern conveniences. Rates range from ¥8,800 ($63) to ¥15,400 ($110) for a single, ¥14,300 ($102) to ¥24,200 ($173) for a twin, and ¥16,500 ($118) to ¥24,200 ($173) for a double. Japanese-style rooms are available for ¥27,500 ($196). Located about a ten-minute walk east of Kyoto Station, the hotel maintains a shuttle-bus service to the south side of Kyoto Station every 15 minutes from 8 a.m. to 9 p.m. Facilities include an indoor swimming pool and sauna, as well as nine superb restaurants popular with Kyoto's residents, including Kyoto's only revolving restaurant. There's an English-language guest relations coordinator ready to assist you, and the hotel also issues its own maps and sightseeing information on Kyoto in English.

Japanese Style

Hiiragiya Ryokan, on the corner of Fuyacho (also spelled Huyacho) and Oike Streets in the heart of old Kyoto, Nakagyo-ku (tel. 075/221-1136), is a fine example of an old Japanese inn. Opened more than 150 years ago as a seafood merchant's shop and becoming an inn in 1861 to cater to visiting merchants, this exquisite ryokan is an excellent choice for foreigners unfamiliar with Japan. The staff is very efficient and accommodating and quite helpful in initiating visitors to the joys of the traditional inn. Surrounded by walls of wood and earth-toned yellow topped by tile roofs, this ryokan makes artful use of wood, bamboo, screens, and stones in creating a haven of simple design. The best room in the house is number 30, with magnificent views of the garden. At ¥88,000 ($630) per person, however, this room is probably a bit out of range for most of us. The next most expensive room is the one I find the most beautiful, a corner room with antiques and plenty of sunshine. It goes for ¥60,000 ($429) per person. Other rooms, with bath and toilet, start at ¥30,000 ($214) per person. All prices include two meals, of course, and Western-style breakfasts are available upon request. The three public baths here, as well as the tubs in the guest rooms, are of Chinese pine, soft to the touch. Guests who have stayed here include princes of the Japanese royal family, former Prime Minister Tojo, Charlie Chaplin, and designer Pierre Cardin.

Across the street from the Hiiragiya is another distinguished and venerable old inn, the **Tawaraya**, Fuyacho, Oike-Sagaru, Nakagyo-ku (tel. 075/221-5566). Since it opened in the first decade of the 1700s, it has been owned and operated by the same family. The present owner is Mrs. Toshi Okazaki Sato, the 11th generation of innkeepers. Unfortunately, fire consumed the original building, so the oldest part of the ryokan now dates back only 175 years. This inn also has an impressive list of former guests, including the king of Sweden, former prime minister of Canada Pierre Trudeau, Leonard Bernstein, Edward Albee, Marlon Brando, Jean-Paul Sartre, Simone de Beauvoir, Walter Cronkite, Alfred Hitchcock, Candice Bergen, and Barbra Streisand. With tranquillity and refined taste reigning supreme, the ryokan has 19 rooms, each one different and exquisitely appointed. Some rooms, for example, have glass sliding doors opening up to a mossy garden of bamboo, stone lanterns, and manicured bushes, with cushions on a wooden veranda from which you can soak in the peacefulness. Per person charges for a room only begin at ¥44,000 ($314). Meals are extra, with dinner ranging from ¥8,800 ($62.86) to ¥27,000 ($193) and breakfast ranging from ¥1,500 ($10.71) to ¥2,700 ($19.29).

Sumiya, Fuyacho-dori, Sanjo-sagaru, Nakagyo-ku (tel. 075/221-2188), is another traditional Japanese inn located on Fuyacho-dori Street south of the two ryokan described above. Like other ryokan in this price range, it offers excellent service amid simple yet elegant surroundings. Some of its 25 rooms have wonderful views of tiny private gardens, with outdoor benches or platforms for sitting. Rates here range from ¥22,000 ($157) to ¥65,000 ($464) per person, including two meals. Western breakfasts are available.

THE MEDIUM BRACKET: Accommodations in this category are numerous and offer excellent value for the money, with prices lower than in Tokyo. All the hotels listed below have private bathrooms connected to all their guest rooms. Some of the ryokan, on the other hand, do not, especially the older ones. However, all ryokan have communal baths and toilets.

Western Style

With the Miyako name behind it, the **New Miyako Hotel**, Hachijo-guchi, Kyoto Station (tel. 075/661-7111), is one of the most popular hotels in this category. Opened in 1975, it's a sister hotel to the older first-class Miyako Hotel and is conveniently located just across the street from Kyoto Station's south side. With lower prices than the first-class Miyako Hotel, a modern exterior, and simple decor, it appeals widely to younger Japanese, group tours, and individual tourists. A ten-story white building shaped like an H, it has 714 rooms and eight restaurants. A beer garden is open on the roof from April to September every evening from 5 to 9 p.m. Rooms are what you'd expect in this price range, coming with TV with English-language broadcasts, radio, refrigerator, and hot-water pot for tea. Single rooms range from ¥6,600 ($47) to ¥8,800 ($63); twins, from ¥10,000 ($71) to ¥20,900 ($149); and doubles, from ¥14,300 ($102) to ¥20,900 ($149). Triples, if you need one, begin at ¥22,000 ($157).

Across the street from Kyoto Station's north side is the **Kyoto New Hankyu Hotel**, Shiokoji-dori, Shimogyo-ku (tel. 075/343-5300), built in 1981 and offering 320 rooms. About 20% of its guests are foreigners, and of particular help to visitors is its information desk in the lobby where the English-speaking staff can answer any questions you might have regarding your stay in Kyoto. The front-desk staff is very efficient and polite. Restaurants include a steakhouse and a Chinese restaurant, as well as a branch of the famous Minokichi Restaurant. Rooms are pleasant, with a decor of subdued colors, and come equipped with the usual fridge, radio, alarm clock, and hot water for tea, as well as a TV with coin-operated video. Rates begin at ¥8,500 ($61) for singles, ¥13,700 ($98) for twins, ¥17,000 ($121) for doubles, and ¥29,800 ($213) for Japanese-style rooms.

Another centrally located hotel is the **Kyoto Century Hotel**, 680 Higashishiokoji-cho, Shiokoji-sagaru, Shimogyo-ku (tel. 075/351-0111). Just east of Kyoto Station, this 243-room brick hotel features a six-story atrium lobby filled with white lights and plants. In addition to an outside swimming pool [which costs ¥1,500 ($10.71)], the hotel has French and Japanese restaurants and a shopping arcade. All rooms include TV with CNN broadcasts and fridge and start at ¥9,300 ($66) for a single; twins range from ¥17,600 ($126) to ¥20,900 ($149), and doubles, from ¥13,700 ($98) to ¥23,000 ($164). Spacious Japanese-style rooms are available, starting at ¥38,000 ($271) for a two-room suite with kitchenette. Ask for a room facing east towards Higashiyama-ku. Although the view is nothing special, it's a lot better than the view towards the west, which looks squarely at the rooms of a neighboring hotel.

Located across the street from the National Museum, the **Kyoto Park Hotel**, Sanjusangendo Side, Higashiyama-ku (tel. 075/525-3111), is a good starting point for strolls throughout the eastern part of Kyoto, including the pleasant walk from nearby Kiyomizu Temple to Heian Shrine. With its stained-glass windows, plants, and statues, it's reminiscent of a European hotel, and there are two gardens on the hotel grounds. One is a rock garden, while the other is a lovely garden with a waterfall, cliff, and pond. Flowered wallpaper brightens up the rooms, which come with TV, hot-water pot, fridge, and clock. Especially nice are the more expensive twin rooms on the fifth floor, which have balconies overlooking the garden. Singles in this hotel are ¥8,500 ($61) to ¥10,700 ($76), doubles are ¥19,200 ($137), and twins run ¥14,800 ($106) to ¥23,600 ($169). To reach the Kyoto Park Hotel, take bus 206 or 208 from Kyoto Station to the Sanjusangendo-mae bus stop.

In the heart of Kyoto on Kawaramachi Dori Avenue, the **Kyoto Royal Hotel**, Kawaramachi, Sanjo, Nakagyo-ku (tel. 075/223-1234), is a typical tourist hotel and is easily reached by taking bus 4 from Kyoto Station to the Kawaramachi-Sanjo bus stop. In addition to Japanese and Chinese restaurants, it also has a Western restaurant on the tenth floor with panoramic views of the city and surrounding hills. Rooms are simple but feature bedside panels for the TV, an alarm clock, hot-water pot, and fridge. Most single rooms face an inner courtyard, which cuts down on noise but also on sunshine. Room rates are ¥8,800 ($63) to ¥10,500 ($75) for singles, ¥14,800 ($106) to ¥22,000 ($157) for doubles, ¥14,800 ($106) to ¥20,900 ($149) for twins, and ¥23,000 ($164) for a triple. Japanese-style rooms are available for ¥24,000 ($171).

Right up the street from the Royal Hotel is the **Kyoto Hotel**, Kawaramachi-Oike, Nakagyo-ku (tel. 075/211-5111). First opened in 1888, the present hotel consists of three different parts, the oldest stemming from 1927 and the newest from 1970. Altogether there are more than 500 rooms and seven restaurants catering to tourists (25% of which are foreigners). On the roof is a beer garden, open from mid-May to the end of August. Rooms have bilingual TV, hot-water pot, and fridge, and half the rooms have balconies. The cheapest singles face an inner courtyard. The older rooms have huge bathrooms—almost larger than the rooms themselves. Singles range from ¥8,200 ($59) to ¥11,000 ($79), twins run ¥14,300 ($102) to ¥33,000 ($236), and doubles cost ¥20,300 ($145) to ¥25,000 ($179). Japanese tatami rooms are also ¥25,000 ($179).

Situated on Oike Dori Avenue, the **Hotel Gimmond**, Takakura Oike Dori, Nakagyo-ku (tel. 075/221-4111), is a smaller hotel, with 145 rooms. Although it calls itself a tourist hotel, its rooms are rather plain and bare, resembling those in business hotels. They come with fridge, alarm clock, and TV with pay video. A good bargain here is the summer evening buffet, offering as much food and beer as you can consume for only ¥4,800 ($34.29), held from 5 to 8 p.m. mid-June through August. All rooms are soundproof, but I still think those that face away from Oike Dori Avenue are quieter. Singles begin at ¥7,700 ($55), and doubles and twins at ¥13,200 ($94). The easiest way to reach the Hotel Gimmond from Kyoto Station is to take the subway to Oike Station; from there it's just a few minutes' walk.

First opening more than 30 years ago, the **International Hotel Kyoto** (called the Kyoto Kokusai Hotel in Japanese), is located on Horikawa-dori Avenue across from Nijo Castle, Nakagyo-ku (tel. 075/222-1111). Despite its name, approximately 90% of the hotel guests are Japanese and the hotel has been somewhat overshadowed by more modern hotels that have opened in Kyoto in the last three decades. Its lobby overlooks a pleasant, lush garden, and rooms are decorated with traditional shoji screens. Singles, none of which face the castle, start at ¥10,500 ($75). You can have a twin facing the castle for ¥15,400 ($110), while doubles with castle views are ¥17,600 ($126). Facilities include five restaurants and bars, as well as a beer garden open in summer from 5 to 9 p.m.

Although it's rather inconveniently located in the northeast corner of Kyoto, far from most of the city's sights, the **Kyoto Holiday Inn**, 36 Nishihiraki-cho, Takano, Sakyo-ku (tel. 075/721-3131), makes up for it by providing facilities normally found only at resort hotels, including indoor and outdoor swimming pools, tennis courts, an indoor ice-skating rink, a sauna and solarium, a golf-driving range, and a 100-lane bowling alley. A restaurant mall features a dozen different restaurants ranging from McDonald's to Chinese to steak, and a rooftop beer garden (open from 5 to 9:30 p.m. in the summer) has barbecue dishes you can cook at your own table. As with all Holiday Inns, the beds are all doubles and children under 12 can stay with their parents free. A number of different kinds of rooms are available, beginning at ¥8,600 ($61) for one person and ¥15,800 ($113) for two. The hotel maintains a shuttle-bus service with runs to Kyoto Station every hour between 8 a.m. and 8 p.m. You can also take public bus 206 from Kyoto Station to the Takano bus stop.

Japanese Style

First opened almost 200 years ago in the early 1800s, **Kinmata** [76], 407 Gokomachi Shijo-agaru, Nakagyo-ku (tel. 075/221-1039), is a beautiful, traditional wooden inn in the heart of Kyoto. Its earliest customers were medicine peddlers, and in the hallway hangs an old sign admonishing the house rules of past centuries—among them no gambling, no prostitution, no mah-jongg, and no noisy parties. The present owner is the seventh generation of innkeepers here. With only seven rooms, Kinmata is exquisite inside and out, complete with an inner courtyard and peaceful garden. The public bath is of cypress. Rates per person start at ¥20,000 ($143), with two meals. You can also stay here for ¥6,600 ($47) per person if you opt to take meals elsewhere—but you'll be missing great meals prepared by the owner himself.

Seikoro, Toiyamachi Gojo, Higashiyama-ku (tel. 075/561-0771), is less than a minute's walk from Gojo Station on the Keihan Electric Railway. Accustomed to foreigners, the manager here speaks good English. The ryokan itself is about 100 years old but its history stretches back 150 years. After passing through a front gate and small courtyard, you'll find yourself in a cozy parlor, which holds an eclectic mixture of both Japanese and Western antiques, including an old grandfather clock. The rooms, also decorated in antiques, are very homey and comfortable and come with a private bathroom. Some rooms overlook a garden. An annex built just before the 1964 Olympics has rooms that are high enough up that you can see over the surrounding rooftops. Per-person rates, including two meals, tax, and service charge, range from ¥22,000 ($157) to ¥50,000 ($357). The management doesn't mind, however, if you prefer to take your meals elsewhere, especially if you're going to be here a while. The charge for two people without meals, tax, or service charge is ¥22,000 ($157) to ¥44,000 ($314).

Located on the approach to Nanzenji Temple, the **Yachiyo Inn**, Nanzenji, Sakyo-ku (tel. 075/771-4148), has a large foreign clientele. Formerly a villa (it became a ryokan after World War II), the building is about 100 years old but has been remodeled so that it seems almost new. All the rooms on the ground floor open up onto a small garden. Less expensive rooms are located on the second floor. There are wooden bathtubs in most rooms, along with showers and Western toilets. Rooms also boast transom carvings and ikebana flower arrangements. This ryokan, which you can reach by taking bus 5 from Kyoto Station, doesn't mind if you prefer to take your meals elsewhere. If you're staying in Kyoto for a few days, you might want to first take breakfast and dinner at the ryokan and then later start going out to Kyoto's many restaurants. Room rates, including tax and service charge, range from ¥14,300 ($102) to ¥23,000 ($164) for one person and ¥17,600 ($126) to ¥26,400 ($189) for two. Rates including two meals, tax, and service range from ¥20,000 ($143) to ¥34,000 ($243) for one person and ¥28,500 ($204) to ¥49,500 ($354) for two.

Located on Shinmonzen shopping street in a quaint neighborhood of small wooden homes and antique shops, **Yoshi-ima**, Shinmonzen Street, Gion (tel. 075/561-2620), is within easy walking distance of both Gion and the Kawaramachi district, with its many restaurants and bars. Much of the ryokan, however, is relatively new and modern, although there are a few older rooms available in a wooden building for the same price. Most of the guests here are booked through the Japan Travel Bureau, including foreigners. In fact, sometimes the whole ryokan is filled with only foreigners. Once a year, for example, a group of writers and artists come from the Soviet Union. There is a total of 20 rooms. Those without private bathroom start at ¥15,900 ($114), including two meals, tax, and service charge. Rooms with private bathroom start at ¥19,200 ($137).

A sister ryokan of the exclusive Hiiragiya Ryokan, the **Hiiragiya Bekkan**, on Gokomachi Dori Street, Nijosagaru, Nakagyo-ku (tel. 075/231-0151), is a very good choice among Kyoto's medium-priced Japanese inns. Run by a very friendly and accommodating staff, this small 14-room ryokan has a warm and home-like feel to it. Opened 25 years ago, it's relatively new by ryokan standards but manages to transmit a traditional atmosphere, as most of the rooms open onto a small garden. The management prefers that you take your meals here, and per-person rates, including breakfast and dinner, tax, and service, run ¥11,000 ($79) to ¥22,000 ($157).

Ryokan Rikiya, Ryozen Kannon-mae, Higashiyama-ku (tel. 075/561-2814), is located in front of Ryozen Kannon between Kiyomizu Temple and Maruyama Park. To reach it, take bus 206 from Kyoto Station to the Yasui bus stop, from which it's a four-minute walk. With ten rooms located in a modern building, this is a quiet, family-run ryokan. The best room is named Daiyu, has its own bathroom, and faces toward the front courtyard. Charges per person without meals are ¥6,600 ($47) for rooms without bathroom and ¥9,300 ($66) for those with bathroom. If you want to take breakfast and dinner here, rooms with bathroom go for ¥19,200 ($137) per person and those without are ¥16,500 ($118).

THE BUDGET CATEGORY: Kyoto abounds in accommodations in this price range, due in part to the large percentage of students and young people who flock to this cultural mecca. The majority of establishments in this category are Japanese style, while the Western hotels are all business hotels. Unless otherwise stated, you can expect the business hotel rooms to have a private bath, but rooms in Japanese-style ryokan do not. Remember also that unless otherwise stated, a 10% tax and 10% service charge will be added to rates above ¥5,000 ($36) per person in Western-style accommodations. Japanese-style ryokan, on the other hand, include tax and service charges in their rates.

Western Style

Kyoto Central Inn, Shijo Kawaramachi, Nishi-iru, Shimogyo-ku (tel. 075/211-1666), as the name implies, is centrally located in the heart of the city. It occupies one of the best spots in town, near the intersection of Shijo and Kawaramachi Streets. Although it's a business hotel, because of its location about 60% of its guests are tourists, including many women. Rooms are small but adequate, and come with TV and radio. The hotel's restaurant and coffeeshop is open from 7 a.m. to 9:30 p.m. Singles are ¥7,000 ($50), twins are ¥10,000 ($71) to ¥12,000 ($86), and doubles are ¥11,000 ($79). Triples begin at ¥13,200 ($94). You can reach the hotel on a number of bus lines from Kyoto Station, including bus 4 and 5.

Located on Kawaramachi Dori Avenue not far from where it meets Sanjo Dori Avenue, the **Hotel Alpha**, Kawaramachi, Sango-agaru (tel. 075/241-2000), is a pleasant business hotel that opened in 1982. To reach it from Kyoto Station, take bus 4, 5, or 205 to the Kawaramachi-Sanjo bus stop. Entrance to the hotel is on a side street called Anekoji Dori. Semi-double-size beds are in all 120 rooms, which also have the usual TV with video, hot-water pot, and fridge. Hair dryers are available on request. Since the cheapest singles face an inner courtyard and are fairly dark, it may be worthwhile to dish out the extra yen for a brighter room. Singles range from ¥5,500 ($39) to ¥6,600 ($47); twins, from ¥11,000 ($79) to ¥14,300 ($102); and doubles, from ¥10,000 ($71) to ¥12,000 ($86). A few Japanese-style rooms are available beginning at ¥22,000 ($157).

It's hard to miss the **Kyoto Tower Hotel**, located right across the street from Kyoto Station's north side at Karasuma Shichijo (tel. 075/361-3211). Topped by a tall tower with an observation platform, this hotel was built just before the 1964 Olympics and is now a kind of cross between a tourist hotel and business hotel. Because of the tower and connecting shops there's a lot of traffic through the hotel's ground floor, but the lobby and restaurant on the eighth floor are a bit more peaceful. Rooms are soundproof and feature shoji screens, refrigerator, hot-water pot, TV, and alarm clock. The bathrooms and tubs are tiny. Room rates are ¥6,300 ($45) to ¥7,900 ($56) for singles, ¥9,700 ($69) to ¥17,500 ($125) for twins, and ¥10,500 ($75) to ¥14,800 ($106) for doubles. Triples begin at ¥16,500 ($118) and Japanese-style tatami rooms are ¥19,800 ($141).

Also located across from Kyoto Station's north side is the **Hotel Hokke Club**, Higashi-Shiokojicho, Shimogyo-ku (tel. 075/361-1251). Part of a business-hotel chain, this one caters to tourists because of its favorable location.

Take off your shoes before entering; the front desk is on the ground floor and the lobby is on the second floor. On the ground floor is also a large tatami room used for Buddhist ceremonies twice a day for the hotel's employees, which you're welcome to observe. There are two public baths, large and bright with windows extending along the length of one wall. You're better off asking for a room on a higher floor. The cheapest Japanese-style tatami rooms without private bathroom go for ¥7,400 ($53). Western-style singles without bath are ¥5,800 ($41). They tend to be rather dark with tiny windows, but have TV, radio, cotton kimono, hot-water pot, and sink. Twins without bathroom are ¥10,500 ($75); with bathroom they're ¥12,700 ($71). Other rooms available include triples beginning at ¥12,500 ($89) and Japanese-style rooms with bathroom at ¥8,500 ($61). All rooms are very simple, with only the basics.

Opened in 1985, **Pension Higashiyama**, Sanjo-sagaru, Shirakawa-suji (tel. 075/882-1181), is a clean and cheerful establishment on a small street banked by the Shirakawa River not far from the Miyako Hotel on Kyoto's east side. Its 14 rooms, some of which overlook the willow-lined stream, are mainly Western style with flowered wallpaper and quilts on the bed, but three Japanese-style tatami rooms are also available. A few rooms have their own private bathroom. Rooms come with coin-operated TV and there's a coin laundry on the premises. Rates are ¥3,900 ($28) for one person, ¥7,900 ($56) for two, and ¥11,000 ($79) for three. Rooms with private bathroom run about ¥800 ($5.71) more. If you want to use a cotton kimono here you can rent one for ¥200 ($1.43). The front doors are locked at 11:30 p.m. To reach it, take bus 206 from Kyoto Station to the Chion-in-mae bus stop, from which it's a two-minute walk.

Kuwacho Ryokan, 231 Shichijo-agaru, Akezu-dori, Shimogy-ku (tel. 075/371-3191), has both Western- and Japanese-style rooms despite its name. Very conveniently located just a three-minute walk north of Kyoto Station near Higashi Honganji Temple, this modern concrete building has 14 rooms, all with private bathroom, coin-operated TV, and cotton kimono. Rooms facing the front even have a small balcony. No meals are served, and rates are ¥4,900 ($35) for single occupancy, ¥7,700 ($55) for double, and ¥11,000 ($79) for triple.

Japanese Style

There isn't much variation in rooms in this category. After all, a tatami room is a tatami room and at this price there usually isn't much else in them. Rooms are fairly bare, with perhaps only a low table, a TV, some cushions, and a futon in the closet which you lay out yourself before retiring. Imparting a feeling of traditional Japan, however, they are highly recommended.

Matsubaya Ryokan, Nishi-iru, Higashitouin, Kamijuzuyamachi Dori Avenue, Shimogyo-ku (tel. 075/351-3727), is conveniently located about a tenminute walk north of Kyoto Station close to Higashi Honganji Temple. A member of the Japanese Inn Group, this traditional ryokan offers excellent value for the money, with singles going for ¥3,800 ($27) and twins for ¥7,000 ($50) to ¥7,700 ($55). There are 11 Japanese-style tatami rooms here, the best ones facing an inner courtyard. These rooms come complete with wooden balconies and a couple of chairs, great places to relax. Another good choice in rooms are those that face a tiny enclosed garden. If you wish to make a reservation here, you must pay a deposit equal to one night's lodging, payable in the form of a cashier's check, international money order, traveler's check, or American Express credit card. Towels and cotton kimonos are provided, and rooms have a coin-operated TV. Facilities include two public baths and a coin laundry. If you want to try a Japanese-style breakfast, you can order one for ¥1,000 ($7.14). Ham and eggs are available for ¥300 ($2.14).

Not far from Matsubaya is **Ryokan Murakamiya**, 270 Sasaya-cho, Shichijo-agaru, Higashinotouin-dori, Shimogyo-ku (tel. 075/371-1260). Small and clean, its seven rooms are nicely decorated, some with old-style ceilings and wood-work. The building itself is about 50 years old. Rates here are ¥3,800 ($27) for a single, ¥7,700 ($55) for a twin, and ¥9,900 ($71) for a triple. Japanese break-fasts are ¥800 ($5.71).

Another inexpensive ryokan in the same general vicinity is **Ryokan Kyoka**, Seisinji-cho, Kaminoguchi-agaru, Kiyamachi Dori (tel. 075/351-7920), about a seven-minute walk from Kyoto Station. Although it doesn't have quite the charm of the other two described above, it also has good prices at ¥3,300 ($24) for one person and ¥6,500 ($46) for two. Some of the rooms are in a nearby annex, where you have a view of the Takase Canal. Although the annex, called Riverside Takase, is farther from the station (about a 15-minute walk away), its location is actually much prettier, with rates the same as at the Kyoka. Japanese- or Western-style breakfasts are available for ¥1,000 ($5). Twice a month, on the first and third Fridays, a tea ceremony and flower-arranging demonstration are held at Kyoka beginning at 1 p.m. at a charge of ¥300 ($2.14).

Hiraiwa Ryokan, 314 Hayao-cho, Kaminoguch-agaru, Ninomiyacho-dori, Shimogyo-ku (tel. 075/351-6748), is one of the best-known ryokan in the Japa-nese Inn Group. Several stories have been published about this inexpensive Jap-anese inn and the couple who run it. They speak almost no English and yet have been welcoming foreigners from all over the world for many years. Spread through the main building and a new annex, rooms are spotless and come with TV, towel, and cotton kimono. Facilities include coin-operated washer and dryer and even heated toilet seats! Breakfasts are communal affairs around the kitchen table, where toast and coffee are available for ¥250 ($1.79). There's a small public bath and showers, but better still is the neighborhood public bath just around the corner, which charges ¥250 ($1.79). Single rooms cost ¥3,300 ($24) and twins are ¥6,500 ($46). This ryokan is about a 15-minute walk from Kyoto Station, but you can also take bus 17 or 205 and get off at the third stop, Kawaramachi Shomen. From there it's a three-minute walk.

In the vicinity of Hiraiwa are a number of other inexpensive Japanese-style accommodations. **Yuhara** [78], Kiyamachi-dori, Shomen-agaru, Shimogyo-ku (tel. 075/371-9583), has been a ryokan for more than 30 years, welcoming guests from all over the world. Pleasantly located beside a tree-lined narrow canal, it's run by an enthusiastic woman who speaks English. Of its nine rooms, one is Western style and three have their own sinks. The rate here is ¥3,300 ($24) per person.

Close by are two more Japanese-style inns, both charging only ¥2,000 ($14) per person. **Sanyu** [79], Kamogawasuji, Shomen-agaru, Shimogyo-ku (tel. 075/371-1968), is the more picturesque. A century old, it's a beautiful old wooden building with traditional latticed windows and railings along the second-floor windows. Some rooms have air-conditioners, while others have only fans, and all rooms are very simple. Unfortunately, the owner isn't sure he'll be able to keep the place open because of financial considerations, so be sure to call first. An alternative is **Ichiume** [80], Higashikiyamachi, Gojo-sagaru, Shimogyo-ku (tel. 075/351-9385). Although the neighborhood is pleas-ant, the building itself is unattractive. Carpets cover the tatami in the rooms, which come with fans instead of air conditioning. The price, however, is right.

Nashinoki Inn, Agaru Imadegawa Nashinoki Street, Kamikyo-ku (tel. 075/241-1543), in a quiet, peaceful neighborhood north of the Kyoto Imperial Pal-ace, is run by a warm and friendly older couple who speak some English and have had the ryokan for 17 years. There are eight tatami rooms here, some of them quite large and adequate for families. The rate for one person is ¥4,800

($34) and for two people it's ¥8,800 ($63). A Japanese or Western breakfast is served for ¥1,000 ($7.14), and Japanese dinners are available for ¥3,800 ($27). To reach this inn, take the subway from Kyoto Station to Imadegawa Station. From there it's about a ten-minute walk.

Rokuharaya Inn [81] 147 Takemuracho Rokuhara, Higashiyama-ku (tel. 075/531-2776), is a basic, inexpensive ryokan located on a small street typical of Kyoto. There are only seven rooms here, and in my opinion the best ones are on the second floor. More foreigners stay here than Japanese. Rooms have coin-operated TVs but not much more—just your average Japanese tatami room. Per-person rates are ¥3,600 ($26) without meals, ¥4,400 ($31.43) with breakfast, and ¥5,500 ($39) with two meals. To reach it, take bus 206 from Kyoto Station to the Gojozaka bus stop, from which it's a three-minute walk.

Another inexpensive lodging is **Hinomoto**, 375 Kotake-cho, Matsubara-agaru, Kawaramachi Dori, Shimogyo-ku (tel. 075/351-4563). Not far from the Kawaramachi-Shijo intersection, its front façade is red brick but the rest is wood. It's a three-minute walk from Kawaramachi Matsubara bus stop, which can be reached by taking bus 17 or 205 from Kyoto Station. Although the couple running this six-room ryokan does not speak any English, they welcome foreigners. Rooms are pleasant, the location is quiet, and the public bath is made of wood. Rates are ¥3,300 ($24) for one person, ¥6,600 ($47) for two, and ¥8,800 ($63) for three. Western breakfasts cost ¥400 ($2.86) and Japanese breakfasts are ¥1,000 ($7.14).

Teradaya Inn, Gojo-bashi Higashi, Higashiyama-ku (tel. 075/561-3821), is located near the sloping approach to Kiyomizu Temple in east Kyoto. A concrete building with only five rooms, it charges ¥3,600 ($26) per person for a room only, ¥4,400 ($31) with breakfast, and ¥5,500 ($39) if you take a room with two meals. Yukata are provided, and televisions and air-conditioners are coin-operated. Rooms on the second floor are the brightest. Facilities include a public bath and coin laundry.

Although it's not as conveniently located as the ryokan listed above, **Rakucho**, Higashihangi-cho, Shimogamo, Sakyo-ku (tel. 075/721-2174), offers pleasant, clean rooms for ¥3,600 ($26) for single occupancy and ¥6,300 ($45) to ¥7,400 ($53) for a double. All rooms have heating and air conditioning and a view of a small, peaceful garden. Rakucho is a ten-minute walk from Kitaoji subway station. You can also reach it by taking bus 205 from Kyoto Station to Furitsu-Daigakumae bus stop, from which it's a one-minute walk away. Entrance to the ryokan is through a well-tended tiny courtyard filled with plants.

Ryokan Mishima Shrine, 539 Kamiuma-machi, Higashioji Higashi-iru, Shibutani-dori, Higashiyama-ku (tel. 075/551-0033), is located on the grounds of Mishima Shrine, a Shinto shrine visited by women who desire children and by women already pregnant who wish to ensure a safe delivery. You can have your picture taken in traditional shrine garb, free if you have your own camera and ¥240 ($1.71) if you have it taken with the shrine's Polaroid. Although the shrine was founded about 150 years ago, the nine Japanese-style rooms are located in a new building that opened in the mid-1980s. Spotless and simple, it caters largely to foreigners in the summer and to Japanese in the winter. Cotton kimonos and towels are provided, and rooms have a coin-operated TV as well as a private toilet. Facilities include four public baths and a coin-operated washing machine. The family running this place speaks some English. If you're alone you'll be charged ¥3,800 ($27), two people are charged ¥6,600 ($47), and three people are charged ¥8,800 ($63). To reach the shrine, take bus 206 from Kyoto Station and get off at the Higashiyama-Umamachi bus stop, from which it's a five-minute walk.

If you want to stay in a Buddhist temple, **Myorenji Temple** [82], Teranouchi

Horikawa, Kamigyo-ku (tel. 075/451-3527), was founded more than 650 years ago, though the present buildings stem from about two centuries ago. To reach it, take bus 9 from Kyoto Station and get off at the Teranouchi bus stop. From there it's a few minutes' walk. Once you enter the temple grounds the building open to guests lies straight ahead. Very peaceful, it's run by a jolly woman named Chizuko-san who speaks a little English. She requests that you make reservations to stay here at least two days in advance, preferably a week before. Sleeping is on futons spread out in large rooms, and the charge of ¥3,300 ($23.57) includes breakfast, dinner, and a ticket to use the neighborhood public bath (there are no bathing facilities on the temple grounds). If you're interested in attending services, they're held every morning at 6:30 a.m. Be sure to check out the rock garden in back of the temple.

If you're looking for lodging at rock-bottom prices, the best place in town is **Tani House**, 8 Daitokujicho, Murasakino, Kita-ku (tel. 075/492-5489). Located close to Daitokuji Temple on the route of several buses from Kyoto Station, including bus 206 (get off at the Kenkunjinja bus stop), the entrance of this 50-year-old wooden house is smothered with bamboo. Mrs. Tani keeps this place tidy and clean, and sleeping is either in private rooms or in communal tatami sleeping rooms separate for men and women. This place has a reputation that extends far beyond Japan's borders. One European staying here told me he heard about Tani House when he was traveling through Russia. Mrs. Tani speaks some English and somehow seems able to cope with the many foreigners who pass through her life daily. You're supposed to leave during the day from 11 a.m. to 3 p.m., but otherwise rules are fairly lenient. The rate is only ¥1,500 ($10.71) per person regardless if you sleep in the dorm or in a private room (if you're the only one in the private room, however, she'll charge you double since they're meant for two people). Although Tani House is a bit far north, the price more than makes up for it.

Of the several youth hostels in and around the Kyoto area, **Higashiyama Youth Hostel**, 112 Shirakawabashi-goken-cho, Sanjo-dori, Higashiyama-ku (tel. 075/761-8135), is the most convenient and the closest to Kyoto Station. A 20-minute bus ride from Kyoto Station on bus 5 to the Higashiyama-Sanjo bus stop, this youth hostel is a modern concrete building that sleeps 130 people in bunkbeds. You have to take breakfast and dinner here, and the charge is ¥3,000 ($21) for youth hostel members and ¥3,200 ($23) for nonmembers. Be sure to call in advance because this place is sometimes booked full with school groups.

A NOTE ON JAPANESE SYMBOLS: Many hotels, restaurants, and other establishments in Japan do not have signs showing their names in English letters. Appendix II lists the Japanese symbols for all such places appearing in this guide. Each establishment name in Japanese symbols is numbered, and the same number appears in brackets in the text following the boldfaced establishment name. For example, in the text the Osaka hotel, Hokke Club [161], is number 161 in the Japanese symbol list in Appendix II.

2. Where to Dine

Most of Kyoto's traditional Japanese restaurants are located in the heart of the city in Nakagyo-ku, spreading to the east in areas called Higashiyama-ku and Sakyo-ku. I have therefore divided Kyoto's restaurants according to district, adding some Western-style restaurants as well. In addition to the restaurants listed here there are also some establishments described in the nightlife section that serve food.

EASTERN KYOTO: Many of the restaurants in this part of town sprang up in connection with the Buddhist temples in the area, serving either vegetarian fare to Buddhist monks and worshippers or traditional Japanese food to sightseers. Kaiseki cuisine and tofu dishes are offered by the majority of restaurants in this area.

Japanese Food

Formerly a villa, **Minoko** [83], 480 Kiyoi-cho, Shimogawara-dori, Gion, Higashiyama-ku (tel. 561-0328), is an enclave of traditional Japan. With its simple, austere exterior and an interior of winding wooden corridors, tatami rooms, and a garden, it's the kind of building that excites curiosity from anyone passing by, making them want to pause and explore further. Opened about 70 years ago by the present owner's father, Minoko does its best to retain the spirit of the tea ceremony. For lunch, for example, you can order an informal box lunch called *chabako-bento*, named after the lacquered box it's served in which is traditionally used to carry tea utensils to outdoor tea ceremonies. Served from 11:30 a.m. to 2:30 p.m., it costs ¥2,700 ($19.29). For lunch you can also order the *hiru-kaiseki*, a mini-kaiseki set, for ¥8,800 ($62.86). Lunch is served communally in a large tatami room with a view of a beautiful tea garden. If you come here for dinner, available by reservation only, you'll eat in your own private tatami room. Elaborate kaiseki dinners begin at ¥10,000 ($71.43), including a special kind of kaiseki, called *cha-kaiseki*, usually served at tea ceremony gatherings. Hours here are from 11:30 a.m. to 11 p.m., with the last order at 8 p.m. It's closed the second and fourth Wednesdays of every month. Minoko is located just a couple minutes' walk south of Yasaka Shrine.

Located right next to the stone torii gate of Yasaka Shrine is **Nakamuraro** [84], Yasaka-jinja-uchi, Gion (tel. 561-0016). Opened 400 years ago to serve worshippers on their way to the shrine, the tiny one-room tea house is said to be the oldest restaurant in Japan. It specializes in *tofu dengaku*, skewers of tofu smothered in miso sauce. Beside the tea house is a handsome wooden restaurant, added in the late 19th century, where meals are served in lovely rooms overlooking a magnificent garden. Now in its 12th generation of restaurateurs, Nakamuraro offers a lunchtime tofu dengaku obento for ¥2,600 ($18.57) and shabu-shabu or sukiyaki for ¥6,600 ($47.14). If you feel like splurging, kaiseki dinners are available starting at ¥15,000 ($197.14). Hours here are 11:30 a.m. to 7:30 p.m. (last order), with lunch served until 3 p.m. Your main problem will be in deciding whether you want to dine in the ancient tea house or the restaurant with its peaceful view of the garden—both have a great atmosphere.

If you're the least bit shy about going into a Japanese restaurant and ordering something without being able to read the menu, the easiest place to enjoy Japanese food is in the internationally known **Miyako Hotel**, Sanjo-Keage (tel. 771-7111). In its Japanese restaurant, Hamasaku, open from noon to 2 p.m. and 5 to 10 p.m., you can have a variety of dishes ranging from tempura, sushi, and eel to kaiseki cuisine. For lunch, why not try a special box lunch of, say, combination sushi or eel and rice for ¥3,000 ($21.43)? Tempura meals range from ¥4,700 ($33.57) to ¥6,300 ($45), while kaiseki menus, which change with the seasons, range from ¥8,800 ($62.86) to ¥13,200 ($94.29).

If you want to come to the Miyako for dinner, another place you can try is Hagoromo. It's open nightly from 5:30 to 9 p.m., serving pork, beef, or chicken sukiyaki beginning at ¥5,500 ($39.29), or *tohbanyaki* (beef, chicken, pork, shrimp, and seasonal vegetables grilled on a porcelain plate) for ¥7,000 ($50).

Minokichi of Kyoto, Sanjo-agaru, Dobutsuen-mae Street, Sakyo-ku (tel. 771-4185), is one of Kyoto's best-known restaurants. First established more than 260 years ago, Minokichi now has several branches in Japan, including a handful in Kyoto, Osaka, and Tokyo. This flagship restaurant consists of various rooms in several buildings, the most enjoyable of which is tatami seating in the oldest building with an open square hearth and views of a graceful bamboo garden. The specialty of the restaurant is Kyoto kaiseki, reflecting the gourmet dining style of the upper classes during the Heian Period more than 800 years ago. Emphasis is on the appearance of the food, with great care given to the selection and preparation of seasonal food from field, mountain, river, and ocean. Although the dishes themselves change, a kaiseki meal here always consists of eight dishes: an appetizer, raw fish, soup, food cooked in delicate broth, steamed food, broiled food, deep-fried food, and vinegared food. Kaiseki meals start at ¥9,300 ($66.43). Other dishes available include sukiyaki or shabu-shabu, beginning at ¥4,600 ($32.86), and tempura or eel, beginning at ¥2,700 ($19.29). There are also special box lunches available with a variety of seasonal dishes, beginning at ¥2,300 ($16.43). Since there's a menu in English, ordering is no problem. This restaurant is open daily from 11:30 a.m. to 9 p.m. (last order), and if you plan on coming for dinner or eating kaiseki be sure to make a reservation. Minokichi is located just a few minutes' walk northwest of the Miyako Hotel.

Another restaurant serving Kyoto kaiseki cuisine is **Awata Sanso** [85], Awataguchi Sanjo Bocho 2-15, Higashiyama-ku (tel. 561-4908). An old Japanese villa, this elegant restaurant, whose private rooms overlook a beautiful garden with flowering bushes, rocks, moss, ferns, and streams, is tucked away on a back street south of Sanjo Dori Avenue not far from the Miyako Hotel. A restaurant since 1937, it has been owned by the Kyoto Hotel since 1950. Entrance to the restaurant sets the mood as you walk past a wooden gate, stone lanterns, and an old well and are ushered into your own private tatami room. If you come here for lunch (served daily from 11:30 a.m. to 2 p.m.) you can order a mini-kaiseki meal starting at ¥11,000 ($78.57) or an obento box lunch for ¥6,500 ($46.43), tax and service charge included. Dinners (served from 5 to 8 p.m.) are much more elaborate affairs and include various kaiseki meals ranging from ¥16,500 ($117.86) to ¥36,000 ($257.14). Although dishes change according to the season, a typical meal may consist of dried mullet roe and sea urchin, halibut, bean-paste soup with grilled rice cake, sea bream with spring vegetables, pork, tempura, cooked crab, turnip and quail egg, turtle soup, assorted Japanese pickles, and fruit. You can also order shabu-shabu for ¥9,300 ($66.43). Reservations are a must.

Hyotei [86], Kusakawa-cho 30-5, Nanzenji (tel. 771-4116), is on the main road leading to Nanzenji Temple (look for a plain façade hidden behind a bamboo fence with a sign shaped like a gourd). This restaurant consists of two parts, one serving expensive kaiseki and the other serving seasonal obento box lunches. Kaiseki meals, which start at ¥16,500 ($117.86) for lunch and ¥22,000 ($157.14) for dinner, are served in separate, tiny houses situated around a beautiful garden with a pond, maple trees, and bushes. The oldest house, which resembles a small tea house, is 350 years old. Seating is on cushions on a tatami floor in your own private room, and your food is brought to you by women in kimonos. The other part of the restaurant serves obento lunch boxes starting at ¥4,400 ($31.43); the menù depends on the season, and seating is at tables and chairs. Obento is served from noon to 4 p.m., while kaiseki is served from 11 a.m. to 7:30 p.m. If you want to eat kaiseki, be sure to make a reservation in advance.

Also on the road leading to Nanzenji Temple is **Junsei**, 60 Kusakawa-cho,

Nanzenji (tel. 761-2311). A restaurant specializing in tofu dishes opened here in 1961, but the grounds and garden were originally part of a private institution established during the shogun era in the 1830s. Although Junsei is popular with tour groups and is tourist-oriented, the food is good and an English menu makes ordering easy. There are several buildings spread throughout the grounds and what you eat determines where you go—as soon as you arrive you will be given a menu and asked what you want to eat. I chose the *yudofu* (tofu) set meal for ¥2,200 ($15.71) and was directed to an older building filled with antiques and tatami mats. My meal came with vegetable tempura and various tofu dishes, including fried tofu on a stick and tofu boiled in a pot at my table. Other dishes available include kaiseki, starting at ¥6,600 ($47.14); turtle dishes, starting at ¥11,000 ($78.57); beef shabu-shabu, beginning at ¥6,500 ($46.43); sukiyaki, from ¥5,500 ($39.29); and tempura for ¥4,400 ($31.43). There are also obento lunch boxes beginning at ¥2,700 ($19.29). Meals are served daily from 11 a.m. and the last orders are taken at 8 p.m. After your meal be sure to take a stroll through the garden.

Located just north of Nanzenji Temple's main gate (called the San Mon Gate), **Okutan** [87], 86-30 Fukuchi-cho, Nanzenji, Sakyo-ku (tel. 771-8709), is one of the oldest, most authentic, and most delightful tofu restaurants in Kyoto. Founded about 350 years ago as a vegetarian restaurant serving Zen dishes to Buddhist monks, this wooden place with a thatched roof serves just one thing, a tofu meal, with the finishing touches provided by a pond, a garden, and peacefulness. Okutan is very simple and rustic, with seating either in tatami rooms or outdoors on platforms. Women dressed in traditional rural clothing bring your food. The tofu set meal for ¥2,700 ($19.29) includes boiled tofu, fried tofu, vegetable tempura, yam soup, and pickled vegetables. If you're still hungry you can order some of the above items à la carte. This restaurant is especially delightful in fine weather. It's open from 10:30 a.m. to 5:30 p.m.; closed Thursday.

On the same road as Okutan (just around the corner to the north) is another vegetarian restaurant, **Koan** [88], this one located on the grounds of the Shotekiin Temple, Fukuchi-cho, Nanzenji (tel. 771-2781). Open from 11:30 a.m. to 4:30 p.m. every day except Wednesday, it offers vegetarian and tofu dishes characteristic of Zen temple meals usually served to monks. The English menu lists yudofu set meals for ¥1,650 ($11.79) and ¥2,600 ($18.57), as well as other vegetarian dishes beginning at ¥3,000 ($21.43).

Goemonjaya [89], 67 Kukasawa-cho, Nanzenji, Sakyo-ku (tel. 751-9638), is an inexpensive restaurant serving tofu dishes, tempura, and noodles. Located across the street from Yachiyo Ryokan on the road leading to Nanzenji Temple, this informal restaurant is easily recognizable by a red lantern beside the road and a display case of plastic food. The restaurant itself is back off the main road, past a red umbrella, a small garden, and a waterfall. Noodles start at ¥500 ($3.57), and other dishes average around ¥2,000 ($14.29). Hours here are 10 a.m. to 8 p.m.; closed the first and third Tuesdays of each month.

Mikaku [90], Kawabata Dori, Shijo-agaru, Gion, Higashiyama-ku (tel. 525-1129), is a Japanese steak restaurant in the heart of Gion. Established about 50 years ago by the present owner's grandfather, the restaurant is located in a 100-year-old building that was once a private house. The specialty of the house is its *aburayaki* meal, which consists of beef filet cooked with various vegetables and seasoned with soy sauce and wine. Sukiyaki, *mizudaki* (similar to shabu-shabu but stronger in taste), and teppanyaki are also served. Meals average ¥8,000 ($57.14). If you order teppanyaki, you'll sit at a counter where the chef will prepare your food in front of you on a hot griddle. Outside the window is a pleasant view of a canal. If you order sukiyaki or mizudaki you'll sit in your own private tatami room on the second floor. This restaurant is open from noon to 10 p.m. (last order is at 9 p.m.) every day except the second and fourth Sundays of the month, and there's an English menu.

If you're in the vicinity of Kiyomizu Temple, on Kiyomizuzaka Street, **Yabu Kozan** [91], Kiyomizu Shinmichi 1-chome (tel. 525-2229), is a convenient place to stop for lunch. Although the noodle restaurant opened only a decade ago, the house itself is about 60 years old, a wooden structure supported by stilts and built into the side of a steeply sloping hill. The entrance is through a wooden gate and up stone steps. Once inside the restaurant, remove your shoes and seat yourself in an airy and pleasant tatami room. *Soba*, or noodles, begin at ¥550 ($3.93), with tempura soba costing ¥1,000 ($7.14). Hours here are from 10 a.m. to 3 p.m.

Maruyama [92], located on the southern edge of Maruyama Park, Ikenohata, Higashiyama-ku (tel. 561-1991), is a convenient place to stop for lunch if you're walking from Kiyomizu Temple to Heian Shrine. Just east of the south entrance to the park, it offers obento lunch boxes, tofu dishes, tempura, and kaiseki cuisine, with most dishes starting at ¥2,000 ($14.29). Open from 10:30 a.m. to 9 p.m. daily, this modern restaurant offers a nice view of the park from its dining room.

Western Food

There aren't many Western restaurants in eastern Kyoto from which to choose, but if you're walking from Kiyomizu Temple to Heian Shrine there's an informal restaurant called **Chorakukan** [93] located near the south entrance of Maruyama Park (tel. 561-0001). Tucked away in a corner of a large stone and brick Western-style building with a huge stone lantern in its driveway, this restaurant is nothing fancy but is restful with classical music playing in the background and a view of some maple trees. The dishes, most in the ¥900 ($6.43) to ¥1,700 ($12.14) range, include fried or grilled shrimp, grilled chicken with bacon, spaghetti, beef or chicken curry, and sandwiches. There are lunch specials averaging ¥1,400 ($10), which change daily. Hours are 11 a.m. to 7:30 p.m. every day of the week.

If you desire more formal dining, try **Versailles**, in the Kyoto Park Hotel, Sanjusangendo, Higashiyama-ku (tel. 525-3111). There aren't many restaurants in this vicinity, and it's the best place to go for lunch or dinner if you're visiting Sanjusangendo Hall or the Kyoto National Museum. Small and intimate, the restaurant overlooks a beautiful garden with a waterfall and pond. The best thing to order is one of the set meals, which change monthly and start at ¥2,200 ($15.71) for lunch and ¥7,000 ($50) for dinner. If you order à la carte for such things as sole, scallops cooked in butter, or steak, expect to spend a minimum of ¥6,000 ($42.86). Service is from 11 a.m. to 3 p.m. and 5 to 9 p.m. (last order) daily.

NAKAGYO-KU (CENTRAL KYOTO): The central part of Kyoto west of the Kamo River and embracing the nightlife district around Kawaramachi-Shijo intersection is called Nakagyo-ku. This area of town has a wide selection of both Japanese and Western restaurants.

Japanese Food

Izumoya [94], Pontocho, Shijo-agaru (tel. 211-2501), is a large, many-storied restaurant on Shijo Dori Avenue right beside the bridge spanning the Kamo River. The backside of the restaurant faces the river, and in the summer months a wooden veranda built on stilts is constructed over the water. Popular with tourists and groups, it serves a wide variety of dishes on its various floors. On the third floor, shabu-shabu and sukiyaki beginning at ¥3,000 ($21.43) are available, while on the second and fourth floors you can dine on set meals of tempura, sashimi, or eel for ¥2,200 ($15.71) and up. Only kaiseki meals, ranging in price from ¥4,000 ($28.57) to ¥6,600 ($47.14), are served on the outdoor veranda, open from 5 to 9:30 p.m. The restaurant itself is open daily from noon to 9:30 p.m.

Kyoshiki, Fuyacho-Dori Street, Sanjo-agaru (tel. 221-4866), is a reasonably priced kaiseki restaurant located just north of Sanjo Dori Avenue on Fuyacho Dori Street. Formerly a private home, it was turned into a restaurant about 15 years ago by English-speaking Shoichi Hirayama, who makes it easy on foreign guests by presenting them with an English menu. Various meals are available, averaging about ¥2,700 ($19.29) for lunch and ¥4,000 ($28.57) for dinner. If you're coming for lunch I recommend the Hisago lunch, which is a variety of seasonal food served in individual dishes that stack neatly on top of each other to form a gourd. You take the bowls apart to eat. The atmosphere here is relaxed and comfortable, with regular customers stopping in for a chat with Mr. Hirayama. The restaurant opens at 11 a.m. and the last order is taken at 8:30 p.m. On Monday and Wednesday free tea and sweets are served with lunch.

If you're hungering for tempura, **Tempura Yoshikawa** is easy to find on Tominokoji Dori Street near Oike Avenue (tel. 221-5544)—its sign is in English. It's a tiny, intimate place with a traditional atmosphere, and the counter seats only 12 so you should make a reservation to eat here. Open every day except Sunday, it serves a tempura lunch for ¥2,200 ($15.71) from 11 a.m. to 2 p.m. and dinner for ¥6,500 ($46.43) from 5 to 9 p.m. You can order side dishes of sashimi to go with your meal.

Another tempura restaurant, this one very chic and modern, **Koyomi-tei** [95] is located on the third floor of the Miyako Club Building, Takoyakushi Dori, Kiyamachi, Nishi-iru (tel. 211-8797). It's behind the Maruzen Book Store on a small street facing the narrow Takase River. A one-room restaurant decorated in bold colors of green and black, it has contemporary furnishings with 21st-century-looking lamps and chairs that resemble unfolded fans. Special teishoku tempura lunches are served from 11:30 a.m. to 2 p.m., starting at ¥2,000 ($14.29). Dinner, served from 5 to 10 p.m., starts at ¥5,500 ($39.29). This restaurant is closed on Tuesday.

Nestled in an inner courtyard off busy Shijo Dori Avenue, **Tagoto** [96], Shijo-Kawaramachi, Nishi-iru, Kitagawa (tel. 221-1811), has been serving a variety of Japanese food at moderate prices for about 100 years. Its entrance is right next to the Kyoto Central Inn (look for a door with a white sign; step through it and follow the passageway to the back courtyard). It's open from 11 a.m. to 8:30 p.m. (closed the third Thursday) with set meals ranging from ¥1,300 ($9.29) to ¥8,800 ($62.86). The menu includes tempura, eel dishes, obento lunch boxes, seasonal kaiseki courses, and sashimi. You can also have noodles beginning at ¥550 ($3.93).

There's a branch of **Minokichi** in the basement under the Bank of Tokyo, Kyoto Fukutoku Building, Karasuma Shijo-agaru (tel. 255-0621). Open for more than a decade, it's the largest Minokichi branch and has prices slightly lower than the main restaurant. With low lighting and latticed wood separating the dining tables from one another, this pleasant restaurant is open daily from 11:30 a.m. to 9 p.m. and serves a variety of typical Japanese cuisine, including shabu-shabu, beginning at ¥3,800 ($27.14); tempura, from ¥2,400 ($17.14); and eel dishes, from ¥1,750 ($12.50). If you want steak, beef teriyaki costs ¥3,800 ($27.14). Kaiseki courses range from ¥5,000 ($35.71) for a mini-meal to ¥7,700 ($55). I selected the mini-kaiseki course. Although it changes monthly, my meal was typical of the variety of dishes you get: appetizer vegetables and sashimi; Japanese potato filled with crabmeat; gelatin with chicken, salmon, and asparagus inside; pumpkin soup; buckwheat noodles with eel and mushroom; a small river fish; tempura; dessert; and Japanese frothy green tea.

Unkai, located on the ground floor of the ANA Hotel Kyoto, Nijo-Castle-Mae, Horikawa-dori Avenue (tel. 231-1155), has a convenient location across from the main entrance of Nijo Castle. With a modern and refined decor, ceiling-to-floor windows, and kimono-clad waitresses, it also has an English menu, making ordering an easy task. What's difficult is deciding what to eat. The varied menu includes a shabu-shabu meal for two persons for ¥7,700 ($55); kaiseki starting at ¥6,600 ($47.14); a vegetarian set meal for ¥4,400 ($31.43); tempura from ¥4,400 ($31.43); and sushi à la carte. Special set lunches start at ¥2,200 ($15.71). Hours here are from 11:30 a.m. to 2:30 p.m. and 5 to 10 p.m.

Ganko Sushi [97], Sanjo-Kawaramachi, Higashi-iru (tel. 255-1126), is a popular, lively sushi restaurant located just to the west of the Kamo River on Sanjo Dori Avenue. The English menu makes ordering here a cinch, with sushi à la carte beginning at ¥260 ($1.86) for two pieces. Available are the usual tuna, eel, bonito, squid, and fish selections, as well as such items as grilled yakitori, grilled asparagus wrapped in bacon, shabu-shabu, tempura, and shrimp or crab dishes. Behind the sushi counter is a fish tank with some rather large specimens, swimming around happily until their number comes up. Hours here are from 11:30 a.m. to 10:30 p.m., closed the first Monday and third Tuesday of every month. Meanwhile, up on the second floor and in the basement are two robatayaki restaurants, with an English menu listing various kinds of grilled vegetables and meats. Popular with office workers when work is over, they're open only in the evenings, from 4:30 to 10:30. At any rate, you can eat at either the sushi or the robatayaki parts of the restaurant for less than ¥3,000 ($21.43), and even cheaper than that if you lay off the beer.

If money is a great concern, however, an even cheaper place for a meal of raw fish can be had at **Musashi**, located on Shijo Dori Avenue just west of the Teramachi covered shopping arcade (tel. 241-3330). Open daily from 11:30 a.m. to 10 p.m., it offers morsels of sushi via a conveyor belt that moves along the counter. Simply reach out and take what you want. Plates with pieces of tuna, octopus, sweet shrimp, eel, or crab salad begin at ¥120 (86¢).

Misoka-an Kawamichiya, Sanjo-agaru, Fuyacho-dori (tel. 221-2525), is a charming, delightful noodle shop with a history that stretches back about 300 years. A tiny affair with a central courtyard and cubbyhole rooms, it offers plain buckwheat noodles for ¥450 ($3.21), as well as noodles with such adornments as tempura or chicken and onions. Its specialty is a one-pot noodle dish called *Hokoro*, which includes such items as chicken, tofu, mushrooms, and vegetables and costs ¥3,000 ($21.43). Closed on Thursday, it's open the rest of the week from 11 a.m. to 8 p.m.

Down the street from Kawamichiya is another noodle shop, **Gontaro** [98] (tel. 221-5810), an upstart that has been serving its own handmade noodles for a mere 70 years. It's located on Fuyacho Dori Street just north of Shijo Dori Avenue—look for a big red lantern outside the front door and a lone pine tree. A small place, with seating at a counter or at your own tatami stall, it offers various noodle (soba) dishes beginning at ¥600 ($4.29). Items you might try include tempura soba, chicken soba, potato soba, and soba sushi. Hours here are 11:30 a.m. to 11 p.m.; closed Wednesday.

One more place you might want to check out for inexpensive Japanese restaurants is the seventh and eighth floors of the **Hankyu department store**, on the corner of Shijo and Kawaramachi. There are lots of restaurants on these two floors serving both Japanese and Western cuisine, and because they have plastic food displays outside their front doors it's easy to choose both a restaurant and what you want to eat. Simply wander around and decide what looks best. These restaurants are open daily from 11 a.m. to 10 p.m.

Western and Foreign Food

Misogi-gawa [99], Sanjo-sagaru, Pontocho, Nakagyo-ku (tel. 221-2270), is a lovely French restaurant on a narrow street called Pontocho which parallels the Kamo River and is one of Kyoto's most famous nightlife districts. Located in a century-old wooden building that used to belong to a geisha as her entertainment house, this exclusive restaurant successfully blends both French and Japanese cuisine into dishes artfully prepared and served on Japanese tableware. In fact, part of the delight of eating here is in receiving the various courses, each one exquisitely arranged as though a work of art. Dining is either at a counter with leg wells or in private tatami rooms, and you have a choice of eating with either chopsticks or knife and fork. The menu changes monthly and ranges from ¥6,500 ($46.43) to ¥22,000 ($157.14) for dinner, served from 4:30 to 9 p.m. daily. There's also a lunch special for ¥7,700 ($55), which includes a glass of wine; it's served daily from 11:30 to 2 p.m. If you want to order à la carte, the menu (written in French) includes such selections as lobster, sole, and various beef dishes—expect to spend about ¥10,000 ($71.43) to ¥18,000 ($128.57) per person. Reservations are strongly recommended.

If you prefer French dining in a Western atmosphere, the **Manyoken**, Fuyacho Shijo, Shimogyo-ku (tel. 221-1022), is one of Kyoto's best-known restaurants and has more than 70 years of experience serving French cuisine. With its chandeliers, fresh roses, white tablecloths, and drawing-room atmosphere, this elegant restaurant serves a lunch for ¥7,700 ($55) and set dinners for ¥8,800 ($62.86) to ¥16,500 ($117.86), all of which change monthly. À la carte selections include such dishes as steak, lobster, fish, and chicken. Perhaps you want to start out with escargot in bourguignonne sauce, followed by onion soup, sirloin steak cooked with a special house sauce, and then baked Alaska or soufflé in Curaçao or chocolate. Expect to spend about ¥15,000 ($107.14) or more per person, excluding wine. Hours are 11:30 a.m. to 3 p.m. and 4:30 to 8:30 p.m. (last order) daily.

If you're looking for French food with a twist, visit **Nijo**, in the basement of the ANA Hotel, which is located across the street from Nijo Castle on Horikawa-dori Avenue (tel. 231-1155). In a successful marriage of French cuisine and kaiseki philosophy, it serves one dish after the other rather than all at once. Portions are small, and each dish is so elegantly and artistically arranged that soon you find youself enjoying the presentation of the food as much as you enjoy eating it. Receiving each course is kind of like opening presents; dining becomes a slow and joyous affair. Ordering is easy because only three set courses, which change with the seasons, are available, beginning at ¥8,800 ($62.86) for dinner. A lunch course is offered for ¥6,600 ($47.14). If you prefer steaks, there's a separate room with a teppanyaki counter, with a set-lunch course costing ¥4,400 ($31.43) and dinner courses beginning at ¥8,800 ($62.86). Hours at Nijo are from 11:30 a.m. to 2:30 p.m. and from 5 to 10 p.m.

Although it's obviously tourist-oriented, **Suehiro**, at the Shijo–Kawaramachi intersection (tel. 221-7188), is dependable for its charcoal-broiled Kobe beef steaks. It has an English menu that makes ordering a snap. You can start with appetizers that might include shrimp or crab cocktail, oysters, and beef sashimi, then move on to various steak dishes ranging from ¥4,700 ($33.57) for filet mignon to ¥15,500 ($110.71) for a prime cut. Steak dinner courses start at ¥6,700 ($47.86). Lunch specials, starting at ¥2,500 ($17.86), are served until 5 p.m. Turning out steaks in Kyoto since 1939, this restaurant, which has several floors of dining space, is open from 11:30 a.m. to 9 p.m. daily.

Tohkasaikan, Shijo Ohashi, Nishizume (tel. 221-1147), is a Chinese restaurant on Shijo Dori Avenue just west of the bridge that spans the Kamo River. A large yellow stone building that dates back more than 60 years, it started out as a Western restaurant and features an ancient elevator, lots of wood paneling, high ceilings, and old-fashioned decor. You have several choices of where to dine. From June to mid-September you can sit outside on a wooden veranda supported by stilts that extends over the Kamo River. If it's winter or raining, consider sitting in the dining room on the fifth floor, which has nice views of the city. The best views, however, are from the rooftop garden, open during the summer months—draft beer here costs ¥500 ($3.57) for a medium and ¥800 ($5.71) for a large. As for food, the English menu lists such dishes as sweet-and-sour pork, cooked shrimp with arrowroot, fried pork meatballs, chicken and green pepper, and pork and vegetable rolled with egg. Most entrées range from ¥1,000 ($7.14) to ¥2,700 ($19.29). It's open from 11 a.m. to 9 p.m. daily.

If you want spicier food, try **Ashoka**, located on the third floor of the Kikusui Building on Teramachi Dori Street just off Shijo Dori Avenue (tel. 241-1318). One of Kyoto's most popular Indian restaurants, Ashoka serves both vegetarian and meat curries including mutton, chicken, fish, vegetable, and shrimp selections. I started out my meal here with mulligatawny Madrasi, a South Indian soup, and followed it with Indian bread stuffed with minced meat along with mutton *sagwala* (mutton and spinach). A meal here averages about ¥2,500 ($17.86) or more. Set lunches start at ¥900 ($6.43), while dinners start at ($17.86). Hours are 11:30 a.m. to 2:30 p.m. and 5 to 9 p.m. every day (on Sunday and holidays, from 11:30 a.m. to 3 p.m. and 5 to 8 p.m.).

Although it's a bit difficult to find, **Sancho** [100] Fuji Ginko Yoko-agaru (tel. 211-0459), is worth a visit for its hearty portions of inexpensive salads. A small establishment with only a long counter and six tables, it's located just north of Shijo Dori Avenue on the first side street that parallels Kawaramachi to the west, which is the same street that runs beside Fuji Bank. Look for the sign that says "Salada House," as well as the plastic display case of salads. Salads cost ¥550 ($3.93) to ¥930 ($6.64) and include such combinations as asparagus and crab salad, shrimp salad and chicken salad. The English menu also lists hamburgers, teriyaki steak, and chicken. Sancho is open from noon to 9 p.m. every day except Wednesday.

From Monday through Saturday from 11 a.m to 3 p.m., **Shakey's**, Teramachi Higashi-iru, Ishibashi (tel. 255-1325), offers an all-you-can-eat pizza buffet for only ¥600 ($4.29). Shakey's is conveniently located in the covered shopping arcade running along Sanjo Dori Avenue, just west of Kawaramachi Dori Avenue.

SHIMOGYU-KU (AROUND KYOTO STATION): Restaurants around Kyoto Station cater to tourists, commuters, and shoppers. Most of these establishments are in the area's many hotels.

Japanese Food

In the basement of the **Kyoto Grand Hotel**, Shiokoji Horikawa (tel. 341-2311), are six restaurants offering a variety of cuisines, all with English menus. Most interesting is Gourmond Tachibana, which serves Japanese-style French cuisine every evening from 5 to 9:30 p.m. It has three set menus for ¥7,700 ($55), ¥11,000 ($78.57), and ¥13,000 ($92.86), which change twice a month. Other restaurants, all open from 11:30 a.m. to 2:30 p.m. and 5 to 9:30 p.m., serve teppanyaki steaks, tempura, eel, sukiyaki, shabu-shabu, traditional

Kyoto cuisine, and Chinese food. The average dinner in these restaurants costs about ¥5,000 ($35.71) and up.

In the **New Hankyo Hotel**, north of Kyoto Station (tel. 343-5300), is a branch of the famous Minokichi restaurant. Designed to resemble a lane in a typical traditional Japanese village, it features waitresses in kimonos and Japanese music playing in the background. The menu includes kaiseki cuisine from ¥7,700 ($55) and typical Kyoto dishes from ¥3,300 ($23.57), as well as such Japanese favorites as tempura, obento lunch boxes, eels, and shabu-shabu. A mini-kaiseki course is available for ¥4,700 ($33.57). Hours here are from 11:30 a.m. to 9 p.m. (last order).

Izusen [101] is an inexpensive restaurant located on the second floor of the Surugaiya Building on Karasuma Dori Avenue just north of the Tourist Information Center (tel. 343-4211). Although the decor is simple, the food is great and beautifully presented and features local Kyoto and vegetarian dishes. There's an English menu, and seating is either at tables or on tatami mats. The best thing to order is one of the specials. A vegetarian meal for ¥1,400 ($10), for example, is a light meal usually served at a tea ceremony. I opted for the Matsu for ¥2,200 ($15.71), which features Kyoto cuisine and included tempura, sashimi, various vegetables, broiled fish, rice, and soup. Other vegetarian dishes and Kyoto specialties start at ¥1,800 ($12.86). Closed on Thursday, it's open the rest of the week from 11 a.m. to 8 p.m.

Western Food

On the 14th floor of the Kyoto Grand Hotel, Shiokoji Horikawa (tel. 341-2311) is **Top of Kyoto**, the city's only revolving restaurant. On clear days you have excellent views over the tops of Kyoto's temples to the mountains surrounding the city. Recently remodeled with marble and decor imported from Italy, this trendy restaurant offers a set lunch menu for ¥4,400 ($31.43) and set dinners beginning at ¥9,900 ($70.71). À la carte orders will average ¥15,000 ($107.14) for meals which might include steak, duckling, rack of spring lamb, veal, sole, lobster, or scallops. Adjoining the restaurant is a comfortable cocktail lounge, where you can relax with a drink after dinner. Food is served from noon to 11:30 p.m. daily.

Next to Kyoto Station is a relatively new building called Renaissance Building, which features several restaurants. On the second floor, for example, is **Gio Giono** (tel. 365-0200), an Italian restaurant. Open from 11:30 a.m. to 10 p.m., it serves pizza starting at ¥850 ($6.07), pasta at ¥880 ($6.29), and seafood. A special lunch menu, available until 2 p.m., gives you a choice of pizza or spaghetti, a salad, dessert, and coffee for ¥880 ($6.29). Other food outlets in the Renaissance Building include a Chinese restaurant, a beer hall with lunches starting at ¥550 ($3.93), and a coffeeshop where you can order the "morning service" for ¥550 ($3.93), which includes coffee, toast, egg, and salad.

3. The Sights

Because Kyoto has 1,500 Buddhist temples, 200 Shinto shrines, and numerous gardens, museums, and other worthwhile sights, it's obvious that you must tailor your itinerary to gain the most satisfaction and enjoyment from your stay. Even the most avid sightseer can become jaded after days of visiting yet another temple or shrine—and after a while how much can your memory retain? Be sure to temper your visits to cultural and historical sights with time spent simply walking around. Kyoto is a city best seen on your own two feet, exploring small alleyways and curio shops, pausing to soak in the beauty of its carefully landscaped gardens. If you spend your days in Kyoto racing around in a taxi or a bus from one temple to another, the essence of this ancient capital and its charm may literally pass you by.

Ideally, you should allow at least four days in Kyoto, allotting a fifth day for a side trip to the even more ancient capital of Nara. Depending on how much you want to cover, that would allow you to select from the list I've compiled below the sights most interesting to you, with time left over for your own explorations. If perchance you have only one day to spend in Kyoto, I recommend that you spend it in East Kyoto, including the stroll from Kiyomizu Temple to Heian Shrine and topping it off with a visit to the Silver Pavilion, and, if time permits, a short stop at the Kyoto Handicraft Center for some shopping—and then start planning for your next trip back to Kyoto. If you have a second day, add Nijo Castle, Ryoanji Temple with its famous rock garden, the Golden Pavilion, and a few other sights of your choosing. Such a two-day tour would present you a well-rounded view of Kyoto by giving you the chance to see temples, a shrine, gardens, and a former shogun's palace.

Before setting out on your walking tours, be sure to stop by the Kyoto Tourist Information Center, located across from Kyoto Station in the Kyoto Tower Building, Higashi-Shiokojicho, Shimogyo-ku (tel. 075/371-5649), to pick up a leaflet called *Walking Tour Courses in Kyoto*. It has four detailed maps for strolling tours of Kyoto, including the walk from Kiyomizu Temple to Heian Shrine and on to the Silver Pavilion, which I've outlined below. The T.I.C. also has city maps and a colorful brochure listing Kyoto's most important sites.

EAST KYOTO: The eastern part of Kyoto, embracing the area of Higashiyama-ku and stretching up all the way to the Silver Pavilion (Ginkakuji Temple), is probably the richest in terms of culture and charm. Although the walking-tour leaflet distributed by the T.I.C. claims you can walk from Kiyomizu Temple to Heian Shrine in 50 minutes, I don't see how it would be possible unless you put on your jogging shoes and ran the whole way. I've walked this route four times and it's always taken me the better part of a day—perhaps I'm slow, but it's a pace I've found does justice to this wonderful area of Kyoto.

The two strolls I've listed below, through Higashiyama-ku and the Philosopher's Stroll, are logical continuations of each other. If you don't finish Higashiyama-ku in one day, therefore, you could start where you left off on the following day and then continue on with the Philosopher's Stroll.

A Stroll Through Higashiyama-ku

Sanjusangendo Hall is the name popularly given to Rengeoin Temple, which is a 20-minute walk east of Kyoto Station or a short ride on bus 206 from the station. The hall is only 50-some feet wide but it stretches almost 400 feet long—and it's filled with more than 1,000 images of the thousand-handed Kannon. There are row upon row of these gold figures glowing in the dark hall, and in the middle is a large seated figure of Kannon, flanked by her 28 disciples. The large Kannon was carved in 1254 by Tankai, a famous sculptor from the Kamakura Period, and the hall itself dates from 1266. At the back of the hall is a 130-yard-long archery range, where a competition is held every January 15. Sanjusangendo is open daily from 8 a.m. to 5 p.m. (4 p.m. in winter) and admission is ¥400 ($2.86).

Across the street and to the northeast of Sanjusangendo Hall is the **Kyoto National Museum** (open from 9 a.m. to 4 p.m.; closed Monday). Established in the latter half of the last century as a repository for art objects and treasures that belonged to both Kyoto's temples and individuals, it displays historical items, artwork, and handcrafts, including a great collection of ceramics, paintings and sculptures. Admission is ¥350 ($2.50).

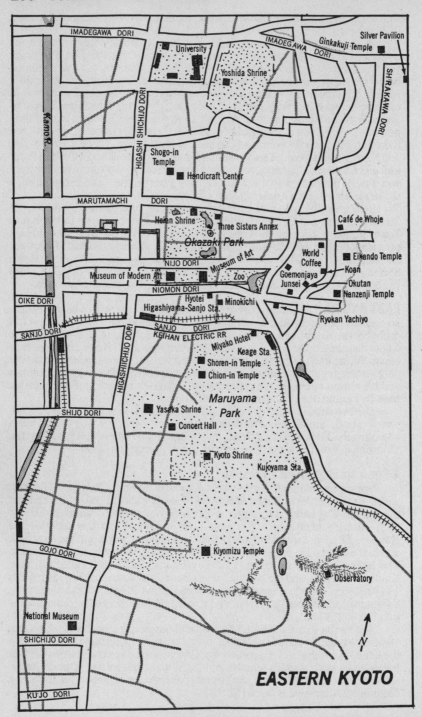

EASTERN KYOTO

From the National Museum, either hop back on bus 206 or walk for about 15 minutes north on Higashioji Dori Avenue to the Gojo-zaka bus stop, where you should take a right and begin climbing up the gradual slope to **Kiyomizu Temple**. You'll pass some pottery shops on your way, but don't go crazy shopping yet—there are many more shops to come. Kiyomizu Temple, first founded in 798 and rebuilt in 1633 by the third Tokugawa shogun, Iemitsu, occupies one of the most exalted spots in all of Kyoto, with a grand view of the city below. The main hall is built over a cliff and features a large wooden veranda supported by 139 pillars, each 49 feet high. The magnificence of the height and view is so well known to the Japanese that the idiom "jumping from the veranda of Kiyomizu Temple" means that they're about to undertake some particularly bold or daring adventure. To appreciate the grandeur of the main hall with its pillars and dark wood, walk the few minutes to the three-story pagoda, which affords the best view of the main hall, built without the use of a single nail. From the pagoda, descend the steps down to Otowa Fall, where you'll see Japanese lined up to drink from the refreshing spring water. Here you'll also find some small pavilions where you can stop for a bowl of noodles and a beer. By all means do (and now you know why this walk takes me all day). If you're lucky to be here in fall, the fiery reds of the maple trees will set the whole place on fire. Kiyomizu Temple is open from 8 a.m. to 6 p.m. Although there is no admission as such, you are expected to give a "donation." About ¥200 ($1.43) to ¥300 ($2.14) is fine, though no one would object if you gave more.

Before departing Kiyomizu temple, be sure to make a stop at **Jishu Shrine**, particularly if you're in need of finding a good mate or thankful that you've found one. This vermillion-colored Shinto shrine is easy to spot and is located just north of Kiyomizu's main temple building. It's regarded as a dwelling place of the deity in charge of love and a good match, a deity you certainly should not slight. There's an explanation of the shrine in English, and you can buy various good-luck charms for everything from a happy marriage to easy delivery of a child to success in passing an examination. On the shrine's grounds are two stones placed about 30 feet apart—if you're able to walk from one stone to the other with your eyes closed, you're supposedly guaranteed success in your love life. It sure doesn't hurt to try.

From Kiyomizu Temple, take the road leading downhill directly in front of the temple's main gate, where you'll find shop after shop selling sweets, pottery, and curios. It's okay to go crazy shopping here, but remember you're going to have to carry whatever you buy. After a few minutes take a right at some steps leading downhill. Called Sannenzaka Slope, it leads past antique and curio shops and wooden buildlings reminiscent of old Kyoto. After passing Ryozen Kannon Temple, with its huge white statue dedicated to Japan's unknown soldiers who died in World War II, look for a tea house on your right called **Kodaiji Rakusho Tea Room** [102] (tel. 561-6892) (if you get all the way to Maruyama Park, you've gone too far). This tea house, one of my favorites in Kyoto, has a 100-year-old garden, which you can glimpse through a gate from the street. There's a pond with some of the largest carp I've ever seen, some of which are 20 years old. Stop for some noodles, tea, or dessert, and refresh yourself with views of the small but beautiful garden.

After you've taken you time strolling through **Maruyama Park** with its ponds, pigeons, gardens, and vendors, you'll come to **Chion-in Temple**, founded in 1234 as a center of the Jodo sect of Buddhism. Famous for its enormous gate rising almost 80 feet, the temple also has Japan's largest bell, weighing 74 tons. Entrance to the temple precincts is free; if you want to go inside the buildings, admission is ¥300 ($2.14), and the hours are 9 a.m. to 4 p.m. Just north of Chion-in is **Shoren-in Temple**, built as a villa for the abbots of a Buddhist sect.

The present buildings date from 1895. The temple has a very impressive garden, constructed in the 15th century and considered to be one of the best in Kyoto. Open from 9 a.m. to 5 p.m., it charges an admission of ¥400 ($2.86).

You'll know you're getting close to Heian Shrine when you see the vermilion-colored *torii* gate straddling a street busy with traffic. Before continuing on to the shrine, however, there are a few museums you might want to stop in on—the **Kyoto Municipal Museum of Art**, the **National Museum of Modern Art**, and the **Kyoto Municipal Museum of Traditional Industry**. The Museum of Traditional Industry is my favorite. Not only is it free, but it sells many of the items displayed. Crafts range from pottery to lacquerware to textiles, bamboo products, damascene jewelry, knives, and dolls. Prices are high, but so is the quality of workmanship. There are also frequent demonstrations by local artists. It's open from 9 a.m. to 4:30 p.m., closed on Monday.

Directly north of the museums is Heian Shrine. If orange and green are your favorite colors, you're going to love this shrine. Although it was built only in 1895 in commemoration of the 1,100th anniversary of the founding of Kyoto, Heian Shrine is a replica of the first imperial palace, built in Kyoto back in 794, giving you some idea of the architecture back then. The most important thing to see here, however, is the garden, the entrance to which is on your left as you face the main hall. Admission is ¥400 ($2.86) and hours are 8:30 a.m. to 4:30 p.m. (5:30 p.m. in summer). Typical of gardens constructed during the Meiji era, it's famous for its weeping cherry trees which blossom in spring, its irises and water lilies in summer, and changing maple leaves in fall.

After visiting Heian Shrine you may want to stop off to do some shopping at the **Kyoto Handicraft Center**, located behind the shrine on its north side. It's open from 9:30 a.m. to 6 p.m. (until 5:30 p.m. December through February). More information is given in the shopping section.

Philosopher's Stroll

North of Nanzenji and Eikando Temples is a narrow canal which runs almost a mile to Ginkakuji Temple, the Silver Pavilion. Lined with cherry, willow, and maple trees, the canal and a small pathway flanking its side are known as "The Path of Philosophy," referring to the fact that throughout the ages philosophers and priests have strolled along the tranquil canal thinking deep thoughts. Allow about two hours to see the sights below and to think your own deep thoughts as you stroll the philosopher's pathway.

Nanzenji Temple, a 20-minute walk southeast of Heian Shrine, is a Rinzai Zen temple set amid a grove of spruce. One of Kyoto's most famous Zen temples, it was founded in 1293. Attached to the main hall is a Zen rock garden, sometimes called "Leaping Tiger Garden" because of the shape of one of the rocks (can you tell which one?). In the building behind the main hall is a famous sliding door with a painting by Kano Tanyu of a tiger drinking water in a bamboo grove. Spread throughout the temple precincts are a dozen other lesser temples and buildings which you can explore if you have the time, including Nanzen-in, which was built about the same time as Nanzenji Temple and served as the emperor's vacation house whenever he visited the temple grounds. As you wander around, here's food for thought: Nanzenji is where a famous outlaw named Goemon Ishikawa hid before being captured and boiled alive along with his son (they certainly didn't fool around back in those days). Admission to the temple grounds is free, but entrance to the main hall, with its Zen rock garden and famous sliding door of the tiger, costs ¥350 ($2.50). For ¥300 ($2.14) more you can have ceremonial green tea and a Japanese sweet served in a tatami room off the main hall with a peaceful view of a waterfall. Hours are 8:30 a.m. to 5 p.m. (4:30 p.m. in winter).

Eikando Temple, also known as Zenrin-ji Temple, was founded in 856. Things to see here include a statue of a Buddha who is turned so that he looks backward instead of forward, a garden, and maple trees. Hours are 9 a.m. to 4 p.m., and entrance is ¥380 ($2.71).

Ginkakuji, the Silver Pavilion, is the crown jewel of this walk—but it isn't silver at all. It was built in 1482 as a retirement villa of Shogun Yoshimasa Ashikaga, who intended to coat the structure with silver in imitation of the Gold Pavilion built by his grandfather. He died before this could be accomplished, however, which is just as well because the wood of the Silver Pavilion is beautiful just as it is. The whole complex is designed for the enjoyment of the tea ceremony, moon viewing, and other aesthetic pursuits, with a beautiful garden of sand, rocks, and moss. One Kyoto resident told me that this was his favorite temple in the whole city (the residence became a temple after Ashikaga's death). At any rate, the splendor, formality, and grandeur of the life of Japan's upper class can easily be imagined as you wander the grounds. Admission is ¥400 ($2.86), and hours are 9 a.m. to 4:30 p.m.

NORTHWESTERN KYOTO: The inspiration for the Silver Pavilion described above was Kinkakuji, the Gold Pavilion, which you can reach by taking bus 205 from Kyoto Station to the Kinkakuji-michi bus stop. One of Kyoto's best-known attractions, it was constructed in the 1390s as a retirement villa for Shogun Yoshimitsu Ashikaga and features a three-story pavilion covered in gold leaf and topped with a bronze phoenix on its roof. If you come here on a clear day the Gold Pavilion shimmers against a blue sky, its reflection captured in the waters of a calm pond. Apparently the retired shogun lived in shameless luxury while the rest of the nation suffered from famine, earthquakes, and plague. Even today Ashikaga is not kindly remembered, but his Gold Pavilion is now enjoyed by the masses of a now-prosperous nation. However, the Gold Pavilion is not the original. In 1950 a disturbed student monk burned the pavilion to the ground, a story told by author Yukio Mishima in his *The Temple of the Golden Pavilion*. The temple was rebuilt in 1955. Be sure to explore the surrounding park with its moss-covered grounds and tea houses. Hours are 9 a.m. to 5 p.m., and admission is ¥400 ($2.86).

About a half-hour walk southwest of the Gold Pavilion is Ryoanji Temple, with what is probably the most famous Zen rock garden in all of Japan. Fifteen rocks set in waves of raked, white pebbles are surrounded on three sides by a wall and on the fourth by a wooden veranda. Sit down here and contemplate what the artist was trying to communicate. The interpretation of what the rocks are supposed to represent is up to the individual (to my mind they look like mountains rising up from the sea.) My only objection to this peaceful place is that unfortunately it's usually not peaceful—a loudspeaker extols the virtue of the garden, destroying any chance for peaceful meditation. If you get here early enough you may be able to escape both the crowds and the noise. After visiting the rock garden, be sure to take a walk around the 1,000-year-old pond. At one corner is a beautiful little restaurant with tatami rooms and screens where you can eat yudofu (boiled tofu with vegetables) for ¥1,400 ($10) or drink a beer and enjoy the view. Note, however, that if you order only a beer, which costs ¥550 ($3.93), an extra ¥300 ($2.14) will be added to the bill. The view, however, is well worth it. Ryoanji is open 8 a.m. to 5 p.m. and admission is ¥350 ($2.50).

Ready for some fun? How about going to the Toei Uzumasa Eiga Mura (Uzamasa Movie Village), where many of Japan's samurai flicks are made? Open from 9 a.m to 5 p.m (9:30 a.m to 4 p.m. from November 16 to March 15) and closed December 21 to January 1, it charges ¥1,400 ($10) admission for adults and ¥650 ($4.64) for children. Popular with school groups and resembling an amusement park more than a movie studio, it does have both outdoor and indoor sets, and if you're lucky you'll see a movie in the making. Reconstructed houses re-create the mood, setting, and atmosphere of feudal Japan while indoor museums show minature castles, houses, and items from the history of Japanese film. Who knows, you may even see a famous star walking around dressed in samurai garb. You can also have a photo taken of yourself decked out in a kimono or samurai gear. Since the Movie Village is clearly a commercial venture, come here only if you have a lot of time or are sick of temples.

CENTRAL KYOTO: Much of central Kyoto has been taken over by the 20th century but there are a few interesting sites worth investigating. **Kyoto Imperial Palace,** near the Imadegawa subway station, was where the imperial family lived from 1331 until 1868, when they moved to Tokyo. The palace was destroyed several times by fire, and the present buildings date from 1855. You need special permission to see the palace, but that can be obtained the day of your intended visit by dropping by the Imperial Household Agency on the palace grounds. A 30-minute tour is held every morning except Sunday at 10 a.m., and you must apply to join this tour by 9:40 a.m. Be sure to bring your passport. Another tour in English is held Monday through Friday at 2 p.m and for this one you must apply by 1:40 p.m. The tours are free.

Whereas the Imperial Palace was where the royal family resided, **Nijo Castle** is where the Tokugawa shogun stayed whenever he left Edo and came to Kyoto for a visit. It was built by the first Tokugawa shogun, Ieyasu, and is considered the quintessence of Momoyama architecture. With delicate transom wood carvings and paintings on sliding doors, the castle has an understated elegance, especially when compared to the castles Europe was building at the same time. The castle has 33 rooms and a total of about 800 tatami mats. All the sliding doors on the outside walls of the castle can be removed in summer, allowing cool breezes to sweep through the building. Winters, on the other hand, must have been dreadfully cold. There was no heating and light was provided only by candles. Typical for Japan at the time, rooms were unfurnished, the mattresses stored in closets.

To protect the shogun from real or imagined enemies, the castle was protected by a moat and stone walls. How deep the shogun's paranoia ran, however, is apparent by the installation of the so-called nightingale floor inside the castle itself. Corridors were fitted with floorboards that squeaked when trod upon to alert against infiltrating assassins, and there were hidden alcoves for bodyguards.

Outside the castle is a garden famous in its own right, designed by famous gardener Kobori Enshu. The original grounds of the castle, however, were without trees—supposedly because the falling of leaves in autumn reminded the shogun and his tough samurai of life's transitory nature, making them terribly sad.

Nijo Castle is open from 8:45 a.m. to 4 p.m.; the garden remains open until 5 p.m. The ¥500 ($3.57) admission covers both the castle and the garden.

About a mile north of Nijo Castle is the **Nishijin Textile Hall (Nishijin-Ori Kaikan)** (tel. 451-9231), dedicated to the centuries of weavers who produced elegant textiles for the imperial family and the nobility. The history of Nishijin textiles began with the history of Kyoto itself back in 794, and by the Edo Period there were an estimated 5,000 weaving factories producing the famous material. The museum has weaving demonstrations, historical displays, and kimono shows held regularly. Admission to the hall itself is free; the kimono show costs ¥200 ($1.43). Hours for the textile hall are 9 a.m to 5 p.m. daily, and it's located on Horikawa-dori Avenue, Imadegawa-minami-iru, Kamigyo-ku.

If you're interested in learning more about the Kyo-Yuzen method for dyeing silk for kimonos, visit **Kodai Yuzen-en** (tel. 811-8101, located a couple minutes' walk northwest of the Horikawa-dori and Gojo Street intersection. It has displays and demonstrations showing the 300-year history of Yuzen dyeing and a shop where Yuzen goods are sold. It's open 9 a.m. to 5 p.m. daily and charges a ¥500 ($3.57) admission. Although it's not as conveniently located—about a five-minute walk from Nishikyogoku Station on the Hankyu electric railway line in the west part of Kyoto—the **Yuzen Cultural Hall (Yuzen Bunka Kaikan)** (tel. 311-0025) also demonstrates the method of Yuzen dyeing. It's open every day except Wednesday from 9 a.m. to 4:30 p.m., and admission is ¥ ($2.14).

Just north of Kyoto Station are two massive temple compounds, **Nishi-Honganji and Higashi-Honganji temples**. They were once joined under one huge religious center called Honganji but split afer a disagreement several centuries ago. Higashi-Honganji is Kyoto's largest wooden structure, while Nishi-Honganji is the older temple and represents an outstanding example of Buddhist architecture. Only parts of both temples are open to the public.

IN KYOTO'S ENVIRONS: If this is your first visit to Kyoto and you're here only a short while, your sightseeing priorities should lie in Kyoto itself, concentrating on the sites described above. If, however, this is your second trip to Kyoto or you're here for an extended period of time, there are a number of worthwhile attractions in the region surrounding Kyoto you should make an effort to see.

Katsura Imperial Villa, Shugakuin Imperial Villa, and Saihoji (popularly called the Moss Temple) all require advance permission to visit. To see the imperial villas you must write or telephone the Imperial Household Agency (tel. 211-1211) at least one week to three months in advance to make an appointment to join a tour—but unfortunately no one at the office speaks English so you'll have to find someone to make the call for you in Japanese. If applying by mail, include your name, age, sex, occupation, and home address. You must be more than 20 years old, and the maximum number of people allowed in your group is four. Tours—in Japanese only—are given at Katsura at 10 a.m. and 2 p.m. and at Shugakuin at 9, 10, and 11 a.m. and 1:30 and 3 p.m. Note that no tours are given on Sunday, national holidays, or *Saturday afternoon*. When specifying your desired date and time, be sure to include several choices. The address of the Imperial Household Agency is 3, Kyoto-Gyoen, Kamigyo-ku, Kyoto, and once you arrive in Kyoto you should drop by the agency (located at the Kyoto Imperial Palace) at least one day prior to the tour to fill out a formal application. Be sure to bring your passport. The tours are free.

Obviously it's somewhat of a hassle to visit the imperial villas, and according to the Tourist Information Office applications by mail are not always acknowledged or successful. Applying by phone is much easier if you can find someone to do so in Japanese. If you're going to be in Japan longer than a week before arriving in Kyoto, you might try calling the Imperial Household Agency as soon as you arrive in Japan. If perchance all time slots are already booked, don't be too disappointed—there are many other sites that are equally enjoyable to visit.

Katsura Imperial Villa
Located about a 15-minute walk from Katsura Station on the Hankyu rail-

way line, Katsura villa is considered the jewel of traditional Japanese architecture and landscape gardening. It was built between 1620 and 1624 by Prince Toshihito, brother of the emperor, with construction continued by Toshihito's son. The garden, markedly influenced by Kobori Enshu, Japan's most famous garden designer, is a "stroll garden" in which each turn of the path brings an entirely new view.

The first thing you notice upon entering Katsura is its simplicity—the buildings are all made of natural materials in which everything was taken into consideration, including the slopes of the roof, the type of various woods used, their grain, texture, and color. A pavilion for viewing the moon, a hall for imperial visits, a tea house, and other buildings are situated around a pond, and as you walk along the pathway you are treated to views that literally change with each step you take. Islets, stone lanterns, various scenes representing the seashore, mountains, and hamlets, manicured trees, and bridges of stone, earth, or wood that arch gracefully over the water—everything is perfectly balanced. No matter where you stand the view is complete and in harmony. Every detail was carefully planned, down to the stones used in the pathways, the way the trees twist, and how scenes are reflected in the water. Little wonder that Katsura villa has influenced architecture not only in Japan but around the world.

Shugakuin Imperial Villa

Located about a 15-minute walk from the Shugakuin-michi bus stop or Shugakuin Station, the Shugakuin Imperial Villa was built in the mid-1600s for Emperor Go-Mizunoo, who became a monk after his abdication. Its stroll garden is among Kyoto's largest and is divided into three levels. The upper garden with its lake, islands, and waterfalls is the largest of the three and uses the principle known as "borrowed landscape," in which the surrounding landscape is incorporated into the overall garden design. The gardens are more spacious than most Japanese-style gardens, and the view of the surrounding countryside is grand.

Saihoji, the Moss Temple

Popularly known as Kokedera, the Moss Temple, Saihoji is famous for its velvety-green moss garden spread underneath the trees. Altogether there are more than 40 different varieties of moss through the grounds, giving off an iridescent and mysterious glow which is at its best just after a rain. Because the monks are afraid that huge numbers of visitors would trample the moss to death, prior permission is needed to visit Saihoji, which you can obtain by writing the temple at least three months in advance. The address is Saiho-ji Temple, Matsuo Kamigaya-cho, Nishikyo-ku, Kyoto, and you should give your name, address, nationality, age, and when you'd like to visit. The cost of a visit to the temple is ¥3,000 ($21.43).

Enryakuji Temple

Along with Mount Koya, south of Osaka, Enryakuji Temple is considered one of the most important centers of Buddhism in Japan. Located atop Mount Hiei, Enryakuji Temple was founded back in 788 at the order of Emperor Kammu to ward off evil spirits that might come from the northeast. At one time Enryakuji Temple consisted of as many as 3,000 buildings and maintained an army of warrior monks that made raids of rival temples. Because of the temple's political and military power, an army organized by Oda Nobunaga attacked Enryakuji and destroyed the temple in 1571. Although some of the temple was subsequently rebuilt, it never again reached its former powerful position. However, there are a number of fine buildings spread out under large cedar trees and a peaceful atmosphere. Enryakuji Temple can be reached either by bus or rail from Kyoto; the trip takes approximately an hour.

Byodoin Temple

Located in the town of Uji about 11 miles southeast of Kyoto, Byodoin temple is a good example of temple architecture of the Heian Period. Most famous is the main hall, known as Phoenix Hall, which was built in 1053. It has three wings, creating an image of the mythical bird of China, the phoenix, and on the gable ends are two bronze phoenixes. On the temple grounds are one of the most famous bells in Japan, as well as a monument to Yorimasa Minamoto, who took his own life here after being defeated by the rival Taira clan.

Fushimi-Inari shrine

A five-minute walk from Inari Station, Fushimi-Inari Shrine has long been popular with merchants and tradesmen who come here to pray for success and prosperity. One of Japan's most celebrated Shinto shrines, it was founded back in 711 and is dedicated to the goddess of rice. The 2½-mile-long pathway to the shrine is lined with more than 10,000 red *torii* gates, presented by worshippers throughout the ages, and there are also stone foxes which are considered messengers of the gods.

Cormorant Fishing in Arashiyama

If you're lucky enough to be in Kyoto during July and August, I highly recommend that you spend one evening drifting in a wooden boat on the Oi River and watching men fishing with trained cormorants. Cormorant fishing is held in Arashiyama every evening (except when there's a full moon) from July 1 to August 31. You can reach Arashiyama by bus from Kyoto Station or electric tram from Shijo Omiya Station in central Kyoto. You should arrive in Arashiyama shortly before 7 p.m. For a fee of ¥1,000 ($7.14) you can board a narrow wooden boat gaily decorated with paper lanterns. Along with dozens of others, your boatsman will pole you down the river so that you can see the fishing boats lit by blazing torches. The cormorants, with rings around their necks so that they don't swallow the fish they catch, dive under the water for *ayu*, a small river fish. Water taxis ply the river offering snacks and beer. I find the whole experience of watching the cormorants and being a part of the flotilla of wooden boats and paper lanterns terribly romantic. It's a lovely way to spend a warm summer's evening.

Trying to find your way around Japan is so difficult that I can't imagine anyone seeking out added aggravation, but if you enjoy frustration at every turn you might want to visit the **Kyoto Daigo Granmaze**, a specially constructed maze for humans. Opened in 1985, the Kyoto Granmaze was the start of the maze craze that has since spread to other parts of Japan. Covering an area about half the size of a football field, this maze features wooden walls about 6½ feet tall, with lookout towers posted every so often to let you survey your position. Although the record time for finding one's way out is eight minutes, it takes most humans about an hour to complete the maze. If you take longer, don't feel bad. The longest time to date belongs to some hapless soul who wandered around for four hours and 34 minutes before reaching the finish line. To get to the Granmaze, take the Keihan Uji Line to Rokujizo Station, from which it's about a seven-minute walk north of the station (make sure you have the right line— otherwise you might well end up in Osaka, with more frustration than you bargained for). The Granmaze opens daily at 9 a.m., and lost souls are flushed out at sunset (10 p.m. July and August). Cost of all this fun: ¥500 ($3.57).

ORGANIZED TOURS: Although I believe that being herded around Kyoto's temples in a large group can never compete with the experience of wandering around at leisure on your own, you may find yourself so short of time that you feel compelled to join an organized tour of Kyoto. Both morning and afternoon tours are offered by **Japan Travel Bureau** (tcl. 361-7241), **Fujita Travel Service** (tel. 343-2304), and **Kintetsu Gray Line** (tel. 691-0903). Sites visited may include the Imperial Palace, Nijo Castle, the Golden Pavilion, Heian Shrine, Sanjusangendo Hall, and Kiyomizu Temple.

One tour that you may consider joining if you have some extra time and you're tired of temples (Kyoto does seem to have more than its fair share of temples) is the **Rapids Shooting Tour**. Flat-bottomed wooden boats depart from Kameoka six times daily March through November, with fewer departures in heated boats during the winter months. The trip lasts about two hours and covers approximately ten miles of the Hozu River, ending in Arashiyama. The rapids are not dangerous (in fact, most of them are nothing more than small riffles), and the trip is a very pleasant and relaxing way to see something of the surrounding countryside with its changing vistas of wooded hills and winding gorge. Cost of the trip is ¥3,300 ($23.57). For more information on the tour or how to get to Kameoka, contact the T.I.C.

4. Notes on Shopping

As the nation's capital for more than 1,000 years, Kyoto became home to a number of crafts and exquisite art forms which evolved to cater to the elaborate tastes of the imperial court and upper classes. Today you can shop for everything from Noh masks to silk to cloisonné and lacquerware in Kyoto.

KYOTO HANDICRAFT CENTER: For one-stop shopping under one roof your best bet is the Kyoto Handicraft Center, Kumano Jinja Higashi, Sakyo-ku (tel. 761-5080), located just north of Heian Shrine. Seven floors of merchandise contain almost everything Japanese imaginable—pearls, lacquerware, dolls, kimonos, woodblock prints, pottery, cameras, cassette players, items made of Japanese paper, swords, lanterns, silk and textile goods, painted scrolls, and music boxes. And that's just for starters. You can even buy socks to be worn with *geta* wooden shoes and *obi* sashes worn with the kimono. You can easily spend an hour or two here wandering around, and there are also demonstrations set up showing artisans at work on various crafts including hand-weaving, woodblock printing, and the production of damascene. The center is open from 9:30 a.m. to 6 p.m. (until 5:30 p.m. December through February); closed December 31 through January 3.

KYOTO CRAFT CENTER: Whereas the Kyoto Handicraft Center described above is good for souvenirs and inexpensive gifts for the folks back home, the Kyoto Craft Center, 275 Gion, Kitagawa, Higashiyama-ku (tel. 561-9660), features beautifully designed and crafted items by local and famous artisans. Located on Shijo Dori Avenue east of the Kamo River in the heart of Gion, the Kyoto Craft Center has a wide range of products, including jewelry, scarves, pottery, glass, fans, damascene, baskets, and much more. This is the place to shop for wedding gifts or something very special for yourself. It's open daily from 11 a.m. to 7 p.m.

DEPARTMENT STORES: Another good place to shop for Japanese items and souvenirs, including pottery, lacquerware, and kimonos, are department stores. They're open from 10 a.m. to 6 p.m., closed one day of the week. **Takashimaya** (tel. 221-8811), closed on Wednesday, and **Hankyu** (tel. 223-2288), closed on Thursday, are both located at the intersection of Shijo and Kawaramachi in the heart of Kyoto; **Daimaru** (tel. 211-8111), closed on Wednesday, is located farther west on Shijo Dori Avenue; **Kintetsu**, located across the street from Kyoto Station's north exit, closed on Thursday.

SPECIALTY SHOPS: There are a number of tiny specialty shops in Kyoto, the majority situated in Gion, along Shijo Dori Avenue and in the area of Kawaramachi Dori Avenue. The square formed by Kawaramachi Dori, Shijo Dori, Sanjo Dori, and Teramachi, for example, includes a covered shopping arcade and specialized shops selling lacquerware, combs and hairpins, knives and swords, tea and tea ceremony implements, and more. If you're looking for antiques and art galleries, head towards Shinmonzen Street in Gion, which parallels Shijo Dori to the north on the east side of the Kamo River. Pottery shops are found in abundance on the roads leading to Kiyomizu Temple in Higashiyama-ku.

If you're interested in Japanese dolls, a good place to go is **Tanakaya**, Yanaginobanba-higashi, on Shijo Dori Avenue (tel. 221-1959), where the shopkeeper speaks English. You can browse for Kyoto-style dolls, Noh masks, and inexpensive miniature animals. It's open from 10 a.m. to 6:30 p.m.; closed Wednesday.

Miyawaki Baisen-an, Tominokoji-nishi, Rokkaku-dori (tel. 221-0181), has specialized in fans since 1823, especially fans characteristic of Kyoto. It's open daily from 9 a.m. to 5 p.m., and English is spoken.

Located on Kawaramachi Dori Avenue next to Maruzen Book Store, Yamato Mingei-ten, Takoyakushi-agaru, Nakagyo-ku (tel. 221-2641), has been selling folkcrafts and folk art from all over Japan for more than four decades. For sale are ceramics, glassware, lacquerware, textiles, paper products, baskets, and other handcrafted items. It's open every day except Friday from 10 a.m. to 8:30 p.m.

Handcrafted boxwood hair combs and ornamental hairpins are on display at **Jusan-ya**, Otabi-cho, Shinkyogoku Higashi-iru, Shimogyo-ku (tel. 221-2008), on Shijo Dori Avenue west of Kawaramachi Dori Avenue. Opened in 1930 by the fifth generation of comb makers, it's open daily from 10 a.m. to 9 p.m.

Komachi House, Ichijo-agaru, Inokuma Dori, Kamigyo-ku (tel. 451-6838), sells old kimonos, obi sashes, and *happi* coats. Located just southeast of the Nishijin Textile Center, it's closed on Sunday but open the rest of the week from 9 a.m. to 5 p.m.

If you want to decorate your garden back home with a Japanese stone lantern, drop by the **Sawakichi Stone Store**, 551 Gojozaka, Higashiyama-ku (tel. 561-2802). Located on a large intersection just west of the approach leading to Kiyomizu Temple, it offers a variety of styles and sizes in stone lanterns and is open daily from 9 a.m. to 7 p.m.

Zohiko Lacquerware, located in Okazaki Park not far from Heian Shrine (tel. 761-0212), carries on the tradition of Kyoto lacquerware, which has been produced in the ancient capital for 1,000 years. The showroom, with various lacquer products for sale, is open from 9:30 a.m. to 5:30 p.m.; closed Sunday and national holidays.

Inaba Cloisonné, Sanjo Shirakawabashi (tel. 761-1161), is one of Japan's most famous shops and has been dealing in cloisonné and artistic enamelware for about a century. Its showroom displays jewelry, vases, trays, and other products. Hours are 9 a.m. to 5:30 p.m.; closed Sunday. There's a workshop here where you can watch women producing various cloisonné wares. The shop is located west of the Miyako Hotel on Sanjo Dori Avenue not far from the Shirakawa River.

TOJI TEMPLE FLEA MARKET: On the 21st of each month a flea market is held at Toji Temple, located about a 15-minute walk southwest of Kyoto Station. Japan's largest monthly market, it's also one of the oldest, with a history stretching back more than 700 years. The market began in the 1200s as pilgrims began flocking to Toji Temple to pay their respects to Kobo Daishi, who founded the Shingon sect of Buddhism. Today Toji Temple is still a center for the Shingon sect, and its monthly market is a colorful affair with booths selling antiques, old kimonos, and other items. Worshippers come to pray before a statue of Kobo Daishi and to have their wishes written on wooden slats by temple calligraphers. Even if you don't buy anything, the festive atmosphere of the market and booths makes a trip here a memorable experience.

5. After Dark in Kyoto

Nothing beats spending a fine summer's evening strolling the streets of Kyoto. From the geisha district of Gion to the bars and restaurants lining the narrow street of Pontocho, Kyoto at night is a city utterly charming and romantic. Begin your evening with a walk along the banks of the Kamo River—it's a favorite place for young couples in love. In the summer, restaurants along the river stretching north and south of Shijo Dori Avenue erect outdoor wooden platforms on stilts over the water. Illuminated with paper lanterns, they look like images from Kyoto's past.

GION: Gion is a small district of Kyoto, an area of plain wooden buildings devoid of flashing neon signs. In fact, as the geisha entertainment district of the city, there's something almost austere and solemn about Gion, as though its raison d'être were infinitely more important and sacred than that of mere entertainment. Gion is a shrine to Kyoto's past, an era when geisha numbered thousands in the city. Now there are only a mere couple of hundred. After all, in today's world of technology, computers, and space travel, few women are willing to undergo the years of training to learn how to conduct the tea ceremony, to play the samisen, or to perform ancient court dances. And contrary to popular Western misconceptions, geisha are not prostitutes. Rather, they are trained experts in conversation and coquettishness, and their primary role is to make men feel like kings while in the soothing enclave of the geisha house.

As you stroll the narrow streets of Gion, perhaps you will see a geisha or *maiko* (a young woman training to be a geisha) clattering in her wooden shoes on her way to her evening appointment. She will be dressed in a brilliant kimono, her face a chalky white and her hair adorned with hairpins and ornaments. From geisha houses music and laughter lilt out from behind paper screens, but you can only surmise the merry scene inside because you cannot enter without being invited. Not even the Japanese will venture inside without proper introductions. If it will satisfy your curiosity, however, I will tell you that on my fourth visit to Kyoto I was finally invited to one of Gion's geisha houses—and found it to be much like any other hostess bar in Japan. The women pour the drinks, the men drink, and everyone is lighthearted and happy.

After strolling around, the best thing to do in Gion is to visit **Gion Corner**, located on the first floor of Yasaka Hall, Hanamikoji Shijo-sagaru (tel. 561-1119), in the heart of Gion. This is where special variety programs are held every night from March 1 to November 29 with demonstrations of the tea ceremony, flower arrangement, *koto* (Japanese harp) music, *gagaku* (ancient court music and dance), *kyogen* (Noh comic play), *kyomai* (Kyoto-style dance) performed by maiko, and *Bunraku* (puppetry). This is an excellent way to see a variety of ancient Japanese entertainment in a short period of time. Admission is ¥2,200 ($15.71) and there are two shows nightly, at 7:40 and again at 8:40 p.m. Reservations are not necessary, but get there early since the 250 seats are on a first-come, first-served basis. Tickets are available at most hotels, travel agencies, and at Gion Corner itself.

The **Minamiza Theater**, on Shijo Dori Avenue just east of the Kamo River, stages Kabuki drama several times a year. Inquire at the Kyoto Tourist Information Center for information on performances, cost, and times. The T.I.C. also has information on Noh performances, which are given at a handful of theaters in Kyoto much of the year.

PONTOCHO AND VICINITY: Pontocho is a narrow street that parallels the Kamo River's west bank and stretches north from Shijo Dori Avenue. Riddled with geisha houses, hostess bars, restaurants, and bars, Pontocho is interesting to walk along and to watch groups of Japanese enjoying themselves. Although many of these restaurants lining the river have outdoor verandas in summer, I was able to include only a couple of them in this book, which you'll find listed in the restaurant section. Most of the restaurants in Pontocho are unfortunately unreceptive to foreigners, and I was turned away from establishment after establishment with the excuse that the place was full—even when I could see that it was not. The Kyoto T.I.C. informed me that they do not recommend Pontocho to foreigners simply because of the cold reception. However, I think it's worth walking through Pontocho because the area is so interesting and so Japanese. Although most of the bars and clubs are virtually impossible to enter without an introduction, you might want to come here for a meal at one of the recommended restaurants in this book. And if you're feeling adventurous and are determined to find seating under the paper lanterns on one of the open verandas, maybe you'll be lucky. Once in a while, restaurants that do not want the publicity of a guidebook will accept the occasional lone foreigner.

If you don't feel like eating but would still like to sit under the stars beside the river, the best thing to do is to go to the north end of Pontocho where it joins Sanjo Dori Avenue and drink a cup of coffee at **Karafuneya**, Pontocho, Sanjo-sagaru (tel. 255-1414). A coffeeshop with an outdoor veranda overlooking the river, it's open 24 hours a day every day, and offers various kinds of coffee, tea, sandwiches, ice cream, sundaes, and desserts, with most items costing ¥600 ($4.29). No alcoholic beverages are served, but it's a pleasant place to sit and watch couples strolling along the riverbanks. Note that the veranda itself is open only in the evenings, from 5 to 11 p.m.

Also on Pontocho, but facing away from the river, **Suishin Honten** [103] (tel. 221-8596) is an inexpensive yakitori-ya very popular with young Japanese. Part of a chain of Suishin yakitori restaurants, it has small mugs of beer that start at ¥400 ($2.86). Three skewers of chicken yakitori or grilled fish (*yakizakana*) cost only ¥270 ($1.93), while a platter of assorted sashimi (called *moriawase*) costs ¥1,300 ($9.29). Open from 4 to 11:30 p.m. every day, it's located on the west side of Pontocho just south of Sanjo Dori Avenue. Look for a big white sign, red curtains hanging outside the front door, and a large display case. This is a good place to stop off for a beer.

Skewer of Nan-Zan, Kawaramachi-Sanjo, Futasugi-agaru (tel. 221-6930), is a friendly yakitori-ya close to the Alpha and Kyoto Royal hotels and just a few steps southeast of the Kawaramachi Catholic Church. It's located on Anekoji

Dori Street in a basement and is open from 5 p.m. to 1 a.m.; closed the third Sunday of the month. The owner has studied English, is a big baseball fan, and is delighted to have foreign guests. The English menu lists various kinds of yakitori, including skewers of beef, chicken, squid, bell pepper, mushroom, and eggplant, with prices averaging ¥330 ($2.36) to ¥1,000 ($7.14) for three to five skewers. Also available is beef sushi, salads, soups, and beef steak cooked Japanese style. I recommend trying grilled wrapped potato—mashed potato with egg, onions, and bacon in it. Beer starts at ¥500 ($3.57) and sake at ¥380 ($2.71).

A comfortable and pleasant bar that caters to a 20- to 30-year-old crowd, **Africa**, Shijo-Kawaramachi (tel. 255-4518), is located on a side street just east of Kawaramachi and north of Shijo Avenues. Open daily from 5 p.m. to 2 a.m., it's filled with all kinds of knickknacks, stuffed animals, masks, junk, and stained-glass lamps. A video screen shows old and recent American movies, TV shows, and rock videos, and there are also a Foosball table and backgammon sets you can use. Beer starts at ¥550 ($3.93) and cocktails at ¥600 ($4.29). Snacks include pizza, gratin, spaghetti, seafood, roast beef, fried chicken, and pilaf.

California Beach, located on Kawaramachi Dori Avenue in front of the Alpha Hotel (tel. 222-2029), does everything it can to imitate sunny California and features a cool white interior with plants, ceiling fans, brass railings, and mirrors. A restaurant-bar, it's open from 7 a.m. for breakfast until midnight on weekdays and until 1:30 a.m. on Friday and Saturday nights. Domestic beer starts at ¥550 ($3.93), imported beer at ¥520 ($3.71), and cocktails at ¥600 ($4.29). Alcoholic drinks are served only after 4 p.m. The English menu lists a wide range of Western fare, including barbecue spareribs, spaghetti, pizza, sandwiches, Mexican tacos, steaks, soups, and salads. Most are in the ¥750 ($5.36) to ¥2,200 ($15.71) range.

If you want to hear live music, head for **Taku Taku** [104], Tominokoji-Bukkoji (tel. 351-1321). Featuring heavy metal, rock, soul, blues, reggae, jazz, and occasionally even performances of avant-garde *buto* dance, this live-entertainment house is located in an old sake warehouse and its decor is rudimentary and plain. It caters mainly to Kyoto's college students and is open daily from 3 to 11 p.m. Live music is usually from 7 to 9 p.m., and the cover charge averages ¥750 ($5.36), rising to as much as ¥4,200 ($30) for bands from England or U.S.A. Beer is ¥550 ($3.93), and sandwiches and various snacks are available. To find Taku Taku, walk south from Shijo Dori Avenue on Tominokoji Dori Street. It's just past the red-and-white spiral of a barbershop on the right-hand side of the street behind a small parking lot. Listen for the music.

Another popular place among Kyoto's college crowd is **Irohanihoheto** [105], Shingoken-cho, Sanjo-kudaru, Yamato-dori, Higashiyama-ku (tel. 541-1683). It's located on Nawate Dori Street on the fifth floor of a white-tiled building just south of Sanjo-Keihan Station (look for a sign on the building's ground floor that says Colorado Coffee Shop). Open daily from 5 p.m. to 5 a.m., this is one of a chain of drinking establishments with headquarters in Hokkaido. Irohanihoheto is known for its rustic decor, which always includes heavy wooden beams held together with ropes to give it a country atmosphere, shoji screens, and crafts hanging down from the ceiling. It's also known for its low prices. Beer starts at ¥330 ($2.36), and the extensive Japanese menu with pictures includes yakitori, sashimi, salads, and vegetables. Most items cost less than ¥400 ($2.86).

Around the corner from Irohanihoheto and directly behind (south of) the Sanjo-Keihan Station is the **Jazz Club Sunnyside**, located on the fifth floor of the

Kyoto Art Center Building, Furumonzen Dori Street, Yamato-oji, Higashi-yama-ku (tel. 525-0910). Informal and cozy with room for only 15 or so people, it's owned by Fumhiro Watanabe, who also provides the entertainment by singing and playing the piano. His repertoire centers on American jazz and popular hits of the 1940s, and there's a tiny dance floor. Closed on Sunday and national holidays, it's open the rest of the week from 8 p.m. to 1 a.m. The ¥2,000 ($14.29) music charge includes one drink, snack, and tip. After that, beer costs ¥500 ($3.57) and cocktails are ¥750 ($5.36).

Catering to a much younger crowd is **China Express**, a disco located in the basement of the Sanjo Terrace Building, Sanjo Kiyamachi-sagaru (tel. 241-3870). It's on the first street south of and paralleling Sanjo Dori Avenue, between Kawaramachi and Kiyamachi Streets. Open from 6:30 p.m. to midnight, it features a wooden dance floor, mirrors in which you can watch yourself dance, and an interesting Chinese-like decor. Admission is ¥3,800 ($27.14) for males and ¥3,300 ($23.57) for females, except on weekends and nights before a holiday, when prices go up ¥500 ($3.57). Included in the admission are 20 tickets you can exchange for drinks; beer costs six tickets, while cocktails are six or seven.

If you like to listen to reggae, one more place worth mentioning is **Rub a Dub**, Sanjo-sagaru, Kiyamachi (tel. 256-3122). It's located on the east side of Kiyamachi Street just a couple shops south of Sanjo Dori Avenue, below a drugstore. A tiny establishment open from 6 p.m. to 2 a.m., this bar is unpretentious and primitive. Beer and cocktails are all a low ¥550 ($3.93). The music isn't live, but prices are cheap.

If you're interested in a quiet place for a cup of coffee or a drink after dinner, the **François Salon de Thé** is on a small street running along the west side of the tiny canal about a minute's walk southwest of the Shijo Avenue Bridge, spanning the Kamo River (tel. 351-4042). More than 50 years old, the outside of the building resembles a miniature castle while the inside has an atmosphere similar to that of an old Viennese coffeehouse. A domed ceiling, dark-wood paneling, stained-glass windows, heavy red-cushioned chairs, and classical music make drinking a cup of coffee here a pleasant and relaxing experience—a good place to escape the crowds. Tea and coffee start at ¥450 ($3.21), cakes start at ¥380 ($2.71), and beer is available for ¥550 ($3.93). It's open from 9:30 a.m. to 11 p.m. daily.

BEER GARDENS: A pleasant and inexpensive way to enjoy a warm summer's night is to spend it under the stars at a rooftop beer garden. On the roof of a restaurant called **Kikusui** [106], Shijo Ohashi (tel. 561-1001), is a beer garden open throughout the summer from 5 until 10 p.m. Monday through Friday, until 10:50 p.m. on Saturday, and until 9:50 p.m. on Sunday. It's atop a five-story stone building right on Shijo Dori Avenue on the east side of the Kamo River and across the street from the Kabuki theater. It's easy to spot because the rooftop is lined with lanterns and has palm trees peeking over the ledge. Beer ranges from ¥450 ($3.21) to ¥770 ($5.50), and various snacks such as yakitori, pizza, and grilled squid are also available.

The **Kyoto Hotel** on Kawaramachi Dori Avenue also has a rooftop beer garden open mid-May to the end of August from 5 to 9 p.m. nightly. It offers a good view of the city, with a nightly buffet of all you can eat and drink for ¥2,700 ($19.29). Included items are yakitori, fried chicken, fried fish, fried noodles, smoked salmon, as well as such drinks as beer, whisky, and sake.

On top of the ANA Hotel is another beer garden, open from May to the end of August nightly from 5:30 to 9 p.m. Beer here begins at ¥550 ($3.93) for a small. And finally, close to Kyoto Station is one more rooftop beer garden, this one atop the **New Miyako Hotel**. It's open from 5 to 9 p.m. throughout the summer months.

6. The ABCs of Kyoto

Below is some practical information on Kyoto that you may need to know during your stay. Remember too that the concierge of your hotel, as well as the Kyoto Tourist Information Center, can probably answer any other questions you may have regarding Kyoto.

BANKS AND MONEY EXCHANGE: Banks are open from 9 a.m. to 3 p.m. Monday through Friday and from 9 a.m. to noon on every Saturday except the second and third Saturdays of the month. If you need to cash a traveler's check outside these hours and your hotel doesn't have the facilities to do so, both the Grand and New Miyako hotels will cash checks even if you are not a hotel guest.

BOOKSTORES: There are two conveniently located stores selling books in English. **Maruzen**, Kawaramachi Takoyakushi-agaru, Nakagyo-ku (tel. 241-2161), is part of a national bookstore chain and has novels as well as books on Japan. Located north of the Shijo–Kawaramachi intersection, it's open from 10 a.m. to 7 p.m. (until 6:30 p.m. on Sunday); closed Wednesday. **Izumiya Book Center** is in the Avanti department store just south of Kyoto Station (tel. 682-5031). It's open from 10 a.m. to 8 p.m. every day except Thursday.

CAR RENTAL: There are many car-rental agencies in Kyoto. Among them are: **Mazda Rent-A-Car**, Kawaramachi-Nishi-Iru, Gojo-dori, Shimogyo-ku (tel. 361-0201); **Nippon Rent-A-Car**, Higashi-Kujo Muromachi (tel. 671-0919); **Nissan Rent-A-Car**, 26, Nishi-Kujo-Inmachi, Minami-ku (tel. 661-2161); and **Toyota Rent-A-Lease**, Sanjo-agaru, Karasuma Dori Avenue, Nakagyo-ku (tel. 241-0100).

CREDIT CARDS: Credit cards are accepted by major tourist shops, restaurants, and hotels. If you need to use your credit card to obtain cash, there are several banks that handle specific credit cards. **Sanwa Bank**, Karasuma Shijo, Shimogyo-ku (tel. 211-1111), has a card-cashing service for American Express; **Tokai Bank**, Shijo Karasuma-agaru, Nakagyo-ku (tel. 221-7061), handles MasterCard; and **Sumitomo Bank** has two locations for those who wish to use VISA—Karasuma Sanjo-agaru, Nakagyo-ku (tel. 211-2111), and Shijo Kawaramachi-nishi, Shimogyo-ku (tel. 223-2811).

DOCTORS AND DENTISTS: The **Kyoto T.I.C.** (tel. 371-5649) has a list of approximately a dozen doctors and half a dozen dentists who speak English. If the T.I.C. is closed or you'd rather talk to a doctor directly, **Dr. Sakabe**, Gokomachi, Nijo-sagaru, Nakagyo-ku (tel. 231-1624), is an internist who speaks excellent English, and he can refer you to other doctors as well.

ELECTRICAL CURRENT: In both Kyoto and Nara it's 100 volts, 60 cycles, almost the same as in the United States (110 volts and 60 cycles).

EMERGENCY: The same all over Japan, the national emergency telephone numbers are 110 for **police** and 119 for both **ambulance** and to report a **fire**.

HOSPITALS: Most hospitals are not equipped to handle emergencies 24 hours a day, but a system has been set up in which hospitals handle emergencies on a rotating basis. If you go by ambulance, it must take you to one of these. The **Kyoto Second Red Cross Hospital (Daini Sekijuji Byoin)**, Marutamachi-sagaru, Kamanza Dori, Kamikyo-ku (tel. 231-5171), is staffed 24 hours a day, but referral by a doctor who knows your problem is expected. English is spoken at **Japan Baptist Hospital (Nihon Baputesuto Byoin)**, 47 Yamanomoto-cho, Kitashirakawa, Sakyo-ku (tel. 781-5191).

LOST PROPERTY: If you left something on the Shinkansen bullet train, the number to call to see whether it's been found is 691-1000. Items lost at Kyoto Station are turned in to the lost and found office (tel. 371-0134). If you lost something along a street or outside, contact the Shichijo Police Station (tel. 371-2111). Forgetting something in a taxi is a bit more complicated because there are several different taxi companies—which means you have to know which taxi company to call. The MK Taxi Company number is 721-4141; the privately owned green taxis all report to 314-4481. Another number to call for items left in taxis is 691-6518. Because it's so difficult to track down items left in taxis, the T.I.C. suggests you visit their office if you have any problems.

POST OFFICE: The **Kyoto Central Post Office** is located just west of Kyoto Station at 843-12 Higashi-shiokoji-cho, Shimogyo-ku (tel. 365-2471). It's open from 9 a.m. to 7 p.m. Monday through Friday, to 5 p.m. on Saturday, and to 12:30 p.m. on Sunday and holidays. You can mail packages bound for international destinations here. You can also have your own mail delivered *Post Restante* here, but you have to pick it up within one month if it's international mail and within ten days if it's domestic.

RAILWAY INFORMATION: For information on train schedules, call the Travel Service Center at Kyoto Station at 371-0036 from 10 a.m. to 6 p.m.

SHOP HOURS: Department stores in Kyoto stay open from 10 a.m. to 6 p.m., while smaller shops in the downtown area remain open from about 10 a.m. to 8 p.m.

STUDENT GUIDES: Students of Kyoto University, Doshisha University, and Kyoto Women's University are happy to act as voluntary guides to tourists in Kyoto (it gives them practice with their English). You must apply at the Tourist Information Center one or two days in advance, and you're expected to pay for the student's transportation, entrance fees to shrines and temples, and lunch.

TELEPHONE AREA CODE: If you're calling from outside Kyoto, the area code for Kyoto is 075.

TOURIST INFORMATION: The **Tourist Information Center (T.I.C.)** is about a minute's walk from Kyoto Station's north side in the Kyoto Tower Building, Higashi-Shiokojicho, Shimogyo-ku (tel. 075/371-5649). Open from 9 a.m. to 5 p.m. Monday through Friday, to noon on Saturday, its staff speaks excellent English and can help you with all your questions regarding Kyoto. The T.I.C.

distributes a great map in English of the city, and has brochures and leaflets not only on Kyoto but on other destinations in Japan as well. Be sure to pick up the leaflet *Walking Tour Courses in Kyoto*.

If the T.I.C. is closed, you can get a map at the **Kyoto City Information Office**, located between the taxi stand and the bus stands on Kyoto Station's north side. Open daily from 8:30 a.m. to 5 p.m., it doesn't have an English-speaking staff but it does have maps in English.

To find out what's going on in Kyoto in terms of festivals, special events, Kabuki or Noh performances, or exhibitions, call the **Teletourist Service** at 361-2911. This service provides 90 seconds of recorded information in English on what's going on during the week.

TOURIST PUBLICATIONS: In addition to the brochures and leaflets distributed by the T.I.C. there are a couple of publications with information on Kyoto. *Discover Kinki,* a monthly distributed free to hotels, travel agencies, and the T.I.C., tells of upcoming events and festivals in Kyoto and the neighboring cities of Osaka, Kobe, and Nara. In addition, a monthly English magazine called *Kansai Time Out* carries information and articles on Kyoto, Kobe, Osaka, and Nara. It's available in Kyoto at both the Maruzen and Izumiya bookstores and at the Gimmond and Miyako Hotels, and costs ¥300 ($2.14).

7. A Side Trip to Nara

In the beginnings of Japanese history, the nation's capital was moved to a new site each time a new emperor came to the throne. In 710, however, the first permanent Japanese capital was set up in Nara. Not that it turned out to be so permanent—after only 74 years the capital was moved first to Nagaoka and shortly thereafter to Kyoto, where it remained for more than 1,000 years. What's important about those 74 years is that they witnessed the birth of Japan's arts, crafts, and literature. Turning to its more advanced neighbor to the west, Nara imported everything from religion to art to architecture from China. Even the city itself was modeled after Chinese concepts, laid out in a rectangular grid pattern. It was during the Nara period that Japan's first historical account, first mythological chronicle, and first poetry anthology (with 4,173 poems) were written. Buddhism flourished and Nara grew as the political and cultural center of the land.

Today Nara is celebrated as the cradle of Japanese culture. Japanese flock here because Nara gives them the feeling that they are communing with their ancestors. Foreigners come here because Nara gives them a glimpse of a Japan that was. For, remarkably enough, many of Nara's buildings and temples remain intact, and long ago someone had enough foresight to enclose many of its historical structures in the quiet and peaceful confines of a large and spacious park. Although most visitors come to Nara on only a day trip from Kyoto, there is more than enough here to occupy two full days. For that reason I've included some recommendations in accommodations. If you stay here overnight, be sure to take advantage of an evening or early-morning stroll through Nara Park.

ORIENTATION: You can pick up brochures and information on Nara before leaving Kyoto at the Kyoto T.I.C. The Kyoto map distributed there also has a map of Nara on the reverse side. Be sure also to pick up the leaflet *Walking Tour Courses in Nara.* In Nara itself there are **tourist information offices** at both the JR Nara Station (tel. 0742/22-9821) and the Kintetsu Nara Station (tel. 0742/24-4858). Both are open from 9:30 a.m. to 5 p.m. daily. These offices have another good brochure and map of Nara issued by the Nara City Tourist Office, with useful information on how to get around Nara by bus. Incidentally, if you'd like to have your own personal guide to show you around, there are volunteer Goodwill Guides who will be glad to show you the sights in exchange for the practice it gives them with their English. One guide each is posted at both the JR and Kintetsu station tourist offices and is available to the first tourists who show up every day except Sunday. If you'd rather not take chances and would like to reserve a guide in advance, call the day before at 0742/44-2207 to arrange a time. The free guide service is available Monday through Saturday from 9:30 a.m. to 3 p.m.

To find out what's going on in Nara by way of festivals and exhibitions, you can call 27-1313 for a two-minute taped recording in English. If you're calling outside Nara, the area code is 0742.

Only 26 miles south of Kyoto, Nara is easily reached in about 33 minutes from Kyoto Station on the Kintetsu Limited Express of Kinki Nippon Railways, which whisks you directly to Nara Kintetsu Station. If you have a railpass you can take the slower JR train from Kyoto Station to the Nara JR Station in about an hour. You can also reach Nara from Osaka in about 30 to 50 minutes, depending on the train and the station from which you leave.

Nara's Kintetsu and JR stations are within a few minutes' walk of each other. Most of Nara's sites are located to the east of the two stations, within easy walking distance. To visit the areas of Horyuji and Nishinokyo, take bus 52 from either the JR or Kintetsu station. It has announcements of its stops recorded in English. Other buses bound for Horyuji and Nishinokyo are shown on the brochure of Nara available at the Nara tourist offices.

The **telephone area code** for Nara is 0742.

THE SIGHTS: The best way to enjoy Nara is to arrive early in the morning before the first tour buses start pulling in. If you don't have much time, the most important sites to see are Todaiji Temple, Kasuga Shrine, and Horyuji Temple.

Around Nara Park

With its ponds, grassy lawns, trees, and temples, Nara Park covers about 1,300 acres. It's home to more than 1,000 deer roaming freely through the park. As you walk east from either the JR or Kintetsu train station, the first temple you reach is **Kofukuji Temple**, founded in 710 as the family temple of the Fujiwaras, the second most powerful clan after the imperial family. At one time as many as 175 buildings were erected on the Kofukuji Temple grounds, but through centuries of civil wars and fires most of the structures were burned. Only a handful of buildings still remain, but even these were rebuilt after the 13th century. Its five-story pagoda, first erected in 730, was burned down five times. The present pagoda dates from 1426 and is an exact replica of its original form. At 164 feet tall, it's the second-tallest pagoda in Japan (the tallest is at Toji Temple in Kyoto). The temple's Treasure House, charging an admission of ¥400 ($2.86) and open from 9 a.m. to 5 p.m., displays many statues and works of art originally contained in the temple's buildings, the most famous of which is a statue of Ashura carved in the eighth century.

To the east of Kofukuji is the **Nara National Museum**, which houses invaluable Buddhist art and archeological relics. Many statues and other items originally contained in Nara's many temples are now housed here. Open every day except Monday from 9 a.m. to 4:30 p.m., it charges ¥300 ($2.14) admission.

Todaiji Temple, along with its **Daibutsu (Great Buddha)**, is Nara's greatest attraction. When Emperor Shomu ordered construction of both the temple and the Daibutsu back in the mid-700s, it was his intention to make Todaiji the headquarters of all Buddhist temples in the land. In his plans to create a Buddhist utopia, he commissioned work on an overwhelmingly huge bronze statue of Buddha. It took eight castings to finally complete the Great Buddha, a remarkable work of art that remains the largest bronze statue of Buddha in Japan. At a height of more than 50 feet, the Daibutsu is made of 437 tons of bronze, 286 pounds of pure gold, 165 pounds of mercury, and 7 tons of vegetable wax. However, because of Japan's frequent natural calamities, the Buddha of today isn't quite what it used to be. In 855, in what must have been a whopper of an earthquake, the Buddha lost its head. It was repaired in 861, but, alas, the huge wooden building housing the Buddha was burned down twice during wars, melting the Buddha's head. The present head dates from 1692, but there's no telling how long he'll be able to hold on to it.

As for the wooden structure, called Daibutsuden, which housed the Great Buddha, it was destroyed several times through the centuries; the present structure dates from 1709. Measuring 161 feet tall, 187 feet long, and 164 feet wide, it's the largest wooden structure in the world. If you can imagine, however, the building is only two-thirds its original size. Be sure to walk in a circle around the Great Buddha to see it from all different angles. Behind the statue is a huge wooden column with a small hole in it near the ground. According to popular belief, if you can manage to crawl through this opening you will be sure to reach enlightenment. The Daibutsuden is open from 7:30 a.m. to 7:30 p.m. from April through September, from 8 a.m. to 4:30 p.m. in winter. Admission is ¥300 ($2.14).

A stroll through Nara Park will bring you to **Kasuga Shrine**, one of my favorite Shinto shrines in all of Japan. Originally the tutelary shrine of the Fujiwara family, it was founded in 768 and, according to Shinto concepts of purity, was torn down and rebuilt every 20 years in its original form until 1863. Nestled in the midst of verdant woods, it's a shrine of vermilion-colored pillars and an astounding 3,000 lanterns, some of them stone and others cast in bronze. The most spectacular time to visit the shrine is in mid-August or the beginning of February, when all 3,000 lanterns are lit. One of the fun things to do at Kasuga Shrine is to pay ¥100 (71¢) for a slip of paper in English with your fortune on it. If the fortune is unfavorable you can conveniently negate it by tying the piece of paper to the twig of a tree.

A ten-minute walk to the southwest of Kasuga Shrine brings you to **Shin-Yakushiji Temple**, built in the middle of the eighth century by the Empress Komyo for the recovery of Emperor Shomu from an eye disease (Yakushi is the name given to the Healing Buddha). Only the main hall remains, the other buildings having been destroyed and rebuilt after the 13th century. The main hall contains a statue of Yakushi-nyorai surrounded by 12 pottery figures, 11 of which are originals and are considered national treasures. Admission is ¥400 ($2.86), and it's open from 8:30 a.m. to 6 p.m., until 5 p.m. in winter.

Incidentally, Nara Park will serve as the site of a special **Silk Road Exposition** to be held April 24 to October 23, 1988. Celebrating the Silk Road, which linked Japan to Persia, it will display relics and items relating to the history of the overland passageway. Contact the Kyoto T.I.C. or Nara tourist information offices for more information.

Horyuji Temple Area

Founded in 607 by Prince Shotoku as a center for Buddhism in Japan, Horyuji Temple is one of Japan's most significant gems in terms of both architecture and art. It was from here that Buddhism blossomed and spread throughout the land. Today about 45 buildings remain, some of them dating from the end of the seventh century and comprising what are probably the oldest wooden structures in the world. At the western end of the grounds is the Golden Hall

(Kondo), a two-story structure 58 feet high which is considered the oldest building at Horyuji Temple. Next to the main hall is a five-story pagoda, which dates from the foundation of the temple. It contains four scenes from the life of Buddha, including Buddha's cremation and entry into Nirvana. The **Great Treasure House** *(Daihozoden)*, a concrete building constructed in 1941, contains temple treasures, including statues and other works of art from the seventh and eighth centuries. On the eastern precincts of Horyuji Temple is an octagonal building built in 739 called **Yumedono Hall**, or Hall of Dreams. Supposedly Prince Shotoku used this building for quiet meditation.

Admission to Horyuji Temple, the Treasure House, and Hall of Dreams is ¥500 ($3.57). The grounds are open from 8 a.m. to 5 p.m. (until 4:30 p.m. in winter), but you must enter at least 30 minutes before closing time.

East of Yumedono is **Chuguji Temple**, a nunnery built for members of the imperial family. It contains two outstanding works of art. The wooden statue of Miroku-bosatsu dates from the seventh century and is noted for the serene and compassionate expression on its face. The Tenjukoku Mandala is the oldest piece of embroidery in Japan. It's a fragment of embroidery originally 16 feet long created by Shotoku's window and her female companions with scenes depicting life of the times. Only a replica of the fragile embroidery is now on display. Admission here is ¥300 ($2.14).

Nishinokyo Area

If you still have time to spend in Nara, it's worth making a trip to the vicinity of Nishinokyo Station to visit two more temples. **Toshodaiji Temple** was founded in 759 by Ganjin, a high priest from China who was invited to Japan by the emperor to help spread Buddhism. Ganjin's first attempts to reach Japan were thwarted by pirate attacks, storms, and five shipwrecks. During one of these voyages Ganjin lost his sight through disease. He finally reached Japan in 754 at the age of 66 and set to work constructing this magnificent temple. Its main hall and lecture hall still stand and are both national treasures. The main hall contains various statues and its front pillars are thought to resemble Greek architecture, the concept of which may have been brought to Japan via the Silk Road. Also on the temple's grounds is Ganjin's tomb.

About 800 yards south of Toshodaiji is **Yakushiji Temple**, which contains more Buddhist statues. Its three-story pagoda is believed to date from 698. It looks as if it has six stories because of the intermediate roofs.

FOOD AND ACCOMMODATION: With a population of more than 300,000, Nara has a number of fine hotels and ryokan in all price categories. One of the most famous is the **Nara Hotel**, Nara-Koen-nai (tel. 0742/26-3300), which was built in 1909 and sits like a palace on top of a hill above several ponds. You have your choice of staying in the old section of the hotel, with its high ceilings and comfortable old-fashioned decor, or in a new addition which opened in 1984, offering pleasant and modern rooms with verandas. Rates range from ¥8,800 ($63) to ¥10,500 ($75) for singles, ¥16,500 ($118) for doubles, and ¥16,200 ($116) to ¥28,600 ($204) for twins. The higher rates are for rooms in the new addition.

The dining room of the Nara Hotel is a good place to come for lunch or dinner. Decorated in old drawing-room fashion with heavy curtains, wood paneling, and a view of a peaceful pond, it has Western-style lunches starting at ¥3,800 ($27.14) from 11:30 a.m. to 2 p.m. and dinner beginning at ¥4,700 ($33.57) from 5:30 to 8 p.m.

If you can't afford to stay at the Nara Hotel, the prices of its **Nara Hotel Annex** (tel. 0742/26-3101) may be more within your budget. Its 34 rooms are located in a building directly above the Kintetsu Station on floors six and seven. Remodeled in 1985, the rooms are bright and cheerful and feature double-paned windows to shut out noise, a hot-water pot for tea, TV, clock, radio, and fridge. Singles cost ¥7,900 ($56) and twins are ¥15,000 ($107).

On the eighth floor of the Nara Hotel Annex is the hotel's restaurant. If you can get a table at the north corner of the restaurant you'll have a good view of Nara Park and the top of Todaiji Temple. Its changing set lunch menu starts at ¥1,000 ($7.14), and dinners cost ¥2,700 ($19.29) to ¥7,700 ($55). À la carte items include sandwiches, spaghetti, lobster, sirloin steak, stewed beef, and pork cutlets. It's open from 11:30 a.m. to 2 p.m. and 5 to 10 p.m. During the summer months, from the end of May to the beginning of September, there's a rooftop beer garden open daily from 5 to 9 p.m.

If you want to stay in a Japanese-style ryokan, **Kikusuiro** [107], 1130 Takahata Bodaimachi (tel. 0742/23-2001), is a lovely 100-year-old inn. An imposing structure surrounded by a white wall not far from Nara Park, it makes good use of various woods to create pleasing forms of decoration in its tatami rooms. It also has a beautiful garden. There are 17 rooms here, eight of which have private bath and toilet. Rates start at ¥33,000 ($236) per person, including two meals, tax, and service. Adjacent to the ryokan are both Western- and Japanese-style restaurants. The Japanese restaurant, open from 11 a.m. to 8 p.m. daily, is new and decorated with bamboo and paper lanterns, and features sukiyaki or shabu-shabu starting at ¥6,000 ($42.86), obento lunch boxes starting at ¥4,000 ($28.57), and kaiseki from ¥16,500 ($117.86).

Shikitei [108], 1163 Takahatacho (tel. 0742/22-5531), is another ryokan situated close to Nara Park. Originally built around the turn of the century, it was remodeled in 1979 and features tatami rooms with all the modern conveniences. Some of its rooms have wooden tubs, and the best rooms overlook either the park or a lake. Rates for the 18 rooms (15 of which have private bath and three of which have toilet only) range from ¥22,000 ($157) to ¥44,000 ($314). You can also come here just for a kaiseki lunch or dinner for ¥11,000 ($78.57) to ¥20,000 ($142.86) per person. The menu changes monthly and you must make a reservation at least two days in advance.

If you're looking for a business hotel, the **Hotel Sunroute Nara**, 1110 Takabatake-cho (tel. 0742/22-5151), is in a residential area south of Kofukuji Temple. With a cheerful lobby, the Sunroute offers a good-sized single, including couch and chairs, for ¥7,700 ($55) to ¥9,900 ($71). Twins range from ¥14,600 ($104) to ¥18,500 ($132). All rooms offer TV, refrigerator, a one-cup water heater with tea bags, private bath, and phone. This 95-room hotel features a pleasant restaurant serving Western breakfast, lunch, and dinner.

For budget travelers, **Ryokan Matsumae**, 28-1 Higashiterabayashi-cho (tel. 0742/22-3686), is a modern Japanese inn that opened in 1985. It's just south of Nara Park, about a ten-minute walk from the Kintetsu Station or a 20-minute walk from the JR Station. All 12 rooms are simple but clean and come with TV, shoji screens, thoughtful touches of artwork, and sink and toilet. A few of the rooms have private bath as well. Rates start at ¥4,900 ($35) for one person, ¥8,800 ($63) for two, and ¥13,200 ($94) for three. If you want to have meals here, Japanese breakfasts cost ¥1,000 ($7.14) and dinners are ¥3,300 ($23.57). If you prefer a Western breakfast, there's a coffeeshop nearby.

Formerly a geisha house, **Mangyoku** [109], Ganrin-in (tel. 22-2265), was remodeled into a comfortable restaurant a few years back, although it retains its wooden floors and old ceiling. It serves a popular lunch special (*higawari teishoku*) every day from noon until 2 p.m. for ¥750 ($5.36), which included grilled fish, rice, soup, and vegetables during my last visit. Dinner, served from 5 to 11 p.m., is surprisingly Western cuisine, including a steak course for ¥3,800

($27.14). Note that this establishment is closed on Thursday. Mangyoku is located about a five-minute walk from Kintetsu Nara Station in the direction of Sarusawa Pond. To reach it, walk through the covered shopping arcade that runs directly in front of the tourist information office. Turn left at the first intersection (called Sanjo Dori Avenue) and then right on a small side street (there's a camera shop on the corner). The restaurant is on the left side of this street, and there's a sign outside that reads "Restaurant."

Chapter VII

THE JAPAN ALPS

1. Takayama
2. Shirakawa-go
3. Matsumoto

LYING IN THE CENTRAL PART of Honshu, the Japan Alps consist of several volcanic mountain ranges. With the exception of Japan's tallest mountain, Mount Fuji, all of Japan's loftiest mountains are in these ranges, making the Japan Alps a popular destination for hikers and nature lovers. Some of the villages nestled in the mountains remain relatively unchanged in architecture, giving visitors the unique opportunity to see how mountain people have lived through the centuries.

1. Takayama

Located in the Hida Mountains of the Japan Alps, Takayama is surrounded by 10,000-foot peaks, making the train ride here breathtaking no matter whether you approach it from the north or the south. The village, located on a wide plateau, was founded back in the 16th century by Lord Kanamori, who selected the site because of the impregnable position afforded by the surrounding Hida Mountains. For centuries Takayama was so remote and difficult to reach that travelers despaired of ever making it here alive.

Because of its isolation Takayama developed its own architecture, food, and craftsmanship, much of it still preserved even today. The heart of Takayama is delightful, with homes of classical design typical of Hida in the 18th century. The streets of the old town are narrow and clean, flanked on both sides by tiny canals of running water. Rising up from the canals are one- and two-story homes and shops of gleaming dark wood with overhanging roofs. Latticed windows and slats of wood play games of light and shadow in the white of the sunshine. Strips of blue cloth flutter in the breeze of open shop doors. As you walk down the streets, you'll notice huge cedar balls hanging from the eaves in front of several shops, indicating a sake factory. Altogether there are eight sake factories in Takayama, most of them small affairs. Go inside, sample the sake, and watch men stirring rice in large vats. Takayama is a village that invites exploration.

ORIENTATION: You no longer have to despair of ever reaching Takayama alive. The easiest way to get here is by direct train from Nagoya, which takes about three hours. There are also a few direct trains from Osaka and Kyoto. Train schedules are listed in a leaflet, *Takayama and Vicinity,* distributed free by the Tourist Information Centers in Tokyo and Kyoto.

Upon arrival in Takayama, stop by the local **tourist office** (tel. 0577/32-

5328), located in a wooden booth on the east side of Takayama Station. You can pick up an English brochure and a map of the village. It's open from 8:30 a.m. to 6:30 p.m. daily (until 5 p.m. in winter).

Most of Takayama's attractions lie to the east of the train station and are easily reached on foot. An alternative is to rent a bicycle from one of the many rental shops ringing the station, the cost of which averages ¥250 ($1.79) per hour or ¥1,300 ($9.29) for the whole day. To reach the Hida Minzoku Mura Folk Village, take bus 4 from Takayama Station.

The **telephone area code** for Takayama is 0577. It lies in Gifu Prefecture.

THE SIGHTS: Takayama's main attraction is its old merchant houses, which are found clustered around Sannomachi and Furuimachinami Streets. Be sure to allow time just for wandering around. Shops in the area sell Takayama's specialties, including sake, yew woodcarvings, and a unique lacquerware called *shunkei-nuri*. Almost all the attractions listed below are closed during the New Year's holidays.

Hida Minzoku Mura Folk Village

Hida Minzoku Mura Folk Village (also called Hida no Sato) is an open-air museum where more than 30 old thatched farmhouses have been set up to show how farmers and craftsmen used to live in the Hida Mountain region. The whole village is very picturesque, with swans swimming in the central pond, green moss growing on the thatched roofs, and flowers blooming in season. Some of the houses have roofs in the *gassho-zukuri* style, built steeply to withstand the heavy snowfalls that often measure six feet deep. The tops of the roofs are said to resemble hands joined in prayer. There are shingle-roofed homes, houses with earthen floors, a woodcutter's hut, a grain storehouse, and a house where the second floor was used as a silkworm nursery. All the structures, which range in age from 100 to 500 years, are open to the public and are filled with utensils, tools, and furniture used in daily life. On display, for example, are old spindles and looms, utensils for cooking and dining, instruments used in the silk industry, farm tools, sleds, and straw boots and capes worn to fend off wet snow.

On one corner of the village grounds is a section devoted to folkcrafts and art where workshops have been set up to demonstrate such crafts as textile dyeing and weaving, lacquerwork, and wood sculpture. Within walking distance of the folk village is the **Hida Folklore Museum (Hida Minzoku-kan)**, with more displays on life in the Hida region. Next to the folklore museum is the **Museum of Mountain Life**, with displays on the history of mountaineering in the Japan Alps and flora and fauna of the region.

Entrance to all the museums and the folk village is included in the one ticket price of ¥500 ($3.57). Hours are 8 a.m. to 5 p.m. daily.

Morning Market

One of the things you should be sure to do in the morning is to head for the east bank of the Miyagawa River, where a colorful local market brings splashes of color as women sell flowers, vegetables, and local produce. It's held daily February through December from 7 a.m. to noon.

Merchants' Houses

In stark contrast to the thatched farmhouses in the Folk Village are two merchants' mansions, which show how the upper class lived. Located side by side on the north end of Ninomachi Street, the **Yoshijima House and Kusakabe Mingeikan** once belonged to two of the richest families in Takayama. Of the two, the Yoshijima House is my favorite. With its exposed attic, heavy crossbeams, sunken fireplace, and sliding doors, it's a masterpiece of geometric design. It was built in 1907 as both the home and factory of the Yoshijima family, well-to-do brewers of sake in Takayama. Notice how the beams and wood of the home gleam, attained through decades of polishing as each generation of women did her share in bringing the wood to a luster.

Not quite as rustic, the Kusakabe Mingeikan merchant house is more refined and imposing, built in 1879 for a merchant dealing in silk, lamp oil, and finance. Its architectural style is considered unique to Hida, and on display are items handed down through the generations.

Both merchant houses are open from 9 a.m. to 5 p.m. (to 4:30 p.m. December through February). From December through February Yoshijima House, which charges ¥200 ($1.43), is closed on Tuesday while the Kusakabe mansion, which charges ¥300 ($2.14), is closed on Friday.

More Museums

Not far from the merchants' houses is the **Takayama Yatai Kaikan**, an exhibition hall where you can see some of the elaborate floats used for Takayama's famous parades, held twice a year in April and October. These are huge floats, most of them from the 17th century and built by famous craftsmen of the village. The exhibition hall is open daily from 8:30 a.m. to 5 p.m. (9 a.m. to 4:30 p.m. December through February) and charges a ¥380 ($2.71) admission.

Other sites of interest in the vicinity of the exhibition hall are **Hachiman Shrine** and **Shishi Kaikan**, an exhibition hall with displays of lion masks used during festivals around Japan.

The **Hida Folk Archeological Museum (Hida Minzoku Kokokan)** in the heart of Takayama on Sannomachi Street is an interesting old house that once belonged to a doctor and contains a number of trick devices, including secret passageways and a hanging ceiling. Imagine inviting an enemy to your home, offering him the best room in the house, and then secretly sneaking upstairs to chop the rope that has been holding up the suspended ceiling. The ceiling plunges down with a loud thud, neatly crushing your enemy to death. Rather dramatic, don't you think? And, of course, very effective. Back in the old days of Japan's constant civil wars, trickery was sometimes the only way to survive the constant power struggles. This museum, with its collection of earthenware and folk tools, is open daily from 7 a.m. to 7 p.m. (8 a.m. to 5 p.m. in winter). The entrance fee is ¥250 ($1.79).

Just down the street from the Folk Archeological Museum is the **Fujii Art Gallery (Fujii Bijutsu Mingei-kan)**, which contains a good and varied collection of furniture, clothing, combs, dolls, pottery, and lacquerware, most dating from the Edo Period. Included are some beautiful *tansu* (chests), smoking utensils, belt pouches with *netsuke*, swords, paper-covered lamps, farming tools, and spinning wheels. Many items are identified in English. A very worthwhile museum, it's open daily from 9 a.m. to 5 p.m. (until 8 p.m. in summer) and charges ¥250 ($179) admission.

The **Takayama Museum of Local History (Takayama Kyodokan)**, on Kami-Ichi-no-Machi Street, is another good museum, displaying antiques and folklore items handed down from generation to generation and work by Hida craftsmen. It charges a ¥200 ($1.43) admission and is open every day except Thursday from 8:30 a.m. to 5 p.m. (to 4:30 p.m. December to March).

Across the street from the history museum is the **Toy Museum (Kyodo Gangu-kan)**, with a collection of toys from around the country. From April through November the museum is open from 8:30 a.m. to 5 p.m., opening at 9 a.m. the rest of the year. Admission is ¥150 ($1.07).

Takayama Jinya, open from 8:45 a.m. to 5 p.m. (to 4:30 p.m. in winter), was once a manor house for administrators in Takayama. It contains a rice granary (rice was collected as a tax), chambers and courts, and historical records. Admission here is ¥300 ($2.14).

WHERE TO STAY: There are by far more minshuku and ryokan in Takayama than hotels, making Takayama the perfect place to stay in a traditional Japanese inn. In fact, staying in a tatami room and sleeping on a futon is the best way to immerse yourself in the life of this small community and partake of its lifestyle. And the best news is that there are places to fit all budgets. All rates below for ryokan and minshuku follow the Japanese system in that they are on a per-person basis and include breakfast, dinner, tax, and service charges. Although the rates given here represent the normal rates, you should be aware that in peak season (August and during festival times in April and October), prices will be higher, generally between 10% and 20% more.

A NOTE ON JAPANESE SYMBOLS: Many hotels, restaurants, and other establishments in Japan do not have signs showing their names in English letters. Appendix II lists the Japanese symbols for all such places appearing in this guide. Each establishment name in Japanese symbols is numbered, and the same number appears in brackets in the text following the boldfaced establishment name. For example, in the text the Osaka hotel, Hokke Club [161], is number 161 in the Japanese symbols list in Appendix II.

Ryokan

Built a little more than a decade ago and possessing all the grace and charm you'd expect from a first-class ryokan, the **Ryokan Hishuya** [110], 2581 Kami-Okamoto-cho (tel. 0577/33-4001), is just a minute's walk from the Hida Minzoku Mura Folk Village on the quiet outskirts of town. Its rooms have views of either the garden surrounding the ryokan or the distant mountain peaks. Five of its 15 rooms here have wooden bathtubs and are more expensive, beginning at ¥16,500 ($118) per person. The other rooms all have the smaller unit bathrooms typically found in business hotels and begin at ¥13,200 ($94), costing about ¥1,000 ($7.14) more during peak season. Dinner is served individually in the guest rooms while breakfast is served in a communal dining hall. If you request it in advance, you'll be greeted in the morning with a Western breakfast of scrambled eggs, toast, ham, coffee, and juice. Shabu-shabu is served to guests who stay a second night.

Another ryokan close to the Folk Village is **Hida Gasshoen** [111], 3-829 Nishinoishiki-cho (tel. 0577/33-4531). Secluded on a hillside, its approach has one of the most impressive stone walls I've ever seen—massive boulders, some of which measure 10 feet high, all neatly piled on top of each other. The main building housing most of the guest rooms was built in 1980 and was designed to resemble an old *gassho-zukuri* farmhouse. Meals are served in a genuine 200-year-old thatched farmhouse. Per-person rates range from ¥7,000 ($50) for rooms without bathrooms to ¥13,200 ($94) for a room in a separate ancient house with its own private bath and toilet. Rates go up here only during festival times.

Kinkikan [112], 48 Asahimachi (tel. 0577/32-3131), is right in the center of old Takayama, set back from a small side street and surrounded by a wall. The entryway of this ryokan is 100 years old, with a small lobby full of furniture made of *shunkei-nuri* lacquerware crafted in Takayama. The lobby opens up over a running stream and a delightful century-old garden, just the kind of place that invites relaxation. Most of the 15 guest rooms were built about a decade ago, each one utilizing Japanese craftsmanship with its own distinctive interior design. One room, for example, has shoji screens and wall trimmings in shunkei-nuri lacquer while another room is decorated with the wood of local trees. Three rooms on the ground floor have peaceful views of the garden. Rooms here start at ¥13,200 ($94), rising to ¥16,500 ($118) in August. All rooms have private toilet, and all but four have private bath as well. As with all ryokan, however, there's a public bath for communal bathing, this one brand new.

A modern ryokan in the center of Takayama, **Seiryu** [113], 6 Hanakawa-cho (tel. 0577/32-0448), has 24 rooms, three of which are combination rooms with both beds and a separate tatami section. Although dinner is served in your own room, breakfast is served in a dining hall with each person receiving his own little tray. Western breakfasts are available on request. Rates here start at ¥8,800 ($63), rising to ¥13,000 ($93) in peak season.

Another modern ryokan is **Asunaro** [114], 2-96-2 Hatsuda-cho (tel. 0577/33-5551), located about a five-minute walk northeast of Takayama Station. Its 32 rooms are fairly standard; 11 of them come with their own bath and all but one have their own toilet. Rates for tatami rooms range from ¥6,500 ($46) to ¥16,500 ($118), and Western breakfasts are available. In August rates begin at ¥13,000 ($93), with the big increase due in part, the management says, to more elaborate meals.

Minshuku

Minshuku Sosuke, 1-64 Okamoto (tel. 0577/32-0818), is a delightful 13-room minshuku about an eight-minute walk southwest of Takayama Station across the street from the Green Hotel. Its entryway resembles farmhouses on display at the Folk Village, filled with country knickknacks and exuding a warm and friendly atmosphere. There's an old open-hearth fireplace, called an *irori,* in the communal room to the left as you enter—if it's chilly you'll be invited to sit down and warm yourself. The couple running this minshuku are outgoing and friendly. Mealtimes are especially fun. Everyone is seated around one long table where each person introduces himself. Since most of the guests are Japanese from other parts of the country, this is a good opportunity to learn about other places in Japan. Although the building housing the minshuku is 150 years old, the inside has been remodeled and all 13 rooms are spotlessly clean. The charge throughout the year is ¥5,800 ($41) per person and includes two meals.

Yamakyu, 58 Tenshoji (tel. 0577/32-3756), has a deserved reputation for serving the best meals in town in its price range. Although it's located a bit far from the station——about a 20-minute walk or a 5-minute taxi ride, it's only a 10-minute walk to the old part of town. As with most minshuku, all 28 Japanese-style rooms are without private bathroom, but the public baths are large and pleasant. Display cases line the corridors, showing off a collection of glass bowls, vases, clocks, and lamps. Per-person rates here with two meals are ¥5,500 ($39), with an additional ¥500 ($3.57) charged in peak season.

Another good choice in minshuku is **Hachibei** [115], 2561 Kami-Okamoto-cho (tel. 0577/33-0573), a few minutes' walk from the Folk Village. A big old house with a new addition and a rather nice and overgrown garden, it also has a pleasant open hearth where guests can sit and socialize in the evening. Most of the guests staying here are young Japanese. The public baths are large and are lined with rock walls. Two of the 33 rooms have their own bathrooms and cost ¥6,600 ($47) per person; otherwise, rates are ¥5,500 ($39).

Matsuyama, 5-11 Hanazato-cho (tel. 0577/32-1608), is conveniently located about a minute's walk from Takayama Station. Its 23 rooms are rather bare and plain, coming with just the basics of coin-operated TV, heater, and fan. Rates are ¥5,500 ($39) per person, rising ¥500 ($3.57) during peak season. If you decide to take your meals elsewhere, you can stay here for ¥3,500 ($25) per person.

Youth Hostel

The **Youth Hostel Tenshoji Temple**, 83 Tenshoji-machi (tel. 0577/32-6345), is located in a temple about 20 minutes east of the station by foot. Unfortunately there is no bus to the hostel. Rooms here are tatami and rates are ¥2,900 ($20.71) for members and ¥3,200 ($22.86) for nonmembers, including two meals.

Hotels

The largest hotel in town is the **Takayama Green Hotel**, about an eight-minute walk from Takayama Station at 2-180 Nishinoishiki-cho (tel. 0577/33-5500). This is the place to stay if you like all the conveniences in one building—restaurants, bar, beer garden, shopping, beauty and barber salons, bike rentals, tennis courts, public bath, tea lounge, and sushi bar. All rooms here are twin-bedded rooms and start at ¥5,000 ($36) for one person and ¥6,000 ($43) for two for the cheapest twin with toilet and sink only. Standard twins with private bathrooms start at ¥15,400 ($110).

About four blocks northeast of Takayama Station, the **Hida Hotel Plaza**, 60, 2-chome, Hanaoka-cho (tel. 0577/33-4600), consists of an older wing built about 15 years ago and a newer wing which opened in 1985. The front desk is housed in this contemporary and high-tech new wing. Rooms in the older wing are very basic and are cheaper: ¥6,500 ($46) for a single and ¥11,000 ($79) for a twin. In the new wing singles cost ¥8,800 ($63) and twins start at ¥16,500 ($118). Japanese-style rooms are also available, beginning at ¥22,000 ($157). All rooms come with TV, radio, refrigerator, hot-water pot and tea bags (and coffee), and private bathroom.

Facilities at the Hida Hotel include an attractive wood-beamed shopping arcade, rental bicycles, a black marble and stainless-steel public bath, a swimming pool, sauna and steambaths, five restaurants, and a bar. During the summer months there's a rooftop beer garden open nightly from 5 to 9 p.m., which offers panoramic views of Takayama and surrounding hills. Prices for beer range from ¥500 ($3.57) for a small to ¥750 ($5.36) for a large.

WHERE TO DINE: For the big splurge, you should dine at **Kakusho** [116], 2-98 Babacho (tel. 32-0174), a restaurant serving local vegetarian fare called *shojin-ryori*. Situated on the slope of a hill on the eastern part of town, this 250-year-old building with heavy wooden beams and ochre-colored walls is surrounded by a mossy garden and clay wall. Only lunch is served here, and hours are 11:30 a.m. to 1:30 p.m., closed Thursday. You must make a reservation to dine here, and there's only one meal available, for ¥9,000 ($64.29), tax and service charge extra. Meals are served in private tiny tatami rooms in a separate old building in the back with its own view of the mossy garden. This place is worth every bite of the various mountain vegetables, mushrooms, nuts, and tofu you'll be served.

A popular restaurant in the center of Takayama is **Suzuya** [117], 24 Hanakawa-cho (tel. 32-2484). Closed on Tuesday but open the rest of the week from 11 a.m. to 8 p.m., it's easy to recognize by its curtains hanging above the front door and the cedar ball hanging from its eaves. Inside, it's darkly lit, with shoji screens covering the windows, wooden beams above, and traditional decor in keeping with the country atmosphere of Takayama. This place is so popular that if you come for lunch between noon and 1 p.m. you'll probably have to wait for a table. There's an English menu, with local specialties of mountain vegetables, fresh river fish, and noodles ranging from ¥660 ($4.64) to ¥2,700 ($19.29). One specialty of Takayama you should try is *hoba-miso*. Usually served for breakfast, it consists of soy-bean paste mixed with dried scallion, ginger, and mushrooms, and cooked on a dry magnolia leaf above a small clay burner. If you're staying at a ryokan or minshuku you'll probably get this for breakfast. Other dishes available include shabu-shabu and *toban-yaki*, a stew of leek, okra, mushrooms, and various chicken parts including liver, gizzard, skin, and meat. Mountain vegetable teishoku begin at ¥1,400 ($10).

If Suzuya is closed or crowded, a restaurant close by is **Bandai Kado Mise** [118], Hanakawa-cho (tel. 33-5166). Located across the street and a few shops down, it doesn't have an English menu so the easiest thing to do is to order one of the obento box meals beginning at ¥1,400 ($10) or the mountain vegetable teishoku for ¥2,200 ($15.71). Tempura or pork teishoku are also available. Bandai is open from 11:30 a.m. to 8 p.m., closed on Wednesday.

If you're looking for an inexpensive meal, there's a fast-food sushi bar at the west end of Kokubunji Dori Street called **Bar Jimbay**, 1-chome, Hanaoka-cho (tel. 35-0863), just a few minutes' walk from the train station. Popular with Takayama's young population, it has various obento lunch boxes of sushi or pork cutlets for ¥440 ($3.14) to ¥1,000 ($7.14), as well as sushi available by the *rollu* for ¥140 ($1) to ¥220 ($1.57). A strange combination, it also serves ice cream and hamburgers. You can either take your meal out or eat it sitting on stools at high tables. If you're into eating sushi or ice cream early in the morning, this is the place to come. It's open daily from 10 a.m. to 11 p.m.

Technically a drinking place because of the dozen different varieties of sake it sells, the **Jizake-ya** [119], Suehiro Nibangai (tel. 34-5001), also serves a wide variety of Japanese food, including tofu steak, tempura, noodles, steamed dumplings, and river fish. Most items cost ¥500 ($3.57) to ¥1,400 ($10). A large room with tatami and low tables, this place has a convivial drinking-hall atmosphere. Hours are 5 p.m. to 2 a.m., closed the third Sunday of the month.

2. Shirakawa-go

With its thatched-roof farmhouses, rice paddies trimmed with flowerbeds, roaring river, and pine-covered mountains rising on all sides, Shirakawa-go is one of the most picturesque regions in Japan. Sure, it has its share of tour buses, especially in May, August, and October. However, because of its rather remote location and because it's accessible only by car or by bus, Shirakawa-go still remains off the beaten path for most tourists in Japan. A visit to this rural region could well be the highlight of your trip.

Stretching almost five miles long beside the Shokawa River and squeezed to a width of only 1.8 miles between towering mountains, Shirakawa-go is a tiny region with a population of 2,000 living in several small communities. The most important village for visitors is Ogimachi, with its 800 residents. It has minshuku, a couple of museums, and an open-air museum of old thatched farmhouses depicting how life used to be in the region before roads opened it up to the rest of the world.

Because Shirakawa-go is hemmed in by mountains, land for growing rice and other crops was always scarce and valuable. As a result, farmhouses were built large enough to hold extended families, sometimes with as many as several dozen family members living under one roof. Because there was not enough land available for young couples to marry and build houses of their own, only the oldest son was allowed to marry. The other children were required to spend their lives living with their parents and helping with the farming. The loss of even one family member meant hardship for the whole family. But even though younger children were not allowed to marry, a man was allowed to choose a young woman, visit her in her parents' home, and father her children. The children then remained with the mother's family, where they would become valuable members of the labor force.

Before the roads came to Shirakawa-go, winter always meant complete isolation as snow six feet deep blanketed the entire region. Open-hearth fireplaces *(irori)* were commonplace in the middle of the communal room. They were used both for cooking and for warmth, and because there were no chimneys smoke simply rose into the levels above. So the family lived on the ground floor, with the upper floors used for silk cultivation and storage of utensils. Because of the heavy snowfall, roofs were constructed at steep angles, known as *gassho-zukuri* in reference to the fact that the tops of the roofs look like hands joined in prayer.

Today there are about 150 thatched farmhouses, barns, and sheds in Shirakawa-go, most of them built about 200 to 300 years ago. The thatched roofs are about two feet thick and last about 50 years. The old roofs are replaced in Shirakawa-go every April when three roofs are replaced on three successive weekends. The whole process involves about 200 people, who can replace one roof in a couple days.

To see how rural people lived in past centuries in the Japan Alps, visit the **Shirakawa-go Gassho no Sato Village**, an open-air museum with 25 gassho-zukuri houses and sheds filled with implements and tools. Many of the old houses were moved to their present site some 20 years ago when construction of a dam threatened to destroy them. In some of the buildings are demonstrations and displays of local crafts, with artisans engaged in woodworking, pottery, basket-weaving, and toy-making. The village is located about a five-minute walk from Ogimachi along a footpath which takes you over a suspension bridge and through a narrow tunnel. Hours are 8:30 a.m. to 5 p.m. most of the year: in the winter from December through March the opening hours are from 9 a.m. to 4 p.m., while in August they're from 8 a.m. to 6 p.m. The entrance fee is ¥500 ($3.57).

In addition to the open-air museum there are several other old farmhouses in Ogimachi open to the public. The **Seikatsu Shiryokan** [120], open daily from 8 a.m. to 5 p.m. March through November, displays farm implements and folkcrafts, including cooking utensils, lacquerware, household items, and clothing. The upstairs is crammed with all kinds of farming tools and items used in everyday life, including mountain backpacks, hatchets, handmade skis, saddles, and implements for silk cultivation. Charging an admission of ¥200 ($1.43), Seikatsu Shiryokan is located on the southern edge of town, past Juemon minshuku.

Myozenji [121] is a 170-year-old house with farm equipment, straw raincoats, palanquins, and other relics on display. You can walk around upstairs and inspect how the roof looks from the inside. If a fire is burning in the downstairs irori, you can also see how smoky the upstairs can get. Attached to the house is the main hall of the Myozenji Temple, which is more than two centuries old. Hours here are generally 7 a.m. to 5 p.m., with shorter hours in winter, and admission is ¥200 ($.143). Myozenji is located in the heart of Ogimachi.

Not far from Myozenji is a relatively new museum, erected in honor of the **Doburoku Matsuri Festival** held in Shirakawa-go every year from October 14 to 19. Centering on a locally produced potent sake made from rice, the festival is held just outside the museum's grounds. The ¥300 ($2.14) entrance fee allows you to see some of the costumes worn during the festival and to try some of the festive sake. The highlight of the museum, however, is the hour-long video that shows the festival activities, including dances, parades, and plenty of drinking. Although the video is kind of corny in parts, it's probably the next best thing to being at the festival itself. The museum is open daily from 8:30 a.m. to 4:30 p.m. (from 9 a.m. to 4 p.m. in winter).

ORIENTATION: The most common way of reaching Ogimachi is by bus from Takayama, with a change of buses in Makido. The entire trip takes a little over 2 ½ hours along winding mountain roads and costs ¥2,900 ($20.71) one way. If you have a JR rail pass, however, you can use it between Makido and Ogimachi, in which case you'll need to buy a ticket only for the stretch between Takayama and Makido. Buses run throughout the year, with about three to five departures from Takayama daily, depending on the season. You can also reach Takayama by bus from Nagoya and Kanazawa.

As for getting around Ogimachi, your own two feet can do it best. You can walk from one end of the village to the other in about ten minutes. There's a **tourist office** (tel. 05769/6-1751) located in a small square in the center of the town. You can reserve a room in a minshuku here if you have not already done so, as well as pick up a pamphlet in English. If you want to make the tourist office your very first stop upon arrival in Shirakawa-go, get off at the bus stop called Gassho-Shuraku. The tourist office is about a minute's walk away and is open from 8:30 a.m. to 5 p.m. daily.

The address for all establishments listed below is Shirakawa Mura, Ogimachi, Ono-gun, Gifu. The **telephone area code** is 05769.

FOOD AND LODGING: Because huge extended families living under one roof are a thing of the past, many residents of Ogimachi have turned their gassho-zukuri homes into minshuku. There are more than two dozen minshuku in Ogimachi, giving visitors the unique chance to stay in a thatched farmhouse with a family that might consist of grandparents, parents, and children. English is limited to the basics of "bath," "breakfast," and "dinner," but smiles go a long way. Most likely the family will drag out their family album with pictures of winter snowfall and the momentous occasion when their thatched roof was repaired. All minshuku charge approximately ¥5,000 ($36) per person, including two meals. Most of them are fairly small affairs, with about five to nine rooms open to guests. Rooms are basic, without bath or toilet, and you're expected to roll out your own futon. Although there's little difference between the minshuku, some of them do not have thatched roofs. Below is a list of those that do.

Magoemon [122] (tel. 05769/6-1167) is located by the suspension bridge on the way to the open-air village. One of its six rooms overlooks the Shokawa River. About 300 years old, it features a cozy living room with open-hearth irori, wooden communal bathtub, and Western-style flush toilets.

Kandaya [123] (tel. 05769/6-1072) is a 200-year-old house. The largest minshuku in Ogimachi, it has nine rooms, some of which are in a separate building. It's located in the middle of the village and has a nicely remodeled bathroom and toilet area with wooden floors and walls.

Close by is **Yosobe** [124] (tel. 05769/6-1172), small, with only five guest rooms. The communal dining area is also small and friendly, with an irori in the middle of the room. The rooms facing the front of the house open onto wooden verandas, polished smooth by years of wear. In case it matters, the toilets here are nonflush in the Japanese style.

Otaya [125] (tel. 05769/6-1172) is located on the northern edge of the village, giving it a little more privacy. A couple of the rooms face a small river that cuts deep into a ravine. A pond outside the front door contains the fish you'll have for dinner.

Juemon [126] (tel. 05769/6-1053), located on the other end of the community on the south edge of Ogimachi, features an irori in the dining room and recently remodeled bathroom facilities. This minshuku is a favorite place for young foreigners traveling in Japan, and the outgoing woman who runs this place is quite a character.

Since all minshuku and ryokan serve breakfast and dinner, the only meal you have to worry about is lunch. **Irori** [127] (tel. 6-1737) is on Ogimachi's main street and is easy to spot because of a huge block of gnarled wood beside its front door. A gassho-zukuri house, the inside is appropriately rustic and even has an irori where you can fry your own fish on a skewer. The menu, in Japanese only, includes fresh river fish, wild mountain vegetables called *sansai*, *hoba miso* (soybean paste cooked on a magnolia leaf over a small clay pot), *unagi donburi* (eel on rice), *yaki-soba* (fried noodles), and *sansai-soba* (mountain vegetables and noodles). I opted for the tofu teishoku set meal, which consists of fried tofu covered with fish flakes, vegetables, rice, and soup. All items on the menu range from ¥450 ($3.21) to ¥1,600 ($11.43). Because this place is open from 10 a.m. to 11 p.m. daily, you might also want to come here for a nightcap. Beer starts at ¥550 ($3.93) and sake at ¥440 ($3.14).

Another large thatched farmhouse that has been turned into a restaurant is **Kitanosho** [128] (tel. 6-1506). It also has an irori, this one in the middle of a large tatami room. From the dining hall you can look out over the Shokawa River. When you finish your meal, climb the steep stairs to have a look at the second floor, where the heavy wooden beams are held together only with rope. Open only from April through November from 10 a.m. to 5 p.m., it offers river fish, bear stew (called *kumanabe teishoku* and available only in spring and autumn), *sansai udon* (noodles and mountain vegetables), curry rice, hoba miso, and *oyakodon* (chicken and egg on rice). The menu is only in Japanese, so look around at what others are eating. Prices range from about ¥500 ($3.57) for noodles to ¥1,650 ($11.79) for teishoku. Kitanosho is located on the southern edge of town, across the street from Juemon minshuku.

Finally, if you're visiting the open-air museum and want a quick lunch or snack, there are a couple of thatched-roof combination modern restaurant and souvenir shops next to the museum's entrance. With hours similar to the museum, they offer noodles, obento box lunches, and sansai or hoba miso teishoku, most in the ¥500 ($3.57) to ¥1,300 ($9.29) price range.

3. Matsumoto

Located in the middle of a wide basin about 660 feet above sea level and surrounded on all sides by mountain ranges, Matsumoto boasts a fine feudal castle with the oldest existing *donjon* (keep) in Japan, as well as an outstanding ukiyoe woodblock print museum. Although the city itself, with a population of 200,000, is modern with little remaining from its castle days, I find the town pleasant, the air fresh, and its people among the nicest I've encountered in Japan. Most travelers pass through Matsumoto on their way to more remote regions of the Japan Alps. Encircled with towering peaks, sparkling mountain lakes, and colorful wild flowers, Matsumoto serves as the gateway to hiking trails in the Japan Alps and in nearby Chubu Sangoku National Park.

ORIENTATION: There's a direct JR line to Matsumoto from Tokyo's Shinjuku Station. The Limited Express Azusa reaches Matsumoto in three hours, while the Express Alps takes a bit longer at about five hours. There's also a direct train from Nagoya, which takes about two hours and 20 minutes.

Before departing Tokyo, be sure to pick up a sheet at the Tourist Information Center called *Matsumoto and Kamikochi*. It gives the latest train schedules as well as information on sights in and around Matsumoto. It also gives recommended hiking trips lasting two to four hours from Kamikochi, a small village which you can reach in a little over two hours via train and bus from Matsumoto.

Once in Matsumoto, stop by the **tourist information window** on the east side of Matsumoto Station (tel. 0263/32-2814). Open from 9:30 a.m. to 6 p.m. (9 a.m. to 5:30 p.m. in winter) daily, it has a map of the city with destinations written in both Japanese and English, and its English-speaking staff will also help with accommodations. As for getting around Matsumoto itself, you can walk to Matsumoto Castle, just a mile northeast of the station, but you'll have to go by bus or taxi to the other sights.

The **telephone area code** for Matsumoto, located in Nagano Prefecture, is 0263.

THE SIGHTS: Originally built in 1504 when Japan was in the throes of bloody civil wars, **Matsumoto Castle** is a fine specimen of a feudal castle with the oldest existing donjon in the country. Surrounded by a willow-lined moat with ducks and white swans, the outside walls of the donjon are black, earning it the nickname of Karasu-jo, or Crow Castle. It's a rather small castle, dark and empty inside. Take your shoes off at the entrance and walk in stocking feet over worn wooden floors and up steep and narrow steps until you finally reach the sixth floor, from which you have a nice view of the city. The castle grounds are open from 8:30 a.m. to 4:30 p.m. Its entrance fee of ¥500 ($3.57) includes admission to the **Japan Folklore Museum**, located next to the castle. A rather eclectic museum, it has displays relating to archeology, history, and the surrounding region, including armor, an ornate palanquin, clothing, farming equipment, butterflies from around the world, insects, animals of the Japan Alps, and a wonderful collection of old clocks from Japan and other nations.

The **Japan Ukiyoe Museum**, 2206-1 Koshiba, Shimadachi (tel. 47-4440), is one of the best museums of woodblock prints in Japan. Privately owned, the museum is in a futuristic and airy building of glass and cement, built in 1982. Inside is the ukiyoe collection of Tokichi Sakai, a collection that dates back five generations to his great-great-grandfather, who was a friend and patron of Hokusai and Hiroshige, two of Japan's greatest woodblock-print artists. The collection contains more than 100,000 prints, including representative masterpieces of all known ukiyoe artists, and is believed to be the largest of its kind in the world. The exhibition changes every two months, so there's always something new to see. On one of my visits, for example, were masterpieces of Hokusai, including his series on famous bridges in Japan and famous waterfalls. A ten-minute slide show with explanations in English introduces the current exhibition, and a pamphlet in English describes the history of the collection and how woodblock prints are made. Closed on Monday, the museum is open from 10 a.m. to 5 p.m. and charges ¥500 ($3.57) admission. Unfortunately, there's no convenient way to get to the museum by public transportation, but the ¥1,000 ($7.14) taxi ride is worth it.

One more museum worth visiting if you have time is the **Matsumoto Folkcraft Museum** [129], located about 15 minutes by bus or taxi from Matsumoto Station (if going by bus, get out at the Shimoganai Mingeikan Guchi bus stop). Open from 9 a.m. to 5 p.m. every day except Monday, it contains products of wood, glass, bamboo, and porcelain from Japan and foreign countries. Particularly beautiful are its wooden chests, and part of the collection is housed in a 100-year-old storehouse. Admission is ¥200 ($1.43).

If perchance you studied violin when you were young, maybe you were one of the countless children around the world who learned by the well-known Suzuki Method. In Matsumoto is the famous **Suzuki Shin-ichi Talent Education Institute**, where young and old alike from around the world come to learn violin, piano, cello, and flute. Dr. Suzuki, founder of the method, is now in his 90s but is still actively involved in the daily lessons of his pupils. Group and private lessons for both pupils and teachers of the Suzuki Method are held throughout the week, and guests are welcome to watch. There are also periodical concerts given by graduating musicians of the institute. For more information, call the institute any time between 9 a.m. and 5 p.m. Monday through Saturday at 32-7171. Dr. Suzuki's group lesson is generally held from 9 to 10:30 a.m., but it would be wise to check the time beforehand.

If you find yourself with extra time on your hands, you might want to take a trip to **Alps Park**, located on one of Matsumoto's surrounding wooded hills, where you'll find the Alps Dream Coaster. I don't know who thinks up these names, but this one is a toboggan run and doesn't allow much time for dreaming. The race down the hill and around curves takes only a few minutes, during which time you swear you're going to fly off course. Being the conscientious researcher that I am, I raced down without applying the brakes to check its safety for you—it was terrifying and fun! Closed in the winter, it's open the rest of the year from 9 a.m. to 5 p.m., and one trip down costs ¥300 ($2.14). To reach Alps Park, take the bus from Matsumoto Station bound for Alps Koen; the trip takes about 25 minutes. Since there are only five buses daily, ask for the timetable at the tourist office. A restaurant and hiking trails are located in the park.

WHERE TO STAY: Because Matsumoto is popular primarily with hikers who are used to roughing it along nature trails, there are no luxury hotels in the city. Rather, facilities are geared mainly toward convenience.

The Medium-Priced Range

Matsumoto Tokyu Inn, 1-3-21 Fukashi (tel. 0263/36-0109), is a practical, clean, and pleasant business hotel conveniently located close to Matsumoto Station. Four kinds of rooms are offered: a nicely decorated single with semi-double-size bed for ¥8,200 ($59); a double-bedded room for ¥14,000 ($100); a twin for ¥14,000 ($100); and a deluxe twin with sofa and chairs and a separate vanity area with its own sink for ¥25,000 ($179). Prices include tax and service. Similar to other business hotels in the nationwide Tokyu Inn chain, its 158 rooms are decorated in beige and brown and come with desk or table, clock, and TV with pay video, including movies from the United States. Facilities include the Shangri-La restaurant, serving Western and Japanese meals, a bar/lounge, and vending machines on the fifth and eighth floors. As a service to the forgetful, rugs in the elevator tell what day of the week it is and are changed daily.

Hotel New Station, 1-1-11 Chuo (tel. 0263/35-3850), is about a two-minute walk from Matsumoto Station. Opened in mid-1985, this 103-room hotel offers a very pleasant and good-sized single for ¥6,000 ($43), with print comforter, large desk, and hot-water heater for tea. Twins go for ¥10,890 ($78). A Japanese-style room with a six-tatami sleeping area is available for two or three persons for ¥14,300 ($102). Prices include tax and service. All rooms have TV. The front-desk personnel are very helpful and accommodating, but not much English is spoken here.

The Budget Range

Matsumoto Tourist Hotel, 2-4-24 Fukashi (tel. 0263/33-9000), is a business hotel about a six-minute walk from the station. Its facilities include a restaurant serving both Western and Japanese food, a public bath, and a vending area. Its staff are very friendly, but again no one speaks much English. All rooms are simple but tastefully decorated, and include TV and hot-water heater for tea. Singles without a bathroom are ¥4,600 ($33), ¥5,720 ($41) with bath. Twins, all with private bathroom, start at ¥10,300 ($73). Also available are Japanese-style tatami rooms, all without private bath but with sink, which go for ¥4,900 ($35) for one person, ¥8,400 ($60) for two, and ¥11,200 ($80) for three. As with most budget accommodations, prices include tax and service.

A bit on the old side, but very reasonably priced and run by friendly people, **Hotel Ikyu** [130], 1-11-13 Honjo (tel. 0263/35-8528), is a concrete building about a ten-minute walk from the train station and is popular with young Japanese. Rates per person are ¥3,800 ($27) without meals and ¥5,500 ($39) including breakfast and dinner. Some of the rooms have a private toilet. Both Japanese-style tatami rooms and Western-style rooms are available, and all rooms come with coin-operated TV, air-conditioner and heater, fridge, and hot-water pot for tea. There are lots of windows in this place and added touches like plants in the stairwell. Meals are served in a small dining hall adjoining the hotel.

Nishiya Ryokan [131], 2-4-12 Ote (tel. 0263/33-4332), is about a six-minute walk from Matsumoto Station in the direction of Matsumoto Castle. No meals are served here and rooms are just basic tatami without private bathrooms. At only ¥3,300 ($24) per person a night, no one is complaining.

The closest youth hostel is the **Asama Onsen Youth Hostel**, 302-1 Asama-Onsen (tel. 0263/46-1335), roughly 20 minutes from Matsumoto Station by bus. There's room for about 150 people here, and the cost of an overnight stay is ¥2,100 ($15) for members and ¥2,600 ($18) for nonmembers. No dinner is served, but Japanese breakfasts are available for ¥450 ($3.21).

WHERE TO DINE: If you feel like treating yourself to a wonderful French meal in rustic yet elegant surroundings, **Taiman**, 4-2-4 Ote (tel. 32-0882), is an excellent choice. Located not far from Matsumoto Castle, it looks as though it were once the hunting château of some European lord but somehow ended up in the Japan Alps. An ivy-covered building, the inside has heavy wooden beams, high ceilings, fresh flowers on the tables, and elaborate cutlery. Full dinners with changing menus are available for ¥8,200 ($58.57) to ¥11,000 ($78.57). There are also less expensive meals of either sole or stewed beef for ¥4,400 ($31.43). If you want to go à la carte for such dishes as roast lamb, steak, chicken, or sole, expect to spend at least ¥8,500 ($60.71).

One way to eat inexpensively is to come for the special lunch for ¥4,400 ($31.43). As an example, my luncheon included bread or rice, and started with an hors d'oeuvre plate of marinated squid, lox, cream cheese, capers, and grated onion. The next course was crab gratin, cooked in a cheese and tomato base, resembling lasagne. The main dish was sautéed pork wrapped in bacon and topped with cheese. Also included in the price were salad, dessert, and coffee. The restaurant is open from 11 a.m. to 9 p.m.; closed the first and third Wednesdays of the month.

If you'd rather have Japanese fare, **Kajika** [132], 1-2-21 Fukashi (tel. 35-7632), is on the fourth floor of the Cosmo Building about a five-minute walk from Matsumoto Station. Open every day except Sunday from 11:30 a.m. to 2 p.m. and 4:30 to 10 p.m., it's a modern restaurant decorated in stained dark wood and cool white walls. The lunch menu is quite reasonable, with various kinds of teishoku available, ranging from ¥1,000 ($7.14) for an obento lunch box to ¥1,600 ($11.43) for steak. Other teishoku offer sashimi, tempura, or soba. At dinnertime kaiseki meals are served, costing from ¥5,500 ($39.29) to ¥11,000 ($78.57). Reservations are required for dinner.

For inexpensive Japanese fare close to Matsumoto Station, try **Shikimi** [133], 1-5-5 Chuo (tel. 72-0968), just a three-minute walk away. Although relatively new, it manages to evoke an atmosphere of old Japan with its traditional tiled roof and cast-iron lanterns hanging from its outside eaves. The inside is a successful blend of the old and new, tastefully decorated with wooden sliding doors, small tatami rooms, a wooden counter, and paper lanterns. Open every day except Thursday from noon to 10:30 p.m., it specializes in eel and sushi. Its *unagi donburi* (eel on rice) costs ¥1,400 ($10) and comes with soup and pickled vegetables, while a platter of assorted sushi, called *moriawase*, is available for ¥1,000 ($7.14) to ¥2,000 ($14.29).

Chapter VIII

THE REST OF HONSHU

IN ADDITION TO TOKYO, Kyoto, and the Japan Alps, Honshu has numerous other towns and attractions well worth a visit. From the bustling modern cities of Osaka and Nagoya to the sacred shrines of Ise-Shima National Park and Miyajima, Honshu has more than enough to satisfy the whims of every traveler.

1. Nagoya

As Japan's fourth-largest city, Nagoya is a place most foreigners never stop to see. True, it doesn't have the attractions of many of the nation's cities, but it does have a castle originally built by the first Tokugawa shogun, as well as one of Japan's most important Shinto shrines. You can visit the world-famous Noritake chinaware factory, and in the area surrounding Nagoya you can observe cormorant fishing during the summer months and visit an open-air architectural museum with structures dating from the Meiji era. Nagoya also serves as the gateway to Toba and Ise-Shima National Park. Incidentally, Nagoya is the birthplace of pachinko, the upright Japanese pinball machine now found in the farthest corners of the islands.

ORIENTATION: Located two hours west of Tokyo by Shinkansen bullet train,

Nagoya has a population of 2.1 million people and supports a wide range of industries, including automobile manufacture, chinaware, shipbuilding, and air-craft construction. Almost completely destroyed during World War II, it was rebuilt with wide and straight streets, many of which actually have names. The city's downtown area is called Sakae and has many shops, restaurants, and department stores.

The area around Nagoya Station is an important center because of its bus terminals, many hotels, and its huge underground shopping arcade. Clustered around the JR Nagoya Station are Shinkansen station, the Meitetsu Bus Terminal, the city bus terminal, and Kintetsu Station.

The easiest way to get around is via the city's subway system, which is simple to use because stations have names written in both English and Japanese. Probably the most important line for tourists is the Meijo Line, which runs through Sakae. It takes you to both Atsuta Jingu Shrine (subway stop: Jingu-Nishi) and to Nagoya Castle (subway stop: Shiyakusho); and if you take this line all the way to the end you'll end up in Ozone—no kidding!

Nagoya has one of the best facilities for foreign tourists of any city I've seen in Japan. Called the **Nagoya International Center**, it's on the third floor of the Nagoya International Center Building, 1-47-1 Nagono (tel. 052/581-5678), about a ten-minute walk from the train station. Open daily from 9 a.m. to 8:30 p.m., this modern and up-to-date facility features an English-speaking staff, cable TV newscasts from the States (a great way to catch up on the news from back home), and a free publication called *Nagoya Calendar,* published monthly with information on what's going on in Nagoya in the way of music, cinema, the stage, sports, art, and more. The center can also tell you anything you need to know regarding sightseeing, shopping, and accommodations. In addition to helping visitors, the center also helps foreign residents by advising them on how to get a visa, where to find an apartment, and which doctors speak English. In short, this facility really makes foreigners feel welcome in Nagoya. Be sure to pick up a map of the city, as well as a map of the underground shopping arcade radiating out from Nagoya Station.

There's also a **tourist information office** at the east exit of Nagoya Station (tel. 541-4301), open from 8:30 a.m. to 6:45 p.m. Although it doesn't have as many pamphlets as the center does, its staff speaks English and distributes maps and information about Nagoya.

The Tourist Information Center in Tokyo or Kyoto distributes a leaflet called *Nagoya and Vicinity,* which has a map of the city and a list of attractions in Nagoya and the surrounding area.

The **telephone area code** for Nagoya, capital of Aichi Prefecture, is 052.

THE SIGHTS: Built for his ninth son by Ieyasu Tokugawa, the first Tokugawa shogun of Japan, **Nagoya Castle** was completed in 1612 and served as both a stronghold and a residence for members of the Tokugawa family for almost 250 years, until the Meiji Restoration ended Tokugawa rule in 1868. As proof of Ieyasu's shrewd wisdom, he forced feudal lords around Japan to contribute to the castle's construction, thereby depleting their resources and making it harder for them to stage rebellions.

Although Nagoya Castle was destroyed in World War II, it was rebuilt in 1959 and is almost a carbon copy of the original. On top of the donjon roof are two golden dolphins, thought to protect the castle from dreaded fires. The dolphins each weigh about 2,650 pounds and are made of cast bronze covered with 18-karat gold scales. The castle is open daily from 9:30 a.m. to 4:30 p.m. and entrance is ¥300 ($2.14).

The 154-foot donjon houses treasures that escaped the bombing during World War II, including beautiful paintings on sliding doors and screens. Like most reconstructed castles in Japan, this one is made of ferroconcrete, and even has an elevator which will zip you up to the fifth floor, from which you have fine views of Nagoya and beyond.

East of the castle is **Ninomaru Garden**, noted as one of the few remaining castle gardens in Japan. Besides providing a beautiful setting, it served as an emergency shelter for the lord in case of enemy attack. Be sure to stop by the Ninomaru Tea House—it's said that if you drink tea here, five years will be added to your life.

If you're interested in seeing personal items that once belonged to the Tokugawa family, the **Tokugawa Art Museum**, 1017 Tokugawa-cho, Higashi-ku (tel. 935-6262), houses thousands of documents, armor, swords, helmets, pottery, lacquerware, and paintings of the shogun and his family. The museum's most famous exhibits are picture scrolls of the *Tale of Genji (Genji Emaki)*—but they're displayed only every five years (the next showing will be in 1990). However, there are plenty of other treasures to warrant a visit. Closed on Monday and during exhibition changes, the museum is open from 10 a.m. to 4:30 p.m.; entrance is ¥800 ($5.71) To reach the museum, take the Meijo subway line to Ozone Station, from which it's a 20-minute walk.

Because it contains one of the Three Sacred Treasures belonging to the emperor, **Atsuta Jingu Shrine** is revered as one of the three most important shrines in Japan. It enshrines the Kusanagi-no-Tsurugi (Grass-Mowing Sword), and even though the sword isn't on public display, Japanese make pilgrimages here to pay their respects. (By the way, the other two sacred treasures are the Sacred Mirror, which is in the Ise Jingu Shrines, and the Jewels, which are kept in the Imperial Palace in Tokyo.)

Atsuta Shrine was founded in the third century and was rebuilt in 1935. According to legend, the Grass-Mowing Sword was presented to an ancient prince by the name of Yamato-Takeru who used it during a campaign against rebels in eastern Japan. The rebels set a field of grass on fire and the prince used the sword to mow down the grass, thereby quelling the fire. *Atsuta* means "hot field" in Japanese.

If you like high places, you may be interested in knowing that the **Nagoya TV Tower** was the first such tower in Japan. Since its opening in 1954, more than 25 million visitors have ridden its glass-enclosed elevators to its observation platform, approximately 300 feet above the ground, for a bird's-eye view of the sprawling city. Used jointly by Nagoya's five television stations, the tower is located about a two-minute walk from Sakae subway station in the heart of Nagoya. Open daily from 10 a.m. to 5:50 p.m., it charges ¥500 ($3.57) for a visit to the observation platform.

Factory Visits

For centuries Nagoya has been a pottery and porcelain production center, and today the city and its vicinity manufacture 50% of Japan's total export chinaware. The largest chinaware company in Japan is Noritake, known the world over for its fine tableware. Founded in 1904, Noritake now exports to 110 nations around the world. The **Nagoya Noritake Factory**, located about a ten-minute walk north of Nagoya Station, offers two free tours daily Monday through Friday. Conducted in English, the tours are at 10 a.m. and 1 p.m. and last about one hour, but you must make reservations by calling beforehand (tel. 562-5072). The tour begins with an excellent film that depicts the history of Noritake and describes the manufacturing and decorating process of porcelain. After the film ends, you're led on a trip through the various production stages of the Diamond Collection, Noritake's best porcelain line. Unlike most modern-day factories where work is largely automated, almost all the work here is still done by hand. You'll be amazed to see how much attention is given to each piece as it moves through the production process. If you're interested in buying some porcelain, there are two shops located next to the plant that sell Noritake ware at reduced prices. Ask your guide to point you in the right direction.

In addition to its chinaware, Nagoya and its vicinity also rank first in the nation in the production of cloisonné. If you're interested in seeing demonstrations of how cloisonné is made, the Nagoya International Center has a 14-minute videotape showing its production. You can also visit the **Shippo-Cho Industrial Hall** (Shippo Sangyou Kaikan), Tojima Shippo-cho (tel. 441-3411). Open every day (except Tuesday and national holidays) from 9 a.m. to 5 p.m., it's free of charge to the public and contains exhibits of cloisonné ware. If you want to see demonstrations of how cloisonné is made, the Industrial Hall can arrange an appointment with one of the area's many cloisonné factories. To reach the Industrial Hall, take the Meitetsu bus from the Meitetsu terminal next to Nagoya Station to the Yasumatsu bus stop. From there it's a 15-minute walk.

Sights in the Vicinity

Meiji Mura: If architecture's your bag, you'll find a lot to delight in at the open-air museum called Meiji Mura. It features more than 50 buildings and structures from around Japan that were constructed during the Meiji Period (1868–1912). Before Japan opened its doors in the mid-1800s, unpainted wooden structures dominated Japanese architecture. After Western influences began infiltrating Japan, however, the nation witnessed a surge in new architectural techniques and materials. Stones, brick, painted wood, towers, turrets, and Victorian features came into play. Contained on the grounds of this 250-acre museum are Western homes that once belonged to foreigners living in Nagasaki and Kobe; official government buildings and schools; two Christian churches; a post office; a Kabuki theater; a brewery; even a prison. One of the most outstanding structures on display is the front façade of the original Imperial Hotel in Tokyo, designed by American architect Frank Lloyd Wright.

To get to Meiji Mura, you can take a direct bus from the Meitetsu Bus Station's third floor in the Melsa Building. Buses leave every 30 minutes (even more frequently on weekends) and the trip to Meiji Mura takes just over one hour. The ¥3,000 ($21.43) fee includes a round-trip bus ticket and entrance to Meija Mura. Meiji Mura is open from 10 a.m. to 5 p.m., closing one hour earlier from November through February.

Cormorant Fishing: There are two places in the vicinity of Nagoya where you can watch cormorant fishing every night (except during a full moon) throughout the summer months. Cormorant fishing is an ancient fishing method in Japan in which trained cormorants dive into the water in search of *ayu*, a small Japanese trout. To ensure that the cormorants don't swallow the fish, the birds are fitted with rings around their necks.

The city of **Gifu** features cormorant fishing on the Nagaragawa River from May 11 to October 15, and you can view the whole spectacle aboard a small wooden boat. To reach Gifu, take the Meitetsu Main Line train from Meitetsu Shin-Nagoya Station to Shin-Gifu Station. From there, switch to a local train heading for Nagara Kitamachi and get off at Nagarabashi Station. You'll be able to see the ticket office (call Nagarabashi Kanransen Jimusyo) after exiting the station. Ticket sales begin at 6 p.m., but you can call in advance to reserve your ticket (tel. 0582/65-0104). The price of a ticket is ¥2,600 ($18.57) during May, September, and October, and ¥2,800 ($20) in June, July, and August.

The other site for cormorant fishing is in the town of **Inuyama**, where the event takes place from June 1 to September 30. To reach Inuyama, take the Inuyama Line of the Meitetsu railways from Meitetsu Shin-Nagoya Station to Inuyama Yuen Station. From there it's a five-minute walk. Tickets are sold throughout the day beginning at 9 a.m. and the action starts after 6:30 p.m. Call ahead to make reservations at 0568/61-0057. Tickets here cost ¥2,400 ($17.14) during June and September, and ¥2,600 ($18.57) in July and August.

WHERE TO STAY: The greatest concentration of hotels is found close to Nagoya Station, with the rest of them spread east of the station close to Sakae and Nagoya Castle. In case you'd rather stay in a ryokan, I've listed a few Japanese inns. As with most cities in Japan, Nagoya does not have many ryokan—the cost of personal service and the price of land is simply too prohibitive.

The Upper Bracket

Western Style: Located between Nagoya Station and Sakae, the **Nagoya Kanko Hotel**, 1-19-30 Nishiki, Naka-ku (tel. 052/231-7711), is a first-class hotel offering many conveniences in one place. Facilities include a shopping arcade, five restaurants serving French, Japanese, and Chinese cuisine, and two lounges. The Aurora restaurant on the 18th floor offers a panoramic view of the city. First opened in 1934 and completely renovated in 1985, this 505-room hotel has a huge lobby featuring white brick, natural woods, brass, and contemporary glass chandeliers. All rooms are nicely appointed and come with TV (bilingual TVs are available upon request) and refrigerator. Singles here range from ¥10,000 ($71) to ¥13,000 ($93), twins run ¥18,500 ($132) to ¥26,000 ($186), and doubles cost ¥19,800 ($141) to ¥26,000 ($186).

Just west of Nagoya Castle is the **Hotel Nagoya Castle**, 3-19 Hinokuchi-cho, Nishi-ku (tel. 052/521-2121). This 253-room hotel boasts an indoor swimming pool, shops, restaurants serving Western, Japanese, and Chinese food, and bars. Guest rooms come equipped with the usual TV (bilingual TVs available) and refrigerator, and those facing east have a wonderful view of Nagoya Castle. Singles, none of which face the castle, start at ¥10,500 ($75). Twins and doubles, all of which have castle views, range from ¥19,800 ($141) to ¥29,000 ($207) and ¥21,000 ($150) to ¥30,000 ($214) respectively.

Japanese Style: About a seven-minute walk from Nagoya Station, **Maizurukan** [134], 1-18-24 Meieki Minami, Nakamura-ku (tel. 052/541-1346), is a modern ryokan. It even has an elevator to deliver you to its five floors. The outside of the building is an uninteresting concrete block, but its rooms have been designed with imagination and each one is different. Some rooms, for example, have tiny rock gardens while others look out onto a ledge decorated with plants. All but two of its 24 rooms have their own private bathroom, but you may want to take advantage of the big public baths here anyway. Rates are ¥15,500 ($111) to ¥22,000 ($157) per person, including two meals.

The Medium-Priced Range

Western Style: About a five-minute walk from Nagoya Station, the **Nagoya Miyako Hotel**, 4-9-10 Meieki, Nakamura-ku (tel. 052/571-3211), is one of the best hotels in this price category. As in all Miyako hotels, service is excellent, and all guest rooms were recently refurbished. Built more than two decades ago, the hotel has an attractive white marble lobby, a rooftop beer garden open in summer, Chinese, Japanese, and Western restaurants, and an underground shopping arcade with passageways to Meitetsu Bus Station and Nagoya Station. Rooms are comfortable, with wooden furniture, fridge, hot-water Thermos, TV, clock, and radio. Rates are based on room size: ¥7,700 ($55) to ¥12,000 ($86) for singles, ¥13,000 ($93) to ¥20,000 ($143) for twins, and ¥14,300 ($102) to ¥20,000 ($143) for doubles. Most of the singles face an inner courtyard—no view, but the rooms are quiet. Japanese-style rooms, some of which have bathtubs made of cypress, range from ¥18,700 ($134) to ¥27,000 ($193).

The **Meitetsu Grand Hotel**, 1-2-4 Meieki, Nakamura-ku (tel. 052/582-2211), is conveniently located right above Meitetsu Station. The check-in desk is on the 11th floor. Built in 1967, this 242-room hotel offers easy access to shops on the third and fourth floors, three restaurants, one lounge, and a beer garden open in the summer. Singles here range from ¥8,200 ($59) to ¥8,800 ($63); the cheapest is a comfortably decorated, good-sized room with semi-double bed, desk, chair, and table. All rooms have TV and refrigerator. Twins range from ¥14,300 ($102) to ¥22,000 ($157); the most expensive is a large room featuring an entry foyer, separate vanity area, semi-double beds, and a sitting area with couch, chairs, and table separated from the sleeping area by a glass partition. Doubles here are ¥16,500 ($118) and Japanese-style rooms are ¥17,600 ($126).

Hotel Castle Plaza, 4-3-25 Meieki, Nakamura-ku (tel. 052/582-2121), a six-minute walk from Nagoya Station, is a sister hotel to the first-class Hotel Nagoya Castle. Less than five years old, this 263-room hostelry has nine restaurants, a shopping plaza, gym, heated swimming pool, sauna, and jogging track. The pool, sauna, gym, and jogging facility can be used for ¥2,700 ($19.29). The hotel is decorated in classy contemporary designs of glass and mauve coloring, and the rooms are bright and cheerful. Singles range from ¥7,000 ($50) to ¥9,000 ($64), and twins are ¥12,100 ($86) to ¥18,500 ($132). The most expensive twins have good views of the city plus a separate entrance foyer and semi-double beds. Doubles start at ¥13,200 ($94).

Mont Blanc Hotel, 3-14-1 Meieki, Nakamura-ku (tel. 052/541-1121), is less than two minutes away from Nagoya Station on foot. It's a business hotel so most of its 281 rooms are singles, but it does have 47 twins and 12 doubles. Built in 1980 and renovated in 1985, it's clean and bright and has both Western and Japanese restaurants. Rooms—which start at ¥5,500 ($39) for a single, ¥9,300 ($66) for a twin, and ¥10,000 ($71) for a double—come with a radio, clock, TV with pay video, and fridge. Bathtubs in the cheapest singles are extremely narrow; if you're a big Westerner you may have trouble taking a bath in one of these.

Opened in 1985, **Hotel Sunroute Nagoya**, 2-35-24 Meieki, Nakamura-ku (tel. 052/571-2221), is one of Nagoya's newest business hotels. A handsome brick building located about a three-minute walk from Nagoya Station, it features a spacious lobby with an atrium and marbled pool and restaurants serving Japanese and Western food. More than 200 of its 276 rooms are singles, ranging in price from ¥6,200 ($44) to ¥8,800 ($63). Twins start at ¥11,000 ($79), while doubles start at ¥13,200 ($94). White walls make the rooms bright and pleasant, while TV with pay video, refrigerator, radio, alarm, and hot water with tea add to the comfort.

The Budget Category

Western Style: The **Chisan Hotel Nagoya**, 1-12-8 Noritake, Nakamura-ku (tel. 052/452-3211), is a business hotel located about a five-minute walk from the west exit of the train station. Opened in 1972, it's a bit worn around the edges but offers simple rooms at a good price. All rooms have TVs, and vending machines are located on several floors. Singles—tiny with even tinier bathrooms—are ¥5,000 ($36); some face an inner courtyard, and since rates are the same I'd advise asking for a room with more of a view. Twins are a little more spacious and go for ¥9,400 ($67). Prices include tax and service. An optional breakfast is ¥880 ($6.29).

Much better is another business hotel, the **Nagoya Daini Washington Hotel**, 3-22-12 Nishiki, Naka-ku (tel. 052/962-7111), located close to Sakae and its restaurants and bars. Unlike most business hotels, which have few facilities, this hotel features four restaurants serving Japanese, Chinese, and Western food and a sauna. Singles range from ¥5,400 ($39) to ¥6,900 ($49); the cheapest rooms manage to maintain an atmosphere of cheerfulness even though they're small and without windows. Twins range from ¥11,500 ($82) to ¥12,000 ($86), and are small but functional, coming with single and narrow beds, a small writing area, and two chairs. Prices include tax and service. Machines selling soda and beer are located on the fifth and eighth floors.

Also located in Sakae, about a three-minute walk from the Sakae subway station, is the **Nagoya Plaza Hotel**, 3-8-21 Nishiki, Naka-ku (tel. 052/951-6311), a business hotel with just the basics but relatively cheap prices. More than 15 years old, the decor could use some updating but the staff is friendly and the location convenient. Rooms come with TV, refrigerator, and desk. Singles start at ¥4,900 ($35) and run to ¥5,500 ($39); the cheapest is rather bare, with just a bed and wall hooks for clothes. Twins are ¥8,400 ($60); doubles range from ¥7,700 ($55) to ¥8,800 ($63). The hotel's one restaurant serves only breakfast, with prices running from ¥660 ($4.71) to ¥750 ($5.36). Room rates include tax and service charges.

Japanese Style: The inexpensive ryokan **Satsuki Honten** [135], 1-18-30 Meieki Minami, Nakamura-ku (tel. 052/551-0052), is about seven minutes by foot from Nagoya Station. The entrance to this 35-year-old ryokan is a little recessed in a tiny courtyard, guarded by a Japanese maple with delicate small leaves. This is a rather eccentric ryokan, filled with all kinds of antiques—Japanese chests sit in the lobby and paper fans, vases, and cast-iron pots decorate the guest rooms. The general atmosphere here is very homey and warm. There's even a small garden with the obligatory carp in the pond (I don't think you can have a pond in Japan without carp). The main drawback of staying here is that there's only one small bath for the ryokan's 11 rooms—which means that you may have to wait in line. One of the rooms does have its own bath—an ancient cypress bath in the shape of a barrel. Once common in Japan, this is one of the few still being used that I've come across in my travels throughout the country. And this room has its own toilet as well. Seven other rooms also have private toilets, and the rest of the rooms come only with a sink. All rooms have an air-conditioner, heater, safety box for valuables, and a coin-operated TV. Rates per person with two meals range from ¥6,900 ($49) to ¥9,300 ($66), tax and service extra. You can also stay here without taking your meals here, for which the rate ranges from ¥4,000 ($29) to ¥6,200 ($44), again excluding tax and service charge.

Oyone Ryokan, 2-2-112 Aoi, Higashi-ku (tel. 052/936-8788), is a member of the Japanese Inn Group and offers inexpensive tatami rooms ranging from ¥3,800 ($27) to ¥4,400 ($31) for one person, ¥6,500 ($46) to ¥7,500 ($54) for two persons, and ¥8,000 ($57) to ¥$10,000 ($71) for three. The building itself is rather characterless, but rooms are clean and come with air-conditioner, heater, and coin-operated TV. Breakfasts are available starting at ¥500 ($3.57), while Japanese dinners start at ¥1,500 ($10.71). To reach Oyone, take the

Higashiyama subway line from Nagoya Station to Chikusa Station (about a seven-minute ride), from which it's a five-minute walk.

Youth Hostels: The **Nagoya Youth Hostel**, 1-50 Kameiri, Tashiro-cho, Chikusa-ku (tel. 052/781-9845), is 16 minutes from Nagoya Station by subway (subway stop: Higashiyama Koen) followed by eight minutes on foot. The charge for both members and nonmembers is ¥1,300 ($9.29) per night. Breakfast is an additional ¥400 ($2.86) and dinner runs ¥600 ($4.29). Like most youth hostels, life is fairly regimented: the front doors close at 9 p.m., lights out at 10 p.m., and rising time is 6:30 a.m.

If you don't have a youth hostel card, it's worth a try calling to see whether there's room at the **Youth Hostel Aichi-ken Seinen-Kaikan**, 1-18-8 Sakae (tel. 052/221-6001). It's so centrally located that it's usually full. Reached in ten minutes by bus from Nagoya Station and three minutes on foot, it charges ¥2,300 ($16.43) for members and ¥3,500 ($25) for nonmembers. A dinner menu has choices ranging from ¥550 ($3.93) to ¥1,300 ($9.29) Breakfast is ¥500 ($3.57).

WHERE TO DINE: One of Nagoya's specialties is *kishimen* noodles (white noodles). It's also famous for its *miso nikomi udon,* which are udon noodles served in a bean-paste soup and flavored with such ingredients as chicken and green onions. There are also fine restaurants serving kaiseki, tempura, and other Japanese cuisine.

Around Nagoya Station

Shoufukuro [136], 2-14-19 Meieki Minami (tel. 586-0005), is a kaiseki restaurant with a sweeping view of the city. Located on the 26th floor of the Sumitomo Building, about a ten-minute walk south of Nagoya Station, this tiny restaurant consists of only eight tables and very simple furnishings, using the dramatic backdrop of the city and its own food arrangements as the focal points for decoration. Service is attentive and gracious from kimono-clad waitresses. The menu changes monthly according to what's in season, and it's best to make a reservation, especially if you want to come for dinner. Kaiseki meals cost ¥11,000 ($78.57), ¥14,300 ($102.14), ¥16,500 ($117.86), and ¥22,000 ($157.14); the differences in price reflect the number of dishes and the type of food served. There's also a ¥5,500 ($39.29) mini-kaiseki available for lunch. Hours are 11:30 a.m. to 3 p.m. and 5 to 9 p.m.; closed Sunday and national holidays.

Also located not far from Nagoya Station, **Restaurant Maizuru**, 1-18-24 Meieki Minami (tel. 541-1346), is run by the Maizurukan Ryokan described above. This modern-looking restaurant utilizes slats of wood in sleek lines to give it both a traditional and contemporary look. Both tatami and table seating are available, and hours are noon to 2 p.m. and 5 to 10 p.m. daily. The cuisine offered includes kaiseki meals ranging from ¥6,500 ($46.43) to ¥11,000 ($78.57), shabu-shabu for ¥6,000 ($42.86), obento lunch boxes starting at ¥1,200 ($8.57), and daily lunch teishoku specials starting at ¥2,800 ($20).

For less expensive dining, try the **Miyako** [137], a restaurant in the basement shopping arcade of the Miyako Hotel, 4-9-10 Meieki (tel. 571-3211). Although its menu is in Japanese, it has a plastic-food display case outside the front door. A typical Japanese-style restaurant popular with the locals, most of its offerings range from ¥1,300 ($9.29) to ¥4,500 ($32.14) for such choices as eel, sushi, and tempura. The Miyako platter includes cucumbers, tuna, and rice rolled in seaweed, sashimi, tempura, and pickled vegetables. If you feel like splurging, a sukiyaki dinner for two is available for ¥8,800 ($62.86). The restaurant is open from 11 a.m. to 9 p.m. daily.

Also in the underground shopping arcade beneath the Miyako Hotel is **Kintetsu Hanten** [137A], (tel. 571-3211), a Chinese restaurant with more than 150 items listed on its English menu. With most servings for one to two people priced between ¥1,900 ($13.57) and ¥2,700 ($19.29), it offers shark's-fin soup, abalone, crab, scallop, squid, shrimp, lobster, fish, beef, pork, chicken, tofu, and vegetable dishes. Selections range from spicy braised shrimp with red peppers to fried crab claws or braised scallops in oyster suace. Hours here are from 11 a.m. to 9 p.m. daily.

You can eat even more cheaply on the roof of the Miyako Hotel at its beer garden, open during the summer months from 5 to 9 p.m. Pop music plays from a loudspeaker and there's a plastic-food display case to help in making your selection of everything from frankfurters to sushi. *Teppanyaki* (strips of beef that you grill at your table) is available for ¥3,500 ($25) per person and includes all the beer or juice you can consume. If you go à la carte, beer starts at ¥550 ($3.93).

Yamamoto-ya Honten [138], is a chain noodle shop specializing in miso nikomi udon. Its noodles, all handmade, are thick, hard, and chewy and are served in a type of bean paste special to Nagoya. If you like your noodles spicy, you can add a mixture of spices to your food from the large bamboo container on your table. A bowl of udon in soup costs ¥600 ($4.29). With chicken (called *Kashiwa iri nikomi udon*) it costs ¥880 ($6.29). A Yamamoto-ya Honten is located just a three-minute walk from Nagoya JR Station on Sakura Dori Street in the basement of the Horiuchi Building (tel. 565-0278). If you want to try these noodles in Sakae, there's another shop just a couple minutes from the Sakae subway station in the basement of the Chu-Nichi Building (tel. 263-7519). Hours for both are 11 a.m. to 8:30 p.m. daily.

In Sakae

A good choice in Sakae's nightlife and restaurant district is **Yaegaki Tempura House** [139], 3-17-28 Nishiki, Naka-ku (tel. 951-3250). This well-established tempura restaurant has been serving fresh seafood and vegetables for more than half a century and features open kitchens so guests can watch the action. The staff here is very friendly and there's an English menu for the offerings in season, which may include shrimp, oyster, smelt, Japanese trout, gingko nuts, or lotus root. It's easiest to order the set dinner, which consists of hors d'oeuvres, four shrimp, six pieces of varied seasonal fish, vegetables, rice, soup, pickled vegetables, and fruit for ¥6,500 ($46.43). This tempura restaurant is open from 11:30 a.m. to 2 p.m. and 5 to 9 p.m.; closed Sunday and national holidays. Reservations are recommended if you want to eat dinner here.

Kisoji [140], 3-20-15 Nishiki, Naka-ku (tel. 951-3755), is a restaurant in Sakae specializing in shabu-shabu. In business for more than 20 years, it evokes a countryside atmosphere with traditional, comfortable decor. You can dine either at tables or on tatami. There's an English menu, but the kimono-clad waitresses are unable to elaborate on what the various courses entail so choose according to your budget. Most dinners range from ¥4,900 ($35) to ¥8,800 ($62.86). The Shabu-Shabu Special incudes hors d'oeuvres, shabu-shabu, rice, pickles, and ice cream, while the Shabu-Shabu Keyaki features hors d'oeuvres, shabu-shabu, sashimi, tempura vegetables, rice, pickles, and dessert. It's open from 11:30 a.m. to 3 p.m. and 5 to 10 p.m.

Kishimentei [141], 3-20-4 Nishiki, Naka-ku (tel. 951-3481), is a small hole-in-the-wall that has been offering Nagoya's specialty for more than 70 years—kishimen noodles. It even sells packages of noodles in case you want to take some home with you. There's no English menu but plastic food is displayed in the window. Meals range from ¥600 ($4.29) to about ¥1,700 ($12.14) and include kishimen noodles with pork, tempura shrimp, or vegetables. It's open Monday through Saturday from 11 a.m. to 8 p.m.

2. Ise-Shima National Park

Blessed with subtropical vegetation, many small islands dotting its shoreline, and the most revered Shinto shrine in all of Japan, Ise-Shima National Park merits a one- or two-night stopover if you're anywhere near the vicinity of Nagoya. Located on Shima Peninsula and covering 200 square miles, this national park is also the home of the Mikimoto pearl, Japan's famous women divers, and thousands of oyster rafts in its many bays and inlets. Although you could conceivably cover the major attractions on a day's outing from Nagoya, I've included some recommended accommodations in case you'd like to take in the sights at a more leisurely pace.

ORIENTATION: Ise-Shima's major attractions are concentrated in the small towns of Ise, Toba, and Kashikojima, all in Mie Prefecture. Ise, for example, is where you'll find the Ise Jingu Shrines; Toba contains the Mikimoto Pearl Island, with a pearl museum and demonstrations by women divers; and in Kashikojima you can visit the Marine Land Aquarium or take boat trips around Ago Bay, considered to be the most scenic spot in the national park.

The easiest way to get to Ise-Shima is from Nagoya on the private Kintetsu Ise-Shima Line (Kinki Nippon Railway), which departs about every 15 minutes or so from the Kintetsu Station right next to the Japan Railways' Nagoya Station. It takes about an hour and 25 minutes to reach Ise (also called Iseshi), about one hour and 40 minutes to reach Toba, and a little more than two hours to reach Kashikojima. A ticket from Nagoya to the end of the line in Kashikojima costs ¥2,700 ($19.29) one way. There are also Kintetsu lines to Shima Peninsula from both Kyoto (two hours and 15 minutes to Toba) and from Osaka's Kintetsu Station in Namba (two hours to Toba).

If you're on a JR railpass, you might be interested to know that you can also reach Ise-Shima by JR, though the trains are not as frequent or convenient. There is only one train from Kyoto, and if you're coming from Nagoya you'll have to change trains in Taki. Note that JR trains pass through Ise and terminate in Toba. If you want to go onward to Kashikojima, therefore, you'll have to switch in Toba to the Kintetsu private line.

Transportation inside Ise-Shima National Park is either by local train or by bus. You might also consider joining a sightseeing tour. Although they're conducted in Japanese only, tours provide a convenient way of seeing the park's far-flung attractions.

Be sure to drop by the Tourist Information Center in Tokyo or Kyoto to pick up the free leaflet *Ise-Shima*. It lists train schedules from Osaka, Kyoto, and Nagoya, and gives information on the national park's main attractions.

THE SIGHTS: The easiest way to see the sights of Ise-Shima National Park is to start in Ise and work your way down the peninsula to Kashikojima.

Ise Jingu Shrines

Ise, the northern gateway to Ise-Shima National Park, is famous for the Ise Jingu Shrines, also called the Grand Shrines of Ise. The shrine grounds consist of the Outer Shrine, the Inner Shrine, and a number of minor shrines.

The **Outer Shrine** *(Geku)* is just a ten-minute walk from either Ujiyamada or Iseshi Station. Founded in 478, it's dedicated to the Shinto goddess of harvest and agriculture. The **Inner Shrine** *(Naiku)* was founded a few centuries earlier and is dedicated to Amaterasu, the sun goddess. Since the shrines lie about four miles apart, you should walk first to the Outer Shrine and then take a bus to the Inner Shrine. Buses make runs between the two shrines about every 15 minutes and the fare is ¥310 ($2.21).

The Ise Jingu Shrines are one of the few Shinto shrines in Japan that do not show any Chinese Buddhist influences. Constructed of plain cypress wood with thick thatched roofs, the shrines are starkly simple and do not have any ornamentation save some gold and copper on the facing of their beams and doors. In fact, if you've come all the way to Shima Peninsula just to see the shrines you may be disappointed—there is nothing much to see. The shrines are considered so sacred that no one is allowed close to them—that is, no one except members of the imperial family and high Shinto priests. Both shrines are surrounded by four wooden fences and we lesser mortals are allowed only as far as the third gate. Because of the fences you can't see much of the shrines, but that doesn't stop the estimated six million Japanese who come here annually. They come because of what the shrines represent, which is an embodiment of the Japanese Shinto religion itself. The Inner Shrine is by far the more important of the two shrines because it's dedicated to the sun goddess, who is considered the legendary ancestress of the imperial family. It contains the Sacred Mirror *(Yata-no-Kagami)*, one of the Three Sacred Treasures of the emperor.

According to legend, the sun goddess sent her grandson to Japan so that he and his descendants could rule over Japan. Before he left she gave him three insignia—a mirror, a sword, and a set of jewels. As she handed him the mirror, she is said to have remarked, "When you look upon this mirror, let it be as if you look upon me." The mirror, therefore, is considered to embody the sun goddess herself and is regarded as the most sacred object in the Shinto religion. The mirror is kept in the deep recesses of the Inner Shrine in a special casket and is never shown to the public. As for the other two treasures, they are also kept locked away. The sword is in the Atsuta Shrine in Nagoya and the jewels are in the Imperial Palace in Tokyo.

Even though you can't see much of the shrines themselves, they're still the most important things you should see in Ise-Shima. The Inner Shrine is surrounded by old cedar trees. Watch how the Japanese stop after crossing the second small bridge on the approach to the shrine to wash and purify their hands and mouth with water from the Isuzu River. Its source lies on the Inner Shrine grounds itself and it's considered to be a sacred stream. You'll also see a couple of white royal horses, kept near the shrine for the use of the sun goddess. Perhaps the most amazing thing about the Outer and Inner Shrines is that even though they were founded centuries upon centuries ago, the buildings themselves are not more than 20 years old. Every twenty years they are completely torn down and rebuilt exactly as they were on neighboring sites. Using the old methods of dowels and interlocking joints, no nails are used. The present buidings were built in 1973 for the 60th time. Keep in mind that no photographs of the shrines themselves are allowed.

Ise-Shima Skyline Highway

Not far from the front entrance of the Inner Shrine are the buses that depart for Toba traveling on the Ise-Shima Skyline highway. About ten miles long, it rises up over Mount Asama, on top of which is **Kongoshoji Temple**. If you want you can get off the bus here, visit the temple, and then catch the next bus on to Toba. Kongoshoji Temple is renowned for the vermilion-painted Moon Bridge, which forms a circle as it reflects in a pond, and for a huge footprint said to be Buddha's. Behind the temple is a pathway lined with poles erected in memory of departed loved ones. The entire ride from the Inner Shrine to Toba takes about 45 minutes and costs ¥1,000 ($7.14).

Toba

Toba's best-known attraction is the **Mikimoto Pearl Island**, just a few minutes' walk from Toba Station and connected to the mainland via a short bridge. Open daily from 8 a.m. to 5 p.m. (from 9:10 a.m. to 4:30 p.m November 20 to February 28) and charging ¥800 ($5.71), it's geared entirely toward tourists but is still quite enjoyable—especially if you have a weakness for pearls or are interested in how they're cultivated. In addition to a pearl museum and a shop, there's a demonstration hall where the process of culturing pearls and the steps involved in sorting and stringing them are explained in live demonstrations. You'll learn more about pearls than you ever thought possible—and possibly more than you ever wanted to know. Most fascinating in my opinion is the **Mikimoto Memorial Hall**, chronicling in flawless English the attempts, failures, and final success of Kokichi Mikimoto to cultivate pearls. The son of a noodle-shop owner, Mikimoto went to Yokohama as a young man and was surprised to see stalls selling pearls with great success. Pearls were produced naturally by oysters around his hometown of Toba. Mikimoto reasoned that if oysters produced pearls as the result of an irritant inside the shell, why couldn't man introduce the irritant himself and thereby induce oysters to make pearls?

It turned out to be harder than it sounded. Oysters used in Mikimoto's experiments kept rejecting the foreign material and dying. It wasn't until 1893, five years after he started his research, that Mikimoto finally succeeded in cultivating his first pearl. In 1905 Mikimoto was able to cultivate his first perfectly round pearl, after which he built what is probably the most successful pearl empire in the world. Mikimoto, who died at the age of 93, was a remarkable man and a real character. His favorite expressions included "Have you anything worth talking about?" and "Make the most of it." Nothing disgusted him more than wastefulness. I'm particularly fond of this quote: "Wisdom is indispensable to success. As is good fortune. But life is the most necessary ingredient of all." I certainly can't argue with that.

The **Special Exhibition Hall** contains various models made with pearls. The Pearl Pagoda, for example, has 12,760 Mikimoto pearls and took 750 craftsmen six months to complete, after which it was exhibited at the Philadelphia World Exhibition in 1926. The Liberty Bell, one-third the size of the original, has 12,250 pearls and was displayed at the New York World's Fair in 1939.

Also at Mikimoto Pearl Island are frequent demonstrations given by women divers. Wearing traditional white diving outfits, these divers demonstrate how women of Shima Peninsula have dived through the ages in search of abalone, seaweed, and other edibles. At one time there used to be thousands of women divers and they were known for their skill in diving to great depths for extended periods of time. Today's tourist brochures say that there are still 3,000 of these women divers left—but the only places I've ever seen divers at work were at demonstrations given for tourists. If you happen to see women divers working in earnest, consider yourself lucky.

If you have more time in Toba, other things to do here include visiting **Toba Aquarium** and **Brazil Maru**, a moored ship that used to take Japanese immigrants to Brazil.

Futamigaura

If you're at all sentimental, you might want to make a trip to Futamigaura, which you can reach by either bus or train from Ise or Toba. There you'll find a pair of large rocks that jut out of the sea not far from shore. Known as the **Wedded Rocks**, they are considered to represent man and wife and are joined by a thick braided rope, the same kind you see extended from *torii* gates at Shinto shrines. If you're an early riser, the best time to visit the rocks is at dawn. In this Land of the Rising Sun, the spectacle of the sun rising between these two rocks is a favorite among Japanese.

Kashikojima

At the southern end of Shima Peninsula and the last stop on the Kintetsu Line is Kashikojima. Here you can visit the **Marine Land Aquarium**, open from 8:30 a.m. to 6 p.m. in summer and 9 a.m. to 5 p.m. the rest of the year. It describes the fish and plant life of the region and also has demonstrations given by women divers. Although explanations are in Japanese only, it's a fun place to visit. Entrance is ¥800 ($5.71). The main attraction of Kashikojima, however, is its **boat cruises of Ago Bay**. Vessels leave from the boat dock about a two-minute walk from the train station. The cost of the cruise is ¥1,500 ($10), and you'll pass oyster rafts, fishing boats, and many small islands along the way. The trip lasts approximately one hour, with boats departing every half hour between 9 a.m. and 3:30 p.m. in the summer. For more information or inquiries about the winter schedule, call the Kintetsu Shima Kanko Kisen Co. at 05994/3-1023.

If you're desperate for a dip in salt water, the most popular beach in the area is **Goza**. The boat from Kashikojima to Goza takes about 25 minutes and costs ¥550 ($3.93) one way, passing oyster rafts, their cultivators, and the sweeping mountainous terrain of the region. The boat ride is very enjoyable but the beach itself is, well, a bit disappointing after coming all that distance. There are certainly prettier beaches in the world, but this one is okay for a quick fix.

FOOD AND ACCOMMODATION: There are resort and hotel establishments throughout Shima Peninsula, which offer the best in seafood dining as well.

In Kashikojima

Sitting atop a hill above Ago Bay with its many oyster rafts, the **Shima Kanko Hotel** in Kashikojima (tel. 05994/3-1211) is a resort hotel with a large outdoor swimming pool and fine Western and Japanese restaurants. A hotel of the old tradition, the service here is impeccable. Although it's just a few minutes' walk from the train station, hotel buses meet each incoming Kintetsu train. Rooms are spacious, and though they have recently been remodeled, they retain a healthy old-fashioned atmosphere with shoji screens and wooden furniture. Some of the twins here have balconies, and rooms that face the bay have splendid views of oyster rafts, water craft, and islands. There are no single rooms. Standard twins range from ¥17,500 ($125) to ¥23,000 ($164) and doubles are ¥18,500 ($132). Japanese-style rooms accommodating up to four persons are available for ¥20,000 ($143) to ¥27,000 ($193). If you come during the peak tourist seasons of July and August or New Year's, expect to pay about ¥3,000 ($21.43) more than the prices quoted above.

Since Kashikojima is surrounded by water, you can safely assume that the seafood here is fresh and excellent. The Shima Kanko Hotel's **La Mer** French restaurant has a well-deserved reputation for serving its own delightful recipes created by its well-known chef. Its specialty is lobster, served in a Western dining hall with chandeliers, wooden floor, white tablecloths, and tables overlooking the bay and oyster rafts. A lobster menu for ¥22,000 ($157) includes abalone, while meals for ¥25,000 ($179) and ¥29,000 ($207) include steak as well. The small à la carte menu offers entrées of lobster, shrimp, or beef, most in the ¥5,500 ($39.29) to ¥8,000 ($57.14) range. Lunch set courses start at ¥11,000 ($78.57), with either beef or seafood as the main dish. In any case, if you want one of the set dinner courses, you should make a reservation beforehand. Incidentally, if you've never had abalone, this is a great, albeit expensive, place to try it. Hours here are 11:30 a.m. to 2 p.m. and 5 to 9 p.m.

The Shima Kanko Hotel has a couple of Japanese restaurants as well, open only in the evenings. **Hamayu** is designed like a country lodge with a high slanted roof of thick beams supported by large pillars and a wooden floor. Open from 6 to 8:30 p.m., it serves a kaiseki dinner for ¥13,500 ($96.43). Other seafood dishes, such as abalone, lobster, shrimp, sashimi, and fried fish, average about ¥2,500 ($17.86) to ¥7,000 ($50).

The hotel also has a sushi bar called **Tsubaki**, open from 6:30 to 10 p.m. The best deal here is the ¥5,500 ($39.29) set meal, which offers a variety of seafood in season.

If you're looking for an expensive place to stay, a good choice is **Ishiyama-So** [142], Yokoyama-jima, Kashikojima (tel. 05995/2-1527). It's located on a small island just a stone's throw from the Kashikojima pier, and the only way to get there is in Ishiyama-So's own private boat. If you call ahead of time they'll even come fetch you at the train station and lead you to their boat. In any case, the trip over the water takes only two minutes, and you pull up right at the ryokan's front door. Although the building itself is concrete, the rooms in this family-run establishment are tatami and feature an air-conditioner, heater, TV, and a safe for valuables. Three of the 12 rooms have their own private bathroom and go for ¥5,500 ($39.29) per person. Other rooms, 3 of which have their own toilet, are ¥4,400 ($31.43) per person. Japanese breakfasts cost ¥500 ($3.57), while Japanese dinners start at ¥1,500 ($10.71). If you want you can swim right off the dock here, and footpaths cross the small island. One of the family members here speaks good English.

In Toba

A good choice in Toba is the **Toba Hotel International**, 1-23-1 Toba (tel. 0599/25-3121). Perched atop a hill about a 20-minute walk or five-minute taxi ride from Toba Station, it has twin and Japanese-style rooms that go for ¥16,500 ($118) off-season, rising to ¥21,000 ($150) in July and August. Combination rooms with both Western-style beds and a separate tatami area go for ¥44,000 ($314). Some rooms have balconies with great views of the water, oyster rafts, fishing boats, and islands.

Facilities here include an outdoor swimming pool and French and Japanese restaurants. Most unique, perhaps, is its floating seafood restaurant, **Shioji**, which features a large fish tank in the middle of its dining room. Your fish couldn't be fresher. The dinner menu, served from 5:30 to 8 p.m., has courses that start at ¥8,800 ($62.86). The Shioji dinner, for example, includes an appetizer, sashimi, tempura, both broiled and boiled shellfish, soup, and fruit. If you're on a budget, consider coming for lunch, served from noon to 2 p.m. for the ¥5,500 ($39.29) set menu.

A conveniently located ryokan in Toba is **Kimpokan** [143], 1-10-38 Toba (tel. 0599/25-2001), just a couple of minutes' walk from Toba Station. With 100 years of history under its belt, it's the oldest ryokan in Toba. The present building, however, is much more recent, a white concrete building catering largely to Japanese groups. All 45 rooms face the water, but because it's located a little inland the views aren't that grand. Rooms come with private bath and Western-style toilet, refrigerator, a safe for valuables, TV with pay video, and shoji screens. Western breakfasts are served on request. Rates here range from ¥11,000 ($79) to ¥22,000 ($157) per person, including two meals, tax, and service.

In Futamigaura

Futamikan, 569-1 Ko, Futami-machi (tel. 05964/3-2003), is a grand, traditional Japanese-style inn which has even played host to the imperial family. The oldest part of the ryokan is more than 100 years old and features beautifully carved transoms and sitting alcoves overlooking the garden. Since they didn't make private bathrooms back then, you might prefer one of the rooms in the newer annex, which also have the additional advantage of a small balcony—ask for a room on the fifth floor, where you have a sweeping view of the sea. But no matter where you stay, be sure to explore. On the second floor of the old building is one of the most beautiful banquet rooms I have ever seen—it has wooden railings outside its sliding glass windows, chandeliers, and 120 tatami mats. As for the town itself, it's small and peaceful. The famous Wedded Rocks are only a five-minute walk away. Rates here range from 16,500 ($118) to ¥33,000 ($236) per person.

In Ise

Not considered as much a resort area as Toba and Kashikojima, Ise has more reasonably priced accommodations. **Saekikan** [144], 6-4 Honmachi (tel. 0596/28-2017), is a rather uninteresting-looking concrete block from the outside, but is conveniently located—about a three-minute walk from Iseshi Station on the road leading to the Outer Shrine. Rooms are very reasonably priced at this ryokan, starting at ¥8,800 ($63) per person with two meals for a room without bath or toilet and rising to ¥13,200 ($94) for rooms with bath and Japanese-style toilet. Western-style breakfasts are available.

More interesting architecturally is the nearby **Yamadakan** [145], 13-1 Honmachi (tel. 0596/28-2532). Built more than 60 years ago, it features old wooden corridors that circle an inner courtyard. There are 28 rooms in all, 6 of which are in a newer annex and have their own bathrooms. Always the romantic, I prefer the older rooms without bathrooms. Rates here range from ¥6,500 ($46) to ¥16,500 ($118).

Catering to a young traveling crowd, **Hoshidekan** [146], 2-15-2 Kawasaki (tel. 0596/28-2377), is less than a ten-minute walk from either Ujiyamada or Iseshi Station. This 70-year-old ryokan has only 13 rooms, all without toilet and bath. Some of the rooms have windows framed with gnarled roots and bamboo (they simply don't make windows like that anymore). Room rates do not include meals: ¥3,300 ($23.57) for one person and ¥6,000 ($43) for two. This inexpensive ryokan is run by a group of women who are strong advocates of **macrobiotic vegetarian cooking**, which they serve in a simple tatami room connected to the ryokan. Open from 11 a.m. to 2 p.m. and 5 to 8 p.m. every day except Sunday, it offers a vegetarian course (*Genmae teishoku*) for ¥750 ($5.36), vegetarian pilaf for ¥550 ($3.93), and such other choices as noodles, tempura, tofu dishes, raw wheat beer, and natural raw sake.

Of the business hotels in the area, your best bet is **Ise City Hotel** [147], 1-11-31 Fukiage (tel. 0596/28-2111). Located between Ujiyamada and Iseshi stations (it's about a three-minute walk from each) and situated right beside the railroad tracks, it opened in 1985. The adequately sized rooms are clean and cheerful, with flowered wallpaper and tiled bathrooms. Amenities include a radio, TV with pay video, clock, push-button phone, and hot water with tea. Single rooms, all of which feature a semi-double bed, go for ¥6,000 ($43) for one and ¥9,600 ($69) if you can squeeze in two. Twins are ¥10,800 ($77). Prices include tax and service.

Youth Hostels

Youth Hostel Taikoji [148], 1659, Ei, Futami-cho (tel. 05964/3-2283), is in a temple four minutes by bus from Futamigaura Station and then five minutes on foot. Tatami mats here accommodate up to 28 persons. The price for card-carrying members is ¥1,800 ($12.86), ¥2,400 ($17.14) for nonmembers. Breakfast and dinner are available for an additional ¥1,000 ($7.14).

Ise-Shima Youth Hostel [149], at 1219-80 Anagawa, Isobe-cho (tel. 05995/ 5-0226), is seven minutes on foot from Anagawa Station and charges ¥2,100 ($15) for an overnight stay. The rules say you have to have a membership card. Breakfast costs ¥400 ($2.86), while dinner is ¥700 ($5).

3. Kanazawa

Located on the northwest coast of Honshu on the Sea of Japan, Kanazawa serves as a gateway to the rugged and sea-swept Noto Peninsula. The second-largest city after Kyoto to escape bombing during World War II, some of the old city has been left intact, including a few samurai houses, old geisha quarters, and tiny narrow streets that run crooked without rhyme or reason, apparently to confuse any enemies foolish enough to attack. Kanazawa is most famous for its Kenrokuen Garden, one of the most celebrated gardens in all of Japan. Considering all its assets, therefore, it's little wonder that Kanazawa has become one of the most popular new destinations for foreigners in Japan. If your time in Japan is limited, however, and you're mainly interested in traditional Japanese buildings and neighborhoods, my own opinion is that Kyoto or Takayama in the Japan Alps have more to offer. On the other hand, if you are a big fan of Japanese gardens, Kenrokuen is one of the best. It's the main reason people come here.

Kanazawa first gained notoriety about 500 years ago when a militant Buddhist sect joined with peasant fanatics to overthrow the feudal lord and establish its own autonomous government, an event unprecedented in Japanese history. The independent republic survived almost 100 years before it was attacked by an army of Nobunaga Oda, who was trying to unite Japan at a time when civil wars wracked the nation. Kanazawa was subsequently granted to one of Nobunaga's retainers, Toshiie Maeda. The Maeda clan continued to rule over Kanazawa for the next 300 years, amassing wealth in the form of rice paddies and encouraging development of the arts. All through the Tokugawa shogunate era the Maedas remained the second most powerful family in Japan after the Tokugawas themselves and controlled the largest domain in the country. About a million *koku* of rice (equaling five million bushels of rice) was produced here annually. The arts of Kutani ware, Yuzen silk dyeing, and Noh theater flourished and enjoy success and popularity even today.

ORIENTATION: The **tourist information window** is located just outside Kanazawa Station as you exit from the east side (tel. 0762/31-6311). Open from 8 a.m. to 8 p.m., it distributes a map in English and will also book hotel rooms for you.

Before leaving Tokyo, be sure to pick up the flyer *Kanazawa and Noto Peninsula* at the Tourist Information Center.

Kanazawa's attractions spread south and southeast from the station. Kenrokuen Garden, for example, is 1½ miles southeast of Kanazawa Station, easily reached by bus 10, 11, or 12 from the station. You can also take a bus from the station to the Kosen Pottery Kiln. Other attractions can be covered on foot in one day.

The **telephone area code** for Kanazawa is 0762. Kanazawa serves as the capital of Ishikawa Prefecture.

THE SIGHTS: Much of Kanazawa's charm lies in the atmosphere of its old neighborhoods. Be sure to wear your good walking shoes, since the best way to explore the city is via your own two feet.

Kenrokuen Garden and Vicinity

At one time Kanazawa possessed an impressive castle belonging to the powerful Maeda clan. Unfortunately, the castle was destroyed by fire in 1881. One of the few structures left standing is the **Ishikawamon Gate**, which used to be the south entrance to the castle. Looking at how big and grand the gate is, you can gain at least a little appreciation of how mighty the Maeda castle once was.

Just south of Ishikawamon Gate is **Kenrokuen Garden**, Kanazawa's main attraction. Along with Kairakuen Garden in Mito and Korakuen Garden in Okayama, Kenrokuen is considered to be one of the best three landscape gardens in Japan. As the largest of the three, it's also considered by many to be the best. Its name can be translated as "a refined garden incorporating six attributes," which are: spaciousness, careful arrangement, seclusion, antiquity, elaborate use of water, and scenic charm. What this all means is that ponds, trees, streams, rocks, mounds, and footpaths have all been combined so aesthetically that the effect is quite spellbinding. No matter the season, you're bound to be captivated by its beauty. Altogether it took about 150 years to complete the garden. The fifth Maeda lord started construction in the 1670s, and through the years each successive lord added to the garden according to his own individual tastes. The garden as we now see it was finished by the 12th Maeda lord in 1822. As the private garden of the Maeda clan, it wasn't until after the Meiji Restoration that the garden was opened to the public in 1875. Admission to the garden is ¥300 ($2.14) and hours are 6:30 a.m. to 6 p.m. daily (8 a.m. to 4:30 p.m. in winter).

As a side note, it may be worth it to arrive either at dawn or near the end of the day, since the garden is a favorite destination of Japanese tour groups, led by guides that explain everything in detail—through loudspeakers. I don't know how they affect you, but loudspeakers drive me to absolute distraction.

In the southeast corner of Kenrokuen Park, and charging a separate admission of ¥400 ($2.86), is **Seisonkaku Villa**, built in 1863 by the 13th Maeda lord as a retirement home for his widowed mother. Of elegant and graceful workmanship, this villa is decidedly feminine in nature with its carved-wood transoms and shoji screens painted with various designs. The villa's bedroom is decorated with tortoises painted on the shoji wainscoting (tortoises were associated with long life, and it must have worked since the mother lived to be 84). Closed on Wednesday, it's open the rest of the week from 8:30 a.m. to 4 p.m.

Next to Seisonkaku Villa is the **Ishikawa Prefectural Museum for Traditional Products and Crafts**, open daily from 9 a.m. to 5 p.m.; closed every third

Thursday from April through November and every Thursday from December through March. Admission is ¥200 ($1.43). Opened in 1984, it houses a good collection of various locally produced lacquerware, woodcarvings, folk toys, pottery, silk, *washi* (Japanese paper), and hats and baskets made from cypress. You can see the famous Kutani pottery here as well, first produced under the patronage of the Maeda clan in the 1600s. There are also displays of Yuzen dyeing, with its bold and clear picturesque designs. A pamphlet and explanations of the various displays in English make a visit here worthwhile.

South of Kenrokuen Park and not far from Seisonkaku Villa are a scattering of more museums to visit if you like museums and you're interested in learning more about Kanazawa's past. The **Ishikawa Prefectural Art Museum**, open daily from 9:30 a.m. to 4:30 p.m. and charging a ¥300 ($2.14) admission, houses a small collection of antique Kutani pottery, samurai costumes, and decorative art, most dating from the Edo Period. Several rooms are also devoted to modern and contemporary paintings, sculptures, and other artwork by local artists, with exhibitions changed monthly. Close by is the **Honda Museum**, which displays samurai outfits, weapons, artwork, and the personal effects of the Honda clan, one of Lord Maeda's chief retainers. Open daily from 9 a.m. to 5 p.m. (closed on Thursday from November through February), it charges ¥500 ($3.57). A third museum, the **Ishikawa Prefecture History Museum**, exhibits artifacts dealing with the history of the prefecture from prehistoric to modern times. Housed in a handsome red-brick building that was built to stock guns and gunpowder before the turn of the century, it contains archeological finds from the region, items from the Edo Period, and folkloric objects. There are even samurai outfits you can try on for size—they weigh up to 44 pounds. Open every day from 9 a.m. to 5 p.m., it charges ¥200 ($1.43).

Since it would be tiring (and expensive) to visit all the museums described above, you might want to limit your selection to one or two. My own personal favorite is the Prefectural Museum for Traditional Products and Crafts.

Nagamachi Samurai District

About a 20-minute walk west of Kenrokuen Garden is an area known as Nagamachi Samurai District. This place should be visited more for absorption of atmosphere than anything else, since most of the homes are still privately owned and are not open to the public. Furthermore, despite the name, many of these homes were built during the Meiji era and never belonged to samurai at all.

The Nagamachi Samurai District is basically just one street, lined with beautiful wooden homes hidden behind gold-colored mud walls. An unhurried stroll in the neighborhood is the main source of entertainment here—perhaps not so different from many neighborhoods in Japan, but certainly different from neighborhoods back home. One home that is open to the public is the **Nomura Samurai House**, open from 8:30 a.m. to 5 p.m. and charging ¥300 ($2.14) admission. Its drawing room is of Japanese cypress with elaborate designs in rosewood, and its shoji screens are painted with landscapes. There's also a small, charming garden with a miniature waterfall, a winding stream, and stone lanterns.

Another old home in the Nagamachi District open to the public has been converted into a Yuzen silk center, where you can watch artists at work painting intricate designs on silk. Closed on Thursday and open the rest of the week from 9 a.m. to noon and 1 to 4:30 p.m., the **Yuzen Silk Center (Saihitsu-an)** charges ¥500 ($3.57) admission, which includes a welcoming tea and a sweet. A video shows the process of Yuzen dyeing, and an English pamphlet describes the steps in detail. It can take up to six months to make one kimono of Yuzen hand-painted silk.

From the Nagamachi District it's just a few minutes' walk to **Oyama Jinja Shrine**, built in 1599 in dedication to the first Maeda lord, Toshiie Maeda. It possesses a three-story gate designed by a Dutchman in 1875, with stained-glass windows on the third floor.

Other Sights

If your interest lies in pottery, it's worth a visit to the **Kosen Pottery Kiln**, 20 minutes by bus from Kanazawa Station to the Nomachi bus stop. It's the only kiln within Kanazawa and shows the entire process of producing Kutani ware. Admission is free, and it's open from 9 a.m. to noon and 1 to 5 p.m.; closed Sunday afternoon.

Myoryuji Temple, 15 minutes by bus from Kanazawa Station to the Nomachi-Hirokoji bus stop and then a five-minute walk, is popularly known as the Ninja-dera (or Temple of the Secret Agents) because of its secret chambers, hidden stairways, tunnels, and trick doors. Although it's very interesting, you must make a reservation to see it (tel. 41-2877) and admission is ¥500 ($3.57). To make sure you don't get lost (which would be quite easy because of all the trick doors), you will be grouped with other visitors and led by a guide who unfortunately describes everything only in Japanese. The tour lasts about 30 minutes and you'll probably be able to make a reservation on the same day of your call. The temple was constructed to serve as an escape route for the Maeda lord in case the castle was attacked. A well at the temple was supposedly connected to the castle via a secret tunnel.

If you're in Kanazawa for more than one day you should consider taking an outing to Yuwaka Spa, where you'll find the **Edo-Mura Village**. About a 40-minute bus ride from Kanazawa Station, this is an open-air architectural museum with a collection of some 20 buildings from the Edo Period, including a samurai mansion, farmhouses, and shops. This museum provides unique insight into how the various social classes lived back in the feudal days. Open from 8 a.m. to 6 p.m. (to 5 p.m. in winter), it charges ¥900 ($6.43).

If you're interested in seeing the **Noto Peninsula**, there are many JR trains and buses that provide transportation throughout the area. The main attraction is the landscape, and various fares and timetables are provided in T.I.C.'s *Kanazawa and Noto Peninsula*.

SHOPPING: The most famous products of Kanazawa are its Kutani pottery, known for its bright five-color overglaze patterns and its hand-painted Yuzen silk. Kanazawa also produces toys, lacquerware, and wooden products. For one-stop shopping, visit the **Ishikawa Prefectural Kanko Bussankan** (tel. 22-7788), located close to Kenrokuen Garden (if you're arriving at Kenrokuen Garden via bus 10, 11, or 12 from Kanazawa Station, you'll get off the bus just a few steps away from the Bussankan). The ground and basement floors sell local products, the second floor is a restaurant, and the third floor houses the Ishikawa Prefectural Museum of Handicrafts, which charges a ¥200 ($1.43) admission to see artisans produce crafts of the area, including Kutani pottery, Japanese cakes, and lacquerware. Hours are from 9 a.m. to 6 p.m., closed Thursdays during the winter.

WHERE TO STAY: Most of Kanazawa's hotels are clustered conveniently around Kanazawa Station. There are also a few ryokan in the city, located in the older sections of town.

The Upper Bracket

Western Style: Conveniently located right in front of Kanazawa Station is the **Kanazawa Miyako Hotel**, 6-10 Konohanacho (tel. 0762/31-2202). First established in the 1960s and remodeled in 1984, it's part of the famous Miyako hotel chain and features 200 comfortable rooms, all well designed with attractive wood furniture and large windows. Each room comes with hot-water pot, alarm clock, double glass windows to shut out offending traffic noise, bilingual TV, and fridge. Singles start at ¥8,000 ($57); doubles, at ¥13,200 ($94); and twins at ¥14,300 ($102). A shopping arcade is connected to the hotel, there are both Western and Japanese restaurants, and there's a beer garden on the roof in the summer.

Holiday Inn Kanazawa, 1-10 Horikawa-cho (tel. 0762/23-1111), is similar to most Holiday Inns in Asia and foreigners should feel readily at home. Single rooms with double-size bed begin at ¥8,200 ($59); if you want a single room with a queen-size bed the cost is ¥11,000 ($79). Twins and doubles range from ¥14,300 ($102) to ¥16,500 ($118), and Japanese-style rooms for one to five persons are available for ¥26,000 ($186). All rooms have TV, refrigerator, a good-sized bathroom, and a water heater and tea bags. Built in the late 1970s, this 174 room hotel has four restaurants, including a Western-style restaurant and bar on the 14th floor with good views of the city, where piano music serenades every evening except Monday.

Opened in 1985, the **Kanazawa Tokyu Hotel** is one of the newest places to stay in town. A 16-story brick building rising from the heart of the city at 2-1-1 Kohrinbo (tel. 0762/31-2411), it's located close to Kanazawa's nightlife and is within walking distance of both the Nagamachi district and Kenrokuen Garden. The lobby and front desk are up on the second floor. Rooms are small and simple but pleasant, with V-shaped windows providing good views of the city. Rates are based on room size as well as height and range from ¥8,200 ($59) to ¥11,000 ($79) for a single, ¥17,600 ($126) to ¥18,700 ($134) for a double, and ¥15,400 ($110) to ¥18,000 ($129) for a twin. Regardless of which price category you select, ask for the highest floor available where the views are much better.

Japanese Style: South of Kanazawa Station in the heart of the city, **Miyabo** [150], Shimo Kakinokibatake 3 (tel. 0762/31-428), is close to Katamachi Shopping Street and within walking distance of Kenrokuen Garden. It boasts one of the oldest private gardens in Kanazawa, and part of the ryokan used to be the private tea house of Kanazawa's first mayor after the feudal age came to an end. Most of the ryokan's building dates from before World War II, although there is also a newer section. Per-person rates including two meals range from ¥11,000 ($79) to ¥30,000 ($214); the lowest price is for a room in the newer section, while the top price is for rooms with private views of the garden and more elaborately prepared meals. My favorite room is the one that used to be the mayor's tea ceremony room. Named "Bunte," with maroon walls, it's off by itself, secluded from the rest of the ryokan right in the middle of the garden. This room usually runs about ¥22,000 ($157) per person with two meals.

The Medium-Priced Range

Located across from the train station next to Miyako Hotel, the **Garden Hotel**, 2-16-16 Honcho (tel. 0762/63-3333), caters primarily to Japanese businessmen. This 147-room hotel opened in the mid-1980s and has a small, contemporary lobby with a restaurant that serves breakfast, lunch, and dinner. It offers tiny but nicely decorated singles with semi-double beds for ¥5,500 ($39) to ¥6,000 ($43), doubles for ¥7,700 ($55) to ¥10,000 ($71), and twins for ¥10,000 ($71) to ¥11,000 ($79). Rooms are equipped with refrigerator, hot-water pot and tea, TV with adult video, music, alarm clock, windows that can be opened, and panels that can be closed for complete darkness.

Just 1½ blocks south of the Garden Hotel with rooms that are similarly equipped is the **Hotel New Kanazawa**, 2-4-10 Honmachi (tel. 0762/23-2255). Another business hotel, this decade-old establishment has a small but homey lobby, a restaurant serving both Japanese and Western food, and a cozy lounge area on the second floor. Vending machines are located on the fifth floor. Rooms are rather plain but comfortable, and start at ¥6,000 ($43) for singles, ¥10,000 ($71) for doubles, ¥11,000 ($79) for twins, and ¥13,200 ($94) for triples.

The Budget Category

Western Style: A practical and attractive business hotel about a three-minute walk from Kanazawa Station, **Kanazawa Castle Inn**, 10-17 Konohanamachi (tel. 0762/23-6300), offers 96 simple but cheerful rooms. The bathtubs are miniature, but otherwise you'll find comfort in the refrigerator, hot-water pot and tea, TV with adult video, and radio. The cheapest singles, which offer a semi-double bed, begin at ¥5,000 ($36), while twins and doubles begin at ¥9,600 ($69). Prices include tax and service.

Less than a block away from Castle Inn and offering the same basic amenities is the **Oka Hotel**, 5-2 Horikawa (tel. 0762/63-5351). Although the front-desk staff doesn't speak much English, they are accommodating and friendly. This simply decorated business hotel which opened in the early 1980s offers singles without bathroom for ¥4,000 ($29) and singles with a private bathroom for ¥5,900 ($42). Doubles, all with bathroom, are ¥9,600 ($69), while twins range from ¥8,300 ($59) for those without bathroom to ¥11,800 ($84) for those with. Triples, in case you're interested, start at ¥10,800 ($77). The hotel's one restaurant serves both Japanese and Western selections, and there's a public bath. All rates include tax and service.

Japanese Style: A 12-minute bus ride from Kanazawa Station and then a three-minute walk, **Ryokan Murataya**, 1-5-2 Katamachi (tel. 0762/63-0455), is in the heart of Kanazawa not far from Katamachi Shopping Street and within walking distance of Kenrokuen Garden. A member of the Japanese Inn Group, it's modern-looking and rather uninteresting from the outside, but comfortable and pleasant on the inside. All 12 rooms are without bath or toilet and cost ¥4,000 ($29) for a single, ¥7,700 ($55) for a twin, and ¥9,900 ($71) for a triple. All rooms come with TV, air conditioning, and heating. Japanese breakfasts only are served, and cost ¥800 ($5.71). As the owner pointed out, there are plenty of coffeeshops nearby if you need your morning coffee to perform.

Yogetsu [151], 1-13-22 Higashiyama (tel. 0762/52-0497), is a delightful little minshuku in the middle of the old Higashiyama geisha district. This district of plain wooden buildings was set aside in the 1820s by the local government as a place where geishas could entertain. Yogetsu is a 100-year-old house that used to belong to a geisha and has only five guest rooms. Run by a jovial woman, it charges ¥5,500 ($39) per person for an overnight stay with two meals and ¥3,800 ($27) without meals. The rooms are rather plain, but the quiet and quaint atmosphere of the surrounding district more than make up for the lack of decor. It's located either a 20-minute walk or a 10-minute bus ride from Kanazawa Station.

Youth Hostels: The **Kanazawa Youth Hostel** [152], 37 Suehiro-cho (tel. 0762/52-3414), is a 25-minute bus ride away from Kanazawa Station and a bit far from all the attractions, but it has a nice location. Rooms here are both tatami and Western, and cost ¥3,500 ($25) for members and ¥4,000 ($29) for nonmembers. Note that nonmembers are not accepted during the busy summer season. Prices include breakfast and dinner.

About 20 minutes from Kanazawa Station is the **Matsui Youth Hostel** [153], 1-9-3 Kata-machi (tel. 0762/21-0275). Take bus 20 to the Katamachi bus stop. For youth-hostel members only, it sleeps 30 persons in tatami rooms (about six people to a room) for ¥2,300 ($16) per person. Nonmembers pay ¥500 ($3.57) more. Breakfast and dinner cost ¥450 ($3.21) and ¥700 ($5) respectively.

WHERE TO DINE: Kanazawa's local specialties are known collectively as *Kaga no aji* and consist of seafood (such as tiny shrimp and winter crabs) as well as freshwater fish and mountain vegetables.

Around Kenrokuen Garden

A great place to try the local Kaga cuisine is right in Kenrokuen Garden itself at the **Miyoshian** [154] (tel. 21-0127). This restaurant was built about 100 years ago and consists of three separate wooden buildings, the best of which was built extending over a pond. This is where you'll probably dine, seated on tatami with a view of an ancient pond and giant carp swimming in the murky waters below. Kaga cuisine here ranges from ¥5,500 ($39.29) to ¥11,000 ($78.57). You can also order à la carte for such dishes as jibuni stew (a chicken and vegetable stew eaten primarily in winter) for ¥770 ($5.50) and shrimp sashimi for ¥550 ($3.93). Set obento lunches range from ¥1,600 ($11.43) to ¥3,300 ($23.57). A jibuni teishoku which includes chicken stew, sashimi, pickled vegetables, rice, and soup is available for ¥1,600 ($11.43). Miyoshian is open from 10 a.m. to 5 p.m.

Another restaurant serving Kaga specialties is **Tozan** [155] (tel. 63-8666), located just outside the north entrance of Kenrokuen Garden. Open from 8 a.m. to 5 p.m. and catering largely to Japanese groups, it has a dining hall on the second floor and features tatami mats, shoji screens, and a wooden ceiling. Outside the front door you'll see the dishes named in English, so ordering is easy here. Meals range from ¥2,000 ($14.29) to ¥5,500 ($39.29). A jibuni stew course is served for ¥1,300 ($9.29).

Also located close to the north entrance of Kenrokuen Garden is an inexpensive udon noodle shop called **Takeda** [156] (tel. 21-3662). A simple restaurant with a few tables and tatami seating, it's located between Kenrokuen Garden's north entrance and the Ishikawa Prefectural Kanko Bussankan. Look for the black curtains hanging at its front door and a plastic-food display case of noodles. Noodles here start at ¥600 ($4.29). Hours are 10:30 a.m. to 6 p.m.; closed Friday.

The second floor of the **Kanko Bussankan** also features a large restaurant area with reasonably priced Japanese food, starting at ¥1,000 ($7.14) for such set courses as sashimi, tempura, noodles, and other common Japanese dishes, including Kaga cuisine. It's open from 11 a.m. to 5 p.m.; closed Thursday from November to March.

Katamachi Area

Just east of the Saigawa Ohashi Bridge is an area of restaurants and drinking establishments radiating out from the Katamachi Shopping and Chuo Dori

Streets. One of Kanazawa's best-known and most exclusive restaurants is **Zeniya** [157], 2-29-7 Katamachi (tel. 33-3331). It serves seasonal kaiseki meals of local specialties in cool, elegant surroundings for ¥11,000 ($78.57) to ¥16,500 ($117.86). Lunch is less expensive, with obento meals starting at ¥3,800 ($27.14) and mini-kaiseki offerings for ¥8,800 ($62.86). The presentation of each dish, naturally, is spectacular, and meals are by reservation only. Lunch is served from 11 a.m. to 2 p.m. and dinner from 5 p.m.; closed Sunday.

Located right down the street from Zeniya on the opposite side of the street is **Hamacho** [158], 2-31-32 Katamachi (tel. 33-3390). Open only in the evenings from 5 p.m. to midnight every day except Sunday and holidays, it offers seafood and vegetables in season. The menu, written on a blackboard unfortunately only in Japanese, changes according to what's fresh and available and may include *imo* (Japanese potatoes), freshly picked mushrooms, vegetables, various seafood selections, and sashimi. Courses are available beginning at ¥3,000 ($21.43), with most averaging ¥5,500 ($39.29). Just tell Mr. Ishigami, the owner and chief chef, how much you want to spend and he'll do the rest. If there's anything you don't like, be sure to tell him. Sit at the counter where you can watch your set course being prepared, which may include grilled fish or shrimp, noodles, tofu, sashimi, soup, and vegetables.

A bit kinder to the traveler's purse is the moderately priced **Kitama** [159], 2-3-3 Katamachi (tel. 61-7176). Sitting on tatami mats, you have a pleasant view of a small, moss-covered 100-year-old garden of tiny pines, stone lanterns, and rocks. I ordered the jibuni teishoku, which came with chicken stew, clear soup, pickled vegetables, rice, and hors d'oeuvres for ¥1,300 ($9.29). My friend opted for the Kojitsu Obento, served in an upright lunchbox; it featured such delicacies as sashimi, small pieces of pork and fish, fried shrimp, soybean patty, and various seasonal vegetables. Most meals here cost less than ¥3,000 ($21.43). The restaurant is closed Wednesday, but open the rest of the week from 11:30 a.m. to 9:30 p.m.

Part of a nationwide chain of inexpensive drinking establishments, **Irohanihoheto** [160], 2-23-7 Katamachi (tel. 21-1683), is located on the ground floor of the Prince Hotel. Decorated with crafts and heavy ceiling beams which are the trademarks of this chain, it's open daily from 5:30 p.m. to a respectable 4 a.m. Most items on the menu are less than ¥400 ($2.86) and include yakitori, grilled tofu, *nikujaga* (beef-and-potato stew), grilled fish, pizza, and salads. Beer starts at ¥350 ($2.50).

In case you feel like going out after dinner, next door to the Prince Hotel is **Ivory Coast** (tel. 22-1212), located in the basement of the Sunrose Katamachi Building. Cashing in on the latest craze for '50s and '60s American music, it features Japanese groups that imitate the real thing, with music ranging from Paul Anka, Neil Sedaka, and the Eagles to the Beatles. Open from 7 p.m. nightly, showtime begins at 8:30 p.m. The admission fee is ¥2,000 ($14.29) for males and ¥1,300 ($9.29) for females. Beer costs ¥500 ($3.57), and cocktails start at ¥650 ($4.64).

Around Kanazawa Station

The **Kanazawa Miyako Hotel**, 6-10 Konohanacho (tel. 31-2202), has both Japanese and Western restaurants on its seventh floor, each with large windows overlooking the city. Kakitsubata serves Japanese kaiseki meals for ¥6,600 ($47.14) and ¥11,000 ($78.57) and sashimi or tempura set courses starting at ¥3,300 ($23.57). You can also come here for lunch, when eel, sashimi or tempura, and obento box lunches are served for ¥1,600 ($11.43) to ¥3,300 ($23.57). Ordering is easy because the menu is in English.

Miyako's Western restaurant, the Belle Vue, is decorated in soft plum colors, with comfortable cushioned chairs and chandeliers providing a romantic setting. Piano music serenades on Saturday and Sunday nights. Dinners here are reasonable, starting at ¥4,400 ($31.43) and going up to ¥8,800 ($62.86). If you want to select your own combination of dishes, most entrées cost from ¥2,500 ($17.86) to ¥3,500 ($25) and include sole, steak, veal, lamb chops, and other seasonal choices. Set lunches range from ¥1,200 ($8.57) to ¥5,500 ($39.29). Hours for both Miyako restaurants are 11:30 a.m. to 2 p.m. and 5 to 10 p.m.

Incidentally, if you're more interested in downing a few pints rather than food, there's a beer garden atop the Miyako Hotel open from mid-May to the end of August every day except rainy ones from 5 to 9 p.m. Beer starts at ¥600 ($4.29) and the view is great.

If you're traveling on a budget, the **Shoan**, on the first floor of the Hotel New Kanazawa, 2-4-10 Honmachi (tel. 23-2255), serves both Western and Japanese dishes from 7:15 a.m. to 9:30 p.m. daily. Comfortably small with brilliant red walls, it offers everything from sashimi and sukiyaki to pork cutlet, lamb, and fish. Most dishes run from ¥1,300 ($9.29) to ¥3,000 ($21.43). It also serves Kaga cuisine for ¥3,800 ($27.14) and up.

4. Osaka

Although Osaka's history stretches back about 1,500 years, it first gained prominence when Hideyoshi Toyotomi built Japan's most magnificent castle here in the 16th century. To develop resources for his castle town, he persuaded merchants from other parts of the nation to resettle in Osaka. During the Edo Period the city became an important distribution center as feudal lords from the surrounding region sent their rice to merchants in Osaka. The merchants in turn sent the rice to Edo (present Tokyo) and other parts of the nation. As the merchants prospered, the town grew and such arts as Kabuki and Bunraku flourished. With money and leisure to spare, the merchants also developed a refined taste for food.

Nowadays Osaka is an industrial city with a population of almost 2.8 million, making it the third-largest city in Japan (after Tokyo and Yokohama). With inklings of its merchant beginnings still present, Osakans are usually characterized as being rather money-minded, and often greet one another with a saying that translates as "Are you making any money?" Today Osaka has a reputation throughout Japan for its food, its castle, and Bunraku puppet theater.

ORIENTATION: Osaka lies on the southern coast of western Honshu about three hours from Tokyo by Shinkansen bullet train. If you arrive in Osaka by Shinkansen, you'll find yourself at Shin-Osaka Station. To get from Shin-Osaka Station to Osaka Station and other points south, the most convenient mode of public transportation is the Midosuji subway line. The name of the subway stop at Osaka Station is called Umeda Station. JR trains also make runs between Shin-Osaka and Osaka stations.

If you arrive by plane at **Osaka International Airport**, you can take one of the airport limousine buses which make frequent runs to Shin-Osaka, Osaka, and Namba Stations. The trip to Osaka (Umeda) Station takes about a half hour and costs ¥360 ($2.57).

For getting around Osaka, there's a convenient subway network that's easy to use because all lines are color-coded and the station names are in English. The Midosuji Line is the most important one for visitors. It passes through Shin-

Osaka Station and then goes to Umeda (close to Osaka Station), Shinsaibashi, Namba, and Tennoji. There's also a JR train called the Osaka Kanjo Line which passes through Osaka Station and makes a loop around the city; take it to visit Osaka Castle.

With regard to hotels, shopping, restaurants, and nightlife, Osaka can be divided into two distinct parts: **Kita-ku**, the North Ward, which embraces the area around Osaka and Umeda stations; and **Minami-ku**, the South Ward, which is in the center of the JR loop train and includes the Shinsaibashi shopping district and a lively eating and entertainment district clustered around a narrow street called Dotonbori. Connecting the two areas is a wide boulevard lined with gingko trees called Midosuji Dori Avenue. It runs from Osaka Station south all the way to Namba Station.

The **Osaka Tourist Information Office** (tel. 06/345-2189) is located at the east exit of Osaka Station, open from 8 a.m. to 7 p.m. Its staff speaks English, gives out good maps of the city, and will also help in securing hotel rooms. Another tourist office is located between the east and central exits of Shin-Osaka Station, on the third floor (tel. 06/305-3311). It's open from 8 a.m. to 8 p.m.

For information on what's going on in Osaka, pick up a copy of *Kansai Time Out,* a monthly magazine with information on sightseeing, festivals, restaurants, and other items of interest pertaining to Osaka, Kobe, and Kyoto. Costing ¥300 ($2.14), it's available at bookstores, restaurants, and places frequented by English-speaking tourists.

The **telephone area code** for Osaka is 06. Osaka is in Osaka Prefecture.

WHAT TO DO: Osaka does not have many tourist sights, which means that you can cover the basics of the city in a one- or two-night stay. Top priority on your list here should be Osaka Castle, Bunraku, and dining.

Osaka Castle

Osaka Castle was built in the 1580s upon the order of Hideyoshi Toyotomi. In constructing the castle he requisitioned materials from his feudal generals, the most conspicuous of which were huge stones. The largest stone measures 19 feet high and 48 feet long, and is known as the "Higo-ishi." Upon its completion Osaka Castle was the largest castle in all of Japan, a magnificent structure used by Hideyoshi as a military stronghold as he waged war against rebellious feudal lords. By the time he died in 1598, Hideyoshi had succeeded in crushing his enemies and unifying Japan under his command.

After Hideyoshi's death, Ieyasu Tokugawa seized power and established his shogunate government in Edo. Toyotomi's heirs, however, still had ideas of their own and, considering Osaka Castle impregnable, they plotted to overthrow the Tokugawa government. In 1615 Ieyasu sent troops to Osaka, where they not only defeated the Toyotomi insurrectionists but destroyed Osaka Castle. Although the Tokugawas rebuilt the castle, they burned it down again in 1868 during the Meiji Restoration as they made their last retreat.

The present Osaka Castle dates from 1931. Built of ferroconcrete, it's not as massive as the original but is still quite large and impressive. Its eight-story donjon, or keep, rises to a height of 130 feet and houses a museum with displays relating to the Toyotomis and old Osaka, including armor, fans, and personal belongings. Hours are 9 a.m. to 4:30 p.m. and admission is ¥400 ($2.86). To reach Osaka Castle, take either the Kanjo loop line to Morinomiya or Osakajokoen Station or the subway to Temmabashi, Tanimachi 4-chome, or Morinomiya Station.

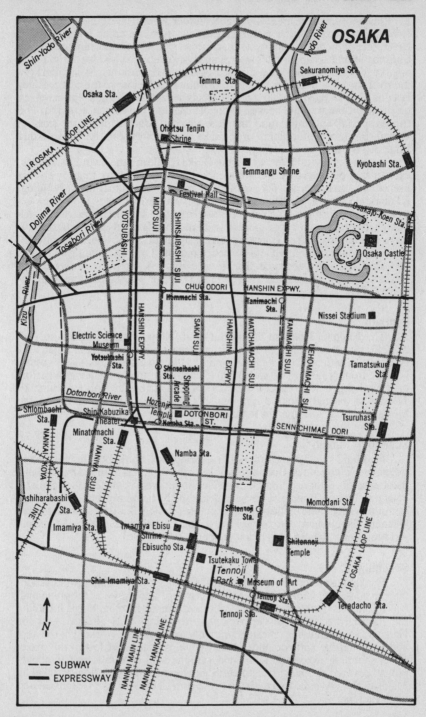

Since you're in the area, you might consider doing a few things in the vicinity of Osaka Castle. Just a few minutes' walk from the castle is the **O-Kawa River**, one of the many waterways that once served as an important avenue for transportation back in Osaka's merchant days. Although O-Kawa doesn't look anything like it used to, glass-enclosed boats (air-conditioned in summer) ply the river throughout the year, departing from a dock close to the castle. Rides last one hour and cost ¥1,500 ($10.71). Boats depart once an hour (at last check on the hour, but it would be wise to double-check) from 10 a.m. to 4 p.m. The trip is especially beautiful (and therefore crowded) during the cherry-blossom season. For more information or to make reservations, call the Osaka Aqua Liner at 444-5000.

Also just a few minutes' walk from Osaka Castle are the Twin 21 buildings, easy to spot because they are two identical-looking buildings that tower over everything. On the second floor of one of them, called National Tower Building, is **Panasonic Square,** a hall filled with electronics of various fields, including electronic communications (such as the TV telephone) and electronic games. Although it's designed for the Japanese (with most things explained in Japanese), there's enough to interest everyone, especially children. A robot, for example, can draw your portrait, while a periscope mounted on the building's roof lets you scan Osaka's panorama. Panasonic Square is open every day except Wednesday from 10 a.m. to 6 p.m., and admission is ¥200. For more information call 949-2122.

Bunraku

The **National Bunraku Theater**, 1-12-10 Nipponbashi, Minami-ku (tel. 212-2531), was completed in 1984 and presents traditional puppet theater six times a year, with most productions running a three-week stretch. Tickets usually range from ¥3,000 ($15) to ¥3,500 ($17.50). To find out whether a performance is being held, contact the Osaka Tourist Office. The National Bunraku Theater is located about a ten-minute walk from Namba Station on the Midosuji subway line or a few minutes from Nipponbashi Station.

Shitennoji Temple

First built in 593 at the order of Prince Shotoku, Shitennoji Temple is considered one of the oldest Buddhist temples in Japan (it was founded more than a decade before Horyuji Temple, outside Nara, was constructed). Popularly known as Tennoji Temple, it has been destroyed by fire many times through the centuries so that none of the original structures remain. Southwest of the temple is **Tennoji Park**, where you can visit a zoo, botanical gardens, and the Municipal Art Museum with both ancient and modern Oriental art.

Shopping

Osaka must rank as one of the world's leading cities in underground shopping arcades. The **Umeda Chika Center** is a huge underground shopping mall which connects Osaka and Umeda stations to a number of buildings, including the Hanshin and Hankyu department stores, Hankyu Sanbangai, and the Hankyu Grand Building. It caters primarily to the people working in the area and is so massive and complicated that you'll probably get lost in the maze. Other shopping areas include the underground mall at **Namba** and an aboveground covered shopping street near Shinsaibashi subway station. Paralleling Midosuji Dori Avenue to the east, it runs south all the way past Dotonbori and on to Namba.

Den Den Town is Osaka's electronics shopping region, similar to Tokyo's Akihabara (*Den* is short for "electric"). The nearest subway station is Nihombashi.

Nightlife

Osaka's liveliest—and most economical—nightlife district radiates from a narrow pedestrian lane called **Dotonbori,** which flanks the south bank of the Dotonbori River. About a five-minute walk from Namba Station, it's lined with restaurants and drinking establishments.

The best place to begin an evening of carousing, however, is not in Dotonbori itself but in the nearby **Nikko Hotel,** 7 Nishinocho (tel. 244-1111), which is located on Midosuji Dori Avenue. Head for the 32nd floor to the **Jet Stream,** where you have a dynamite view of the city, perfect for watching the sun go down and the lights of the city come on. More than 360 feet high, the Nikko Hotel is the tallest building in the area. Romantic with soft candlelight, it offers what it calls its Twilight Dinner every day from 5 to 7 p.m. A bargain at just ¥2,200 ($15.71), it offers a choice of entrée, salad, bread, and coffee.

From 7:30 to 11 p.m., Jet Stream features live jazz and popular music, for which it levies a ¥1,000 ($7.14) cover charge. On the second Friday of the month, the dance floor is expanded and a full band comes in to serenade dance tunes, for which the charge is ¥2,200 ($15.71). And on the fourth Saturday of the month it stages a big show with top personalities, charging an admission fee of about ¥4,000 ($28.57) per person. Beer starts at ¥700 ($5) and most cocktails average ¥1,100 ($7.86). Food is also available, with most entrées averaging between ¥2,000 ($14.29) and ¥5,500 ($39.29) for fried chicken, steak teriyaki, sautéed beef with green asparagus, and scallops gratin with mushroom sauce. There are also set dinners for ¥7,500 ($53.57), ¥8,800 ($62.86), and ¥11,000 ($78.57).

At the more frenzied end of the scale is **Maharaja,** located on the fifth floor of the Diamond Building, 24 Soemoncho (tel. 213-7090). Serving the needs of disco maniacs, it's open daily from 5:30 p.m. to midnight, charging ¥4,500 ($32.14) for males and ¥4,000 ($28.57) for females [on Saturday night and the eve before a holiday, rates go up ¥500 ($3.57)]. The entrance fee buys you ten tickets which you then trade in for drinks, which average about two tickets. The music is loud, and there are lots of mirrors so you can watch yourself dance. Maharaja is located on the first street paralleling Dotonbori River to the north, identified by a big sign that says "Soemon-Cho."

If all you want to do is drink, the **Pig and Whistle,** on the second floor of the Is Building at 43 Tatmiya-cho (tel. 213-6911), is probably the best-known expatriate bar in Osaka. However, because there aren't that many foreigners living in the city, the majority of customers here are Japanese. This bar used to be housed in a much more modest location but became so successful and popular that it moved to its present contemporary site in 1985. It's open from 4 p.m. to midnight (to 1 a.m. on weekends). A large beer here costs ¥650 ($4.64), and whisky and water is ¥500 ($3.57). Munchies include pizza and fish and chips.

Much newer and trendier is **Newz Bar,** 20-1 Mitsutera-cho (tel. 212-6063). It's located right on Midosuji Dori Avenue, just north of the Holiday Inn on the same side of the street, in a building called intriguingly enough Gourmet Tower Across—but across from what remains a mystery. Fashionable, with bare white walls, a marbled floor from Italy, and a large cactus in the corner, it's a good place from which to observe the world go stumbling by. Open from 11 a.m. to a formidable 6 a.m., it offers beer starting at ¥500 ($3.57), cocktails at ¥750 ($5.36), and wine from ¥550 ($3.93) a glass. Its food, mostly in the ¥600

($4.29) to ¥900 ($6.43) price range, includes pasta, pilafs, pizzas, sandwiches, and snacks.

Part of a chain that has 14 locations in Japan, the **Wine Bar,** on the third floor of the Awajiya Building, Soemon-cho (tel. 211-7736), serves wine by the glass beginning at ¥400 ($2.86) and is popular with young Japanese. A half liter of Suntory wine (a Japanese brand) begins at ¥1,100 ($7.86). It's located on the first street paralleling the Dotonbori River to the north (on the same street as Maharaja described above) and is open daily from 5 p.m. to 1 a.m. Along with wines from France, Germany, and California, it also offers such dishes as grilled spareribs, salads, short-neck clams simmered in white wine, quiche Lorraine, and a Spanish omelet.

If you happen to be much farther north, in the vicinity of Osaka Station, try **Studebaker's,** 2-4-12 Nakazakinishi (tel. 372-1950), located next to Umeda Center. Open daily from 11 a.m. to 4 p.m. and again from 5 p.m. to midnight (closed the third Sunday of every month), it's an enthusiastic re-creation of an American 1950s diner, complete with lots of chrome, red, white, and blue, as well as booths and counters. A sister shop to similar diners in Houston and Dallas, it offers a set lunch for ¥750 ($5.36) until 2 p.m. After 5 p.m. there's a ¥1,000 ($7.14) admission charge, which from 5 to 7 p.m. includes an all-you-can-eat buffet. A disc jockey plays golden oldies, and in an attempt to make this diner upscale, only persons older than 23 are admitted and jeans, sweat shirts, and tennis shoes are not allowed.

WHERE TO STAY: Like Tokyo, Osaka has a wide range of hotels, from first-class accommodations to business hotels. The majority are concentrated around Osaka Station, while the rest stretch to the south and around Shin-Osaka Station.

The Upper Bracket

Opened in 1984, the **ANA-Sheraton Hotel,** 1-3-1 Dojimahama, Kita-ku (tel. 06/347-1112), is a sleek white first-class hotel about a 15-minute walk south of Osaka Station. Its architectural philosophy is based on the concepts of running water, greenery, and ample sunlight, evident as soon as you enter the impressive lobby. An inner courtyard stretches up to a skylight on the sixth floor, from which water trickles along extended chains to a pond below. Facilities include a number of fine restaurants, a swimming pool and sauna, and an excellent guest relations desk where the staff will help in everything from directions to recommending nightspots in the vicinity. During July and August you can down beer on the hotel's outdoor patio. Its guest rooms are large and comfortably designed, and feature bilingual TVs with an English channel of sightseeing information and news, plug-in hot-water Thermos, English-language newspapers delivered both morning and afternoon, and excellent room service. Single rooms range from ¥13,200 ($94) to ¥17,600 ($126), twins run ¥22,000 ($157) to ¥27,500 ($196), and doubles cost ¥22,000 ($157) to ¥26,000 ($186).

The **Miyako Hotel Osaka,** 6-1-55 Uehommachi, Tennoji-ku (tel. 06/773-1111), opened in autumn 1985. Located close to Uehommachi Station of the Kintetsu Line, it was designed by the well-known Japanese architect Togo Murano, renowned for his ability to combine Japanese simplicity and tradition with modern efficiency. He recently died at the age of 91, so this Miyako Hotel was his last complete architectural achievement. It's a sister hotel to the famous Miyako Hotel in Kyoto, and the service is excellent. Facilities include a health club with swimming pool, racquetball courts, sauna, and serving everything from Japanese to Chinese to French cuisine. La Mer is an exclusive and expensive seafood restaurant specializing in seafood, while the Ciel Bleu up on the 21st floor offers French dishes and a view. In the basement are inexpensive restaurants, including those specializing in buckwheat noodles, tofu, and *okonomiyaki,* a local dish described later in the dining section. Guest rooms come with all the comforts you'd expect from a first-class hotel, including bilingual TV with CNN cable broadcasts from the United States, packets of soup and coffee along with tea, a stocked refrigerator, delivery of English-language newspapers twice a day, and semi-double beds in most rooms. Beds are decked with quilts instead of the usual heavy blankets. Rates start at ¥12,000 ($86) for a single, ¥18,700 ($134) for a double, and ¥22,000 ($157) for a twin.

Another new hotel—and Osaka seems to have a lot of them—is the **Hotel New Otani Osaka,** 1-4 Shiromi, Higashi-ku (tel. 06/941-1111). Located close to Osaka Castle, everything about this hotel is visually pleasing, right down to the elevators. The marbled lobby boasts a four-story atrium with a clever use of mirrors and skylights to give it an added airiness. Its fitness club facilities include indoor and outdoor swimming pools and four tennis courts, and although as with most hotel sports clubs a fee is charged, hotel guests can use the outdoor pool free during weekdays in the summer. Rooms are pleasant and comfortable and are equipped with semi-double beds, bilingual TVs with CNN newscasts from the United States, a radio, a mini-bar, a hair dryer, and windows that open. Rates are based on room size and whether you get a view of the castle. Singles range from ¥16,500 ($118) to ¥18,000 ($129), twins from ¥24,000 ($171) to ¥29,000 ($207), and doubles from ¥25,000 ($179) to ¥29,000 ($207). Among its many restaurants is the ever popular Trader Vic's.

Not to be outdone is the **Osaka Hilton International,** 1-8-8 Umeda, Kita-ku (tel. 06/347-7111), which opened in 1986. Conveniently located just a five-minute walk from the Central Exit of Osaka Station in the heart of the city, it has 553 double, twin, and suite rooms, with rates based on height and therefore view. Single occupancy ranges from ¥17,600 ($126) to ¥26,000 ($186), while double occupancy ranges from ¥21,500 ($154) to ¥32,000 ($220). Decorated in subtle blends of Japanese and Western styles, rooms feature soothing color combinations of pale peach and celadon green, shoji screens, bilingual TV with CNN newscasts and remote control, a radio, a mini-bar, and large full-length mirrors. Facilities include a fitness center with pool, tennis court, sauna, and gym; a multitude of restaurants; and an adjoining shopping arcade.

Just a few years older than the newer hotels, the elegant **Hotel Nikko Osaka,** 7 Nishinocho, Daihoji-machi, Minami-ku (tel. 06/244-1111), is owned by Japan Air Lines. Located on fashionable Midosuji Boulevard, it has a striking architectural design with slanted walls. It's only a seven-minute walk from the hotel to Dotonbori Street, the heart of Osaka's nightlife district with its many restaurants. The hotel's service is excellent and there's a guest relations desk to answer any questions you may have regarding Osaka or the hotel. About 30% to 40% of hotel guests are foreigners, mainly Americans. Rooms are equipped with bilingual TV featuring CNN, with movies shown on weekends. On the 27th floor are rooms designed by Hanae Mori, one of Japan's best-known fashion designers. Rates range from ¥13,200 ($94) to ¥18,000 ($129) for a single, ¥22,500 ($161) to ¥28,000 ($200) for a twin, and ¥22,000 ($157) to ¥26,000 ($186) for a double.

One of Osaka's most established hostelries is the **Royal Hotel,** 5-3-68 Nakanoshima, Kita-ku (tel. 448-1121). First opened about 40 years ago but now completely remodeled, it's located on an island called Nakanoshima in the middle of a river in the heart of Osaka. One of the largest hotels in Osaka, it boasts

1,300 guest rooms, almost two dozen restaurants, two beautifully designed swimming pools and a health club, and a shopping arcade with more than 40 boutiques. The lobby has views of a waterfall surrounded by trees. Its rooms sport large windows, bilingual TVs with CNN, and English-language newspapers delivered twice daily. Singles start at ¥13,700 ($98), twins and doubles both at ¥25,000 ($179). The nearest subway stop is Yodoyabashi Station on the Midosuji Line; free shuttle buses make runs between this station and the hotel every 15 minutes.

The **Plaza**, 2-2-49 Oyodo-Minami, Oyodo-ku (tel. 06/453-1111), was one of Osaka's first deluxe hotels (it opened in 1970). It's about a seven-minute taxi ride west of Osaka Station. Facilities here include an outdoor swimming pool, six restaurants, two lounges, and three bars. Its Rendezvous French restaurant on the 23rd floor is one of Osaka's best. Foreigners constitute about 30% of the hotel's guests. Rooms are large and come with the usual amenities of hot-water pot, bilingual TV with CNN, mini-bar, and radio. Rates begin at ¥10,500 ($75) for a single, ¥20,000 ($143) for a twin, and ¥18,700 ($134) for a double.

The Medium-Priced Range

Since it's right beside Osaka Station, the **Osaka Terminal Hotel**, 3-1-1 Umeda, Kita-ku (tel. 06/344-1234), is very convenient for a one-night stay in the city. But because its lobby is on the ground floor with doors that open right into the train station, it's also very hectic and busy. Thankfully, its 665 guest rooms are located above all this confusion up on the 21st to 26th floors. Opened in 1983, this tourist hotel caters to a 20% foreign clientele and has nine restaurants and bars, many of them located on the 19th floor with grand views of the city. Rooms are cheerful and have double-pane windows, a pot for heating water, radio, alarm clock, refrigerator, and TV with CNN. The cheapest singles and twins face an inner courtyard—they're quieter, but you're missing a great view of the city. Rates range from ¥9,300 ($66) to ¥12,000 ($86) for a single, ¥16,500 ($118) to ¥24,000 ($171) for a double, and ¥17,600 ($126) to ¥26,400 ($189) for a twin.

Hotel New Hankyu, 1-1-35 Shibata, Kita-ku (tel. 06/372-5101), opened in 1964 but is so well maintained it doesn't seem nearly that old. As part of the conglomerate that owns Hankyu Railways, Hankyu department stores, restaurants, and even a baseball team, this hotel is located just north of Hankyu Station next to Osaka Station. There are more than 1,000 rooms here, all with TV with pay video, clock, music, and double-pane windows. Vending machines dispense soda and beer. The decor is simple and resembles that found in business hotels. Altogether there are 21 bars and restaurants in the hotel and in the neighboring Hankyu complex. You'll pay ¥8,200 ($59) to ¥11,000 ($79) for a single, ¥14,300 ($102) to ¥19,800 ($141) for a twin, and ¥16,500 ($118) to ¥19,200 ($137) for a double. Triples are available for ¥23,000 ($164) and Japanese-style tatami rooms start at ¥20,000 ($143) for double occupancy.

Part of a nationwide hotel chain, the **Osaka Tokyu Inn**, 2 Doyama-cho, Kita-ku (tel. 06/315-0109), is your typical standard business hotel. Its one restaurant serves Western food, and its 402 rooms are quiet and clean, featuring clock, desk, TV, fridge, and small bathroom. Vending machines are on the seventh floor. Singles start at ¥8,400 ($60), and twins and doubles at ¥14,000 ($100), tax and service included. The Tokyu is about a ten-minute walk east of Osaka Station, but it's a bit confusing to find because the most direct way to get there is via an underground passageway lined with shops. Follow the signs that say "Ogimachi" until they bring you above ground—you should be able to spot the Tokyu from there.

The **Holiday Inn Nankai**, 28-1 Kuzaemon-cho, Minami-ku (tel. 06/213-8281), has a very convenient location close to Dotonbori and Osaka's nightlife district. The lobby is on the fifth floor, and the rooftop pool, open free to hotel guests during the summer months, is a plus. There's also an outdoor beer garden on the third floor, open daily from 5 to 9 p.m. from the end of May to the end of August. Four restaurants serve French, Chinese, American, and Japanese cuisine. As with all Holiday Inns, all beds are doubles, even those in single rooms, and the rooms are large. Rates for one person start at ¥12,000 ($86), for two persons, at ¥19,800 ($141).

Hotel Osaka Grand, 2-3-18 Nakanoshima, Kita-ku (tel. 06/202-1212), is a fine, medium-priced hotel located on the island of Nakanoshima in a river in the heart of Osaka. Dating from 1960, it's also one of Osaka's older hotels and has aged gracefully. The lobby is small and cozy and evokes an atmosphere of decades past with its high ceiling and old decor. Its 357 rooms start at ¥10,200 ($73) for a single, ¥17,600 ($126) for a twin and ¥18,000 ($129) for a double. As proof of its age, the bathrooms are covered with tile instead of the usual plastic, and all rooms come with radio, clock, TV with bedside control buttons, and a pot for hot water. I prefer the rooms that face the river—although there's no traffic on the river and there's nothing to see, it at least affords a bit of spaciousness.

The **Tennoji Miyako Hotel**, 10-48 Hidein-cho, Tennoji-ku (tel. 06/779-1501), is a medium-priced tourist hotel belonging to the Miyako hotel chain. It's right over the train tracks of Tennoji Station, which you can reach via the Midosuji subway line from either Shin-Osaka or Osaka Station. The front desk is on the fifth floor. A small hotel with only 150 rooms, it first opened in 1960 but has been renovated frequently. Even the single rooms here are spacious. Bathrooms are tiled and large, and wide windows let in a lot of sunshine. Decor is simple but tasteful, and rooms are equipped with a pot for hot water, TV, clock, and double-pane windows. The hotel's one restaurant serves Western food. Rooms without private bathroom are ¥6,000 ($43) for a single and ¥11,000 ($79) for a twin. Rooms with private bathroom start at ¥8,200 ($59) for a single, ¥13,000 ($93) for a twin, and ¥13,700 ($98) for a double. Japanese-style rooms start at ¥13,000 ($93).

Hotel California, 24 Nishinocho, Daihoji-cho, Minami-ku (tel. 06/243-0333), tries to evoke images of sunny California through its use of whites and greens, plants, and brass railings. Rooms are cheerfully decorated in soft pastels with rattan furniture, and come with TV with pay video, radio, clock, hot-water pot, and refrigerator. Rates start at ¥6,600 ($47) for a single, ¥10,000 ($71) for a double, and ¥12,000 ($86) for a twin. The California is conveniently located in Minami-ku, not far from the Nikko Hotel and between the Yotsubashi and Shinsaibashi subway stations.

There are a few hotels located close to Shin-Osaka Station, but because the area is unexciting and industrial I suggest staying at one of the hotels listed above. If you find it more convenient to stay close to the Shinkansen station, however, try the **New Osaka Hotel**, 5-14-10 Nishi-Nakajima, Yodogawa-ku (tel. 06/305-2345). It's about a two-minute walk from the central exit of the station and caters almost exclusively to Japanese businessmen (most of its 304 rooms are singles). Rooms are simply decorated and come with refrigerator and TV with pay video. Because the building is sandwiched in between two other buildings, all but 76 of the rooms face a wall. If you want to have more of a view, be sure to ask. Singles range from ¥5,500 ($39) to ¥7,000 ($50), twins are ¥11,500 ($82), doubles are ¥11,000 ($79), and Japanese-style rooms are ¥12,500 ($89). A restaurant on the 13th floor serves Chinese and Western food.

Another business hotel close to Shin-Osaka Station, the **Chisan Hotel**, 6-2-19 Nishi-Nakajima, Yodogawa-ku (tel. 06/302-5571), is about a seven-minute walk from the central exit of the station. Part of a business-hotel chain, this Chisan is older than most and its rooms are little more than just that. If all you want is a bed and a coin-operated TV, this is the place for you. Rooms are tiny, bathrooms are minuscule, and windows are small. Rates start at ¥6,000 ($43) for a single and ¥9,600 ($69) for a twin, tax and service included.

If you find yourself with a stopover at Osaka International Airport, try the **Osaka Airport Hotel**, located right in the airport terminal building (tel. 06/855-4621). There are 105 rooms here, and they come with TV, fridge, and a pot for hot water. Singles start at ¥9,300 ($66), and twins and doubles, at ¥16,500 ($118).

The Budget Category

Hotel Hokke Club [161], 12-19 Togano-cho, Kita-ku (tel. 06/313-3171), first opened about 37 years ago and is one of Osaka's oldest business hotels. Located about a ten-minute walk east of Osaka Station, it has rooms without private bathrooms, but there are large public baths separate for men and women. Rooms are small but adequate. If you're taking a single, request a corner room since the other singles face an inner courtyard and are dark. Rooms are available in either Western or Japanese style, and go for ¥5,900 ($42) for a single and ¥10,000 ($71) for a twin. Prices include tax, service, and buffet-style breakfast. If you elect to take your breakfast elsewhere, rates are ¥800 ($5.71) cheaper.

Ebisu-so, 1-7-33 Nipponbashi-Nishi, Naniwa-ku (tel. 06/643-4861) is a Japanese-style inn located a 10-minute walk from the Kintetsu Nipponbashi Station, a 15-minute walk from Namba Station, or a 5-minute walk from the Ebiso-cho subway station. A member of the Japanese Inn Group, it's more cluttered and run-down than most (it's been an inn for 30 years). There are 13 tatami rooms, all without private bathroom, but of course there's a public bath. This inn reminds me of a small apartment house where young single Japanese often live—a narrow corridor flanked on both sides with 4½- and 6-tatami rooms. I have friends who say they like living in a 4½-tatami room because they can reach everything without having to move. At any rate, rates here are certainly cheap: singles go for ¥3,300 ($23); twins, for ¥5,500 ($39); and triples, for ¥8,200 ($59). Rooms come with coin-operated TV, fan, and heater.

Another inexpensive Japanese-style accommodation is **Masumi**, 2-12-4 Miyakojima-Hondori, Miyakojima-ku (tel. 921-0597). All but eight of the rooms have their own private bathroom, and since there's no public bath facilities here, don't take the bathless room for ¥3,000 ($21) unless you're broke, clean, or are willing to go to a public bath, which will cost about ¥200 ($1.43) anyway. You're better off taking a room with bath which goes for ¥3,300 ($24) per person. Breakfasts are available for ¥500 ($3.57). Rooms could do with a bit of cheering up and a good spring cleaning. Masumi is a three-minute walk from Miyakojima Station on the Tanimachi subway line.

If you want to stay near Shin-Osaka Station, **Shin-Osaka Sen-i City** [162], 2-2-17 Nishi-Miyahara, Yodogawa-ku (tel. 06/394-3331), is a very simple business hotel with 70 rooms. It's about an eight-minute walk north of the station, and is easy to spot with its green-and-blue sign and clock on the top of the building. The lobby is on the sixth floor and guest rooms are on the sixth and seventh floors. The rooms are a few decades away from being modern, but they're clean, good for the price, and fairly large as far as business hotels go. They come with refrigerator and coin-operated TV with pay video. All the singles and most twins are bathless, and go for ¥4,100 ($29) and ¥7,000 ($50) respectively, but there are public baths. Eight twins with Western-style toilet and Japanese-style bathtub are ¥7,700 ($55). Although there's no tax levied on prices, this establishment is different from most hotels in this category in that it adds a 10% service charge.

A business hotel about a five-minute walk from Osaka International Airport is **Kurebe**, 1-9-6 Kuko, Ikeda-shi (tel. 06/843-7201). A lot of business people stay here if they have an early-morning flight. Simple, with just the basics of a bed and TV, singles here range from ¥6,000 ($43) to ¥7,700 ($55). Twins run ¥11,000 ($79) to ¥14,300 ($102), and doubles are ¥14,300 ($102).

Youth Hostels: The **Osaka-Shiritsu Nagai Youth Hostel** [163], 450 Higashinagai-cho, Higashi-sumiyoshi (tel. 06/699-5632), is located on municipal sports grounds which even have a swimming pool. You don't have to have a membership card to stay here, and the overnight price of ¥1,500 ($10.71) is the same for both members and nonmembers. Sheets rent for ¥200 ($1.43), while air conditioning costs are an additional ¥250 ($1.79). Breakfast costs ¥350 ($2.50) and dinner is ¥600 ($4.29). To reach the youth hostel, take the Midosuji subway line to Nagai Station (about a 20-minute ride from Umeda Station); from there it's a 15-minute walk.

Hattori Ryokuchi Youth Hostel [164], 1-3 Hattori-ryokuchi, Toyonaka-shi (tel. 06/862-0600), is a 45-minute subway ride on the Midosuji Line from Umeda Station. Get off at Ryokuchi-koen Station and from there it's a ten-minute walk. Both members and nonmembers are charged ¥1,500 ($10.71) for an overnight stay. Breakfast costs ¥300 ($2.14) and dinner is ¥500 ($3.57). Sheets are an extra ¥100 (71¢).

WHERE TO DINE: There's a saying among Japanese that whereas a Kyotoite will spend his last yen on a fine kimono, an Osakan will spend it on food. You don't have to spend a lot of money to enjoy good food in Osaka, however. Most of Osaka's restaurants are found either in Kita-ku near Osaka Station or in Minami-ku on or near Dotonbori Street. The best Western-style restaurants are in Osaka's first-class hotels. Be sure to check the nightlife section.

In Kita-ku

Japanese Style: At 1-1-11 Sonezaki-shinchi (tel. 341-2381), **Kagaman** [165] is a kaiseki restaurant located a few minutes' walk north of the ANA-Sheraton Hotel. It has a simple interior but is very popular because of the excellent quality of its cuisine. In fact, it's sometimes so full at night that you should make reservations if you want to come for dinner. Although the menu is in Japanese only, there are set meals available which make ordering easy. Full kaiseki courses of seasonal food cost ¥14,300 ($102), ¥17,600 ($126), and ¥22,000 ($157). Mini-kaiseki courses are available for ¥6,000 ($43), ¥7,700 ($55), and ¥11,000 ($79), served until 3 p.m. Hours here are 11:30 a.m. to 10:30 p.m.; closed Sunday and national holidays.

Part of the Suehiro chain of steak restaurants in Japan, **Suehiro Asahi** [166], 1-5-2 Sonezaki-shinchi (tel. 341-1610), is conveniently located about a seven-minute walk south of Osaka Station. Serving Matsuzaka beef as well as beef imported from the United States, it offers shabu-shabu and sukiyaki specials ranging from ¥4,400 ($31.43) to ¥11,000 ($78.57). Prices for steak range widely depending on the weight and cut. Sirloin starts at ¥6,000 ($43), while tenderloin steak starts at ¥4,500 ($32.14). If you come for lunch you can also order such dishes as fried shrimp, beef stew, beef or pork cutlet, a hamburger, or fried fish, priced from ¥600 ($4.29) to ¥1,800 ($12.86).

Serving everything from sushi to tempura to shabu-shabu, **Unkai**, on the sixth floor of the ANA-Sheraton Hotel, 1-3-1 Dojimahama (tel. 347-1112), is a good place to go if you can't decide on just one type of cuisine. Open daily from 11:30 a.m. to 2:30 p.m. and 5:30 to 10 p.m., this simple and pleasant restaurant has both a sushi and a tempura counter where the food is prepared in front of the guests, as well as individual tables and chairs. Tempura ranges from ¥4,400 ($31.43) to ¥7,700 ($55), while the sushi runs from ¥1,000 ($7.14) to ¥2,000 ($14.29) for two pieces. A sushi teishoku set meal is served at lunch only for ¥2,200 ($15.71). Shabu-shabu is available for ¥7,000 ($50), and kaiseki dinners range from ¥8,800 ($62.86) to ¥16,500 ($117.86).

A specialty of Osaka is *okonomiyaki,* which literally means "as you like it." Its origins date from about 1700 when a type of thin flour cake cooked on a hot plate was served during Buddhist ceremonies. The cake was filled with a bean paste called *miso.* It wasn't until this century that it became popular among the masses, primarily during food shortages. At first it was a simple dish consisting only of flour, water, and a sauce, but gradually other ingredients such as pork, egg, and vegetables were added.

Osaka is literally riddled with okonomiyaki restaurants offering very inexpensive dining. One of the best-known establishments in **Botejyu**, a chain store with one shop located in the second basement of the Hankyu Sanbangai Building, next to Osaka Station (tel. 374-2254), open from 11 a.m. to 10 p.m. (except the third Wednesday of the month). Most of its dishes range from ¥600 ($4.29) to ¥1,200 ($8.57). Its window display shows okonomiyaki filled with pork and egg, squid, rice and shrimp, noodles and pork, and many other ingredients in various combinations. I tried the *oma soba,* a type of omelet filled with cabbage, wheat noodles, and pork and smothered in ketchup and mayonnaise. Cooking is done on a hot griddle right in front of you, and dishes are served on sheets of aluminum foil.

Probably a bit easier to find is **Okonomiyaki Madonna**, located in the second basement of the Hilton Plaza next to the Hilton Hotel. 1-8-8 Umeda (tel. 347-7371). Following the recent trend of modern and with-it okonomiyaki restaurants, Madonna is open daily from 11 a.m. to 11 p.m. Ingredients for its okonomiyaki change with the seasons but may include pork, beef, squid, octopus, shrimp, potato, mushroom, or oyster. Okonomiyaki with one ingredient is ¥1,000 ($7.14), with two it's ¥1,250 ($8.93), and with three it's ¥1,500 ($10.71). Fried noodles are also available. Madonna is located across from Victoria Station, described later in this chapter.

If you want inexpensive dining with a view, there are many restaurants on the top floors of the **Hankyu Grand Building** near Osaka Station. On the 28th floor, for example, there are restaurants serving everything from shabu-shabu to tonkatsu (pork cutlet) to noodles to tempura and sashimi. Prices are generally low, with most meals costing about ¥1,500 ($10.71) to ¥2,000 ($14.29). All the restaurants have plastic-food displays, so ordering is no problem. Hours for most are 11 a.m. to 8:45 p.m.

Western Style: The ANA-Sheraton Hotel's **Rose Room**, 1-3-1 Dojimahama (tel. 347-1112), is an elegant French restaurant serving nouvelle cuisine. Popular with local Osakans, its chef, Tomoyoshi Yokota, studied French cooking in France for six years and worked as a chef at the well-known Le Rendezvous in the Osaka Plaza Hotel before joining the Sheraton as grand chef in 1984. Small, with seating for only 59 diners, it features a huge bouquet of roses as its focal point and makes dining intimate with low lighting and candles. You might want to start your meal with one of the hotel's specially made cocktails. Rose d'Or uses a mixture of three different kinds of wines, while Symphonie en Rose is made from Campari and white wine.

For dinner you might want to start out with Norwegian smoked salmon with capers or a light soufflé of escargots served with garlic-scented parsley, followed by chilled lobster soup with sour cream or mousse of red pimento gazpacho soup. The seafood selection includes soufflé of turbot with sea urchin, steamed slices of sea bass, and lobster gratin with spinach. Entrées include hashed duck and sweetbread with mashed potatoes, roasted rack of lamb, duck, veal, and steak. Expect to spend about ¥15,000 ($107.14) and up per person for dinner. There are also set dinners ranging from ¥10,000 ($71.43) to ¥17,600 ($125.71). Set lunches start at ¥5,500 ($39.29). The Rose Room is open daily from 11:30 a.m. to 2:30 p.m. and 5:30 to 10 p.m.

Another popular and well-known French restaurant in Osaka is **Le Rendezvous**, on the 23rd floor of the Plaza Hotel, 2-2-49 Oyodo-Minami, Oyodo-ku (tel. 453-1111). Advising on its creations are internationally known chefs Paul Bocuse and Louis Outhier. Outhier is the owner and chef of L'Oasis on the Côte d'Azur, which has a three-star rating from Michelin. Le Rendezvous is the only Asian member of Traditions et Qualité, a prestigious gastronomical association of French restaurants. With windows overlooking Osaka, this restaurant serves such à la carte selections as Kobe sirloin and tenderloin steaks, duck, sole stuffed with artichoke and basil, and young rabbit leg, with meals running ¥13,000 ($92.86) per person and more. Le Rendezvous is open daily from 11:30 a.m. to 2:30 p.m. and 5:30 to 10:30 p.m.

If you're looking for more casual and cheaper dining, **Victoria Station**, in the second basement of the Hilton Plaza next to the Hilton Hotel (tel. 347-7470), serves a mean hamburger with a trip to the salad bar for ¥1,000 ($7.14) daily until 4:30 p.m. Other lunch selections include teriyaki beef steak beginning at ¥880 ($6.29), sirloin steak beginning at ¥1,700 ($12.14), and seafood quiche, beef rib, and chicken, all for ¥1,000 ($7.14). The dinner menu also includes steaks, roast prime rib, and chicken, most under ¥2,200 ($15.71). Set dinner courses, which include a trip to the salad bar, soup, and more start at ¥4,200 ($30). Victoria Station is open from 11 a.m. to 11 p.m. daily.

There are a couple of medium-priced hotels that have inexpensive lunch buffets at very good prices. Up on the 19th floor of the **Osaka Terminal Hotel**, 3-1-1 Umeda, above Osaka Station (tel. 344-1234), is a daily smörgåsbord at the Pub Restaurant from 11 a.m. to 2 p.m. with a wide selection of dishes. Very popular with Osaka's residents, it costs only ¥1,000 ($7.14). You can dine here with a great view of the city, but get here by 11:30 a.m. if you don't want to wait for a table.

The Osaka Grand Hotel, 2-3-18 Nakanoshima (tel. 202-1212), offers both lunch and dinner buffets in its Grand Sky restaurant on the 14th floor. The lunch smörgåsbord, served from 11:30 a.m. to 2 p.m. every day except Sunday and national holidays, cost ¥2,400 ($17.14). A dinner buffet is served daily from 5 to 9:30 p.m., costing ¥5,400 ($38.57).

Minami-ku

Dotonbori Street, a narrow pedestrian lane flanking the south bank of the Dotonbori River, is lined with restaurants and drinking establishments. One of the best-known restaurants on Dotonbori is **Kuidaore** [167], 1-8-25 Dotonbori (tel. 211-5300). It's famous for its clown model outside the front door, which has been beating a drum and wriggling its eyebrows ever since the place first opened in 1949. This restaurant offers eight floors of dining at inexpensive prices, and can serve up to 700 persons at one time. There's an extensive plastic-food display case by the front door, and an English menu is available. It serves a wide variety of Japanese cuisine, including tempura, sashimi, charcoal-broiled beef, shabu-shabu, eel, sukiyaki, yakitori, and noodles. Meals start at ¥1,400 ($10) for a tempura dinner and go up to ¥6,500 ($46.43) for its special sukiyaki dinner. Pieces of sushi range from ¥160 ($1.14) to ¥330 ($2.36) for such delicacies as raw tuna, shrimp, octopus, squid, yellowtail, or salmon roe. There are also combination sushi plates starting at ¥1,000 ($7.14) as well as kaiseki courses which change monthly for ¥5,500 ($39.29) and ¥7,700 ($55). Hours are 10:30 a.m. to 10:30 p.m.

Also on Dotonbori is another well-known restaurant, **Kani Doraku** [168], 1-6-18 Dotonbori (tel. 211-8975). Open from 11 a.m. to 11 p.m. daily, its specialty is crab *(kani)*. You can't miss this place because it has a huge model crab on its façade which moves its legs and claws. The restaurant is part of a chain originating in Osaka a couple of decades ago with more than 50 stores now spread throughout Japan. Its dishes range from crab-suki and crab-chiri (a kind of crab sukiyaki) for ¥4,400 ($31.43) to fried crab dishes starting at ¥2,700 ($19.29). Other offerings include boiled hairy crab with vinegar starting at ¥3,800 ($27.14), crab tempura starting at ¥1,300 ($9.29), and various combinations of crab sushi.

Under the same ownership as Kani Doraku, but specializing in shrimp, **Ebi Doraku** [169] is also on Dotonbori Street at 1-6-2 Dotonbori (tel. 211-1633). *Ebi* is the Japanese word for shrimp. Opened about 20 years ago, this restaurant has a big wriggling shrimp on its façade and a dining room overlooking the canal and its fountains. There's no English menu here, so make your selections from the plastic-food display case. It's open from 11 a.m. to 11 p.m. daily. Most dishes range from ¥1,500 ($10.71) to ¥4,500 ($32.14) and include ebi-shi (a shrimp sukiyaki), ebi tempura, fried shrimp, and shrimp sushi. If you feel like overdosing on shrimp, the kaiseki ebi teishoku for ¥6,200 ($44.29) features nine different kinds of shrimp dishes.

Located on Dotonbori Street almost directly in front of Kuidaore and beside Kani Doraku, the Dohton Biru Building, 1-6-15 Dotonbori, has several different kinds of restaurants. On the second floor is another **Botejyu** (tel. 211-3641), selling okonomiyaki from 11:30 a.m. to 10:30 p.m. daily. Also on the second floor is a **Shakey's** (tel. 213-7624) pizza parlor with its all-you-can-eat lunch special from 11 a.m. to 2:30 p.m. Monday through Saturday for ¥600 ($4.29). On the third floor is **Moti** (tel. 211-6878), an Indian restaurant open from 11:30 a.m. to 10 p.m. daily with various meat and vegetable curries from ¥1,000 ($7.14) and tandoori from ¥1,370 ($9.79).

Near the Castle

If you find yourself in the vicinity of the castle come lunchtime, a good choice is **Trader Vic's,** open daily from noon to midnight in the New Otani Hotel, 1-4 Shiromi (tel. 941-1111). It serves a daily luncheon special until 3 p.m. for ¥2,000 ($14.29), as well as a champagne brunch on Sunday for ¥3,800 ($27.14). Dinners offer a wider selection, including salads, a good selection of vegetable side dishes, curries, steaks, seafood, and Chinese dishes.

5. Kobe

Blessed with the calm waters of the Seto Inland Sea, Kobe has served Japan as an important port town for centuries. Even today its port is the heart of the city, its raison d'être, and the people of Kobe seem to possess those special qualities of pride and contentment with their city, of being satisfied with where they are. As one of the first ports to begin accepting foreign traders in 1868 following Japan's 200-some years of isolation, Kobe is quite cosmopolitan, with 45,000 foreigners living in this vibrant city of 1.5 million inhabitants. There are a number of fine restaurants serving Western, Japanese, Chinese, Korean, and Indian food, not to mention the many steakhouses offering the famous Kobe beef. Equally famous is Kobe's wonderful nightlife, crammed into a small, navigable, and rather intimate quarter of neon lights, cozy bars, brawling pubs, and sophisticated nightclubs. As one resident of Kobe told me, "We don't have a lot of tourist sights in Kobe, so we make up for it in nightlife."

ORIENTATION: Squeezed in between hills rising in the north and the shores of the sea in the south, Kobe stretches long and thin along the coastline. The city is about 18 miles from east to west—but in many places less than two miles wide—and is made up of many wards *(ku)*, such as Nada-ku, Chuo-ku, and Hyogo-ku. The heart of the city lies around the Sannomiya and Motomachi stations in the Chuo-ku ward. It's here that you'll find the city's nightlife, its port, its restaurants and shopping district, and most of its hotels. Many of the major streets here have names with signs posted in English. Because the city is not very wide, you can walk to most points north and south of Sannomiya Station. South of Sannomiya Station are the Sannomiya Center Gai covered-arcade shopping street and a flower-lined road leading straight south, towards the port—called appropriately enough Flower Road. North of Sannomiya Station are bars and restaurants clustered around narrow streets like Higashimon Street and Kitano Dori. About a ten-minute walk west of Sannomiya Station is Motomachi Station, south of which lies Chinatown.

Only 3½ hours from Tokyo by Shinkansen bullet train, Kobe's Shinkansen station is called Shin-Kobe, which lies about a mile northwest of Sannomiya Station. Shin-Kobe is easily linked to Sannomiya Station via a three-minute subway ride. If you're arriving in Kobe from nearby Osaka, Himeji, or Okayama, however, it's easiest to take a local commuter train that stops directly at Sannomiya Station. Incidentally, there are several terminals in Sannomiya, including stations for JR, Hankyu, and Hanshin. There are also buses from Sannomiya bound for Osaka International Airport, leaving approximately every 20 minutes. The trip takes 40 minutes and costs ¥680 ($4.86).

There are **tourist information offices** in both Shin-Kobe and Sannomiya Stations where you can pick up a map and ask for directions to your hotel. They're open from 9 a.m. to 5 p.m. (The tourist office at Sannomiya Station is on the second floor of the Kobe Kotsu Center and is rather difficult to find; if you get lost, the telephone number is 392-0020.) English maps in more detail are available at major hotels and bookstores for ¥700 ($5). Current information on Kobe's sights, festivals, and attractions appears in a monthly magazine called *Kansai Time Out*, which you can pick up at bookstores, restaurants, and tourist-oriented locations for ¥300 ($2.14).

If you're calling from outside Kobe, the **telephone area code** is 078. Kobe lies in Hyogo Prefecture.

THE SIGHTS: I find Kobe's port fascinating. Unlike many harbor cities where the port is located far away from the center of town, Kobe's port is right there, demanding attention and getting it. For a bird's-eye view of the whole operation, go to Naka Tottei Pier where you'll find **Port Tower**. Opened in 1963, it's

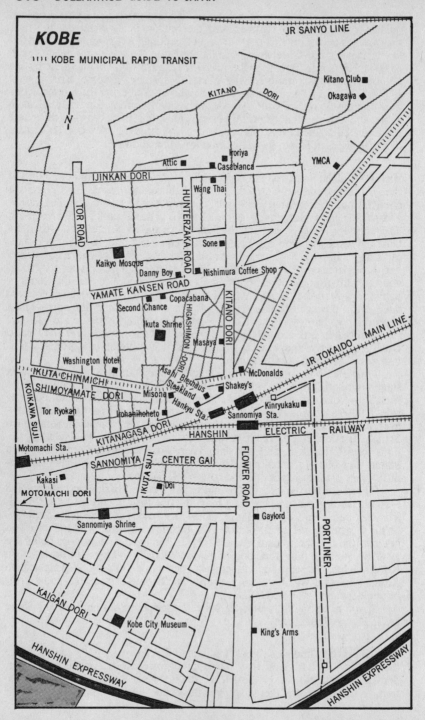

designed to resemble a Japanese drum, a cylindrical shape with the middle squeezed together. Almost 600 feet tall, its glass-enclosed, five-story observatory can be reached by two elevators. It's open from 10 a.m. to 9 p.m. Right beside the Port Tower is the newly developed **Meriken Park**, along with the **Kobe Maritime Museum**, which has a roof shaped like a ship. Open every day except Monday from 10 a.m. to 5 p.m., the museum's exhibits show the history of Kobe's port, as well as ports and harbors around the world. Models of port activities spring to life with a push of a button, along with a spoken commentary in English. A combination ticket for both the Port Tower and the Maritime Museum is ¥700 ($5). If you buy the tickets separately, they're ¥500 ($3.57) each. The closest station is Motomachi Station.

Next to Port Tower are boats offering **cruises of the harbor**. Costing ¥1,100 ($7.86), the trip lasts 50 minutes and takes you to Kawasaki and Mitsubishi shipyards, the container yard, Port Terminal, and Port Island. Although the commentary is only in Japanese, it's well worth it. Departures are every hour on the hour from 10 a.m. to 4 p.m. on weekdays, and every 30 minutes on Sunday and holidays. For more information call 391-8633.

Another interesting way to see the harbor is by taking the unmanned, computer-controlled **Portliner monorail** from Sannomiya Station out to **Port Island**. Port Island is an artificial island complete with amusement park, luxury hotel, condominiums, exhibition grounds, and convention halls. This is a great ride even if you don't get off the monorail. It takes about a half hour to make the whole loop around the island, passing bridges, ships, tankers, tugboats, barges, and stacked containers along the way. If you're up to an outing, I suggest you get off at Shimin Hiroba Station and go to Portopia Hotel for a meal or cup of coffee. It's quite an interesting hotel with a dramatic lobby. From there you can walk to the amusement park. The monorail costs ¥210 ($1.50) no matter how far you go, and announcements are in English.

If you want to learn more about the history of Kobe, visit the **Kobe City Museum**, located next to the Oriental Hotel about a 10-minute walk south of Sannomiya Station. Open from 10 a.m. to 5 p.m. every day except Monday, it displays the history and folklore of Kobe, including Japanese paintings and art objects of the 16th and 17th centuries showing decidedly European influences. Admission here is ¥200 ($1.43). Chinese bronzes, ceramics, and lacquerware are displayed at the **Hakutsuru Art Museum**, a 15-minute walk from Mikage Station on the Hankyu Line, while the **Hyogo Prefecture Ceramic Museum**, with a collection of Japanese ceramics, is just a 3-minute walk from Motomachi Station.

Another point of interest are some wooden houses in Kitano-cho, north of Sannomiya Station, where foreigners used to live after Kobe became an international port. You might also want to travel to **Sakagura**, where you can visit the Sawanotsuru Collection Hall, once a sake cellar and now a museum displaying tools used in sake brewing during the Edo Period. This hall, open free to the public, is close to Oishi Station on the Hanshin Line. It's closed on Wednesday and open the rest of the week from 10 a.m. to 4 p.m.

Farther away, **Mount Rokkosan** is a resort high in the peaks with hiking, golfing, eating, and relaxation the main forms of entertainment. Serving mainly as an escape for residents of Osaka and Kobe, it has little of interest to the short-term visitor but is worth a day's outing if you're here for an extended length of time. More convenient for a quick getaway are the hills directly behind Shin-Kobe Station. Hiking trails lace through an area of woods and streams. You can reach Nunobiki Falls (called *Nunobiki-no-taki* in Japanese) in less than an hour.

NIGHTLIFE: Kobe has a wide selection of English-style pubs, bars, expatriate hangouts, and nightclubs. All the establishments below are easily accessible to foreigners and are within walking distance of Sannomiya Station. Have fun!

Live Music

The **Casablanca Club**, 3-1-6 Kitano-cho on Yamamoto Dori Avenue (also called Ijinki Dori Avenue) (tel. 241-0200), is actually a membership club with a great dinner special available also to nonmembers for slightly more. As a non-member you pay a ¥1,000 ($7.14) cover charge, but the dinner is only ¥2,200 ($15.71) and includes your choice of chicken, fish, veal, or beef, plus soup, salad, rice or pita bread, dessert, and coffee. The interior is an elegant cool white with a grand piano, palm trees, and pictures of Bogart and Bacall. There's nightly entertainment and dancing. Hours are 5 p.m. to midnight on weekdays, until 1 a.m. on weekends.

Much older and more established is **Sone**, 1-24-10 Nakayamate Dori (tel. 221-2055), which has been a jazz hangout for more than 20 years. It has its own in-house jazz band, which plays mainly classics and well-known tunes to an appreciative Japanese audience. Open daily from 5 p.m. to 2 a.m. (until midnight on Sundays), it offers beer for ¥750 ($5.36) and cocktails starting at ¥900 ($6.43), as well as snacks and sandwiches.

If you want a place that's a lot more lively, the **Paladium**, 1-13-7 Nakayamate (tel. 391-6640), showcases black bands from the United States. There's a tiny dance floor where you can bump away to the latest popular tunes, but the privilege for doing so is rather steep. Admission is ¥3,800 ($27.14) for guys and ¥3,300 ($23.57) for gals. Drinks are purchased with special tickets—a set of ¥2,500 ($17.86) worth of tickets will buy you about three drinks. Paladium, which is located on Yamate Kansen Road across from the Nishimura Coffee Shop, is open daily from 7 p.m. to 3 a.m.

With 17 locations in Japan, **Kento's**, 3-10-18 Shimoyamate Dori (tel. 392-2181), has been a great hit among the Japanese, with live bands playing oldies but goodies from the 1950s and '60s. Located on Tor Road just north of where it intersects with Ikuta Shinmichi Street, it's open from 5 p.m. to 1 a.m. daily and charges a ¥1,200 ($8.57) music and table fee. Guests must buy one drink and one food item; beer starts at ¥550 ($3.93) and dishes of spaghetti, salads, seafood, desserts, and snacks average ¥900 ($6.43).

Pubs and Bars

King's Arms, 4-2-15 Isobedori (tel. 221-3774), is an English-style pub popular with Kobe's foreigners. Located south of Sannomiya Station on Flower Road not far from New Port Hotel, it started out in 1950 as an exclusive club for American and British military personnel. After it went public it became a favorite hangout for sailors and travelers passing through town, and has since mellowed into a cozy and well-established eating and drinking spot catering to all kinds of people, including the businessmen who stop here after work for a drink and a study of the daily newspaper. Its walls are decorated with beer coasters, bills of various currencies from around the world (including a U.S. $2 bill), and business cards of former patrons. Churchill's portrait gazes sternly down upon the bar where beer starting at ¥550 ($3.93) and cocktails at ¥850 ($6.07) are dispensed to customers. While the first floor is for serious drinking, the second floor is for dining—on stewed beef, grilled chicken, roast beef sandwiches, and such. Steaks start at ¥4,400 ($31.43), and the ¥9,300 ($66.43) Kobe steak set menu includes appetizer, soup, fish, bread, salad, dessert, and coffee. À la carte entrées are in the ¥1,650 ($11.79) to ¥2,200 ($15.71) range. Lunch specials begin at ¥900 ($6.43). Hours here are 11:30 a.m. to 10 p.m., with the last order for food taken at 9 p.m.

An English-style pub popular with the Japanese, **Danny Boy**, located north of Sannomiya Station at the corner of Hunter-Zaka and Yamate Kansen Roads at 2-10-1 Nakayamate Dori (tel. 231-6566), is a quiet place to escape the noisy crowds of Kobe's nightlife. There's an English menu here with such choices as pizza, teriyaki steak, and beef Stroganoff starting at ¥900 ($6.43). Beer starts at ¥500 ($3.57) and cocktails at ¥770 ($5.50). A respectable and somewhat plush establishment, it's open from 11:30 a.m. until 1 a.m. daily.

Another pleasant retreat in Kobe's nightlife district is **The Studio**, on the sixth floor of the Palais de Kitanozaka, 4-7-11 Kano-cho (tel. 392-3908), on Kitano Dori Street. The owners here are a Canadian-Japanese couple and a mother-in-law, and with its comfortable and cozy atmosphere and mellow music, this is a good place to relax and reminisce. The owners consider their bar an "extension of their homes." Highly recommended, the Studio is open daily from 7 p.m. to whenever, which is sometimes as late as 1 a.m. Table charge is ¥550 ($3.93), beer starts at ¥660 ($4.71), and cocktails are ¥880 ($6.29) and up.

The Attic, 4-1-12 Kitano-cho (tel. 222-1586), is located in the Ijinkan Club Building on the—where else—top floor. It's crammed with all kinds of things often relegated to the attic and then promptly forgotten—tennis shoes, racquets, football helmets, license plates, an American flag, a cello, guitars, and assorted junk. It's owned by local celebrity Marty Kuehnert, a broadcaster of English-language sport shows. This is also a membership club, so as a nonmember a 20% service charge will be added to your bill, and on weekends there's an additional ¥550 ($3.93) cover charge. Munchies include hamburgers, barbecued chicken, and steak sandwiches, with most entrées about ¥1,000 ($7.17). Hours here are from 6 p.m. to 2 a.m. daily.

If your ambition is to stay up until dawn, head toward **Second Chance**, second floor of the Takashima Building at 2-1-12 Nakayamate Dori (tel. 391-3544), on Yamate Kansen Road. Open from 6 p.m. to 6 a.m., this all-nighter is a small, one-room bar favored by young night owls who don't mind the rather sparse furnishings. I must admit my own recollections of this place are a bit fuzzy, but I do remember music ranging from the Doors to the Talking Heads. This is where people congregate when the other bars have had the good sense to close down for the night. Cocktails start at ¥750 ($5.36).

Nightlife Miscellany

One of Kobe's most famous entertainment hot spots is **Copacabana**, 2-1-13 Nakayamate Dori (tel. 332-6694), in the basement of the Akai Fusha-no-Aru Building on Yamate Kansen Road north of Sannomiya Station (next to Second Chance). It features Brazilian and other Latin American music, but the real draw is probably the almost-nude female dancer who entertains the large number of sailors who come here. The place is small with a brightly colored red interior. Open from 6 p.m. to 3 a.m. except for a day of rest on Sunday, it charges a ¥770 ($5.50) entrance fee and a ¥330 ($2.36) obligatory table snack. Beer starts at ¥770 ($5.50) and cocktails are ¥1,100 ($7.86).

A Japanese interpretation of a German beer hall can be found at the **Asahi Bierhaus**, located north of the Hankyu Sannomiya Station in the basement of the Eki Mae Building (tel. 332-0593). It's a good place for a hearty beer or two, with prices starting at ¥400 ($2.86) for a small mug. The hall is designed to resemble a German establishment with all kinds of corny statements in German— one translation reads "In heaven there's no beer, that's why I drink it here."

German beer-garden music serenades in the background and the waitresses here even wear dirndls. If you're hungry, the menu includes roulade, sausage and sauerkraut, German fried potatoes, and pizza, with most items under ¥1,300 ($6.50). It's open daily from noon to 10 p.m., except from November through April when it closes the third Tuesday of every month.

If you're looking for a typical Japanese drinking establishment, **Doi Yakitori**, 1-chome Sannomiya-cho (tel. 391-4401), is an inexpensive place favored by the local working crowd. South of Sannomiya Station, it's on a street paralleling Sannomiya Center Gai shopping street to the south. This is a very simple two-story place consisting of counters and food cooked over a charcoal grill—there are no frills here, just good food and drinking. There's an English menu that tells you skewers cost about ¥120 (86¢) per yakitori stick, with about a dozen different kinds available. You can order chicken breast, by far the most popular, or if you're more adventurous you might try "greasy chicken skin" or "ovaries." Perhaps something's lost in the translations. Other dishes include barbecued chicken and *laver* (seaweed) on rice for ¥550 ($3.93). Lunch teishoku specials for ¥750 ($5.36) get you five skewers, rice, and soup. Closed the first and third Wednesdays of the month, it's open the rest of the week from 11:30 a.m. to 10 p.m. Beer starts at ¥450 ($3.21).

Located just north of Hankyu Sannomiya Station on a small side street is an inexpensive yakitori-ya called **Irohanihoheto**, 1-9-17 Kitanagasa Dori (tel. 321-1688). A chain group of drinking establishments that caters primarily to young Japanese, it's identified outside its door with a sign that says "Antique Pub Restaurant," but there's nothing antique about it. Its prices are cheap, with most dishes of fish, sashimi, soup, yakitori, and more available for less than ¥400 ($2.86). Beer starts at ¥400 ($2.86). Hours here are from 5:30 p.m. to 5 a.m.

If you've had your fill of alcohol, **Nishimura**, 1-26-3 Nakayamate Dori (tel. 221-1872), is a good place to go for a cup of coffee. Located on the corner of Hunter-Zaka and Yamate Kansen Roads, it's open from 8:30 a.m. to 11 p.m. with coffee starting at ¥380 ($2.71) for such blends as Colombian, mocha, and Jamaican. In addition to this branch there are six other Nishimura coffeehouses in Kobe.

WHERE TO STAY: Most of Kobe's tourist and business hotels radiate north and south of Sannomiya Station within easy reach of Kobe's many restaurants and bars.

The Upper Bracket

Kobe's most famous and ritziest hotel is the **Kobe Portopia Hotel**, 6-10-2 Minatojima, Nakamachi, Chuo-ku (tel. 078/302-1111). Opened in 1981, this first-class hotel on Port Island is sleek, tall, and white, looking like some futuristic ship slicing through the landscape. With waterfalls, fountains, lots of brass, marble, plants, and 27 name-brand shops like Nina Ricci and Givenchy, this impressive hotel flaunts ample space and brightness. It offers visitors 15 restaurants, lounges, and coffeeshops, plus indoor and outdoor swimming pools, a gym, and tennis courts. The most dramatic way to arrive at the hotel is via monorail. Otherwise it's about a 15-minute taxi ride from Shin-Kobe Station or a 10-minute ride from Sannomiya Station.

Its 770 rooms, whose large windows face either the sea or Kobe city, are elegantly designed with all the amenities and plushness you'd expect from a first-rate hotel, including bilingual TVs with CNN satellite newscasts from the United States. Singles range from ¥9,300 ($66) to ¥15,400 ($110), twins run

¥19,800 ($141) to ¥26,500 ($189), and doubles cost ¥22,000 ($157) to ¥26,000 ($186). There are also Japanese-style rooms available for ¥35,000 ($250).

The **Oriental Hotel**, at 25 Kyomachi Street, Chuo-ku (tel. 078/331-8111), is about a 5-minute taxi ride or 15-minute walk south of Sannomiya Station. A handsome brick building, it's one of Kobe's older hotels and has aged well. It has 190 rooms and seven restaurants, serving everything from Italian to Chinese to French to kaiseki cuisine. Its guest rooms are small but comfortable and pleasant, and come with TV, fridge, clock, and radio. Room rates begin at ¥8,800 ($63) for a single and ¥15,400 ($110) for a twin or double.

The Medium-Priced Range

You can't get any closer to Sannomiya Station than the **Sannomiya Terminal Hotel**, Kumoi-Dori 8-chome, Chuo-ku (tel. 078/291-0001). Located practically on top of the JR Sannomiya Station, it's a very convenient and upper-scale business hotel with check-in at 1 p.m. instead of 3 p.m. as with most business hotels. Singles start at ¥7,400 ($53), doubles at ¥13,700 ($98), and twins at ¥14,600 ($104). Rooms are fairly large and spotlessly clean, and feature TV with CNN cable, radio, a pot for heating water, and double-pane windows to shut out noise from train traffic. Long-staying guests are provided with scales—perhaps so they can monitor their weight gain as they gorge themselves on Kobe's scrumptious food in the Japanese and French restaurants. Only the twins, doubles, and deluxe singles have refrigerators, but there are vending machines in case you're searching for liquid other than water.

Opened more than 20 years ago, the **New Port Hotel**, 3-13-6 Hamabe-Dori, Chuo-ku (tel. 078/231-4171), is being renovated. About half of its rooms have been outfitted with new wallpaper and carpet, but the remainder of the rooms are rather scruffed up. The hotel has been here so long it's as much a part of the cityscape as the Port Tower, and a plus is that it has a cozy revolving French restaurant on the 15th floor with excellent views of the city and port. Singles start at ¥6,600 ($47); twins and doubles run ¥13,700 ($98) and up. Rooms come equipped with stocked refrigerators, piped-in music, and TV with pay video. The three restaurants dish out Japanese, French, and Chinese cuisine. The New Port is about a 15-minute walk south of Sannomiya Station on Flower Road.

As part of a nationwide business hotel chain, the **Kobe Washington Hotel**, 2-11-5 Shimoyamatedori, Chuo-ku (tel. 078/331-6111), is a reliable and high-quality business hotel about a seven-minute walk northwest of Sannomiya Station on Ikuta Shinmichi Street. The rooms are tiny but nicely decorated with modern furniture and come with refrigerators, TV with pay video (bilingual in twins and doubles), clock, and piped-in music. Panels on the windows slide shut for complete darkness. Three restaurants serve Japanese and Western food. Rates for single rooms start at ¥6,000 ($43); twins are ¥11,000 ($79) and doubles are ¥12,000 ($86).

Opened in 1986, **Hana Hotel**, 4-2-7 Nunobiki-cho, Chuo-ku (tel. 078/221-1087), is a cheerful, airy business hotel located just a two-minute walk north of JR Sannomiya Station. *Hana* means flower in Japanese, and that's the motif here. A small, personable business hotel with only 6 rooms on each floor, its 42 rooms are nicely furnished with refrigerators, radio, TV with pay video, alarm clock, hair dryer, and windows that open. Facilities include one steak restaurant, one coffeeshop, and one bar. The front desk is on the second floor, and the staff is accommodating and courteous. Singles are ¥7,700 ($55), doubles are ¥11,000 ($79), and twins are ¥13,900 ($99). Note that prices include tax and service.

Hotel Sannomiya Central [170], 4-2-1 Nunobiki-cho, Chuo-ku (tel. 078/

241-5031), is a Japanese-style business hotel with rooms of tatami mats. Located next to Hana Hotel, also just a two-minute walk from Sannomiya Station, its building, rooms, and especially bathrooms show its more than 15 years of business, but the place is clean enough and charges only ¥6,500 ($46) for one person and ¥12,000 ($86) for two, including tax and service charge. Six of the hotel's 30 rooms come with beds instead of futons, but I think you're better off with the tatami rooms. All rooms come with TV and private bath and toilet.

Remodeled in 1985, the **Kitagami Hotel** [171], 3-2-3 Kano-cho, Chuo-ku (tel. 078/391-8781), started out primarily as a business hotel but is trying to change its image to attract tourists—most of the 42 rooms are twins that go for ¥10,500 ($75) to ¥13,900 ($99). Triple rooms start at ¥15,400 ($110). Prices include tax and service. Western-style breakfasts are available for ¥750 ($5.36). Rooms are simple but bright, with large windows. The Kitagami is less than a five-minute walk north of Sannomiya Station.

Kobe Union Hotel, 2-1-9 Nunobiki-cho, Chuo-ku (tel. 078/222-6500), is located between Sannomiya and Shin-Kobe stations, about a ten-minute walk to each. It's next to Lawson Food Store, a 24-hour convenience store. They're used to foreigners here and have one Western restaurant. Rooms are simple but pleasant with large double-pane windows, TV with video, coin-operated hair dryer, and hot-water pot. Check-in is at 1 p.m. Rates are ¥6,000 ($43) for a single and ¥10,500 ($75) for a twin, including tax and service.

There's not a lot you can say about the Green Hill Hotels 1 and 2 except that they're both located between Sannomiya and Shin-Kobe stations and are your typical clean and sparsely furnished business hotels. **Green Hill Hotel 1**, 2-5-16 Kano-cho, Chuo-ku (tel. 078/222-1221), is slightly older and cheaper, with singles beginning at ¥6,600 ($47) and twins and doubles at ¥12,000 ($86). **Green Hill Hotel 2**, 2-8-3 Kano-cho (tel. 078/222-0909), sports more modern rooms, which feature shoji screens, refrigerator, and TV with pay video. Singles here are ¥7,500 ($54), while twins begin at ¥13,900 ($99). All rates include tax and service. Green Hill Hotel 2 even has a chapel and Japanese wedding room in case you want to tie the knot while staying here (weddings constitute a big part of the business in Japanese hotels, sometimes as much as 25% of the hotel's profit).

The Budget Category

A good choice in this category, **Tor Ryokan**, 3-12-11 Kitanagasa Dori, Chuo-ku (tel. 078/331-3590), is a member of the Japanese Inn Group. It has a great location, just a three-minute walk from Motomachi Station or a seven-minute walk from Sannomiya Station, just off Tor Road. Owned by an older couple, this small establishment has 12 rooms. Half have their own private bathroom and two of them come with beds instead of futons. If you can do without a private bathroom, room rates are ¥4,400 ($31) for one person and ¥8,800 ($63) for two. Rooms with a bathroom go for ¥5,000 ($36) for one person and ¥9,900 ($71) for two. Rates include tax and service charge. Rooms are simple with a tatami, futons, a low table, coin-operated TV, and a clothes rack and mirror. There's a public bath and coin-operated washer and dryer in the hotel. A bell at the front door signals your coming and going, at which point one of your hosts appears to either take your shoes or give them back. Some may not like the attention; others welcome the homey atmosphere.

The **Kobe YMCA Hotel**, 2-7-15 Kano-cho, Chuo-ku (tel. 078/241-7205), between Sannomiya and Shin-Kobe stations, is sandwiched in between the two Green Hill Hotels. Used primarily for banquets, weddings (yes, you can get married here at the YMCA), and for teaching classes, it has only four single rooms beginning at ¥5,000 ($39) and ten twins starting at ¥9,900 ($71), including breakfast, tax, and service charge. Rooms have a bare, dormitory look to them, but all have a minuscule bathroom, coin-operated TV, and a pot for heating water. Men, women, and families are welcome, and if you're a YMCA member you get a ¥300 ($2.14) discount.

Youth Hostels: There are no conveniently located youth hostels in Kobe. **Youth Hostel Kobe Mudoji** [172], 100 Shinchi, Fukuchi, Yamada-cho, Kita-ku (tel. 078/581-0250), is reached via bus from Minotani Station followed by ten minutes on foot. The cost is ¥2,800 ($20) for members and ¥3,300 ($24) for nonmembers, including two meals.

WHERE TO DINE: In addition to the many Japanese and Western restaurants listed below, be sure to read the nightlife section. Many bars serve meals and snacks that are sometimes cheaper than those served at restaurants.

Japanese Food

Kobe is famous for its beef, and one of Kobe's most famous steakhouses is **Misono**, 1-7-6 Kitanagasa Dori (tel. 331-2890). It claims to have originated teppanyaki steak back in 1945, a style of cooking that uses flat hot plates. Today teppanyaki steak is a favorite not only in Japan but in other countries as well. Misono uses Kobe beef from cattle raised in mountain villages about 40 miles north of the city.

Unlike Western countries where cattle graze in open fields, in these mountain villages the cattle are hand-fed barley, corn, rice, bran, molasses, rapeseed oil, and soybean meal. The rumor that cattle are fed beer is untrue—they may, however, get one bottle each as a farewell present just before being sent off to the slaughterhouse. There are only a few head of cattle per household, so each gets a lot of individual attention. For exercise the cattle are used for labor, and after the workout are washed and massaged with water and straw brushes.

Misono serves its teppanyaki steaks from 11:30 a.m. to 2 p.m. and again from 5 to 10 p.m. (open throughout the day on Sunday). As you sit around a small table, your chef will prepare your steak right before your eyes. Set dinners cost ¥11,000 ($78.57) to ¥16,500 ($117.86), while special lunch menus are available for ¥2,200 ($15.71). Misono is located a couple minutes northwest of Sannomiya Station on Ikuta Shinmichi Street, across from Higashimon Street.

Iroriya, 3-chome Kitano-cho (tel. 231-6777), a rather formal establishment, is another well-known restaurant serving Kobe beef, but specializing in shabu-shabu and sukiyaki. Here you take off your shoes at the front entryway, where a man will quickly whisk them out of sight. Then a kimono-clad woman will lead you through this rather large restaurant to your dining table with your own private hearth. All interior artwork is done by the owner of the restaurant. Meals begin at ¥4,000 ($28.57) for sukiyaki or shabu-shabu and ¥2,750 ($19.64) for *udon suki* (noodles, seafood, and vegetables cooked together and eaten straight out of the pot). Iroriya is about a 10- to 15-minute walk north of Sannomiya Station on Kitano-zaka Road, and is open daily from noon to 10 p.m. (last order at 9:30 p.m.).

Okagawa, 1-115-2 Kitano-cho (tel. 222-3511), occupies a rather new and dignified building up on the bluffs of Kitano not far from Shin-Kobe Station and about a five-minute taxi ride from Sannomiya Station. It specializes in tempura, offered for ¥4,400 ($31.43) at lunch and ¥8,800 ($62.86) at dinner. You can also order shabu-shabu or sukiyaki for ¥7,700 ($55) and a kaiseki menu for ¥11,000 ($78.57). Okagawa is in a modern building that follows the traditional Japanese design of simplicity with latticed wood, shoji screens, and flower arrangements—coolly elegant. In addition to various tatami rooms, its two tempura counters command good views of the city. Hours here are 11 a.m. to 9 p.m. daily.

Conveniently located just north of and across the street from Hankyu Sannomiya Station is **Rakuchin** [173], 2-12-10 Kitanagasa Dori (tel. 321-5200), which specializes in kaiseki and shabu-shabu. It even offers a tofu kaiseki course which features bean-curd dishes prepared in various ways. Prices here begin at ¥3,500 ($25) for a monthly teishoku, with shabu-shabu priced at ¥4,900 ($35) and kaiseki starting at ¥6,600 ($47.14). Located on the fourth floor, this modern yet traditionally decorated restaurant is divided into individual tatami-matted rooms, complete with kimono-clad waitresses and classical Japanese music.

Budget Selections: If you want to eat teppanyaki steak but can't afford the high prices of Kobe beef, one of the cheapest places you can go is **Steakland Kobe** [174], 1-2-8 Kitanagasa Dori (tel. 332-1787), on the street facing the north side of Hankyu Sannomiya Station. Lunch specials, served from 11 a.m. to 3 p.m., begin at only ¥1,300 ($9.29) for steak cooked on the hot plate in front of you, miso soup, rice, Japanese pickles, and a vegetable. At dinner, served until 10 p.m., you can have steaks beginning at ¥2,500 ($17.86). If you opt for Kobe beef, these steak dinners begin at ¥4,600 ($32.86).

Yamada no Kakasi, 3-9-6 Sannomiya-cho (tel. 391-0363), is a cozy kushikatsu restaurant on the western edge of Sannomiya Center Gai covered-shopping arcade. A very narrow and small establishment, it consists of a long counter and some tables in the back. All the wood gleams with a shine, and added touches of pottery make you feel you're in the country instead of in the middle of Kobe. The man who has been operating this eatery for the past quarter of a century makes 25 different kinds of kushikatsu, the kinds dependent on the season. Skewers here average ¥150 (75¢) to ¥270 ($1.35), but the easiest thing to do is simply to order the "Kakasi Course" set menu for ¥1,500 ($10.71), which consists of ten sticks. Your man behind the counter will select the ingredients himself, and since the food is supposed to be eaten hot, he'll serve one stick at a time. If you're still hungry at the end of the meal you can always order a few skewers more. The specialty here is the delicately breaded shrimp and garlic skewer. Other morsels include asparagus wrapped in bacon, mushrooms, potatoes with cheese, chicken wrapped in mint leaf, and lotus root. Closed on Tuesday, it's open from 11 a.m. to 3 p.m. and 5 to 9 p.m. every day except Sunday and holidays, when it stays open throughout the day.

A well-known noodle restaurant in Kobe, **Masaya Honten**, 1-8-21 Nakayamate Dori (tel. 331-4178), is a few minutes' walk north of Sannomiya Station. It has been dishing out noodles for more than 30 years and is easy to spot by the waterwheel outside its front door and its plastic-food display case of noodles (there's another display case inside). Since the menu is in Japanese only, make your choice from one of these cases before sitting down. Dishes available include tempura with noodles (*tempura soba*), pork cutlet with noodles (*tonkatsu soba*), and curry noodles, each less than ¥1,000 ($7.14). Sukiyaki served with noodles is available for ¥2,700 ($19.29). A good place for night owls, it's open daily from 11 a.m. to 1 a.m.

International Restaurants

French and Continental Cuisine: For elegant French dining, **Alain Chapel**, on the 31st floor of the Portopia Hotel, 6-10-2 Minatojima, on Port Island (tel. 302-1111), is an excellent choice. In a stately drawing-room setting of square pillars, chandeliers, flowers, and white tapered candles on each table, this restaurant serves the creations of French chef Alain Chapel. Set lunches, served from 11:30 a.m. to 2 p.m., are priced at ¥6,600 ($47.14), while set dinners, offered from 5 to 9:30 p.m., range from ¥11,000 ($78.57) to ¥17,600 ($125.71). If you decide to dine à la carte, you might start with lobster salad and then try either Kobe beef or duck in foie gras. Average dinner checks including wine, tax, and service are generally around ¥17,000 ($121.43) per person. Top off your meal with a drink or coffee at **Plein d'Etoiles**, which is a floor below Alain Chapel. This lounge features piano music and a band every night, for which it charges a ¥650 ($4.64) cover charge. Cocktails, served until 11:30 p.m., start at ¥800 ($5.71).

Another fine Western restaurant is the **Sky Restaurant**, on the 11th floor of the Oriental Hotel, on Kyomachi Street (tel. 331-8111). Open from noon to 2 p.m. and 5 to 10 p.m., the restaurant has three walls of glass, letting the port and city serve as the decorative background. Piano music nightly adds to the mood. Set dinner menus include steaks with truffle sauce and lobster for ¥13,200 ($94.29) to ¥16,500 ($117.86). If you're ordering à la carte, I recommend the roast rib of Kobe beef. Other dishes include seafood, chicken, veal, and lamb. If you order from the menu expect to spend about ¥11,000 ($78.57). A monthly lunch special is available for ¥3,800 ($27.14).

At the New Port Hotel, 3-13-6 Hamabe-Dori, the elegantly old-fashioned revolving restaurant **Naruto** (tel. 231-4171), on the 15th floor, also offers good views of the city. Open only in the evenings from 5 to 11 p.m., it offers set dinner courses from ¥5,500 ($39.29) to ¥13,200 ($94.29). Specialties are Kobe steaks and seafood.

One more place with a view is **Kitano**, 1-5-7 Kitano-cho (tel. 222-5123), located on a hill overlooking the city about a ten-minute walk from Shin-Kobe Station. Lunches, served daily from 11 a.m. to 2:30 p.m., include set steak meals for ¥5,500 ($39.29) and the daily lunch special, known as the Queen's Lunch, for ¥3,300 ($23.57). It's especially popular with middle-aged Japanese women, but, yes, you guys can order it too. Open for dinner from 5 to 10:30 p.m., it serves sole, turbot, lobster, chicken, filet mignon, scallops, and steaks, with set courses starting at ¥5,500 ($39.29).

Indian Restaurants: With a sizable Indian population, Kobe has a number of excellent Indian restaurants. One of the best known is **Gaylord**, in the basement of the Meiji Seimi Building at 8-3-7 Isogami Dori (tel. 251-4359), on Flower Road between the Sanwa and Kyowa banks and across from the Flower Clock. With its low lighting, candles, wood-paneled ceiling, Indian artwork, and piped-in sitar music, this place is classier than your usual Indian restaurant. Other Gaylord restaurants are in Bombay, New Delhi, Hong Kong, London, San Francisco, and Los Angeles. It has an extensive menu, with such delights as shrimp cooked in mild gravy with coconut, marinated lamb pieces cooked in cream spices, and tandoori fish, chicken, or mutton. Vegetarian selections include saffron-flavored rice with nuts and fruit, Bengal beans cooked in sharp spices, spiced lentils cooked with cream, and spinach and cheese cooked in spices. Most dishes range from ¥1,400 ($10) to ¥2,000 ($14.29), and it's customary to order one dish per person and then share. If you're by yourself, a good way to sample various dishes is to order one of the set menus starting at ¥3,300 ($23.57). Since that was my case, I ordered the mini-tandoori set course, which came with fish and chicken tandoori, shish kebab, Indian bread, salad, chicken curry, a dry vegetable dish (in this case potato and cabbage), rice, and tea or coffee. Lunch specials are served every day except Sunday and holidays for ¥1,300 ($9.29). The restaurant is open daily from 11:30 a.m. to 2:30 p.m.

and 5 to 9:30 p.m., except on Saturday, Sunday, and holidays, when it remains open throughout the day.

Raja, 2-7-4 Sakaemachi Dori (tel. 332-5253), is located south of Motomachi Station and just west of Chinatown. Open every day except Wednesday from 11:30 a.m. to 2:30 p.m. and from 5 to 9 p.m., this small establishment is rather trendy in its simplicity; my only complaint is that the tables are squeezed too closely together. Perhaps it's just a reflection of the demand. At any rate, the menu offers the usual tandoori chicken, seafood, mutton, and vegetable curries, with most priced around ¥1,200 ($8.57). Set lunch courses start at ¥1,000 ($7.14), while set dinner courses begin at ¥2,700 ($19.29).

Gandhara, on the fourth floor of the Nikaku Building, 1-2-3 Kitanagsa Dori (tel. 391-4975), is an Indian restaurant conveniently located just north of Sannomiya Station next to Shakey's. Its portions are not as generous as those described above, but it is easy to find and the curries are slightly cheaper, with most averaging around ¥1,000 ($7.14). Dinners range from ¥2,700 ($19.29) to ¥5,500 ($39.29), but the best deal is the lunch special for ¥1,650 ($11.79), which comes with a choice of mutton or chicken curry, vegetable curry, rice, Indian bread, shish kebab, salad, and dessert. Decorated with Indian knickknacks you never see in restaurants in India, this place is open from 11 a.m. to 10 p.m. daily. Other Gandhara restaurants in Kobe are located in Kitano and Sannomiya Center Gai shopping arcade.

Thai Food: Claiming to be the first Thai restaurant in the Kansai area (which encompasses Kobe, Osaka, and Kyoto), **Wang Thai**, on the second floor of the President Arcade at 2-14-22 Yamamoto Dori Avenue (tel. 222-2507), offers an extensive menu in English with almost 100 items. With most dishes priced between ¥1,000 ($7.14) and ¥1,900 ($13.57), it serves pork, beef, seafood, rice, noodle, and vegetarian selections. Most popular is the chicken wrapped in bamboo leaf, but I found the chicken curry with peanuts, potatoes, and herbs equally delicious. Closed Wednesday and national holidays, it's open the rest of the week from 11 a.m. to 2:30 p.m. and from 5:30 to 9:30 p.m. It's located across the street from the Casablanca Club.

Chinese Food: Chinatown, called Nankinmachi by the locals, is located south of Motomachi Station. Occupying the former hot spot of sailor bars and pubs, this pedestrian-laned area boasts about 30 restaurants, most with plastic-food displays outside their doors. Simply walk around and pick one.

For dining in Sannomiya, **Kinrykaku** (tel. 221-1616) is located on the seventh floor of the Kobe Shinbun Kaikan Building just southwest of Sannomiya Station. The English translation of its name is "Golden Dragon," and it's more luxurious than the usual Chinese restaurant. It serves Cantonese food from 11:30 a.m. to 8:30 p.m. daily. The chef is Chinese and the dishes include many different varieties of pork, chicken, seafood, vegetables, and noodles. Set dinner courses for two persons start at ¥8,800 ($62.86). Much cheaper is the set lunch menu available every day except Sunday and holidays for ¥1,000 ($7.14), which allows you to select two main dishes from a list of ten, plus pickles, soup, and rice. Since most à la carte dishes are meant for two to three persons, ask for the Japanese menu if you're dining alone—it offers smaller portions with dishes averaging ¥700 ($5).

Budget Selections: Kobe also has its share of inexpensive fast-food joints. **Shakey's**, which serves an all-you-can-eat lunch from 11 a.m. to 3 p.m. every day except Sunday and holidays for only ¥600 ($4.29), is located just north of Sannomiya Station. In the same vicinity is a McDonald's.

6. Mt. Koya

The sacred mountain of Mt. Koya is the place to go if you've harbored visions of wooden temples nestled in among the trees whenever you've thought of Japan. It's all there—head-shaven monks, religious chantings at the crack of dawn, the wafting of incense, temples, towering cypress trees, tombs, and early-morning mist rising above the treetops. Mt. Koya, called Koyasan by the Japanese, is one of Japan's most sacred places and is the mecca of the Shingon Esoteric sect of Buddhism. Standing 3,000 feet above the world, the top of Mt. Koya is home to about 120 Shingon Buddhist Temples scattered through the mountain forests. Some 50 of these temples offer accommodations to visitors. So it's one of the best places in Japan to observe temple life first-hand.

Koyasan became a place of meditation and religious learning more than 1,150 years ago when Kukai, known posthumously as Kobo Daishi, was granted the mountaintop by the imperial court in 816 as a place to establish his Shingon sect of Buddhism. Kobo Daishi was a charismatic priest who spent two years in China studying Esoteric Buddhism and introduced the Shingon sect in Japan upon his return. Revered for his excellent calligraphy, his humanitarianism, and his teachings, Kobo Daishi remains today one of the most beloved figures in Japanese Buddhist history. When he died in the ninth century, he was laid to rest in a mausoleum on Mt. Koya. His followers believe that Kobo Daishi is not dead but is simply in a deep state of meditation, awaiting the arrival of the last Buddha messiahs. According to popular belief, priests opening his mausoleum decades after his death found his body still warm. Through the centuries many of Kobo Daishi's followers, wishing to be close at hand when the great priest awakens, have had huge tombs or tablets constructed close to Kobo Daishi's mausoleum, and many have had their ashes interred here. Pilgrims over the last thousand years have included emperors, nobles, and common people, all climbing to the top of the mountain to pay their respects. Women were barred from entering the sacred grounds of Koyasan until 1872.

ORIENTATION: The easiest way to get to Koyasan is from Osaka. Ordinary express *(kyuko)* trains of the Nankai Line depart from Osaka's Namba Station every half hour and cost ¥1,060 ($7.57) one way. The trip takes about one hour and 40 minutes. If you want to ride in luxury you can also take one of the limited express cars with reserved seats. These cost an extra ¥700 ($5) and take about one hour and 20 minutes. After the train ride (the last stop is called Gokurakubashi) you continue your trip to the top of Mt. Koya by cable car. The price of the cable car is included in your train ticket.

At the top of Koyasan is a connecting bus which goes through the main street of Koyasan all the way to the Okunoin-mae or Ichinohashi bus stops. It passes almost all the sites along the way as well as most temples accommodating visitors. It also passes the **Koyasan Tourist Association** (tel. 0736/56-2616), located approximately in the center of Koyasan. Here you can pick up an English brochure with a map and arrange for accommodation in a temple if you have not already done so. The office is open from 8:30 a.m. to 5 p.m. daily, with slightly shorter hours in winter.

The **telephone area code** for Mt. Koya is 0736. Mt. Koya is located in Wakayama Prefecture, the complete address for which is 600 Koya-san, Koya-cho, Ito-gun, Wakayama Prefecture.

THE SIGHTS: The most awe-inspiring and magnificent of Koyasan's many structures and temples, **Okunoin** contains the mausoleum of Kobo Daishi. The most dramatic way to approach Okunoin is from the Ichinohashi bus stop, where a pathway leads one mile to the mausoleum. Swathed in a respectful darkness of huge cypress trees which form a canopy overhead are monument after monument, tomb after tomb, all belonging to faithful followers from past centuries. I don't know whether being here will affect you the same way, but I was awestruck by the hundreds of tombs, the iridescent green moss, the shafts of light streaking through the treetops, the stone lanterns, and the gnarled bark of the old cypress trees. Together they present a dramatic picture representing a thousand years of Japanese Buddhist history—a picture that has engraved itself upon my mind forever. If you're lucky you won't meet many people along this pathway. (Tour buses fortunately park at a newer entrance to the mausoleum at the bus stop called Okunoin-mae. I absolutely forbid you to take this newer and shorter route, since its crowds lessen the impact of this place considerably. Rather, make sure you take the path to the farthest left, which begins near Ichinohashi bus stop. Much less traveled, it's also much more impressive). At any rate, be sure to return to the mausoleum at night—the stone lanterns are lit (now electrically), creating an effect both mysterious and powerful.

At the end of the pathway is the **Lantern Hall**, which houses about 11,000 lanterns. Two sacred fires which have been burning reportedly since the 11th century are kept safely inside. The mausoleum itself is *behind* the Lantern Hall. Buy a white candle, light it, and wish for anything you want. Then sit back and watch respectfully as Buddhists come to chant and pay respects to one of Japan's greatest Buddhist leaders.

As for other things to see, **Kongobuji Temple** is close to the tourist office and is the headquarters of the Shingon sect in Japan. The entrance fee of ¥350 ($2.50) allows you to wander around the old wooden structure. On the temple grounds is a large and magnificent rock garden. Imagine the effort spent in getting those huge boulders to their present site. If it's raining, consider yourself lucky—the wetness adds a sheen and color to the rocks.

Another important site is the **Danjogaran Complex**, an impressive sight with a huge main hall *(kondo)*, a large pagoda which many consider to be Koyasan's most magnificent structure, and the oldest building on Mt. Koya, the Fudodo, built in 1198. Next to the complex is the **Reihokan Museum**, with such treasures of Koyasan on display as scrolls, pictures, art, and implements. It's open from 9 a.m. to 4 p.m. (until 5 p.m. in summer), and admission is ¥500 ($3.57).

A little out of the way from the other sites are the **Tokugawa Mausolea**, where two Tokugawa shoguns were laid to rest. There's nothing spectacular about them, especially since they're surrounded by a wooden fence and wall, obscuring a close look. Come only if you're a Tokugawa fan.

FOOD AND LODGING: Because about 7,000 people live on Mt. Koya, the community has the usual stores, schools, and offices of any small town. However, what is unusual is the fact that there are no hotels here—the only place you can stay at is a temple, and I strongly suggest you do so. Japanese who come here have almost always made reservations beforehand, so you should do the same. You can make a reservation by calling the temple directly or through travel agencies such as JTB. You can also make reservations upon arrival in Koyasan at the tourist association, but that may be a bit risky during peak travel seasons. At last check, the Koyasan Tourist Association indicated it would make reservations only for those who come in personally to its office.

Prices for an overnight stay, including two vegetarian meals, are the same for all temples on Koyasan and range from ¥7,000 ($50) to ¥11,000 ($79) per person.

Your room will be tatami and may include a nice view of a garden. Living at the temple are high school students and college students attending Koyasan's Buddhist university, who will bring your meals to your room, make up your futon, and clean your room. The morning service is at 6 a.m. (You don't have to attend but I recommend that you do.) Both baths and toilets are communal, and meals are at set times. Because the students must leave for school, breakfast is usually served by 7:30 a.m. Incidentally, Buddhist monks are vegetarians, not teetotalers, and because beer and sake are made of rice and grain they're readily available at the temples for an extra charge. Below are just a few of the dozens of temples open for overnight guests.

Shojoshinin [175] (tel. 0736/56-2006) has a good location right at the beginning of the tomb-lined pathway to Okunoin, making it convenient for your late-night stroll to the mausoleum. The present temple buildings date from about 150 years ago, but the temple was first founded about 1,000 years ago. A large wooden structure with rooms overlooking a small garden and pond, it's usually full in August and peak seasons, so make reservations early.

Also located near Shojoshinin near the Ichinohashi bus stop is **Ekoin** [176] (tel. 0736/56-2514). This 100-year-old temple has beautiful grounds and is nestled in a wooded slope.

Fumonin Temple [177] (tel. 0736/56-2224) is centrally located close to the tourist association and has a small but beautiful garden created by the same person who designed the garden at Nijo Castle in Kyoto. (Other temples with famous gardens include Hosenin and Tentokuin.)

Rengejoin Temple [178] (tel. 0736/56-2233) is owned by a priest whose wife and son speak English, so a lot of foreigners are directed here and it's a good place to meet people. There's also a nice garden here, and this is one of the few temples that will probably take you in if you show up without a reservation.

Even the **Henjoson-in Youth Hostel** [179] (tel. 0736/56-2434) is located in a temple, about 50 years old. An overnight stay here for members is ¥3,400 ($24.29); nonmembers pay ¥500 ($3.57) more. Breakfast and dinner are included. Reservations can be made by postcard only. The address is 303, Koyasan, Koya-cho, Ito-gun, Wakayama-ken 648-02.

7. Himeji

THE SIGHTS: The main reason tourists come to Himeji is to see its beautiful castle, which embodies better than any other the best in Japan's military architecture. It is also one of the few castles in Japan that has remained virtually undamaged since its completion centuries ago, surviving even the World War II bombings that laid Himeji city in ruins. Perhaps the most beautiful castle in all of Japan, it is nicknamed White Heron Castle in reference to the fact that its white walls stretching out on either side of the main donjon resemble a white heron poised in flight over the plain. Whether it looks to you like a heron or just a castle, the view of the white five-story donjon under a blue sky is striking.

Originating as a fort in the 14th century, Himeji Castle took a more majestic form in 1581, when a three-story donjon was built by Hideyoshi Toyotomi during one of his military campaigns in the district. In the early 1600s the castle became the residence of Terumasa Ikeda, one of Hideyoshi's generals and a son-in-law of Ieyasu Tokugawa. He remodeled the castle into its present five-story structure. With its extensive gates, three moats, and turrets, it had one of the most sophisticated defense systems in Japan. The maze of passageways leading to the donjon were so complicated that intruders would find themselves trapped in dead ends. The castle walls were constructed with square or circular holes to allow muzzles of guns to poke through; the rectangular holes were for archers. There were also drop chutes where stones or boiling water could be dumped on enemies trying to scale the walls.

Open daily from 9 a.m. to 4 p.m. (5 p.m. in summer), the castle charges a ¥400 ($2.86) admission fee. On weekends there are sometimes volunteer guides hanging around the ticket office who are willing to give you a guided tour of the castle for free. It gives them an opportunity to practice their English. Often college students, they can tell you the history of the castle and relate old castle gossip. But even if you go on your own, you won't have any problems learning about the history of the castle, since the city of Himeji has done a fine job in placing English explanations throughout the castle grounds. Allow about 1½ hours to see the castle.

Just behind Himeji Castle to the northeast is the **Hyogo Prefectural Museum of History**. If you're coming here from the castle, take the Karamete Exit from the castle, follow the circular drive to the right, and then turn left in front of the red-brick building (the city art museum). The history museum is straight ahead. Open every day except Monday from 10 a.m. to 5 p.m. and charging a ¥200 ($1.43) admission, it exhibits materials from prehistorical times to the present day, with many explanations in English. Some of the displays give hands-on experience, such as traditional Japanese toys and Bunraku puppets with strings you can pull to move eyebrows and other facial features. If you're here at 2 p.m. Tuesday through Saturday or 11 a.m. to 2 p.m. on Sunday, you can even try on a samurai period costume (samurai outfits were amazingly heavy). One room is devoted to castles in Japan and around the world, and videos in English describe the structure and layout of Himeji Castle; children's games of yesteryear; and Shoshazan Enkyoji, a famous temple complex on nearby Enkyo Mountain.

Incidentally, near Himeji Castle's main southern gate at the small zoo are bicycles you can ride for free for up to three hours between 9 a.m. and 4:30 p.m. daily (you must pick the bike up by 3 p.m.). Called the **Rental Cycle Center**, it has maps with cycling paths, with one path circling the castle and passing through the pleasant, overgrown park behind the castle. All you have to do to rent the bicycle is leave some identification such as your driver's license. Keys for the bikes are available at the zoo's entry window.

If you have time for an excursion, board bus 8 from in front of Himeji Station (to the right after exiting from the station's central exit) and ride it for 25 minutes to **Shoshazan Enkyoji**. Founded in the Heian Period (12th century), this large complex of temples contains a thousand years of Buddhist history in its precincts, including the Kongo Satta Buddha sculpted in 1395 and the Yakushido, the oldest surviving structure dating from the Kamakura Period (early 14th century). The easiest way to reach the temple complex from the bus stop (called Shosha) is by ropeway, which costs ¥300 ($2.14) one way. There are also horse-drawn carriages available for the same price.

ORIENTATION: Himeji is located about four hours from Tokyo, one hour from Kyoto, and a half hour from Okayama by the Shinkansen bullet train. The **Himeji City Tourist Information Center** (tel. 0792/85-3792) is at a central exit of the station's north side to the left after you exit form the ticket gate. It's open from 9 a.m. to 8 p.m. daily and offers rudimentary maps in English. (The Japanese map is much better and is worth having if you're going to spend much time here.) If you're stopping in Himeji only for a few hours, to see the castle, deposit your luggage in the coin lockers just beside the tourist office. Himeji Castle is about a ten-minute walk straight north of the station. You can see it immediately upon leaving the station.

The **telephone area code** for Himeji is 0792. Himeji is in Hyogo Prefecture.

WHERE TO STAY: Himeji lacks an adequate supply of good accommodations. In fact, some of the worst hotels I've seen in Japan are in Himeji. Your safest bet is to stick to the recommendations listed below.

Banryu [180] 135 Shimodera-machi (tel. 0792/85-2112), is a traditional ryokan about a 10-minute taxi ride from Himeji Station and about a 15-minute walk to Himeji Castle. Surrounded by a wood-and-stone wall and possessing a modest but peaceful garden, this Japanese-style inn has 20 rooms and is used to catering to foreigners. A pleasant place with large rooms and some antiques, it's about 30 years old. Rates per person, including two meals, start at ¥12,000 ($79) for rooms without a bathroom and ¥16,500 ($118) for rooms with a bathroom and views of the garden. Western breakfasts are served upon request.

Himeji Castle Hotel, 210 Hojyo (tel. 0792/84-3311), opened in 1975, is considered to be one of Himeji's best tourist hotels. A ten-minute walk from the south exit of the station (which is also the Shinkansen exit), it charges ¥7,400 ($53) to ¥7,640 ($55) for a single, ¥9,600 ($69) to ¥16,500 ($118) for a double, and ¥12,000 ($86) to ¥19,200 ($137) for a twin. Rooms are okay but nothing exciting. A plus, however, is that all prices include tax and service charge. The hotel's Restaurant Castle, open from 11 a.m. to 9:30 p.m. daily, serves Western lunches starting at ¥1,500 ($10.71) and dinners starting at ¥4,200 ($30).

A business hotel, **Hotel Himeji Plaza**, 158 Toyozawa-cho (tel. 0792/81-9000), is your best bet for a good hotel close to the station. Located about a minute away from the south exit of the station, it's a white building with a clock on the front façade. Its 230 rooms are bright and cheerful and come with mini-bar, hot-water pot for tea, TV with pay video, clock, and semi-double beds. The windows are glazed but can be opened. Singles start at ¥6,400 ($46) and twins and doubles begin at ¥10,500 ($75), all with a private bathroom. There are also cheaper singles for ¥6,000 ($43) with a toilet but no bathtub. Prices include tax and service. There's a coin-operated laundry in the hotel, a public bath and sauna (for men only), soda and beer machines, and one Western-style restaurant. The staff is friendly and courteous.

Hotel Sunroute Himeji [181], 195-9 Ekimae-cho (tel. 0792/85-0811), is a white building located within a minute's walk to the right after exiting from Himeji Station's central exit on the north side. The front desk and lobby are up on the fourth floor. Opened in the mid-1970s, it features rooms with heavy curtains that can be drawn to shut out any light, a hot-water pot for tea, a clock, refrigerator, and TV with pay video. Rooms facing the railroad tracks are fitted with double-pane windows to screen out train noises. During summer months there's a rooftop beer garden here open daily from 5 to 9 p.m., with mugs of beer starting at ¥500 ($3.57). The hotel's one restaurant serves Japanese food, plus a Western-style breakfast for ¥1,000 ($7.14). Room rates begin at ¥6,500 ($46) for a single, ¥11,000 ($79) for a twin, ¥13,200 ($94) for a double, and ¥16,000 ($114) for a triple.

Hotel Sunroute New Himeji [182], 241 Ekimae-cho (tel. 0792/23-1111), opened in 1983, when it took over an existing hotel. Facilities have recently been renovated, including a Chinese restaurant and cheerful coffeeshop. Windows are large, with sliding panels for complete darkness, and rooms are equipped with the usual alarm clock, refrigerator, hot-water pot and tea, and TV with pay video. The cheapest singles have tiny glazed windows that can't open, so if sunshine is important to you, pay the higher price. Rates are ¥5,500 ($39) to

¥7,000 ($50) for a single, ¥12,000 ($86) to ¥15,400 ($110) for a twin, and ¥13,200 ($94) for a double. Japanese-style rooms start at ¥14,300 ($102). This hotel is located right across the street from Himeji Station's central exit. During summer months there's a rooftop beer garden here open daily from 5 to 9 p.m.

Youth Hostel Tegarayama Seinen-no-Ie, 58 Nishi-nobuse (tel. 0792/93-2716), is very inexpensive at only ¥1,200 ($8.57) a night. However, no meals are served, no one here speaks English, and the woman I talked to was not very receptive. If you're still undaunted (or broke), you can reach this youth hostel by taking a bus from Himeji Station for ten minutes and then walking for another ten minutes. Youth hostel cards aren't required.

WHERE TO EAT: Paralleling and to the right of the main drag from Himeji Station to the castle is a covered shopping arcade called **Miyukidori**, with lots of restaurants and coffeeshops. There's even a McDonald's if you're interested.

I suggest, however, that you try **Fukutei** [183], Kameimachi (tel. 23-0981). If you're walking from the station, it's about halfway down the arcade on the left-hand side on the corner just before McDonald's. It has white lanterns hanging outside, a take-out sushi counter, and a glass display case with plastic reproductions of sashimi, tempura, noodles, eel, and sushi. A meal here will probably cost you between ¥1,000 ($7.14) and ¥2,000 ($14.29). A great deal is the hearty teishoku lunch for around ¥900 ($6.43), served until 2 p.m. It usually includes sashimi, tempura, soup, rice, and pickled vegetables. At any rate, the menu is only in Japanese so it's best to make up your mind what you want before entering. Inside you'll find a sushi counter to the right with the rest of the restaurant divided into tables and tatami made private by lots of wooden latticed screens. A refuge for shoppers, Fukutei has soothing Japanese instrumental music playing in the background. It's closed on Thursday and is open the rest of the week from 11 a.m. to 8 p.m.

About a five-minute walk from Himeji Station is a small neighborhood noodle shop called **Minato-an** [184], Tatemachi (tel. 22-1171). It's on a back street to the west of the main street leading from the station to the castle. Across from a tiny shrine and located on a corner, the restaurant has pictures of a black-and-red bucket, and a plastic-food display case outside. The specialty here is udon noodles served in a wooden bucket. Other noodle dishes include somen, ramen, tempura udon, and curry udon, with most in the ¥500 ($3.57) to ¥650 ($4.64) price range. The menu is only in Japanese, so make your choice from the plastic goodies on display. Hours here are from 11 a.m. to 9 p.m.; closed Wednesday.

Mampuku [185], Hakurocho (tel. 22-3501), is a small and plain-looking restaurant located on the left-hand side of the street leading from the station to the castle. It's just before the last stoplight leading to the castle grounds. It has blue curtains in front of its door and a plastic-food display case. It's an eel shop, but also has noodles, sushi, tempura, and other Japanese food, with most dishes priced below ¥1,500 ($10.71). This place is open from 10 a.m. to 5 p.m., closed Thursday.

Beside Mampuku is an obento counter selling box lunches of eel, curry rice, hamburgers, and more for about ¥450 ($3.21) per lunch. You might want to buy your lunch here for a picnic on the castle's park grounds.

Not far from Mampuku and the castle but this time on the other side of the Miyukidori shopping arcade is **C.P. News**. Gofukumachi 16 (tel. 82-7510 and 84-1774), one of the trendiest restaurant/bars in town. It looks like it was imported from Tokyo, with its sparse, art-deco style, triangular tables, young staff, and young clientele. Open from 9:30 a.m. to midnight, it offers sandwiches, spaghetti, pizza, salads, curry rice, and more, all around ¥600 ($4.28) to ¥800 ($5.71). It also serves coffee, tea, beer, and alcoholic concoctions.

And finally, if you're here during the summer months, there are **beer gardens** located on the roofs of Hotel Sunroute Himeji, Hotel Sunroute New Himeji, and Festa department store, which is right above Himeji Station itself. Hours for all are 5 to 9 p.m., and snacks are available in addition to beer.

8. Okayama

With the opening of the Seto Ohashi Bridge in the spring of 1988, Okayama Prefecture has leaped into the tourism spotlight. Japanese from all over the country have come to marvel over this bridge measuring almost six miles in length and connecting Okayama Prefecture on Honshu island with Sakaide on Shikoku island. Whereas it used to take one hour by ferry to reach Shikoku, the double-decker bridge for trains and cars cuts travel time down to just ten minutes. For the Japanese, the Seto Ohashi Bridge is one of the most important attractions of Okayama Prefecture and the Seto Inland Sea.

For those of you less interested in bridges, Okayama is important for other reasons as well. In Okayama city, there's a garden considered to be one of the most beautiful in Japan. And in nearby Kurashiki, covered later in this chapter, there's an old section of the town that's one of the most picturesque places in the country.

ORIENTATION: Okayama lies on the Shinkansen line about four hours from Tokyo and 1½ hours west of Kyoto. The **Okayama Tourist Office** (tel. 0862/22-2912) is inside the Okayama Station building, located near the central exit of the east side (if you're arriving by Shinkansen, take the east exit). The tourist office window is well marked in English and is open from 8:30 a.m. to 8 p.m. daily. They're well prepared for foreign visitors with brochures and a map in English.

Okayama's sights are all clustered within walking distance of each other and are located to the east of Okayama Station. The easiest way to sightsee is to take a streetcar from Okayama Station bound for Higashiyama, and to disembark after about eight minutes at the Shirojita tram stop. From there you can walk to the Orient Museum and then Korakuen Park, Okayama Castle, and the Hayashibara Art Museum. It should take about four or five hours to tour all of these sights. Before leaving Tokyo, stop by the T.I.C. and pick up a leaflet called *Okayama and Kurashiki*.

If you're calling outside Okayama, the **telephone area code** for the city is 0862. Okayama city is located in Okayama Prefecture.

THE SIGHTS: Okayama's claim to fame is its **Korakuen Park**, considered to be one of Japan's three most beautiful landscape gardens (the other two are in Kanazawa and Mito). Completed in 1700 after 14 years of work, its 28 acres are graced with a pond, running streams, pine trees, plum and cherry trees, bamboo groves, and tea plantations. The surrounding hills, as well as Okayama's famous black castle, are incorporated into the design of the garden. The garden's name, Korakuen, means "the garden for taking pleasure later," which has its origins in an old saying: "Bear sorrow before the people; take pleasure after them." This garden is different from most gardens in that it has large expanses of grassy open areas, a rarity in crowded Japan. Entrance to Korakuen is ¥250 ($1.79), and it's open from 7:30 a.m. to 6 p.m. April through September, from 8 a.m. 5 p.m. October through March.

Across the river from Korakuen and over a footbridge, **Okayama Castle**, open from 9 a.m. to 5 p.m. daily, was originally built in the 16th century. Destroyed in World War II and rebuilt in 1966, this unique castle has earned the nickname of Crow Castle because of its black color. It seems that the lord of this castle had some sense of humor, since he deliberately painted his castle black to contrast with neighboring Himeji's famous White Heron castle. At any rate, like most castles this one houses swords, samurai gear, and palanquins. Unlike castles of yore, however, this one comes with an elevator that whisks you up to the top floor of the donjon from which you have a view of the park and the city beyond. If you feel like indulging in whimsical fantasies deserving of children's fairy tales, you can rent paddleboats in the shape of swans or tea cups in the river below the castle. Admission is ¥200 ($1.43).

The **Orient Museum**, open every day except Monday from 9 a.m. to 5 p.m., exhibits about 2,000 items of artwork from the ancient Orient, including pottery, glassware, and metalwork from Asia, Iran, Syria, and ancient Mesopotamia. Admission is ¥200 ($1.43). Another museum worth visiting is the **Hayashibara Art Museum**, about a five-minute walk from Okayama Castle. Open daily from 9 a.m. to 5 p.m. and charging an entrance fee of ¥200 ($1.43), it contains relics belonging to the former feudal owners of the castle, the Ikeda clan, including furniture, swords, pottery, lacquerware, and armor.

SHOPPING: A sampling of products and crafts made in Okayama Prefecture can be seen at the **Okayama Prefectural Product Center (Okayama-ken Bussan Tenjijo)** [186], 1-3-1 Tamachi (tel. 25-4765), about a ten-minute walk from Okayama Station. It features Bizen pottery, rush-grass mats *(igusa)*, woodcarvings, colorful wooden masks, spirits and papier-mâché toys, and more. Closed Sunday and holidays, it's open the rest of the week from 9 a.m. to 5 p.m.

For general shopping, at Okayama Station there's a large underground shopping arcade with boutiques selling clothing, shoes, and accessories, and the Takashimaya department store located across from the station.

WHERE TO STAY: A Western-style hotel with a resort-like holiday atmosphere, the **Okayama Kokusai Hotel**, 4-1-16 Kadota Honmachi (tel. 0862/73-7311), is located above the city on a wooded hill about a 15-minute taxi ride from the station. It features a rooftop beer garden with romantic views of the city lights, open from mid-June through August, and an outdoor swimming pool open from mid-July to the end of August. Built in 1973, this hotel also has the most psychedelic elevators I've ever seen—colorful silk threads in wavy patterns. Rooms face either the city or the woods—with the view of the city being the most dramatic. The cheapest single rooms face the woods, but twins and doubles have views of the city. Rates range from ¥7,000 ($50) to ¥10,400 ($74) for a single, are ¥17,600 ($126) for a double, and start at ¥14,300 ($102) for a twin. Rooms are comfortable and feature a radio, free English newspapers, an alarm clock, and a refrigerator stocked with everything from beer to "titbits"—which turns out to be nuts. The television has a video channel you can view for an extra charge, including movies in English, sports, and adult movies which the management assures "can be put off at your inconvenience." Ah, the joys of Japanese English. The staff here is friendly and courteous, and restaurants serve Japanese, French, and Chinese cuisine.

Hotel New Okayama, 1-1-25 Ekimae-cho (tel. 0862/23-8211), is a spacious hotel located right across from Okayama Station's east exit. The large lobby is on the sixth floor. Rooms are luxuriously appointed, with large windows covered with shoji-like screens, a mini-bar, semi-double beds, radio, refrigerator, and alarm clocks. Rates here range from ¥11,000 ($79) to ¥14,300 ($102) for a single, ¥20,000 ($143) to ¥26,000 ($186) for a twin, and are ¥17,600 ($126) for a double. The cheapest singles face an inner courtyard and have absolutely no view, so it may be worth it to spring for the higher-priced rooms. The hotel has both Japanese and Western restaurants, and from May to mid-August there's a beer garden on the hotel's roof from 5 to 9 p.m.

Located right beside Okayama Station to the right as you exit from the east side is the **Okayama Terminal Hotel**, 1-5 Ekimoto-cho (tel. 0862/33-3131). Your average business hotel, this white building houses rooms with TV, hot water for tea, radio, and clocks, which begin at ¥6,200 ($44) for a single, ¥11,000 ($79) for a twin, and ¥11,600 ($83) for a double. The front desk is on the third floor, and rooms feature double-pane windows to shut out traffic noise.

Hotel Sunroute [187], 1-3-12 Shimoishi (tel. 0862/32-2345), is a chain business hotel about a ten-minute walk from the station. Look for a red-brick building. Rooms are basic, coming with TV with pay video, clock, hot-water pot, and tea bags. Singles are ¥5,500 ($39), doubles are ¥8,500 ($61), twins run ¥9,400 ($67), and triples cost ¥14,800 ($106).

About a five-minute taxi ride from the station, **Culture Hotel**, 1-3-2 Gankunan-cho (tel. 0862/55-1122), is an excellent choice for a modestly priced hotel. A rather striking white building which opened in 1983, its lobby uses white bricks in a number of imaginative ways—chipped to form patterns, buckled, or pulled out from the wall in relief. Water from an inside fountain empties into a stream which runs through the lobby lounge to an outside waterfall and small garden. I wish other hotels in this price category would take their cue from this establishment and put as much excitement into their designs as this one does.

Rooms here are pleasantly decorated with cheerful flowered wallpaper and have a clock, radio, and hot-water pot. They cost ¥5,500 ($39) for a single, ¥10,000 ($71) for a twin, and ¥11,000 ($79) for a double. There are also eight Japanese-style rooms that range from ¥11,000 ($79) to ¥16,500 ($118). Used primarily by wedding parties in preparation for elaborate receptions held at the hotel, some of them look onto a small private garden. The hotel's one restaurant serves Western food.

Okayama Plaza Hotel, 2-3-12 Hama (tel. 0862/72-1201), is right next to Korakuen Park, about a ten-minute taxi ride from the station. The lobby features a gigantic wind chime—glass chandeliers in front of the main door which sway in the breeze and make a music of their own. Rooms are large with semi-double beds, but the bathrooms are fairly small. You'll pay ¥6,000 ($43) for a single, ¥11,000 ($79) for a twin, and ¥13,200 ($94) for a double.

The Budget Category

Matsunoki [188], 19-1 Ekimotocho (tel. 0862/53-4111), is located just a two-minute walk from the west side of Okayama Station. A gleaming white building that was built in 1987, it's situated behind the New Station Hotel. Owned and managed by a friendly family, it has 15 Japanese-style tatami rooms and 5 Western-style singles and twins. All rooms are equipped with deep Japanese tubs, Western toilets, hair dryers, TV, and air conditioning, and those that face east toward the station even have little balconies. Rates are on a per-person basis and are ¥5,500 ($39) with two meals and ¥4,400 ($31) without meals. If there are two or more of you sharing a room, the rate without meals drops to ¥3,500 ($25) per person. Meals are served in a cheerful, communal dining hall. Incidentally, there are 10 more Japanese-style rooms in an older annex next door. All without private bathroom, these go for about ¥300 ($2.14) less.

The **Youth Hostel Okayama-ken Seinen Kaikan** [189], 1-7-6 Tsukura-cho (tel. 0862/52-0651), is about a 20-minute walk from Okayama Station. Its 13 rooms sleep three to ten persons per room, for a total capacity of 80 persons. Members are charged ¥2,000 ($14.29) and nonmembers pay ¥2,750 ($19.64). Breakfasts cost ¥400 ($2.86), and dinners, ¥650 ($4.64).

WHERE TO DINE: As with all cities in Japan, you won't have any problems finding restaurants in Okayama. Many Japanese restaurants are clustered around Okayama Station, while the best Western restaurants are located in the hotels.

Japanese Food

If you're hungry for sushi, you can't go wrong with **Gonta** [190], 1-2-1 Nodaya-cho (tel. 23-6442). The prices are reasonable, the food is excellent, and the atmosphere is typical sushi bar with a long counter and sushi experts dressed in traditional garb with twisted headbands. Sushi set meals range from ¥880 ($6.29) to ¥2,200 ($15.71). I had the Nigiri Matsu for ¥1,850 ($13.21), which came with nigiri-zushi of conger eel, shrimp, squid, sea bream, tuna, and fish from the Seto Inland Sea, and three *norimaki* (edible seaweed rolled around rice and pickled vegetables). If you order sushi à la carte, it will be served to you on large shiny leaves. Other choices include seafood kaiseki starting at ¥5,000 ($35.71) and the *Okayama Barazushi* set for ¥1,400 ($10). Traditionally served during festive occasions, this Okayama specialty consists of a rice casserole laced with shredded ginger and cooked egg yolk and topped with a variety of goodies, including conger eel, shrimp, fish, lotus root, and bamboo. Lunch teishoku sets are also available beginning at ¥1,000 ($7.14). They also sell sushi to go here starting at ¥500 ($3.57). Hours are 10:30 a.m. to 11 p.m.; closed the second and fourth Mondays of the month. This sushi bar is about a five-minute walk from Okayama Station. To reach it, take the Ekimae Shotengai covered shopping arcade from the station, walk all the way through, and after emerging from the arcade you'll come to a busy street. Gonta is across this street on the left corner, recognizable by its white lanterns hanging in front of the door and green sign.

There are lots of inexpensive restaurants in the basement of the Dai-ichi Central Building across from Okayama Station's east exit. Among the restaurants selling pizza, plus Chinese and Japanese cuisine, is **Suishin** [191] (tel. 32-5101), which specializes in *kamameshi* (rice casserole dishes), with prices starting at ¥660 ($4.71). This is a chain restaurant with headquarters in Hiroshima. Being a great fan of eel dishes, I chose the eel kamameshi, which came laced with bits of conger eel, ginger, and boiled egg yolk with Japanese pickles on the side. The Japanese menu shows pictures of other dishes served, including cold shabu-shabu, tempura, and sushi. Most dishes cost under ¥2,000 ($14.29). A simply furnished and popular place, it gets quite busy at lunchtime. It's open from 11 a.m. to 9 p.m.; closed Wednesday.

Although it sounds as if it should be French, **C'est La Vie** [192], located in the basement of the Honmachi Building, Honmachi (tel. 31-6155), is a Japanese restaurant specializing in kaiseki meals beginning at ¥8,800 ($62.86), and vegetarian offerings beginning at ¥5,500 ($39.29). You can also order elaborate obento meals, which come in large round lacquered boxes for ¥3,300 ($23.57) and up. Closed Wednesday, it's open for dinner from 5 to 9 p.m. During lunch hours from 11 a.m. to 3 p.m. it serves teishoku specials ranging from ¥1,650 ($11.79) to ¥3,300 ($23.57) for tempura, tofu, sashimi, or eel. This restaurant is located about a three-minute walk from Okayama Station.

Western Food

For relaxed and intimate dining, head for the Okayama **Kokusai Hotel,** 4-1-16 Kadota Honmachi, to eat at its French restaurant on the 13th floor. Called **L'Arc en Ciel** (tel. 73-7311), it has sweeping views of the city (beautiful at sunset) and is open daily from 11:30 a.m. to 2 p.m. and 5 to 10 p.m. If you order à la carte for such dishes as filet of steak with green peppers, creamed shrimp and scallops, chicken sauté with morels, creamed lobster in vegetables, or steak, you can expect to spend about ¥7,000 ($50) per person for a full-course meal. Dishes here are imaginative and fun. I chose the sole filet in white cream sauce and was surprised to see it arrive with small squid, a shrimp, and shredded crab and carrots on top. There are also set meals ranging from ¥5,500 ($39.29) to ¥11,000 ($78.57).

Akatogarashi [193], 6-27 Togiya-cho (tel. 25-7966), means "hot pepper" in Japanese and is the name of an inexpensive Italian restaurant about a ten-minute walk from Okayama Station. To reach it, walk east from the station on Momotaro Dori Street (the street on which the streetcar runs). Akatogarashi is on a side street—the third right after crossing over the canal (there's a stoplight on the corner). A one-room place with white stucco walls, heavy ceiling beams, and Italian wine bottles as decoration, it's small and personable, and for some reason attracts mainly young Japanese females, which the manager here figures make up about 80% of its clientele. Open every day except Sunday from 11 a.m. to 3 p.m. and 5 to 10 p.m., it serves different kinds of spaghetti starting at ¥800 ($5.71), pizzas from ¥850 ($6.07), and entrées of chicken, beef, lamb, and fish that average ¥1,400 ($10) to ¥2,000 ($14.29). There are also set dinners ranging from ¥2,700 ($19.29) to ¥5,500 ($39.29) and a lunch teishoku for ¥750 ($5.36).

For inexpensive French dining, try **Puchi Marie** [194], 6-7 Nishikimachi (tel. 22-9066), located about a five-minute walk east of Okayama Station. A tiny one-room establishment that's so popular customers line up outside, the interior is kind of corny but the food is fun, with most of its dishes costing less than ¥2,500 ($17.86). A beef stew cooked in red wine is popular, as is the set lunch which costs ¥700 ($5). Hours here are from 11:15 a.m. to 2:45 p.m. (last order) and from 5 to 9 p.m. (last order). It's closed on Wednesday.

If you're in the vicinity of Korakuen Park, you might want to try the ninth-floor restaurant of the **Okayama Plaza Hotel** (tel. 72-1201), open daily from 7 a.m. to 9 p.m. Its huge windows give this Western restaurant a bright and spacious look. The à la carte menu includes steaks, sole, chicken sautéed in garlic, ox-tongue stew, and scallops, as well as spaghetti, pilaf, and curry rice. Best bet is the Chef's Suggestion, a changing full-course meal which usually costs about ¥5,500 ($39.29). There are also special Western and Japanese set lunches for ¥1,650 ($11.79) and up.

9. Kurashiki

If I were forced to select what I consider to be the most picturesque town in Japan, Kurashiki would certainly be a top contender. In the heart of the city clustered around a willow-fringed canal is a delightful area of old buildings and ryokan perfect for camera buffs. As an administrative center of the shogunate in the 17th century, Kurashiki blossomed into a prosperous marketing town where rice, sake, and cotton were collected from the surrounding region and shipped off to Osaka and beyond. Back in those days wealth was measured in rice, and large granaries were built in which to store the mountains of granules passing through the town. Canals were dug so that barges laden with grain could work their way to ships anchored in the Seto Inland Sea. "Kurashiki," in fact, means Warehouse Village. It's these warehouses still standing that give Kurashiki its distinctive charm.

ORIENTATION: Before leaving Tokyo, pick up the leaflet *Okayama and Kurashiki* at the Tourist Information Center. In Kurashiki, the **tourist information office** (tel. 26-8681) at Kurashiki Station passes out maps in English and will point you in the right direction to your hotel. It's located on the second floor of the station near the south exit and is open daily from 8:40 a.m. to 5 p.m.

The willow-lined canal with all the museums is only a ten-minute walk south of Kurashiki Station. There's another tourist information office, called the Kurashiki-Kan (tel. 22-0542), located right on the canal, which also has maps and brochures. It's open from 9 a.m. to 6 p.m. (to 5:30 p.m. in winter) and is the only Western-looking wooden building in the area.

Note that if you're arriving in Kurashiki by Shinkansen (which takes about 4½ hours from Tokyo and almost two hours from Kyoto), you'll arrive at Shin-Kurashiki Station, which is about six miles west of Kurashiki Station and the heart of the city. The local train between the stations runs about every 20 minutes. If you're coming to Kurashiki from the east, it's easier to disembark from the Shinkansen in Okayama and transfer to a local train for the 17-minute ride directly to Kurashiki Station.

The **telephone area code** for Kurashiki is 0864, and the town is located in Okayama Prefecture.

THE SIGHTS: Kurashiki's old town is small, consisting of a canal lined with graceful willows and 200-year-old granaries. The granaries are made of black-tile walls topped with white mortar, and many of them have been turned into museums, ryokan, restaurants, and boutiques selling hand-blown glass, papier-mâché toys, and mats and handbags made of *igusa* (rush grass). Street vendors sell jewelry, their wares laid out beside the canal, and healthy young boys stand ready to give visitors rides in rickshaws. "I hear they're imported from Hong Kong," explains a resident who feels impelled to stop and point out Kurashiki's museums spread out along the canal. He's anxious that I don't miss a thing. Another Kurashiki resident advises me that because of the crowds that descend upon Kurashiki during the day (about four million tourists come here a year), I should get up early in the morning before the shops and museums open and explore this tiny area while it's still under the magic of the early-morning glow. "Real lovers of Kurashiki come on Monday," he adds, "because that's when most everything is closed and there are less people." But no matter when you come you're likely to fall under the city's spell. Even rain only enhances the contrasting black and white of the buildings. In other words, one of the most rewarding things to do in Kurashiki is simply to explore.

The Museums

A highlight of Kurashiki's old town is its many fine museums. Foremost in this cultural oasis is the **Ohara Art Museum**, which first opened in 1930 and is located right on the canal. The main building, a two-story stone structure that looks like a transplanted Greek temple, is small but manages to contain the works of such European greats as Picasso, Matisse, Vlaminck, Chagall, Manet, Monet, Degas, Pissarro, Sisley, Toulouse-Lautrec, Gauguin, Cézanne, El Greco, Renoir, Corot, and Rodin. The founder of the museum, Magosaburo Ohara, believed that people even in remote Kurashiki should have the opportunity to view great works of art. Other galleries on the museum grounds hold modern Japanese paintings, ceramics, and woodblock prints, including prints by the famous Japanese artist Shiko Munakata and ceramics by Shoji Hamada. The entrance fee of ¥600 ($4.29) allows entry to all galleries, and hours are 9 a.m. to 5 p.m. Note that along with most museums in Kurashiki, this one is closed on Monday.

Incidentally, after visiting the Ohara Art Museum you might wish to stop in at **El Greco coffeehouse** (tel. 22-0297) next door. An ivy-covered stone building, it's Kurashiki's most famous coffeeshop and is simply decorated with a wooden floor, wooden tables and benches, and vases of fresh flowers. It serves coffee, green tea, milkshakes, ice cream, and cake from 10 a.m. to 5 p.m. Like the museums, it's closed Monday.

Continuing along the same side of the canal as the Ohara Art Museum and rounding the curve to the right, you'll come to the **Kurashiki Museum of Folkcraft**, easily identified by its sign in English. With the slogan "Useability Equals Beauty," the museum contains folkcrafts not only from Japan but from various countries around the world, giving a unique glimpse at the similarities and differences in cultures as reflected in the items they make and use in daily life. There are baskets, for example, made of straw, bamboo, willow, and other materials from such diverse cultures as Taiwan, Hawaii, Mexico, Sweden, Indonesia, England, Portugal, Germany, and Japan. There are also ceramics, glass, textiles, and woodwork. The displays are housed in three old rice granaries, virtual museum pieces in themselves. Admission is ¥400 ($2.86), and hours are 9 a.m. to 5 p.m. (to 4 p.m. December through February); closed Monday.

Almost next to the Folkcraft Museum is the **Japanese Rural Toy Museum**, a delightful and colorful display of traditional and antique toys from all over Japan, as well as dolls from various countries (the United States is represented by the cornhusk doll). Included in the museum are miniature floats, spinning tops, masks, and kites—2,000 items in all. It's open every day from 8 a.m. to 5 p.m., which means you can drop by even on a Monday, and admission is ¥300 ($2.14). A store at the entrance sells toys in case your appetite has been whetted by all those wonderful creations.

Other museums worth exploring include the **Archeological Museum**, with objects unearthed in the surrounding region as well as relics of the Incas and Chinese, and the **Ohashi House**, built in 1796 by a wealthy merchant family that made its fortune in rice and salt.

Ivy Square

A few minutes' walk from the canal and museums is a complex called Ivy Square. Built as a cotton mill by a local spinning company in 1888, this handsome red-brick complex shrouded in ivy has been renovated into a hotel, restaurants, museums, and a few boutiques and galleries selling crafts. It's especially romantic in the evening, when from the end of June to the end of August there's a beer garden in the inner courtyard open from 5:30 to 9:30 p.m. daily. Classical music wafts from loudspeakers built into the brick floors of the courtyard.

As for museums at Ivy Square, **The Kurabo Memorial Hall** shows the history of the old spinning company, a company that was Kurashiki's biggest employer for decades, providing jobs for many young women in the area. Perhaps the most interesting thing to see in this museum is a tape made more than 70 years ago showing life at the factory, including the women's dormitory where many of the single women lived. The tape is located towards the end of the museum and is activated with the push of a button.

Nearby is **Ivy Gakkan**, a museum with a curious mixture of reproductions of the world's famous paintings (perhaps for art students who can't afford trips to see the real thing) and a section devoted to the history of Kurashiki. Interesting here are photographs of the city taken in the early 1900s.

WHERE TO STAY: One of the great things about staying in Kurashiki is that it offers some really interesting places to stay with a wide selection of choices in all price ranges. The hard part is in selecting just one of them to stay in.

Ryokan

The best place to stay to get a feeling of old Kurashiki is right in the heart of it in one of the old warehouses. **Ryokan Kurashiki** [195], 4-1 Honmachi (tel. 0864/22-0730), is made up of an old mansion and three converted rice-and-sugar warehouses more than 250 years old. Located right on Kurashiki's picturesque willow-lined canal and filled with antiques, this ryokan has long, narrow corridors, nooks and crannies, and the peaceful sanctuary of an inner garden. There's no other ryokan in Japan quite like this one—it's fun simply walking through the corridors and looking at all the antiques. No two rooms are alike, and at the Terrace de Ryokan Kurashiki you can sip ceremonial green tea while looking out over a small garden. Even if you don't stay at this ryokan, you may wish to come treat yourself to green tea, which costs ¥500 ($3.57). Those of the ryokan's 20 rooms without their own private bath and toilet start at ¥15,400 ($110) per person, including two meals, while rooms with their own bathroom start at ¥18,000 ($129). It goes without saying that there are public communal baths. Western-style breakfasts are available.

A NOTE ON JAPANESE SYMBOLS: Many hotels, restaurants, and other establishments in Japan do not have signs showing their names in English letters. Appendix II lists the Japanese symbols for all such places appearing in this guide. Each establishment name in Japanese symbols is numbered, and the same number appears in brackets in the text following the boldfaced establishment name. For example, in the text the Osaka hotel, Hokke Club [161], is number 161 in the Japanese symbol list in Appendix II.

Another old building located right on the canal that has been converted into a ryokan is **Tsurugata** [196], 1-3-15 Chuo (tel. 0864/24-1635). About 240 years old, it was once a merchant's house and shop selling rice, cotton, and cooking oil. All 13 rooms here have toilets but only three come with bath as well. There are public baths, however, with instructions in English on how to use them, indicating that they're accustomed to foreign guests here. Rustic furniture, gleaming wood, and high ceilings are trademarks of this ryokan. Rates per person range from ¥17,500 ($125) to ¥30,000 ($214), including Japanese breakfast and dinner. The kaiseki dinners here are lovely, beautifully arranged on various dishes and as delicious as they look. Tsurugata also maintains its own small restaurant, serving kaiseki, tempura, and sashimi. Open from 10 a.m. to 2 p.m. and 5 to 7 p.m. (from 10 a.m. straight through to 7 p.m. on weekends), it's a good place to stop off for lunch. Kaiseki starts at ¥4,400 ($31.43), while sashimi teishoku is ¥1,500 ($10.71).

Minshuku

Kamoi [197], 1-24 Honmachi (tel. 0864/22-4898), is a minshuku located on a slope leading toward Tsurugatayama Park and Achi Shrine. About a 15-minute walk from Kurashiki Station, this pleasant establishment can be found right beside the stone *torii* gate leading to Achi Shrine. Charging only ¥5,000 ($35.71) per person, including two meals (Western breakfast served upon request), this one is popular among young people and its fourth-floor rooms have good views of the city. Since the owner of this minshuku is also owner and chef of a restaurant, you can be assured that the food served here is especially good. Although the building was built about a decade ago, it follows an architectural style befitting old Kurashiki. Rooms are simple, with coin-operated TV, and are without private bathrooms. If you take your meals elsewhere, the charge for a room only starts at ¥3,500 ($25).

Located on a tiny side street just off the Kurashiki canal and not far from the Rural Toy Museum, the **Minshuku Kawakami** [198], 1-10-13 Chuo (tel. 0864/24-1221), has six Japanese-style rooms. Rooms are simple and without private bathroom, but they have coin-operated TVs and are air-conditioned. Rates per person here are ¥5,000 ($36) with two meals (Western-style breakfasts available) and ¥3,800 ($27) without.

Another minshuku which caters mainly to young Japanese is **Tokusan Kan** [199], 6-1 Motomachi (tel. 0864/25-3056), located between the canal and Ivy Square. Rooms are divided into two separate buildings, one 90 years old and the other 200 years old, but both interiors have been totally renovated and are modern. The older building serves lunches to tour groups of Japanese, which can be quite noisy, assuming you want to hang around in your room. There are a total of 19 Japanese-style rooms, all but one without private bathrooms. The per-person charges here are ¥5,500 ($27) with two meals and ¥4,500 ($32) without. Dinners, served in your room, are ¥750 ($5.36), while breakfasts are served in a communal dining hall for ¥300 ($2.14).

If you prefer to stay closer to the station, **Kokumin Ryokan Ohguma**, 3-1-2 Achi (tel. 0864/22-0250), is located just across from Kurashiki Station. The entry to this small establishment with 13 Japanese-style rooms is through a narrow, pedestrian-covered shopping arcade (located to the right of the main road leading from the station, not the more obvious, large arcade located to the left). The ryokan first opened more than 60 years ago, but most of the building dates from about 15 years ago. Rooms with two meals start at ¥6,500 ($46) per person, while room-only rates start at ¥3,600 ($27) per person. One of the rooms has its own private bathroom, which without meals goes for ¥6,000 ($43) per person.

Hotels

The Top Choice: If you prefer to sleep in a bed rather than on a futon, the **Kurashiki Kokusai Hotel**, 1-1-44 Chuo (tel. 0864/22-5141), is Kurashiki's most popular Western-style hotel—and it's easy to see why. This delightful 106-room hotel built in 1963 blends into its surroundings, with walls of black tiles set in white mortar. Inside the hotel's lobby are two huge woodblock prints by Japanese artist Shiko Munakata. Commissioned by the hotel, the work is titled *Great Barriers of the Universe,* and constitutes his largest piece. The atmosphere of the hotel is decidedly a little old-fashioned, which only adds to the charm. Located behind Ohara Art Museum about a ten-minute walk from Kurashiki Station, the hotel's back rooms have a pleasant view of the museum, greenery, and the black-tile roofs of the old granaries. It's a convenient location for exploring the old town, and facilities include a pleasant Western-style restaurant, a Japanese-style restaurant with a tempura corner, a bar, and a beer garden in the backyard from mid-July to the end of August. All rooms come with radio, TV, refrigerator, hot-water pot, and tea bags. Rates range from ¥7,400 ($53) to ¥8,000 ($57) for a single, ¥11,500 ($82) to ¥12,000 ($86) for a double and ¥13,200 ($94) to ¥18,700 ($134) for a twin. The more expensive rooms are those that face the back of the hotel, which have the most pleasant views.

The Medium-Priced Range: Another interesting place to stay, and a good choice in this price category, the **Ivy Hotel** (tel. 0864/22-0011) is located in the converted cotton mill on Ivy Square. The hotel opened in 1974 with 180 rooms that have a somewhat stark but country feel to them. Much of the architectural style of the old mill has been left intact. Rooms come with the usual TV, fridge, clock, and hot water for tea, and all rooms have a toilet. Singles without a bath-tub start at ¥5,500 ($39), while those with bath are ¥8,200 ($59). Twins without bath start at ¥9,000 ($64), and those with bath begin at ¥11,500 ($82). All doubles have baths and are ¥15,400 ($110), while triples are without bath and start at ¥12,000 ($86). The best rooms are those that face a tiny expanse of green grass and an ivy-covered wall.

If you prefer to stay in a place close to Kurashiki Station, you can't get any closer than the **Hotel Kurashiki**, a business hotel located right above the train station (tel. 0864/26-6111) and part of the Japan Railways group. To find it, take the south exit from the station, go outside, and turn right. The entrance to the hotel is on the ground level, and check-in time is 2 p.m. A modern, spotless, and attractive hotel, its rooms are pleasantly decorated with flowered bedspreads and cheerful pastels of green or pink and have nicely tiled bathrooms instead of the usual one-unit cubbyholes of most business hotels. Windows are double-pane glass to shut out noise, and there are both Japanese and Western restaurants. Singles here are ¥6,200 ($44), twins begin at ¥11,500 ($82), and triples are ¥16,500 ($118).

Another business hotel close to the station is the **Kurashiki Terminal Hotel** [200], 1-7-2 Achi (tel. 0864/26-1111). After emerging from the south exit of Kurashiki Station, look for the red-brick building immediately to the right with the name of the hotel written at the top of the building. The lobby is on the ninth floor, and its 212 rooms are spread between the 10th and 12th floors. The rooms come with TV with pay video, a mini-bar, an alarm clock, and double-pane windows. On the ninth floor is a restaurant serving both Japanese and Western food, as well as a buffet-style breakfast costing ¥1,000 ($7.14). Vending machines dispense beer and soda, and hot water for tea is free. Room rates start at ¥6,000 ($43) for one person, ¥8,800 ($63) for two, and ¥17,000 ($121) for three.

The Budget Category: About a two-minute walk from the south exit of Kurashiki Station, the **Kurashiki Station Hotel** [201], 2-8-2 Achi (tel. 0864/25-2525), is slightly older than the business hotels listed above but is also cheaper: single rooms begin at ¥4,800 ($34), doubles at ¥9,300 ($66), twins at ¥10,500 ($75), and triples at ¥13,200 ($94). Rooms are unimaginative but clean, and come with coin-operated TV and private bathroom. The hotel lobby is on the fifth floor, and its one restaurant in the basement serves only Japanese breakfasts, which cost ¥800 ($5.71).

If all the hostelries suggested above are full, you might try a rather different kind of place called **Young Inn Kurashiki**, 1-14-8 Achi (tel. 0864/25-3411). A red-brick building about a one-minute walk from the south exit of Kurashiki Station behind the Terminal Hotel, it has a youth-hostel feel to it and reminds me more of places in Europe than in Japan. Painted in bright primary colors, it looks as though it might have been rather chic at one time but has faded somewhat with neglect. Informal, it caters mainly to young people, with two to three beds per room; the beds arranged are on different levels in bunk-bed style. In fact, the three-bed rooms on the fifth floor have to be seen to be believed—the third bed is about ten feet off the floor and you have to climb a ladder to reach it. Definitely for the nimble unafraid of heights. There are no single rooms here, but single occupancy rates are ¥3,600 ($26) for a twin without a bathroom and ¥5,200 for one with a bathroom. Double occupancy rates per person are ¥3,100 ($22) and ¥4,600 ($33) respectively.

The **Kurashiki Youth Hostel**, Mukoyama (tel. 0864/22-7355), has a policy of accepting card-carrying members only, but has been known to let in unknowing foreign nonmembers who show up forlornly on their doorstep. What you do with that bit of information is up to you. It's located 30 minutes from the station —on foot, there are no buses that go there. There are eight persons to a room with 80 beds total. The price is ¥2,300 ($16.43) per night, ¥700 ($5) for dinner, and ¥450 ($3.21) for breakfast. If you don't have a membership card and they accept you, expect to spend about ¥500 ($3.57) more for your overnight stay.

WHERE TO DINE: Kamoi [202], 1-3-17 Chuo (tel. 22-0606), is a sushi restaurant run by the man who has a minshuku of the same name. It's located in a 200-year-old rice granary along Kurashiki's willow-fringed canal across from the Ohara Art Museum. Inside, the stark-white walls and dark wooden beams are decorated with such antiques as cast-iron teapots, old rifles, gourds, and samurai hats. Since the menu is in Japanese, you can select from the plastic display outside the front door. Set meals range from ¥1,000 ($7.14) to ¥2,000 ($14.29), and in addition to sushi there's also tempura, eel, and *daikonzushi*, a local rice dish covered with vegetables and seafood commonly served during festivals. During winter the same dish is served warm and is called *nukuzushi*. The cost of both rice casseroles is ¥750 ($5.36). Closed, along with the museums, on Monday, it's open the rest of the week from 9 a.m. to 7:30 p.m.

Kiyutei, 1-2-20 Chuo (tel. 22-5141), is also located across from the main entrance of the Ohara Art Museum at the head of the canal. Enter through the front gate, pass through the small courtyard, and enter a small room dominated by a counter with cooks grilling steaks, the specialty of the house. Steak dinners, which come with soup, salad, and rice or roll, range from ¥2,200 ($15.71) to ¥6,600 ($47.14). The English à la carte menu lists such dishes as grilled lobster or salmon, stewed beef with soup, hamburger steak, spaghetti, fried shrimp, and grilled chicken, with most dishes around ¥1,000 ($7.14) to ¥2,000 ($14.29). Closed on Monday, it's open other days from 11 a.m. to 9 p.m.

For more Western dining close to the canal, **Wisteria** (tel. 22-5141), in the Kurashiki Kokusai Hotel, offers a pleasant setting with large windows. Lunch, served daily from 11 a.m. to 2 p.m., includes such selections as seafood, salads, spaghetti, sandwiches, and beef or shrimp curry, with most dishes between ¥1,000 ($7.14) and ¥1,800 ($12.86). Lunch set meals begin at ¥1,650 ($11.79). Dinner, served from 6 to 9 p.m., includes seafood, roasted duck with peach, stewed beef, grilled salmon, lobster, and steaks. If available, try the *sawara* in champagne, a locally caught fish. Set dinner courses begin at ¥4,500 ($32.14).

In Ivy Square you might try **Tsuta** (tel. 22-0011), which means "ivy" in Japanese. It serves local Kurashiki specialties, including special rice dishes, fish, obento, sukiyaki, shabu-shabu, and farm products. Set in the converted spinning factory, it has high ceilings and is airy and bright. Most set meals here range from ¥1,000 ($7.14) to ¥3,000 ($21.43). The most popular dish consists of rice with red beans, sashimi, fried tofu, and vegetables and is called *obento rikyu*. It's open from 11:30 a.m. to 2 p.m. and 5 to 9:30 p.m. daily.

Next to Tsuta in Ivy Square is **Coffee House Ivy** (tel. 22-0011), which serves

Western fare. It's open from 7:30 a.m. to 9:30 p.m. daily. Decorated on an ivy theme, even the tablecloths and napkins are green with designs of vines. It also has the high ceiling of the original factory. Set menus start at ¥2,000 ($14.29) for a hamburger course, going up to ¥4,500 ($32.14) for sirloin or tenderloin steak dinners. À la carte entrées average ¥2,000 ($14.29) and include salmon or sole filet, scallops, chicken, fried shrimp, beef teriyaki, or beef stew. Less expensive dishes include beef or shrimp curry, mixed pilaf, spaghetti, and sandwiches for ¥880 ($6.29) to ¥1,200 ($8.57).

10. Matsue

With a population of about 140,000, Matsue lies near the northern coast of western Honshu. It's off the beaten track of most foreign tourists, who keep to a southerly route in their travels toward Kyushu. The Japanese, however, are quite fond of Matsue, and a fair number of them choose to spend their summer vacation at this pleasant small town. I'll always remember Matsue as the place where the local schoolchildren greet foreigners with *"konnichiwa"* instead of the usual *"haro"* (hello), testimony to the fact that foreigners are still few and far between. At last check with the Japan National Tourist Organization, only one of the more than 130 group tours organized by foreign tour operators included Matsue in its itinerary of Japan. And yet Matsue, hugging the shores of Lake Shinji, has a number of cultural assets that make a trip here worthwhile.

ORIENTATION: The easiest way to reach Matsue is from Okayama via a three-hour train ride. There's also one daily express to Matsue directly from Hiroshima. Upon arrival at Matsue Station, stop off at one of the **tourist information offices**. One is located inside the station itself and is open daily from 8:30 a.m. to 7 p.m. An additional information office is located to the left after you leave the station by the north exit, and it's open from 9:30 a.m. to 5:30 p.m. daily. Both locations have an English brochure with a map of the city—but it's terribly out of date and needs to be revised. Who knows, maybe with luck that will happen before you get there. If not, please note that the Shimane Product and Handcraft Center is incorrectly identified at number 23. Ten years ago it was moved and now occupies the spot identified by the number 24, next to Ichibata Department Store. If you have any questions, call the tourist office (tel. 27-2598).

Matsue's attractions lie to the north of the station, and although buses run virtually everywhere, you can easily cover the distances on foot. At the Tokyo or Kyoto T.I.C. be sure to pick up the leaflet *Matsue and Izumo-Taisha Shrine.*

The **telephone area code** for Matsue is 0852, and it's located in Shimane Prefecture.

THE SIGHTS: Although Matsue's sights are concentrated in one area of town and are easy to find on your own, you may wish to apply for a "goodwill guide" to show you around, especially if you're going to Izumo-Taisha Shrine. Established by the Japan National Tourist Organization, the goodwill guide network is composed of volunteers with foreign-language abilities who act as guides in their city. All you have to do is pay the entrance fees into museums, etc., and it's nice if you buy them lunch, too. If you wish to have guides (they're always assigned in pairs), apply the day before at one of the tourist information offices listed above before 4 p.m.

First built in 1611 and partly reconstructed in 1642, **Matsue Castle** was the only castle along this northern stretch of coast built for warfare rather than merely as a residence. It's also one of Japan's few original castles—that is, it's not a reconstruction of ferroconcrete as many castles are. Rising up from a hill with a good view of the city about one mile northwest of Matsue Station, the five-story donjon houses the usual daimyo and samurai gear, including armor, swords, and helmets. Lafcadio Hearn, a European who lived in Matsue in the 1890s, adopted Japanese citizenship, and wrote extensively about Japan and the Japanese, wrote this about Matsue Castle: "Crested at its summit, like a feudal helmet, with two colossal fishes of bronze lifting their curved bodies skyward from either angle of the roof and bristling with horned gables and gargoyled eaves and tilted puzzles of tiles roofing at every storey, the creation is a veritable architectural dragon, made up of magnificent monstrosities." As you walk through the castle up to the top floor, notice the staircase. Although it looks sturdy, it's light enough that it could be pulled up to halt enemy intrusions back in the feudal days. And to think that the castle almost met its demise during the Meiji Restoration, when the ministry of armed forces auctioned it off. Luckily, former vassals of the clan pooled their resources and bought the castle keep. In 1927 the castle grounds were donated to the city. It is open daily from 8:30 a.m. to 4:30 p.m. (until 5 p.m. in the summer), and admission is ¥300 ($2.14).

Just south of Matsue Castle is the **Matsue Cultural Museum (Matsue Kyodo-kan)** [203], a white Western-style building built in honor of Emperor Meiji in 1903. Open from 8:30 a.m. to 5 p.m. and charging ¥150 ($1.07) admission, it displays crafts, utensils, and implements of everyday life from the Meiji era beginning in 1868 through the early part of this century. There are old photographs, manuscripts, old obento lunch boxes, combs and hairpins, and tea ceremony objects.

If you walk from Matsue Castle north along its moat, in about five minutes you'll come to a number of attractions. Stop off at **Teahouse Meimei-an** [204], one of Japan's most renowned and well-preserved tea houses, which was built in 1779. It's located at the top of a flight of stairs from which you have a good view of Matsue Castle. For the entrance fee of ¥150 ($1.07) and an additional ¥300 ($2.14) you can have the bitter Japanese green tea and sweets served to you before moving off to your next destination. It's open from 9 a.m. to 5 p.m. daily.

Buke Yashiki [205], a few minutes' walk from the tea house, is an ancient samurai house open daily to the public from 8:30 a.m. to 5 p.m. Facing the castle moat, it was built in 1730 and belonged to the Shiomi family, one of the chief retainers of the feudal lord residing in the castle. High-ranking samurai, the Shiomi family lived pretty much like kings themselves, with a separate servants' quarters and even a shed for their palanquin. As you walk around this house, peering into rooms with their wooden walls slid open to the outside breeze, you'll see furniture and objects used in daily life by samurai during the Edo Period. Admission is ¥150 ($1.07).

On the same street as this samurai house are two more attractions. The **Tanabe Art Museum** [206] is a modern building housing changing exhibits of ceramics and artwork, open every day from 9 a.m. to 5 p.m. except Monday and days of exhibit changes. Its admission ranges from ¥500 ($3.57) to ¥750 ($5.36), depending on the exhibit. The **Hearn Memorial Hall** contains memorabilia of writer Lafcadio Hearn (1850–1904), including his desk, manuscripts, and smoking pipes. The Japanese are fascinated with this man who married a Japanese, took on Japanese citizenship, and adopted the name Koizumi Yakumo. Writing a number of books about Japan, he was one of the first writers to give the Japanese the chance to see themselves through the eyes of a foreigner. His books still provide insight into Japanese life at the turn of the century and are available at all bookstores in Japan with an English section. Since most

Japanese will assume it's out of respect for Hearn that you've come to Matsue, you may want to read one of his books before coming here. His volume *Glimpses of Unfamiliar Japan* contains an essay called "In a Japanese Garden" in which he gives his impressions of Matsue, where he lived for 15 months before moving to Kumamoto to teach English. This memorial is open daily from 8:30 a.m. to 5 p.m. and admission is ¥150 ($1.07). Near the memorial is a Japanese-style house where Hearn lived. Charging ¥100 (71¢), it's open from 9 a.m. to 4:30 p.m. (until 5 p.m. in summer); closed Wednesday.

About a 15-minute walk west of Matsue Castle is **Gesshoji Temple** [207], the family temple of the Matsudaira, clan. It was established back in 1664 by Naomasa Matsudaira, whose grandfather was the powerful Ieyasu Tokugawa. Generations of the Matsudaira clan are buried here. It's open from 8 a.m. to 6 p.m. (5 p.m. in winter), and admission is ¥300 ($2.14).

The most important religious structure in the vicinity of Matsue, however, is **Izumo-Taisha Shrine.** It takes 55 minutes from Matsue-onsen Station to Izumo-Taisha-mae Station, with a change of trains required at Kawato Station. The shrine is important, however, because its site is the oldest in Japan and is probably the most popular attraction in the area. But as with most things in Japan, the present shrine buildings date only from 1744 and 1874. Dedicated to the Shinto deity responsible for medicine and farming, the shrine is constructed in an ancient style, simple and dignified.

SHOPPING: For one-stop shopping for locally crafted goods, visit the **Shimane Product and Handcraft Center (Shimane-ken Bussankanko-kan)** [208], Tonomachi (tel. 22-5758), located just southeast of Matsue Castle close to the Ichibata department store. It sells everything from ceramics to furniture to toys and foodstuffs, all products of Shimane Prefecture. It's open from 9:30 a.m. to 6 p.m. daily.

More products of Shimane Prefecture are for sale at the **Matsue Meisan Center** [209], Chidori-cho (tel. 21-5252), located next to Ichibata Hotel in an area of town called Matsue Onsen. Open daily from 9 a.m. to 9 p.m., it also features a stage on the fourth floor where shows of music, dance, and other traditional performing arts are given four times every day except December. The cost is ¥400 ($2.86). Inquire at the tourist office for current showtimes.

FOOD AND LODGING: Accommodation in Matsue includes ryokan, tourist hotels, and business hotels, most of them within walking distance of Matsue Station.

Ryokan

Minami-kan [210], located off Kyomise covered shopping arcade at 14 Suetsugu Honmachi (tel. 0852/21-5131), has 12 Japanese-style rooms facing Lake Shinji, nine of which have a private bathroom. Completely remodeled in 1985, its modern rooms come with TV and fridge, and cost ¥16,500 ($118) to ¥27,000 ($193) per person. As with most ryokan, prices include two meals, tax, and service charge. Western breakfasts are available. If you want to feel special, there are two rooms in a separate little house right beside the lake that cost up to ¥22,000 ($157) per person.

Minami-kan is also renowned for its restaurant, which overlooks a gravel garden and the water of the lake beyond. Open daily from 11:30 a.m. to 2:30 p.m. and 5 to 9 p.m., it serves lunch menus beginning at ¥1,400 ($10). I particularly recommend the mini-kaiseki Hanagoromo set lunch for ¥2,500 ($17.86) with its various dishes of bite-sized morsels. For dinner there are set meals of various local specialties ranging from ¥3,300 ($23.57) to ¥8,800 ($62.86).

An older ryokan tucked away on a side street not far from Matsue Castle, the 50-year-old **Horaiso** [211], Tonomachi (tel. 0852/21-4337), is guarded by a wall, an imposing wooden gateway, and a pine tree. It has 10 rooms, each one different and facing an inner courtyard garden. Rates here, per person, including two meals, range from ¥11,000 ($79) to ¥22,000 ($157). This is one of the few ryokan that doesn't mind if you want to take your meals elsewhere, in which case it's ¥8,000 ($57) to ¥10,000 ($71) per person, depending on the room. The higher-priced rooms are those with a private bathroom.

Another ryokan with a good location is **Ohashi-kan** [212], 40 Suetsugu Honmachi (tel. 0852/21-5168). On the bank of a river that empties into Lake Shinji just off Ohashi Bridge, it has 29 rooms located in a wooden building constructed in 1938 and in a newer annex. Personally, I prefer the rooms in the older building. Only one of these comes with its own bathroom; costing ¥15,000 ($107) per person, including two meals, it's made of wood and has wooden railings running outside its windows, typical of older Japanese buildings. Otherwise per-person rates at this ryokan, including two meals, begin at ¥8,800 ($63) for rooms facing inland to ¥22,000 ($157) for large corner rooms with windows on two sides and a private bathroom.

Hotels

Tokyu Inn, 590 Asahimachi (tel. 0852/27-0109), one of Matsue's newer business hotels and part of a national chain, is located across the street from Matsue Station's north exit. Its 181 rooms are of adequate size and come with TV and clock. Vending machines dispense beer, cold coffee, soda, and whisky. The front desk is courteous and facilities include a restaurant, which serves both Western and Japanese dishes. Called the Shangri-La, it's open for lunch from 11 a.m. to 2 p.m. and offers seafood, spaghetti, and sandwiches, as well as set courses beginning at ¥880 ($6.29). Japanese-style obento lunch boxes cost ¥1,000 ($7.14) and ¥1,600 ($11.43), while a filet mignon steak lunch with salad, roll or rice, coffee, and dessert is ¥1,600 ($11.43). Dinner, served from 5 to 9 p.m., offers set steak courses beginning at ¥3,300 ($23.57), as well as Japanese courses starting at ¥2,200 ($15.71), including tempura. If you're on a budget or like sitting outside, Tokyu Inn also has a rooftop beer garden open in summer from 5:30 to 9 p.m. Beer starts at ¥550 ($3.93), and the food menu includes yakitori, fried noodles, and chicken steak. Singles at this hotel begin at ¥7,000 ($50), and twins and doubles at ¥13,000 ($93), tax and service included.

Matsue Urban Hotel [213], 590-3 Asahimachi (tel. 0852/22-0002), is a red building located to the right of the Tokyu Inn. Its 60 single rooms go for ¥4,900 ($35) and its 10 twins for ¥8,800 ($63). Although the single rooms are rather small, with tiny windows, all beds are semi-doubles in size, and the twin rooms are all corner rooms with large windows. Rooms are pleasant, with a fridge, clock, and TV with pay video, but large people may have trouble fitting into the tiny tubs. There's a Japanese restaurant as well as a Western restaurant which serves spaghetti and pilaf. The front desk is located up on the second floor.

Matsue's best-known tourist hotel is the **Hotel Ichibata**, 30 Chidori-cho (tel. 0852/22-0188), located in a part of town called Matsue Onsen, a hot-spring spa. It's not very conveniently located, since it's about a 30-minute hike from the station and a 20-minute walk to Matsue Castle. In addition, built in 1968, it's seen better days. Still, it does have hot-spring public baths on the seventh floor with views over the lake. Right next to Lake Shinji, it also has a summertime beer garden on its front lawn and one restaurant serving both Japanese and

Western fare. Rooms, equipped with TV, clock, refrigerator, radio, and hot-water pot for tea, begin at ¥5,500 ($39) for a single and ¥12,000 ($86) for a double—but none of these face the lake. Twins facing the lake begin at ¥15,400 ($110), while those that face inland start at ¥11,000 ($86). All the Japanese-style rooms, which begin at ¥17,500 ($125) for two, have views of the lake, as do the combination-style rooms for ¥18,700 ($134) for two.

There are a couple of business hotels located at the south exit of Matsue Station. **The Matsue Plaza Hotel** [214], 469-1 Asahimachi (tel. 0852/26-6650), is a red-brick and brown building across the street from the station. The front desk is located on the second floor. The carpets here are a little worn and the rooms are small, but they're cheap—beginning at ¥4,000 ($29) for a single and ¥7,700 ($55) for a double or twin. On weekends, when business traffic is at its slowest, the price for single rooms drops a couple hundred yen. No rooms have a great view, but those on the top floor are best. All rooms have a private bathroom, windows that open, TV with pay video, clock, and hot-water pot. Both Japanese and Western restaurants are located in the hotel building.

To the right of Plaza Hotel is a white building on a corner that contains the **Matsue Minami Guchi Hotel** [215], 470-1 Asahimachi (tel. 0852/27-2000). Its name means "South Exit Hotel." The people working the front desk (on the second floor) are accommodating, and the guest rooms are typical business hotel rooms with TV, bathroom, fridge, and clock, beginning at ¥4,400 ($31) for one person and ¥8,200 ($59) for two.

Youth Hostel

The **Matsue Youth Hostel** [216], 1546 Kososhicho (tel. 0852/36-8620), is open only to youth hostel members. It's located about a ten-minute walk from Furue Station, and instructions in English on how to get there are available at the Matsue tourist offices at the train station. Rates are ¥4,400 ($31) with two meals, ¥2,300 ($16.43) if you take your meals elsewhere.

More Dining

For dining outside hotel or ryokan facilities, try **Kaneyasu** [217], Otesemba-cho (tel. 21-0550). Located about two minutes directly north of Matsue Station, this is an unpretentious and modest one-counter place with good food run by motherly women bustling behind the counter and back in the kitchen. It's been around for more than 20 years, and about 80% of its customers are local working people. It has a great lunch teishoku for ¥550 ($3.93) that includes a piece of *yakizakana* (grilled fish), vegetable, soup, tofu, rice, and tea. It's served from 10:30 a.m. to "whenever"; I came at 3 p.m. and still got the lunch special. Since it's popular with local regulars, avoid the noontime rush. If you come for dinner and indulge in sake, sashimi, and grilled fish, expect to spend about ¥3,000 ($21.43). Hours here are 10:30 a.m. to 9 p.m.; closed Sunday and holidays.

Also just a few minutes' walk from Matsue Station is **Ginsen** [218], Asahimachi (tel. 21-2381), located on the street that runs right in front of the station's north side. One of Matsue's most well known and popular restaurants, it's open every day except Sunday from 11 a.m. to 10 p.m. Its specialty is *kamameshi* (rice casseroles), which change with the season and may include such toppings as red snapper, oysters, eel, and other delicacies. A kamameshi teishoku which includes sashimi, soup, rice, and numerous side dishes begins at ¥2,500 ($17.86), but kamameshi alone costs less than ¥1,000 ($7.14).

A wonderful place to stop off for lunch if you're sightseeing north of

Matsue Castle, **Yagumoan** [219], (tel. 22-2400), is located between the Buke Yashiki samurai house and the Tanabe Art Museum on the road bordering the castle moat. Open from 9 a.m. to 6 p.m. daily, this is a lovely soba shop with a tea house-like atmosphere surrounded by bamboo, bonsai trees, a Japanese garden, and a pond. The noodles here are all handmade and start at ¥450 ($3.21). Surrounded by a stone wall with a large wooden entryway, part of this restaurant is 200 years old and is a former samurai residence. A plastic-food display case is located to the left as you step through the entryway.

Another soba restaurant, **Kososhi** [220], 5 Horomachi (tel. 22-1435), is a family-run affair, a modest one-room place decorated with an old spinning wheel, straw capes, and other knickknacks. It's been selling noodles for more than 17 years. Prices for most dishes are less than ¥550 ($3.93); beer starts at ¥270 ($1.93). Closed on Sunday, it begins serving noodles at 11:30 a.m. and closes according to the grandmother's whim, usually between 3 and 5 p.m. It's located north of Kyomise shopping arcade, just off the canal's north side.

A good choice of an inexpensive evening eatery is **Murasaki** [221], located right in the Kyomise shopping arcade (tel. 27-8070). It's easy to spot, with its red-paper lantern hanging outside the front door and a mock thatched roof. Open daily from 5 p.m. to midnight, it offers lots of dishes for less than ¥400 ($2.86), including yakitori, sashimi, and salads. For those of you who are weight watchers, most dishes list calorie content.

11. Hiroshima

With a population of approximately one million, Hiroshima looks just like any other up-and-coming city in Japan. Modern buildings, industry, the manufacture of cars and ships—the city is full of vitality and purpose, with a steady flow of both Japanese and foreign businessmen in and out of the city.

But unlike other cities, Hiroshima's past is clouded: it has the unfortunate distinction of being the first city ever destroyed by an atomic bomb (the second city, and hopefully the last, was Nagasaki). It happened one clear summer morning at 8:15 on August 6, 1945, when three B-29s approached Hiroshima from the northeast. One of them passed over the central part of the city, dropped the bomb, and then sped off at full speed. The bomb exploded 43 seconds later at an altitude of 1,900 feet in a huge fireball, followed by a mushroom cloud of smoke which rose 29,700 feet in the air.

There were approximately 400,000 people living in Hiroshima at the time of the bombing and about half of them lost their lives. The heat from the blast was so intense that it seared people's skin, while the pressure caused by the explosion tore clothes off bodies and caused the rupture and explosion of intestines and other internal organs. Flying glass tore through flesh like bullets and fires broke out over the city. But that wasn't the end of it. Victims who survived the blast were subsequently exposed to huge doses of radioactivity. Their hair fell out, their gums bled, white blood cells decreased, and many died of leukemia or other forms of cancer. Even people who showed no outward signs of sickness suddenly died, creating a feeling of panic and helplessness in the survivors. And today people still continue to suffer from the effects of the bomb, including a high incidence of cancer, disfigurement, scars, and keloid skin tissue. Hiroshima's most important event is the peace demonstration held here every year on August 6.

ORIENTATION: Before leaving Tokyo, pick up a copy of the leaflet *Hiroshima and Miyajima* at the T.I.C. The Hiroshima city tourist offices are located both at

Hiroshima Station (open daily from 9 a.m. to 5:30 p.m.) and in the Rest House at the north end of Peace Memorial Park (open from 9:30 a.m. to 6 p.m. April through September and from 8:30 a.m. to 5 p.m. October through March). Both locations have a brochure and map in English. If you have any questions, call the tourist office at 082/249-9329.

There are tram and bus lines running through the city, but you can make the circuit between Shukkei-en Garden, Hiroshima Castle, and Peace Memorial Park on foot. Shukkei-en Garden is 15 minutes from Hiroshima Station; Hiroshima Castle is five minutes from the garden; and from the castle to the park it's another 15-minute walk, passing the A-Bomb Dome on the way. Hondori covered shopping arcade and its neighboring streets are considered the heart of the city and are located to the east of Peace Park. Close by is Nagarikawa, Hiroshima's nightlife district.

The **telephone area code** for Hiroshima is 082, and Hiroshima is located in the prefecture of the same name.

THE SIGHTS: As you walk around Hiroshima today it's hard to imagine that it was the scene of such widespread horror and destruction a little more than 42 years ago. On the other hand, Hiroshima does not have the old buildings, temples, and historical structures other cities have. But even though there are not many tourist sights in Hiroshima, it draws a steady flow of travelers who come to see Peace Memorial Park, the city's best-known landmark. Hiroshima is also the most popular gateway for cruises of the Seto Inland Sea and for trips to Miyajima, a jewel of an island covered later in this chapter.

Peace Memorial Park

The main focus of Peace Memorial Park located in the center of the city is **Peace Memorial Museum**. The exhibit begins by describing the atomic bomb used to destroy the city, the route of the American B-29s, and the intensity of the blast's epicenter. It then goes on to show in graphic detail the effects of the blast on bodies, buildings, and materials. Most of the photographs in the exhibit are of burned and seared skin, charred remains of bodies, and people with open wounds. There's a bronze Buddha that was half melted in the blast and melted glass and ceramics. There are also some granite steps that show a dark shadow where someone had been sitting at the time of the explosion—the shadow is all that remains of that person's life.

Opening at 9 a.m., the museum closes at 5:30 p.m. May through November and at 4:30 p.m. December through April. Admission fee is ¥50 (36¢). The exhibits all have explanations in English, but if you want more information you can rent portable cassette players with cassettes in English for ¥120 (86¢).

Next to the museum is the **Peace Memorial Hall**, where two documentaries in English are shown throughout the day on the second floor. One focuses on Hiroshima and the results of the bombing while the second film takes a more scientific look at the atomic bombs in both Hiroshima and Nagasaki.

To the north of the museum is the **Memorial Cenotaph**, designed by Japan's famous architect Kenzo Tange (who also designed Tokyo's Akasaka Prince Hotel). Shaped like a figurine clay saddle found in ancient tombs, it contains a stone chest which in turn holds the names of those killed by the bomb. An epitaph, written in Japanese, carries the hopeful phrase, "Repose ye in Peace, for the error shall not be repeated." If you stand in front of the cenotaph you have a view through the hollow arch of the Peace Flame and the Atomic-Bomb Dome. The **Peace Flame** will continue to burn until all atomic weapons vanish from the face of the earth and nuclear war is no longer a threat to mankind. The **A-Bomb**

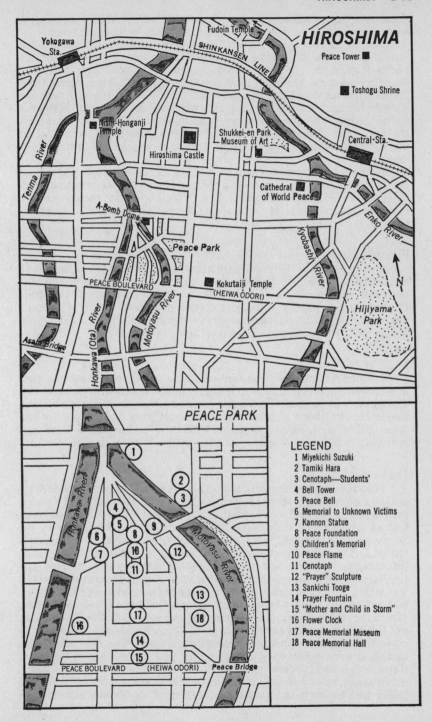

HIROSHIMA

Fudoin Temple

Yokogawa Sta.

SHINKANSEN LINE

Peace Tower

Toshogu Shrine

Nishi-Honganji Temple

Shukkei-en Park
Museum of Art

Central Sta.

Hiroshima Castle

Tenma River

Cathedral of World Peace

A-Bomb Dome

Enko River

Peace Park

Kyobashi River

PEACE BOULEVARD

Kokutaiji Temple
(HEIWA ODORI)

N

Honkawa (Ota) River

Motoyasu River

Hijiyama Park

Asahi Bridge

PEACE PARK

LEGEND
1 Miyekichi Suzuki
2 Tamiki Hara
3 Cenotaph—Students'
4 Bell Tower
5 Peace Bell
6 Memorial to Unknown Victims
7 Kannon Statue
8 Peace Foundation
9 Children's Memorial
10 Peace Flame
11 Cenotaph
12 "Prayer" Sculpture
13 Sankichi Tooge
14 Prayer Fountain
15 "Mother and Child in Storm"
16 Flower Clock
17 Peace Memorial Museum
18 Peace Memorial Hall

Honkawa River

Motoyasu River

PEACE BOULEVARD   (HEIWA ODORI)   Peace Bridge

Dome is the skeletal ruins of the former Industrial Promotion Hall—it was left as a visual reminder of the death and destruction caused by the single bomb.

Also in the park is the **Statue of the A-Bomb Children**, dedicated to the war's most innocent victims who died instantly in the blast or afterward from the effects of radiation. The statue is of a girl with outstretched arms, and rising above her is a crane, symbol of happiness and longevity in Japan. The statue is based on the true story of a young girl who suffered from the effects of radiation after the bombing in Hiroshima. She believed that if she could fold 1,000 paper cranes she would become well again. After folding her 964th crane, however, she died. Today all Japanese children are familiar with her story, and around the memorial are streamers of paper cranes donated by schoolchildren from all over Japan.

Needless to say, visiting Peace Memorial Park is a rather sobering and depressing experience, but it's perhaps a necessary one. Every concerned individual should be informed of the effects of an atomic bomb and should be aware that what was dropped on Hiroshima is small compared to the hydrogen bombs of today.

Hiroshima Castle

Originally built in 1593 but destroyed in the atomic blast, Hiroshima Castle was reconstructed in 1958. Its five-story donjon, or keep, is a faithful reproduction of the original one. It's open from 9 a.m. to 5:30 p.m. (to 4:30 p.m. from October through March). Although the castle now serves as a local museum, there are plans to convert it into a history museum on the castle's 400th birthday, in 1989, with a collection focusing on Japan's feudal days.

Shukkei-en Garden

Located close to Hiroshima Station, Shukkei-en Garden was first laid out in 1620 with a pond constructed in imitation of a famous lake in China, Si Hu. The garden's name means "landscape garden in miniature." The park is situated on the Ota River and includes streams, ponds, islets, and bridges—a pleasant respite from city traffic. Charging a ¥150 ($1.07) admission, Shukkei-en is open daily from 9 a.m. to 6 p.m. (until 5 p.m. from October through March).

The Seto Inland Sea

Hiroshima is also the usual departure point for day cruises on the Seto Inland Sea. Stretching between Honshu and the islands of Shikoku and Kyushu, the Inland Sea is dotted with more than 3,000 pine-covered islands and islets. Cruises are operated daily from March to the end of November by the Setonaikai Kisen steamship company (tel. 253-1212), and advance booking is required. One cruise departs from Hiroshima at 9:30 a.m. on Monday, Friday, Saturday, and Sunday, and visits Etajima, Ondonoseto, Kure Bay, and Enoshima before arriving back in Hiroshima at 3:10 p.m. The cost of this tour is ¥11,000 ($78.57). Another boat leaves every day from Miyajima at 8:40 a.m. with a stop in Hiroshima before heading on to Omishima Island and Setoda. The trip from Miyajima or Hiroshima to Setoda is ¥6,200 ($44.29) one way, and English interpreters are on board on Monday, Wednesday, and Friday. If it's winter or you're simply more interested in a shorter cruise, Setonaikai Kisen also offers three cruises daily throughout the year to the island of Miyajima. Departures from Hiroshima are at 10:30 a.m. and again at 12:30 p.m., with a sunset cruise offered at 6:30 p.m. Cost of the round-trip cruise is ¥1,790 ($12.79) for the morning trip, ¥2,000 ($14.29) for the mid-day trip which includes lunch, and ¥2,000 ($14.29) for the sunset cruise. One-way tickets are also available, a good option since the cruises do not allow any time for sightseeing on Miyajima.

All the above cruises must be booked in advance, which you can do at several hotels, including the ANA Hotel Hiroshima. More information on these cruises is given in a leaflet called *Inland Sea and Shikoku,* available from the T.I.C. in either Tokyo or Kyoto.

WHERE TO STAY: The most common accommodation in Hiroshima is Western-style hotels. There are also Japanese-style inns, mainly in the budget category.

The Upper Bracket

Western Style: Opened in 1983, the **ANA Hotel Hiroshima**, 7-20 Nakamachi (tel. 082/241-1111), is on wide Peace Boulevard *(Heiwa Odori)* just a few minutes' walk from Peace Memorial Park. The lobby, overlooking a tiny garden with waterfalls, is carpeted and subdued, with a menagerie of glass birds hanging from the ceiling. Some 20% of the hotel's guests are foreigners, the majority of them Americans. Therefore, rooms have facilities Westerners will appreciate, such as bilingual TV with one channel devoted to Kyodo news service in English, FEN English radio station, and free delivery of the Japan Times. Rooms are large and comfortable, with all the amenities you'd expect from a first-class hotel. Singles here range from ¥9,300 ($66) to ¥11,000 ($79); doubles, from ¥14,800 ($106) to ¥17,500 ($125); and twins, from ¥16,500 ($118) to ¥18,500 ($132). There are also four Japanese suites for ¥33,000 ($236), which sleep up to four persons. Facilities at the hotel include Japanese, Chinese, and Western restaurants and a rooftop beer garden (open in summer months from 5:30 to 9 p.m.). There are two bars on the 22nd floor, one of which features live piano music nightly. The hotel's health club charges ¥5,500 ($39.29) for use of its swimming pool, exercise equipment, and sauna.

Japanese Style: The nine-room **Mitakiso** [222], 1-7 Mitaki-cho, Nishi-ku (tel. 082/237-1402), offers visitors the memorable experience of staying in a traditional Japanese inn. The oldest part of the ryokan is more than 70 years old, and its rooms are spread along an exquisite landscape garden with stunted pines, ponds, tiny maple trees, stone lanterns, and meandering streams. Well known for its excellent cuisine, it charges ¥16,500 ($118) to ¥38,000 ($271) per person, including two meals, tax, and service charge. The best rooms are elegant and private, with sliding doors that open onto the garden. The least expensive rooms face away from the garden toward the street, but if you're traveling off-season you may be upgraded to a room with a garden view. Rooms come with toilet only, but there are public baths. The ryokan is about a 15-minute taxi ride from Hiroshima Station, and entrance is past a high stone wall and a massive stone lantern.

The Medium Range

Western Style: Part of a nationwide chain of business hotels, the **Tokyu Inn**, 3-17 Komachi (tel. 082/244-0109), is a good and reliable medium-priced hotel. About 80% of its clientele are Japanese businessmen. Located close to Peace Memorial Park not far from the ANA Hotel, it has 284 rooms, which start at

¥6,800 ($49) for a single, ¥9,300 ($66) for a double, and ¥10,600 ($76) for a twin, tax and service charge included. The hotel's restaurant serves a buffet-style Japanese and Western breakfast for ¥1,000 ($7.14), lunches for ¥550 ($3.93) to ¥2,700 ($19.29), and dinners from about ¥1,500 ($10.71). Because *Tokyu* means "109," there are special lunches served on the 19th of each month, consisting of sirloin steak, rice or bread, salad, and coffee for just ¥1,090 ($5.45). Served from 11 a.m. to 2 p.m., they're real bargains. To reach Tokyu Inn from Hiroshima Station, take streetcar no. 1 and disembark at the stop called Jugoku-denryoku-mae, a trip which takes about 15 minutes. The hotel is located close to the Rijo Dori and Peace Boulevard interjunction.

Hotel Hokke Club, 7-7 Nakamachi (tel. 082/248-3371), is another business hotel close to the ANA Hotel and Peace Park. Singles (there are no double rooms) are ¥6,000 ($43), twins run ¥10,400 ($74), and prices include tax and service charge. Rooms are just the basics of TV, radio, and private bathroom. There's a public bath and sauna, but sorry, ladies—it's for men only.

Hotel Silk Plaza, 14-1 Hatchobori (tel. 082/227-8111), is located on Hakushima Dori Avenue close to three department stores. You can reach it in about ten minutes from Hiroshima Station by taking streetcar no. 1, 2, or 6 and getting off at the Hatchobori stop. A locally owned hotel rather than part of a chain, it started out in 1974 as a business hotel, but after five years began catering to wedding receptions and now attracts foreign tourists as well. Singles range from ¥5,800 ($41) to ¥6,000 ($43); doubles and twins are ¥11,000 ($79). The cheaper singles are not recommended, since they open toward another wall with windows of other guest rooms just two feet away. They also tend to be dark. The rooms facing the outside are much better. All rooms are very simple—TV with pay video, clock, refrigerator, and phone. There are both Western and Japanese restaurants, and a buffet-style breakfast is served for ¥1,000 ($7.14).

Built in 1966, the **Hiroshima Kokusai Hotel**, 3-13 Tatemachi (tel. 082/248-2323), is a well-known and established hotel in the center of Hiroshima. Rooms are rather crowded in appearance and their furniture is old, but they're comfortable and come with refrigerator, TV with pay video, clock and radio. Room charges begin at ¥6,300 ($45) for a single ¥11,000 ($79) for a twin, and ¥12,000 ($86) for a double. If two of you can fit onto a semi-double-size bed, you can have it for ¥9,600 ($69). Japanese rooms are available beginning at ¥7,100 ($51) for one person and ¥9,600 ($69) for two. There are both Japanese and Western restaurants, and smörgåsbord breakfasts are served for ¥1,100 ($7.86).

Located on one of Hiroshima's six rivers that run into Hiroshima Bay, the **Hiroshima Central Hotel** [223], 1-8 Kanayama-cho (tel. 082/243-2222), is a business hotel located about a 13-minute walk from Hiroshima Station. Of its 137 guest rooms, two are Japanese style, five are doubles, 16 are twins, and the rest are singles. Although rooms are rather small, the windows are large, and those that face the river have pleasant views. Equipped with hair dryers, hair tonic, stocked refrigerators, TV with pay video, alarm clocks, and deep Japanese-style tubs, rooms are ¥6,500 ($46) for a single, ¥6,850 ($49) to ¥8,400 ($60) for a semi-double-sized bed, and ¥10,600 ($76) for a double or twin including tax and service. Breakfasts are ¥700 ($5).

Japanese Style: A modern ryokan, **Sera Bekkan** [224], 4-20 Mikawa-cho (tel. 082/248-2251), is located in the center of the city just off Namiki Dori Avenue. All 27 rooms are Japanese style with the usual shoji screens, TV, and safe for valuables. Although there are large public baths, all rooms have a private bathroom. Dinner is served in your room but breakfast is served in a communal dining room, and Western-style breakfasts are available. Charges per person range from ¥12,000 ($86) to ¥27,000 ($193), depending on the meal you order for dinner and the number of people staying in the rooms.

The Budget Category

An excellent place to stay at if there's room is **Rijyo Kaikan** [225], 1-5-3 Otemachi (tel. 082/245-2322). Located close to the Hondori covered shopping arcade and Peace Memorial Park, it's intended primarily as lodging for government office employees, but anyone can stay here. Opened in 1985, it's a modern structure of glass and brown tiles in an unusual shape—because of a sloping side wall it looks like a triangle when viewed from the front. Check-in isn't until 4 p.m. here, and the front counter is located to the left as you enter the building. Per-person rates range from ¥4,400 ($31) to ¥5,500 ($39) for a single, and ¥4,000 ($29) to ¥6,600 ($47) for a twin. The rooms here are great for the price —bright, white, and cheerful with hot-water pot, phone, radio, TV, clock, toilet, and deep tub. There are both Japanese and Western restaurants and a self-service cafeteria where you can get a cup of coffee for only ¥200 ($1.43). Breakfast, consisting of ham and eggs, bread, soup, salad, and coffee, is served for ¥700 ($5). If you want to stay here it's safest to make a reservation one to two months in advance. The weekends are usually fully booked, but weekdays are generally not so full.

Mikawa Ryokan, 9-6 Kyobashi-cho, Minami-ku (tel. 082/261-2719), is about a seven-minute walk from Hiroshima Station. A member of the Japanese Inn Group, this 13-room accommodation prefers advance reservations. Rooms are simple tatami and come with coin-operated TV and air conditioning. Singles are ¥3,300 ($24), doubles are ¥6,000 ($43), and triples run ¥9,000 ($64). Check-in is at 5 p.m. and the front doors close at 11 p.m. A Japanese breakfast is available for ¥500 ($3.57).

Minshuku Ikedaya, 6-36 Dobashi-cho (tel. 082/231-3329), a few minutes' walk west of Peace Memorial Park, is also a member of the Japanese Inn Group. The tourist office at Hiroshima Station has maps showing how to get there by streetcar 2 or 6. This establishment is decorated with wooden rice spoons which, like horseshoes, are considered to bring good luck. Even your door key is attached to a wooden spoon. There are 16 tatami rooms located in a main building and its annex, all without bath or toilet. Rooms come with TV and air conditioning, which you can run free until midnight but thereafter costs ¥100 (71¢) per hour. There's a communal fridge, a vending machine with beer and soda, and a coin-operated washer and dryer. Check-in is at 3 p.m. and check-out is at 10 a.m. Rooms cost ¥3,300 ($24) for a single and ¥6,200 ($44) for a twin. Only Japanese breakfasts are available, for ¥500 ($3.57).

Youth Hostel: Just 15 minutes from Hiroshima Station by bus, the **Hiroshima Youth Hostel** [226], 1-13-6 Ushitashi-machi (tel. 082/221-5343), is very easy to find. The bus even announces the youth-hostel shop in English, from which there are signs directing you to the hostel. Located partway up a hill with good views, it accepts nonmembers. An overnight stay is ¥1,700 ($12.14) in spring and fall, and ¥1,880 ($13.43) in summer and winter because of extra heating and cooling costs. The price includes sheets. Breakfast is ¥400 ($2.86) and dinner is ¥600 ($4.29). The staff all speak English, and they're enthusiastic about accepting foreigners. Doors close at 9:30 p.m., but it's worth it to get back by 9 p.m., when a movie in English is shown every night.

WHERE TO EAT: In addition to the Japanese and Western restaurants listed below, the hotel section above also gives some information about buffets and meals.

Japanese Food

Even if you don't stay at the **Mitakiso** ryokan, 1-7 Mitaki-cho, Nishi-ku (tel. 237-1402), described under upper-bracket accommodations, you may want to come here for a meal in a tatami room overlooking the garden. All you have to do is call at least a couple of hours in advance to make the reservation. They serve kaiseki cuisine. Lunch is served from 11:30 a.m. to 2 p.m. and starts at ¥16,500 ($118). Dinner, which is served anytime by appointment, begins at ¥22,000 ($157) per person.

Amagi [227], 10-10 Kaminobori-cho (tel. 221-2375), is a well-known restaurant specializing in kaiseki meals. Recently remodeled, it offers informal dining up on the second floor in a setting of cool and simple elegance. The lunch menu, available from 11 a.m. to 2 p.m., includes obento lunch boxes from ¥3,300 ($23.57), mini-kaiseki courses from ¥3,800 ($27.14), and Japanese-style steak courses for ¥4,900 ($35). Full kaiseki courses start at ¥6,600 ($47.14). Dinner, served from 5 to 9 p.m. (last order at 8 p.m.), offers kaiseki courses beginning at ¥11,000 ($78.57). If you feel like splurging, you can reserve your own private tatami room in the back of the restaurant in what used to be a ryokan years ago. You should make reservations for kaiseki meals here, which start at ¥11,000 ($78.57) for lunch and ¥16,500 ($117.86) for dinner, at least three days in advance; charges for your own private room are ¥1,000 ($7.14) per person. Amagi is closed on Sunday and national holidays.

Unkai, on the fifth floor of the ANA Hotel, 7-20 Nakamachi (tel. 241-1111), is a Japanese restaurant which overlooks a garden of stunted pine trees, azalea bushes, neatly arranged stones, and a pond full of golden carp. The arrangement of this garden is said to resemble Shukkei-en Garden. There's an English menu here, with such à la carte choices as tempura shrimp, abalone in butter served in its own shell, sashimi, rice porridge, and even the head of red snapper boiled in soy sauce, costing between ¥1,500 ($10.71) and ¥3,000 ($21.43). There are also set meals ranging from ¥4,400 ($31.43) to ¥13,200 ($94.29) for such fare as shabu-shabu, tempura, kaiseki, and red snapper sashimi, delivered still jumping and twitching to your table. I had the Miyajima Course, which came with sashimi, sardines, clear soup, eggs of red snapper, a locally caught fish from the Seto Inland Sea, tempura, vegetables, bean-paste soup, Japanese pickles, rice, and fruit. A lunch teishoku, served until 2 p.m. for ¥3,000 ($21.43), offers soup, sashimi, tempura, pickles, rice, and dessert. There are also other set lunches ranging from ¥1,400 ($10) to ¥3,800 ($27.14) for such dishes as noodles, Japanese steak, or obento lunch boxes. The restaurant is open daily from 11:30 a.m. to 10 p.m.

There are 10,000 rafts cultivating oysters in Hiroshima Bay with a yearly output of 30,000 tons of shelled oysters. Needless to say, oysters are a Hiroshima specialty, and one of the best places to enjoy them is at **Kanawa** [228] (tel. 241-7416), a houseboat moored on the Motoyasu River just off Peace Boulevard not far from Peace Memorial Park. Although winter is the best time to enjoy fresh oysters, the owner of this restaurant has his own oyster rafts and freezes his best stock in January so that he's able to serve excellent oysters even in summer. This floating restaurant has been here for 20 years, and dining is in tatami rooms with views of the river. Although the menu is in Japanese only, you can have oysters here cooked about any way you like (it might help to have someone at your hotel write out your choice of cooking style in Japanese). À la carte dishes range from ¥900 ($6.43) to ¥2,200 ($15.71) for the popular baked oyster in its shell with lemon, tempura oyster, or oyster soup. Set menus range from ¥5,500 ($39.29) to ¥11,000 ($78.57); one course features just oysters cooked in various ways, including in the shell, fried, in soup, and steamed. Open from 11 a.m. to 10:30 p.m., this restaurant is closed every first and third Sunday except in December (peak oyster season).

Suishin [229], 6-7 Tatemachi (tel. 247-4411), is the main shop of a locally owned restaurant chain specializing in *kamameshi* (rice casseroles). First opened in 1950, this chain now has six locations in Hiroshima alone. The main shop has five floors of dining, and though the decor is rather simple, this place is very popular for its rice casseroles topped with such Hiroshima delicacies as oysters, mushrooms, sea bream, sea eels, shrimp, and chestnuts. It sells about 800 kamameshi per day, a number which swells to as many as 2,000 on Sunday. To deal with the demand, the restaurant owner invented his own conveyor-belt oven, which can cook 180 kamameshi in one hour. Kamameshi starts at ¥660 ($4.71). Other dishes include oysters, eel, globe fish, stingfish, flatfish, and sardines. Most choices range from ¥1,000 ($7.14) to ¥2,500 ($17.86). Lunch specials change daily and are available for ¥600 ($4.29) from 11:30 a.m. to 3 p.m. There are also take-out boxes of seafood and vegetables for ¥1,000 ($7.14) to ¥3,800 ($27.14), making this a good place to buy your picnic lunch. Closed on Wednesday, the restaurant is open the rest of the week from 11:20 a.m. to 10 p.m. (last order is 9 p.m.).

Masui, located close to Chugoku Bank, which is close to the Silk Plaza Hotel (tel. 227-2983), is a very inexpensive and popular restaurant serving beef dishes. Individual small servings of shabu-shabu, for example, start at only ¥770 ($5.50) for pork and ¥1,300 ($9.29) for beef, while sukiyaki goes for ¥880 ($6.29) and ¥1,400 ($10). Steaks start at ¥2,000 ($14.29). This two-story restaurant is especially crowded during lunchtime when it churns out plate after plate of teishoku specials. The ¥700 ($5) teishoku gets you a hamburger patty, ham, omelet, pork cutlet, and rice, but if that's too expensive you can forgo the hamburger and get the other items for ¥600 ($4.29). Open from 11 a.m. to 9 p.m., it's closed every Wednesday and the second Tuesday of the month.

Western Food

Castle View, on the 22nd floor of the ANA Hotel, 7-20 Nakamachi (tel. 241-1111), is named for the view you have here of the castle, but you have to look pretty hard to find it. Still, this is the tallest building in Hiroshima and you *do* have a fine view of the city. A small and elegant restaurant decorated in gold and light pink, with comfortable chairs and a single rose on each table, this establishment has set dinners for ¥6,000 ($42.86) and ¥13,200 ($94.29) and a lunch for ¥2,750 ($19.64). If you're ordering à la carte you might begin your dinner with an avocado and shrimp salad followed by clear turtle soup or lobster bisque, topped with steak tartare, sole, steak cooked in red wine, or lamb. For dessert you might choose baked Alaska or café diable. Expect to spend about ¥10,000 ($71.43) and up per person if you order from the menu. Hours here are from 11:30 a.m. to 2:30 p.m. and from 5:30 to 10 p.m.

The **Kokusai Sky Lounge,** on the 14th floor of the Kokusai Hotel, 3-13 Tatemachi (tel. 248-2323), is Hiroshima's only revolving restaurant—after lunch, that is. It doesn't start revolving until 2 p.m., when it begins to make a full turn every 30 minutes (a little too fast for me). It's reasonably priced and each table is beside the window, making for privacy with a view. With a dark-blue interior, white tablecloths, and potted palms, it has entrées of such dishes as grilled lobster, sirloin steak, grilled chicken, beef stew, or hamburger steak served with either oysters, pineapples, or fried onion rings. Most meals average about ¥3,500 ($25) per person. There are also set dinners for ¥2,200 ($15.71) to ¥3,600 ($25.71), and a lunch course served from 11:30 a.m. to 1:30 p.m. every day except Sunday and national holidays for ¥850 ($6.07). In case you want to come here for an after-dinner drink, cocktails are ¥750 ($5.36) and beer starts at ¥550 ($3.93). Hours here are 11:30 a.m. to 1 a.m. every day (11 p.m. on Sunday).

For other hotel dining, the Hotel Silk Plaza's **Caspi** restaurant, 14-1 Hatchobori (tel. 227-8111), serves a good lunch bargain daily from 11 a.m. to 2 p.m. for ¥850 ($6.07). Its menu changes daily, but when I was there the special consisted of soup, salad, pork cutlet with vegetables, and coffee, with unlimited portions of salad. **Rijyo**, in the Rijyo Kaikan, 1-5-3 Otemachi (tel. 245-2322), described under budget accommodations, is a bright and modern restaurant made cheerful by colorful wall hangings. It serves a variety of inexpensive dishes, including salmon steak, hamburger steak, roast beef, sirloin and tenderloin steaks, beef curry, pizza toast, sandwiches, and spaghetti. Lunches start at ¥660 ($4.71) and dinners at ¥1,650 ($11.79). It's open daily from 9 a.m. to 9 p.m.

Anderson Kitchen, 7-1 Hondori (tel. 247-2403), is located on a corner of the Hondori covered shopping arcade not far from Peace Park. It's a popular cafeteria above its own bakery with the same name. Altogether there are five counters serving different types of food. One counter, for example, sells Chinese food, while other counters specialize in salads and sandwiches, fried dishes such as grilled chicken, or desserts. Just pick up a tray and select the items you want. You pay at the end of each counter. Most items are between ¥500 ($3.57) and ¥1,000 ($7.14). Closed the third Tuesday of every month, it's open otherwise from 11 a.m. to 5 p.m. A small corner of the restaurant, however, stays open until 10 p.m.

Incidentally, at Hondori shopping arcade you'll also find a number of inexpensive and fast-food places, including McDonald's and Mister Donut.

12. Miyajima

Easily reached in about 45 minutes from Hiroshima, Miyajima is a treasure of an island only 1.2 miles off the mainland in the Seto Inland Sea. No doubt you've seen pictures of its most famous landmark—a huge red *torii*, or shrine gate, rising up out of the water. Erected in 1875 and made of camphor wood, it's the largest torii in Japan, measuring more than 53 feet tall, and guards Miyajima's main attraction, Itsukushima Shrine.

Miyajima is considered one of the most scenic spots in Japan. It is an exceptionally beautiful island that has been held sacred since ancient times. In the olden days no one was allowed to do anything so human as to give birth or die on the island, with the result that both the pregnant and the ill were quickly ferried across to the mainland. Even today there's no cemetery on Miyajima. Covered with cherry trees which illuminate the island with their snowy petals in spring and maple trees which emblazon it in reds in autumn, Miyajima is home to tame deer which roam freely through the village and to monkeys which swing through the woods. It's a delightful island on which to stroll around—but avoid coming on a weekend.

ORIENTATION: Before leaving Tokyo or Kyoto, drop by the T.I.C. for a copy of *Hiroshima and Miyajima.* You can reach Miyajima directly by ferry from Hiroshima Ujina Port. The **Setonaikai Kisen steamship company** (tel. 253-1212), for example, offers several cruises daily throughout the year aboard its Galaxy luxury boat complete with French and seafood restaurants. Cost of the round-trip cruise is ¥1,790 ($12.79) for the morning trip departing from Ujina Port at 10:30 and ¥2,000 ($14.29) for the 12:30 p.m. boat, which includes lunch. Unfortunately, neither cruise allows much of a stopover, but one-way tickets are also available. You may wish to take the early cruise to Miyajima and return with the afternoon boat or else return to Hiroshima by a different route.

You can, for example, also travel from Hiroshima by train, streetcar, or bus, all of which deposit you at Miyajimaguchi, from which it's just a ten-minute ferry ride to the island of Miyajima. If you have a JR rail pass, you can ride the JR ferry for free, which leaves from the pier right in front of the train station.

In Miyajima stop off at the **Tourist Information Office** (tel. 44-0008), located on the second floor of the JR ferry terminal. Open from 8:30 a.m. to 5 p.m. every day except Sunday and national holidays, it has a brochure in English with a map.

The **telephone area code** for Miyajima is 0829, and Miyajima is located in Hiroshima Prefecture.

THE SIGHTS: **Itsukushima Shrine** is less than a ten-minute walk from the ferry pier along a narrow street lined with souvenir shops and restaurants. Founded back in 592 to honor three female deities, the shrine is built out over the water so that when the tide is in it appears as though the shrine is floating. A brilliant vermilion, it contrasts starkly with the wooded hills in the background and the blue of the sky above, casting its reflection in the waters below. The majority of the buildings are thought to date from the 16th century, preserving the original style of 12th-century architecture. Since the shrine is made of wood, it's been repaired repeatedly through the centuries. Most of the buildings of the shrine are closed, but from 6:30 a.m. to 6 p.m. daily (5 p.m. in winter) for ¥200 ($1.43) you can walk along the 770-foot covered dock that threads its way past the outer part of the main shrine and the oldest Noh stage in Japan. From the shrine you have a good view of the red torii standing in the water. If you're lucky you might get to see *bugako* put on for one of the many tour groups which pass through. An ancient musical court dance, bugako was introduced to Japan centuries ago from India through China and Korea. The costume of the dancer is orange, matching the shrine around him.

Incidentally, I should also add that if you happen to witness Itsukushima Shrine when the tide is in and it's seemingly floating on water, you should consider yourself very lucky indeed. Most of the time the lovely shrine is floating above nothing more glamorous than mud. That's when a little imagination comes in handy.

As you exit from the shrine, you'll find the **Miyajima Museum of Historic Treasures**, which contains replicas of national treasures (the real ones are safely locked away), old books, armor, and household items. Perhaps of more interest is the **Miyajima Municipal History and Folklore Museum**, a few minutes' walk from the shrine. This one has explanations in English to guide you through the 150-year-old house, which once belonged to a wealthy merchant. Open from 8:30 a.m. to 5 p.m. daily, it features farm equipment, water jars, cooking objects, carved-wood boxes, furniture, and items used in daily life. Admission is ¥270 ($1.93).

Other attractions on Miyajima include an aquarium, 1,750-foot-high **Mount Misen**, the largest peak on the island and easily reached by cable car from Momijidani Park, and beaches for swimming.

FOOD AND LODGING: Although you can visit Miyajima in a day from Hiroshima, it's a pleasant experience to stay overnight in a ryokan (there are no Western-style hotels).

The most famous ryokan on the island is **Iwaso Ryokan** [230] (tel. 0829/44-2233), which has a history spanning more than 130 years since it became the first ryokan to open on the island. Most of its rooms range in price from ¥16,500 ($118) to ¥30,000 ($214) per person, including two meals, tax, and service charge, with the price determined by the room, its view, and the meals you select. There are four price levels of dinners, and Western breakfasts are served on request. The newest part of the ryokan was built in 1981, and though some of its rooms have very peaceful and relaxing views of a stream and woods, I prefer the rooms dating from about 50 years ago (they have more individuality than the newer rooms). But if you really want to splurge and live in style, there are also a couple of separate cottages more than 70 years old that are exquisitely decorated and come with old wooden tubs. You can open your shoji screens here to see maples, a gurgling brook, and woods, all in utter privacy. You'll be treated like royalty here, but of course you have to pay for it—these cottages cost up to ¥40,000 ($286) per person.

Even if you don't stay at Iwaso you can stop off for lunch at its restaurant, **Momiji** [231], open from 11 a.m. to 2 p.m. This is a very pleasant modern restaurant with clusters of paper-covered lanterns hanging from the ceiling and windows opening onto woods and a stream below. The specialty here is mini-kaiseki lunches for ¥2,000 ($14.29) and ¥3,300 ($23.57). Momiji also serves an *anagomeshi* (barbecued conger eel on rice) teishoku for ¥950 ($6.79).

The **Miyajima Grand Hotel** (tel. 0829/44-2411) was completely renovated and reopened in 1985 with 67 rooms, 10 of which are combination rooms with both twin beds and separate tatami areas. This ryokan doesn't differ from other modern ryokan, except that in its lobby there's a rather unusual mix of green, light purple, and pink in the decor. Rates here average about ¥18,000 ($129) per person, and Western breakfasts are served on request.

If you're looking for a ryokan that's a bit more moderately priced, a good choice is **Jyukeiso** [232] (tel. 0829/44-0300). Although it's about a 20-minute hike from the ferry pier (located in the same vicinity as Miyajima Lodge listed below), it has the advantage of sitting atop a small hill, with some pleasant views of Miyajima. In addition, the owner here speaks English. The ryokan was started some 50 years ago by his grandmother, though the present building is much more modern. All but one of the rooms are Japanese tatami rooms, and two have their own private bathroom. Rates here, which include two meals (Western breakfast on request), tax, and service, range from ¥8,800 ($63) to ¥16,500 ($118) per person.

For lower-priced accommodation, try **Miyajima Lodge** [233] (tel. 0829/44-0430). Located about a 25-minute walk from Miyajima Pier beside Omoto Park, the 30 rooms of this people's lodge are the do-it-yourself kind in which you lay out your futon yourself. Sheets, a cotton kimono, and TV are provided in each room. The simply decorated rooms without private bathroom are ¥5,500 ($39), and those with bathroom are ¥6,500 ($46) per person, including two meals. Tax and service charge are extra.

Fujitaya [234] (tel. 4-0151) is a pleasant restaurant located on the right side of the road leading toward Mount Misen and Daishoin as you exit from Itsukushima Shrine. It's open from 11 a.m. to 5 p.m. daily. It has a history of 80 years, but although the building itself is recent, the management has done a good job of maintaining a traditional atmosphere with wooden ceiling, shoji lamps, and a back courtyard with a maple tree, moss-covered rocks, and water running from a bamboo pipe into a pool carved into a flat rock. I had the house special here, *anagomeshi* (barbecued conger eel on rice). Costing ¥1,300 ($9.29), it comes with pickled vegetables, soup, and tea. There's also a sashimi lunch for ¥1,500 ($10.71) and noodles or rice with chicken for around ¥600 ($4.29). If you really want to go all out on eel, you can order an eel specialty in which it will be cooked and served in a variety of ways starting at ¥4,000 ($28.57). However, you must reserve this meal five days in advance.

Chapter IX

SHIKOKU

1. Takamatsu
2. Matsuyama

THE SMALLEST of Japan's four main islands, Shikoku is also one of the least visited by foreigners making a trek through Japan. That's surprising considering the natural beauty of its rugged mountains, its mild climate, and its most famous monuments—88 sacred Buddhist temples. It's the wish of many Japanese to make a pilgrimage to all 88 temples at least once in their lifetime as a tribute to the great Buddhist priest Kobo Daishi, who was born in Shikoku in 774 and who founded the Shingon sect of Buddhism. Such a pilgrimage has been popular since the Edo Period in the belief that a successful completion of the tour releases Buddhist followers from having to go through rebirth. It used to take several months to visit all 88 temples on foot, and even today you can see the pilgrims making their rounds dressed in white—only now they go by bus, which cuts traveling time down to two weeks. Many Japanese make the trip upon retirement.

I suggest you visit Shikoku on your travels through southern Japan. You could, for example, travel through Honshu to Kyushu and from Kyushu start back north via Shikoku, or vice versa. Ferries connect Shikoku to Beppu on Kyushu island, as well as to Tokyo, Osaka, Kobe, and Hiroshima on Honshu island. Although traditionally the most common way of reaching Shikoku has been to take the Shinkansen bullet train to Okayama, change to a local train bound for Uno and from Uno take a ferry to Takamatsu, the expected completion of one of the longest bridges in the world will change all that. Due for completion in March 1988 and therefore probably opened by the time you read this, the Seto Ohashi Bridge measures 5.83 miles from shore to shore and connects Kojima on Honshu with Sakaide on Shikoku. Those of you aboard the Shinkansen, therefore, need only change trains in Okayama for trains bound for either Takamatsu or Matsuyama on Shikoku. Whereas the journey from Tokyo Station to Shikoku used to take six to seven hours, you can now cover the same distance in about 4½ hours. Incidentally, the Seto Ohashi Bridge took ten years to construct and actually consists of six separate bridges that connect various islands of the Seto Inland Sea. The people of Shikoku are very proud of this bridge connecting their once-isolated island with Honshu and consider it one of their major tourist attractions. Since the bridge is double-decker and can also accommodate cars, buses, and trucks, this easier access to Shikoku will undoubtedly change the nature of the island and open it up to further development.

1. Takamatsu

Shikoku's second-largest town, Takamatsu is on the northeastern coast of the island overlooking the Seto Inland Sea. Takamatsu means "high pine," and the city served as the feudal capital of the powerful Matsudaira clan from 1642 until the Meiji Restoration in 1868. Takamatsu's most famous site is Ritsurin Park, one of the most outstanding gardens in Japan.

ORIENTATION: The Takamatsu train station is located on the coast of the Seto Inland Sea, only a few minutes' walk from the pier where ferries depart for Honshu and Shodo islands. The **Takamatsu City Information Office** (tel. 0878/51-2009) is located directly in the train station and is open every day except New Year's from 9 a.m. to 5 p.m. Stop here for a map of the city and directions to your hotel. If you want more detailed information on Shikoku, be sure to drop by the Tourist Information Center in Tokyo or Kyoto for a leaflet called *Inland Sea and Shikoku*.

All of the hotels and restaurants listed below, as well as Ritsurin Park, are located south and southeast of the train station. Chuo-dori Street is the town's main avenue and runs south from the train station past Ritsurin Park, passing Takamatsu Grand Hotel, Tokyu Inn, and Hotel Rich on the way. Buses and trams depart from in front of the station. The tram station is located across the street from the train station right beside the Takamatsu Grand Hotel. If you're taking the tram to Ritsurin Park, get off at the stop called Ritsurin-koen.

The **telephone area code** for Takamatsu is 0878. If you're writing to one of the hotels in Takamatsu, add Kagawa Prefecture 760 to the addresses given below.

THE SIGHTS: The main attractions of Takamatsu are spread out in the city but are easily reached by bus, tram, or train from the train station.

Ritsurin Park

Ritsurin Park was once the summer retreat of the Matsudaira family. Work on the park began in the 1600s, and it took about 100 years to complete. Using the backdrop of adjacent Mount Shiun in a principle known as "borrowed landscaping," the park incorporates the mountain into its overall design. Basically the garden can be divided into two parts: a traditional, classical southern garden and a modern northern garden with wide grassy lawns.

The southern garden holds the most interest to visitors. Arranged around the prescribed six ponds and 13 scenic mounds, it represents what is called a strolling garden in which each bend of the footpath—indeed, every new step—brings another perspective into view, another combination of rock, tree, and mountain. The garden is absolutely exquisite, and when I was there a mist was rolling off Mount Shiun, lending a mysteriousness to the landscape. After all, what better fits the image of traditional Japan than mist and pine trees? Altogether there are 1,500 pine trees and 500 cherry trees in Ritsurin Park, which you should tour in a counterclockwise fashion to appreciate fully the changing views.

Also in the park are a museum of local folk art and handcrafts, a zoo, and a shop where local products of Kagawa Prefecture are sold, including kites, masks, woodcarvings, umbrellas, fans, and bamboo vases. Be sure also to stop off at the park's tea house for a cup of frothy green tea. Called Kikugetsu-tei, the tea house dates from feudal days. There's a separate entrance charge of ¥300 ($2.14); a cup of ceremonial tea costs another ¥300.

Ritsurin Park is open every day of the year from sunrise to sunset, which is approximately from 7 a.m. to 5 p.m. in winter and 5:30 a.m. to 7 p.m. June through August. The admission fee to the park is ¥300 ($2.14), and the park is located about ten minutes from Takamatsu train station by bus or tram.

Shikoku Mura Village

Shikoku Mura Village is an open-air museum of 21 houses dating from the Edo Period and brought to Takamatsu from all parts of Shikoku. The houses, which are picturesquely situated on the slope of Yashima Hill, include thatched-roof homes of farmers and fishermen, a 150-year-old rural Kabuki stage, a tea ceremony house, and sheds for pressing sugar and for producing paper out of mulberry bark. There's also a suspended bridge made of vines which used to be a familiar sight in Shikoku as a means for crossing the island's many gorges and ravines—if you look closely, however, you'll see that this one is reinforced by cables.

It takes at least an hour to stroll through the village, which is open daily from 8:30 a.m. to 4:30 p.m. (until 5 p.m. in summer). The admission fee is ¥500 ($3.57). I heartily recommend this village if you have not had the opportunity to see similar villages in Takayama or Kawasaki, since they convey better than anything else what it must have been like to live in rural Japan in centuries past. Shikoku Mura Village is about a 20-minute tram ride from the main tram station, which is across the square from Takamatsu Station.

Other Sights

From Yashima Station close to Shikoku Mura Village you can take a cable car to the top of Yashima Plateau, where you'll find **Yashimaji Temple**, 84th of Shikoku's 88 sacred temples. Yashima is also famous as the site of a 12th-century battle between the rival clans of Taira and Minamoto as they fought for control over Japan. The Minamoto clan eventually won and established its shogunate court in Kamakura.

If you have some extra time and want to rest a few minutes, visit **Tamamo Park**, which is located behind the Takamatsu Grand Hotel close to the Takamatsu train station. The moats, gardens, and several three-story turrets are all that remain of what used to be an imposing castle belonging to the local warlords. There isn't a lot to see, but it's a pleasant place for a stroll or a picnic lunch if you're waiting for the next train.

If you're spending several days in Takamatsu, there are several attractions in the surrounding countryside worthy of your attention. **Shodo Island** (called *Shodoshima* in Japanese) is the second-largest island in the Seto Inland Sea and is easily reached from the ferry pier close to the Takamatsu train station in about an hour. Most visitors come to Shodo Island to see its natural wonders, including Kankakei Gorge, which measures 3.7 miles long, a monkey park with more than 700 wild monkeys, and Shihozashi Lookout, with its panoramic views of the Inland Sea. An extensive network of public buses crisscrosses the island, but if you're on a tight schedule you may wish to join one of the full or half-day sightseeing tours available. More information on Shodo Island can be obtained by calling the Shodoshima Tourist Office at 0879/62-1111.

If your interests run more along the lines of history, one of the best side trips you can take is to **Kotohira**, home of Kotohiragu Shrine as well as the oldest Kabuki theater in Japan. It takes about an hour to reach Kotohira by train from Takamatsu station, but that isn't the end of it—the shrine itself is at the top of 785 granite steps. If that's too much for you, you can hire porters who will take you only to the main gate (called *Omon* in Japanese), which is reached after climbing 365 steps. The cost of riding in one of these palanquins is ¥4,500 ($32.14) if you ride it one way and ¥5,500 ($39.29) if you're carried back down.

At any rate, the long trek up to Kotohiragu Shrine begins by exiting from the Kotohira train station's only exit, taking a left after passing under the first *torii* gate, and then right on a narrow, shop-lined street. Presently you'll reach the first flight of stairs. If you're making a detour to the Kabuki theater described below, turn left after the twenty-second step, from which the theater is only a 3-minute walk away. Otherwise continue climbing upwards—you should reach the main shrine after a 30-minute workout. You'll be rewarded with a sweeping view of the surrounding countryside, as well as the shrine itself. Popularly known as Kompira-San, the Kotohiragu Shrine was originally founded in the 11th century but has been rebuilt many times, with the main shrine buildings re-erected about 100 years ago. Considered one of the biggest and oldest Shinto shrines in the country, it's a popular shrine for fishermen, who come here to pray for safe journeys at sea. Part of the shrine complex is filled with boat models and photographs of ships that have been placed under the deity's care. Notice also the paper cranes, symbolizing good luck, as well as the small slats of wood hanging from the beams. If you wish, you can buy one of these slats and write a wish upon it. On my last visit, I saw a plea for a better profit in a family's business, as well as a wish to become smarter. I'm sure you lack in something that you can wish for, too.

Since you're in the vicinity, I highly recommend a visit to **Kompira Grand Playhouse**, known as *Kompira O-Shibai* [235] in Japanese. Open every day except Tuesday from 9 a.m. to 5 p.m. and charging an admission fee of ¥300 ($2.14), it is stunning in its simplicity and delightful in its construction. Since there was no electricity back in 1835, when it was built, the sides of the hall are rows of shoji screens and wooden coverings, which could be opened and closed to control the amount of light reaching the stage. Notice the tatami seating, the paper lanterns, and the revolving stage which was turned by eight men sweating it out in the basement. You can also tour the various makeup and dressing rooms behind the stage. Most curious is the fact that although all actors in Kabuki are men, there's a separate dressing room for the actor who impersonated and played the part of a woman. Actual Kabuki plays are staged once a year in April, but as you may well imagine, tickets are hard to come by. I'm sure it's a beautiful and moving sight.

WHERE TO STAY: Because Takamatsu is not a big tourist destination it doesn't have a wide selection of accommodations. Prices for rooms, however, are much lower here than in most cities in Japan.

Hotels
In terms of location, price, and view, one of the best deals in town is the **Takamatsu Grand Hotel**, 1-5-10 Kotobuki-cho (tel. 0878/51-5757). A striped building on Chuo-dori Street, it's conveniently located about a minute's walk from Takamatsu Station, the main artery for trains to the rest of Shikoku and for ferries from Honshu and Kyushu. Built in 1971 and having 136 rooms, the hotel sits on the edge of Tamamo Park, formerly the site of Takamatsu Castle and now an oasis of pine trees, three-story turrets, moats, and a classical garden. Both the lobby on the third floor and the Yashima Sky Restaurant on the seventh floor command sweeping views of the park, a welcome respite after a day of sightseeing. Rooms are a little worn but come equipped with a mini-bar, clock, and TV. Singles range from ¥5,500 ($39) to ¥6,700 ($48), twins run ¥ 11,000

($79) to ¥20,000 ($143), while doubles are ¥ 12,500 ($89). The higher-priced rooms face the park and have the nicest views. There are nine restaurants as well as a shopping arcade located in the hotel complex.

A NOTE ON JAPANESE SYMBOLS: Many hotels, restaurants, and other establishments in Japan do not have signs showing their names in English letters. Appendix II lists the Japanese symbols for all such places appearing in this guide. Each establishment name in Japanese symbols is numbered, and the same number appears in brackets in the text following the boldfaced establishment name. For example, in the text the Osaka hotel, Hokke Club [161], is number 161 in the Japanese list in Appendix II.

The **Takamatsu Tokyu Inn**, 9-9 Hyogo-machi (tel. 0878/21-0106), was built in 1982 and still remains one of the newest hotels in town. A brown building, it's about a seven-minute walk from Takamatsu train station on Chuo-dori Street, beside the Hyogomachi covered shopping arcade. The lobby is on the second floor, and its one restaurant serves Western fare. Its 64 rooms begin at ¥6,700 ($48) for a single and ¥13,600 ($97) for a twin or double. Rooms are clean, simple, and small but have all the usual business-hotel amenities, including clock, TV, and cotton kimono. Rooms facing Chuo-dori Street are fitted with double-paned glass to shut out traffic noise. None of the views are spectacular, but given a choice I'd chose a room on a top floor facing the west and the sea, far in the distance.

Located almost directly across the street from Tokyu Inn on Chuo-dori Street is **Hotel Rich**, 9-1 Furujinmachi (tel. 0878/22-3555). A beige-brick building, it features three restaurants, serving Japanese, Chinese, and French cuisine, as well as a bar. Rooms are similar to those in Tokyu Inn and range from ¥6,000 ($43) to ¥7,700 ($55) for a single and ¥12,000 ($86) to ¥16,500 ($118) for a double or twin.

If the above hotels are full, **Takamatsu Plaza Hotel** [236] 7-Banchi, Tamamo-cho (tel. 0878/51-3655) is an inexpensive, ten-story business hotel just a five-minute walk from Takamatsu train station. Rooms are of adequate size, with the difference in price based on room size—so I recommend you ask for a room on a higher floor with a view of either the sea or Tamamo Park. Singles here are ¥5,200 ($37), doubles are ¥8,800 ($63), and twins are ¥5,500 ($39) and ¥8,800 ($63). The twin rooms don't have closets; instead there are hooks on the wall for hanging clothes, just like in olden days in Japan.

Ryokan

Hotel Kawaroku, Hyakken-cho (tel. 0878/21-5666), first opened as a ryokan 110 years ago, was destroyed during an air raid in World War II, and is now a modern structure with 49 Japanese-style rooms and 21 Western-style rooms. A ten-minute walk from Takamatsu Station, it's located close to the Mitsukoshi department store and several shopping arcades right in the heart of the city. All rooms come with private bathroom, safe, mini-bar, and TV. The Western-style rooms are white, bright, and clean, while the Japanese-style rooms are simply furnished and have that wonderful earthy smell of tatami. The hotel's one restaurant serves French cuisine; if you want Japanese food, it will be served in your room. The rate per person, including Japanese dinner and breakfast, is ¥14,300 ($102). If you decide to take your meals elsewhere, the room charge for Western-style rooms begins at ¥6,600 ($47) for a single and ¥11,000 ($79) for a twin, while Japanese-style rooms begin at ¥8,800 ($63) for one person and ¥12,000 ($86) for two.

A traditional Japanese ryokan, **Tokiwa Honkan** [237], 1-8-1 Tokiwa-cho (tel. 0878/61-5577), has a delightful inner courtyard reminiscent of those found around tea houses, with a pond, dwarf pine trees, golden carp, stone lanterns, wooden passageways, and vermilion railings. The ryokan is topped with a donjon, making it look like a shogun's castle. Built in 1954, the ryokan at first catered almost exclusively to foreigners, but as Western-style hotels began making their appearance it lost many of its foreign customers. Now the ryokan receives only about 20 foreign guests a year. Rooms were completely renovated in 1987, with the result that all now have private toilet. Only half the rooms are equipped with private bathtub, but public baths are located on each floor. There are also large communal baths separated for men and women.

Unlike most ryokan, this one gives you the choice of whether you want to take your meals here. If you do, it's ¥13,200 ($94) to ¥20,000 ($143) if you're taking a room alone and ¥11,000 ($79) to ¥20,000 ($143) per person if there are two of you. Rooms without meals are about 30 percent less. You may also pay separately for your meals. Western breakfasts are ¥1,650 ($12), while dinners of tempura or sukiyaki range from ¥3,300 ($24) to ¥6,600 ($47) per person.

Youth Hostel

The **Takamatsu Yuai-Sanso Youth Hostel** [238] is just a ten-minute walk from Takamatsu Station at 2-4-14 Nishiki-cho (tel. 0878/22-3656). It's small—only five rooms accommodating 32 persons. Rates are ¥1,850 ($13), with an additional ¥200 ($1.43) charged in summer and winter for heating or air conditioning expenses. Breakfasts are available for ¥450 ($3.21) and dinners for ¥660 ($4.71). If you're not a card-carrying youth hostel member, you can still stay here, though you'll be charged an extra ¥500 ($3.57) per night.

WHERE TO DINE: Takamatsu is known throughout Japan for its *sanuki udon*, which are thick white noodles made from wheat flour. With Takamatsu as the center of the industry, there are as many as 400 sanuki manufacturers and more than 2,000 noodle shops in Kagawa Prefecture. It's been estimated that about 10% of the population eats sanuki noodles every day, a percentage that's about five times higher than in any other area of Japan. Takamatsu also has a fresh supply of fish from the Seto Inland Sea.

Japanese Food

If you want to watch sanuki udon being made, the best place to observe it is at **Kanaizumi** [239], Daikumachi (tel. 21-6688), located about a 15-minute walk from Takamatsu Station. It's a bit classier than your usual noodle shop, and is easily recognizable from the outside by a huge paper lantern hanging in front of the restaurant and a front window where sanuki noodles are being made by hand. Although the menu is in Japanese, pictures accompany each set meal, making it easy to order. These come with noodles and a combination of various vegetables and meats, and range from ¥550 ($3.93) to ¥3,000 ($21.43). If you want just a bowl of noodles without side dishes, it will cost about ¥380 ($2.71). I had a set meal called Niku-nabe Udon, which cost ¥1,100 ($7.86) and consisted of a bowl of noodles, leek, thin slices of beef, and rice cake in hot broth. Before eating each morsel I dipped it first into a mixture of raw egg, just as one does with sukiyaki. It was good, but rice cakes take forever to chew. Be prepared also for slippery noodles and all that good-natured slurping that accompanies a meal in a noodle shop. Hours here are 10 a.m. to 1 a.m.; closed the second and fourth Mondays of the month.

Another noodle restaurant you might want to try—especially if you're going to Shikoku Mura Village—is **Zaigoudon-waraya** (tel. 43-3115). It's located next to and just below the village in a 100-year-old thatched house (look for the water wheel and tables for outdoor seating) and is open daily from 10 a.m. to 7 p.m. Its handmade udon ranges in price from ¥450 ($3.21) to ¥2,500 ($17.86). The combination udon and tempura dish is especially popular.

A well-known tempura and sushi restaurant in town is **Tenkatsu** [240], Hyogomachi (tel. 21-5380). To reach it from Takamatsu Station, walk south on Chuo-dori Street until it intersects with a large covered pedestrian shopping arcade called Hyogomachi. Turn right, walk all the way through the arcade, and upon emerging you'll find the restaurant immediately on your left. It's a modern-looking building with a plastic-food display case and a window where a chef prepares sushi. Inside the restaurant are tatami mats and tables, but I suggest sitting at the counter, which encircles a large pool filled with fish, mainly flatfish. As customers order their meals, fish are swooped out of the tanks with nets—they certainly couldn't be fresher. In fact I saw some customers served a fish that was still quivering even though it had been sliced for sashimi. Although the menu here is in Japanese only, there are pictures accompanying some of the tempura and sushi courses. Most dishes range from ¥1,000 ($7.14) to ¥2,000 ($14.29). If you feel like splurging, there's a meal for ¥3,500 ($25) that features Japanese food in season, changing every month. Another specialty of the house is wine, served every month with something different in it, usually flower petals. In March, for example, it's peach blossoms and in April cherry blossoms. Hours are 11 a.m. to 10 p.m. daily.

Hansuke [241] is located just around the corner from Tokyu Inn in the Hygomachi shopping arcade (tel. 51-5653). Unlike many of the other shops in the covered arcade, this yakitoria-ya has been in operation in this same spot for more than 30 years, making it one of the oldest—if not the oldest—yakitori shops in town. Simple and cheap, it's a greasy spoon in the true sense of the word; the grill looks like it's been here from the beginning. The yakitori, however, is excellent and costs ¥350 ($2.50) for four skewers of chicken wedged between slices of onion. The establishment also serves eel, with *kabayaki*, a filet of eel, costing ¥1,300 ($9.29). The real specialty of Hansuke, however, is its namesake, *hansuke*, which according to the shop owner means "heads of eel stuck on a skewer." Both I and the Japanese I was with thought it was one of the most unappetizing sights we had ever seen, but in a spontaneous burst of adventure we decided to try it. I don't want to spoil your own experiences by telling you what it was like, but be prepared for lots of bones. A skewer of hansuke is a bargain at only ¥80 (57¢) a stick. This locale is open every day except Sunday and national holidays from 11:30 a.m. to 1 p.m. and again from 4 to 10 p.m.

Western Food

If you want Western food in Takamatsu your best bet is to dine at a hotel. **Le Bon 6** is a French restaurant located on the ground floor of the Hotel Kawaroku, Hyakken-cho (tel. 21-5666). The Japanese chef here studied and worked for many years in both France and Belgium and, representing Japan, won a gold medal in 1982 at a world food contest held in Luxembourg. The emphasis at this restaurant is on food rather than on decor, including seafood, beef, and lamb dishes. Entrées range from about ¥2,300 ($16.43) to ¥6,000 ($42.86) for most dishes. The chef takes special pride in his creations for the set meals, which change monthly and cost ¥6,500 ($46.43) and ¥8,800 ($62.86). Hours here are 11 a.m. to 2 p.m. and 4 to 9 p.m. daily.

On the seventh floor of the Takamatsu Grand Hotel, 1-5-10 Kotobuki-cho, is the **Yashima Sky Restaurant** (tel. 51-5757). Enclosed on three sides by glass, it affords panoramic views of Tamamo Park and the harbor full of boats and ferries coming and going. Lunch, served from 11:30 a.m. to 2 p.m., has set meals available for ¥900 ($6.43), ¥2,000 ($14.29) and ¥2,750 ($19.64). Dinners, served from 5 to 8:30 p.m., range from ¥2,500 ($17.86) to ¥6,000 ($42.86). The à la carte menu is varied with such items as fondue, steak tartare, lobster thermidor, tenderloin and sirloin steaks, filet mignon, wienerschnitzel, shrimp pilaf, and sandwiches. Most dishes are in the ¥1,500 ($10.71) to ¥3,000 ($21.43) price range.

The **Takamatsu Plaza Hotel**, 7-Banchi, Tamamo-cho (tel. 51-3655), also has a restaurant, this one on the tenth floor with views of the harbor. It's open from 11 a.m. to 2 p.m. and 5 to 9 p.m. Dishes are slightly cheaper and include spaghetti, pork, beef, and chicken entrées averaging ¥1,000 ($7.14).

2. Matsuyama

Although Matsuyama is Shikoku's largest town, with a population of more than 420,000, it has the relaxed atmosphere of a small town. Located on the island's northwest coast, about a three-hour train ride from Takamatsu, Matsuyama features one of Japan's best-preserved feudal castles and what I consider to be the most delightful public bathhouse in the country.

ORIENTATION: With the completion of the Seto Ohashi Bridge in the spring of 1988, the easiest way to reach Matsuyama is by train from Okayama on Honshu island. Matsuyama is also linked to various ports, including Beppu on Kyushu and Hiroshima on Honshu.

The **Matsuyama City Tourist Information Office** (tel. 0899/31-3914) is located inside the Matsuyama JR Train Station and can be spotted easily with its sign in English. Open daily from 8:30 a.m. to 7:30 p.m., it has an excellent pamphlet and map in English. The train station itself is situated on the west end of town, with most points of interest spreading to the east. Streetcars depart from the front of the station to such places as Dogo Spa and the Okaido Shopping Arcade, a covered pedestrian passageway lined with restaurants and shops, considered to be the heart of the city. Matsuyama Castle lies just northwest of Okaido. Many buses and commuter trains bound for the suburbs depart from Matsuyama City Station, called *Shi-eki* in Japanese, which is linked to Matsuyama JR Train Station via streetcar. More information on how to reach Matsuyama and places of interest can be obtained in a leaflet called *Inland Sea and Shikoku*, available at the T.I.C. in either Tokyo or Kyoto.

The **telephone area code** for Matsuyama is 0899. Matsuyama lies in Ehime Prefecture, and its postal code is 790.

THE SIGHTS: Matsuyama Castle crowns the top of Katsuyama Hill right in the heart of the city. It was built by feudal lord Kato Yoshiakira about 385 years ago, later falling into the hands of the powerful Matsudaira family. Like most structures in Japan, Matsuyama Castle has suffered fire and destruction through the ages, but unlike many other castles (such as those in Osaka and Nagoya) this one is the real thing rather than a replica made of ferroconcrete. There's only one entrance to the castle, a pathway leading through a series of gates which could be swung shut to trap attacking enemies. The three-story donjon houses a museum where you can see armor and swords that used to belong to the Matsudaira family. Surrounding the castle is a park, and if you're feeling energetic you can walk to the castle in about 15 minutes. Otherwise there's a chair lift and a cable car on the east side of Katsuyama Hill. A ticket for ¥550 ($3.93) includes the round-trip ride to the top of the hill and entrance to the castle. The castle is open daily from 9 a.m. to 4:30 p.m.

Dogo Spa, with a history of 3,000 years, claims to be the oldest hot-spring spa in Japan, certainly an impressive record. Located in the northeast part of the city about a 20-minute tram ride from Matsuyama Station, Dogo Spa can accommodate about 9,000 people in 62 hotels and ryokan, which means that the narrow streets resound at night with the clatter of *geta* (wooden shoes) as vacationers go to the various bathhouses.

Most of the hotels and ryokan in Dogo have their own *onsen* (hot-spring bath), but I suggest that no matter where you stay you make at least one trip to **Dogo Onsen Honkan,** a wonderful three-story public bathhouse built in 1894. A wooden structure with shoji screens, tatami rooms, creaking wooden stairways, and a white heron topping the crest of the roof, Shinrokaku is as much a social institution as it is a place to soak and scrub. On busy days as many as 4,000 people will pass through its front doors. The water here is transparent, colorless, tasteless, and alkaline. The hottest spring water coming into the spa is 120°F and coolest is 70°F—but don't worry, the waters are mixed to achieve a comfortable 108°F.

Bathing, however, is just a small part of the experience here. Most people come to relax, socialize, and while away an hour or more, and I suggest that you do the same. Although you can bathe for as little as ¥250 ($1.79), it's worth it to pay extra for the privilege of relaxing on tatami mats in a communal room on the second floor, dressed in a rented *yukata* (kimono), drinking tea from a lacquered tea set, and eating Japanese sweets. If the weather is fine, all the shoji screens are pushed open to let in a breeze, and as you sprawl out on the tatami, drinking your tea and listening to the clang of the streetcar and the clatter of wooden shoes, you can almost imagine you've somehow landed in ancient Japan. To my mind the whole scene resembles an old woodblock print that has suddenly sprung to life. Cost of the bath, yukata, sweets, and tea is ¥660 ($4.71). A smaller and therefore more private bath and lounging area where tea and sweets are also served costs ¥1,000 ($7.14). And if you really want to splurge, you can rent your own private tatami room on the third floor, which also comes with tea, sweets, and yukata, for ¥1,300 ($9.29).

Connected to the spa is another building built in 1899 for the imperial family (the present emperor has visited this spa twice), and you can take a tour of these rooms for a couple hundred yen. The spa is open from 6:30 a.m. (which is the arrival time of the first streetcar) until 11 p.m., but you must enter by 10 p.m. The ticket window for sweets, yukata, and tea closes at 9 p.m.

After your bath, you may want to visit **Ishiteji Temple**, about half a mile east of Dogo. Built in 1318, it's the 51st of Shikoku's 88 sacred temples and is a good example of architecture of the Kamakura Period with its blend of Chinese and Japanese styles. Notice the many straw sandals hanging on the temple gate. They are placed there by older Japanese in hopes of regaining new strength in their legs. There are, incidentally, seven other temples in Matsuyama that belong to the sacred 88, but Ishiteji is the most important and popular.

Crafts and Culture

Matsuyama is famous for several crafts, one of which is *Iyo Kasuri*, a cotton cloth dyed with Japanese indigo and worn traditionally as working clothes by farm housewives. The history of the cloth stretches back to the early 1800s, when it was originated by a woman named Kana Kagiya. If you're interested in seeing first-hand how this cloth is produced, then and now, you can visit **Mingei Iyo Kasuri Kaikan** [242], Kumanodai 1165 (tel. 22-0405), a small factory you can reach by bus from the JR Train Station. Open from 8:10 a.m. to 4:55 p.m.

daily, it charges a small admission fee of ¥50 (36¢) and displays the process of dyeing, machine weaving, and hand-weaving the blue cloth. You can even dye your own handkerchief for an extra ¥800 ($5.71). A shop sells various products made from Kasuri cloth, including pillowcases, purses, clothing, hats, and bolts of cloth.

Another product of Ehime Prefecture is Tobe pottery, called *Tobe-yaki* in Japanese. Noted for its thick white porcelain painted with cobalt blue designs, Tobe pottery is produced in the town of Tobe, which you can reach by bus in about 40 minutes from Matsuyama Shi-eki. There are several kilns open to the public, the most well known of which is **Umeno Seito-jo** [243], tel. 62-2311. It's open every day except Monday from 9 a.m. to 5 p.m. Tobe-yaki is also on display at **Tobe-yaki Kanko Center** [244], tel. 62-2070, with the same open hours. At both places you can try your hand in a workshop.

If you'd like to see Kasuri cloth or Tobe-yaki but don't have the time to visit the places where they are made, you can see both at the **Ehime Prefectural Products Hall (Ehime no Bussan)** [245], located at Ichibancho 4-chome not far from the ANA Zenniku Hotel (tel. 41-7584). Open every day from 8:30 a.m. to 5 p.m. except Sunday and national holidays, it sells the products of Ehime Prefecture, including such foodstuffs as sweets and honey, as well as Tobe-yaki, Kasuri cloth, masks, bamboo vases, lacquer, cultivated pearls, and dolls. Notice how the dolls are shaped in an oval. Known as the princess doll, they are made in the image of Empess Jingu, who came to Dogo Spa way back in the second century when she was pregnant.

If you're interested in the performing arts, you should check whether there's anything going on in the newly opened **Ehime Prefectural Convention and Cultural Hall.** Designed by Kenzo Tange, this bright, modern hall has frequent concerts, dramas, and performances. Check with your hotel or the tourist office for information on current productions.

Uchiko

If you have time for a side trip around Ehime Prefecture, I strongly recommend an excursion to the village of Uchiko. With a population of less than 13,000, it has some fine old homes and buildings dating back to the Edo Period and the turn of the century. Whereas about 70% of Matsuyama was destroyed during World War II, Uchiko was left intact and a tiny part of the old city is a living memorial to the days of yore. Even the train ride from Matsuyama JR Station is enjoyable as you weave through valleys of wooded hills. The train trip takes about 50 minutes. Be sure to pick up a map of the village at the Uchiko train station, even though it's in Japanese. A walk through the old part of town, known as *Yokaichi*, should take about an hour or two, depending on how often you stop along the way. Most of the older homes are clustered along one narrow street—there isn't a whole lot to see, but the walk is pleasant and some of the scenes make good photo essays. Note that most museums and buildings in Uchiko are closed on Wednesday.

The first important building on a walking tour of the city is **Uchikoza** [246], which is a Kabuki theater built back in 1916. It was recently restored and though it's not as grand as the one near Takamatsu described earlier in this chapter, it's a good example of how townspeople used to enjoy themselves years ago. It features a revolving stage and many windows that can be opened and closed to control the amount of light reaching the stage.

Other places of interest in Yokaichi include **Machi-ya Shiryokan** and **Kamihaga House**, old homes which have been restored and are open to the public. Built in 1894, Kamihaga House is especially grand, having once belonged to a merchant who made his fortune by exporting wax. During the Edo Period,

Uchiko gained fame as a center of candlemaking and wax production, used both for lighting and for the styling of elaborate hairdos. Later the wax was applied to thread used in weaving and as an ingredient in vanishing cream, pomade, and shoe polish. At the world fairs of 1894 in Chicago and 1900 in Paris, Uchiko wax won first prize for quality.

Today only one man carries on this waxing tradition, a man named Omori Yataro who represents the fifth generation of candlemakers. Following the same techniques as those developed by his ancestors 200 years ago, he even collects his own *haze* berries (a kind of sumac) and makes his candles by hand. His workshop is open to the public, and in the mornings you can observe him at work.

FOOD AND LODGING: There are plenty of choices of both hotels and ryokan in Matsuyama and in Dogo Spa.

The Top Choice

Matsuyama's premier hotel is the **ANA Zenniku Hotel**, 3-2-1 Ichiban-cho (tel. 0899/33-5511). About a ten-minute taxi ride from the train station, it is in a good location for visiting both Matsuyama and Dogo Spa. It's only a five-minute walk to the cable car going up to the castle, and streetcars heading for Dogo pass right in front of the hotel. Built in 1979, the hotel is spacious, cheerfully decorated, and offers 52 boutiques on four floors for shopping. Its 334 rooms, which start at ¥8,500 ($61) for singles and ¥16,500 ($118) for twins and doubles, are large and well appointed with TV, mini-bar, radio, clock, and desk.

The hotel also offers a good selection in dining. The **Unkai** is a Japanese restaurant offering a variety of food, including sukiyaki, shabu-shabu, tempura, and sashimi. Although the menu is in Japanese only, there are pictures accompanying most of the set meals, which average about ¥4,000 ($28.57). À la carte dinners usually run about ¥6,000 ($42.86) per person; lunches start at ¥1,000 ($7.14). The restaurant overlooks a small garden with a stream that is lit up at night.

If you'd rather have Western food, the **Castle Grill**, on the 14th floor, serves seafood and steaks, with the cost of an average dinner coming to about ¥6,000 ($42.86) to ¥8,000 ($57.18). There are also dinner specials for ¥5,500 ($39.29), ¥6,600 ($47.14), and ¥9,300 ($66.43). Dinner is romantic, with candles and flowers on each table and a view in the valley below of a European-style castle built by a former lord. Lunch courses start at ¥1,600 ($11.43).

Both Unkai and Castle Grill are open daily from 11:45 a.m. to 2:30 p.m. and 5 to 9:30 p.m. Located next to Castle Grill is a bar where you can retire for drinks after dinner.

If you're on a budget or simply want to sit out under the sun or stars, try the ANA Zenniku's **rooftop beer garden**. Open May to September from 5 to 9:30 p.m., this place serves snacks and dishes at about ¥550 ($3.93) to ¥800 ($5.71) a plate. Choices include chicken, pizza, and Japanese dishes. Mugs of beer go for ¥500 ($3.57) and ¥850 ($6.07), and cocktails are ¥650 ($4.64). Buy your food and drink tickets at the front counter. After you seat yourself, the waiter will collect your ticket and deliver your order.

A Medium-Priced Hotel

A small and pleasant medium-priced hotel not far from the ANA Zenniku Hotel, the **Kokusai International Hotel**, 1-13 Ichiban-cho (tel. 0899/32-5111), has 80 rooms with radio, clock, TV, mini-bar, and large windows that let in lots of light. Rooms start at ¥6,000 ($43) for one person and ¥7,300 ($52) for two. Even single rooms here have double beds, and some rooms have views of Matsuyama Castle. **Yoshicho**, the hotel's Japanese restaurant, serves such specialties as kushikatsu, sashimi, sukiyaki, and tempura, with the average meal costing ¥3,000 ($21.43) to ¥5,000 ($35.71). Restaurant hours are 7 a.m. to 10 p.m. daily. The hotel's Western restaurant, open from 7 a.m. to 10 p.m., offers sandwiches, fish, beef curry, spaghetti, and set meals, as well as teppanyaki steaks. Expect to spend about ¥3,000 ($21.43) for a meal.

Ryokan

If you want to stay in a ryokan, head for Dogo. A good choice here is **Funaya** [247], Dogo Yunamachi (tel. 0899/47-0278). Although it doesn't look like much from the outside, the inside is comfortable and pleasant. The present building dates from 1963 but the ryokan itself has a history extending almost 140 years. This is where the imperial family stays on visits to Dogo. The lobby and many of its rooms look out onto a garden. Of the ryokan's 43 rooms, 38 are tatami, two are furnished with twin beds, and three are combinations with both beds and tatami areas, which is ideal if you want the feel of a ryokan but don't relish sleeping on the floor. Rates here are ¥22,000 ($157) per person, which includes breakfast, dinner, tax, and service charge.

Another ryokan in Dogo is **Kasugaen** [248], 3-1 Saigidani-cho (tel. 0899/41-9156). It has both Japanese-style rooms as well as rooms fitted with both twin beds and tatami. Amenities include mini-bar, TV, and safe. The price of a room, which includes two meals, tax, and service charge, is ¥20,000 ($143) per person.

The Budget Category

A red-brick building about a five-minute walk from the Matsuyama JR Train Station, **Hotel Sunroute**, Miyatacho (tel. 0899/33-2811), opened in 1986 with a total of 110 rooms. Its rooms are reasonably priced and feature a TV with coin-operated videos, radio, clock, hot-water pot for tea, and double-paned windows to shut out noises from the train station. The best views are from those rooms on the top floors facing east, which have a glimpse of the distant castle. Singles are ¥5,500 ($39), while doubles and twins begin at ¥8,800 ($63). On the hotel's roof is a covered beer garden, open rain or shine from 5 to 9 p.m. March through September. After paying an initial charge of 2,700 ($19.29), you can eat and drink as much as you like.

Business Hotel Taihei [249], 3-1-15 Heiwa Dori (tel. 0899/43-3560), is a rather interesting establishment located at the northern base of Katsuyama Hill about a 15-minute taxi ride from Matsuyama Station. Unlike the plastic impersonal atmosphere of most business hotels, this one is rather eccentric—most rooms are decorated with old-fashioned wallpaper, worn flowered bedspreads, curtains, and shaggy rugs. The effect is cozy and pleasant, and rooms are great for the price. Singles are ¥4,400 ($31), twins are ¥7,700 ($55), doubles run ¥8,800 ($63), and triples go for ¥10,000 ($71) and up. There are also Japanese-style rooms available for ¥6,500 ($46). All rooms have bathrooms. Buffet breakfasts for ¥550 ($3.93) and dinners for ¥880 ($6.29) are served in a cheerful dining area. There's a public bath and sauna, but it's only for men. If women happen to be in the majority, it becomes a women's-only facility, but I have the feeling that happens only rarely.

The **Matsuyama Shinsen-en Youth Hostel** [250], 22-3 Dogohimezaka Otsu (tel. 0899/33-6366), is an eight-minute walk from Dogo Spa Station. A one-night's stay here costs ¥2,200 ($15.71), breakfast is ¥440 ($3.14), and dinner runs ¥660 ($4.71). If you're not a youth hostel member, you can still stay here but you'll be charged an extra ¥500 ($3.57) per night.

More Dining

Hyakkumi [251], 2 Sanbancho (tel. 45-1893), is just off Okaido pedestrian shopping lane close to the ANA Zenniku Hotel. Although it doesn't have an English menu, it has a plastic-food display case outside showing tempura, shabu-shabu, somen, kamameshi, and other dishes. Most items are ¥800 ($5.71) to ¥2,700 ($19.29). I've had the Bochan Teishoku, a rice casserole dish served with fish, soup, egg custard, and tea, for ¥1,850 ($13.21). The topping for your rice casserole is your choice—how about crab, shrimp, or fish? I've also tried the *Higawari teishoku*, which means daily special and which changes every day. It's available until 2 p.m. every day except Sunday and national holidays and costs ¥900 ($6.43). It usually consists of a variety of small dishes, and included soup, sashimi, tempura, pickled vegetables, beef, egg custard, and rice during my last visit. The ground floor provides counter seating, but I find the little cubicles with either tatami or table seating on the first floor much more festive. The hours here are from 11:30 a.m. to 9:30 p.m., closed on Tuesday. If Tuesday is a national holiday, the restaurant stays open but closes the following Wednesday.

Shinhamasaku [252], Sanbancho 4-chome (tel. 33-3030), is a modern restaurant serving fresh seafood from the Seto Inland Sea and other local specialties, as well as shabu-shabu, kamameshi, and crab and eel dishes. The menu is in Japanese only but has pictures of the various set courses, most of which range from ¥1,000 ($7.14) to ¥3,000 ($21). Popular is the *Seiro bento* for ¥2,700 ($19.29), which includes about 20 different bite-size morsels, all served in a wooden box. It's open from 11 a.m. to 3 p.m. and from 4:30 to 8:30 p.m. daily.

Chapter X

KYUSHU

AS THE SOUTHERNMOST of Japan's four main islands, Kyushu offers a mild climate, hot-spring spas such as Beppu and Ibusuki, beautiful countryside, national parks, and warm, friendly people. Historians believe that Japan's earliest inhabitants lived in Kyushu before gradually pushing northward, and according to Japanese legend it was from Kyushu that the first emperor, Jimmu, began his campaign to unify Japan. Kyushu is therefore considered to be the cradle of Japanese civilization. And because Kyushu is the island closest to Korea and China, it has served through the centuries as a point of influx for both people and ideas from abroad, including those from the West. Christian missionaries such as St. Francis Xavier succeeded in converting many Kyushu Japanese to Christianity. And in Nagasaki, small communities of Dutch and Chinese merchants were allowed to remain throughout Japan's 200-some years of isolation from the West. In short, Kyushu should be high on the list of any visitor to Japan. From its hot sand baths to its volcanic peaks to its beaches and cosmopolitan cities, Kyushu offers some of the best attractions in Japan.

1. Fukuoka

With a population of more than one million, Fukuoka is Kyushu's largest city and serves as a major gateway to the island, both internationally and domestically. With international direct flights from Pusan, Seoul, Taipei, Manila, Hong Kong, and Honolulu, Fukuoka is also the last stop on the Shinkansen bullet train from Tokyo, about seven hours away; Hiroshima is just 1½ hours away.

During Japan's feudal days, Fukuoka was actually divided into two distinct towns separated by the Nakagawa River. Fukuoka was where the samurai lived, since it was the castle town of the local feudal lord. Across the river in Hakata was where the merchants lived, making it the commercial center of the area.

Both cities were joined into one town in 1889 under the common name of Fukuoka. Fukuoka's main train station, however, is in Hakata and is therefore called Hakata Station.

In Japanese history books, Fukuoka's main claim to fame lies in the 13th century, when it was selected by Mongol forces under Kublai Khan as the most convenient place to invade Japan. The first invasion occurred in 1274, but the Japanese were able to repel the enemy. The second attempt came in 1281, but the Japanese had not been idle and were well prepared for the attack. They had built a stone wall along the coast almost ten feet high. Not only did the Mongols find the wall impossible to scale, but a typhoon blew in and destroyed the entire Mongol fleet. The Japanese called this gift from heaven "divine wind," or *kamikaze*, a word that took on quite a different meaning when young Japanese pilots crashed their planes into American ships during World War II in an attempt to turn the tide of war in Japan's favor.

As an industrial and business center of Kyushu, Fukuoka is not considered much of a destination on the tourist circuit. However, you may find yourself making a one-night stopover here after an international flight or a day's train ride from Tokyo.

ORIENTATION: Before leaving Tokyo or Kyoto, drop by the Tourist Information Center to pick up a leaflet called *Fukuoka*. It lists the major sights of the city.

The **Fukuoka Tourist Information Office** (tel. 431-3003) is in Hakata Station. Open from 9 a.m. to 7 p.m., it has maps in English. If you're going to spend any amount of time in Fukuoka Prefecture, pick up a copy of *Fantastic Fukuoka*, available for ¥300 ($2.14) at the Fukuoka Kotsu Center on the fourth floor next to Hakata Station. By the way, an **international post office** is also located next to Hakata Station.

Although Hakata Station is the terminus for the Shinkansen bullet train and has most of Fukuoka's hotels clustered in its vicinity, the heart of Fukuoka is actually in an area of town called **Tenjin**. Serving as the business center for the city, it's also home to several department stores, a large underground shopping arcade, coffeeshops, and restaurants. Less than a ten-minute walk from Tenjin is **Nakasu**, Fukuoka's largest nightlife district with lots of bars, restaurants, and small clubs.

As for getting around Fukuoka, the easiest method of transportation is by subway. One convenient subway line, for example, runs from Hakata Station to Tenjin (the third stop), passing Nakasukawabata on the way, which is the stop for the Nakasu nightlife district. If you stay on this same line, it will also take you to Ohori-Koen Park. Fukuoka also has bus lines; the city's two bus terminals are located in Tenjin and at Hakata Station. And whereas Hakata Station serves as the terminus for the Shinkansen and JR trains departing for the rest of Kyushu, Tenjin has its own station, called the Nishitetsu Fukuoka Station. This is where you board the train if you're going to Dazaifu.

The **telephone area code** for Fukuoka is 092, and Fukuoka is located in the prefecture of the same name.

THE SIGHTS: **Shofukuji Temple** is just a ten-minute walk northwest of Hakata Station. Thought to be the oldest Zen Buddhist temple in Japan, it was founded in 1195 by a priest named Eisai, who was the first to introduce Zen and tea seeds into Japan after studying four years in China.

Located about 15 minutes by foot from Hakata Station is **Sumiyoshi-jinja Shrine**. With buildings dating from about 400 years ago, it's one of Kyushu's oldest Shinto shrines and is dedicated to the guardians of seafarers. As it's favored by the Japanese as a good place for wedding ceremonies, you may be lucky and witness a traditional wedding in progress.

If you feel like being completely and wickedly lazy, take the subway line from Hakata Station to the Ohori-Koen subway stop, just ten minutes away. There you'll find **Ohori-Koen Park**, built on part of the outer defenses of the former Fukuoka Castle. Laid around a lake with small islands connected with bridges, it's a perfect place to relax with a picnic lunch. On the south side of the park is a traditional Japanese garden—constructed not centuries ago but in 1984.

If you start feeling guilty for being so lazy, visit the nearby **Fukuoka City Art Museum**, in the southeastern part of the park facing the lake. It contains modern and Buddhist art as well as tea ceremony utensils, ancient weapons, and armor. Closed on Monday, it's open the rest of the week from 9:30 a.m. to 5:30 p.m. Admission is ¥150 ($1.07).

If you have time, the most popular thing to do in Fukuoka is to take a side trip to **Dazaifu Temmangu Shrine**, which you can reach in 35 minutes by taking the Nishi Nippon Tetsudo Line (called Nishitetsu for short) from Nishitetsu Fukuoka Station in Tenjin. Trains depart every 30 minutes and the station stop is called Dazaifu Station. Dazaifu Temmangu Shrine was established in 905, although the present main hall dates from 1590. It's dedicated to the god of scholarship, which is one reason why the shrine is so popular—high school students flock here to pray that they pass the tough entrance exams into universities. Planted with lots of plum trees, camphor trees, and irises, the extensive grounds surrounding the shrine can be explored on a rented bicycle.

SHOPPING: You don't have to venture far from Hakata Station to go shopping. In fact, the Izutsuya department store is located right above the station itself. Incidentally, on top of the department store is a rooftop beer garden open mid-April through August from 5 to 10 p.m. Radiating out from the station are underground shopping arcades. Deitos is located under the Shinkansen tracks and comprises of various souvenir shops selling cakes, woven handbags, and Hakata's famous clay *ningyo* dolls.

Another large shopping area is in Tenjin, third stop on the subway line from Hakata Station. There's a huge underground shopping mall here, called Tenjin Chikagai, which stretches some 1,300 feet north to south. There are also many boutiques, department stores, specialty shops, coffeeshops, and restaurants in the area.

FOOD AND LODGING: Because most people make a stopover in Fukuoka for only one night, I've listed accommodations conveniently located within walking distance of Hakata Station.

The Upper Bracket

One of the finest places to stay in town is the **ANA Zenniku Hotel Hakata,** 3-3-3 Hakata-ekimae (tel. 092/471-7111). It's about a five-minute walk from what is called the Hakata Guchi Exit of the station. A modern and sparkling-clean first-class hotel, it has everything you'd expect from a hotel of this stature. Its lobby is large and spacious and its 363 rooms are bright and comfortable, with the usual pay video channels on TV, mini-bar, radio, and large bathroom. Singles range from ¥9,300 ($66) to ¥13,200 ($94), doubles run ¥13,700 ($98) to ¥20,900 ($149), and twins cost ¥17,500 ($125) to ¥26,500 ($189). Japanese-style rooms with all the modern conveniences cost ¥24,000 ($171) and sleep two to three persons.

The ANA Zenniku Hotel also offers fine dining. Most hotels feature Western restaurants on their top floors, but this hotel has given its Japanese restaurant, **Tsukushino**, the premier spot on the 15th floor. A beautifully sculpted bonsai pine graces the entrance to the restaurant, constructed in such a fashion that it looks like the lane of a village. Overhanging eaves topped with traditional tiled roofs extend down from the ceiling above the walls, and in the center of the restaurant is a glass-enclosed courtyard with raked gravel and bushes. As soon as you can tear your eyes away from your immediate surroundings you'll notice the city spread beyond the windowpanes. The English menu describes each dish. Mizutaki, for example, is a Fukuoka specialty described as chicken boiled in light broth with various Japanese vegetables and tofu. Kaiseki offerings, which change every two months, are ¥6,600 ($47.14) to ¥16,500 ($117.86). There's also shabu-shabu, sashimi dishes, and a separate tempura counter. Most set meals cost ¥6,000 ($42.86) and up, but you can do it much cheaper if you come here for lunch, served until 2 p.m. Teishoku specials begin at ¥1,000 ($7.14). The most popular is the Tsukushino obento box lunch for ¥2,400 ($17.14), which includes sashimi, boiled vegetables, and lots more. The restaurant is open from 11:30 a.m. to 10 p.m. daily.

Other facilities at the hotel include an outside sidewalk café open from 5 to 9:30 p.m. during summer months, a health club with pool, sauna, and exercise equipment which you can use for ¥5,500 ($39.29), cocktail lounges, and Chinese and Western restaurants.

The **Hakata Miyako Hotel**, 2-1 Hakata-eki Higashi (tel. 092/441-3111), is just in front of the Shinkansen bullet train exit of Hakata Station, on the south side. With the good name and legendary service of the Miyako hotel chain behind it, this hostelry has well-appointed rooms (some with bilingual TV) beginning at ¥8,200 ($59) for a single, ¥13,200 ($94) for a twin, and ¥14,300 ($102) for a double. The hotel's six Japanese-style rooms, used most often as waiting rooms before wedding ceremonies and receptions held at the hotel, have cypress bathtubs and cost ¥17,500 ($125).

Western dining at the Miyako Hotel is done in style at the 12th-floor **Starlight**, open only for dinner from 5 to 10 p.m. There's music nightly from the large white piano and at one end of the restaurant is a cocktail bar, where you can retire for drinks after dinner. Set courses range from ¥5,500 ($39.29) to ¥13,200 ($94.29). If you order seafood or steak entrées from the large leatherbound menu, expect to spend about ¥10,000 ($71.43) per person.

With the Miyako chain's most famous hotel located in Kyoto, it's not surprising that this hotel's Japanese restaurant, **Shikitei**, specializes in Kyoto-style dishes. Set meals start at ¥3,300 ($23.57) for sashimi, tempura, and mizutaki and rise to ¥5,500 ($39.29) for shabu-shabu and sukiyaki. Kyoto kaiseki selections start at ¥6,600 ($47.14). Particularly delightful is a meal called the *Nodate*, which is served in an upright wooden box with food arranged in boxes and bowls that are pulled out like drawers. Such boxes are used in traditional tea ceremonies. This meal costs ¥4,000 ($28.57) and includes sashimi, tempura, seasonal vegetables, rice, and soup. During lunch there are also obento lunchbox specials for ¥1,650 ($11.79) and ¥2,750 ($19.64). Shikitei is open from 11:30 a.m. to 2 p.m. and 5 to 9:30 p.m.

The Medium-Priced Range

One of Fukuoka's newest hotels is **Clio Court**, 5-3 Hakataeki-Chuogai (tel. 092/472-1111), which is located beside the Shinkansen exit of Hakata Station. A sleek modern hotel with lots of chrome, mirrors, marble, and bright white, its lobby is up on the third floor and its 203 guest rooms are doubles and twins decorated in art-deco styles. Few rooms have the same interior design, which were the creation of well-known female architect Rei Kurokawa. Rooms are large; even the bathrooms are roomy. Single occupancy rates range from ¥6,600 ($47) to ¥11,000 ($79) for double rooms and ¥7,700 ($55) to ¥15,400 ($110) for twins. Double occupancy rates range from ¥7,700 ($55) to ¥13,200 ($94) for double rooms and ¥8,800 ($63) to ¥18,700 ($134) for twins. The cheapest rooms, however, don't have any windows.

Restaurants in the hotel serve French, Chinese, or Japanese cuisine, and there's a steakhouse on the top floor. In the basement is an interesting setup called **Clio Seven**, which is essentially one large room cleverly divided into seven different bars and restaurants, including a sushi bar, a yakitori-ya, and an English-style pub. Clio Seven is open daily from 5 p.m. to 1 a.m.

Another new hotel in Fukuoka is **Hotel Centraza Hakata**, 4-23 Hakataeki-Chuogai (tel. 092/461-0111), located just across the square from Clio Court. Its spacious and marbled lobby is up on the second floor, and all its rooms are equipped with semi-double- or double-size beds, a TV control panel beside the bed, radio, clock, refrigerator, and hot-water pot. There's a small outdoor swimming pool. Singles here begin at ¥7,000 ($50), doubles at ¥9,300 ($66), and twins at ¥13,200 ($94).

In the basement of Hotel Centraza is **Gourmet City**, with approximately a dozen establishments offering everything from sushi Chinese food, and steaks to ice cream and beer. All of the restaurants, open from 11 a.m. to 11 p.m. daily, have plastic-food displays, with lunch specials offered for less than ¥1,500 ($10.71). Restaurants are chic and well-designed, a welcome addition to the dining scene around Hakata Station.

On the other side of Hakata Station are several more business hotels, among them the **Chisan Hotel Hakata** [253], 2-8-11 Hakata-ekimae (tel. 092/411-3211). To reach it, take the Hakata Guchi Exit, keep walking straight ahead for about seven minutes, and look for a white-tiled triangular building to your right. It's an efficient and dependable hotel with good service and a friendly staff, and the rooms come with TV with pay video, radio, clock, mini-bar, and hot-water pot for tea. The hotel's one restaurant serves a buffet breakfast of Japanese and Western food for ¥880 ($6.29). Tax and service charge included, rates here are ¥6,000 ($43) for a single, ¥8,800 ($63) for a double, and ¥10,900 ($78) to ¥12,000 ($86) for a twin. The best rooms are the higher-priced twins. Located in the curve of the hotel's front facade, they offer large rounded windows and lots of space.

Next to Chisan Hotel is another business hotel, the **Mitsui Urban Hotel** [254], 2-8-15 Hakata-ekimae (tel. 092/451-5111). Part of a nationwide hotel chain, this one was built more than a decade ago but still looks relatively new. The rooms are small but the windows are large. Singles start at ¥5,700 ($41) and doubles and twins are ¥9,900 ($79), tax and service charge extra.

Toyo Hotel, 1-9-36 Hakata-eki Higashi (tel. 092/474-1121), is a comfortable business hotel a few minutes' walk from the Shinkansen exit of the station. All beds in the hotel are semi-doubles, and prices include tax and service charge. Singles are ¥5,700 ($41), doubles are ¥7,700 ($55), and twins run ¥9,300 ($66). The sofa in the twin rooms can be made into an extra bed for a third person, in which case the room goes for ¥11,500 ($82). Some of the twin rooms on lower floors face another building, making them rather dark. Ask for a room higher up; those facing north have the best view. Since this is a Japanese businessman's hotel, don't be too surprised to find vending machines selling magazines of questionable taste.

Not far from the Toyo Hotel are the **Hakata Green Hotels 1 and 2**, 4-4

Hakataeki-Chuogai (tel. 092/451-4111), a minute's walk from the station. Green Hotel 1 is slightly older and has mainly singles starting at ¥4,900 ($35). In my opinion it's worth it to spend the extra couple of bucks to stay in the newer Green Hotel 2. It also has mainly singles, but some twins and doubles are available. Prices here are ¥5,500 ($39) for a single, ¥7,900 ($56) for a twin, and ¥7,200 ($51) for a double, including tax and service. Rooms, tiny and without closets, are white, bright, and clean, and come with coin-operated TV, clock, a plug-in pressing board to keep businessmen's pants nicely pressed (you can also use it on skirts), and large windows that open. There's a tiny drying rack in the bathrooms to hang up wet clothes. Machines in the hallway dispense free hot tea.

On the ground floor is a Japanese restaurant called **Ginroku**. Decorated with Japanese kites and traditional decor, the music is most likely to be modern pop. Open daily from 11 a.m. to 2 p.m. and 5 to 11 p.m., it offers such dishes as yakitori, sashimi, baked potatoes, flatfish, and corn on the cob. You can eat here for less than ¥1,000 ($7.14).

The Budget Category

As for youth hostels in the area, there isn't one in Fukuoka itself. The **Dazaifu Youth Hostel** [218], 1553-3 Oaza-Dazaifu, Dazaifu-machi (tel. 092/922-8740), is about a 12-minute walk from Dazaifu Station. An overnight stay costs ¥2,300 ($16.43), breakfast is ¥450 ($3.21), and dinner runs ¥750 ($5.36). If you're a nonmember, you can stay here but you'll be charged extra for a one-night guest card, which is ¥600 ($4.29). There's another youth hostel about a 50-minute bus ride from Nishitetsu-Fukuoka Bus Center in Tenjin called the **Yakiyama Youth Hostel**, Yakiyama, Izuka City (tel. 09482/2-6385).

More Dining

A Japanese restaurant specializing in Japanese seafood, **Gyosai** [256], 3-chome Hakata-ekimae (tel. 441-9780), is located across the street from the Chisan Hotel about a seven-minute walk from Hakata Station. Actually it's one of four Gyosai restaurants in Fukuoka—two are in the Tenjin shopping area and another one is located not far from Hakata Station. There's even a Gyosai in New York City. You can get a plate of assorted sashimi here for ¥1,400 ($10); most other dishes of fried fish and more sashimi cost between ¥900 ($6.43) and ¥2,200 ($15.71). The menu is in Japanese only, so the easiest thing to do is order a set meal. There's a brochure with pictures of dishes ranging from ¥4,000 ($28.57) to ¥7,000 ($50). The lunch teishoku, served from 11:30 a.m. to 1:30 p.m., is very reasonable at ¥600 ($4.29) and consists of fried and raw fish, vegetables, pickles, soup, and rice. Hours are 11:30 a.m. to 1:30 p.m. and 5 to 10:30 p.m.

2. Beppu

Twelve million people come to Beppu every year to relax and rejuvenate themselves, and they do so in a number of unique ways. They sit in mud baths up to their necks. They bury themselves in hot black sand. They soak in hot springs, and on New Year's they bathe in water filled with floating orange peels. With more than 3,000 hot springs spewing forth 140,000 tons of water daily, and a total of 168 public bathhouses, Beppu is one of Japan's best-known spa resorts. Whether it's in mud, sand, or water, bathing reigns supreme here—and I suggest you join in the fun. After all, visiting Beppu without enjoying the baths would be like going to a famous restaurant with your own TV dinner.

Beppu itself is not a very large town. Situated on Kyushu's east coast in a curve of Beppu Bay, its 150,000 inhabitants are bounded on one side by the sea and on the other by steep hills and mountains. Steam rises everywhere throughout the city, escaping from springs and pipes and giving the town an otherworldly appearance. Indeed, eight of the hot springs look so much like hell that that's what they're called—Jigoku, the Hells. But rather than a place most people try to avoid, the Hells are a major tourist attraction. In fact, everything in Beppu is geared toward tourism, and if you're interested in rubbing elbows with Japanese on vacation, this is one of the best places to do so.

ORIENTATION: The Tourist Information Centers in Tokyo and Kyoto have a free leaflet called *Beppu, Aso, Kumamoto* with information on these three places in Kyushu as well as on transportation in the area. The trip from Tokyo takes about seven to eight hours, with the usual route involving a change of trains in Kokura from the Shinkansen to a limited express bound for Beppu. The nearest airport is Oita, just a short distance away, which ANA flights can reach from Tokyo's Haneda airport in about 1½ hours. There are also ferries making regular runs between Beppu and Osaka, Hiroshima, Takamatsu, and Matsuyama.

Once in Beppu be sure to stop by the **Beppu Tourist Information Office** (tel. 0977/24-2838), which is located at Beppu Station and is open daily from 9 a.m. to 6 p.m. You can pick up an excellent brochure called *The Smile of Japan—Beppu*, with such useful information as what to see in the area, which local buses to take, the opening and closing hours for the major sights, and a map of the city. Another information office, called the **Foreign Tourist Information Service**, is located about a five-minute walk from Beppu Station on the third floor of the Kitahama Center Building, 2-9-23 Kitahama (tel. 23-1999). It's operated by English-speaking volunteers and offers tourist information and advice.

The easiest ways to get around Beppu are bus and taxi. If you plan on doing a lot of sightseeing by bus, there's a one-day bus pass with the strange name of "My Beppu Free" which nonetheless costs ¥700 ($5) and allows unlimited travel on Kamenoi Company buses within the city. If you're short of time you may want to join one of the many organized tours.

The **telephone area code** for Beppu is 0977. Beppu is located in Oita Prefecture and the postal code is 874.

WHAT TO DO: There are many kinds of springs and baths with various mineral contents that help in ailments from rheumatism to skin disease. If you have a specific ailment, call the hot-springs section of the tourist office (tel. 21-1111) to ask which baths would help you most. The pamphlet *The Smile of Japan*, described above, also has information on the various baths and their specific benefits. Otherwise, if you're simply here for the experience of the baths, there are two I particularly recommend.

Suginoi Palace

Most of the Japanese inns, hotels, and even private homes are tapped into Beppu's hot springs, but no matter where you stay you should visit Suginoi Palace, which adjoins the Suginoi Hotel. This is one of the most fantastic and fantasy-provoking baths in all of Japan, and also one of the largest. Gigantic affairs in what look like airplane hangars, there are actually two separate bathing areas, one for men and one for women. Filled with lush tropical plants and pools of various sizes and temperatures, one of the baths features a benevolent-looking Buddha sitting atop a giant fish bowl full of carp, while the other bath boasts a large red *torii* gate similar to ones you see at Shinto shrines. The women's and men's baths alternate, so if you come two days in a row you can see both. Other features of the baths here include a steam room, sauna, a Korean-style heated floor upon which you can lie down and relax, a pit with hot sand in which to bury yourself, and even a so-called "coffee bath" with real coffee in it, thought to aid the complexion.

The baths are open daily to the public from 9 a.m. to 9 p.m. The cost is ¥1,750 ($12.50) Monday through Saturday and ¥2,000 ($14.29) on Sunday. If you're staying at the Suginoi Hotel, you can use the baths daily for free from 7 a.m. to 10:30 p.m.

In addition to its huge bathhouses, Suginoi Palace offers quite a few other diversions as well, including an outdoor waterfall and pond filled with greedy carp (buy some fish food and you'll see what I mean—they almost jump out of the water in their feeding frenzy). There's also a small landscaped garden, a beautiful display of bonsai plants, a play area with amusement-park rides for children, a miniature golf course, and bowling lanes. There's even a variety show with two performances daily. Especially good is the **Suginoi Museum**, which charges a separate admission fee of ¥200 ($1.43). Its collection is worth more than ¥10 billion and includes a varied selection of samurai armor, Japanese antique weapons, toilet sets, ceramics, lacquerware, religious artifacts, clocks, and other items dating from the Edo Period. The museum is small but gives a good overview of objects used in Japan in centuries past.

A Hot-Sand Bath

One of the unique things you can do in Beppu is take a bath in hot sand, and one of the best places to do it is at **Takegawara Bathhouse**. Built in 1879, it's one of the oldest public baths in the city. The inside of the building resembles an ancient gymnasium. Bathing areas are separate for men and women, and are dominated by a pit filled with black sand. The attendants are used to foreigners here and will instruct you to strip, wash yourself down, and then lie down in a hollow they've dug in the sand. You should bring your own towel, which you should use to cover your vital parts. An attendant will then shovel sand on top of you and pack you in until only your head and feet are sticking out. I personally didn't find the sand all that hot, but it is relaxing as the heat soaks into your body. You stay buried for ten minutes, contemplating the wooden ceiling high above and hoping you don't get an itch somewhere. When the time is up, the attendant will tell you to stand up, shake off the sand, and then jump into a bath of hot water. The cost of this bathing experience is ¥600 ($4.71), and hours are 6:30 a.m. to 9 p.m. daily.

Open-air sand baths are also offered at Beppu Beach, known as *Shoningahama* in Japanese and reportedly good for muscle pain, rheumatism, and neuralgia. You keep on your *yukata* for the burial here, and the experience costs ¥660 ($4.71). Hours are 8:30 a.m. to 6 p.m., with slightly shorter hours in winter.

The Hells

As for sightseeing, you might as well join everyone else and go to the Hells. These Hells are actually boiling ponds created by volcanic activity. Six of them are clustered close together within walking distance of each other and can be toured in about an hour or so. One ¥1,200 ($8.57) ticket allows entrance to all eight Hells. Otherwise, the separate entrance fee to each one is ¥250 ($1.79).

You can also join a two-hour tour of the Hells for ¥2,900 ($20.71), but it's conducted in Japanese only. Each Hell has its own attraction. Umi Jigoku, or Sea Hell, has the color of sea water. Chinoike Jigoku, the Blood-Pond Hell, is blood-red in color because of the red clay dissolved in the hot water. Yama Jigoku features animals living in its hot spring and Oniyama Jigoku is where crocodiles are bred. Tatsumaki Jigoku, Waterspout Hell, has one of the largest geysers in Japan, and with a temperature of 221°F it's hotter than any other hot spring in Beppu.

Takasakiyama Mountain

On Beppu's southern border, about a 15-minute bus ride from Beppu Station, rises Takasakiyama Mountain. Its peak is home to more than 1,800 monkeys, which come down every day to feed, returning to their home by late afternoon. They wander freely among the visitors, and humans are advised not to challenge them by looking directly into their eyes. Admission to this attraction is ¥300 ($2.14), and hours are 8:30 a.m. to 5 p.m.

African Safari

If you have children traveling with you or simply are fond of zoos, you may be interested in visiting African Safari, a drive-through nature park with a road that winds through bare grassland. Bears, baboons, elephants, rhinos, zebras, camels, bison, giraffes, lions, tigers, and other exotic animals are allowed to roam in their own restricted areas, separated by fences so that they don't eat each other. Humans are confined to their cars or special buses.

Entrance to the park is ¥2,000 ($14.29), while bus rides through the park cost ¥400 ($2.86). Best, however, is to pay extra for the ¥1,000 ($7.14) caged bus that features slots of food for the various animals so that you can watch them eat at close range. Caged buses depart at 10 a.m., 12:30 p.m., 2:15, and 3:30 Monday through Friday, with more trips made on Sunday and holidays. The prices for children are ¥1,000 ($7.14) for admission and ¥750 ($5.36) for the caged bus. The zoo, which features 1,300 animals belonging to 69 different species, is open every day from 9 a.m. to 5 p.m. (9:30 a.m. to 4 p.m. from November 16 to March 15).

To reach African Safari, take bus no. 41 or 43 from Beppu Station. The trip takes about 50 minutes. Incidentally, the bus passes through an interesting part of Beppu called Myoban, where you'll notice a number of straw huts along the side of the road. These huts are built above hot springs and protect the formation of white powder-like deposits called *yunohana* in Japanese. You can buy the powder and add it to your bath at home for an instant hot-spring experience.

WHERE TO STAY: Since Beppu is a resort town, there are many accommodations in all price ranges, including hotels, ryokan, and minshuku.

The Top Choices

Probably the best-known hotel in Beppu is the **Suginoi Hotel**, Kankaiji (tel. 0977/24-1141), famous for its gigantic baths. A huge complex situated on a wooded hill with a sweeping view of the city and sea below, it's one of the most popular places to stay for both Japanese and foreign visitors. Popular also with group tours, it's a lively and noisy hotel filled with good-natured vacationers. In other words, if you like being in the middle of the action, this is the place for you. Although this place calls itself a hotel, only 88 of its 590 rooms are Western style. The rest are all Japanese tatami rooms. The drawback to Western-style rooms is that they face inland, though some combination-style rooms that feature both beds and a separate tatami area are also available that have fantastic views of the sea.

Room rates without meals are ¥11,000 ($78.57) for one person and ¥13,200 ($94.29) for two in Western-style rooms, while in the Japanese-style rooms they begin at ¥15,400 ($110) and ¥17,500 ($125) respectively. If you want rates that include breakfast and dinner served buffet style in both Japanese and Western restaurants, Western rooms go for ¥13,200 ($94.29) per person if there are two of you and ¥17,500 ($125) if you're alone. Japanese-style rooms with meals start at ¥24,000 ($171) for one person and ¥16,500 ($118) per person for two. All rooms are modestly furnished and come with private bathroom, TV, and a safe for valuables. Note that rates with meals include tax and service charge, as do those in a ryokan, while room-only rates do not.

If it's peace and quiet you're searching for, **Kannawaen** [257], Kannawa (tel. 0977/66-2111), is a wonderful ryokan hidden away on a lushly landscaped hill. Consisting of six separate houses spread around its grounds, the ryokan's tatami rooms with shoji screens look out onto carefully tended gardens, hot springs, bamboo, streams, bonsai, stone lanterns, and flowers. This is the perfect place to escape the crowds and to relax in an open-air bath set among rocks and trees. Rates range from ¥16,500 ($118) to ¥30,000 ($214) per person, depending on the room, and include breakfast, dinner, tax, and service charge. Rooms do not have private bathrooms, but the beauty of the surrounding countryside more than makes up for it. I highly recommend this place.

Nanmeiso [258], 7-8 Aoyama-cho (tel. 0977/22-2221), is a modern ryokan not far from Beppu Station in the center of the city. It has about 100 Japanese-style rooms with and without private bath as well as Western-style rooms with private bath. The staff here is friendly and particularly eager to welcome foreigners. A plus is the rooftop beer garden, open during the summer months, with good views of the surrounding city. Rates here are ¥9,000 ($64) to ¥13,000 ($93) per person, and as with most ryokan, include two meals, tax, and service.

Minshuku

If you're on a budget, one of the best places to stay is **Sakaeya** [259], Ida, Kannawa (tel. 0977/66-6234), a minshuku with an 82-year history and the oldest minshuku in the city. The oldest rooms date from the Meiji Period (1868–1912) and are furnished with old radiators heated naturally from hot springs. Another relic is the stone oven in the open courtyard which utilizes steam from hot springs for cooking (many older homes in Beppu still use such ovens). Use of the oven is free in case you want to cook your own meals; there's also a modern kitchen you can use. There are 35 rooms here, all with TV, air-conditioner, and kimono; most have sinks as well. Three of the rooms have their own toilet, but none have private baths. Room rates here are only ¥2,750 ($20) to ¥3,300 ($24) per person. Meals here are especially good, with set Japanese courses available for ¥3,000 ($21) to ¥5,500 ($39.28). Western or Japanese breakfasts cost ¥900 ($6.43). Sakaeya is about a ten-minute taxi ride from Beppu Station, but as you might imagine, this establishment is popular with young Japanese, especially during Golden Week at the beginning of May and during New Year's. If the minshuku is full, the owner here said he'd be happy to relocate you in another minshuku close by.

About a two-minute walk from Beppu Station is **Kokage**, 8-9 Ekimaecho (tel. 0977/23-1753). In operation for almost 20 years, it is run by a friendly older gentleman who speaks a few words of English and welcomes foreign guests. There are 11 Japanese-style rooms, 1 combination room with bed and tatami area, 3 twin rooms, and 1 double room. Rooms are old and a bit worn but are furnished with kimono, towels, hot water for tea, coin-operated air-conditioners and televisions, and 10 rooms have private bathrooms. In any case there's a public hot-spring bath and prices are unbeatable. Rates for rooms only are ¥3,300 ($24), while rates with two meals are ¥5,500 ($39) and ¥6,500 ($46) per person. Meals are served in a homey dining room with a cluttered but interesting collection of hanging lamps and clocks.

Budget Hotels

About a ten-minute walk from Beppu Station, **Nippaku Hotel**, 26-12-3 Kitahama (tel. 0977/23-2291), is a reasonably priced tourist hotel. Welcoming more than 1,000 foreign guests a year, they're used to foreigners here and the front-desk staff speak English. Rooms are nicely but modestly furnished, and facilities include a restaurant and hot-spring public baths. Both Japanese- and Western-style rooms are available. Those without private bathroom are ¥5,200 ($37) for one person and ¥9,100 ($65) for two. Rooms with private bathroom are ¥5,700 ($41) for one person and ¥10,100 ($72) for two. Prices include tax and service.

Green Hotel [260], 1-3-11 Kitahama (tel. 0977/25-2244), is a relatively new business hotel located just a couple of minutes' walk from Beppu Station with rooms much larger than the average business hotel. All 56 rooms come with coin-operated TV, radio, and private bathroom and cost ¥4,400 ($31) for a single, ¥6,000 ($43) for a double, and ¥7,500 ($54) for a twin. Rooms facing the front of the hotel have tiny balconies.

Youth Hostel

The **Beppu Youth Hostel** is close to the Suginoi Hotel at Kankaiji 2 (tel. 0977/23-4116), about a 20-minute bus ride from Beppu Station. It's small, with only four tatami rooms accommodating about six persons per room. Accommodation only costs ¥2,000 ($14.29) if you have a youth hostel card and ¥500 ($3.57) more if you don't. Breakfasts are ¥400 ($2.86) and dinners are ¥750 ($5.36).

In Yufuin

Although it's a 40-minute bus ride from Beppu Station, Yufuin has become a popular place to stay, particularly among young Japanese. Accommodations are cheaper than in Beppu, and both of the establishments below offer the advantage of the *roten buro*, or open-air bath. The ride to Yufuin is lovely, along the same Trans-Kyushu Highway described in the next section on Mount Aso. In fact, if you're on your way to Aso, you might consider making a stopover here. While in Yufuin be sure to visit **Mingei Mura**, a crafts village where you can watch artisans handmaking Japanese paper, knives, bamboo products, spinning tops, glassware, and other products.

Established in 1977, **Pension Yufuin** (tel. 0977/85-3311) is about a five-minute walk from the station and is the oldest pension in town. A pension in Japan is similar to a minshuku in that it's a small establishment offering two meals, except that all rooms are with beds instead of tatami and futons. In any case, this pension is located across the lane from a lazy river and is very cheerful and pleasant, with lots of plants, both real and plastic. The walls both inside and out are painted with more flowers and woodland nymphs. The ten rooms, two of which have their own private bathroom, start at ¥7,400 ($52) per person, including two Western meals, tax, and service.

If you want Japanese-style accommodation, **Makibanoie** [261] (tel. 0977/ 84-2138) charges ¥5,500 ($39) per person, which includes breakfast, dinner, tax, and service. Most of the eight rooms here are freestanding under their own roof, and meals are served in an old-fashioned dining hall with a hibachi at one end. The outdoor public bath is especially large and sits in the middle of a rice field, with a view of the mountains in the distance. If you plan to come to Yufuin during August or another busy time of year, be sure to make a reservation.

WHERE TO DINE: An economically priced restaurant, **Chikuden** [262], 1-6-1 Kitahama (tel. 25-2277), is about a 15-minute walk from Beppu Station. It serves a variety of sashimi, including fugu, sea bream, and abalone, and is a good place to go if you want to sample a variety of raw seafood without spending a small fortune. The menu is in Japanese only, but if you want a plate with a variety of sashimi, ask for the *Mori-a-wa-se,* which costs ¥2,700 ($19.29) per person. A plate of fugu costs ¥2,700 ($19.29). Sukiyaki is also served. The ground floor has tatami and counter seating, while the second floor has four private tatami rooms for groups. The restaurant is open from 5 p.m. to 1 a.m. every day of the week.

In addition to fugu, another specialty of Beppu is flat noodles. A popular noodle restaurant, **Amamijaya** [263], 1-4 Jissoji (tel. 67-6024), means "Sugar Tea House." Filled with local crafts and toys hanging on its walls, this inexpensive shop is about a 15-minute walk from the cluster of six Hells. Most items on the Japanese menu are ¥380 ($2.71) to ¥450 ($3.21), and all the noodles are made by hand by the owner. Dishes include *dangojiro* (flat noodles and vegetable soup), *yaseiuma* (a sweet dish of flat noodles covered with powdered soy beans and sugar), *mochi* (Japanese rice cake), and *zosui* (rice porridge with plums). Closed on Wednesday, it's open the rest of the week from 10:30 a.m. to 10:30 p.m.

If you're hungering for Western food, **Bistro Soen** [264], 1-1 Higashi-soen-cho (tel. 26-0583), is a small, pleasant informal restaurant located on the second floor above a bakery. As you may guess, the bread here is fresh. The menu is in Japanese only and includes à la carte entres of spaghetti, crêpes, fish, and steak, ranging from ¥1,000 ($7.14) to ¥2,500 ($17.86). There are also set menus ranging from ¥2,750 ($19.64) to ¥8,200 ($58.57), and a special lunch teishoku for ¥1,000 ($7.14) to ¥1,650 ($11.79). Hours here are 11 a.m. to 10 p.m., closed Tuesday.

3. Mt. Aso

In the center of Kyushu between Beppu and Kumamoto is the **Mt. Aso National Park.** The park encompasses two groups of mountains, volcanic Mt. Aso and Mt. Kuju, as well as grasslands, forests, and hot springs. Although Mt. Kuju is the largest mountain on the island, the chief attraction of the park is Mt. Aso—it has the honor of possessing the largest crater basin in the world. Measuring 11 miles from east to west, almost 15 miles from north to south, and 74½ miles in circumference, Mt. Aso must have been one mighty mountain before blowing its stack, larger even than Mt. Fuji. Today five volcanic cones sit in the Mt. Aso crater basin. One of them, Nakadake, is still active, constantly spewing forth high-temperature gas and sulfurous fumes. Every once in a while it even explodes (the latest eruption occurring in 1979). At the base of Nakadake at Aso West Station is the **Mt. Aso Volcanic Museum.** The entrance fee is ¥800 ($5.71), and the highlights are two cameras that have been placed on the walls of the active volcanic cone so that you can see the latest activity. There's also a 15-minute show depicting Mt. Aso National Park during the various seasons.

ORIENTATION: There are several resort towns at Mt. Aso circling Nakadake, including Aso, Takamori, and Aso-Shimoda. If you're interested in going to the top of Nakadake, the approach is from Aso Station in Aso. Aso Station is one hour from Kumamoto and 2½ hours from Beppu. From Aso Station you can board a bus for the 40-minute ride to Aso West Station (Asosan Nishi), from which you can take a ropeway to the top of the crater. There are seven buses daily running both ways between Aso Station and Aso West Station. The last bus departs Aso West Station at 5 p.m., but you'd be wise to check on this.

Trans-Kyushu Highway

Although you can reach Aso by rail, the most popular and pleasant route is by bus along the 186-mile-long Trans-Kyushu Highway, which links Beppu with Mt. Aso, Kumamoto, and Nagasaki. Sightseeing buses departing several times daily from both Kumamoto and Beppu are operated by the Kyushu Kokusai Kanko Bus Company. A timetable for buses departing from both Beppu and Kumamoto is provided in the leaflet *Beppu, Aso, Kumamoto*, available at the Tourist Information Centers in Kyoto and Tokyo.

The buses pass through rice paddies, tobacco and wheat fields, and bamboo groves, and skirt around waterfalls, streams, and hot springs. They all stop at Aso Station and allow a half hour for sightseeing at Mt. Aso's West Station. Since this is hardly enough time to visit both the museum there and take the cable car to the summit, if you're a volcano buff you may want to purchase a one-way ticket to Mt. Aso, spend an hour or two at the top, and then take one of the local buses back down to Aso Station.

FOOD AND LODGING: Because of its high altitude Mt. Aso National Park is an ideal summer retreat, with a number of hot-spring resorts spread throughout the Aso crater basin.

In Aso and Vicinity

About a ten-minute ride from Aso Station, **Ryokan Mimura** [265], Uchinomaki, Aso-machi (tel. 0967/32-0835), is a new and elegant ryokan that spreads along the ridge of a hill. This peaceful 17-room establishment is the epitome of simplified beauty with flower arrangements in each room and wooden beams. Four rooms have twin beds with separate tatami areas for those who prefer to sleep in beds. Some of the rooms also have Japanese-style deep wooden tubs, which smell wonderful when filled with piping hot water. There are also separate hot-spring baths for men and women, with large windows overlooking the countryside below.

Rooms here cost ¥13,200 ($94) to ¥27,500 ($196) per person, depending on the meals you order for breakfast and dinner. But no matter the price range, the food served is as elegant as the ryokan itself and is the highlight of a stay here. The meals are beautifully displayed using items from nature—a sprig from an azalea bush may serve as a chopstick holder, while cedar leaves or a delicate maple leaf may be used to enhance individual dishes. My sashimi came in a small ice igloo complete with pebbles in the bottom. My meal also included *basashi* (raw horse meat), considered a great delicacy in Kyushu. Diced crab was served in its shell, which acted as its bowl, and fish was fried on a hot flat stone. Each plate that arrived was another culinary and visual surprise.

If the above ryokan is too expensive, too full, or for some reason you want to stay closer to Aso Station, you might want to try **Aso no Tsukasa Villa Park**

Hotel, Kurokawa, Aso-machi (tel. 0967/34-0811). Located about three minutes by taxi or ten minutes on foot from Aso Station, this modern brick hotel first opened more than 20 years ago but was completely rebuilt and renovated in 1984. It charges ¥8,800 ($63) to ¥33,000 ($236) per person including two meals, tax, and service, with the difference in price reflected in room size, furnishings, and meals. The cheapest rooms have no private bathroom, while the most expensive ones feature wooden tubs. Most of the 128 rooms are Japanese style, but there are also combination rooms with a bedroom, living room, and separate tatami area, large enough for the whole family.

Facilities at the hotel include hot-spring baths, tennis courts, an outdoor pool, and horses for rent. There's also a restaurant where you might want to go for lunch called **Steak House Ban**, which features local beef from the Aso area, known as "Higo beef." This restaurant buys whole cows so that it can slice the beef itself. The texture of the meat is unique, and is much different from the beef back home. The menu is in Japanese only, with steak courses starting at ¥2,000 ($14.29), which includes soup, rice, and salad. If you want to go à la carte and add your own soup and salad, tenderloin starts at ¥3,000 ($21.43) for 150 grams, while sirloin starts at ¥3,300 ($23.57) for 200 grams. Also available is raw Higo beef and smoked salmon. This restaurant is open from noon to 9 p.m. daily.

Not far from Aso near a small town called Uchinomaki are a dozen or so Western-style pensions. They differ from minshuku in that their rooms contain beds instead of futons, but they are also small, family-run affairs with only a handful of rooms. The owner of **Pension Aso no Tokei-dai**, Uchinomaki, Aso-machi (tel. 0967/32-2236), speaks some English and will refer you to one of the other nearby pensions if his place is full. Rooms in all the pensions average about ¥7,000 ($50) per person, including two meals, tax, and service. This "Pension Mura" as the locals call it (which means Pension Village), is located about five minutes by taxi from Uchinomaki Station, but if you call from the station, someone from the pension will come pick you up.

Also in Aso is the **Aso Youth Hostel** [266], 9222-2, Bochu, Asomachi (tel. 0967/34-0804), about a five-minute walk or five-minute bus ride from Aso Station. Accommodating 64 people, it charges ¥2,000 ($14.29) per night without meals and ¥3,000 ($21.43) if you want breakfast and dinner for both members and nonmembers.

In Takamori

On the other side of Mt. Aso is another resort town called Takamori. Since there's no bus service from here to the summit, this place is better for those who appreciate the beauty of massive volcanoes from afar.

In Takamori is a National Vacation Village called **Minami Aso Kokumin Kyuka Mura** [267] (tel. 0967/62-2111). Popular with school groups and families because of the great view it commands of Mount Aso, it features tennis courts, bikes for rent, public baths, and a botanical garden. The rooms are typical of national vacation villages—simple tatami rooms with a TV, futon and sheets, yukata cotton kimono, and private bathroom. The cost of a room per person is ¥4,400 ($31), but with meals it usually comes out to about ¥8,800 ($63). The 81 rooms are usually packed during July and August, but otherwise you should be able to get a room. It's wise to make reservations in advance.

A wonderful restaurant in Takamori is **Dengaku no Sato** [268] (tel. 62-1899), about a five-minute taxi ride from Takamori Station. Housed in a 120-year-old thatched farmhouse, this rustic, country restaurant has tatami seating around individual hibachis built into the wooden floor. Its specialty is *dengaku* (food skewered on sticks). You cook your dengaku yourself by sticking the skewers into the ashes surrounding the blaze in your hibachi. Order the dengaku teishoku for ¥1,500 ($10.71), and you'll have a variety of skewered items, including fish, taro, tofu, and mountain crabs which you pop whole into your mouth—delicious and crunchy. You can also order *kappozake* (sake heated in a hollow bamboo) beside your fire. Hours are 10 a.m. to 7:30 p.m.

In Aso-Shimoda

Near Aso-Shimoda you'll find a People's Lodge, the **Minami Aso Kokumin Shukusha** [269] (tel. 0967/67-0078). Its rates are cheaper than the National Vacation Village described above: an overnight's stay, including two meals, comes to ¥5,500 ($39). If you don't want meals it's only ¥3,000 ($21). There are only three buses daily from Aso-Shimoda Station so it might be best to take a 15-minute taxi ride. All the rooms have balconies, some with splendid views, and come with coin-operated TV, yukata cotton kimono, sheets, and futon. Not far from the lodge is a picturesque open-air bath beside a pounding waterfall. Men and women bathe together here.

4. Kumamoto

Located roughly in the middle of Kyushu about 1½ hours south of Fukuoka, Kumamoto boasts a fine castle and a landscape garden, both with origins stretching back to the first half of the 17th century. Once one of Japan's most important castle towns, Kumamoto today is a progressive city with a population of more than half a million. In an effort to attract both domestic and foreign enterprises, the city is planning a technopolis—a technological research city—to be built close to its airport by 1995. With other technopoli being planned for such cities in Kyushu as Kagoshima, Oita, and Miyazaki, the island has given itself a nickname: Silicon Island.

ORIENTATION: Upon arrival at Kumamoto Station, stop by the **tourist information center** (tel. 096/352-3743) to pick up a good English map and brochure of the city. It's open from 9 a.m. to 5:30 p.m. daily.

The leaflet *Beppu, Aso, Kumamoto* distributed by the Tourist Information Centers in Kyoto and Tokyo contains information on how to get to Kumamoto and places of interest in the city.

Kumamoto Station is not in the city's downtown section but it's easy to get there by streetcar 2, which departs from in front of the station. Downtown is considered to be the area south and southeast of Kumamoto Castle, centered around several covered shopping arcades called Shimotori and Sunroad Shinshigai. There are many shops, bars, and restaurants in the area. Nearby is Kotsu Center, from which all buses in the city depart, and the location of several business hotels listed below. Streetcar 2, which runs from Kumamoto Station and passes Kotsu Center, will also take you to both the castle (stop: Kumamoto-jo-mae) and the Suizenji Garden (stop: Suizenji-Koen-mae).

The **telephone area code** for Kumamoto is 096, and it's located in Kumamoto Prefecture.

THE SIGHTS: Completed in 1607, **Kumamoto Castle** is massive—it took seven years to build. It was constructed under the direction of Kiyomasa Kato, a great warrior who fought alongside Ieyasu Tokugawa in a battle in 1600 and who was rewarded for his loyalty with land in what is today Kumamoto. To make the castle walls impossible for enemies to scale, they were built with curves and topped with an overhang. Furthermore, the castle was built atop a hill and had three main buildings, 49 towers, 29 gates, and 18 two-story gatehouses. Passing into the possession of the Hosokawa family in 1632, the castle remained an important stronghold for the Tokugawa shogunate throughout its 250 years of rule, particularly in campaigns against powerful and independent-minded lords in southern Kyushu.

Unfortunately, much of the castle was destroyed in 1877 during the Seinan Rebellion led by Takamori Saigo. A samurai disgruntled with the new policies of the Meiji government in which ancient samurai rights were rescinded, Saigo led a troop of samurai in an attack on the castle and its imperial troops. The battle raged for 50 days before government reinforcements finally arrived and quelled the rebellion. When the smoke cleared, most of the castle lay in smoldering ruins, ravaged by fire.

The castle was reconstructed in 1960 of ferroconcrete and although it's not nearly as massive as before, it's still quite impressive. The interior houses a museum with elaborately decorated palanquins, armor of feudal lords, swords, former possessions of both Kiyomasa Kato and the Hosokawa family, and artifacts from the Seinan Rebellion. There are also displays of such locally made products as pottery and toys. Open from 8:30 a.m. to 5:30 p.m. (until 4:30 p.m. in winter), it charges an admission of ¥100 (71¢) for the castle grounds. If you want to go inside the castle, it costs ¥200 ($1.43) more.

Not far from the castle are two museums worth seeing. The **Kumamoto Prefectural Art Museum**, open every day except Monday from 9:30 a.m. to 5 p.m., displays fine art, as well as replicas of burial tombs that have been excavated in the prefecture. Nearby is the **Kumamoto Municipal Museum**, open every day except Monday from 9 a.m. to 5 p.m. It houses collections devoted to the humanities and the natural and physical sciences, and also contains a planetarium.

Suizenji Garden, laid out in 1632 by the Hosokawa family, wraps itself around a cold spring-fed lake. Incorporated into the design of the garden are famous scenes in miniature from the 53 stages of the ancient Tokaido Highway, which connected Kyoto and Tokyo and which were immortalized in Hiroshige's famous woodblock prints. Most recognizable is cone-shaped Mount Fuji. Considering the fact that the real Mount Fuji is often cloaked in clouds, this reproduction may be the closest you'll get to seeing the famous peak. The park is small—almost disappointingly so. One wishes it stretched on and on. To assuage disappointment, stop off at the 400-year-old thatched-roof tea house beside the pond, transported from the imperial grounds in Kyoto. Inside ceremonial green tea is served while you sit and contemplate the view. If you want to sit on tatami inside the tea house, it costs ¥500 ($3.57). If you're content sitting outside at a table under the shelter of trees, it costs ¥400 ($2.86). Entrance to the park is ¥100 (71¢) between 7:30 a.m. and 6 p.m. (from 8:30 a.m. and 5 p.m. in winter); after that it's free, but only the north gate remains open. If you want to do some moon gazing, this is the place.

Although it's located on the outskirts of Kumamoto, about 30 minutes by bus from Kotsu Center, if you're at all interested in handcrafted items used in everyday life from various countries around the world you'll enjoy the **Kumamoto International Folk Art Museum**, Tatsuda machi-Kamitatsuda (tel. 096/338-7504). Located in a 140-year-old sake warehouse which once stood in Okayama, this museum displays furniture, pottery, weavings, toys, and other handcrafted items from such diverse countries as India, Peru, Greece, Korea, Mexico, Egypt, and Japan. As items used in everyday life both now and in former times, many of them are rustic but beautifully made. The museum is open every day except Monday from 9 a.m. to 4 p.m. and charges an admission of ¥300 ($2.14). If going by bus, get off at Sannomiya bus stop.

SHOPPING: One of Kumamoto's most famous products is its damascene, in which gold and silver are inlaid on an iron plate to form patterns of flowers, bamboo, and other designs. Originally used to adorn armor, damascene today is used in such accessories as jewelry and tie clasps. Another Kumamoto product is the Yamaga lantern, made of gold paper and used during the Yamaga Lighted Lantern Festival held in August. Other products include Amakusa pearls, pottery, toys, and bamboo items.

A wonderful place to see Kumamoto Prefecture's products and learn about their production is the **Kumamoto Traditional Crafts Center** [270], located at 3-35 Chiba-jo (tel. 324-4930), next to Kumamoto Castle, not far from Kumamoto Castle Hotel. Confusingly enough, it's identified on the English map given out by the tourist office as Industrial Art Museum—hopefully someone will get around to correcting this someday. A spacious and attractive brick building constructed in 1982, the center's second floor is devoted to handmade craftwork from all over the prefecture, along with displays on how the items are made. The displays are so well laid-out and the room is so bright and cheerful that it doesn't matter that the explanations are only in Japanese. By looking at the display on the bow and arrow, for example, you can see for yourself the intricate steps involved in their production. Wander around and look at pottery, bamboo products, fans (haven't you ever wondered how they're made?), bows and arrows, toys, furniture, wooden rice barrels, damascene, and kitchen knives sharp enough to chop through bone. The products are so well designed that you can't help but gain a wider appreciation of the beauty and simplicity of Japanese design. Most items aren't hidden away behind glass but are out in the open. Entrance here is ¥150 ($1.07) and worth every yen.

The first floor of the Traditional Crafts Center is free and serves as a gallery at which locally made products are sold, including those wonderful kitchen knives, furniture, ceramics, toys, paper lanterns, and damascene. Unfortunately, the center can ship only purchases that have a total value less than ¥60,000 ($429) and even then only to about eight large cities in the United States. The center is open from 9 a.m. to 5 p.m.; closed Monday.

Another place selling local products is the **Display Hall of Kumamoto Products (Kumamoto-ken Bussankan)** [271], on the third floor of the Sangyo Bunka Kaikan Building downtown next to the Kotsu Center. This store, open from 10 a.m. to 6:30 p.m. (except on the second and fourth Mondays of the month), sells pottery, toys, knives, paper lanterns, damascene, Amakusa pearls, spirits, and confectioneries.

For more shopping, in the heart of downtown there are covered shopping arcades, called **Shimotori** and **Sunroad Shinshigai**, where you'll find the usual clothing boutiques, gift shops, shoe stores, restaurants, and coffeeshops.

WHERE TO STAY: Accommodations in Kumamoto are hotels rather than ryokan. Many of the hotels, however, have Japanese-style rooms in case you'd rather sleep on futon and tatami. There are also some inexpensive minshuku.

The Upper Bracket

A 25-story high-rise about a ten-minute walk from Kumamoto Station, **New Sky Hotel**, 2 Higashiamidaji-cho (tel. 096/354-2111), is one of Kumamoto's best hotels. Its 358 rooms are divided between an older west wing and a more modern east wing. Its guest rooms are stocked with a lot of thoughtful amenities: a laundry rope in the bathroom (a welcome sight if you've been on the road a while), a hot-water pot for tea, bilingual TV (in the new wing only), mini-bar, alarm clock, radio, bedside control panels, an extra phone in the bathroom, and the *Japan Times* delivered to your room in the morning (it's always a day late in Kyushu). Facilities of the hotel itself include Japanese, Chinese, and Western restaurants, a beauty salon and a barbershop, and a health club with workout equipment and indoor swimming pool, sauna, and hot bath. Single rooms, which are located only in the older west wing, begin at ¥7,000 ($50), while twins begin at ¥16,500 ($118). Doubles are ¥14,300 ($102). There are also 40 Japanese-style rooms available for ¥12,000 ($86) for two people.

The **Kumamoto Castle Hotel**, 4-2 Joto-cho (tel. 096/326-3311), is a tall brick building next to the Kumamoto Castle grounds, which means that some of its rooms have good views of the city's most famous landmark. A more subdued, quiet, and conservative hotel than the New Sky, its rooms come with the usual TV (Japanese only), fridge, and hot-water pot, and start at ¥8,200 ($59) for a single, ¥11,800 ($82) for a double, and ¥14,800 ($106) for a twin. Japanese-style rooms are ¥27,000 ($193). Restaurants in the hotel serve Western, French, and Chinese cuisine.

Business Hotels

There are several medium- and budget-priced business hotels located in the downtown section close to Kotsu Center bus depot. Newest of these and first on my list is **Chisan Hotel Kumamoto**, 4-39 Karashimacho (tel. 096/322-3911), which opened in 1984, part of the Chisan hotel chain. Its lobby is pleasantly decorated with marble, brass railings, and stained glass, and the rooms are simply but tastefully decorated and come with stocked fridge, TV, and hot-water pot for tea. The electricity in the room works only when you insert your key into a pocket beside the door (this not only saves energy but saves time searching for misplaced keys). The hotel's one restaurant, decorated with masks from Africa, serves Western food. It offers a buffet lunch from 11:30 a.m. to 2 p.m. at a price of ¥880 ($6.29) per person. Room rates begin at ¥6,000 ($43) for a single, ¥7,700 ($55) for a double, and ¥9,600 ($69) for a twin.

Tokyu Inn, 7-25 Shinshigai (tel. 096/322-0109), is a business hotel located across the street from the Kotsu Center right next to the Sunroad Shinshigai covered shopping arcade. Its rooms are small but contain everything you need, including TV, refrigerator, and cotton kimono. Single rooms are ¥6,600 ($47), doubles are ¥8,200 ($59), and twins are ¥9,900 ($71). There's a Western as well as a Japanese/Korean restaurant.

Located right in the Kotsu Center itself is the **Kotsu Center Hotel**, 3-10 Sakuramachi (tel. 096/354-1111). Its lobby is on the third floor of the center and is usually buzzing with activity from Japanese or Chinese group tours. The hotel's French restaurant serves a buffet-style lunch of French and Chinese cuisine Thursday for ¥2,700 ($19.29). There's also a Chinese Szechuan restaurant, and from April to September there's a rooftop beer garden open daily from 5 to 9:30 p.m. Rooms are basic but comfortable, and for some reason each room is decorated with two different kinds of wallpaper. Singles range from ¥4,800 ($34) to ¥7,000 ($50), but the lowest-priced rooms don't have windows and aren't recommended. Doubles are ¥9,600 ($69), twins begin at ¥13,200 ($94), and triples run ¥14,300 ($102). There are eight Japanese-style rooms that go for ¥11,600 ($83) for one person, ¥14,300 ($102) for two, and ¥16,500 ($118) for three.

For a business hotel close to Kumamoto Station, the **Kumamoto Station Hotel** [272], 1-3-6 Nihongi (tel. 096/325-2001), is a three-minute walk from the station. A typical business hotel, its 50 single rooms go for ¥5,000 ($36), its 17 twins and doubles run ¥10,700 ($76), and its three Japanese-style rooms cost ¥11,000 ($79) for two people and ¥14,300 ($102) for three. Breakfast is available for ¥550 ($3.93). To reach this business hotel, walk straight out from Kumamoto Station, pass over the bridge you see in front of you, and then turn immediately right. Kumamoto Station Hotel is the first building to your right and is located right beside the small river.

Inexpensive Japanese Style

A member of the Japanese Inn Group, **Maruko Hotel**, 11-10 Kamitori-cho (tel. 096/353-1241), is larger than most members of this group, with a total of 45 rooms. Completely renovated in 1985, this brick building is located in the heart of the city just off the Kamitori covered shopping arcade. To reach it, take streetcar 2 from Kumamoto Station, disembarking at Tetori-Honcho stop, from which it's an eight-minute walk. Owned and managed by a petite, gracious woman who is happy to receive foreign guests, it charges ¥6,600 ($47) for single occupancy, ¥12,000 ($86) for a double, and ¥14,300 ($102) for a triple. Forty-one of its rooms are Japanese tatami rooms, with a pleasant sitting alcove next to large windows. There are also a couple Western-style rooms and a couple combination rooms with both beds and tatami. All rooms come with private bathroom, TV with video, hot water for tea, a safe for valuables, refrigerator, kimono, and air conditioning. Both breakfast and dinner are available.

Just a couple minutes' walk to the left after exiting from Kumamoto Station, **Tsukasa Besso** [273], 1-12-20 Kasuga (tel. 096/354-3700), is a family-run minshuku with a total of 12 rooms, most of them Japanese style. The family members here are very friendly, and the daughter speaks English. Although the building itself is a bit old, the atmosphere makes up for it, as does the price at ¥6,000 ($43) per person, which includes two meals, tax, and service charge. About half of the rooms have their own private toilet, and some of them have private tubs as well. In any case, there are two public baths. Meals are served in a communal dining hall.

Youth Hostels

Suizenji Youth Hostel [274], 1-2-10 Hakusan (tel. 096/371-9193), can be reached by taking tram 2 from the station to tram stop Misotenjin, about a 25-minute ride. From there it's a 2-minute walk. It has one room with six beds and five Japanese-style rooms with a total capacity of 38 people. A one-night stay is ¥2,000 ($14.29) if you're a card-carrying member and ¥2,500 ($17.86) if you're not. Breakfast is ¥400 ($2.86).

Kumamoto Shiritsu Youth Hostel [275], 5-15-55 Shimazaki-machi (tel. 096/ 352-2441), can be reached by taking a bus leaving from platform 36 of the Kotsu Center bus terminal. Get off at the Kuriyama Youth Hostel Mae bus stop. The price here is the same whether you're a youth hostel member or not: room charges are ¥1,600 ($11.43), breakfasts are ¥400 ($2.86), and dinners are ¥660 ($4.71). In summer and winter you'll be charged an extra ¥200 ($1.43) for air conditioning or heating. This hostel has 32 beds for women and 32 beds for men. Incidentally, on the map issued by the tourist office, this establishment is identified as the Municipal Youth Hostel, and the man in charge here speaks English.

WHERE TO DINE: Kumamoto's special dishes include *dengaku* (delicacies such as fish, taro, and tofu coated with bean paste and grilled at a fire), *karashi renkon* (lotus root that has been boiled, filled with a mixture of bean paste and mustard, and then deep-fried), and *basashi* (raw horse meat that is sliced thin and then dipped in soy sauce flavored with ginger or garlic).

Japanese Food

You can try Kumamoto's local dishes at **Senri** [276] (tel. 384-1824), located right in Suizenji Garden. A good place to stop off for lunch or dinner while visiting the famous garden, it's open every day from 11 a.m. to 9 p.m. Although the menu is in Japanese only, there's a pamphlet available with pictures. Teishoku set lunches cost ¥2,000 ($14.29) each and choices include eel, river fish, tempura, or basashi. Along with your choice of main dish are side dishes of a vegetable, soup, rice, and tea. Dinners cost ¥3,300 ($23.57) to ¥6,500 ($46.43) and include the same items as in the lunch teishoku, plus extra dishes. Dining is in small tatami rooms, located to the right after you enter the front door. The choice rooms face the garden. It's best to make a reservation to dine here.

Not far away and also located in Suizenji Garden is **Kimura-so** [277] (tel. 384-1864). Open from 11 a.m. to 9 p.m. daily, it features inexpensive dining outside on a pavilion built over a pond, with a partial view of the garden. Carp is its specialty, which you can have raw or fried for ¥550 ($3.93). Also on the menu are grilled shrimp, eel, tonkatsu, and basashi.

Aoyagi [278], 1-2-10 Shimotori (tel. 353-0311), is just off the Shimotori shopping arcade in downtown Kumamoto. It has a plastic-food display case outside its front door with dishes of sushi, tempura, basashi, and *kamameshi* (rice casseroles). Set meals range from ¥700 ($5) to ¥2,500 ($17.86). You can also take out box lunches of sushi for ¥740 ($5.29) and up. Hours are 11:30 a.m. to 11 p.m. daily, and there are three floors of dining.

Located in the same vicinity is **Goemon** [279], 1-7-3 Shimotori (tel. 354-2266). Since it's open only in the evening from 5 p.m. to 2 a.m. this is technically a drinking establishment, but it serves a variety of inexpensive dishes and is popular with a lively young crowd, especially on weekends. À la carte dishes of dengaku, flatfish, sashimi, green-tea noodles, and much more range from a mere ¥80 (57¢) for pickled vegetables to ¥500 ($3.57) for raw tuna. Most items cost ¥200 ($1.43) to ¥300 ($2.14). There are also set meals for ¥1,000 ($7.14) to ¥2,750 ($19.64). The menu is only in Japanese but it has some pictures; the best thing to do is simply to look around at what others are eating. This establishment has a rustic feel to it, and although it's tatami seating, some of the tables have leg wells underneath for your feet. Take off your shoes at the front door and deposit them in a locker, just as you would at a bathhouse.

The **New Sky Hotel**, 2 Higashiamidaji-cho, has an excellent Japanese restaurant called **Kohrin** (tel. 354-2111), open from 11 a.m. to 10 p.m. The menu is in Japanese only, but set meals range from ¥3,300 ($23.57) to ¥11,000 ($78.57) and include sushi, tempura, and seasonal kaiseki dishes. I highly recommend the course of *seishoho-yaki*—Japanese steak wrapped in bamboo and served with side dishes of basashi, mustard lotus, sashimi, red snapper, pickled vegetables from the region of Mount Aso, and rice. Top off your meal with shochu, for which Kumamoto is famous. If you come here for lunch, you can have noodles, which are served from 11 a.m. to 5 p.m.—try the tempura soba for ¥1,000 ($7.14). Another good lunchtime choice is the Kohrin teishoku, for ¥2,000 ($14.29), which includes sashimi, tempura, sushi, soba noodles, and side dishes.

Another hotel restaurant serving Japanese food, **Ginnan** (tel. 326-3311) is located in Kumamoto Castle Hotel, 4-2 Joto-cho. A fish tank at the restaurant's entrance displays shrimp, flatfish, and eels happily swimming around, unaware of their impending fate. The Japanese menu has pictures of its offerings, most of which range from ¥3,000 ($21.43) to ¥6,000 ($42.86). The tempura dinner is most popular. Set teishoku lunches run ¥1,100 ($7.86) to ¥3,800 ($27.14).

If the weather's warm and you're more interested in drinking beer while sitting outside, head for the roof of the **Kotsu Center Hotel** (tel. 354-1111), conveniently located at the Kotsu Center bus depot. Open from April to mid-September from 5 to 9:30 p.m., this beer garden has its share of fake palm trees and Astro-turf, but it also offers panoramic views of the city. Beer starts at ¥400 ($2.86) and snacks include grilled chicken, sausage, french fries, *edamame* (soy beans), and other fare, most of it under ¥500 ($3.57).

Western Food

For elegant dining, go to **Leodor**, the New Sky Hotel's tower restaurant on the 25th floor at 2 Higashiamidaji-cho (tel. 354-2111). A white piano (with nightly entertainment from 7 to 9:30 p.m.) dominates the powder-blue room. Elaborate tableware and flowers on every table enhance meals of steak, fish, or lamb, with most entrées ranging from ¥2,750 ($19.64) to ¥7,000 ($50). Expect to spend about ¥12,000 ($85.71) per person for dinner, including wine. There are also set dinners for ¥6,600 ($47.14) and ¥7,700 ($55), and a set lunch menu for ¥3,800 ($27.14). Hours are 11 a.m. to 2 p.m. and 5 to 10 p.m.

Another place to go for Western food is the **Loire**, on the 11th floor of the Kumamoto Castle Hotel, 4-2 Joto-cho (tel. 326-3311). While dining here you can look out over Kumamoto Castle. The menu is short, offering primarily set meals ranging from ¥4,200 ($30) to ¥11,000 ($79). The offerings are changed every four months to match the changing seasons, but usually include seafood and beef dishes. Dinner is served from 5 p.m. to midnight. From 11:30 a.m. to 2 p.m. set lunches are served, ranging in price from ¥1,100 ($7.86) to ¥5,500 ($39.29).

5. Nagasaki

Unlike Kumamoto, Kagoshima, or many other well-known cities in Japan, Nagasaki does not have a castle or famous landscape garden. Rather, Nagasaki's charm is much more subtle, lying in the city itself. Many people in Japan— including foreign residents—consider Nagasaki one of the country's most beautiful cities. It's a town of hills rising from the harbor, of houses perched on terraced slopes, of small streets, distinctive neighborhoods, and a people extremely proud of their city. Without a doubt it's one of Japan's most liveable cities.

Perhaps to the untrained foreign eye Nagasaki may look like any other modern Japanese town. In truth, however, there's no other city in Japan quite like Nagasaki. In a nation as homogeneous as Japan, Nagasaki from a historical perspective is its most cosmopolitan city, with a unique blend of outside cultures interwoven into its architecture, food, and festivals. Centuries ago, Nagasaki's bay, sheltered by islands, made it a natural as a safe place to anchor ships. It opened its harbor to European vessels in 1571 and became a port of call for Portuguese and Dutch ships. Chinese merchants moved here and set up their own community. Along with traders came Christian missionaries, primarily from Portugal and Spain, who found many converts among the Japanese in Nagasaki. And during Japan's more than 200 years of isolation, only Nagasaki was allowed to conduct trade with the outside world and thus served as the nation's window on the rest of the world. Even today Japanese come to Nagasaki for a dose of the city's intermingled cultures.

If you're looking for a typical Japanese city, Nagasaki isn't the place. If you're searching for something more than just typical—something special— then Nagasaki won't disappoint you.

ORIENTATION: Nagasaki lies on the northwest coast of Kyushu about 2½ hours from Fukuoka and 9½ hours from Tokyo. At Nagasaki Station the **Naga-**

saki City Office of Tourist Information (tel. 0958/23-7423) maintains an information window, located to the left after you exit from the ticket gate, which distributes maps in English. It's open from 9 a.m. to 5 p.m. daily. An even better map, however, is available just across the street from the train station in the **Nagasaki Prefecture Tourist Federation** office (tel. 0958/26-9407), on the second floor of the Kotsu Sangyo Building. This office can provide information on all of Nagasaki Prefecture, including Unzen. In many hotels and restaurants catering to foreigners you can pick up a copy of *Harbor Light,* an English-language monthly newsletter costing ¥200 ($1.43), with information on what's going on in Nagasaki. More information on Nagasaki and its attractions is given in *Nagasaki and Unzen,* available at the Tourist Information centers in Tokyo and Kyoto.

Nagasaki Station is not considered the downtown part of the city. Rather, the majority of nightspots, shops, and restaurants are located southeast of the station clustered around an area that contains Shianbashi, Kanko Dori Street, and the Hamanomachi shopping arcade. Peace Park and its museum on the atomic bomb are located north of Nagasaki Station.

The easiest way to get around the city is by streetcar. Five lines run through the heart of the city and most stops are written in English. The streetcars are ancient, one-wagon affairs, retired to Nagasaki from other cities that considered them too slow and old-fashioned a mode of transportation. And yet in Nagasaki streetcars have their own lanes of traffic so that during rush hour they're usually the fastest things on the road. It costs a mere ¥100 (71¢) to ride one; pay at the front when you get off. You can also buy a ¥500 ($3.57) ticket at major hotels that allows unlimited rides for one day on the city's streetcars. If you're buying individual tickets, you're allowed to transfer to another line only at Tsukimachi Station. Otherwise you must buy a separate ticket each time you board a tram.

You can also get around Nagasaki easily by foot, certainly the most intimate way to experience the city and its atmosphere. You can walk from the Hamanomachi shopping district to Glover Garden, for example, in 15 to 20 minutes. In any case, along with Kobe and Sapporo, Nagasaki is one of Japan's most navigable cities, and there are lots of signs in English that point the way to attractions. Nagasaki also has buses, but destinations are only in Japanese and who knows where the heck they're going. Stick to the streetcars.

The **telephone area code** for Nagasaki is 0958 and the prefecture is Nagasaki Prefecture.

THE SIGHTS: All of Nagasaki's major attractions are connected with the city's diversified and sometimes tragic past. The city is perhaps best known as the second city—and, we hope, the last city—to be destroyed by an atomic bomb.

Nishizaka Hill

After Nagasaki opened its port to European vessels, Christian missionaries began coming to the city to convert Japanese to Christianity. Gradually, however, the Japanese rulers began to fear that these Christian missionaries would try to exert influence in Japan through their converts. After all, Christian churches in Europe held vast political and financial power in Europe, and who wasn't to say that conversion to Christianity was just the first step toward colonialization? So in 1587 the shogun Hideyoshi Toyotomi officially banned Christianity. In 1597, 26 Christians (20 Japanese and 6 foreigners) were arrested in Kyoto and Osaka, marched through the snow to Nagasaki, and crucified on Nishizaka Hill as examples of what would happen to offenders. Through the ensuing years there were more than 600 documented cases of Christians being put to death in the Nishizaka area. In 1862 the 26 martyrs were named saints by the pope.

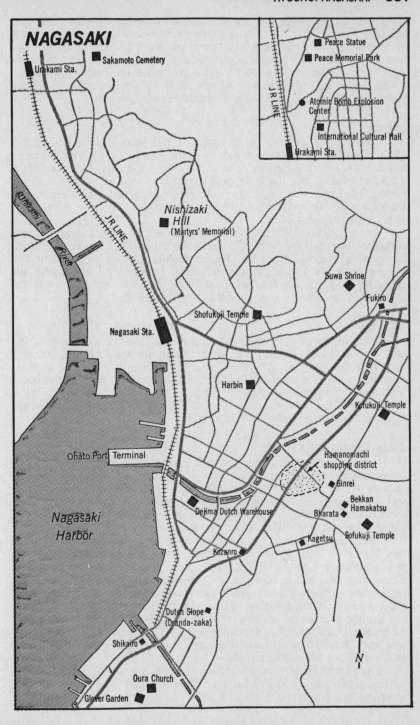

NAGASAKI

Sakamoto Cemetery

Urakami Sta.

Peace Statue

Peace Memorial Park

J R LINE

Atomic Bomb Explosion Center

International Cultural Hall

Urakami Sta.

Urakami River

J R LINE

Nishizaki Hill
(Martyrs' Memorial)

Suwa Shrine

Fukiro

Shofukuji Temple

Nagasaki Sta.

Harbin

Kofukuji Temple

Ohato Port Terminal

Hamanomachi shopping district

Ginrei

Nagasaki Harbor

Bekkan Hamakatsu

Dejima Dutch Warehouse

Bharata

Sofukuji Temple

Kagetsu

Kozanro

Dutch Slope (Oranda-zaka)

Shikairo

N

Oura Church

Glover Garden

Today on Nishizaka Hill, about a three-minute walk from Nagasaki Station, there's a monument dedicated to the saints with statues of the 26 martyrs carved in stone relief. There's also a small museum housing artifacts relating to the history of Christianity in Japan and ashes of three of the saints. Perhaps most amazing about the history of Christianity in Japan is that the religion was practiced secretly by the faithful throughout Japan's isolation policy, surviving more than 200 years underground without the benefits of a church or clergy.

Dejima

When the Tokugawa shogunate adopted a national policy of isolation in the 1630s, only Nagasaki was allowed to remain open as a port of trade with foreigners. Since the Portuguese and Spaniards were associated with the outlawed Christian religion, only the Dutch and the Chinese were allowed to continue trading. The Dutch were confined to a tiny man-made island called Dejima, and the only people allowed to cross the bridge into the Dutch community were Japanese prostitutes and traders.

Today Dejima is little more than a streetcar stop, having long ago become part of the mainland in the city's land reclamation projects. If you're interested, however, the **Nagasaki Municipal Dejima Museum** in Dejima houses materials relating to the Dutch during their seclusion on the island. It's free and is open every day except Monday from 9 a.m. to 5 p.m. Behind the museum is a model of how the island used to look when the Dutch lived here.

The Port

If you're interested in seeing the results of Nagasaki's history as a trading port, walk to nearby Ohato Port Terminal and board a boat for a 50-minute trip through the town's modern harbor. The never-ending commentary is in Japanese, but you can see for yourself the Mitsubishi shipyards where massive boats are both built and repaired. Boats depart daily at 11:40 a.m. and 3:15 p.m., with more boats added in peak season, but you'd be wise to check the schedule beforehand. Cost of the cruise is ¥800 ($5.71).

Glover Garden and Vicinity

After Japan opened its doors to the rest of the world, Nagasaki emerged as one of the more progressive cities in the country, with many foreign residents. A number of Western-style houses built during the Meiji Period (1868–1912) still survive and have been moved to a large park called Glover Garden on a hill overlooking Nagasaki and the harbor. The stone and clapboard houses have sweeping verandas, Western parlors, the most modern conveniences of the time —and Japanese-style roofs. The most famous of the houses is the **Glover Mansion**, built in 1863 and romanticized as the home of Madame Butterfly (a fictitious character). Thomas Glover, married to a Japanese, was a remarkable Englishman who among other things financially backed and managed shiprepair yards in Nagasaki, brought the first steam locomotive to Japan, opened the first mint in Japan, sold guns and ships, and exported tea.

Also located on the grounds is the **Nagasaki Traditional Performing Arts Museum**, which displays floats and dragons used in Nagasaki's most famous festival, the Okunchi Festival, held in autumn. The highlight of the museum is an excellent film of the colorful parade.

Entrance to Glover Garden and the museum is ¥600 ($4.29), and hours are 8 a.m. to 6 p.m. (8:30 a.m. to 5 p.m. December through February). After entering the grounds you might be a little shocked to see a moving escalator carved into the hillside. While an outdoor escalator in a garden might seem a little bizarre, the Japanese point out that it's there for the benefit of senior citizens who might find the climb up the hill too strenuous. At any rate, the views from here are among the best in the city, offering a good look at both the town, its harbor, and the shipyards.

Next to Glover Garden is the **16th Mansion (Jurokuban-kan Mansion)**, built in 1860 by the American government as the first mansion in Japan for its consular staff. It houses many relics of Nagasaki's early years, including glassware, chinaware, and religious objects. Some of the Imari chinaware on display has pictures of Europeans on it. Destined for Western markets, they prove that the Japanese were willing and able to adapt their products for an outside market even then. The entrance fee is ¥400 ($2.86), and hours are 8:30 a.m. to 5 p.m.

Within a few minutes' walk from Glover Garden are the **Oura Catholic Church**, Japan's oldest Gothic wooden church, built in 1865 to commemorate the 26 Christian martyrs, and **Dutch Slope (Oranda-zaka)**, a cobbled road lined with wooden houses built by former Dutch residents. Also within a few minutes' walk is the **Nagasaki City Museum of History and Folklore**, located at the base of the hill from the Oura Church past the Tokyu Hotel. This museum is housed in an interesting building constructed in 1908 for the Hongkong Shanghai Bank and is open free to the public from 9 a.m. to 5 p.m. every day except Monday. Usually empty and ignored by the throngs marching past on their way to Glover Garden, it exhibits crafts and daily utensils common in Nagasaki between the mid-18th and mid-20th centuries, including hand mirrors, hair ornaments, Chinese objects, some lacquerware, old furniture, gramophones, and even a plastic-food replica of Nagasaki's most famous meal, the *shippoku*. The museum occupies the first and second floors.

Temples and Shrines

The legacy left by Nagasaki's many Chinese residents is best enjoyed at the city's many Chinese restaurants (refer to the dining section) and best seen at its Chinese-style temples. Not far from the Oura Church described above is the colorful **Confucius Shrine** and the **Historical Museum of China**, which charges an admission of ¥500 ($3.57) to see its artifacts, on loan from the Chinese National Museum of History in Peking. Nagasaki's most famous temple, however, is **Sofukuji Temple**, which dates back to 1629 and is known for its Ming Dynasty architecture. It's located about a seven-minute walk from the Hamanomachi downtown shopping district. From Sofukuji Temple I recommend a pleasant 20-minute walk along narrow streets to **Kofukuji Temple**, the first Obaku-Zen Buddhist temple in Japan, founded by a Chinese priest in 1629.

Although the Okunchi Festival has Chinese roots, it's celebrated at **Suwa Shrine**, a Shinto shrine that was built to promote Shintoism when the feudal government was trying to stamp out Christianity. Today the shrine symbolizes better than anything else the spiritual heart of the Japanese community. When Japanese women turn 33 and men turn 40, they come here to pray for good health and a long life. The shrine has fortunes in English. If you're satisfied with your fortune, keep it. If you're not, tie it to the branch of a tree and the fortune is conveniently negated.

Peace Park

On August 9, 1945, at 11:02 a.m., American forces dropped an atomic bomb over Nagasaki, three days after they had dropped a bomb over Hiroshima. Exploding 1,600 feet above ground, it destroyed about one-third of the city, killed an estimated 75,000 people, and injured 75,000 more. Today Nagasaki's citizens are among the most vigorous peace activists in the world, and Peace Park, located north of Nagasaki Station, serves as a reminder of that fateful day and as a warning to the destructiveness of the atomic bomb. Every year on the anniversary of the bombing a peace demonstration is held in Peace Park. As the director of the Peace Park's museum told me, "When the atomic bomb was produced, human beings entered an era when they should stop killing each other. If a nuclear war breaks out, humans will be annihilated. The problems of starvation, religion, and education are all connected to peace."

At one end of Peace Park a black stone pillar marks the exact epicenter of the atomic blast. Ironically enough, the bomb exploded almost directly over a Catholic church. At the other end of the park is the Peace Statue, a 30-foot-high statue of a male deity. Although the exact meaning of the statue is left to individual interpretation, one hand points to the sky from whence the bomb came (meant as a warning?) and the other hand points to the horizon (representing the future?).

Next to Peace Park is a museum, the **Nagasaki International Cultural Hall**. It contains objects, photos, and artifacts showing the devastation caused by the atomic bomb. It's by no means pleasant, but something every concerned individual should see. An estimated one million people visit the museum every year, including about 50,000 foreigners. The International Cultural Hall is open from 9 a.m. to 6 p.m. April through October, closing one hour earlier November through March. Entrance fee is ¥50 (36¢). Located in the basement of the same building but containing an entirely different kind of collection is the **Nagasaki Municipal Museum**, which charges a ¥100 (71¢) admission. It features artifacts relating to Nagasaki's history, especially the Edo Period. Peace Park can be reached by streetcar 1 or 3; disembark at Matsuyama tram stop.

Nagasaki Holland Village

If you're in Nagasaki for more than one day and you want to take a side trip, you might want to visit one of Nagasaki's newest attractions—Nagasaki Holland Village, a living proof of how adept the Japanese are at imitation. They have reconstructed a replica of a Dutch village, with each building a faithful copy of an original back in the Netherlands. Although I was a bit skeptical about visiting an imitation Dutch village in Japan, I must admit that the grounds and craftsmanship are beautifully done. Even Holland itself doesn't always look this pristine. Contained in the village are a porcelain museum, with an exact replica of a room in West Berlin's Charlottenburg Palace that has an elaborate display of china made in both China and Arita, Japan; a museum dedicated to the Dutch in Nagasaki's history; churches; and an abundance of shops. There are china shops, craft shops, souvenir boutiques, and more. There's even a cheese shop selling Dutch imports, which once managed to sell three tons of cheese in one day. That could well be a world record.

At any rate, Nagasaki Holland Village is one hour away by bus from Nagasaki Station. Admission is a bit steep at ¥2,700 ($19.29), and bus fare is ¥550 ($3.93). There's a special information office for the Holland Village at Nagasaki Station, where you can buy your ticket, called a "passport." The best time to visit is of course in the spring, when—what else?—it's tulip season.

SHOPPING: Locally made Nagasaki products include cultured pearls, coral objects, and tortoiseshell jewelry. Keep in mind, however, that U.S. customs forbids tortoiseshell imports. At any rate, a convenient place to shop for Nagasaki products is the **Local Products Hall (Nagasaki-ken Bussankan)**, across the street from Nagasaki Station on the second floor of the Kotsu Sangyo Building. Look for the sign outside that says "Nagasaki Prefecture Tourist Federation."

Another good place for shopping is the **Hamanomachi shopping arcade**, close to the Nishi-Hamanomachi and Kanko Dori streetcar stops. Located centrally downtown, this covered arcade has clothing boutiques, restaurants, accessory stores, and shops specializing in tortoiseshell products and other local handcrafts.

Another famous product of Nagasaki is its castella *(kasutera)*, a sponge cake with Portuguese origins. Japanese visitors to Nagasaki can't leave Nagasaki without buying castella for co-workers and friends back home. There are cake shops throughout the city. The most famous one is **Fukusaya**, 3-1 Funadaiku-machi (tel. 21-2938), not far from the Hamanomachi shopping arcade. Fukusaya is located in a 200-year-old building and has a history that stretches back even further. It's open from 8:30 a.m. to 8 p.m.; closed Monday.

WHERE TO STAY: Nagasaki has very reasonably priced hotels. The busiest time of the year is in May, when Nagasaki is brimming with busloads of schoolchildren who come here on class excursions from other cities.

The Upper and Medium-Priced Range

Nagasaki Grand Hotel, 5-3 Manzai-machi (tel. 0958/23-1234), is a fine older hotel conveniently located not far from the Hamanomachi shopping district. Its 126 rooms are soothingly decorated in soft pastels of mauve or pea green and come with what you'd expect from a hotel of this category—TV, hot-water pot, alarm clock, and mini-bar. The single rooms, with unusual layouts utilizing space to its utmost, are especially pleasant. In addition to three restaurants, there's also a great beer garden right outside the lobby that is surrounded by palm trees and azaleas. It's open mid-April to the end of August from 5 to 10 p.m. Rooms in this hotel start at ¥7,300 ($52) for singles and ¥14,300 ($102) for doubles and twins. There are also three Japanese-style rooms, starting at ¥20,900 ($149) for one person and ¥22,000 ($157) for two.

Hotel New Tanda, 2-24 Tokiwa-machi (tel. 0958/27-6121), is a brick hotel located at the bottom of Dutch Slope about a seven-minute walk to either Glover Garden or the Hamanomachi shopping district. Popular with foreign visitors, it has one Western-style restaurant as well as a beer garden on its roof (open in summer), where you can look out over the harbor. Room rates, which are based on location, view, and furnishings, range from ¥6,800 ($49) to ¥8,200 ($59) for a single, ¥12,000 ($86) to ¥15,400 ($110) for a double, and ¥13,700 ($98) to ¥15,900 ($114) for a twin. Triples are ¥17,000 ($121).

Also located close to Glover Garden is the **Nagasaki Tokyu Hotel**, 1-18 Minamiyamate-machi (tel. 0958/25-1501). Although the lobby is sparsely furnished, the rooms are comfortable and come with tiny balconies and bilingual TVs. Since rates are based on room size rather than view, ask for a room facing Glover Garden. Singles start at ¥10,700 ($76), and twins and doubles start at ¥17,300 ($124). Restaurants in the hotel serve Western, Japanese, and Chinese cuisine.

Opened in 1984, the **Holiday Inn**, 6-24 Doza-machi (tel. 0958/28-1234), is conveniently located just off Kanko Dori Street close to the Hamanomachi shopping arcade. You can walk from the hotel to most sites, including Glover Mansion and Sofukuji and Kofukuji temples. All 84 rooms have double-, queen-, or king-size beds, and start at ¥7,400 ($53) for one and ¥9,600 ($69) for two. Rooms are large and bright, and come with the usual TV, fridge, and alarm clock. The hotel restaurant serves Japanese food.

Park Side Hotel, 14-1 Heiwa-machi (tel. 0958/45-3191), is a pleasant and small hotel located next to Peace Park. Long-term guests like the place because it's quiet and because they can jog early in the morning in the park. The Western-style restaurant has big windows overlooking the greenery of the park, which is ablaze with cherry blossoms in spring. Since this hotel is the tallest building in the area, its rooftop beer garden (open March to mid-September from 5 to 9 p.m.) gives a good view of the vicinity and of the surrounding hills radiating into the distance. The 56 rooms have semi-double beds and double-pane windows. Single rooms are ¥6,200 ($44) and twins and doubles run ¥11,000 ($79).

Hotel Station Ajisai [280], 7-3 Daikoku-machi (tel. 0958/22-2222), a modern brick building across the street from Nagasaki Station, is a cross between a business and a tourist hotel. Locally owned by a Japanese who has five hotel properties in Nagasaki, its 83 rooms come with just the basics, including double-pane windows to shut out train traffic. Singles here are ¥6,000 ($43), doubles cost ¥8,800 ($63), and twins range from ¥9,600 ($69) to ¥11,000 ($79). The most expensive twins are large corner rooms with big windows that open onto a balcony and offer sweeping views. The best deal, however, is a Japanese-style room. It's large, has two beds plus a separate tatami area, and is good for a family, large group, or entertaining friends. Rates for this room are ¥15,400 ($110) to ¥17,600 ($126) for two people and ¥2,000 ($10) for each additional individual up to eight persons. The hotel has one coffeeshop and one Japanese-style restaurant.

Nagasaki Washington Hotel, 9-1 Shinchi-machi (tel. 0958/28-1211), is a chain hotel located on the edge of the city's tiny Chinatown, about a minute's walk from Hamanomachi shopping district. The rooms in this ten-story brick building are slightly more expensive than in the average business hotel, but the rooms are large and come equipped with TV, alarm clock, fridge, radio, and Japanese-style deep tubs. Panels in the windows can be closed for complete darkness. To save energy, electricity is generated only when the key card is inserted into the bedside panel. Singles here start at ¥6,700 ($48), doubles begin at ¥11,000 ($79), and twins go up from ¥13,200 ($94).

If you want to stay in a ryokan, **Sakamoto-ya** [281], Kanaya-machi (tel. 0958/26-8211) is a beautiful 90-year-old ryokan located right in the heart of the city, about five minutes from the station—a wonderful place to stay. Nagasaki's oldest ryokan, most of its 19 rooms have Japanese-style bathtubs made of wood, as well as artwork on the walls. The best room is the Pine Room (Matsu No Ma), which even has its own private little garden. Rates here vary according to the room and the meals served, and range from ¥13,200 ($94) to ¥27,000 ($193) per person, including tax and service charge. If you want you can order *shippoku*, a Nagasaki specialty consisting of a variety of dishes showing European and Chinese influences, for ¥5,000 ($36) more. Western breakfasts are also served.

A bit out of the way, but offering fantastic views of the city, **Yataro**, 2-1 Kazagashira-machi (tel. 0958/22-8166), is perched high on a wooded hillside, a rambling complex offering both Japanese- and Western-style rooms, all with balconies. However, because it's about a 20-minute bus ride from the station (bus stop: Kazagashira) or a ¥1,200 ($6) taxi ride, I advise staying here only if you can get a view facing the harbor. The sweeping view from atop this hill is great, but if you don't have that view you're better off staying in a room closer to the heart of the city. Rates vary according to the season but generally are

¥13,200 ($94) to ¥20,000 ($143) per person, including breakfast, dinner, tax, and service charge. Off-season rates are ¥10,000 ($71). Meals are served in your room and Western breakfasts are available.

The Budget Category

Hotel Ibis, 8-19 Kabasima-machi (tel. 0958/24-2171), is a reasonably priced business hotel about a ten-minute walk from Nagasaki Station. Rooms are simple, and rates start at ¥5,000 ($36) for a single, ¥8,300 ($59) for a double, ¥9,200 ($66) for a twin, and ¥11,300 ($81) for a triple. Western breakfasts are served for ¥750 ($5.36).

Another business hotel you might try is the **Nishikyushu Daiichi Hotel** [282], 2-1 Daikoku-machi (tel. 0958/21-1711), located across the street from Nagasaki Station. Rooms are comfortable, with the usual TV with pay video for adult entertainment and alarm clock, but the bathrooms are minuscule. Singles start at ¥4,800 ($34), but because the windows are shaded by an adjoining building you're better off paying ¥5,300 ($38) for singles with more light. These higher-priced singles come with either a sofa or a semi-double bed. I suggest taking the larger bed since the sofas are uselessly tucked away in a corner and simply make the rooms more crowded. Twins and doubles here start at ¥8,200 ($59), and triples are ¥11,500 ($82). The hotel's restaurant serves a Western breakfast for ¥750 ($5.36).

An inexpensive ryokan about a five-minute walk from Nagasaki Station, **Terada** [283], 1-7 Goto-machi (tel. 0958/22-6178), is more than 20 years old and has a rather unusual feature—a dusty shell museum on the ground floor. The owner here speaks English and is glad to initiate foreigners into the intricacies of staying in a Japanese-style inn. All 18 rooms are tatami, and are equipped with Japanese-style toilets; some have bathtubs as well. Rates per person are ¥3,300 ($24) to ¥4,500 ($32), depending on the size of the room, but in the off-season they're willing to bargain here. Rates do not include meals, but the ryokan has a small and informal Japanese seafood restaurant which serves set meals from ¥2,200 ($15.71).

Another inexpensive Japanese-style accommodation just a few minutes' walk from Nagasaki Station is **Sansui-so** [284], 2-25 Ebisu-machi (tel. 0958/24-0070). All of its 30 rooms have private bathrooms, and the charge here is ¥5,000 ($36) per person without meals and ¥7,700 ($55) including breakfast and dinner. Off-season you can bargain for cheaper rates. Five of the rooms are Western-style but I find them much more dreary than the simpler tatami rooms. All rooms are outfitted with coin-operated TV and air-conditioner.

If you're on a tight budget or prefer the intimacy of a minshuku, one of the best places to stay is **Minshuku Siebold** (sometimes pronounced "Shibolt" by the Japanese), 1-2-11 Sakurababa (tel. 0958/22-5623). There are only five Japanese-style rooms here, all without private bathrooms, and rates are low at only ¥3,300 ($24) per person for rooms without meals. ¥3,800 ($27) including breakfast, and ¥4,900 ($35) with two meals. The woman who runs the place doesn't speak much English, but her husband, who works at a travel agency, does and is happy to recommend inexpensive yakitori-ya in the neighborhood. To reach Siebold, take streetcar 3 from the station and disembark at Shindaiku Machi, which is the fourth stop. Siebold is just a minute's walk from the tram stop on a back street.

Yataro Inn, 2-1 Kazagashira-machi (tel. 0958/22-8166), is an inexpensive accommodation located next to Yataro, described above under medium-priced lodgings. Yataro Inn caters primarily to schoolchildren on excursions, and although it's fairly far away from the heart of the city, prices are very good.

Rooms with private bathrooms are ¥7,400 ($53) per person; those without are ¥5,200 ($37). Rooms with toilets only are ¥6,300 ($45). These prices include buffet-style breakfast, dinner, tax, and service charge. Rooms are both Japanese and Western style and come with balconies, some with great views. Facilities include large public baths and an inexpensive restaurant with a great view of Nagasaki's harbor.

Youth Hostels

There are four youth hostels in Nagasaki. The most conveniently located is the **Nagasaki Kenritsu Youth Hostel** [285], 2 Tateyama-cho (tel. 0952/23-5032), about a 12-minute walk from Nagasaki Station. There are 90 beds, and you don't have to be a youth hostel member to stay here. A one-night stay costs ¥1,800 ($13) for both members and nonmembers, breakfast is ¥400 ($2.86), and dinner runs ¥600 ($4.29). Sheets can be rented for ¥200 ($1.43).

Nagasaki Oranda-Zaka Youth Hostel [286], 6-14 Higashiyamate-cho (tel. 0952/22-2730), can accommodate 50 persons and is located about a three-minute walk from the Ishibashi streetcar stop. Members are charged ¥3,000 ($21) per night, which includes breakfast and dinner, while nonmembers are charged ¥3,500 ($25).

Other youth hostels in Nagasaki are **Uragami-ga-oka Youth Hostel**, 6-14 Miyoshi-machi (tel. 0952/47-8473), and **Nagasaki Nanpoen Youth Hostel**, 320 Hamahira-cho (tel. 0952/23-5526), both about 20 minutes from Nagasaki Station by bus.

WHERE TO EAT: Nagasaki's most famous food is actually a whole meal of various dishes with Chinese, European, and Japanese influences. Called *shippoku*, it's a feast generally shared by a group of four or more persons and includes such dishes as fish soup, sashimi, and fried, boiled, and vinegared seasonal delicacies from land and sea. Another Nagasaki specialty is *champon*, a thick Chinese noodle usually served in soup.

Japanese and Chinese Food

A wonderful place to try shippoku, **Kagetsu** [287], Maruyama-cho (tel. 22-0191), was first established in 1618 and is one of Japan's longest-running restaurants. The oldest part of the present building is about 300 years old. A wooden structure set back from the road of Nagasaki's night scene of sailors' bars and strip cabarets, Kagetsu is an oasis of dignified old Japan, with kimono-clad waitresses shuffling down wooden corridors and serving guests in tatami rooms. Formerly a geisha house, it even has a stone-floored room designed for a table and chairs where foreign patrons could be entertained. In the back of the restaurant is a 300-year-old garden. I'll never forget my evening stroll here as a half moon rose above gnarled stunted pines. The back of the restaurant, consisting mainly of glass, was all lit up so I could see into a multitude of private tatami rooms all on different levels. Guests were seated on the floor on cushions and women in kimonos were playing the gracious hostess, pouring drinks and laughing behind their hands, and from the eaves outside the wooden restaurant hung lighted lanterns. If it weren't for the fact that the men were in business suits, I would have sworn it looked exactly like a woodblock print of old Japan.

Needless to say, this restaurant is very popular and reservations should be made at least a week in advance, though sometimes it is booked up to a full month in advance. There must be at least two of you if you want to eat shippoku. Lunch or dinner of either shippoku or kaiseki cuisine usually costs about

¥20,000 ($142.86) per person, including tax and service charge. It's open from noon to 8 p.m. and is usually closed on either Sunday or Monday.

Another elegant old wooden restaurant, **Fukiro** [288], 146 Kami Nishiyama-machi (tel. 22-0253), sits perched on a small cliff not far from Suwa Shrine. In a building 180 years old, it specializes in shippoku served in private tatami rooms. Lunch (from 11 a.m. to 3 p.m.) costs ¥5,000 ($36), while dinner (served from 5:30 to 8:30 p.m.) runs from about ¥8,000 ($57) to ¥16,500 ($118). The restaurant is open daily and reservations are a must.

If sitting on the floor puts your legs to sleep, you can enjoy a shippoku meal in Western surroundings at the **Dejima Restaurant**, on the seventh floor of the Grand Hotel, 5-3 Manzai-machi (tel. 23-1234). Open from 11 a.m. to 9 p.m., it has set meals of steak, daily specials, and shippoku, all starting at ¥5,000 ($36). If you order the shippoku here you'll get swordfish in diced soybean sauce, various seasonal hors d'oeuvres, minced veal soup, fresh seafood, brisket of pork, seafood and vegetable fritter, chicken hollandaise, cold beef, Chinese pilaf, dessert, and coffee.

Another hotel restaurant serving shippoku is the **Ohura** restaurant in the Tokyu Hotel, 1-18 Minamiyamate-machi (tel. 25-1501). It also serves Japanese and Chinese selections, including tempura, fried sweet-and-sour pork, shredded pork with green pepper, and assorted fried noodles Nagasaki style. Shippoku courses start at ¥2,800 ($20) for a small selection of dishes and go to ¥9,600 ($68.57) for an all-out feast. Colorful pictures depict each course. Ohura is open daily from 11:30 a.m. to 2:30 p.m. and 5 to 9:30 p.m. Located just a few minutes' walk from Glover Garden, it's a convenient and quiet place to stop for a meal if you're in the area.

Another inexpensive place to try shippoku is at a modern restaurant called **Hamakatsu** [289], 6-50 Kajiya-machi (tel. 26-8321), located just a minute's walk from the Hamanomachi covered shopping arcade. There must be at least two of you to order shippoku meals, which start at ¥4,100 ($29.28) per person. If you're by yourself you can order a smaller set menu for ¥2,750 ($19.64) that will give you a variety of local specialties including tempura with green tea noodles, fried and boiled dishes, sashimi, and more. Set meals are served on the second floor; the first floor is devoted to inexpensive à la carte dishes of both Japanese and Chinese origin, with most items under ¥700 ($3.50). Although the menu is in Japanese and changes seasonally, each dish is accompanied by a photo and may include such items as steamed dumplings, tofu dishes, cold chicken, raw beef, or chili shrimp. Opening daily at 11:30 a.m., this restaurant's second floor takes last orders at 8:30 p.m., but the inexpensive first floor serves food until 8:50 p.m.

If you're interested in eating champon Chinese noodles, **Shikairo**, 4-5 Matsugae-cho (tel. 22-1296), is the Chinese restaurant which created these Nagasaki noodles. First opened back in 1899, it moved into its present building in 1973. Located close to the Tokyu Hotel and Glover Garden, it's a large white building topped with a rounded dome and offering five floors of dining. It can accommodate as many as 1,500 people, and caters to large groups and receptions. Knowing where to go for a meal would be confusing if it weren't for the welcoming committee on the ground floor who are eager to point the way. Come to think of it, however, you might still be confused because the numbers for floors in the elevator are written in kanji only. Assuming that you do eventually end up in the right dining hall, you'll find yourself in a large and noisy room surrounded by lots of other hungry souls.

Champon starts at ¥500 ($3.57) and dinner courses start at about ¥2,700 ($19.29). There are more than 30 items on the English menu, including barbecued pork, braised shark fin with shredded meat, chicken with bamboo shoots and onion, fried noodles, and of course, champon. Hours here are 11:30 a.m. to 9:30 p.m. daily, with the last orders taken at 8 p.m.

Another popular Chinese restaurant is **Kozanro** [290], 12-1 Shinchi-machi (tel. 21-3735), located in the heart of Nagasaki's small Chinatown. Most of its foreign clientele is Chinese (which speaks highly of the restaurant), and its most popular dish is champon, ranging in price from ¥550 ($3.93) to ¥770 ($5.50). If you order such à la carte dishes as spring rolls, champon, or sweet-and-sour pork, most of which are under ¥1,000 ($7.14), you'll dine in the restaurant's simply furnished ground-floor dining area of tables and chairs. You may wish to order a set meal of various dishes, which range in price from ¥2,200 ($15.71) to ¥8,800 ($62.86), in which case you have the option of being escorted upstairs to your private tatami room. Kozanro is open from 11 a.m. to 9 p.m. with last orders taken at 8:40 p.m. It's usually closed the first Monday of the month, but since that can vary you're better off calling first.

If you're on a budget there are a lot of inexpensive restaurants in the Hamonomachi shopping district. **Kurukuru Shiragiku** [291] (tel. 22-8900) is in the covered shopping arcade close to Mr. Donut. It's an informal sushi bar with inexpensive dishes that move along the counter on a conveyor belt. Simply pick out any items that catch your fancy. Most plates cost only ¥100 (71¢), though a few cost ¥200 ($1.43) and ¥300 ($2.14). In any case, plates are color coded, but if you're not sure, ask. It's open from 10 a.m. to 8 p.m., closed some Thursdays.

Nagasaki's nightlife district centers on a small street known as Shianbashi Dori, which begins just off the streetcar stop of the same name and is easily recognizable by its neon arch of a bridge and palm trees. Lined with pink plastic flowers, this street shimmers with the lights of various drinking establishments and yakitori-ya, which are often the cheapest places to go for a light dinner. **Yagura-chaya** [292], 6-38 Motoshikkui-machi (tel. 22-0984) is one such place and is located right next to a live-music house called Kento's. Open from 5 p.m. to midnight daily, Yagura-chaya sports dark-stained heavy wooden beams that give it a respectable farmhouse feeling, an atmosphere amplified by the dolls, straw sandals, kites, paper lanterns, umbrellas, and other things suspended from the walls and ceiling. The menu is extensive but unfortunately written only in Japanese, and includes baked fish, skewers of yakitori, chicken nuggets, sashimi, baked corn, pizza, tomato gratin, salads, tofu, and much more. Most dishes are priced under ¥550 ($3.92); beer starts at ¥400 ($2.86) and shochu at ¥300 ($2.14).

Incidentally, **Kento's** (tel. 21-3453) next door features "oldies but goodies," primarily American hits from the 1950s and '60s, sung by Japanese bands. Admission fee is ¥1,000 ($7.14), after which each customer is required to buy at least one food dish and one drink. Dishes range from ice cream to spaghetti and salads, all under ¥1,000 ($7.14). This place is open from 6 p.m. to 2 a.m., and the music is loud.

Foreign Restaurants

Established in 1959, **Harbin**, 2-27 Kozen-machi (tel. 22-7443), is a family-run restaurant serving a unique blend of French and Russian cuisine. The owner, Mitsuru Kubota, was born in Manchuria and named his restaurant after a town close to his birthplace which was once an international city of Russian, Chinese, and Japanese residents. The restaurant itself looks as if it belongs to another era. It has the atmosphere of an old house, mellowed and comfortable with age, with dark-wood paneling and antiques. You might start your dinner here with borscht, followed by skewered lamb, beef Stroganoff, scallops and shrimp in curry sauce, filet of duck in orange sauce, or lamb chops in mint sauce. À la carte dinners generally run about ¥8,000 ($57.14) per person. Set dinners range from ¥5,000 ($35.71) to ¥9,500 ($67.86). The inexpensive set lunches, at ¥1,000 ($7.14) to ¥2,700 ($19.29), are a good bargain. The restaurant opens at 11 a.m. and takes last orders at 9 p.m. It generally closes the third Sunday of the month, but as with many restaurants in Nagasaki this can vary, so be sure to call beforehand.

Another Western-style restaurant with a solid reputation and a faithful clientele, **Ginrei**, 2-11 Kajiya-cho (tel. 21-2073), is close to the Hamanomachi shopping district on Kajiya-machi Street. Open from 10 a.m. to 9 p.m. daily, it resembles an English country cottage, packed full of antique glass and pottery the owner spent half a century collecting. The building itself is 100 years old and from the outside looks like a miniature castle covered in ivy. Although the menu is in Japanese only, there's a lighted display board at the restaurant's entrance with pictures of various dishes. Steaks are the specialty here, with tenderloin and sirloin dishes running about ¥5,000 ($35.71) to ¥6,000 ($42.86).

Obinata, 3-19 Funadaiku-machi (tel. 26-1437), has a warm, earthy feel to it, due perhaps to its heavy wooden beams, large bouquets of flowers, candelabra, and classical music playing softly in the background. An oasis of old Europe in the heart of Kyushu, the atmosphere is cozy and the service is a delight. The menu, a cheerful production illustrated with bright water-colors, lists such entrées as steaks, southern fried chicken with bacon, filet of beef goulash, Japanese steak, spaghetti, lasagne, and pizza. Dishes are creative and fun, the restaurant's own interpretations. Expect to pay about ¥6,000 ($42.86) if you go all out and order appetizers, entrées, and wine (there's a wide selection of Bordeaux, Moselle, and Rhine wines), but you can eat more cheaply if you stick to pastas, which range from ¥900 ($6.43) to ¥1,300 ($9.29). It's open from 5 p.m. to 1 a.m. daily.

Although it's one of Nagasaki's newer and trendy restaurants, **Sakura House**, 6-15 Kajiya-machi (tel. 26-0229), resembles a much older establishment from the 1930s or '40s. Decorated with half-paneled walls, wooden floors, and a wooden bar counter, it's located close to Hamanomachi not far from Ginrei, described above. Its menu lists soups, salads, seafood, chicken, duck, beef, pork, and lamb selections, with set dinner courses starting at ¥3,600 ($25.71). Since it calls itself a restaurant/bar you can also come here for just a drink and listen to background music of jazz or swing. It's open daily from 11:30 a.m. to 1 a.m., but the last order is taken at midnight.

A craving for hot and spicy food can be satisfied at **Bharata**, 2-10 Yasaka St., Aburaya-machi (tel. 24-9194), located close to Hamanomachi shopping arcade just off Kajiya-machi Street on the second floor of a white building. An inexpensive establishment with modest decor, it serves Indian food with curry dishes of beef, chicken, kofta (meatballs), shrimp, or fish running about ¥1,000 ($7.14), including Indian bread or pilaf, chutney, and salad. There's a set vegetarian meal with various small dishes for ¥1,300 ($9.29) and a nonvegetarian meal for ¥2,500 ($17.86).

On weekdays this restaurant is open from 11:30 a.m. to 3 p.m. and 5 to 10 p.m., while on weekends it's open the whole day from 11 a.m. to 10 p.m. It's closed the first and third Thursdays of the month.

A young crowd gravitates toward **Infinity**, on the second floor of the Meganebashi Building just off Meganebashi Bridge, Furukawa-machi (tel. 23-9526). Playing reggae and rock music, this bar/restaurant doesn't start hopping until around 9 p.m., but it serves a cheap lunch plate of the day for only ¥600 ($4.28) from noon to 2 p.m. It also serves spaghetti, salads, and rice dishes for about ¥700 ($5) each. Beer runs ¥450 ($3.21) and cocktails are about ¥660 ($4.71). It's open from 11 a.m. to midnight every day except Sunday when it doesn't open until 5 p.m. It's closed the first Wednesday of the month.

And finally, if you're having a Big Mac attack, you'll find **McDonald's** on Kanko Dori Avenue next to the Holiday Inn in the Hamanomachi shopping district.

6. Unzen

Unzen Spa is a small resort town 2,385 feet above sea level in the pine-covered hills of the Shimabara Peninsula. Because of its high altitude and cool mountain air, its great scenery and hot sulfur springs, Unzen became popular as a summer resort for foreigners back in the 1880s. American and European missionaries, businessmen, and government officials and their families came from as far away as Shanghai, Hong Kong, and Singapore to escape the oppressive humid summer heat. They arrived in Unzen by bamboo palanquin from Obama, seven miles away. The fact that there were foreigners here explains why Unzen has one of Japan's oldest golf courses, dating from 1913.

In 1934 the area around Unzen became **Unzen National Park**, named after an extinct volcano, Mt. Unzen. Unzen Spa itself, however, still bubbles with activity as sulfurous hot springs erupt into surface cauldrons of scalding water in an area known as "The Hells" (Jigoku). Indeed, in the 1600s these cauldrons were used for hellish punishment as Christians were boiled alive here after Christianity was outlawed in Japan. Today Unzen Spa has more than 30 solfataras and fumaroles. The Hells are a favorite hangout of huge black ravens, and the barren land has been baked a chalky white through the centuries. There are pathways leading through the hot springs where sulfur vapors rise thick to veil pine trees from surrounding hills. Old women in bonnets sell eggs that have been boiled in the hot springs for ¥50 (36¢) apiece. They also sell corn on the cob for ¥350 ($2.50) an ear.

I like Unzen Spa because it's small and navigable. It consists basically of just a few streets with hotels and ryokan spread along them, a welcome relief if you've been spending a few hectic weeks rushing through big cities and catching buses and trains. Only 1,600 people live here, and from the town a number of hiking paths wind into the tree-covered hills. If you feel like taking an excursion, buses leave about every hour for **Nitta Pass**, about a 20-minute ride away. The fare is ¥300 ($2.14) one way. From Nitta Pass you can take a ropeway up higher to **Mount Myoken** for a better view, but the best thing to do in my opinion is to take the footpath that runs from Nitta Pass and skirts the mountain along a tree-shaded path. The first 15 or 20 minutes of the path is fairly easy, and that's all you may care to exert yourself. If you're ready for some real climbing, however, continue along the path for another half hour or so where it leads starkly uphill to the summit of **Mount Fugen**, Unzen's highest peak at 4,462 feet above sea level. There you'll be rewarded with splendid views of other volcanic peaks as far away as Mount Aso in the middle of Kyushu. Also on Mount Fugen is Fugen Shrine, which is about a 20-minute hike from the peak. Allow at least two hours for the hike from Nitta Pass to Mount Fugen and back.

For sports, you can play golf at Unzen's famous and Japan's oldest public golf course (tel. 73-3368), open from 8 a.m. to 5 p.m. Total charge for the nine-hole course, including greens fees, tax, and caddy, is ¥7,300 ($52.14) on weekdays and ¥9,500 ($67.86) on weekends and holidays. There's also a shorter nine-hole course (good for beginners) charging ¥2,900 ($20.71). Unzen Spa also has public tennis courts that are free—your only obligation is to rake the dirt court when you finish playing.

Keep in mind that, as with many resort areas in Japan, Unzen tends to be crowded during Golden Week in early May, during New Year's, and in July and August. The best times of year are late April to June, when the azalea bushes are in glorious bloom, and in late October and early November, when the maple leaves turn brilliant reds.

ORIENTATION: Before leaving Tokyo or Kyoto, be sure to pick up the free leaflet *Nagasaki and Unzen,* which describes places of interest in Unzen and the Shimabara Peninsula. The easiest way to get to Unzen is by Kenci Bus from Nagasaki. Buses leave about every hour or so from the bus terminal across the street from Nagasaki Station. The ride takes about two hours and costs ¥1,700 ($12.14) one way. The **Unzen tourist office** (tel. 0957/73-3434) is located in the heart of Unzen Spa not far from The Hells. Open daily from 9 a.m. to 5 p.m., it has a rudimentary but adequate map in English of Unzen and the surrounding area. Not far away is the **Unzen Visitor's Center** with natural history displays of the national park.

The **telephone area code** for Unzen is 0957, and Unzen is located in Nagasaki Prefecture.

FOOD AND LODGING: If you're the least bit of a romantic you won't be able to resist staying at the **Unzen Kanko Hotel** (0957/73-3263). Built in 1935, a year after the establishment of Unzen National Park, it's an old-fashioned mountain lodge of stone and wood covered in ivy. The rooms are rustic and old-fashioned too, with heavy ceiling-to-floor curtains tied back to reveal a balcony, brass doorsills, high ceilings, and wooden beams. There are 50 Western-style rooms here which start at ¥7,700 ($55) for a single and ¥11,000 ($79) for a double or twin. There are also newer Japanese-style tatami rooms starting at ¥13,200 ($94), and combination rooms that come with both bed and tatami area for ¥22,000 ($157). Facilities at the hotel include hot-spring sulfur baths, billiard tables, table tennis, and electronic games. The hotel also has a couple of racquets you can use in case you want to swing at balls down at the public tennis courts.

Even if you don't stay at the hotel you may want to come here for a meal. The dining hall is large, with wooden paneling and wooden floors, white tablecloths, and flowers on each table. Open for lunch from noon to 1:30 p.m. and for dinner starting at 6 p.m., with last orders taken at 8 p.m., it serves set menus of both Japanese and Western selections starting at ¥4,400 ($31.43). The Western set meal for ¥5,500 ($39.29), for example, will bring you hors d'oeuvres, soup, lobster, sautéed chicken and vegetables, a salad, ice cream, a roll or rice, and coffee or tea. There's also a small à la carte menu that includes such dishes as filet mignon, Japanese beefsteak, chicken, pork cutlets, lobster, fried shrimp, and spaghetti.

Also on the hotel grounds is a tempura restaurant called **Gyo En**, located just to the right as you enter the hotel's cedar-lined driveway. A small house with one room for dining, it's open from 5 to 8:30 p.m. daily with set meals ranging from ¥4,400 ($31.43) to ¥6,500 ($46.43).

Miyazaki Ryokan [293] (tel. 0957/73-3331) is one of the largest Japanese inns in Unzen, a modern structure with a lobby overlooking a manicured traditional garden and hills and sulfur vapors rising in the background. All 110 rooms come with TV with pay video, a safe for valuables, alarm clock, fridge, and private bathroom. Japanese-style rooms start at ¥18,000 ($129) per person. There are also combination rooms with twin or double bed and a separate tatami area for ¥25,000 ($179) per person. Rates include two excellent meals, tax, and service charge. Breakfasts (Western style, if desired) are served in a communal dining area, but dinners are served in the individual guest rooms in true ryokan fashion. Room prices are the same regardless of which direction the rooms face, so I'd advise one facing the hot springs and wooded hills rather than the village. The views from these rooms are among the best in Unzen. As expected, this ryokan has large hot-spring public bath facilities.

First opened during the Meiji Period about 100 years ago by the present owner's grandfather, **Yumei Hotel** (tel. 0957/73-3206), is a moderately priced ryokan in Unzen. With the present building constructed in 1973, rates begin at ¥8,800 ($63) per person on weekdays, ranging from ¥11,000 ($79) to ¥22,000 ($157) on weekends and during peak season. All rooms come with private bathroom, a safe for valuables, refrigerator, and TV with adult video. Rooms on the fifth floor have the extra advantage of a large balcony at no extra cost, clearly the best deal. Although most of the 72 rooms are Japanese-style, 20 of the rooms are combination style, with both beds and a separate tatami area, going for ¥13,200 ($94) per person. Dinners are served in each guest's room, while breakfasts are served in a communal dining room. Facilities include hot-spring baths open 24 hours a day, a pool open from July through August, a bowling alley, and public tennis courts next door.

A more economically priced ryokan, **Kaseya Ryokan** [294] (tel. 0957/73-3321) charges ¥6,600 ($47) to ¥11,000 ($79) per person, including two meals (Western-style breakfasts available), tax, and service charge. Although none of the rooms here has a private toilet, the higher-priced rooms have bathtubs. The ryokan, which dates back to 1909, has been totally remodeled so that it appears new and modern. All 13 rooms are Japanese style and are simply decorated, with high ceilings and flower arrangements in each room. There are three communal public sulfur baths, one each for men and for women, and a smaller bath for families.

Formerly a youth hostel, **Seiunso Kokumin Shukusha** [295] (tel. 0957/73-3273) still offers the least expensive accommodation in Unzen Spa. Although it is located about a 30-minute walk from Unzen Spa, the staff will pick guests up if they telephone from the bus stop in Unzen. It has 52 tatami-style rooms, which range in price from ¥5,100 ($36) to ¥6,300 ($45) per person, including two meals, tax, and service charge. The higher-priced rooms have their own private bathroom and balcony, but the view from the cheaper rooms is no less grand. There's a hot-spring public bath, and the most crowded times of the year here are during New Year's and in August, during which times you should try to make reservations three months in advance. There's a public outdoor bath not far from Seiunso.

7. Kagoshima

With a population of more than half a million, Kagoshima in southern Kyushu is a city of palm trees, flowering trees and bushes, wide avenues, and people that are like the weather—warm, mild-tempered, relaxed, and easygoing. In addition, because of its relative isolation at the southern tip of Japan far away from the capitals of Kyoto and Tokyo, Kagoshima through the centuries has developed a mind of its own, an independent spirit that fostered a number of great men and accomplishments. Foremost in Kagoshima's history is the Shimazu clan, a remarkable family that for 29 generations (695 years) ruled over Kagoshima and its vicinity before the Meiji Restoration in 1868. Much of Japan's early contact with the outside world was via Kagoshima, first with China and then with the Western world. Japan's first contact with Christianity, for example, occurred in Kagoshima when St. Francis Xavier landed here in 1549. Although he stayed only ten months, he converted more than 600 Japanese to Christianity.

By the mid-19th century, as the Tokugawa shogunate began losing strength and the confidence of the people, the Shimazu family was already looking toward the future and the modernization of Japan. In the mid-1850s the Shimazus built the first Western-style factory in the country, employing 200 men to make cannons, glass, ceramics, landmines, ships, and farming tools. In 1865, while Japan's doors were still officially closed to the outside world and all contact with foreigners was forbidden, the Shimazus smuggled 17 young men to Britain so that they could learn foreign languages and technology—certainly an act of defiance in the first degree. After these men returned to Japan, they became a driving force in the Meiji Restoration and the modernization of Japan.

Another historical figure who played a major role during the Meiji Restoration was Takamori Saigo, who was born in Kagoshima Prefecture. A philosopher, scholar, educator, and poet, he helped restore Emperor Meiji to power, but because he was also a samurai he subsequently became disillusioned when the ancient rights of the samurai class were rescinded and the wearing of swords was forbidden. He led a force of samurai against the government in what is called the Seinan Rebellion, but suffered defeat. He then withdrew to Shiroyama in Kagoshima, where he committed suicide in 1877. Today Saigo has many fans among the Japanese, and on Shiroyama hill you can visit the cave where he committed suicide.

ORIENTATION: Information on Kagoshima is given in *Southern Kyushu*, a leaflet distributed by the Tourist Information Centers in Tokyo and Kyoto. In Kagoshima there are **tourist information centers** at both Nishi Kagoshima Station (tel. 0992/53-2500) and Kagoshima Station (tel. 0992/22-2500), as well as at the airport. The staffs speak English and have good maps of the city. Tourist information centers are open every day from 8:30 a.m. to 5 p.m.

Kagoshima's international airport connects Kyushu with Hong Kong, Singapore, Bangkok, Guam, and Sydney, while domestic flights give easy access to such cities as Tokyo, Nagoya, Osaka, and Hiroshima. Travel by train takes about 12 hours from Tokyo, 8 hours from Osaka, and about 5 hours from Fukuoka. All trains passing through Kagoshima make two stops, at both Kagoshima Station and Nishi Kagoshima Station. Kagoshima Station is the closest station to Iso Garden, the Sakurajima Ferry Terminal, Shigetomiso, Hirayama Ryokan, and Shiroyama Kanko Hotel, listed below. If you're heading for any of the other hotels described below, you should get off the train at Nishi Kagoshima Station, where you'll also find an international post office.

The downtown section of Kagoshima is the area between Nishi Kagoshima and Kagoshima stations, with Tenmonkan Dori Street serving as the heart of the city. You can walk from one station to the other in less than 30 minutes, but there is also a streetcar connecting the two. If you think you'll be doing a lot of traveling by streetcar, you might want to invest in a one-day pass for ¥550 ($3.93), valid for travel on trams and some city buses and which gives a 20% discount in the admission fee at Iso Garden.

The **telephone area code** for Kagoshima is 0992, and Kagoshima is located in Kagoshima Prefecture.

THE SIGHTS: With ties to Naples, Italy, as its sister city, Kagoshima bills itself as the "Naples of the Orient." That's perhaps stretching things a bit too far, but Kagoshima is balmy and it even has its own Mount Vesuvius—**Mount Sakurajima**, an active volcano across Kinko Bay which continuously puffs steam into the sky and occasionally covers the city with fine soot and ash. In 1914 Sakurajima had a whopper of an eruption in which it belched up three billion tons of lava. When the eruption was over, the townspeople were surprised to discover that the flow of lava had been so great that it blocked the 1,666-foot-wide channel separating the volcano from a neighboring peninsula. Sakurajima, which had once been an island, was now part of the mainland.

Magnificent from far away and impressive if you're near the top, Sakurajima can be visited by a ferry that leaves every 15 minutes from a pier close to Kagoshima Station. It takes 15 minutes to reach Sakurajima. Oddities of Sakurajima include the fact that its rich soil produces both the world's largest radishes and the world's smallest oranges. Although Sakurajima radishes average about 37 pounds, occasionally they weigh more than 80 pounds. The oranges, on the other hand, are only 1.2 inches in diameter.

There are walking paths through lava fields close to Sakurajima's ferry pier, but because Sakurajima is sparsely populated with only limited public transportation, you might want to join a tour operated by Japan Railways that visits lava fields and lookouts around the volcano in one hour and 45 minutes. JR buses depart Nishi Kagoshima Station three times daily at 9:03 a.m., 11:05 a.m., and 1:24 p.m. You can also catch the bus at the ferry dock on Sakurajima. It would be prudent to check the departure times to make sure they haven't changed. Price of the tour is ¥800 ($5.71), but if you have a Japan Rail Pass you can go for free.

Whereas Sakurajima, rising dramatically across the bay, is Kagoshima's best-known landmark, **Iso Garden** is its most widely visited attraction. These gardens of the Shimazu clan were laid out more than 300 years ago with Sakurajima and Kinko Bay incorporated into the design scheme. Open from 8:30 a.m. to 5:30 p.m. daily (until 5 p.m. in winter) with an admission fee of ¥500 ($3.57), the garden features a particularly idyllic spot where the 21st lord of the Shimazu family held famous poem-composing garden parties. Guests seated themselves on stones beside a gently meandering rivulet and were requested to have completed a poem by the time a cup filled with sake came drifting by in the tiny brook. Ah, those were the days!

Next to Iso Garden, and included in its entrance fee, is the **Shokoshuseikan Museum**, built in the mid-1850s as Japan's first modern factory. It houses about 300 items relating to the almost 700-year history of the Shimazu clan, including palanquins used to carry lords to far-away Edo (present Tokyo). There are also everyday items the family used and photographs. I find the photographs showing the Shimazu family dressed in Western-style fashions particularly interesting. Iso Garden is located about 10 minutes by bus from Kagoshima Station and 30 minutes by bus from Nishi Kagoshima Station.

Another museum worth visiting is the **City Art Museum (Kagoshima Shiritsu Bijutsukan)**, which has a collection of contemporary paintings by artists born in Kagoshima Prefecture, including Seiki Kuroda, Takeji Fujishima, and Wada Eisaku. A small selection of paintings by Western artists is also displayed, as well as pottery, glass, bronzes, and other works of art. The permanent exhibition is small, but special exhibitions are also held here. Hours here are 9 a.m. to 5 p.m.; closed Monday.

Only a couple minutes' walk away is the **Kagoshima Prefectural Museum of Culture (Reimeikan)**, also open from 9 a.m. to 5 p.m. every day except Monday. It's one of the finest prefectural museums in the country and was built on the former site of Tsurumaru Castle, of which only the moat remains. The museum traces the history of the people of Kagoshima over the last 40,000 years, with exhibits devoted to topography and natural history, archeological finds, and the society and culture of old Satsuma.

Chiran

If you have an extra morning or afternoon, I suggest taking an excursion to Chiran, a small village 19 miles south of Kagoshima. Surrounded by wooded hills and rows of neatly cultivated tea plantations, it's one of the 102 castle towns that once bordered the Shimazu kingdom during the Edo Period. Although the castle is no longer standing, six old gardens and samurai houses have been carefully preserved by descendants.

Apparently the village headman of Chiran had the opportunity to travel with his lord Shimazu in the mid-1700s to Kyoto and Edo, taking along with him some of his local samurai as retainers. The headman and his retainers were so impressed with the sophisticated culture of Kyoto and Edo that they invited gardeners to Chiran to construct a series of gardens on the samurai estates surrounding the castle.

Some of these gardens remain intact, and are located on a delightful road called Samurai Lane, which is lined with moss-covered stone walls and hedges. Since descendants of the samurai are still living in the houses, only the gardens are open to the public. There are three types of gardens here: the miniature artificial hill style, in which a central pond symbolizes the sea and rocks the mountains; the "dry" garden, in which the sea is symbolized not by water but by white sand that is raked to give it rippling movements of water; and the "borrowed scenery" garden, in which surrounding mountains and scenery are incorporated into the general garden design. Although the gardens are small, they are exquisite and charming. Notice, for example, how the tops of hedges are cut to resemble rolling hills, blending with the shapes of mountains in the background.

The six gardens open to the public are indicated by a white marker in front of each entry gate. All six can be visited for ¥300 ($2.14), and it should take about an hour to see them all. Pay the entry fee for all six at the first garden you visit; you'll be given a pamphlet containing a map and a description of the gardens in English.

Chiran can be reached in about 75 minutes from Yamagataya Bus Station next to the Yamagataya department store in downtown Kagoshima. Although Chiran is located midway between Ibusuki and Kagoshima, there are unfortunately no buses going onward to Ibusuki. If you want to visit Chiran and continue on to Ibusuki, it's best to join one of the organized tours that depart from Kagoshima, stop in Chiran, and end in Ibusuki. The cost of such a tour, conducted in Japanese only, is ¥3,940 ($28.14). Tour buses depart from Nishi Kagoshima Station at 10:10 a.m. and include stops at Lake Ikeda, Mount Kaimon, and the Ibusuki Jungle Bath at the Ibusuki Kanko Hotel, in addition to Chiran. The tour ends at 7:14 p.m. at Ibusuki Station.

SHOPPING: If you're interested in shopping in Kagoshima, local products include *Oshima pongee,* Japanese silk made into such items as clothing, handbags, and wallets; *shochu,* an alcoholic drink made from such ingredients as sweet potatoes and drunk either cold on the rocks or mixed with boiling water; furniture, statues, and chests made from *yaku* cedar; and Satsuma pottery. Satsuma pottery is probably Kagoshima's most famous product. It's been produced in the Kagoshima area for more than 380 years, first by Korean potters brought here to practice their trade. Satsuma pottery comes in two styles—black and white. White Satsuma pottery is more elegant and was used by former lords; the black pottery, on the other hand, was used by the townspeople in everyday life.

In Kagoshima's downtown area are several department stores—Yamagataya, Mitsukoshi, and Takashimaya—where you can shop for local products. There are also souvenir shops in the downtown area, including a covered shopping arcade.

Another good place to shop for local items is the **Display Hall of Kagoshima Products,** 9-1 Meizancho, Sangyo Kaikan (tel. 25-6120). Open from Monday to Friday from 8:30 a.m. to 5 p.m. and on Saturday until 12:30 p.m., this one-room shop is located in Kagoshima's downtown and sells such goods as tinware, handmade knives, Satsuma pottery, glassware, Oshima pongee, yaku cedar, shochu, and other items from Kagoshima Prefecture. Incidentally, the **Kagoshima Prefectural Tourist Office** is located in the same building up on the fourth floor (tel. 23-5771) where you can obtain information on the city as well as the prefecture, including Ibusuki and Chiran.

If you're interested in pottery, there are many Satsuma pottery factories in the Kagoshima area. Most easily accessible is **Kinko Togei,** 2-2-3 Taniyama-cho (tel. 61-0037). Open from 8:30 a.m. to 5:15 p.m. daily, it can be reached by train or tram from Nishi Kagoshima Station. If you're going by train, get off at Sakanoue Station; from there it's either a 20-minute walk or a 5-minute taxi ride. If you want to go by streetcar, get off at Taniyama Station; from there it's a 10-minute taxi ride. You can observe production of Satsuma pottery here and make purchases from its showroom. The factory will ship or airmail your purchases home.

FOOD AND LODGING: In addition to accommodations, hotels in Kagoshima offer a good selection of dining for both Japanese and Western cuisine. In case you wish to eat a few meals outside a hotel, more restaurants are listed at the end of this section, along with recommendations of local food specialties you should try.

The Upper Bracket

Japanese Style: One of Kagoshima's most beautiful ryokan is **Shigetomiso** [296], 31-7 Shimazu-machi (tel. 0992/47-3155), once a villa for the ruling Shimazu clan. Spreading along a gentle slope of a hill in a profusion of flowering plants with a garden and a waterfall, this enchanting ryokan overlooks the bay in a storybook setting. Its oldest rooms date from the 1820s, and through the decades a number of stories, myths, and legends have arisen to add to its mystique. One room, for example, is said to have belonged to the lord's mistress; here you can see a wooden pillar marred by tiny holes—apparently made by the mistress as she stabbed it with her hairpin out of frustration caused by the lord's too infrequent visits. Another room is colored a unique reddish tinge, derived from the blood of pigs brought from Okinawa. There's a closet where the clan could hide during attack, and the ceiling of one hallway was constructed deliberately low to thwart downward blows of enemy swords. In more recent history, the James Bond movie *You Only Live Twice* has a sequence filmed in one of the ryokan's rooms. In short the whole ryokan is a museum in itself and contains antiques that once belonged to the Shimazu family. All rooms come with private bathroom, peace, and tranquillity for ¥14,300 ($102) to ¥55,000 ($393) per person, including two meals, tax, and service charge. Highly recommended if you can afford it.

Western Style: Kagoshima's foremost hotel is the **Shiroyama Kanko Hotel,** 41-1 Shinshoin-cho (tel. 0992/24-2211), which sits 353 feet high on wood-covered Shiroyama hill commanding a fine view of the city below and Sakurajima across the bay. Rooms start at ¥7,700 ($55) for a single, ¥11,000

($79) for a double, and ¥14,800 ($106) for a twin, with the best rooms facing the volcano. Rooms are pleasant and comfortable, although the singles are slightly small. Facilities at the hotel include a pool and sauna; souvenir shops selling such locally made products as silk pongee, Satsuma pottery, yaku cedar, and confectioneries; an art gallery; a pleasant outdoor beer garden open during the summer months; and Japanese, Western, and Chinese restaurants.

The **Sky Lounge**, on the seventh floor of the Shiroyama Kanko Hotel, is open from 11 a.m. to 11:30 p.m. Its à la carte selections include fried or grilled shrimp, sole filet, lobster thermidor, green pepper steak, veal cutlet, spaghetti, and sandwiches. Most entrées run between ¥1,200 ($8.57) and ¥3,000 ($21.43). There are also set menus for ¥3,800 ($27.14) to ¥7,700 ($55). The restaurant affords a good view of the city and volcano, especially at dusk as the lights come on below and Sakurajima slowly fades into darkness.

Taki-no-Chaya is Shiroyama Kanko Hotel's Japanese restaurant, serving sashimi, tempura, sukiyaki, kaiseki, and Japanese barbecue dishes from 11 a.m. to 10 p.m., with a beautiful view of a garden. Most dishes cost ¥2,000 ($14.29) to ¥5,000 ($35.71). If you feel like splurging, one section of the restaurant, called Kappo Lakusui, serves local selections of seafood and vegetables. The setting here is impressive, with an indoor pond and individual tatami rooms constructed as though they were tiny huts in a village. Dinners here run anywhere from ¥6,500 ($46.43) and up, and you should make a reservation if you want to dine in this section. Lunch courses start at ¥3,500 ($25).

The Medium-Priced Range

Kagoshima Tokyu Hotel, 22-1 Shinmachi, Kamoike (tel. 0992/57-2411), is a first-rate medium-priced hotel located in a new section of town which sports immaculate, modern buildings and wide avenues. Its only drawback is that it's a bit far from the center, but city buses departing from Nishi Kagoshima Station reach the hotel in 15 minutes. Built right on the waterfront with a good view of the volcano, its 206 rooms range from ¥6,900 ($49) to ¥9,000 ($64) for a single, ¥13,200 ($94) to ¥15,500 ($111) for a twin, and ¥17,000 ($121) for a double. The twins and doubles face the water and have verandas, great for sitting out in the morning and watching the sun rise over Sakurajima. Singles all face inland and do not have balconies.

The hotel's Japanese restaurant, **Yamabuki**, serves tempura, sashimi, and local dishes; its Western restaurant, **Hibiscus**, serves steaks, lobster, sandwiches, curries, and pilaf. If you're in the mood for teppanyaki steak, try the hotel's **Steak House Fresia**, where the chef prepares your food before your very eyes. Steaks here cost between ¥4,000 ($28.57) and ¥8,000 ($57.14).

Kagoshima Sun Royal Hotel, 1-8-10 Yojiro (tel. 0992/53-2020), is also located in the new section of Kagoshima, not far from the Tokyu Hotel. Its rooms come with TV with pay video, clock, music, and refrigerator, and all the double, twin, and Japanese-style rooms face the sea and have balconies. Singles, which face only inland and do not have balconies, start at ¥4,300 ($31) without bathroom and ¥5,700 ($41) with. Twins are ¥7,700 ($55) without bathroom and ¥11,000 ($79) with bathroom. The doubles all have bathrooms and cost ¥11,000 ($79). I personally prefer the Japanese-style rooms with their tatami sitting alcoves beside the balcony. They go for ¥12,000 ($86) and up. There's a great *onsen* (hot-spring bath) on the 13th floor, separated for men and women. You can look out over Mount Sakurajima as you bathe.

For meals, try the **Phoenix Sky Lounge** on the 13th floor, open from 11:30 a.m. to 2 p.m. and from 5:30 p.m. to 11:30 p.m. It's very pleasant, with a drawing-room ambience in colors of pale pink and green. Entrées include grilled chicken, steak, beef Stroganoff, wienerschnitzel, grilled lobster, pilaf, and spaghetti and start at ¥660 ($4.71). There are set steak courses for ¥4,400 ($31.43) and ¥6,600 ($47.14).

The hotel also has a Japanese restaurant, where kaiseki and local dishes are served for about ¥3,000 ($21.43) to ¥6,000 ($42.86).

Located right in the heart of downtown, the **Kagoshima Hayashida Hotel**, 12-11 Higashisengoku-cho (tel. 0992/24-4111), is about a ten-minute walk from either Nishi Kagoshima or Kagoshima Station. Following what appears to be a Space Age theme, it's built around an inner garden atrium called Space Garden, and the inside guest rooms possess views of the atrium through one-way mirrors. Although these rooms facing the inside tend to be dark, they're much quieter than those facing the outside streets. Rooms are of modern design, though small, and are equipped with TV, clock, and radio. All have a private bathroom. Single rooms start at ¥7,000 ($50), doubles begin at ¥9,350 ($67), and twins run ¥11,550 ($82.50) and up.

Inside Space Garden, with its sunroof, plants, and trees, are four restaurants serving Japanese, Cantonese, French, and Western cuisine. Meals average about ¥3,000 ($21.43) and up, and hours are 11 a.m. to 2:30 p.m. and 5 to 10 p.m. daily. A Filipino band performs in the center of the atrium five times a day.

The Budget Category

The past few years have witnessed the opening of a number of business hotels in Kagoshima, most of them located close to Nishi Kagoshima Station. **Park Hotel** [297], 15-24 Chuo-cho (tel. 0992/51-1100), is one of these and can be reached in two minutes on foot from the station. All of its 70 rooms are Western style and come with semi-double-size beds, TV with adult videos, windows that can be opened, hot water for tea, and bathrooms that are larger than in most business hotels. All but 12 of its rooms are single, which are ¥5,500 ($39). There are six doubles, which go for ¥8,800 ($63), and six twins, which cost ¥10,000 ($71). Its one restaurant serves both Western and Japanese food, with selections including shabu-shabu, obento lunch boxes, spaghetti, sirloin steak, and hamburger steak.

Also about a two-minute walk from Nishi Kagoshima Station but much older is **Station Hotel New Kagoshima**, 6-5 Chuo-cho (tel. 0992/53-5353). Its 210 rooms are basic but adequate, and all come with private bathroom. Single rooms start at ¥5,200 ($37), doubles begin at ¥8,200 ($59), and twins go for ¥8,800 ($63) and up, tax and service charge included. Eight Japanese-style rooms are also available beginning at ¥8,800 ($63) for two. A restaurant on the eighth floor called Star Dust serves both Japanese and Western food. The ninth floor boasts a beer garden (open in summer).

About a three-minute walk from Nishi Kagoshima Station is **Business Hotel Gasthof**, 7-3 Chuo-cho (tel. 0992/52-1401). Although it looks rather uninteresting from the outside, the lobby is quite another story. It reminds me of some forgotten pawnshop, with glass cases packed with antiques, old knives, ceramics and pottery, and fish tanks. More likely than not four small dogs will greet you from atop the check-in counter. None of the stuff is for sale—it's all there simply for your viewing pleasure. The rooms are very basic and a bit worn, but are adequate enough and most come with bathroom. For one person the charge is ¥3,800 ($27) for singles with private bath, but if you can do without your own bathtub there are singles with toilets only for ¥2,700 ($19). Doubles are ¥4,400 ($31), twins are ¥6,500 ($46), and triples are ¥10,000 ($71). Charges include tax and service, and breakfasts are available for ¥400 ($2.86).

Close to the city's other train station, Kagoshima Station, is **Hirayama**

[298], 6-7 Meizancho (tel. 0992/22-4489), about five minutes away. All 18 rooms here are Japanese style and only two come with their own private bathroom. The hallways could use a good vacuuming, but the tatami rooms are fine and come with coin-operated TV and air conditioning. Rates are on a per-person basis and are ¥3,300 ($24) for a room without meals, ¥3,800 ($27) for a room with breakfast, and ¥5,500 ($39) including two meals. Meals are Japanese and are served in a dining hall.

If you're a youth hosteler, try **Kagoshima Fujin Kaikan Youth Hostel,** Shimoarata 2-27-12 (tel. 0992/51-1087). To reach it, take bus 13 from Nishi Kagoshima Station and get off at bus stop Shimoatara Fujin Kaikan Mae. There are eight Japanese-style rooms here, and the price including two meals is ¥2,900 ($21). Nonmembers can stay for ¥3,800 ($27).

Another youth hostel is the **Sakurajima Youth Hostel** [299], Hakama-goshi (tel. 0992/93-2150). It's on the slope of the Sakurajima volcano, about a five-minute walk from the ferry terminal. The charge of ¥3,000 ($21) brings you bed, breakfast, and dinner and is the same for both members and nonmembers.

More Dining

While in Kagoshima, be sure to try its local dishes, known as *Satsuma* cooking (Satsuma was the original name of the Kagoshima area). This style of cooking supposedly has its origins in food cooked on battlefields centuries ago, but if that's the case I'm sure it's improved greatly since then.

A good place to try local Satsuma dishes is **Kumasotei** [300], 6-10 Higashisengoku-cho (tel. 22-6356), located in the center of town between Nishi Kagoshima and Kagoshima stations. Hours here are 11 a.m. to 10 p.m. This restaurant is well known in Kagoshima and reminds me more of a private home or ryokan, since dining is in individual tatami rooms. As soon as you enter you are ushered into its recesses, and if there isn't a crowd you'll probably have your own private room; otherwise you'll share. The main menu is in Japanese, but there's a smaller menu in English listing two courses for ¥2,700 ($19.29) and ¥4,400 ($31.43) that feature Satsuma cooking. There are also kaiseki courses starting from ¥3,800 ($27.14) and some à la carte selections. Satsuma specialties include *satsume-age* (ground fish that has been deep-fried), *torisashi* (raw chicken, and not as bad as it sounds), tonkotsu (pork that has been boiled for several hours in shochu and brown sugar—absolutely delicious), *zakezushi* (rice that has been soaked in sake all day and is then mixed with such things as vegetables and shrimp), bonito baked with salt, *awameshi* (rice mixed with wheat and undoubtedly very healthy), and *Satsume-jiru* (miso soup with chicken and locally grown vegetables). *Kibinago* is a small fish belonging to the herring family caught in the waters around Kagoshima. A silver color with brown stripes, it is often eaten raw arranged on a dish so that it looks like a chrysanthemum.

A more modestly priced restaurant serving Satsuma food, **Satsuma** [301], 10-4 Chuo-chu (tel. 52-2661), is right across the street from Nishi Kagoshima Station. Look for a tiny restaurant with a large red lantern and white curtains outside its door. Open from 10 a.m. to 3 p.m. and from 5:30 to 10 p.m. every day except Monday, this cozy establishment has room for about only ten people on its ground floor and another ten people on the second floor. Such items as torisashi, kibinago, Satsuma-jiru soup, Satsuma-age, and tonkotsu cost between ¥550 ($3.93) and ¥1,000 ($7.14), and there are also set meals ranging from ¥550 ($3.93) to ¥2,750 ($19.64).

Another popular and inexpensive dining place is **Noboruya** [302], 2-15 Horie-cho (tel. 26-6690). This is Kagoshima's best-known ramen, or noodle, shop, and since there's only one dish there's no problem ordering. Costing ¥880 ($6.29), a big bowl of ramen comes with noodles (made fresh every day) and slices of pork and is seasoned with garlic. You also get pickled radish (supposedly good for the stomach) and tea. Open from 11 a.m. to 7 p.m. every day except Sunday, it's in the center of town about a 15-minute hike from Kagoshima Station. As you eat your ramen at the counter, you can watch women peeling garlic and cooking huge pots of noodles over gas flames.

8. Ibusuki

Located about an hour from Kagoshima by train at the southern tip of the Satsuma Peninsula, Ibusuki (pronounced "ee-*boo*-ski"), with a population of 33,000, is southern Kyushu's most famous hot-spring resort. With a pleasant average temperature of 64.5°F, it's a region of lush vegetation, flowers, and palm trees—and of course, hot springs.

ORIENTATION: Be sure to get the leaflet *Southern Kyushu* from the T.I.C. in Tokyo or Kyoto. Upon arrival in Ibusuki, stop by the **tourist information counter** at Ibusuki Station to pick up a map in Japanese with some English on it. There's also an English brochure available with a brief rundown of sightseeing attractions in the area around Ibusuki. The information counter is open daily from 8:30 a.m. to 7:30 p.m.

The town of Ibusuki is spread along the coast, and there are public buses that run through the main streets. In any case, the town isn't large, and taxis are readily available.

The **telephone area code** for Ibusuki is 09932. Ibusuki is located in Kagoshima Prefecture.

WHAT TO DO: The most popular thing to do is to have yourself buried up to your neck in hot black sand, and the best place to do this is at **Surigahama Public Beach**, located about five minutes from Ibusuki Station by bus. After paying ¥500 ($3.57) you'll be supplied with a yukata cotton kimono and towel. Change into the yukata in the changing room and then walk down to the beach. One of the women there will dig you a shallow grave. Lie down, arrange your yukata so that no vulnerable areas are left exposed, and then lie still while she piles sand on top of you. It's quite a funny sight, actually, to see nothing but heads sticking out of the ground. Bodies are heated by hot springs that surface close to the ground before running into the sea. It's best to go when the tide is low so you can get closer to the sea. The water is alkali saline, a hot 185° Fahrenheit, and helps in gastroenteric troubles, neuralgia, and female disorders. Many of the older people you see here are not tourists but are living in Ibusuki and come here every day for treatment. After your sand bath, go indoors for a hot-spring bath. The Surigahama sand baths are open every day from 8:30 a.m. to 9 p.m. (until 8 p.m. in the winter).

Other hot-spring and sand baths are found in the spa hotels spread along Ibusuki's six-mile-long beach. The biggest indoor baths are the **Ibusuki Kanko Hotel's Jungle Bath**, a huge affair with pools of various shapes and sizes surrounded by tropical plants. If you've been to Beppu's Suginoi Palace baths, however, this one may be somewhat of a letdown. The women's baths are much smaller than the men's, although no one objects if women want to use the men's baths instead. Use of the Jungle Bath is free to hotel guests; all others must pay a ¥1,600 ($11.43) entrance fee. There are also indoor hot-sand baths here, for which everyone (including hotel guests) must pay an extra ¥1,000 ($7.14).

To visit the area surrounding Ibusuki, it's best to either join a tour group (conducted in Japanese only) or rent a car. Public bus lines are neither extensive nor frequent. Popular destinations include **Nagasakibana Point**, Kyushu's southernmost point and the location of a bird and animal park with variety shows; and **Lake Ikeda**, Kyushu's largest lake with a depth of 265 meters (820 feet) and gigantic eels. Some of these eels weigh 33 pounds and measure about six feet in length. If you're interested in seeing these creatures, souvenir shops and stops along the lake have some on display in big tanks.

Another destination is **Kaimon Natural Park**, located at the foot of Mount Kaimon. There's a rest house here serving snacks and inexpensive food, and an 18-hole golf course. Greens fees are ¥8,300 ($59.29) on weekdays, ¥12,700 ($90.71) on Saturday, and ¥15,700 ($112.14) on Sunday and holidays. For more information on golfing, call the golf course at 2-3141.

FOOD AND LODGING: Most of Ibusuki's hotels are located along its six-mile beach. Because this is a resort area, accommodations are more expensive than in the cities.

Ibusuki's best-known spa hotel is the **Ibusuki Kanko Hotel**, 3755 Juni-cho (tel. 09932/2-2131). It's a self-contained resort with everything from outdoor swimming pools to tennis courts, a bowling arcade, shopping arcade, its own private beach, and the huge hot-spring baths described above. It even has a delightful small art museum with French and Japanese paintings by such artists as Henri Matisse, Seiki Kuroda, and Takeji Fujishima. Next to the art museum and connected to it by an underground passageway is a newly opened museum featuring art and antiques from Japan and China, including cloisonné, ivory, and ceramics. The architecture of the two buildings is innovative and impressive, with an imaginativeness and creativity rarely expressed in bare concrete. The museums are open daily from 8 a.m. to 6 p.m. and are in themselves worth a trip to the Kanko Hotel.

As for the hotel itself, it's situated on 125 acres of lush tropical grounds with pleasant walking trails throughout. The hotel is very popular with Japanese tour groups and is a good place to rub elbows with Japanese on vacation. It tries to look as much as possible as though it's in Hawaii—the staff even wears Hawaiian shirts to help create the mood. The hotel has 460 Western-style twin rooms (there are no singles) and 167 Japanese tatami rooms. Twins range from ¥11,000 ($79) to ¥16,500 ($118) for single occupancy and ¥13,200 ($94) to ¥18,700 ($134) for a double. All the rooms have either a full or partial view of the sea and come with balconies—the best rooms in my opinion are the ones that face the acres of garden. The Japanese-style rooms, which are located in an older building with a less magnificent view, are ¥11,000 ($79) for those without bathrooms and ¥15,900 ($114) for those with bathrooms, with rates based on double occupancy.

Nights at the Kanko Hotel are nice, with the sound of the waves and the frogs croaking in the lotus pond.

Altogether the restaurant has eight food-and-beverage outlets. For Western dining, try the **Sky Lounge** on the 10th floor, with a sweeping panoramic view of the water. Open from 7 a.m. to 11:20 p.m., it serves a variety of dishes including salmon, lobster, sole, and sirloin steak. The average dinner costs about ¥5,000 ($35.71). The Japanese restaurant, **Okonomi**, serves tempura, sushi, and local dishes. A particularly entertaining place to dine is the **Jungle Park Restaurant Theater**. It features live variety shows usually from—you guessed it—Hawaii. Although a new theater may be built in the near future, the present one is massive, holding up to 1,500 people in an airplane-hangar-size building filled with tropical plants. The Japanese guests show up in an outfit provided in the hotel rooms—blue-flowered pajama-like shirts and shorts for the men and pink-flowered shifts for the women. If you really want to join in the fun, wear the same. Most of the Japanese here are with tour groups. The food is Japanese barbecue style, and you cook your thin slices of beef and vegetables at your table on a hot griddle over a gas flame. Dinner begins at ¥4,000 ($28.57) and show time is 6:30 to 8 p.m.

If you want to stay in a ryokan, **Shusuien** [303], 5-27-27 Yunohama (tel. 09932/3-4141), is renowned both for its excellent service and its cuisine. In 1985 and 1986 competitions held by Japanese travel agencies in which 100 top accommodations were rated, Shusuien won first prize for its cooking, fourth for its service, and third overall. Although it has only 50 rooms, Shusuien employs a staff of 120.

This is a good place to stay if you want to be pampered and don't want to spend your holidays with group tours of jovial vacationers. Rates per person range from ¥16,500 ($118) to ¥55,000 ($393), including two meals, tax, and service charge. The most expensive rooms face the sea, have balconies, and are higher up. The less expensive rooms face inland and have no balcony. Needless to say, this ryokan is elegant yet refined in its setting. Used to foreign businessmen, it serves Western-style breakfasts on request.

Ibusuki Park Hotel Hakusuikan [304], Tarahama-kaigon (tel. 09932/2-3131), has a long driveway lined with pine trees, which immediately sets the mood for this reasonably priced hotel on the beach. On the hotel grounds are three swimming pools, an indoor hot-sand bath, a beer garden (open in summer), and an outdoor hot spring, with separate areas for men and women. Of the 208 rooms, 38 are Western-style twin rooms and 77 are combination rooms with both beds and separate tatami areas. The rest are Japanese-style tatami rooms. The best rooms are those on the sixth and seventh floors that face the sea—they have their own balconies. Rates range from ¥11,000 ($79) to ¥33,000 ($236) per person, with two meals, tax, and service charge included. Breakfasts are Western-style buffets. This is a very pleasant place to stay.

An inexpensive place to stay is **Hotel Kairakuen**, 5-26-4 Yunohama (tel. 09932/2-3121). About a 20-minute walk from Ibusuki Station or a five-minute taxi ride, it's located right next to the Surigahama sand baths on the beach. Of its 21 rooms, two are Western style and four are combination rooms with both beds and tatami areas. Although the hotel's building is old and a bit run-down, the price is right at ¥7,700 ($55) per person, including two meals, tax, and service. Since rates are the same for all rooms, be sure to request a room facing the sea. The best room of all is room 408, which is located on a corner of the building with lots of windows and features both beds and a tatami area, making it perfect for families. All private baths feature water directly from the hot springs, and rooms facing the sea have windows above the tubs so you can look out on the water as you bathe. Dinner is served in your room, while Japanese breakfasts are served in a communal dining area.

Even less expensive is **Marutomi** [305], 5-24-15 Yunohama (tel. 09932/2-5579). It's also located close to Surigahama sand baths, on a tiny road that leads inland just across the street from the baths. This establishment is a family-run minshuku, and since the owner here is a fisherman you can count on fresh seafood. Rates here are ¥5,000 ($36) per person including two meals. There are only seven Japanese-style rooms, all without private bathroom but featuring coin-operated TV, coin-operated air-conditioners, and chips of camphor wood which give the rooms a pleasant, outdoor smell. There's a small tiled bathtub with water from a hot spring.

Another place to try if you're on a budget is **Ibusuki Kokumin Kyuka-son** [306], Higashikata, Shiomi-cho (tel. 09932/2-3211), a National People's Village. It's located right at the water's edge and is very reasonable, charging ¥6,240 ($45) per person, including meals, tax, and service charge, for rooms without bathrooms and ¥8,000 ($57) for those with baths. You can do it even cheaper if you don't take meals here and your room is without a bathroom—that costs only

¥2,500 ($18) per person. With tennis courts, rental bikes, and windsurfing boards available, this place is very popular and is full during the summer vacation months of July and August, on New Year's, in March during spring vacation, and in May during school trips. Otherwise, you can probably get a room here. Rooms are basic, with TV and safe for valuables, and those that face the sea even have balconies. Eight of the 77 rooms are Western style. You can reach the village by the village's own bus, recognizable by three circles of green, red, and blue, which is the symbol of National People's Villages. Buses depart from in front of Ibusuki Station following every train arrival. Otherwise, it's about a ten-minute taxi ride.

The **Ibusuki Youth Hostel,** 12-Cho 836 (tel. 09932/2-2758), recently moved into these new quarters, with a total of five rooms that each have air conditioning, heater, and TV. Prices, which include two meals, are ¥3,300 ($24) for members and ¥4,400 ($31) for nonmembers.

If you're looking for a place to eat lunch, the best place in town is probably **Shimazu-han,** located in Shusuien ryokan, described above (tel. 3-4141). In fact, Shimazu-han is so well known among the Japanese that visitors staying in other ryokan in Ibusuki will request room-only rates so that they can enjoy dinner here at Shimazu-han. Shusuien has won awards for its cuisine, and though the food served in its restaurant is not as extensive or expensive as that served to its ryokan guests, meals here are a pleasure, served in private tatami rooms on plates that have been chosen with care to match both the seasons and the food displayed. Dishes are served in courses rather than all at once and start at ¥1,600 ($11.43) for lunch and ¥3,800 ($27.14) for dinner. Since there are only eight small rooms, you should make a reservation. Although the menu is in Japanese only, there are photos for each course. The most popular set meal is the Shimazu Gozen for ¥3,300 ($23.57), which includes sashimi, tempura, fish, soup, egg custard, vegetables, rice, and other dishes. Be sure to order a cup of plum shochu (*ume shu*)—it's the best shochu I've ever had. Shimazu-han is open from noon to 2 p.m. and from 6 to 11 p.m.

If you're adventurous, there's a very fun restaurant in the countryside called **Chozyuan** [307], Kaimon-cho, Tosenkyo (tel. 2-3155). Eight buses depart daily from Ibusuki Station and the ride lasts about 30 minutes. This restaurant is also a lunch stop for some of the organized tours of the area and is a unique *somen,* or cold noodle place. Seating is under a pavilion beside a man-made waterfall, so you eat to the accompaniment of running water and Japanese traditional music playing in the background. In the middle of your table is a large round container with water swirling around in a circle. When you get your basket of noodles, dump them into the cold water; then fish them out with your chopsticks, dip them in soy sauce, and enjoy. There are four set menus for ¥1,000 ($7.14) to ¥2,500 ($17.86) which come with such things as grilled trout, vegetables, and soup. You can also try carp sashimi. Be sure to keep the wrapper your chopstick came in—it can be used as a bookmark. Hours are 9 a.m. to 9 p.m. July and August, 9 a.m. to 7 p.m. May and June, and 9 a.m. to 5:30 p.m. September through April.

9. Miyazaki

With a population of 280,000, Miyazaki is one of the largest and most important cities in southern Kyushu and serves as the government seat of Miyazaki Prefecture. Yet Miyazaki feels isolated and somewhat neglected by the rest of Japan. Tokyo seems far away, and most foreigners who happen to land at Kagoshima's international airport tend to head north for Kumamoto, missing Miyazaki altogether. Japanese honeymooners, who used to favor Miyazaki over most other destinations a decade ago, are now flocking to the shores of Hawaii.

And yet Miyazaki is a perfect place to relax, swim in the Pacific Ocean, get in some rounds of golf, and savor some of the local delicacies. Temperatures here are the second-warmest in Japan, after Okinawa, and flowers bloom throughout the year. You won't see many foreigners here, and the natives will treat you warmly and kindly. If you want to unwind and pamper yourself for a few days, Miyazaki is a good place to do it. And if you have the energy for sightseeing, Miyazaki Prefecture has some historical and natural attractions to occupy your time.

ORIENTATION: It takes more than 12 hours to reach Miyazaki from Tokyo by train. The trip by plane takes only 1½ hours, after which it's about a 15-minute ride to the center of town.

For a map of the city in English, stop off at the **tourist information centers** at either the airport or JR Miyazaki Station, open from 8:30 a.m. to 5 p.m. every day except Sunday.

The main street in town is Tachibana-dori Street, lined with shops, department stores, and restaurants. Many buses serving other parts of town as well as Miyazaki Prefecture make stops along this main thoroughfare. There's also a large bus terminal south of the Oyodo River close to Minami Miyazaki Station.

For detailed information on Miyazaki Prefecture, drop by the **prefectural tourist office** (called *kankyo kyokai* in Japanese), located just off Tachibana-dori Street at 1-6 Miyata-cho (tel. 0985/25-4676. Open from 8:30 a.m. to 6 p.m. Monday through Friday and 8:30 a.m. to 1:30 on Saturday, it has information on Aya, Aoshima, Udo Shrine, and other attractions. This is also a good place to shop for locally made products in its adjoining shop. You can purchase wooden trays, bowls, ceramics, masks, haniwa clay reproductions, swords, lacquerware, and other crafts made in Miyazaki Prefecture.

Before leaving Tokyo or Kyoto, be sure to pick up the leaflet *Southern Kyushu,* which has information on Miyazaki. The **telephone area code** for Miyazaki is 0985.

THE SIGHTS: Although all of the sights listed below are accessible by public transportation, they are quite spread out. You may, therefore, want to join an organized tour even though it will be conducted only in Japanese. At least it gets you to each destination and you won't have to worry about time schedules and bus stops. A tour operated by Miyazaki Kotsu Bus Company which departs at 8:50 a.m. daily from the bus terminal near Minami Miyazaki Station visits Miyazaki Shrine, Haniwa Garden, Aoshima island, Horikiri Pass, Cactus Park, and Udo Shrine. The tour lasts seven hours and costs ¥4,650 ($33.21).

The most important shrine in town is **Miyazaki Shrine,** dedicated to the first emperor of Japan, Emperor Jimmu, who was the first leader of the Yamoto courts. Peacefully surrounded by woods and cedar trees and about a 15-minute bus ride from Tachibana-dori Street, the shrine is austerely plain and is built from cedar. Be sure to visit the nearby **Miyazaki Prefectural Museum (Miyazaki-ken Sogo Hakubutsukan),** open every day except Monday from 9 a.m. to 4:30 p.m. Its collections of ancient clay images, stone implements, ancient pottery, folklore, and other items depict the natural history, ancient history, and arts of Miyazaki Prefecture.

Archeological digs in Miyazaki Prefecture have unearthed a multiple of ancient burial mounds and clay figures knowns as *haniwa.* Replicas of both these ancient mounds and haniwa clay figures can been seen in **Haniwa Garden,** most easily reached by taxi in about 15 minutes from Miyazaki Station. Approximately 400 of these clay figures have been placed between trees on mounds covered with moss. Even though they are replicas, the impact of seeing so many images together is quite effective. I especially like the hamiwa with the simple face and body with the O-shaped mouth, said to be that of a dancing woman. A one-room exhibition house displays some items found in ancient burial mounds, and if you want you can buy a small clay replica to take home with you.

Heiwadai Garden is located in a large park called Heiwadai Park, in which you'll also find the **Tower of Peace.** Having a pedestal built with stones donated from countries around the world, it was constructed with the help of volunteers and was finished—ironically enough—in 1940.

If you want to see real burial mounds, head for Saitobaru, where there are more than 300 ancient tombs constructed mostly in the fifth and sixth centuries. Most of the mounds are now covered with grass and trees, so there isn't a lot to see. There is, however, the **Saitobaru Museum,** with a display of excavated artifacts taken from the tombs, including swords, mirrors, bead jewelry, clay pots, stone coffins, tools, and haniwa. The haniwa were buried along with deceased lords to symbolize court retainers who would serve him after death. There are also scale models of several of the burial mounds, including models of the two largest mounds, where the Emperor's ancestors were buried. Saitobaru can be reached in about an hour by bus from the bus terminal near Minami Miyazaki Station or from downtown.

Also an hour's bus ride from Miyazaki is **Aya,** a village of 7,300 people. Known for its production of traditional handcrafts, Aya boasts about 13 kilns, more than 10 woodcarving shops, 2 bamboo-crafts makers, and 3 weaving shops. All these products are now gathered under one roof in a recently constructed crafts center, which with its native wooden beams and clay walls, is just as interesting as the products for sale. Next to the crafts center is a workshop where you can make your own pottery piece for ¥1,000 ($7.14), which includes the price of shipment of your masterpiece to the United States. There's also a weaving workshop, where you can fashion your own coaster for about ¥300 ($2.14).

Next to the crafts center is **Aya Castle,** a reproduction of the original Aya castle built 650 years ago. Made of fir trees, the castle is tiny compared to most in Japan and contains just a few artifacts, such as samurai uniforms and swords. Because both the castle and the crafts center are small and are located an hour away from Miyazaki, I suggest you visit Aya only if you have a special interest in crafts or have no other chance to see a Japanese castle. Both the center and castle are located about a ten-minute walk from the center of Aya town on top of a peaceful wooded hill. Hours are 9:30 a.m. to 5:30 p.m. and the entrance fee is ¥300 ($2.14).

One of the most famous sights associated with Miyazaki is **Aoshima,** a tiny island less than a mile in circumference and connected to the mainland via a walkway. Although Aoshima is located about 25 minutes south by train from Miyazaki Station, it's considered part of Miyazaki city. There's a small shrine on the island, and the beaches nearby are the most popular among the people of Miyazaki for swimming. It seems everything in Japan has its own special season, and the season for swimming here is July and August.

If you follow the coast from Aoshima farther south, you'll come to **Nichinan Coast,** famous for its eroded, rippling waves of rock, which resemble a washboard. There's a local bus from Miyazaki that travels along this beautiful coastline (and passes through Aoshima), going all the way to Udo in about 1½ hours (the name of the bus stop is "Udo"). Here you'll find **Udo Shrine,** located about a 15-minute walk from the bus stop. Dedicated to the father of Emperor

Jimmu, this vermilion-colored shrine is actually located in a cave beside the ocean, and the view, in my opinion, is exhilerating. Udo Shrine is famous among young couples who come here to pray for success and harmony in marriage. Up until 60 years ago, the trek to the shrine was not so easy, requiring climbs over mountain passes and along beaches. At any rate, behind the shrine are cave formations thought to resemble breasts, and milk candy is a specialty of the shops near the shrine.

FOOD AND LODGING: The most relaxing and luxurious places to stay in Miyazaki are Sun Hotel Phoenix and Seaside Hotel Phoenix, located side-by-side about a 15-minute taxi ride from Miyazaki Station at 3083 Hamayama Shioji. Under the same ownership, both of the hotels are isolated, surrounded by many acres of land and by the sea. Facilities include tennis courts, bowling lanes, a zoo, a children's playground, an outdoor swimming pool (open in summer only), a golf course, and a public bath. The 27-hole golf course is famous in Japan and is much cheaper than courses near Tokyo. Green fees including tax and caddy are ¥15,400 ($110) on weekdays, ¥18,000 ($129) on Saturday, and ¥20,000 ($143) on Sunday. Club rentals are about ¥2,000 ($14.29). The hotel has a much cheaper course in the mountains, where weekday fees including caddies are ¥9,400 ($67.14). Next to the hotel complex is a wonderful area of woods and ponds, and bicycles are available for rent.

Built about 15 years ago, the **Sun Hotel Phoenix** (tel. 0985/39-3131) is the more expensive of the two hotels, with rates per person beginning at ¥13,200 ($94) per person including buffet-style breakfast and dinner, tax, and service. Room-only rates are also available, beginning at ¥9,300 ($66) for one person and ¥11,500 ($82) for two in the Western-style rooms and ¥14,300 ($102) for one and ¥16,500 ($118) for two in the Japanese-style rooms. Higher prices are charged for rooms facing the sea. Western-style rooms are roomy, with bedside reading lamps, a hair dryer, stocked fridge, clock, radio, and kimono.

The Sun Hotel Phoenix's **Restaurant Ski Blue,** up on the ninth floor, has unobstructed views of the Pacific, pine woods, and the golf course below. Open from 11 a.m. to 3 p.m. and 5 to 10 p.m., it offers lunch courses starting at ¥2,000 ($14.29) and dinner courses from ¥3,300 ($23.57) for steaks or seafood. The à-la-carte menu includes gratin, sandwiches, seafood, stewed beef, pilaf, curry, and spaghetti. The hotel's Japanese restaurant on the second floor features seafood and sashimi, with teishoku beginning at ¥3,300 ($23.57).

Two years older is **Seaside Hotel Phoenix** (tel. 0985/39-1111), with both Western and Japanese rooms. Rates including two meals, tax, and service begin at ¥11,000 ($79). Rooms without meals start at ¥7,000 ($50) for a single and ¥9,300 ($66) for a double, while Japanese rooms start at ¥12,000 ($86) for one person and ¥14,300 ($102) for two.

Also under the same ownership, but in town, is the **Hotel Phoenix,** 2-1-1 Matsuyama (tel. 0985/23-6111). Located right beside the Oyodo River about a seven-minute taxi ride from Miyazaki Station, its Western-style rooms begin at ¥7,700 ($55) for a single and ¥10,000 ($71) for a double, while Japanese-style rooms start at ¥11,000 ($79) for one person and ¥13,200 ($94) for two. Rates with two meals begin at ¥11,000 ($79) per person. Rooms that face the river cost slightly more. There's a small outdoor pool open in July and August, which is unfortunately located right outside the lobby's window, there's no hiding those extra pounds. A beer garden on the roof, open from May to September 15 from 5:30 to 9 p.m., has a great view of the river, city, and the hills beyond. Beer starts at ¥600 ($4.29).

If you're looking for a business hotel, the **Miyazaki Oriental Hotel,** 2-10-22

Hiroshima (tel. 0985/27-3111), is just a two-minute walk from Miyazaki Station. Built in 1975, its rooms are a bit old but are reasonable at ¥4,600 ($33) for a single, ¥7,700 ($55) and ¥8,800 ($63) for a twin. Ninety of its 104 rooms are single, and rates with meals are also available. There's someone at the front desk who speaks English, and the hotel's one restaurant serves Chinese food. Single rooms come with stocked fridge, hair dryer, a pants-presser, and clock, while some of the twins have a separate toilet and shower area.

If you're a sun worshipper, you may want to stay at the **Aoshima Kokumin Shukusha** [308], located at 2-12-36 Aoshima (tel. 0985/65-1533) right next to the tiny island. All of its rooms face the ocean, and the beach for swimming is only a five-minute walk away. All of its 45 Japanese-style rooms (5 of which have private bathrooms) have balconies, but its 8 Western-style rooms do not. Popular with Japanese families, this kokumin shukusha is heavily booked during New Year's, Golden Week in May, and July and August, so book ahead if you plan to travel during these times. Rates per person begin at ¥3,200 ($22.86) for Japanese rooms without bathroom and ¥4,600 ($32.86) for Japanese rooms with bath and for Western rooms. Breakfasts are ¥750 ($5.36), while suppers begin at ¥1,600 ($11.43). Aoshima can be reached in about 25 minutes by train from Miyazaki Station, after which it's about a three-minute walk.

More Dining

Miyazaki's subtropical climate is conducive to the growth of a number of vegetables and fruits, including sweet pumpkins, oranges, cucumbers, green peppers, *shiitake* mushrooms, and chestnuts. Especially popular is *shochu*, made from sweet potatoes, buckwheat, or corn. Both of the restaurants listed below specialize in dishes made with locally grown vegetables, fruit, and other produce, used imaginatively in unique creations by their own chefs. They are located close together just off Tachibana-dori Street near the prefecture tourist office, about a 15-minute walk from JR Miyazaki Station.

Although the stairwell doesn't look like much as you walk down into the basement of the Shokokaikan Building, **Gyosantei** [309], Higashi 1-chome (tel. 24-7070), is an attractive restaurant with wooden floors, tatami mats, leg wells under the tables, and waitresses dressed in kimonos. Notice the two little mounds of salt on either side of the restaurant's door—they symbolize purification. Just as in the olden days, there's a split length of bamboo inside the leg well on which to rest your stockinged feet, and the menu is written on a scroll. I suggest you order one of the courses featuring local food, which range from ¥3,800 ($27.14) to ¥6,000 ($42.86). The *Himukazen* course, for example, which means "facing the sun," changes according to what's in season and what the cook decides to create, but it always includes as its main course a pumpkin filled with chicken and radish and topped with hard-boiled egg yolk, with a raw yolk plopped on top (which nevertheless slowly cooks from the heat)—meant to resemble the sun. Side dishes might include salmon rolled inside Japanese radish, raw flying fish served with freshly grated *wasabi* (horseradish), fried prawn with dried mushrooms used as a coating instead of flour, or Miyazaki melon. It's truly a restaurant of culinary surprises, making dining here a pleasure and an experience. It's open from 11:30 a.m. to 2 p.m. and from 5 to 10 p.m., closed the first and third Sundays of the month.

Not far away is **Sugi no Ko** [310], Tachibana-dori 2-1-4 (tel. 22-5798), located up on the third floor. The owner of this restaurant creates all his own dishes and has even produced a book with his recipes. The dining area displays *haniwa* dolls and other crafts of Miyazaki Prefecture, and there are also private tatami rooms. The menu is written in Japanese only, and lists lunch teishoku for

¥1,000 ($7.14) to ¥2,200 ($15.71) and dinner courses from ¥3,800 ($27.14) to ¥8,800 ($62.86). The lunch Miyazaki Gyuu Teishoku, for example, comes with Miyazaki beef seasoned with soy sauce and served with four different sauces, vegetables, soup, rice, and fruit. One of the side dishes featured during my visit was delicate tofu filled with pungent mustard. Sugi no Ko is open from 11:30 a.m. to 11:30 p.m., closed the second and fourth Sundays of the month.

Chapter XI

NORTHERN JAPAN

1. Matsushima
2. Hakodate
3. Sapporo
4. The National Parks of Hokkaido

BECAUSE SO MANY of Japan's historical events took place in Kyoto, Tokyo, and other cities in southern Honshu, most tourists to Japan never venture farther north than Tokyo. True, northern Japan does not have the temples, shrines, gardens, and castles of southern Japan. It does have spectacular scenery, however. Matsushima, about three hours north of Tokyo, is considered one of Japan's most scenic spots, with pine-covered islets dotting its bay. Farther north is Hokkaido, the northernmost of Japan's four main islands.

HOKKAIDO: Hokkaido's landscape is strikingly different from any other place in Japan. With more than 30,000 square miles, Hokkaido makes up about 21% of Japan's total land mass and yet it has only 5% of Japan's population. In other words, Hokkaido has what the rest of Japan doesn't, and that's space. Considered Japan's last frontier, Hokkaido didn't begin opening up to development until after the Meiji Restoration in 1868 when the government began encouraging Japanese to migrate to the island. Even today Hokkaido has a frontier feel to it, attracting lots of young Japanese who come here to backpack, ski, camp, and tour across the countryside on motorcycles or bicycles. There are dairy farms and silos and broad fields of flat land clothed in wheat, corn, potatoes, and rice. Then the land puckers up to craggy and bare volcanoes, gorges, and hills covered densely with trees. There are clear spring lakes, mountain ranges, rugged wilderness, wild animals, and rare plants. About 7% of Hokkaido is preserved as national and prefectural parks. An English photographer I know who has lived in Japan for six years and traveled the length and breadth of the country says that Hokkaido is her favorite place in all of Japan.

With winters that are long, cold, and severe, Hokkaido's main tourist season is in August, when days are cool and pleasant with an average temperature of 70°F. And while the rest of the nation is under the deluge of the rainy season, Hokkaido's summers are usually bright and clear. However, even winter is not an idle time in Hokkaido. Ski enthusiasts flock to slopes near Sapporo and to resorts such as Daisetsuzan National Park. And February marks the annual Sapporo Snow Festival, with its huge ice and snow sculptures.

As for the people of Hokkaido, they are considered to be as open and hearty as the wide expanse of land around them. Hokkaido is also home of the Ainu, the native inhabitants of the island. Not much is known about their origins, but the Ainu arrived in Hokkaido approximately 800 years ago. It's not even clear wheather they're Asian or Caucasian, but at any rate they're of different racial stock than the Japanese. They are round-eyed and light-skinned, and Ainu males can grow thick beards and mustaches. Traditionally the Ainu lived as hunters and fishermen, but after Hokkaido opened up to development they were gradually assimilated into Japanese society, taking Japanese names and adopting the Japanese language and clothing. Like American Indians, they were often discriminated against and their culture was largely destroyed. Today there are an estimated 15,000 Ainu still living in Hokkaido. Some of them earn their living from tourism, selling Ainu woodcarvings and other crafts, and performing traditional dances and songs.

TRAVELING AROUND HOKKAIDO: Getting around Hokkaido is by train and bus. In addition to regular bus lines there are also sightseeing buses linking national parks and major attractions. Although they are more expensive than trains and regular buses, they offer unparalleled views of the countryside. Keep in mind that bus schedules fluctuate with the seasons, as some lines cease operations altogether during the snowy winter months.

If you plan to do a lot of traveling in Hokkaido and you are not traveling by Japan Railpass, you can purchase a special pass issued by Japan Railways that allows unlimited travel on its trains and buses in Hokkaido. The pass can be purchased in Japan, and there are several options available. A 20-day Hokkaido JR Pass, for example, costs ¥42,000 ($300) and includes a round-trip ticket from the place of departure (say, Tokyo) to Hokkaido. A 5-day pass costs ¥14,000 ($100) and a 10-day pass costs ¥22,600 ($161). These allow 20% discounts on round-trip tickets from the place of departure to Hokkaido.

Because distances are long and traffic is rather light, Hokkaido is one of the few places in Japan where driving your own car is actually recommended. Because it's expensive, however, it's economical only if there are several of you. The rate for three days of car rental generally starts at about ¥20,000 ($142.86) for the first 260 miles. After that it's about ¥30 (21¢) per mile. Car-rental agencies are found throughout Hokkaido as well as at Chitose Airport outside Sapporo.

Incidentally, travel to Hokkaido by land is generally via Shinkansen bullet train from Tokyo to Morioka, followed by limited express from Morioka to Aomori on the northern tip of Honshu island. For centuries the only way to continue from Aomori to Hokkaido was by boat, but in April 1988 the expected opening of the Seikan Tunnel will allow the entire trip to be made by train. Whereas the ferry ride to Hakodate, on Hokkaido, used to take four hours, the train ride by tunnel will take only two—but even that seems like a remarkably long time to be in a tunnel. At any rate, the entire trip from Tokyo to Hakodate via train should take about eight hours. The fastest way to reach Hokkaido, of course, is to fly.

1. Matsushima

Because the trip to Hokkaido is such a long one, the most pleasant way to travel is to break up the journey with an overnight stay in Matsushima in northern Honshu. Matsushima means "Pine-clad Islands," and that's exactly what this region is. More than 200 pine-covered islets and islands dot Matsushima Bay, giving it the appearance of a giant pond in a Japanese landscape garden. Twisted and gnarled pines sweep upward from volcanic tuff and white sandstone, creating a wonderland of bizarre and beautiful shapes. Matsushima is so dear to Japanese hearts that it is considered one of the three most scenic spots in

Japan (the other two are Miyajima in Hiroshima Bay and Amanohashidate on the north coast of Honshu). Basho (1644–1694), the famous Japanese haiku poet, was so struck by Matsushima's beauty that it's almost as though he were at a loss for words when he wrote: "Matsushima, Ah! Matsushima! Matsushima!"

I have no doubt that Matsushima was indeed awesomely and strikingly beautiful during Basho's time, as well as during the time it was selected as one of Japan's three most scenic spots about 270 years ago in a book written by a Confucian philosopher of the Edo government. But motorboats have been invented since then, and although they offer the closest view of the islands, all those boats plying the water somehow detract from the mood that evoked such ecstasy in Basho long ago. Still, Matsushima itself is a pleasant small town on the waters of Matsushima Bay and makes a worthwhile stop if you're on your way north to Hokkaido.

ORIENTATION: Before leaving Tokyo, be sure to pick up from the T.I.C. a sheet called *Sendai, Matsushima, and Hiraizumi*. It has a map of Matsushima Bay and tells of attractions in and around Matsushima. From Tokyo you can take the Tohoku Shinkansen from Ueno Station to Sendai, which will take from 2 to 2½ hours, depending on the number of stops your train makes. In Sendai, change to the JR Senseki Line—it's well marked in English so you shouldn't have any difficulty changing trains in Sendai. It takes about 25 minutes by express train to reach Matsushima Kaigan Station, which is where you disembark. You can also arrive in Matsushima by boat (described in the sightseeing section below).

Once in Matsushima, stop off at one of the **Matsushima Tourist Association Offices**, located at both Matsushima Kaigan train station and at Matsushima Kaigan Pier (tel. 022/354-2168). You can pick up a brochure with a map in English and get directions to your hotel. Hours for both are 8:30 a.m. to 5 p.m. The train station and pier are about a ten-minute walk apart. As for Matsushima itself, all its major attractions are within walking distance of both the train station and the pier. You can cover the whole area on foot in half a day of leisurely sightseeing.

The **telephone area code** for both Matsushima and Sendai is 022, and both are located in Miyagi Prefecture.

WHAT TO SEE: Your sightseeing trip around Matsushima can begin even before you reach your destination. A popular way to get to Matsushima is to take the Senseki Line from Sendai only as far as Hon-Shiogama (about 18 minutes by express). From there you can catch a sightseeing boat to Matsushima Kaigan Pier. Passing pine-covered islands and oyster rafts along the way, it's a good introduction to the bay and costs ¥1,500 ($10.71) for the one-hour trip. Unfortunately, the commentary is in Japanese only (a good time to break out the Walkman unless you've become oblivious to noise by now). And believe it or not, a couple of the boats have been disguised as either a peacock or a dragon. Boats leave from both Hon-Shiogama and Matsushima Kaigan piers about every half hour between 8 a.m. and 4 p.m. in summer, but only four times a day in winter. If you're going in the off-season, be sure to check the schedule (tel.022/366-5111).

Even if you don't arrive by boat you might still want to take a boat trip in the bay (if you can't beat 'em, join 'em, right?). Regular sightseeing boats make 40-minute trips around the bay and back and charge ¥1,500 ($10.71) per person. You can also charter smaller motorboats which, judging by the number of them leaving the pier every few minutes, seems to be the most popular way to see Matsushima. Charter motorboats cost ¥4,500 ($32.14) for a tour lasting 30 minutes, ¥6,500 ($46.43) for 50 minutes, and ¥16,500 ($117.86) for two hours. You can see more of the islands on these smaller craft than you can on the regular sightseeing boats.

In addition to the boat trips, there are four spots spread around Matsushima Bay historically considered the best for viewing Matsushima's islands. These spots are called Otakamori, Tomiyama, Tamonzan, and Ogidani. The closest is **Ogidani**, a ten-minute taxi ride away from the pier. However, I personally don't think it's worth the time or effort to make it to each of these four lookouts. You can get as much a feel for Matsushima's beauty simply by visiting the more easily accessible attractions listed below. If you feel like hiking to a lookout, **Sokanzan Lookout** is about a 30-minute walk from Matsushima Kaigan Pier and offers a panoramic view of the region.

Matsushima's best-known structure is **Zuiganji Temple** [311], the most famous Zen temple in the northern part of Japan. Located right in front of Matsushima Kaigan Pier just a few minutes' walk away, its entrance is shaded by tall cedar trees. On the right side of the pathway leading to the temple are caves and grottoes dug out by priests long ago. Adorned with Buddhist statues and memorial tablets, they were used for practicing *zazen* (sitting meditation). Zuiganji Temple was founded in 1606 by the order of Masamune Date, the most powerful and important lord of northern Honshu. Unifying the region known as Tohoku, Date built his castle in nearby Sendai and today almost all sites in and around Sendai and Matsushima are tied to the Date family. At any rate, it took hundreds of workers six years to build the temple, which was constructed in the *shoin-zukuri* style typical of the Momoyama Period. The temple served as the family temple of the Date clan.

An adjoining treasure hall, the **Seiryuden**, displays items belonging to the temple and the Date family, while the main hall contains elaborately carved wooden doors, transoms, and painted sliding doors—and this is one of the few temples that still allows flash photography. Admission is ¥500 ($3.57) and hours vary according to the season. The longest hours are from April to mid-September, when it's open from 7:30 a.m. to 5 p.m. In winter, hours are reduced to 8 a.m. to 3:30 or 4 p.m.

Next to Zuiganji Temple (to the left if you're facing Zuiganji) is **Entsuin** [312], a lesser-known temple also built more than 300 years ago by the Date clan. Open from 8 a.m. to 5 p.m. throughout the year and charging a ¥300 ($2.14) admission, it features a small rock garden, a beautiful rose garden, and a small temple housing an elaborate statue of Lord Mitsumune Date, grandson of Lord Masamune Date who founded the Sendai fief. Depicted here on horseback, Mitsumune was reportedly poisoned and died at the tender age of 19. The statues surrounding him represent retainers who committed ritual suicide to follow their master into death. At any rate, the statues and small temple are located at the back of the temple grounds, past the rose garden. Tour groups seem to bypass this temple, making it a peaceful retreat away from the crowds that sometimes descend on Matsushima.

Under the supervision of Zuiganji Temple is **Godaido**, a small wooden worship hall on a tiny island not far from the pier. Connected to the mainland by a short bridge, it's open night and day and is free, but there's not much to see. The interior is closed to the public, open only every 33 years. (It won't be open again until August 20, 2006.) Godaido is often featured on brochures of Matsushima, making this delicate wooden temple one of the town's best-known landmarks.

Kanrantei, the "Water-Viewing Pavilion," is just a short walk from the pier. A simple wooden tea house, it was used by generations of the Date family for such aesthetic pursuits as viewing the moon and watching the ripples on the tide. Originally it belonged to warlord Hideyoshi Toyotomi as part of his estate at Fushimi Castle near Kyoto, but he presented it to the Date family at the end of the 16th century. Kanrantei is open from 8 a.m. to 5 p.m. The entrance fee is ¥200 ($1.43). For an additional ¥300 ($2.14) you can drink ceremonial green tea while seated upon the tatami of the tea house and contemplating the bay, its islands, and the boats carving ribbons through the water. After drinking your tea, wander through the small museum, which contains artifacts belonging to the Date family. I found particularly interesting a screen painted long ago showing Matsushima—even then there were boats winding between the islands. Realizing how quaint those wooden boats powered by men in straw hats look to us now, it occurred to me that the Matsushima of today with its motorboats may one day look quaint and old-fashioned to generations hence.

Just a couple of minutes beyond Kanrantei on the southern edge of Matsushima is **Oshima**, a small island once used as a retreat by priests. At one time there used to be many caves with carvings of scriptures, Buddhist images, and sutras, but today the island and its remaining stone images and structures are rather neglected and forgotten. There's no fee, no gate, and the island never closes. It's a nice quiet spot to sit and view the harbor. While you're sitting here, think about the fact that because it was a Buddhist retreat, women were forbidden to enter Oshima until after the Meiji Restoration in 1868. Think also about the fact that if a place like this were left unguarded in America, it would have long ago been vandalized.

Next to Oshima is the **Matsushima Aquarium**, open from 9 a.m. to 5 p.m. and charging ¥800 ($5.71) admission. It has a large variety of freshwater and saltwater fish and animals and a lot of attractions for kids, including rides on a miniature train and carousel.

At the other end of Matsushima is **Fukuurajima**, another island connected to the mainland, this time by a long red concrete bridge with orange-colored railings. It's a botanical garden of sorts, with several hundred labeled plants and trees, but mostly it's unkempt and overgrown—which comes as a surprise in cultivated Japan. It takes less than an hour to walk completely around the island. Between the hours of 8 a.m. and 6 p.m. (4 p.m. in winter) you must pay ¥100 (71¢) admittance; after hours you can enter for free.

As for destinations outside Matsushima, if you have time you may want to visit **Kinkazan Island**, accessible in about two hours by ferry from Ishinomaki. Kinkazan is small with a pyramid-shaped mountain on it and has woods inhabited by deer and monkeys. A shrine called Koganeyama is located halfway up the mountain.

FOOD AND LODGING: Because this is a tourist town, accommodation in Matsushima is not cheap, especially during the peak months of May through November. During the Tanabata Festival, held August 6 to 8 in Sendai, and the Toronagashi Festival, on August 15 and 16, in Matsushima, rooms are usually fully booked a half year in advance. Rates are generally cheaper during the off-season months (from December through April). Almost all accommodations here are in ryokan, which means you're generally expected to take your dinner and breakfast at the ryokan. Unless otherwise stated, all prices quoted below include two meals. Because Matsushima tends to be expensive, I've included some budget accommodations in nearby Sendai at the end of this section.

In Matsushima

Accommodating 1,500 people, **Taikanso** [313], 10-76 Aza Inuta (tel. 022/354-2161), sprawls atop a plateau surrounded by pine-covered hills and offers the best view in town. Even its public baths overlook the island-studded bay, so you can wash contemplating the beauty of Matsushima. The hotel, located five minutes by taxi or 15 minutes on foot from Matsushima Kaigan Station, has a nightclub with floor shows nightly and an outdoor swimming pool. Both Western- and Japanese-style rooms are available, most with private bathroom. Pleasantly bright, they come with fridge, TV with pay video, and a safe for valuables. Rates vary according to the season and whether your room faces the sea or the wooded mountains (which are also quite nice), has tatami or beds. Rates during the tourist season (May through November) start at ¥15,400 ($110) for Japanese-style rooms (all of which face the sea): Western-style twins start at ¥14,300 ($102) for those facing the mountains and ¥16,500 ($118) for those with views of the sea. Combination-style rooms with both beds and tatami areas start at ¥17,600 ($125). On Saturday night and evenings just before public holidays during peak season, you should expect to spend about ¥3,000 ($21) more than the rates quoted above. During off-season months, however, prices are ¥3,000 ($21) less than the quoted rates. Prices are per person and include two meals.

Restaurants in Taikanso include a noodle shop with noodle dishes starting at ¥700 ($5), a Japanese seafood restaurant serving sashimi and tempura ranging in price from about ¥900 ($6.43) to ¥2,200 ($15.71), and a Western restaurant, called **Shiosai**, on the seventh floor with fine views of both Matsushima Bay and the surrounding pine-covered hills. In fact, the view from here is probably the best in town and is worth the 30-minute walk from Matsushima's pier. The food itself is nothing to write home about but is reasonably priced, with entrées of curry, pilaf, spaghetti, and seafood and Japanese dishes priced less than ¥1,600 ($11.43). Steak dinners start at ¥3,800 ($27.14), while a daily lunch special is available for ¥1,600 ($11.43). Hours are from 11 a.m. to 9 p.m.

Matsushima Century Hotel, 9 Aza Senzui (tel. 022/354-4111), is a glittering white hotel that opened on the shore of Matsushima in 1984. A cool oasis in the middle of town with a convenient location between the pier and Fukuurajima Island, it's a sleek hotel appealing especially to the young. Its disco charges a ¥2,700 ($19.29) cover, which includes one free drink. Another plus of this hotel is its outdoor swimming pool, and its modern and beautiful public baths and sauna, all of which overlook the bay.

A NOTE ON JAPANESE SYMBOLS: Many hotels, restaurants, and other establishments in Japan do not have signs showing their names in English letters. Appendix II lists the Japanese symbols for all such places appearing in this guide. Each establishment name in Japanese symbols is numbered, and the same number appears in brackets in the text following the boldfaced establishment name. For example, in the text the Osaka hotel, Hokke Club [161], is number 161 in the Japanese symbol list in Appendix II.

The rooms here are sunny and cheerful and decorated in pastels and white. The Japanese-style rooms, all of which face the bay and have balconies, cost ¥22,000 ($157) per person with two meals during tourist season and ¥13,200 ($94) during the winter months. Western-style rooms, which face only inland and have no balconies, are very reasonable. Prices for these rooms do not include meals and run ¥6,000 ($43) for a single and ¥13,200 ($94) for a twin all year round.

The Century Hotel is also a good place to come for lunch or dinner at **La**

Saison. Open from 11 a.m. to 1:30 p.m. and from 5 to 8:30 p.m., this Western seafood restaurant is decorated with white latticed wood and ferns. You can order such dishes as sole, fried shrimp, scallops, steaks, and beef stroganoff à la carte, but especially good are the set courses, ranging from ¥2,400 ($17.14) to ¥11,000 ($78.57). Although courses change frequently, the ¥6,600 course, for example, may include duck pâté, oysters, shrimp crevette, grilled steak, salad, ice cream, bread or rice, and coffee.

Hotel Sohkan, Isozaki, Aza Hama 1-1 (tel. 022/354-2181), is a modern and comfortable ryokan located on the edge of Matsushima about a five-minute taxi ride from the pier. Catering mainly to Japanese groups, it offers a koto concert in the early evening in its lobby, played by a woman in a traditional kimono. Facilities include public baths, a couple of golf holes for practice or beginners, and a 210-foot-high tower from which for ¥350 ($2.50) you can have a view over all of Matsushima. Its disco, with live bands, is a fun place to watch the Japanese enjoying themselves—there's even *karaoke* here, in which people from the audience stand up and sing while accompanied by background music. There is a total of 76 rooms, all with private bathroom. Two of the rooms are Western style, can sleep four people, and even have bilingual TV. Rates per person at this ryokan range from ¥13,200 ($94) to ¥20,000 ($143) during peak season and ¥11,000 ($79) to ¥16,500 ($118) during the off-season. You have your choice of Japanese or Western breakfast and dinner.

If you want to stay in an old-fashioned ryokan, the best choice in town is the **Matsushima Kanko Hotel** [314], near Matsushima Kaigan Pier (tel. 022/354-2121), popularly called Matsushima-jo, which means Matsushima Castle. Indeed, as Matsushima's oldest ryokan (built about 100 years ago), it does rather resemble a castle with its sloping tiled roof, white walls, and red railings. Inside it's airy and delightful, with old wooden banisters polished from decades of human hands. Its walls are decorated with woodblock prints by the famous artist Hiroshige, as well as photographs of stern-faced Japanese who have stayed here in the past. Because the building was built before the advent of modern plumbing, only eight of the 28 rooms have bathrooms, and the communal toilets are Japanese style. Keep in mind also that rooms come only with fans, not air conditioning, and tend to be drafty in winter. However, rooms do have a sink, coin-operated TV, and fridge, and those on the third floor are high enough to see over the rooftops to the water beyond. It has a convenient location directly behind Godaido worship hall just a minute from Matsushima Kaigan Pier. Rates throughout the year range from ¥8,800 ($63) to ¥27,000 ($193) per person with two meals. Off-season you can also stay here without taking meals, in which case rates begin at only ¥6,500 ($46) per person. The public bath is unique: it mixes underground salt water with tap water. Western breakfasts are served on request.

Konnoya [315], 38-1 Fugendo (tel. 022/354-3006), is a moderately priced, clean, modern ryokan about a five-minute walk inland from the pier and a 15-minute walk from Matsushima Kaigan train station. All 14 rooms are Japanese style and come with a private toilet; 12 rooms also have their own bathtub. Per-person rates here are ¥16,500 ($118) in peak times and ¥11,000 ($79) off-season.

Ryokan Kozakura [316], near Matsushima Kaigan Pier on the town's main street (tel. 022/354-2518), is a simple concrete Japanese-style inn with inexpensive rooms. About a ten-minute walk from the train station, it has a total of 12 tatami rooms, some with their own private bathrooms that go for ¥8,800 ($63) per person including two meals; rooms without bathrooms are ¥6,500 ($46). If you want to take your meals elsewhere, you can stay here for as little as ¥3,800

($27) per person. In summer months and on Saturday night, rates increase by ¥2,000 ($14). Rooms are simple but come with coin-operated TV, air-conditioner, heater and refrigerator, and meals are served in your own room.

The **Matsushima Youth Hostel** [317] is located not in Matsushima itself but on Miyato Island, Narusei-cho (tel. 022/588-2220). From Matsushima Kaigan Station take the Senseki Line 15 minutes to Nobiru Station. From there it's about a 15-minute walk. The hostel sleeps on the average eight persons per room in bunk beds. Members pay ¥2,000 ($14.29) while nonmembers pay ¥500 ($3.57) more. Breakfast costs ¥400 ($2.86) and dinner is ¥700 ($5).

Since all ryokan serve breakfast and dinner, the only meal you probably have to think about is lunch. There are several restaurants in Matsushima and you shouldn't have any trouble locating one. If you want a specific recommendation, however, **Okunohosomichi** [318], Zuiganji Tenrin-in (tel. 354-5806), is a small and attractive restaurant located on a street running behind Kanrantei not far from Tenrin-in Temple. The menu is in Japanese only, but includes sashimi, tempura, fried shrimp, fried oyster, obento, various fish, and eel. Most teishoku range from about ¥1,650 ($11.79) to ¥3,000 ($21.43). Hours are 11 a.m. to 9 p.m.; closed the first and third Wednesdays of the month except during summer, when it remains open throughout the week. A convenient place for a light, inexpensive lunch is **Donjiki** [319], located right across the street from Entsuin Temple (tel. 354-5855). Easy to spot because of its thatched roof, it was built about 300 years ago and offers tatami seating and sliding doors pushed wide open in the summertime. It serves noodles beginning at ¥500 ($3.57) as well as its specialty of *odango*, which are pounded rice balls covered with sesame, red-bean, or soy sauce. Although rice balls tend to be chewy, these are surprisingly light. Open from 9:30 a.m. to 5 p.m. throughout the summer, in the winter it's open only on weekends and holidays.

In Sendai

Although Matsushima is where most of the attractions are, because it's a resort area it may be too expensive for your budget. In that case the most convenient alternative would be to spend the night in Sendai and make a day trip to Matsushima, only 25 minutes away. There are two inexpensive ryokan located close to Sendai Station, which offer basically the same facilities of tatami rooms at moderate prices, coin-operated TV, and public baths. Both are members of the Japanese Inn Group and are happy to receive foreigners. Rates are for room charge only and do *not* include meals.

A five-minute walk from the station is **Isuzu Ryokan**, 1-148 Kakyoin (tel. 022/222-6430), which has nine Japanese-style rooms. Rates here start at ¥3,300 ($24) for a single, ¥6,000 ($43) for a twin, and ¥8,000 ($57) for a triple. The ryokan will also serve a tempura or sukiyaki dinner for ¥1,650 ($11.78). **Japanese Inn Aisaki**, 5-6 Kitame-machi (tel. 022/264-0700), is a ten-minute walk from the station behind the Sendai Central Post Office. It has both Japanese- and Western-style rooms, starting at ¥3,800 ($27) for a single and ¥7,000 ($50) for a twin.

There are also four youth hostels in Sendai: **Sendai Chitose Youth Hostel**, 6-3-8 Odawawra (tel. 022/222-6329), 10 minutes by bus from Sendai Station and then three minutes on foot; **Youth Hostel Sendai Akamon**, 61 Kawauchi-Kawamae-cho (tel. 022/264-1405), 15 minutes by bus from Sendai Station and then a 5-minute walk; **Sendai Onai Youth Hostel**, 1-9-35 Kashiwagi (tel. 022/234-3922), 15 minutes by bus and 2 minutes on foot; and **Sendai-Dochuan Youth Hostel**, 31 Kitayashiki, Onoda (tel. 022/247-0511), 12 minutes by subway from the station and 8 minutes on foot. Count on spending about ¥3,300 ($24) per person per night, including two meals. Nonmembers pay ¥500 ($3.57) more.

2. Hakodate

The southern gateway to Hokkaido, Hakodate is about as far as you can get in one day if you're arriving in Hokkaido from Tokyo by train. Not a destination in and of itself, Hakodate makes a good one-night stopover because it has one nighttime attraction and one early-morning attraction, which means that you can easily see a little of the city before setting out to your next destination.

Hakodate is probably most famous for its night view from atop **Mount Hakodate**, which rises 1,100 feet just 1¾ miles southwest of Hakodate Station. Few vacationing Japanese spend the night in Hakodate without taking the cable car to the top of this lava cone, which was formed by the eruption of an undersea volcano. From the peak, the lights of Hakodate shimmer and glitter like jewels spilled on black velvet. You can reach the foot of Mount Hakodate via streetcar from Hakodate Station. The name of the stop is Jyujigai, and it's a five-minute trip from the station. From there you can take the cable car to the top for ¥1,200 ($8.57) round trip. From mid-April to mid-October it runs every 20 minutes from 9 a.m. to 10 p.m., with shorter hours during the cold winter season.

The next morning you can get up and visit the **morning market** before taking the train out of town. The market spreads out just south of the train station and is held every morning except Sunday from about 4 a.m. to noon. Walk around and look at the various vegetables and fish for sale, especially the hairy crabs for which Hokkaido is famous.

If you have some extra time you might consider a one-hour boat trip around the harbor. Hakodate, along with Nagasaki, Kobe, and Yokohama, was one of the first ports open to foreigners in 1859 following Japan's more than 200 years of isolation. Boats leave three times a day from the end of April to the end of September and cost ¥1,300 ($9.29). At last check, boats left at 11 a.m., 1 p.m., and 3 p.m., but contact the tourist office to confirm this.

ORIENTATION: Connected by rail to northern Honshu with the completion of the Seikan Tunnel in the spring of 1988, Hakodate can be reached in less than ten hours by train from Tokyo and from four to five hours by train from Sapporo, Hokkaido's largest town. The **Hakodate tourist office** (tel. 0138/23-5440) is just to the right after you exit from the Hakodate train station. Open from 9 a.m. to 7 p.m. (to 5 p.m. in winter), the tourist office has information and a map of Hakodate written in English. Before leaving Tokyo or Kyoto, be sure to pick up a flyer called *Southern Hokkaido*. It gives a couple of recommended strolling tours in Hakodate in case you're interested in seeing some old Western-looking buildings constructed back in the days when the town first opened as an international port.

The **telephone area code** for Hakodate is 0138.

FOOD AND LODGING: Because it's not a tourist destination, Hakodate does not have a lot in the way of accommodations. Most of its hotels are conveniently located within walking distance of the train station.

The Top Choice

Although located in a part of town full of junkyards and roads with potholes, the **Hakodate Kokusai Hotel**, 5-10 Otemachi (tel. 0138/23-8751), is the city's most expensive hotel. About a five-minute walk from the station close to the water's edge, it has both Japanese- and Western-style rooms that are a good value for the money. Singles range from ¥8,200 ($59) to ¥11,000 ($79), twins run ¥14,300 ($102) to ¥21,000 ($150), and doubles cost ¥17,600 ($126) to ¥21,000 ($150). Tatami rooms range from ¥13,200 ($94) to ¥18,700 ($134). All rooms come with their own bathrooms, TV, clock, radio, and refrigerator. This is also one of the few hotels to have air conditioning (most hotels in Hokkaido forgo air-conditioners because it's hot only one month of the year). The most expensive twins and doubles are deluxe rooms which face the busy harbor, are slightly larger in size than standard rooms, and offer semi-double-size beds in the twin rooms.

On the eighth floor of the Kokusai Hotel are both a Japanese and a Western restaurant, both with good views of the harbor. **Matsumae**, open from 11:30 a.m. to 9 p.m., is a Japanese seafood restaurant offering a variety of dishes from sashimi to tempura to broiled flatfish and squid, with à la carte prices starting at about ¥900 ($6.43). With translations straight from the dictionary, there are also such mouth-watering temptations as "salted guts" of salmon or squid. In addition, there are a variety of set teishoku meals of tempura, sashimi, and more, with prices ranging from ¥1,600 ($11.43) to ¥6,000 ($42.86).

The crab meal for ¥6,000 ($42.86), for example, includes hors d'oeuvres, clear soup, sliced crabmeat, fried tempura crab, vinegared crab, rice, pickled vegetable, and fruit. Ordering is easy here because the menu is in English.

Harbour View, the hotel's Western restaurant, is the perfect place to come for a late dinner because it's open from 5 p.m. to 1:30 a.m. You might want to come here after an evening stroll atop Mount Hakodate. Its à la carte menu lists seafood, steaks, and pastas ranging from ¥1,000 ($7.14) to ¥3,300 ($23.57). Dinner courses start at ¥4,400 ($31.43).

A Medium-Range Hotel

One of Hakodate's newest business hotels is the **Hotel 2nd Ocean**, located across the street from the Hakodate train station (tel. 0138/27-2700). Opened in 1984, this business hotel is clean, easy to find, and conveniently located for a one-night stopover. All 152 rooms come with their own bathroom, double-pane windows to shut out noise, window panels you can close for complete darkness, fridge, and TV with pay video. Some of the rooms are on a high enough floor that you can see the harbor and Mount Hakodate in the distance. It has a pleasant restaurant on the second floor called **Sea Gull**, serving inexpensive Western food. Singles here are ¥6,000 ($43), twins and doubles are ¥12,000 ($86), and Japanese-style rooms are ¥12,000 ($86).

The Budget Category

Just a three-minute walk from Hakodate Station is a very reasonably priced place to stay called the **Hotel Kikuya**, 8-23 Wakamatsucho (tel. 0138/26-1144). The front desk is on the second floor and various kinds of rooms are available. Singles without bathroom are ¥4,000 ($29); with bathroom, ¥4,600 ($33). Twins without bathroom are ¥7,700 ($55); with bathroom they're ¥8,800 ($63) and ¥9,600 ($69). Japanese-style rooms start at ¥4,900 ($35) for one person and ¥8,200 ($59) for two for rooms with toilet but no bathtub. Rooms are small but adequate, and come with coin-operated TV and clock. The hotel's small restaurant serves both Japanese and Western food.

A conveniently located minshuku is **Minshuku Fukuiso** [320], 30-16 Wakamatsucho (tel. 0138/26-8239). It's about a five-minute walk from Hakodate Station. To reach it, turn left on the road in front of the station (the one with the tram rails). Fukuiso is a couple of blocks down on the left side, past the crossroad with the planted medium. There are 12 rooms here, all Japanese style without private bathroom. Simply decorated and with the basics of air conditioning, heater, coin-operated TV, and cotton kimono, it charges ¥3,300 ($24) per person for a room only. If you want to dine here, the rate is ¥5,000 ($36) per person with breakfast and dinner. Although the proprietor here doesn't speak much English, things are pretty self-explanatory. The minshuku has its own public baths.

For even cheaper accommodation, **Business Hotel Rizabu** [321], 25-20 Wakamatsucho (tel. 0138/23-2719), offers some of the lowest rates in town. About a five-minute walk from Hakodate Station, it's located on Koensen Avenue right next to the Hokkaido Sogo Ginko Bank. The front desk is on the second floor, and no English is spoken. Most of the 20 rooms here are singles, all without private bathrooms and about as small as you can get. There's barely enough room here for the bed, but the rate is only ¥2,800 ($20). If you're claustrophobic, you may opt to stay in a double room for ¥3,300 ($24) single occupancy, which has the additional advantage of its own tiny bathroom. Otherwise rates for a double with two people is ¥6,500 ($46), while twins go for ¥5,500 ($39). Although single rooms do not have their own heating, transoms above the door can be opened for heat or circulation—which also means you can hear noisy neighbors. This place is old, but the price is right.

Youth Hostel

The **Hokusei-so Youth Hostel** [322], 1-16-23 Yunokawa-machi (tel. 0138/57-3212), is in a part of Hakodate called Yunokawa. It's a 25-minute bus ride from Hakodate Station and then just a couple of minutes' walk. There are both beds and tatami rooms here, accommodating about 100 persons. The ¥3,500 ($25) rate includes two meals. If you're not a hostel member you can still stay here for ¥500 ($3.57) more.

3. Sapporo

Sapporo is one of Japan's newest cities. Unlike other Japanese cities such as Kyoto, Osaka, or Nagasaki which were founded centuries ago, just a little more than a century ago Sapporo was nothing more than a scattering of huts belonging to a handful of Ainu and Japanese families. All of Hokkaido, in fact, was a vast wilderness, untamed, largely unsettled, rich in timber and land. With the dawning of the Meiji Era, however, the government decided to colonize the island and established the Colonization Commission in 1869. The area of Sapporo, which comes from the Ainu word meaning "big, dry river," was chosen as the site for the new capital from which to administer the land. In 1871 construction of the city began.

During the Meiji Era Japan looked eagerly toward the West for instruction in technology, for ideas and education, and Hokkaido was no exception. Foreign technicians and experts who had had experience in colonization were brought to this Japanese wilderness to aid in the island's development. Between 1871 and 1884, 76 foreigners were brought to Hokkaido to share their expertise, including 46 Americans. Sapporo was laid out in a grid pattern of uniform blocks similar to American cities. In 1875 the Sapporo Agricultural College was founded to train youths in skills useful to Hokkaido's colonization and development. Among the Americans invited to Hokkaido was Dr. William S. Clark, who taught one year at the agricultural college. He is most remembered for what he said upon leaving: "Boys, be ambitious."

Ambitious they were. The Sapporo of today has grown to 1.5 million residents, making it the largest city north of Tokyo. In 1972 Sapporo was introduced

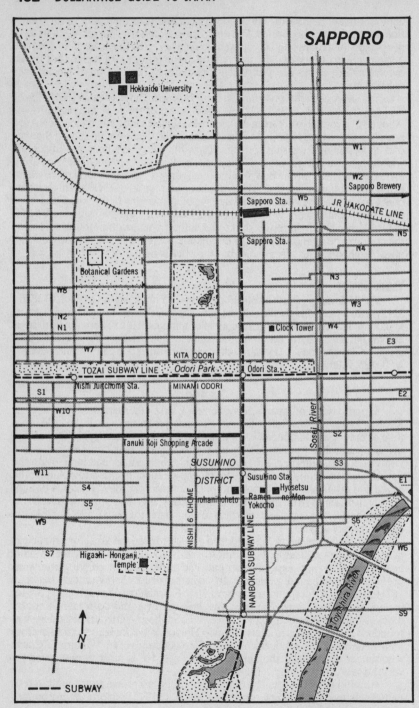

SAPPORO

Hokkaido University

W1

W2
Sapporo Brewery

Sapporo Sta. W5 JR HAKODATE LINE

N5

Sapporo Sta. N4

Botanical Gardens N3

W8 W3

N2 W4
N1 ■ Clock Tower

W7 E3

KITA ODORI
TOZAI SUBWAY LINE Odori Park Odori Sta.
Nishi Juichome Sta. MINAMI ODORI E2
S1

W10

Tanuki Koji Shopping Arcade S2

SUSUKINO
W11 S3
DISTRICT Susukino Sta.
S4 Hyosetsu E1
Irohanihoheto Ramen no-Mon
S5 Yokocho
W9 S6

S7 Higashi- Honganji W6
Temple

S9

↑
N

－－－ SUBWAY

to the world when the Winter Olympics were held here. Its many fine ski slopes continue to attract winter vacationers, and its annual Snow Festival, with its mammoth snow and ice sculptures, has attracted visitors from around the world. In August, when the rest of Japan is sweltering under uncomfortably humid temperatures, Sapporo stays pleasantly cool. With its nearby Chitose Airport, Sapporo serves as a springboard to Hokkaido's national parks and lakes. And yet despite all Sapporo has to offer and despite its size and importance, I've seen few foreigners in Sapporo even in August. For most visitors to Japan, Sapporo and the rest of Hokkaido remain virtually undiscovered.

ORIENTATION: After the jumble of most Japanese cities with their incomprehensible address systems, Sapporo will come as a welcome surprise. Because its streets are laid out in a grid pattern, Sapporo ranks as one of the easiest Japanese cities to find your way around in. Addresses in Sapporo refer to blocks which follow each other in logical, numerical order. The center of Sapporo is considered to be Odori (Main Street), a tree-lined avenue which bisects the city into north and south sections. North 1st, therefore, refers to the street one block north of Odori as well as the entire block to the north of that street. Addresses in Sapporo are generally given by block. N1 W4, for example, is the address for the Sapporo Grand Hotel and means that it's located a block north of Odori and four blocks west of West 1st Street. If you want to be more technical about it, the entire, formal address would read N1-jo W1-chome. "Jo" runs from north to south, while "chome" goes from east to west. Street signs are in English.

Most of Sapporo's attractions and hotels lie south of Sapporo Station. Transportation in Sapporo is via bus, a few subway lines, and one streetcar line. Sapporo is also easy to cover on foot. You can, for example, walk south from Sapporo Station to Odori Park in less than ten minutes and on to Susukino, Sapporo's nightlife district, in another seven or eight minutes.

If you're arriving at Sapporo's Chitose Airport, you can reach downtown Sapporo by either the airport limousine bus or by train from JR's Chitose Airport Station.

For information on Sapporo, be sure to pick up a flyer called *Sapporo and Vicinity* from the T.I.C. in either Tokyo or Kyoto. There are two **Sapporo tourist offices** at Sapporo Station, both located at the south exit. One is underground, past the ticket wickets, while the second one is on ground level. Hours for both are from 9 a.m. to 5 p.m. daily, and they both have an excellent brochure in English titled *Welcome to Sapporo*, with a very good map, information on sightseeing, and other helpful advice. If you have any questions during your stay, call the **Sapporo Tourism Department** at 211-2376.

The **telephone area code** for Sapporo is 011.

WHAT TO SEE: One of the first things you should do in Sapporo is simply walk around. Starting from Sapporo Station, take the street leading directly south called **Eki-mae Dori Street** (which is also West 4). This is one of Sapporo's main thoroughfares, and takes you through the heart of the city. Four blocks south of the station, turn left on N1 and after a block you'll find Sapporo's most famous landmark, **Clock Tower**. This Western-style wooden building was built back in 1878 as a drill hall for the Sapporo Agricultural College (present Hokkaido University). The large clock at the top of the tower was made in Boston and was installed in 1881. Chiming away ever since, during the summer months it attracts tourists even at night, who hang around the outside gates just to listen to it strike the hour. Inside the tower is a local history museum with some old photographs of Sapporo and displays outlining the city's development. Although the explanations are only in Japanese, the museum is free so you might as well go in and pay your respects. It's open from 9 a.m. to 4 p.m. every day except Monday and national holidays.

If you continue walking one block south of the Clock Tower, you'll reach **Odori**, a wide boulevard stretching almost a mile from east to west. In the middle of the boulevard is a wide median strip that has been turned into a park with trees, flower beds, and fountains. This is where much of the Sapporo Snow Festival is held in early February, when snow is packed together and then carved to form statues, palaces, and fantasies. One snow structure may require as much as 300 six-ton truckloads of snow, brought in from the surrounding mountains. The Snow Festival also displays intricate ice carvings, done with such a flourishing degree of detail that it's almost a crime the carvings must melt. First begun in 1950 to add a bit of spice and life to the cold winter days, the snow festival now features about 150 large and small snow statues and draws about 1.9 million visitors a year. The festival is always held from the first Wednesday to the first Sunday of February.

Odori Park is also the scene of the Summer Festival, celebrated with beer gardens set up the length of the park from July 20 to August 10 every evening beginning at 5 p.m. Various Japanese beer companies set up their own booths and tables under the trees, while vendors set up stalls selling fried noodles, corn on the cob, and other goodies. Stages with live bands serenade the beer drinkers under the stars. It all resembles the cheerful confusion of a German beer garden, which isn't surprising considering the fact that Munich is one of Sapporo's sister cities (Portland, Oregon, is another one).

From Odori Park you can continue your walk either above or below ground. Appreciated especially during inclement weather and during Hokkaido's long cold winters are two underground shopping arcades. Underneath Odori Park from Odori Subway Station all the way to the TV tower in the east is **Aurora Town**, with its boutiques and restaurants. Even longer is **Pole Town**, 1,300 feet of shop after shop, almost 100 in all. Pole Town extends from Odori Subway Station south all the way to Susukino, Sapporo's nightlife amusement center where you can find many restaurants and pubs (refer to the dining section). Before reaching Susukino, however, you may want to emerge at **Sanchome** (you'll see escalators going up), where you'll find more shopping at the Tanuki-koji covered shopping arcade.

Backtracking now toward the station, your last stop should be the **Botanical Garden (Shokubutsu-en)**, the entrance to which is at N3 W8. Open every day except Monday from 9 a.m. to 4 p.m. from April 29 to November 3, it has 5,000 varieties of plants arranged in marshland, herb, and alpine gardens, a greenhouse, and other sections. With lots of trees and grassy lawns, it's a good place for a summer afternoon picnic. Admission is ¥250 ($1.79). In winter only the greenhouse is open.

On the Botanical Garden grounds is the **University Museum**, a natural history museum with collections of stuffed animals, plants, and minerals of Hokkaido.

Other Things to Do

Although not within easy walking distance of Sapporo Station, you should make the **Sapporo Beer Factory** part of your sightseeing itinerary. You can reach the beer factory from Sapporo Station in about ten minutes by bus. Sapporo Beer is famous throughout Japan, and the brew has been produced here in Sapporo ever since the first factory opened in 1876. Tours are held daily throughout the year, with the first tour starting at 8:40 a.m. and the last at 4:40 p.m. during peak summer months. It's best to make reservations beforehand to avoid having to wait (tel. 731-4368). Although tours are conducted only in Japanese, a few of the guides speak English, so ask whether it's possible to have an English interpreter at the time you make your reservation. Free of charge, tours last approximately one hour.

More than 200,000 people tour the brewery each year, and during peak time in August as many as 3,000 people may come in one day. The tour begins with a walk through the brewery, where you'll be struck by how empty the whole factory is of human help. The process is fully automated in assembly lines —the human's main function is merely to watch to make sure nothing goes haywire. Following the brewery tour is a short stop in the **Sapporo Museum**, where you'll see old beer posters, photographs, and other memorabilia. Then comes the fun part—you get to sample the brew. If after the tour you want to stick around and drink more of it (it often seems to work that way), on the brewery grounds is the Sapporo Beer Hall, and in summer months there's even an outdoor beer garden. Refer to the dining section for more mouth-watering details.

If you have time you should also consider visiting **Nopporo Forest Park (Nopporo Shinrin Koen)**, where you'll find a 330-foot tower (built in 1970 to commemorate Hokkaido's centennial) and two other attractions. The **Historical Museum of Hokkaido (Kaitaku Kinenkan)** houses collections detailing Hokkaido's development from prehistoric to modern times. The admission charge is ¥250 ($1.79) and hours are 9:30 a.m. to 4:30 p.m.; closed Monday and national holidays. The **Historical Village of Hokkaido (Kaitaku-no-Mura)** is an open-air museum of various houses from the pages of Hokkaido's history, including homes, farmhouses, a school, hostel, and shrine. With the same hours as the Historical Museum, it charges ¥400 ($2.86) admission [¥300 ($2.14) in winter]. You can reach Nopporo Park via the JR bus from Sapporo Station in 50 minutes.

Skiing

The slopes around Sapporo offer skiing from early December to late April. Since you can fly directly to Sapporo from many cities in Japan, it's a popular winter destination. The **Teine Olympia Ski Grounds** are located about an hour from Sapporo by bus. This was the site of the alpine, bobsled, and toboggan events in the Sapporo Winter Olympic Games of 1972. Other skiing areas within 30 minutes of Sapporo are **Mount Moiwa, Mount Arai**, and **Maruyama**. Most sites provide ski-rental equipment for approximately ¥3,500 ($25) per day, but keep in mind that sizes are generally smaller than in the West.

ACCOMMODATIONS: Because of the 1972 Olympics held in Sapporo, the city has a large selection of fine hotels in various price categories. Sapporo's heaviest tourist season is during the summer months and during the annual Snow Festival held in early February. If you plan to attend the Snow Festival, book your hotel room at least six months in advance. At other times during the year you should have no problem finding a room, but if you're coming in August you'd be wise to make a reservation. During winter (excluding the time of the Snow Festival) some upper- and medium-priced hotels lower their room rates, sometimes as much as 40%. That should come as welcome news to you ski enthusiasts. Unless otherwise stated, rooms come with private bathroom.

The Upper Bracket

Sapporo Grand Hotel, N1 W4 (tel. 011/261-3311), is usually where VIPs stay when they come to Sapporo. About a six-minute walk south of Sapporo Station, this dignified hotel with more than 50 years of excellent service behind it has an exceptional French restaurant, a beer hall, several bars, Japanese restaurants, and a shopping arcade. Rooms in the new annex (which opened in 1984) are very chic, with contemporary furniture, a mini-bar built into a wood cabinet, bilingual televisions with pay video, large desks with lots of working space, semi-double beds, and tiled bathrooms with marble-topped counters. These rooms go for ¥13,200 ($94) for a single and ¥21,000 ($150) for a twin. Rooms in the older part of the hotel are also very nice and are less expensive, going for ¥11,000 ($79) for a single, ¥18,000 ($129) for a double, and ¥18,500 ($132) for a twin. Eight Japanese-style rooms are available for ¥20,000 ($143).

Less than a five-minute walk from Sapporo Station, the **ANA Hotel Sapporo** (in Japanese, the **Zenniku Hotel** [323]), N1 W3 (tel. 011/221-4411), is a gleaming white building rising high in the skyline of Sapporo. It has the kind of room travelers can appreciate: five lamps in its larger rooms so you don't have to read in the dark, bilingual TVs that swivel and have pay video, an extra phone in the bathroom, two layers of curtains for complete darkness, and such facilities as a mini-bar, hot-water pot for tea, radio, and alarm clock. Rates here range from ¥10,500 ($75) to ¥11,500 ($82) for a single, ¥17,000 ($121) to ¥23,000 ($164) for a twin, and ¥18,700 ($134) for a double. Facilities include Japanese and French restaurants on the 25th and 26th floor with views of the city, and a beer garden off the lobby's second floor (open July to mid-August from 5 to 9 p.m.). The beer garden offers a Hokkaido specialty, Genghis Khan, which is thin strips of mutton, onions, green peppers, and other seasonal vegetables cooked in an iron pot at your table. For ¥3,300 ($24) you can have all the Genghis Khan and beer you can consume. On the 26th floor of the hotel is the sky lounge Sapporo View, where there's piano music every night except Sunday starting at 7:30 p.m. Cocktails here start at ¥750 ($5.36).

Next to the ANA Hotel is the **New Otani**, N2 W1 (tel. 011/222-1111). Also a five-minute walk from the train station, it opened in 1982 with a wide range of facilities, including a medical center, the Asahi Culture Center, with traditional art exhibitions, and two restaurants. One restaurant, The Four Seasons, offers French, Chinese, and Japanese cuisine, while the other one, Rendezvous, is a convenient lobby coffee shop open from 7 a.m. to 10:30 p.m. (the hot tuna sandwich, by the way, is delicious). Also available at the New Otani are rental bicycles and skis. Rooms, decorated in soothing pastels, have bilingual TV with pay video, radio, alarm clock, fridge, double-pane windows that open, and bathrooms with larger-than-average tubs. Singles start at ¥12,000 ($86), while twins and doubles start at ¥21,000 ($150).

Just a few minutes west of Sapporo Station, the **Keio Plaza Hotel**, N5 W7 (tel. 011/271-0111), is a graceful hostelry that made its debut in 1982. Its white and light-green lobby gives way to bold colors in the bedrooms, which are accented with striped bedspreads in primary colors. It features 11 bars and restaurants, and a sauna and indoor pool hotel guests can use for ¥3,000 ($21.43). Rooms are what you'd expect in an upper-class hotel, including double-pane windows to block out noise, TV with pay video, mini-bar, hot-water pot, clock, and radio. The sink area has lots of room to spread out. It's an attractive hotel all around. Singles start at ¥10,500 ($75), twins at ¥18,700 ($134), and doubles at ¥21,000 ($150). Winter rates are as much as 40% lower than in summer.

The Medium-Priced Range

The **Century Royal Hotel**, N5 W5 (tel. 011/221-2121), has an excellent location, right next to the train station—which is the main selling point of the hotel. Another selling point is its revolving restaurant on the 23rd floor. Otherwise, rooms are fairly basic, with fridge, TV, music, and alarm clock, and windows are double-pane to shut out noise. In summer the rates start at ¥9,600 ($69) for a single and ¥18,000 ($129) for a twin, but in winter they go down to ¥7,400 ($53) and ¥14,300 ($102) respectively.

The **Sapporo International Hotel** (known as the Kanko Hotel in Japanese) is right across the street from Sapporo Station at N4 W4 (tel. 011/222-3811), above the All Nippon Airways office. The front desk is on the second floor. Opened in time for the Sapporo Olympics, it's a no-frills medium-priced hotel with rooms that are of good size for the price but otherwise pretty basic. Guest rooms have TV, radio, alarm clock, fridge, hot-water pot, and double-pane windows. Rates here start at ¥8,800 ($63) for a single, ¥15,400 ($110) for a double, and ¥15,900 ($114) for a twin. On the hotel premises are both a French and a Chinese restaurant and an American-style coffeeshop. Winter rates average about ¥3,000 ($21) less than summer rates.

Part of a reliable national hotel chain, the Washington Hotel has two locations in Sapporo, both close to the train station. **Washington Hotel 2**, N5 W6 (tel. 011/222-3311), is the newer of the two and therefore a bit nicer and more pleasant in its facilities. A three-minute walk southwest of the station, its guest rooms have rattan furniture, TV with video, fridge, hot-water pot, music, and alarm clock. Unlike most business hotels with check-in at 3 or 4 p.m., the Washington's check-in is 2 p.m. Singles start at ¥7,900 ($56), and twins and doubles begin at ¥15,900 ($114). Winter rates are ¥6,000 ($43) for a single and ¥12,000 ($86) for a double or twin.

Washington Hotel 1, N4 W4 (tel. 011/251-3211), is right across the street from the station. Its lobby is on the second floor up the escalator. Although the cheapest singles go for a low ¥5,200 ($37), I don't advise them unless you hate sunshine (they have no windows and are extremely dark). Singles for ¥6,900 ($49) face a rather drab inside courtyard, but at least you have a window. Why not splurge and go for the best singles in the house for ¥8,200 ($59), which are larger and face toward the outside? Twins start at ¥14,300 ($102); doubles, at ¥16,500 ($118). In the winter you can get a twin for ¥11,000 ($79). All rates include tax and service charge.

Rooms have TV with pay video, hot-water pot and tea, and a tiny one-piece plastic bathroom; those that face the station have double-pane windows to shut out noise. Vending machines in the hallways dispense beer, snacks, and soft drinks.

Chisan Hotel Sapporoshinkan, N2 W2 (tel. 011/222-6611), opened in 1984 as an annex to an older Chisan hotel. A pleasant business hotel about a five-minute walk from Sapporo Station, its rooms come with the usual dark furniture and purple- and pink-striped bedcover that is the trademark of Chisan chain hotels. Panels close over the windows for darkness, and other facilities include coin-operated TV with pay video, fridge, and semi-double beds. Prices here are ¥8,200 ($59) for a single and ¥15,400 ($110) for a twin, going down to ¥7,000 ($50) and ¥13,200 ($94) respectively in winter. The hotel contains one Japanese restaurant.

Don't confuse this hotel with the older **Chisan**, where prices are ¥5,800 ($41) for a single and ¥11,000 ($79) for a twin. Winter rates here are ¥1,000 ($7.14) less per person. Located just 30 seconds from the newer branch, its rooms are more dated and less cheerful. If you can afford it, therefore, you're better off staying in the newer Chisan.

Hotel Rich, N1 W3 (tel. 011/231-7891), is a seven-minute walk south of Sapporo Station. Simply decorated, this business hotel has 167 rooms—mostly singles but there are also 31 twins. It has a Western-style restaurant and vending machines in the halls. Rooms have TV with pay video, hot-water pot for tea, clock, radio, and double-pane windows. Both the rooms and the bathrooms are tiny and a bit old, and the carpet could use replacement. The cheapest singles and twins face an inside courtyard, with other windows, and aren't very cheerful. Since the price is almost the same, try to get a room facing the outside.

Rates, the same year round, are reasonable: singles go for ¥6,300 ($45) to ¥6,800 ($49); twins range from ¥12,000 ($86) to ¥13,200 ($94).

If you want to be close to the nightlife action in Susukino, the **Sapporo Tokyu Inn**, at S4 W5 (tel. 011/531-0109), is your best choice in the area. A member of the Tokyu hotel chain, this red-brick business hotel is only a one-minute walk from the Susukino subway station. Altogether there are 18 restaurants in the hotel and the adjoining basement shopping arcade. The guest rooms are spotlessly clean and tastefully decorated in muted browns, and come with TV and clock. Vending machines with beer and soda are located in the hallways. Prices remain the same year round: ¥7,700 ($55) to ¥8,300 ($59) for a single; ¥14,500 ($104) to ¥16,500 ($118) for a double, and ¥15,000 ($107) to ¥17,000 ($121) for a twin. Rates include tax and service charge. Notice the tiny dots beside each door, which are the room number in Braille. They're for the hotel's masseurs, who are often blind in Japan.

If you want to stay in a ryokan, **Nakamuraya Ryokan** [324], N3 W7 (tel. 011/241-2111), is a comfortable and modern Japanese inn located about a seven-minute walk southwest of Sapporo Station next to the entrance of the Botanical Garden. It has 32 rooms, mostly Japanese style, all of which come with bathroom, fridge, TV, and clock. I prefer the Japanese rooms to the Western ones—their simplicity is in sharp contrast to the old carpeting and odd color combination in the Western rooms. Rates for Western or Japanese rooms are ¥7,700 ($55) for one person and ¥15,400 ($110) for two, without meals. Those are the rates, anyway, that Japanese pay. This ryokan is a member of the Japanese Inn Group, so if you make a booking in advance and mention Japanese Inn Group, you'll receive a much lower rate as a foreigner. In this case rooms start at ¥6,000 ($43) for one person and ¥11,000 ($79) for two. Prices do not include meals, but there's a cafeteria in the ryokan and Japanese dinners are served starting at ¥2,600 ($18.57). Although rooms have their own tubs, you might want to take advantage of the public baths here.

Located in the heart of the Susukino nightlife district, **Hotel Sunflower Sapporo**, S5 W3 (tel. 011/512-5533), is a good place to stay if you like carousing through the bars at night—it's not far to crawl back to your hotel. Based on its facilities and atmosphere I would classify this establishment as strictly a business hotel, but because of its location it caters to both businessmen and tourists. The rooms are tiny and unexciting, coming with TV with pay video and a minuscule bathroom. The single rooms have glazed windows so you can't see out, but even if you open the windows there isn't much to see, so I guess it doesn't matter. The hotel serves a popular and good buffet dinner which offers a variety of Western, Japanese, Chinese, and local Hokkaido specialties for only ¥2,400 ($17.14) from 5 to 9 p.m. Rates here are ¥6,600 ($47) for a single, ¥8,800 ($63) for a double, and ¥12,000 ($86) for a twin. Prices include tax and service and are about 10% lower in winter.

The Budget Category

Approximately a five-minute walk from the Susukino subway station is **Yoshizumi** [325], S4 W9 (tel. 011/231-3853). There are eight tatami rooms here, all without bathroom but with TV and fan. This ryokan is 30-some years old, and the owner speaks English. The price is ¥4,400 ($31) per person, including breakfast. It's worth it to also take dinner here, in which case the rate is only slightly higher at ¥5,000 ($36) per person.

The closest youth hostel to Sapporo Station is **Sapporo House Youth Hostel**, N6 W6 (tel. 011/726-4235), about a seven-minute walk from the station. A white concrete building, the sign outside is in Japanese only, but look for the sign with

"YH" on it. More than 200 people can be accommodated here in both tatami and Western-style rooms, and even in August they often have space. Prices are ¥2,300 ($16.43) for members and ¥3,000 ($21.43) for nonmembers. Breakfast is ¥450 ($3.21) and dinner runs ¥600 ($4.29).

Although farther away, if the above youth hostel is full there are a couple alternatives in the vicinity of Sapporo. **Sapporo Miyagaoka Youth Hostel**, N1 14-chome Miyanomori (tel. 011/611-9016), can be reached by subway and bus from Sapporo station in about 30 minutes. Closed from October through June, it charges both members and nonmembers ¥2,900 ($20.71) for an overnight stay including two meals. If you eat elsewhere, the rate is only ¥1,700 ($12.14). **Sapporo Shiritsu Lions Youth Hostel**, N1 18-chome Miyanomori (tel. 011/611-4709), is about 40 minutes away from Sapporo Station by bus and subway. Open throughout the year, it charges ¥2,000 ($14.29) for members and ¥2,700 ($19.29) for nonmembers. Breakfast is ¥450 ($3.21) and dinner is ¥600 ($4.29).

WHERE TO DINE: Hokkaido's specialties include crab, corn on the cob, potatoes, Genghis Khan, Chinese noodles, and frozen salmon. As for Western food, your best bet is to dine in one of the many fine restaurants in Sapporo's top hotels.

Japanese Food

I can't imagine going to Sapporo without dropping by the **Sapporo Bier Garten**, N6 E9 (tel. 742-1531). Open from June through August every day from 5 to 9 p.m., the beer garden is spread out under broad-leafed acacia trees. If it's winter or early in the day, you can dine in the Sapporo Beer Hall, an old ivy-covered brick building built in 1889 as the Sapporo brewery. The interior is also brick with a wood floor and wood beams, making for a very congenial atmosphere. I personally prefer the second floor of this establishment, where you dine underneath a huge old mash tub once used in brewing beer. Since the eatery is on the grounds of Sapporo brewery itself, you can raise your mugs unabashedly here. By the way, though I haven't seen it myself, the management tells me that from January 20 to mid-February there's a snow igloo built outside in which you can sit and drink beer too—that is, if it's cold enough so the snow doesn't melt. Anyway, if it gets too cold for you there's sure to be a roaring fire inside the hall itself, which is open daily from 11:30 a.m. to 9 p.m.

The specialty of the house is Genghis Khan, a plateful of mutton, cabbage, bean sprouts, green pepper, and onion that you cook yourself on a hot skillet at your table. Look at the skillet closely. Recognize the shape? It's a map of Hokkaido. The best deal in the house is the King Viking, which for ¥3,200 ($23) gives you as much Genghis Khan and as much draft beer as you can consume in a two-hour period. If you don't feel like gorging yourself for two hours, a regular serving of Genghis Khan is ¥1,000 ($7.14). Other dishes include such Hokkaido favorites as buttered corn on the cob, potatoes, and crab. Draft beer starts at ¥450 ($3.21) for a small mug.

Not to be outdone is **Suntory**, which opened its own Suntory Beer Benizakura Garden at Sumikawa 389-769, Minami-ku (tel. 582-4411), in 1985. It's located on the south edge of town just a five-minute taxi ride from the Makomanai Subway Station on the Nanboku Line. Buses run between the subway station and the beer garden every 30 minutes. Open daily from 11:30 a.m. to 9 p.m., this establishment also offers Genghis Khan for ¥1,000 ($7.14), and Suntory beer starts at ¥450 ($3.21). For ¥3,200 ($22.86) you can eat all the Genghis Khan and drink as much beer as you want over a two-hour time period.

Sauces for dipping morsels of mutton and vegetables are available either mild or spicy. Although the building itself is bright and airy, dining outside by the lotus pond is great in fine weather. Be sure to wander through the gardens, which extend back behind the restaurant. Created about 30 years ago, they consist of ponds and a waterfall, a pleasant respite from the city.

Another well-known restaurant in Sapporo is **Hyosetsu-no-Mon** [326], S5 W2 (tel. 521-3046), which specializes in giant king crab caught in the Japan Sea north of Hokkaido. Actually there are three restaurants here side by side in Sapporo's Susukino nightlife district. The main shop is the one farthest west (the first one you'll reach if you're walking from the Susukino subway station). The menu is easy enough—it's almost entirely of king crab, which comes in a variety of styles with prices to match. Set meals start at ¥2,200 ($15.71) and include a cooked crab, sashimi, crab soup, crab tempura, and vegetables. Other meals range all the way up to ¥13,200 ($94.29), increasing the portion of crab and number of side dishes. You can also order à la carte for fried king crab claws, deep-fried king crab, tempura king crab, grilled king crab, and crabmeat chowder with prices ranging from ¥820 ($5.86) to ¥4,400 ($31.43). Other à la carte selections include various sashimi, raw sea urchin, salmon eggs, and raw crab organs. This main shop is open daily from 11 a.m. to 11 p.m., while its two annex shops described below are open evenings only from 5 to 11 p.m.

Next to the main restaurant is its Western restaurant, which serves king crab à la carte dishes ranging from ¥450 ($3.21) to ¥3,300 ($23.57). Other dishes include spaghetti, steaks, sausage, pork, and potatoes, with prices mostly under ¥1,000 ($7.14).

A small band provides entertainment nightly. The interior of this place is imitation European, although exactly which country it's imitating is hard to say. Hanging on its walls are menus collected from various countries by the manager, who has a passion for easy-to-read menus. His menus here all come with photographs so that foreigners have no problems ordering.

The third Hyosetsu-no-Mon restaurant serves the same food as in the main shop, but this one has a floor show as well. There are two shows nightly, and it's best to make a reservation. One show starts at 6 and the second show is at 8:15 p.m. The show costs only ¥900 ($6.43) so it's worth coming here for dinner. This establishment is filled with Japanese tourists on holiday in Hokkaido and is great fun. You sit on the floor here to eat your meal in a dining hall reminiscent of old Kabuki theaters. The show starts off with a classical dance followed by contemporary and folk dances.

Another good nightspot in the Susukino area is **Irohanihoheto** [327], S5 W4 (tel. 521-1682). Open from 5 p.m. to 12:30 a.m. daily, this eating and drinking establishment is part of a chain which originated in Sapporo and has since spread all over Japan. It's popular everywhere with young Japanese because of its low and affordable prices. As in all Irohanihoheto shops, this one is decorated in a rustic country style with painted shoji screens and folkcraft hanging from the rafters. The menu is in Japanese only, but there are some pictures; an alternative is to look at what others are eating around you. There are nearly 100 items on the menu, all within the ¥150 ($1.07) to ¥550 ($3.93) price range, so you don't have to worry that what you order will bankrupt you. Beer starts at ¥380 ($2.71). Items include yakitori, tofu dishes, oden, sashimi, vegetables, sausage, nikujaga (potato and beef stew), salads, buttered corn, fried fish, and more. Other Irohanihoheto branches in Sapporo can be found at S4 W2 and at S6 W3, both in the Susukino area, and at N3 W3 just a few minutes' walk south of Sapporo Station.

Sapporo is famous for its *ramen* (Chinese noodles), and the most popular place to eat them is on a tiny, narrow street in Susukino popularly known as **Ramen Yokocho**. Located just one block east of Susukino subway station before you get to the Hotel Sunflower, it's an alleyway of noodle shop after noodle shop—16 in all. It doesn't matter which one you choose—just look to see where there's an empty seat. The shops are all very small affairs consisting of a counter and some chairs. Most are open from 11 a.m. to 3 a.m. and their closed days are staggered so you're sure to find some open. Noodles generally begin at ¥600 ($4.29) for a steaming bowlful.

Closer to Sapporo Station, in the basement of the ANA Hotel (the Zenniku), N1 W3 (tel. 221-4411), is a restaurant called **Satohoro** [328] serving Hokkaido specialties at reasonable prices. Simply decorated with wood and bamboo, it serves such items as frozen salmon (*benishake ruibe*), potatoes in butter (*imo batta*), crab salad, local fish, and other dishes, starting at ¥750 ($5.36). There are also set meals starting at ¥4,500 ($32.14), including a hairy crab kaiseki for ¥8,800 ($62.86) which includes sliced crab, raw crab, boiled crab, crab gratin, crab porridge, fruit, pickled vegetables, soup, shrimp, and potatoes. Hours are 11:30 a.m. to 10 p.m.

If you want to dine in more elegant surroundings with a view of the city, the Zenniku's 25th floor has both a Japanese and a Chinese restaurant. **Kurumaya**, the Japanese restaurant, has an English menu and includes such things as a shabu-shabu dinner for ¥5,300 ($37.86), a sukiyaki meal for ¥5,800 ($41.43), or broiled Matsuzaka beef with Japanese peppers for ¥3,800 ($21.14). Other items include tempura, sashimi, salmon, noodles, rice porridge, and kaiseki. You can pay as little as ¥600 ($4.29) or as much as ¥12,000 ($86), according to what your pocketbook dictates. Hours here are 11:30 a.m. to 10:30 p.m.

Western Food

On the 26th floor of the ANA Hotel (the Zenniku) is a French restaurant called **Top of Sapporo**, open only for dinner from 5 to 11 p.m. This small, intimate, and tastefully decorated restaurant has meals beginning at ¥7,000 ($50), which change every two months and which include Hokkaido delicacies cooked in a French style. À la carte dishes, for which you'll probably spend ¥8,000 ($57.14) for a complete meal, include broiled lobster, king crab cream style, with sea urchin, roast lamb, and steaks.

Another excellent French restaurant in town is the **Grand Chef**, located in the Grand Hotel, N1 W4 (tel. 261-3311). Elegantly and cheerfully decorated in pink, white, and gray, this superb restaurant specializes in Hokkaido food cooked Western style. Lunch is served from 11:30 a.m. to 2 p.m. with various courses available for ¥2,200 ($15.71) and up. Dinners, served from 5 to 10 p.m., has an à la carte menu which changes annually but always includes selections of seafood such as scallops, sole, or sea urchin; steaks; and lamb, chicken, and duck. The average dinner will cost around ¥6,500 ($46.43) to ¥11,000 ($78.57). There are also special dinner courses for ¥8,800 ($62.86) to ¥16,500 ($117.86).

If you're fond of revolving restaurants, there's one atop the Century Royal Hotel, N5 W5 (tel. 221-2121), on the 23rd floor. Called **Rondo**, it's open from 11:30 a.m. to 11 p.m. and has an English menu complete with photos. It revolves a complete turn in one hour, and tables are all located at windows so everyone gets the best view in the house. Even if you don't eat here, it's a good place to come on a fine clear day for a cup of coffee or an evening cocktail. The varied menu includes spaghetti, sandwiches, curry rice, grilled half chicken, pork chops, steak, sole gratin, and lobster gratin. Choices start at ¥1,300 ($9.29). Cocktails are ¥880 ($6.29).

4. The National Parks of Hokkaido

Much of Hokkaido's wilderness has been set aside in national parks. Of these, Shikotsu-Toya, Daisetsuzan, and Akan national parks are the best known, offering a wide range of activities from hiking to skiing to bathing at hot-spring resorts.

SHIKOTSU-TOYA NATIONAL PARK: If you have only a couple of days to spare to visit a national park in Hokkaido, Shikotsu-Toya National Park is the closest to Sapporo and therefore the easiest for the short-term visitor. It's also the first national park you'll reach if you've entered Hokkaido via ferry in Hakodate. With 381 square miles, this national park encompasses lakes, volcanoes, and the famous hot-spring resorts of Toyako Spa and Noboribetsu Spa. In the village of Shiraoi a museum and village have been erected commemorating the native Ainu and their culture.

Be sure to pick up a copy of *Southern Hokkaido,* put out by the Tourist Information Center in either Tokyo or Kyoto. It lists places of interest throughout the national park. As for traveling to and within the park, there's a bus from Sapporo that goes directly to Toyako Spa on Lake Toya. From Toyako Spa you can then proceed by bus to Noboribetsu; from Noboribetsu you can take a train to Shiraoi and back to Sapporo. There are also trains that run directly from Hakodate to Toya Station (from Toya Station it's a 15-minute bus ride to Lake Toya), and on to Noboribetsu, Shiraoi, and Sapporo.

Toyako Spa

Hugging the shores of Lake Toya, Toyako Spa (also called Toyako Onsen; *onsen* means spa in Japanese) is a small resort town with a sprinkling of ryokan, souvenir shops, and not much more. However, you don't come here for Toyako Spa itself. Rather, you come here for what it gives access to, which is **Lake Toya,** the shining blue jewel of Shikotsu-Toya National Park. Surrounded on all sides by hills, Lake Toya is almost perfectly round. It is a typical caldera lake—that is, a lake that has formed within the collapsed crater of an extinct volcano. Approximately 590 feet deep, Lake Toya is invitingly clear and cool and never freezes over even in the dead of winter. In the middle of the lake are four thickly wooded islets, casting mirror images of themselves in the water below.

Orientation: If you're arriving by train from Sapporo (about two hours) or from Hakodate (a little over two hours), you'll arrive at Toya Station. Toyako Onsen on Lake Toya is located about 4½ miles northwest of Toya Station, easily reached by bus in about 15 minutes. (If you decide to splurge and take a taxi, the fare from Toya Station to Toyako Onsen is about ¥2,000, or ($14.29). You can also reach Toyako Onsen directly by either Donan or Jotetsu Bus Company from Sapporo. The trip takes two hours and 40 minutes and costs ¥2,750 ($19.64).

Since there is no train station in Toyako Onsen itself, you'll arrive by bus at Toyako Onsen bus terminal. The **tourist association** (tel. 01427/5-2446) is down the hill toward the lake about a minute's walk away from the bus terminal. It's open from 9 a.m. to 5 p.m. and can help with room reservations. Unfortunately there's no map in English, but the spa is so small you shouldn't have any difficulty finding your way around. Your own two feet are your best mode of transportation. The town stretches along one main road which follows the curve of the lake. Buses for Showa-Shinzan and Camp Takinoue depart from the bus terminal, so inquire there about the schedule. Buses aren't very frequent, so if you find yourself stuck somewhere, stick out your thumb. Hitching in Hokkaido is safe and easy, especially since people realize that public transportation is sometimes a bit inconvenient out here in the "wilderness."

Most people stay in Toyako Onsen only one night. It's enough time to relax and do the few things the place has to offer. If you happen to stay two nights, you'll find your ryokan deserted after check-out time until the next crowd arrives at check-in time.

The **telephone area code** is 01427.

The Sights: With the water such a strong lure, it's probably no surprise that the most popular thing to do is take a **boat ride** across the clear lake to a couple of the islands in the middle. Charging ¥1,000 ($7.14), the boat pulls into two small docks, the first at an island where there are some deer and winding footpaths, the second at another island where there's a natural history museum (which, unfortunately, has explanations only in Japanese and is therefore of little interest to foreign visitors). If you decide to disembark at either of these islands, you can catch the next boat in about a half hour. Otherwise, if you don't disembark but simply stay on the boat for the entire trip, it takes about an hour. Along the shore of Toyako Spa are also several docks where you can rent rowboats and paddleboats.

If it's August and hot, the temptation to simply jump into the lake and cool off will be almost too hard to resist. To your astonishment, however, you won't find any swimming facilities in Toyako Spa itself. In fact, hardly any lakes in Hokkaido allow swimming, the reason being that they are too cold and dangerous for humans. Desperate for a swim and unwilling to leave the lake until its coolness swallowed me up, I took a bus ride 20 minutes around the lake to **Takinoue Camp** (tel. 01426/6-2121), one of the few places where swimming is allowed. There's a small sandy beach here and a few parents playing with their children, making it a good place to jump in and play too. Incidentally, you can also camp here for ¥300 ($2.14) per person. There are even tents for rent at ¥850 ($6.07), but you must have your own sleeping bag and camping supplies.

There are two very active volcanoes on the shores of Lake Toya not far from Toyako Spa. **Mount Usu**, which towers up above the tiny spa, erupted in August 1977, blanketing 80% of Hokkaido in volcanic ash and dumping enough ash on Toyako Onsen itself that the people literally had to dig their way out of it. Chronicling Mount Usu's eruption is the **Abuta Volcano Science Museum (Abuta Kazan Kagaku-kan)**, conveniently located right above the Toyako Onsen bus terminal. Open from 9 a.m. to 5 p.m. and charging ¥400 ($2.86) admission, it depicts the 1977 eruption with photographs, lava rocks displays, and even exhibits the mayor's car covered in rubble. Although explanations are in Japanese, a pamphlet is available in English which explains important facts. The most interesting aspect of the museum is the "experience room," which seats 350 persons around a large panoramic model of Lake Toya and Mount Usu. At the beginning of the "experience" the lights are turned out and a rumbling begins directly below you, followed by vibrations so that your whole seat shakes and shimmies. Then the model begins erupting, the vibrations continue, and the rumbling gets louder, giving at least a little insight into what it must feel like to see a volcano blow its top. Following is a film (again, only in Japanese) showing the Usu eruption, the evacuation of Toyako Onsen, and the ashes covering the town. The whole experience brings home the fact that all of Japan is basically volcanic in origin and that its people have lived in the shadows of volcanoes and earthquakes from the beginning of time.

The other famous volcano in the vicinity is **Showa-Shinzan**, somewhat of an upstart which made its debut only in 1945. Before then it was nothing more than a flat farm field. Over a period of two years, however, the ground began to rise, volcanic eruptions shook the area, and lava rose, resulting in the fledgling volcano. Showa-Shinzan still spouts billowing clouds of smoke. If you're interested in getting a closeup view, you can reach Showa-Shinzan by buses which depart from the Toyako Onsen bus terminal. A small museum at the foot of the volcano documents its birth. You can also catch a glimpse of the volcano from afar if you take the boat ride out onto Lake Toya.

One other thing worth mentioning are the nightly **fireworks** displays put on by the town of Toyako Onsen from June through August—that is, if they're still going on. Although the town has managed to put on fantastic shows the past few years, such displays are extremely costly and as of now it's not certain whether they'll be carried on during the summers of 1988 and 1989. If so, however, they're worth seeing. The show begins at 9 p.m. and fireworks are set off from boats in the lake.

Where to Stay: Because the town of Toyako Spa itself is not very interesting, the best rooms are those that face the lake with views of the picturesque islands in the middle. Of course, these rooms are also the most expensive. This being a resort town for the Japanese, accommodations are largely Japanese-style inns in which you're expected to take your dinner and breakfast at the ryokan. So all prices given below include two meals, unless otherwise stated. The busiest tourist season is from May to October; rates are generally higher during these months.

The **Sun Palace Hotel** (tel. 01427/5-4126) is the most elaborate and conspicuous hotel in Toyako Onsen. Isolated on the edge of the small town on the shores of the lake, it's about a 30-minute walk from the bus terminal. Since buses are infrequent, the easiest way to reach it if you have baggage is by taxi. Its lobby features a spectacular light fixture made of gold-colored twisted metal sheets that rise out of a pond and spread up and out into the ceiling. This resort hotel also has the largest public bath in town, open only to hotel guests. Filled with tropical plants, the hot baths meander both indoors and out, and have waterslides, spaceships, and other play objects for kids. There's also a large indoor pool. The children I saw here were racing excitedly about, obviously enthralled with the whole setup. For older kids there's an electronic game room with sophisticated machinery, while for adults there's a disco with a live band. This is a good family hotel that appeals widely to both adults and kids. Its 500 rooms are both Japanese- and Western-style, and you don't have to worry about a lake view here—all rooms face the lake. Rooms come with TV, a safe for valuables, and a fridge. The cheapest rooms are quite simple, while the more expensive rooms are larger and more nicely furnished. The main thing you're paying for at this hotel are its public facilities. Rates per person range from ¥15,400 ($110) to ¥26,000 ($186). In the off-season, rooms go down to as little as ¥11,000 ($79) per person.

Another first-class hotel in town, **Manseikaku** [329] (tel. 01427/5-2171) is a large, handsome brown-brick building at the water's edge. Rooms are modern and comfortable, and some even have balconies. Most of the rooms are Japanese-style tatami. There are also Western-style rooms with beds, most of which face inland. The hotel has its own tennis court and large indoor public baths. Right beside the hotel is a boat dock where you can rent paddleboats and take charter motorboats around the lake. High-season rates range from ¥16,500 ($118) to ¥60,000 ($429) per person, decreasing to ¥12,000 ($86) to ¥36,000 ($257) October through April.

Less than a five-minute walk from the bus terminal, the **Park Hotel** (tel. 01427/5-2445) boasts tennis courts, a pleasant public bath filled with tropical plants, a game room, bowling lanes, and a bar with laser shows. Located right beside the water, half the rooms facing the water have verandas of sorts—but you have to crawl over the windowsill to get outside. The other rooms have only windows. Since the hotel's Western-style rooms—all twins—face only inland, the Japanese rooms here are better by far, especially since they're the same price. You're much better off going native. All with private bathroom, they're ¥11,000 ($79) to ¥16,500 ($118) per person. There are also Japanese rooms without bathrooms facing inland for as little as ¥8,800 ($63). During the off-season, rooms are available for about ¥2,000 ($14.29) to ¥4,000 ($28.57) less.

A somewhat older medium-range ryokan is the **Toyako Onsen Hotel** (tel. 01427/5-2222). The only facilities for guests are small public baths, but rooms were recently renovated with new wallpaper and tatami mats. The big plus here is that all rooms facing the lake have balconies, perfect for watching the summertime fireworks. All rooms have toilets, and the more expensive rooms have tubs as well. Although 11 Western-style rooms are available, none of them face the lake; a few combination rooms with both beds and tatami area, however, do have lake views. Prices here are ¥12,000 ($86) to ¥16,500 ($118) in summer season, ¥10,000 ($71) off-season.

If you want to stay in Toyako Onsen but can't afford a hotel on the lake's edge, a good choice of accommodations is **Kofuen** (tel. 01427/5-2231). About a two-block walk from the lake and just a couple of minutes from the bus terminal, this older concrete ryokan has 53 Japanese-style rooms, all without bath or toilet. Rates range from ¥5,500 ($39) to ¥8,800 ($63). The more expensive rooms are those on the third floor, where you can see a little of the lake above the rooftops. Otherwise, rooms on the second floor facing back toward the mountains are nice—bright and sunny, they look onto an empty and overgrown back lot (which is much better than concrete if you ask me). The men's public bath here is fairly large; the women's is smaller. In the men's bath there's even an ancient-looking tiled pool that's narrow and long. Built decades ago, it's good for swimming laps. Rooms come with TV, and about half have fridge.

Another inexpensive accommodation is the **Hotel New Toyako** [330] (tel. 01427/5-2818), located a block downhill from the bus depot. A combination business hotel/minshuku, its 15 rooms are very clean and basic and consist of 12 Japanese-style rooms, two twins, and one double. Only the twin rooms have a private bath and toilet. Rates are the same for all rooms the whole year round: ¥5,500 ($39) to ¥8,800 ($63) per person, including two meals.

The closest youth hostel is the **Showa-Shinzan Youth Hostel** [331], 103 Sobetsu-onsen, Sobetsu-cho (tel. 01427/5-2283). Sleeping some 60 people on tatami, it's about a seven-minute bus ride from Toyako Onsen bus terminal. Get off at the Showa-Shinzan Toza-an Guchi bus stop. Both nonmembers and members pay ¥3,300 ($23.57), including two meals.

Nearby is the **Toya Kankokan Youth Hostel**, 83 Sobetsu-onsen, Sobetsu-cho (tel. 01427/5-2649). Also about a seven-minute bus ride from Toyako Onsen bus terminal, it's located in front of the Sobetsu-onsen bus stop. Accommodating 200 persons, it charges ¥1,800 ($12.86) for nonmembers, while members pay an additional ¥700 ($5). Dinner is ¥800 ($5.71), breakfast is ¥400 ($2.86), and use of the hot-spring baths is an extra ¥150 ($1.07).

Where to Dine: Since you'll be taking dinner and breakfast at your hotel, you have only lunch to worry about. **Oshima** [332] (tel. 5-4111) is on the second floor of the Wakasaimo Honten Building on the water's edge just west of the main boat dock. In this pleasant and attractive modern restaurant you sit on tatami beside huge windows overlooking the lake. The menu is in Japanese only, but you can make your selection from the plastic-food display case. This is primarily a tempura and soba restaurant, with a variety of other selections as well. Set meals average about ¥1,300 ($9.29), to ¥1,600 ($11.43), with such main dishes as pork cutlet, shrimp tempura, salmon teishoku, obento box lunch, or tempura soba. My favorite is the kani soba for ¥1,300 ($9.29), which consists of crab and a variety of fresh vegetables piled on top of noodles. Hours here are 11 a.m. to 8 p.m. (11 a.m. to 6 p.m. in winter) daily.

Another good choice is **Nagisa**, a floating houseboat moored outside the Sun Palace Hotel (tel. 5-4126). Open from 11 a.m. to 2 p.m. and 6 to 10 p.m., it's a light, airy, bright place for a meal. The specialties here are Genghis Khan (strips of mutton and vegetables) for ¥1,300 ($9.29) and barbecued meat dishes starting at ¥2,000 ($14.29) all of which you cook at your own table top grill. The barbecued meat dishes include mountains of fresh vegetables and seafood, enough to feed a small army.

Not far from the tourist office, **Boyotei** (tel. 5-2311) is a rather interesting-looking café set back from the town's main road behind an overgrown garden. A wooden sign hanging outside over the sidewalk says "Kafe Restaurant." Opened about 40 years ago before the large hotels across the street were built to block the view, it now seems rather hidden and forgotten. The interior looks as if it hasn't changed much over the decades and is filled with knickknacks. A good, cozy place for a morning coffee, lunch, or an evening drink, it's open from 10 a.m. to 10 p.m. daily (until 7 p.m. in winter) and even has some tables and chairs outside. The menu includes pork chops, hamburger steak, fried salmon, macaroni chicken gratin, macaroni crabmeat gratin, beef curry, spaghetti, and sandwiches, with prices ranging from ¥700 ($5) to ¥1,750 ($12.50). There are also set lunches and dinners for ¥1,400 ($10) to ¥5,500 ($39.29). Various kinds of coffees start at ¥380 ($2.71), and beer starts at ¥550 ($3.93). They even have Guinness.

One more inexpensive place for lunch is **Restaurant Park** in the Park Hotel (tel. 5-2445). Open only from 10 a.m. to 3 p.m., this informal and simply decorated place serves hamburger steak, curry dishes, noodles, and other choices for ¥600 ($4.29) to ¥1,650 ($11.79).

Noboribetsu

Famous for the variety of its hot-water springs, Noboribetsu Spa (called *Noboribetsu Onsen* in Japanese) is one of Japan's best-known spa resorts. It boasts 11 different types of hot water gushing 10,000 tons a day. With temperatures ranging between 113° and 197° Fahrenheit, the waters contain all kinds of minerals, including sulfur, salt, iron, and gypsum, and are thought to help relieve such disorders as high blood pressure, rheumatism, arthritis, eczema, and even constipation. Noboribetsu gets its name from the Ainu word meaning simply "white muddy river."

Orientation: Noboribetsu Onsen is about a 15-minute bus ride from the town of Noboribetsu and its Noboribetsu Station, which is where you'll arrive if you come by train. There are also direct buses from Sapporo to Noboribetsu Onsen.

The **tourist office** (tel. 01438/4-2068) is on Noboribetsu Onsen's main street just a minute north of the bus depot. It's open from 9 a.m. to 5 p.m. weekdays, to noon on Saturday; closed Sunday. There's a pamphlet and map in English, but I've never encountered anyone here who speaks English. Luckily, the town is so small that you shouldn't have any problem getting around. The busiest tourist season is May to October and during New Year's, which is when hotel rates are at their highest.

The **telephone area code** for Noboribetsu Onsen is 01438.

What to Do: Although all the spa hotels and ryokan have their own taps into the spring water, the most famous hotel bath in town is at the **Daiichi Takimotokan**, a monstrous bathing hall with more than a dozen pools containing different mineral contents at various temperatures. Recently remodeled, it's an elaborate affair with hot-spring baths both indoors and out, a Jacuzzi, saunas, steam rooms, and waterfall massage (the waterfall massage is one of my favorites—you simply sit under the shooting water and let it pummel your neck and shoulders). The baths are separated for men and women, but there's an indoor pool with mixed bathing, so be sure to bring your swimsuit. My only complaint is that the workers cleaning the walls and floors of the bathhouses are men, a couple of whom were none too discreet in their stares. The Japanese women paid them no attention, so I guess we're supposed to do the same. At any rate, visiting the baths here is the best favor you can do yourself while in Noboribetsu. If you're staying at the Daiichi Takimotokan Hotel, you can use the baths free of charge at any time. Otherwise, the baths are open to the public only from 9 a.m. to 3 p.m. (that is, you must enter by 3 p.m.). The charge is ¥1,600 ($11.43).

To get an idea of what all this hot water looks like, visit **Hell Valley (Jigokudani)**, at the north edge of town past the Daiichi Takimotokan hotel. A volcanic crater 1,485 feet in diameter, the huge depression is full of bubbling and boiling hot water and rock formations of orange and brown. If you walk along the concrete path that winds along the left side of the crater and follow it until it swings farther to the left, you'll soon see a narrow footpath that leads off to the right through lush woods. If you follow it for about ten minutes, you'll come to a lookout point overlooking a large pond of hot bubbling water (the lookout is across the highway). If you want to take a different route back, follow the path that leads to the right after you recross the highway. This pathway traces the backbone of several ridges all the way back into town, passing a number of small stone deities on the way.

Another attraction is **Lake Kuttara**. It's an unspoiled caldera lake a few miles from Noboribetsu Onsen and is ranked the second clearest in Japan (the clearest is considered to be Masshu in Akan National Park). Because the water is very cold, swimming is forbidden. However, you can rent rowboats for ¥550 ($3.93) per half hour. The water is beautiful and wooded hills rise on all sides. There's also a small restaurant where you can eat ramen, tempura, soba, and trout, at prices ranging from ¥600 ($4.29) to ¥1,600 ($11.43). Unfortunately, there are only two buses a day that come here from Noboribetsu Onsen, the first one leaving the onsen at 10:30 a.m. and the second at 1:30 p.m. Each bus makes a 25-minute stop at the lake before returning to Noboribetsu Onsen. If this isn't enough time for you, you might want to take the early bus to the lake and return on the later one. Be sure to check on the latest schedule. Buses run from June 1 to October 20 only.

If you find yourself at Noboribetsu Station with some time on your hands, you might want to check out the Hokkaido Marine Park, about ten minutes from the station on foot. Scheduled for opening sometime in the summer of 1988, it is one of the largest aquariums in eastern Japan.

Food and Lodging: Because of its large bathing hall with the various pools, the **Daiichi Takimotokan** (tel. 01438/4-2111) is Noboribetsu Onsen's best-known ryokan and first opened 130 years ago. Guests are entitled to use the pools free anytime night or day. The ryokan's present modern structure houses

336 rooms: 8 rooms have beds, and the rest are all Japanese-style tatami. As with most first-class ryokan in Hokkaido's resort areas, rooms come with fan, TV with pay video, fridge, and a safe for valuables. Rates here during peak season average ¥20,000 ($143) per person in both twin and tatami rooms, including two meals. Off-season, Japanese rooms with toilets only cost ¥13,200 ($94), while twin rooms are ¥17,500 ($125) per person.

Across the street from Daiichi Takimotokan is its Western-style counterpart, **Takimoto Inn** (tel. 01438/4-2205). A small, comfortable, and moderately priced hotel, it has only 47 rooms, all twins. Rooms are colorfully decorated, some with larger-than-life-size flowers splashed onto wallpaper, but otherwise are fairly basic with a small bathroom and TV with pay video. The main advantage to staying here is that you can use Daiichi Takimotokan's famous baths for free. From late spring through early autumn, all weekends, and during New Year's, rooms cost ¥14,300 ($102) per person including two meals, decreasing to ¥11,000 ($79) other times of the year. If you'd rather not take your meals here, rooms are available for about 30% less.

Rivaling Daiichi Takimotokan in terms of size, facilities, and comfort is the **Grand Hotel** (tel. 01438/4-2101). Spreading along the slope of a hill just above the bus terminal, it has 261 rooms, 85 of which are twins. Per-person rates for these Western-style rooms are ¥11,000 ($71) including two meals, or ¥15,400 ($110) for two persons without meals. Japanese rooms are ¥15,500 ($111) per person for rooms with a private bathroom and two meals. Rates are the same throughout the year, although they increase by about ¥1,000 ($7.14) per person on Saturday night. This hotel sports a nice public bath. Though not as large as Takimotokan's, it is more elegant. The men's section has baths both indoors and outdoors, complete with waterfall and Roman goddess statues. As for the women's section, sorry—no outdoor pool, waterfall, or goddesses. However, it's large and bright, and there are saunas for both sexes.

A small, reasonably priced, and very friendly ryokan is **Kiyomizu** (tel. 01438/4-2145). Located on Noboribetsu Onsen's main street just a couple of minutes' walk from the bus terminal, its 20 Japanese-style rooms are modestly furnished and are all without bathroom. Singles range from ¥4,400 ($31) to ¥6,000 ($43), twins run ¥7,200 ($51) to ¥9,900 ($71), and triples cost ¥11,500 ($82) to ¥15,000 ($107). Prices are room rates only, without meals. If you opt for food, Japanese or Western breakfasts cost an additional ¥800 ($5.71), while dinner ranges from ¥1,600 ($11.43) to ¥2,200 ($15.71). Meals are served in your room. The owner, Mr. Iwai, speaks very good English and can answer your questions regarding Noboribetsu and the surrounding area. There are small hot-spring baths in the ryokan and the public toilets are Japanese style. Incidentally, Mr. Iwai plans to add another 40 rooms in a nearby annex. Slated for completion by the summer of 1989, it will feature a hot-spring bath on the seventh floor, with views of the surrounding countryside. Rates here for tatami rooms will start at around ¥10,000 ($71).

Although they're a bit far from Noboribetsu Onsen, if you're on a budget you might consider staying at either Kikusui or Noboribetsu-so. Both are minshuku run by families who also manage adjoining temples. **Kikusui** [333] (tel. 01438/4-2437) is run by a woman whose husband is a Buddhist monk. There are a total of nine tatami rooms here, all without bath. Close by is **Noboribetsu-so** [334] (tel. 01438/4-3352), smaller, with only five tatami rooms, all without bath. Both minshuku charge ¥5,500 ($39) per person, including two meals. There's infrequent bus service, which deposits you within a few minutes' walk of either minshuku; otherwise it's about a 30-minute hike from the bus terminal. Since these minshuku do not have hot-spring baths, you'll have to hike into town to Takimotokan if you want the real thing.

There are three youth hostels in Noboribetsu Onsen. **Kannonji** [335] (tel. 01438/4-2359) is run by a very friendly group of people who delight in receiving foreign guests. Accommodating 25 persons in tatami rooms, it has its own hot-spring bath and coffee is available free in the small dining room. Members are charged ¥2,000 ($14.29) and nonmembers pay ¥2,600 ($18.57). Japanese breakfasts cost ¥400 ($2.86), while dinners are ¥700 ($5). It's located about a seven-minute walk from the bus terminal.

Another good choice in youth hostels is **Akashiya Youth Hostel** [336] (tel. 01438/4-2616). Just a couple of minutes' walk from the bus terminal, it sleeps 55 persons in both beds and tatami. The charge of ¥3,400 ($24.28) for members and ¥3,900 ($27.86) for nonmembers includes two meals. Use of the hot-spring baths here costs an extra ¥100 (71/).

If these two places are full, there's another youth hostel located a few minutes farther out of town called **Youth Hostel Ryokan Kanefuku** [337] (tel. 01438/4-2565), with prices similar to those given above. Unfortunately, there is no hot-spring bath here—only baths with water of the regular kind.

If you find yourself looking for a place to stop for lunch, or a draft beer, or coffee, the Takimoto Inn's **Poplar Restaurant** serves inexpensive Western dishes from 11 a.m. to 2:30 p.m. The English menu lists such choices as beefsteak, pork chops, hamburger steak, fried shrimp, salmon meunière, fried scallops, crab croquette, curry rice, shrimp gratin, and spaghetti. All are in the ¥650 ($4.64) to ¥1,600 ($11.43) range.

Shiraoi

On your way between Sapporo and Noboribetsu you might wish to visit Shiraoi, where a mock Ainu village has been set up. The village consists of thatched houses with demonstrations and dances performed by Ainu. Particularly interesting is the museum, which contains crafts, utensils, and clothing of the Ainu. Explanations are in English and the displays realistically depict what life was like for the Ainu before the Japanese assimilated them into their society. If you want to know more about the Ainu, pick up a booklet called *The Ainu Museum* for ¥400 ($2.86), which describes their lifestyle, religious beliefs, and customs. Entrance fee to the Ainu village is ¥500 ($3.57), and hours are 8 a.m. to 5 p.m. daily (8:30 a.m. to 4:30 p.m. in winter).

DAISETSUZAN NATIONAL PARK: Although I find it difficult to rank nature in terms of beauty, there are some who maintain that Daisetsuzan National Park is the most spectacular of Hokkaido's parks. With its tall mountains covered with fir and birch trees and sprinkled with wildflowers, its river gorge laced with waterfalls and hiking trails throughout, Daisetsuzan National Park is the perfect place to come if you've been itching to get some exercise in a relatively unspoiled countryside. Lying in the center of Hokkaido, the national park contains three volcanic mountain groups, including the highest mountain in Hokkaido, Mount Asahi, at 7,513 feet. Hiking in summer and skiing in winter are the primary pursuits of the region.

The perfect base for exploring the national park is Sounkyo Onsen, nestled at the very edge of Sounkyo Gorge, Daisetsuzan's most famous natural attraction. A tiny village of ryokan and minshuku, it's a good starting point for seeing both the gorge and for ascending the mountains. Although the town itself is rather unattractive, with its cluster of souvenir shops and unimaginative buildings, its soothing hot springs and magnificent scenic backdrop make coming here worthwhile. Not only that, Sounkyo Onsen serves as the starting point for bicycle trips along Sounkyo Gorge and for the cable car trip to the top of a neighboring peak. Sounkyo is one of my favorite places in all of Hokkaido.

Orientation

The only way to reach Sounkyo Onsen by public transportation is by bus. If you're coming from Sapporo, take the train as far as Kamikawa (2 ½ hours) and from there transfer to a bus for a 30-minute ride that will take you directly to Sounkyo. There are also buses connecting Sounkyo Onsen with Asahigawa and Rubeshibe, both a 2-hour ride away. The **tourist information office** is located in a modern-looking wooden building downhill from the bus station. You can see it from the bus depot, and it's called the PR Center (tel. 01658/5-3350). No one speaks English here and maps are only in Japanese, but the staff can point you in the direction of your ryokan or even make ryokan reservations for you. It's open daily from 9 a.m. to 5 p.m. (from 10 a.m. to 4 p.m. November through April). In any case, the village is so tiny you won't have any difficulty getting around.

The **telephone area code** for Sounkyo Onsen is 01658.

What to Do

Sounkyo Gorge is a river valley hemmed in on both sides by rock walls rising almost 500 feet high. Almost perpendicular in places, the gorge extends for about 12 miles, offering spectacular views with each bending curve. The best way to see the gorge is on a bicycle, which you can rent from stalls beside the bus terminal and a number of other places for ¥1,200 ($8.57) a day. There's a designated route you're supposed to follow, and altogether the trip to the end of the route and back should take no longer than two hours. The first part of the trip by bicycle is unfortunately on a sidewalk next to a highway, with a string of cars. (Since you probably already think I'm degenerate, I might as well tell you that I wore my Walkman while riding on the sidewalk here to block out traffic noise. What the heck, I was by myself anyway and had no one else to talk to.) The highway winds along a rushing river passing a couple of waterfalls until finally the highway disappears into a dark tunnel—which is where I'm convinced it belongs anyway. At this point the gorge belongs to cyclists and hikers, and becomes quite narrow. You then pass through a tunnel yourself and emerge at the turning point of your trip where you'll find—what else?—souvenir shops, soda machines, and vendors selling corn on the cob. This is where tour buses pull in for a quick look.

If you're interested in hiking, or even if you're not, take the cable car from Sounkyo Onsen to the lofty peak of **Kuro-dake Mountain**. The trip takes seven minutes and costs ¥650 ($4.64) one way. From the cable-car station, walk a few minutes farther up the mountain where you'll come to a chair lift. This costs ¥210 ($1.50) one way and takes 15 minutes, swinging you past lush forests of fir and birch. At the end of the lift where the hiking paths begin, there's a hut here where you sign your name and give your route so that tabs can be kept on people who are on the mountain. If you're not feeling overly ambitious you can hike an hour and reach the peak of Kuro-dake, 6,500 feet high, where if the weather is clear you'll be rewarded with views of the surrounding mountain ranges.

If you feel like taking a day's hike, there's a circular path along the top of mountain ridges that you can hike in about seven hours. And if you're really into hiking and wish to carry your backpack with you, a popular route is to walk from the Sounkyo chair lift over Mount Asahi, Hokkaido's tallest mountain, and on to another chair lift that will take you down to Asahidake Onsen, spa where you can spend the night. This trip takes eight to ten hours, so set out early. Be sure to pick up a map showing the hiking trails. It's in Japanese only, but since the trails are marked in Japanese only, having an English map wouldn't do you much good. The hiking path isn't considered that strenuous, but you do need sturdy walking shoes. If you're going for just a short hike, tennis shoes are fine. The tops of the mountains are really beautiful here, covered with wildflowers and alpine plant life. It would be a shame to come to Sounkyo and not spend at least a few hours amid its lofty peaks.

During the winter season the mountains become a skier's haven from November to May. Although you can rent skis up on the mountain at the cable-car station, keep in mind that your feet may be too big. Skis and boots rent for ¥3,300 ($23.57) and up. A day's cable-car and chair-lift ticket costs ¥2,700 ($19.29). The lift operations vary according to the month, but are open from about 8 or 9 a.m. to 4 or 4:30 p.m. in winter and from 6 a.m. to 7 p.m. in summer months. Please note that the lifts shut down entirely for two weeks beginning in mid-February for maintenance work.

If you have time to kill, you might also consider dropping in on the **Sounkyo Museum Daisetsuzan National Park**. Its explanations are in Japanese only, and you'll see some aerial reliefs of the area, stuffed animals, butterflies, insects, and birds. Admission is ¥200 ($1.43).

Food and Lodging

As in all resort areas in Japan, Sounkyo Onsen's hotels, ryokan, and minshuku all include breakfast and dinner in their rates. Unless otherwise stated, therefore, all prices quoted below are on a per-person basis and include two meals. If you want to stay here in August, make reservations in advance. Incidentally, most families who live here run several operations that might include a ryokan, an adjoining restaurant, and a souvenir shop. As for the army of young Japanese college-age guys you see waiting tables, hustling customers at the bicycle stalls, and working in ryokan kitchens and souvenir shops in the summertime, they're not locals. Rather, they come from other parts of Japan and are working in Sounkyo for a summer job. They may not know a lot about the area, but most of them speak some English.

If you can get a room on a top floor facing the gorge, one of the best places to stay in town is the **Taisetsu Hotel** (tel. 01658/5-3211). A large white hotel atop a hill above the town, this 250-room property is about a seven-minute walk from the bus terminal. Depending on the size of your room and its view, rates here range from ¥11,000 ($79) to ¥16,500 ($118) per person; rates are about 20% cheaper in the wintertime. The most expensive rooms face the gorge, while the cheapest rooms have toilets but no baths. Western breakfasts are available on request. Most rooms are tatami, but three Western-style rooms are also available. The hot-spring public baths here are large and consist of several different pools. As is often the case, however, the men's bath commands a better view than the women's.

Just across the street from the Taisetsu is the **Sounkyo Prince Hotel Choyotei** (tel. 01658/5-3241), which made its debut in 1987. Boasting a good view of the gorge from its location atop a ridge, it offers 271 rooms, all with private bathroom. With both Japanese-style and combination rooms available, its rooms are pleasant and elegantly simple and come with refrigerator, a safe for valuables, and TV with adult video. Rates average ¥16,500 ($118) to ¥22,000 ($157) per person with two meals, with the higher rates charged for rooms with views of the gorge. Rates are about 20% cheaper in winter. Facilities include a modern, comfortable lobby with views of a rock garden, an electronic-game room, a souvenir shop, noodle and sushi counters, and public baths on the top floor overlooking the gorge.

Situated beside the highway that runs through Sounkyo Gorge, the **Grand**

Hotel [338] (tel. 01658/5-3111) is an older hotel which recently received a much-needed face-lift. The lobby, with its marbled pillars and white walls, is cheerful though a bit overdone; the public spa baths are quite nice, with large windows, white tile, and stone. There are also outdoor baths, separated for men and women. All of its 208 rooms come with private bathroom and start at ¥8,800 ($63), with ¥13,200 ($94) the average price paid for a room on a top floor with a view of the surrounding mountain ranges. During winter the rates are about 10% lower.

A relatively new ryokan that opened in 1984, **Kumoi** [339] (tel. 01658/5-3553) is a brick building easily recognizable by the V-shaped blue façade above its top windows. All 22 rooms are tatami, six of which have a private bathroom. The rest have a sink and toilet. If you ask me, your own bathtub shouldn't be much of a concern since the communal public bath is natural hot springs and you'll probably want to bathe there anyway. They'll serve you a Western breakfast if you order it the day before. Rooms are clean, new, and simple. Summer rates here are ¥8,800 ($63) to ¥16,500 ($118); winter rates are the same.

Right next to Kumoi is **Matsubara** [340] (tel. 01658/5-3015), a ryokan run by friendly and personable people. The woman in charge speaks a little English. Tiny, with only ten rooms, this establishment opened back in 1961 so it's one of the oldtimers around here. None of the rooms here, which are all tatami, has a toilet or bath, but some do have a sink. Rates are ¥5,500 ($39) to ¥8,800 ($63), and Western breakfasts are available. The public bath's water is from the hot springs.

Pension Yukara [341] (tel. 01658/5-3216) opened in 1985 in a spotlessly clean, white, bright, and cute style meant to appeal to young Japanese girls. Its seven rooms, all without bathroom, include both twins and tatami rooms and are decorated with flowered wallpaper, feminine furniture, and lots of pink. There's a coin laundry here, but the drawback to this place is that it doesn't have a hot-spring bath—just regular bath water. Breakfast is Western style. Rates are ¥7,500 ($54) throughout the year, except in August when they're ¥8,000 ($57).

Tsuchiya [342] (tel. 01658/5-3517) prides itself on being the largest minshuku in Hokkaido, for whatever that's worth. It has 50 rooms in a main building and an annex, all without bathrooms. It charges ¥5,500 ($39) throughout the year. Facilities include hot-spring baths, coin laundry, and very clean rooms. Western breakfasts are available.

Kitagawa [343] (tel. 01658/5-3515) is another minshuku which attracts mainly young Japanese. It has 12 Japanese-style rooms without bathrooms and is located above a souvenir shop and restaurant of the same name. It has both a coin laundry and hot-spring baths. Clean and pleasant, it charges ¥5,500 ($39) per person.

There are two youth hostels in Sounkyo Onsen. **Sounkyo Youth Hostel** [344] (tel. 01658/5-3418) is located on top of a hill past the Taisetsu Hotel, about a ten-minute walk from the station, a pleasant location. It has both beds and futon and charges ¥3,190 ($23), including two meals, for both members and nonmembers. The other youth hostel, **Ginsenkaku Youth Hostel** [345] (tel. 01658/5-3003) is located in town just a few minutes' walk from the bus terminal. It charges ¥3,500 ($25) for hostel members, while nonmembers pay ¥500 ($3.57) more. Prices include two meals. This youth hostel also has its own hot-spring bath, for which it charges an extra ¥150 ($1.07).

AKAN NATIONAL PARKS: Spreading through the eastern end of Hokkaido, Akan National Park features volcanic mountains, dense forests of subarctic primeval trees, and three caldera lakes, including Lake Akan. The best place to stay in the park is at Akanko Onsen, a small hot-spring resort on the edge of Lake Akan. It makes a good base from which to explore both the Akan National Park and the Red-Crested Crane National Park nearby.

Orientation

Because Akan National Park lies at the eastern extremity of Hokkaido, you may wish to fly back to Tokyo. **Kushiro Airport** is one hour and 20 minutes away by bus from Akanko Onsen. The plane trip from Kushiro to Tokyo takes about 1½ hours.

Since there's no train station at Akanko, transportation to the resort town is by bus. Sightseeing buses are the best way to see the park, described in more detail below. If you have any questions concerning Akan National Park, drop by the **Visitor's Center,** with displays (unfortunately only in Japanese) of natural wonders pertaining to the park. You can also stop at the **tourist association** (tel. 0154/67-2254), located in a log cabin-like building on Akanko Onsen's main street just next to the fire station and across the street from the New Akan Hotel Crystal. It's open from 8:30 a.m. to 4:30 p.m. daily. There's also a small tourist window next to the boat pier where you buy tickets for boat rides on Lake Akan.

As for Akanko Onsen itself, it's small and walking is the best way to get around. It consists primarily of one main street that snakes along the lake, with ryokan and souvenir shops on both sides.

The **telephone area code** for Akanko Onsen is 0154.

What to Do

Your sightseeing in Akan National Park should begin before reaching Akanko Onsen, which lies in the southern part of the park. The best way to see the park, if you're not renting a car, is to board an **Akan sightseeing bus** in Bihoro, which is north of the park. That way you'll travel all the way through the park and see the most important natural wonders. The bus trip takes five hours, making stops at several scenic spots along the way, including Kussharo and Mashu lakes. Kussharo is one of Japan's largest mountain lakes, while Mashu is considered to be one of the most beautiful. A deep crater lake with the clearest water in Japan, Mashu was called "lake of the devil" by the Ainu because of the mysterious fact that no water flows either into it or out of it. Surely Mashu is one of Japan's least-spoiled lakes—because of its steep, 660-foot-high rock walls ringing the lake, it has remained inaccessible to mankind (the bus stops at two observation platforms high above the lake). The bus trip costs ¥5,700 ($40.71) and is called the Panorama Course. At last check buses departed from Bihoro four times daily, at 8 a.m., 9:30 a.m., 10:55 a.m., and 12:45 p.m. from the end of April to the end of October. During the winter months only one bus departs daily. In any case, be sure to check departures ahead of time, since bus schedules change. For more information, call 0152/3-4182.

As for things to do in Akanko, the most popular activity is to take a **boat cruise** around **Lake Akan.** Lake Akan is famous for its very rare spherical green weed, called *marimo.* It's a sponge-like ball of duckweed that grows two to five inches in diameter. Found only a couple places in the world, marimo is formed when many separate and stringy pieces of weed at the bottom of the lake roll around and eventually come together to form a ball. The ball grows larger and larger until sooner or later it breaks apart, whereby the whole process starts over again. On your boat cruise you'll make a stop at a small island on the lake where a marimo museum has been set up, consisting of duckweed in a few tanks with explanations of how they're formed. Supposedly, when the sun shines the marimo rises to the surface of the water, giving Lake Akan a wonderful green shimmer. However, the only marimo I ever saw was in the museum's tanks and in tanks of souvenir shops around town even though the sun was shining. Perhaps you'll have better luck. The boat trip takes 1½ hours and costs ¥1,000 ($7.14).

While you're out on your boat trip you'll notice two cone-shaped **volcanoes**, O-Akan to the east and Me-Akan to the south. Both are popular destinations for hikers. O-Akan is dormant and it's about a 4 ½ hour hike to the summit from Akanko Onsen. Me-Akan, the highest mountain in the Akan area, is active and is covered with primeval forests of spruce and fir. There's a trail leading to Me-Akan from the west end of the town, and it takes about four hours to reach the top, from which you have panoramic views of the surrounding area.

A shorter hike follows a trail to Mount Hakutozan, from which you also have a good view of the town and lake. It takes about two hours to reach Akan's skiing area and another 30 minutes to reach Mount Hakutozan, a grassy and moss-covered knobby hill that remains warm throughout the year because of thermal activity just below the surface. The woods of birch and pine here are beautiful, and what's more, you'll probably find yourself all alone.

Incidentally, behind the Visitor's Center described under the orientation section is a catwalk leading through marshy woods and connecting with a trail that terminates on the lake's shore. Here you'll find some bubbly hot-mud ponds, a grassy area good for picnics, and a rock-enclosed hot-spring that empties right into the lake. You can take a soaking here if you like, and no one would object if you wear your swimsuit.

If you're in Akan in the winter, you may want to take advantage of its artificial snow atop the town's one skiing hill. The season runs from about the end of November until May and the two runs are good for beginners.

If you haven't seen any Ainu dances yet, you might want to pay a visit to **Ainu Kotan Village**. Actually this isn't a village at all. It's a souvenir-shop-lined street leading to a thatched-roof lodge where you can see Ainu performing traditional dances. Costing ¥600 ($4.29), shows are performed about five times a day from May to the end of October and last half an hour.

Red-crested cranes are the prefectural birds of Hokkaido, and south of Akan is a breeding ground for these graceful and beautiful animals. **Tanchozuru Shizen Koen (Red-crested Crane Natural Park**; tel. 0154/56-2219) is a marshy area set aside for breeding and raising the crane. Open throughout the year from 9 a.m. to 5 p.m. (to 4 p.m. in winter), it charges ¥200 ($1.43) for visitors to observe the birds behind high mesh fences. You'll be surprised at how large these birds actually are. The crane park is one hour and 15 minutes by bus from the Akanko Onsen bus terminal; get off at the Tsuru-koen bus stop. By the way, this is the same bus that goes from Akanko to Kushiro Airport. The bus makes a five-minute stop at this park, which is enough time to jump out and take a quick look at the birds before continuing on to the airport.

If you happen to be in Akan in the winter, you'll have the extra delight of visiting **Tancho-no-Sato**, private grounds where red-crested cranes court, mate, and live in the winter months from November to March. This is the best place to photograph the birds in action. It's a 42-minute bus ride from Akanko Onsen bus terminal.

Food and Lodging

Unless otherwise stated, all prices include two meals and are per person.

Ryokan and Hotels: Situated on a shady spot beside **Lake Akan,** the **New**

Akan Hotel (tel. 0154/67-2121) is a 296-room property winding along the curve of the lake in a series of wings built at various stages in the past 20 years. The newest addition is the Annex Crystal, with very pleasant rooms featuring bay windows looking out on shade trees and the lake beyond. Rooms cost about ¥22,000 ($157) to ¥27,000 ($193) per person in summer and as little as ¥13,200 ($94) in winter. These rooms have nicely finished tile bathrooms, hair dryers, fridge, radio, clock, hot-water pot, TV with coin video, and even a pants presser for pants and skirts. Both Japanese-style and Western-style rooms are available. Rooms in the older wings are more modestly priced, beginning at ¥16,500 ($118) per person for rooms facing the lake and ¥11,000 ($79) for those facing inland.

Facilities at the hotel include souvenir shops, large public hot-spring baths, a bar, and a few restaurants. **Crystal Restaurant** in the Annex Crystal is a good place to come for lunch. It offers sandwiches, spaghetti, beef curry, shrimp or crab pilaf, noodles, and more, at ¥700 ($5) to ¥1,500 ($10.71) for most items, as well as daily specials for ¥2,200 ($15.71). The restaurant has a very nice view of shade trees and is open from 11 a.m. to 9 p.m.

Located right next to the boat dock on the water's edge, **Hotel Akankoso** (tel. 0154/67-2231) has a variety of Western- and Japanese-style rooms, as well as combination rooms, with and without bathroom, all with a variety of prices to match. The best rooms face the lake and come with a private bathroom, at ¥16,500 ($118) while the least expensive are Western-style twins or Japanese-style rooms without a bathroom facing inland at ¥13,200 ($94). During winter, rates drop down to ¥13,200 ($94) and ¥11,000 ($79) respectively. The hotel's large communal hot-spring baths on the fifth floor are nicely laid out in brick with views of the lake.

Robata is the hotel's Japanese restaurant, overlooking a small lawn and the bay with its sightseeing boats coming and going. When the weather is fine you can even dine outdoors under the shade of umbrellas. Open from 11 a.m. to 2 p.m., it offers various fish choices from ¥1,650 ($11.79), as well as *toban-yaki* (beef cooked on a grill at your table) for ¥2,000 ($14.29). Although the menu is in Japanese, it has pictures of dishes and there's a small display case outside the restaurant door.

Opened in 1984, the **Akan View Hotel** (tel. 0154/67-3131) is the spa's newest and despite its name is one of the few hotels without a view of the lake.

It's back from the waterfront, more inland than the other hotels, and all 200 rooms are Western-style twins with private bathrooms. Rates here range from ¥11,000 ($79) to ¥13,200 ($94) per person during peak season, dropping down to ¥6,600 ($47) in winter. One of the best things about this hotel is that it has large indoor pools, one for swimming laps and one for children, as well as the usual hot-spring baths, open from 7 a.m. to 9 p.m. Even if you're not staying at the hotel you can use the facilities for ¥750 ($5.36) on weekdays and ¥1,100 ($7.86) on weekends and holidays. Other facilities include tennis courts and bicycles for rent. Although none of the rooms has a view of the water, the best rooms, in my opinion, are those that face east, where there are some woods and a creek.

A much older hotel, the **Hotel Ichikawa** [346] (tel. 0154/67-2011) is an 89-room ryokan that opened back in 1961. Located right on the water's edge, it's a very reasonably priced place to stay and the front-desk personnel are nice and friendly. One advantage to staying here is Shigeru Dameon Takada, a young Japanese man who studied in Canada and speaks very good English. Since this ryokan is a family-run affair, he told me he would be staying here the rest of his life. He also said he'd be very happy to help foreigners with any questions they might have regarding Akan, which could be quite useful since hardly anyone in Akan speaks English. All rooms are Japanese style except two twins, and rates are ¥8,800 ($63) per person for rooms facing inland and ¥12,000 ($86) for those with a view of the lake. During winter the rates go down to ¥7,000 ($50) and ¥8,800 ($63) respectively. Rooms on the top (sixth) floor command the best views. The hot-spring public baths on the first floor are very modern and face the lake. If you're here in summer, be sure to go out on the hotel's tatami-floored boat, gaily decorated with lanterns. It goes out for about 40 minutes at night serenaded by Japanese music. The trip costs ¥1,500 ($10.71) per person and includes one drink with a snack.

The hotel also maintains a pontoon boat for two-hour sunset cruises on the lake, complete with barbecue dinner and a glass of wine for ¥3,300 ($23.57) per person. The hotel can make arrangements for fishing, waterskiing, or snow skiing and will even tailor day trips to other lakes and hiking destinations to your own desires.

Right next to Ichikawa is the **Akan Grand Hotel** [347] (tel. 0154/67-2531), also right on the water's edge. This white hotel has Japanese-style tatami and combination rooms, all with bathroom. Rooms with a lake view cost ¥14,300 ($102) to ¥22,000 ($157), while those facing inland are ¥13,200 ($94) to ¥16,500 ($118). Winter rates are ¥2,000 ($14.29) to ¥4,000 ($28.57) lower. Rooms are modern and clean, and come with the usual TV with pay video, fridge, and clock. The public baths here are fairly unique and have a large fish tank built into the wall.

Minshuku: In addition to the large hotels and ryokan there are a number of inexpensive minshuku in Akanko Onsen. Rooms are simple and are without private bathroom but offer good value for the money. The charge for all the minshuku listed below is ¥5,000 ($36) per person, with two meals.

Minshuku Yamaguchi Fujino [348] (tel. 0154/67-2555) is located on the west edge of town. As with most minshuku, this family-run lodge is small, with just ten Japanese-style rooms. The advantage to staying here is that it has a hot-spring communal bath. Rooms come with coin-operated TV and are simple but cozy. From the dining room you have a peaceful view of some woods and, in winter when the leaves are gone, a view of the lake.

Across the street from Yamaguchi is **Minshuku Ginrei** [349] (tel. 0154/67-2597). There are nine rooms here, again simple, with coin-operated TV. There's no view and no hot-spring bath, but the man who runs this place is used to foreigners and welcomes them.

One more minshuku is **Minshuku Kiri** (tel. 0154/67-2755), located across the street from the Ichikawa Hotel. Look for the wooden sign hanging above the door with the English written very small. The eight Japanese-style rooms are simple, with coin-operated TV. The bathtubs here are wooden and the water is from hot springs.

Youth Hostels: The **Akankohan Youth Hostel** (tel. 0154/67-2241) is right next to the boat sightseeing dock. Old and a bit run-down, it charges ¥3,000 ($21.43) for hostel members, including two meals, while nonmembers pay ¥500 ($3.57) more. Its sign is in English, and it's conveniently located about a four-minute walk from the bus terminal. More than 25 years old, it has a rather uncertain future, so it would be wise to call beforehand to make sure it's still in operation.

The **Angel Youth Hostel** [350] (tel. 0154/67-2309) is farther out of town, about a 15- to 20-minute walk from the bus terminal, but the building is newer and in better shape. If you call from the bus terminal, someone will come pick you up. There are also bicycles for rent here, making it easy to get back and forth to town. Rates here with two meals are ¥3,300 ($23.57) for members and ¥3,800 ($27.14) for nonmembers.

Closer to the bus terminal is **Choritsu Akanko Youth Hostel** [351] (tel. 0154/ 67-2445), about a five-minute walk away. It charges ¥3,400 ($24.29) for both members and nonmembers, which includes two meals.

Chapter XII

HONG KONG

EVERY TIME I GO TO HONG KONG I feel as though I've wandered onto a movie set. Perhaps I'm an incurable romantic, but whenever I stand at the railing of the famous Star Ferry as it glides across the harbor, crouch upon the wooden bench of a rickety old tram as it winds its way across Hong Kong Island, or clutch the side of the funicular as it groans its way up to Victoria Peak, I can't help but think I must have somehow landed in the middle of an epic drama where the past has melted into the present. So many images float by— wooden boats bobbing up and down in the harbor beside huge ocean liners; narrow streets and old crumbling buildings standing next to modern high-rises; abacuses being sold alongside pocket calculators. There are neon lights, markets, crowds of people, and noise. Certainly it's one of the most vibrant cities in the world. But that doesn't say it all.

A British colony, Hong Kong was founded as a place to conduct business and to trade, and that has been its raison d'être ever since. The world's third-largest financial center after New York and London, Hong Kong is the Wall Street of Asia, with banking, international insurance, advertising, and publishing among its biggest concerns. Hong Kong is also the world's leading exporter of toys and garments and is one of the largest manufacturers of watches and electronics.

A duty-free port, Hong Kong attracts more than three million tourists a year, making tourism its third-largest industry. Shopping is one of the main reasons people come here, and at first glance Hong Kong does seem rather like one huge department store. But there's much more to Hong Kong than shopping. Whether it's dining, wining, sightseeing, or relaxing that you're looking for, one thing is certain—the more you search, the more you'll find. And before long you too will be swept up in the drama.

1. Introducing Hong Kong

GEOGRAPHY: Located at the southeastern tip of the People's Republic of China, Hong Kong is just south of the Tropic of Cancer, at the same latitude as Mexico City, the Bahamas, and Hawaii. Covering 404 square miles, Hong Kong can be divided into four distinct parts: Hong Kong Island, Kowloon Peninsula, the New Territories, and 235 outlying islands.

Hong Kong Island is where the colony's financial and business district is located, in a modern area known as the Central District. East of the Central District are Wanchai, formerly the reputed haunt of Suzie Wong and women of the night, and Causeway Bay, an area of restaurants and shops. Victoria Peak crowns the center of the island, and on the southern coast can be found Aberdeen with its boat population, Repulse Bay with its long stretch of beach, and Stanley with its famous market.

North across the harbor from Hong Kong Island is Kowloon Peninsula, the tip of which is called Tsimshatsui (also written Tsim Sha Tsui). This is where most of Hong Kong's tourist hotels, shops, and restaurants are located. The New Territories stretch north of Kowloon to the border of China. Once a vast area of peaceful little villages, fields, and duck farms, in the past decade the New Territories have witnessed a remarkable mushrooming of satellite towns with huge public-housing estates.

HISTORY: Records show that Hong Kong Island has been inhabited since ancient times, evidenced by the recovery of stone, bronze, and iron artifacts, and more than 100 Neolithic and Bronze Age sites have been identified on Hong Kong and its 235 islands.

Hong Kong's modern history, however, begins in 1841 when Hong Kong Island was ceded to the British as a spoil of the first Opium War. The Opium War was fought basically because the British were determined to sell bars of opium to the Chinese, while the Chinese emperor was determined to keep the British from doing so. Opium, after all, was damaging Chinese society and was draining the country of silver traded to support the drug habit. China lost the struggle, however, and in a treaty it never recognized, was forced to cede in perpetuity Hong Kong Island to the British.

Kowloon Peninsula and Stonecutters Island were added to the colony in 1860 as a result of the second Opium War, and in 1898 the New Territories, including the 235 outlying islands, were leased to Britain for 99 years.

When the British moved in to occupy Hong Kong Island in 1841, it was so empty that the British Lord Palmerston described it as "a barren island with hardly a house upon it." It didn't stay that way for long. The British were interested in Hong Kong Island as an entrepôt and stronghold in Asia, and by 1846 the population was an astonishing 24,000. By the turn of the century the number had swelled to 300,000.

Hong Kong's growth this century has been no less astonishing, in terms of both its trade and its population. In 1911 the overthrow of the Manchu Empire in China sent a flood of refugees into Hong Kong, followed in 1938 with an additional 500,000 Chinese refugees. Another mass influx of Chinese refugees took place after the fall of Shanghai to the Communists in 1950. From this wave of immigrants emerged the beginnings of Hong Kong's now-famous textile industry.

In 1978 Vietnamese refugees started pouring into Hong Kong at the rate of 600 a day, and a year later more than 550,000 Vietnamese were living in camps

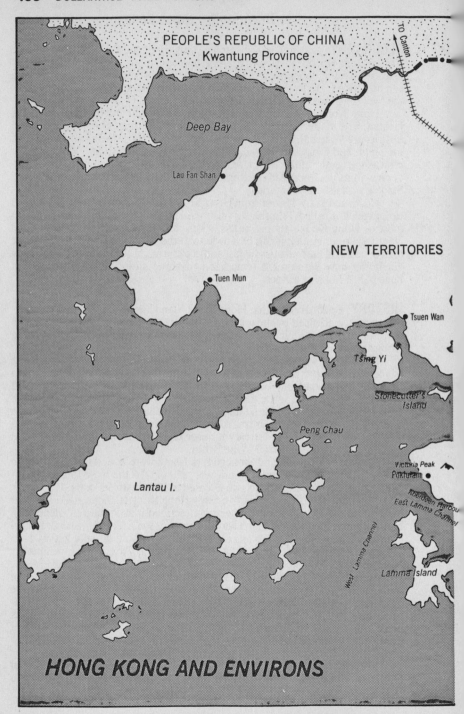

HONG KONG AND ENVIRONS

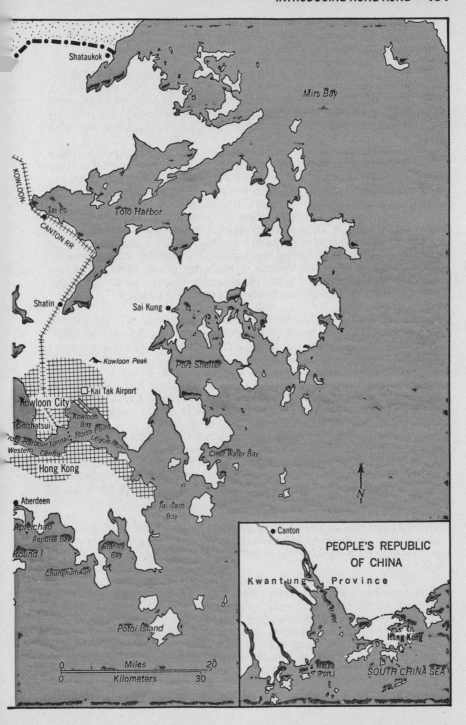

Shataukok

KOWLOON-

Mirs Bay

CANTON RR

Tai Po

Tolo Harbor

Shatin

Sai Kung

Kowloon Peak

Port Shelter

Kai Tak Airport

Kowloon City

Tsimshatsui

Kowloon Bay

Cross-Harbour Tunnel

North Point

Leiyuemon

Western

Central

Clear Water Bay

Hong Kong

Aberdeen

Tai Tam Bay

N

Apleichau

Repulse Bay

Round I

Stanley Bay

Chunghumwan

Potoi Island

Canton

PEOPLE'S REPUBLIC
OF CHINA

Kwantung   Province

Hong Kong

Miles   20

Macau
(Port.)

SOUTH CHINA SEA

Kilometers   30

around the colony. Finding itself no longer able to support additional refugees, Hong Kong now has a policy whereby illegal immigrants from China are immediately sent back and Vietnamese are sent elsewhere as soon as possible.

THE PEOPLE: With a population of 5½ million, Hong Kong is one of the most densely populated areas in the world. The vast majority—98%—are Chinese, more than half of whom were born in Hong Kong. The other 2%, known in Cantonese as *gwailo*—which literally means "foreign devils"—are primarily British, followed by Americans, Australians, Canadians, Indians, and other Asians.

The Chinese are by nature a very hard-working, pragmatic people. There are many stories of refugees who arrived with nothing in their pockets, set up a small sidewalk business, worked diligently until they had their own store, and then expanded it into a modest chain. In such a business-oriented society, success is everything and failure accounts for nothing.

People often ask me whether there is much difference between the Japanese and the Chinese. There probably couldn't be two more dissimilar peoples. While the Japanese tend to be quiet, reserved, restrained, and restricted, the Chinese are noisy, less inhibited, less orderly, and probably more gregarious. Many Japanese have told me that Hong Kong is too much for them— accustomed to orderliness, they find Hong Kong too chaotic, too confusing, and too unpredictable. And it is for exactly these reasons that I like it.

RELIGION: The practical nature of the Chinese is also evident in the role religion plays in their lives. Most Hong Kong Chinese are both Taoist and Buddhist, something they do not find incongruous. There are about 360 Chinese temples scattered throughout Hong Kong.

Whereas Buddhism is concerned with the afterlife, Taoism is a folk faith that believes in luck and in currying its favor. In Taoism gods must be worshipped and spirits appeased, and the most popular of these is Tin Hau, goddess of the sea and protectress of fishermen. There are at least 24 temples erected in her honor in Hong Kong.

Another Taoist belief is that before a house can be built, a tree chopped down, or a boulder moved, a specialist must be called in to make certain that the spirits inhabiting the place are not disturbed. In New Year celebrations, door gods are placed on the front door for good luck and all lights are switched on to ward off monster spirits. On New Year's Day, the house is not swept for fear of whisking away good luck.

THE FUTURE: As a Crown Colony governed by the British, Hong Kong has always lived very much in the present. However, with the expiration of the 99-year lease on the New Territories in 1997, the future of Hong Kong is on everyone's mind.

On July 1, 1997, Britain will transfer all of capitalist Hong Kong to Chinese Communist rule. According to the pact drawn up for the transfer, China guarantees that it will preserve Hong Kong's capitalist lifestyle and social system for at least 50 years after 1997. But whether Hong Kong nonetheless will undergo a great change once China takes over is a subject of hot debate in the Crown Colony. As Britain pulls out, many of Hong Kong's foreign community will go with her. Many Chinese who can afford to emigrate are already looking for viable new homes, with Singapore and North America high on the list. As one Hong Kong Chinese told me, his family fled China to escape Communist rule—why remain after 1997?

The vast majority of Chinese, however, will stay. They point out that Hong Kong has had a strong relationship with China for a long time and is dependent on the mainland for much of its food and even its water. China, on the other hand, has much to gain by keeping Hong Kong as it is, especially since China is opening up more and more to foreigners and seems eager to compete in the world market.

2. Getting There and Getting Around

GETTING THERE: Unless you've joined a luxury liner or are trekking across China, most likely you'll arrive in Hong Kong by plane. As described in Chapter I in the section on getting to Japan, the best thing to do if you plan to visit both Japan and Hong Kong is to purchase a ticket to Hong Kong that allows stopovers in Japan. The fares listed below are for Japan Air Lines, and all flights originating in North America stop in Japan before continuing on to Hong Kong. The fares quoted are as of August 1987 and are subject to change. Be sure to contact a travel agent or JAL once you've decided on your itinerary.

Plane Fares

If you want to travel in luxury, JAL's first-class round-trip ticket to Hong Kong is $4,326 from New York, $4,324 from Chicago, and $3,626 from Seattle, San Francisco, or Los Angeles. The normal economy, all-year round-trip fare, which allows you to travel in the private business-class cabin, is $2,466 from New York, $2,464 from Chicago, and $1,884 from airports on the West Coast. The special economy round-trip fare, which has some restrictions, is $2,246, $2,244, and $1,664 respectively.

If you're traveling on a budget, you can save money by purchasing a Super Saver ticket. Reservations, ticketing, and payment must be completed prior to departure. There is no minimum period of stay and the trip must be completed within one year. Two stopovers are permitted along the way for regular Super Saver fares, but no stopover is permitted (except at the point of turnaround) for midweek Super Saver fares. There is a 25% cancellation penalty. You should check with your travel agent for any other restrictions or changes. Rates for regular Super Saver tickets during the basic season (November 1 through May 31) are $1,197 from New York or Chicago and $969 from the West Coast. During peak season (June 1 through October 31) the rates rise to $1,308 and $1,094 respectively. Midweek (Monday through Thursday) Super Saver fares for the basic season are $1,099 from New York or Chicago and $850 from the West Coast cities, while for peak season these fares are $1,149 and $900 respectively.

Kai Tak Airport

Hong Kong's Kai Tak Airport (tel. 3-7697531) is located in densely populated Kowloon Peninsula and has one of the most spectacular runways in the world—built right out into the middle of the bay. From the airport it's about a 20- to 30-minute ride to Tsimshatsui and a 40-minute ride to Central, though during rush hours (8 to 9:30 a.m. and again from 4 to 6:30 p.m.) it can take as long as an hour.

The cheapest and one of the easiest ways to travel between the airport and Hong Kong's major hotels is by Airbus. There are three different routes, with buses traveling every 15 minutes between 7 a.m. and 11 p.m. Airbus A1 goes to Tsimshatsui and costs HK$5 (65¢), delivering passengers to such hotels as the

Ambassador, Empress, Grand, Holiday Inn Golden Mile, Hyatt Regency, Imperial, International, Kowloon, Miramar, New World, Park, Peninsula, Regent, Shangri-La, and Sheraton.

Airbus A2, which costs HK$7 (91¢), travels through Wanchai and Central before terminating at the Macau Ferry Pier, making stops at or near the Furama, Harbour, Harbour View International House, Hilton, Mandarin, New Harbour, and Victoria along the way. Airbus A3 also charges HK$7 for the trip to Causeway Bay and makes stops at the Caravelle, Excelsior, Lee Gardens, and Park Lane.

There are also **hotel shuttle buses** that pick up arriving passengers at Kai Tak and deliver them to major hotels. Fares differ depending on how far you're going, but it cost me HK$15 ($1.95) to get to Tshimshatsui.

Since these shuttle buses do not make regular and continuous rounds to hotels, you should use the Airbus or a taxi to get back to the airport. A taxi to the airport costs about HK$30 ($3.90) from Tsimshatsui and HK$45 ($5.84) to HK$55 ($7.15) from the Central District. Departure tax at the airport is HK$120 ($15.58) for adults and HK$60 ($7.79) for children aged 2 to 11.

GETTING AROUND: If you've been traveling in Japan, getting around in Hong Kong will seem like a breeze. For one thing, the streets here have names, they're written in English, and fares for public transport are generally quite low. In addition, public transportation is extensive and varied, and even the novice traveler should have no problem getting around. One thing you should keep in mind, however, is that buses and trams require the exact fare. It's therefore imperative to have a lot of loose change with you whenever you go out. Even though the ferries and subways will give change, you'll find it more convenient if you have the exact change, especially during rush hours. If you plan to do a lot of traveling by public transport, pick up a brochure called *Places of Interest by Public Transport,* available free at Hong Kong Tourist Association offices.

By Ferry

Without a doubt the ferries of the Star Ferry Company are among the most famous and celebrated boats in the world. And well they should be. Carrying passengers back and forth between Hong Kong Island and Kowloon ever since 1898, these boats have come to symbolize Hong Kong itself, and are almost always featured in travel articles on Hong Kong.

The familiar white-and-green ferries ply the waters daily from 6:30 a.m. to 11:30 p.m. between Hong Kong Island's Central District and the tip of Kowloon's Tsimshatsui, offering a seven-minute ride that is one of the best in the world, and certainly one of the cheapest. It costs only HK$.50 (6¢) for ordinary (second) class; if you really want to splurge, first class is HK$.70 (9¢). First class is on the upper deck and is a good idea if it's raining because it has glass windows surrounding it. Otherwise I find ordinary class much more colorful and entertaining because it's the one the locals use. Signs admonish passengers to watch out for pickpockets, to refrain from spitting on the deck, and to remain seated until the ferry docks.

To ride the ferry, simply drop your money into the ancient-looking turnstile, follow the crowd in front of you down the ramp, walk over the gangway, and find a seat on one of the polished wooden benches. A whistle will blow, a man will haul up the gangway, and you're off, dodging fishing boats, tugboats, and barges as you make your way across the harbor. Except for early in the morning or late at night, ferries depart every few minutes.

In addition to the Star Ferry, there are also many ferries to other parts of the colony. Ferries from the Central District, for example, also go to Kowloon's Hung Hom, where the railway station is located, and to the Yaumatei Ferry Pier, close to Jordan Road. If you want to go to one of Hong Kong's outlying islands, most ferries depart from the Outlying Islands Ferry Pier located west of Central's Star Ferry terminus. Operated by the Hong Kong Yaumatei Ferry Company (HYF), these boats vary in fares and departure times. The latest schedules and fares are available in a list compiled by the Hong Kong Tourist Association (HKTA) or by calling HYF at 5-423081. One thing to keep in mind is that on weekends the ferries are unbelievably crowded and fares often go up. It's best, therefore, to travel on a weekday.

By Tram

Another colorful way to get around is by tram, and these are found only on Hong Kong Island. Set up in 1904, these are old, narrow, double-decker affairs that clank their way slowly along the northern part of the island from Kennedy Town in the West to Shau Kei Wan in the east, with one branch making a detour to Happy Valley. Passing through the Central District, Wanchai, and Causeway Bay on Des Voeux, Queensway, and Hennessy Roads, they can't be beat for atmosphere and are easy to ride since most of them go on only one line (those branching off to Happy Valley are clearly marked).

Enter trams from the back and go immediately up the winding stairs to the top deck. Try to get a seat at the very front of the tram and from there you'll have an unparalleled view of Hong Kong: laundry hanging from second-story windows, markets down side streets, crowded sidewalks, and people darting in front of the tram who you'll swear couldn't have made it. When you've had enough, go downstairs to the front of the tram and pay the exact fare of HK$.60 (7¢) into a little tin box next to the driver as you exit. Trams run from 5:40 a.m. to 1 a.m.

By Subway

Hong Kong's Mass Transit Railway (MTR) is modern, efficient, clean, and easy to use. The only hard thing about it is trying to remain seated on its slick stainless-steel seats (you may laugh now, but wait till you've tried it). Built primarily to transport commuters to and from work, it runs under the harbor to link Hong Kong Island with Kowloon and has replaced ferries, trams, and buses as the fastest way to travel. Lines begin on Kowloon at Tsuen Wan and Kwun Tong, run down the length of Nathan Road through Tsimshatsui, go underneath the harbor, and emerge on Hong Kong Island at Admiralty. From there they either go one stop west to the Central District or go east through Wanchai and Causeway Bay to Chai Wan.

Buy your plastic credit-card-size ticket at a vending machine at the station, where signs in English will tell you how much to pay. The fare begins at HK$2 (26¢), and no change is given. If you don't have the right amount, there are change machines close by for coins and information desks for bills. As you enter the turnstile, insert your ticket into a slot and pick it up after it shoots out the other end of the turnstile. Be sure to save your ticket for the end of your journey, when you will again insert your ticket, but this time you won't get it back.

If you think you're going to be doing a lot of traveling on the MTR, then buy the **MTR Tourist Ticket**, available upon presentation of your passport at HKTA offices or at the mini-banks located in many of the subway stations. It costs HK$15 ($1.94) and gives you HK$15-worth of transportation on the subway. Used just like a regular ticket, it's valid for a year, and the computerized gate will show how much you have left on your ticket as you exit the station. Remember to collect your ticket as you leave.

The subway is in operation from 6 a.m. to 1 a.m. Also, take note that there are no public toilets at any of the stations or on the trains, and that smoking, drinking, and eating are prohibited.

By Bus

Buses are good for traveling to places where other forms of public transport don't go, such as to the southern part of Hong Kong Island or up into parts of Kowloon and the New Territories. Depending on the route, buses run from about 6 a.m. until midnight, and fares range from HK$.80 (10¢) to HK$8 ($1.04). You must have the exact fare, which you pay as you get on. Drivers often do not speak English, so you may want to have someone at your hotel write down your destination in Chinese. You can pick up leaflets indicating bus routes to some of the major tourist spots at HKTA offices.

By Minibus

These are a bit confusing for the tourist. Although the destination is written in both Chinese and English, you almost need a magnifying glass to identify the English, and by then the minibus has probably already whizzed past. There are two types of minibuses, distinguishable by color, and they both hold up to 14 persons. The green-and-yellow ones follow fixed routes, range in price from HK$1 (13¢) to HK$4 (52¢), depending on the route, and are paid for as you enter.

The red-and-yellow minibuses follow no fixed route and can be hailed from almost anywhere except in some restricted areas in the Central District. Fares begin at HK$1 (13¢) and you pay as you exit. Just yell when you want to get off.

By Taxi

As a rule taxi drivers in Hong Kong are strictly controlled and are fairly honest. If they're free to pick up passengers, a red "For Hire" flag will be raised in the windshield or at night their "Taxi" sign will be lighted on the roof. You can hail them from the street, but since most drivers do not speak English it's a good idea to have your destination written in Chinese. Taxis are generally abundant anytime except rainy days, during shift change (which is usually at 4 p.m.), and on horse-racing days.

Taxis on **Hong Kong Island and Kowloon** are red and start at a low HK$5.50 (72¢), plus HK$.70 (9¢) for each 275 yards. Waiting time is HK$.70 (9¢) for every 90 seconds, and if you go through the harbor tunnel you'll be charged an extra HK$20 ($2.59). The luggage charge is HK$2 (26¢) per piece.

Taxis in the **New Territories** are green and white, and rates begin at HK$4 (52¢) at flag fall.

If you have a complaint about a taxi driver, call the police at 5-277177, but make sure you have the taxi's license number.

By Rental Car

Rental cars are not advisable in Hong Kong. For one thing, nothing is so far away that you can't get there easily and quickly by taxi or public transport. In addition, there will probably be no place to park once you get there. If you want a chauffeur-driven car, many of the major hotels have their own private fleet you can hire. But if you are still determined to rent, the familiar self-drive firms have branches here—**Avis**, **Budget**, and **Hertz**—along with a couple of dozen local firms. A valid overseas driver's license is required.

By Train

There's only one train line in Hong Kong and it goes from Hung Hom in East Tsimshatsui in Kowloon up to Sheung Shui in the New Territories. That is, Sheung Shui is where you have to get off if you don't have a visa to go any farther into China; if you do have a visa you can continue to the border, change trains, and travel into the mainland. Known as the Kowloon–Canton Railway, it passes through Mongkok, Kowloon Tong, Tai Wai, Shatin, Fo Tan, University, Tai Po Market, and Fanling before reaching Sheung Shui. The whole journey takes about a half hour on Hong Kong's new electric trains and costs HK$5.20 (68¢) one way for ordinary (second) class and HK$10.40 ($1.35) for first class.

By Rickshaw

Once the most common form of transport in the colony, rickshaws are almost a thing of the past—no new licenses are being issued. A few ancient-looking men hang around the Star Ferry terminal in the Central District, but usually they're either snoozing or reading the paper. I've never once seen them hauling a customer. They'll charge you about HK$50 ($6.49) to take you around the block, clearly the most expensive form of transportation in Hong Kong, and by the look of them that's about as far as they can go. Probably the most humane thing you can do is take their picture—they'll charge you about HK$10 ($1.30) to HK$20 ($2.60) just for that. If you still want to take a ride, be sure to settle the price before climbing in.

3. Accommodations

For many years hotel managers in Hong Kong were in the enviable position of having too many guests and not enough rooms to accommodate them. Because of this high demand and low supply, prices for hotel rooms skyrocketed a few years back, with many hotels raising their room rates as much as 20% each year. A surplus in visitors to Hong Kong also led to a flurry of new hotel projects. In December 1985, the Hong Kong Tourist Association reported a total of 18,180 hotel rooms in the colony. By the end of 1989, when the last of the new hotels has been completed, this figure will have risen to an astounding 27,948.

Luckily for tourists, this mushrooming of new hotels has caused fierce competition among the existing hotels. Room rates have stabilized, first-class hotels are offering all kinds of incentives, and medium-priced hotels are all remodeling and upgrading their facilities. Admittedly, the price of hotel rooms in Hong Kong is not inexpensive and can be compared to hotel prices of major cities around the world. On the brighter side, however, dining and shopping in Hong Kong remain very much a bargain.

The biggest hotel crunches occur twice a year, from March to early June and again from October to early December. If you plan to travel during these months, you'd be wise to reserve your room at least two months in advance. You should also know that some hotels, especially those in the medium- and budget-price ranges, raise their rates during peak season. If you're traveling off-season, it doesn't hurt to bargain for a cheaper rate, or at the very least to ask whether you can be upgraded to a better room.

Generally speaking, the price of a room in Hong Kong is governed not only by the season but also by the view and location. Not surprisingly, rooms with a view of the famous Victoria Harbour are the most expensive, as well as those on higher floors. In contrast to Japan, room size often has little to do with price, and rooms here are much larger than they are in Japan. You should also note that prices listed in this section are for *room rates only*—with the exception of some of the budget hotels, a 10% service charge and 5% government tax will be added to your hotel bill.

Most of the hotels I am including in this section are members of the Hong Kong Hotel Association (HKHA). All of Hong Kong's deluxe and upper-range hotels are members of this organization, as well as the best of the medium range. The benefit of staying in one of these hotels is that if you have a complaint, you can lodge it directly with the Hong Kong Tourist Association. In addition, the HKHA maintains a counter at Kai Tak Airport where you can reserve a room in one of its member hotels at no extra charge. Incidentally, new hotels opening in the latter half of 1988 include the Ramada Renaissance in Kowloon, the Grand Hyatt in Wanchai, and the Marriot Hotel on Queensway. Since room rates were unavailable at the time this book went to press, consult a travel agency or contact the Hong Kong Tourist Association if you're interested in staying in one of these new hotels.

Realizing that HKHA hotels are among the first to fill up during peak season, I am also including what I consider to be a few good alternatives in the budget range, as well as some rock-bottom recommendations. Unless otherwise specified, all rooms in the deluxe through budget categories are air-conditioned and come with private bath.

KOWLOON: Kowloon Peninsula, including its tip, known as Tsimshatsui, has the greatest concentration of hotels in Hong Kong. Many travelers prefer to stay in this area because it abounds in shops of all kinds, restaurants, and nightlife. In any case, Hong Kong Island is just across the harbor, a short subway or ferry ride away. Unless a subway station or bus route is given, you can assume that the hotels listed below are within walking distance of the Star Ferry and Tsimshatsui MTR station.

The Deluxe Hotels

The Peninsula, Salisbury Road (tel. 3-666251), is to Hong Kong what Raffles is to Singapore. An imposing and grand edifice facing Victoria Harbour, the Peninsula has remained Hong Kong's most famous and most elegant hotel ever since it was built back in 1928, and it exudes more of a colonial atmosphere than any other hotel in Hong Kong. This is where you should stay if you are an incurable romantic, have a penchant for the historical, and have enough money to afford its high prices. The hotel prides itself on service, and room attendants will even draw your bath if you ask them. All rooms were renovated in 1987.

Rooms for both single and double occupancy range from HK$1,480 ($192) to HK$2,150 ($279), with the higher rate charged for rooms with a harbor view. Sadly enough, however, that view has all but disappeared with the construction of the Space Museum on reclaimed land across the street. That's progress Hong Kong style, but the Peninsula is worth a visit even if you don't stay here. Lobby-sitting at the Peninsula has always been high on the list of things to do in Hong Kong, so put on your finest and go for a cup of coffee in a lobby reminiscent of a Parisian palace with high gilded ceilings, pillars, and ferns. The Peninsula is also famous for its restaurant, Gaddi's, described in the dining section.

The Regent, Salisbury Road (tel. 3-7211211), has replaced the Peninsula as the deluxe hotel with the best view of the water. In fact, you can't get much closer to the water than at the Regent—the hotel is located on a projection of land and sits on more than 120 pylons sunk into the harbor. Built in 1981 on reclaimed land, 70% of the hotel's 585 rooms command sweeping views of the harbor, and all come with sunken bathtubs, separate rooms for both shower and toilet, three phones, and a butler for every six rooms.

Special features of the hotel include a magnificent free-standing staircase of white Carrara marble, a large outdoor heated swimming pool, and lobby and restaurants with great views of the harbor. Although the Regent is a relative newcomer, already 52% of the people staying here are repeat guests, which speaks highly of the hotel's service and facilities. Rates here, the same for single or double occupancy, begin at HK$1,160 ($151). Rooms with a view of the harbor begin at HK$1,600 ($208).

Shangri-La, 64 Mody Rd., East Tsimshatsui (tel. 3-7212111), is a deluxe hotel designed for business travelers, who make up 85% of the hotel's guests. A Westin hotel, it is situated on the waterfront of East Tsimshatsui and features large and luxuriously appointed rooms with ceiling-to-floor bay windows overlooking the harbor, a health club with free use of the swimming pool and whirlpool, an executive business center with secretarial services, and five superb restaurants. The hotel also has a nonsmoking floor, where even the room attendants are nonsmokers. Service throughout the hotel is discreet and excellent. Rooms here begin at HK$1,125 ($146) for a single and HK$1,225 ($159) for a double, increasing to HK$1,925 ($250) and HK$2,025 ($263) respectively for rooms with harbor views.

The Upper Bracket

Located on Nathan Road only a five-minute walk from the Star Ferry and a one-minute walk from the Tsimshatsui subway station, the **Hyatt Regency Hong Kong**, 67 Nathan Rd. (tel. 3-662321), was established in 1969 as Hyatt's first property in Asia. All 728 of its rooms were renovated in 1985–1986 and feature colors of apricot and celadon with natural teakwood furniture. Hints of local culture are represented with a lacquered Chinese chest housing a television and Chinese brush paintings on the walls. Special features of the new rooms include double-glazed windows and insulated walls to reduce outside noise, mini-bars, telephones in the bathroom and at the bedside with an extra plug-in socket at the desk, and in all rooms safe-deposit boxes large enough for a briefcase. Bathrooms, designed with Italian marble, all come equipped with hair dryers. The hotel boasts five food-and-beverage outlets, including the original Hugo's, and a fortune teller in the lobby who will read your palm between noon and 6 p.m. every day except Sunday—if you've always wanted to have your palm read, this is the place to do it. A single room here starts at HK$800 ($104), while doubles and twins begin at HK$870 ($113).

The **Royal Garden**, 69 Mody Rd., East Tsimshatsui (tel. 3-7215215), is a small hotel with a lot of architectural surprises. The middle of the lobby looks down on an open area of fountains and water, while from the 3rd to the 15th floors an open atrium reaches up to the ceiling. Plants hang down from balconies ringing the atrium, glass-enclosed elevators glide up the wall, a piano sits on an island in the middle of a pool, and the sound of rushing water adds a freshness and coolness.

With only 433 rooms, the Royal Garden is one of the best choices in this category, but is also one of the most expensive. Its rooms, which begin at HK$850 ($110) for a standard single or a double and rise to HK$1,290 ($168) for a room with a partial harbor view, are decorated in an Oriental theme with Chinese furniture and dark russet colors. (In case you're wondering, "a partial harbor view" means either that other buildings are obstructing part of your view or that your windows do not squarely face the water.) Facilities at the hotel include both Chinese and Western restaurants and a disco that charges HK$77 ($10) on weekdays and HK$99 ($12.86) on weekends.

One of East Tsimshatsui's newest hotels is the **Hotel Nikko**, 72 Mody Rd. (tel. 3-7391111), which opened at the end of 1986. Affiliated with Japan Air Lines, it features 461 rooms and suites decorated with furniture carved from American maple and with either Japanese works of art or Dutch maps of the Far East. An electronic bedside panel enables guests to set the alarm clock, control the television, and open or shut the curtains. Bathrooms, finished in black-veined white Italian Carrera marble, come equipped with separate bathtubs and showers, hair dryers, and bathrobes and cotton kimonos.

Rates for single occupancy start at HK$930 ($121), with HK$1,500 ($195) charged for rooms with a view of the harbor. Double occupancy is an extra HK$100 ($13) added to the rates above. Restaurants serve Chinese, Japanese, and French cuisine, while the Sky Lounge on the fifteenth floor offers drinks, dancing, and a view of Hong Kong's lights.

The **Sheraton Hong Kong Hotel**, 20 Nathan Rd. (tel. 3-691111), is an attractive hotel situated on the waterfront at the corner of Nathan and Salisbury Roads—certainly one of the choicest spots on Kowloon Peninsula. Its rooms are tastefully decorated in bright earth tones and come with the usual radio, fridge, and color TV. Although single rooms are available, they are small and face an inner courtyard. A rooftop swimming pool, heated in winter, is free to hotel guests. There's also a health club. Rooms here start at HK$820 ($107) for a single and HK$1,130 ($147) for a double, with HK$1,260 ($164) and HK$1,350 ($175) charged respectively for rooms with a harbor view. If you feel like splurging, rooms on the 16th- and 17th- floors are known as the Sheraton Towers and include such extras as complimentary continental breakfast, evening cocktails, personalized stationery, and their own check-in lounge. Rates for these rooms begin at HK$990 ($129) for a single and HK$1,400 ($182) for a double, with harbor views costing HK$1,550 ($201) and HK$1,600 ($208) respectively.

Holiday Inn Harbour View, 70 Mody Rd., East Tsimshatsui (tel. 3-7215161), is one of the farthest of a string of hotels that stretches from the Star Ferry through East Tsimshatsui. Because it's close to Hong Kong's coliseum, a number of stars have stayed here, including David Bowie, Elton John, and John McEnroe. Its rooms are comfortable and cheerful, although the least expensive ones, which begin at HK$950 ($123) for one person and HK$1,040 ($135) for two, have windows that open rather unceremoniously onto a facing windowless wall. Those with a harbor view start at HK$1,320 ($171) for a single and HK$1,400 ($182) for a double. Some of the rooms come equipped with sofa beds in consideration of female executives who might feel uncomfortable about hosting a business meeting in a hotel room. A plus in this hotel is its rooftop swimming pool.

Another member of this chain in Hong Kong is the **Holiday Inn Golden Mile**, 50 Nathan Rd. (tel. 3-69311), named after the so-called Golden Mile of shopping on Nathan Road. Very clean and decorated with modern furnishings, the rooms start at HK$700 ($91) for single or double occupancy. Within the hotel complex are three floors of shopping arcades, a rooftop swimming pool, restaurants, bars, and a delicatessen. The hotel lobby is used as a departure point for a number of tours throughout the colony, which means that it's convenient if you want to join tours during your stay but rather noisy and bothersome if you don't.

The **Hotel Regal Meridien**, 71 Mody Rd. (tel. 3-7221818), is a French-owned hotel that does a good job of blending the East and the West. In the lobby and elsewhere in the hotel, 18th- century French antiques and Louis XV–style furniture stand alongside Chinese works of art. Its 589 rooms, all sound-proof and containing two phones, a mini-bar, color TV, clock, and radio, are variations of soft pastels of peach and celadon green. A French restaurant and a brasserie are among the eating establishments in the hotel. Room rates start at HK$1,030 ($134) for a single and HK$1,090 ($142) for a double, but these rooms have no view at all, since they face another building. Deluxe rooms, some of which have a partial harbor view, go for HK$1,250 ($162) for a single and HK$1,300 ($169) for a double.

The **Hongkong Hotel**, 3 Canton Rd. (tel. 3-676011), is the closest hotel to the Star Ferry. A member of the Marco Polo International group of hotels, it's connected to three shopping centers by air-conditioned walkways and sports an outdoor pool, 14 restaurants and bars, and 790 guest rooms. Its marbled lobby is spacious and comfortable and its rooms combine both Western and Eastern decor in muted colors. Rooms without a harbor view start at HK$600 ($78) for single occupancy and HK$910 ($118) for double. The deluxe room, which offers a partial view of the harbor that is better if you get a room on a higher floor, is HK$1,040 ($135) for a single and HK$1,100 ($143) for a double. A full harbor view here will cost HK$1,320 ($171) and offers a great look at harbor activity, including the ocean liners that sometimes dock right next door.

The **Marco Polo**, Harbour City, Canton Road (tel. 3-7215111), offers no views from its windows, but it's a comfortable hotel located in the middle of the Harbour City shopping complex, a shopping mall of 600 shops and boutiques not far from the Star Ferry. It caters mainly to business travelers, so the rooms feature desks with a large work space, stocked refrigerators, and large bath-rooms. With a friendly and efficient staff, this hotel prices its rooms according to location and noise level—those that face Canton Road tend to be somewhat noisier. Rates start at HK$640 ($83) for singles and HK$690 ($90) for doubles for rooms on the lower floors and go to HK$990 ($129) for deluxe twins at the top. There is no swimming pool in the hotel itself, but since it's part of the Marco Polo group of hotels guests are free to use the pool at the nearby Hongkong Hotel.

Another Marco Polo International hotel, the **Prince Hotel**, Harbour City, Canton Road (tel. 3-7227333), is also located in the huge Harbour City shopping complex. It's a small hotel with a gleaming white marble lobby, and its 402 rooms all feature queen-size beds, even in the twin rooms. The economy rooms, which cost HK$640 ($83) for single occupancy and HK$690 ($90) for double, are on the lower floors. Superior rooms are higher up and therefore quieter, and go for HK$860 ($112) single and HK$910 ($118) double; a few of these rooms even give minute glimpses of the harbor at no extra cost, so ask for the highest room with a view. As with the Marco Polo, guests wishing to swim will have to go to the sister Hongkong Hotel.

Farther up Nathan Road across from Kowloon Park is the **Hotel Miramar**, 130 Nathan Rd. (tel. 3-681111). It's strategically located in the midst of a shop-ping area, including the relatively new Park Lane shopping arcades. An older hotel once known for its showy exterior and flashy gold-colored decor, it has joined the recent trend in renovating and updating its facilities and guest rooms, a process that will take several years. Catering primarily to group tourists from Japan and mainland China, it charges HK$680 ($88) to HK$1,010 ($131) for singles and HK$750 ($97) to HK$1,080 ($140) for twins.

If you have only one or two nights to spend in Hong Kong and you'd rather stay close to the airport, the **Regal Meridien Airport Hotel**, San Po Road, Kowloon (tel. 3-7180333), is as close as you can get. Linked directly to the airport by an air-conditioned conveyor-belt walkway, this hotel features rooms with soundproof windows and TV screens with flight information. A free shuttle-bus service transports guests to the Star Ferry about every half hour. Rates are the same for single or double occupancy and range from HK$770 ($100) to HK$990 ($129).

The Medium Bracket

Opened in 1986 and under the same management as the Peninsula Hotel, **Kowloon Hotel**, 19-21 Nathan Rd. (tel. 3-698698), is a modern, glass-walled structure situated right behind the older edifice of the Peninsula. Although its 742 rooms are fairly small, they're built at such an angle that their V-shaped bay windows allow unobstructed views up and down the street. Conceived with the business executive in mind, the hotel features what it calls a "Telecenter" in each room, which is a combination television and computer. Equipped with a simplified keyboard, it allows access to pages of computerized information files, including airline telephone numbers, the weather report, and tourist sightseeing information. At the touch of a button, guests can also call up any messages they may have received as well as their hotel bills. Single occupancy begins at HK$560 ($73), doubles are HK$590 ($77), and twins are HK$640 ($83). Rooms on the top floors are high enough to offer views of the harbor and cost HK$640 ($83) for a single and HK$690 ($90) for a double.

Another new hotel is the **Guangdong Hotel**, 18 Prat Ave. (tel. 3-7393311), located about a ten-minute walk from the Star Ferry. Its rooms are pleasant and clean, with rates based on size. If you want to be away from the din of traffic, ask for a room on a higher floor. Its marbled lobby is spacious and bare, reflecting the latest look in Hong Kong's hotels. Singles here range from HK$460 ($60) to HK$570 ($74), while twins range from HK$490 ($64) to HK$600 ($78). Restaurants serve Japanese and Chinese food.

The **New World Hotel**, 22 Salisbury Rd. (tel. 3-6941111), is a 740-room hotel that is part of the New World complex, which includes more than 400 shops and boutiques. But even though it's situated in a prime location right on the waterfront, not one of its rooms faces the harbor. Resembling a Japanese business hotel with economy rooms not much larger than its beds, the New World is modern, clean, and functional, and is conveniently located. Facilities include an outdoor swimming pool, restaurants and cocktail lounges, and Faces, a popular disco in Tsimshatsui. The smallest rooms cost HK$580 ($75) for a single and HK$630 ($82) for a double during peak season, falling to HK$500 ($65) and HK$550 ($71) respectively off-season. The hotel's larger standard rooms go for HK$910 ($118) for a single and HK$960 ($125) for a double, with bargain rates of HK$790 ($103) and HK$840 ($109) respectively off-season.

The **Ambassador**, 4 Middle Rd. (tel. 3-666321), has a great location between the Sheraton and Holiday Inn hotels on Nathan Road and is a good choice in this category. Its rooms are bright, cheerful, and roomy, and come with the usual color TV, fridge, phone, radio, and desk. The staff is young and friendly, and dim sum are served daily in one of its restaurants. Its cheaper rooms, which range from HK$570 ($74) to HK$710 ($92) for single occupancy and HK$690 ($90) to HK$840 ($109) for double, all face the back of the hotel and are priced according to which floor you're on, with higher rates charged for the higher floors. However, since the windows are glazed and you can't see out, the discrepancy in price doesn't make much sense. The only difference may be in the level of traffic noise. Rooms that face towards the front of the hotel are larger and have views of Nathan Road, with HK$780 ($101) charged for single occupancy and HK$910 ($118) for double.

Almost right next door to the Ambassador is the **Imperial Hotel**, 30-34 Nathan Rd. (tel. 3-662201). Conveniently located, its rooms are simple but come with radio, fridge, phone, color TV, desk, and large bathrooms. Economy rooms, which cost HK$330 ($43) for a single and HK$370 ($48) for a twin or double, face the back side of Chungking Mansion, notorious for its cheap and often uninviting rooms. Although the view is not what you'd call stunning, it is enlightening, with laundry strung everywhere and garbage piled up below, apparently tossed unconcernedly from the windows up above. If that doesn't appeal to your sense of adventure, some of the standard rooms face Nathan Road and begin at HK$460 ($60) for a single and HK$500 ($65) for a double or twin. Since some standards also face Chungking Mansion, be sure to ask if it's important to you. Be aware, however, that rooms that face the road get the brunt of the traffic noise below. Rooms high enough to offer a view of the harbor are HK$800 ($104) for a single and HK$825 ($107) for a double or twin.

Although located a good 20-minute hike from the Star Ferry, the **Ritz Hotel**, 122 Austin Rd. (tel. 3-692282), is one of the best choices among hotels of comparable price. In 1984 it became one of the first medium-range hotels to renovate its rooms with modern facilities in both rooms and bathrooms, setting an example for other hotels that have since followed suit in the face of stiff competition. With only 60 rooms, the Ritz is small and personable and is a favorite with visiting businessmen from Japan and France. In fact, it's such a popular choice with a high number of repeat guests that it's almost mandatory to reserve a room here at least two weeks in advance during peak season. Off-season rates start at HK$280 ($36) for a single and HK$350 ($45) for a double, rising to HK$390 ($51) and HK$460 ($60) respectively during peak season. The closest MTR subway station is Jordan Station, about two minutes away.

Built in the early 1960s, the **Park Hotel**, 61-65 Chatham Rd. South (tel. 3-661371), is one of the best-known medium-priced hotels on Kowloon. Especially popular with Australians, it has what are probably the largest rooms in this category, certainly a plus if you're tired of cramped quarters. What's more, all guest rooms received a much-needed face-lift in 1987 so that now it doesn't even look like the same hotel. Future plans call for complete remodeling of the lobby. A comfortable and clean hotel, you can't go wrong staying here. Singles range from HK$550 ($71) to HK$880 ($114), and twins run HK$660 ($86) to HK$990 ($129).

The **Grand Hotel**, 14 Carnarvon Rd. (tel. 3-669331), is another older hotel built in the early '60s with rooms refurbished in 1985. Guest rooms come with a mini-bar, digital clock, radio, and color TV and are bright and cheerful. Located in the heart of Tsimshatsui off Nathan Road, this hotel serves a popular lunch buffet for HK$85 ($11.04) from noon to 3 p.m. and a dinner buffet for HK$108 ($14) from 6 to 10:30 p.m. Depending on the size and location of the room, a person traveling alone will pay from HK$460 ($60) to HK$790 ($103) for accommodation, while two people can expect to spend HK$520 ($67) to HK$850 ($110). Triples are available for HK$990 ($129).

Located at the corner of Chatham and Mody Roads about a ten-minute walk from the Star Ferry, the **Empress Hotel**, 17-19 Chatham Rd. (tel. 3-660211), is a 189-room property which is slowly being renovated. An older hotel, it boasts a good location and a personable staff. Its deluxe rooms are a good bargain at HK$800 ($104) for single occupancy and HK$880 ($114) for double; they feature a large balcony with glass sliding doors and a view of the harbor. Otherwise, rooms begin at HK$550 ($71) for a single and HK$600 ($78) for a twin. Incidentally, if you want to sit outside on the deluxe room balcony, you can request outdoor chairs from housekeeping.

Farther up Nathan Road a few blocks past the Jordan subway station is the **Hotel Fortuna**, 355 Nathan Rd. (tel. 3-851011), where 24 single rooms are available for HK$410 ($53). Although they're nicely furnished, some people may find them too claustrophobic because they don't have windows. Much larger rooms with windows are available beginning at HK$520 ($67) for single occupancy and HK$570 ($74) for double. The corridors here tend to be dark because of a dark-wood paneling, but there's a counter on every floor staffed by a floor attendant. The staff here is friendly and helpful, and the hotel caters largely to group tours from Southeast Asia.

Located close to the Jordan subway station, the **Shamrock Hotel**, 223 Nathan Rd. (tel. 3-675786), is an older hotel built in the early 1950s that caters mainly to visitors from Asia. It's a pioneer member of the HKHA. The most remarkable thing about this hotel is its lobby—although small, the ceiling is covered with about two dozen chandeliers and lights of all different designs. You don't have to worry about darkness here. Guest rooms are rather small, but high ceilings give them a bit more feeling of spaciousness. Singles begin at HK$290 ($38), doubles at HK$350 ($45), and twins at HK$370 ($48).

Off Nathan Road on a quiet side street not far from the Shamrock, the 70-room **Bangkok Royal Hotel**, 2-12 Pilkem St. (tel. 3-679181), not surprisingly considering its name, has a popular Thai restaurant. The only drawback to this hotel is that its bathrooms are quite small and its sinks minute. In an attempt to upgrade itself, however, rooms are slowly being renovated. During peak season, singles range from HK$300 ($39) to HK$340 ($44) and doubles from HK$370 ($48) to HK$460 ($60), with the higher rates charged for renovated rooms. Off-season rates start at HK$280 ($36) for a single and HK$300 ($39) for a double.

The **International Hotel**, 33 Cameron Rd. (tel. 3-663381), is more than 35 years old and looks it. Someone loves orange here, for that's the color of the rooms. However, the hotel is well located—only 15 minutes or so away from the Star Ferry—and the size of its rooms are adequate. Only international guests are accepted at the International, and all rooms come with the usual color TV, radio, phone, and desk, but there's no fridge. Some of the double rooms even have balconies, although the view is nothing to write home about. Rooms that face towards the back of the hotel have glazed windows. Depending on the season and the size of the room, single rates range from HK$280 ($36) to HK$560 ($73) and double rates run HK$380 ($49) to HK$740 ($96).

Although not a member of HKHA, **Jade Hotel**, 23 Cameron Rd. (tel. 3-697491), is conveniently located in the middle of Tsimshatsui and is worth a try if other hotels are full. The wallpaper, shag carpeting, and rattan furniture are a bit old, but the prices are reasonable: HK$250 ($32) to HK$290 ($38) for a single, HK$270 ($35) for a double, and HK$290 ($38) to HK$330 ($43) for a twin. Prices are slightly lower off-season.

Located close to Hotel Fortuna north of the Jordan subway station, **Nathan Hotel**, 378 Nathan Rd. (tel. 3-885141), is popular with Southeast Asians. Its furniture is a bit old and there's nothing remarkable about the rooms, but they're large and come with everything you need, including color TV and mini-bar. Singles rent for HK$330 ($43) to HK$410 ($53) and doubles go for HK$400 ($52) to HK$590 ($77).

The Budget Category

The overwhelmingly number-one choice in this category is the **YMCA** on Salisbury Road (tel. 3-692211), which has the good fortune of being right next door to the Peninsula on the waterfront. Not surprisingly, it's almost always full, although 132 additional rooms were added in 1987. To be safe it's a good idea to book a room here two or three months in advance. Families and women are welcome. Facilities include a swimming pool, Jacuzzi, gymnasium, sauna, tennis courts, and a rooftop garden where you can sit outside and look out over the harbor.

The best rooms, in my opinion, are the 14 twins in the old wing that have a balcony overlooking the harbor, although they don't come with private bath or toilet. These go for HK$240 ($31). Rooms without balcony or private bathroom in the old wing are HK$180 ($23) for a single and HK$200 ($26) for a twin. Rooms in the new wing are more modern and have the comforts of a private bathroom, carpeting, and color TV. There are no singles here, but twins are HK$330 ($43). Ask for a room on one of the top floors, where the view is better. Dormitory beds, which you can't book in advance and are available only on a first-come, first-served basis, cost HK$65 ($8.44) per night. All these rates include service charge, and there is no tax.

Caritas Bianchi Lodge, 4 Cliff Rd., Yaumati (tel. 3-881111), is another good choice in this price range. Although it's a bit far from the Star Ferry, it's close to the Yaumatei subway station and is located next to the Salvation Army. Its 90 rooms come with mini-bar, color TV, phone, and a private bath, and most rooms face a cliff with a few trees, certainly a more pleasant view than most hotels can boast. Try to get a room on a higher floor. Rates here are HK$240 ($31) for a single, HK$330 ($43) for a double or twin, and HK$400 ($52) for a triple.

Fuji Hotel, 140-142 Austin Rd. (tel. 3-678111), has 60 rooms with bath, color TV, and phone, and is not a member of HKHA. A bit run-down, it caters mainly to a younger Asian crowd, including many Japanese, and has a young staff as well. Only those rooms facing the front street have a window, and although they are certainly brighter, they are also much noisier. Single rooms here cost HK$300 ($39), while doubles are HK$330 ($43). Twin rooms are slightly larger and go for HK$360 ($47). This hotel has a variety of different rooms, so if you don't like the one you're shown, ask to see another one. The nearest subway station is Jordan Station.

Located near the Yaumatei subway station, **King's Hotel**, 473 Nathan Rd. (tel. 3-7801281), is just a basic hotel with no frills, its rooms supplied with color TV, stocked fridge, phone, and bath. It caters primarily to Asians, including mainland Chinese, and has a good Thai restaurant. Singles begin at HK$230 ($30) and twins at HK$250 ($32).

The **YMCA International House**, 23 Waterloo Rd. (tel. 3-7719111), is near the Yaumatei subway station and accepts both males and females. It seems to appeal more to Asians (most Westerners seem to opt for the YMCA on Salisbury Road). All rooms come with air conditioning and private bathroom, costing HK$325 ($42) for a single and HK$360 ($47) for a double.

Inconveniently located but with reasonable prices, the **YWCA Guest House**, 5 Man Fuk Rd., Waterloo Hill (tel. 3-7139211), can be reached by bus 8 from the Star Ferry. Both men and women are welcome, and all rooms are air-conditioned. Singles without private bathroom are HK$145 ($19), while those with are HK$266 ($35). Double rooms are HK$300 ($39). The fourth floor has a pleasant roof garden where you can sit outside from 9 a.m. to 5 p.m.

Rock-Bottom Choices

Getting down to the rock-bottom choices, most notorious is **Chungking Mansion**, which occupies a prime spot at 40 Nathan Rd. between the Holiday Inn and the Imperial Hotel. Actually a huge and meandering concrete high-rise rather than one single hotel, Chungking Mansion consists of an extensive and cheap shopping arcade on the ground floor and a variety of eating and sleeping establishments on the many floors above, a majority of which seem to be owned by Indians living in Hong Kong. A couple of the so-called hotels are passable; most are not.

I stayed in Chungking Mansion on my first trip to Hong Kong a few years back, living in a neon-colored cell that contained only two sagging beds, a night table, and a closet. In the shared bathroom down the hall lived the biggest spider I have ever seen, a hairy thing that nevertheless behaved itself quite well whenever I was there—it never moved an inch the whole time I took a shower, but when I returned the next night it was always motionless in another part of the room. I figured it survived only by being unobtrusive and I wouldn't be surprised if it's still there. I shared my room with another woman and we paid about $5 (U.S.) each.

These are the kinds of places that have made Chungking notorious, but luckily not all are quite as colorful as where I stayed (too bad I didn't have this book). Most well-known in the building is **Chungking House** (tel. 3-665362), on the fourth and fifth floors of A Block (Chungking Mansion is divided into sections A through E, each with its own elevator). It's the only one in the building that's a member of HKHA, and all rooms here have private bath, air conditioning, phone, and radio, and some even have a TV. It's a bit dreary, but prices are reasonable. Often fully booked, rooms here start at HK$140 ($18) in a single and HK$190 ($25) in a double.

On the 13th floor of B Block is the **New Washington Guest House** (tel. 3-665798), which has ten rooms and has been in operation for more than 20 years. Rooms are simple and clean, but none have private bathrooms. The cheapest rooms go for HK$55 ($7) and come with TV and fan, while air-conditioned rooms are priced at HK$88 ($11). This establishment is one of the best in its price category.

New Asia Guest House (tel. 3-7240426) is located on the eighth floor of A Block and offers a variety of rooms ranging from HK$88 ($11) to HK$165 ($21), most with private bathroom and air conditioning. Rooms are clean and the owners are friendly.

Not quite up to the standards of the above establishments, **Capital Guest House** on the 13th floor of A Block (tel. 3-663455) is worth a try if the other places are full. All seven rooms here have air conditioning and TV, and some have private bathroom as well. Be sure to take a look at what's available, since some rooms are brighter than others. Rates here range from HK$75 ($10) to HK$165 ($21).

Popular with the backpacking crowd, the **Traveller's Hostel** is on the 16th floor of A Block (tel. 3-682505) at Chungking Mansion. A dormitory bunkbed costs HK$24 ($3.12), singles go for HK$75 ($10), and doubles run HK$90 ($12). Toilets and showers are shared and there's a canteen selling breakfast for HK$9 ($1.15) and sandwiches for HK$5.50 (75¢). It's basic, but the fact that it's so high up and has so many windows means that it's bright and sunny. Perhaps the main drawback is that it's a bit messy, with everyone's belongings strewn everywhere. On the other hand, it's a good place to stay if you want to meet other travelers, and there's even a travel service here that specializes in arranging trips to China.

If staying in Chungking Mansion doesn't appeal to you, another option is the **Hong Kong Hostel**, which offers 18 dormitory beds for only HK$25 ($3.25) a night. Located on the 11th floor at 230 Nathan Rd. (tel. 3-678925), its two rooms of crowded bunk beds don't leave much room for personal belongings, but there's a small locker for valuables. Mostly Europeans, North Americans, and Australians stay here, and there's a kitchen for cooking and a small table for eating and socializing. This place is located near Jordan MTR subway station.

One other rock-bottom place worth mentioning is the **International Youth Accommodation Centre**, on the sixth floor at 21A Lock Rd. (tel. 3-663419), behind the Hyatt Regency. Not for the squeamish, it's a chaotic but mellow place with backpacks, belongings, and unidentifiable objects strewn all over the place. It certainly could be cleaner, but people who have stayed here swear that it has the best atmosphere in town. Of course, it should be mentioned that these are long-term travelers, mostly Europeans, who have been roughing it for who knows how many years. There are 26 bunkbeds here that rent for HK$26 ($3.40) a night.

WANCHAI/CAUSEWAY BAY: If the thought of jostling elbows with other tourists in Kowloon in an area that is obviously tourist-oriented does not appeal to you, then consider staying in a hotel across the harbor in Wanchai or Causeway Bay on Hong Kong Island. This is where the locals themselves come to shop and to eat. Prices are lower, and the area has much more of a Chinese feel to it. Although redevelopment is slowly gobbling up old neighborhoods here too, there are still old buildings, side streets with markets, street vendors, and narrow, winding roads.

The Upper Bracket

The **Excelsior**, Causeway Bay (tel. 5-767365), is the most exclusive hotel in the area. A Mandarin Oriental Associate hotel, it sits on the waterfront with a view of the Hong Kong Yacht Club and Kowloon across the harbor. Although it doesn't have a swimming pool, it has rooftop tennis courts and seven restaurants and bars, including the comfortable Dickens Bar and the Talk of the Town disco. All rooms are the same size with the same decor, but those with a harbor view are more expensive.

Comfortably decorated with small sofas in front of the windows, a large desk area, and a black-and-white tiled bathroom, each room costs the same regardless of single or double occupancy, starting at HK$880 ($114). Deluxe rooms, which have partial harbor views, cost HK$1,200 ($156). The best of these face the Central District and Victoria Peak. If you want a full harbor view, expect to pay HK$1,370 ($178).

Park Lane Radisson Hotel (formerly called the Park Lane Hotel), 310 Gloucester Rd., Causeway Bay (tel. 5-7901021), is affiliated with Japan Air Lines and is popular with visiting groups from Japan. All rooms have recently been renovated and feature marble tabletops and marble bathrooms. Room rates, which vary according to location (the lower floors are cheapest), begin at HK$930 ($121) for both single and double occupancy. If you feel like splurging, the hotel's deluxe rooms, which go for HK$1,200 ($156), are located on the top floors and have views of either the harbor or Victoria Park.

Another hotel that caters mostly to Japanese groups is **Lee Gardens**, Hysan Avenue, Causeway Bay (tel. 5-8953311), located inland a bit. The prices of its rooms are based on size, decor, and floor number rather than view. Decorated on a South Pacific theme with bamboo furniture and soothing colors of beige and bisque, the rooms are pleasant and bright, and run HK$700 ($91) to HK$1,000 ($130) for single or double occupancy. Restaurants in the hotel serve Chinese, Korean, Japanese, and Western food, and a shuttle bus transports guests to the Central District.

The Medium-Priced Bracket

Totally renovated and reopened in 1986 under a new name, **Hotel New Harbour**, 41-49 Hennessy Rd. (tel. 5-8611166), is a pleasant hotel catering largely to Japanese businessmen. Although located on a busy street in the heart of Wanchai, rooms are quiet and come with stocked refrigerator, TV, and direct-dial telephone service. Rates are based on both room size and height, with the cheapest singles going for HK$380 ($49) and doubles for HK$450 ($58). Deluxe rooms are on the 18th floor, and some of these offer glimpses of the harbor at a price of HK$580 ($75) for single occupancy and HK$650 ($84) for double.

The **New Hong Kong Cathay Hotel**, 17 Tung Lo Wan Rd., Causeway Bay (tel. 5-778211), is a 142-room hotel built in 1967 and catering mainly to visitors from Southeast Asia. Rooms are large, bright, and modestly furnished with the basics of color TV, stocked refrigerators, and large desks. Rates begin at HK$340 ($44) for single occupancy and HK$380 ($49) for double. By far the best rooms here are those on the tenth floor—they come with large balconies that are great for looking out on the city below. Since decor and carpeting at this hotel are rather old, the management plans to start a gradual renovation—after which rates will rise. It might be prudent to check prices beforehand.

Harbour Hotel, 116-122 Gloucester Rd. (tel. 5-748211), sits slightly back from the waterfront and offers some harbor-view rooms at a reasonable price. Popular with groups of visiting businessmen from mainland China, its cheapest rooms rent for HK$330 ($43) single or double, and come with color TV, phone, radio, desk, and private bath, but they're small and windowless and a bit claustrophobic. Next up the scale are singles for HK$390 ($51) and doubles or twins for HK$440 ($57) that feature windows opening onto a quiet back street. The largest rooms are deluxe rooms with a partial harbor view, which rent for HK$550 ($71) and come with a small empty fridge you can stock yourself. There are 33 of these rooms and since they're all the same price, ask for one on a higher floor where the view is better.

If you've come to Hong Kong primarily for the horse races, the **Caravelle Hotel**, 84 Morrison Hill Rd., Happy Valley (tel. 5-754455), is where you may want to stay. It's located just across the street from Happy Valley racetrack and its front rooms even have views of the racecourse. It's a small hotel with only ten rooms on each floor and the corridors are dimly lit, but there's an attendant on every floor. The rooms are bright enough and come with the usual color TV, radio, empty fridge, desk, and phone, though furnishings are old. Most guests here are Japanese and British. Singles begin at HK$390 ($51) and twins at HK$440 ($57). Rates are the same for those facing the track, so be sure to ask if you're interested in the races.

The Budget Category

Opened in 1986, the **Harbour View International House**, 4 Harbour Rd., Wanchai (tel. 5-201111), is owned and operated by YMCA and occupies a prime spot right by the harbor. Located next to the Hong Kong Arts Centre, it's a 20-story building with 320 rooms, all simply decorated but very functional with TV, carpeting, international direct-dial telephone, refrigerator, radio and in-house music, and tiny but private bathrooms. Facilities include a coffeeshop, one restaurant with a view of the harbor, room service, laundry service, and telex. But the best thing about the hotel is that more than half of its rooms face the harbor and go for HK$440 ($57) for a twin and HK$460 ($60) for a double (there are no single rooms). Twin rooms facing inland are HK$380 ($49).

Although not a member of HKHA, **Hua Long Lodge**, 53 Gloucester Rd.,

Wanchai (tel. 5-299219), offers reasonable rates in the heart of Wanchai. The smallest rooms—all of which face towards the back with enlightening views of how the local people live—go for HK$220 ($29), while the larger rooms face the water and cost HK$270 ($35). If you opt for one of the larger rooms, be sure to ask for one on a higher floor where you can catch a glimpse of the harbor. Old with furniture to match, this hotel caters largely to Chinese, Indians, and Pakistanis, some of whom rent by the month. Sheets are changed twice a week, and all rooms come with air conditioning, TV, phone, bathroom, and a small kitchenette, where you can heat water for tea or coffee.

CENTRAL DISTRICT: The business area of Hong Kong, Central District has only a few hotels and tends to empty out and shut down after dark, but it serves as a good base for exploring the rest of Hong Kong. Trams, most Hong Kong Island buses, Victoria Peak tram, the Star Ferry, the subway, and ferries to the outlying islands pass through or begin in the Central District.

Deluxe Choices

Famed for its service and consistently rated as one of the top hotels in the world, the **Mandarin**, 5 Connaught Rd. (tel. 5-220111), maintains a staff of 1,100 for its 545 rooms. Located in front of the Star Ferry, its clientele is primarily businessmen and its rooms are the most expensive in Hong Kong. Spacious and decorated on an Oriental theme, all rooms have balconies and range from HK$1,430 ($186) for those facing inland and HK$1,730 ($225) to HK$1,920 ($249) for those with a view of the harbor. Rooms have an understated elegance and include all amenities you could possibly want—but if you are still in need of something the staff will make every effort to fulfill your wishes. The lobby is decorated with a stunning glass light fixture and woodcarvings from China. Several of its restaurants have well-deserved reputations for serving excellent cuisine, including the Mandarin Grill for seafood, Man Wah for Cantonese food, and the Pierrot for specialties from France.

The Upper Bracket

Hong Kong Hilton, 2 Queen's Rd. (tel. 5-233111), is at the junction of Queen's and Garden Roads not far from the Victoria Peak tram. One of the few hotels on Hong Kong Island with an outdoor heated swimming pool, the Hilton has 821 rooms plus eight restaurants and bars. All rooms, decorated in mauve or smoky green, have large windows extending the full width of the exterior wall, three phones, a marble bathroom, well-stocked mini-bar, and a sitting area with settee and desk. Singles range from HK$1,010 ($131) for a standard to HK$1,400 ($182) for a deluxe room on a top floor with a harbor view, while twins or doubles begin at HK$1,080 ($140) and go up to HK$1,510 ($196) for a deluxe overlooking the water. Special features of the Hilton include five floors of "Executive Rooms" with their own reception desk and free breakfast, and cocktails (priced the same as deluxe rooms); a business center; packing and mailing service; a health club you can use at an extra charge; and an 110-foot brigantine, a faithful reproduction of British pirate-chasers in the 1840s. Service at the hotel is excellent.

The lobby of the **Hotel Furama**, 1 Connaught Rd. (tel. 5-255111), is on the second floor and faces beautiful Chater Garden. Famous for its revolving restaurant, La Ronda, on the 30th floor, this hotel equips all its guest rooms with a safe, bathrobe, hair dryer, and mini-bar. Rooms begin at HK$880 ($114) for single occupancy and HK$1,000 ($130) for double, while rooms with a harbor view are HK$1,100 ($143) and HK$1,200 ($156) respectively.

Opened in 1986, **Hotel Victoria**, Shun Tak Centre, Connaught Road (tel. 5-407228), is located in the same complex that also houses the new Macau Ferry Terminal and the entrance to the Sheung Wan MTR subway station. You can walk all the way from Hotel Victoria to the Star Ferry terminal in the heart of Central via an elevated walkway in about 15 to 20 minutes. Occupying the top 15 floors of a 40-story building, Hotel Victoria offers 540 rooms with spacious sitting areas close to the large windows, large writing tables (reflective of the hotel's high percentage of business clientele), and marbled bathrooms with lots of room to spread out. Rates range from HK$1,000 ($130) for rooms facing inland to HK$1,300 ($169) for deluxe rooms with great views of the harbor. Facilities include an outdoor swimming pool, two floodlit tennis courts, a business center, and restaurants serving Cantonese and Western cuisine. Room discounts are offered during the off-season months of January, February, March, June, July, August, September, and December, when prices are lowered 10% to 15%.

YOUTH HOSTELS AND CAMPSITES: Hong Kong and its territories have a number of youth hostels and camping sites available, offering the cheapest rates around. The most conveniently located youth hostel is **Ma Wui Hall**, located on the top of Mount Davis on Hong Kong Island (tel. 5-8175715). As with all the other youth hostels in Hong Kong, it charges HK$10 ($1.30) a night [nonmembers pay HK$15 ($1.95) more]. Seven other youth hostels are spread on some of the outlying islands and in the New Territories. For more information on Hong Kong's youth hostels, contact the **Hong Kong Youth Hostels Association**, 1408A Watson's Estate, Causeway Bay (tel. 5-700985 or 5-706222). You may also purchase a youth hostel card here for HK$90 ($11.69).

There are **camping** facilities on some of the outlying islands, ranging in price from free to about HK$33 ($4.28). You must bring your own tent, but some of the camps provide sheets and blankets. The more primitive campsites lack water or latrine facilities—but they're free. For more information on campsites, contact the HKTA.

4. Where to Dine

With an estimated 19,000 restaurants, Hong Kong has what is probably the greatest concentration of Chinese restaurants in the world. In fact, the food is so good and the prices are so reasonable that dining out ranks high as one of *the* things to do while in Hong Kong.

Traditionally speaking, Chinese restaurants tend to be noisy and crowded affairs, the patrons much more interested in food than decor. Recent years, however, have witnessed an explosion in chic, trendy, and fashionable Chinese restaurants, outfitted in styles reminiscent of art deco. In any case, dining is usually in large groups; the basic rule is to order one dish for each person and then to share each dish as it comes. If you want to be correct about it, a Chinese meal usually begins with a cold dish, followed by dishes of beef, pork, vegetables, seafood, soup, and noodles or rice. Many of the dishes are accompanied by sauces, the most common being soy sauce, chili sauce, and hot mustard. Tea is often provided whether you ask for it or not (if you want more tea, simply take the lid off the teapot—someone will come around to refill it), and the beginning and end of your meal is heralded with a round of hot towels, a wonderful custom that you'll soon grow addicted to and wish would be imported to restaurants in the United States.

The most common styles of Chinese cooking in Hong Kong are Cantonese, Peking, Szechuan (also called Sichuan), and Shanghai, though Cantonese is by far the most popular since most Hong Kong Chinese are originally from the area of Canton in China. It's also the most common style of Chinese cooking around the world and is probably the one with which you're most familiar. **Cantonese food** is either steamed or fried and prepared without spices in the belief that the natural flavor of the various ingredients should be prevalent and enjoyed. Popular dishes include roast duck or pigeon, pan-fried lemon chicken, shark's-fin soup, slices of garoupa (a local fish) with ham and bamboo shoots, and sweet-and-sour pork.

Another popular Cantonese dish is *dim sum*, which means "light snack" and is eaten for breakfast and lunch and with afternoon tea. Dim sum consists primarily of finely chopped meat, seafood, and vegetables wrapped in thin dough and then either steamed, fried, boiled, or braised.

Many Cantonese restaurants offer dim sum from about 7:30 a.m. until 4 p.m., served from trolleys wheeled between the tables. Just point at what you want. Some of my favorite dishes are *shiu mai* (steamed minced pork and shrimp dumpling), *har gau* (steamed shrimp dumpling), *au yuk* (steamed minced beef balls), *fun gwor* (steamed rice-flour dumpling filled with pork, shrimp, and bamboo shoots), and *tsun guen* (deep-fried spring roll filled with shredded pork, chicken, mushrooms, bamboo shoots, and bean sprouts). A serving of dim sum usually comes three to four on a plate and averages about HK$5 (65¢) to HK$8 ($1.04). Your bill is figured at the end of your meal by the number of plates on your table or by a card that was stamped each time you ordered a dish.

Peking food, much of which originated in the imperial courts of emperors and empresses, uses a liberal amount of peppers, garlic, ginger, leek, and coriander. Noodles and dumplings are more common than rice, the food is richer than Cantonese cuisine, and roasting is the preferred method of cooking. Most famous among Peking-style dishes is Peking duck, which is air-dried and then coated with a mixture of syrup and soy sauce before roasting. It's best to have at least four people to order this dish, and it's served by wrapping thin slivers of duck in a thin pancake together with spring onion, radish, and sweet plum sauce.

Other popular cuisine includes "drunken chicken," a cold dish of chicken in wine sauce; "beggar's chicken," a whole chicken stuffed with mushrooms, pickled Chinese cabbage, herbs, and onions, sealed in clay and baked all day; sautéed beef with spring onions served on a sizzling platter; and Mongolian hotpots, with dumplings, meat, noodles, and vegetables.

Szechuan food is my favorite Chinese cuisine, as it's the spiciest, hottest, and most fiery style of cooking. Seasoning is done with chili-bean paste and peppercorns, and Szechuan specialties include pan-fried shrimp in spicy sauce, sour-and-peppery soup, smoked duck with camphor and tea flavoring, and sautéed diced chicken in chili-bean paste.

Shanghai food is heavier, richer, sweeter, and oilier than either Cantonese or Peking food (technically speaking, Shanghai does not have a cuisine of its own but is rather a composite of various cooking styles). Some dishes are rather heavy on the garlic and portions tend to be enormous. The most popular Shanghai dish in Hong Kong is freshwater hairy crab, flown in from Shanghai in autumn. Other foods you might consider trying include eel, sautéed shrimp in spicy tomato sauce over crispy rice, and sautéed shredded beef and green pepper.

One other type of Chinese food worth mentioning that is not very well known is **Chiu Chow**. The name refers to the people, dialect, and food of the area of Swatow in southeast Canton. The food is rich in protein, light and tasty, and sauces are liberally applied. Dishes include steamed lobster, deep-fried shrimp balls, sautéed slices of whelk, fried goose blood, and bird's nest in coconut milk. Chiu Chow tea, popularly called Iron Buddha, is probably the world's strongest and bitterest tea. Drink some of this stuff and you'll be humming for hours.

Of course, there are many other dishes you can eat in addition to the ones I've mentioned above. It's said that the Chinese will eat anything that swims, flies, or crawls, and though that may not be entirely true, if you're adventurous enough you may want to try such delicacies as snake soup, pig's brain, bird's nest soup (derived from the saliva of swallows), or eel heads simmered with Chinese herbs.

If you want to know more about the great variety of Chinese food available, there's an excellent booklet called *Visitor's Guide to Chinese Food in Hong Kong* available at HKTA offices. You're safe eating anywhere in Hong Kong, but residents warn foreigners never to eat local oysters—there have been too many instances of oyster poisoning. Eat oysters only if they're imported, say, from Australia. The good restaurants will clearly stipulate in the menu that their oysters are imported.

Another thing you should watch in eating Chinese food is your reaction to monosodium glutamate (MSG), used to enhance flavor in Chinese cooking. Some people react strongly to this spice, reporting bouts of nausea and headaches and a feeling of being bloated. Although you can try requesting dishes without MSG, much of the food has been prepared beforehand and may already include liberal doses. Fortunately, however, in the past couple of years there has been an increased awareness in Hong Kong about the detrimental side effects of MSG, with the result that many of the top Chinese restaurants (especially those in hotels) have either cut down in its usage or stopped using it altogether.

In addition to Chinese restaurants, I've also included a good selection of Western restaurants that could easily stand on their own anywhere in the world. Keep in mind, however, that Western restaurants tend to be more expensive than Chinese ones, and that wine is especially expensive. To keep costs down, stick with beer: the two most popular brands are San Miguel or Tsingtao.

In addition to the restaurants listed below, there are also bars and pubs in the "Hong Kong After Dark" section that serve food. In any case, keep in mind that in addition to the prices I've given below a 10% service charge will be added to your bill.

THE UPPER BRACKET: By far Hong Kong's best and most exclusive restaurants, both Chinese and Western, are in the hotels. That's not surprising when you realize that first-class hotels are used to catering to well-traveled visitors who demand high quality in service, cuisine, and decor.

Chinese Food

The **Man Wah**, on the 25th floor of the Mandarin Hotel, 5 Connaught Rd. in the Central District (tel. 5-220111), is the place to go if you're tired of the usual noisy Chinese restaurant and feel like splurging on elegant dining with a good view of the harbor. A 600-year-old screen from the Ming Dynasty, woodcarvings, pink tablecloths, exquisite chinaware, fresh flowers and candles on every table, and Chinese instrumental music playing softly in the background set the mood for a romantic dinner of Cantonese cuisine.

Although the menu changes often, dishes might include such specialties as braised pigeon with bamboo shoots and mushrooms in oyster sauce, deep-fried scallops with minced shrimp, sautéed diced chicken with chili, roast duck Peking style (order it in advance), sweet-and-sour pork, shark's-fin soup with crab roe, or spicy pork spareribs. For soup I can personally recommend the spicy-and-sour soup, piquant and full of noodles, tofu, and mushrooms. Dinner here averages about HK$220 ($28.57) à la carte. Lunch is served from noon to 3 p.m. and dinner from 6:30 to 11 p.m. Seating is for 55 people only, and if you want to be assured of having a window seat, be sure to say so when you call for reservations.

Perched on the top floor of the Hilton hotel at 2 Queen's Rd. (tel. 5-233111) is the **Eagle's Nest**, from which you have a bird's-eye view of Central District around you and Kowloon across the harbor. Recently redecorated with art deco lamps and accented with fresh flowers and candles on every table, it looks like a European restaurant—only the chopsticks betray the fact that the Eagle's Nest dishes out superb Cantonese cuisine. Open daily from 7:30 p.m. to 1 a.m. to the accompaniment of a small dance band, it serves a wide selection of abalone, chicken, pigeon, duck, beef, pork, seafood, and vegetarian dishes. Specialties of the restaurant include Vagabond (beggar's) chicken, fresh lobster salad, roast duck with plum sauce, double-boiled shark's fin with shredded chicken, baked stuffed sea whelk in the shell with curry sauce, steamed garoupa, and roasted Peking duck. An especially good deal is the special menu for HK$218 ($28.31) per person, which allows you to select as many dishes as you want from a list of about 70 items. A vegetarian dim sum platter is available for HK$55 ($7.14).

One of the most elaborately decorated Chinese restaurants in Hong Kong is the **Shang Palace** in the Shangri-La Hotel, 64 Mody Rd., East Tsimshatsui (tel. 3-7212111). The entrance to the restaurant is past two red-lacquered elephants and rows of red columns, which are cleverly multiplied with the use of mirrors to give the illusion of a long corridor. The walls are of red lacquerware carved in designs, and Chinese lanterns hang from the ceiling.

The menu is quite extensive, with a large variety of seafood, chicken, duck, pigeon, beef, and pork cooked Cantonese style. Most dishes are for two to four persons, and average HK$40 ($5.19) to HK$100 ($12.98). If you really want to splurge you can order bamboo fungus with crabmeat, mixed vegetables, bird's nest, or crab roe, which are all priced at HK$350 ($45.45) or more. Other specialties include shark's-fin soup, barbecued pork, Peking duck, and pan-fried minced pigeon with lettuce. Expect to spend about HK$220 ($28.57) per person for dinner, served daily from 6:30 to 11 p.m.

Shang Palace also serves lunch from noon to 3 p.m. (from 11 a.m. on Sunday and holidays), and although the menu changes every two weeks, it always includes more than a dozen varieties of dim sum for HK$8.80 ($1.14) and HK$13 ($1.69) a plate. Because the menu is in English this is a great place to try dim sum for the first time, not to mention the fact that it's also some of the best dim sum in town. There's also a set lunch for two for HK$105 ($13.64), a particularly good deal.

Lai Ching Heen, in the Regent, on Salisbury Road, Kowloon (tel. 3-7211211), is a deluxe Cantonese restaurant that emphasizes the beauty of stark simplicity. Bonsai trees and a color scheme of rose and pale gray offset beautiful jade table settings and ivory and silver chopsticks. Dishes are traditional Cantonese as well as creations of the executive chef that border on Chinese nouvelle cuisine. Lunch is served from noon to 3 p.m. and dinner from 6 to 11:30 p.m. Dinner will probably be about HK$350 ($45.45) and lunch about HK$200 ($26). The menu changes with each lunar month.

Opened in 1986 on the sixth floor of the Hongkong Hotel at 3 Canton Rd. (tel. 3-7226565) in Kowloon, the **Golden Unicorn Restaurant** is one of the forerunners of the recent trend to uplift Chinese food into a modern and more formal setting. Serving Cantonese cuisine with a Western flair, this restaurant uses

Wedgwood china and Christofle silverware in its presentation of such specialties as drunken shrimp, deep-fried chicken, duck, pork, and seafood selections. Ordering à la carte will probably amount to a bill of HK$330 ($42.86), but if you're by yourself you'll probably want to order the set menu for HK$184 ($23.90), which changes monthly. Hours here are from noon to midnight daily.

Western Food

Gaddi's, in the Peninsula Hotel, on Salisbury Road in Kowloon (tel. 3-666251), has long had a reputation for being the best European restaurant in town. Although that is now being challenged by some pretty stiff competition from other hotels, the service is still excellent, the waiters are all professionals, and the food is always beyond reproof. The atmosphere is that of an elegant dining room, with two crystal-and-silver chandeliers, a pure wool Tai Ping carpet in royal blue, and plenty of space between the tables. There's live music and dancing at night, and although the menu changes every six months, it always includes steak and seafood. A full-course dinner here, including wine, will set you back about HK$600 ($77.92) per person, but it's definitely worth it if you can afford it since Gaddi's is as much a part of Hong Kong as the Peninsula Hotel. If you don't want to splurge for dinner, come for the set lunch menu at HK$120 ($15.58). Hours are noon to 3 p.m. and 7 to 11 p.m. daily. Jacket and tie required.

I personally prefer the **Verandah Grill**, also located in the Peninsula Hotel. It's less pretentious than Gaddi's and is the restaurant you see under the light-blue-and-green canopy on the second floor if you walk past the front of the hotel. Its big windows wrap themselves around the U-shaped front façade of the hotel, offering a view of the harbor that is unfortunately blocked to some extent by the Space Museum. An airy, bright, and cheerful place that does give an illusion of being a veranda, this place offers seafood, grilled steaks, and veal dishes beginning at HK$100 ($12.99). If you want to splurge you can order fresh beluga caviar or lobster soup, but the best deal is undoubtedly the light luncheon set menu for HK$104 ($13.51), which includes a salad or soup, entrée, dessert, and coffee or tea. Otherwise, meals here average about HK$220 ($28.57) per person. The Verandah is open for business from 7 to 11 a.m., noon to 3 p.m., and 6:30 to 11 p.m. Dress is casual during the day, but jacket and tie are recommended for dinner.

The Hyatt Regency's **Hugo's**, 67 Nathan Rd. (tel. 3-662321), was the first Hugo's to open in Asia. A good example of a great restaurant in a hotel, this place is noted for its superb continental cuisine and excellent service. The decor is very masculine, with swords on the walls, huge leather-bound menus, and big green water glasses. Needless to say, men need a coat and tie here. Filipino musicians serenade in the evenings, and the specialty of the house is U.S. prime rib of beef, with the rest of the menu changing every six months. If lobster bisque is on the menu, you can't go wrong ordering it, and the desserts are always spectacular. Depending on the wine you choose, dinner will range from about HK$400 ($51.94) to HK$500 ($64.93) and is served from 7 p.m. to 11 p.m. You can do it cheaper if you go for lunch between noon and 2:30 p.m. and order the set meal for HK$108 ($14.03).

Serving continental food with an emphasis on French nouvelle cuisine, **Margaux**, in the Shangri-La Hotel, 64 Mody Rd., East Tsimshatsui (tel. 3-7212111), is decorated in brass and teakwood and has an inspiring view of the harbor. Margaux offers the usual beef, veal, and seafood dishes, and I particularly recommend the lobster bisque, sole rolled with salmon mousse, grilled veal médaillons with a morel cream sauce, and sautéed scallops. Dinner, by candlelight and requiring both coat and tie, will cost about HK$330 ($42.85) if you don't order wine and HK$550 ($71.42) and up if you do. The wine list is fairly extensive; Château Margaux is widely featured, so it may be hard to resist. There's a six-course dinner priced at HK$310 ($40.26) and a lunch special for a reasonable HK$96 ($12.46). Lunch is considerably more casual, but jeans are frowned upon. Lunch is served from noon to 3 p.m. every day except Sunday, and dinner is from 7 to 11:30 p.m. daily.

Some people consider the **Plume**, in the Regent Hotel, on Salisbury Road in Kowloon (tel. 3-7211211), to be the best European restaurant in Hong Kong. Certainly it feels like a great restaurant, sitting right over the water with a grand view of Hong Kong Island and serving nouvelle cuisine.

It's open only for dinner from 6 to 11 p.m. The evening here begins with a complimentary glass of champagne Mir (champagne with a hint of blackberry liqueur), Indian bread, and goose-liver pâté. The menu, which contains only original creations, is printed anew every day but always includes the house specialty: a delicate cream of artichoke with beluga. Most entrées run around HK$145 ($18.83), but a full dinner with appetizer, soup, and dessert may cost up to HK$450 ($58.44), excluding wine. As expected, coat and tie are required.

The **Mandarin's Pierrot** on the 25th floor, 5 Connaught Rd. (tel. 5-220111), was the first hotel restaurant to introduce Hong Kong gourmets to a year-round menu of nouvelle cuisine and has remained one of the city's favorites. Its name and decor inspired by Picasso's painting of his son in a pierrot costume, this restaurant offers a great view of the harbor and a menu that changes twice a year. Selections may include such dishes as marinated Scotch salmon and Beluga caviar served with potato galette; panfried goose liver; garoupa; poached chicken accompanied by a truffle sauce; and white chocolate mousse. Dinners here average about HK$450 ($58.44). Hours here are from noon to 3 p.m. every day except weekends and holidays and from 7 p.m. to midnight daily. After dinner you may wish to retire to the Harlequin Bar for a cocktail, open from 11 a.m. to midnight.

If you absolutely refuse to dine in a hotel, then **Au Trou Normand**, 6 Carnarvon Rd. (tel. 3-668754), may be for you. With prices slightly lower than the hotel restaurants listed above, dinner here will run about HK$250 ($32.47), including wine. There's a lunch special for HK$66 ($8.57), which includes a buffet appetizer table, choice of entrée, dessert, and a complimentary glass of wine. The French owner and chef, Bernard Vigneau, is always there and makes frequent appearances, a plus for any restaurant. It's decorated in the style of a farmhouse in Normandy, and the menu includes such things as pork and duck liver, grilled steaks, sautéed frogs' legs, an excellent cheese board, and sublimely superb chocolate mousse. A mainstay in Hong Kong since it opened back in 1964, this restaurant serves food from noon to 3 p.m. and 7 to 11 p.m.

With a cheeky reference to Hong Kong's future, **Nineteen 97**, 9 Lan Kwai Fong in Central District (tel. 5-260303), is a high-tech café/restaurant/bar that offers a pleasant place to while away the evening. Located up on the first floor, it sports a ceiling covered with draped cloth, which gives the place a cozy, tent-like atmosphere, while artwork of local and overseas artists is exhibited on the walls. Open daily from noon to 3 p.m. and from 7 to 11 p.m., this place offers a fun and innovative menu, with such delights as finely sliced beef filet presented on fresh asparagus tips with olive oil and pork filet stuffed with herbs and pistachio nuts baked in banana leaves and accompanied by a lightly curried sauté. There are separate lunch and dinner menus, with lunches averaging about HK$120 ($15.58) and dinners about HK$220 ($28.57).

If you can't decide whether you want Western or Chinese food, then head for **La Ronda** (tel. 5-255111) for its buffet lunch or dinner. Located on the 30th floor of the Furama Hotel at 1 Connaught Rd., this is a revolving restaurant with stunning views of Hong Kong Island, the harbor, and Kowloon. Taking about 70 minutes to make a complete turn, La Ronda features Chinese, Indian, Japanese, and Western dishes, and charges HK$120 ($15.58) for lunch served from noon to 3 p.m. and HK$175 ($22.73) for dinner from 7 to 11 p.m. There's a live band and dancing in the evenings, and if you want a window table, be sure to call ahead for reservations.

As part of London's famous chain of seafood restaurants, **Bentley's** opened in 1987 in the basement of the Prince's Building, Statue Square, in the Central District (tel. 5-8680881). It specializes in oysters (usually from Scotland), including oysters on the half shell or served with sauces like curry and tomato or a light champagne-and-cream sauce. Also on the menu are selections of soups, crab or lobster bisque, Dover sole, scallops, and baked crab. Expect to spend at least HK$250 ($32.47) per person. It's open every day except Sunday and holidays from noon to 3 p.m. and from 6 to 11 p.m.

THE MEDIUM-PRICED RANGE: Most of Hong Kong's better restaurants outside hotels fall into this category, which means that you don't have to spend a lot of money to have a good meal. Although the decor in many of the Chinese restaurants may not be very exciting, good food in generous portions more than makes up for it. The Western restaurants, on the other hand, go much more for atmosphere and are pretty much the same as what you'd find back home. In addition to the restaurants listed below, there are some in the upper bracket above that offer very reasonable lunches, including Shang Palace, Gaddi's, Hugo's, Verandah Grill, Margaux, Au Trou Normand, and La Ronda. If you feel like splurging, lunch in an expensive restaurant may be the way you want to go.

Chinese Food

One Chinese restaurant that rates high on both food and decor is **Luk Yu Tea House**, 24-26 Stanley St., Central District (tel. 5-235464). With ceiling fans, individual wooden booths for couples, marble tabletops, wood paneling, and stained-glass windows, Luk Yu is the most famous tea house remaining in Hong Kong (it originally opened in 1925 and moved to its present site a few years back). It's one of the best places to try a few Chinese teas. *Bo lai* (a black tea) is the favorite drink with dim sum. Other teas here include jasmine, *lung ching* (a green tea), and *sui sin* (narcissus or daffodil).

A Cantonese restaurant, Luk Yu is well known for its dim sum, which is served from 7 a.m. to 5 p.m. Although dishes are very reasonable at HK$9 ($1.17) to HK$16 ($2.08) a plate, the problem here is that the place is always packed during the day with regular customers who all have their own special places to sit. And if you come after 11 a.m. dim sum is no longer served by trolley but from a menu, which is written only in Chinese. If you want to come during the day (certainly when it's at its most colorful), try to get a Chinese to go with you.

Otherwise, consider going for dinner, which is served from 5 to 10 p.m. There are more than 200 items on the English menu, which includes all the Cantonese favorites. Dishes start at HK$35 ($4.50) and you can probably have dinner here for less than HK$120 ($15.58).

No doubt you've heard about Hong Kong's floating restaurants in Aberdeen. Although they are often included in Hong Kong's nighttime organized tours, they are no longer touted by the tourist office as one of the places every tourist has to see—there are simply too many other restaurants that are less touristy, more authentic, better priced, with better food. However, if it's been your lifetime fantasy to eat in a floating restaurant in Aberdeen, try **Tai Pak**

Seafood Restaurant, in Aberdeen. (tel. 5-525953). The atmosphere here is of a huge, high-ceilinged dining room with traditional Chinese decor. The Cantonese menu is diverse with lots of choices, and portions are hearty. Specialties include shark's-fin soup, baked lobster with onion sauce, braised garoupa (a local fish), sautéed scallops, crabmeat omelet, sliced beef in oyster sauce, and steamed chicken with vegetables. Dinner here will cost at least HK$150 ($19.48) per person, though there's also a set menu for HK$80 ($10.39). Hours here are from 11 a.m. to 11 p.m. daily.

Decorated in stark black and white with a blend of art deco and modern Chinese decor, **The Chinese**, in the Hyatt Regency, 67 Nathan Rd. in Kowloon (tel. 3-662321), features walls lined with wooden booths, reminiscent of Chinese tea houses of the 1920s. Serving dim sum and Cantonese favorites, it's open from noon to 3 p.m. and from 6 to 11 p.m. Recommended is the dim sum lunch special which gives you four different varieties for HK$35 ($4.55). A seasonal menu lists selections of beef, pork, pigeon, chicken, duck, shellfish, fish, abalone, and vegetables, with most dinners averaging about HK$160 ($20.78). If available, deep-fried crispy chicken skin, minced pigeon with butter lettuce, and fried lobster balls are all equally delicious.

A popular restaurant for decades, **Yung Kee Restaurant**, 32-40 Wellington St. in Central District (tel. 5-221624), started out as a small shop selling roasted goose. Its goose became so much in demand that it was transformed into a Cantonese restaurant, specializing in roasted goose with plum sauce. Other specialties include bean curd combined with shrimp, shredded chicken, or other delicacies; filet of garoupa sauté; and hundred-year-old eggs (which come automatically with each meal). Meals here average about HK$70 ($9.09) and are served up on the first floor. If all you want is a bowl of congee or other rice dishes, join the office workers who pour in for a quick meal on the ground floor. Hours here are from 11 a.m. to 11:30 p.m. daily, with dim sum served from 2 to 5:30 p.m.

An upper-end Cantonese restaurant serving good food at moderate prices in a small dining room that simulates the courtyard of a Chinese village is the **Lychee Village**, 9-11A Cameron Rd., Tsimshatsui (tel. 3-686544). Serving dim sum beginning at HK$5 (65¢) from 7:30 a.m. to 6 p.m. and à la carte dishes until midnight, this pleasant and rather sophisticated-looking restaurant offers more quiet dining in a less chaotic atmosphere than many other Cantonese restaurants. The 100-item menu has the usual pigeon, abalone, duck, chicken, and vegetable dishes, and dinner will run about HK$120 ($15.58). There's also a set menu at HK$55 ($7.14) per person, good if you're alone.

With its pink tablecloths and modern decor, **Full Moon**, 102 Barnton Court in Harbour City, just off Canton Road in Tsimshatsui (tel. 3-679131), is another one of Hong Kong's new Chinese restaurants. Opened in 1985, it offers more than 100 items on its Cantonese menu. Its specialty is dancing prawn, which are supposedly drowned in Chinese yellow wine and than cooked in a soup at HK$38 ($4.93) per person. Roasted Peking duck is HK$130 ($16.89). Dim sum is served from 11 a.m. to 4 p.m., while dinner is served from 6 p.m. to midnight.

United Restaurant, conveniently located above the Admiralty MTR subway station on the fifth and sixth floors of United Centre (tel. 5-295010), is a gigantic Cantonese restaurant with seating for 2,400 persons. Popular for large banquets and private parties, it has many private rooms for the Chinese game of mah-jongg. The decor is simple but the food is good, and dinners average about HK$100 ($12.99). Open daily from 7 a.m. to midnight, specialties here include barbecued whole suckling pig, baked lobster in supreme soup, and deep-fried shrimp balls.

Popular with local Chinese on a night out on the town, Food Street in

Causeway Bay is a pedestrian lane bordered on both sides by restaurant after restaurant serving all kinds of different food, from Chinese to Japanese to Western to fast foods. Altogether there are about 28 food outlets, so there's lots to choose from. A good Cantonese restaurant here is **Riverside Restaurant** (tel. 5-779733), located at the end of Food Street at 13-15 Cleveland. Open from 11 a.m. to 3 p.m. and 5:30 p.m. to midnight Monday through Friday and from 11 a.m. straight through to midnight on the weekends and holidays, this restaurant has a very Chinese feel to it, with bright reds and greens and Chinese paintings. I recommend the roasted chicken, steamed shrimp with garlic sauce, deep-fried stuffed crab claws, boneless duck with mashed lotus taro, or garoupa balls sauté. Dim sum is available for lunch. Otherwise lunches average about HK$50 ($6.49), while dinners are usually around HK$130 ($16.88).

Another restaurant in the area that enjoys popularity with the locals is the **Cleveland Szechuan Restaurant**, 6 Cleveland St. (tel. 5-763876). A favorite of families with children, this spicy Szechuan restaurant has rather plain decor but very good prices, with meals here running from about HK$70 ($9.09) to HK$100 ($12.99). The main specialty of the house is its smoked duck with camphor tea. Other dishes highly recommended are fried king shrimp on a sizzling plate, fried diced chicken with black beans and pepper, deep-fried fish with sweet-and-sour sauce, and beef filet with hot garlic sauce served on a hot plate. Most dishes come in three sizes, small, medium and large: the small one is good for 2 people, the medium for 4, and the large for 12. Hours are from 10:30 a.m. to 2:30 p.m. and again from 5:30 p.m. to midnight Monday through Friday, open throughout the day on weekends.

One of my favorite Szechuan restaurants in Hong Kong is the **Red Pepper**, 7 Lan Fong Rd. in Causeway Bay (tel. 5-768046), which has a large following among the colony's expatriates. It's a very relaxing, smaller restaurant, though its decor is fairly elegant: Chinese lanterns, Chinese straight-backed chairs, and a red ceiling with gold dragon motifs. Since it's so popular with Western residents living in Hong Kong, I strongly recommend that you make reservations for this place if you want to come for dinner. Open since 1970, Red Pepper specializes in fried shrimp with chili sauce on a sizzling platter, sour-pepper soup, and dry fried string beans. Hours are noon to midnight daily, and you can expect to spend HK$100 ($12.99) to HK$120 ($15.58) for a meal.

Sze Chuen Lau Restaurant is located at 466 Lockhart Rd. in Wanchai (tel. 5-8919027) and is open from 11:30 a.m. to 11:30 p.m. daily. A real plus in this restaurant is the set lunch for HK$40 ($5.19), for two persons. If you order à la carte to sample such Szechuan specialties as chili shrimp on a sizzling plate, smoked duck, smoked pigeon, braised eel, or cold chicken with chili-sesame sauce, your meal will come to about HK$100 ($12.99) per person.

Reportedly one of the most expensive Szechuan restaurants in Hong Kong, **Sichuan Garden** (tel. 5-214433) is located on the third floor of the chic Landmark Building in the Central District, which probably explains why the restaurant is so expensive (somebody has to pay the rent). In its defense, though, it should also be said that the food here is excellent, the service attentive, and the atmosphere bright and elegantly simple. Open every day from 11:30 a.m. to 3 p.m. and again from 6 p.m. to midnight, it's a very popular restaurant and almost always crowded. The hot-and-spicy dishes are indicated on the 150-item menu to help the uninitiated, with small plates beginning at HK$39 ($5.06) and medium at HK$60 ($7.79). You might try the hot-and-sour soup, fried shrimp with chili sauce, shredded pork in hot garlic sauce, or the pigeon smoked in camphor wood and tea leaves. I had the latter and found it quite good, but I was unprepared for the decapitated pigeon head that came on the platter as decoration (at least I assumed it wasn't for consumption). Dinner here can cost HK$150 ($19.48) per person, though you can do it for about half that if you select your dishes with care and don't drink alcohol.

Opened in 1984, Ziyang, 45D Chatham Rd. on the corner of Prat Avenue in Tsimshatsui (tel. 3-687177), is an up-market Szechuan restaurant with gray suede and pink-marble walls, chairs imported from Italy, and caged parakeets. With most meals averaging HK$120 ($15.58), it offers bean-curd rolls, fried prawn with chili and hot garlic sauce, beef in hot pepper sauce, and selections of pork, chicken, and seafood dishes. Spicy dishes are noted on the menu, and hours are from 11 a.m. to 3 p.m. and from 6 p.m. to midnight.

Another new Szechuan restaurant with a modern decor is Lotus Pond, 15 Harbour City, Canton Road in Tsimshatsui (tel. 3-7241088). Open from 11 a.m. to midnight daily, it lists more than 100 dishes on its menu, including such specialties as fried shrimp in chili sauce, fried chicken Szechuan style, smoked duck, and shark's-fin soup. Average checks here range from about HK$100 ($12.99) to HK$200 ($25.97), though you can eat for less if your wallet dictates. Small dishes are available for less than HK$40 ($5.19).

Spring Deer Restaurant, 42 Mody Rd. in Kowloon (tel. 3-664012), offers excellent Peking food at reasonable prices and is an old standby favorite in Hong Kong. Nothing fancy, the restaurant is likely to give you a table with a cloth that is clean but has some holes in it, but that doesn't deter the fans who come here obviously to enjoy themselves. Spring Deer is cheerful and very easy and accessible to foreigners, and is one of the best places to come if you want to try its specialty—Peking duck. Since you'll probably have to wait 40 minutes for the duck if you order it during peak time (between 7:30 and 9:30 p.m.), it's best to arrive either before or after the rush (the restaurant is open daily from noon to 3 p.m. and 6 to 11 p.m.). Chicken dishes are also well liked, including the deep-fried chicken in soy sauce, and the handmade noodles are excellent. Most dishes come in small, medium, and large sizes, and meals range from HK$100 ($12.98) to HK$130 ($16.88) per person.

Despite its name, the American Restaurant, 20 Lockhart Rd., Wanchai (tel. 5-271000), is another restaurant serving Peking food. Easily spotted from the outside by its bright green-and-red façade, this restaurant is popular with both Chinese and Western residents as well as with visitors, and is an updated version of one of the few original Peking restaurants (it opened in the 1940s after World War II). The waiters don't speak English but the menu, with almost 200 dishes, is in English and includes barbecued Peking duck, beggar's chicken, and various beef, chicken, pork, and seafood dishes. Open every day from 11:30 a.m. to 11:30 p.m., the restaurant serves its selections in three sizes: most small dishes good for one person range from HK$20 ($2.60) to HK$33 ($4.28); medium, from HK$25 ($3.24) to HK$50 ($6.49); and large, from HK$38 ($4.93) to HK$65 ($8.44). Peking duck comes in one size only—at HK$110 ($14.28)—and can be shared between two or more persons.

Established in 1958, the Great Shanghai at 26-36 Prat Ave. (tel. 3-662693) is a well-known restaurant in Tsimshatsui serving Shanghai food. A big dining hall with bright lights, white tablecloths, and plenty of waiters in white shirts and black bow ties, this restaurant has more than 300 items on its menu, including chop suey with fried noodles, shrimp in chili sauce, diced chicken with cashew nuts, cold chicken in wine sauce, hot-and-sour soup, Peking duck, and beggar's chicken. Although the restaurant is open daily from 11 a.m. to 3 p.m. and 6 p.m. to midnight, beggar's chicken is available only at night and it's necessary to call in your order by midafternoon. Being by myself, I could manage only one dish, braised eel, which was cooked in an oily garlic sauce that I found excellent. Average cost of a meal here will be HK$65 ($8.44) to HK$90 ($11.68).

Another popular restaurant serving Shanghai cuisine is Wu Kong, the address for which is 27 Nathan Rd. but whose entrance is around the corner on Peking Road (tel. 3-667244). Usually packed during mealtimes, it's open from 11:30 a.m. to midnight daily and with its soothing green-and-white color scheme is more upscale than most Shanghai restaurants. Its menu includes a variety of shark's-fin dishes, as well as the usual pigeon in wine sauce, sautéed fresh shrimp, braised shredded eels, and other dishes common to Shanghai cuisine. Dinner here will average about HK$80 ($10.39) to HK$100 ($12.99).

On the other side of the harbor is **Shanghai Garden**, located in the Hutchison House next to the Furama Hotel in the Central District (tel. 5-238322). Although it's primarily a restaurant specializing in Shanghai food, it also serves dishes from Peking, Nanking, Sichuan, and Hangchow. The menu is extensive, including such soups as hot-and-sour shredded meat and fish soup, such cold dishes as spiced duck or sautéed shredded eels in garlic sauce, and such entrées as sautéed shrimps with tea leaves, quick-fried shredded eels with ginger, stewed shrimps with tomato sauce and crispy rice, and fried noodles Shanghai-style. The average check here is HK$100 ($12.99), and hours are 11 a.m. to 3 p.m. and 6 to 11 p.m. daily.

If you want to try the little-known Chiu Chow cuisine, **City Chiuchow Restaurant**, in the East Ocean Centre at 98 Granville Rd., East Tsimshatsui (tel. 3-7236226), is a spacious dining room overlooking the gardens that lead down to a major promenade. With seating for 500, it's decorated in gold and red and features a big tank with fresh fish to choose from.

Famous dishes here include Chiu Chow shark's-fin soup, much thicker and stronger tasting than the Cantonese style; double-boiled shark's-fin-and-chicken soup, not as strong but equally popular; sliced soy goose, fried chicken with a black spicy sauce; and seafood dishes, including lobster. I particularly recommend the cold sliced lobster in a special honey sauce—it's not on the menu but it's available year round. This restaurant also serves Chiu Chow and Cantonese dim sum until 3 p.m. Monday through Saturday and 5 p.m. on Sunday at HK$10 ($1.29) for a plate of six pieces. Hours for the restaurant are 11 a.m. to midnight, but during weekdays it closes for afternoon siesta from 3 to 5 p.m. Expect to spend about HK$165 ($21.42) if you have drinks, HK$90 ($11.64) if you don't.

Well-known for its vegetarian lunch buffet, the **Jade Lotus** in the Hilton Hotel, 2 Queen's Rd. (tel. 5-233111), serves a variety of delectable Western, Chinese, and Indian foods. This is a real bargain at HK$99 ($12.86)—but don't forget the automatic 10% service charge—and is served from noon to 3 p.m.

Western and Non-Chinese Food

The Hilton Hotel, 2 Queen's Rd. (tel. 5-233111), also has another lunch buffet at the **Dragon Boat** from noon to 2:30 p.m. Monday through Friday, including such choices as roast beef, Peking duck, and salad bar, and desserts. The price is HK$88 ($11.43). Meanwhile, in the basement of the Hilton is **The Den**, decorated in a Mediterranean theme with a stone floor and cloth draped from the ceiling in imitation of a tent. There are various buffets here at different price ranges, including a selection of Mediterranean "mezze" cold dishes for HK$48 ($6.23) or a selection of curries for HK$59 ($7.66). If you want to go all out and eat everything in sight, a full buffet of Mediterranean dishes, curries, dessert, and coffee costs HK$93 ($12.08). Closed Sunday and holidays, The Den is open the rest of the week from noon to 3 p.m. and 6 to 10 p.m.

Another popular buffet lunch is served in **Nathans** at the Hyatt Regency, 67 Nathan Rd. in Kowloon (tel. 3-662321), from noon to 3 p.m. daily. The specialty here is Indian tandoori, and it's all reasonably priced at HK$55 ($7.14).

For Italian food, **Rigoletto**, 14-16 Fenwick St. in Wanchai (tel. 5-277144), is the restaurant most frequently recommended by Hong Kong residents. The presence of Italian owner and musician Ugo Conta gives the restaurant its special Italian flair, and even though the decor is a bit overdone with Italian pendants and souvenirs hanging around and rather loud orange and green tablecloths, the lighting is pleasantly dark and wide windows offer an interesting perspective on the action of Wanchai on Fenwick and Lockhart Roads.

Dinner here might open with one of the spaghettis which begin at HK$33 ($4.29), lasagne at HK$40 ($5.19), risottos at HK$45 ($5.84), or pizza at HK$38 ($4.93). Entrées consist mainly of northern Italian dishes and include calves' liver, veal, steaks, and seafood. A full-course dinner here will run about HK$180 ($23.38). Rigoletto is open for lunch every day except Sunday from noon to 3 p.m. and for dinner from 6 p.m. to midnight daily.

First opened more than two decades ago, **La Taverna**, 1-2 On Hing Terrace, Central District (tel. 5-228904), is Italian-owned and employs an Italian chef to cook up its daily specials, as well as such favorites as homemade pasta, thinly sliced beef tenderloin in olive oil and rosemary dressing, veal, chicken, seafood, and pizza. A pleasant restaurant located just off Wyndham Street, its front facade resembles a sidewalk café, with glass doors that can be pushed open in fine weather. A guitar player serenades in the evenings, while candles on all the tables bathe the restaurant in a warm, soft glow. Set lunches are available starting at HK$55 ($7.14) and are served daily from 11:30 a.m. to 3 p.m. Dinner, served from 6:30 to 11 p.m., averages about HK$170 ($22.07). If you're on the Kowloon side, another La Taverna is located at 36-38 Ashley Rd., Tsimshatsui (tel. 3-691945), with the same opening hours.

Despite its name, **Seasons Bar & Café**, 17 On Lan St., Central District (tel. 5-268429) is also a restaurant. Opened in 1985 and decorated in pine wood and pastels, this small establishment serves cocktails and lunch in its upstairs, while the downstairs features live music (jazz on Monday and Wednesday nights and classical music on Saturday night) and its own creative specials. The menu changes frequently but may include such dishes as grilled chicken breast stuffed with wild mushrooms and Emmenthaler cheese, grilled pork chops, garlic king shrimp, salmon, or steak. A business lunch is available for HK$72 ($9.35), while a set dinner for HK$82 ($10.65) is served on Tuesday, Thursday, and Friday evenings. Cocktails start at HK$24 ($3.17) and beer at HK$13 ($1.69), but from 5 to 7:30 p.m. and again from 10 to 11 p.m. there's a happy hour when you can buy two drinks for the price of one. Open every day except Sunday, it's open from 11 a.m. to 3 p.m. and 5 p.m. to midnight.

First opened in 1928, **Jimmy's Kitchen** had several homes before moving to its present site in the 1960s on Wyndham Street in the Central District (tel. 5-265293). The atmosphere here reminds me of an American steakhouse, with white tablecloths, dark-wood paneling, and grocery-store music, but it's a favorite with foreigners living in Hong Kong and serves dependably good European food.

Open noon to 11 p.m. every day, it features daily specials written on a blackboard and a large à la carte menu offering seafood, steaks, salads and soups, chicken, spaghettis, and curries. You can have oysters imported from Australia, and there's a large selection of seafood, including sole, scallops, and the local garoupa. A glass of house wine or beer begins at HK$13 ($1.69). If you decide to go the works, dinner here will range from HK$150 ($19.48) to HK$180 ($23.38). A second Jimmy's Kitchen is located across the harbor at 29 Ashley Rd., Tsimshatsui (tel. 3-684027), with the same menu. Hours for both are noon to 11 p.m. seven days a week.

Landau's, owned by the same company as Jimmy's Kitchen, opened in 1976 at 257 Gloucester Rd. in Causeway Bay (tel. 5-7902901). I personally prefer the menu and atmosphere of this restaurant to Jimmy's Kitchen, finding it somehow more intimate, romantic, and sophisticated. Blackboards throughout the place announce daily specials, but a general meal may begin with a soup such as chilled cream of avocado, lobster bisque, cream of tomato, or baked onion, which range from HK$20 ($2.60) to HK$27 ($3.51). Entrées, which generally cost HK$60 ($7.79) to HK$80 ($10.39), include such specialties as black pepper steak, port wine duck, New Zealand lamb chops, wienerschnitzel, beef Stroganoff, Australian rock oysters, paprika veal goulash, and corned beef and cabbage. House wine begins at HK$12 ($1.56) a glass. The management estimates that the cost of an average meal here, including wine, runs about HK$200 ($25.97). Landau's is open for business from noon to 3 p.m. and 7 p.m. to midnight.

Although located in the elegant Regent hotel, on Salisbury Road, **Harbour Side** (tel. 3-7211211) is an informal dining hall with a view of the harbor and is open daily from 6 a.m. to midnight. Rather plain and bare with a brick floor and wooden chairs, it serves hamburgers, poached sole with leeks, chicken and shrimp curry, and other dishes listed on a menu printed daily. Most entrées are between HK$38 ($4.93) and HK$80 ($10.39), a cup of coffee is HK$15 ($1.95), and cocktails average HK$29 ($3.77).

Thai food is very popular in Hong Kong these days, and one of the better-known Thai restaurants is the **Golden Elephant Thai Restaurant**, located in Harbour City towards the back of Barnton Court near the cinemas (tel. 3-692733). A member of HKTA and affiliated with Thai Airways, this restaurant serves both spicy and mild foods in meals that will probably cost less than HK$100 ($12.99) per person. A lunch buffet is a good bargain at HK$63 ($8.18), but if you opt for an à la carte meal, perhaps you want to start out with such appetizers as Thai crispy rice served with minced pork and shrimp sauce or Thai shrimp crackers. Main courses include such delectables as boiled beef with satay sauce, fried diced chicken with red chili and hot basil leaf, Thai fish cake, steamed fish with plum sauce and ginger, and fried beef with chili sauce. Hours here are 11 a.m. to 3 p.m. and 6 to 11 p.m. daily.

THE BUDGET CATEGORY: Hong Kong has an almost endless number of inexpensive restaurants, food stalls, and tiny holes-in-the-wall where you can eat quite well and quite a lot at very reasonable prices. Keep in mind that in addition to the restaurants listed below, there are a number of Cantonese restaurants that serve dim sum through much of the day, a real bargain for those on a budget. Restaurants listed in the medium-range section above serving dim sum are The Chinese, Lychee Village, Full Moon, United Restaurant, City Chiuchow Restaurant, and Luk Yu Tea House.

Chinese Food

Glorious Restaurant, 41-51 Lockhart Rd. in Wanchai (tel. 5-281128), is a good name for this Cantonese restaurant. It's everything a dim sum place should be—huge, noisy, tastefully decorated, and usually packed, which is always a good sign. If you ask me, everyone who comes to Hong Kong should experience a dim sum place like this at least once. Served from 7 a.m. to 5 p.m. daily, most of the dim sum here costs HK$4 (51¢) to HK$13 ($1.69) a plate. Just choose what you want from the trolleys that roll by. The type of dim sum available will vary depending on whether it's breakfast, lunch, or afternoon tea. If you decide to come here for dinner, served daily from 6 to 11 p.m., expect to spend about HK$75 ($9.74) per person for such specialties as grilled duck with lemon, shark's-fin soup with shredded chicken, honey-roast duck, steamed garoupa, or roasted suckling pig.

Dim Sum Kitchen is one of the many restaurants located on Food Street in Causeway Bay, described earlier in the medium-priced restaurant section. Simple and cheap, this cafeteria serves dim sum beginning at HK$4.70 (61¢), as well as such other dishes as barbecued pork with rice or soy-sauce chicken, both of which costs HK$12 ($1.56). Simply pay for what you want beforehand at the ticket window and then present your food ticket to someone at the counter. Hours here are from 7:30 a.m. to midnight.

Another dim sum restaurant that is more conveniently located but probably a bit overdone on decor is **Golden Crown**, 66-70 Nathan Rd., Tsimshatsui (tel. 3-666291). To get to this place you have to walk up to the second floor past red-and-gold dragons with lighted white eyes, but the dining room is mercifully more subdued. Ancient-looking women push the trolley carts here, and when you choose something they mark it on a tab kept on your table. To pay your bill, just pick it up and wave it until someone sees you. Dim sum prices here begin at HK$4.60 (60¢) a plate, and it's served daily from 7:30 a.m. to 5 p.m.

Offering what is probably the cheapest dim sum in Tsimshatsui is the **Capital Restaurant**, located in Chungking Mansion at 40-44 Nathan Rd. (tel. 3-681844). Serving dim sum from 7 a.m. to 5 p.m., it charges HK$3.80 (49¢) to HK$12 ($1.59) a plate until 3 p.m., after which the price goes down to only HK$2.70 ($35¢). Dim sum is served up on the second floor (which would be the third floor in the United States).

A rather bare-looking but popular and usually crowded Szechuan restaurant, **Fung Lum Restaurant**, 23 Granville Rd. in Tsimshatsui (tel. 3-678919), is a small restaurant seating only about 80 persons. It's been here more than a quarter of a century, surviving so far the onslaught of clothing stores that now occupy sites of former restaurants that used to line the street. It's open from 11 a.m. to 11 p.m. daily, with specialties that include Szechuan chicken, shrimp with chili and garlic sauce, sliced pork in garlic and chili sauce, beef filet with pepper and hot garlic sauce, scallops in garlic and onion sauce, and frogs' legs with chili. Small dishes average about HK$33 ($4.29) to HK$55 ($7.14), and larger ones run up to HK$60 ($7.79).

Sanno King Shing, 3-5 Cornwall Ave. in Tsimshatsui (tel. 3-672995), is a simple restaurant with excellent Shanghai cuisine as well as Szechuan food. Try the chicken in wine sauce, shredded braised eels, dry braised bamboo sprouts with chili sauce, spiced fried duck, or deep-fried chicken. There are more than 300 items on the menu as well as specials that aren't, so be sure to ask the waiter what he recommends. Dinner here should average about HK$55 ($7.14) per person.

One of Hong Kong's oldtimers, **Wishful Cottage Vegetarian Restaurant**, 336-340 Lockhart Rd., Wanchai (tel. 5-735645), opened in 1967. Ornately decorated with Chinese lanterns and a Buddhist statue, it serves seasonal vegetables, noodles, and bean-curd dishes. The most expensive thing on the menu is bamboo fungus for HK$130 ($16.89), but otherwise you should be able to eat here for about HK$45 ($5.84) per person.

If you don't know very much about Chinese food, feel that you should try it, but still aren't very keen on the idea, head for one of the **Jade Garden Chinese** restaurants. There are eight of these Cantonese restaurants altogether, the most convenient being: Swire House, Central District (tel. 5-239966); Star House, fourth floor, Kowloon (tel. 3-7226888); and 25-31 Carnarvon Rd., Kowloon (tel. 3-698311). Geared toward the Chinese-food novice, these places have the traditional decor of reds and blacks that one would expect of a Chinese restaurant and offer fine food at reasonable prices.

Open daily from 11:30 a.m. to midnight, each restaurant serves the typical dim sum lunch, with women offering steaming bamboo bowlfuls of rice, shrimp in wonton, and many other dishes, as well as sautéed-to-order pork cakes, shrimp tofu, tripe stew, and other items. Most dim sum here average between HK$5 (65¢) and HK$12 ($1.59). Lunch at these places can be rather a free-for-all: you watch for the carts, look, and then order fast. An alternative is to order dishes from the menu, but you have to find the waiter. Specialties include braised shark's fin, sautéed chicken with oyster sauce, barbecued Peking duck, braised abalone in oyster sauce, roasted pigeon, beggar's chicken, and sweet-and-sour pork. Set menus are available for HK$100 ($12.99) per person, but you can eat here for much less. Three of us shared about five different dishes for HK$60 ($7.79) a piece.

Western Food

If you're looking for spaghetti or pizza cooked American style, the **Spaghetti House** is your best bet. There are six of them in Hong Kong located at 5 Sharp St. East, Causeway Bay (tel. 5-7952245); at Hennessy and Luard Roads, Wanchai (tel. 5-290901); Malahon Centre, 10 Stanley St., Central District (tel. 5-231372); 3B Cameron Rd., Tsimshatsui (tel. 3-688635); and Barnton Court, ground floor, Harbour City Tsimshatsui (tel. 3-7220260). Similar to American pizza parlors in atmosphere and decor, these restaurants have 13 different kinds of spaghetti beginning at HK$17 ($2.21), pizza beginning at HK$20 ($2.60) for a small size, chili con carne, sandwiches, fried chicken, and lasagne. Hours are 11:30 a.m. to 11:30 p.m. daily.

Rick's Café, 4 Hart Ave., Tsimshatsui (tel. 3-672939), is the place to go if you're going through withdrawal symptoms for Mexican food. Taking its name from the movie *Casablanca*, it sports potted palm trees, ceiling fans, and posters of Humphrey Bogart and Ingrid Bergman. Although it's more of a bar than a restaurant, it serves great tacos, enchiladas, chili con carne, sandwiches, seafood satay, Moroccan kebabs, African ribs, and other exotic fare for HK$25 ($3.25) to HK$45 ($5.84) per plate. Drinks are a little steep, with cocktails starting at HK$30 ($3.89), but until 9 p.m. there's happy hour when they cost about 30% less. After 9 p.m. until about 10:30 there's live entertainment, with jazz, rock, folk, or rhythm and blues; the cover charge varies, depending on the show. Call before hand to inquire about the schedule. The hours of this place are 11:30 a.m. to 4 a.m. every day except Sunday, when it doesn't open until 6 p.m.

La Tortilla, 26-28 Cameron Rd., Tsimshatsui (tel. 3-7233870), is a Mexican restaurant that draws a large Chinese clientele for its popular lunch specials priced at only HK$26 ($3.38), which usually includes a soup or salad, entrée, and coffee. The food isn't exactly like the Mexican food served in the United States, but the waiters are attentive and enthusiastic and the prices are good. The à la carte menu has everything you'd expect from a regular Mexican place, including enchiladas, chili relleno, burritos, tostadas, chili con carne, and of course, tacos. There are also such things as chili shrimp, seafood, and steaks, and a good wine list. Dinner will run about HK$70 ($9.09) here—and be prepared for the corny Mexican music. Hours are noon to midnight.

Considering the fact that many of the shops and hostels in Chungking Mansion are run by Indians, you'd expect that the complex would contain at least a few cheap Indian restaurants. **Sheri Punjab Club Mess**, Block B, on the third floor of Chungking Mansion at 36-44 Nathan Rd. (tel. 3-680859), is one of the most popular among travelers on a tight budget. A bare, clean, and simple room, and some tables and chairs are the only decorations. The menu consists of things like chicken curry, mutton masala, mutton vindaloo, mixed vegetable, tendouri, and muglai chicken, with prices ranging from HK$10 ($1.29) to HK$30 ($3.90) a plate. You'll need to order at least two plates per person, and the plates here are plastic. Hours are 11:30 a.m. to 3 p.m. and 6:30 to 11 p.m.

The local fast-food chain in Hong Kong is **Maxim's**, branches of which can be found all over Hong Kong. You can eat in or take out, and the hours are generally 7:30 a.m. to 9 p.m. The menu offers such items as chicken legs, hamburgers, and sandwiches, with prices averaging HK$6.50 (84¢) and less. A lunch box for HK$7.50 (97¢) changes every day.

In case you're interested, there are also plenty of **McDonald's** available. A hamburger costs HK$3.60 (47¢) and a Big Mac is HK$8 ($1.03).

READER'S EATING SUGGESTION: "Next door to the Park Hotel on Cameron Road is a restaurant I highly recommend to people or families in a budget, the **Can Do Restaurant.** It is popular with locals and with tourists. They serve breakfast through dinner, they have an English menu and the waiters speak some English. They even offer some traditional Australian foods if you have had enough Chinese. Also, they have Western sandwiches and Western-type food, but they do offer a full line of Chinese food and seafood. You can dine in the HK$20 ($2.60) to HK$30 ($3.90) range easily" (John Cross, Atlanta, Ga.).

5. What to See

THE FOUR MUSTS: There are four things every visitor to Hong Kong should do, and they all involve the colony's public transportation system. They are: ride the Star Ferry across the harbor; take a rickety old tram on Hong Kong Island; go up to Victoria Peak in the Peak tram; and ride one of the ferries to the outlying islands. Nothing can beat the thrill of these four experiences, nor give better insight into the essence of Hong Kong and its people; riding the ferries and trams are trips in themselves and all are inexpensive.

For tips on using the Star Ferry and Hong Kong's tram system, refer to the "Getting Around" section of this chapter. The Peak tram will be described later in this section, while ferries to outlying islands are outined in "Exploring the Territories and Environs." You might also want to pick up two free brochures at Hong Kong Tourist Association (HKTA) offices called *Places of Interest by Public Transport* and *Outlying Islands*.

JUST WALKING AROUND: Surprisingly compact, Hong Kong is an easy city to explore by foot. Walking affords a more intimate relationship with your surroundings, allows chance encounters with the unexpected, and lets you discover that vegetable market, temple, or shop you otherwise never would have seen. If, for example, you're in the Central District and want to eat dinner on Food Street in Causeway Bay, you can walk there in less than an hour, passing through colorful Wanchai on the way. Causeway Bay is good for unstructured exploring since it's full of little sidewalk markets, street vendors, restaurants, and shops patronized by the locals. A walk up Nathan Road from the harbor to the Yaumatei subway station takes less than 30 minutes, although it would be hard to resist all the shops and department stores you pass on the way. If you don't mind dishing out HK$10 ($1.30), you can purchase a nifty booklet put out by the Hong Kong Tourist Association called *Central and Western District Walking Tour*. Complete with detailed maps, it describes a three-hour walk through Hong Kong Island's Central and Western districts, including Cloth Alley, with its stalls selling fabrics; Egg Street, with its variety of eggs bound for Hong Kong's restaurants; Bonham Strand, with Chinese medicinal shops; and Cat Street, with its junk and antiques. The booklet explains things you'll see on the way and is highly recommended.

CHINESE CULTURAL SHOWS: The HKTA provides **free cultural entertainment** for visitors throughout the month. The program and location of the shows vary. Programs may be demonstrations of Chinese magic and acrobatics, folk songs and dances, Fukienese string puppetry, Chinese martial arts, Chinese instrumental music, shadow puppetry, or Chinese opera. The shows, which last an hour, take place at two locations: Cityplaza on Hong Kong Island and New World Centre on Kowloon. For information on what's being shown, times, and locations, contact the HKTA.

Chinese opera, with its elaborate costumes and stage settings, has a worldwide reputation. Unfortunately, this ancient form of entertainment is so popular in Hong Kong that it is almost impossible for visiting tourists to get tickets. The best performers are from mainland China, and tickets sell out well in advance.

If you're still determined to see a performance, contact the HKTA to see whether anything is going on or check with the weekly *Hong Kong*, a tourist publication available free in hotels and at HKTA offices.

Other cultural activities in which you may be interested include performances by the **Hong Kong Philharmonic Orchestra** or entertainment at the **Arts Center and Academy for Performing Arts** at Wanchai, which offers everything from live theater and pop concerts to avant-garde films. Hong Kong also has two arts festivals, one in February and one in October.

For information on what's going on, check Hong Kong's two **newspapers**, the *South China Morning Post* and the *Hong Kong Standard;* the two tourist newspapers, *Orient* and *Hong Kong;* and the *Official Hong Kong Guide.*

HONG KONG ISLAND: With about 30 square miles, Hong Kong Island holds the most attractions for the visitor. This is where the colony's history began, and there's everything here from the high-rises of the Central District to the beaches on the southern coast.

Victoria Peak

At 1,308 feet, Victoria Peak is the island's tallest hill and offers the best and most spectacular views of Hong Kong. It's always been one of the colony's most exclusive places to live, since in the days before air conditioning the peak was usually a few degrees cooler than the sweltering city below. A hundred years ago the rich reached the peak after a three-hour trip in sedan chairs (which were carried to the top by coolies). Then, in 1888, the **peak tram** opened, cutting the journey from three hours to eight minutes.

The easiest way to reach the peak tram, located on Garden Road just behind the Hilton Hotel, is to take one of the free shuttle buses that operate between the tram terminal and the Star Ferry. Shuttle buses run between 9 a.m. and 7 p.m. daily at 20-minute intervals.

As for the peak tram, it costs HK$6 (78¢) one way, HK$10 ($1.30) round trip. The green cast-iron funicular cars with mahogany seats depart every ten minutes and are in operation daily from 7 a.m. to midnight. The tram climbs almost vertically to the top of the peak and—don't worry—there's never been an accident. At the top there's the **Peak Tower**, where you will find a restaurant, observation deck, and the Peak Tower Village, with more than 30 booths selling Chinese arts and crafts from 9:30 a.m. to 7 p.m. daily.

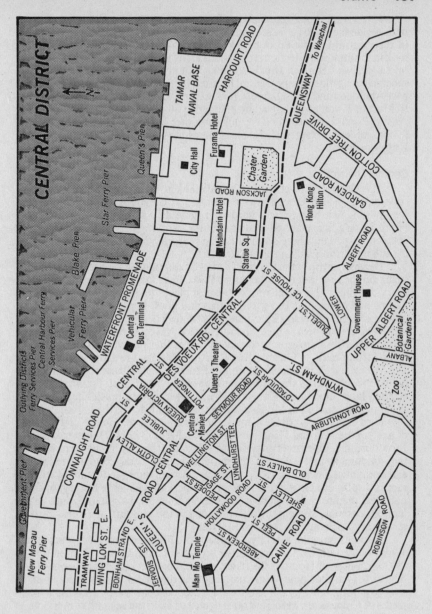

If you want to do some walking there are a couple of possibilities. A foot-path beside the Peak Tower snakes along the side of the cliff, offering great views of the Central District down below, the harbor, and Kowloon. If you want a look in the opposite direction, you can circle the top of the peak in about an hour on Lugard and Harlech Roads. Although in my opinion the views are not as spectacular as those on the Central District side, on really clear days you can see past Aberdeen and the islands of Cheung Chau, Lantau, and Lamma all the way to Macau. If you're feeling really energetic you might want to hike up Mount Austin Road to where the governor's summer lodge used to stand. Only the formal gardens remain, but it's a pleasant respite from the crowdedness of Hong Kong down below.

Central District

The Central District used to be called Victoria and had elegant colonial-style buildings with sweeping verandas and narrow streets filled with pigtailed men pulling rickshaws. That's hard to imagine if you look at it now. Today it's Hong Kong's financial and business center, with high-rise office buildings of glass and concrete. There's almost nothing to remind one of the olden days, but it's still interesting walking around here a bit.

Begin your trip in the Central District by stopping off for a relaxing drink or snack on the upper deck of the public **Blake Pier**, located just west of the Star Ferry terminal. This is one of the cheapest places to enjoy a great view of the harbor and of the Star Ferry as it comes and goes. Popular at lunchtime with office personnel, the snackbar here sells sandwiches, spaghetti, and salads as well as ice cream, beer, coffee, and soft drinks. As you sit there soaking up some of the waterfront ambience, consider the fact that the waterfront used to be much farther back, at Queen's Road. In the 1800s land reclamation added first Des Voeux and then Connaught Roads. Land reclamation has also been carried on extensively across the harbor on Kowloon—all of East Tsimshatsui is re-claimed land. One Hong Kong local I met joked that so much land was being reclaimed it wouldn't be long before you could walk across the harbor.

Next on your tour of the Central District could be the **Hong Kong Museum of Art**, on the 10th and 11th floors of City Hall (tel. 5-224127), just east of Star Ferry terminal. Open every day except Thursday from 10 a.m. to 6 p.m. (from 1 p.m. on Sunday and holidays), the museum houses a collection of Chinese art and antiquities, including jade, cloisonné, lacquerware, and paintings. Its ceramics display has pieces from nearly every period in Chinese history, while its historical picture collection consists of more than 800 paintings, prints, draw-ings, lithographs, and engravings. Included in the museum are works by con-temporary Asian artists. Admission is free.

Another museum worth your time is the **Flagstaff House Museum of Tea Ware**, located off Cotton Tree Drive up the hill from Chater Garden (tel. 5-299390). Flagstaff House is the oldest colonial building in Hong Kong—it was built in 1844 as the home of the commander of the British forces. Open from 10 a.m. to 5 p.m. daily except Wednesday, the museum is free and displays 500 pieces of Chinese tea ware of various dynasties from the seventh century on.

From Flagstaff House, retrace your steps to Queensway Road, where you'll find the tram tracks. Take a left and follow the tracks onto **Des Voeux Road Central**. As you walk along Des Voeux, you'll pass smart-looking fashion bou-tiques, banks, and office buildings as well as the Landmark with its designer shops and restaurants. Presently you'll reach **Li Yuen Street East and Li Yuen Street West**, which rise up steeply to your left and are packed with street vendors selling clothing and accessories. After you've explored these two streets, continue walking down Des Voeux until you reach **Central Market**, a four-story Victorian-looking square building where fresh produce—everything from vegetables and eels to live chickens—is sold. It's open from 6 a.m. to 2 p.m. and again from 4:30 to 8 p.m.

The next interesting place to look for is **Wing On Street**, locally known as Cloth Alley because of the long string of stalls selling fabrics from around the world. Next comes **Wing Sing Street**, also called Egg Street, which is the first left off Wing Lok Street. All different kinds of eggs are sold here in the morning, from century-old eggs to salted eggs. Century-old eggs are actually only a few weeks old, having first been treated with tea leaves, salt, and chemicals before being covered with mud and rice husks.

At the end of Wing Sing Street, take a right onto Queen's Road Central, and keep going straight onto Bonham Strand. From here take an immediate left onto Jervois Street. On **Jervois** and **Hillier Streets** you'll find snake shops. Eaten in autumn as protection against the winter cold, snakes are favored also for their gall bladders, which are mixed with Chinese wine as cures for rheumatism. The mixture is also believed to be an aphrodisiac.

Back on Bonham Strand, you'll pass several rattan shops, followed by Chinese herb and medicinal shops on Bonham Strand West, where you'll see everything from ginseng to deer antlers for sale. From Bonham Strand cut back inland (south) until you reach **Hollywood Road**. Hollywood Road is a strange mixture of shops selling coffins and other things for funerals and furniture and curio antique shops, offering real antiques as well as excellent imitations. Next to Ladder Street, an extremely steep flight of stairs, is **Man Mo Temple**, Hong Kong Island's oldest and most famous temple. It was around this area that the movie *The World of Suzie Wong* was shot. The temple, which dates back to 1847 and is open daily from 7 a.m. to 5 p.m., is dedicated to two deities, a third-century statesman representing the god of literature and a second-century soldier, the god of war. Two ornately carved sedan chairs are kept in the temple which are used to carry the two gods around during festivals. Incidentally, the deity representing the soldier is said to find patronage among members of the underworld—as well as the police force.

If you follow the steps leading downhill on Ladder Street, you'll see **Upper Lascar Row** leading off to the left, better known as Cat Street. Pleasant with potted palms, this pedestrian lane offers a fantastic study in junk, with most dealers laying their wares out on the street. Browse here for old bits of china, snuff bottles, watches, pictures, and other odds and ends.

Museum of Chinese Historical Relics

If you're in Wanchai, be sure to stop off at the Museum of Chinese Historical Relics, Causeway Centre, 28 Harbour Rd. (tel. 5-8320411). Open daily from 10 a.m. to 6 p.m. and charging an admission of HK$12 ($1.56), it contains artifacts and treasures from China dating over a span of a thousand years, with both permanent and temporary exhibitions.

Zoological and Botanical Gardens

Established in 1864, these gardens are located on the side of Victoria Peak past the Hilton on Garden Road. They are free to the public, and exploring them is a pleasant way to spend an hour or so if you're tired of the Central District and its traffic. Flowers are almost always in bloom, from azaleas in spring to wisteria and bauhinea in summer and fall. In addition to Jaguars, orangutans, and monkeys, there's an aviary with about 800 birds representing 300 species.

Included are Palawan peacocks, birds of paradise from Papua New Guinea, cranes, and Mandarin ducks.

Aw Boon Haw Gardens (Tiger Balm Gardens)

These are probably the most bizarre gardens you'll ever see. Built in 1935 by Chinese millionaire Aw Boon Haw, who made his fortune with a cure-all called Tiger Balm, the 7½ acres of these gardens feature colorfully painted statues from Chinese mythology. Some of the figures are rather grotesque, especially those depicting unfortunate souls being tortured in hell. However, the place is free and is open daily from 9 a.m. to 4 p.m. Because the gardens are so colorfully you can get some great photographs here to show the folks back home. Sometimes in the near future (and perhaps by the time you read this), the ground floor of the Aw Mansion will be opened to the public with a display of antique jade carvings. Aw Boon Haw Gardens is located off Tai Hang Road, which you can reach by bus 11 from the Central Bus Terminal.

Noon Day Gun

It's not worth going out of your way for, but if you're in the neighborhood of the Excelsior Hotel, look for a small garden opposite the hotel with a gun planted in it. Fired every day at noon, this gun was immortalized in Noël Coward's "Mad Dogs and Englishmen": "In Hong Kong they strike a gong and fire off the noon day gun." The tradition started in the last century when the Jardines trading company fired off a double-gun salute to returning bosses. This perturbed a British senior naval officer who ordered as punishment that Jardines fire the gun every day at noon.

Aberdeen

A naturally protected harbor on the south side of Hong Kong Island, Aberdeen used to be a charming fishing village famous for its several thousand junks and boat people. Many of the boat people, however, have been moved to massive housing projects, and the waterfront surrounding Aberdeen is crowded with high-rises. Still, Aberdeen continues to be popular with the tourist crowd because of its remaining boat population and floating restaurants. Women operating sampans will vie for your dollars to tour you around the harbor, which is definitely worth the cost since it's about the only thing to do here and is the best way to see the junks. A 20-minute tour will cost HK$35 ($4.55) per person and is offered daily between 8 a.m. and 6 p.m. You'll pass huge boats housing extending families and you'll be amazed at what you see: men repairing fishing nets, women hanging out their laundry, dogs barking and children playing, families eating and people fishing in the murky waters. There was a time when a boat person could be born, live, marry, and die on board without ever setting foot on shore. Nowadays, however, young people are moving to shore to take advantage of job opportunities.

Ocean Park

If you're a kid or a kid at heart, you'll love Ocean Park and its attractions, open every day from 10 a.m. to 6 p.m. except on Sunday and holidays, when it opens earlier at 9 a.m. Situated along a rocky and dramatic coastline on the island's southern shore, the park is divided into "lowland" and "highland" areas, which are linked together by a spectacular ten-minute ride by cable car. The lowland boasts a botanical garden and the Golden Pagoda, with more varieties of goldfish than you ever imagined possible, most of them from China. For children there's a children's zoo, a dolphin pool where you can feed the dolphins, and a playground that includes trampolines and air balloons to get rid of excess energy.

The highland area has an artificial wave cove which is home to seals, walruses, sea lions, and penguins, as well as various thrill rides which include a roller coaster that turns upside down. Ocean Theatre features shows by talented dolphins, sea lions, and a killer whale. But most impressive of all, in my opinion, is the Atoll Reef, the world's largest aquarium. The observation passageway circles three stories around the outside of the aquarium, giving you views from different angles of everything from giant turtles to schools of tropical fish. Ocean Park's most recent addition is its impressive aviary, with approximately 150 species of birds.

Entrance fee to Ocean Park is HK$80 ($10.39) for adults, half price for children. For more information, call 5-555222.

Water World

This attraction is located next to Ocean Park and is a good place to cool off on a hot summer's day. Open from 9 a.m. to 10:30 p.m. daily (until 5 p.m. in spring and autumn). Water World is a conglomeration of several pools with various slides and diving platforms, and it even has a pool with a sandy beach and real waves. Open from April to the end of October only, it costs HK$30 ($3.90) to HK$40 ($5.19), depending on the time and the day (Sunday is the most expensive). Children are half price. Be sure to bring your bathing suit.

KOWLOON: Kowloon gets its name from *Gau Lung,* which means "nine dragons." Legend has it that about 800 years ago a boy emperor counted eight hills on Kowloon and remarked that there must be eight dragons living here, since dragons were known to inhabit hills. His prime minister answered that in actuality there must be nine dragons, since an emperor is also considered to be a dragon.

You'd have a lot of trouble trying to find eight hills in Kowloon today. Most of the peninsula has been taken over by housing and industrial estates, and doesn't offer much to the tourist other than shopping. However, there are a few attractions you may wish to visit, especially if it's a humid or rainy day and you're looking for some respite.

Space Museum

Located on Salisbury Road in front of the Peninsula Hotel on the Tsimshatsui waterfront, this museum is easy to spot, with its white-domed planetarium. The museum is divided into three parts—the Space Theatre's planetarium, where the film is projected onto the 75-foot domed roof, the Hall of Solar Sciences on solar phenomena, and an exhibition hall that explores man's progress in astronomy and space. Shows at Space Theatre are held throughout the afternoon and early evening and cost HK$15 ($1.95) per person. English headsets with simultaneous translations are provided free of charge for the hour-long show. Space Museum is open every day except Tuesday until 9:30 p.m., opening at 2 p.m. on weekdays, at 1 p.m. on Saturday, and noon on Sunday. Call 3-721236 for more information on show times.

Museum of History

In Kowloon Park, the Museum of History (tel. 3-671124) outlines the history of the colony through displays of archeological finds, ethnographic collections, and historical photographs. Included in the collection is an exhibition of

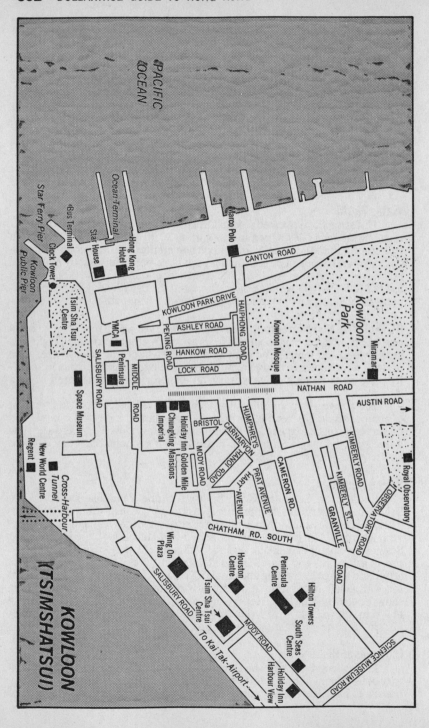

PACIFIC OCEAN

Star Ferry Pier

Ocean Terminal

Bus Terminal

Clock Tower

Kowloon Public Pier

Star House

Hong Kong Hotel

Marco Polo

CANTON ROAD

Tsim Sha Tsui Centre

Kowloon Park Drive

HAIPHONG ROAD

Kowloon Park

YMCA

PEKING ROAD

ASHLEY ROAD

HANKOW ROAD

LOCK ROAD

Kowloon Mosque

Miramar

SALISBURY ROAD

Peninsula

MIDDLE ROAD

NATHAN ROAD

AUSTIN ROAD →

Space Museum

BRISTOL

Chungking Mansions

Imperial

Holiday Inn Golden Mile

MODY ROAD

HUMPHREY'S

CARNARVON

HART AVENUE

PRAT AVENUE

CAMERON RD.

KIMBERLY ROAD

KIMBERLEY ST.

GRANVILLE

OBSERVATORY ROAD

Royal Observatory

Regent

New World Centre

Cross-Harbour Tunnel

CHATHAM RD. SOUTH

Wing On Plaza

SALISBURY ROAD

Tsim Sha Tsui Centre

To Kai Tak Airport →

Houston Centre

Peninsula Centre

Hilton Towers

South Seas Centre

MODY ROAD

Holiday Inn Harbour View

ROAD

SCIENCE MUSEUM ROAD

KOWLOON (TSIMSHATSUI)

model junks. The museum is free of charge and open every day except Friday from 10 a.m. to 6 p.m. (on Sunday and holidays from 1 to 6 p.m.).

Jade Market

Every morning at 10 a.m. and continuing until 4 p.m., buyers, traders, and sellers of jade converge on Kansu Street in Kowloon's Yaumatei District. Laying out their wares on everything from cloth spread out on the sidewalk to satin-lined display cases, vendors sell jade to Chinese who know the market. In other words, unless you know what you're looking for and can tell good jade from worthless, you're better off coming here just for a look. It's possible to infuse jade with color so that inferior stones acquire the brightness and translucence associated with more expensive jade. If you want a souvenir, pick up a pendant or bangle but don't spend more than a few dollars for it. Pearls are also sold.

Jade has long been important to the Chinese, who consider it a symbol of youth and regeneration. Jade comes in a variety of colors, including, red, white, and black. Green, however, is the color you usually see. Watch how the Chinese bargain at the market—they do it secretly so that no one standing around and watching will know the final price. More information is available in a free pamphlet put out by HKTA called *Yau Ma Tei & Jade Market*.

Sung Dynasty Village

This is a re-creation of how a village might have looked in China 1,000 years ago during the Sung Dynasty. Built at a cost of two million U.S. dollars, it took five years to construct the village with close attention given to architectural detail. The village consists of various open-fronted wooden shops, stalls, and buildings grouped around a willow-lined stream. Staffed by villagers dressed in Sung Dynasty costumes, each shop is based on a different theme with a different product, from almond cookies and Chinese tea to hand-painted fans and incense. Demonstrations are given to show how the items are made. There's a rice-wine shop, an herbal medicine shop, a Chinese restaurant, and a replica of a rich man's house. There's also entertainment, from a monkey show to Chinese acrobatics and opera.

Included in the village is Hong Kong's largest wax museum, with famous personalities from Chinese history. Be sure to read the explanations that accompany each figure as they're quite entertaining. We learn, for example, that Pao Szu, the favorite concubine of Emperor Chou Yu, was a great beauty but that it was very difficult to make her laugh. Kou Chien, who lived around 421 B.C., suffered defeat by his enemies and as self-punishment "he slept on faggots and constantly tasted gall." It must have worked because we're told that after 20 years he finally succeeded in defeating his enemy.

If you're interested in visiting Sung Dynasty Village, it's best to join an organized tour, the information for which is given below. Otherwise, if you want to go on your own, you can do so only on Saturday or Sunday from 12:30 to 5 p.m. Admission is HK$35 ($4.54), and to get there take either bus 6A from the Star Ferry or the Mass Transit Railway (MTR) to Mei Fou Station.

ORGANIZED TOURS: Hong Kong is well developed in the organized-tour department, and if you're pressed for time this is the best way to go. The Hong Kong Island Tour, for example, is a three- to four-hour trip offered both morning and afternoon to such places as Victoria Peak, Tiger Balm Gardens, Repulse Bay, and Aberdeen. **Watertours** is the largest tour organizer of boat and junk cruises around the harbor and to outlying islands, offering about 20 various trips from which to choose. There are also tours of factories making everything from clothing to brassware, porcelain, and silk. For information on night tours, refer to Section 7, "Hong Kong After Dark." You can contact Water Tours directly through your hotel or call 5-254808 or 5-263538.

Another tour operator, **The Gray Line**, offers a variety of tours to Hong Kong Island, Kowloon and the New Territories, Macau, and China, with tour outlets at most first- and medium-class hotels. The Hilton even offers its own cruise aboard its 110-foot brigantine named the *Wan Fu*, built in Taiwan in 1959. Breakfast, luncheon, dinner, and sunset cruises are offered. For more information call the Hilton at 5-233111.

HKTA also offers several tours, including one to Sung Dynasty Village described above. Tours to the village that include lunch or dinner are HK$180 ($23.38) for adults and HK$125 ($16.23) for children. Afternoon tours, including a snack only, are HK$140 ($18.18) and HK$105 ($13.64) respectively. Another HKTA tour is "The Land Between" Tour, which takes guests via air-conditioned motorcoach on a trip through the New Territories. This seven-hour trip includes lunch in a Cantonese restaurant and visits to a Buddhist temple and a produce market at HK$198 ($25.71) for adults and HK$155 ($20.13) for children under 12.

You can also join an HKTA tour for a visit to the racetrack on Wednesday, Saturday, and an occasional Sunday from September through May. This is an exciting trip if you get in on the betting, and you don't have to bet much— HK$10 ($1.30) per race is enough. This tour costs HK$220 ($28.57), includes lunch or dinner, and is limited to tourists over 18 who have been in Hong Kong fewer than 21 days.

Sports enthusiasts may want to take advantage of the Sports and Recreation Tour, which involves a day spent at the Clearwater Bay Golf and Country Club. The tour price of HK$210 ($27.27) for adults and HK$165 ($21.42) for children includes transportation to and from the club, lunch, and the admission fee to the club. Facilities at the club include golf courses, tennis courts, swimming pool, saunas, and a Jacuzzi. There's a greens fee of HK$240 ($31.17) charged for golf, tennis courts rent from HK$33 ($4.29) per hour, and both clubs and racquets are available for hire. Use of the pool, saunas, and Jacuzzi is free.

All tours can be booked through your hotel, a travel agent, or HKTA.

SPORTS: Despite the fact that Hong Kong is rather small with a sizable population, there's enough open space to pursue everything from golf to hiking to windsurfing. For the hard-working Chinese and expatriates, recreation and leisure are important for winding down after a tiring week. With that in mind, try to schedule your golfing, swimming, or hiking trips on weekdays unless you enjoy jostling elbows with the crowds.

Horse Races

If you'd rather watch sports than play, and if you're in Hong Kong anytime from September through May, join the rest of Hong Kong at the horse races. Horse racing got its start in the colony in Happy Valley more than 100 years ago, making the Happy Valley track the oldest racecourse in Asia outside China. Without a doubt, horse racing is by far the most popular sporting event in Hong Kong. The Chinese love to gamble and there are even off-course betting offices around the city for those unable to make it to the races. There are two tracks in Hong Kong, the older one in Happy Valley and a new, modern one in Shatin in the New Territories, with races held at one or the other on Wednesday nights and on Saturday and Sunday afternoons.

The cheapest admission fee is HK$10 ($1.30), which is for the general public and is standing room only. If you want to watch from the Hong Kong Royal Jockey Club members' stand, are over 18 years old, and have been in Hong Kong fewer than 21 days, you can purchase a member's badge for HK$50 ($6.49). It's available upon display of your passport at either the Badge Enquiry Office at both tracks' main entrance to the members' private enclosure or at off-course betting centers. Tickets are sold on a first-come, first-served basis. If you don't want to go to the races but would still like to bet on the outcomes, you can place bets at one of the many off-course betting centers. Two convenient off-course centers are at the Star Ferry concourse in the Central District and 2-4 Prat Ave. in Tsimshatsui. On the other hand, the most effortless way to see the races is to join an HKTA tour to the horse races, described in the tour section above.

Golf

The **Royal Hong Kong Golf Club** welcomes visitors during weekdays at courses in both Fanling and Deep Water Bay. There are three 18-hole courses at Fanling, with greens fees at HK$390 ($50.65). Deep Water Bay charges HK$110 ($14.29) for its nine holes (weekdays only) with clubs renting for HK$5 (65¢). For more information, call the Royal Hong Kong Golf Club at 0-901211.

The **Discovery Bay Golf Club** (tel. 5-9877271) on Lantau Island has a beautiful 18-hole course developed by Robert Trent Jones, Jr., with great views of the water. Visitors are allowed to play here from Monday to Friday with the exception of public holidays, and greens fees are HK$165 ($21.43).

Another scenic course is operated near Sai Kung by the **Clearwater Bay Golf and Country Club** (tel. 3-7192454). Visitors' green fees are HK$260 ($33.77). On weekends, guests must be signed in by a member, but green fees remain the same. If you're interested in playing golf here but want to let someone else worry about arranging transportation, contact HKTA for its Sports and Recreation Tour, described in the organized tour section above.

Beaches

There are about 40 beaches in Hong Kong open for public use, most of which have lifeguards on duty in the summer, changing rooms, and snack stands or restaurants. Even on Hong Kong Island itself you can find a number of beaches, including Big Wave Bay and Shek O on the east coast, and Stanley, Deep Water Bay, and Repulse Bay on the southern coast. Repulse Bay is by far the most popular beach in Hong Kong and gets unbelievably crowded on a summer weekend. Prettier beaches are found on the outlying islands, including Hung Shing Ye on Lamma, Tung Wan on Cheung Chau, and Cheung Sha on Lantau.

Windsurfing boards can be rented at many of the beaches, including Stanley and Tung Wan. Although prices may vary slightly, cost of a board for one hour is HK$45 ($5.85) to HK$60 ($7.79) at Stanley.

Hiking

There are many trails of varying levels of difficulty throughout Hong Kong. Serious hikers, for example, may want to consider the MacLehose Trail in Sai Kung in the New Territories, which stretches about 60 miles through eight country parks, or Lantau Trail, a 43-mile circular trail on Lantau Island. The Lantau Trail begins and ends at Mui Wo (also called Silvermine Bay), passing several popular scenic spots along the way. Both the MacLehose and Lantau trails are divided into smaller sections of varying difficulty, which means you can tailor your hike to suit your own abilities. For more information about hiking in Hong Kong, contact HKTA.

FESTIVALS: Hong Kong has 17 public holidays a year. Although some of them are British holidays, the majority are Chinese and follow the Chinese lunar calendar, which means that they do not fall on the same date each year. Most shops and restaurants stay open during holidays, with the exception of Chinese New Year. Below are a few of the most popular festivals.

Chinese New Year
The most important Chinese holiday, this is a family festival with visits paid to friends and relatives. Falling in either late January or February, it's a time for settling debts, visiting fortune tellers, and worshipping ancestors. Shops close down for two to three days, streets are decorated, and a fireworks display is held over the harbor. Since this festival is a family affair, it holds little interest to the tourist. In fact, you should remember that if you're planning a side trip into China this is the worst time to go, since all routes to the mainland are clogged with Chinese going back to their homeland to visit relatives. Dates for the Chinese New Year are February 17 in 1988 and February 6 in 1989.

Tin Hau Festival
This is one of Hong Kong's most colorful festivals. Tin Hau, Hong Kong's most popular deity among fishing folk, is goddess of the sea. Legend has it that she was a fisherman's daughter who guided a fishing fleet to shore in the midst of a terrible storm. To pay tribute to Tin Hau, fishing boats are decorated with colorful flags and family shrines are carried to shore to be blessed by Taoist priests. This festival falls on May 8 in 1988 and on April 28 in 1989.

Cheung Chau Bun Festival
Held in May on the island of Cheung Chau, this three-day affair is to appease restless ghosts and spirits. Activities include street parades and prayers in the temples, and in front of Pak Tai Temple three scaffolds holding buns are erected. These buns supposedly bring good luck to those who receive them. The 1988 and 1989 dates for this festival have not yet been set.

Dragon Boat Races
Races of long and narrow boats gaily painted and powered by oarsmen are held every year around June. It's an exciting event, and tour operators run cruises so that visitors can watch the events from a junk, ferry, or cruiser. Upcoming dates are June 18, 1988, and June 8, 1989.

Mid-Autumn Festival
Held in early autumn, this festival celebrates the harvest and the brightest moon of the year. In honor of the event, locals light lanterns and eat mooncakes. The Urban Council organizes lantern carnivals in parks on both Hong Kong Island and Kowloon, where you can join the Chinese for strolls under hundreds of lanterns. This festival falls on September 25, 1988, and September 14, 1989.

6. Where to Shop
One of the main reasons people come to Hong Kong is to shop. In fact, Hong Kong is such a popular shopping destination that many luxury cruise lin-

ers dock longer in Hong Kong than they do anywhere else on their tour. According to the Hong Kong Tourist Association (HKTA), visitors to the colony spend approximately 50% of their money on shopping. As a duty-free port, all imported goods are free of duty in Hong Kong with the exception of tobacco, alcohol, perfume, cosmetics, cars, and some petroleum products. This means that you can get many items cheaper in Hong Kong than you can in the country where they were made.

However, Hong Kong is a buyer-beware market. Name brands are sometimes fakes and equipment may not work. To make things worse, goods usually are not returnable and deposits are not refundable. To be on the safe side, try to make your major purchases at HKTA member stores. Altogether there are more than 750 member shops, listed in a directory provided free by HKTA offices called *The Official Guide to Shopping, Eating Out and Services in Hong Kong*. This booklet gives the names, addresses, and phone numbers of shops for everything from audio-video equipment to musical instruments and hairpieces. HKTA member stores, which display the HKTA logo (a round circle with a red junk in the middle), are required to give accurate representation of the products they sell and prompt rectification of justified complaints. If you have any complaints against a member store, contact the Membership Department of HKTA, 35th floor, Connaught Centre, Central District (tel. 5-244191).

In any case, if you're buying an imported good such as a camera or electronic item, be sure to ask for a guarantee, which should include a description of the model and serial number, date of purchase, name and address of the shop where you bought it, and the shop's official stamp. You should also ask for a receipt detailing a description of your purchase.

And before you buy anything, be sure to shop around. Unless you're in a department store or an expensive boutique you'll probably be able to bargain—and prices for items can vary drastically.

WHAT TO BUY: If you've looked at the labels of clothes sold in your own hometown stores and shopping malls, you've probably noticed that "Made in Hong Kong" is a common label. It shouldn't come as a surprise, therefore, to learn that Hong Kong is one of the best places in the world to buy clothes. Both custom-made and designer clothes are a real bargain in Hong Kong, including three-piece business suits, leather outfits, furs, and jeans. Other good buys include shoes, jewelry, watches, clocks, stereo equipment, leather goods, luggage, handbags, briefcases, shoes, Chinese herbs, and eyeglasses. And, of course, if you're interested in fake name-brand watches, handbags, or clothing to impress the folks back home, you've come to the right place. Although illegal, fake name-brand items were still being sold at Hong Kong's night markets during my last visit. The vendors are simply a little more cautious, ready to flee at the first sight of officials.

You can buy products from the People's Republic of China sometimes cheaper in Hong Kong than you can in China, including porcelain, jade, cloisonné, silk clothing, jewelry, and artwork. Hong Kong is also the center for arts and crafts from other parts of Asia, including Indonesia, the Philippines, India, and Thailand.

SHOPPING DISTRICTS: Tsimshatsui has the greatest concentration of shops in Hong Kong. **Nathan Road**, which extends up the backbone of Kowloon for 2½ miles from the harbor to the border of the New Territories, is lined with stores selling clothes, jewelry, cameras and electronic goods, crafts from China, shoes, handbags, luggage, watches, and more. There are tailors tattoo artists, and even shops that will carve your name into a wooden chop (I saw a sign that was probably more truthful than most that advertised "chop craving"). There are also department stores and shopping arcades. Be sure to explore the side streets radiating off Nathan Road, as well as the three huge shopping malls spread along the waterfront of Tsimshatsui, which are described under their own section below.

Another shopping district is **Causeway Bay** on Hong Kong Island. In contrast to Tsimshatsui, it caters more to a local market rather than to tourists, and prices are generally quite low. In addition to small shops selling everything from shoes to clothing to Chinese herbs, there are Japanese department stores, a Lane Crawford department store, and the China Products store with imports from mainland China. On the other side of Hong Kong Island is Stanley Market, a fun, interesting, and inexpensive shopping destination described in more detail later in this chapter.

TAILORS: The 24-hour suit is a thing of the past, but you can still have clothes made to fit in a few days. Tailors in Hong Kong will make anything you want, from business suits to evening gowns and wedding dresses. Some stores will let you bring in your own fabric while others require that you buy theirs. Take a picture or drawing along with you to show what you want. As for price, it will cost about the same as what you'd pay for it ready-made back home, but the difference, of course, is that this one should fit you perfectly. If it doesn't, the tailor should make alterations—but make sure beforehand that they're included in the original price. If you still don't like the finished product, you don't have to accept it. However, you'll forfeit the deposit that you were required to pay before the tailor began working. For that reason, don't pay more than 20% as a deposit.

With more than 2,500 tailoring establishments in Hong Kong, it shouldn't be any problem finding one. If your hotel has a shopping arcade you may even be able to find one there. Otherwise, check the list in the *Official Guide to Shopping, Eating Out and Services in Hong Kong*.

EXPENSIVE DESIGNER BOUTIQUES: If you're looking for international name brands and don't care about price, check out the boutiques in the Peninsula Hotel in Tsimshatsui and the Landmark, Swire House, and Prince's Building in the Central District. The Landmark, for example, has shops for Gucci, Hermès, Louis Vuitton, Givenchy, Lanvin, Christian Dior, Chloë, and Bally. The Swire House has Japanese fashions from such designers as Matsuda, Issey Miyake, and Yohji Yamamoto. The Prince's Building, located across from the Mandarin Hotel, showcases boutiques by Dunhill, Cartier, Cerruti, Chanel, Christian Dior, Daks Simpson, Nina Ricci, and Diane Freis, while the Peninsula Hotel across the water boasts a shopping arcade with designer boutiques by Charles Jourdan, Louis Vuitton, Loewe, Bally, Chanel, and Dunhill, to name only a few. Expect to pay a lot of money and you won't be disappointed.

FACTORY OUTLETS: Shoppers in the know head for Hong Kong's factory outlets to buy their clothes. Most outlets are either in the Central District on Hong Kong Island or in Hung Hom and Tsimshatsui in Kowloon. Clothes sold here are excess stock, overruns, and quality control rejects which sell at unbelievably low prices. Because they are made for the export market, sizes are Western. HKTA puts out a list of some of the factory outlets. Most shops are open from about 9 a.m. to 5:30 or 6 p.m. Monday through Friday, and some shops are also open on Saturday and Sunday. Bargains include clothes made of silk, cashmere, leather, cotton, and wool, and some outlets have men's clothing as well. These are great places to buy well-tailored and expensive-looking business outfits.

DEPARTMENT STORES: Department stores in Hong Kong sometimes have great sales. Wing On and Lane Crawford are two up-market chain department stores with a good selection of clothing, accessories, local and imported designer fashions, gift items, and cosmetics. Japanese department stores have also made great headway in Hong Kong and are very popular with the locals. In Causeway Bay, for example, there are Daimaru, Matsuzakaya, and Mitsukoshi stores, while Kowloon has Isetan and Tokyu department stores.

For addresses of department stores, consult the *Official Guide to Shopping, Eating Out and Services in Hong Kong.*

SHOPPING MALLS: Kowloon has the four largest shopping malls in Hong Kong. Three of them are only a minute's walk away from the Star Ferry on Canton Road and are called **Ocean Terminal, Ocean Centre,** and **Harbour City.** All interconnected by air-conditioned walkways, they have shops selling clothing, accessories, jewelry, cosmetics, antiques, electronic goods, furniture, housewares, Asian arts and crafts, etc. Altogether there are 600 outlets in the whole complex, enough to keep you occupied on a rainy or humid day when you'd rather be inside than out. Most shops are open from about 10 a.m. to 7 or 8 p.m. Another shopping mall is located in the **New World Centre** in East Tsimshatsui.

CHINESE PRODUCTS: Three names to watch out for if you're looking for imports from China are Chinese Products Co., Chinese Arts & Crafts Ltd., and Yue Hwa Chinese Products Emporium Ltd. As I said before, you can buy some products from China more cheaply in Hong Kong than in China itself.

Chinese Arts & Crafts Ltd. is the top upper-end shop for Chinese arts and crafts. This is probably the best and safest place to buy jade, and you can also buy silk dresses and blouses, antiques, carpets, cloisonné, furs, Chinese medicine, rosewood furniture, and embroidered linen tablecloths or pillowcases. There are several stores in Hong Kong, including the Star House next to the Star Ferry in Tsimshatsui and at Queen's Road and Wyndham Street in the Central District. This chain's newest store is in the Silvercord Building, located across from the Harbour City complex in Tsimshatsui. This three-story shop claims to be the largest emporium of China-made goods in Hong Kong. In addition to traditional jade and rosewood carvings, antique Chinese jewelry, paintings, and silk fashions, there are also garments by Pierre Cardin manufactured in a factory in China. The Silvercord shop is open from 10 a.m. to 6:30 p.m. every day except Sunday, when it's open from noon to 6 p.m.

China Products Co. sells more ordinary everyday household items, including household goods and appliances, kimonos, porcelain, clothes, shoes, and furniture. **Yue Hwa** is more of the same. It was here that I bought some friends a gag wedding gift—Chinese whisky with preserved lizards in it, all for only HK$20 ($2.60). Definitely a bargain.

Check *The Official Guide to Shopping, Eating Out and Services in Hong Kong* for the many addresses of these stores.

MARKETS: These are where you can get some of the best deals in Hong Kong, though a lot depends on how well you can bargain. If you're good at it you might be able to get items for 25% off the originally quoted price.

Li Yuen Street East and West

These two streets are pedestrian lanes in the Central District. They're packed full with stalls selling handbags, clothes, scarves, sweaters, toys, bolts of cloth, knickknacks, and even brassieres. They're popular with locals and sometimes human traffic is quite slow. Don't neglect the open-fronted shops behind the stalls. Some of these are boutiques selling fashionable but cheap clothing as well as shoes, purses, and accessories.

Stanley Market

Stanley Market is probably the most popular market in Hong Kong and it's a trendy place for foreign residents to live. Located on the southern coast of Hong Kong Island on a small peninsula, it's a great place to pick up jeans and clothing for a song. Some of the shops are remodeling and becoming more chic, but you can still find good bargains in silk clothing as well as arts and crafts. It seems as though no one who comes here can leave without bundles and bags of purchases. Most shopkeepers seem reluctant to bargain but it's still worth a try, especially if you're purchasing more than one item. To reach Stanley, take bus 6 or 260 from the Central Bus Terminal by the Star Ferry. The bus ride to Stanley takes approximately 30 minutes.

Night Markets

Both **Temple Street** in Kowloon and **Poor Man's Nightclub** on Hong Kong Island are night markets that open up when the sun goes down. They sell the usual stuff street vendors sell, including T-shirts, jeans, watches, lighters, socks, jewelry and jewelry boxes, cassette tapes, sweaters, and imitation Lacoste shirts. Be sure to bargain fiercely, and check products to make sure they're not faulty or poorly made.

Antiques

In addition to the Chinese products department stores, you can also find antiques in the Hollywood Road area above the Central District. There are shops selling porcelain, silver, rosewood and blackwood furniture, as well as fakes and curios. Cat Street Galleries on neighboring Lok Kwu Road has arts and crafts and expensive antiques.

7. Hong Kong After Dark

Although not as varied and extensive as Tokyo's nightlife, Hong Kong does offer the visitor a steady stream of British pubs, topless bars, discos, and cocktail lounges from which to choose. Keep in mind that one of the finest traditions in Hong Kong is its "happy hour," when some bars offer drinks at half price, two for the price of one, or simply at lower prices. Happy hour generally is from 5 to 7 p.m., sometimes longer. Remember also that a 10% service charge will be added to your bill.

COCKTAIL LOUNGES: The Sheraton Hotel's **Sky Lounge**, 20 Nathan Rd. in Kowloon (tel. 3-691111), has what I consider to be the best and most romantic view of Hong Kong Island glittering across the harbor. Take the glass-enclosed capsule elevator up to the 18th floor just as dusk approaches, grab a window seat, and watch the colors of the day fade as lights turn on one by one in the Central District and Wanchai. Open from 11 a.m. to 1 a.m. daily (to 2 a.m. on Friday and Saturday), the Sky Lounge charges HK$22 ($2.86) for most of its beers and HK$29 ($3.77) for most of its cocktails. Unfortunately, there's no happy hour here, and from 8 p.m. onward there's a minimum drink charge of HK$66 ($8.57) per person. Soft, live music begins at 5:30 and serenades until midnight, 1 a.m. on weekends.

Another cocktail lounge on the Kowloon side is the **Tiara**, on the 21st floor of the Shangri-La, 64 Mody Rd., East Tsimshatsui (tel. 3-7212111). Open daily from 5 p.m. to 2 a.m., it's best to get here right when it opens if you want to be assured of a window seat overlooking the harbor. Piano music sets the mood for this intimate and cozy lounge where beer starts at HK$20 ($2.59) and cocktails at HK$31 ($4.03). There's a minimum drink charge here of HK$65 per person after 8 p.m.

On the Hong Kong side, a lounge offering spectacular closeup views of the Central District and of the harbor and Kowloon beyond is **La Ronda Bar**, on the 30th floor of the Furama Hotel, 1 Connaught Rd. (tel. 5-255111). Although it's located next to a revolving restaurant, the bar itself is stationary. With cocktails averaging HK$30 ($3.90), it's open from 5:30 p.m. to midnight every day. On Friday and Saturday nights and the eve before a public holiday, there's a minimum drink charge of HK$52 ($6.75).

PUBS AND BARS: One of the most interesting developments in Hong Kong's night scene in recent years is the modest mushrooming of some bars and pubs in the area of Lan Kwai Fong and D'Aguilar Streets in Hong Kong Island's Central District. Catering more to Hong Kong's foreign and Chinese young residents than to tourists, who tend to stick to Tsimshatsui, it's a welcome relief in the Central District, which has always tended to shut down as soon as the offices closed up. One of the most chic bars here is **California**, Lan Kwai Fong (tel. 5-211345), whose owner is, nonetheless Canadian. This is the place to see and be seen, the place of the young nouveaux riches in search of a definition. The atmosphere is modern and sophisticated, with silent TV screens showing movies almost everywhere you look. It's open from noon to 1 a.m. every night except Wednesday, Friday, and Saturday, when California turns into a disco from 11:30 p.m. until 4 a.m. Cover charge for the disco is HK$93 ($12.08) which includes two drinks, but on Wednesday women can get in for free. Otherwise, drinks here begin at HK$16.50 ($2.14) for beer and HK$33 ($4.29) for cocktails, except during happy hour, from 5 to 7 p.m., when you can get two drinks for the price of one. If you're interested in lunch or dinner, the menu lists everything from hamburgers (the house specialty) to pastas, seafood, and chicken.

Close to Lan Kwai Fong is **MadDogs**, 33 Wyndham St. (tel. 5-252383), one of Hong Kong's most pleasant English pubs, which caters to a mellow and professional working crowd. A favorite with local expatriates who drop by on their way home from work. MadDogs is located in an old building and consists of a ground floor, basement, and small patio courtyard out back. With traditional decor that includes a stern picture of Queen Victoria, cane chairs, and ceiling fans, the pub is open for business from 11:30 a.m. to 1 a.m. (2 a.m. on Friday and Saturday), and offers a glass of beer for less than HK$10 ($1.29) and snacks of sandwiches, meat pies, and salads. If you want to get away from Queen Victoria's gaze, the downstairs area is a little less staid, the music tends to be louder, and the atmosphere a bit livelier. Incidentally, the easiest way to get to MadDogs is via the side-door entry just off D'Aguilar and Lan Kwai Fong streets, especially if you're walking from the nightlife area around Lan Kwai Fong.

Serving German draft beers, sauerkraut, sausages and other German fare, **Schnurrbart** is a serious drinking establishment located at 29 D'Aguilar St. (tel. 5-234700). Popular with German expatriates, it's open from noon to 2 a.m. every day except Sunday. German beer starts at HK$16.50 ($2.14), and the food menu changes weekly. By the way, a second Schnurrbart (which means "moustache" in German) is located across the harbor at 6-6A Hart, Tsimshatsui (tel. 5-234700).

The **Bull and Bear**, on the ground floor of Hutchinson House at 10 Harcourt Rd., Central District (tel. 5-257436), was one of the first English pubs to open in Hong Kong back in 1974, and it has been notorious from the beginning. A huge, sprawling place with dart boards and waitresses in long skirts and frilly white blouses, this pub gets pretty rowdy on weekend nights, and draws everyone from businessmen in suits to servicemen on leave. Having had to fight off the attentions of a rather inebriated sailor with tattoos up and down his arms, I can state that it's not a particularly comfortable place for a woman alone; however, for those who are interested there are definitely more men here than women. (You may also be interested in knowing that a British woman living in Hong Kong described this place as a meat market.) If that's what you're looking for, HK$9 ($1.17) will buy you a small beer, and in case you're so so uncultured as to ask for a cocktail in an English pub, they start at HK$22 ($2.86). Hours are 11:30 a.m. to 1 a.m. every day except Sunday, when it's open from 6 p.m. to midnight, and bank holidays, when it remains closed. The menu includes items like chili con carne, steak-and-kidney pie, salads, sandwiches, and daily specials.

A much quieter and more refined English pub, **The Jockey**, in the Swire House, Central District (tel. 5-261478), is popular with bankers, lawyers, and office people. Its theme is obviously racing and jockeys, with a very masculine decor. Open every day except Sunday from 11:30 a.m. to 11:30 p.m., the Jockey prices its beer from HK$9.30 ($1.21) to HK$19 ($2.47), and cocktails run HK$20 ($2.60).

Rivaling the Jockey for elegance is **Dicken's Bar**, located in the basement of the Excelsior Hotel, Causeway Bay (tel. 5-767365). A classy place with darkwood paneling, softly lit lamps, and live music from 9 p.m. to 1 a.m., this English pub serves snacks of soups and sandwiches as well as a curry buffet lunch from noon to 2 p.m. every day except Saturday and public holidays for HK$52 ($6.75). Draft beer begins at HK$10.50 ($1.36) for a half pint and cocktails start at HK$26 ($3.38). Particularly recommended is a jazz band that plays every Sunday afternoon from 3 to 6 p.m.

The **Captain's Bar**, on the ground floor of the Mandarin Hotel, 5 Connaught Rd. in the Central District (tel. 5-220111), is popular with Hong Kong's professional working crowd. Seating is at the bar or on couches, and live music begins nightly at 9. It's open from 11 a.m. to 2 a.m. every day. Cocktails are HK$35 ($4.55) and beer starts at HK$17 ($2.21).

Old China Hand, 104 Lockhart Rd. in Wanchai (tel. 5-279174), is an informal English pub with dart boards, a picture of Queen Elizabeth, and a lot of kitsch on the walls. A sign warns customers: "Sorry, we don't serve women—you have to bring your own." A small draft here starts at HK$7.50 (97¢) and spirits at HK$14 ($1.82). In the tradition of the pub lunch, meals are also served, including steak-and-kidney pie, fish and chips, sandwiches, salads, chili con carne, and moussaka, with most items costing less than HK$25 ($3.25). It's open from 11 a.m. to 2 a.m. daily.

White Stag, 72 Canton Rd., Tsimshatsui (tel. 3-684612), is an English-style pub that caters to a large Chinese clientele. A nice, quiet place where you can actually hear yourself talk, this place sports wooden tables and a few deer heads and antlers, with beer beginning at HK$7 (90¢) for a half pint. A blackboard tells of entrées for the day, which might include such things as corned beef hash and eggs, spring rolls, Shanghai fried noodles, or tuna-fish salad, and it's open for business from 10 a.m. to 2 a.m. Monday through Saturday.

Just down the road at 76 Canton Rd. is **Beefy's Tavern** (tel. 3-674697), open from 5 p.m. to 5 a.m. daily. With no money wasted on decor, it looks like any bar anywhere. A sign at the counter with a quote from W. C. Fields reads, "Work is the curse of the drinking class." One I like says, "The best man for the job is a woman." A half-pint of beer here costs HK$10 ($1.30). Until 10 p.m., spirits cost only HK$11 ($1.43); after that they go up to HK$20 ($2.60). There's a live Filipino band from 10:15 p.m. until 4 a.m. (5 a.m. on weekends) every night except Monday, when the house band performs. As you might guess, the action here starts late.

Ned Kelly's Last Stand, 11A Ashley Rd. in Tsimshatsui (tel. 3-660562), is an Australian pub with live Dixieland jazz or swing nightly from 9 p.m. to 2 a.m. Resembling a saloon, it opens its doors at 11:30 a.m. and serves beer beginning at HK$7 (91¢) until 7 p.m., after which it costs HK$12 ($1.56). The food here ranges from HK$19 ($2.47) to HK$50 ($6.49) and includes juicy pork sausages from Australia served with mashed potatoes and onion gravy; stew; liver, bacon, and fried onions; Australian sirloin steak; and meat pie with mashed potatoes and onion gravy.

One of Tsimshatsui's most popular watering holes is **Someplace Else**, located in the basement of the Sheraton Hotel, 20 Nathan Rd. (tel. 3-691111). It's standing room only from 4 to 7 p.m., when you can buy two drinks for the price of one. Most drinks are priced at HK$30 ($3.90), while draft beer starts at HK$15.50 ($2.01). Open from 11 a.m. to 1 a.m. daily (until 2 a.m. on weekends), this establishment is divided into two levels and decorated with stained-glass lampshades and ceiling fans. If you're hungry, there's a great menu with everything from satay, samosas, and taco salad to fish and chips, spareribs and hamburgers. From 11 a.m. to 3 p.m. there's a salad bar available for HK$33 ($4.29).

THE TOPLESS BARS: Wanchai was the world of Suzie Wong, a world of bars and two-bit hotels, narrow streets, and dark alleyways, where men came to drink and to brawl and spend money for women. Sailors came here when they landed in port, followed by American soldiers on leave from Vietnam, and it was a place of neon lights and buzzing activity, excitement, the unspoken and the whispered.

Much of the nightlife district has given way to new buildings and high-rises. However, it's still interesting to walk around Wanchai along Lockhart Road, where you'll find food stalls, tattoo parlors, neon lights galore, and plenty of nighttime activity.

Much of Hong Kong's nightlife, however, has moved to Tsimshatsui, where topless bars, so-called nightclubs, and hostess establishments try to part customers from their dollars. Japanese men are big customers here, perhaps because they're used to hostess bars in their own country. At any rate, you've been warned.

The best place to go if you want to go to a topless joint is **Bottoms Up**, 14 Hankow Rd., Tsimshatsui (tel. 3-675696). Despite the lewd pictures in the entranceway, this place is actually rather innocuous and welcomes tourists, couples, men, and women. Used as a location shot in the James Bond movie *Man with the Golden Gun*, it features four round counters with a topless waitress in the middle of each, with soft, red lighting. I don't know what was in the men's bathroom, but the women's room had some posters of Burt Reynolds in sexy poses. Open from 4 p.m. to 3 a.m. daily (5 p.m. to 2:30 a.m. Sunday), it has one of the longest happy hours in Hong Kong—from 4 to 9 p.m., when beer is HK$13.50 ($1.75) and other drinks average about HK$18 ($2.33). After 9 p.m. prices double.

DISCOS: Disco fever hit Hong Kong in the late 1970s and the first to cash in on the craze was **Disco Disco Underground**, 38 D'Aguilar St., Central District (tel. 5-248809). Now under new management, it may change its name and its image to keep up with the stiff competition, but at last check the establishment drew a wide mixture of clientele, including gays, straights, expatriates, and Chinese. From Sunday through Thursday it's open from 9:30 p.m. to 3 a.m. and charges a HK$70 ($9.09) cover; women can get in for free on Wednesday and for half price other weekdays. On Friday and Saturday nights, cover charge increases to HK$95 ($12.34). Included in the cover charge are two standard drinks. After that, beer costs HK$30 ($3.90), while cocktails are HK$38 ($4.93). There are separate rooms for dancing and drinking, and the dance floor is surrounded with mirrors so you can watch yourself if so inclined.

Not far away is **Club 97**, located on the ground floor under the restaurant Nineteen 97 at 9 Lan Kwai Fong (tel. 5-260303). This small, rather eclectically decorated disco opens its doors at 10 p.m., closing at 4 a.m. Monday through Thursday and 5 a.m. on weekends. It's closed on Sunday. There's no entrance fee. Cocktails are around HK$38 ($4.93).

Also on Hong Kong Island but over in Causeway Bay is **Talk of the Town**, on the 30th floor of the Excelsior Hotel (tel. 5-767365). This disco, recently redecorated in art deco style, has a fantastic view of the harbor and Kowloon and features a Filipino band. If you're a hotel guest there's no cover charge; otherwise it costs HK$88 ($11.43) on weekdays and HK$110 ($14.29) on weekends, which includes two free drinks. Talk of the Town is also open for happy hour, when beers go for HK$15.50 ($2.01) and cocktails run HK$29 ($3.77).

On the other side of the harbor is another popular hotel disco which caters to a young and trendy crowd. Called **Hollywood East**, it's located in the basement of the Regal Meridien at 71 Mody Rd. in Tsimshatsui (tel. 5-8936460). Decorated on a Hollywood theme with backlighting fixtures, posters of movie stars, and 12 screens that depict the history of Hollywood, this disco charges HK$110 ($14.28) at the door but it includes two drinks. Hours are 9 p.m. to 2:30 a.m. (to 4 a.m. on the weekends).

One of Hong Kong's hottest and most innovative discos is **Canton**, located next to the Prince Hotel on Canton Road in Harbour City, Tsimshatsui (tel. 3-7210209). It changes its look often so that the locals keep coming back—and judging by the crowds, it's highly successful. Complete with a dance cage where you can watch a professional performer go at it, TV video screens with Canton's own in-house videos, and Chinese poster advertisements from the 1920s, it boasts a dance floor with lots of technical gadgets and lights. Open from 9 p.m. until 3 a.m. weekdays and 4 a.m. Friday and Saturday, it charges a cover of HK$82 ($10.65) on weekdays and HK$96 ($12.47) weekends, which includes two drinks. After that, concoctions cost HK$36 ($4.68).

Down the road is **Hot Gossip**, also located in Harbour City on Canton Road (tel. 3-7216884). The ground floor is a high-tech restaurant and bar, while the disco is located in the basement. The disco is huge, with three laser shows nightly, and the entrance charge of HK$96 ($12.47) on weekdays and HK$108 ($14.03) on weekends includes two drinks. On Monday women are admitted free. The disco is open from 9 p.m. to 2:30 a.m. (until 3:30 a.m. weekends), but the restaurant, which serves soups, salads, sandwiches, burgers, spaghetti, and more, opens at noon.

The Cavern, 35-39 Hankow Rd., Tsimshatsui (tel. 3-677790), is the place a lot of people gravitate to after the other establishments close. Open from 4 p.m. until 6 a.m., it features pictures of the Beatles on its walls and a live band every night except Sunday from 2 to 5 a.m. The crowds don't start pouring in until after midnight, after which things can become quite wild and hectic. Admittance for males is HK$66 ($8.57), which includes two drinks, while females are charged HK$33 ($4.29), which includes one drink. This place is popular with people in their 20s, including Chinese, Filipinos, and other expatriates.

The **Music Room,** in the Shangri-La Hotel, 64 Mody Rd., East Tsimshatsui (tel. 3-7212111), is the place to go if you think you're too old for the discos described above but aren't quite ready for the rest home. Aiming for an older, sophisticated crowd, it's designed more for socializing and conversation than for wild partying. It's a relaxing place that looks like a living room, with plush carpets and sofas, and the music is concentrated on the dance floor. Open from 5 p.m. to 2 a.m. daily, it charges an entrance fee of HK$80 ($10.39) on Friday and HK$93 ($12.08) on Saturday (hotel guests get in free). Cocktails costs HK$30 ($3.90) until 9 p.m.; after that they're HK$38 ($4.93).

NIGHT MARKETS: Shopping is one of the things you can do in Hong Kong in the evenings, since many shops stay open until 10 p.m. But if you're looking for some atmosphere, head for one of the night markets. **Temple Street market** on the Kowloon side extends for several blocks and has stalls selling clothing, accessories, toys, cassettes, household items, and much more. Bargain fiercely here, and be sure to check the merchandise to make sure it isn't going to fall apart in two weeks. Be sure also to follow Temple Street to its northern end and beyond where you'll find palm readers, musicians, and street singers. Cantonese pop songs and operas are among the favorites in their repertoire.

Another market is the **Poor Man's Nightclub** on Hong Kong Island, which was unfortunately drastically reduced in size with the completion of the Macau Ferry Terminal next to it. Still, you can pick up some good buys here, with stalls selling everything from imitation Lacoste shirts to belts, jeans, wallets, jewelry boxes, and noodle soup. The night markets are open from approximately 6 to 11 p.m.

NIGHT TOURS: If you have only one or two nights in Hong Kong, I suggest taking an organized night tour. **Watertours** offers eight different tours of Hong Kong by night which combine harbor cruises with various land activities. The tram and dinner cruise, for example, starts out with a tram ride from Causeway Bay through Wanchai to the Central District, followed by a stroll through Poor Man's Nightclub and then either a Chinese dinner and cruise through the harbor or a Western buffet meal in La Ronda Revolving Restaurant. The price for this tour is HK$330 ($42.86). Other tours might include a trip up Victoria Peak, dinner in an Aberdeen floating restaurant, a cruise in a traditional Chinese junk, or a ride in an open-top bus. You can make reservations for tours through your hotel or by calling Watertours directly at 5-254808.

If you like having some guidance in making your plans but prefer to carry them out on your own, you might want to take advantage of a do-it-yourself night tour organized by the HKTA which lets you select from a number of discos, pubs, bars, and establishments that are members of HKTA. You decide which ones to visit, when, and for how long, though there are some restrictions.

Two options are available. With the Grand Tour, you receive two coupons for your choice of two pubs, bars, or nightclubs, where you can have one or two standard drinks free as well as one disco coupon good for one standard drink. Cost of the Grand Tour is HK$165 ($21.43). If you opt for the De Luxe Tour package for HK$290 ($37.66), you receive one coupon good for one or two standard drinks at a pub, bar, or nightclub as well as one hostess club coupon good for two standard drinks, a fruit plate, and one hour with a hostess. For more information, contact HKTA.

8. The ABCs of Hong Kong

Arriving in a new city is never very easy, especially if it's at the other end of the earth where the language, culture, and people are different from your own. This section is designed to answer some questions you might have before departing on your trip, to make your immersion into Hong Kong life easier, and to help you with unforeseen questions or emergencies that might arise during your stay.

Remember that the concierge of your hotel is usually a valuable source of information for everything from where the nearest bank is to how to get to a certain destination. The Hong Kong Tourist Association (HKTA) is also very proficient in answering visitors' questions.

AMERICAN EXPRESS: The most convenient office in the Central District is opposite Connaught Centre at 8 Connaught Rd. in the Swire House (tel. 5-243151). On the Kowloon side it's 119 Nathan Rd. (tel. 3-7210179 or 3-683245). Hours for the Central District office are 9:30 a.m. to 4 p.m. Monday through Friday and 9:30 a.m. to noon on Saturday. The Kowloon office has slightly longer hours and is open from 9 a.m. to 5 p.m. Monday through Saturday.

BABYSITTERS: Most of the upper-class hotels have babysitting services. For a full list of hotels providing this service, contact the Hong Kong Tourist Association.

BANKING HOURS: The average banking hours are from 9:30 or 10 a.m. to 3 p.m. Monday through Friday and 9:30 a.m. to noon on Saturday. However, some branches stay open longer. Hong Kong and Shanghai banks, Hong Kong's two major banks, stay open from 9 a.m. to 4:30 p.m. weekdays and 9 a.m. to 12:30 p.m. on Saturday.

BUS TERMINALS: The two major bus terminals are at both ends of the Star Ferry, in the Central District on Hong Kong Island and in Tsimshatsui in Kowloon. HKTA has a free leaflet helpful for getting around on buses: *Places of Interest by Public Transport*, which tells how to get to such major destinations as Stanley or Aberdeen.

CLIMATE: Because of its subtropical location, Hong Kong's weather is generally mild in winter and hot and humid in summer. Peak tourist seasons are spring and autumn, a time when many hotels raise their rates and accommodations become tight. Late September to early December is considered the most pleasant time of year, with clear skies and temperatures ranging in the 70s. January and February are the coldest months, when temperatures in the 50s mean you should bring along a jacket or sweater. In spring the humidity rises, the temperature goes up to about 70, and it's often cloudy and misty. By summer temperatures are in the 90s, humidity is 90%, and there's little or no relief even at night. Summer is also typhoon season, but Hong Kong has a very good warning system so there's no need to worry. Most of Hong Kong's rain falls in summer, but it's a good idea to bring along an umbrella any time of year.

CONSULATES: The American Consulate is at 26 Garden Rd., Central District (tel. 5-239011). Hours are 8:30 a.m. to 12:30 p.m. and 1:30 to 5:30 p.m. weekdays. If you need to go to the passport section, it's open weekdays only from 8:30 a.m. to noon and again from 1:30 to 5 p.m. The Canadian Consulate, Tower One, Exchange Square, Connaught Road, Central District (tel. 5-8104321), is open Monday through Friday from 8:30 a.m. to noon. The Australian Consulate is on the 23rd and 24th floors of Harbour Centre, 25 Harbour Rd., Wanchai, on Hong Kong Island (tel. 5-731881), and is open weekdays from 9 to 11:30 a.m. and 1 to 4 p.m. Matters pertaining to Britain are c/o Overseas Visa Section, Hong Kong Immigration Dept., Upper Basement, Mirror Tower, 61 Mody Rd., East Tsimshatsui (tel. 3-7333111). Hours here are 8:45 a.m. to 4:30 p.m. Monday to Friday and 9 to 11:30 a.m. on Saturday.

CREDIT CARDS: Most shops accept international credit cards, although some of the smaller ones may not. Look to see whether there are credit-card signs in the shop. Credit cards readily accepted include American Express, VISA, and MasterCard. American Express cardholders also have access to Jetco automated-teller machines and can withdraw local currency and traveler's checks at Express Cash automated tellers. Holders of VISA cards can obtain local currency from the Hongkong Bank automated-teller machines at the airport and approximately ten other convenient locations.

CRIME: Hong Kong is relatively safe for the tourist, especially if you use common sense and stick to such tourist areas as Tsimshatsui or Causeway Bay at night. However, you do have to guard against pickpockets. Although on the decline, they often work in groups to pick men's pockets or slit open a woman's purse, quickly taking the valuables and then relaying them on to accomplices who disappear in the crowd. Japanese tourists, used to the safety in their own country, are easy targets since they usually carry large amounts of cash with them, and favored places are Tsimshatsui, Causeway Bay, and Wanchai. To be on the safe side, keep your valuables in your hotel's safety deposit box.

CURRENCY: The basic unit of currency in the colony is the Hong Kong dollar. Notes are issued by two local banks for HK$10, HK$20, HK$50, HK$100, HK$500, and HK$1,000. In 1985 new notes began circulation and are smaller than the older notes, which are still being used. Coins are minted in England in bronze for 5-, 10-, 20-, and 50-cent pieces and in silver for HK$1, HK$2, and HK$5.

Throughout Hong Kong the dollar sign ("$") refers to Hong Kong dollars, but the same symbol is most familiar to readers of these guides as indicating U.S. dollars. In order to prevent confusion, *in this guide Hong Kong dollars are always identified by the symbol "HK$."*

Although rates fluctuate, all conversions in this book are based on HK$7.7 $1 U.S. If the exchange rate has changed drastically, plan your budget accordingly.

The best deal for money exchange is at banks, since they don't charge a commission, except on traveler's checks. Hotels give a slightly less favorable exchange rate but are convenient. Money changers are found in the tourist areas, especially in Tsimshatsui. Avoid them if you can. They often charge a commission or a "changing fee." If you exchange money at Kai Tak airport, you'll be charged a 5% service fee. If you want to exchange cash or cash American Express traveler's checks at the American Express office, therefore, change at the airport only what you need to get into town—$10 (U.S.) should more than do it.

CUSTOMS: You're allowed to bring into Hong Kong duty-free a one-liter (34-ounce) bottle of alcohol, 200 cigarettes or 50 cigars, and a reasonable quantity of cosmetics and perfumes in opened bottles for personal use.

DRUGSTORES: There are no 24-hour drugstores in Hong Kong, so if you need something urgently in the middle of the night you should contact one of the hospitals listed below.

One of the best-known pharmacies in Hong Kong is **Watson's**, which first opened in the 1880s. Today there are more than 30 Watson's drugstores in Hong Kong, most of them open from 10 a.m. to 10 p.m. Locations for some of them are Star House next to the Star Ferry on the Kowloon side (tel. 3-7231832); Haiphong Road in Tsimshatsui (tel. 3-686381); Paterson Plaza on Paterson Street, Causeway Bay (tel. 5-7954008); the Hilton Hotel and the Pedder Building on Pedder Street (tel. 5-215531), both in the Central District.

ELECTRICITY: The electricity used in Hong Kong is 200 volts, alternating current (AC), 50 cycles. Most hotels have adapters to fit shavers of different plugs and voltages, but for other gadgets you'll need transformers and plug adapters. Better yet, buy travel hair dryers or irons that can be used both in the United States and abroad.

EMERGENCIES: All emergency calls are free—just **dial 999** for police, fire, or ambulance.

FIRST FLOOR: The floors of Hong Kong buildings are under the British system. That is, what we would call the first floor in the United States is called the ground floor in Hong Kong. Our second floor, therefore, is called the first floor in Hong Kong.

HOLIDAYS: The Chinese New Year, which falls according to the Chinese lunar calendar in either late January or in February, is the only time of year when most shops close in Hong Kong. They stay closed for two to four days, but some restaurants and shops do stay open to cater to tourists.

HOSPITALS: The following hospitals can help you around the clock: **Queen Mary Hospital**, Pokfulam Road, Hong Kong Island (tel. 5-8192111); **Hong Kong Adventist Hospital**, 40 Stubbs Rd., Hong Kong Island (tel. 5-746211); **Queen Elizabeth Hospital**, Wylie Road, Kowloon (tel. 3-7102111).

LANGUAGES: Both Chinese and English are spoken in Hong Kong, with Cantonese the most common Chinese dialect. Although English is understood in the hotels and tourist shops, few Chinese understand it outside these areas, including taxi drivers, bus drivers, and waiters in many Chinese restaurants. To avoid confusion, have someone in your hotel write out your destination in Chinese so that you can show it to the taxi or bus driver.

LAUNDRY: Most hotels provide same-day laundry service.

LITERATURE: If you want to know something about Hong Kong before setting out on your trip, I recommend reading *A History of Hong Kong* by G. B. Endacott, which gives a thorough account of the history of the colony. A more intimate view of Hong Kong is given in *Borrowed Place, Borrowed Time* by Richard Hughes, a *Sunday Times* correspondent who has lived in Hong Kong for several decades. Fictional accounts that depict the flavor of Hong Kong are Richard Mason's *The World of Suzie Wong* and James Clavell's *Taipan*.

MAIL DELIVERY: If you don't know where you're going to be staying in Hong Kong, you can still receive mail. Have it sent to you "Post Restante" at the **General Post Office**, 2 Connaught Pl., Central District, Hong Kong Island, which is located just to the right as you exit from the Star Ferry. They'll hold your mail for you here for two months, and the counter is on the ground floor.

NEWSPAPERS: Five English-language newspapers are printed in Hong Kong: *South China Morning Post, Hong Kong Standard, Asian Wall Street Journal, International Herald Tribune*, and the *Evening Standard*.

PASSPORTS AND VISAS: Visas are not necessary for most tourists entering Hong Kong, only a valid passport. Americans can stay up to one month without a visa. Australians, Canadians, and other British Commonwealth citizens can stay for three months, while those from the United Kingdom can stay for six months without a visa. If you have any questions regarding visas once you're in Hong Kong, contact the **Hong Kong Immigration Dept.**, 61 Mody Rd., East Tsimshatsui (tel. 3-7333111).

POST OFFICES: Post offices are open from 8 a.m. to 6 p.m. Monday through Saturday; closed Sunday and holidays. On Hong Kong Island the **main post office** is at 2 Connaught Pl., where stamps are sold on the first floor (what we would call the second floor in the United States). On the Kowloon side, post offices are located at 405 Nathan Rd. between the Jordan and Yaumatei subway stations, and at 10 Middle Rd., which is one block north of Salisbury Road.

SHOP HOURS: Most shops are open seven days a week, although some department stores are closed on Sunday. Shops in the Central District are generally open from 10 a.m. to 6 p.m.; in Causeway Bay and Wanchai from 10 a.m. to about 9:30 p.m.; in Tsimshatsui from 10 a.m. to 9 or 10 p.m., some even later than that; and in East Tsimshatsui from 10 a.m. to 7:30 p.m.

STUDENT INFORMATION: If you're a student, the **Hong Kong Student Travel Bureau** can help you with sightseeing tours of the city, visas and trips to China, cheap flights to other destinations, and even rail passes for both Europe and Japan. Even if you're not a student you can take advantage of some of their services. They have two conveniently located offices: on the tenth floor of Star House in Tsimshatsui next to the Star Ferry (tel. 3-7213269) which is open from 9 a.m. to 7 p.m. Monday through Saturday, and on the 13th floor of the Entertainment Building, 30 Queen's Rd., Central District (tel. 5-8107272), open the same hours.

TAXES AND SERVICE CHARGES: Hotels will add to your bill a 10% service charge and a 5% government tax. Restaurants and bars will automatically add a 10% service charge. There's an airport departure tax of HK$120 ($15.58) for adults and HK$60 ($7.79) for children aged 2 to 11. If you're taking the boat to Macau, you have to pay a Hong Kong departure tax of HK$15 ($1.95).

TELEPHONES AND TELEGRAMS: Telephones are free for local calls made from homes, offices, shops, restaurants, and most hotel lobbies, so don't feel shy about asking to use the phone. From some hotel lobbies, hotel rooms, and in public phone booths a local call costs HK$1 (13¢).

Telephone prefix numbers are like our area codes. Hong Kong Island has a "5" prefix, Kowloon a "3" prefix, and the New Territories a "0". *If you're calling within an area, don't dial the prefix number.* For example, if you're on Hong Kong Island, don't dial the 5 prefix if you're calling a Hong Kong Island number. For directory assistance, dial 108.

Most hotels in Hong Kong will handle overseas calls and offer direct dialing. Otherwise long-distance calls and telegrams can be made from Cables and Wireless offices. Open 24 hours a day including public holidays, the Cables and Wireless office is at Room 102A Exchange Square Tower I, Connaught Place, Central District. On the Kowloon side there's an office in the Hermes House, Middle Road, Tsimshatsui. International collect calls can be made from any public or private phone by dialing 011.

TIPPING: Even though restaurants and bars will automatically add a 10% service charge to your bill, you're still expected to leave your small change for the waiter. A general rule of thumb is to leave 5%, but in most Chinese restaurants where meals are usually quite low it's acceptable to leave change up to HK$2 (25¢).

You're also expected to tip taxi drivers, bellboys, barbers, and beauticians. For taxi drivers, simply round up to the nearest HK$1 or add a HK$1 (13¢) tip. Tip people who cut your hair 5% or 10%, and give bellboys HK$5 (65¢) to HK$10 ($1.30), depending on the number of bags.

TOURIST INFORMATION: The Hong Kong Tourist Association is a well-organized and efficient outfit designed to make your trip to Hong Kong pleasant and enjoyable. If you'd like information and literature before leaving on your trip, contact one of the HKTA offices in the United States: 548 Fifth Ave., New York, NY 10036-5092 (tel. 212/869-5008); Suite 2422, 333 N. Michigan Ave., Chicago, IL 60601 (tel. 312/782-3872); Suite 200, 421 Powell St., San Francisco, CA 94102-1568 (tel. 415/781-4582).

Once you arrive in Hong Kong you will find four HKTA offices ready to serve you. In Hong Kong's International Airport at Kai Tak in the arrival hall the HKTA is open from 8 a.m. to 10:30 p.m. daily. The Kowloon Information

Centre is in the Star Ferry terminal and hours here are 8 a.m. to 6 p.m. Monday through Friday, to 1 p.m. on Saturday and Sunday. In East Tsimshatsui there's a new office at G8 Empire Centre, 68 Mody Rd., open daily from 9 a.m. to 6 p.m.

The main HKTA office is on Hong Kong Island on the 35th floor of Connaught Centre in the Central District to the right as you exit the Star Ferry (tel. 5-244191). It's closed on Sunday and public holidays, but is open Monday through Friday from 8 a.m. to 6 p.m. and on Saturday until 1 p.m.

The HKTA also operates a hotline to answer any questions you might have. Call 3-7225555 Monday through Friday from 8 a.m. to 6 p.m., on weekends to 1 p.m. If you call after office hours an answering machine should ask for your telephone number and the staff will return your call the next day.

There's quite a bit of free literature available on Hong Kong you can pick up at HKTA offices, which should help you during your stay. I recommend *The Quick Guide to Hong Kong, Places of Interest by Public Transport, Museums & Arts & Crafts, Outlying Islands,* and *The Official Guide to Shopping, Eating Out and Services in Hong Kong.*

You can also ask HKTA for a free map of Tsimshatsui and northern Hong Kong Island. *The Official Hong Kong Guide,* published monthly, is available free in most upper- and medium-range hotels, and has a lot of practical information and sightseeing advice on the colony. It's also available at HKTA offices for HK$10 ($1.30).

Two tourist tabloids distributed free in hotel lobbies and tourist places are *Hong Kong* and *Orient.* Although they're filled mostly with advertisements, they're published weekly and have some information on what's going on in Hong Kong. *Hong Kong Visitor,* published by the *South China Morning Post,* is also valuable for information on what's happening in the colony.

9. Exploring the Territories and Environs

Mention Hong Kong and most people think of Hong Kong Island and Kowloon, of shops, nightclubs, and neon signs. What they don't realize is that Hong Kong Island and Kowloon are rather minute in the scheme of things—the New Territories and outlying islands make up a whopping 90% of the colony.

If you have a day or two to spare, or even just an afternoon, I suggest spending it on a trip outside the city in one of Hong Kong's rural areas. After all, it's in the small villages and in the countryside that you have the chance to glimpse an older and a slower way of life, where traditions still reign supreme and where lifestyles have a rhythm of their own.

THE NEW TERRITORIES: Before the 1980s the New Territories were a peaceful countryside, with duck farms, fields, and old villages. No longer. A vast area that stretches 281 square miles between Kowloon and the border of China, the New Territories is Hong Kong's answer to its population and refugee crunch. Huge government housing projects have mushroomed throughout the Territories, turning once-sleepy villages into satellite concrete jungles.

However, the Territories is so big that not all of it has been turned into housing, and it still makes an interesting day trip for first-timers to the colony.

"The Land Between" Tour

The easiest and best way to get a roundup view of the New Territories is to join a tour organized by the Hong Kong Tourist Association called "The Land Between." A seven-hour trip via air-conditioned coach, the tour takes you past satellite towns into a countryside dotted with ponds, duck farms, and small vegetable gardens planted with Chinese kale, chives, onions, and tomatoes. Every inch of land in the valley is used; only the barren hills are empty. Stops on the tour include Cheuk Lam Sim Yuen, a Buddhist monastery housing three of the largest "precious Buddha" statues in Hong Kong, and the indoor market of Luen Wo in Fanling.

Lunch is at Yucca de Lac Restaurant, a pleasant establishment built on a hill overlooking Tolo Harbour. The food is Cantonese, with lots of dishes that might include fried chicken with lemon sauce, diced pork with cashew nuts, or fried filet of garoupa with green pepper. Cost of the tour, which is operated on weekdays only, is HK$180 ($21.42) for adults and HK$140 ($15.58) for children.

Kowloon–Canton Railway

For years the thing every visitor did in the New Territories was to take the train to the border for a look into forbidden and mysterious China. Now, of course, it's easy to get permission to enter China, so the border lookout has lost its appeal and the view was never very exciting anyway. Still, you might want to take the train up into the New Territories just for the experience. Starting from the Kowloon railway station, the Kowloon–Canton Railway will take you along 20 miles of track, passing through towns like Shatin, University Station, Tai Po Kau, and Fanling before reaching Sheung Shui about a half hour later. Sheung Shui is your last stop unless you have a visa to go farther into China. Altogether the train makes eight stops along the way, making it possible to get out and do some exploring on your own.

Shatin: Shatin is Hong Kong's prime example of a budding satellite town. It's also home to Hong Kong's new and modern racetrack. The most interesting thing for the tourist here, though, is the **Temple of 10,000 Buddhas**, located on a hill west of the Shatin railway station. It will take about a half hour to walk there, and be prepared for the more than 300 stairs you have to climb to get to the top. The temple was founded by a monk named Yuet Kai, who is still there. Well, he's kind of still there—he's been embalmed in gold leaf and sits behind a glass case for all to see. The other attraction of the temple is the Buddha statues. Actually there are more than 10,000 of them. There are 12,800 Buddha statues lining the walls, and no two are exactly alike. Included on the grounds is a nine-story pink pagoda. The temple affords a good view of the surrounding countryside.

University Station: This stop serves students going to Chinese University. It's also where you get off if you want to go to the Art Gallery. From the train station, catch a bus going to Chinese University and get off at the second stop, called Science Centre. There you will find the **Art Gallery** (tel. 0-6952402), a museum that contains more than 1,000 paintings and examples of calligraphy from the Ming Period to the present. Also in the collection are bronze seals, jade flower carvings, and Chinese ceramics. The museum is open daily from 10 a.m. to 4:30 p.m. (from 12:30 to 4:30 p.m. on Sunday), and admission is free.

University Station is also where you get off if you want to take a **ferry around Tolo Harbour**. From the station it's a five-minute walk to Ma Liu Shui, where you board the ferry for a leisurely trip to six villages around the harbor. The ferry leaves only two times a day, at 7:25 a.m. and at 3:15 p.m. Since the first ferry may be a little too early for you and doesn't allow you to disembark for sightseeing, I suggest taking the afternoon cruise. The ferry makes a stop at Tap Mun at 4:50 p.m., goes on to some other villages, and then returns to Tap Mun about 45 minutes later. This gives you time to do some sightseeing, but make sure you make it back to the ferry by 5:45 p.m. because there are no hotels here. The ferry gets back into Ma Liu Shui at 7:10 p.m.

Tai Po Market: The **Tai Ping Carpet Factory** allows visitors to come watch the intricate process of producing its beautiful carpets. Visiting hours are 2 to 4 p.m. only, Monday through Thursday. You have to make an appointment here, which you can do by calling 0-6565161, extension 211. The factory is located on Lot No. 1687, Tai Ping Industrial Park, Ting Kok Road, Tai Po Market.

Fanling: The **Luen Wo Market** in the middle of Fanling (included in "The Land Between" Tour) is interesting if you've never seen a Chinese country market. Covering one square block, this indoor market is a maze of tiny passageways and various stalls selling everything from live chickens to deer heads (honest).

Sheung Shui: Sheung Shui Heung is an ancient village located about 300 yards north of the main town. Although much of its charm has been lost with the construction of modern buildings all around it, it's still more peaceful than other old villages that are more on the beaten path. A home belonging to a prominent family, the Liu family, has recently been renovated and is open to the public.

Kam Tin Walled Villages

During the Ming Dynasty (1368–1644), some of the clans in the area of the New Territories built walls around their homes to protect themselves against roving bandits and invaders. Six of these walled villages still exist today. The most famous of these is Kut Hing Wei, popularly known as Kam Tin. About 400 descendants of the Tang clan who built the village back in the 1600s still live here. Although it's the best preserved of the walled villages, it's crowded with souvenir stands and the locals don't like it if you wander off the main passageway.

Other villages in the area are Shui Tau, Kam Hing Wai, Kam Tsin Wai, and Shek Tsin Wai. They are inhabited by Hakka people, and Hakka women are easily recognizable by their straw hats with hanging black fringe. They hate to have their photographs taken because they think it steals something from their spirit, so it might be a good idea to show respect for their beliefs by putting away your camera when visiting these villages.

Closer to Kowloon in Tsuen Wan is another walled village, once deserted but restored in 1987. Built in the 18th century by members of the Hakka Chan clan, it's a tiny oasis of single-story, tile-roofed houses in the midst of modern high-rises. You can reach Tsuen Wan by subway.

Where to Eat

I suggest that you eat at the same restaurant HKTA selected for its "The Land Between" Tour, **Yucca de Lac Restaurant**, in Ma Liu Shui (tel. 0611630). The easiest way to get here is by taxi from Shatin Station. You can sit outside on a terrace overlooking the harbor, which gives it a slightly European atmosphere. The Cantonese menu has more than 200 items, including duck, pigeon, pork, beef, chicken, seafood, and tofu dishes. Selections average HK$25 ($3.25) to HK$65 ($8.44), and the restaurant is open daily from 11 a.m. to 11 p.m.

OUTLYING ISLANDS: In addition to Hong Kong Island there are 235 outlying islands, most of them barren and uninhabited. Because construction in the New Territories is booming, the islands of Hong Kong now offer the best opportunity for observing rural Chinese life. Three of the most accessible islands are Lantau, Cheung Chau, and Lamma. Ferries are cheap (less than HK$10, or $1.30) and depart about every hour from the Outlying Islands Pier in Hong Kong Island's Central District. Some of the ferries have an open area in the back of the first-class deck, which is a great place to sit when the weather is fine, enjoy a beer or coffee, and watch Hong Kong and the harbor float past. Remember to avoid going to the islands on a Sunday, when ferries are packed with city folks on family outings.

Be sure to pick up the *Outlying Islands* leaflet provided free by HKTA. HKTA also has information on the latest ferry schedules. If you plan on doing some extensive hiking on the islands, inexpensive maps are available at the Government Publications Centre, located just west of the Central District Star Ferry terminal.

Lantau

Twice the size of Hong Kong Island, Lantau is the colony's largest island. But whereas Hong Kong Island has a population of more than a million, Lantau has less than 30,000 residents.

Taking a ferry from Hong Kong Island, you'll arrive in **Silvermine Bay**, known as Mui Wo in Chinese. There's not much of interest here, but in front of the ferry pier is where you can catch buses around the island.

If you've arrived in time for lunch, first stop on your itinerary should be **Po Lin Monastery** (tel. 5-9857426), largest and most famous of the 135 Buddhist monasteries located on Lantau. Situated on the plateau of Ngong Ping at an elevation of 2,460 feet, this place has what many consider to be the best vegetarian meals in Hong Kong. The big dining hall serves steaming dishes of vegetables and rice daily from noon to 6:30 p.m. for HK$27 ($3.51).

If you don't mind rather austere surroundings, you can also spend the night here. For HK$110 ($14.29) you can sleep on a hard mat and eat three vegetarian meals. No matter that lunch and dinner look pretty much the same, that lights were out at 6:30 p.m. the night I was there, and that breakfast is served at 7:30 a.m. The landscape around the monastery is empty and peaceful, good for long solitary walks, and if you want you can climb to Lantau Peak (3,064 feet above sea level) to watch the sunrise. Close to the monastery is a tea plantation you might want to visit, and that monstrosity they're building on the side of the hill is Southeast Asia's tallest Buddha, more than 100 feet tall and costing HK$20 million ($2.6 million). They've been working on it for several years, so maybe it will be done by the time you see it.

From Po Lin Monastery you can catch a bus, or, as I suggest, walk the two hours to the village of **Tai O**, Lantau's most interesting village. Tai O wraps itself around the muddy waters of a bay on the west coast of the island. There are no cars on the narrow, twisting streets, no neon signs, no high-rises of concrete and steel. Instead there are one-story wooden houses resting on stilts above the mud of the bay. Life is unhurried and relaxed. You can hear the click-clicking of adults playing mah-jongg all day long.

There are several temples in Tai O, the best known of which is Kwan Ti, on Market Street. There are also some fish-processing shops and open-fronted stores selling Chinese herbs and hardware. The village is divided in two by a creek, and the only way to get across is by a flat-bottom boat which is pulled along a rope strung across the water.

From Tai O the bus back to Silvermine Bay takes about 45 minutes. You might want to cool off here with a swim at **Cheung Sha beach**, a two-mile-long white sandy beach with changing rooms, showers, and toilets. Cheung Sha is about ten minutes away from Silvermine Bay by bus.

Where to Eat: In addition to the vegetarian meals served at the Po Lin Monastery described above, there are a couple of other places you might want to try. In Silvermine Bay, Cantonese dishes are served at the **Silvermine Beach Hotel** (tel. 5-9848295) from 7:30 a.m. to 10 p.m. daily. There's an English menu and lunch costs around HK$60 ($7.79), while dinner averages about HK$140 ($18.18). From the restaurant you have a view of Silvermine Beach, and an outside terrace serves drinks in case you want to relax outside after your meal.

At the other end of the island in Tai O there's the **Tai O Seafood Restaurant**, 15 Wing On St. (tel. 5-9857094), open from 5:30 a.m. for all those early-rising fisherfolk until 12:30 a.m. Serving Cantonese food as well as seafood, it specializes in clam dishes, and there's an English menu to choose from. There are tables outside for dining where you have a view of some fish ponds. Lunch here will range from HK$60 ($7.79) to HK$80 ($10.39), and dinner averages HK$100 ($13) to HK$130 ($16.88).

Cheung Chau

If you have only a few hours to spare and don't want to worry about catching buses and finding your way around, Cheung Chau is your best bet. It's a tiny island only a square mile in area, but 50,000 people live here in a thriving fishing village. There are no cars on the island, making it a delightful place for walking around and exploring.

The waterfront where the ferry lands, known as the **Praya**, buzzes with activity as vendors sell fish, lobsters, and vegetables. About 10% of Cheung Chau's people live on junks in the harbor, and one of the things to do here is to take a *kai do*, or water taxi, past the junks to **Sai Wan**. I like this harbor more than Aberdeen, and I find it amazing how many families keep dogs on board their boats. At Sai Wan there's a temple dedicated to Tin Hau, goddess of the sea, from which it's about a 30-minute walk back to the Praya.

As for the village itself, it's threaded through with tiny alleys and with shops offering noodles and rice, teakwood coffins, and haircuts. Through open doors you can see tailor shops, basket weaving, soy sauce manufacturing, and jade carving. Junks are built on Cheung Chau after a design hardly changed in centuries, entirely from memory and without the aid of blueprints. If you walk down narrow Tung Wan Road, you'll pass lots of open-fronted shops, finally reaching **Tung Wan Beach**, the most popular beach on the island.

Food and Lodging: If you want to spend a few nights away from the hustle and bustle of Hong Kong to unwind and relax, the **Warwick Hotel** (tel. 5-981-0081) is the best place to do it. It's located on the south end of Tung Wan Beach. Although its 70 rooms are slightly small, they are tastefully decorated in a tropical theme and come with color TV, clock, radio, phone, air conditioning, marble-top counters, and balconies. Although rooms facing the beach are slightly more expensive at HK$410 ($53), they're worth it. Those that don't have water views go for HK$370 ($48). Prices are 10% to 15% higher on weekends. Facilities at the hotel include a bar/disco, windsurfing boards and paddleboats that rent for HK$22 ($2.86) an hour, and a swimming pool with sunken stools and a bar in the water.

The Warwick is also a good place to come for a meal. Its two restaurants serve Western and Chinese food, and you can sit outside on a veranda with a good view of the beach for either a meal or cocktails. The Western restaurant, open from 7:30 a.m. to 10:30 p.m., serves spaghetti, curries, chicken, and sandwiches for lunch and such dishes as grilled fresh shrimp, sole, garoupa, and beef stroganoff for dinner. The Chinese restaurant, open from noon to 3 p.m. and 6 to 10:30 p.m., offers sautéed chicken with soy bean and chili, roasted crisp chicken, sautéed sliced beef in oyster sauce, sautéed shrimp with garlic, and more. Cost of a meal at the Warwick averages about HK$85 ($11.04) at both restaurants.

The **Sea Pearl** (tel. 5-9818153) is a gaily painted floating restaurant anchored in Cheung Chau's harbor. It specializes in fresh Cantonese seafood, but also serves such dishes as roasted chicken or pigeon, sweet-and-sour pork, or sliced beef with noodles. You can spend as little as HK$25 ($3.26) or as much as HK$110 ($14.29). Very popular with vacationing Chinese, it's open from noon to 9 p.m. daily. To reach the restaurant, take the free shuttle service from the public pier (located to the right as you disembark from the ferry from Hong Kong Island). The shuttle boat won't have any English sign on it, but look for the yellow flag with red Chinese characters written on it that it flies on its roof.

Easy to find right on Cheung Chau's waterfront (and located just to the right as you disembark from the Hong Kong Island ferry), **Amego Café**, at 31 Praya St. (tel. 5-9810710), is open from 11 a.m. to 11 p.m. daily. It serves easy-to-prepare snacks and Western dishes, including sandwiches, spaghetti, omelets, milk shakes, and daily specials, most priced under HK$15 ($1.95).

Not far away is **King's Café** (tel. 5-9810878), 25 Praya St., to the left as you disembark from the Hong Kong Island ferry. Like the Amego Café described above, it serves Western-style food and snacks such as spaghetti, curry rice, soups, omelets, salads, ice cream, shakes, and beer. Although the food isn't great, prices are cheap: most dishes average HK$10 ($1.30) to HK$25 ($3.25), and there are some tables and chairs outside where you have a wonderful view of the action on the Praya and on the junks anchored close by. Closed on Wednesday, it's open the rest of the week from noon to midnight.

The local foreigner hangout is the **Village Tree Inn**, 18 Tung Wan Rd. (tel. 5-9817363), where you can get such things as noodle soup, spaghetti, omelets, sandwiches, or meat pies for HK$5 (65¢) to HK$12 ($1.56). Beer starts at HK$8 ($1.04). It's closed Monday and open other days from noon to midnight, though hours can vary.

Next to Village Tree Inn at 16 Tung Wan Rd. is the **Bor Kee Restaurant** (tel. 5-9812328). With its open façade and cafeteria-like appearance it doesn't look like much, but what it lacks in character is more than made up for by its seafood. It has a long menu in English, but most prices aren't given so it's best just to ask what's fresh and available. Expect to pay about HK$50 ($6.50) for a meal. It's open every day from 9 a.m. to 10 p.m.

Although it's actually located on nearby Lantau Island, the **Frog and Toad**, Tai Long Village (tel. 5-9892300), is a restaurant/bar most easily reached via a 20-minute sampan ride from Cheung Chau. Simply tell the sampan driver "Tai Long Wan," which means Big Wave Bay. Cost of the trip will be about HK$30 ($3.90), but be sure to bargain and settle the fee beforehand. You'll find yourself deposited at a pier on a seemingly deserted beach, but if you follow a trail leading inland from the middle of the beach (where you'll also see a sign), you'll soon come to a tiny settlement and the Frog and Toad. Owned by several expatriates, this mellow establishment serves as a day-trip getaway for people in the know, many of whom come here to relax in the rural setting. Open from 11 a.m. until the last customer leaves, it serves a barbecue special for HK$60 ($7.79) which includes ribs, chicken wings, sausage, and salad. If you want fresh seafood, you can order it by calling beforehand—it will then be bought in Cheung Chau. In fact, it might be a good idea to call beforehand anyway, simply to make sure they're open. This place is so far out of the way you might well be the only customer. There's a veranda where you can sit outside on fine days, and when you're ready to leave simply tell the man behind the bar. He'll call Cheung Chau and have a sampan sent on its way.

Lamma

If you want to do some pleasant hiking Lamma is the island to visit. The closest of the outlying islands, Lamma is Hong Kong's third-largest island and has a population of only 9,000, with much of its area still undeveloped. There are no cars on the island and a two-hour hiking trail connects Lamma's two main villages, Sok Kwu Wan and Yung Shue Wan.

From Sok Kwu Wan the hiking trail winds around the harbor through lush and verdant valleys and over barren and windswept hills. Large "armchair" graves dot the hillsides, and as you get closer to Yung Shue Wan the grasses give way to vegetable patches and green quilts of neatly cultivated fields. Watch for the villagers who water their fields by swinging back and forth two watering cans balanced on a pole slung across their shoulders.

There are a number of good beaches on Lamma. **Hung Shing Ye Beach** is the island's most popular, and is located about 20 minutes outside Yung Shue Wan on the hiking path described above. It has changing facilities, showers, and toilets, and lifeguards on duty during the summer.

You might also want to try out **Mo Tat Wan Beach**, about a 20-minute walk east of Sok Kwu Wan, but there are no lifeguards on duty here. While you're in the area, check out the village of **Mo Tat**, about 400 years old and the oldest settlement on the island. It consists of a handful of crumbling old houses inhabited mainly by old people and sits picturesquely amid banana trees and lush countryside.

Where to Eat: Try to schedule your outing on Lamma so that you can eat in Sok Kwu Wan. A fishing village, Sok Kwu Wan is well known for its seafood restaurants, many of which sit over the water on stilts with views of the harbor. I suggest you just walk along the waterfront and choose one that strikes your fancy, but if you want a specific recommendation, try **Sum Kee Restaurant**, 26 1st St. (tel. 5-9828241). Facing the sea and partly built on stilts, it offers outside dining in a covered area with a view of the harbor. It's open from noon until late in the evening and serves Cantonese-style seafood. An English menu is available and specialties include spicy shrimp and chili crab dishes. The average cost of a meal is about HK$85 ($11.04).

Another restaurant you might try is **Peach Garden Sea Food Restaurant**, 11 Sok Kwu Wan (tel. 5-9828581). Open from 10 a.m. to 10 p.m., it also has outside dining with a view of the water and serves seafood Cantonese style. Try its baked, buttered lobster or spicy squid. A meal here costs about HK$60 ($7.79).

If you end up in Yung Shue Wan and decide to eat there instead, a restaurant with a variety of seafood and Cantonese dishes is **Man Fung Restaurant**, 5 Yung Shue Wan St. (tel. 5-9820719). This restaurant also has outdoor seating where you have a view of the sea, and there's an English menu available with such specialties as pigeon, locally caught seafood, and dim sum. It's open from 8 a.m. to 10 p.m. Lunch runs about HK$80 ($10.39) while dinner costs about twice as much.

MACAU: Presently under Portuguese rule but reverting to Chinese authority in 1999, Macau is located on the southeastern coast of China and has a total land area of only six square miles. Although Portuguese is the official language, 98% of its 400,000 residents are Cantonese, which means that you hardly ever hear the official language.

Portuguese ships first landed in Macau in 1513, acquiring it from the Chinese in 1557. It became Portugal's most important trading center in Asia and was once the Orient's greatest port. As Hong Kong came onto the scene, however, Macau lost its importance and slowly sank into obscurity. Today its main attractions are its casinos, and Hong Kong residents and foreigners alike flock here to try their luck at the gambling tables.

With its mixture of Portuguese and Chinese influences, Macau has a charm all its own and boasts a number of churches, temples, and government buildings that reflect Portugal's 400 years of rule. The most famous structure is the ruin of St. Paul's, which was designed by an Italian Jesuit and built with the help of Japanese Christians who had fled persecution in Nagasaki in the 1600s. In 1835 during a typhoon the church caught fire and burned to the ground, leaving its now famous façade.

Before leaving for Macau, visit the **Macau Tourist Information Bureau** at the Macau Terminal, 305 Shun Tak Centre Shopping Mall, 200 Connaught Rd., Central District (tel. 5-408180). Open from 9 a.m. to 1 p.m. and from 2 to 5 p.m. Monday through Friday and from 9 a.m. to 1 p.m. on Saturday, the bureau can supply you with a map and brochures outlining Macau's historical and architectural attractions.

Located only 40 miles from Hong Kong, Macau is easily accessible by jetfoil, jetcat, hydrofoil, or ferry, all of which leave from the New Macau Terminal on Hong Kong Island. No visas are required for Americans, Canadians, Australians, or the British, but you will have to pay a HK$15 ($1.95) departure tax upon leaving Hong Kong. Although the pataca is Macau's official currency, you can use your Hong Kong dollars everywhere in Macau, even in buses and for taxis. Hotels will add a 10% service charge and 5% government tax to room prices, while restaurants will add a 10% service charge to your bill.

Where to Stay

The **Macau Oriental**, Avenida da Amizade (tel. 567888), is a Mandarin International Hotel and one of Macau's most expensive hotels, but it's still much cheaper here than in Hong Kong. Rooms begin at HK$550 ($71), and those facing the sea go for HK$790 ($103). Opened in 1984, the Excelsior is elegantly decorated throughout with imports from Portugal, including blue and white tiles, chandeliers, tapestries, and artwork. Recreation facilities include an outdoor swimming pool, two tennis courts, two air-conditioned squash courts, and a health center with sauna and massage. There's also a small casino in the hotel.

Opened in 1983, the **Hyatt Regency Macau** on Taipa Island (tel. 27000) has 356 rooms that were shipped in units from the United States and assembled in Macau like a jigsaw puzzle. Rooms are bright with all the usual amenities, and begin at HK$550 ($71), HK$770 ($100) for rooms with ocean views. The Hyatt has the island's most popular disco, the Green Parrot, and a sports and recreational center that includes a swimming pool, jogging track, tennis and squash courts, gym, and a small lake.

The **Pousada de São Tiago**, Avenida da República (tel. 78111), is a delightful small hotel built around the ruins of the Portuguese Fortress da Barra, which dates from 1629. The entrance to the hotel is quite dramatic—a flight of stairs leads through a cave-like tunnel with a small stream running alongside. There are only 23 guest rooms in the hotel, and all bedroom furniture is imported from Portugal, including the carved-wood beds. Rooms begin at HK$650 ($84); those with balconies cost HK$770 ($100). With a staff of over 100, service here is excellent.

If you're coming to Macau to gamble, you can't get much closer to the action than at the **Hotel Lisboa**, Avenida da Amizade (tel. 77666). Its large casino, the most popular in town, is open 24 hours a day. Built in 1969, the hotel is a bit on the garish side and seems old-fashioned by today's standards. Rooms are large but the furniture is a bit old, and bathrooms are overdone in pink. Still, this is the place to be if you want to be in the thick of it. Singles are HK$200 ($26) and twins start at HK$330 ($43).

A hostelry of a bygone era, the **Bela Vista**, 8 Rua do Comendador Kou Ho Neng (tel. 573821), built in 1892, is an old, rambling eccentric-looking hotel standing on a hill overlooking the water. Although its carpets are worn, its walls are cracking, and its paint is blistering, the Bela Vista is rather like a museum piece and is the place to stay if you're at all nostalgic. There are only 23 rooms in this two-story hotel: singles are priced at HK$175 ($23) and doubles start at HK$220 ($29). The best room in the hotel, and the one I'd recommend, is Room 209, a corner room with a dramatically high ceiling and its own private veranda overlooking the water. It costs HK$410 ($53).

Where to Eat

Macau's best dining is in the hotels, and its cuisine shows Portuguese, African, and Indian influences. Specialties include caldeirada (seafood stew), spicy giant shrimp, grilled Macau sole, and feijoada (pork with red beans). Portuguese wine is inexpensive and a great bargain here.

Afonso's, in the Hyatt Regency, specializes in Portuguese food, with an emphasis on fresh seafood. In addition to the daily specials and dessert buffet, Afonso's also serves such authentic dishes as plain grilled fresh tuna steak with seasonal vegetables and marinated pork with clams, coriander, and paprika. Lunch is served from noon to 3 p.m. and dinner from 7 to 11 p.m., and there is live music every evening to set the mood. A meal here will average about HK$80 ($10.39) to HK$200 ($25.97) depending on what you order and what you drink.

The **Grill Fortaleza**, in the Pousada de São Tiago, is a pleasant place to come for lunch or dinner because it's small and intimate, with seating for only 40 persons. A half-oval room with heavy red curtains drawn back to reveal a full view of the ocean, the Grill Fortaleza serves both Portuguese and continental cuisine, with most dishes ranging from HK$55 ($7.15) to HK$100 ($13). The menu includes shredded cod, braised rabbit in red wine sauce, duck terrine with cherry sauce, spicy African chicken, Macau sole, and grilled U.S. sirloin. Hours here are noon to 3 p.m. and 7 to 11 p.m. daily.

A good place for lunch when the weather is balmy is the **Bela Vista**, which offers outside dining on its veranda and terrace with sweeping views of the ocean, tugboats, and barges. A great place to while away the afternoon, it offers chicken, seafood, and curry dishes. I had fish chowder and baked crab in the shell, which I can heartily recommend. Most dishes range from about HK$30 ($3.90) to HK$55 ($7.14). It's open from noon to 3 p.m. and 6 to 11:30 p.m. daily.

If you don't feel like dining out in a hotel, try **Henri's Galley Maxim's**, 4 Avenida da República (tel. 76207). Open from 11 a.m. to 11 p.m. daily, it's owned by Henri Wong, who used to be a chief steward on a galley job at sea. A jovial and friendly man who speaks English well, he has decorated his café-like restaurant with things reminiscent of a galley. The staff is attentive and there are a few seats outside under umbrellas. Specialties of the house include fried Macau sole, African chicken, Portuguese baked chicken, fresh crab curry, and stuffed crabmeat in its shell. The average meal will cost about HK$77 ($10) per person.

TRIPS TO CHINA: Hong Kong is a major gateway for travelers going to the People's Republic of China. Most visitors join organized tours to the mainland that last anywhere from one day to a week or more. **China Travel Service** is probably the biggest and best-known company organizing tours to China. On

Hong Kong Island its office is at 77 Queen's Rd., Central District (tel. 5-252284). On the Kowloon side its office is at 27-33 Nathan Rd. (tel. 3-7219826). Office hours are from 9 a.m. to 6:30 p.m. Monday through Friday, 9 a.m. to 5:30 p.m. on Saturday, and from 9 a.m. to 1 p.m. and again from 2 to 5 p.m. on Sunday and holidays. CTS can arrange for your visa, but be sure to make your visa application at least two working days prior to departure.

JAPANESE VOCABULARY

NEEDLESS TO SAY, it takes years to become fluent in Japanese, particularly in written Japanese with its thousands of *kanji,* or Chinese characters, and many *hiragana* and *katakana* characters. Knowing just a few words of Japanese, however, is not only useful but will also delight the Japanese you meet during your trip.

In pronouncing the following vocabulary, keep in mind that there's very little stress on individual syllables (pronunciation of Japanese is often compared to Italian). Here is an approximation of some of the sounds of Japanese:

a as in f*a*ther
e as in p*e*n
i as in s*ee*
o as in *o*h
oo long o as in *ooo*h
u as in b*oo*k
g as in *g*ift at the beginning of words; like *ng* in si*ng* in the middle or at the end of words

Vowel sounds are always short unless they are pronounced double, in which case you hold the vowel a bit longer. Similarly, double consonants are given more emphasis than only one consonant by itself. *Okashi,* for example, means "a sweet," whereas *okashii* means "strange." As you can see, even slight mispronunciation of a word can result in confusion or hilarity. Incidentally, jokes in Japanese are nearly always plays on words.

General Words and Phrases

Good morning	Ohayo gozaimasu
Good afternoon	Kon-nichi-wa
Good evening	Kon-ban-wa
Good night	Oyasumi-nasai
Hello	Haro (or Kon-nichi-wa)
Good-bye	Sayonara (or bye-bye!)
Excuse me, I'm sorry	Sumimasen
Thank you	Domo arigatoo
You're welcome	Doo-itashi-mashite
Please (go ahead)	Doozo
Yes	Hai
No	I-ie

Foreigner	Gaijin
Japanese person	Nihonjin
Japanese language	Nihongo
American person	Amerikajin
English language	Eigo
Do you understand?	Wakarimasu ka?
I understand	Wakarimasu
I don't understand	Wakarimasen
Just a minute, please	Chotto matte kudasai
How much?	Ikura desu ka?
Where?	Doko desu ka?
When?	Itsu desu ka?
Expensive	Takai
Cheap	Yasui
I like it	Suki desu (pronounced "ski")

Traveling

Train station	Eki
Airport	Kuukoo
Subway	Chika-tetsu
Bus	Bus-u
Taxi	Takushi
Airplane	Hikooki
Ferry	Ferri
Train	Densha
Bullet train	Shinkansen
Limited express train	Tokkyu
Ordinary express train	Kyuko
Local train	Futsu
Ticket	Kippu
Exit	Deguchi
Entrance	Iriguchi
North	Kita
South	Minami
East	Higashi
West	Nishi
Left	Hidari
Right	Migi
Straight ahead	Massugu (or zutto)
Far	Toi
Near	Chikai
Can I walk there?	Aruite ikemasu ka?
Street	Dori (or michi)
Tourist information office	Kanko annaijo
Map	Chizu
Police box	Koban
Post office	Yubin-kyoku
Stamp	Kitte
Bank	Ginko

Hospital	Byooin
Toilet	Toire
	Ben joh
	Goh fu joh
	O teh ahmai
Spa	Onsen
Bath	Ofuro
Public bath	Sento

Food and Lodging

Restaurant	Resutoran
I'd like to make a reservation	Yoyaku onegai shimasu
Menu	Menyu
Tea	Ocha
Coffee	Koohi
Water	Mizu
Lunch or daily special	Teishoku
Delicious	Oishii
Thank you for the meal	Gochisoo-sama deshita
Hotel	Hoteru
Japanese-style inn	Ryokan
Youth hostel	Yusu hosuteru
Cotton kimono	Yukata
Room	Heya
Does that include meals?	Shokuji wa tsuite imasu ka?
Key	Kagi
Balcony	Baranda

Time

Now	Ima
Later	Ato de
Today	Kyoo
Tomorrow	Ashita
Day after tomorrow	Asatte
Yesterday	Kinoo
Which day?	Nan-nichi desu ka?
Daytime	Hiruma
Morning	Asa
Night	Yoru
Afternoon	Gogo
Sunday	Nichiyoobi
Monday	Getsuyoobi
Tuesday	Kayoobi
Wednesday	Suiyoobi
Thursday	Mokuyoobi

Friday	Kinyoobi
Saturday	Doyoobi
January	Ichi-gatsu
February	Ni-gatsu
March	San-gatsu
April	Shi-gatsu
May	Go-gatsu
June	Roku-gatsu
July	Shichi-gatsu
August	Hachi-gatsu
September	Kyuu-gatsu
October	Juu-gatsu
November	Juuichi-gatsu
December	Juuni-gatsu

Numbers

1	Ichi
2	Ni
3	San
4	Shi
5	Go
6	Roku
7	Shichi (or nana)
8	Hachi
9	Kyuu
10	Juu
11	Juuichi
12	Juuni
20	Nijuu
30	Sanjuu
40	Shijuu or yonjuu
50	Gojuu
60	Rokujuu
70	Nanajuu
80	Hachijuu
90	Kyuuju
100	Hyaku
1,000	Sen

JAPANESE SYMBOL LISTINGS

IN JAPAN, many hotels, restaurants, and other establishments do not have signs showing their names in English letters. This appendix lists the Japanese symbols for all such places appearing in this guide.

Each establishment name in Japanese symbols is numbered, and the same number appears in brackets in the text following the boldfaced establishment name. For example, in the text the Osaka hotel, Hokke Club [161], is number **161** in this list.

Tokyo

1. Seifuso
   聖富荘

2. Shimizu Bekkan
   しみず別館

3. Meguro Gajoen
   目黒雅叙園

4. National YWCA of Japan
   日本YWCA

5. Tokyo YWCA Sadowara Hostel
   東京YWCA砂土原ホステル

6. Keiunso
   景雲荘

7. Takamura
   簞

8. Kakiden
   柿傳

9. Tamura
   田村

10. Hayashi
    はやし

11. Shirakawago
    白川郷

12. Furusato
    ふるさと

13. Inakaya
    田舎家

14. Fukuzushi
    福鮨

15. Sushiko
    寿司幸

16. Zakuro
    ざくろ

17. Sushi Sei
    寿司清

18. Edogin
    江戸銀

19. Tentake
    天竹

20. Hassan
八山

21. Shabu Zen
しゃぶ禅

22. Chinya
ちんや

23. Komagato Dojo
駒形どじょう

24. Mugitoro
むぎとろ業り

25. Gonin Byakusho
五人百姓

26. Hayashi
はやし

27. Ohmatsuya
大松屋

28. Tsunahachi
つな八

29. Suehiro
スエヒロ

30. Kushi Colza
串コルザ

31. Ganchan
がんちゃん

32. Tatsumiya
東南屋

33. Irohanihoheto
いろはにほへと

34. Uogashi
魚がし

35. Sushi Dai
寿司大

36. Genrokusushi
元禄寿司

37. Torigin
鳥ぎん

38. Atariya
当りや

39. Torijoh
鳥上

40. Kushinobo
串の坊

41. Tonki
とんき

42. Hyotanya
ひょうたん屋

43. Keyaki
欅

44. Donto
どんと

45. Yabu-Soba
やぶそば

46. Tanuki
狸穴そば

47. Namiki
並木薮

48. Roppongi Shokudo
六本木食堂

49. Ichioku
一億

50. Tenmi
天味

51. Kuremutsu
暮六つ

52. Ichimon
一文

53. Club Maiko
クラブ舞妓

54. Lupin
ルパン

55. Yagura Chaya
櫓茶屋

56. Volga
ボルガ

57. Daisansoku
第三倉庫

Kamakura

58. Raitei
櫑亭

59. Monzen
門前

60. Miyokawa
御代川

61. Kayagi-ya
茅木屋

62. Nakamura-an
なかむら庵

63. Kamakura Hotel
鎌倉ホテル

Yokohama

64. Yokaro
陽華楼

65. Kaseiro
華正楼

66. Janomeya
じゃのめや

Hakone

67. Ichinoyu
一の湯

68. Hakone Prince Hotel
箱根プリンスホテル

69. Ryuguden
龍宮殿

70. Sugiyoshi Ryokan
杉よし旅館

Atami

71. Kiunkaku
起雲閣

72. Hotel New Akao
ホテルニューアカオ

Shimoda

73. Haji
はじ

Dogashima

74. Ginsuiso
銀水荘

75. Kaikomaru
海晃丸

Kyoto

76. Kinmata
近又

77. Rikiya
力彌

78. Yuhara
ゆはら

79. Sanyu
三友

80. Ichiume
一梅

81. Rokuharaya Inn
六波羅屋

82. Myorenji
妙蓮寺

83. Minoko
美濃幸

84. Nakamuraro
中村樓

85. Awata Sanso
粟田山荘

86. Hyotei
瓢亭

87. Okutan
奥丹

88. Koan
高庵

89. Goemonjaya
五衛ェ門茶屋

90. Mikaku
みかく

91. Yabu Kozan
やぶ高山

92. Maruyama
円山

93. Chorakukan
長楽館

94. Izumoya
いづもや

95. Koyomi-tei
暦亭

96. Tagoto
田ごと

97. Ganko Sushi
がんこ寿司

98. Gontaro
権太呂

99. Misogi-gawa
禊川

100. Sancho
サンチョ

101. Izusen
泉仙

102. Rakusho Tea Room
洛匠

103. Suishin Honten
酔心本店

104. Taku Taku
磔磔

105. Irohanihoheto
いろはにほへと

106. Kikusui
菊水

Nara

107. Kikusuiro
菊水楼

108. Shikitei
四季亭

109. Mangyoku
まんぎょく

Takayama

110. Hishuya
飛州屋

111. Hida Gasshoen
飛驒合掌苑

112. Kinkikan
金亀館

113. Seiryu
清龍

114. Asunaro
あすなろ

115. Hachibei
八兵衛

116. Kakusho
角正

117. Suzuya
寿々や

118. Bandai Kado Mise
萬代角店

119. Jizake-ya
地酒屋

Shirakawa-go

120. Seikatsu Shiryokan
生活資料館

121. Myozenji
明善寺

122. Magoemon
孫右ェ門

123. Kandaya
かんだ屋

124. Yosobe
よそべえ

125. Otaya
大田屋

126. Juemon
十右ェ門

127. Irori
いろり

128. Kitanosho
基太の庄

Matsumoto

129. Matsumoto Folkcraft Museum
松本民芸館

130. Ikyu
一休

131. Nishiya
西屋旅館

132. Kajika
かじか

133. Shikimi
しき美

Nagoya

134. Maizurukan
舞鶴館

135. Satsuki Honten
五月本店

136. Shoufukuro
招福楼

137. Miyako
みやこ

137A. Kintetsu Hanten
近鉄飯店

138. Yamamoto-ya Honten
山本屋本店

139. Yaegaki
八重垣

140. Kisoji
木曽路

141. Kishimentei
きしめん亭

Ise-shima National Park

142. Ishiyama-So
石山荘

143. Kimpokan
錦浦館

144. Saekikan
佐伯館

145. Yamadakan
山田館

146. Hoshidekan
星出館

147. Ise City Hotel
伊勢シティホテル

148. Youth Hostel Taikoji
ユースホステル 太江寺

149. Ise-Shima Youth Hostel
伊勢志摩ユースホステル

Kanazawa

150. Miyabo
みやぼ

151. Yogetsu
陽月

152. Kanazawa Youth Hostel
金沢ユースホステル

153. Matsui Youth Hostel
松井ユースホステル

154. Miyoshian
三芳庵

155. Tozan
東山

156. Takeda
竹田

157. Zeniya
銭屋

158. Hamacho
浜長

159. Kitama
きたま

160. Irohanihoheto
いろはにほへと

Osaka

161. Hotel Hokke Club
ホテル法華クラブ

162. Sen-i City
センイ シティ ホテル

163. Osaka-Shiritsu Nagai Youth Hostel
大阪市立長居ユースホステル

164. Hattori Ryokuchi Youth Hostel
服部緑地ユースホステル

165. Kagaman
かが万

166. Suehiro Asahi
スエヒロ朝日

167. Kuidaore
くいだおれ

168. Kani Doraku
かに道楽

169. Ebi Doraku
えび道楽

Kobe

170. Hotel Sannomiya Central
ホテル三宮セントラル

171. Kitagami Hotel
北上ホテル

172. Youth Hostel Kobe Mudoji
ユースホステル神戸無動寺

173. Rakuchin
楽珍

174. Steakland Kobe
ステーキランド KOBE

Mt. Koya
175. Shojoshinin
清浄心院

176. Ekoin
恵光院

177. Fumonin
霊峰高野山

178. Rengejoin
蓮華定院

179. Henjoson-in Youth Hostel
遍照尊院ユースホステル

Himeji
180. Banryu
播龍

181. Hotel Sunroute Himeji
ホテル サンルート姫路

182. Hotel Sunroute New Himeji
ホテル サンルート ニュー姫路

183. Fukutei
福亭

184. Minato-an
三七十庵

185. Mampuku
万福

Okayama
186. Okayama-ken Bussan Tenjijo
岡山県物産展示場

187. Hotel Sunroute
ホテル サンルート岡山

188. Matsunoki
まつのき旅館

189. Youth Hostel Okayama-ken Seinen Kaikan
ユースホステル 岡山県青年会館

190. Gonta
権太寿し

191. Suishin
酔心

192. C'est La Vie
瀬良備

193. Akatogarashi
赤とうがらし

194. Puchi Marie
プチマリエ

Kurashiki
195. Ryokan Kurashiki
旅館くらしき

196. Tsurugata
鶴形

197. Kamoi
カモ井

198. Minshuku Kawakami
民宿かわかみ

199. Tokusan Kan
特産館

200. Kurashiki Terminal Hotel
倉敷ターミナルホテル

201. Kurashiki Station Hotel
倉敷ステェーションホテル

202. Kamoi
カモ井

Matsue

203. Matsue Kyodo-kan
松江郷土館

204. Meimei-an Teahouse
明々庵

205. Buke Yashiki
武家屋敷

206. Tanabe Art Museum
田部美術館

207. Gesshoji Temple
月照寺

208. Shimane-ken
Bussankanko-kan
島根県物産観光館

209. Matsue Meisan Center
松江名産センター

210. Minami-kan
皆美館

211. Horaiso
蓬莱荘

212. Ohashi-kan
大橋館

213. Matsue Urban Hotel
松江アーバンホテル

214. Matsue Plaza Hotel
松江プラザホテル

215. Matsue Minami Guchi
Hotel
松江南口ホテル

216. Matsue Youth Hostel
松江ユース・ホステル

217. Kaneyasu
かねやす

218. Ginsen
銀扇

219. Yagumoan
八雲庵

220. Kososhi
こそし

221. Murasaki
村さ来

Hiroshima

222. Mitakiso
三瀧荘

223. Hiroshima Central
Hotel
広島セントラルホテル

224. Sera Bekkan
世羅別館

225. Rijyo Kaikan
鯉城会館

226. Hiroshima Youth
Hostel
広島ユースホステル

227. Amagi
あまぎ

228. Kanawa
かなわ

229. Suishin
酔心

Miyajima

230. Iwaso Ryokan
岩惣旅館

231. Momiji
もみじ

232. Jyukeiso
聚景荘

233. Miyajima Lodge
宮島ロッジ

234. Fujitaya
ふじたや

Takamatsu
235. Kompira O-shibai
金毘羅大芝居

236. Takamatsu Plaza Hotel
高松プラザホテル

237. Tokiwa Honkan
常磐本館

238. Takamatsu Yuai-Sanso
Youth Hostel
高松友愛荘ホステル

239. Kanaizumi
かな泉

240. Tenkatsu
天勝

241. Hansuke
半助

Matsuyama
242. Mingei Iyo Kasuri
Kaikan
民芸伊予かすり会館

243. Umeno Seito-jo
梅野精陶所

244. Tobe-yaki Kanko Center
砥部焼観光センター

245. Ehime no Bussan
愛媛の物産

246. Uchikoza
内子座

247. Funaya
ふなや

248. Kasugaen
春日園

249. Business Hotel Taihei
ビジネスホテル泰平

250. Matsuyama Shinsen-en
Youth Hostel
松山神泉園ユースホステル

251. Hyakkumi
佰味

252. Shinhamasaku
新浜作

Fukuoka
253. Chisan Hotel Hakata
チサンホテル博多

254. Mitsui Urban Hotel
三井アーバンホテル

255. Dazaifu Youth Hostel
太宰府ユースホステル

256. Gyosai
魚菜

Beppu
257. Kannawaen
神和苑

258. Nanmeiso
南明荘

259. Sakaeya
サカエ屋

260. Green Hotel
グリーン ビジネス ホテル

261. Makibanoie
牧場乃家

262. Chikuden
ちくでん

263. Amamijaya
甘味茶屋

264. Bistro Soen
びすとろ そうえん

Mt. Aso
265. Ryokan Mimura
旅館みむら

266. Aso Youth Hostel
阿蘇ユースホステル

267. Minami Aso Kokumin
Kyuka Mura
南阿蘇国民休暇村

268. Dengaku no Sato
田楽の里

269. Minami Aso Kokumin
Shukusha
南阿蘇国民宿舎

Kumamoto
270. Kumamoto Traditional
Crafts Center
熊本県伝統工芸館

271. Kumamoto-ken
Bussankan
熊本県物産館

272. Kumamoto Station
Hotel
熊本ステーションホテル

273. Tsukasa Besso
司別荘

274. Suizenji Youth Hostel
水前寺ユースホステル

275. Kumamoto Shiritsu
Youth Hostel
熊本市立ユースホステル

276. Senri
泉里

277. Kimura-so
きむら荘

278. Aoyagi
青柳

279. Goemon
五右衛門

Nagasaki
280. Hotel Station Ajisai
ホテル ステーション あじさい

281. Sakamoto-ya
坂本屋

282. Nishikyushu Daiichi
Hotel
西九州第一ホテル

283. Terada
てらだ

284. Sansui-so
山水荘

285. Nagasaki Kenritsu
Youth Hostel
長崎県立ユースホステル

286. Nagasaki Oranda-Zaka
Youth Hostel
長崎オランダ坂ユースホステル

287. Kagetsu
花月

288. Fukiro
富貴楼

289. Hamakatsu
浜勝

290. Kozanro
江山楼

291. Kurukuru Shiragiku
くるくる しらぎく

292. Yagura-chaya
やぐら茶屋

Unzen

293. Miyazaki Ryokan
雲仙 宮崎旅館

294. Kaseya Ryokan
かせや旅館

295. Seiunso
青雲荘ユースホステル

Kagoshima

296. Shigetomiso
重富荘

297. Park Hotel
パークホテル

298. Hirayama Ryokan
ひらやま旅館

299. Sakurajima Youth Hostel
桜島ユースホステル

300. Kumasotei
熊襲亭

301. Satsuma
さつま

302. Noboruya
のぼる屋

Ibusuki

303. Shusuien
秀水園

304. Ibusuki Park Hotel Hakusuikan
ホテル白水

305. Marutomi
丸富

306. Ibusuki Kokumin Kyuka-son
指宿国民休暇村

307. Chozyuan
長寿庵

308. Aoshima Kokumin Shukusha
青島国民宿舎

309. Gyosantei
魚山亭

310. Sugi no Ko
杉の子

Matsushima

311. Zuiganji Temple
瑞巌寺

312. Entsuin
円通院

313. Taikanso
大観荘

314. Matsushima Kanko Hotel
松島観光ホテル

315. Konnoya
今野屋

316. Ryokan Kozakura
旅館小櫻

317. Matsushima Youth Hostel
松島ユースホステル

318. Okunohosomichi
奥の細道

319. Donjiki
どんじき茶屋

Hakodate
320. Minshuku Fukuiso
民宿ふくい荘

321. Business Hotel Rizabu
リザーブ

322. Hokusei-so Youth Hostel
北星荘ユースホステル

Sapporo
323. Zenniku
全日空

324. Nakamuraya Ryokan
中村屋旅館

325. Yoshizumi
芳住

326. Hyosetsu-no-Mon
氷雪の門

327. Irohanihoheto
いろはにほへと

328. Satohoro
さとほろ

Shikotsu-Toya National Park
329. Manseikaku
万世閣

330. Hotel New Toyako
ホテルニュー洞爺湖

331. Showa-Shinzan Youth Hostel
昭和新山ユースホステル

332. Oshima
大島

333. Kikusui
菊水

334. Noboribetsu-so
のぼりべつ荘

335. Kannonji
観音寺

336. Akashiya Youth Hostel
あかしやユースホステル

337. Ryokan Kanefuku
旅館金福

Daisetsuzan National Park
338. Grand Hotel
グランドホテル

339. Kumoi
雲井

340. Matsubara
松原

341. Pension Yukara
ペンション ユーカラ

342. Tsuchiya
つちや

343. Kitagawa
北川

344. Sounkyo Youth Hostel
層雲峡ユースホステル

345. Ginsenkaku Youth Hostel
銀泉閣ユースホステル

Akan National Park

346. Hotel Ichikawa
ホテル市川

347. Akan Grand Hotel
阿寒グランドホテル

348. Minshuku Yamaguchi Fujino
民宿山口ふじの

349. Minshuku Ginrei
民宿ぎんれい

350. Angel Youth Hostel
エンジェル ユースホステル

351. Choritsu Akanko Youth Hostel
町立阿寒ユースホステル

Date_____

FROMMER BOOKS
PRENTICE HALL PRESS
ONE GULF + WESTERN PLAZA
NEW YORK, NY 10023

Friends:

Please send me the books checked below:

FROMMER'S $-A-DAY GUIDES™
(In-depth guides to sightseeing and low-cost tourist accommodations and facilities.)

☐ Europe on $30 a Day $13.95	☐ New Zealand on $40 a Day $11.95
☐ Australia on $30 a Day $11.95	☐ New York on $50 a Day............. $10.95
☐ Eastern Europe on $25 a Day $10.95	☐ Scandinavia on $50 a Day............ $10.95
☐ England on $40 a Day.............. $11.95	☐ Scotland and Wales on $40 a Day..... $11.95
☐ Greece on $30 a Day............... $11.95	☐ South America on $30 a Day $10.95
☐ Hawaii on $50 a Day............... $11.95	☐ Spain and Morocco (plus the Canary
☐ India on $25 a Day $10.95	Is.) on $40 a Day $10.95
☐ Ireland on $30 a Day.............. $10.95	☐ Turkey on $25 a Day $10.95
☐ Israel on $30 & $35 a Day $11.95	☐ Washington, D.C., & Historic Va. on
☐ Mexico (plus Belize & Guatemala)	$40 a Day $11.95
on $20 a Day..................... $10.95	

FROMMER'S DOLLARWISE GUIDES™
(Guides to sightseeing and tourist accommodations and facilities from budget to deluxe, with emphasis on the medium-priced.)

☐ Alaska............................ $12.95	☐ Cruises (incl. Alaska, Carib, Mex,
☐ Austria & Hungary $11.95	Hawaii, Panama, Canada, & US) $12.95
☐ Belgium, Holland, Luxembourg $11.95	☐ California & Las Vegas $11.95
☐ Egypt............................ $11.95	☐ Florida........................... $11.95
☐ England & Scotland $11.95	☐ Mid-Atlantic States $12.95
☐ France........................... $11.95	☐ New England....................... $12.95
☐ Germany.......................... $12.95	☐ New York State $12.95
☐ Italy............................. $11.95	☐ Northwest......................... $11.95
☐ Japan & Hong Kong $13.95	☐ Skiing in Europe $12.95
☐ Portugal, Madeira, & the Azores $12.95	☐ Skiing USA—East $11.95
☐ South Pacific...................... $12.95	☐ Skiing USA—West $11.95
☐ Switzerland & Liechtenstein $12.95	☐ Southeast & New Orleans........... $11.95
☐ Bermuda & The Bahamas........... $11.95	☐ Southwest......................... $11.95
☐ Canada $12.95	☐ Texas............................. $11.95
☐ Caribbean $13.95	

FROMMER'S TOURING GUIDES™
(Color illustrated guides that include walking tours, cultural & historic sites, and other vital travel information.)

☐ Egypt............................ $8.95	☐ Paris $8.95
☐ Florence $8.95	☐ Venice $8.95
☐ London $8.95	

TURN PAGE FOR ADDITIONAL BOOKS AND ORDER FORM.

THE ARTHUR FROMMER GUIDES™

(Pocket-size guides to sightseeing and tourist accommodations and facilities in all price ranges.)

☐ Amsterdam/Holland	$5.95	☐ Mexico City/Acapulco	$5.95
☐ Athens	$5.95	☐ Minneapolis/St. Paul	$5.95
☐ Atlantic City/Cape May	$5.95	☐ Montreal/Quebec City	$5.95
☐ Boston	$5.95	☐ New Orleans	$5.95
☐ Cancún/Cozumel/Yucatán	$5.95	☐ New York	$5.95
☐ Dublin/Ireland	$5.95	☐ Orlando/Disney World/EPCOT	$5.95
☐ Hawaii	$5.95	☐ Paris	$5.95
☐ Las Vegas	$5.95	☐ Philadelphia	$5.95
☐ Lisbon/Madrid/Costa del Sol	$5.95	☐ Rome	$5.95
☐ London	$5.95	☐ San Francisco	$5.95
☐ Los Angeles	$5.95	☐ Washington, D.C.	$5.95

SPECIAL EDITIONS

☐ A Shopper's Guide to the Caribbean	$12.95	☐ Motorist's Phrase Book (Fr/Ger/Sp)	$4.95
☐ Bed & Breakfast—N. America	$8.95	☐ Swap and Go (Home Exchanging)	$10.95
☐ Guide to Honeymoon Destinations (US, Canada, Mexico, & Carib)	$12.95	☐ The Candy Apple (NY for Kids)	$11.95
		☐ Travel Diary and Record Book	$5.95
☐ Beat the High Cost of Travel	$6.95	☐ Where to Stay USA (Lodging from $3 to $30 a night)	$10.95
☐ Marilyn Wood's Wonderful Weekends (NY, Conn, Mass, RI, Vt, NH, NJ, Del, Pa)	$11.95		

☐ Arthur Frommer's New World of Travel (Annual sourcebook previewing: new travel trends, new modes of travel, and the latest cost-cutting strategies for savvy travelers) $12.95

SERIOUS SHOPPER'S GUIDES

(Illustrated guides listing hundreds of stores, conveniently organized alphabetically by category.)

☐ Italy	$15.95	☐ Los Angeles	$14.95
☐ London	$15.95	☐ Paris	$15.95

ORDER NOW!

In U.S. include $1.50 shipping UPS for 1st book; 50¢ ea. add'l book. Outside U.S. $2 and 50¢, respectively.

Enclosed is my check or money order for $_____

NAME _____

ADDRESS _____

CITY _____ STATE _____ ZIP _____

It's 2 am.
It's far from home.
It's more than
a tummyache.

American Express Cardmembers can get emergency medical and legal referrals, worldwide. Simply by calling Global Assist.ᔆᴹ

What if it really is more than a tummyache? What if your back goes out? What if you get into a legal fix?

Call Global Assist – a new emergency referral service for the exclusive use of American Express Cardmembers. Just call. Toll-free. 24 hours a day. Every day. Virtually anywhere in the world.

Your call helps find a doctor, lawyer, dentist, optician, chiropractor, nurse, pharmacist, or an interpreter.

All this costs nothing, except for the medical and legal bills you would normally expect to pay.

Global Assist. One more reason to have the American Express® Card. Or, to get one.

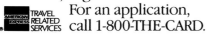 For an application, call 1-800-THE-CARD.

Don't leave home without it.®